THIRD REVISED EDITION

THE RESTAURANT MANAGER'S HANDBOOK

**How to Set Up, Operate and Manage A
Financially Successful Food Service Operation**

Douglas Robert Brown

Published By:
ATLANTIC PUBLISHING GROUP, INC

THE RESTAURANT MANAGER'S HANDBOOK
How to Set Up, Operate and Manage a Financially Successful Food Service Operation

By Douglas Robert Brown

Published by **ATLANTIC PUBLISHING GROUP, INC**

ATLANTIC PUBLISHING GROUP, INC • 1210 S.W. 23rd Place • Ocala, FL 34474-7014

800-541-1336 • http://www.atlantic-pub.com • sales@atlantic-pub.com

SAN Number :268-1250

Member American Library Association
Copyright 2003, All Rights Reserved

Library of Congress Cataloging-in-Publication Data

Brown, Douglas Robert, 1960-

The restaurant manager's handbook : how to set up, operate, and manage a financially successful food service operation / by Douglas Robert Brown.-- 3rd ed.

p. cm.

Includes bibliographical references and index.

ISBN 0-910627-09-6 (Hardcover : alk. paper)

1. Restaurant management. I. Title.

TX911.3.M27 B76 2003

647.95'068--dc21

2002011299   CIP

WARNING DISCLAIMER

This book is designed to provide information in regard to the subject matter covered. It is sold with the understanding that the publisher and author are not engaged in rendering legal, accounting or other professional services. If legal or other expert assistance is required, the services of a competent professional should be sought.

It is not the purpose of this manual to reprint all the information that is otherwise available to the author and/or publisher but to compliment, amplify and supplement other texts.

Every effort has been made to make this manual as complete and as accurate as possible. However, there may be mistakes both typographical and in content. Therefore, this text should be used only as a general guide and not as the ultimate source of information.

The purpose of this manual is to educate and entertain. The author and the publisher shall have neither liability nor responsibility to any person or entity with respect to any loss or damage caused or alleged to be caused directly or indirectly by the information contained in this book.

TABLE OF CONTENTS

CHAPTER 1
SUCCESSFUL PRE-OPENING ACTIVITIES FOR A NEW RESTAURANT VENTURE

CHAPTER 2
THE BASICS OF BUYING & SELLING A RESTAURANT

CHAPTER 3
HOW TO ANALYZE & INVEST IN A RESTAURANT
FRANCHISE OPPORTUNITY

CHAPTER 4
BASIC COST CONTROL FOR FOOD SERVICE OPERATIONS—AN OVERVIEW

CHAPTER 5
PROFITABLE MENU PLANNING—FOR MAXIMUM RESULTS

CHAPTER 6
SUCCESSFUL KITCHEN MANAGEMENT & CONTROL PROCEDURES—FOR MAXIMUM EFFICIENCY

CHAPTER 7
THE ESSENTIALS OF FOOD SAFETY, HACCP & SANITATION PRACTICES

CHAPTER 8
SUCCESSFUL BAR MANAGEMENT & OPERATIONS

CHAPTER 9
SUCCESSFUL WINE MANAGEMENT & OPERATIONS

CHAPTER 10
SUCCESSFUL MANAGEMENT OF OPERATIONAL COSTS & SUPPLIES

CHAPTER 11
COMPUTERS & YOUR FOOD-SERVICE OPERATION—HOW TO USE THEM & PROFIT FROM THEM

CHAPTER 12
MANAGING THE DINING ROOM & WAITSTAFF PERSONNEL FOR MAXIMUM SERVICE & PRODUCTIVITY

CHAPTER 13
SUCCESSFUL EMPLOYEE RELATIONS & LABOR COST CONTROLS

CHAPTER 14
PUBLIC RELATIONS FOR YOUR RESTAURANT—HOW TO GET CUSTOMERS IN THE DOOR WITH LITTLE OR NO COST

CHAPTER 15
INTERNAL RESTAURANT MARKETING – HOW TO KEEP CUSTOMERS COMING BACK TO YOUR ESTABLISHMENT

CHAPTER 16
INTERNAL BOOKKEEPING—ACCOUNTING FOR SALES & COSTS— WHERE DID IT ALL GO?

CHAPTER 17
SUCCESSFUL BUDGETING & PROFIT PLANNING—FOR MAXIMUM RESULTS

CHAPTER 18
HOW TO PREPARE THE MONTHLY AUDIT & COST PROJECTIONS—PUTTING IT ALL TOGETHER

CHAPTER 19
HOW TO PERFORM AN INTERNAL AUDIT ON A RESTAURANT/BAR OPERATION—LOCATE & FIX PROFIT LEAKING AREAS

ADDITIONAL INFORMATION

Glossary of Terms

Index

List of State Restaurant Associations

List of Industry Publications

Atlantic Publishing Order Form

The Food Service Professional's Directory of Food Service Suppliers, Manufacturers and Distributors

DIRECTORY OF FORMS & CHARTS

CHAPTER 9—SUCCESSFUL WINE MANAGEMENT & OPERATIONS

CHAPTER 10—SUCCESSFUL MANAGEMENT OF OPERATIONAL COSTS & SUPPLIES

CHAPTER 13—SUCCESSFUL EMPLOYEE RELATIONS & LABOR COST CONTROLS

CHAPTER 16—INTERNAL BOOKKEEPING—ACCOUNTING FOR SALES & COSTS—WHERE DID IT ALL GO?

CHAPTER 17—SUCCESSFUL BUDGETING & PROFIT PLANNING—FOR MAXIMUM RESULTS

CHAPTER 18—HOW TO PREPARE THE MONTHLY AUDIT & COST PROJECTIONS—PUTTING IT ALL TOGETHER

INTRODUCTION

In the years 1998 through 2001, 23,211 restaurants failed and/or closed in this country alone. Countless others are losing money and on the verge of closing. According to the Small Business Administration, 27 percent of all new restaurants fail in their first year, and 60 percent after just five years. These are, of course, only the failures actually reported. Although the reasons for these unfortunate statistics are many and varied, they can be pinpointed to one main fact; there hasn't been any comprehensive source of information about the subject of restaurant management to guide the prospective restaurateur prior to the original publication of this book.

Virtually everyone, at one time or another, has been tempted to run, or at least considered running, his or her own restaurant. This may be due to a number of reasons. Perhaps the prospective restaurateur is accomplished in the kitchen, or so his spouse and friends tell him. Perhaps the motivation was derived from an unfortunate experience at a local restaurant, and the "I can do this much better" syndrome has set in. Or, perhaps he feels his town could use a good seafood restaurant. The reasons for starting a restaurant are varied. However, most have one factor in common: they end in financial disaster due to a lack of pertinent knowledge about setting up, operating and managing a financially successful restaurant.

Americans enjoy eating out, and the pace of development of the modern lifestyle indicates that they will continue to eat out more in the future. Higher economic levels, more mobility and more women in the workforce will all lead to a continuing growth in the industry in the next decade. A preview of the 2002 Restaurant Industry Forecast available from the National Restaurant Association indicates the nation's 858,000 restaurants will hit $407.8 billion in sales in 2002, an increase of almost 4 percent over 2001. The average annual household expenditure for food away from home in 1998 was $2,030, or $812 per person. More than 4 out of 10 adults were restaurant patrons on a typical day in 2000.

Food service continues to lead other industries, such as housing, automaking and electronics, in total sales. The food service industry continues to gain a greater share of all food dollars spent in America. Between 1970 and 2001 restaurant-industry sales posted a compound annual growth rate of 7.5 percent. In 2001, the restaurant industry posted its tenth consecutive year of real (inflation-adjusted) sales growth, moving up another point to 45 percent versus 55 percent for retail food; a gain of 20 share points since 1960. The average family's weekly expenditure on food away from home is at an all time high at $31.72.

As these figures clearly show, there is room for entry into the restaurant marketplace. Profits, however, can only be realized from the application of modern management procedures. Food service is a complex business. The preparation and the serving of food entails warehousing, manufacturing and selling. It is one of the few retail trades where the product is manufactured, sold and consumed on the premises.

Properly armed with the right information and entrepreneurial drive, one will find that the restaurant business can be very rewarding both financially and through a sense of personal achievement.

This manual will arm you with the right information. Keep it on your desk for constant reference. The many valuable forms contained in this work are available on the companion CD-ROM. There is no other publication as comprehensive as *The Restaurant Manager's Handbook*. This book truly is appropriately titled.

Good reading and good luck!

Sincerely,

Douglas R. Brown

ACKNOWLEDGEMENTS

Many people helped to make this new edition of *THE RESTAURANT MANAGER'S HANDBOOK* possible. Some were inspirational and some provided valuable information, while others provided editorial talent, encouragement and support. Without the assistance of the individuals listed below, this book would never have become a reality. I sincerely thank all these fine people and organizations:

- Sherri Lyn Brown
- Halowell & Jean E. Brown
- Bruce & Vonda Brown
- Kim Hendrickson
- Ed Manley; IFSEA
- Robert Baker
- Diana Toomalatai
- Hal & Charlanne Brown
- Lynn & Jim Durante
- Dr. Joseph E. Gelety
- Robert M. & Nancy Frazier

- Richard Meade, CPA
- Meg Buchner
- Amy L. Chamberlain
- Jackie Ness
- Jackie Sullivan
- Ghislaine René de Cotret
- Mr. Ed Larson; Superior Products
- National Restaurant Association
- The Small Business Administration

- The Internal Revenue Service
- The U.S. Department Of Labor
- Ocala Public Library
- University of Florida Library
- Central Florida Community College & Library
- Gizmo Graphics Web Design www.gizwebs.com
- Corbie Morrow; Superior Products - Next Gourmet

Cover and interior design by Meg Buchner of Megadesign
www.mega-designs.com • e-mail: megadesn@mhtc.net • 608-734-3259

1

SUCCESSFUL PRE-OPENING ACTIVITIES FOR A NEW RESTAURANT VENTURE

INTRODUCTION

The purpose of this chapter is to list and describe the activities fundamental to opening a restaurant. Each restaurant offers its own unique and challenging problems. The following chapter will make the prospective restaurateur aware of all the pre-opening procedures that must be completed for any restaurant. Before engaging in any business activity seek the guidance of a lawyer. You will undoubtedly have many legal questions and you will need legal counseling during the opening period. The services of a local accountant or C.P.A. should also be retained. The accountant will be instrumental in setting up the business and can provide you with a great deal of financial advice to inform your decision making. Perhaps the most important task to accomplish right now is writing the formal business plan, which will be your road map for success.

ELEMENTS OF A BUSINESS PLAN

I.   **Cover sheet**

II. **Statement of purpose**

III. **Table of contents**

IV. **The Business**
   A. Description of business
   B. Marketing
   C. Competition
   D. Operating procedures
   E. Personnel
   F. Business insurance
   G. Financial data

V.   **Financial Data**

A. Loan applications

B. Capital equipment and supply list

C. Balance sheet

D. Breakeven analysis

E. Pro-forma income projections (profit and loss statements)
   1. Three-year summary
   2. Detail by month, first year
   3. Detail by quarters, second and third years
   4. Assumptions upon which projections were based

F. Pro-forma cash flow
   1. Follow guidelines for number 5.

VI. Supporting Documents

A. Tax returns of principals for last three years

B. Personal financial statement (all banks have these forms)

C. In the case of a franchised business, a copy of franchise contract and all supporting documents provided by the franchisor

D. Copy of proposed lease or purchase agreement for building space

E. Copy of licenses and other legal documents

F. Copy of resumes of all principals

G. Copies of letters of intent from suppliers, etc.

THE BUSINESS PLAN — What It Includes

What goes in a business plan? This is an excellent question. And, it is one that many new and potential small business owners should ask, but often times don't. The body of the business plan can be divided into four distinct sections:

1. The description of the business

2. The marketing plan

3. The management plan

4. The financial management plan

Addenda to the business plan should include the executive summary, supporting documents and financial projections.

THE BUSINESS PLAN — Description of the Business

The business description section is divided into three primary sections. Section 1 actually describes your business, Section 2 the product or service you will be offering, and Section 3 the location of your business and why this location is desirable (if you have a franchise, some franchisors assist in site selection). When describing your business, generally you should explain:

1. **Legalities.** Business form: proprietorship, partnership or corporation. What licenses or permits you will need.

2. **Business type.**

3. **What your product or service is.** Perhaps the sample menu could be included.

4. **Business character.** Is it a new independent business, a takeover, an expansion, a franchise?

5. **Why your business will be profitable.** What are the growth opportunities? Will franchising impact on growth opportunities?

6 **When your business will be open.** What days? hours?

7. **What you have learned about your kind of business from outside sources** (trade suppliers, bankers, other franchise owners, franchisor, publications).

A cover sheet goes before the description. It includes the name, address and telephone number of the business and the names of all principals. In the description of your business, describe the unique aspects and how or why they will appeal to consumers. Emphasize any special features that you feel will appeal to customers and explain how and why these features are appealing.

The description of your business should clearly identify goals and objectives and it should clarify why you are, or why you want to be, in business.

PRODUCT/SERVICES

Try to describe the benefits of your goods and services from your customers' perspective. Successful business owners know or at least have an idea of what their customers want or expect from them. This type of anticipation can be helpful in building customer satisfaction and loyalty. And, it certainly is a good strategy for beating the competition or retaining your competitiveness. Describe:

1. What you are selling—include your menu here.

2. How your product or service will benefit the customer.

3. Which food and beverage products/services are in demand.

4. What is different about the product or service your business is offering.

THE LOCATION

The location of your business can play a decisive role in its success or failure. Remember the old maxim "Location, Location, Location." Your location should be built around your customers, it should be accessible, and it should provide a sense of security. Consider these questions when addressing this section of your business plan:

1. What are your location needs?

2. What kind of space will you need?

3. Why is the area desirable? the building desirable?

4. Is it easily accessible? Is public transportation available? Is street lighting adequate?

5. Are market shifts or demographic shifts occurring?

It may be a good idea to make a checklist of questions you identify when developing your business plan. Categorize your questions and, as you answer each question, remove it from your list.

THE BUSINESS PLAN — The Marketing Plan

Marketing plays a vital role in successful business ventures. How well you market your business, along with a few other considerations, will ultimately determine your degree of success or failure. The key element of a successful marketing plan is to know your customers—their likes, dislikes and expectations. By identifying these factors, you can develop a marketing strategy that will allow you to arouse and fulfill their needs.

Identify your customers by their age, sex, income/educational level and residence. At first, target only those customers who are more likely to purchase your product or service. As your customer base expands, you may need to consider modifying the marketing plan to include other customers.

Develop a marketing plan for your business by answering these questions. (Potential franchise owners will have to use the marketing strategy the franchisor has developed.) Your marketing plan should be included in your business plan and contain answers to the questions outlined below.

1. Who are your customers? Define your target market(s).

2. Are your markets growing? steady? declining?

3. Is your market share growing? steady? declining?

4. If a franchise, how is your market segmented?

5. Are your markets large enough to expand?

6. How will you attract, hold, increase your market share? If a franchise, will the franchisor provide assistance in this area? based on the franchisor's strategy? How will you promote your sales?

7. What pricing strategy have you devised?

COMPETITION

Competition is a way of life. We compete for jobs, promotions, scholarships to institutes of higher learning, in sports—and in almost every aspect of our lives. Nations compete for the consumer in the global marketplace, as do individual business owners. Advances in technology can send the profit margins of a successful business into a tailspin causing them to plummet overnight or within a few hours. When considering these and other factors, we can conclude that business is a highly competitive, volatile arena. Because of this volatility and competitiveness, it is important to know your competitors.

Questions like these can help you:

1. Who are your five nearest direct competitors?

2. Who are your indirect competitors?

3. How is their business: steady? increasing? decreasing?

4. What have you learned from their operations? from their advertising?

5. What are their strengths and weaknesses?

6. How does their menu or service differ from yours?

Start a file on each of your competitors. Keep manila envelopes of their advertising and promotional materials and their pricing strategy techniques. Review these files periodically, determining when and how often they advertise, sponsor promotions and offer sales. Study the copy used in the advertising and promotional materials and their sales strategy. For example, is their copy short? descriptive? catchy? How much do they reduce prices for sales? Using this technique can help you to better understand your competitors and how they operate their businesses.

PRICING AND SALES

Your pricing strategy is another marketing technique you can use to improve your overall competitiveness. Get a feel for the pricing strategy your competitors are using. That way you can determine if your prices are in line with competitors in your market area and if they are in line with industry averages.

Some of the pricing considerations are:

- Menu cost and pricing

- Competitive position

- Pricing below competition

- Pricing above competition

- Price lining

- Multiple pricing

- Service components

- Material costs

- Labor costs

- Overhead costs

The key to success is to have a well-planned strategy, to establish your policies and to constantly monitor prices and operating costs to ensure profits. Even in a franchise where the franchisor provides operational procedures and materials, it is a good policy to keep abreast of the changes in the marketplace because these changes can affect your competitiveness and profit margins.

ADVERTISING AND PUBLIC RELATIONS

How you advertise and promote your restaurant may make or break your business. Having a good product or service and not advertising and promoting it is like not having a business at all. Many business owners operate under the mistaken concept that the business will promote itself, and channel money that should be used for advertising and promotions to other areas of the business. Advertising and promotions, however, is the lifeline of a business and should be treated as such. We have devoted a whole chapter to marketing your restaurant and promoting your restaurant.

Devise a plan that uses advertising and networking as a means to promote your business. Develop short, descriptive copy (text material) that clearly identifies your goods or services, its location and price. Use catchy phrases to arouse the interest of your readers, listeners or viewers. In the case of a franchise, the franchisor will provide advertising and promotional materials as part of the franchise package; you may need approval to use any materials that you and your staff develop. Whether or not this is the case, as a courtesy, allow the franchisor the opportunity to review, comment on and, if required, approve these materials before using them. Make sure the advertisements you create are consistent with the image the franchisor is trying to project. Remember the more care and attention you devote to your marketing program, the more successful your business will be.

THE BUSINESS PLAN — The Management Plan

Managing a business requires more than just the desire to be your own boss. It demands dedication, persistence, the ability to make decisions and the ability to manage both employees and finances. Your management plan, along with your marketing and financial management plans, sets the foundation for and facilitates the success of your business.

People are the most valuable resources a business has. You will soon discover that employees and staff will play an important role in the total operation of your business. Consequently, it's imperative that you know what skills you possess and what you don't, since you will have to hire personnel to supply the skills that you lack. Additionally, it is imperative that you know how to manage and treat your employees. Make them a part of the team. Keep them informed of, and get their feedback regarding, changes. Employees oftentimes have excellent ideas that can lead to new market areas, innovations to existing products or services or new product lines or services that can improve your overall competitiveness.

Your management plan should answer questions such as:

- How does your background/business experience help you in this business?

- What are your weaknesses and how can you compensate for them?

- Who will be on the management team?

- What are their strengths/weaknesses?

- What are their duties?

- Are these duties clearly defined?

- If a franchise, what type of assistance can you expect from the franchisor?

- Will this assistance be ongoing?

- What are your current personnel needs?

- What are your plans for hiring and training personnel?

- What salaries, benefits, vacations and holidays will you offer? If a franchise, are these issues covered in the management package the franchisor will provide?

- What benefits, if any, can you afford at this point?

If the business is to be a franchise, the operating procedures, manuals and materials devised by the franchisor should be included in this section of the business plan. Study these documents carefully when writing your business plan, and be sure to incorporate this material. The franchisor should assist you with managing your franchise. Take advantage of his or her expertise and develop a management plan that will ensure the success for your franchise and satisfy the needs and expectations of employees, as well as those of the franchisor.

THE BUSINESS PLAN — The Financial Management Plan

Sound financial management is one of the best ways for your business to remain profitable and solvent. How well you manage the finances of your business is the cornerstone of every successful business venture. Each year thousands of potentially successful businesses fail because of poor financial management. As a business owner, you will need to identify and implement policies that will lead to and ensure that you will meet your financial obligations.

To effectively manage your finances, plan a sound, realistic budget by determining the actual amount of money needed to open your business (start-up costs) and the amount needed to keep it open (operating costs). The first step to building a sound financial plan is to devise a start-up budget. Your start-up budget will usually include such one-time-only costs as major equipment, utility deposits, down payments, etc.

START-UP BUDGET

The start-up budget should allow for these expenses:

- Personnel (costs prior to opening)
- Occupancy
- Equipment
- Supplies
- Salaries/Wages
- Income
- Payroll expenses

- Legal/Professional fees
- Licenses/Permits
- Insurance
- Advertising/Promotions
- Accounting
- Utilities

OPERATING BUDGET

An operating budget is prepared when you are actually ready to open for business. The operating budget will reflect your priorities in terms of how you spend your money, the expenses you will incur and how you will meet those expenses (income). Your operating budget also should include money to cover the first three to six months of operation.

It should allow for the following expenses:

- Personnel
- Rent
- Loan payments
- Legal/Accounting

- Insurance
- Depreciation
- Advertising/Promotions
- Miscellaneous expenses

- Supplies
- Salaries/Wages
- Dues/Subscriptions/Membership Fees
- Repairs/Maintenance

- Payroll expenses
- Utilities
- Taxes

The financial section of your business plan should include any loan applications you've filed, a capital equipment and supply list, balance sheet, breakeven analysis, pro-forma income projections (profit and loss statement) and pro-forma cash flow. The income statement and cash-flow projections should include a three-year summary, detail by month for the first year, and detail by quarter for the second and third years.

The accounting system and the inventory control system that you will be using are generally addressed in this section of the business plan also. If a franchise, the franchisor may stipulate in the franchise contract the type of accounting and inventory systems you may use. If this is the case, he or she should have a system already intact and you will be required to adopt this system. Whether you develop the accounting and inventory systems yourself, have an outside financial advisor develop the systems, or the franchisor provides these systems, you will need to acquire a thorough understanding of each segment and how it operates. Your financial advisor can assist you in developing this section of your business plan.

The following questions should help you determine the amount of start-up capital you will need to purchase and open a franchise.

- How much money do you have?

- How much money will you need to purchase the franchise?

- How much money will you need for start-up?

- How much money will you need to stay in business?

Other questions that you will need to consider are:

- What type of accounting system will you use? Is it a single entry or dual entry system?

- What will your sales goals and profit goals for the coming year be? If a franchise, will the franchisor set your sales and profit goals? Or will he or she expect you to reach and retain a certain sales level and profit margin?

- What financial projections will you need to include in your business plan?

- What kind of inventory control system will you use?

Your plan should include an explanation of all projections. Unless you are thoroughly familiar with financial statements, get help in preparing your cash-flow and income statements and your balance sheet. Your aim is not to become a financial wizard, but to understand the financial tools well enough to gain their benefits. Your accountant or financial advisor can help you accomplish this goal.

TYPES OF BUSINESS ORGANIZATIONS

When organizing a new business, one of the most important decisions to be made is choosing the structure of the business. Factors influencing your decision about your business organization include:

- Legal restrictions

- Liabilities assumed

- Type of business operation

- Earnings distribution

- Capital needs

- Number of employees

- Tax advantages or disadvantages

- Length of business operation

The advantages and disadvantages of sole proprietorship, partnership, corporation, and the new hybrid Limited Liability Company are listed below.

SOLE PROPRIETORSHIP

This is the easiest and least costly way of starting a business. A sole proprietorship can be formed by simply finding a location and opening the door for business. There are likely to be fees to obtain business name registration, a fictitious name certificate and other necessary licenses. Attorney's fees for starting the business will be less than those of the other business forms because less preparation of documents is required and the owner has absolute authority over all business decisions.

PARTNERSHIP

There are several types of partnerships. The two most common types are general and limited partnerships. A general partnership can be formed simply by an oral agreement between two or more persons, but a legal partnership agreement drawn up by an attorney is highly recommended. Legal fees for drawing up a partnership agreement are higher than those for a sole proprietorship, but may be lower than incorporating. A partnership agreement could be helpful in solving any disputes. However, partners are responsible for the other partner's business actions, as well as their own.

A partnership agreement should include the following:

- Type of business

- Amount of equity invested by each partner

- Division of profit or loss

- Partners compensation

- Distribution of assets on dissolution

- Duration of partnership

- Provisions for changes or dissolving the partnership

- Dispute settlement clause

- Restrictions of authority and expenditures

- Settlement in case of death or incapacitation

CORPORATION

A business may incorporate without an attorney, but legal advice is highly recommended. The corporate structure is usually the most complex and is more costly to organize than the other two business forms. Control depends on stock ownership. Persons with the largest stock ownership, not the total number of shareholders, control the corporation. With control of stock shares or 51 percent of stock, a person or group is able to make policy decisions. Control is exercised through regular board of directors' meetings and annual stockholders' meetings. Records must be kept to document decisions made by the board of directors. Small, closely held corporations can operate more informally, but record keeping cannot be eliminated entirely. Officers of a corporation can be liable to stockholders for improper actions. Liability is generally limited to stock ownership, except where fraud is involved. You may want to incorporate as a "C" or "S" corporation.

LIMITED LIABILITY COMPANY (LLC)

The LLC is not a corporation, but it offers many of the same advantages. Many small business owners and entrepreneurs prefer LLCs because they combine the limited liability protection of a corporation with the "pass through" taxation of a sole proprietorship or partnership.

- LLCs have additional advantages over corporations.

- LLCs allow greater flexibility in management and business organization.

- LLCs do not have the ownership restrictions of S Corporations, making them ideal business structures for foreign investors.

- LLCs accomplish these aims without the IRS's restrictions for an S Corporation.

LLCs are now available in all 50 states and Washington, D.C. If you have other questions regarding LLCs, be sure to speak with a qualified legal and/or financial advisor.

SELECTING THE RESTAURANT SITE LOCATION

After determining a likely area best suited for the restaurant, be sure to obtain as many facts as you can about it: e.g., How many restaurants of the same kind are located in the area? Can you find out something about their sales volume? Since restaurants attract primarily local inhabitants, what is the population of the area? Is the trend of population increasing, stationary or declining? Are the people native-born, mixed or chiefly foreign? What do they do for a living? Are they predominantly laborers, clerks, executives or retired persons? Are they all ages or principally old, middle-aged or young? To help you gauge their buying power find out the average sales price and rental rates for homes in the area, the average real estate taxes for homes, the number of telephones, number of automobiles, and, if the figure is available, the per capita income. The zoning ordinances, parking availability, transportation facilities and natural barriers—such as hills and bridges—are important in considering the location of the restaurant.

Possible sources for this information are the Chamber of Commerce, trade associations, real estate companies, local newspapers, banks, city officials, and personal observations. If the United States Bureau of the Census has developed census tract information for the area in which you are interested, you will find this especially helpful. A census tract is a small, permanently established geographical area within a large city and its environs. The Census Bureau provides population and housing characteristics for each tract; their Web site is located at *http://www.census.gov*. This information can be valuable in measuring your market or service potential. Use the score sheet below to help in determining the best site location.

SCORE SHEET ON SITES

Grade each factor: "A" for excellent, "B" for good, "C" for fair and "D" for poor.

FACTOR	GRADE	FACTOR	GRADE
1. Centrally located to reach the market		10. Taxation burden	
2. Merchandise or raw materials available readily		11. Quality of police and fire protection	
3. Nearby competition situation		12. Housing availability for employees	
4. Transportation availability and rates		13. Environmental factors (schools, cultural, community activities, enterprise of business people)	
5. Quality of available employees			
6. Prevailing rates of employee wages		14. Physical suitability of building	
7. Parking facilities		15. Type and cost of lease	
8. Adequacy of utilities (sewer, water, power, gas)		16. Proven for future expansion	
9. Traffic flow		17. Estimate of overall quality of site in 10 years	

GOVERNMENTAL LAWS, REGULATIONS AND LICENSES

STATE REGISTRATION

Contact the Secretary of State's Office as early as possible and discuss your plans of opening a new business. All states have different regulations. This office will be able to describe all of the state's legal requirements and direct you to local and county offices for further registration. There is generally a fee required for registering a new business; most often it is less than $100. The city, county and/or state agency will most likely run a check to make certain no other businesses are currently using your particular business name. You may also be required to file and publish a fictitious name statement in a newspaper of general circulation in the area. You must renew this fictitious name periodically in order to legally protect it.

Should your state have an income tax on wages, request from the State Department of Labor or Taxation all pertinent information. This would include all required forms, tax tables and tax guides. Also contact the State Department of Employee Compensation for their regulations and filing procedures.

CITY BUSINESS LICENSE

Contact the city Business Department. Almost all cities and most counties require a permit to operate a business. Your application will be checked by the zoning board to make certain that the business conforms to all local regulations. Purchasing an existing restaurant will eliminate most of these clearances.

SALES TAX

Contact the state revenue or taxation agency concerning registry and collection procedures. Each state has its own various methods of taxation on the sale of food products. Most states which require collection on food and beverage sales also require an advance deposit or bond to be posted against future taxes to be collected. The state revenue agency will often waive the deposit and accept instead a surety bond from your insurance company. The cost of this insurance is usually around 5 percent of the bond.

Sales tax is collected only on the retail price paid by the end user. Thus when purchasing raw food products to produce menu items it will not be necessary to pay sales tax on the wholesale amount. However, you must present the wholesaler with your sales tax permit or number when placing orders, and sign a tax release card for their files. A thorough investigation into this area will be required for your particular state's requirements.

Certain counties and/or cities may also assess an additional sales tax in addition to the state sales tax. Hotels and resorts often have a separate room, or bed, tax. This entire issue needs to be thoroughly researched, as an audit in the future could present you with a considerable tax liability.

HEALTH DEPARTMENT LICENSE

The Health Department should be contacted as early as possible. A personal visit to discuss your plans and their needs would be in order. It would be to your advantage to show cooperation and compliance from the very beginning. The Health Department can and will close your facility until you comply with its regulations. A restaurant shut down by the Health Department will almost surely be ruined if the closure becomes public knowledge. Prior to opening day, the Health Department will inspect the restaurant. If the facilities pass the thorough inspection they will issue the license enabling the restaurant to open. The cost of the license is usually less than $50. Should they find faults in your facility, you will be required to have them corrected before they will issue a license.

Periodically during the year the Health Department will make unannounced inspections of the restaurant. An examination form will be filled out outlining their findings. You must have all violations rectified before their next inspection. You can be certain that they will be back to see if you have complied.

Many health inspections are brought about by customer complaints. The Health Department will investigate every call they receive. Depending upon the number of calls and the similarity among the complaints, a pattern will be formulated. They will then trace the health problem to its source. Usually the problem is a result of some mishandling of a food product by a member of the staff. However, the problem can sometimes be traced to your supplier.

Although the Health Department can at times seem like a terrific nuisance, they really are on your side; their goals and yours are the same. Cooperation between both sides will resolve all the restaurant's health problems and make it a safe environment.

Many states now have laws requiring that at least the manager—and in some states the entire staff—goes through and passes an approved health and sanitation program. Check with your state restaurant association. A list of all associations is located in the back of this book. The most common approved program is the ServSafe program developed by the NRA Educational Foundation. Materials may be purchased at *http://www.atlantic-pub.com* or by calling 800-541-1336. The ServSafe products, including instructor guides, answer sheets, instructor slides, manager training, food safety CD-ROMs and instructor tool kits, are available in English and Spanish.

FIRE DEPARTMENT PERMIT

A permit from the Fire Department, also referred to as an occupational permit, will be required prior to opening. As with the Health Department, contact the Fire Department as early as possible, preferably in person, and learn of their regulations and needs. The Fire Department inspectors will be interested in checking exhaust hoods, fire exits, extinguisher placements and the hood and sprinkler systems. Many city Fire Departments do not permit the use of open-flame candles, flaming foods or flaming liquor in the building. If this was your intention it would be best to ask in advance.

Based upon the size of the building, the local and national fire code, and the number of exits, the fire inspectors will establish a "capacity number" of people permitted in the building at one time. Follow their guidelines strictly, even if this means turning away customers because you've reached capacity.

BUILDING AND CONSTRUCTION PERMIT

Should you plan on doing any renovating to the restaurant that is going to change the structural nature of the building, you may need a local building permit.

Building permits are generally issued from the local Building and Zoning Board. The fee is usually around $100, or it may be based on a percentage of the total cost of the project. You will need to approach the building inspector with your blueprints or plans to initially determine if a permit is required. Should a permit be required he will inspect your plans ensuring that they meet all the local and federal ordinances and codes. Once the plans are approved a building permit will be issued. The building inspector will make periodic inspections of your work at various stages of completion to ensure that the actual construction is conforming to the approved plans.

SIGN PERMITS

Many local city governments are beginning to institute sign ordinances and restrictions. These ordinances restrict the sign's size, type, location and lighting, and the proximity of the sign to the business. The owners or managers of a shopping mall or shopping center may also further restrict the use and placement of signs.

STATE LIQUOR LICENSE

The state liquor license requires extensive investigation because of its complexity. Many states do not allow the sale of liquor in restaurants; others allow only beer and wine. Certain states vary the restrictions on sales of alcoholic beverages by county. A license to sell liquor in some states may cost but a few hundred dollars; in others a license can cost upwards of $100,000. Several states are on quota systems and licenses are not even available. Certain counties in some states prohibit liquor sales entirely. A thorough investigation concerning your particular state, possibly with your lawyer, is in order.

Once you do obtain a license, it is imperative that you adhere to its laws and regulations. Most states have several thousand rules, so many in fact that they must be put into book form to contain them all. Most are just based on common sense, and they all have a designated purpose. You can easily lose the license due to an infraction: obviously this would be disastrous and could spell ruin for your organization.

Make certain all employees are thoroughly familiar with all the liquor laws. Carefully train new employees; test them if necessary. Constantly reiterate the laws. Employees will become lax if they are not often reminded of this big responsibility.

FEDERAL IDENTIFICATION NUMBER

All employers, partnerships and corporations must have a Federal Identification Number. This number will be used to identify the business on all tax forms and other licenses. To obtain a federal identification number fill out Form 55-4, obtainable from the IRS. There is no charge. Also at this time request from the IRS the following publications, or you can download them via the Internet at *http://www.irs.gov:*

1. Publication #15, circular "Employer's Tax Guide."

2. Several copies of Form W-4, "Employer Withholding Allowance Certificate." Each new employee must fill out one of these forms.

3. Publication 334, "Tax Guide for Small Businesses."

4. From the Occupational Safety and Health Administration, request free copies of "All about O.S.H.A." and "O.S.H.A. Handbook for Small Businesses." Depending upon the number of employees you have, you will be subject to certain regulations from this agency. Their address is: O.S.H.A., U.S. Department of Labor, Washington, D.C. 20210, *http://osha.gov/.*

5. From the Department of Labor, request a free copy of "Handy Reference Guide to the Fair Labor Act." Contact: Department of Labor, Washington, D.C. 20210, *http://www.dol.gov.*

INTERNAL REVENUE REGISTRATION

In conjunction with the liquor license, you may also need to obtain from the Internal Revenue Service their tax stamps. Simply call the local IRS office and have them send you application Form 11 *(http://www.irs.gov).* Based on the information about the restaurant you supply on the form, the IRS will assess a fee. This application makes the IRS aware that you are engaging in the retail sale of liquor.

OPENING THE RESTAURANT BANK ACCOUNT

Opening a business bank account is a great deal more important than at first it may appear. If you received your financing through a local commercial bank, it is suggested you also use this bank for your business account, if it fills all your needs.

Whichever bank you decide to use, it is important that it can provide you with these services:

- Night deposits.

- All credit-card services (if you will be accepting them).

- Change service (coins, small bills).

- A line of credit to certain suppliers.

- Nearby location for daily transactions.

It is very important that you get to know all the bank personnel on a first-name basis, particularly the manager. You will be in the bank every day. Make an effort to meet them and introduce yourself. Their assistance in obtaining future loans and gaining credit references will be invaluable. It would be my suggestion to use a smaller bank, if it provides all your needs. Your account will mean a lot more to them than a larger bank.

Take plenty of time to shop around for the bank that will serve you the best. When you go into a prospective bank, ask to see the bank manager, tell him of your plans and what your needs are. All banks specialize in certain services. Look at what they charge for each transaction, and all other service charges. Compare very closely the handling charges on charge card deposits. A small percentage over thousands of dollars over a couple of years adds up to a great deal of money. Look at the whole picture very carefully. After you have selected a bank, you should order:

A. Checks

B. Deposit slips

C. Deposit book

D. Night deposit bags and keys

E. Coin wrappers for all change

F. Small bank envelopes

INSURANCE

Properly insuring a restaurant is similar to the coverage of any business enterprise where members of the public are in frequent attendance. Liability protection is of the utmost concern. Product liability is also desirable, as the consumption of food and beverages always presents a hazard. Described in this section are all the different types of insurance coverage applicable to all types of restaurants. By no means is it recommended that you should obtain all of this insurance, for you would probably be overinsured if you did. A discussion with your agent is needed to determine under which insurance coverages you should be placed. Any policy written, however, should contain a basic business plan of Fire/Theft/Liability/Workers' Compensation.

FIRE

Covers the buildings and all permanent fixtures belonging to and constituting a part of the structures. Coverage usually includes machinery used in building services such as air-conditioning systems, boilers, elevators, etc. Personal property may also be covered.

REPLACEMENT COST ENDORSEMENT

Provides for full reimbursement for the actual cost of repair or replacement of an insured building.

EXTENDED COVERAGE ENDORSEMENT

Covers property for the same amount as the fire policy against damage caused by wind, hail, explosion, riot, aircraft, vehicles and smoke.

VANDALISM

Covers loss or damage caused by vandalism or malicious mischief.

GLASS INSURANCE

Covers replacement of show windows, glass counters, mirrors, and structural interior glass broken accidentally or maliciously.

SPRINKLER DAMAGE

Insures against all direct loss to buildings or contents as a result of leakage, freezing, or breaking of sprinkler installations.

FLOOD INSURANCE

Flood insurance is written in areas declared eligible by the Federal Insurance Administration. Federally subsidized flood insurance is available under the National Flood Insurance Program.

EARTHQUAKE INSURANCE

Covers losses caused by earthquakes.

CONTENTS AND PERSONAL PROPERTY DAMAGE

- General property form
- Improvements and betterments ins.
- Extended coverage endorsement
- Replacement cost endorsement
- Boiler and machinery insurance
- Direct damage insurance

- Vandalism
- Consequential damage endorsement
- Business interruption (use and occupancy)

BUSINESS OPERATIONS INSURANCE

- Valuable papers
- Motor truck cargo owner's
- General liability
- Extra expense
- Owner's protective liability
- Umbrella liability
- License bonds
- Fiduciary liability
- Partnership
- Health insurance
- Major medical
- Dishonesty, Destruction and Disappearance
- Electrical signs
- Time element
- Earnings insurance
- Contractual liability
- Lease hold interest
- Fidelity bonds
- Liquor liability
- Life insurance
- Travel/Accident
- Comprehensive general liability
- Endorsement extending period of indemnity
- Transportation policy
- Business interruption
- Product liability
- Rental value insurance
- Personal injury vehicle
- Crime
- Business legal expense
- Group life insurance
- Key man insurance

WORKERS' COMPENSATION INSURANCE

Workers' Compensation insurance covers loss due to statutory liability as a result of personal injury or death suffered by an employee in the course of his or her employment. This insurance coverage pays all medical treatment and costs plus a percentage of the employee's salary due to missed time resulting from the injury. Workers' Compensation insurance is highly regulated by both state and federal agencies, particularly O.S.H.A. Be certain to obtain all the information that pertains to your particular state. Workers' Compensation insurance is mandatory in most states.

ORGANIZING THE PRE-OPENING ACTIVITIES

Opening a restaurant or any business is a great test of anyone's organizational and managerial abilities. It is imperative that communication be maintained with your key personnel. The best way to do this is to utilize the form at the back of this chapter. Keep track of the assignments that need to be completed, who the assignments are delegated to, and when they must be completed. Allow plenty of time for assignments and projects to be accomplished. Even the seemingly simplest task may uncover a web of tangles and delays. Delegate responsibilities whenever possible, but above all else, keep organized.

Maintain a collective composure and deal with people and problems on a level and consistent basis, and you'll be off to a great start.

FIRST-PRIORITY ITEMS

Suggested items that must be completed well ahead of opening date are:

1. List the restaurant's name and number in the phone book and yellow pages.

2. Order and install an employee time clock or appropriate software.

3. Allow shipping and lead time for:

    A. China, tables, chairs, settings, etc.
    B. Silverware.
    C. Equipment.
    D. Drop safe for office.
    E. Printing: menus, stationery, business cards, matches, napkins, etc.

4. Develop a list of all construction projects. It should include who is completing them, when they will be completed and a list of materials needed.

5. Set up a large calendar on the wall with deadlines, when deliveries will be expected, construction projects finished, equipment installed, meetings, and of course, the opening date.

6. Contact the art galleries or artists' groups in your area. They may be able to supply you with artwork to be displayed in the restaurant on a consignment basis.

PRE-OPENING PROMOTION

Described below are some pre-opening promotional ideas. It should be noted that there is a definite distinction between promotion and advertising. Promotion involves creating an interest in a new project usually at little or no cost.

As soon as possible, put up the new restaurant sign or a temporary sign explaining briefly the name of the new restaurant, type of restaurant, hours of operation and the opening date. People by nature are most interested in what is occurring in their neighborhood; give them something to start talking about. This is perhaps the best and least expensive promotion you can do.

1. Meet with the advertising representatives for the local papers. Determine advertising costs and look into getting a small news story published describing the restaurant.

2. Have plenty of the restaurant's matches and business cards on hand as soon as possible: they're a great source of publicity.

3. Join the Better Business Bureau and the local Chamber of Commerce. Besides lending credibility to your organization, they often can supply you with some very good free publicity.

4. When you place your employment ad in the classified section always list the type of restaurant and location. This inexpensive classified advertising will help spread the word. Many people in the restaurant industry also love to find new restaurants to try out.

INITIALLY CONTACTING PURVEYORS AND SUPPLIERS

Approximately six to eight weeks prior to the scheduled opening date, it will be necessary to contact all the local suppliers and meet with their sales representatives. It would be advisable to have the kitchen and bar managers present if possible. These companies will be supplying the restaurant with its raw materials. Make certain each sales representative understands that quality products are your top consideration. Competition is fierce among both sales representatives and suppliers. Let each know you are considering all companies equally. Never become locked into using one purveyor only. Shop around, so to speak, and always be willing to talk with new sales representatives.

Consider these points when choosing a purveyor:

1. Quality of products. Accept nothing but A-1.

2. Reliability.

3. Delivery days. All deliveries should arrive at a designated time.

4. Is the salesperson really interested in your business?

5. Does he seem to believe in what he sells?

6. Terms in billing (interest, credit, etc.).

7. Is the company local—for emergencies?

8. From the first meeting with the sales representative you should obtain:

   A. Credit applications to be filled out and returned.

   B. Product lists or catalogues describing all the products.

   C. References of the restaurants they are currently servicing in the area. Check them out!

You should supply them with a list of the products you will be purchasing, with estimates as to the amount of each item you will be using every week.

Emphasize to the sales representative that price is certainly an important consideration, but not your only one, when selecting a supplier. Point out to the sales representative the other concerns you have about using their company. Indicate that you do intend to compare prices among the various companies but wouldn't necessarily switch suppliers due to a one-time price undercutting. Loyalty is important to sales representatives; they need to expect that order from you each week. But at the same time let them know they must be on their toes and earn your business.

Most companies offer a discount to restaurants once they purchase a certain number of cases. Keep this in mind when comparing prices and suppliers. Choosing a supplier is often a difficult task, with so many variable factors to consider. Begin to analyze these problems in terms of the overall picture, and your purchasing decisions will become consistently more accurate.

PAYROLL

Prior to the opening date there will be many people on the payroll. You will need the assistance of personnel to assemble chairs, do odd painting, hang pictures, and do anything required so that the opening date may be achieved. Many of these temporary employees may be utilized for various jobs in the restaurant after opening. The time clock should certainly be used during this period for better control. Overtime must be carefully monitored, and if at all possible, avoided. This will require a great deal of organization between assignments and scheduling.

Many of these jobs will be boring and tedious. Compensate these employees well for their efforts. Having a free lunch or dinner available would certainly be greatly appreciated. These small tokens on your behalf will be returned in gratitude many times over the small cost incurred.

In most restaurants the Internal Bookkeeper calculates and prepares the payroll. We highly recommend the use of Quickbooks computer software, Peachtree or other competing software for payroll processing. In addition, Quickbooks will be very useful in other parts of your business and in your business planning. Quickbooks can be located at *http://www.quickbooks.com*, Peachtree at *http://www.peachtree.com.*

However, like many companies you may prefer to use a computerized payroll service or your accountant. All computerized payroll service companies operate in a similar manner. The bookkeeper totals the number of hours each employee worked for the pay period from the time cards. This information is transmitted to the computer company via telephone, or data input sheets may be picked up from your office as part of the service. Using the rate and number of hours worked, the computer calculates the gross pay, overtime, social security, federal and state taxes, other miscellaneous deductions, and the net check amount. Based upon this information, each check will be printed along with a corresponding stub. The checks are verified and returned, often within 24 hours. Payroll checks are issued out of a special checking account which will be set up with your bank. This will enable you to transfer only the exact funds needed for the payroll as a safety measure. The service will also provide a report detailing the amounts withheld from each check. This will enable you to easily prepare the IRS Form 941, ""Employers Federal Quarterly Tax Return." Use the information on Form 941 to compute your quarterly state unemployment compensation form. Annually, the service will also prepare a W-2 form for each employee who received wages during the year. The utilization of a computerized payroll service is highly recommended. Look ahead to the section on payroll preparation in Chapter 16, "Internal Bookkeeping."

PUBLIC UTILITIES

Notify public utility companies of your intention to be operating by a certain date. Allow plenty of lead time for completion. Don't lose valuable time because the utilities are not hooked up yet. Some of these companies may require a deposit before they will issue service. Every company and city has different policies, so be sure to investigate yours thoroughly.

PHONE COMPANY

You will need at least two phone lines for any restaurant and probably three to four for a restaurant that takes reservations. Don't forget about data lines and a fax line. Don't loose customers because they can't get through. You should have two to three phones in the offices, one to two extensions at the entrance area, one to two extensions in the bar, and a public pay phone. The phones in the entrance area and bar may be wired so that they cannot call long distance. This prevents misuse by customers and employees. Place local emergency numbers at all phones.

You will need some sort of intercom, handheld radio system and/or paging system throughout the restaurant, so you can speak from your position to key areas for any information you may need to communicate. A discussion with your local phone company business office about your needs will reveal your many options. A music intercom paging system is also available; see the discussion in the section on music.

GAS AND ELECTRIC COMPANIES

All major equipment need special hookups that can only be completed by trained technicians of either the gas or electric company or by authorized representatives. These technicians should be contacted as early as possible to come evaluate the amount of work required. In many cases they will need to schedule the work several weeks ahead of time.

Many gas and electric companies have service contracts that may be purchased. If available, it is highly recommended that you purchase them. Equipment that is maintained to the manufacturer's specifications will last longer and operate both more effectively and efficiently. One particular item that should be in any service contract is the calibrating of the kitchen ovens. It is critical that all ovens register their temperatures accurately for consistent cooking results. Most ovens need to be calibrated every month.

Set up a loose-leaf binder to contain all the information on your equipment and its maintenance schedules. Included in this binder should be warranties, brochures, equipment schematics, operating instructions, maintenance schedules, part lists, order forms, past service records, manufacturers' phone numbers, a chart showing which circuit breaker operates each piece of equipment, etc. Keep this manual up to date from the very beginning. Become aware of your equipment's needs and act accordingly. Train your employees thoroughly in the proper use of all equipment, and it will serve the restaurant well for many years.

WATER

Water is different in all parts of the country due to the type of chemical particles it contains. Water that has been subjected to a chemical treatment plant may contain a high level of chlorine. Water taken directly from the water table will contain any number of additives depending upon the geological makeup of the soil where it came from. Different types of water can give different results when used in cooking. The state Department of Natural Resources can give you information concerning the water's chemical makeup in the local area.

Chemical particles in the water can have a particularly bad effect in the brewing of fresh coffee. Food recipes using water and cocktails made with water will also be affected.

Several companies now have on the market filtering devices which attach directly to the water lines. If prescribed, filters need only be connected to the water lines that are used for drinking/cooking water. Bathroom and dishwasher lines would not require a filter. Filtering devices are usually tube-shaped canisters which contain charcoal or a special filtering paper. Discuss your particular situation with the state Department of Natural Resources and the sales representative for your coffee supplier.

SERVICE PERSONNEL NEEDED

LOCKSMITH

A registered or certified locksmith must be contacted to change over the locks as soon as you occupy the building. Keys to locked areas should be issued on a "need to have" basis. Only employees that need to have access to a locked area to perform their jobs should have keys to that lock. The locksmith can set door locks so that certain keys may open some doors, but not others. Only the owner and manager should have a master key to open every door. Each key will have its own identification number and "Do Not Duplicate" stamped on it. Should there be a security breach, you can easily see who had access to that particular area. The restaurant should be entirely rekeyed when key-holding personnel leave or someone looses his or her keys. Safe combinations should periodically be changed by the locksmith.

Below is an example of a key system chart which should be made up and kept in a secure place in the office. In the example, the key code corresponds to a particular key that only opens doors with a similar letter. By determining who should have access to an area and who shouldn't, you will be able to develop an airtight security system. It is important that no one has a key to the liquor, wine or china storage areas. It is important to develop a control system which has as its basis the knowledge that no one but the manager has a key to these areas.

KEY SYSTEM CHART AREA	KEY CODE	ISSUED TO (Employee)
Front Door	A	#2
Back Door	A	#2
Food Storage (Dry)	B	#6
Freezer	B	#6
Walk-Ins	B	#6
Reach-In	B	#6
Liquor Storage	**	Manager Only
Wine Storage	**	Manager Only
Bar Area	C	#3, 4
China Storage	**	Manager Only
Cleaning Supplies	D	#2, 3, 5, 6
Offices	E	#2, 3, 6, 7
Safe Combination	-	#7

** Manager Master Key   Janitors – 5   Dining Room Manager – 2
Kitchen Director – 6   Bar Manager – 3   Bookkeeper – 7
Bartenders – 4

FIRE AND INTRUSION ALARMS

Every restaurant should have two separate alarm systems: a system for fire, smoke and heat detection and one for intrusion and holdup.

The fire detection system consists of smoke monitors and heat sensors, strategically placed around the building. This system must be audible for evacuations and directly connected to either the Fire Department or a private company with 24-hour monitoring service. In newer buildings the sensors also activate the sprinkler system. Most cities and states also require restaurants to install a hood system in the kitchen areas. This consists of a sprinkler-type system situated above equipment with an exposed cooking surface or flame. The system may be operated either automatically or manually. When released, a chemical foam is immediately sprayed out over the area. This is particularly effective in stopping grease fires. Once activated the system will automatically shut off the gas or electric service to the equipment. In order to regain service the company which installed the system must reset it. As previously indicated, check with the local Fire Department for further recommendations. They may also direct you towards a reputable fire and safety service company.

An intrusion alarm system is recommended for any restaurant. Begin to research this subject by initially contacting the Police Department and advising them of your intentions. Contact several of the recommended companies and ask for a survey and proposal (usually at no charge) of the building and your needs.

The security system should contain magnetic contact switches on the main doors, windows, internal doors, and other places of entry such as trapdoors and roof hatches. Don't overlook the air conditioner vents. The interior of the building should be monitored by strategically placed motion detectors that are zoned so that if one fails, the entire system will continue to function. The safe and/or the area around the safe should most definitely be monitored. The locking-type holdup buttons, which may only be released with a key, are an excellent option and should be placed in the cashier area, bar and the office. Video monitors can also be provided by most alarm companies.

Another recommended option to obtain from a private monitoring service is the monitoring of the temperature in the freezers and walk-ins. A temperature-sensitive device may be installed in the freezer and walk-ins. When the temperature rises to a certain level, it will set off an alarm at the monitoring station. The operator may then call the restaurant manager or dispatch the refrigeration repairman. Some of these security service companies may also provide other services including guard service in the lounge area and escort service to the bank. These companies must of course be bonded, licensed and insured.

As previously indicated, the installation of an alarm system in the restaurant is almost a necessity. The loss of business and profits due to burglary, vandalism or arson is not to be gambled upon. As a side note, the installation of an alarm system will increase the value of the property, and a 24-hour monitored system may make you eligible with your insurance company for a rate reduction of 5 to 10 percent on the insurance premium.

DISHWASHER CHEMICAL COMPANY

Contact all the dishwasher chemical suppliers in the area and meet with their representatives. In most areas there will be four to five companies which may provide the dishwasher with the service it requires. Several of these companies maintain large research staffs that are constantly developing innovative chemicals and devices which will lower the machine's energy usage and chemical use and subsequently reduce your overall operational cost. Their field service people are experts due to the extensive in-house training they have had. They will monitor the entire system making sure the machine and staff are working together for maximum efficiency. A local company supplying the chemicals and service as a sideline cannot possibly maintain the service offered by these national companies. Clean dishes and silverware are an absolute necessity for a restaurant. Don't gamble on the outcome by not using an expert.

KNIFE SHARPENER

The services of a professional knife sharpener should be utilized in any restaurant. Sharp knives are essential. Generally a service contract may be purchased so that all knives and the blades of the cutting and slicing machines will be sharpened on a regular basis. In between servicing, the staff may keep the blades honed on a sharpening oil stone or ceramic sharpening sword.

SANITATION SERVICE

In most counties, a private business must provide its own garbage pickup. A restaurant of any size has a great deal of waste. In order to preserve a proper health environment, the services of a trash removal or sanitation service company will be required.

Receive quotes from all the sanitation companies in the area. Prices may vary considerably depending upon who purchases the dumpsters. You may wish to get the advice from your Health Department for the selection. Any service contract should contain provisions for the following:

1. Dumpsters with locking tops;

2. Periodic steam cleaning of the dumpsters;

3. Fly pesticide sprayed on the inside of the dumpster;

4. Number of days for pickup; and

5. Extra pickups for holidays and weekends.

Some restaurant waste may actually be used by manufacturers in the area. Soap manufacturers would be interested in purchasing all the meat and fat scraps for a few cents a pound. Pig farmers may buy all the food scraps. These companies will provide special containers to store the products. Scrap glass from empty liquor bottles may also be sold or donated to the local recycling or ecology project.

PARKING LOT MAINTENANCE

Parking lots will need periodic maintenance besides the daily duty of light sweeping and picking up of any trash. Painting new lines for the parking spaces should be done annually. Blacktop surfaces will also require a sealant to be spread over the surface periodically. This stops water from seeping into it. Winter climates will require snow removal and possibly salting and sanding of the lot. Most of these services may be purchased under contract.

PLUMBER

A local plumber will be needed to handle any miscellaneous work and emergencies that may come up. The plumber must have 24-hour emergency service. Make every effort possible to retain the plumber that did the original work on the building. He will be thoroughly familiar with the plumbing and know why certain procedures were performed. This can be a terrific advantage.

Due to the large amount of grease that must go through the restaurant's plumbing, clogs and backups will be the major problem. Extra-wide pipes should be fitted to the dishwasher and sink drains. Grease will collect in the elbows and fittings along the plumbing. When cold water is put through the drain the grease will solidify, closing the inside diameter of the pipe. Food products or paper may then lodge into these areas causing a clog which will result in a backup. The plumber must have an electric snake and the necessary acids to remove the clog. A hand snake and plunger should always be on hand in the kitchen.

ELECTRICIAN

As with the plumber it would be a great advantage to retain the original electrician who worked on the building. An electrician will be needed when equipment is moved or installed. If it has not been done already, the electrician should check out and label all the circuits and breakers in the building. The electrician should also be on 24-hour emergency service.

REFRIGERATION SERVICE

The most important consideration when choosing a refrigeration company is how fast they can respond to emergencies. At any given time the refrigeration systems and freezer could go out, which may result in the loss of several thousand dollars in food. Make certain any prospective company understands this crucial point. They must have 24-hour service.

In some situations, there may be no hope in getting the refrigeration units back to work in time, usually because of a broken part that must be replaced. Short of losing all the food, there are some possible solutions. You might contact the purveyors you use who have large refrigeration units. They may be able to store the food temporarily. Call the tractor trailer companies in the area: they may have an empty refrigeration truck which could be rented; simply transfer the perishables into it for storage.

A fully loaded freezer will usually stay cold enough to keep frozen foods frozen for two days if the cabinet is not opened. In a cabinet with less than half a load, food may not stay frozen for more than a day.

If normal operation cannot be resumed before the food will start to thaw, use dry ice. If dry ice is placed in the freezer soon after the power is off, 125 pounds should keep the temperature below freezing for two to three days in a 10-cubic-foot cabinet with half a load, three to four days in a loaded cabinet.

Place dry ice on cardboard or small boards on top of the packages, and do not open the freezer again except to put in more dry ice or to remove it when normal operation is resumed. Monitor the temperature with an accurate recording device.

EXTERMINATOR

Exterminators must be licensed professionals with references from the other restaurants they service. You may wish to consult the Health Department for their recommendations. Exterminators can eliminate any pest-control problems, such as rats, cockroaches, ants, termites, flies, etc. Have several companies come in to appraise the building. They are experts and can read the "telltale" signs that might otherwise be missed. Take their suggestions. The company selected should be signed to a service contract as soon as possible. This is not an area to cut corners or try to do yourself—it won't pay in the long run.

PLANT MAINTENANCE

If the restaurant contains a lot of large expensive plants, and many do, you may need the services of a plant maintenance company. A professional plant-care person can provide all the necessary services to protect these investments: watering, pruning, transplanting, arranging, etc. Contact the companies in the area and get their opinions, quotes and references. They must be made aware that they are working in an environment where toxic sprays may only be used with the approval of the Health Department, and even then very cautiously.

OUTSIDE LANDSCAPING

You may desire to have the exterior areas of the restaurant professionally designed and landscaped. An appealing exterior is at least as important as the interior. You may have little room to work with, but a landscaper can put together a design that can be very appealing. Contact the local landscapers and get their opinions, designs, quotes and references.

FLORIST

Should you decide to have fresh cut flowers, you will need to contact a local florist. Each week the florist will set aside a selection of cut flowers of your choice. Many restaurants use only a single flower or rose in a long-stem vase with some fern for backing. Should you decide to do this, make sure there is a large supply of backup flowers. Some customers will take them home when they leave. Adding fresh water with a little dissolved sugar or a chemical provided by the florist to the vases every day will keep the flowers fresh-looking for a week or more.

EXHAUST HOOD CLEANING SERVICE

Contact a company which specializes in the cleaning of exhaust hoods and ventilation systems. They should appraise and inspect the whole ventilation system prior to opening. Depending upon the amount and type of cooking performed, they will recommend a service which will keep the system free from grease and carbon buildup. Usually twice-a-year cleaning is required. Without this service, the exhaust hoods and vents will become saturated with grease, causing a dangerous fire hazard. All that would be necessary to ignite a fire would be a hot spark landing on the grease-saturated hood. Most of these companies also offer grease and fat (deep fryer oil) removal.

HEATING AND AIR-CONDITIONING

You will need the services of a company that can respond 24 hours a day at a moment's notice. Losing the heating system in the winter or the air-conditioning in the summer will force the restaurant to close. Make certain the company is reliable with many references.

Heating and air-conditioning systems need regular service and preventative maintenance to ensure they function at maximum efficiency. Energy and money will be wasted if the system is not operating correctly. A service contract should be developed with these companies to ensure the machines are being serviced to the manufacturer's schedule. Keep the contract and all additional information in the equipment manual previously described.

JANITORIAL AND MAINTENANCE SERVICE

Depending upon the size and operating hours of the restaurant, you may wish to use the services of a professional cleaning company. This is highly recommended. Restaurant cleanliness is such an important area, it shouldn't be left to chance by having an amateur responsible for it.

The cleaning service usually arrives during the night after closing time. They will clean and maintain the areas previously agreed upon in the service contract. Their work is guaranteed. Never will a customer enter the restaurant and see a dirty fork left on the floor from the night before.

Cleanliness also has an important effect upon the employees. A spotless restaurant will create the environment for positive employee work habits. They will become more organized, neater and cleaner in their jobs and the areas they affect. The maintenance service company selected must have impeccable references. The company should be insured against liability and employee pilferage. Employees should be bonded. You will probably need to give the owner of the company her own keys to the entrance, maintenance closets, security system, and possibly the office, for cleaning. It must be made very clear that food and liquor are completely off limits to maintenance employees.

Some important factors to consider when choosing a maintenance company:

    A. Can they assist with cleaning prior to opening?

B. Bids for the job. They vary widely: look at the contracts and proposals closely.

C. The hours they will be in the restaurant.

D. Cleaning supplies: who buys the soaps, chemicals, etc.

E. Have a trial period written into the contract.

F. Have your lawyer examine the contract before signing.

G. How will you communicate to discuss problems?

H. References from other restaurants.

I. Make them aware that no toxic chemicals are allowed in the kitchen.

J. Inexperienced companies can cause damage to items by cleaning them incorrectly. Use a company with a track record.

K. All doors should be locked once the employees are inside. The perimeter alarm system should also be on.

L. Garbage emptied from the offices should be kept in dated plastic garbage bags and saved for one week. They may contain important information or papers accidentally thrown away.

M. Listed below are some basic maintenance functions any service contract should contain. This is just a basic outline, the actual contract must contain specific items that must be cleaned and when. Both yourself and the maintenance company's supervisor should have a check-off list of everything that must be completed each night. The morning following the service, walk through the restaurant spot-checking from the check-off sheet that all items have been completed as prescribed. Notify the supervisor immediately of any unsatisfactory work. At first, it may take a great deal of communication to get the desired results. Once operating a few months however, it will run smoothly.

Items to be cleaned daily:

1. All floors washed and treated.

2. Vacuum entire restaurant.

3. Dust: windowsills, woodwork, pictures, chairs, tables, etc.

4. Outside area—sweep and clean; patrol parking lot for trash.

5. Public bathrooms—clean, sanitize and deodorize; replace supplies: toilet paper, soap, napkins, tampons, etc.

6. Trash containers—empty, sterilize.

7. All sinks and floor drains cleaned.

8. Maintenance room—clean and organize.

Weekly services:

1. All windows cleaned inside and out.

2. Polish all chairs and woodwork.

3. Strip, wax and polish decorative floors.

Annually:

1. Steam clean all carpets.

As previously indicated, these examples describe a generalized outline of some of the major points a service contract should contain. All of these areas plus the ones that pertain to your restaurant need to be expanded to detail precisely how, when and what needs to be done.

Some manufacturers include in their equipment detailed instructions for the cleaning of their product. Special cleaners must be used on some equipment. Improperly cleaning a piece of equipment can ruin it forever. Keep all of this information in a loose-leaf binder in the office. The cleaning supervisor should have access to this manual and must be thoroughly familiar with its contents.

OTHER SERVICES AND SYSTEMS

CIGARETTE MACHINES/CIGARS/ELECTRONIC GAMES

Cigarettes, cigars and electronic games can provide a small additional source of revenue for the restaurant with little or no investment if they are pertinent to the restaurant's environment. Cigarettes and cigars are provided as a service to customers and should always be available; electronic games are not a necessity and should be utilized only if they are compatible with the restaurant's atmosphere. Distributors for all of these products may be found in the yellow pages of most city directories.

Cigarette machines are usually installed in the restaurant for free. The distributor will service the machine, refilling the cigarettes and removing the change. Some distributors may only carry certain types of cigarettes. Periodically they will issue the restaurant a check for a small percentage of the total sales or a specified amount for each pack sold.

Cigars for the bar and entrance area may also be purchased from these same distributors. Most cigars have fixed prices already printed on them; you may not exceed this price. Cigars are usually bought wholesale for about half the manufacturer's predetermined retail price.

Depending upon the type of clientele and the image of the establishment, you might look into the leasing of electronic games. There are numerous types of games available. You may choose from the more traditional games, like the pinball machine, or a whole new array of computerized video games. Some of these games have become extremely popular and can contribute a good sum of additional revenue.

Most companies lease the machines to the restaurant. There will be various terms from which to choose for each machine. Service to the games should be included in any contract. Many of these companies can also provide TVs, wide-picture screens, and movies with projection equipment.

Prior to contracting for any of these electronic games or video equipment, carefully consider the pros and cons. If the restaurant's atmosphere is right, some of these games can bring in substantial additional income. However, keep in mind that you are primarily in the restaurant business—the last thing you want to do is turn away any of your regular restaurant customers.

COFFEE EQUIPMENT

All major coffee distributors offer the same basic plan to restaurants. They will provide all the equipment necessary for coffee service including: brewing machines, filters, pots and maintenance and installation of all equipment. All that is required from you is to sign a contract stating that you will buy their coffee exclusively. The price of all the equipment and maintenance is included in the price of the coffee.

You could buy all your own equipment and pay to have someone install and maintain it. This would enable you to purchase coffee from any company at reduced prices. However, a large capital outlay would be necessary. Since there is no great advantage to doing this, it is recommended that most restaurants use the coffee distributor contract method.

There are many different coffee blends available. Coffee is an extremely important part of any dining experience: get the finest and most popular blend available. Have the restaurant employees try the different blends under consideration in a blind tasting. When negotiating with the coffee salespeople, inform them that you want brand-new equipment. They are competing for your business, but once you sign the contract you will be locked in to it. Use this leverage now while you have it. Placing the coffee machines in the main and service bars for the making of coffee drinks would increase efficiency greatly. Various specialty teas may be purchased from these distributors. Sugar packets and sugar substitute packages may also be purchased from these companies. For an additional charge your restaurant's name and logo can be imprinted on the outside of each packet.

SODA AND DRAFT BEER SYSTEMS

Soda and draft beer systems may be contracted in the same manner as the coffee arrangement. National brand soda and beer distributors will connect all the hoses, valves, taps and guns needed to operate the bar, generally at no cost. You will be obligated to sign a contract stating that you will purchase their products exclusively. The price of the system is passed on to you as you purchase soda canisters and kegs of beer. The distributor will also provide promotional material such as wall plaques, neon lights, drink coasters, etc.

These systems do occasionally break down, so maintain at least two cases of each type of soda in bottles or cans, and three to four cases of beer in the storeroom. Draught beer and soda lines must be flushed out every week. The cost of this service is usually put upon the restaurant. You may do this yourself, and many people do; however, it is recommended that the services of a professional be used. They are experts and have the proper equipment to do the job thoroughly. Cleaning these lines is not something which should be experimented with. Soda and beer is no better than the lines through which it flows. The distributors can recommend a service.

ICE CREAM FREEZERS/MILK DISPENSERS

Many other companies offer similar contracts for the use of equipment when you guarantee to purchase their product exclusively. Ice cream freezers, milk dispensers and various other kitchen equipment is available. Your sales representative will have all the information about the equipment available.

These arrangements may be very beneficial for small restaurants that have limited capital. Whatever your financial situation is, do a thorough, careful investigation into the terms of the service contract. In some cases, the price of the product may be so high you would be better off purchasing equipment. You should always compare competitive prices of the products after several months of operation. The free equipment may not justify the total cost of the product. Should you decide to sign the contract and use the free equipment, remember that you may be locked in for a long time. Be sure to request new equipment from the sales representative.

All the freezers and dispensers that are to be left in the open should have some sort of locking device on them for better control. Small ice cream freezers are also available for use in the bar should you serve a lot of cocktails made with ice cream.

LINEN SERVICE

When tablecloths and napkins are used on the tables the services of a linen company will be needed to clean and press them. Tablecloths and napkins are an integral part of the table setting. They must be spotless and wrinkle free. A poorly folded or soiled tablecloth will make a lasting negative impression on the customer. There are various options and methods for accomplishing this important service. In choosing a linen service, you must look carefully at your restaurant's available capital and sales volume. These factors will determine which option is the most economical for the establishment.

The linen service will provide the restaurant with tablecloths, napkins, uniforms and bar towels. They will pick up dirty linen and leave clean ready-to-use items, ensuring they have left enough linen to carry you through until the next delivery. Generally there are two fees for this service. The restaurant will be charged for the use of the linen and for cleaning and pressing. You may also be charged for linen that is torn or soiled from misuse. Many medium to large restaurants purchase their own linen from their food-service supplier. The linen company would then be used to service the used linen. If you have the capital to spend on purchasing all your own linen, this way is usually advantageous. During the course of a year new linen will be needed to replace torn and soiled items. Remember to allocate funds for this and to compute this figure into the total cost when examining the options.

Many large-volume restaurants install their own in-house laundry systems. Hotels have been doing this for years. Restaurants can under the right circumstances save a great deal of money. There are many different machines and systems available. Some are very good and have built solid reputations, while many others have just entered this growing market and do not seem to have all the mechanical bugs quite worked out.

Examine all machines that are available. In making a choice about which laundry system and machines to use, get as many references as possible. Call other restaurants and hotels; see what machines they are using. They will tell you quite honestly if they are satisfied with the results. Service warranties and the machine's load capacity are two important considerations. Machines use a great deal of electricity or gas and a lot of hot water. Compute these additional costs into the total projection. Detergents and soaps must also be considered in these costs. A complete detergent system may be set up by the dishwashing chemical supplier. You will also need to hire a person to do the laundry every day. This employee must be trained precisely in the operation and maintenance of the equipment.

The big development in the in-house laundry market came a few years ago with the introduction of Visa material. Visa requires no ironing or pressing when washed and dried. The material is ideal for tablecloths and napkins. Visa is extremely strong and durable. Perhaps the only disadvantage it may have over conventional material is that water tends to bead on it, rather than absorb into it. The napkins are smoother and more likely to slide off one's lap than conventional cloth.

When ordering tablecloths and napkins figure approximately six times the number of seats for napkins, and six times the number of tables for tablecloths. You will need one set for the initial setting; two to three more sets for changing during the evening (adjust figure for your needs); and one to two sets will be either at the cleaners or in the laundry room.

A complete in-house laundry system costs several thousand dollars to set up and get into operation. A thorough examination of all costs and available capital is required to see if the investment can be made. Over a number of years the system will easily recoup the initial investment many times over in savings.

MUSIC

Music in the background of the restaurant sets the mood and enhances the atmosphere. Music is a very important part of any dining experience.

The most inexpensive way to provide a music system for the restaurant is to set it up yourself. Contact a local stereo dealer. After examining the acoustics in the building he will be able to suggest a system which will best meet your needs. Take care to camouflage the speakers into the surroundings. Place the cassette deck in an area where usually there is an employee stationed, such as the bar or cashier stand. The speakers should have individual volume controls for each area. Long-playing cassettes with the type of music that befits the restaurant's atmosphere should be used. A radio station should never be used. The problem with this system is that tapes must be changed periodically. There will be a pause whenever a tape runs out and is being changed.

There are systems available that use special CD players, long-playing tapes or multiple CD changers which play for several hours then start all over again without pausing. Tapes are available for every musical category. The entire system in many cases may be leased. A paging system can also be installed.

Live music is also a consideration for the restaurant. Live music and entertainment is usually centered in the bar and lounge area. Music generated throughout the restaurant will create an interest, drawing customers back into the lounge after dining. Most customers would not mind waiting for a table in the lounge, knowing they will be entertained. Live music will draw restaurant diners looking for entertainment or dancing after dinner. The restaurant will also attract customers for the lounge and bar business, usually late at night. Some restaurant managers affix a cover charge or a drink minimum for people who wish to come in for the live entertainment only.

Live music must be consistent with the restaurant's atmosphere and type of clientele. Rather than attracting customers you can easily turn them away by not having the right group or band. Remember that your establishment is a restaurant first and a lounge second. Personally sit in on the band's audition to make certain the right group is employed. Go over all the material they will be playing. The group should maintain a certain volume level during the night; music should be in the background, not domineering.

Live music will be rather expensive. An average band will cost an upwards of a thousand dollars for three or four nights. However, if they blend in well and attract customers, the additional expense may be recouped many times over through increased food and liquor sales. Drawing customers only to the lounge may not seem like a benefit at first, but this will expose potential customers to the restaurant. Live entertainment can be a great source of additional publicity.

MUSIC LICENSING

If you are interested in playing recorded music in the restaurant you will need permission (a license) to play records, CDs or tapes in your establishment. Although most people buy a tape or CD thinking it becomes their property, there is a distinction in the law between owning a copy of the CD and owning the songs on the CD. There is also a difference between a private performance of copyrighted music and a public performance. Most people recognize that purchasing a CD doesn't give them the right to make copies of it to give or sell to others. The record company and music publishers retain those rights. Similarly, the music on the CDs and tapes still belongs to the songwriter, composer or music publisher of the work. When you buy a tape or CD, the purchase price covers only your private listening use, similar to the "home" use of "home videos." When you play these tapes or CDs in your restaurant it becomes a public performance. Songwriters, composers and music publishers have the exclusive right of public performance of their musical works under U.S. copyright law. There are some distinctions in the law if the performance is by means of public communication of TV or radio transmissions and played by eating, drinking, retail and certain other establishments of a certain size which use a limited number of speakers or TVs. Further, the reception must not be further transmitted from the place where it is received (to another room, for example), and there must be no admission charged.

There are two licensing agencies in the United States: BMI and ASCAP. You can contact ASCAP at 800-95-ASCAP (*http://www.ascap.com*) and BMI at 212-586-2000 (*http://www.bmi.com/home.asp*). We highly recommend that you contact both BMI and ASCAP to ensure your compliance.

HOW MUCH CHINA AND SILVERWARE TO ORDER

The following chart is based on an average dining room in a moderately priced restaurant. To compute, multiply the number indicated by the number of seats in the restaurant. Keep in mind that all dishwashers and machines work at different speeds. Use this as a guide in ordering.

This chart will provide a basic outline to indicate what will be required in an average dinner restaurant. Not maintaining enough stock will slow up service. Too much stock will cause you to store it in the restaurant, tying up cash. Figures will need to be adjusted depending on the menu and how many uses you have for the same piece of china or silverware.

Bar glasses are diversified and it is difficult to estimate the usage of each. If you have a mechanical dishwasher in the bar area, you will not require as much stemware.

CHINA	FLATWARE	GLASSES
Dinner plate...................2	Teaspoon 5	Water glass 3
Bread plate....................3	Soup spoon 1	Wineglass 1
Salad bowl 2	Tablespoon ....½	
Soup bowl 2	Iced-tea spoon ....½	
Sauce dish 1½	Fork 3	
Dessert plate.................2	Salad fork 2	
Cup/Mug.........................3	Oyster fork 1	
Saucer 3	Knife 2	
	Steak knife 1	

WORKSHEETS

The following worksheets, provided courtesy of the Small Business Administration, will aid the restaurant manager greatly in estimating start-up costs and expenses.

HOW MUCH MONEY DO YOU NEED?

To help you estimate the amount of financing you will need to get your venture off the ground, use the following chart. Keep in mind, however, that not every category applies to all businesses. Estimate monthly amount.

Salary of Owner-Manager (if applicable)	
All Other Salaries and Wages	
Rent	
Advertising	
Delivery Expenses	
Supplies	
Telephone	
Utilities	
Insurance	
Taxes, Including Social Security	
Interest	
Maintenance (Facilities/Equipment)	
Legal and Other Professional Fees	
Dues/Subscriptions	
Leases (Equipment/Furniture/Etc.)	
Inventory Purchases	
Miscellaneous	
One-Time Start-Up Costs	
Fixtures/Equipment/Furniture	
Remodeling	
Installation of Fixtures/Equipment/Furniture	
Starting Inventory	
Deposits with Public Utilities	
Legal and Other Professional Fees	
Licenses and Permits	
Advertising and Promotion for Opening	
Accounts Receivable	
Cash Reserve/Operating Capital	
Other	
TOTAL—Your total amount will depend upon how many months of preparation you want to allow before actually beginning operations.	

FURNITURE / FIXTURES / EQUIPMENT

	If you plan pay cash in full, enter the full amount below & in the last column	If you are going to pay by installments, fill out the columns below. Enter in the last column your down payment plus at least one installment			Estimate of the cash you need for furniture, fixtures & equipment
		PRICE	DOWN PAYMENT	AMOUNT OF EACH INSTALLMENT	
COUNTERS					
STORAGE SHELVES					
DISPLAY STANDS, SHELVES, TABLES					
CASH REGISTER					
SAFE					
WINDOW DISPLAY FIXTURES					
SPECIAL LIGHTING					
OUTSIDE SIGN					
DELIVERY EQUIPMENT IF NEEDED					

TOTAL FURNITURE, FIXTURES & EQUIPMENT

NECESSARY MISCELLANEOUS RESTAURANT, RESORT & HOTEL SUPPLIES

A

accounting & financial
   services

advertising services,
   materials &
   electronic catalogs

air cleaners/purifiers

air conditioning &
   heating eqt. sales

air curtains

air pollution control
   systems

air purification & dust
   collection eqt.

air screens/air curtains
   for entranceways

alcoholic beverages

alligator/alligator
   meat

aluminum foil

animated displays

antioxidants for
   fruits & vegetables

antiques

apparel

appetizers

appliances: food service
   machines

aprons

aquariums/lobster
   tanks

architects/engineers

art

artificial flowers &
   plants

ashtrays & stands

associations, trade

ATMs—automated teller
   machines

attorney at law

audiovisual eqt. &
   systems

awards, plaques &
   certificates

awnings, canopies &
   poles

B

bacon

badges/name badges

bags & covers: paper,
   plastic, cheesecloth
   & scented

bags, cooking

bags, food: paper
   & plastic

bains marie

baked goods:
   fresh & frozen breads,
   rolls, pastries, etc.

bakers eqt. & supplies

baking ingredients

baking supplies

balers

balloons

banners & flags

banquet service eqt.

bar codes/uniform
   product codes

bar eqt. & supplies

barbeque pits, machines,
   eqt. & supplies

bars, liquor service

bars, portable
   & folding bases
   & legs, tables
   & boothes

baskets, bread & roll

bathrobes & bathroom
   accessories

bathroom accessories
   & eqt.

bathroom eqt.
   & baby changing
   stations

batter: doughnut,
   pancake & waffle

beds: bedspreads
   & blankets

beer & ale

beer brewing eqt.

beer service eqt.

beverage service eqt.

beverage/coffee servers

beverages,
   concentrated fruit

beverages,
   nonalcoholic

beverages: beer/ale/wine

beverages, carbonated
   & noncarbonated

beverages:
   liquors/liqueurs

bibs, adult & child

binders

bins, ingredient

bins, silverware

bins, storage

biscuits, fancy & soda

blackboards

blenders

bookkeeping systems

books, educational
   & technical

books, reservation

booths & chairs, tables,
   bases & legs

bowls: mixing, salad
   & serving

brass fittings & tubing

bread & rolls

bread specialties

bread sticks

breading machines

breadings & batters:
   seafood & poultry

brochures & postcards

broilers, electric & gas

broilers, infrared

broilers, charcoal
   & conveyor

broilers, charcoal,
   electric & gas

brooms

brushes, cleaning

buffalo products

buffet products:
   chafers, fuel, etc.

buildings, modular

bulletin boards

bulletin boards:
   changeable letters

butchers eqt. & supplies

butter, margarine
   & cooking oils

C

cabinets: food
   warming
   & conveying

cabinets: miscellaneous

cafeteria eqt.

cakes & cake
decorations; cookies
& pastries

can openers: electric
& hand-operated

candelabra & candle
holders

candies, chocolates
& confectioneries

candle light,
nonflammable

candle warmers for
food & beverages

candles & tapers

canned foods: fish,
fruits & vegetables,
meat & poultry

canopies

canopies: ventilation

cappuccino coffee eqt.

carbon dioxide

carbonators

carbonic gas/bulk co2

carpet sweepers

carpets & rugs

carriers, food
& beverage insulated

carts, espresso & coffee

carts, food-service

carts, hospital
food-service

carts, transport

carts, storage
& serving

cash register
supplies: tape, ribbon,
etc.

cash registers
& control systems

casters

catalogues
& directories

catering supplies
& banquet service eqt.

catering
trucks/delivery
trucks

caviar

ceilings: acoustical,
tin, wood, etc.

ceramic dinnerware

ceramics

cereals, ready-to-serve
& uncooked

chafing dishes

chairs, folding or
stacking

chairs, infant

chairs, restaurant

chairs, upholstered

check recovery services

cheese

cheese, grated

children's premiums
& party supplies

children's rides
& amusements

chillers

china, table

chinese foods

chocolate

choppers: electric for
food & meat

chopping blocks

cigars, cigarettes,
tobacco products:
display & storage
systems

citrus products/citrus
syrups

cleaners for grills, griddles,
pans, etc.

cleaners, hand

cleaners, multipurpose

cleaners, ovens

cleaners, rug
& upholstery

cleaners, window

cleaning eqt., materials,
services & supplies

cleaning systems,
pressurized

cleaning: exhaust
maintenance

clocks, electric

coasters, beverage

coat & hat checking
eqt.

cocktail mixes

cocktail stirrers

cocoa

coffee

coffee-brewers, glass
& filters

coffee mills

coffee urns & makers

coin sorters
& handling eqt.

cold plates

communication
systems, services & eqt.

compactors, waste

computer aided design
(cad) systems

computer furniture

computer software:
accounting,
administrative,
hospitality, etc.

computer software:
hospitality
& cost control

computer supplies

computerized
food service
systems

computerized
restaurant
management systems

computerized systems,
wireless

computers/internet

concession eqt.
& supplies

condiments
& condiment holders

confectionery &
chocolate products

connectors:
gas/water/steam

construction:
materials/renovation

consulting services

containers, food

containers, microwave

containers, ovenable
paperboard

containers: aluminum,
plastic & glass

conveyors & subveyors

conveyors, belt

cookies

cooking computers
or timers

cooking eqt., electric
& gas

cooking eqt., induction

cooking eqt., outdoor

cooking heat/warmers

cooking wines
& marinades

cookware, induction

cookware: pots, pans
& microwave

coolers, beverage

copperware

costumes

cotton candy
machines

counters & tabletops

counters, cafeteria

covers, rack

crackers

creamers

credit cards: card
processing/
authorization

crepe-making machines

croutons

crushers, can & bottle,
electric

cups: disposable,
portion, thermal, etc.

custom-built kitchen
eqt.

cutlery: chef's eqt.
& supplies

cutlery, disposable

cutlery, silver-plated
& stainless steel

cutters, food

cutting boards

D

dairy substitutes

dance floors, portable

data processing eqt.,
services & supplies

decaffeinated
beverages

decor & display
materials

decorations: holiday,
party favors,
balloons, etc.

degreasers & non-slip
treatment products

deli products

deodorizers

designers/decorators

dessert products

dicers, hand-operated

dicers, vegetable-
cutting, power

dietetic foods

dinnerware, heat
resistant, glass

dinnerware, metal

dinnerware: china,
stainless steel,
plastic or disposable

disco equipment

dishtables

dishwashers/ware:
washer eqt. & supplies

dishwashing compounds

disinfectants
& cleaning supplies

dispensers for
concentrates

dispensers, carbonated
beverage

dispensers, condiment

dispensers: controls
& timers

dispensers, cup

dispensers, custom

dispensers, french fries

dispensers, glove

dispensers, ice

dispensers, ice cream

dispensers: liquor, beer
& wine

dispensers, malted milk

dispensers, napkins

dispensers, noncarbonated
beverage dispensers,

dispensers, salad dressing

dispensers: self-leveling
for dishes & trays

dispensers, snack

dispensers, soap
& detergent

dispensers, straw

dispensers, toilet paper

dispensers, water—
hot and/or cold

dispensers, whipped
cream

dispensers, wine

dispensers: liquids,
beverages, cream/milk,
syrup & dressings

display cases

display cases, heated

display cases,
refrigerated

distributor, food
& beverage

distributor, food eqt.

doilies: paper or plastic

doors: cold storage &
freezer

doors: hinged,
revolving & swinging

dough dividers/rounders

dough: prepared,
frozen & canned

doughnut machines

doughnut mix

drain cleaners/line
maintenance

draperies, curtains
& hangings

draperies, stage

drapery & curtain
hardware

dressings, salad

drive-thru service eqt.

drug testing

dry grocery items:
staples

dry ice

dryers, clothes

dryers, dish/tray

E

eggs/egg products/
egg substitutes/
boilers & timers

electric utility services/
energy conservation

electronic data
capture

electronic funds
transfer

embroidered apparel

employee benefit services

employee scheduling
& services

employment agencies,
services & leasing

enclosures, patio &
pool

energy conservation eqt.

energy cost analysts

entertainment, sports-
   themed

entertainment/
   entertainment
   systems

entrees, fresh & frozen

environmental
   products

equipment, cook/chill

equipment,
   dish handling

equipment,
   drain cleaning

equipment, exercise

equipment,
   food forming

equipment, front office

equipment, heating—
   boilers, furnaces,
   radiators, etc.

equipment,
   hot-chocolate
   making

equipment, leasing

equipment, marinade

equipment: preventive
   maintenance
   programs

equipment:
   repairs/parts/
   installation

equipment, rug cleaning

equipment,
   sales & service

equipment, under-bar

equipment, upholstery
   cleaning
   & shampooing

espresso coffee
   & coffee eqt.

ethnic foods

executive recruiters,
   hospitality industry

exhaust fans

exhaust maintenance
   cleaning

extractors, fruit juice

extracts, flavoring

F

fabrication, stainless
   steel

fabrication, wood

fabrics

fabrics, fire resistant

fans, electric
   & ventilating

fats & oils, cooking

fats & oils: eqt. Systems
   & supplies

faucets

filters, air-conditioning

filters: coffee makers

filters, cooking oil

filters, exhaust systems

filters, grease
   extracting

filters, water

financial services/
   financial
   consultants

financial: tax
   & legal planning

fire alarm systems

fire protection systems:
   extinguishers/
   suppression/sales/service

first-aid eqt. & supplies

fish: canned, fresh,
   frozen, pre-portioned
   & smoked

flagpoles, flags
   & accessories

flatware carts & trays
   for storage
   & dispensing

flatware, disposable

flatware: recovery
   machines

flatware: silver/gold
   plated, stainless
   & disposable

floor cleaning
   & maintenance eqt.

floor drain treatment

flooring tile: vitrified
   or ceramic

flooring: floor
   treatments, non-slip
   preparations
   & coating

flour & flour sifters

flowers, foliage
   & plants

food containers:
   aluminum, plastic

& glass

food covers

food, dehydrated

food delivery
   & catering eqt.

food eqt.: Service
   & parts

food: frozen—
   cooked/precooked

food photography

food portioning eqt.

food processors:
   grinders & slicers,
   electric & manual

food products:
   deli/ethnic,
   import/export

food products:
   prepared, canned
   or frozen

food reproduction
   & replication/props

food safety training

food thawing device

food waste disposers

food, processed

footwear

forms: guest checks
   & business forms

fountain syrups
   & flavors

fountains, beverage

fountains, ornamental
   & display

franchise consultants

freezers/refrigeration
   eqt.: service & parts

freezers, portable

frequent dining
   programs/clubs

frozen breakfast food

frozen cocktail
   machines

frozen food reconstitutor

fruit juices: canned,
   concentrated,
   fresh & frozen

fruit syrups

fruits & vegetables:
   candied, brandied
   & pickled

fruits & vegetables:
   canned, fresh & frozen

fryers, convection
fryers, deep fat
& pressure
fryers, oil-less
fuel: synthetic/alternative
furniture design
furniture, health care
furniture: fiberglass,
metal, plastic,
upholstered & wood
furniture: lawn,
garden, patio
& casual
furniture,
portable/folding

G/H

games
garbage can liners
garbage containers:
metal, plastic
or concrete; waste
receptacles
& compactors
gas, propane
gas: service/supplier
& natural
gelatin
gelato
gift basket packaging
glass replacement
service
glass washers
glass, beveled
& tempered
glass, decorative
glassware chiller
& froster
glassware, service
glazes
gloves: cloth
or synthetic
gourmet foods
gravy mix or base
grease exhaust systems:
cleaning
& maintenance
grease traps: cleaning,
maintenance, elimina
tion & analysis
griddles & grills
groceries
guest checks

guest questionnaires,
comment cards
& boxes
guest services
HAACP training
hair dryers
hand dryers
hand trucks
handicapped: aids
& accessories
hangers, clothes
health foods
healthcare products
& eqt.
heat lamps
heaters, water
heaters, patio
& outdoor/indoor
herbs
high chairs
holloware: plated,
silver plated
& stainless steel
hoods
hors d'oeuvres
hoses: flexible gas
connectors
hot chocolate mix
hot dog grills/cookers
hot food tables
hot plates, electric & gas
hotel & restaurant
supplies
hotel amenities
hotel eqt. & supplies
hotel/motel
management
hotel/motel planning
& development
hotel/motel supplies

I/J

ice bins, buckets, carts
& containers
ice cream
ice cream cabinets
ice cream dishes
ice cream freezers
ice cream makers
& soft serve machines
ice cream, toppings,
syrups & cones

ice crushers, cubers
& shavers
ice machine repairs,
service
& maintenance
ice makers, bins,
dispensers, crushers
& cubers
ice transport systems
Ice: ice eqt. & supplies
incentive programs
information service
infrared ovens, ranges
& broilers
insect traps
insecticides
inserts, steam table
insulation materials:
hot & cold
insurance
interior decor/
interior design
international
marketer/distributor:
food eqt.
inventory control
eqt.
inventory systems: eqt.
& supplies
investigative services
janitorial:
cleaning/sanitizing
janitorial supplies
japanese foods
juice fountains
juicers/extractors

K/L

kettles, steam
key & lock systems
key tags
kitchen accessories
kitchen fabrication
kitchen layout
& design
knife sharpeners
kosher food/products
ladles
laminated plastic for
counters, etc.
laminating services
& products
lamps: floor, table,

electric, battery,
candle, infrared & oil

lampshades

laundry eqt. & supplies

laundry machinery

lawn care services

led message displays

legal services

legumes

lighting fixtures

lighting systems,
emergency

lighting, fluorescent
& neon

lights: flood, spot, etc.

linen products

linen products, rental

liquor substitutes

liquor supplies
& liqueurs

lobster

lobster tanks

lockers

locks

M/N

machines, soft ice
cream & milk shake

magazines & newspapers

management services

management systems

marinades

markers, chalks
& crayons

marketing materials
& services

marketing research

marketing:
promotional items
& public relations

matches/matchbooks

mats, floor

mats, rubber
& composition

mattresses & bedsprings

mayonnaise

meat analogs

meat cookers

meatball machines

meats: fresh, frozen,
canned, pre-

portioned
& processed

menu accessories

menu covers & holders

menu display

menu planning
& development

menu price changers

menus, menu boards &
menu card systems

mesquite wood

metal polish

metal work:
kitchen eqt.

mexican foods

microwave accessories

microwave food

microwave ovens
& cookware

mini bars

mints: hospitality
& printed

mirrors, murals
& wall decorations

mixers, drink

mixers, food—electric

mixes, cocktail

mixes, food

mixes: prepared
flour/dough

mobile restaurants

money counters

mops & mopping eqt.

motivational incentives,
employee contests
& games

muffin depositor

murals & wall
decorations

mushrooms

music & sound systems

music licensing:
organizations &
copyright law

music systems

music videos

musical instruments

name badges/tags

napkin rings

napkins, disposable

napkins, fabric

nondairy creamers

nutrition services
& information

nuts: specialty nut meats

O

office machines

office supplies

oils, cooking—fats & oils

olives

on-line services

onion rings

onions, dehydrated

ordering systems

organizers: calendars,
notebooks & seating
charts

ovens & ranges: cooking
eqt., parts & service

ovens, baking & roasting

ovens, brick

ovens, combination
convection/steam

ovens: convection,
conveyor, infrared,
low temperature,
microwave, quartz,
vapor & wood burning

ovenware: china or glass

P/Q

packaging & wrap: foil,
plastic & paper

packaging materials:
wrapping

packaging, take-out

paging systems
& employee call systems

paint markers or strippers

pan liners & coatings

paneling & partitions,
acoustical

paper goods & disposable
tabletop items

parking lot maintenance

partitions or walls,
movable

pasta cookers

pasta making
eqt./machines

pasta: fresh, frozen,
flavored, homemade
& processed

pastry products
pates
payroll companies
payroll processing
   services
peanut butter
pepper mills
personnel services:
   recruitment, leasing
   & consultants
pest control services
   & products
photographic services
   & eqt.
pickles & pickled
   products
pie fillings
pie making machines
pies, baked & frozen
pillows
pitchers
pizza eqt. & supplies
pizza products
place mats
plants, flowers & greenery
plastic signs
plasticware, disposable
   & nondisposable
plasticware, disposable,
   molded
plates, disposable
platforms & risers,
   portable
platters
playground equipment
plumbing fixtures & eqt.
point-of-sale eqt.,
   materials & supplies
polishes & waxes, floor
popcorn equipment
portable toilets
   & sanitation
posters & poster systems
pot & pan washing eqt.
potato products
potatoes, processed
pots & pans
poultry information
poultry: fresh, frozen,
   canned & pre-portioned
powders, fry-kettle
precooked frozen food

pre-portioned foods:
   jam, cheese, salt,
   pepper, etc.
pre-portioned meat, fish
   & poultry
pre-washing machines
premiums & incentives
pressure cookers
pressure fryers
pretzels
printing & design
printing forms, notices,
   etc.
produce: fruits
   & vegetables
property management
   systems
prosciutto
public address systems
public cold storage
pushcarts
quality control

R

racks, coat & hat
racks, dish & glass
racks, dishwashing
racks, drying
racks, luggage
racks, shelving
   & storage
railings: brass, chrome,
   stainless steel, wood, etc.
ramekins
ranges, electric & gas
real estate: analysis,
   brokerage
   & financing
recipe card indexers
recipes: new ideas
recycling containers,
   eqt. & services
refinishing services:
   tableware
refrigeration eqt.:
   display
refrigeration eqt.:
   reach-in
refrigeration eqt.:
   repair & service
refrigeration eqt.:
   walk-ins

relishes, chutneys, etc.
rendering services
rental: supplies & eqt.
rentals & leasing: cars
   & trucks
rentals & leasing
   party supplies
reservation services
responsible vendor
   training
restaurant
   consultants
restaurant eqt.
   & supplies
restoration
rice/rice products
room service products
rotisseries

S

safes & vaults
safety products
salad dressings
salad dryers
salad oils
salads & salad bars:
   eqt. & supplies
sandwich & salad
   units, refrigerated
sandwiches
sanitation eqt.
   & supplies
sauces & sauce bases
saunas
sausage
saws, meat cutting—
   power
scales, food
schools &
   educational services
scouring pads
seafood & seafood
   products
seafood steaming eqt.
seasonings & spices
seating systems: charts
   & wait lists
seating, auditorium
   & theater
seating, food court
secret shopper service
security eqt. systems

& services

septic tank cleaning,
    repairs & maintenance

serving dishes

sharpening services:
    knives & eqt.

sheets & pillow cases

shelf liners

shellfish tools/mesh
    steaming bags

shelving, plastic

shelving, steel & wood

shopping service/
    mystery shopper

shortening

shower curtains

signs, changeable
    letter

signs, electrical
    & electronic

signs, painted

signs, tabletop

signs, wooden

signs: engraved, led,
    & neon

silver burnishers,
    cleaners
    & compounds

silver plating

sinks, kitchen

sinks, under-bar

slicers, food—
    electric

slicers, mechanical/
    hand-operated

slush machines

smoked meats & sausage:
    manufacturer

snack bar units

snack foods: candies,
    chips & nuts

sneeze guards

soap, toilet & bath

soaps: detergents &
    cleaning compounds

soda fountain supplies

soda fountains & eqt.

soft serve eqt.
    & products

sorbet

sound systems

soups: condensed,
    dehydrated & ready-

to-serve

soups, frozen

soups & soup bases

souvenirs, novelties
    & party favors

specialty foods

stages, mobile & fold-
    ing; dance floors

stainless steel

stanchions
    & decorative rope

staples

starch, cooking

steam cleaning services

steam cookers

steam tables

sterilizers

stirrers: wood
    or plastic

straws, sipping

strip doors

sugar & sugar
    products

supplies: electronic
    machines—paper, rolls
    & ribbon

sweetening products

swimming pool eqt.

syrups & toppings

systems, intercom

T

table covers, disposable

table padding

table toys & table games

table: skirting, linens,
    napkins, etc.

tables, bakers'

tables, banquet room
    & folding

tables & counters,
    restaurant

tables, kitchen

tables, outdoor

tables, pedestal

tables, room service

tables: hot/cold food;
    serving & folding

tableware, disposable

takeout service/
    delivery service

tea making
    & dispensing eqt.

tea & iced tea

technical research

telecommunication
    services

telephone pay

telephone systems,
    sales & service

television, closed
    circuit

television, satellite

tenderizers

tents & canopies

testing & evaluation
    services: safety
    & sanitation

textured vegetable
    protein product

theme party supplies

thermo delivery
    pouches

thermometers

thermoware

tiling

tilting skillets

time keeping eqt.
    & supplies

time recorders

tissues, disposable

toasters, automatic—
    gas or electric

tobacco products

toilet paper

toilet seat covers

tomato products

tools: garnishing,
    ice carving, etc.

toothpicks & party
    picks

toppings

tortilla press

tortilla products

touch screens

towels: cotton or
    linen

towels, paper

trade publications

training films
    & filmstrips

training materials

tray covers

tray stands
tray washers
trays, baking
trays, foam
trays, paper
trays, plastic
trays, restaurant
trays: storage, serving
& display
trucks for folding
tables, chairs
& mattresses
trucks, baggage
trucks, delivery
trucks, dish & food
trucks, laundry & linen
supply
trucks, maid

U/V

umbrellas, aluminum
outdoor
uniform emblems:
imprinted
or embroidered
uniforms: clothing
uniforms: hats & caps
uniforms: protective
apparel
upholstery cleaners
utensils,
cooking/kitchen
utility, analysis, con-
trol & distributions
vacuum cleaner
vacuum-packed/vacuum-
sealed bags & pouches
vegetable cutters
& peelers
vegetable juice
vehicles, maintenance
vehicles, personnel
vending machines
vending products
vending vehicles
ventilating systems,
kitchen
ventilators
& ventilating eqt.
vinegars
visitor guides,
in-room guides, travel

guides & maps

W

waffle irons & cone
makers
waffles
wait staff call system
walk-in coolers
& freezers—
wall covering
wall panels, tile,
wallboard, etc.
wall cleaners
& maintenance
walls, movable
warehousing
warmers, beverage
warmers, dish/plate
warmers, food
warmers, fudge—
electric
wash cloths
waste disposal systems
waste grease
collection
waste reduction eqt.
& services
waste reduction/
waste disposal
wastebaskets
& receptacles
water conditioner
& softener eqt.
& supplies
water machines:
heating & cooling
water purification/
filtration
water vacuums/brooms
water, bottled
water, mineral
water & water
dispensers
whipping eqt.: cream,
sour cream & toppings
whipping eqt.:
accessories
wholesale club
windows
wine accessories
wine cellers

wine consultants
& distributors
wine service eqt.
wines
wipes
wire accessories
woks, electric
& nonelectric
woodenware, bowls
& kitchen utensils
work tables, kitchen
wraps: lemon, stem, etc.

Y

yogurt eqt.
yogurt: frozen, fresh
& soft-serve

LAYOUT AND FLOWCHART OF A TYPICAL FAMILY-TYPE RESTAURANT

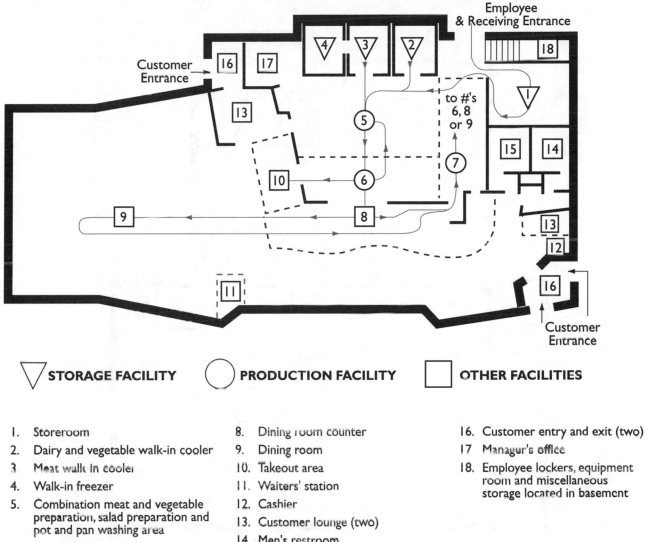

△ **STORAGE FACILITY**   ◯ **PRODUCTION FACILITY**   ▢ **OTHER FACILITIES**

1. Storeroom
2. Dairy and vegetable walk-in cooler
3. Meat walk-in cooler
4. Walk-in freezer
5. Combination meat and vegetable preparation, salad preparation and pot and pan washing area
6. Meat and vegetable cooking area
7. Dish room

8. Dining room counter
9. Dining room
10. Takeout area
11. Waiters' station
12. Cashier
13. Customer lounge (two)
14. Men's restroom
15. Women's restroom

16. Customer entry and exit (two)
17. Manager's office
18. Employee lockers, equipment room and miscellaneous storage located in basement

---

LAYOUT AND FLOWCHART OF A TYPICAL OCCASIONAL-TYPE RESTAURANT

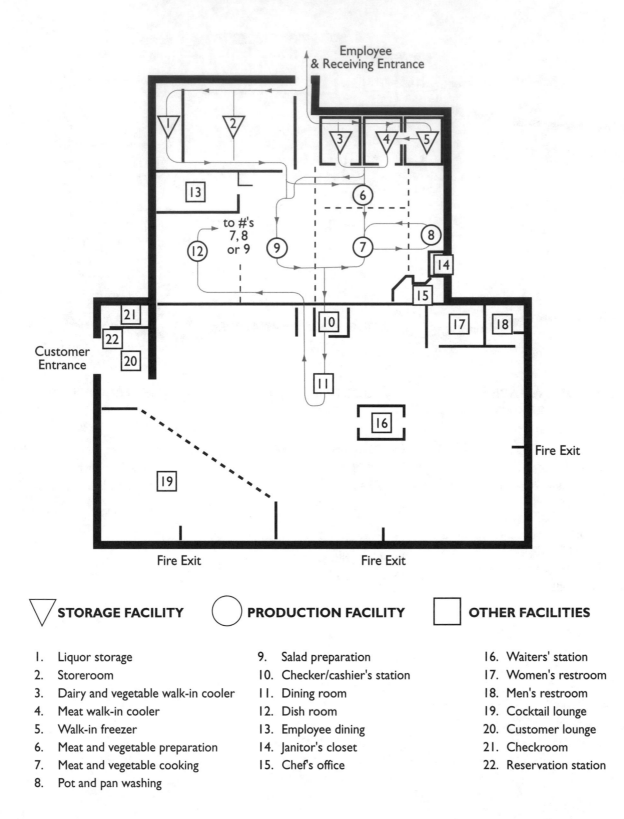

▽ **STORAGE FACILITY**   ○ **PRODUCTION FACILITY**   ☐ **OTHER FACILITIES**

1. Liquor storage
2. Storeroom
3. Dairy and vegetable walk-in cooler
4. Meat walk-in cooler
5. Walk-in freezer
6. Meat and vegetable preparation
7. Meat and vegetable cooking
8. Pot and pan washing

9. Salad preparation
10. Checker/cashier's station
11. Dining room
12. Dish room
13. Employee dining
14. Janitor's closet
15. Chef's office

16. Waiters' station
17. Women's restroom
18. Men's restroom
19. Cocktail lounge
20. Customer lounge
21. Checkroom
22. Reservation station

LAYOUT FOR RECEIVING, STORAGE AND EMPLOYEE DINING AREAS

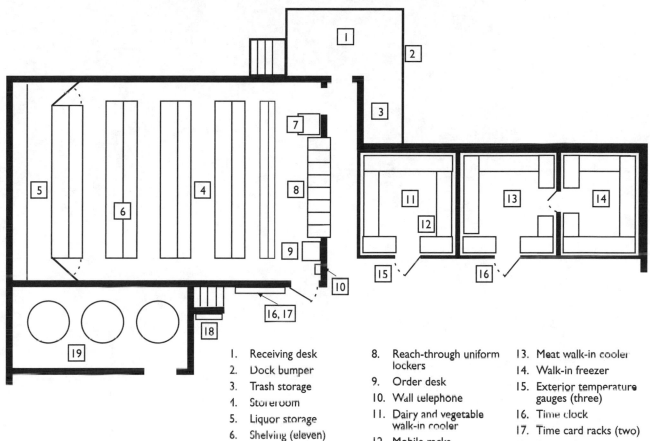

1. Receiving desk
2. Dock bumper
3. Trash storage
4. Storeroom
5. Liquor storage
6. Shelving (eleven)
7. Platform scale

8. Reach-through uniform lockers
9. Order desk
10. Wall telephone
11. Dairy and vegetable walk-in cooler
12. Mobile racks (fourteen)

13. Meat walk-in cooler
14. Walk-in freezer
15. Exterior temperature gauges (three)
16. Time clock
17. Time card racks (two)
18. Bulletin board
19. Employee dining

2

THE BASICS OF
BUYING & SELLING A RESTAURANT

INTRODUCTION

The real estate property of a restaurant is often its most valuable feature. In many cases the real estate is a bigger attraction to the buyer than the business itself. In fact, many restaurants are bought and sold without the real property being part of the operation. These are cases where the restaurant leases its property from a landlord who has no involvement in the business itself. "Real estate" is the land itself and any permanent improvements made on the land, such as utility connections, parking lots, buildings, etc. Real estate is a reversion asset, which means that it's expected to retain most or all of its value, regardless of whether the business run on it is successful. The value of real estate is one of the major assets that need to be calculated when determining a food-service operation's value. Generally there are three procedures for determining the value of a restaurant: Market Approach, Cost Approach and Income Approach.

DETERMINING THE RESTAURANT'S VALUE

MARKET APPROACH

The Market Approach is based on the idea of substitution. Basically, this means that the value of a property is determined by comparing it to like pieces of property in similar areas. Since these comparable properties are usually not exactly the same as the property you are trying to value, you'll need to make adjustments to place an accurate market value. The determining of these adjustments is a subjective process at best, and at worst it is impossible, because owners of similar properties are extremely unlikely to tell you the details of their businesses. For these reasons the Market Approach is generally not used to estimate the value of a restaurant's real estate. However, if you are selling land only or the land portion of a restaurant, the market approach can be an accurate determiner of value, since there are considerably fewer adjustments to make.

COST APPROACH

The Cost Approach is based on the idea of replacement. In simple terms, the property is valued on what it would cost to replace it completely. To determine this you must add the replacement costs of all the assets in your establishment. Obtain purchase prices for new equipment and assets that exactly match your existing ones. In the case of equipment that is no longer made, add the price of what a new piece of equipment that provides the same utility would cost. Include all taxes, freight and installation in your quotes, and factor in depreciation. The Cost Approach is not widely used to estimate the value of a restaurant's real estate, but is used mostly by insurance companies while processing a claim.

INCOME APPROACH

The Income Approach bases its valuation on the anticipation of future income to be derived from the property. The real estate value, then, is the present value of the estimated future net income, plus the present value of the estimated profit to be earned when the property is sold. This is the preferred approach when determining an accurate sales price for an income-producing property. This is because investors are concerned with the amount of income they can earn while using a property's assets, not with what it would cost to replace those assets.

There are other approaches to value as well. If your property was recently assessed for tax purposes the Assessed Value may be a useful estimate to you, even if the valuation doesn't match current market conditions. The Book Value Approach is based on the initial purchase price for the property, minus accrued depreciation. This value will no doubt have very little to do with current market conditions, but it can be useful if you want to compute a low estimate of value for other reasons. The Underwriter Approach is used by lenders to determine the amount of loan proceeds an income property can support. This is determined by multiplying the DSC, or debt-service-coverage, ratio (the amount of income available for debt service, divided by the annual amount of debt-service payment demanded by the lender) by the loan constant, then dividing this sum by the annual income available for debt service.

It is often useful to use several valuation procedures to determine the most likely sales price. This is because establishments may have separate aspects of their business that can be valued separately. For instance, a bar may have its real property as well as its tavern license. The real estate may be valued through the Income Approach, and the license through the Market Approach.

THE VALUE OF OTHER ASSETS

A restaurant's assets are often broken down into three categories: real estate, other reversion assets and the business. A reversion asset is one that retains its value regardless of the success or failure of the business. These are assets like the real estate, equipment, inventories, receivables, prepaid expenses (deposits, taxes, advertising, etc.), lease-hold interest, antiques, licenses, franchises and exclusive distributorships like lottery ticket sales. These assets keep their value even if a business goes under, and they can be sold at market value. Therefore it is in an owner's best interest to own as many reversion assets as possible, because these assets increase the business's value to sellers.

The business itself consists of everything the owner wishes to sell. Usually this means the furniture, fixtures, equipment, leasehold improvements, etc. It may also include tax credits, favorable operating expenses, customer lists and name recognition. The price for a food-service business is usually 40 to 70 percent of the operation's 12-month food-and-beverage sales volume. The seller usually will set the sale price at the high end of this percentage, and the prospective buyer will set it at the low end.

Setting a sales price is not, of course, a straightforward process, and there are many other factors that need to be considered. Here are a few:

- **Profitability.** This has the most influence on sales price and salability of a restaurant. The most common way to determine profitability is to examine the net operating income figure. If a restaurant earns an average net operating income, its most probable sales price will be equal to 50 percent of the previous 12 months' food-and-beverage sales. The net income should be compared to the industry standard and the regional standard for that type of operation.

- **Leasehold terms and conditions.** The term remaining on the property lease and the monthly payment will affect the sales price greatly. Buyers normally want five-year leases, and a seller should be prepared to assign the existing lease or help in negotiating a new lease with the landlord. Buyers who can't get a minimum five-year lease are usually not interested in buying a restaurant unless it's very prof-itable or priced very low. In addition to a five-year lease, most buyers also need a reasonable monthly payment and a reasonable common area maintenance pay-ment. This should not exceed 6–8 percent of the monthly food-and-beverage sales.

- **Track record.** Businesses need to show acceptable track records to entice buyers. This usually means the business must be at least a year old. The track record will be used to project the business's future prospects. If a business depends on the work of highly skilled employees such as a well-known chef, this too can affect the price because it makes the business more difficult to expand and more expensive to operate.

- **Other income.** Most restaurants don't earn much other income—usually less than 2 percent. But there are rebates, interest on bank deposits, vending machines, salvage from aluminum, grease and cardboard, etc. All of these can make an impact—in the case of vending machines, a considerable one—and need to be taken into consideration when valuing a restaurant.

- **Below-market financing.** When a restaurant is sold, usually the buyer puts up a small down payment and the seller then carries back the remainder of the sales price at favorable terms. Seller financing is almost always below market, and the buyer avoids the fees associated with bank loans.

- **Personal goodwill.** If enough of a restaurant's business is depends on the personal relationships between staff and management who won't be staying on, then the sales price will probably be diminished.

- **Franchise affiliation.** If a restaurant is part of a large franchise the sale price will increase significantly. This is truer of the larger national franchises than the regional ones.

- **Number of buyers and sellers.** A seller should plan to market his business when there are as many potential buyers as possible. This means early spring and summer—especially if it's a tourist business—or after legislation limiting construction has passed, taxes are lowered, etc.

- **Contingent liabilities.** Contingent liabilities reduce a restaurant's net income. These may be coupons issued by the previous owner, dining club memberships, or pension plans that eat into your net profit margin. If a buyer cannot eliminate these expenses, they most likely represent a negative value that should be factored into the offering price.

- **Grandfather clauses.** New owners are expected to meet fire, health and safety codes that the previous owner may have been able to avoid because of being "grandfathered in" when the regulations were passed. Grandfather clauses usually expire when a business changes hands. If this is the case, the seller or buyer may need to bring the building up to code. If the buyer is responsible for this, she will usually ask that the expense be deducted from the sale price. If the cost is very high, this could affect the salability of the business altogether.

GOODWILL

The IRS determines goodwill as the amount of money paid for a restaurant in excess of the current book value of the physical assets. Most investors, however, look at excess earnings as attributable to positive goodwill, and deficient earnings to negative goodwill. In order to compute the goodwill value, the restaurant's income statement from the past 12 months must be reconstructed. The idea behind this is to develop a financial statement that reflects what could have happened if a wise and knowledgeable restaurateur had been running the business. The best model to use for this process is the National Restaurant Association's Annual Restaurant Industry Operations Report, which itemizes in detail the following income and expense areas:

- Food sales
- Other income
- Payroll
- Direct operating expenses
- Advertising and promotion

- Beverage sales
- Cost of sales
- Employee benefits
- Music and entertainment
- Utilities

- Administrative and general
- Occupation costs
- Depreciation
- Maintenance and repairs
- Interest expense

The sales volume is the most critical one here, because the most likely sales price is tied into the previous 12 months' net food-and-beverage sales volume. The sales volume is doubly important because a seller will have to adhere to the figure supported in the sales reports. Buyers generally are not interested in hearing about phantom buried income or optimistic forecasts of future sales. In some cases a solid case for a net sales increase can be made, but usually a buyer will not allow a seller to profit from something the seller didn't create.

In order to arrive at a credible goodwill value, a seller needs to work with the existing income/expense figures and only make changes that can be supported. In most cases sales volume figures cannot be supported, but expense adjustments usually can. These can include the expenses owners usually list on their tax returns—travel, cars, supplies and unwarranted employee benefits that are unrelated to the business. The flip side to this is that a seller may increase payroll and benefits if they are artificially low due to the owner's taking salaries directly from profits.

A buyer may be willing to pay for goodwill, but a seller should expect the buyer to downplay its value in order to lower the sale price as much as possible. A few other complications with goodwill can arise:

- There is a difference between personal goodwill and goodwill attributable to the business itself. Unless the appropriate staff has agreed to stay on, personal goodwill isn't transferable to the next owner. It is up to the buyer to distinguish between transferable goodwill and goodwill that disappears with the previous owner.

- Sellers must be able to convince the buyer that the excess net income that is positive goodwill will not decrease after the business changes hands. It is in the seller's interest to prove that positive goodwill is due to something like a great location, and to point out that the new owner should generally operate according to the established standards and practices that generated or supported that positive goodwill.

- The IRS does not allow the buyer to depreciate goodwill. In most cases a buyer will assign the value of the goodwill to a non-competition agreement with the seller, and therefore be able to rescue the goodwill amount in a tax shelter.

- If the restaurant is less than a year old it is very difficult to project a stabilized annual net income. Reasonable estimates are the best thing here. A buyer will not want to talk about goodwill unless the numbers are based on reasonable projections of revenues and expenses.

- If a restaurant has negative goodwill, the seller is in the difficult position of making a convincing argument that the buyer should purchase a marginally profitable business. The best argument here is to point out the existing reversion assets that are part of the sale price. If there aren't any reversion assets, it's very difficult to point out the potential of future earnings without begging the question as to why the seller didn't capitalize on that potential. In many cases, pointing out the elimination of excessive start-up costs by purchasing an already running business is the only option. This really only holds water if there is a reasonable expectation that the business's net income will improve significantly.

- Judges and arbitrators who settle disputes usually don't consider goodwill. They like to deal strictly with the book value of tangible assets. As a result, it can be difficult for restaurateurs to receive fair compensation for their investment.

TERMS, CONDITIONS AND PRICE

In most cases sellers will determine likely sales price, terms and conditions, and then pad those somewhat to create room for negotiation and compromise. In general, unrealistic asking prices generate unrealistic offerings, or none at all. Sellers should prepare a pragmatic and well-documented solicitation and then search for buyers who will appreciate these considerations.

As much as possible, anticipating every potential problem that may arise during negotiations will put sellers in a good position to offer solutions to a buyer's objections. It is a good idea for a seller to hire an attorney, accountant or business broker when preparing a preferred sales price, terms and conditions. The savvy buyer and seller also incorporate their transaction costs—brokerage fees, lawyers, etc.—into the prices she is asking or offering. In most cases there are higher transaction fees for the seller. It is a good practice for the seller to enumerate all the assets that are included in the sale of the restaurant. At the least this will garner respect from potential buyers, and it may give the seller a leg up during initial negotiations.

TERMS

The terms of sale are the procedures used by the buyer to pay the seller. A buyer is usually willing to accept a proposed sales price if the seller will accept the buyer's terms. In most cases sellers receive a minimal down payment and the remainder of the purchase price over a three-to-five-year period. All-cash offers are rare, and seller financing is usually necessary to attract buyers. In most cases it's in the seller's interest to receive a large down payment because this demonstrates the buyer's commitment to the long haul. Sellers are also more likely to grant favorable terms to a buyer making a substantial down payment because the financial risk is lessened.

Sometimes buyers will want to pay with property or corporate stock instead of cash. These can be great from a tax perspective, but stock can be problematic because it can decrease in value, and usually the stock used for this type of deal cannot be sold for a year or more, and often only in small amounts.

Seller financing is probably the most desirable aspect of the investment in a restaurant, and most buyers want to assume favorable loans. Sellers offering favorable terms must be sure they receive adequate compensation in the form of a higher sales price. Seller financing is negotiable, but usually the marketplace suggests typical loan amounts and terms. The loan payments should not be tied into sales volume or any other performance measures, because the seller doesn't want to suffer if a new owner drives the business under. The only instance where loan payments should be tied into performance measures is in an "earn-out agreement," where the premium part of the sales price is contingent on its future performance.

CONDITIONS

There are several conditions the seller and buyer will attach to most sales contracts. Sometimes they are separate agreements, but most of the time they are part of the sales contract. The following lists conditions of the largest concern to the seller:

- **Conclusion of sale.** Sellers want to finish the transaction as fast as possible because delays give buyers time to second-guess. Sellers want the new owners into the operation as quickly as possible.

- **Buyer access.** Sellers generally want minimal contact with the buyer while waiting for the transaction to close, and they don't want the buyer spending time with the restaurant staff. It's good for a seller to provide the needed assistance for the ownership transition, but it should only be after the buyer has taken possession of the business.

- **Guarantees.** Sellers usually have to guarantee the condition of assets. Sometimes sellers have to guarantee that buyers can assume some of the restaurant's current contracts. Sellers should never guarantee things they don't have total control over. Imprecise language should also be avoided here. If the seller is making guarantees, then buying the relevant insurance to back up these claims is prudent.

- **Indemnification.** Sellers will want to be compensated if a buyer backs out of the deal. Sellers should also be protected for expenses paid to fix code violations, or for legal expenses if the seller needs to sue the buyer to uphold an agreement.

- **Escrow agent.** Independent escrow agents are usually hired to supervise transactions. These agents see that all terms and conditions are met, and that after that point ownership can be transferred. The seller should insist that the buyer agree to an independent third-party escrow agent. This ensures the many details of this transaction are handled well and legally.

- **Legal requirements.** Seller and buyer must agree to comply with all pertinent laws and statutes. Escrow agents ensure that all current creditors are notified of the restaurant's sale, and that all legal requirements are met. This ensures that the buyer can begin with a clean slate, without any of the seller's responsibilities to creditors.

- **Buyer's credit history.** Before agreeing to seller financing, the seller must investigate the buyer's credit history. It is standard for buyers to give personal financial statements, resumes, references, and permission to run a credit report. Serious buyers have no problem with this because it secures the seller's respect and encourages the revealing of confidential information.

- **Security for seller financing.** Many deals go bad because buyer and seller can't agree on financing. If a seller agrees to hold paper, the buyer must sign a promissory note and security agreement. The note represents the buyer's promise to pay, and the security agreement is the collateral pledged to secure the loan. If the seller is the only lender, a clause should be added that requires his approval before the new owner can obtain additional financing. The promissory note should contain a default provision that the lender can foreclose if loan payments are not met, in addition to other specific provisions pertinent to the business. These might be that the seller can foreclose if the new owner doesn't maintain a required balance sheet, or if she does not produce previously agreed upon menu items.

- **Assumable loans and leases.** Buyers will want to assume any contract that calls for below-market payments. Sellers should do everything possible to ensure a favorable transition, because many deals rest on buyers being able to assume outstanding contracts.

- **Life and disability insurance.** If the seller carries the paper, the buyer should be required to purchase the appropriate insurance naming the seller as beneficiary. If the buyer refuses to purchase this, the seller should. If the new owner dies or becomes ill, without insurance, the previous owner would potentially lose his investment.

- **Collection of receivables.** It is reasonable for the owner to receive a modest fee for the collection of receivables. This can be true for business booked prior to the change of ownership.

- **Inventory sale.** This is usually handled at the close of escrow. Physical inventory of all food, beverages and supplies should be taken by an independent service and a separate bill of sale prepared for the agreed-upon price of this merchandise.

- **Non-compete clause.** This is quite common in the sale of an ongoing business, because the new owner doesn't want the seller to open up a competing business near by. Sellers try to avoid these, but understand they're inevitable. Smart sellers make sure the agreement only covers the same type of food operation; so if they're selling a pizza parlor, they're not prohibited from opening a five-star bistro.

- **Repurchase agreement.** Sellers often include agreements that grant them the option to buy the restaurant back within a certain time period. This usually notes the purchase price and terms of the sale. If the restaurant becomes incredibly valuable all of a sudden, the former owner can buy it back or sell the repurchase agreement to someone else.

- **Employment contract.** If a seller agrees to remain as an employee of the new restaurant, a very specific contract should be drafted. Most sellers have no interest in these contracts and just want out. However, his offering to stay on may increase his potential for selling the restaurant, and he could enjoy a good salary during this time.

- **Consulting contract.** This may be a more acceptable employment contract that gives the new owner a tax-deductible expense but doesn't burden the former owner, either.

- **Conditions not met.** Often buyers cannot meet every sales condition. Sellers can use this as a way to back out of the deal. However, the seller should also reserve the right to proceed with the sale even if certain conditions are not met.

DETERMINING PRICE FROM A BUYER'S PERSPECTIVE

Potential buyers must do a thorough financial analysis of the restaurant. They should carefully study its current profitability and use this information to determine its potential capacity for generating revenue. Because there is a very close relationship between a restaurant's current profitability and its likely sales price, the buyer should examine this income very carefully. Understandably, sellers are not particularly eager to divulge their financial records to buyers. However, if a seller is forthcoming with this information it can signal to the buyer that he has nothing to hide.

It's a good idea for the buyer to hire a good accountant to assist in this financial analysis. This will help determine whether the deal meets the buyer's investment requirements. Buyers should also consider hiring other specialists to work with contracts, unemployment compensation and insurance and banking. If the buyer qualifies, Small Business Development Centers (SBDC) throughout the country offer free consulting services to businesses with fewer than 500 employees.

The buyers should also complete at least a rough market and competition survey before performing her financial evaluation. This will ensure her familiarity with the restaurant's location and will help her estimate future revenues and expenses. If the buyer is unfamiliar with the area, an independent consulting service can be hired to provide a useful survey.

A seller expects a written offer with price, terms, conditions and an earnest money deposit before he will allow a potential buyer to review confidential financial information. It must be agreed that the buyer can withdraw if she's unhappy with the financial records. This is because the earnest deposit is at risk unless the right to retract the offer is in place. When reviewing the sellers' financial records, buyers should expect that an independent CPA has never audited them. This is because auditing is a costly process, and most small businesses don't do it unless they absolutely have to. A lucky buyer is one who is given audited financial statements.

Buyers need to reconstruct historical financial statements to show what they could have been had the buyer been operating the business. This is usually done from only the previous year's statement. Patience is important here. This is a time-consuming process, and if errors are made, the estimate of the restaurant's sales price may be inaccurate. Sellers will tend to overestimate customer counts and check averages and underestimate utilities and other expenses. The inexperienced buyer should be wary when evaluating these numbers and may want to hire professional counsel.

Also, it is important to be aware that sellers will usually include only the financial details they initially want to reveal. These numbers are usually pretty optimistic, but can give the buyer a good idea of whether the restaurant matches her investment needs. The typical listing agreement contains the asking price, financing possibilities, current sales volume, current expenses, and age and size of the restaurant. Buyers should evaluate this information carefully, with special attention to the apparent net cash flow, before spending a lot of time and money on detailed analysis.

During this analysis, it's important to note that the typical restaurant purchase will not appear to generate enough money to provide sufficient cash flow, give the buyer an appropriate salary and ensure a return on the initial investment. Don't be put off too quickly, however. Solid analysis often reveals that a change in ownership can considerably enhance a restaurant's profitability.

This analysis should examine all relevant tax filings to determine the most likely annual sales volume that the restaurant will generate. The profit figures included in these filings will be used to determine an accurate sales price. The payroll costs will be used to predict future personnel and payroll requirements and minimal tax liabilities. Personnel records are crucial in determining if there have been any Department of Labor judgments against the current owner or if there are any pending judgments that could impede the transfer of ownership. It is a good idea to meet with a DOL representative to find out if the restaurant is currently under investigation.

Cost of food, beverages and supplies is a restaurant's biggest expense. The potential buyer should take a random sample of canceled invoices and check their consistency with the cost of goods sold and direct operating-supplies expenses listed on the current income statement. If these numbers match, the buyer has a good idea of what product and supply expenses the restaurant will incur if no organizational and operational changes are made. The canceled invoices are also a good test of the current owner's purchasing skills. If invoices show higher prices than those of competing suppliers, the buyer can expect to decrease those expenses.

Most lenders require a cash budget to be prepared by buyers. This will point out the operation's daily cash requirements and the times of year when short-term money must be borrowed to cover brief shortages.

Potential buyers also should analyze balance sheets and income statements carefully. Balance sheets can reveal the anxiety level of a seller, and can indicate the current management's ability. If this ability is in question, this could predict greater earnings under sound management. Income statements are used by the buyer to determine whether the restaurant could have satisfied salary demands and provided a return on the initial investment, had it been under the buyer's management for the previous 12 months. Most sellers require a pro forma income statement for the coming year as part of the loan application process. Because a buyer is basing her price on current income, but purchasing the operation's future revenue-making ability, this is one of the most critical tasks the buyer will perform.

INITIAL INVESTMENT

Equally as important as price, terms and conditions is the total amount of money required to begin operating. Restaurants require large amounts of cash when starting, and buyers must estimate as accurately as possible the total initial investment needed to get their businesses up and running the way they envision them. Many restaurants that could have been successful failed because they were undercapitalized. For exactly this reason, one of the very appealing aspects of purchasing an existing restaurant is that many start-up costs are avoided. There are, however, a number of start-up costs even with transfer of ownership. Here are a number to be aware of:

- **Investigation costs.** Buyers must be willing to spend time and money to thoroughly examine the opportunities that are available. Typical buyers want to begin running their new establishment as soon as possible and don't want to be bothered with extensive analysis. By contrast, restaurant developers or chain-restaurant companies spend great time and effort before investing in a property. Many investors falsely believe that once initial development work is complete, the start-up costs are eliminated. While they usually are reduced considerably, these costs still exist, and wise investors calculate them in their analysis.

- **Down payment.** Standard down payment is usually around a quarter of the sales price. Buyers who offer this down payment usually can expect the seller to provide below-market financing for the remainder of the sales price. The down payment can affect the sales price, and in many cases sellers will accept a lower sales price with a larger down payment and vice versa.

- **Transaction costs.** Escrow agents will prorate insurance, payroll, vacation pay, license renewal fees, advertising costs, etc. on the close-of-escrow date. The buyer usually will have a debit balance that the escrow agent will transfer to the seller. The fees paid to the escrow company and for the drawing of documents needed to close the transaction constitute the closing costs.

- **Working capital.** Buyers must budget necessary amounts of money to ensure sufficient supplies are on hand to run the restaurant.

- **Deposits.** Most creditors require cash deposits as assurance they will be paid for their products and services. Utility, telephone, sales-tax, payroll-tax and lease deposits all must be factored in.

- **Licenses and permits.** Most restaurants must have a slew of retail, health and government permits. All required operating licenses and permits should be budgeted as start-up expenses.

- **Legal fees.** Competent legal advice is a very good idea for buyers. Escrow agents should not be counted on to draw papers correctly and to make sure that the interests of various parties have been represented. A buyer should have her own counsel looking out for her interests solely, and fees for these services should be budgeted in.

- **Renovations and utensils.** There may be building code violations to rectify or large renovations necessary to bring the restaurant into a competitive position. It may also be necessary to purchase new china, glass, silver and utensils to replace worn older ones.

- **Advertising.** Promoting an opening or reopening, rebuilding signage and offering promotional discounts or other incentives can be good ways to build patronage for a new establishment.

- **Fictitious name registration.** If the name of a restaurant is fictitious, the name usually must be registered at the local courthouse or County Recorder's Office.

- **Loan fees.** Buyers who are not acquiring seller financing will accrue loan fees from the lending parties.

- **Equity fees.** Buyers who want to sell common stock to a few investors will incur attorney, document preparation and registration fees.

- **Insurance.** A lender will require a borrower to have appropriate life and disability insurance and that the lender be named sole beneficiary.

- **Franchise fees.** Buyers acquiring an existing franchise will be required to pay the franchise a transfer-of-ownership fee. This fee pays the franchiser for the costs of evaluating the new owner for the franchise. It is paid in up front and in cash before the new franchise can begin operations.

- **Distributorship fees.** Buyers who assume exclusive distributorship licenses or want to discontinue a current license agreement may incur costs similar to franchise fees. Exclusive distributorships are usually granted to individuals, but some are given to business locations, and in this instance a buyer can assume the license with little out-of-pocket expense.

- **Pre-opening labor.** This is one of the expenses that are greatly minimized by purchasing an existing operation instead of starting one from scratch. Buyers usually plan to make some personnel changes, and a portion of current staff members should be expected to leave during the change of management.

- **Accounting fees.** Fees for assistance in the evaluation of a restaurant purchase need to be budgeted.

- **Other consulting fees.** A restaurant owner's primary consultants are her attorney and her accountant, but several other consultants should be retained if the buyer needs specific advice. Menu consultants, labor-relations specialists and computer consultants can all be retained to support management.

- **Other prepaid expenses.** When new ownership takes over an existing business it is not uncommon for creditors to demand a form of prepayment.

- **Sales taxes.** Property may be subject to a transfer tax, and non-food supplies are often subject to sales tax.

- **Locksmith.** Most buyers will change all the locks on a restaurant after the sale is concluded.

- **Security.** A typical buyer will transfer the current security service into her business. If one doesn't exist, the buyer should invest in one to protect her new business.

- **Contingency.** Successful restaurateurs suggest having a contingency fund large enough for the first six months' operating expenses. Among other things, it is often necessary to over-hire and over-schedule employees before an effective sales distribution pattern emerges, so operators incur incredibly high expenses during the first six months of operation.

STRATEGIES FOR SELLING

A strategy of clearly stated sales objectives will ensure that an acceptable sale is made, and as a seller, you won't give the business away. Sellers need to prioritize their sales objectives and consider what trade-offs may help achieve them. Deciding what is most important to hold onto, and the ability to be flexible in other areas, will support your overall selling goals. For example, if a high asking price is important, being flexible on the down payment is a likely trade-off, and vice versa. The following is a list of typical sales objectives:

- **Selling quickly.** Once an owner decides to sell, his enthusiasm for the business can fade, and this can hurt his bottom line. Unfortunately most restaurant sales take around 8 to 15 months to complete. However, most of the attention a restaurant gets when it goes on the market is in the first 3 to 4 weeks, so it is important that the business be attractively priced to capitalize on this initial attention. Sellers should also be ready to respond to offers from the moment the restaurant goes on sale. Chances of selling are not good if buyers are interested but the seller does not have a well-prepared sales solicitation ready.

- **Best present-value sales price.** The sales price needs to be incorporated in the terms and conditions. Otherwise you won't have a business that is representing its present value. You may sell quickly at a very high price if your terms and conditions are favorable. Price, terms and conditions are interrelated. If one changes the others do as well. Sellers must determine the price, terms and conditions that must be met so that they can have a baseline to operate from. This is particularly important because different buyers will want very different prices, terms and conditions. The seller who has determined multiple variable scenarios of what he absolutely requires for his price and from the terms and conditions is preparing himself well for negotiations.

- **Large down payment.** The bigger the down payment the lower the probability the seller will need to foreclose on the new operation. This is because investors who have put in large amounts of equity are considerably less likely to abandon an investment if troubles arise. Thus, sellers are often willing to reduce sales prices by as much as 50 percent if the buyer will make a large down payment.

LOOKING FOR THE RIGHT BUYER

Sellers should look for buyers who will manage the restaurant well. The only way a seller should sell their business to a new restaurateur is if the buyer cashes out the seller. A seller wants a competent buyer who will run the business and prevent the need for repossession. Sellers want their business to stay sold.

Sellers should learn as much as possible about potential buyers. Reference checks can be helpful in determining if a buyer is seriously interested, but they don't tell you what their motivations are. As much as is humanly possible, the sellers should try and understand what is motivating their buyers, and these factors should be highlighted in negotiations. Are they looking for the property only? Do they want the prestige of owning a restaurant right in town? Are they looking for a consistent return on their investment? Savvy sellers answer these questions as much as possible and then push the appropriate attributes of the business.

Sellers should develop a professional property information package that will entice buyers. This package should contain just enough information for buyers to see if the business meets their investment requirements. If a buyer wants more information, she is expected to prepare an offer and pay an earnest money deposit before the seller will provide it. This brochure is often an investor's first view of the property and, as such, is a crucial tool for the seller. Sellers should devote considerable time and effort to its preparation. An effective brochure doesn't reveal more than the seller wants to divulge, while enticing buyers. It should be printed on high-quality card stock and have the following data:

- **Pictures of the restaurant.**

- **Confidential inquiries.** Seller's name and contact information and other sources such as broker, answering service, etc.

- **Description of the restaurant.** Concept, theme, hours of operation, square footage, etc.

- **Map/Description of neighborhood.** Types of businesses, attractions, residential makeup. The map should be easy to read, and the business's location should be highlighted.

- **Real estate description.** Property's legal description, common description and the tax assessor's most recent valuation figure—unless it contrasts with the seller's estimate.

- **Summary of leasehold improvements.** China, glass and utensils. Original cost, current book value and estimated replacement cost of these assets.

- **Income analysis.** Monthly profit and loss statements from the previous 12 months.

- **Real-property lease review.** Remaining term, monthly base rent, percentage-rent clause, common-area maintenance fees, insurance requirements, options and rate adjustments.

- **Personal-property lease review.** Remaining term, monthly base rent, maintenance costs, insurance requirements, options and amount of final payment that must be made if lease is rent-to-own.

- **Financing availability.** Amount, interest rate, terms and conditions of both assumable and seller financing.

- **Market survey.** Summary data on the restaurant's target area.

- **Competition survey.** Summary data on the restaurant's current and pending direct competition.

- **Initial investment summary.** Includes estimate of the initial investment required to buy and manage the restaurant.

- **Summary of seller's solicitation.** Asking price and down payment. Should also highlight the assets included in the sale and the availability of assumable and seller financing.

Sellers can be contacted directly or through an intermediary. Most sellers prefer to use an intermediary in order to keep a professional distance and attract buyers through an established system. Intermediaries also help to weed the serious investors from the suspect. A good broker protects the seller's privacy and knows how to sell a business. There are drawbacks to intermediaries, though. Brokers need to be paid—often as much as 10 percent of the restaurant's sales price—and conflicts of interest can arise. Due diligence in selecting a broker is recommended.

STRATEGIES FOR BUYING

Before contacting sellers, potential buyers should prepare a document that outlines for themselves their desired sales price, terms and conditions. A close examination on the buyer's part of how the seller is arriving at his sales price, terms and conditions is also invaluable. This will give you, the buyer, considerable flexibility in negotiations and the ability to anticipate the seller and effectively counteroffer. Through careful preparation you will be able to take your desired sales price, terms, conditions, initial investment and revenue goals from the page to a signed contract on a business that has a high probability of meeting those goals. This plan, however, needs to be flexible enough to adapt to different possible investments, because there are many types of restaurants available and an infinite range of prices, terms and conditions. You must determine the type of restaurant that is right for you. Consider the restaurant's investment yield, taxes and the effect the business will have on your personal life. Basically, buyers should be looking for restaurants that will meet their numbers, and ones that they are going to be happy working at 12 to14 hours a day.

As sellers must, so should buyers prioritize their objectives and consider the trade-offs that must be made to attain them. Buyers generally want to accomplish the flowing objectives:

- **Best possible sales price.** Serious buyers and sellers compromise on the sales price, terms and conditions in order to reach a mutually satisfying end, and buyers are almost always willing to trade price for terms and conditions. Most buyers will draw the line at a sales price that exceeds the restaurant's replacement cost.

- **Reasonable down payment.** Most serious buyers are willing to maintain a 1:1 debt-to-equity ratio. A typical down payment is, then, the amount of money that when added to other initial investment charges, will total 50 percent of the total investment needed to acquire and run the business. Many buyers want to lower their down payments to reduce risk and unfortunately find themselves with businesses that cannot support their debt load.

- **Reasonable initial investment.** Serious buyers are willing to equally match dollars of debt with dollars of personal equity. Buyers do want most of their equity to go towards the down payment.

- **Maximum future profits.** Buyers are buying a restaurant's current financial performance but are always looking for the highest potential revenue-generating business.

- **Reduced possibility of failure.** Only one out of five established businesses that are purchased go under. That is much better than the four-out-of-five failure rate of new businesses. The typical buyer of an existing business is an optimist with real-world experience.

- **Enhancement of borrowing power.** Most lenders prefer financing an existing, profitable operation to a new venture.

- **Minimizing tax liabilities.** Buyers need to be aware of the tax consequences of the restaurants they're buying. Both buyer and seller should work at minimizing taxes. The only way to ensure that this happens is for both parties to hire accountants. Most buyers focus on deferring income-tax liabilities through asking sellers to accept a lower sales price in exchange for a higher interest rate on seller financing. The interest can then be deducted over the life of the loan.

Buyers, too, should develop a purchase plan that lists potential sellers, analyzes their motivations for selling, analyzes restaurants and develops planned responses to counteroffers. Research into a seller's motivation is crucial here, and can serve the buyer in myriad ways. The following is a list of six major seller motivations:

- **Owners who want to retire.** These folks usually want to move out of the area and receive a retirement income. They usually seek acceptable seller financing or an annuity arrangement.

- **Disillusioned owners.** Neophytes or absentee owners often decide to get out of the business when it starts going poorly. Often the business is not as profitable or fun as they had thought, and they don't know what to do to remedy those problems.

- **Owners with tax problems.** Once depreciation expenses and interest expenses have evaporated, owners often sell in order to move into a larger operation and to reinstate these tax shelters.

- **Owners with other investment opportunities.** Often owners want to use the money received from the sale of their restaurants for investments elsewhere or, if the market is favorable, just to cash out at a very good price.

- **Owners with distressed properties.** Struggling properties often do not throw off enough profit to fund necessary remodeling or overhaul.

- **Distressed owners.** Often profitable operations are run by people having troubled relationships with their business or marital partners or their shareholders. In some cases one of these parties has died. These can give serious cause for an owner to leave a profitable operation.

Once a buyer has responded to a sales solicitation she will receive enough information to determine if the restaurant meets or exceeds her investment requirements. The buyer should do more preliminary work to find out further specifics about whether a restaurant is or is not a good opportunity. Experienced buyers know almost immediately from the sales brochure if the restaurant will meet their needs. One of the ways they determine this is through the real-property lease payment. If it's less than or equals 6 percent of the restaurant's total sales volume, most buyers know it's worth further investigation. Buyers also consider future sales volume and profit-generating capacity.

When a buyer decides to pursue more research, she should tour the facility; learn the lease highlights and other purchase options; and evaluate the neighborhood, the competition, the customer viewpoint, the history of ownership and the owner's reason for selling. After doing a deeper analysis of the restaurant, the buyer must once again determine if it meets her investment requirements. If she determines that it does, an earnest money deposit and offer should be delivered to the seller in return for detailed information on the restaurant.

FINANCING

The typical offer and acceptance agreement includes several conditions necessary for the deal's completion. Most of these are met easily, but there are two that are difficult to meet. The buyer's qualification for financing and the attainment all necessary permits and licenses are the two most common impediments. There is little you as a buyer can do if you don't qualify for permits, unless you need to fix only simple code violations to qualify. In the financing realm, however, the seller and buyer have more control and can adjust the final sales contract to suit the buyer's needs. Buyers should beware that there is no bigger threat to their success than inadequate or inappropriate financing. Excessive debt burden is one of the most consistent reasons restaurants go under.

EQUITY FUNDS

Equity is capital that is at risk. Owners invest this money without any guarantee on a return. There are several types of equity financing techniques. The following are the most common:

- **Personal equity.** These are ventures that are funded entirely with personal equity or with a combination of personal equity and lease and debt financing.

- **Partnerships.** Many restaurateurs solicit funds by getting partners to invest. Typical partnership arrangements are general or limited. General partnerships usually mean both parties will be involved in the operation and both have food-service experience. Limited partnerships are usually only formed if the restaurant includes the real estate as well. In these cases there is usually a general partner and one or more inactive, limited partners, with the general partner acting as manager and the limited partners as passive investors.

- **Corporation.** Corporate ownership can be a great way to raise capital. Generally it is done through a stock offering—in the case of a large corporation, to the public, and in a small company, to private investors.

- **Venture capital.** Venture capitalists normally do not fund a venture unless it has expansion potential and is well run. Venture capitalists are interested in long-term financial gain and are less interested in the net operating profits of a new establishment. Buyers intending to purchase chain restaurants might be able to obtain venture capital because of the high earning potential.

SBA FINANCIAL PROGRAMS

The Small Business Administration (SBA) offers a variety of financing options for small businesses. Whether you are looking for a long-term loan for machinery and equipment, a general working capital loan, a revolving line of credit or a microloan, the SBA has a financing program to fit your needs. These programs are discussed in detail on SBA's Web site at *http://www.sba.gov.*

SBA ASSISTANCE

SBA is the largest source of long-term small-business financing in the nation. In order to determine whether you qualify or whether an SBA business loan best suits your financing needs, contact your banker, one of the active SBA-guaranteed lenders or an SBA loan officer.

THE 7(A) LOAN GUARANTY PROGRAM

The 7(a) Loan Guaranty Program is the SBA's primary loan program. The SBA reduces risk to lenders by guaranteeing major portions of loans made to small businesses. This enables the lenders to provide financing to small businesses when funding is otherwise unavailable at reasonable terms. The eligibility requirements and credit criteria of the program are very broad in order to accommodate a wide range of financing needs.

When a small business applies to a lending institution for a loan, the lender reviews the application and decides if it merits a loan on its own or if it requires additional support in the form of an SBA guarantee. The lender then requests SBA backing on the loan. In guaranteeing the loan, the SBA assures the lender that, in the event the borrower does not repay the loan, the government will reimburse the lending institution for a portion of its loss. By providing this guarantee, the SBA is able to help tens of thousands of small businesses every year get financing they could not otherwise obtain.

To qualify for an SBA guarantee, a small business must meet the 7(a) criteria, and the lender must certify that it could not provide funding on reasonable terms except with an SBA guarantee. The SBA can then guarantee as much as 85 percent on loans of up to $150,000 and 75 percent on loans of more than $150,000. In most cases, the maximum guarantee is $1 million. Exceptions are the International Trade, DELTA and 504 loan programs, which have higher loan limits. The maximum total loan size under the 7(a) program is $2 million.

FRIENDS AND RELATIVES

Many entrepreneurs look to private sources such as friends and family when starting out in a business venture. Often, money is loaned interest free or at a low interest rate, which can be quite beneficial when getting started.

BANKS AND CREDIT UNIONS

The most common sources of funding, banks and credit unions, will provide a loan if you can show that your business proposal is sound.

BORROWING MONEY

It is often said that small business people have a difficult time borrowing money. This is not necessarily true. Banks make money by lending money. However, the inexperience of many small business owners in financial matters often prompts banks to deny loan requests. Requesting a loan when you are not properly prepared sends a signal to your lender. That message is: High Risk!

To be successful in obtaining a loan, you must be prepared and organized. You must know exactly how much money you need, why you need it and how you will pay it back. You must be able to convince your lender that you are a good credit risk.

HOW TO WRITE A LOAN PROPOSAL

Approval of your loan request depends on how well you present yourself, your business and your financial needs to a lender. Remember, lenders want to make loans, but they must make loans they know will be repaid. The best way to improve your chances of obtaining a loan is to prepare a written proposal. A well-written loan proposal contains:

GENERAL INFORMATION
- Business name, names of principals, Social Security Number for each principal and business address.

- Purpose of the loan. Exactly what the loan will be used for and why it is needed.

- Amount required. The exact amount you need to achieve your purpose.

BUSINESS DESCRIPTION
- History and nature of the business. What kind of business it is, its age, number of employees and current business assets.

- Ownership structure. Details of your company's legal structure.

MANAGEMENT PROFILE

- Provide a short statement about each principal in your business. Include background, education, experience, skills and accomplishments.

MARKET INFORMATION

- Clearly define your company's products as well as your markets.

- Identify your competition and explain how your business competes in the marketplace.

- Profile your customers and explain how your business can satisfy their needs.

FINANCIAL INFORMATION

- Financial statements: balance sheets and income statements for the past three years. If you are starting out, provide a projected balance sheet and income statement.

- Personal financial statements on yourself and other principal owners of the business.

- Collateral you are willing to pledge as security for the loan.

HOW YOUR LOAN REQUEST WILL BE REVIEWED

When reviewing a loan request, the lender is primarily concerned about repayment. To help determine your ability to repay, many loan officers will order a copy of your business credit report from a credit-reporting agency. Therefore, you should work with these agencies to help them present an accurate picture of your business. Using the credit report and the information you have provided, the lending officer will consider the following issues:

- Have you invested savings or personal equity in your business totaling at least 25 to 50 percent of the loan you are requesting? (Remember, a lender or investor will not finance 100 percent of your business.)

- Do you have a sound record of credit-worthiness as indicated by your credit report, work history and letters of recommendation? This is very important.

- Do you have sufficient experience and training to operate a successful business?

- Have you prepared a loan proposal and business plan that demonstrate your understanding of, and commitment to the success of, the business?

- Does the business have sufficient cash flow to make the monthly payments?

CLOSING THE SALE

Once buyer and seller have agreed on the particulars, they will commit themselves to a binding sales contract and transfer ownership. There are often lawyers, brokers, accountants, lenders, escrow agents, government officials, trade unions, family members and other people involved in this transaction. It usually takes 30 to 60 days to finish the ownership transfer.

The close of escrow happens when all the documents necessary to complete the sale are recorded at the County Recorder's Office. This usually happens the morning after the closing date.

The documents usually recorded:

- Deed
- Mortgage or deed of trust
- Sales contract
- Bill of sale
- Request for notice

- Promissory note
- Other security agreements
- Option
- Assignments
- Notice of completion of work

If the new owner doesn't make payments on an assumable loan, the seller will want to be notified. If they have made the request for notification in advance—and made it part of public record—it will happen. The notice of completion of work is also included in these filings because many people will record guarantees and warranties to make sure there are no questions regarding their dates of expiration.

3

❧❦

HOW TO ANALYZE & INVEST IN A RESTAURANT FRANCHISE OPPORTUNITY

INTRODUCTION

Many restaurant owners have been helped in getting a sound start by investing in a franchise. According to the U.S. Department of Commerce, buying a franchise is the average persons most viable avenue to owning a business. You may want to consider such an investment. Franchising can minimize your risk. It will enable you to start your business under a name and trademark that has already gained public acceptance. You will have access to training and management assistance from experienced people in the restaurant industry. Sometimes, you can obtain financial assistance; this allows you to start your business with less cash than you would ordinarily need.

On the other hand you must make some sacrifices when entering a franchised operation. You lose a certain amount of control of the business. You will no longer truly be your own boss in some situations. And, of course, you must pay a fee or share profits with the franchisor. This chapter will present some of the advantages and disadvantages of franchises, and how to evaluate one.

DEFINITION OF FRANCHISING

Essentially, franchising is a plan of distribution under which an individually owned business is operated as though it were a part of a large chain. Products are standardized. Standardized trademarks, symbols, design elements and equipment are used. A supplier (the franchisor) gives the individual dealer (the franchisee) the right to sell, distribute and market the franchisor's product by using the franchisor's name, reputation and selling techniques. The franchise agreement (or contract) usually gives the exclusive right to sell, or otherwise represent the franchisor, in a specified market or geographical area. In return for this exclusive right the franchisee agrees to pay a sum of money (a franchise fee) or a percentage of gross sales or to buy equipment or supplies from the franchisor—often these options are variously combined.

ADVANTAGES OF FRANCHISING

As a franchisee you have the luxury of starting a business with:

1. **Limited experience.** You are taking advantage of the franchisor's experience, experience which you probably would have gained the hard way—through trial and error.

2. **A relatively small amount of capital** and a strengthened financial and credit standing. Sometimes the franchisor will give financial assistance to enable you to start with less than the usual amount of cash. For example, the franchisor may accept a down payment with your note for the balance of the needed capital. Or the franchisor may allow you to delay in making payments on royalties or other fees in order to help you over the "rough spots." With the name of a well-known, successful franchisor behind you, your standing with financial institutions will be strengthened.

3. **A well-developed image and consumer support** of proven products and services. The goods and services of the franchisor are proven and widely known. Therefore, your business has "instant" pulling power. To develop such pulling power on your own might take years of promotion and considerable investment.

4. **Competently designed facilities, layout, displays and fixtures.** The franchising company has designed effectively facilities, layout, displays and fixtures based upon experience with many dealers.

5. **Chain buying power.** You may receive savings through chain-style purchasing of products, equipment, supplies, advertising materials and other business needs.

6. **The opportunity for business training and continued assistance** from experienced management in proven methods of doing business. You can normally expect to be trained in the mechanics of the restaurant business and guided in its day-to-day operation until you are proficient at the job. Moreover, management consulting services are provided by the franchisor on a continuing basis. This often includes help with record keeping as well as other accounting assistance.

7. **National or regional promotion and publicity.** The national or regional promotion of the franchisor will help your business. Also, you will receive help and guidance with local advertising. The franchisor's program of research and development will assist you in keeping up with competition and changing times.

All of these factors can help increase your income and lower your risk of failure.

DISADVANTAGES OF FRANCHISING

1. **Submission to imposed standardized operations.** You cannot make all the rules. Contrary to the "be your own boss" lures in franchise advertisements, you may not be your only boss. In addition, you must subjugate your personal identity to the name of the franchisor. Obviously, if you would like your operation to be known by your own name, a franchise is not for you. The franchisor exerts fundamental control and obligates you to 1) conform to standardized procedure; 2) handle specific products or services which may not be particularly profitable in your marketing area; and 3) follow other policies which may benefit others in the chain but not you. This means that you forfeit the freedom to make many decisions—to be your own boss.

2. **Sharing of profits with the franchisor.** The franchisor nearly always charges a royalty of a percentage of gross sales. This royalty fee must ultimately come out of the profits of the franchisee—or be paid whether the franchisee makes a profit or not. Sometimes such fees are exorbitantly out of proportion to the profit. Royalty payments in the fast-food franchising industry ranging from a low of 1 percent to a high of 18 percent of gross sales. The average royalty fee is about 4 percent of gross sales.

3. **Required purchases.** Merchandise, supplies or equipment that the franchisor requires you to buy from the corporation might be obtained elsewhere for less. A recent government study indicated that in fast-food franchising many franchisees who were required to buy a large proportion of supplies from their franchisors were paying higher prices than they could obtain on their own. Additionally, you might pay more to the franchisor than other franchisees for the same services.

4. **Lack of freedom to meet local competition.** Under a franchise you may be restricted in establishing selling prices and in introducing additional products or services or dropping unprofitable ones, even in the face of insidious local competition.

5. **Danger of contracts being slanted to the advantage of the franchisor.** Clauses in some contracts imposed by the franchisor provide for unreasonably high sales quotas, mandatory working hours, cancellation or termination of the franchise for minor infringements, and/or restrictions on the franchisee in transferring his franchise or recovering his investment. The territory assigned the franchisee may overlap with that of another franchisee or may be otherwise inequitable. In settling disputes of any kind the bargaining power of the franchisor is usually greater.

For example, the same study referred to above showed fast-food franchisees working a median of 60 hours a week, with some families working as much as 120 hours. The power imbalance in favor of the franchisor is due not only to the franchisee's smaller financial resources but to his lack of the information the franchisor has. For example, the franchisor understands thoroughly the implications of the agreement she, herself, has devised and she has experience in negotiating under this agreement.

6. **Time consumed in preparing reports required by the franchisor.** Franchisors require specific reports. The time and effort of preparing these may be inordinately burdensome. On the other hand, you should recognize that if these reports are helpful to the franchisor they probably will help you to manage your business more effectively.

7. **Sharing the burden of the franchisor's faults.** While ordinarily the franchisor's chain will have developed goodwill among consumers, there may be instances in which ill will has been developed. For example, if a customer has been served a stale roll, a burnt hamburger or received poor service in one outlet he or she is apt to become disgruntled with the whole chain. As one outlet in the chain, you will suffer regardless of the excellence of your particular unit. Furthermore, the franchisor may fail. You must bear the brunt of the chain's mistakes as well as share the glory of its good performances.

MINORITY PARTICIPATION IN FRANCHISING

A number of franchise systems have developed special programs for minority individuals who seek to go into business for themselves. One such program asks the minority individual for a down payment of only 2 percent. The franchisor matches this with 98 percent financing and up to a year of training. Another program is a joint venture between a minority-owned business and an established franchising company. This joint venture is not a merger of the two companies. Rather, it is a plan whereby each company contributes an equal amount of dollars, but all responsibility for day-to-day operations is left with the minority-owned company.

FRANCHISE FINANCING

There are a growing number of alternatives for individuals and investors who want to enter franchising or expand their current market position. More and more local and regional banks, along with national non-bank lenders, are offering franchise financing. Lending institutions have a greater appreciation for the importance of franchising in the marketplace, for its future growth and for its stability as a distribution method.

For example, the International Franchise Association lists more than 30 bank and non-bank franchise lenders in its Franchise Opportunities Guide this year. The U.S. Small Business Administration, which last year backed more than 60,000 small-business loans totaling $14.75 billion, works with local and regional banks to offer its guaranteed loan program to start-up franchisees.

EVALUATING A FRANCHISE OPPORTUNITY

A franchise costs money. One can be purchased for as little as a few hundred dollars, or as much as a quarter of a million dollars or more. Hence it is vital that you investigate and evaluate carefully any franchise before you invest.

Beware of the "fast buck" artists. The popularity of franchising has attracted an unsavory group of operators who will take you if they can. Sometimes known as "front money men" they usually offer nothing more than the sale of equipment and a catchy business name. Once they sell you the equipment they do not care whether you succeed or fail. If you are promised tremendous profits in a short period of time, be wary.

The following checklist will aid you in selecting the right franchise. Check each question when the answer is "yes." Most, if not all, questions should be checked before you sign a franchise contract.

QUESTIONS TO ANSWER AFFIRMATIVELY BEFORE GOING INTO FRANCHISING (Check if answer is yes.)

THE FRANCHISOR

1. Has the franchisor been in business long enough (five years or more) to have established a good reputation?

2. Have you checked Better Business Bureaus, Chambers of Commerce, Dun and Bradstreet and bankers to find out about the franchisor's business reputation and credit ratings?

3. Did the above investigations reveal that the franchisor has a good reputation and credit rating?

4. Does the franchising firm appear to be financed adequately so that it can carry out its stated plan of financial assistance and expansion?

5. Have you discovered how many franchisees are now operating?

6. Have you ascertained the "mortality," or failure, rate among franchisees?

7. Is the failure rate small?

8. Have you checked with some franchisees and found that the franchisor has a reputation for honesty and fair dealing among those who currently hold franchises?

9. Has the franchisor shown you certified figures indicating exact net profits of one or more going operations which you have personally checked?

10. Has the franchisor given you a specimen contract to study with the advice of your legal counsel?

11. Will the franchisor assist you with:
    A. A management training program?
    B. An employee training program?
    C. A public relations program?
    D. Obtaining capital?
    E. Good credit terms?
    F. Merchandising ideas?
    G. Designing store layout and displays?
    H. Inventory control methods?
    I.   Analyzing financial statements?

12. Does the franchisor provide continuing assistance for franchisees through super-visors who visit regularly?

13. Does the franchising firm have an experienced manager with in-depth training?

14. Will the franchisor assist you in finding a good location for your business?

15. Has the franchising company investigated you carefully enough to assure itself that you can successfully operate one of its franchises at a profit both to it and to you?

16. Have you determined exactly what the franchisor can do for you that you cannot do yourself?

17. Does the franchise comply with all applicable laws?

18. If a product must be purchased exclusively from the franchisor or a designated supplier, are the prices to you, as the franchisee, competitive?

19. Does the franchise fee seem reasonable?

20. Do continuing royalty or percent-of-gross-sales payment requirements appear reasonable?

21. Are the total cash investment required and the terms for financing the balance satisfactory?

22. Does the cash investment include payment for fixtures and equipment?

23. If you will be required to participate in company-sponsored promotions and pub-licity by contributing to an advertising fund, will you have the right to veto an increase in contributions required?

24. Will you be free to buy the amount of merchandise you believe you need rather than a required amount?

25. Can merchandise be returned for credit?

26. Would you be free to engage in other business activities?

27. If there is an annual sales quota, can you retain your franchise if it is not met?

28. Does the contract give you an exclusive territory for the length of the franchise?

29. Is your territory protected?

30. Is the franchise agreement renewable?

31. Can you terminate your agreement if you are not happy for some reason?

32. Is the franchisor prohibited from selling the franchise out from under you?

33. May you sell the business to whomever you please?

34. If you sell your franchise, will you be compensated for the good will you have built into the business?

35. Does the contract obligate the franchisor to give you continuing assistance while you are operating the business?

36. Are you permitted a choice in determining whether you will sell any new products introduced by the franchisor after you have opened your business?

37. Is there anything with respect to the franchise or its operation that would make you ineligible for special financial assistance and other benefits accorded to small business concerns by federal, state or local governments?

38. Did your lawyer approve the franchise contract after he or she studied it paragraph by paragraph?

39. Is the contract free and clear of requirements compelling you at any point to take steps that are, according to your lawyer, unwise or illegal in your state, county or city?

40. Does the contract cover all aspects of your agreement with the franchisor?

41. Does the contract really benefit both you and the franchisor?

YOUR MARKET

42. Are the territorial boundaries of your market completely, accurately and understandably defined?

43. Have you done a study to determine whether the product you propose to sell has a market in your territory at the prices you will have to charge?

44. Does the territory provide adequate sales potential?

45. Will the population in your territory increase over the next five years?

46. Will the average per capita income in the territory remain the same or increase over the next five years?

47. Do you know that existing competition in your territory is not well entrenched?

YOU—THE FRANCHISEE

48. Do you know where you will go to get the equity capital you will need?

49. Have you compared what it will take to start your own restaurant with the price you must pay for the franchise?

50. Have you made a business plan? For example: Have you worked out what income from sales or services you can reasonably expect in the first six months? the first year? the second year?

51. Have you made a forecast of expenses including a regular salary for yourself?

52. Are you prepared to give up some independence of action to secure the advantages offered by the franchise?

53. Are you capable of accepting supervision, even though you presumably will be your own boss?

54. Are you prepared to accept rules and regulations with which you may not agree?

55. Can you afford the period of training involved?

56. Are you ready to spend much or all of the remainder of your business life with this franchisor, offering his product or service to the public?

CONCLUSION

Franchising creates distinct opportunities for the prospective small business owner. Without franchising it is doubtful that thousands of small business investors could ever have started. The system permits goods to be marketed by a small business owner in a way that otherwise can done only with the vast sums of money and number of managerial people possessed by large corporations. As a new owner you can draw from the experience and resources—promotional, managerial, structural and material—of a large, established parent company.

Unfortunately, not even the help of a good franchisor can guarantee success. You will still be primarily responsible for the success or failure of your venture. As in any other type of business your return will be related directly to the amount and effectiveness of your investment in time and money.

BASIC COST CONTROL FOR FOOD-SERVICE OPERATIONS — AN OVERVIEW

INTRODUCTION

This chapter will introduce you to the basic cost control concepts that we will be developing in detail throughout the rest of this book. This chapter is being introduced now so that prior to developing the menu and menu items you can start to visualize the entire control process.

COST CONTROLS ARE CRUCIAL

Presently, throughout the entire food-service industry, operating expenses are up and income is down. After taxes and expenses, restaurants that make money, according to the National Restaurant Association, have bottom lines at 0.5–3.0 percent of sales. This tiny percentage is the difference between being profitable and going under, and it drives home the importance of controlling your costs.

A lot can be done to control costs, and it begins with planning. Cost control is about numbers. It is about collecting, organizing, interpreting and comparing the numbers that impact your bottom line. This is not a job that can be delegated, because these numbers are your controls. They are what tell you the real story of what's going on in your restaurant. Some operators may need outside assistance in interpreting these numbers such as an accountant or food service consultant.

Understanding this story and its implications on your bottom line comes only with constant review and the resulting familiarity with the relationships between these numbers and the workings of the business. This may seem like drudgery, but it is in fact your key to understanding the meaning behind your numbers. Once you have mastered the numbers they'll tell you the story behind your labor productivity, portion control, purchase prices, marketing promotions, new menu items and competitive strategy. This knowledge will free you to run the best, most profitable operation you can.

According to government statistics, a restaurant investor has a 1-in-20 chance of getting his money back in five years. Furthermore, the consensus of many successful restaurateurs is that 80 percent of the success of a restaurant is determined before it opens. This means you must prepare. And part of that preparation is integrating an ongoing cost control program into your business.

This can be doubly important if you are fortunate enough to start out doing great business. This is because high profits can hide many inefficiencies that will surely expose themselves during times of low sales. Too many people become cost-control converts only after suffering losses. This is shortsighted. The primary purpose of cost controls is to maximize profits, not minimize losses. Controlling costs works—all the time—because it focuses on getting the most value from the least cost in every aspect of your operation. By keeping costs under control you can charge less than the competition or make more money from charging the same price.

These are huge operating freedoms and opportunities that are not afforded you if you don't know what you're spending and therefore can't control that spending. Furthermore, most of the waste that occurs in restaurants can't be detected by the naked eye. It takes records and reports—whose meanings you've mastered interpreting— to tell you the size of the inefficiencies that are taking place.

Cost control is not accounting or bookkeeping: these are the information-gathering tools of cost control. Cost control can be defined by explaining its purposes:

- To provide management with information needed for making day-to-day operations decisions.

- To monitor department and individual efficiency.

- To inform management of expenses being incurred and incomes received and whether they fall within standards and budgets.

- To prevent fraud and theft.

- To provide the ground for the business's goals (not for discovering where it has been).

- To emphasize prevention, not correction.

- To maximize profits, not minimize losses.

This idea of prevention versus correction is fundamental. Prevention occurs through advanced planning. Your primary job is not to put out fires, it's to prevent them—and to maximize profits in the process.

The larger the distance between an owner or manager and the actual restaurant, the greater the need for effective cost control records. This is how franchisors of restaurant chains keep their eyes on thousands of units across the world. Many managers of individual operations assume that since they're on the premises during operating hours, a detailed system of cost control is unnecessary. Tiny family operations often see controls the same way and view any device for theft prevention as a sign of distrust towards their staff. This is shortsighted, because the main purpose of cost control is to provide infor-

THE RESTAURANT MANAGER'S HANDBOOK

mation to management about daily operations. Prevention of theft is a secondary function. Cost controls are about knowing where you are going. Furthermore, most waste and inefficiencies cannot be seen; they need to be understood through the numbers.

Understanding those numbers means interpreting them. To do this effectively you need to understand the difference between control and reduction. Control is achieved through the assembly and interpretation of data and ratios on your revenue and expenses. Reduction is the actual action taken to bring costs within your predetermined standards. Effective cost control starts at the top of an organization. Management must establish, support and enforce its standards and procedures.

There are ten primary areas that are central to any food and beverage operation and are therefore crucial elements of cost control records:

- **Purchasing.** Your inventory system is the critical component of purchasing. Before placing an order with a supplier you need to know what you have on hand and how much will be used. Allow for a cushion of inventory so you won't run out between deliveries. Once purchasing has been standardized, the manager simply orders from your suppliers. Records show supplier, prices, unit of purchase, product specifications, etc. This information needs to be kept on paper.

- **Receiving.** This is how you verify that everything you ordered has arrived. Check for correct brands, grades, varieties, quantities, correct prices, etc. Incorrect receivables need to be noted and either returned or credited to your account. Products purchased by weight or count need to be checked.

- **Storage.** All food is stored until it's used. Doing so in an orderly fashion ensures easy inventory. Doing so properly, with regard to temperature, ventilation and freedom from contamination, ensures food products remain in optimum condition until being used. Expensive items need to be guarded from theft.

- **Issuing.** Procedures for removing inventory from storage are part of the cost control process. Head chefs and bartenders have authority to take or "issue" stock from storage to the appropriate place. This is a much more important aspect of cost control than it seems, because in order to know your food and beverage costs you need to know a) your beginning inventory, b) how much was sold, and c) your ending inventory. Without this data you can't determine accurate sales figures.

- **Rough preparation.** How your staff minimizes waste during the preliminary processing of inventory is critical.

- **Preparation for service.** Roughly prepared ingredients are finished off prior to plating. The quality and care with which this is done determines the amount of waste generated in preparation of standard recipes.

- **Portioning/Transfer.** Food can be lost through over portioning. Final preparation should be monitored regularly to ensure quality and quantity standards are being adhered to. This is such a crucial element to cost control that management must be assigned to monitor order times, portions, presentation, and food quality with an eagle eye.

- **Order taking/Guest check.** Every item sold or issued from the kitchen needs to be recorded. This can be done by paper check or computer. Basically, it needs to be impossible for anyone to get food or drinks without having them entered into the system. No verbal orders for food or beverages should be accepted by or from anybody—including management and owners.

- **Cash receipts.** Monitoring sales is crucial to cost controls. Under-/overcharging, falsification of tips and lost checks must be investigated after every shift. Sales information from each meal period must be compiled to build a historical financial record. This record helps you forecast the future.

- **Bank deposits/Accounts payable.** Proper auditing of bank deposits and charge slips must be conducted.

Cost control is an ongoing process that must be part of the basic moment-to-moment breathing of your business. A continuous appraisal of this process is equally as integral to the functioning of your restaurant. There are five key elements to an effective cost control strategy:

1. Planning in advance.

2. Procedures and devices that aid the control process.

3. Implementation of your cost control program.

4. Employee compliance.

5. Management's ongoing enforcement and reassessment.

Furthermore, your program should be assessed with the following questions:

1. Do your cost controls provide relevant information?

2. Is the information timely?

3. Is it easily assembled, organized and interpreted?

4. Are the benefits and savings greater than the cost of the controls?

This last point is especially important. When the expense of the controls exceeds the savings, that's waste, not control. Spending $30,000 on a computer system that will save you $5,000 in waste is ineffective.

Standards are key to any cost control program. Predetermined points of comparison must be set, against which you will measure your actual results. The difference between planned resources and resources actually used is the variance. Management can then monitor for negative or positive variances between standards and actual performance and will know where specifically to make corrections. These five steps illustrate the uses of standards:

1. Performance standards should be established for all individuals and departments.

2. Individuals must see it as the responsibility of each to prevent waste and inefficiency.

3. Adherence—or lack of adherence—to standards must be monitored.

4. Actual performance must be compared against established standards.

5. When deviations from standards are discovered, appropriate action must be taken.

Your job is to make sure standards are adhered to. Is your staff using measuring scoops and ladles and sized bowls, glasses and cups, weighing portions individually, portioning by count, and pre-portioning? These are all useful tools to make sure standards are met and your cost control program implemented effectively.

OST RATIOS

Owners and managers need to be on the same page in terms of the meaning and calculation of the many ratios used to analyze food, beverage, and labor costs. It's important to understand how your ratios are being calculated, so you can get a true indication of the cost or profit activity in your restaurant. Numerous cost control software programs are available with built-in formulas for calculating ratios and percentages. The Uniform System of Accounts for Restaurants (USAR), published by the National Restaurant Association, is an essential guide for restaurant accounting. It establishes a common industry language that allows you to compare ratios and percentages across industry lines. The goal of this comparison is to create financial statements that are management tools, not just IRS reports. Cost control is not just the calculation of these numbers. It's the interpretation of them and the appropriate (re)actions taken to bring your numbers within set standards.

FOOD COST PERCENTAGE

This basic ratio is often misinterpreted because it can be calculated so many ways. Basically, it is food cost divided by food sales. However, whether your food cost is determined by food sold or consumed is a crucial difference. Also, for your food cost percentage to be accurate, a month-end inventory must be taken. Without this figure your food cost statement is inaccurate and therefore basically useless. This is because your inventory will vary month to month—even in the most stable environment (which yours probably won't be initially)—because months end on different days of the week.

Distinguishing between food sold and consumed is important because all food consumed is not sold. Food consumed includes all food used, sold, wasted, stolen or given away to customers and employees. Food not sold is determined by subtracting all food bought at full price from the total food consumed.

Maximum allowable food cost percentage (MFC) is the most food can cost and still return your profit goal. If at the end of the month your food cost percentage is over your maximum allowable percentage, you won't meet your profit expectations. This is how you calculate it:

1. Write your dollar amounts of labor costs and overhead expenses and exclude food costs. Refer to past accounting periods and yearly averages to get realistic cost estimates.

2. Add your monthly profit goal as either a dollar amount or a percentage of sales.

3. Convert dollar values of expenses to percentages by dividing by food sales for the periods used for expenses. Generally, don't use your highest or lowest sales figures for calculating your operating expenses. Subtract the total of the percentages from 100%. The remainder is your maximum allowable food cost percentage (MFC). For example:

$$100 - \left(\frac{\text{Monthly Expenses (– Food Costs) + Profit Goal} \times 100}{\text{Monthly Food Sales}}\right) = \% \text{ MFC}$$

Actual food cost percentage (AFC) is the percentage you're actually operating at. It's calculated by dividing food cost by food sales. If you are deducting employee meals from your income statement, then you are calculating cost of food sold. If there is no deduction of employee meals—which is true for most operations—then the food cost you're reading is food consumed. This is always a higher cost than food sold, and if inventory is not being taken, the food cost on your income statement is just an estimate based on purchases and isn't accurate.

Potential food cost percentage (PFC) is also called your theoretical food cost. This is the lowest your food cost can be because it assumes that all food consumed is sold, and that there is no waste whatsoever. It is found by multiplying the number sold of each menu item by the ideal recipe cost.

Standard food cost (SFC) is how you adjust for the unrealistically low PFC. This percentage includes unavoidable waste, employee meals, etc. This food cost percentage is compared to the AFC, and is the standard management must meet.

Prime food cost includes with the food cost the cost of direct labor. This is labor incurred because the item is made from scratch—baking pies and bread, trimming steaks, etc. When the food cost is determined for these items, the cost of the labor needed to prepare them is added. So prime cost is food cost plus necessary direct labor. This costing method is applied to every menu item needing extensive direct labor before it is served to the customer. Indirect labor cannot be attributed to any particular menu item, and is therefore overhead. Prime cost is the total cost of food and beverage sold, payroll, and employee benefits costs.

THE RESTAURANT MANAGER'S HANDBOOK

Beverage cost ratio is calculated when alcoholic beverages are sold. It is determined by dividing costs by sales—calculated the same way as food consumed. A single beverage ratio can't be standardized because the percentage will vary depending on the mix of hard alcohol, wine and beer. Spirits run a lower cost percentage than wine and beer, and as such, it is recommended that alcoholic beverages be split into their three categories.

Beverage sales do not include coffee, tea, milk or juice, which are usually considered food. Wherever you include soft drinks, know that it will reduce the food cost, since the ratio of cost to selling price is so low.

Check average is not just total food and beverage sales divided by customers served. Of course this is one way to determine your check average, but it is important to see how this figure compares to the check average you need to meet your daily sales goals. If you are coming in under what you need, you should look at your prices. Check average should be determined by each meal period, especially when different menus are served for each meal. Standards need to be set on how customers who order only a drink and no food are counted.

Seat turnover is how many times you can fill a chair during a meal period with another customer. Restaurants with low check averages need high seat turnover.

Inventory turnover is calculated by dividing cost of food consumed by your average inventory (This is simply your beginning inventory plus your ending inventory, divided by 2).

Ratio of food to beverage sales is simply the ratio of their percentages of your total sales. In restaurants with a higher percentage of beverage than food sales, profits are generally higher, because there is a greater profit margin on beverages.

Sales mix is the number of each menu item sold. This is crucial to cost analysis because each item impacts food cost differently. If your Wendy's does a huge breakfast business, and the one down the street does a big lunch, your food costs are going to be different than theirs.

Breakeven point (BEP) is simply when sales equal expenses, period. Businesses can operate forever at breakeven if there are no investors looking for a return on their money.

Contribution margin is your gross profit. It is what remains after all expenses have been subtracted from 100 percent net.

Closing point is when the cost of being open for a given time period is more expensive than revenue earned. This means that if it cost you $2,000 to open today, and you only made $1,800, your closing point expense will be $200.

CONTROLLING FOOD COSTS

In order to control food costs effectively, there are four things you need to do:

1. Forecast how much and what you are going to sell.

2. Purchase and prepare according to these forecasts.

3. Portion effectively.

4. Control waste and theft.

In order to do these effectively, you must have standards to which you rigorously adhere. Here are two main standards that will help you sustain quality, consistency and low cost:

- **Standardized recipes.** Since the recipe is the basis for determining the cost of a menu item, standard recipes will assure consistent quality and cost. Standardized recipes include ingredients, preparation methods, yield, equipment used and plate presentation.

- **Standardized purchase specifications.** These are detailed descriptions of the ingredients used in your standardized recipes. Quality and price of all ingredients are known and agreed upon before purchases are made, making the recipe's cost consistent from unit to unit and week to week.

YIELD COSTS

Once you have standardized recipes in place, you can determine the per plate cost of every dish. In order to do this you need to know what the basic ingredients cost and the edible yield of those ingredients for each dish. There are a number of necessary terms for this process:

- **As-Purchased (AP) Weight.** The weight of the product as delivered, including bones, trim, etc.

- **Edible Portion (EP) Weight.** The amount of weight or volume that is available to be portioned after carving or cooking.

- **Waste.** The amount of usable product that is lost due to processing, cooking, or portioning, as well as usable by-products that have no salable value.

- **Usable Trim.** Processing by-products that can be sold as other menu items. These recover a portion or all of their cost.

- **Yield.** The net weight or volume of food after processing but before portioning.

- **Standard Yield.** The yield generated by standardized recipes and portioning procedures—how much usable product there is after processing and cooking.

- **Standard Portion.** The size of the portion according to the standardized recipe, also the basis for determining the cost of the plated portion.

- **Convenience Foods.** Items where at least a portion of the preparation labor is done before delivery. These can include precut chicken, ready-made dough, etc.

These factors allow you to calculate plate costs. The food cost of convenience foods is higher than if you made them from scratch, but once you factor in labor, necessary equipment, inventories of ingredients, more complicated purchasing and storage, etc., you may find that these foods offer considerable savings.

To cost convenience foods you simply count, weigh or measure the portion size and determine how many portions there are. Then divide the number of servable portions into the as-purchased price. Even with their pre-preparation, a small allowance for normal waste must be factored in, often as little as 2 percent per yield.

Costing items from scratch is a little more complex. Most menu items require processing that causes shrinkage of some kind. As a result, if the weight or volume of the cooked product is less than the as-purchased (AP) weight, the edible portion (EP) cost will be higher than the AP price. It's a simple addition of the labor involved and the amount of saleable product being reduced. Through this process, your buyer uses yields to determine quantities to purchase, and your chef discovers optimum quantities to order that result in the highest yield and the least waste.

MENU SALES MIX

The menu is where you begin to design a restaurant. If you have a specific menu idea, your restaurant's location must be carefully planned to ensure customer traffic will support your concept. This also works the other way: if you already have the location, design your menu around the customers you want to attract.

Once your concept is decided, your equipment and kitchen space requirements should be designed around the recipes on your menu. Once a kitchen has been built, there is of course some flexibility to menu changes, but new pieces of equipment may be impossible to add without high costs or renovations. To design right, you need to visualize delivery, processing, preparation, presentation and washing. To do this you must be intimately familiar with each menu item.

When shopping for equipment, choose based on the best equipment for your needs, not price. Only when you have decided if you need a small fryer or an industrial one, two ovens or five, and then which specific brand will meet your needs, should you begin to find the best price. This is true for equipment all the way down to pots, pans, dishes and utensils.

THE MENU ITSELF

Your menu should not just be a list of the dishes you sell, it should positively affect the revenue and operational efficiency of your restaurant. Start by selecting dishes that reflect your customer's preferences and emphasize what your staff does well. Attempting to cater to everyone generally has you doing nothing particularly well and doesn't distinguish your restaurant. Your menu should be a major communicator of the concept and personality of your restaurant, as well as an important cost control.

A well-designed menu creates an accurate image of the restaurant in a customer's head, even before she's been inside. It also directs her attention to certain selections and increases the chances of them being ordered. Your menu also determines, depending upon its complexity and sophistication, how detailed your cost control system needs to be.

An effective menu does five key things:

1. Emphasizes what customers want and what you do best.

2. Is an effective communication, merchandising and cost control tool.

3. Obtains the necessary check average for sales and profits.

4. Uses staff and equipment efficiently.

5. Makes forecasting sales more consistent and accurate for purchasing, preparation and scheduling.

The design of your menu will directly affect whether or not it achieves these goals. Don't leave this to chance. Plan to have a menu that works for you. Certain practices can influence the choices your guests make. Instead of randomly placing items on the menu, single out and emphasize the items you want to sell. These will generally be dishes with low food cost and high profits that are easy to prepare. Once you have chosen these dishes, use design—print style, paper color and graphic design—to direct the reader's attention to these items. In general, a customer's eye will fall to the middle of the page first. This is an important factor. However, design elements used to draw a reader's eye to another part of the menu can be effective as well. Also, customers remember the first and last things they read more than anything else, so when you draw their eyes to specific items is also important.

Once you have an effective menu design, analyzing your sales mix to determine the impact each item has on sales, costs and profits is an important practice. If you have costs and waste under control, looking at your menu sales mix can help you further reduce costs and boost profits. You will find that some items need to be promoted more aggressively, while others need to be dropped altogether. Classifying your menu items is necessary for making those decisions. Here are some suggested classifications:

- **Primes.** These are popular items that are low in food cost and high in profit. Have them stand out on your menu.

- **Standards.** Items with high food costs and high profit margins. You can possibly raise the price on this item and push it as a signature.

- **Sleepers.** Slow selling low food cost items with low profit margins. Work to increase the likelihood that these will be seen and ordered through more prominent menu display, featuring on menu boards, lowered prices, etc.

- **Problems.** High in food cost and low in profits. If you can, raise the price and lower production cost. If you can't, hide them on the menu. If sales don't pick up, get rid of them altogether.

PRICING

Pricing is an important aspect of your revenues and customer counts. Prices that are too high will drive customers away, and prices that are too low will kill your profits. But pricing is not the simple matter of an appropriate markup over cost; it combines other factors as well.

Price can either be market driven or demand driven. **Market-driven** prices must be responsive to your competitor's prices. Common dishes that both you and the place down the road sell need to be priced competitively. This is also true when you're introducing new items that a demand has not been developed for. Opposite to these are **demand-driven** items, which customers ask for and where demand exceeds your supply. You have a short-term monopoly on these items, and therefore price is driven up until demand slows or competitors begin to sell similar items.

However you determine your price, the actual marking up of items is an interesting process. A combination of methods is usually a good idea, since each menu item is usually different. Two basic theories are: a) charge as much as you can, and b) charge as little as you can. Each has its pluses and minuses. Obviously, if you charge as much as you can, you increase the chance of greater profits. You do, however, run the risk of needing to offer a product that customers feel is worth the price; otherwise you will lose them because they won't think you're a good value. Charging the lowest price you can gives customers a great sense of value but lowers your profit margin per item.

Prices are generally determined by competition and demand. Your prices must be in line with the category customers put you in. Burrito joints don't price like a five-star restaurant, and vice versa. Both would lose their customer base if they did. While this is an exaggeration, the point is still the same. You want your customers to know your image and your prices to fit into that picture.

Here are four ways to determine prices:

1. **Competitive pricing.** Simply based on meeting or beating your competition's prices. This is an ineffective method, since it assumes diners are making their choice on price alone, and not food quality, ambiance, service, etc.

2. **Intuitive pricing.** This means you don't want to take the time to find out what your competition is charging, so you are charging based on what you feel guests are willing to pay. If your sense of the value of your product is good, then it works. Otherwise, it can be problematic.

3. **Psychological pricing.** Price is more of a factor to lower-income customers who go to lower priced restaurants. If they don't know an item is good, they assume it is if it's expensive. If you change your prices, remember the order in which buyers see them also affects their perceptions. If an item was initially more expensive, it will be viewed as a bargain, and vice versa.

4. **Trial-and-error pricing.** This is based on customer reactions to prices. It is not practical in terms of determining your overall prices, but can be effective with individual items to bring them closer to the price a customer is willing to pay, or to distinguish them from similar menu items with a higher or lower food cost.

There are still other factors that help determine prices. Whether customers view you as a leader or a follower can make a big difference on how they view your prices. If people think of you as the best seafood restaurant in the area, they'll be willing to pay a little more to eat with you. Service also determines people's sense of value. This is even truer when the difference in actual food quality between you and the competition is negligible. If your customers order at a counter and buss their own tables, this lack of service cost needs to be reflected in your prices. Also, in a competitive market, providing great service can be a factor that puts you in a leadership position and allows you to charge a higher price. Your location, ambience, customer base, product presentation and desired check average all factor into what you feel you can charge and what you need to in order to make a profit.

FINANCIAL ANALYSIS

In order to make profits, you need to plan for profits. Many restaurants offering great food, great atmosphere and great service still go out of business. The reason for this is they fail to manage the financial aspects of the business. This means that poor cost control management will be fatal to your business. Furthermore, good financial management is about interpreting financial statements and reports, not simply preparing them.

A few distinctions need to be made in order to understand the language we are now using. Financial accounting is primarily for external groups to assess taxes, the status of your establishment, etc. Managerial accounting provides information to internal users that becomes the basis for managing day-to-day operations. This data is very specific, emphasizes departmental operations and uses nonfinancial data like customer counts, menu sales mix and labor hours. These internal reports break down revenues and expenses by department, day and meal period so they can be easily interpreted, and areas that need attention can be seen. Daily and weekly reports must be made and analyzed in order to determine emerging trends.

INTERNAL CONTROLS

It is estimated that about five cents on every dollar spent in U.S. restaurants is lost to theft. Clearly established and followed controls can lessen this percentage. Begin by separating duties and recording every transaction. If these basic systems are in place, then workers know at each step of the way that they will be held responsible for shrinkage. Management Information Systems (MISs) are common tools for accumulating, analyzing and reporting data. They help establish proper rules for consistent and prompt reporting and set up efficient flows of paperwork and data collection. In short, their goal is to prevent fraud on all levels. While no system is perfect, a good MIS will show where fraud or loss is occurring, allowing you to remedy the situation.

In most restaurants the majority of theft occurs at the bar. In tightly run establishments cash is more likely to be taken by management than hourly workers, because managers and some waitstaff as well as bartenders have access to it and know the system well. Hourly workers tend to steal products, not cash, because that's what they can get their hands on. Keeping food away from the back door and notifying your employees when you are aware of theft and are investigating can have a deterring effect.

The key to statistical control however, is entering transactions into the system. This can be done electronically or by hand—either way, if food or beverages can be consumed without being entered into the system, your system is flawed, and control is compromised. Five other cost control concepts are crucial to your control system:

1. **Documentation** of tasks, activities and transactions must be required.

2. **Supervision and review of employees** by management intimately familiar with set performance standards.

3. **Splitting of duties** so no single person is involved in all parts of the task cycle.

4. **Timeliness.** All tasks must be done within set time guidelines, comparisons then made at established control points, and reports made at scheduled times to detect problems.

5. **Cost-benefit relationships.** Cost of procedures used to benefits gained must exceed the cost of implementing the controls.

The basic control procedure is an independent verification at a control point during and after the completion of a task. This is often done through written or electronic reports. This verification determines if the person performing the task has the authority to do so and if the quantity of product or cash and performance results meet set standards.

Point-of-sale systems are also crucial for reducing loss. If your servers simply can't obtain any food or beverage without a hard-copy check, or without entering the sale electronically, you have eliminated most of their opportunity to steal. Many electronic systems are available in the industry, and once initial training and intimidation are overcome, they can seriously reduce the amount of theft and shrinkage in your restaurant.

These systems also allow you to instantly see which items are selling best at different times of the day. This enables you to order more efficiently and keep inventory to a minimum. They also allow you automatically subtract from inventory all the ingredients used in the items you sold. These can be invaluable tools for tracking employee productivity, initiating promotions and contests and generating weekly, daily, by-meal or hourly sales reports. Point-of-sale systems collect invaluable data for you to interpret.

PURCHASING AND ORDERING

What exactly is the difference? Purchasing is setting the policy on which suppliers, brands, grades and varieties of products will be ordered. These are your standardized purchase specifications; the specifics of how items are delivered, paid for, returned, etc., are negotiated between management and distributors. Basically, purchasing is what you order and from whom. Ordering, then, is simply the act of contacting the suppliers and notifying them of the quantity you require. This is a simpler, lower-level task.

Once menus have been created that meet your customer's satisfaction and your profit needs, a purchasing program designed to assure your profit margins can be developed. An efficient purchasing program incorporates:

- Standard purchase specifications; based on

- Standardized recipes; resulting in

- Standardized yields; that, with portion control, allow for

- Accurate costs based on portions actually served.

Once these criteria are met, to order the necessary supplies, your operator needs to be able to predict how much will be needed to maintain purchase specifications, follow standard recipes and enforce portioning standards. When these are done well, optimum quantities can be kept on hand.

Buying also has its own distinctions. Open, or informal, buying is face-to-face or by over-the-phone contact and uses largely oral negotiations and purchase specifics. In formal buying terms are put in writing, and payment invoices are stated as conditions for price quotes and customer-service commitments. Its customer service is possibly the most important aspect of the supplier you choose, because good sales representatives know their products, have an understanding of your needs and offer helpful suggestions.

INVENTORY

Ordering effectively is impossible unless you know your inventory. Before an order is placed, counts of stock should be made. Many software programs are able to determine order quantities directly from sales reports, but without this kind of system you must inventory what you have on hand before ordering. The taking of inventory must be streamlined, because it must be done as frequently as you order. It mustn't be an unpleasant late-night debacle that is done only rarely, and only when it has to be.

Whether your inventory system is by hand or computer, its purpose is to accomplish the following:

- Provide records of what you need.

- Provide records of product specifications.

- Provide records of suppliers.

- Provide records of prices and unit of purchase.

- Provide a record of product use levels.

- Facilitate efficient ordering.

- Increase the accuracy of inventory.

- Facilitate the inventory process.

- Make it easy to detect variance levels in inventory.

With such a system, the records generated and kept are extensive and valuable. You will have records of what you purchased, product specifications, your primary and alternative suppliers, price and unit of purchase. Equally important, reports will indicate the usage level of the product between deliveries. These statistics allow for month-to-month comparisons to be made between units in a multiunit operation.

LABOR PRODUCTIVITY

Labor costs and turnover are serious concerns in today's restaurant market. Increasing labor costs cannot be offset by continuously higher prices without turning customers away. Maximizing worker productivity so few can do more has become a key challenge to the restaurateur. This is especially true since the food-service industry continues to be an entry-level arena for the unskilled and uneducated. Qualified applicants are still few in the restaurant industry.

A few of the causes of high labor costs and low productivity are poor layout and design of your operation, lack of labor saving equipment, poor scheduling and no regular detailed system to collect and analyze payroll data. The following are some suggested ways management could improve these areas for greater efficiency:

- **Scheduling.** The key to controlling labor costs is not a low average hourly wage, but proper scheduling of productive employees. Place your best servers, cooks, etc., where you need them most. This requires knowing the strengths and weaknesses of your employees. Staggering the arrival and departure of employees is a good way to follow the volume of expected customers and minimize labor costs during slow times.

- **On-call scheduling.** When your forecasted customer counts are inaccurate, scheduled labor must be adjusted up or down to meet productivity standards. Employees simply wait at home to be called if they are needed for work. If they don't receive a call by a certain time, they know they're not needed. Employees prefer this greatly to coming in only to be sent home, especially tipped staff who don't want to work when business is slow.

- **On-break schedules.** When you can't send someone home, you can put him on a 30-minute break and give him a meal. The 30 minutes is deducted from his time-card, and you can take a credit for the cost of the meal against the minimum wage.

BEVERAGE CONTROLS

Pricing of beverages is not just a cost-markup exercise. The markup of alcohol in restaurants is lower than in bars where liquor makes up the majority of sales. Prices reflect the uniqueness of an operation and the overhead operating costs.

In order to monitor your liquor costs accurately, you need to record the sales of each type of beverage separately. Separate keys for wine, beer and spirits on your register or a point-of-sale system need to be used. Unless an electronic system is used, however, a detailed sales mix is difficult to obtain.

Your alcoholic beverage purchaser or buyer is responsible for ensuring adequate amounts of required spirits are on hand. Unlike food and supplies, they are not required to shop around for the best deal for the following reasons:

- Specific brands are only sold by specific dealers.

- Wholesaling of alcohol is state regulated and controlled.

- Prices are published in monthly journals, and there is little change from month to month.

- Only quantity discounts are available.

- Purchase is done by brand name.

Purchasing and ordering alcohol is therefore much simpler than purchasing and ordering food, but the need to inventory correctly is no less crucial. In fact, alcohol needs to be guarded and inventoried more rigorously because of its cost, ease of theft and possible abuses. Liquor inventory should be kept locked in different storerooms, cages or walk-ins than other inventory. Only authorized individuals should have access to these areas, and requisitions must be filled out to record withdrawals.

We recommend replenishing your stock by trading stamped empty bottles for stamped full bottles. These prevent bartenders from bringing their own bottles in and selling them. If this does occur, it's virtually impossible to detect without marked bottles, because there will be no inventory shortages. If you have drops in sales levels of $50 to $100 in one night, this is a sign of phantom bottles in your inventory.

Inventories need to be audited to ensure your liquor is actually in the storeroom, and deliveries need to be checked for accuracy. It is recommended that a purchase order—and not the driver's invoice—be used to verify deliveries. Controls for determining dispensing costs, recording sales and accounting for consumed beverages can be done three different ways:

1. **Automated systems that dispense and count.** These range from mechanical dispensers attached to each bottle, to magnetic pourers that can only be activated by the register. These systems are exact, reduce spillage and cannot give free drinks. Basically, liquor can't be dispensed without being put into the system.

2. **Ounce or drink controls.** This requires establishing standard glassware and recipes; recording each drink sold; determining costs of each drink; comparing actual use levels to potential consumption levels; and comparing actual drink cost percent to potential cost percent.

3. **Par stock or bottle control.** This is a matter of keeping the maximum amount of each type of liquor behind the bar, then turning in all empty bottles for full ones. No full bottles are given without an empty one coming in. A standard sales value per bottle is determined based on the drinks it makes. A sales value is determined from consumption and compared to actual sales for variances. If less was sold than consumed, investigate.

Standards at the bar are as important as in the kitchen. Dispensers, jiggers or other measuring devices should be mandated to assure portion controls. Regular inventory also needs to be done to watch for fraud and theft, and management needs to be expected to meet set standards. Whenever there is a managerial shift change, you must verify inventory to make sure that numbers reported are actual and haven't been adjusted to meet costs.

5

PROFITABLE MENU PLANNING — FOR MAXIMUM RESULTS

INTRODUCTION

The prosperity of any restaurant is often directly attributable to its menu. A restaurant is the culmination of food, atmosphere and service. Many restaurants can thrive without a fanciful atmosphere or quality service, but none can survive without exceptional food. The restaurant manager must examine his restaurant's atmosphere and clientele carefully. Based upon these observations he can then design a menu that will be effective.

The objective of this chapter is to present the restaurant manager with complete guidelines for planning a successful and profitable menu. It would be impractical in these pages to list specific examples of potential menu items. There are many excellent cookbooks that describe menu and recipe ideas in detail. The following sections will illustrate a basic outline, from which you can plan your own exclusive menu. Each of the procedures described play an integral part in developing your cost control system. The procedures and systems will unfold as the book progresses. Some of these procedures may be adapted for your own particular needs. However, the underlying, fundamental purpose of each cannot be altered, else management will be in danger of losing control over the restaurant's costs.

MENU STYLE

Menu style describes how much or how little variety the menu offers. Do you serve a limited or expansive menu? The things that may influence whether or not you offer a limited menu include kitchen size and labor cost control. Menus with more options, however, do have a broader appeal. Limited-limited menus are generally offered by fast-food operations. These menus allow them to keep production simple and maintain a tight rein on food and labor costs.

Extensive-limited menus are offered by restaurants that serve three meals a day, such as coffee shops. While they offer more items, they limit the number of ways these items are prepared. Specialty restaurants (TGI Friday's, Ruby Tuesday and ethnic restaurants) have limited-extensive menus. By preparing and combining the same ingredients in different ways, these establishments are able to offer many more choices but still control inventory and costs. Fine dining restaurants offer extensive-extensive menus. These establishments offer a great variety of choices in items prepared and methods of preparation.

There are advantages to both the limited menu and extensive menu styles:

LIMITED

- You need less equipment and less kitchen space.

- Food prep is simplified and can be speedy.

- You need fewer and less skilled kitchen employees.

- Purchasing your inventory is easier and less time-consuming.

- Space needed for inventory is lessened.

- Cost controls and quality control are simpler.

- Operating costs are lower.

- Table turnover can be increased because transaction time is quicker.

EXTENSIVE

- You can appeal to a broader customer base.

- New customers will be intrigued.

- Regulars will return more often because they have a greater number of options to choose from.

- The menu can be more responsive to customer taste.

- The menu is more flexible.

- You can charge higher prices for specialty items.

So, how many menu items should you offer? You want to provide the customer with variety, but not at the expense of your ability to control inventory and cost, nor by over-taxing your production or serving staffs. Research has shown that 60 to 75 percent of menu items sold are the same 8 to 12 items, regardless of the number of choices offered. Keeping this in mind, it is probably wise to offer somewhere between 18 and 24 options.

FORMATTING YOUR MENU

After you have defined your establishment's goals and determined the style of your menu, you must decide what items will go on your menu. This can be done in a four-step process:

1. You must decide what menu groups you will offer. Groups are appetizers, entrees, soups, desserts, etc.

2. Decide what categories to offer within these groups. For entree choices, for example, you could offer the following categories: beef, poultry, seafood, pork, lamb, veal and vegetarian. Decide how many dishes you will offer in each category. You may have four beef dishes, three seafood entrees, two poultry and two vegetarian, for example.

3. After deciding the groups and categories that will go on your menu, you need to decide on the specifics of the dish. Will you be serving ground, cubed, solid, roast, baked, grilled, broiled or fried?

4. Finally you must decide on the dish itself. If you are offering three beef entrees, you may choose to serve two solid beef dishes and one ground. Your actual menu items may be a strip steak, a filet mignon and a hamburger.

While this may sound like an onerous task, by keeping these four steps in mind you will be able to maintain variety in your menu and control cost factors.

DEVELOPING THE MENU SELECTIONS

All menu items selected must fit into the physical workings of the restaurant. Thus, the menu should be finalized prior to designing, selecting equipment for and laying out the kitchen. This is necessary for maximum efficiency of time, labor and equipment. The design and layout of the kitchen and work areas must meet the needs of the menu. If it doesn't, the entire operation will become slow, disorganized and inefficient. Inefficiency can only result in a drop in employee morale and in the restaurant's profit margin.

Just as the kitchen must meet the demands of the menu, the personnel employed to prepare the menu items must be selected to fit into the design of the kitchen. Careful consideration must be given to the number and type of employees needed. Is the menu simple enough for inexperienced workers to prepare, or are the skills of a professional, more experienced chef needed? Will the food be prepared ahead of time, or upon receipt of the order? When will these employees be needed, and for how long? Will there be enough room in the kitchen for everyone to work at the same time? Who will supervise them?

Planning the restaurant menu is a lot more than merely selecting menu items that are enjoyed and demanded by the restaurant's clientele. Menu planning includes arranging equipment, personnel and food products into an efficient unit that will be affordable and in demand by the public. Successful, growing restaurants have accomplished this blending—the ones that failed, hadn't.

Most restaurants employ, at least to some degree, a separate cooking and preparation staff. The largest restaurants may employ an upwards of 30 employees for each staff. Each staff may then be divided into smaller departments. For example, the preparation staff may be divided into baking, meat cutting and cold food preparation; and the cooking staff could be divided into broiling, frying and carving. Smaller restaurants assign combinations of these responsibilities to a few employees on each staff. The smallest restaurant may employ one individual who arrives several hours prior to opening to prepare all of the food items and then performs a cook's duties. Having separate preparation and cooking staffs is the most efficient method for producing a large number of consistent products at the least expense. Since this is the method used in most establishments, it will be the one described and referred to in this book.

Constant communication between the preparation and cooking staff is required for success. These groups of employees will be working toward the same end—at different times. An entree incorrectly prepared by the preparation staff will destroy the normal procession and organization in the kitchen, sending repercussions throughout the restaurant. The cooking staff are dependent upon the products that the preparation staff readies for them. Management's responsibility under this arrangement is increased, as it must provide the necessary communication between the two groups in order for each to operate effectively. The benefits derived under this system—such as consistent final products, lower labor costs, lower food costs and an overall increase in the organization and efficiency of the kitchen—far outweigh any disadvantages.

The major points to consider when selecting menu items:

1. The menu item must be of superior quality.

2. The raw materials used in preparing the item must be readily available year-round at a relatively stable price.

3. The menu item must be affordable and demanded by your clientele.

4. The menu item must be acceptable to the preparation and cooking staff system you use.

5. The raw materials used in preparing the menu item must be easily portioned by weight.

6. All menu items must have consistent cooking results.

7. All menu items must have a long shelf life. Food items prepared ahead of time and not utilized may not be sold for as long as 36 hours.

8. All menu items must have similar cooking times (approximately 8 to 15 minutes), as any entree requiring a longer cooking time will not be completed when the other orders are ready to serve.

9. The storage facilities must accommodate the raw materials used in preparing the menu items.

10. Menu items should be creative and not readily available in other restaurants.

LIMITING THE MENU

Begin to develop the menu by compiling those recipes and ideas that meet the requirements set forth in the previous section. Consider only the items that are compatible with the restaurant's atmosphere, decor and anticipated clientele. Based upon these guidelines, you should have little trouble compiling a considerable list of acceptable choices. The trick is to limit the menu to only those items for which the kitchen is equipped and organized and that the staff can easily execute—while still allowing for an interesting menu with plenty of varied selections.

All too often, a new restaurant will list numerous menu selections simply to round out the menu or offer token items that are on almost every menu. New restaurants should move toward specializing and serving only those menu items that they can prepare better than the other establishments in the area. It is simply not justifiable to create a diversified menu for the sole sake of offering a multitude of items. Specialization in the restaurant business is the key to building a solid reputation. Word of mouth is the most effective form of advertising available to the restaurant manager. Develop the menu with only those items for which you have the trained staff and equipment to properly prepare and serve. A successful menu is one that is honed to build a reputation for excellence.

Limiting the menu in the manner described will create many advantages for the entire restaurant. The kitchen staff will become more experienced and skilled at preparing each item, as there will be a smaller selection for customers to choose from. The waitstaff can then concentrate on promoting and recommending those items that the restaurant specializes in. From an administrative standpoint, a smaller menu will be easier to control. Purchasing will center on only a few major food products; thus the buyer may utilize his large purchasing power to obtain price breaks, discounts and above-average service.

Side dishes and desserts must meet all of the same qualifications as the entrees. The number and kinds of side dishes and desserts should be limited only to those items which are exceptional and slightly out of the ordinary, so they may be promoted as house specialties as well.

Always try to include some menu selections that are produced in the local area. Maine lobster, Cajun cooking, Texas beef, Gulf shrimp, key lime pie and San Francisco sourdough bread are some examples. The tourist trade is an important source of revenue for most restaurants. In fact, many establishments depend on it. With a little promotion this could be an important new avenue for sales.

Once the menu is finalized, it will be necessary for management to become thoroughly familiar with every aspect of each menu item. Extensive experimentation in the kitchen will be needed to discover the precise recipe ingredients, amounts and preparation procedures. Take the time to find out everything there is to know about the menu items. Determine where the raw products come from; which is the best type or brand to purchase; and how the kitchen staff can best handle and store the products. How do other restaurants in the area serve similar dishes?

The rule for developing a portion size is to use the largest portion feasible but charge accordingly. It is far better to serve too much food than too little. The crucial element, which must be constantly reinforced, is that every menu item—entrees, side dishes and some desserts—must be a specific weight and size. Portion control is the basis for the restaurant's entire cost control program. Its importance cannot be overstated.

Portion-controlling all food items is an effective way to control food costs, but it also serves another important function. It maintains consistency in the final product. Once the precise recipe is developed, the completed menu item should look and taste exactly the same regardless of who prepared it. A dinner presented to a customer on Tuesday must be exactly the same as it was on Saturday night.

Portions may have a variance of up to, but not exceeding, half an ounce. Thus if the set portion size for a steak is 12.5-ounces, the steak may range from 12 to 13 ounces. Any amount over 13 ounces must be trimmed. A light steak should be utilized for something else. Although a 1/2-ounce variance may seem like a small amount, in actuality it will add up very quickly. In fact, many restaurants allow a variance of only 1/8 of an ounce!

Since portion-controlling is such a vital kitchen function, purchase the best scales available. A good digital ounce scale will cost upwards of $200. However, this investment will be recouped many times over from the food cost savings it will provide. Purchase at least two ounce-graduated scales for the kitchen and always keep a third available in reserve. One floor-type pound scale with at least a 150-pound capacity will be needed. This scale will be used to verify deliveries and raw yields. All scales should have a temperature-compensating device. Maintain these scales per the manufacturer's instructions; clean them periodically and oil when necessary, and they will provide years of service. To ensure the accuracy of the scales test them periodically with an item of known weight. Most good scales come with a calibration kit.

For practical reasons some food items, such as dressings, sauces and butter, are portioned by weight. However, they should still be portion-controlled by using proper-size spoons and ladles. Soups and condiments must be placed in proper-size serving containers.

At each work area of the kitchen, place a chart listing the portion sizes and other portion control practices. All employees must use the measuring cups and spoons and the recipe manual when following recipes. Remember, that the basis for the food cost program you are developing is based upon the knowledge that every item has a precise portion size. Management has the responsibility to ensure that these standards are being practiced and adhered to.

TRUTH AND ACCURACY IN THE MENU

Careful consideration must be taken when writing the final menu to ensure its complete accuracy. Few restaurant managers would purposely deceive their customers, as the restaurant would only suffer in the long run. However, you must become aware of the unintentional inaccuracies you may have in the menu and the governmental regulations regarding this.

Due to the actions of a few unscrupulous restaurant operators in recent years, a crackdown on the whole food-service industry has been declared by certain regulatory agencies. All states have one or more laws that basically say that any organization selling a product must not misrepresent the product in any manner with intent to deceive. Many states have specific "truth in menu" legislation.

Every statement made, whether it be orally by the waiter or waitress or written in the menu description, must be completely accurate. For example, "fresh bay scallops" must never be frozen; they must be bay—not sea or ocean—scallops. "Real maple syrup" must be 100 percent–real maple syrup. "Imported baby spring lamb" must be imported, baby, spring lamb. Words and descriptions to watch are: fresh, real, imported, baby, 100 percent, B-B-Q or barbeque, pure, natural, homemade, etc. The description printed on the menu must be exactly the product you are serving.

You may be wondering how you can possibly write an enticing menu (that will not read like a grocery list) and yet still remain within the boundaries of the law. The trick is to be creative in writing the descriptions. State precisely what the product is, but modify the sentences to make the product sound enticing. Creative printing and the use of artwork will boost the appeal of the menu.

The following is an example of how to dress up the most fundamental menu item—salad—and yet still describe exactly the products for sale.

SAMPLE MENU

Salads
Included with Entrees

Spinach Salad
Fresh spinach with bacon, egg and mushrooms.

Green Salad
Crisp green lettuce with tomatoes, onions, cucumbers and sprouts.

Garden Salad
The above green salad served with a greater variety of fresh vegetables.

Fresh Fruit Salad
A variety of fresh fruits in season served on a bed of crisp greens and topped with our yogurt dressing.

Choice of Dressings
Our own recipes made daily
- Danish Blue
- Italian
- Yogurt Dressing
- 1000 Island
- Creamy Cucumber
- Oil & Vinegar

Many restaurants, in order to limit liability, will print what is called a disclaimer. A disclaimer is simply a statement that what you have printed is accurate to the best of your knowledge but that the restaurant cannot be held responsible for any actions beyond its immediate control. Here's one type of disclaimer:

> *Due to the inclement weather this week, local Bay Scallops were not harvested. However, we were able to import some frozen Sea Scallops from Nova Scotia. These scallops are equal or superior to our regular fare.*

Some restaurants print a general disclaimer at the bottom of the menu:

> *We serve only the finest food available. However, at certain times during the year we may not be able to obtain the exact product desired; therefore, we may substitute a similar product that will be equal or superior to the original item. Should this be the case your waiter/waitress will inform you of the substitution.*

Carefully analyze your menu for possible misrepresentations. Self-regulation in the food industry is the key to maintaining the high standards and reputation it enjoys.

You will find a copy of the Accuracy in Menu Checklist at the end of this chapter.

NUTRITIONAL CLAIMS ON MENUS

If you want to include menu items that are marketed as healthy (i.e., heart-healthy, low-fat, reduced-fat, cholesterol-free, etc.), make sure you have the nutritional information for these items readily accessible. Items described as "fresh" are included in this category.

Since 1997 restaurants have been included in the FDA's nutrition labeling laws. Any restaurant that uses health or nutrient-content claims on its menu must comply with these regulations. The FDA defines "restaurant" as "a place that serves food ready for consumption, including typical sit-down and carryout venues as well as institutional food service, delicatessens and catering operations" (Restaurants USA, October 1996). If you use a symbol to designate these dishes, such as a heart shape, the regulations still apply.

Basically, the FDA regulations state that if you make health/nutrition claims on your menu you must be able to demonstrate there is a reasonable basis for making them. There is some flexibility in how restaurants may support the claim, but basically they must be able to show customers and officials that their claims are consistent with the claims established under the Nutrition Labeling and Education Act.

Some establishments are beginning to list ingredients and "Nutritional Facts" labels on the menu for the convenience of their customers. Such a label indicates the item's value in calories, total fat, cholesterol, sodium, carbohydrates, protein, etc. Some states now require food purchased for take-out to be labeled in this manner. If your restaurant manufactures a product (your famous salad dressing, salsa, tomato sauce, etc.) for off-site consumption you may need to comply with the "Nutritional Facts" laws applied to packaged food. There are several software programs available that will perform these calculations for you and print labels. Please review these programs at *http://www.atlantic-pub.com*.

If you decide to include items on your menu that will have health claims, you must decide on the best way to communicate the nutrition information to your customer. Here are some things to consider:

- Information should be correct and clear.

- You may not need to include all the nutritional information on the menu; you may only need to have it available. For example, many of the fast-food chains simply list this information on a poster in a public area in the restaurant. Depending on your menu format, you may not want to clutter the space with this information. If you find that your typical customer is requesting this information, it may be better to include it on the menu.

MENU SIZE AND COVER

The menu cover should reflect your restaurant's image as well as its identity. It can include graphics (the restaurant's logo) and copy. If your restaurant is in a historic building, for instance, you may want to include a drawing or photo of the building on your cover. If you are operating a family restaurant that has been in existence for generations, you may want to put a paragraph or two of copy about your family's history or food philosophy. Remember, the cover is the first step in the menu's role as a communication tool, and it's the first place on paper you can communicate your identity to the customer. The menu is the only item that the customer is guaranteed to pay attention to when she walks into your establishment.

According to the National Restaurant Association, the ideal menu dimensions are 9 inches wide by 12 inches tall. Of course, other sizes can work as well, and the number of items on the menu will partially determine the menu size. Keep in mind that the menu size should be manageable for the customer. Remember that they are often maneuvering in a limited space that includes water and wine glasses, candles, table tents and flowers.

The cover should be of some durable material; part of its function is to protect interior pages. It can be leather, vinyl, laminated paper or plastic. Your establishment's identity will help you choose the appropriate cover material. A fine-dining restaurant would not use plastic sleeves, but for a mid-price family restaurant plastic-sleeve menu covers would be appropriate. The cover's color should also be chosen with care. The color should tie into the theme and décor of your restaurant; but remember, color does have a psychological impact, so you will want colors that will evoke pleasant images and feelings. Bear in mind that the more colors you use for your menu, the more expensive the printing process becomes.

You may want also to include general information on the cover, such as your hours of operation, address, telephone number, the forms of payment you accept and any special services you provide. While your regular customers may not need this information, new customers will appreciate it, and it will make it easier for them to return if they know when you are open and how to find you again.

MENU DESIGN SOFTWARE

With the advent of the personal computer there have been a few menu design software programs developed in recent years. The software is generally very easy to use, having built-in templates, artwork, etc. Your finalized menu can be printed out on a laser printer. Color, artwork and graphics may be added.

Table tents and other promotional devices can also be utilized. The initial cost of the software will be easily recouped as you save in design and printing costs. In addition, you will have complete control over the design process. Changes can be made instantly. Daily menus can be created, which is great way to accommodate special purchases that might have been made. The ability to generate new menus easily allows for instant price changes to reflect market conditions. One such software program is Menu Pro™. An extensive demonstration of the software may be found at *http://www.atlantic-pub.com*. Call 800-541-1336 for information.

COPYRIGHTING THE MENU

Prior to printing the menu you would be wise to obtain a copyright. Copyrighting the menu protects it from being reproduced in any form without your written permission. This would be extremely important if you were to prepare original artwork or write the menu in an interesting and novel way. Obtaining a copyright is a very simple procedure.

One of the pages of the menu, preferably the first or second, must contain the copyright registration. This notice must include the following three elements:

1. The name of the copyright owner.

2. The year of publication.

3. The symbol © and/or the word "Copyright."
   e.g., COPYRIGHT 2003 ABC Restaurant Corporation

The Copyright Application Form TX may be found at the end of this chapter or at this Web site: *http://www.loc.gov/copyright/*. The registration process normally takes about four weeks and currently costs $30.

PRINTING THE MENU

As indicated in the previous section, creatively printing the menu will have a marked effect upon the marketing of your offerings. The menus in restaurants across the country are probably more diverse than the food itself. Menus range from freehand writing on a white piece of 8 1/2"- by-11" paper to menus printed on boards, tables, walls and bottles, to menus spoken verbally. As you can see, the menu can be easily turned into a promotional vehicle for your restaurant; it's a crucial internal marketing tool. It is the way you communicate to your customer your objectives and identity. Your menu design will directly impact guest-check averages, so it can help you achieve your profit goals. A well-designed menu can attract a customer's attention to specific items and increase the chances that the customer will purchase those items. For instance, if you put an item in a box on the menu, the customer's eye will be drawn to this area of the menu.

Regardless of how creatively the menu is utilized, it should be typeset and printed either by a professional or with the professional menu software previously described. Simply using an unusual type style will dress up any menu. Discuss the possibilities with your local printer or graphic-art person, or contact a company specializing in menu production.

Artwork should be used if at all possible; use the restaurant's logo if nothing else. Your local printer may have an artist on staff or know of some freelancers in the area who can help. Listed are some of the various types of printing styles and sizes available.

Why reinvent the wheel? Atlantic Publishing has several books dedicated to menu design. There are at least four books that contain nothing but sample menus in four colors from other restaurants around the country. These menus, many of which are award winners from the National Restaurant Association's Annual Menu Contest, will give you some great ideas. You can find these resources at *http://www.atlantic-pub.com*.

VARIOUS PRINTING STYLES AND SIZES FOR MENU PREPARATION

Gill Sans	**Gill Sans Bold**	*Gill Sans Italic*
Branding Iron	University	Amaze
Giovanni Book	**Giovanni Bold**	**Giovanni Black**
COPPERPLATE GOTHIC BOLD	COPPERPLATE GOTHIC LIGHT	Brush
Helios	OLD ENGLISH	Nuptial Script
Brophy Script	**Antique Olive Medium**	Antique Olive
Park Avenue	**Impact**	Optim
Futura Book	*Futura Book Italic*	**Futura Condensed**

6 pt   8 pt   10 pt   12 pt   18 pt   24 pt   28 pt

36 pt   48 pt   60 pt

RECIPE AND PROCEDURE MANUAL

Your Recipe and Procedure Manual will contain all the restaurant's recipes, preparation procedures, handling instructions and ordering specifications. This manual, if properly used, will ensure perfection and consistency every time the menu item is prepared.

The Recipe and Procedure Manual must be available to the kitchen personnel at all times. Recipes should never be prepared from memory. The employee, without constant reinforcement from the manual, will tend to forget the exact proportions, and may even eventually leave an entire ingredient out of the recipe. For this reason and to ensure consistency, the Recipe and Procedure Manual should be open and in front of anyone

RECIPE AND PROCEDURE MANUAL

MENU ITEM:	Baked Haddock	
INGREDIENTS	**PORTION/AMOUNT**	**CURRENT COST**
Haddock	12.5 oz.	5.25
Lemon Juice	$1/4$ tsp.	0.05
Bread Crumbs	$1/2$ tsp.	0.10
Butter	$1/2$ tsp.	0.14
Garlic Salt	$1/4$ tsp.	0.02
Salt & Pepper	$1/4$ tsp.	0.01
Tartar Sauce	0.5 oz.	0.05
Garnishes:		0.10
Parsley		
Tomato Wedge		
Lemon Slices	$1/4$ lemon	0.06
Salad Bar		1.85
Misc. Expense		0.55
TOTAL COST		**$8.18**

PREPARATION PROCEDURE	Remove skin and bones. Cut into 12.5 oz. portion. Place on aluminum foil; fold aluminum foil tightly around fish. Sprinkle with lemon juice and cover with slices. Lightly cover with bread crumbs.
COOKING PROCEDURE	Bake in oven at 350° for 10–13 minutes. Fish is done when flaked with fork.
ORDERING INFORMATION	Use only fresh North Atlantic Haddock.
PRESENTATION	Remove aluminum foil. Place on #10 dinner plate. Arrange tartar sauce and garnishes (tomato wedge, lemon slices and parsley).
ADDITIONAL COMMENTS	Fish must be served hot. Fast service required.

preparing a food product. The pages of this manual should be sealed in plastic to protect them while in the kitchen.

The facing example Recipe and Procedure Manual page shows the type of information this manual should contain. A separate page will be necessary for all entrees, side dishes, desserts, dressings and sauces. In the example, the "Current Cost" column may be omitted if you do not wish the employees to know the recipe's food costs. However, the inclusion of this information will increase your employees' awareness of the amount of "money" they are handling and responsible for every day. Under "Additional Comments" list all the accompaniments that a customer might request when ordering dinner. For example: if the entree is a steak dinner, the customer may request A.1. Steak Sauce, L&P Sauce, Tabasco sauce or ketchup. These are items you will need to have available.

ORDERING MANUAL

The ordering manual contains all of the products that will need to be reordered. You will find an example of an ordering manual page **Food Ordering Form** at the end of this chapter. The completed Recipe and Procedure Manual will list all of the food items you will need to order. Simply transfer these food items onto the order forms in alphabetical order. It is a good idea to group similar food items together, such as dry goods, seafood, poultry, dairy products, produce and so forth. The "Build To Amount" column will be described in detail in Chapter 6, "Successful Kitchen Management and Control Procedures."

PROJECTING MENU COSTS

In order to accurately assess the price you must charge for a menu item, you must know the exact food cost of that item. Projecting menu costs is simply a matter of mathematics.

You will need the completed Recipe and Procedure Manual and the current price lists from your purveyors. From your sales representative obtain projections on the average yearly prices for the major food items you order, such as meat products, seafood products, poultry, dairy and produce.

Using the Recipe and Procedure Manual and the current price lists and price projections, compute the cost of each recipe item and place the amount in the column under current cost. Round all the amounts off to the nearest cent. Should estimates need to be given, it is better to figure a little high in order to cover yourself. Should your restaurant have a salad bar, estimate the average cost you can expect for each customer. Allow yourself 25 cents per person over your estimate to cover everything.

The "Miscellaneous" column covers all the condiments and accompaniments not listed. Enter into this column approximately 5 percent of the total entree cost to cover these expenses. Adjust accordingly for each entree. If coffee, dessert or any side orders are included in the price of an entrée, add a larger percentage to the total miscellaneous cost. Once open and operating you will be able to fix an average cost per customer for all miscellaneous costs and for the salad bar.

When computing the portion costs for items such as meat, fish and poultry, you must consider the waste from cutting and trimming into the cost. The amount of usable portions you get when you're finished trimming or cutting a piece of food is the yield.

TO COMPUTE THE YIELD PERCENTAGE:

1. Compute the gross starting weight in ounces.

2. Compute the net ending weight (yield) in ounces (This is the number of ounces yielded after the item is portioned).

3. Divide the net yield (in ounces) by the gross starting weight (in ounces). The resulting figure is the yield percentage.

TO COMPUTE THE ACTUAL PORTION OF A PRODUCT:

1. Divide the price per pound by the average yield percentage (This is the actual price per pound after waste).

2. Divide the actual price per pound by 16 to get the actual price per ounce.

3. Multiply the actual price per ounce by the average portion size: this figure is the actual portion cost.

Total all the current costs for each item. This figure is the estimated total portion cost. This cost figure is, of course, not completely accurate because of the large number of variable factors used in the computations. However, this figure is an educated estimate from which you may accurately set your menu prices. Remember that the costs listed here are food costs only; no other costs (such as labor, paper products, plates, etc.) are factored in at this point.

PROJECTING THE ACTUAL AVERAGE COST PER CUSTOMER

Once set up and operating, it will be relatively easy to compute the actual average cost per customer. The actual average cost per customer should be projected once every month. This ensures that the estimates used in computing the menu costs are accurate. Also, this is an extremely important procedure for restaurants that offer a salad bar. Restaurants offering a buffet service or "all you can eat" specials must project their actual average cost per customer at least once a month, or better yet, biweekly.

TO PROJECT THE ACTUAL AVERAGE COST PER CUSTOMER:

Keep a list of all the food items you do not charge for during a specific test period and their prices. You can develop this list from the invoices, which detail daily purchases. Add into this figure the dollar amount of food you have on hand at the beginning of the test period. This pertains only to the food that you are not directly charging for. At the end of the test period subtract the amount on hand from the total. Divide the total cost by the number of customers served during that period. This figure is the average actual cost per customer. Use it in projecting menu costs in place of any estimates you have made with this figure.

PROJECTING MENU PRICES

Projecting menu prices is a complex procedure because of the number of factors that must be considered. In order to operate profitably most restaurants must achieve and maintain their food cost of sales at 25–40 percent. The food cost percentage is the total food cost divided by the total food sales for a given period. For example: if the total food sales for a given period was $100,000 and the total food cost was $40,000 for that same period, the kitchen would be operating at a food cost of sales of 40 percent. One percentage point in this example would be worth $1,000.

Computing what you must charge for each entree item is relatively easy. You will need the estimated total portion costs from the preceding section. The total portion cost (food cost) divided by the menu price (food sales) must equal a food cost percentage of between .25 (25 percent) and .40 (40 percent).

Portion Costs ÷ Menu Price x 100 = 25–40%

Simply plug different menu prices into the formula until you reach the desired food cost percentage.

The complications result when you've determined the price you must charge in order to make the desired profit. Some of the prices you'd need to charge would be simply too high. No one would ever purchase the item at that price. What you must do in these cases is balance out the menu with high and low food cost items. The average cost of the menu must then be in the food-cost-percentage range desired. Poultry and seafood entrees will usually have a lower food cost percentage than meat entrees. Try to promote these lower food cost items to offset the higher ones.

Find out what other restaurants in the area are charging for similar dishes. Your clientele will dictate what the market will bear. The restaurant manager must set menu prices based on what customers will spend and what he or she must charge in order to make the desired profit margin.

Appetizers, side orders, beverages and desserts can be priced at a very low food cost percentage. These items will contribute to a large percentage of your food sales and will lower your overall food cost percentage. Some restaurant managers, realizing this important point, have set up promotional contests awarding prizes or money to the waiter or waitress who sells the largest percentage of side orders. This can be very effective if the waitstaff do not "hard sell" the items, but rather suggest the accompaniments to their customers.

Maintaining the food cost percentage is critical to maintaining your profit level. However, the food cost percentage does not tell the entire story. You must also be interested in getting the largest guest checks possible, to bring the largest percentage of gross profit to your bottom line. For example, which would you rather sell:

A. An item that sells for $5 and has a food cost of 35 percent (a gross profit of $3.25), or

B. An item that sells for $10 and has a food cost of 50 percent (a gross profit of $5.00)?

Here is an example of a higher-food-cost-percentage item actually bringing a higher gross profit. Consider this important point when pricing out the menu!

Our baked haddock dinner detailed above has a total food cost of $8.18, so if you were to charge $17.95 you would have a food cost percentage of 45.6 percent. Should the percentage be too high or the retail price too high you can reduce the portion size and the retail price. Some establishments might charge separately for the salad bar or side item. Should the retail price be lower than current market conditions or competing restaurants you can match the higher price and run a lower food cost on this entree to balance out higher food cost entree items, such as a prime rib dinner.

If you are not reaching your food cost goals or are not getting as high a check average as you'd like, it may be because of your menu design. Not all items on your menu can be low cost and high profit. Your menu is likely a mix. Your menu design may be emphasizing high food cost or low profit items. Fixing this will help decrease food cost and increase profits. Remember, if you sell too many high cost items your food cost will go up, because many of these (such as beef and seafood) have a high cost as well. On the other hand, if you sell too many low cost items, your check averages and gross profits will decline. Keep this in mind when designing your menu; you want to have a sales mix of both these types of items.

THE BEGINNING INVENTORY

The beginning inventory is the total dollar value of supplies on hand when the restaurant opens. This figure represents the starting point from which you can then compute individual costs. Each category—food, liquor, wine and operational supplies—has its own beginning inventory figure.

A cost for each of these categories will be determined every month. To determine the cost for each area, simply add the beginning inventory value with the total purchases of that category for the month. Inventory the amount left at the end of the month and subtract it from total of the beginning inventory and purchases. The percentage of cost is the total cost divided by the total sales. Projecting costs and inventory procedures are described in Chapter 18. The important thing here is to compute an accurate beginning inventory figure for your starting point.

Computing the beginning inventory is a simple calculation. If you are purchasing all new food products, simply total all your food purchases prior to opening day. This figure will be the beginning inventory.

If you are opening an existing restaurant and will be using some of the old supplies, first take an inventory of the old supplies. (See inventory procedures in Chapter 18.) Add the dollar value of these supplies with all your new food purchases prior to opening day. From the food order sheets, enter onto the inventory form all food items in alphabetical order. An example of an **Inventory Form** may be found at the end of the chapter.

Under the "Size" heading list the unit size of the product in your inventory. If two different sizes of the same product are used, list the item twice. For example, ketchup may be listed in the bulk, gallon size and in the individual service-bottle size. When extending a price for each unit it will be imperative that the cost corresponds to the appropriate size. The cost column, too, will be described in a later chapter.

The important consideration at this point is that all the food items you will be using are listed. All entrees, side orders, desserts, condiments, beverages—every food item in any form—must be on the inventory sheets in order for you to project an accurate food cost. The inventory pages will be used later to calculate the dollar amount of unused stock at the end of the month. Leave at least a half-page blank on the last inventory sheet for any food items that may have been left out. You can write the additional items in as you inventory them.

Each category—food, liquor, wine and operational supplies—will have its own inventory pages. We are concentrating on food now so that you will have all the information you need at this point.

ACCURACY IN MENU CHECKLIST

Determine the accuracy of your own menu by using this checklist
and answering the sample questions.

QUANTITY REPRESENTATION

YES   NO

——   ——   1. When merchandising steaks by weight, do I use the generally accepted
practice of referring to the steak's weight prior to cooking?

——   ——   2. Are my double martinis really twice the size of a single drink?

——   ——   3. Are my breaded shrimp at least 50% shrimp, as government
regulations require?

——   ——   4. Is my "3-egg omelette" really made with three eggs?

——   ——   5. Are my "jumbo" eggs really "jumbo," the nationally recognized egg size, or
are they actually "large?"

——   ——   6. When I say "choice sirloin of beef" do I really refer to "USDA Choice
Grade Sirloin of Beef," as I've implied?

——   ——   7. Do I realize that it's OK to use the words "prime rib" to describe a cut of
beef (i.e., the "primal" ribs: 6th to 12th ribs), but when I combine this term
with "USDA" (USDA Prime Ribs), I'm implying a *grade* of beef, not a *cut* of
beef?

——   ——   8. Do I realize that "ground beef" is just what the name implies—ground
beef with no extra fat (the fat limit is 30%), water, extenders or binders?

——   ——   9. Do I understand that terms like "Prime," "Grade A," "Good," "No. 1,"
"Choice," "Fancy," "Grade AA" and "Extra Standard" are all descriptions of
grades as set by federal and state standards?

PRICE REPRESENTATION

——   ——   10. If my pricing structure includes a cover charge, service charge or gratuity,
have I brought these items to my customers' attention?

——   ——   11. Do I clearly define any restrictions regarding the use of coupons or premium promotions?

——   ——   12. If extra charges are made for special requests like "all white meat" or
"no-ice drinks," are these charges clearly stated at time of ordering?

YES   NO

———   ———   13. Are my house brands really manufactured to my own specifications, even if they are prepared off premises?

———   ———   14. Am I careful when advertising brand names that the brand advertised is always the brand sold?

———   ———   15. When substitutions are necessary for whatever reason (non-delivery, availability, price, etc.), do I realize these substitutions must be reflected on my menu?

Some such substitutions:

- Maple syrup and maple-flavored syrup
- Baked ham and boiled ham
- Chopped veal cutlets and shaped veal patties
- Ice milk and ice cream
- Fresh eggs and powdered eggs
- Picnic-style pork shoulder and ham
- Milk and skim milk
- Pure jams and pectin jams
- Whipped cream and whipped topping
- Turkey and chicken
- Hereford beef and Black Angus beef
- Peanut oil and corn oil
- Beef liver and calf's liver
- Cream and half-and-half
- Cream and nondairy creamer
- Butter and margarine
- Ground beef and ground sirloin of beef
- Capon and chicken
- Standard ice cream and French-style ice cream
- Cod and haddock
- Noodles and egg noodles
- White-meat tuna and light-meat tuna
- Haddock and pollack
- Flounder and sole
- Cheese food and processed cheese
- Cream sauce and nondairy cream sauce
- Bonita and tuna fish
- Roquefort cheese and blue cheese
- Tenderloin tips and diced beef
- Mayonnaise and salad dressing

YES   NO

—— —— 16. Can I back up the following descriptions with package labels, invoices or other supplier-produced documentation to prove point of origin?
- Lake Superior Whitefish
- Maine Lobster
- Puget Sound Sockeye Salmon
- Gulf Shrimp
- Smithfield Ham
- Idaho Potatoes
- Imported Swiss Cheese
- Bay Scallops
- Florida Orange Juice
- Wisconsin Cheese

—— —— 17. Do I realize that it is all right to use the following terminology in the generic sense to describe a method of preparation or service?
- New England Clam Chowder
- Irish Stew
- French Fries
- Russian Service
- Swiss Cheese
- Country Fried Steak
- French Dip
- German Potato Salad
- Manhattan Clam Chowder
- Russian Dressing
- Country Ham
- Danish Pastries
- English Muffins
- French Toast
- Denver Sandwich
- Swiss Steak
- French Service
- Florida Fresh Juice

—— —— 18. Do I use the term "fresh juice" only for a juice without additives and prepared from the original fruit within 12 hours of sale?

MERCHANDISING TERMS

—— —— 19. Instead of using the term "homemade," do I use more accurate terminology, like "home-style," "homemade-style," "made on the premises" or "our own?"

—— —— 20. If I use any of the following terms, am I sure I can substantiate them?
- Fresh Daily
- Flown In Daily
- Center-Cut Ham
- Aged Steaks
- Slept in Chesapeake Bay
- Corn-Fed Porkers
- Finest Quality
- Black Angus Beef
- Low Calorie
- Fresh-Roasted
- Kosher Meat
- Own Special Sauce
- Milk-Fed Chicken

MEANS OF PRESERVATION

—— —— 21. Am I careful not to misrepresent canned orange juice as frozen or canned applesauce as homemade?

—— —— 22. Do I use food preserved by the commonly accepted means: canned, chilled, bottled, frozen and dehydrated?

——— ———   23. Am I always absolutely accurate in the terminology used to describe the method by which the food is prepared?

Some preparation methods:

- Charcoal-Broiled
- Barbecued
- Broiled
- Fried in Butter
- Deep Fried
- Baked
- Roasted
- Prepared from Scratch
- Sauteed
- Smoked
- Poached

VERBAL AND VISUAL REPRESENTATION

——— ———   24. Do my menus, wall placard or other advertising materials containing pictorial representations always portray the actual product with true accuracy?

——— ———   25. For instance, am I careful not to:

A. Use mushroom pieces in a sauce when the picture depicts mushroom caps?

B. Use sliced strawberries on a shortcake when the picture depicts whole strawberries?

C. Use four shrimps when the picture shows five?

D. Use a plain bun when the photo depicts a sesame-topped bun?

E. Let my waiter/waitress offer "butter or sour cream" when, in actuality, I'm using imitation sour cream or margarine?

F. Let my waiter/waitress tell a customer, "The pies are baked in our own kitchen," when in fact they purchased prebaked, institutional pies?

DIETARY OR NUTRITIONAL CLAIMS

——— ———   26. Am I sure I never risk the public's health by misrepresenting the dietary or nutritional content of a food?

——— ———   27. Do "salt-free" and "sugar-free" mean just that?

——— ———   28. Can I substantiate with specific data any special nutrition claims or claims of "low calories?"

NOTE: If you cannot answer "yes" to all these questions, it is time to revise your menu to avoid misrepresentations and potential customer misconceptions about your food.

FORM TX

For a Nondramatic Literary Work
UNITED STATES COPYRIGHT OFFICE

REGISTRATION NUMBER

TX	TXU

EFFECTIVE DATE OF REGISTRATION

Month	Day	Year

DO NOT WRITE ABOVE THIS LINE. IF YOU NEED MORE SPACE, USE A SEPARATE CONTINUATION SHEET.

1

TITLE OF THIS WORK ▼

PREVIOUS OR ALTERNATIVE TITLES ▼

PUBLICATION AS A CONTRIBUTION If this work was published as a contribution to a periodical, serial, or collection, give information about the collective work in which the contribution appeared.   **Title of Collective Work ▼**

If published in a periodical or serial give: **Volume ▼**   **Number ▼**   **Issue Date ▼**   **On Pages ▼**

2

a

NAME OF AUTHOR ▼

DATES OF BIRTH AND DEATH
Year Born ▼   Year Died ▼

Was this contribution to the work a "work made for hire"?
☐ Yes
☐ No

AUTHOR'S NATIONALITY OR DOMICILE
Name of Country
OR { Citizen of ▶ _____
Domiciled in ▶ _____

WAS THIS AUTHOR'S CONTRIBUTION TO THE WORK
Anonymous?   ☐ Yes ☐ No
Pseudonymous?   ☐ Yes ☐ No

If the answer to either of these questions is "Yes," see detailed instructions.

NATURE OF AUTHORSHIP Briefly describe nature of material created by this author in which copyright is claimed. ▼

NOTE

Under the law, the "author" of a "work made for hire" is generally the employer, not the employee (see instructions). For any part of this work that was "made for hire" check "Yes" in the space provided, give the employer (or other person for whom the work was prepared) as "Author" of that part, and leave the space for dates of birth and death blank.

b

NAME OF AUTHOR ▼

DATES OF BIRTH AND DEATH
Year Born ▼   Year Died ▼

Was this contribution to the work a "work made for hire"?
☐ Yes
☐ No

AUTHOR'S NATIONALITY OR DOMICILE
Name of Country
OR { Citizen of ▶ _____
Domiciled in ▶ _____

WAS THIS AUTHOR'S CONTRIBUTION TO THE WORK
Anonymous?   ☐ Yes ☐ No
Pseudonymous?   ☐ Yes ☐ No

If the answer to either of these questions is "Yes," see detailed instructions.

NATURE OF AUTHORSHIP Briefly describe nature of material created by this author in which copyright is claimed. ▼

c

NAME OF AUTHOR ▼

DATES OF BIRTH AND DEATH
Year Born ▼   Year Died ▼

Was this contribution to the work a "work made for hire"?
☐ Yes
☐ No

AUTHOR'S NATIONALITY OR DOMICILE
Name of Country
OR { Citizen of ▶ _____
Domiciled in ▶ _____

WAS THIS AUTHOR'S CONTRIBUTION TO THE WORK
Anonymous?   ☐ Yes ☐ No
Pseudonymous?   ☐ Yes ☐ No

If the answer to either of these questions is "Yes," see detailed instructions.

NATURE OF AUTHORSHIP Briefly describe nature of material created by this author in which copyright is claimed. ▼

3

a
YEAR IN WHICH CREATION OF THIS WORK WAS COMPLETED This information must be given in all cases.
◀ Year

b
DATE AND NATION OF FIRST PUBLICATION OF THIS PARTICULAR WORK
Complete this information ONLY if this work has been published.
Month ▶ _____ Day ▶ _____ Year ▶ _____
◀ Nation

4

See instructions before completing this space.

COPYRIGHT CLAIMANT(S) Name and address must be given even if the claimant is the same as the author given in space 2. ▼

TRANSFER If the claimant(s) named here in space 4 is (are) different from the author(s) named in space 2, give a brief statement of how the claimant(s) obtained ownership of the copyright. ▼

APPLICATION RECEIVED

ONE DEPOSIT RECEIVED

TWO DEPOSITS RECEIVED

FUNDS RECEIVED

DO NOT WRITE HERE
OFFICE USE ONLY

MORE ON BACK ▶ • Complete all applicable spaces (numbers 5-9) on the reverse side of this page.
  • See detailed instructions.   • Sign the form at line 8.

DO NOT WRITE HERE
Page 1 of _____ pages

DO NOT WRITE ABOVE THIS LINE. IF YOU NEED MORE SPACE, USE A SEPARATE CONTINUATION SHEET.

PREVIOUS REGISTRATION Has registration for this work, or for an earlier version of this work, already been made in the Copyright Office?

☐ **Yes** ☐ **No** If your answer is "Yes," why is another registration being sought? (Check appropriate box.) ▼

a. ☐ This is the first published edition of a work previously registered in unpublished form.

b. ☐ This is the first application submitted by this author as copyright claimant.

c. ☐ This is a changed version of the work, as shown by space 6 on this application.

If your answer is "Yes," give: **Previous Registration Number** ▶   **Year of Registration** ▶

5

DERIVATIVE WORK OR COMPILATION

Preexisting Material Identify any preexisting work or works that this work is based on or incorporates. ▼

a

6

See instructions before completing this space.

Material Added to This Work Give a brief, general statement of the material that has been added to this work and in which copyright is claimed. ▼

b

DEPOSIT ACCOUNT If the registration fee is to be charged to a Deposit Account established in the Copyright Office, give name and number of Account.

Name ▼   **Account Number** ▼

a

7

CORRESPONDENCE Give name and address to which correspondence about this application should be sent. Name/Address/Apt/City/State/ZIP ▼

b

Area code and daytime telephone number ▶   Fax number ▶

Email ▶

CERTIFICATION* I, the undersigned, hereby certify that I am the

Check only one ▶

☐ author
☐ other copyright claimant
☐ owner of exclusive right(s)
☐ authorized agent of _____

of the work identified in this application and that the statements made by me in this application are correct to the best of my knowledge.

Name of author or other copyright claimant, or owner of exclusive right(s) ▲

8

Typed or printed name and date ▼ If this application gives a date of publication in space 3, do not sign and submit it before that date.

_____ Date ▶

Handwritten signature (X) ▼

X _____

9

Certificate will be mailed in window envelope to this address:	Name ▼
	Number/Street/Apt ▼
	City/State/ZIP ▼

YOU MUST:
• Complete all necessary spaces
• Sign your application in space 8

SEND ALL 3 ELEMENTS IN THE SAME PACKAGE:
1. Application form
2. Nonrefundable filing fee in check or money order payable to *Register of Copyrights*
3. Deposit material

MAIL TO:
Library of Congress
Copyright Office
101 Independence Avenue, S.E.
Washington, D.C. 20559-6000

Fees are subject to change. For current fees, check the Copyright Office website at www.copyright.gov, write the Copyright Office, or call (202) 707-3000.

Rev: June 2002—20,000   Web Rev: June 2002   ♻ Printed on recycled paper   U.S. Government Printing Office: 2000-461-113/20,021

INVENTORY FORM

ITEM	SIZE	DATE				TOTAL	COST	EXTENSION
							TOTAL	

FOOD ORDERING FORM

ITEM	BUILD TO AMT.	ON HAND									

SUCCESSFUL KITCHEN MANAGEMENT & CONTROL PROCEDURES — FOR MAXIMUM EFFICIENCY

INTRODUCTION

This chapter on kitchen management is divided into three separate sections: personnel, procedures and controls. HACCP and food-safety sanitation practices are covered in Chapter 7.

The personnel section describes the duties, functions and responsibilities of the various employees that are found in any restaurant. Every restaurant is unique in the way it operates. Some adaptation of these positions may be necessary in meet your own restaurant's needs. A list of specific job responsibilities provides details of some of the more critical positions.

The last part of the personnel section combines the functions into an organizational flowchart. This chart illustrates how kitchen employees unite their individual efforts and talents to present the final product to the customer.

The kitchen procedures section describes the basic day-to-day operational policies of the kitchen. Described are the procedures for purchasing, receiving, storing, rotating and issuing all food items. Several sample forms are given at the end of this chapter illustrate each of the procedures. These sample forms are also used in the control section and are an integral part of the control system.

Finally, the kitchen controls section combines all of the personnel and procedures previously described into a system of checks and balances. This section will enable the restaurant manager, through the use of the sample forms and simple procedures, to know exactly where every food item and every cent the restaurant business spent went. The last few pages of this section consolidate all the personnel, procedures and sample forms into a sequence of daily events. This illustrates how every food item is controlled, from the initial purchasing stage to when the cashier rings up the sale.

Although Chapter 7 addresses HACCP food safety and sanitation, the kitchen controls section of this chapter describes basic sanitation practices with which every restaurant manager and every employee must be thoroughly familiar. This section is perhaps the most important. Improper handling of food items or disregarding sanitation procedures will undoubtedly lead to hazardous health conditions. There are numerous cases where restaurants have caused or were held responsible for the spread of severe sickness and infectious diseases that have even, in certain instances, led to death. There is no excuse for neglecting any health or sanitation procedure. It is the responsibility of the restaurant manager to guarantee the wholesomeness of the restaurant's product.

ITCHEN PERSONNEL

THE KITCHEN DIRECTOR

JOB DESCRIPTION

A kitchen director, head cook or head chef position can usually be found in any medium- to large-volume restaurant. Although job descriptions differ among various establishments, the primary objective of the kitchen director is to establish the maximum operational efficiency and food quality of the kitchen. The director is responsible for all the kitchen personnel and their training. Her foremost responsibility is to ensure that all food products are of the highest quality obtainable. She must set an example to other employees through her work habits and mannerisms.

The restaurant manager must have complete faith in the ability of the kitchen director. The kitchen director must possess the same goals and desires as that of the restaurant's manager: primarily a total dedication to serve only the finest food possible at the lowest cost.

Your kitchen director must be available during both the day and evening. During the day she must oversee the preparation cooks and ensure that all food products are ordered and accounted for. She would also be responsible for any breakfast, lunch, brunch or catering functions. During the evening the director must make certain the kitchen is properly staffed and take any measures needed, including working in the kitchen behind the line to ensure positive results.

The restaurant manager cannot possibly spend the necessary time to supervise the kitchen and attend to all the minute details. Therefore it is highly recommended that a competent kitchen director be employed.

KITCHEN DIRECTOR'S AREAS OF RESPONSIBILITY

1. All personnel in the kitchen.

2. Food quality.

3. Controlling waste and food cost.

4. Ordering, receiving, storing and issuing all food products.

5. Training of kitchen personnel.

6. Morale of the kitchen staff.

7. Health and safety regulation enforcement.

8. Communicating possible problem areas to the manager.

9. Scheduling all kitchen personnel.

10. Scheduling his/her own time.

11. Maintaining a clean and safe kitchen.

12. Holding kitchen staff meetings.

13. Filling out all forms for prescribed kitchen controls.

PREPARATION COOK

JOB DESCRIPTION

The preparation ("prep") cook generally is part of a team of other preparation cooks. Their primary responsibility is to prepare all the food items in the restaurant in accordance with the preparation methods prescribed. The kitchen director trains, supervises and is responsible for the preparation cooks. The preparation cooks are directly involved in determining the outcome and quality of the final food product. This area is where the greatest amount of waste occurs; the kitchen director must monitor preparation closely. Preparation cooks must follow the Recipe and Procedure Manual exactly as it is printed in order to ensure consistent products and food costs.

SOME RESPONSIBILITIES OF PREPARATION COOKS

1. Prepare all food products according to the prescribed methods.

2. Maintain the highest level of food quality obtainable.

3. Receive and store all products as prescribed.

4. Maintain a clean and safe kitchen.

5. Follow all health and safety regulations.

6. Follow all restaurant regulations.

7. Control waste.

8. Communicate all problems and ideas for improvement to management.

9. Communicate and work together with coworkers as a team.

10. Arrive on time and ready to work.

11. Attend all meetings.

12. Fill out all forms as prescribed.

13. Maintain all equipment and utensils.

14. Organize all areas of the kitchen.

15. Follow proper rotation procedures.

16. Label and date all products prepared. For resources visit *http://www.dissolveaway.com* or call 800-847-0101.

17. Follow management's instructions and suggestions.

COOKING STAFF

JOB DESCRIPTION

The cooking staff arrives one to two hours before the restaurant is open for business. Their primary responsibility is to cook the prepared food items in the prescribed method. The cooking staff may be made up of regular line cooks or highly skilled chefs, depending on the complexity of the menu. They must ensure that all food products have been prepared correctly before cooking. They are the last quality-control check before the food is presented to the waitstaff and the public. It is imperative that the cooking staff work together as a team and communicate with one another. A group effort is needed to keep the kitchen operating at maximum efficiency.

SOME RESPONSIBILITIES OF THE COOKING STAFF

1. Arrive on time and ready to work.

2. Ensure that proper preparation procedures have been completed.

3. Prepare the cooking areas for the shift.

4. Maintain the highest level of food quality obtainable.

5. Communicate with coworkers, waitstaff and management.

6. Become aware of what is happening in the dining room (e.g. arrival of a large group).

7. Account for every food item used.

8. Maintain a clean and safe kitchen.

9. Follow all health and safety regulations prescribed.

10. Follow all the restaurant regulations prescribed.

11. Control and limit waste.

12. Communicate problems and ideas to management.

13. Attend all meetings.

14. Fill out all forms required.

15. Maintain all kitchen equipment and utensils.

16. Keep every area of the kitchen clean and organized.

17. Follow the proper rotation procedures.

18. Label and date all products used. For resources visit *http://www.dissolveaway.com* or call 800-847-0101.

19. Follow management's instructions and suggestions.

THE EXPEDITER

JOB DESCRIPTION

Sets the pace and flow in the kitchen. The expediter receives the order ticket from a waiter or waitress or from a printer in the kitchen and communicates which menu items need to be cooked to the cooking staff. Each cook performs a specific cooking function at his or her station, such as broiling, deep-frying, cooking pasta, sauteing or carving.

The expediter can regulate the pace in the kitchen by holding an order ticket for a few minutes before reading it to the cooking staff. This is particularly useful when the cooks are bogged down in work.

The expediter is also responsible for laying out and garnishing all the plates. He makes certain that each member of the waitstaff receives the correct plates with the correct items on them. As a double check, each waitstaff member must check his or her order ticket against the actual prepared plates before taking them out of the kitchen. The expediter must make certain that every food item that leaves the kitchen has had an order ticket written for it. Under no circumstance is the expediter to instruct the cook to start the cooking of an item unless there is a written order ticket—it is crucial to the success of this control system. All order tickets are to be held by the expediter for reference at the end of the night.

SOME RESPONSIBILITIES OF THE EXPEDITER

1. Communicate with everyone in the kitchen.

2. Always get an order ticket from a waiter/waitress or kitchen printer.

3. Ensure all food leaving the kitchen is of the level of quality prescribed.

4. Make certain all plates are hot and garnished correctly.

5. Make certain that every food item is accounted for.

6. Safely store all food order tickets for later reference.

7. Fill out all required forms appropriately.

8. Maintain all equipment and utensils.

9. Keep own work area of the kitchen organized.

10. Follow all rotation procedures.

11. Label and date all products used. For resources visit *http://www.dissolveaway.com* or call 800-847-0101.

12. Follow management's instructions and suggestions.

SALAD PREPARER

JOB DESCRIPTION

The salad preparer fixes and portions salads from the ingredients prepared during the day. A salad preparer is used when the restaurant has salad table service. For better control, this person may also be assigned to issue desserts. A salad preparer can be a great aid in speeding up service and controlling food cost.

Smaller restaurants that cannot justify the employment a salad preparer should use the waitstaff or cooks to prepare the salads. In this case, all dessert tickets must go to the expediter before the desserts are issued.

DISHWASHER

JOB DESCRIPTION

The dishwasher position is unfortunately often thought of as an unimportant position that anyone can be trained to perform quickly and cheaply. However, a dishwasher is as important as any other employee in the restaurant. She is responsible for supplying spotless, sanitized dishes to the dining room and clean kitchen utensils to the cooks. A slowdown in the dishwashing process will send repercussions throughout the restaurant. Improperly cleaned china, glassware or flatware can ruin an otherwise enjoyable dining experience. How many times have you sat at a table with a dirty fork or a glass with lipstick residue? The dishwasher handles thousands of dollars of china and glassware every day. Accidentally dropping a tray of dishes can erase a day's profits.

All glassware, china, flatware and kitchen utensils have special washing requirements. The correct chemicals and dishwashing racks must be used in order to achieve the desired results. Your dishwasher chemical company can supply you with all the training. Your salesperson can set up a training session with your staff. He will instruct your staff on how to: operate the dishwasher correctly; set up systems to alleviate breakage; use the chemicals correctly; and set up the proper daily maintenance needed on the machine.

KITCHEN PROCEDURES

PURCHASING

The goal of purchasing is to supply the restaurant with the best goods at the lowest possible cost. There are many ways to achieve this. The buyer must have favorable working relations with all suppliers and vendors. A large amount of time must be spent meeting with prospective sales representatives and companies. The buyer's responsibility is to evaluate and decide how to best make each of the purchases for the restaurant. Purchasing is a complex area that must be managed by someone who is completely familiar with all of the restaurant's needs. The kitchen director or manager would be the best choice to do the purchasing. It is preferable to have one or two people do all the purchasing for all areas of the restaurant. There are several advantages to this, such as greater buying power and better overall control.

Provided the buyer completes the necessary research and evaluates all of the possible purchasing options, she can easily recoup a large part of her salary from the savings made. The most critical element to grasp when purchasing is the overall picture. Price is not the top priority and is only one of the considerations in deciding how and where to place an order. Review the purveyor section in the first chapter for a list of points you must consider when choosing a purveyor.

INVENTORY LEVELS

The first step in computing what item and how much of it to order is to determine the inventory level, or the amount needed on hand at all times. This is a simple procedure, and it requires that the order sheets are prepared as described in Chapter 5. To determine the amount you need to order, you must first know the amount you have in inventory. Walk through the storage areas and mark in the On Hand column the amounts that are there. To determine the Build To Amount, you will need to know when regularly scheduled deliveries arrive for that item and the amount used in the period between deliveries. Add on about 25 percent to the average amount used; this will cover unexpected usage, a late delivery or a backorder at the vendor. The amount you need to order is the difference between the Build To Amount and the amount On Hand. Experience and food demand will reveal the amount an average order should contain. By purchasing too little, the restaurant may run out of supplies before the next delivery. Ordering too much will result in tying up money, putting a drain on the restaurant's cash flow. Buying up items in large amounts can save money, but you must consider the cash-flow costs.

A buying schedule should be set up and adhered to. This would consist of a calendar showing:

- Which day's orders need to be placed.

- When deliveries will be arriving.

- What items will be arriving from which company and when.

- Phone numbers of sales representatives to contact for each company.

- The price the sales representative quoted.

Post the buying schedule on the office wall. When a delivery doesn't arrive as scheduled, the buyer should place a phone call to the salesperson or company immediately. Don't wait until the end of the day when offices are closed.

A **Want Sheet** (See the example at the end of this chapter) may be placed on a clipboard in the kitchen. This sheet is made available for employees to write in any items they may need to do their jobs more efficiently. This is a very effective form of communication; employees should be encouraged to use it. The buyer should consult this sheet every day. A request might be as simple as a commercial-grade carrot peeler. If, for example, the last one broke, and the preparation staff has been using the back of a knife instead, the small investment could save you from an increase in labor and food costs.

COOPERATIVE PURCHASING

Many restaurants have formed cooperative purchasing groups to increase their purchasing power. Many items are commonly used by all food service operators. By cooperatively joining together to place large orders, restaurants can usually get substantial price reductions. Some organizations even purchase their own trucks and warehouses and hire personnel to pick up deliveries. This can be quite advantageous for restaurants that are in the proximity of a major supplier or shipping center. Many items, such as produce, dairy products, seafood and meat, may be purchased this way. Chain-restaurant organizations have a centralized purchasing department and, often, large self-distribution centers.

RECEIVING AND STORING

Most deliveries will be arriving at the restaurant during the day. Deliveries should only be received during the prescribed time periods: before and after the lunch period. The preparation crew is normally responsible for receiving and storing all items (excluding liquor, beer and wine). The buyer should also be present to ensure that each item is of the specification ordered.

Receiving and storing each product is a critical responsibility. Costly mistakes can come about from a staff member who was not properly trained in the correct procedures. Listed below are some policies and procedures for receiving and storing all deliveries. A slight inaccuracy in an invoice or improper storing of a perishable item could cost the restaurant hundreds of dollars.

Watch for a common area of internal theft. A collusion could develop between the delivery person and the employee receiving the products. Items checked as being received and accounted for may not have been delivered at all. The driver simply keeps the items. In an upcoming section we will discuss how to guard against internal theft.

All products delivered to the restaurant must:

1. Be checked against the actual order sheet.

2. Be the exact specification ordered (weight, size, quantity).

3. Be checked against the invoice.

4. Be accompanied by an invoice containing: current price, totals, date, company name and receiver's signature.

5. Have their individual weights verified on the pound scale.

6. Be dated, rotated and put in the proper storage area immediately. For resources visit *http://www.dissolveaway.com* or call 800-847-0101.

7. Be locked in their storage areas securely.

Credit slips must be issued or prices subtracted from the invoice when an error occurs. The delivery person must sign over the correction.

Keep an invoice box (a small mailbox) in the kitchen to store all invoices and packing slips received during the day. Mount the box on the wall, away from work areas. Prior to leaving for the day, the receiver must bring the invoices to the manager's office and place them in a designated spot. Extreme care must be taken to ensure that all invoices are handled correctly. A missing invoice will throw off the bookkeeping and financial records and statements.

ROTATION PROCEDURES

1. New items go to the back and on the bottom.

2. Older items move to the front and to the left.

3. In any part of the restaurant: the first item used should always be the oldest.

4. Date and label everything. For resources visit *http://www.dissolveaway.com* or call 800-847-0101.

TEMPERATURE RANGES FOR PERISHABLE ITEMS

All frozen items...-10–0° F

Fresh meat and poultry ....31–35° F

Produce ....33–38° F

Fresh seafood ....33–38° F

Dairy products..33–38° F

Beer...40–60° F

Wine (Chablis, rosé) ....45–55° F

Wine (most reds) ....55–65° F

ISSUING

All raw materials from which portionable entrees are prepared, such as meat, seafood and poultry, must be issued on a daily basis. Whenever one of these bulk items is removed from a freezer or walk-in, it must be signed out. An example of a **Sign-out Sheet** may be found at the end of this chapter. When a part of a case or box is removed, the weight of the portion removed must be recorded in the "Amount" column. The Sign-out Sheet should be on a clipboard affixed to the walk-in or freezer. Once the item is signed out, the weight must be placed in the "Amount Ordered or Defrosted" column on the **Preparation Form.** An example of a Preparation Form may be found at the end of this chapter. This will show that the items signed out were actually used in the restaurant. From this information, the kitchen director can compute a daily yield on each item prepared. This yield will show that the portions were weighed out accurately and the bulk product that was used to prepare menu items. At any one of these steps pilferage can occur. The signing-out procedure will eliminate pilferage. Products such as dry goods or cleaning supplies may be issued in a similar manner. If these or other items were being stolen, the cost of each would show up in the cost projections at the end of the month.

KITCHEN CLEANLINESS

Kitchen cleanliness must always be of constant concern to both management and employees. A maintenance company should do little cleaning in the kitchen. They have not been trained in the cleaning procedures that must be used in the kitchen to maintain food safety requirements. A maintenance company should only be used, perhaps, for cleaning and washing the kitchen floor. All the rest of the kitchen cleaning and maintenance is the responsibility of the staff.

All employees must be made aware that their daily cleanups are as critical as any of their other responsibilities—perhaps more so. A complete section on food safety can be found in the next chapter. Every employee must be completely familiar with its contents.

The most effective cleanup policy to institute is to make each employee responsible for his or her own area. Every workstation must have its own cleaning check-off sheet for the end of each shift. (See the example below.) These sheets should be sealed in plastic, so that a grease pencil can be used to check off each completed item. Every employee must have his or her cleanup checked by a manager. You must inspect employee cleanup carefully and thoroughly. Once a precedent is set for each cleanup it must be maintained. At the end of a long shift some employees may need a little prodding to get the desired results.

THE RESTAURANT MANAGER'S HANDBOOK

CLEAN-UP SHEET FOR EACH COOK

Place a check mark on all completed items.

   ___   1. Turn off all equipment and pilots.

   ___   2. Take all pots, pans and utensils to the dishwasher.

   ___   3. Wrap, date and rotate all leftover food.

   ___   4. Clean out the refrigerator units.

   ___   5. Clean all shelves.

   ___   6. Wipe down all walls.

   ___   7. Spot clean the exhaust hoods.

   ___   8. Clean and polish all stainless steel in your area.

   ___   9. Clean out all sinks.

   ___   10. Take out all trash. Break down boxes to conserve space in dumpster.

   ___   11. Sweep the floor in your area.

   ___   12. Replace all clean pots, pans and utensils.

   ___   13. Check to see if your coworkers need assistance.

   ___   14. Check out with the manager.

COOK _____ MANAGER _____

TIME OF LEAVING _____

KITCHEN CONTROLS

The following section will present a system of kitchen controls. Combining these controls with the procedures and policies already set forth will enable you to establish an airtight food cost control system. The key to controlling food cost is reconciliation. Every step or action taken is checked and reconciled with another person. Management's responsibility is, once these systems are set up, to monitor them with daily involvement. Should all the steps and procedures be adhered to, you will know exactly where every dollar and ounce of food went. There are no loopholes. Management must be involved in the training and supervision of all employees. Daily involvement and communication is needed in order to succeed. Employees must follow all procedures precisely. If they do not, they must be informed of their specific deviations from these procedures and correct them. Any control initiated is only as good as the manager who follows up and enforces it. The total amount of time a manager needs to complete all of the work that will be described in this section is less than one hour a day. There is no excuse for not completing each procedure every day. A deviation in your controls or involvement can only lead to a loss over the control of the restaurant's costs. Please note: although a simple manual system is detailed here, many of these functions can be implemented into your computerized accounting system. Many of the basic purchasing and receiving functions are found in virtually all off-the-shelf accounting programs.

PREPARATION FORM

The Preparation Form is used by the preparation cooks. See the example form at the end of this chapter. It should be filled out as follows:

A. The first procedure performed each morning by the preparation cook is counting the number of items on hand. These are food items left from the previous night. The number of each item left is placed in the "Beginning Amount" column. Every item that needs to be prepared must be on this sheet: all entrees, side orders, desserts, salad items, etc. This sheet will be used as a reference guide throughout the day to determine which items need to be prepared.

B. List the minimum amount needed for the day from the Minimum Amount Needed Form. This is the form that sets the minimum amount you need to have prepared for the cooking staff. Each day will show a different amount, depending upon the amount of customers you anticipate serving. The minimum amount needed is computed by management based on the number of items previously sold on an average day in the past. Procedures for calculating the Minimum Amount Needed are discussed in the following section.

C. Subtract the Beginning Amount from the Minimum Amount Needed. This figure will be the amount that needs to be prepared for that particular item. Based on this figure you can then compute the amount of food that must be either ordered or removed from the freezer to defrost. All portion-controlled items must be signed out on the Sign-out Sheet before removed from the freezer or walk-in.

D. All items entered on the Sign-out Sheet must also be entered in the "Amount Ordered or Defrosted" column on the Preparation Form. This information is entered here so that the kitchen director will be able to compute a yield on all the items prepared. This column will also be used by the manager to calculate the daily perpetual inventory, which will be discussed later in this chapter.

E. As the day progresses, items will be prepared, dated, wrapped, rotated and placed in the walk-in for use that night. The number of portions prepared for each item is recorded in the "Amount Prepared" column.

F. The Amount Prepared plus the Beginning Amount equals the starting total. The starting total must be equal to or greater than the minimum amount needed. When all items are completed, the preparation sheet is placed in the manager's office.

MINIMUM AMOUNT NEEDED FORM

The purpose of the Minimum Amount Needed Form is to guide the preparation cook in determining the amount of food that will need to be prepared for each day. An example of the **Minimum Amount Needed Form** can be found at the end of this chapter. The Minimum Amount Needed must be large enough so that the restaurant will not run out of any food during the next shift. However, too much prepared food will quickly lose its freshness and may spoil altogether.

To compute the Minimum Amount Needed of each item for each particular day, consult the Food Itemization Form, described in Chapter 16, "Internal Bookkeeping." This form will list the actual number of each menu item sold for every day of the past month. It will also indicate the percentage sold of that item in relation to the rest of the menu items for the month and for each day. Examine the last two months' product mixture figures. Based on this information you should get a relatively accurate depiction of the amount of each item sold on each particular day of the week. Based on the average amount sold each day and the percentage sold in relation to the total menu, you will be able to project the minimum amount needed for the following months.

EXAMPLE

According to the Food Itemization Form last month the restaurant sold between 20 and 25 shrimp dinners each Saturday night. The restaurant served between 200 and 300 dinners for each of these nights, so about 10 percent of the menu selections sold were shrimp dinners. To project next month's Minimum Amount Needed for an average Saturday evening, estimate the average number of dinners you expect to serve.

Let's assume 250 dinners will be sold on an average Saturday evening. Multiply this figure (250) by the average percentage of the menu sold (10 percent, or .10)—the answer (25) would be the approximate number of shrimp dinners you would sell on an average Saturday for the next month. This is, of course, only an educated guess; add 30 percent to the figure you projected to cover a busy night or an unusually high demand for that particular item. In the example, this extra 30 percent is 8 more dinners: 33 shrimp dinners is the minimum amount needed for Saturday night. Holidays and seasonal business changes need to be considered when setting minimum amounts.

DAILY YIELDS

Daily yields represent the actual usage of a product from its raw purchased form to the prepared menu item. The yield percentage is a measure of how efficiently this was accomplished, or how effectively a preparation cook eliminated waste. The higher the yield percentage, the more usable material was obtained from that product.

All meat, seafood and poultry products must have a yield percentage computed for each entree every day. Yields are extremely important when determining menu prices. They are also a very useful tool in controlling food cost. Daily yields should be computed by the kitchen director. An example of a daily **Yield Sheet** can be found at the end of this chapter.

Yield sheets should be kept for several months: they may become useful in analyzing other problem areas. All the information to compute each yield can be obtained from the daily Preparation Form.

TO COMPUTE THE YIELD PERCENTAGE:

1. From the "Amount Ordered or Defrosted" column compute the total amount of ounces used. Verify the amount in this column against the Sign-out Sheet. This figure is the starting weight in ounces.

2. The "Amount Prepared" column contains the number of portions yielded. Enter this figure on the Yield Sheet.

3. To compute the yield percentage, divide the Total Portion Weight (in ounces) by the Total Starting Weight (in ounces).

Yields should be consistent regardless of who prepares the item. If there is a substantial variance in the yield percentages—4–10 percent—consider these questions:

1. Are the preparation cooks carefully portioning all products? Over the months have they gotten lax in these methods?

2. Are you purchasing the same brands of the product? Different brands may have different yields!

3. Are all the items signed out on the Sign-out Sheet actually being used in preparing the menu items? Is it possible some of the product is being stolen after it is issued and before it is prepared? Do certain employees preparing the food items have consistently lower yields than others?

4. Is the staff properly trained in cutting, trimming and butchering the raw products? Do they know all the points of eliminating waste?

Periodically compare the average yield percentage to the percentage used in projecting the menu costs. If the average yield has dropped, you may need to review the menu prices.

PERPETUAL INVENTORY

The perpetual inventory is a check on the daily usage of items from the freezers and walk-ins. This form is used in conjunction with the Sign-out Sheet. An example of the **Perpetual Inventory Form** may be found at the end of this chapter. When completed, the perpetual inventory will ensure that no bulk products have been stolen from the freezer or walk-ins. List all the food items that are listed on the Sign-out Sheet and Yield Sheet. In the "Size" column list the unit size that the item is packaged in. The contents of most cases of food are packed in units such as 5-pound boxes or 2-pound bags. Meat is usually packed by the number of pieces in a case and the case's weight. The size listed on the perpetual inventory must correspond to the size the preparation cooks are signing out of the freezer and walk-ins.

In the "Start" column, enter the number of each item listed. For example, if shrimp is packed in 5-pound boxes and you have two 50-pound cases, there are 20 boxes. Enter 20 in the start column. Each number along the top corresponds to each day of the month. At the end of each day, count all the items on hand and enter this figure on the "=" line. Compare this figure to the "Amount Ordered or Defrosted" column on the Preparation Form; these amounts must be the same. Place the total number of each item on the "–" line. If there were any deliveries, place this total on the "+" line.

Check the invoices every day for the items delivered that are in your perpetual inventory. Ensure that all items signed off as being delivered are actually in the storage areas. Should there be a discrepancy, check with the employee that signed the invoice. The number of items you start with (20) plus the number you received in deliveries (5), minus the amount signed out by the preparation cooks (1), must equal the number on hand (24). If there is a discrepancy, you may have a thief.

Should you suspect a theft in the restaurant, record the names of all employees who worked that particular day. If thefts continue to occur, a pattern will develop among the employees who were working on all the days in question. Compute the perpetual inventory or other controls you are having a problem with at different times of the day, before and after each shift. This will pinpoint the area and shift in which the theft is occurring. Sometimes, placing a notice to all employees that you are aware of a theft problem in the restaurant will resolve the problem. Make it clear that any employee caught stealing will be terminated.

GUEST TICKETS AND THE CASHIER

There are various methods of controlling cash and guest tickets. The following section will describe an airtight system of checks and balances for controlling cash, tickets and prepared food. Certain modifications may be needed to implement these controls in your own restaurant. Many of the cash registers and POS (point-of-sale) systems available on the market can eliminate most of the manual work and calculations. The systems described in this section are based on the simplest and least expensive cash register available. The register must have three separate subtotal keys for food, liquor and wine sales and a grand-total key for the total guest check. Sales tax is then computed on this amount. The register used must also calculate the food, liquor and wine totals for the shift. These are basic functions that most machines have. Guest tickets must be of the type that is divided into two parts. The first section is the heavy paper part listing the menu items. At the bottom is a space for the subtotals, grand total, tax and a tear-away customer receipt. The second section is a carbon copy of the first. The carbon copy is given to the expediter, who then issues it to the cooks, who start the cooking process. Some restaurants utilize handheld ordering computers, and/or the tickets may be printed in the kitchen at the time of entry into the POS system or register. Regardless, the expediter must receive a ticket in order to issue any food.

The tickets must have individual identification numbers printed in sequence on both parts and the tear-away receipt. They must also have a space for the waitperson's name, the date, table number and the number of people at the table. This information will be used by the expediter and bookkeeper in tracking down lost tickets and/or food items.

Each member of the waitstaff is issued a certain number of tickets each shift. These tickets are in numbered sequence.

For example, a waiter may be issued 25 tickets from 007575 to 007600. At the end of the shift he must return to the cashier the same total number of tickets. No ticket should ever become lost; it is the responsibility of the waitstaff to ensure this. Should there be a mistake on a ticket, the cashier must void out all parts. This ticket must be turned in with the others after being approved and signed by the manager. The manager should issue tickets to each individual waiter and waitress. An example of a **Ticket Issuance Form** can be found at the end of this chapter. In certain instances, the manager may approve of giving away menu items at no charge. The manager must also approve of the discarding of food that cannot be served. A ticket must be written to record all of these transactions. Listed below are some examples of these types of situations:

- **Manager food.** All food that is issued free of charge to managers, owners and officers of the company.

- **Complimentary food.** All food issued to a customer compliments of the restaurant. This includes all food given away as part of a promotional campaign.

- **Housed food.** All food of which is not servable, such as spoiled, burned or incorrect orders.

All of these tickets should be filled out as usual, listing the items and the prices. The cashier should not ring up these tickets, but record them on the Cashier's Report Form. Write the word "manager," "complimentary" or "housed" over the top of the ticket.

The manager issues cash drawers, or "bank," to the cashier. The drawers are prepared by the bookkeeper. Inside the cashier drawer is the Cashier's Report itemizing the breakdown of the money it contains. An example of the **Cashier's Report Form** can be found at the end of this chapter. The accuracy of the Cashier's Report is the responsibility of both the cashier and the manager. Upon receiving the cash drawer, the cashier must count the money in the cash drawer with the manager to verify its contents. After verification, the cashier will be responsible for the cash register. The cashier should be the only employee allowed to operate it.

Each member of the waitstaff will bring his or her guest ticket to the cashier for totaling. The cashier must examine the ticket to ensure:

- All items were charged for.

- All items have the correct price.

- All the bar and wine tabs are included.

- Subtotals and grand total are correct.
- Sales tax is entered correctly.

The cashier is responsible for filling out the charge-card forms and ensuring their accuracy. Charge-card procedures are described in Chapter 16. The cashier will return the customer's charge card and receipt to the appropriate member of the waitstaff.

At the end of each shift, the cashier must cash out with the manager. List all the cash in the "Cash Out" columns. Enter the breakdown of sales into separate categories. Do not include sales tax. Enter all complimentary, housed and manager amounts. Itemize all checks on back. Itemize each ticket for total sales and total dinner count. Break down and enter all charged sales.

The total amount of cash taken in plus the charge sales must equal the total itemized ticket sales. Itemize all checks on the back of the Cashier's Report and stamp "FOR DEPOSIT ONLY"; the stamp should include the restaurant's bank name and account number.

Should a customer charge a tip, you may give the waiter or waitress a "cash paid out" from the register. When the payment comes in you can then deposit the whole amount into your account. Miscellaneous paid-outs are for any items that may need to be purchased throughout the shift. List all of them on the back and staple the receipts to the page.

When everything is checked out and balanced, the sheet must be signed by the cashier and manager. The manager should then deposit all tickets, register tapes, cash, charges and forms into the safe for the bookkeeper the next morning. The cash on hand must equal the register receipt readings.

COOK'S FORM

The Cook's Form is used in conjunction with the Preparation Form. When both of these forms are completed, you will have complete accountability for all menu items. An example of the **Cook's Form** can be found at the end of this chapter. In the "Item" column list all the entrees, side orders and desserts. These items should be in the same sequence as in the Preparation Form for ease of comparison. In the "Start" column list all the items that were left over from the day before. Look at the dates to ensure that all the items used first are the oldest.

The "Additions" column contains the items that were prepared that day. The "Starting Balance" column contains the total of the Start amount plus the Additions. This figure represents the total number of starting items for the shift.

At the beginning of each cook's shift, the manager will compare the total starting figure on the Cook's Form to the total starting figures on the Preparation Form. All numbers must match. If any of the items do not match, the cook must go back and recount that item. You must be certain that both the Cook's Form and the Preparation Form are accurate. Recount the items yourself if necessary. Should there still be a discrepancy, you must consider whether there has been a theft sometime after the preparation cooks finished and before the cooking staff completed their form.

When the cooking shift is completed, the cooks will recount all the items not used. These figures are placed in the "Balance Ending" column. The difference between the Starting and the Balance Ending is the number sold. Once completed, the cooks will turn the sheet over to the expediter. The expediter will verify that the number of items sold equals the number of items cooked. To compare these two figures he must itemize the carbon copy part of the tickets that were given to him by the waitstaff. An example of this **Ticket Itemization Form** can be found at the end of this chapter.

To itemize the tickets, place an "X" in the column next to the corresponding item. The total number of "X" marks equals the total number of tickets received for that item. Enter this figure in the "# Sold" column. The Total Sold from the Ticket Itemization Form must equal the total amount sold on the Cook's and Cashier's Report Forms. If there is a discrepancy:

A. The expediter must reitemize all tickets.

B. The cooks must recount the ending balance.

C. Make certain you considered all house, complimentary and manager tickets.

Should there still be a discrepancy, the manager must recheck all the calculations and make certain all the tickets are accounted for. If the differences remain unresolved, you must consider that theft may be the reason. Either the item left the kitchen without a ticket, or the item was taken without the cooking staff realizing it. The latter is unlikely, since the cooks are usually at their stations for the entire shift.

Once the Cook's Form is reconciled, return it to the office. All the Preparation, Cook's and Ticket Itemization Forms should be kept in a loose-leaf binder for several weeks for reference.

Each morning the manager will compare the cook's Balance Ending figure with the preparation cook's Beginning Amount. This will verify that all the items from last night are still there the following morning. This completes the daily cycle of checks and balances. The bookkeeper will further break down and analyze the forms, cash and tickets. These procedures, too, are described in Chapter 16.

SUMMARY

To enable you to envision precisely how the personnel procedures and controls combine to control the restaurant's food cost, a summary of the key points are listed in this section in sequence of events. In the example you will trace 25 pounds of shrimp through a typical day's operation, from the initial purchasing to the final product. The first column in each of the example forms are filled out so you will be able to see how they are used and why each one is a critical part in the overall control system. I would recommend that the manager put the following list in the form of a check-off sheet for his own organizational purposes.

SEQUENCE OF EVENTS

____ 1. Determine the need to purchase shrimp.

____ 2. Purchase the amount needed. In example: 25 pounds.

____ 3. Shrimp is delivered. Follow the receiving and storing procedures.

____ 4. Enter on the Perpetual Inventory Form the amount delivered. In example: 5 boxes of 5 pounds each.

____ 5. Preparation cooks compute the opening counts. In example: 25 shrimp dinners is the beginning count.

____ 6. Determine the Minimum Amount Needed: 33. The preparation cooks need to prepare 8 more dinners for that night. They remove 5 pounds, or 1 box, of shrimp from the freezer.

____ 7. Sign out the 5 pounds of shrimp on the Sign-out Sheet.

____ 8. Place the amount, 5 pounds, in the "Amount Ordered or Defrosted" column on the Preparation Form.

____ 9. Prepare the shrimp as prescribed in the Recipe and Procedure Manual.

____ 10. The number of dinners prepared is 9; enter this figure in the "Amount Prepared" column. The starting total would be 34 (9 + 25). Enter these figures on the Preparation Form.

____ 11. The Preparation Form is completed and given to the kitchen director. All storage areas are locked before leaving. The invoices are brought to the manager's office.

____ 12. The kitchen director computes the yields.

____ 13. The cooks enter and count all the items for the Starting Total.

____ 14. The manager verifies that the Starting Total on the Preparation Form is the same as on the Cook's Form.

____ 15. The manager issues the tickets to the waitstaff. The manager issues the cashier drawer to the cashier and verifies the starting amount.

____ 16. The manager checks the perpetual inventory.

____ 17. The waitstaff gives the order tickets to the expediter.

____ 18. The expediter reads off the items to the cooks who start the cooking of the menu items.

____ 19. When completed, the waiter/waitress takes the dinner to the customer.

____ 20. The bill is totaled and given to the customer.

____ 21. The cashier verifies the amount and collects the money or charge.

____ 22. The cooks count the Balance Ending. In example: Starting Total is 34, and the ending balance is 21, leaving 13 as sold.

_____ 23. The expediter itemizes the carbon copies: 13 shrimp dinners sold.

_____ 24. The manager cashes out with the cashier. Ticket itemization: 13 sold.

_____ 25. All three figures verified: cooks to expediter to cashier.

_____ 26. The following morning the manager verifies the ending balance of the Cook's Form (21) to the Beginning Amount of the Preparation Form.

_____ 27. The bookkeeper rechecks and verifies all the transactions of the previous night.

DETAILED LAYOUT OF DISHROOM EQUIPMENT

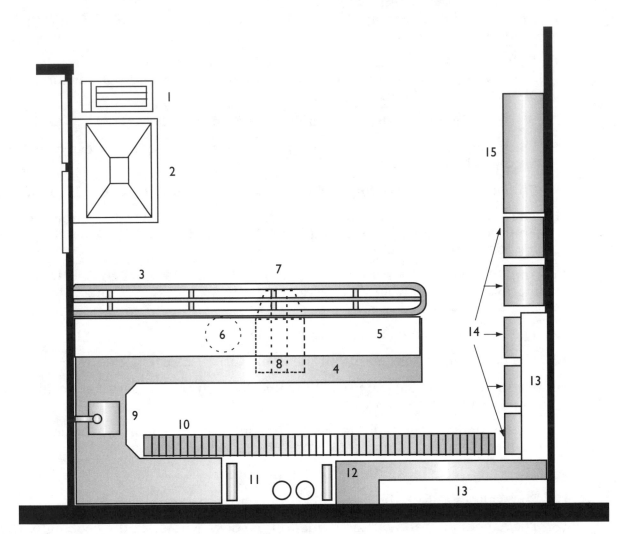

1. Silver burnisher	6. Disposal (3 h.p. hammermill type) and scrap chute	10. Dish-rack conveyor
2. Linen hamper	7. Silverware chute	11. Dish machine
3. Tray rail	8. Silverware soak tank	12. Clean-dish table
4. Soiled-dish table	9. Prerinse sink with flexible spray arm	13. Overshelves (two)
5. Glass rack overshelf		14. Dish-rack dollies (five)
		15. Storage cabinet

THE RESTAURANT MANAGER'S HANDBOOK

DETAILED LAYOUT OF KITCHEN EQUIPMENT
IN A FAMILY RESTAURANT

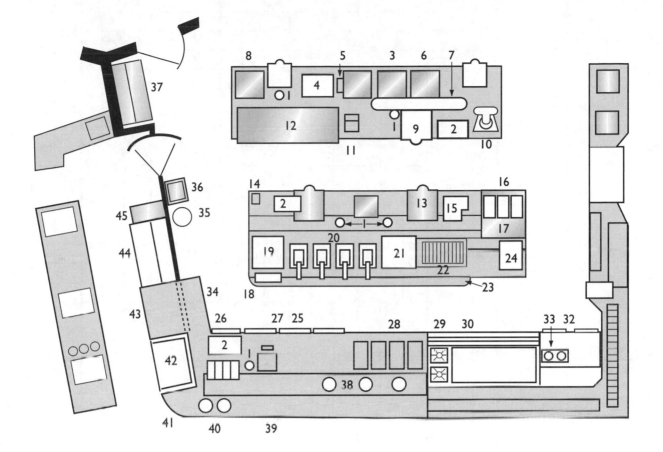

1. Knife wells (five)	14. Can opener	30. Wooden cutting board
2. Composition cutting boards (three)	15. Slicer	31. Griddle
3. Stainless-steel combination pot and pan washing table with three-compartment sink and meat and vegetable drawers (two)	16. Closed-top range	32. Base cabinet refrigerator
	17. Exhaust canopy	33. Waffle grill
	18. Wooden cutting board	34. Pass-through window
4. Disposal (3 h.p. hammermill type)	19. Microwave oven	35. Trash can
5. Recirculating centrifugal pump	20. Deep fat fryers (four)	36. Wash basin
6. Flexible spray rinse arm	21. Griddle	37. Ice machine
7. Overhead pot rack	22. Open-top broiler	38. Heat lamps (two)
8. Single-compartment sink	23. Base cabinet refrigerator with overshelf	39. Waitstaff pickup counter
9. Stainless-steel salad preparation work table with undershelf		40. Soup wells (two)
	24. Steamer	41. Soup bowl lowerators
10. 12-quart mixer on mobile stand	25. Base cabinet refrigerator	42. Reach-in refrigerator, sliding-door type
11. Portion scale	26. Cold food wells (eight)	
12. Reach-in refrigerator	27. Sandwich grill	43. Customer takeout back counter
13. Stainless-steel meat and vegetable preparation worktable with angle-compartment sink, drawers (two), overshelf and undershelf.	28. Hot food wells (four) and undercounter dish storage.	44. Fountain
		45. Milkshake machine
	29. Open-top burners (two)	

PERPETUAL INVENTORY FORM

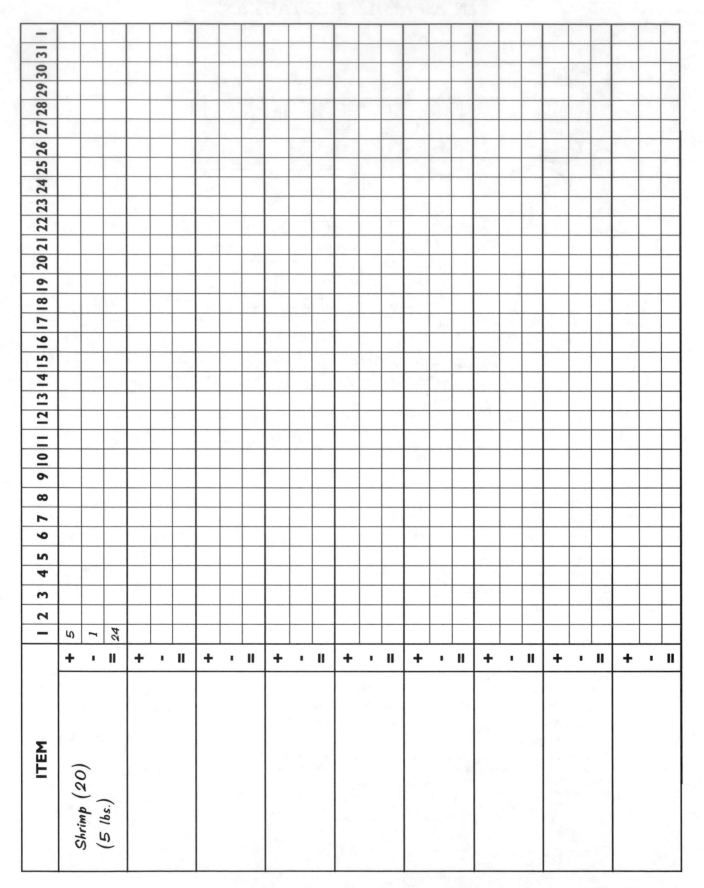

THE RESTAURANT MANAGER'S HANDBOOK

SIGN-OUT SHEET

ITEM	DATE	AMOUNT/WT.	EMPLOYEE
Shrimp-box	11-30	1-5 lb. box	Joe B.

PREPARATION FORM

ITEM	MINIMUM AMOUNT	AMOUNT DEF./ORD.	BEGINNING AMOUNT	AMOUNT PREPPED	STARTING TOTAL
Shrimp	33	5 lbs.	25	9	34

MINIMUM AMOUNT NEEDED FORM

ITEM	MON	TUE	WED	THU	FRI	SAT	SUN
Shrimp dinners						33	

YIELD SHEET

ITEM	STARTING WEIGHT (OZ.)	# OF PORTIONS	TOTAL PORTION WEIGHT (OZ.)	YIELD %	PREP. COOK
Shrimp dinner	80.0	9	9 x 8.0oz ≈ 72 oz.	90%	Bob S.

THE RESTAURANT MANAGER'S HANDBOOK

CASHIER'S REPORT FORM

Prepared By: _____

Date: _____ **Day:** _____ **Shift:** _____

		BAR REGISTER		SERVICE REGISTER		TOTAL
		Day	Night	Day	Night	All Shifts
1	**BANK DEPOSIT** Part I					
2	Currency					
3	Silver					
4	Checks					
5	**SUB TOTAL**					
6	**CREDIT CARDS:**					
7	MasterCard/Visa					
8	American Express					
9	Diners Club					
10	Other					
11	**OTHER RECEIPTS:**					
12	**TOTAL BANK DEPOSIT**					
13	**CASH SUMMARY** Part II					
14	Sales per Register					
15	Sales Tax per Register					
16	**ADJUSTMENTS:**					
17	Over/Under Rings					
18	Other: Complimentaries					
19	Other					
20	**TOTAL ADJUSTMENTS**					
21	Sales to Be Accounted For					
22	Sales Tax to Be Acctd. For					
23	Accounts Collected					
24	Other Receipts:					
25						
26						
27	**TIPS CHARGED:**					
28	MasterCard/Visa					
29	American Express					
30	Diners Club					
31	Other					
32	House Accounts-Tips					
33	**TOTAL RECEIPTS**					
34	**DEDUCT: PAID OUTS**					
35	Tips Paid Out					
36	House Charges					
37	Total Deductions					
38	**NET CASH RECEIPTS**					
39	**BANK DEPOSIT** (Line 12)					
40	**OVER or SHORT**					

TICKET ISSUANCE FORM

WAITPERSON	TOT #	#THRU	INITIALS	RETURN # VERIFIED
			TOTAL	

COOK'S FORM

ITEM	START	ADDITIONS	STARTING BALANCE	BALANCE ENDING	# SOLD
Shrimp dinners	25	9	34	21	13
				TOTAL	

TICKET ITEMIZATION FORM

ITEM	USE A ✔ MARK TO DESIGNATE ONE SOLD	TOTAL SOLD
Shrimp dinner	✓ ✓ ✓ ✓ ✓ ✓ ✓ ✓ ✓ ✓ ✓	*13*
	TOTAL	

WANT SHEET

ITEM	EMPLOYEE	APPROVED	ORDERED ON	RECEIVED

7

THE ESSENTIALS OF FOOD SAFETY, HACCP & SANITATION PRACTICES

INTRODUCTION

Every restaurant employee is responsible for preparing and serving quality and safe food products. Each employee must be thoroughly familiar with basic food safety and sanitation practices. This chapter will describe the fundamental methods and procedures that must be practiced in order to control food contamination, the spread of infectious diseases and personal safety practices.

Management must provide employees with the training, knowledge and tools that will enable them to establish and practice proper food handling and sanitation procedures. Through the use of this section, and under the guidance of your local Department of Health, you and your staff can obtain training and knowledge. First, however, the restaurant must be equipped with the proper tools and training and working conditions. Employees will never establish good sanitation procedures if they do not first have the proper environment in which to practice them.

Aside from what is required by law, the management should provide training materials, proper training sessions or clinics, hand sinks at every station, hand and nail brushes, labels for dating and rotation procedures, disposable towels, gloves, first-aid kits, germicidal hand soaps, employee bathrooms and lockers, scrub brushes, uniforms, hairnets, thermometers, test kits and quality, color-coded utensils.

Food-service establishments may harbor all types of bacteria, bugs and animal pests. Restaurants can attract these health hazards with the three basic ingredients necessary to sustain life: food, water and warmth. Any environment that provides these three elements for an extended period of time will become host to these intruders. In order to eliminate contamination, all that is necessary is to make the living conditions unfavorable for these unwanted intruders.

WHAT IS HACCP?

Hazard Analysis of Critical Control Points (HACCP) is a system for monitoring the food service process to reduce the risk of food-borne illness. HACCP focuses on how food flows through the process—from purchasing to serving. At each step in the food-preparation process there are a variety of potential hazards. HACCP provides managers with a framework for implementing control procedures for each hazard. It does this through identifying critical control points (or CCPs). These are points in the process where bacteria or other harmful organisms may grow or food may become contaminated.

WHY USE HACCP IN YOUR FACILITY

As a food service manager, you are responsible for protecting your customers by serving safe and wholesome food. To accomplish this, you have to educate your employees and motivate them to put into practice at every step what they've learned about food safety. To do this, you need a systematic process for identifying potential hazards; for putting safety procedures in place; and for monitoring the success of your safety system on an ongoing basis. HACCP helps you do all of these things.

Using HACCP, you can identify potentially hazardous foods and places in the food-preparation process where bacterial contamination, survival and growth can occur. Then you can take action to minimize the danger.

USING HACCP

HACCP is based on this principle: If the raw ingredients are safe, and the process is safe, then the finished product is safe.

Implementing HACCP involves seven key steps. As you proceed through these steps, you will:

1. Assess the hazards.

2. Identify "critical control points."

3. Establish "critical limits."

4. Monitor the "critical control points."

5. Take corrective action as needed.

6. Develop a record-keeping system.

7. Verify your system's effectiveness.

HACCP STEP 1: ASSESS THE HAZARDS

To assess the hazards present at each stage of the preparation process, track each HACCP food from purchasing and receiving through serving and reheating.

To begin, review your menus. Identify all potentially hazardous foods, as well as those foods that may become contaminated during the process.

At this point, you may even want to reduce risks by removing highly hazardous food items from your menu. For example, you may want to avoid egg salad sandwiches if sandwiches must be transported and held before being served.

Once you have surveyed the foods on your menu, evaluate general preparation and cooking procedures to isolate any points where contamination might occur. Next, rank these hazards in terms of severity (how serious are the consequences) and probability (how likely are they to occur).

HACCP STEP 2: IDENTIFY "CRITICAL CONTROL POINTS"

Identify the points in the process where hazards can be controlled or prevented. Develop a flowchart, or list the steps involved in preparing each potentially hazardous food. Then, identify procedures to prevent, reduce and eliminate recontamination hazards at each step you have listed.

In general, food-service workers can reduce the risk of food-borne illness by:

1. Practicing good personal hygiene.

2. Avoiding cross-contamination.

3. Using proper cooking and cooling procedures.

4. Reducing the number of steps involved in preparing and serving.

HACCP STEP 3: ESTABLISH "CRITICAL LIMITS"

In order to be sure a food passes safely through a critical control point, you need to establish critical limits that must be met. These critical limits should be standards that are observable and measurable. They should include precise time, temperature and sensory requirements.

Specify exactly what should be done to meet each particular standard. For example, instead of saying that a "food must be thoroughly cooked," the standard might say, "Heat rapidly to an internal temperature of 165° F within two hours." In addition, make sure employees have calibrated, metal-stemmed or digital thermometers and that they use them routinely.

Make sure recipes state: 1) end-cooking, reheating, and hot-holding temperatures and 2) specific times for thawing, cooking and cooling foods. Schedule sufficient staff in peak hours to prepare and serve foods safely.

HACCP STEP 4: MONITOR THE "CRITICAL CONTROL POINTS"

Using your flowcharts or lists, follow potentially hazardous foods through every step in the process. Compare your operation's performance with the requirements you have set. Identify any areas of deficiency.

HACCP STEP 5: TAKE CORRECTIVE ACTION

Take corrective action as needed. For example, if products' temperatures are unacceptable when received, reject the shipment. Similarly, if...

A. Food is contaminated by hands or equipment, rewash or discard it.

B. Food temperature is not high enough after cooking, continue cooking to the required temperature.

C. Food temperature exceeds 55° F during cold prep or serving, discard it.

HACCP STEP 6: DEVELOP A RECORD-KEEPING SYSTEM

Develop a record-keeping system to document the HACCP process and monitor your results. This may be any simple, quick system, such as a log, in which employees can record their compliance with standards at critical control points. These records are crucial and may provide proof that a food-borne illness did not originate at your establishment.

HACCP STEP 7: VERIFY YOUR SYSTEM'S EFFECTIVENESS

Verify that the HACCP process in your facility works. You can do this in a number of ways.

For starters, be alert to how often you need to take corrective actions. If you need to take corrective actions frequently, this may indicate a need to change, or at least fine-tune, your system. In addition, think of tests you can do, like measuring the strength of your sanitizing solution. Also, examine your records and make sure employees are entering actual, valid data. An inspection by the Board of Health can provide a good assessment of whether or not your process is working.

On the following pages, you'll find a sample HACCP checklist. Use this checklist to determine areas in your operation that require action. Once a month, make observations during production and take corrective action if needed.

HACCP'S 8 KEY STEPS OF THE FOOD-SERVICE PROCESS

In order, we'll look at:

1. Purchasing

2. Receiving

3. Storing

4. Preparing

5. Cooking

5. Serving and holding

6. Cooling

7. Reheating

There are multiple hazards at, and specific preventative measures for, each step.

STEP 1: PURCHASING

The goal of purchasing is to obtain wholesome, safe foods to meet your menu requirements. Safety at this step is primarily the responsibility of your vendors. It's your job to choose your vendors wisely. Suppliers must meet federal and state health standards. They should use the HACCP system in their operations and train their employees in sanitation. Delivery trucks should have adequate refrigeration and freezer units, and foods should be packaged in protective, leakproof, durable packaging. Let vendors know up front what you expect from them. Put food safety standards in your purchase specification agreements. Ask to see their most recent Board of Health Sanitation Reports, and tell them you will be inspecting trucks on a quarterly basis.

Good vendors will cooperate with your inspections and should adjust their delivery schedules to avoid your busy periods so that incoming foods can be received and inspected properly.

STEP 2: RECEIVING

The goals of receiving are: 1) to make sure foods are fresh and safe when they enter your facility and 2) to transfer them to proper storage as quickly as possible.

Let's look more closely at two important parts of receiving:

1. Getting ready to receive food, and

2. Inspecting the food when the delivery truck arrives.

There are several important guidelines to keep in mind and tasks to complete as you get ready to receive food:

- Make sure your receiving area is equipped with sanitary carts for transporting goods.

- Plan ahead for deliveries to ensure sufficient refrigerator and freezer space.

- Mark all items for storage with the date of arrival or the "use by" date.

- Keep the receiving area well lit and clean to discourage pests.

- Remove empty containers and packing materials immediately to a separate trash area.

- Keep all flooring clean of food particles and debris.

When the delivery truck arrives, make sure it looks and smells clean and is equipped with the proper food storage equipment. Then inspect foods immediately:

- Check expiration dates of milk, eggs and other perishable goods.

- Make sure shelf-life dates have not expired.

- Make sure frozen foods are in airtight, moisture-proof wrappings.

- Reject foods that have been thawed and refrozen. Look for signs of thawing and refreezing such as large crystals, solid areas of ice or excessive ice in containers.

- Reject cans that have any of the following: swollen sides or ends; flawed seals or seams; dents or rust. Also reject any cans with foamy or bad smelling contents.

- Check temperature of refrigerated and frozen foods, especially eggs and dairy products, fresh meat, and fish and poultry products.

- Look for content damage and insect infestations.

- Reject dairy, bakery and other foods delivered in flats or crates that are dirty.

STEP 3: STORING

In general, there are four possible ways to store food:

1. In dry storage, for longer holding of less perishable items.

2. In refrigeration, for short-term storage of perishable items.

3. In specially designed deep-chilling units for short periods.

4. In a freezer, for longer-term storage of perishable foods.

Each type of storage has its own sanitation and safety requirements.

DRY STORAGE

There are many items that can be safely held in a sanitary storeroom. These include, for example, canned goods, baking supplies (such as salt and sugar), grain products (such as rice and cereals) and other dry items. In addition, some fruits (such as bananas, avocados, and pears) ripen best at room temperature. Some vegetables, such as onions, potatoes and tomatoes, also store best in dry storage. A dry-storage room should be clean and orderly, with good ventilation to control temperature and humidity and retard the growth of bacteria and mold. Keep in mind the following:

- For maximum shelf life, dry foods should be held at 50° F, but 60–70 °F is adequate for most products.

- Use a wall thermometer to check the temperature of your dry-storage facility regularly.

- To ensure freshness, store opened items in tightly covered containers. Use the "first in, first out" (FIFO) rotation method, dating packages and placing incoming supplies in the back so that older supplies will be used first.

- To avoid pest infestation and cross-contamination, clean up all spills immediately and do not store trash or garbage cans in food storage areas.

- Do not place any items—including paper products—on the floor. Make sure the bottom shelf of the dry-storage room is at least 6 inches above the ground.

To avoid chemical contamination: Never use or store cleaning materials or other chemicals where they might contaminate foods! Store them, labeled, in their own section in the storeroom away from all food supplies.

REFRIGERATED STORAGE

Keep fresh meat, poultry, seafood, dairy products, most fresh fruit and vegetables and hot leftovers in the refrigerator at internal temperatures of below 40° F. Although no food can last forever, refrigeration increases the shelf life of most products. Most importantly, because refrigeration slows bacterial growth, the colder a food is, the safer it is.

Your refrigeration unit should contain open, slotted shelving to allow cold air to circulate around food. Do not line shelves with foil or paper. Also do not overload the refrigerator, and be sure to leave space between items to further improve air circulation.

- All refrigerated foods should be dated and properly sealed. In addition:

- Use clean, nonabsorbent, covered containers that are approved for food storage.

- Store dairy products separately from foods with strong odors like onions, cabbage and seafood.

- To avoid cross-contamination, store raw or uncooked food away from and below prepared or ready-to-eat food.

- Never allow fluids from raw poultry, fish or meat to come into contact with other foods.

- Keeping perishable items at the proper temperature is a key factor in preventing food-borne illness. Check the temperature of your refrigeration unit regularly to make sure it stays below 40° F. Keep in mind that opening and closing the refrigerator door too often can affect temperature.

Many commercial refrigerators are equipped with externally mounted or built-in thermometers. These are convenient when they work, but it is important to have a backup. It's a good idea to have several thermometers in different parts of the refrigerator to ensure consistent temperature and accuracy of instruments. Record the temperature of each refrigerator on a chart preferably once a day.

DEEP CHILLING

Deep or super chilling—that is, storing foods at temperatures between 26° F and 32° F—has been found to decrease bacterial growth. This method can be used to increase the shelf life of fresh foods, such as poultry, meat, seafood, and other protein items, without compromising their quality by freezing. You can deep-chill foods in specially designed units or in a refrigerator set to deep-chilling temperature.

FROZEN STORAGE

Frozen meats, poultry, seafood, fruits and vegetables and some dairy products, such as ice cream, should be stored in a freezer at 0° F to keep them fresh and safe for an extended period of time.

As a rule, you should use your freezer primarily to store foods that are frozen when you receive them. Freezing refrigerated foods can damage the quality of perishable items. It's important to store frozen foods immediately. It's also important to remember that storing foods in the freezer for too long increases the likelihood of contamination and spoilage. Like your refrigeration unit, the freezer should allow cold air to circulate around foods easily. Be sure to:

- Store frozen foods in moisture proof material or containers to minimize loss of flavor, as well as discoloration, dehydration and odor absorption.

- Monitor temperature regularly, using several thermometers to ensure accuracy and consistent temperatures. Record the temperature of each freezer on a chart.

Remember that frequently opening and closing the freezer's door can raise the temperature, as can placing warm foods in the freezer. To minimize heat gain, open freezer doors only when necessary and remove as many items at one time as possible. You can also use a freezer "cold curtain" to help guard against heat gain.

STEP 4: PREPARING

THAWING AND MARINATING

Freezing food keeps most bacteria from multiplying, but it does not kill them. Bacteria that are present when food is removed from the freezer may multiply rapidly if thawed at room temperature. Thus, it is critical to thaw foods out of the "temperature danger zone." NEVER thaw foods on a counter or in any other nonrefrigerated area!

Some foods, such as frozen vegetables and pre-formed hamburger patties and chicken nuggets, can be cooked from the frozen state. It is important to note, however, that this method depends on the size of the item. For example, cooking from frozen is not recommended for large foods like a 20-pound turkey.

The two best methods for thawing foods are:

1. In refrigeration at a temperature below 40° F, placed in a pan on the lowest shelf so juices cannot drip on other foods.

2. Under clean, drinkable running water at a temperature of 70° F or less for no more than two hours, or just until the product is thawed.

Always marinate meat, fish and poultry in the refrigerator—Never at room temperature. Never save and reuse marinade. With all methods, be careful not to cross-contaminate!

CAUTIONS FOR COLD FOODS

When you are preparing cold foods, you are at one of the most hazardous points in the food-preparation process. There are two key reasons for this: First, cold food preparation usually takes place at room temperature. Second, cold food is one of the most common points of contamination and cross-contamination.

Chicken salad, tuna salad, potato salad with eggs and other protein-rich salads are common sources of food-borne illness. Sandwiches prepared in advance and held unrefrigerated are also dangerous.

Because cold foods such as these receive no further cooking, it is essential that all ingredients used in them are properly cleaned, prepared and, where applicable, cooked. It is a good idea to chill meats and other ingredients and combine them while chilled.

Here are several other important precautions to keep in mind:

*   Prepare foods no further in advance than necessary.

*   Prepare foods in small batches and place in cold storage immediately. This will

prevent holding food too long in the "temperature danger zone."

- Always hold prepared cold foods below 40° F.

- Wash fresh fruits and vegetables with plain water to remove surface pesticide residues and other impurities, such as soil particles.

- Use a brush to scrub thick-skinned produce, if desired.

- Beware of CROSS-CONTAMINATION! It's crucial to:
  - Keep raw products separate from ready-to-serve foods.
  - Sanitize cutting boards, knives and other food contact surfaces after each contact with a potentially hazardous food.
  - Discard any leftover batter, breading or marinade after it has been used with potentially hazardous foods.

STEP 5: COOKING

Even when potentially hazardous foods are properly thawed, bacteria and other contaminants may still be present. Cooking foods to the proper internal temperature will kill any existing bacteria and make food safe.

It's important to remember, however, that conventional cooking procedures cannot destroy bacterial spores nor deactivate their toxins.

Keep in mind the following "safe cooking" tips:

- Stir foods cooked in deep pots frequently to ensure thorough cooking.

- When deep-frying potentially hazardous foods, make sure fryers are not overloaded, and make sure the oil temperature returns to the required level before adding the next batch. Use a hot-oil thermometer designed for this special application.

- Regulate size and thickness of each portion to make cooking time predictable and uniform.

- Allow cooking equipment to heat up between batches.

- Never interrupt the cooking process. Partially cooking poultry or meat, for example, may produce conditions that encourage bacterial growth.

Monitor the accuracy of heating equipment with each use by using thermometers. In addition, always use a thermometer to ensure food reaches the proper temperature during cooking. Use a sanitized metal-stemmed, numerically scaled thermometer (accurate to plus or minus 2° F) or a digital thermometer. Check food temperature in several places, especially in the thickest parts, to make sure the food is thoroughly cooked. To avoid getting a false reading, be careful not to touch the pan or bone with the thermometer. Always cook food to an internal temperature of 165°F.

STEP 6: SERVING AND HOLDING

Food that has been cooked isn't necessarily safe. In fact, many outbreaks occur because improper procedures were used following cooking. Although it may be tempting to hold food at temperatures just hot enough to serve, it is essential to keep prepared foods out of the "temperature danger zone." This means, specifically:

- Always keep HOT foods in hot-holding equipment above 140° F.

- Always keep COLD foods in a refrigeration unit or surrounded by ice below 40° F.

For safer serving and holding:

- Use hot-holding equipment, such as steam tables and hot-food carts, during service but never for reheating.

- Stir foods at reasonable intervals to ensure even heating.

- Check temperatures with a food thermometer every 30 minutes.

- Sanitize the thermometer before each use, or use a digital infrared thermometer that never touches the food.

- Cover hot-holding equipment to retain heat and to guard against contamination.

- Monitor the temperature of hot-holding equipment with each use.

- DISCARD any food held in the "temperature danger zone" for more than four hours!

To avoid contamination: Never add fresh food to a serving pan containing foods that have already been out for serving!

SOME KEY POINTS

1. Always wash hands with soap and warm water for at least 20 seconds before serving food.

2. Use cleaned and sanitized long-handled ladles and spoons so bare hands do not touch food.

3. Never touch the parts of glasses, cups, plates or tableware that will come into contact with food.

4. Never touch the parts of dishes that will come into contact with the customer's mouth.

5. Wear gloves if serving food by hand.

6. Cover cuts or infections with bandages, and if on hands, wear gloves.

7. Discard gloves whenever they touch an unsanitary surface.

8. Use tongs or wear gloves to dispense rolls and bread.

9. Clean and sanitize equipment and utensils thoroughly after each use.

10. Use lids and sneeze guards to protect prepared food from contamination.

To avoid contamination: Always wash hands, utensils and other food-contact surfaces after contact with raw meat or poultry and before contact with cooked meat or poultry. For example, do not reuse a serving pan used to hold raw chicken to serve the same chicken after it's cooked, unless the pan has been thoroughly cleaned and sanitized.

SANITARY SELF-SERVICE

Like workers, customers can also act as a source of contamination. Unlike workers, customers—especially children—are, generally, not educated about food sanitation and may do the following unsanitary things:

1. Use the same plate twice.

2. Touch food with their hands.

3. Touch the edges of serving dishes.

4. Sneeze or cough into food.

5. Pick up foods, such as rolls or carrot sticks, with their fingers.

6. Eat in the food line.

7. Dip their fingers into foods to taste them.

8. Return food items to avoid waste.

9. Put their heads under sneeze guards to reach items in the back.

Be sure to: Observe customer behavior and remove any foods that may have been contaminated. Also, as a precautionary measure, serve sealed packages of crackers, breadsticks and condiments, and prewrap, date and label sandwiches if possible.

STEP 7: COOLING

Here, as at other critical points, every move you make can mean the difference between the safe and the unsafe.

It is often necessary to prepare foods in advance or use leftover foods. Unfortunately, this can easily lead to problems, unless proper precautions are taken. In fact, problems at this stage are the number-one cause of food-borne illness. The two key precautions for preventing food-borne illness at this point in the process are rapid cooling and protection from contamination.

CHILLING IT QUICKLY

All potentially hazardous, cooked leftovers should be chilled to an internal temperature of below 40° F. Quick-chill any leftovers larger than half a gallon or 2 pounds.

Quick-chilling involves five simple steps:

1. **Reduce food mass**. Smaller amounts of food will chill more quickly than larger amounts, so cut large items into pieces or divide food among several containers or shallow pans. Use shallow, prechilled pans (no more than 4 inches deep). Use stainless-steel containers when possible; stainless steel transfers heat better and cools faster than plastic.

2. **Chill.** Ideally, place food in an ice-water bath or quick-chill unit (26–32° F) rather than a refrigerator. These options are best for two reasons:

   • First, water is a much better heat conductor than air. As a result, foods can cool much more quickly in an ice bath than they can in a refrigerator.

   • Second, refrigeration units are designed to keep cold foods cold rather than to chill hot foods. They can take too long to cool foods to safe temperatures.

   • Another option is to prechill foods in a freezer for about 30 minutes before refrigerating.

   • Separate food items so air can flow freely around them. Do not stack shallow pans. NEVER cool at room temperature.

3. **Stir frequently.** Stirring accelerates cooling and helps to ensure that cold air reaches all parts of the food.

4. **Measure temperature periodically**. Food should reach a temperature of 70° F within two hours and 40° F within four hours. It's important to note that this time must be reduced if food has already spent time in the "temperature danger zone" at any other point in the preparation and serving process.

5. **Tightly cover and label cooled foods**. On labels, include preparation dates and times.

To avoid contamination: Be aware that although uncovered foods cool faster, they are at increased risk for cross-contamination. Be sure to store uncovered cooked and cooled foods on the upper shelves of the cooler, and cover them when they reach 45° F. Never store them beneath raw foods.

STEP 8: REHEATING

While assuming leftovers are safe might seem reasonable, it's not. In reheating and serving leftovers—just as in all phases of the food-preparation process—you must be careful to avoid contamination.

To safely reheat and serve leftovers, be sure to:

- Boil sauces, soups and gravies, and heat other foods to a minimum of 165° F within two hours of taking the food out of the refrigerator.

- Never reheat food in hot-holding equipment.

- Never mix a leftover batch of food with a fresh batch of food.

- Never reheat food more than once.

THE DIFFERENCE BETWEEN CLEAN & SANITARY

Heat or chemicals can be used to reduce the number of bacteria to acceptable levels. They can also be used for certain other harmful microorganisms.

Heat sanitizing involves exposing equipment to high heat for an adequate length of time. This may be done manually by immersing equipment in water maintained at a temperature of 170–195° F for at least 30 seconds, or in a dishwashing machine that washes at 150° F and rinses at 180° F.

For any method, it is important to check water temperature frequently. Thermometers and heat-sensitive tapes and labels are available for determining whether adequate sanitation temperatures have been achieved.

Chemical sanitizing can be accomplished by immersing an object in, or wiping it down with, bleach or sanitizing solution. For bleaching, use 1/2 ounce or 1 tablespoon of 5-percent bleach per gallon of water. For using commercial products, follow the manufacturers' instructions.

Chemical sanitizers are regulated by the EPA, and manufacturers must follow strict labeling requirements regarding what concentrations to use, data on minimum effectiveness and warnings of possible health hazards. Chemical test strips are available for testing the strength of the sanitizing solution. Because sanitizing agents become less effective as they kill bacteria and are exposed to air, it is important to test the sanitizing solution frequently.

SANITIZING PORTABLE EQUIPMENT

To properly clean and sanitize portable equipment you must have a sink with three separate compartments: for cleaning, rinsing and sanitizing. There should be a separate area for scraping and rinsing food and debris into a garbage container or disposer before washing, and separate drain boards for clean and soiled items.

To sanitize a piece of equipment, use the following procedure:

1. Clean and sanitize sinks and work surfaces.

2. Scrape and rinse food into garbage or disposal. Presoak items, such as silverware, as necessary.

3. In the first sink, immerse the equipment in a clean detergent solution at about 120° F. Use a brush or a cloth to loosen and remove any remaining visible soil.

4. Rinse in the second sink using clear, clean water between 120° F and 140° F to remove all traces of food, debris and detergent.

5. Sanitize in the third sink by immersing items in hot water at 170° F for 30 seconds or in a chemical sanitizing solution for one minute. Be sure to cover all surfaces of the equipment with hot water or the sanitizing solution and keep them in contact with it for the appropriate amount of time.

6. If soapsuds disappear in the first compartment or remain in the second, if the water temperature cools, or if water in any compartment becomes dirty and cloudy, empty the compartment and refill it.

7. Air dry. Wiping can recontaminate equipment and can remove the sanitizing solution from the surfaces before it has finished working.

8. Make certain all equipment is dry before putting it into storage; moisture can foster bacterial growth.

SANITIZING IN-PLACE EQUIPMENT

Larger and immobile equipment should also be washed, rinsed and sanitized. Use the following procedure:

1. Unplug electrically powered equipment, such as meat slicers.

2. Remove fallen food particles and scraps.

3. Wash, rinse and sanitize any removable parts using the manual immersion method described in steps 3 through 5 above.

4. Wash the remaining food-contact surfaces and rinse with clean water. Wipe down with a chemical sanitizing solution mixed according to the manufacturer's directions.

5. Wipe down all non-food contact surfaces with a sanitized cloth, and allow all parts to air dry before reassembling. Sanitize cloth before and during sanitizing by rinsing it in sanitizing solution.

6. Resanitize the external food-contact surfaces of the parts that were handled during reassembling.

7. Scrub wooden surfaces, such as cutting boards, with a detergent solution and a stiff-bristled nylon brush; then rinse in clear, clean water; and wipe down with a sanitizing solution after every use.

A FIRST-RATE FACILITY

Safe and sanitary food service begins with a facility that is clean and in good repair. The entire facility—work areas as well as equipment—should be designed for easy cleaning and maintenance.

It's important to eliminate hard-to-clean work areas, as well as faulty or overloaded refrigerators or other equipment. Also get rid of dirty surroundings and any conditions that will attract pests. Remember, the easier the workplace is to clean, the more likely it will stay clean.

FLOORS, WALLS AND CEILINGS

Floors, walls and ceilings should be free of dirt, litter and moisture. Clean walls regularly by swabbing with a cleaning solution or by spraying with a pressure nozzle. Sweep floors, then clean them using a spray method or by mopping. Swab ceilings, instead of spraying them, to avoid soaking lights and ceiling fans. And don't forget corners and hard-to-reach places!

VENTILATION

Good ventilation is a critical factor in maintaining a clean food-service environment. Ventilation removes steam, smoke, grease and heat from food-preparation areas and equipment. This helps maintain indoor air quality and reduces the possibility of fires from accumulated grease. In addition, good ventilation eliminates condensation and other airborne contaminants. It also:

- Reduces the accumulation of dirt in the food-preparation area.

- Reduces odors, gases and fumes.

- Reduces mold growth by reducing humidity.

To ensure good ventilation, be sure to:

- Use exhaust fans to remove odors and smoke.

- Use hoods over cooking areas and dishwashing equipment.

- Check exhaust fans and hoods regularly to make sure they are clean and operating properly.

- Clean hood filters routinely according to the instructions provided by the hood manufacturer.

STOREROOMS

Like all areas of the facility, storerooms must be kept clean and litter-free. To accomplish this, be sure to sweep and scrub walls, ceilings, floors, shelves, light fixtures and racks on a routine basis. Check all storage areas frequently—this includes your refrigerator and freezer as well as your dry-storage room. In checking storage areas:

1. Look for damaged or spoiled foods, broken or torn packages and bulging or leaking cans.

2. Remove any potentially spoiled foods immediately, and clean the area thoroughly.

3. Make sure foods and other supplies are stored at least 6 inches from the walls and above the floor.

To avoid chemical contamination: Store cleaning supplies and chemicals in a separate area away from food supply areas and other chemicals so they do not pose a hazard to food or people.

RESTROOMS

Restrooms should be convenient, sanitary and adequately stocked with the following:

- Toilet paper

- Liquid soap

- Disposable paper towels and/or air blowers

- Covered trash receptacles (The trash receptacle lid should open with a foot pedal.)

Scrub restrooms daily and keep the doors closed. You may also want to provide brushes to wash fingernails and sanitizing solution for soaking the brushes.

BACTERIA

Bacteria are everywhere: in the air, in all areas of the restaurant and all over one's body. Most bacteria are microscopic and of no harm to people. Many forms of bacteria are actually beneficial, aiding in the production of such things as cheese, bread, butter, alcoholic beverages, etc. Only a small percentage of bacteria will cause food to spoil and can generate a form of food poisoning when consumed.

Bacteria need food, water and warmth in order to survive. Their growth rate depends upon how favorable these conditions are. Bacteria prefer to ingest moisture-saturated foods, such as meats, dairy products and produce. They will not grow as readily on dry foods such as cereals, sugar or flour.

Bacteria will grow most rapidly when the temperature is between 85° F and 100° F. In most cases, the growth rate will slow down drastically if the temperature is hotter or colder than this. Thus, it is vitally important that perishable food items are refrigerated before bacteria have a chance to establish themselves and multiply. Certain bacteria can survive in extreme hot- and cold-temperature ranges. By placing these bacteria in severe temperatures you will be slowing down their growth rate, but not necessarily killing them.

The greatest problem in controlling bacteria is their rapid reproduction cycle. Approximately every 15 minutes the bacteria count will double under optimal conditions. The more bacteria present, the greater the chance of bacterial infection. This is why food products that must be subjected to conditions favorable to bacteria are done so for the shortest period possible.

An important consideration when handling food products is that bacteria need several hours to adjust to a new environment before they are able to begin rapidly multiplying. Thus, if you had removed a food product from the walk-in refrigerator and had inadvertently introduced bacteria to it, advanced growth would not begin for several hours. If you had immediately placed the item back into the walk-in, the temperature would have killed the bacteria before it became established.

Bacterial forms do not have a means of transportation; they must be introduced to an area by some other vehicle. People are primarily responsible for transporting bacteria to new areas. The body temperature of 98.6° F is perfect for bacterial existence and proliferation. A person coughing, sneezing or wiping their hands on a counter can introduce bacteria to an area. Bacteria may be transmitted also by insects, air, water and articles onto which they have attached themselves, such as boxes, blades, knives and cutting boards.

DANGEROUS FORMS OF BACTERIA

The following section describes a number of harmful bacteria that may be found in a restaurant. The technical names and jargon are given for your own information. The important points to retain are the causes and preventive actions for each.

CLOSTRIDIUM PERFRINGENS

Clostridium perfringens is one of a group of bacterial infectious diseases that will cause a poisoning effect. These bacteria are extremely dangerous because they are tasteless, odorless and colorless, and therefore nearly impossible to detect.

Clostridium perfringens bacteria are usually found in meat or seafood that was previously cooked and then held at room temperature for a period of time. These perfringens are anaerobic. They do not need air in order to survive. They can thrive in masses of food or in canned foods in the form of botulism. In order to survive, the bacterium will form a spore and surround itself. The spore will protect the bacterium from exposure to the air and give it a much wider temperature range for survival than normal bacteria: 65–120° F. These bacterial forms may survive through long periods of extreme temperature and then multiply when the conditions are more favorable.

Keeping cooked food consistently above 148° F or below 40° F eliminates clostridium perfringens bacteria.

CLOSTRIDIUM BOTULISM

This is another of the poisoning forms of bacteria. Botulism is a rare infectious disease but it is far more lethal than the other types. *Botulism bacteria* exist only in an airfree environment like that of canned goods. These bacteria are most often found in home-canned goods; however, several national food packers have reported outbreaks in their operations.

Symptoms such as vomiting, double vision, abdominal pain and shock may occur anytime from three to four hours after ingestion to eight days later. Examine all canned goods closely before using. Look for dented, leaking cans and swollen cans or jar tops.

STAPHYLOCOCCI POISONING

Staphylococci bacteria (Staph) are perhaps the most common cause of food poisoning. Staph bacteria can be found everywhere, particularly in the human nose. The bacteria by themselves are harmless. The problem arises when they are left uncontrolled to grow in food items. Food that has been left out, unrefrigerated, for just a few hours can produce the poisonous toxins of Staph bacteria.

Symptoms will appear two to six hours after consumption. Common symptoms are vomiting, muscle weakness, cramps and diarrhea. The sickness ranges from very severe cases—sometimes lethal—to a relatively mild illness. To prevent Staph poisoning follow refrigeration procedures precisely. Only remove the refrigerated food items that you will be using right away.

SALMONELLA INFECTION

Salmonella infection is caused directly by the bacteria themselves, after consumption by a human. In certain cases, death has resulted; however, usually *Salmonella* cause severe—but temporary—illness. Symptoms are vomiting, fever, abdominal pain and cramps. Symptoms usually show up 12 to 24 hours after consumption and may last for several days.

Salmonella are found in the intestinal tract of some animals. They have been discovered in some packaged foods, eggs, poultry, seafood and meat. Thorough cooking and following refrigeration procedures can keep *Salmonella* growth to a minimal amount.

Hepatitis, dysentery and diphtheria are some of the other infectious diseases that are bacterially derived.

CONTROLLING BACTERIA

The first step in controlling bacteria is to limit their access to the restaurant. Make certain that all products entering the restaurant are clean. Follow the prescribed bug-exterminating procedures to stop bacteria from being transported into the restaurant. Keep all food products stored and refrigerated as prescribed. Clean up any spills as you go along, making the environment unsuitable for bacteria to live. Keep all food refrigerated until needed, and cook it as soon as possible.

The quality known as "pH" indicates how acidic or alkaline ("basic") a food or other substance is. The pH scale ranges from 0.0 to 14.0—7.0 being exactly neutral. Distilled water, for example, has a neutral pH of 7.0. Bacteria grow best in foods that are neutral or slightly acidic, in the pH range of 4.6 to 7.0. Highly acidic foods, such as vinegar and most fresh fruits, inhibit bacterial growth. Meats and many other foods have an optimal pH for bacterial growth. On the other hand, some foods normally considered hazardous, such as mayonnaise and custard filling, can be safely stored at room temperature if their pH is below 4.6.

Lowering the pH of foods by adding acidic ingredients, such as making sauerkraut from cabbage or pickles from cucumbers, may render them non–potentially hazardous. This is not a foolproof prevention method, however. For example, although commercially prepared mayonnaise has a pH below 4.6, adding mayonnaise to a meat salad will not inhibit bacteria. The moisture in the meat and the meat's pH are likely to raise the pH of the salad to a point where bacteria can multiply.

ACIDITY VS. ALKALINITY — pH Levels of Some Common Foods			
Vinegar	2.2	Carrots	5.0
Lemons	2.2	White bread	5.1
Cola drinks	2.3	Tuna	6.0
Commercial Mayonnaise	3.0	Green peas	6.0
Grapefruit	3.1	Potatoes	6.1
Dill pickles	3.2	Chicken	6.2
Orange juice	3.7	Corn	6.3
Pears	3.9	Steamed rice	6.4
Tomatoes	4.2	Fresh meat	6.4
Buttermilk	4.5	Milk	6.6

AVOID BACTERIAL CROSS-CONTAMINATION

One of the most common causes of food-borne illness is cross-contamination: the transfer of bacteria from food to food, hand to food or equipment to food.

Food to food. Raw, contaminated ingredients may be added to foods, or fluids from raw foods may drip into foods that receive no further cooking. A common mistake is to leave thawing meat on a top shelf in the refrigerator where it can drip down onto prepared foods stored below.

Hand to food. Bacteria are found throughout the body: in the hair, on the skin, in clothing, in the mouth, nose and throat, in the intestinal tract and on scabs or scars from skin wounds. These bacteria often end up on the hands where they can easily spread to food. People can also pick up bacteria by touching raw food, then transfer it to cooked or ready-to-eat food.

Equipment to food. Bacteria may pass from equipment to food when equipment that has touched contaminated food is then used to prepare other food without proper cleaning and sanitizing. For example, cross-contamination can occur when surfaces used for cutting raw poultry are then used to cut foods that will be eaten raw, such as fresh vegetables.

Coverings, such as plastic wrap and holding and serving containers, can also harbor bacteria that can spread to food. A can opener, a plastic-wrap box or a food slicer can also become a source of cross-contamination if not properly sanitized between uses.

Personal hygiene is the best way to stop bacteria from contaminating and spreading into new areas. Hands are the greatest source of contamination. Hands must be washed constantly throughout the day. Every time an individual scratches her head or sneezes, she is exposing her hands to bacteria and will spread it to anything she touches, such as food, equipment and clothes. Hand and nail brushes, antibacterial soaps and disposable gloves should be a part of every restaurant, even if not required by law. Proper training and management follow-up is also critical.

Every employee must practice good basic hygiene:

    A.   Short hair, and/or hair contained in a net.

    B.   Facial hair contained in a net or clean shaven.

    C.   Clean clothes/uniforms.

    D.   Clean hands and short nails.

    E.   No unnecessary jewelry.

    F.   A daily shower or bath.

    G.   No smoking in or near the kitchen.

    H.   Hand washing prior to starting work, periodically, and after handling any foreign object: head, face, ears, money, food, boxes or trash.

An employee who has the symptoms of the common cold or any open cuts or infections should not go to work. By simply breathing, he or she may be inadvertently exposing the environment to bacteria. Although it is rarely practiced in the food industry, all employees should be required to have a complete medical examination as a condition of employment. This should include blood and urine tests. A seemingly healthy individual may unknowingly be the carrier of a latent communicable disease.

"ARE YOUR HANDS REALLY CLEAN?"

Hand washing is perhaps the most critical aspect of good personal hygiene in food serv-ice. Workers should wash their hands with soap and warm water for 20 seconds. When working with food, they should wash gloved hands as often as bare hands. Hand wash-ing is such a simple—yet very effective—method for eliminating cross-contamination. I recommend the following exercise:

You'll need a fluorescent substance and a black light. (One possible source for these is Atlantic Publishing's Glo Germ Training Kit. See *http://www.atlantic-pub.com* or call 800-541-1336.) Using these materials you can show trainees the "invisible dirt" that may be hiding on their hands:

1. Have employees dip their hands in the fluorescent substance.

2. Tell employees to wash their hands.

3. Have employees hold their hands under the black light to see how much "dirt" is still there.

4. Explain proper hand-washing technique.

5. Have employees wash their hands again, this time using the proper hand-wash-ing technique.

6. Have employees once again hold their hands under the black light.

AIDS

AIDS is not an airborne, waterborne or food-borne disease. It cannot be transmitted through air, water or food. The only medically documented manner in which HIV, the virus which is believed to cause AIDS, can be contracted is by sexual contact, by shared needles (usually associated with drug addiction), by infusion of contaminated blood or through the placenta from mother to fetus.

*   You cannot contract AIDS through casual, social contact.

*   You cannot catch AIDS by touching people.

*   You cannot catch AIDS through shared bathroom facilities.

*   You cannot catch AIDS by breathing air in which people have sneezed or coughed.

*   You cannot catch AIDS by sharing food, beverages or eating utensils.

*   This means that, with regard to AIDS, food-service operations are safe places to work and dine.

BUGS, INSECTS AND ANIMAL PESTS

Bug and insect infestation in a restaurant is the result of poor sanitation practices. Aside from being a nuisance, they are a threat to food safety. Flies, cockroaches and other insects all carry bacteria, and many, because of where they get their food, carry disease. Bugs, insects and animals require the same three basic necessities of life as bacteria do: food, water and warmth. When healthful, thriving bugs and insects are visible, this is an indicator that proper sanitation procedures have not been carried out. Eliminate the environment that these pests need to live, and you will be eliminating their existence. Combining proper sanitation practices with periodic extermination spraying will stop any problems before they start.

To prevent the spread of flies in your establishment, keep all doors, windows and screens closed at all times. Ensure that garbage is sealed in airtight containers and is picked up regularly. All trash must be cleaned off the ground: flies can deposit their eggs on the thinnest scrap of food. Dumpsters must be periodically steam cleaned and deodorized. They should never contain any decaying food scraps.

All doorjambs and building cracks, even the thinnest ones, must be sealed. Be cautious when receiving deliveries. Bugs may be in the boxes or crates. The greatest protection against cockroaches is your exterminator (Review Chapter 1). Of course, the exterminator will be of little value if you do not already have good sanitary practices in place. Select an exterminator who is currently servicing other restaurants. Chemicals sprayed in a restaurant must be of the nonresidual type. These are safe and approved for use in food-service establishments. Rodents are prolific breeders, producing as many as 50 offspring in a life span of one year. They tend to hide during the day, but they can be discovered by their telltale signs. These signs include the following:

- Droppings

- Holes

- Nesting materials

- Gnawing

- Tracks on dusty surfaces

Animal pests, such as rats and mice, may be very serious problems for the restaurant operator. These rodents can eat through a cement wall to gain access to your building. They are filthy animals that will eat any sort of garbage or decaying food available. Rats are infested with bacteria and, often, disease. They have been known to bite people, as have their fleas, which also spread their bacteria and disease. Rats and mice have evolved into creatures highly developed for survival. Many scientists suggest that when mankind perishes, the rats will dominate the planet. Once they have become settled in an area, they are very difficult to get rid of. They are prolific breeders and spread rapidly.

Rats and mice, like flies, are attracted to exposed garbage. They are extremely strong and can easily gain access to a building through a crack or hole no larger than a quarter. Ensure that your building's foundation is airtight. Keep all food products at least 6 inches off the floor; this enables the exterminator to get under the shelving to spray. Rat bait, a poisoning capsule resembling food, is particularly effective when spread around the building and dumpsters. As with any poison or chemical you use, make certain that it is labeled clearly and stored away from food-storage areas.

KITCHEN SAFETY

By its nature, the food-service environment is full of potential hazards to employees' safety. Knives, slicers, grinders, glass, hot surfaces and wet or greasy floors are only a few of the hazards food-service workers face every day. Fortunately, most accidents also involve human error and, therefore, can be prevented.

HEAT AND BURNS

There are many ways employees can get burned in a food-service environment unless they're very careful. Burns can result from contact with hot surfaces such as grills, ovens, burners, fryers and other heating equipment. Burns can also be caused by escaping steam or by hot food or drinks that are splattered, splashed or spilled.

To prevent burns:

- Use thick, dry potholders or mitts, and stir food with long-handled spoons or paddles.

- Turn on hot-water faucets cautiously. Wear insulated rubber gloves for rinse water that is 170° F. Follow instructions for the use of cooking equipment—particularly steam equipment. Be sure all steam is expelled from steamers before opening the doors.

- Lift cooking lids and similar equipment away from yourself to avoid burns from steam.

- To avoid splattering and splashing, don't fill kettles too full. Also, don't allow food to boil over.

- Remember that oil and water don't mix, so be sure food is DRY before you place it in a fryer.

- Point pan handles away from foot traffic, but also within reach, to avoid knocking over other pans.

- Do not crowd cooking surfaces with hot pans. Remove cooked foods from cooking surfaces immediately.

- Allow oil to cool and use extreme caution when cleaning fryers.

- Use caution when removing hot pans from the oven. Wear insulated gloves or mitts, and be certain no one is in the removal path.

- Do not wear clothing that may drape onto a hot spot and catch on fire.

CUTS

Just as they need to take precautions to prevent being burned, food-service workers also need to be careful not to get cut. And it's not just knives that can cause trouble.

Workers can hurt themselves—or their coworkers—with the sharp edges of equipment and supplies or with broken glass. Nails and staples used in food packaging can also be dangerous.

To prevent cuts, take the following precautions:

- Use appropriate tools (not bare hands) to pick up and dispose of broken glass. Immediately place broken glass into a separate, clearly marked garbage container.

- Take care when cutting rolls of kitchen wrap with the cutter.

- Be careful with can openers and the edges of open cans. Never use a knife to open cans or to pry items loose.

- Use a pusher to feed food into a grinder.

- Turn off and unplug slicers and grinders when removing food and cleaning.

- Use guards on grinders and slicers.

- Replace equipment blades as soon as they are cleaned.

- Be aware that left-handed people need to take extra care when working with slicers and similar equipment. This is because the safety features on this equipment are designed for right-handed people.

In addition:

- Keep knives sharp. Dull blades are harder to work with and cause more cuts than sharp ones.

- Never leave knives or equipment blades in the bottom of a sink.

- Carry knives by the handle with the tip pointed away from you. Never try to catch a falling knife.

- Cut away from yourself on a cutting board.

- Slice, do not hack.

Also, when you're storing or cleaning equipment, be sure to:

- Store knives and other sharp tools in special places when not in use.

- Wash dishes and glasses separately to help prevent them from being crushed by heavier objects and breaking in the dishwasher or sink.

- Do not stack glasses or cups inside one another.

- Watch out for nails, staples and protruding sharp edges while unpacking boxes and crates.

ELECTRICAL SHOCK

Because of the variety of electrical equipment used in food service, electrical shock is a common concern.

To prevent electrical shock:

- Properly ground all electrical equipment.

- Ensure that employees can reach switches without touching or leaning against metal tables or counters.

- Replace all worn or frayed electrical cords.

- Use electrical equipment only when hands are dry.

- Unplug equipment before cleaning.

- Locate electrical switches and breakers to permit rapid shutdown in the event of an emergency.

STRAINS

Carrying equipment or food items that are too heavy can result in strains to the arms, legs or back.

To prevent strains:

- Store heavy items on lower shelves.

- Use dollies or carts to move objects that are too heavy to carry.

- To move objects from one area to another, use carts with firm shelves and properly operating wheels or casters.

- Don't carry too many objects at one time; instead, use a cart.

- Don't try to lift large or heavy objects by yourself.

- Use proper lifting techniques. Remember to bend from your knees, not your back.

SLIPPING AND FALLING

Anyone who slips and falls onto the floor can be badly hurt. Be sure your facility does not have hazards that put workers at risk.

To prevent slips and falls:

- Clean up wet spots and spills immediately.

- Let people know when floors are wet. Use signs that signal caution, and prominently display them. Wear shoes that have no-slip soles.

- Do not stack boxes or other objects too high. They can fall and cause people to trip.

- Keep items such as boxes, ladders, step stools and carts out of the paths of foot traffic.

FIRES

More fires occur in food service than in any other type of operation. Fire extinguishers should be available in all areas where fires are likely, especially in the kitchen near grills and deep fryers. But be careful—don't keep extinguishers so close to the equipment that they will be inaccessible in the event of a fire.

All employees should be trained in avoiding fires as well as in the use of fire extinguishers and in evacuation procedures. REMEMBER: Always call the fire department before using a fire extinguisher!

CHOKING

As kids, probably we all heard our parents say: "Don't eat so fast! Chew your food properly!" They may have added, "Don't talk while you're eating," and "Drink your milk carefully!"

It's good advice for children—and for adults. Anyone can choke on food if he or she is not careful. That's why an important part of food-service safety is being alert to your customers.

Here's what to look for, and what to do:

- If a person has both hands to the throat and cannot speak or cough, it is likely he or she is choking.

- If this person can talk, cough or breathe, do not pat him or her on the back or interfere in any way.

- If this person cannot talk, cough or breathe, you will need to take action. Use the Heimlich maneuver, and call for help immediately.

All food-service employees should be trained in the use of the Heimlich maneuver, and posters with instructions on how to perform it should be posted near the employee dining area.

EXPOSURE TO HAZARDOUS CHEMICALS

Improper exposure to cleaning agents, chemical pesticides and chemical sanitizers may cause injury to the skin or poisoning. To protect workers from exposure to hazardous materials, special precautions need to be taken, including certain steps that are required by law.

For example, the U.S. Department of Labor's Occupational Safety and Health Administration—commonly known as OSHA—requires food-service establishments to keep a current inventory of all hazardous materials.

Manufacturers are required to make sure hazardous chemicals are properly labeled and must supply a Material Safety Data Sheet (MSDS) to be kept on file at the food-service facility. The MSDS provides the chemical name of the product and physical hazards, health hazards and emergency procedures in case of exposure.

Information about each chemical—including its common name, when it is used, who is authorized to use it, and information from the MSDS—must also be provided to workers.

To prevent improper exposure to hazardous materials, make sure:

- Only properly trained workers handle hazardous chemicals.

- Employees have safety equipment to use when working with hazardous chemicals.

- Employees wear nonporous gloves and eye goggles when working with sanitizing agents and other cleaners.

Improper handling of food products or neglecting sanitation and safety procedures will certainly lead to health problems and/or personal injury. A successful restaurant must develop a reputation for serving quality food in a safe environment. Should there ever be a question in your customers' minds as to the wholesomeness or quality of a product, the restaurant will quickly lose its hard-earned reputation. The sanitation and safety procedures described in this section are very simple to initiate, but management must follow up and enforce them.

MANAGER SELF-INSPECTION CHECKLIST

DATE _____ OBSERVER _____

PERSONAL DRESS AND HYGIENE

Employees wear proper uniform including proper shoes.
❏ YES ❏ NO Corrective Action _____

Hair restraint is worn.
❏ YES ❏ NO Corrective Action _____

Fingernails are short, unpolished and clean.
❏ YES ❏ NO Corrective Action _____

Jewelry is limited to watch, simple earrings and plain ring.
❏ YES ❏ NO Corrective Action _____

Hands are washed or gloves are changed at critical points.
❏ YES ❏ NO Corrective Action _____

Open sores, cuts, splints or bandages on hands are completely covered while handling food.
❏ YES ❏ NO Corrective Action _____

Hands are washed thoroughly using proper hand-washing techniques at critical points.
❏ YES ❏ NO Corrective Action _____

Smoking is observed only in designated areas away from preparation, service, storage and warewashing areas.
❏ YES ❏ NO Corrective Action _____

Eating, drinking and chewing gum are observed only in designated areas away from work areas.
❏ YES ❏ NO Corrective Action _____

Employees take appropriate action when coughing or sneezing.
❏ YES ❏ NO Corrective Action _____

Disposable tissues are used and disposed of when coughing/blowing nose.
❏ YES ❏ NO Corrective Action _____

LARGE EQUIPMENT

Food slicer is clean to sight and touch.
❏ YES ❏ NO Corrective Action _____

Food slicer is sanitized between uses when used with potentially hazardous foods.
❏ YES ❏ NO Corrective Action _____

All other pieces of equipment are clean to sight and touch — equipment on serving lines, storage shelves, cabinets, ovens, ranges, fryers and steam equipment.
❏ YES ❏ NO Corrective Action _____

Exhaust hood and filters are clean.
❏ YES ❏ NO Corrective Action _____

REFRIGERATOR, FREEZER AND MILK COOLER

Thermometer is conspicuous and accurate.
❏ YES ❏ NO Corrective Action _____

Temperature is accurate for piece of equipment.
❏ YES ❏ NO Corrective Action _____

Food is stored 6 inches off floor in walk-ins.
❏ YES ❏ NO Corrective Action _____

Unit is clean.
❏ YES ❏ NO Corrective Action _____

Proper chilling procedures have been practiced.
❏ YES ❏ NO Corrective Action _____

All food is properly wrapped, labeled and dated.
❏ YES ❏ NO Corrective Action _____

FIFO (First In, First Out) inventory is being practiced.
❏ YES ❏ NO Corrective Action _____

FOOD STORAGE AND DRY STORAGE

Temperature is between 50° F and 70° F.
❏ YES ❏ NO Corrective Action _____

All food and paper supplies are 6 to 8 inches off the floor.
❏ YES ❏ NO Corrective Action _____

All food is labeled with name and delivery date.
❏ YES ❏ NO Corrective Action _____

FIFO (First In, First Out) inventory is being practiced.
❏ YES ❏ NO Corrective Action _____

There are no bulging or leaking canned goods in storage.
❏ YES ❏ NO Corrective Action _____

Food is protected from contamination.
❏ YES ❏ NO Corrective Action _____

All surfaces and floors are clean.
❏ YES ❏ NO Corrective Action _____

Chemicals are stored away from food and other food-related supplies.
❏ YES ❏ NO Corrective Action _____

HOT HOLDING

Unit is clean.
❏ YES ❏ NO Corrective Action _____

Food is heated to 165° F before placing in hot holding.
❏ YES ❏ NO Corrective Action _____

Temperature of food being held is above 140° F.
❏ YES ❏ NO Corrective Action _____

Food is protected from contamination.
❏ YES ❏ NO Corrective Action _____

FOOD HANDLING

Frozen food is thawed under refrigeration or in cold running water.
❏ YES ❏ NO Corrective Action _____

Food is not allowed to be in the "temperature danger zone" for more than 4 hours.
❏ YES ❏ NO Corrective Action _____

Food is tasted using proper method.
❏ YES ❏ NO Corrective Action _____

Food is not allowed to become cross-contaminated.
❏ YES ❏ NO Corrective Action _____

Food is handled with utensils, clean-gloved hands or clean hands.
❏ YES ❏ NO Corrective Action _____

Utensils are handled to avoid touching parts that will be in direct contact with food.
❏ YES ❏ NO Corrective Action _____

Reusable towels are used only for sanitizing equipment surfaces and not for drying hands, utensils, floor, etc.
❏ YES ❏ NO Corrective Action _____

UTENSILS AND EQUIPMENT

All small equipment and utensils, including cutting boards, are sanitized between uses.
❏ YES ❏ NO Corrective Action _____

Small equipment and utensils are air dried.
❏ YES ❏ NO Corrective Action _____

Work surfaces are clean to sight and touch.
❏ YES ❏ NO Corrective Action _____

Work surfaces are sanitized between uses.
❏ YES ❏ NO Corrective Action _____

Thermometers are washed and sanitized between each use.
❏ YES ❏ NO Corrective Action _____

Can opener is clean to sight and touch.
❏ YES ❏ NO Corrective Action _____

Drawers and racks are clean.
❏ YES ❏ NO Corrective Action _____

Small equipment is inverted, covered or otherwise protected from dust and contamination when stored.
❏ YES ❏ NO Corrective Action _____

CLEANING AND SANITIZING

Three-compartment sink is used.
❏ YES ❏ NO Corrective Action _____

Three-compartment sink is properly set up for warewashing (wash, rinse, sanitize).
❏ YES ❏ NO Corrective Action _____

Chlorine test kit or thermometer is used to check sanitizing process.
❏ YES ❏ NO Corrective Action _____

The water temperatures are accurate.
❏ YES ❏ NO Corrective Action _____

If heat-sanitizing, the utensils are allowed to remain immersed in 170° F water for 30 seconds.
❏ YES ❏ NO Corrective Action _____

If using chemical sanitizer, it is the proper dilution.
❏ YES ❏ NO Corrective Action _____

The water is clean and free of grease and food particles.
❏ YES ❏ NO Corrective Action _____

The utensils are allowed to air dry.
❏ YES ❏ NO Corrective Action _____

Wiping clothes are stored in sanitizing solution while in use.
❏ YES ❏ NO Corrective Action _____

GARBAGE STORAGE AND DISPOSAL

Kitchen garbage cans are clean.
❏ YES ❏ NO Corrective Action _____

Garbage cans are emptied as necessary.
❏ YES ❏ NO Corrective Action _____

Boxes and containers are removed from site.
❏ YES ❏ NO Corrective Action _____

Loading dock and are around dumpster are clean.
❏ YES ❏ NO Corrective Action _____

Dumpster is closed.
❏ YES ❏ NO Corrective Action _____

PEST CONTROL

Screen on open windows and doors are in good repair.
❏ YES ❏ NO Corrective Action _____

No evidence of pests is present
❏ YES ❏ NO Corrective Action _____

TEMPERATURE LOG

Month: _____ Freezer: _____ Refrigerator: _____

DATE	TIME	TEMP	INITIALS	DATE	TIME	TEMP	INITIALS

8

⊰⊱

SUCCESSFUL BAR
MANAGEMENT & OPERATIONS

INTRODUCTION

This chapter on bar management is divided into four major sections:

SECTION 1 describes the various types of liquor and other alcoholic beverages that the restaurant manager must become familiar with. Guidelines are established as to the types and amounts of each to stock

SECTION 2 describes the physical "nuts and bolts" operation of the bar. These sections contain a drink recipe manual and cover liquor ordering, inventory control, pouring procedures, setting bar prices, establishing a "Happy Hour," and how to initiate some inexpensive professional touches of showmanship gathered from bars across the country, that will separate your lounge from the rest.

SECTION 3 on bar personnel describes the job descriptions, procedures, responsibilities and scope of all bar personnel.

SECTION 4 covers bar controls and combines the three preceding sections into a streamlined and profitable bar operation. In addition, this section will deal with receiving and storing procedures, restocking and reconciliation of all liquor and how to set up inventory security, and it details a system of checks and balances which will ensure that all products and sales are accounted for and reconciled.

SECTION 1 DESCRIPTION OF LIQUOR & ALCOHOLIC BEVERAGES

The following section contains definitions and descriptions of the various types of liquor the restaurant manager must become familiar with. Below each description are some suggestions as to the type and number of each to stock.

All liquor served in the restaurant can be divided into two basic categories: well items and call items. Some restaurants establish a three-tier system: well, call and premium liquor. Premium liquor would have an additional surcharge.

Well items are the house liquors the restaurant serves. They are called well items because they are in a well speed rack in front of the bartender. Well liquors are used when a customer orders a particular drink without specifying a brand: e.g a scotch and soda or a bourbon and water. For each major type of liquor, such as bourbon, gin, vodka, scotch, tequila, rum, brandy and rye, you will need to select a well or house brand. The well liquor you select must be a popular and recognized brand which is moderately priced.

Call items are the more expensive, higher-quality types of liquor. These a customer orders by the particular brand name: for example, a Cutty Sark scotch and soda or a Jack Daniel's bourbon and water. Call items are sometimes called back bar items because they are usually stored on the shelves behind the bar.

WHISKEY

All whiskeys are distilled from fermented grains. Commonly used grains are barley, rye, corn and wheat. All whiskeys are aged in oak barrels. From this aging process they obtain their characteristic color, flavor and aroma.

Most whiskey consumed in this country is produced in either the United States, Canada, Scotland or Ireland. Each country produces its very own distinctive whiskeys. Whiskey can be divided into two basic types: straight whiskey and blended whiskey.

Straight whiskey is a whiskey that has never been mixed with other types of whiskey or with any neutral grain spirits. Straight whiskey itself has four major types, discussed below.

Blended whiskey is a blend of straight whiskeys and/or neutral grain spirits. It must contain at least 20 percent, by volume, of a straight whiskey and be bottled at no less than 80 proof.

STRAIGHT WHISKEY
Bourbon whiskey—Its name is derived from Bourbon County in Kentucky, where the whiskey was originally produced. Bourbon must be distilled from grain mash containing at least 51 percent corn. (Suggested: 1 well bourbon and 3–6 call items.)

Rye whiskey—Rye has the similar amber color of bourbon, but the flavor and aroma are different. Rye whiskey must be distilled from a fermented mash of grain containing at least 51 percent rye. (Suggested: 1 well rye and 1–2 call items.)

Corn whiskey—Corn whiskey must be distilled from fermented mash of grain containing at least 80 percent corn. (Suggested: 1 call item only.)

Bottled-in-bond whiskey—Usually a rye or bourbon whiskey that is produced under the supervision of the United States Government. The government ensures the following:

1. That the whiskey is aged at least four years.

2. That it is bottled at 100 proof.

3. That it is produced in one distilling by a single distiller.

4. That it is bottled and stored under government supervision.

Since the government bonds these steps, the whiskey referred to as "bottled in bond." The government does not guarantee the quality of the whiskey; it only ensures that these steps have been completed under its supervision. (Suggested: 1–2 call items.)

BLENDED WHISKEYS

Canadian whiskey Canadian whiskey is a blend produced under the supervision of the Canadian Government. This whiskey is usually lighter bodied than most American whiskeys. (Suggested: 1 well and 3–6 call items.)

Scotch whiskey—Scotch whiskey is produced only in Scotland. All Scotch blends contain malt and grain whiskeys. The unique smoky flavor of Scotch is derived from drying malted barley over open peat fires. In recent years the popularity of single malt scotch and other whiskeys has grown phenomenally. Many bars have a vast selection of hard-to-find single malts, and they are very expensive and profitable. Single malt whisky is the product from a single distillery and has not been blended with any other whiskies. Only water is added before it is bottled, and in the case of "cask strength" bottlings, not even that. There are bottlings with an alcohol-percentage of over 60 available! (Suggested: 1 well scotch and 4–8 call items.)

Irish whiskey—Irish whiskey is produced only in Ireland. This whiskey is usually heavier and fuller bodied than most Scotch blends. The malted barley used in the distilling process is dried over coal-fired kilns. This drying process has little or no affect on the whiskey's taste. (Suggested: 2–3 call items.)

OTHER LIQUOR

VODKA

Vodka was originally produced in Russia from distilled potatoes. Now, produced in various countries, vodka is commonly made from a variety of grains, the most common of which are wheat and corn. It is bottled at no less than 80 and no higher than 110 proof. During the distillation process it is highly refined and filtered, usually through activated charcoal. Vodka is not aged. It is colorless, odorless and virtually tasteless. Because of these traits, it is a very versatile liquor that can be mixed with almost anything. In addition, it can be served straight, chilled to taste. (Suggested: 1 well brand at 80 proof and one at 110 proof and 2–3 call items, 1–2 of which should be imported.)

GIN

Gin is distilled from a variety of grains and is bottled at 80 proof. Every gin manufactured has its own distinctive flavor and aroma. The aroma is derived from a recipe of juniper berries and other assorted plants. Gin is usually colorless and is most often used in making the popular martini cocktail. Vacuum-distilled gin is distilled in a glass-lined vacuum at lower than normal distilling temperature. This process tends to eliminate the bitterness found in some gins. (Suggested: 1 well and 3–4 call items, 1–2 of which should be imported.)

RUM

Rum is distilled from cane syrup, which is the fermented juice of sugarcane and molasses. It is bottled at no less than 80 proof. Most rums are a blend of many different types of aged rums. Dark rums often have caramel syrup added for color. Rums can be classified into two major types:

Light-bodied—Light-bodied rums are dry and light in color due to a lack of molasses. Among the light-bodied rums are two varieties, gold label and white label. The gold is often of slightly better quality and is darker and sweeter; the white is paler and slightly stronger in flavor. (Suggested:1 well 80 proof and 1–2 call items.)

Heavy-bodied—Heavy-bodied rums have been distilled by a different and slower process. Because of this process, the rum contains more molasses, which makes the rum darker, sweeter and richer. (Suggested: 1 well 80 proof, 2–3 call items and 1–2 high-proof items.)

BRANDY

Brandy is traditionally distilled from a mash of fermented grapes but may be produced from other fruits. There are many different types available.

Cognac—Cognac is perhaps the finest of distilled brandies. It is produced only in the Cognac region of France. Usually it is a blend of many different types of distilled cognac of the region. Cognac may be aged for as long as 50 years or more.

Armagnac—This brandy is similar to cognac but slightly drier in taste. It is produced only in the Armagnac region of France.

Apple Jack—This brandy is distilled from the cider of crushed apples. Calvados (an apple brandy) is produced only in Normandy, France. In the United States, Apple Jack is often bottled in bond.

Fruit-flavored brandies—These brandies have a distilled brandy base with a flavor ingredient added. These are commonly used in blended cocktails. A good selection of the more popular types will be needed.

TEQUILA

Tequila is usually produced in Mexico or the American Southwest. It is distilled from the fermented mash of the aqua or century plants, which are cacti. Tequila is usually clear, although some types may have a gold tint. The smell and taste are distinctive. Tequila is used primarily in making margarita cocktails. In recent years there has been a wide increase in the variety of "premium" tequilas. Tequila can also be chilled and served straight as a "shooter" with a beer chaser. (Suggested: 1 well and 2–3 imported call items.)

CORDIALS AND LIQUEURS

Cordials and liqueurs are created by the mixing or pre-distilling of neutral grain spirits with fruits, flowers or plants, to which sweeteners have been added. Cordials and liqueurs are all colorful and very sweet in taste, which is why they are usually served as after-dinner drinks. There are a wide variety of cordials and liqueurs available. A good selection of cordials and liqueurs would include 15 to 25 of these. There are approximately 10 to 12 different types that you must stock because of their popularity or because they are used in making certain cocktails. A list of the popular liqueurs for your area will be available from your local liquor distributor. (All cordials and liqueurs should be call items).

VERMOUTH

Vermouth is not classified as liqueur or liquor at all, but is actually a wine flavored with roots, berries or various types of plants. Vermouth is used almost exclusively in making martinis and manhattans. There are two basic types:

Dry—Dry vermouth is usually produced in America or France. This variety has a clear to light goldish color. It is used primarily in martini cocktails. One good well item is all that is required.

Sweet—Sweet vermouth is a darker reddish wine with a richer, sweeter flavor. It is most often produced in Italy. Sweet vermouth is primarily used in making manhattan cocktails. One good well item is all you'll need.

BEER

Whether packaged in bottles or kegs, beer should be treated as a food product. Always keep in mind that it is a perishable commodity with a limited life span. To ensure the freshness and full flavor of bottled beer, it's essential to adhere to a few simple procedures. The two biggest enemies of beer are exposure to light and temperature extremes, and the best way to combat them is to store beer in a dark, relatively cool place.

There are five basic categories for the hundreds of brands of beer produced. They are: lagers, the most popular type produced today; ales, which contain more hops and are stronger in flavor; and porter, stout and bock beers, which are all heavier, darker, richer and sweeter than the first two.

Beer is available in bottles, cans or on a draught keg system. Of the hundreds of brands available, fewer than a dozen are primarily demanded by customers. However, it should be noted that the popularity of "microbrewed" beers has come on very strong. There are many independent restaurants and at least two national chains that use a microbrewery in their own establishment as a marketing vehicle. It is suggested that your most popular beer be on draught—most customers prefer it that way, and it is cheaper for you. Beer is a perishable item, so you'll want to buy the other, less popular brands you'll carry in bottles or cans to preserve their freshness. Most draft systems can handle three separate kegs; if your business warrants it, use all of them. If your restaurant serves ethnic or international food it's a nice touch to include some beer selections produced in that region or country.

Imported beers have gained increasing popularity in recent years. Although they are 50–100 percent more expensive than domestic beers, customers still demand the more popular ones. There are 3–4 of these imported beers that you should always stock.

Light beer is produced with fewer calories than other beer and has developed a great demand within the past five years. One to two light beers should be included on your list.

COMMON BAR TERMS

ALCOHOL—There are several types of alcohol. Ethyl alcohol is the type found in all alcoholic beverages.

PROOF—Proof is the measurement of alcohol in an alcoholic beverage. Each degree of proof represents a half percent of alcohol. For example, a bottle of liquor distilled at 90 proof is 45-percent alcohol.

GRAIN NEUTRAL SPIRITS—This is a colorless, tasteless, usually odorless ethyl alcohol distilled from grain at a minimum of 190 proof. Grain neutral spirits are used in blending whiskies and in making other types of liquor/liqueur.

SHOT or **JIGGER**—A shot, or jigger, is a unit of liquor ranging from $3/4$ ounce to 2 ounces. Most restaurants pour shots of $1^1/4$ to $1^1/2$ ounces for cocktails and add slightly less to blended drinks.

STRAIGHT UP refers to a cocktail that is served with no ice—usually a martini, manhattan or margarita. A special chilled long-stem straight-up glass should be used. Liqueurs and cordials that are served straight up may be poured into pony glasses.

ON THE ROCKS refers to a cocktail—usually a straight liquor, such as a scotch, or a cordial—served over ice. Although most cocktails are served over ice anyway, certain cocktails and liquors are just as commonly served without ice. In such cases the bartender or cocktail waitress must ask the customer which way he or she prefers.

TWIST, **WEDGE** and **SLICE** refer to the fruit that garnishes the cocktail glass. A twist is a lemon peel. A wedge or slice is usually a piece of lime or orange.

PRESS—Use a fruit press to squeeze the juice of a fruit garnish into the cocktail.

BITTERS is a commercially produced liquid made from roots, berries or a variety of herbs. It is, indeed, bitter, and a dash or two is used in some cocktails.

VIRGIN refers to a drink that contains no alcoholic beverage, such as a virgin piña colada or a virgin Bloody Mary.

BACK—Usually refers to either a water or coffee back. This indicates that along with the cocktail ordered, the customer would also like a separate glass of water or cup of coffee.

RIMMED—Place either salt, sugar or celery salt around the rim of a cocktail glass. Usually bloody marys, margaritas and salty dogs are served this way. The bartender prepares a rimmed glass by wetting the rim of the glass with a wedge of fruit then twirling the glass in a bowl of the salt or sugar desired.

SHAKEN refers to a cocktail that is shaken in the mixing glass before being strained.

STIRRED refers to a cocktail that is stirred (not shaken) in the mixing glass with a spoon before being strained.

SECTION 2 BAR OPERATIONS

LIQUOR AND BEER ORDERING

Liquor ordering is not as involved as purchasing food items, as there are fewer problem areas to contend with. Liquor has a long shelf life and will rarely turn bad, which enables it to be ordered in large quantities on a less frequent basis. Moreover the quality is always consistent among distributors: they all carry the same products. Thus, it is far simpler to compare prices and terms knowing that each supplier has the same item. Once you establish which well and call brands you wish to serve, ordering should only involve projecting your needs and purchasing from the distributor with the best overall terms.

Each state has its own laws and regulations regarding the sale and distribution of alcoholic beverages. States may be divided into one of two classifications: those that permit private businesses to sell and distribute liquor and those that have a monopoly on the sale of liquor (usually excluding beer and wine) and sell through state-run stores. There are advantages and disadvantages to both situations.

State-operated liquor stores purchase their inventories in large quantities from distributors. Because they purchase vast amounts and eliminate most middlemen, their prices are often substantially less than that of privately owned stores. However, there are two distinct disadvantages for the wholesale user (restaurants) under this system.

The first disadvantage to buying from a state-run store is that the service provided cannot compare to that of a store in the private sector. Delivery arrangements and credit terms are difficult, if not impossible, to work out. No matter how efficiently its store is operated and how friendly the people working there, the state will not have the same interest in serving customers as would a private owner.

The second disadvantage to a state-operated store is its pricing system for wholesale users. Price discounts are usually given on purchasing full cases, but there is often no discount allowed when purchasing several or more cases. Thus you pay the same price for one case as you would for a hundred of the same.

In many of the states with private operations, liquor distributors may not have the right to sell some brands of liquor. This arrangement between the producer and the distributor is similar to a franchising agreement. Should this be the case in your area, you may have to purchase from many of the local distributors in order to stock all of the brands of liquor you wish to serve. This can be advantageous, as there will be a high level of competition among distributors for the common liquors each carry. However, if you spread your business out among several distributors, your individual account may not be very important to each supplier. Since you are not a prime customer you will probably not get the best terms, prices or service from any one supplier.

Liquor salespeople are mostly interested in obtaining a bar's well items for their accounts. Well liquor is poured at least five times as often as call items. Since the price you pay for liquor will depend directly upon the amount you use and purchase, this will be a very important consideration. Allow plenty of time for your selection of both the well brands and the distributor from whom you choose to purchase them.

In almost all states, beer is distributed by local suppliers, each of whom have a franchising agreement to sell a particular brewer's product. In most cases the distributor is only allowed to sell one manufacturer's products at a time. However, each manufacturer usually produces several brands of beer under different labels.

Since each distributor sells only a few types of beer, you will probably need to use all of the suppliers in your area to stock all the different types you want. Since all distributors have different products, there is little or no competition among them regarding pricing. However, there is a very high level of competition among distributors to get their manufacturer's products into your restaurant. This is why they are willing to install the restaurant's draught system for free in exchange for your exclusive use of their products.

The distributor you select to purchase the draught beer from will be your biggest supplier. Draught beer will outsell bottles and cans three to one, if not more. This large volume of keg beer will enable you to get considerable discounts on your supplier's other products. The draft beer distributor should carry many of the other brands of beer you wish to serve, so that you may take advantage of this purchasing power.

A large part of your liquor order will be for nonalcoholic juices, garnishes and mixers. Most liquor distributors and food-service suppliers can provide you with everything you will need; consider carefully from which supplier you will purchase these additional items.

Juices and mixers must be of the best quality you can afford. It makes little sense to pour quality liquor into a cocktail made with a low-quality juice or mix. Juices must be 100 percent real—no substitutes added. Mixers can be of any brand that has the quality level you are striving for. It is often advantageous to use brand-name items even if they cost a little more. Customers who sit at the bar should see that you are using high-quality recognized liquors, juices and mixers.

There will be a high level of competition among the various suppliers for this part of your business. This is due in part to the fact that these products have a high profit margin. All suppliers stock at least some of these products. When comparing prices, remember to look at the whole picture. Consider how much this extra business will mean to each supplier. Due to the increase in volume, how will this affect the prices of the other items you purchase from the supplier? Are the services and delivery arrangements to your satisfaction? What are the credit terms? What is the finance charge? How much is the overall purchase actually costing?

SOME COMMONLY USED BAR MIXERS, JUICES & GARNISHES

JUICES

Orange juice

Cranberry juice

Pineapple juice

Grapefruit juice

Tomato juice

Lime juice

Lemon juice

FRESH FRUIT

Oranges

Limes

Bananas

Cherries

Strawberries

Lemon peels

Lemons

Pineapple

SODA (See Chapter 1)
WATER

Coke or Pepsi

Diet Coke or Diet Pepsi

Sprite or 7-Up

Ginger ale

Tonic water

Soda water

Sparkling or mineral water

Purified water

GARNISHES

Cherries

Stuffed olives

Cocktail onions

Kosher salt

Celery salt

Super-fine bar sugar

MIXERS, MISC.

Sweet-and-sour bar mix

Coconut cream concentrate

Grenadine

Bitters

Orgeat syrup

Worcestershire sauce

Tabasco sauce

Sugar-saturated water

Once you establish which liquor, beer, mixer and garnishes you will be using, transfer them onto the order sheets. List them alphabetically and by category on the order sheet. An example of a **Liquor Order Form** may be found at the end of this chapter. The liquor order form is filled out and used exactly the same way as the Food Ordering Form.

The storing, receiving and rotating procedures described in the last chapter for food items also pertains to liquor and all other items delivered to the restaurant. The manager and, if possible, the person who placed the order should always be present when the delivery is received. Immediately after the order is checked for accuracy, it must be locked and secured in its separate room. As explained in Chapter 1, the manager must be the only individual who has the key to the liquor storage room. Liquor may be stored at room temperature as long as the temperature remains relatively constant.

LIQUOR INVENTORY FORM—BEGINNING INVENTORY

The Liquor Inventory Form is similar to the Inventory Form described in Chapter 5. It, too, is used to count each item in the restaurant at the end of each month. Based on this figure (the ending inventory) and others described in the upcoming chapters, you will be able to project operating costs for each area: food, liquor, wine and operational supplies.

As with food items, transfer contents of the completed order sheet to the inventory form. In the "Size" column list the size bottle each item comes in. The size listed on the inventory sheet must correspond to the size in inventory. (Example: Scotch 750 ml, Vodka 5th etc.) An example of the **Liquor Inventory Form** may be found at the end of this chapter. The steps for calculating the beginning inventory for liquor are identical to those used for food. Again, the beginning inventory is the total dollar amount of a category's (liquor) supplies that are on hand opening day. This represents the starting point from which you may later determine what you have used and, therefore, the costs for the past month in that category.

To compute the beginning inventory for liquor, simply total all the liquor purchases prior to opening day. If you are opening an existing restaurant and will be using some of the old stock, add the dollar value of the old stock to that which you have purchased. To compute the value of the old stock you must first, of course, take an inventory of it to record the amount on hand. Inventory procedures are described in an upcoming chapter.

POURING PROCEDURES

Liquor, as all food items, must be portioned in order to control costs and maintain consistency in the final product. Liquor is portioned not by weight but by volume. Volume is measured in shots or jiggers, which are liquid measurements ranging from $3/4$ ounce to 2 ounces. Most restaurants pour between $1^1/_4$ and $1^1/_2$ ounces per cocktail and slightly less—$1^1/_8$ to $1^1/_4$ ounces—for blended drinks.

The first step in developing consistent pouring procedures is to determine the amount of liquor each drink will contain. It is suggested that you use the amount stated above for each shot. More than $1\frac{1}{2}$ ounces of liquor in a cocktail will make it too strong and dominated by the liquor's flavor, which many people do not care for. A cocktail containing less than $1\frac{1}{8}$ ounces of liquor will be too weak and may give customers the impression that you are trying to cut corners.

There are two basic ways to portion-control liquor: a computerized bar gun and a free-pouring bartender. Both systems have advantages and disadvantages.

A computerized bar gun is by far the best way to control and account for every shot of liquor poured. Although there are many different types and models available, all basically operate the same. Each well item is hooked up to a hose that runs to the bar. The well items are hidden either underneath the bar or behind the back wall in an adjacent room. The hose at the bar is hooked into a gun which is similar to the one used for the soda canisters. Small buttons on the face of the gun indicate each of the well items. When the bartender presses a button the exact measurement of liquor is dispensed. The number of shots and type of liquor poured is automatically recorded and written up with the correct price. A tape is simultaneously run showing the updated number and type of cocktails poured over the night. As previously stated, there are many variations on this system, but they can all determine if there has been any loss of liquor or revenue. There are also liquor pour spouts available that are simply placed on the bottle and dispense only one shot at a time. These are effective, but by simply turning the bottle upright again, the bartender can dispense another shot.

There are two distinct disadvantages to the computerized bar gun. First and foremost, the bar tends to loose its aesthetic value. Computerized bars may be applauded by accountants and restaurant owners, but they are generally frowned upon by the public. The restaurant and lounge should be a place where a person can go to get away from the hustle and bustle of the modern world. She should be able to get a cocktail made by a professional and enjoy it with her companions in a warm atmosphere and comfortable environment. The last thing most customers wish to see is some unknown liquor dribble out of a hose into a glass while a set of digital lights flash across the register. The art and showmanship of mixology is an important part of the atmosphere of a restaurant. A computerized bar may eliminate this integral part of the dining experience.

The second disadvantage to the computerized bar is the substantial investment needed to purchase one. Although it may pay for itself over a period of time, it is still an expensive start-up cost. Perhaps this is the reason bar guns are not, as of yet, universally used throughout the food-service industry.

These two disadvantages of the computerized bar are the primary advantages of the free pour system. The cost of operation is negligible: a few shot glasses and a pouring spout for each bottle is all that is required. The aesthetic value gained is immeasurable. It is impossible to put a value on atmosphere and taste. A good compromise is the use of the pour spots that dispense an exact portion.

The main disadvantage to the free pour system is, of course, the lack of control over and accountability for each shot poured. However, if bartenders are properly trained and supervised in the procedures described, there will be little problem in controlling the cost and the consistency of the product. Bartenders, as all other employees in the restaurant, may become lax in using all the procedures they were trained to. This is why, if a consistent, profitable operation is to be maintained, management must follow up, note and review all procedures with each and every employee.

FREE-POURING PROCEDURES

There are two basic methods for free-pouring liquor. The first method is used primarily by beginners and inexperienced free pour bartenders. This technique uses a fluted shot glass with a line drawn across the top of the glass at the level of the shot desired. The bartender simply places the shot glass on the bar or spill mat and pours until the liquid reaches the line. Then he pours the contents of the shot glass into the cocktail glass over the ice. This method is very accurate, but it is much slower and far less aesthetically pleasing than the second.

The second technique requires several weeks of full-time practice to master. Use an empty liquor bottle filled with water to practice pouring. This method gives the customer the impression that you have filled the shot glass once and then, after you have emptied the shot, continued to pour more liquor into the cocktail. In fact, what you did was measure out approximately $3/4$ of an ounce into the shot glass, emptied it into the cocktail, then made up the difference by pouring directly from the bottle into the drink, measuring by silently counting off, until you have reached the full shot.

To pour:

A.   Grasp the bottle around the neck with your right hand (reverse if left-handed). Place your index finger around the pour spout.

B.   Hold the $3/4$-ounce shot glass in your left hand above the cocktail glass and place the pour spout into the shot glass. Begin to pour. As you are pouring, angle the shot glass downward. When it nears capacity, spill the contents into the cocktail glass. Continue to point the pour spout into the glass while pouring. At this point you will have poured slightly less than $3/4$ of an ounce.

C.   The difference will now be made up by pouring directly into the cocktail glass from the bottle. In order to measure exactly the amount to pour into the cocktail glass directly, count to yourself while pouring. To determine the correct count for the remaining $1/2$ to $3/4$ ounce, experiment by counting while pouring into a lined shot glass.

Bartenders should be tested periodically to ensure they are pouring the required number of shots from each bottle. This is the figure that directly determines the price of each drink. To compute the number of shots you should get from each bottle, divide the bottle volume in ounces by the size of the average shot poured. Bottle spouts are available in a variety of speeds: fast, medium and slow; there's also a wide-mouthed juice spout. The speed at which the liquor flows is determined by the size of the air hole in the spout stopper. Partially covering this hole while pouring will regulate the flow. Fast-pour spouts should be used on liquors that are thick and syrupy, such as cordials. Medium pourers should be used on most bottles. Slow spouts may be used on any liquor that is poured in a shot containing less than $1\frac{1}{8}$ ounces. Some expensive brandies and cordials are often poured at only one ounce. A slow pourer will give the effect of a long pour.

Some hints on bar organization:

1. Set up glasses and ice first.

2. Make blended drinks next.

3. Once you pick up the shot glass, don't put it down until everything is poured

4. Once you pick up a bottle, pour into all the glasses needed.

5. Allow at least $\frac{1}{4}$ inch of space at the top of each cocktail to allow for garnishes, straws, etc.

POURING DRAUGHT BEER

Draught beer should be poured so that it produces a head that rises just above the top of the glass or pitcher. This will settle down to about $\frac{3}{4}$ of an inch in a few minutes. This head or foam has both great economical and aesthetic value.

The size of the head is controlled by the angle of the glass or mug to the spout when you begin to pour. Should the head be too small, you will be pouring more beer into each glass; this will lead to a lower than expected yield on each keg. Since the customer is swallowing the CO_2 gas that would normally escape from the head, the customer will probably drink less. A head that is too large may give the customer the impression that you are attempting to cut corners on quality.

The most important consideration in serving beer is to use cold, spotless glasses or mugs. Glasses that appear clean may have a residual buildup of soap or grease. The slightest trace of these agents will break down the head and bubbles in the beer leaving a stale-looking product. Every glass used should be rinsed with cold fresh water before filling. Always use a new glass for each beer ordered.

The temperature at which beer is served is also a crucial element. To ensure that the proper flavor is released, all beer should be served at 40° F. When beer is served below 38° F it looses its distinct taste and aroma. Beer served above 42° F may turn cloudy and will loose its zest and flavor. Draught beer is not pasteurized, so it must always be held at a constant temperature. All beer coolers should be set at 38° F so that the proper serving temperature can be maintained. Remember to always use chilled glasses and mugs (with thick glass and handles) to help keep the beer at a cool, constant temperature.

Beer lines must be flushed out weekly, just as soda lines must. Beer is only as good as the lines through which it flows. The service of a professional tap and line cleaner are needed weekly. Your beer distributor can recommend a reputable company.

TO POUR A PERFECT DRAFT:

Pouring a perfect beer with every pull of the tap handle takes some skill, but it can be easily mastered with practice. The procedures listed below offer some tips for maximizing draft beer service.

- Start with a "beer clean" glass.

- The size of the head is determined by the angle at which the glass is held under the spout at the start of the draw (never let the glass come in direct contact with the spout itself). If the glass is held at a sharp angle so that the beer flows down the side of the glass there will be little or no head. Conversely, if the glass is held straight so that the beer splashes directly into the bottom of the glass, there will be a large head.

- For flat-bottomed glassware (such as an hourglass): Open the tap all the way by grasping the handle at its base and pulling it quickly (grasping at the top of the tap handle will result in too slow an open and the beer will come out overly foamy). Tilt the glass at about a 45-degree angle at the beginning of the pour and then straighten it up so that the beer splashes directly into the glass. The resulting head should be about $1/2$ to 1 inch thick.

- For wide-bottomed glassware (such as a schooner or goblet): Don't tilt the glass at all. Open the tap as indicated above and allow the beer to pour directly into the bottom of the glass. The result should be a $1/2$- to 1-inch head.

- Note that unchilled glassware will have a warming effect on beer. A thin, room-temperature glass will increase the temperature of the beer about 2° F. An unchilled mug will raise the temperature of the beer about 4° to 6° F.

TROUBLESHOOTING

Loose Foam (settles quickly)

- Beer line system/coils not as cold as beer in barrel

- Pressure required does not correspond to beer temperature (unbalanced system)

- Beer dispensed through small diameter tubing into large shanks and faucets

Flat Beer

- Glasses are not "beer clean"
- Pressure shut off at closing
- Leak in pressure tubing or barrels
- Defective pressure-check valve in tap
- Obstruction in line near barrel
- Oily air from compressor or kitchen

- Not enough CO_2 pressure
- Cooler or dispensing system too cold
- Loose tap or pressure connections
- Sluggish pressure regulator
- Compressor too small or inefficient
- Long exposure to air instead of CO_2 gas pressure.

Unpalatable Beer

- Dirty faucets
- Failure to leave water in beer lines overnight
- Unsanitary conditions at bar
- Foul air or dirt in lines or air tank
- Improper location, maintenance and lubrication of air pump
- Temperature of beer in barrel too warm
- Failure to provide fresh air inlet for air pump

- Dirty beer system
- Failure to flush beer lines with water after each empty barrel
- Coils not cleaned properly
- Oily air from kitchen
- Failure to purge condensation from compressor storage tank
- Dry glasses

Sour Beer

If the problem is sour beer, the difficulty is due to the temperature of the keg itself, either in the restaurant or bar, at the distributor's warehouse or en route. The beer should always be maintained at between 36° and 38° F under normal operation. It should never be allowed to warm to 50° F or more for any length of time, since this may begin a secondary fermentation.

HOW MUCH BEER IN A KEG?

A barrel of beer contains 31 gallons, or the equivalent of 13.8 cases of 12-ounce bottles (24 bottles to a case). (Each case contains approximately 2.25 gallons of beer.) Typically, the kegs of draft beer that are used at most on-premise establishments are actually half-barrels. Assuming a one-inch head, there are approximately 200 12-ounce servings per keg or about 150 16-ounce servings, varying slightly with the type of glass used.

BAR RECIPE AND PROCEDURE MANUAL

The purpose of the Bar Recipe and Procedure Manual is to ensure that the recipes and-methods of preparing all cocktails are consistent among your bartenders. Most drinks can be prepared in many different ways. Therefore, it is imperative that all recipes and procedures are standardized to ensure that both the final product and cost is consistent.

Of the hundreds of varieties of cocktails, less than 25 are ordered 90 percent of the time. In order to obtain consistency among them, a recipe and procedure manual should be developed. This manual should contain the following information: cocktail ingredients and amounts, which cocktail glass should be used, garnishes, pertinent serving instructions and preparation procedures. An example of a **Bar Recipe and Procedure Manual** may be found at the end of this chapter.

There are several excellent bartender guides available that list all the various cocktails and how to prepare them. One of these books should be kept at the bar. Occasionally a customer will order a drink that you will not know, nor will it be listed in the book. Usually this is because the customer is pronouncing it wrong, or it is some variation of another cocktail. Politely inform the customer that you are not familiar with the cocktail; many times she can tell you how to prepare it.

Twenty-five of the most commonly ordered cocktails:

• Screwdriver	• Sombrero	• Mai-Tai	• Piña Colada
• Old Fashioned	• Tequila Sunrise	• Gimlet	• Margarita
• Martini	• Cosmopolitan	• Manhattan	• Gibson
• Bloody Mary	• Stingers	• Coffee	• Collins drinks
• Fizzes	• Daiquiris	• Sours	• White Russian
• Black Russian	• Black Russian	• Gin and tonic	• Juice/punch drinks
• Long Island iced tea			

The majority of drinks require no mixing, stirring or blending. These cocktails are often made from a well or call item poured "on the rocks" or added to juice or a mixer.

SETTING BAR PRICES

Setting proper bar prices is an easier process than that of establishing menu prices. The procedures are basically the same; however, there are fewer cost factors to contend with in projecting liquor costs. The bar should operate at 18–25 percent cost of sales. Costs of sales is determined by dividing the total liquor cost by total liquor sales. This figure excludes wine, as it is considered a separate category and projected as such. As stated in Chapter 5, "Profitable Menu Planning," the cost of sales is the total cost over a given period of time, usually one month, divided by total sales. For example, if the monthly total liquor cost was $10,000 and the total sales was $50,000, the cost percentage would be 20 percent.

In order to set the proper bar prices, it is necessary to calculate first the cost of the cocktail. The cost in this instance refers to the liquor, mixes, garnishes and so forth used to make the cocktail. Labor, ice and glassware are not actual liquor costs and are thus computed in other categories. There are two cost factors to consider when computing the cost of a cocktail: 1) the cost of the shot of alcohol poured and 2) the cost of all the miscellaneous nonalcoholic ingredients, such as mixers, juices, garnishes, etc.

TO PROJECT THE COST OF EACH SHOT POURED:

A. Using the conversion chart convert the metric measurement of each bottle into ounces.

B. Calculate the number of shots that should be yielded from each bottle by dividing the bottle volume (in ounces) by the size (in ounces) of the average shot poured.

C. Divide the cost of the bottle by the number of shots it should yield to compute the cost per shot.

CONVERSION CHART FOR LIQUID MEASURES			
METRIC SIZE	**FLUID OUNCES**	**U.S. MEASURE**	**FLUID OUNCES**
50 ml	7.0	Miniature	1.6
200 ml	6.8	$\frac{1}{2}$ Pint	8.0
500 ml	16.9	1 Pint	16.0
50 ml	25.4	$\frac{4}{5}$ Quart	25.6
1 Liter	33.8	1 Quart	32.0
1.75 Liters	59.2	$\frac{1}{2}$ Gallon	64.0

Again, in order to project the exact cost for each cocktail it is necessary to calculate the cost of the nonalcoholic ingredients that are added. Since this would entail many hours of computation it is far simpler and nearly as precise to assess an average miscellaneous expense for all drinks. The average miscellaneous cost would thus account for the additional cost of juices, mixers, garnishes, soda and so forth. This miscellaneous-expense figure would not be applied to beer or wine since there is no additional cost to the final product.

Research shows that the average miscellaneous expense fluctuates between 5 and 20 percent of the cost of each shot poured. Of course, this figure will depend upon the type and number of drinks you serve. Blended drinks will have a high percentage of cost since they contain several different ingredients. To compensate for this additional cost, most restaurants pour a smaller shot ($1\frac{1}{8}$ to $1\frac{1}{4}$ ounces). Straight drinks and beer will help balance out this cost since they have little or no additional ingredients. Based upon this information it would be accurate enough to assess the miscellaneous expense at 10 percent of the shot cost. Thus, the cost of each shot plus the average miscellaneous expense (10 percent of the shot cost) will equal the estimated total cost of the drink.

To compute what must be charged for each drink, simply plug different prices into the formula listed below until you reach the desired liquor cost-of-sales percentage:

Total Drink Cost ÷ Price = 18–25% Liquor Cost of Sales

Certain expensive liquors, when priced out to get the desired cost-of-sales percentage, will be too expensive. Customers may not pay the price you would need to charge to reach the desired 18–25 percent.

Analyze what other restaurants in the area are charging for cocktails. When you first open, customers tend to be cautious. A reputation for high- or overpriced drinks can be detrimental to your restaurant business. Should you have entertainment in the lounge, you may raise drink prices to offset the entertainment expense. This is a common and generally accepted practice.

Try to set as few different bar prices as possible. Bartenders and cocktail waitresses will have a difficult time remembering all the different prices and may inadvertently charge the wrong price. The ideal pricing structure would be to have one price for each category of liquor: well items, call items and cordials and liqueurs. Beer may also be grouped into three basic price categories: domestic, imported and draft. Categorical prices may be set by averaging the high- and low-priced drinks and considering the number sold of each. The high-cost sale items will be offset by the sale of the lower-cost ones, resulting in the average cost-of-sales percentage desired.

Juice and soda prices should assimilate those set by area restaurants. These items are often compared by customers, as they are sold in all restaurants. Soda can be used as a promotional tool to attract teenagers and adults with children. Free soda with dinner and free refills are commonly used inducements. The small cost factor involved in initiating these promotions makes them a good promotional vehicle.

The "Happy Hour," a period of time when drink prices are generally reduced, can be an effective means of increasing bar sales. However, to be substantiated, it must draw a large volume of customers. "Happy Hours" are most often run prior to opening the dining room, usually between 4:00 and 6:00 p.m. Drinks are sold at half-price or at a substantial discount. Hors d'oeuvres and salty snacks, which will induce the customers' thirst, are often served.

In order to offset the enormous increase in the cost of sales due to the lower drink prices, total liquor sales must be increased substantially. A restaurant that lowers all drink prices by 50 percent during "Happy Hour" will be simultaneously doubling its cost of sales.

When analyzing the feasibility of a "Happy Hour" you must also consider the additional cost of labor during a nonoperating period; the food cost of hors d'oeuvres and other snacks; and any variable costs, such as the use of additional utilities.

The gross profit margin during any "Happy Hour" is small, though it can be substantiated with sufficient sales. An increase in revenue, small as it may be, will be created where none had previously existed.

There are other possible benefits from initiating a "Happy Hour." Lounge customers will be exposed to the restaurant and may wish to return at a later date to try the dining room. Customers may stay past the "Happy Hour" period and purchase cocktails at the full price or remain for dinner.

Employees will also benefit from a "Happy Hour" by an increase in income through increased hours and tips. This point is an important consideration, as employees may become discouraged during periods of slow or seasonal business. A "Happy Hour" that may not provide the restaurant with the desired profit may be deemed worthwhile for increasing employee morale and decreasing job turnover, eliminating the costly expenditure of rehiring and retraining new personnel.

SOME ENHANCING TOUCHES OF QUALITY

Sometimes the only element which separates successful restaurants from those that fail is in the small professional touches of excellence. These extra touches imply that a tremendous effort has been made all around to attain the highest level of quality possible. These subtle signs of concern are most important in the bar and lounge area, where the product is prepared and served in the open under the watchful and interested eyes of the customer. Professional bartenders and courteous cocktail waitresses can be found in any well-managed restaurant. However, it is the small undemanded touches and extra procedures that separate good lounges from superb ones. Described in this section are some simple, inexpensive suggestions that will give your bar and lounge the extra touches—the finesse—that will separate it from the rest.

HEATED SNIFTERS
Snifter glasses should be warmed prior to pouring brandy and certain cordials. Brandy heated in a warm glass has a stronger aroma and flavor that is preferred by most people.

To heat the brandy snifter, pour near-boiling water into the bottom third of the glass. Let it sit for two to three minutes. Before using, wipe the entire glass dry with a clean bar towel. Coffee drink glasses and mugs should also be preheated as described to maintain the coffee's temperature. You may also preheat glasses by filling them with tap water and microwaving them for 15 to 30 seconds.

FROSTED BEER MUGS
Beer mugs and glasses should be frosted prior to use. Aside from adding aesthetic value

to the beer, chilled glasses help maintain it at the proper drinking temperature.

Stock a supply of the mugs in a cooler set at 31–33° F. When the mugs are removed from the cooler, condensation will occur, leaving the frosted glass with a thin layer of ice. Mugs must be dry when placed in the cooler. Should they contain droplets from a recent washing, this excess water will freeze onto the mug. When defrosted by the warmth of the beer, this ice will melt, diluting the beer, and depriving the customer of its delicate flavor.

CHILLED COCKTAIL STRAIGHT-UP GLASSES

Chilled cocktail straight glasses must be kept ice-cold, as the cocktails themselves contain no ice. These glasses are used almost exclusively for straight-up martinis, manhattans, Gibsons and margaritas. If there is no cooler space available to keep a supply chilled, bury them stem-up in crushed ice. Glasses must be shaken dry before using.

FLAMING LIQUOR

Certain cocktails require that they be set aflame prior to serving. Extreme care must be used by employees and customers when handling these cocktails. Preheat the glass and warm the entire cocktail before attempting to ignite it. Remove a teaspoon of the cocktail and set it aflame. Pour the flaming liquid carefully back into the cocktail.

Fire regulations in your area may prohibit any open flames, such as those from candles, flaming food and flaming liquor. Contact the local Fire Department to learn of its restrictions.

FRESH FRUIT DAIQUIRIS

Fresh fruit daiquiris are incomparable in quality to daiquiris that are made from fruit-flavored liqueurs. Unfortunately, most bars prepare the latter. Aside from being a misrepresentation, substituting fruit-flavored liqueurs for real fruit is unnecessary. Fresh fruit is available in most places year-round. The small additional cost and bother is outweighed by the resulting quality of the cocktail.

Glassware is an important consideration when promoting specialty drinks. The proper glass for each cocktail is essential. The appearance and the presentation are almost as important as the drink's taste. As a final touch, use a piece of freshly cut fruit to garnish the rim.

Fresh fruit daiquiris and other specialty drinks should be promoted; these cocktails are very popular and profitable items. Be creative: develop some house specialties and give them exotic names. Employees must become enthusiastic about a promotion in order for it to become a success. Encourage them through monetary incentives to sell. Let them try the different specialty drinks; if they enjoy them they will promote them with vigor. Point out that the larger the average check, the larger the tip the employee will receive.

FLOATING CORDIALS—POUSSE CAFE

The most attractive cordial served uses a variety of liqueurs which are floating in layers, one on top of the other in the same glass. This presentation amazes customers and will bring praise to the bartender and restaurant. Although it appears complicated—if not impossible—to create, the floating cordial is actually rather simple. Liqueurs and cordials have different densities, thus enabling liqueurs with lower densities to float atop those with higher densities. The trick is to pour the liqueur carefully on top of the preceding one. This can be best accomplished by pouring each liqueur over an inverted spoon. The rounded bottom of the spoon will diffuse the liquid over the one below and no mixing will occur. Be certain that all ingredients given in the recipe are poured in the exact order listed.

CREATING THE PEACOCK EFFECT WITH NAPKINS

Undoubtedly you have seen in fancy bars the stacks of cocktail napkins displayed like the feathers of a peacock, all jutting out in a different circular direction. Although this appears to be a painstakingly difficult and time-consuming task, in actuality it is easily and quickly created. The bartender can prepare an entire night's napkins in less than five minutes.

Place a two-inch-high stack of cocktail napkins on the bar. Place a small highball glass on its side in the middle of the stack. Press down on the glass and rotate it two to three inches to the left. Move the glass around to each side until the napkins are all feathered out evenly. This is an extremely simple procedure which results in elegant-looking napkins.

RECIPES

Bloody Mary Mix Recipe

Manufactured premixed bloody mary mix can be purchased from most liquor distributors, and most restaurants do so. However, preparing your own mix can be less expensive, and you will make a substantially better bloody mary if you do.

A bartender or preparation cook can concoct a batch of bloody mary mix in 15 minutes that will last for several days. The quality of the final product will outweigh the additional amount of time and cost needed to prepare the batch. Once the recipe is formulated, type it up and give a copy to all the employees responsible for preparing it. Enter a copy into the recipe and procedure manual. This will encourage proper and consistent preparation of all batches.

Some ingredients that may be used:

- Tomato or V-8 juice
- Worcestershire sauce
- Lime or lemon juice
- Salt and pepper
- Garlic salt
- A.1. steak sauce
- Tabasco or hot sauce
- Horseradish
- Celery salt

- Celery seed
- Minced onions
- Vegetable juices
- Assorted spices
- Minced hot peppers

Experiment with different ingredients and develop your own unique recipe. Inform the cocktail waitresses and waiters that the bar is preparing its own unique mix; they can help promote it. Garnish bloody marys with a rim of celery salt, a lime or lemon wedge and a celery stalk.

Some restaurants that serve Sunday brunch have even set up a small "Bloody Mary Bar" where patrons can add their own ingredients.

Sweet-and-Sour Bar Mix
Sweet-and-sour bar mix is used in all sour drinks and some blended cocktails. This mix, too, may be purchased in a premixed form or prepared from scratch. The easiest way to develop a recipe is to start with one of the commercially prepared powders or liquids as a base and then add your own ingredients.

Some of the ingredients that may be used:

- Sugar
- Water
- Lemon juice
- Egg whites (to hold the mixture together)
- Foam additive
- Lime juice
- Bitters
- Honey
- Orange juice
- Mint flavoring

Real Whipped Cream
All coffee drinks and many blended drinks use whipped cream as a topping or garnish. Real whipped cream is simple and inexpensive to prepare. The alternative to real whipped cream is the widely used aerosol can of (usually nondairy) whipped cream. Real whipped cream is superior to the canned variety. The taste, texture and quality of the ingredients are, in my opinion, incomparable.

Though there are many recipes, real whipped cream is made primarily with sugar, vanilla and heavy or whipping cream. Real whipped cream is often used in the kitchen for topping desserts and other items. To prepare, whip these ingredients in a mixing bowl for several minutes. Care must be taken not to overwhip. Real whipped cream can also be made by whipping the ingredients in the blender at the bar.

FRESHLY SQUEEZED JUICES
A most impressive demonstration of quality is the use of freshly squeezed juices. Throughout the evening the bartender can extract fresh juice for cocktails that use the juice of oranges, grapefruits, lemons and limes. The additional cost of using fresh juices is passed on to the customer through higher drink prices.

Any of the major food-service distributors can supply a juice extractor. Advise your produce supplier of your intentions; make certain he or she can furnish the restaurant with fresh fruit year-round at an affordable price. The produce supplier should be able to get a discount on bruised or damaged fruit that, because of its appearance, cannot be sold as A-1 eating grade but may be used for juicing.

GARNISHES

Garnishes sell drinks. Garnishes are part of the entertainment of drinking. There is nothing worse than a customer seeing less-than-fresh garnishes laying in a tray from the previous night that are about to go into her drink. They look bad and cost operators money in waste. Calculate how much is needed and cut just enough.

Heads turn when customers glimpse a pair of sunglasses or plastic animals hanging off a cocktail. Try using dry ice; a triple garnish of orange, lime and lemon slices; a cluster of grapes for the glass of wine; a choice of olives, such as almond- or garlic-stuffed; a lemon twist wrapped around a coffee bean; a skewer of oversized cherries; or a pickled okra sprout. Garnishes add finesse and style and can become your trademark. Be creative: review some food-garnishing books and let your inventive chef have a crack at some ideas.

BAR TAB PROCEDURES

To allow bar tabs or not is a policy that can be debated from both sides with sound reasoning. Many restaurants have been victimized by customers who walk out and do not pay their bar tabs. A policy of no bar tabs will alleviate the initial problem, but it will certainly be inconvenient—and possibly insulting—to some customers.

A bar tab should always be run if the customer so desires. The lounge is a place where the customer may relax and enjoy a cocktail before dinner. He should not be inconvenienced by paying for each drink he orders as he goes along. Drinks should also be automatically added to the dinner bill unless the customer wishes otherwise.

A system must be established to ensure that the bar tabs get appropriated to the correct diners. There are a variety of ways to execute this; the best way depends upon the layout of the restaurant. Each bar tab should have the customer's name and table number written on the back so that misplaced tickets can be traced. Inevitability, some bar tabs will be lost, and occasionally some unprincipled customer will sneak out before paying her bill. However, this loss in revenue and extra inconvenience is far outweighed by the benefits derived from having relaxed, unhurried and completely comfortable customers.

SECTION 3 — BAR PERSONNEL

THE BARTENDER

JOB DESCRIPTION

A proficient professional bartender must be thoroughly familiar with all alcoholic beverages and know how to prepare them in a polished, efficient and relaxed manner. Aside from these traits he or she must at times borrow some of the qualities found in psychologists, policeman and members of the clergy. Bartenders must know when to converse and when to be quiet and listen. No other position in the restaurant has more control over the final product than does the bartender's. They prepare the drinks from raw materials, make the final product and often serve it themselves. No single employee carries so much financial responsibility as does the bartender.

RESPONSIBILITIES

1. Adhere to the basic procedures of personal hygiene such as neat, clean and pressed clothes, styled hair and manicured hands.

2. Always greet customers with a smile and, if possible, by name. Recognizing new customers is critical; if you are busy, acknowledge them and indicate that you will be with them in a moment. Always place a cocktail napkin in front of a customer to show that he or she has been waited on.

3. When applicable, suggest the house specialty drinks and appetizers or offer the menu for perusing.

4. Be attentive to your customers. Clean ashtrays, light cigarettes and keep the bar and stools neat and clean. Watch for empty glasses; politely ask customers if they would like another. Always ask before removing empty glasses.

5. Know how to operate the cash register correctly. You are responsible for accounting for every drink poured. Record all incorrect, manager and complimentary cocktails accurately.

6. Make sure the cocktail waitresses'/waiters' tickets are accurate and complete. Do not fill any order until the prices are entered and totaled correctly.

7. Know all the bar prices.

8. Check questionable customers' I.D.s to ensure they are of legal drinking age.

9. Communicate with coworkers throughout your shift.

10. Follow all the health and safety regulations prescribed.

11. Follow all of the restaurant regulations prescribed.

12. Control and limit waste.

13. Communicate problems and ideas to management.

14. Attend all meetings.

15. Fill out all forms as prescribed.

16. Maintain all equipment and tools.

17. Follow all rotation procedures to ensure freshness of all products.

18. Follow management's instructions and suggestions.

COCKTAIL WAITRESSES/WAITERS

JOB DESCRIPTION

The primary function of the cocktail waitresses/waiters is to serve cocktails to the customers in the lounge and dining rooms. Although this is their main responsibility they also contribute other valuable services to the restaurant.

Cocktail waitresses and waiters are usually the first service employees the customer meets, thus their approach, attitude and appearance will set a tone in the customer's mind that will last throughout the evening. This is why it is essential they be proficient, congenial and able to put customers in a relaxed mood prior to going into the dining room. These points arc all equally as important as the quality of the cocktail served.

RESPONSIBILITIES

1. Maintain a neat, clean and attractive appearance.

2. Ensure that all customers are relaxed and receptive prior to their meals.

3. Ensure that all customers are served quickly. Always greet customers with a smile and, if possible, by name. Always acknowledge new customers; if you are busy, indicate that you will be with them in a few moments. Place a cocktail napkin in front of each customer; this will indicate that the customer has been waited on.

4. When applicable, suggest the house specialty drinks and appetizers or offer the menu for perusing.

5. Know all bar prices.

6. Write tickets neatly and accurately. Fill in all prices and totals before issuing to the bartender. Make a notation to the bartender when wine is served.

7. Be attentive to your customers. Clean ashtrays and keep the tables and chairs neat and clean. Watch for empty glasses and politely suggest another drink. Always ask before removing empty glasses.

8. Ensure that all bar tabs are forwarded to the correct dinner check.

9. Always add the cost of cocktails served in the dining room onto the dinner

check. It will undoubtedly be an annoyance to the customer to stop eating in order to pay for drinks.

10. Always count out change by repeating the total ticket amount, then "count up": beginning with coins, name each denomination until you reach the amount received.

11. Assist the bartender in any way possible.

12. Check questionable customers' I.D.s to ensure that they are of legal drinking age.

13. Communicate to coworkers throughout your shift.

14. Follow all health and safety regulations prescribed.

15. Follow all restaurant regulations prescribed.

16. Control and limit waste.

17. Communicate problems and ideas to management.

18. Attend all meetings.

19. Fill out all forms as prescribed.

20. Maintain all equipment and tools.

21. Follow all rotation procedures to ensure freshness of products.

22. Follow management's instructions and suggestions.

SECTION 4 | BAR CONTROLS

Controlling liquor and its cost is a continual battle for the restaurant manager. As I mentioned earlier, liquor is one of the most commonly pilfered items in the restaurant. Every employee has access to it at some time. It's valuable, desirable and very difficult to account for. Unlike food items, liquor is not generally in exact portions, so it is difficult to determine if a small amount is missing except when using the computerized bar. However, even here I have seen some very creative ways to manipulate the machines. Only one person—the bartender—controls the portion size; no one generally checks on his pouring until it is too late. The greatest control you can establish in the bar is to employ honest, mature and concerned employees.

Described in this section is a system where every bottle is accounted for so you will be able to determine if one is missing. However, when the bartender is pouring he is controlling the cost. Every month a liquor cost of sales will be projected, but should there be a cost problem, you will not realize it until the end of the month. Management must take an active daily involvement in the bar in order for it to be a financial success. The systems outlined in this section are based upon this crucial point.

FIRST STEP: SECURITY

The first step in developing control over liquor cost is to ensure that it is received and stored properly. The manager must be present and take an active part in receiving the liquor delivery. Once verified the delivery must be placed immediately into the locking storage room. With the exception of wine, nothing but liquor should be stored in the liquor storage room. Again, the manager must be the only person (apart from the owner) with a key to the storage room; the control system described in this section is based upon this certainty. The door to the storage area must have nonremovable hinges and a sliding bolt lock.

Juices, mixers and other bar items of this nature may be stored at the bar or in the food dry storage area. They cannot be kept in the liquor storage room, as the bartender will not have access to this room. The manager should not get into the habit of lending out her keys; if an article is needed from a locked storage room, she should retrieve it or accompany the employee retrieving it

The bar itself needs to be as secure as the storage room. Every bottle must be locked up at the end of each shift. Many bars have sliding doors or removable panels that can be locked to cover the shelves of liquor. These are excellent devices, but make certain the hinges are nonremovable and on the inside. Locks and latches should be commercial grade and of tempered steel. Refrigerators and coolers usually have locks on the handles, but most of these are weak and can be jimmied with a knife blade: replace them with latches and locks.

The walk-in where the beer and kegs are stored must be separated from the food area. If you do not have the room or capital to build a separate walk-in, divide off a section for the exclusive use of the bar. Screened partitions with lockable doors can be purchased from your food-service supplier or made locally by a welder. If the beer system does not already have one, install a cut-off valve in the walk-in. This will enable the system to be shut off after each shift.

The number of bottles of liquor stored at the bar is an integral part of the control system. Each type of liquor and each brand must have only two bottles at the bar at any time: one opened bottle and one unopened bottle for backup. Unless you have an extremely busy lounge, this amount will suffice. Should the bar run out of a particular bottle, the manager will have to go to the storage room to retrieve one.

BARTENDER'S PROCEDURES

Once an open bottle is exhausted, remove the pouring spout and place the spout on the unopened backup bottle. Do not throw the empty bottle out. Store it in a box along with the others under the bar.

At the end of the shift, complete a **Liquor Used and Restocked Form**, an example of which you will find at the end of this chapter. List the exhausted bottles and the number of each under the appropriate columns. The "Restocked" column of this form will be completed by the manager. Double-check to be sure that the empty bottles correspond to the ones listed on the form. Give this form to the manager when closing out.

LIQUOR RESTOCKING

On a daily basis the manager must restock, from the storage room, all the liquor used the night before at the bar. First, compare the Liquor Used and Restocking Form completed by the bartender with the empty bottles at the bar. Each entry on the list must correspond to an empty bottle in the case. This will ensure that the bottle was actually used at the bar. After verification, the empty bottles may be thrown away or stored for the recycle center. Using the list completed by the bartender, restock the bottles needed from the storage room. Under the "Restocked" column of the form, fill in the number of bottles restocked. When the restocking is completed there should be two bottles for each type of liquor at the bar. Should there be fewer than two, either the bartender made an error or, more likely, a theft has occurred.

This system of restocking replaces every emptied bottle with a new one. Since the manager is doing the actual restocking, no bottle will ever become lost or stolen from storage. This system enables you to pinpoint areas that are cost problems. If the liquor cost-of-sales percentage is high at the end of the month, you can be certain that the bartender is responsible. He is either overpouring or not following some other procedure, which resulted in a cost increase. You can base this assumption on the fact that every bottle delivered to the bar was accounted for; only under the bartender's control did the cost problem arise.

ACCOUNTING FOR BAR SALES

There are many different ways to control or account for liquor sales. This section will outline some basic operating procedures that may be instituted in any restaurant.

Liquor sales are derived from three sources: 1) customers at the bar, which the bartender governs, 2) orders from the lounge, which are usually handled by the cocktail waitress/waiter, and 3) customers in the dining room. The control system for accounting for each liquor sale will be similar to the one used in the dining room for food items. Substitute the cocktail waiter for the waitress and the cashier, the bartender for the cook and dishwasher, and it is exactly the same setup as food sales.

Only one person—the bartender—is responsible for operating and accounting for the cash register. The manager will issue the cash drawer, bar tickets and bar keys to the bartender at the same time the cashier drawer and waitstaff tickets are issued to the cashier. The bartender's report is similar to the cashier's report. It lists all the information necessary to account for all sales received at the register and to break them down into accountable terms for the bookkeeper. The cash drawer is prepared by the bookkeeper, and cash figures must be verified by the manager and bartender at the beginning and end of each shift. An example of the **Bartender's Report** may be found at the end of this chapter. At the bottom of this form spaces for verifying and issuing the bar tickets are listed.

Liquor, wine and food sales must be kept separate when entered into the register: use a separate key for each. The sale of cigars and so forth may be recorded under the "Misc." Sales column; itemize each sale on the back of the report.

Bar tickets may be the same as those used in the dining room. They should consist of two parts, the first being the heavy paper copy on which the order and other pertinent information is written. The bottom section is the tear-away customer receipt. The second is a carbon copy of the first; this is the slip from which the bartender prepares the order. Before starting any order the bartender must make certain that the prices entered on the ticket are accurate and the bill is totaled.

Drink orders received at the bar by the bartender must be written like regular orders. The stiff paper copy of the ticket should be placed in front of the customer. Additional drinks may be written below the first one; this will ensure that all drinks are recorded on a ticket. A common ploy used by dishonest bartenders is to not write the order on a ticket at all—when the tab is paid, the bartender pockets the money. Prevent this problem by making it a mandatory procedure to record every drink served on a ticket and to place the ticket in front of the customer. A periodic swing by the bar to make sure all customers have bar-tab tickets is all that is needed to enforce this policy.

The easiest system to account for sales in the lounge is to keep a running tab of each customer at the bar. When the customer is finished, the cocktail waiter will pick up the money and the tab and give them to the bartender, who will ring the sale into the register. This system is impressively accurate; there is no possible way a sale could become lost. The disadvantage to this arrangement is that it tends to slow the bartender down, as he will spend more time at the register.

Many busy restaurants resolve this problem by giving each cocktail waiter and waitress his and her own money bank. When a customer is finished, the cocktail waiter totals the tab and makes change from the bank on his tray. This system frees the bartender but will slow down the service in the lounge. More responsibility is given to the cocktail waiter under this system, as he must now account for his own money and fill out all the necessary paperwork. Additional bookkeeping hours will be required, as each bank must be audited after every shift. Remember that the simplest system is often the best: if applicable, use the first system described above.

As I stated in the beginning of this section, the best control you can establish in the bar is to have honest, mature and concerned employees. All controls are effective to a point, but if an employee is determined to steal from you, she will. The employee with the greatest opportunity to steal and least chance of being discovered is the bartender. Many operators who have a suspected problem in the bar will hire spotters to sit at the bar and look over the bartender's procedures; if your bar control problem remains unsolved, you may find yourself forced to use this unfortunate—but highly effective—tactic.

Aside from the habitually criminal employee, most employees steal from their employers as a way to get even for some injustice. Either they are unhappy with their pay scale or feel they are being otherwise treated unfairly. They compensate themselves by stealing. The easiest way to avoid this atmosphere of deceit and mistrust is to make certain that all employees are treated equally and fairly. Grievances should be aired before bad feelings can develop. More on this topic in Chapter 13, "Successful Employee Relations and Labor Cost Controls."

Get employees on your side by involving them in monthly inventories. Let them see what your costs are and that you are very concerned with what is taking place in the bar. Monthly bonuses or other incentives for maintaining consistent cost-of-sales percentages will compel the bartenders to become involved and concerned with controlling costs.

LAYOUT OF A TYPICAL BAR

1. Bar cash registers (two)
2. Locked liquor storage cabinet
3. Liquor display
4. Base cabinet refrigerator, back bar
5. Three-compartment sinks (two)
6. Disposals (two)
7. Blenders (two)
8. Glass racks (four)
9. Ice bin
10. Glass chiller
11. Soda cabinet (under bar)
12. Planter

ITEM _____

INGREDIENTS: **PROCEDURE:**   **GLASS:**

_____   _____   _____

_____   _____   _____

_____   _____   **GARNISH:**

_____   _____   _____

_____   _____   _____

_____   _____   _____

_____   _____   _____

_____   _____   _____

_____   _____   _____

ITEM _____

INGREDIENTS: **PROCEDURE:**   **GLASS:**

_____   _____   _____

_____   _____   _____

_____   _____   **GARNISH:**

_____   _____   _____

_____   _____   _____

_____   _____   _____

_____   _____   _____

_____   _____   _____

BARTENDER'S REPORT

BARTENDER _____

MANAGER _____

BOOKKEEPER _____

BARTENDER _____

MANAGER _____

BOOKKEEPER _____

CASH IN

$100.00 _____		$1.00 _____	
$50.00 _____		$0.50 _____	
$20.00 _____		$0.25 _____	
$10.00 _____		$0.10 _____	
$5.00 _____		$0.05 _____	
$1.00 _____		$0.01 _____	

| TOTAL | | TOTAL | |

CASH OUT

$100.00 _____		$1.00 _____	
$50.00 _____		$0.50 _____	
$20.00 _____		$0.25 _____	
$10.00 _____		$0.10 _____	
$5.00 _____		$0.05 _____	
$1.00 _____		$0.01 _____	

| TOTAL | | TOTAL | |

CHARGES

1. _____
2. _____
3. _____
4. _____
5. _____
6. _____

| TOTAL | |

SALES SUMMARY

LIQUOR SALES _____

FOOD SALES _____

WINE SALES _____

MISC. SALES _____

| TOTAL | |

SALES TAX _____

VOID SALES _____

Note: Itemize checks separately on back.
Enter figure in sale and sales breakdown.

ITEM	LIQUOR	WINE
Housed	_____	_____
Manager	_____	_____
Comp	_____	_____

EMPLOYEE _____

Total # _____ #__# _____ Initial ____

Return _____ Verify _____

EMPLOYEE _____

Total # _____ #__# _____ Initial ____

Return _____ Verify _____

EMPLOYEE _____

Total # _____ #__# _____ Initial ____

Return _____ Verify _____

LIQUOR ORDER FORM

ITEM	BUILD TO AMT.	DATE										

LIQUOR INVENTORY FORM

ITEM	SIZE	QUANTITY				TOTAL	COST	EXTENSION

THE RESTAURANT MANAGER'S HANDBOOK

LIQUOR USED AND RESTOCKED FORM

LIQUOR	USED	RESTOCKED	LIQUOR	USED	RESTOCKED

9

SUCCESSFUL WINE MANAGEMENT & OPERATIONS

INTRODUCTION

Just a few years ago, many restaurants offered only two choices of wine: white or red. With the popularity of wine drinkers soaring, many restaurants now have extensive wine lists, ranging from the common to the rare. As wine's popularity continues to grow, on-premise consumption continues to expand beyond the traditional restaurants. Sales are being further increased by well-publicized and documented studies that indicate that wine can be good for one's health if consumed in moderation.

Serving wine in the restaurant may be as simplistic or as elaborate as you wish it to be. Some restaurants stock hundreds of bottles, many of rare vintages and kept in elaborate cellars. Others serve only a house wine or, even simpler, none at all. Wine, regardless of the vintage or cost, will always improve the customer's evening by enhancing the flavor of the entrees and making dinner a festive event. The purpose of this chapter is not to delve into the intricacies of wine, but to demonstrate how to develop and promote a sensible wine list. By developing such a wine list, you will not only increase your customers' enjoyment of wine, but will increase the restaurant's profits, as well. Developing the wine list is just the start, however, of a wine program; server training is imperative. Wine education is way down on the list of things that the restaurateur has the time to think about; however, wine is one of the items that could impact the restaurateur's bottom line the most significantly.

SELECTING WINES FOR THE RESTAURANT

Wines selected for the restaurant must be a logical extension of, and compliment to, the menu. Obviously, a large assortment of Spanish wines in a French restaurant would be improper. Should your menu consist of predominantly ethnic foods, select wines that represent the theme of the menu. Offer as wide a selection of wines as feasible. Wine is a very profitable product that requires little handling or preparation. The more wines listed, the greater the interest you will arouse in wine tasting. A distinction must be made between stocking a large number of wines and a large selection of wines. As with liquor and food items, the fewer you have, the easier it is to control them. Stock enough wine to represent all categories. An insufficient variety of wine is like a menu that consists of only appetizers and desserts. That is not to say you must become a wine expert in order to develop a notable wine list. Through the use of this section and your wine merchant it will be easy to write a good representative wine list which will please everyone. Described below are the basic classifications of wine; what menu items are best served with them; and the approximate number to stock in order to represent each category adequately.

	NUMBER TO STOCK
RED WINE	
Light-bodied—RED MEATS	4
Full-bodied—ALL RED MEATS, DUCK	4
Semi-sweet—DESSERT. Never before dinner, as the sweetness will spoil the customer's appetite.	4
WHITE WINE	**NUMBER TO STOCK**
Dry light-bodied—SHELLFISH, SOME SEAFOOD	2
Semi-sweet—SEAFOOD	4
Full-bodied—WHITE MEATS, SEAFOOD	4
ROSÉ	**NUMBER TO STOCK**
Dry light-bodied—Can be served in place of either dry white or red wines.	1
SPARKLING WINES	**NUMBER TO STOCK**
Dry—May be served in place of dry white wines.	1
Semi-sweet—May be served in place of semi-sweet whites.	1
CHAMPAGNE	**NUMBER TO STOCK**
Dry—WITH ANY ITEM	1
Extra-dry (Brut)—WITH ANY ITEM	1

DEFINITIONS OF WINE CLASSIFICATIONS

LIGHT—Refers to the wine's body and/or alcohol content.

BODY—Refers to the fullness of the wine—its substantiality—which is described as light, medium or full.

DRY—Refers to the lack of sweetness in the wine.

SEMI-SWEET—Refers to the underlying sweetness of a wine.

Your wine merchant or salesperson will be able to point out which wines will fit into these classifications; it is not imperative that you understand or can taste the difference between each. What is important is that each group is represented in your final list.

Wine is an interesting and fun hobby to pursue. If you are interested in learning more about it, there are a number of excellent books covering all phases of the subject.

A representative wine list must include wines of different prices and of different origins for each classification. There should be at least one moderately and one more expensively priced bottle for each classification. This allows customers who appreciate the better and more expensive bottles to do so, yet it allows the patron who may not know or care about the difference to enjoy some wine at a better price. A distinction should be made between moderately priced and cheap wines.

Although they have become increasingly popular, never use a wine that has a screw top. There is actually nothing wrong with the screw top itself, but it usually indicates a very cheap bottle of wine. Also, the serving procedure for opening wine bottles is a very important part of the total dining experience that will be lost if a screw-top bottle is used.

At least one domestic and one imported wine should be listed for each classification. Imported wines are usually the more expensive bottles. In recent years many of the notable California wines have been rivaling or exceeding the quality (and price) of the imported bottles. Wines from several different countries should be listed to give the customer the impression of a well-rounded and balanced list. Each of the wine-producing countries specializes in a particular wine variety. Your wine merchant will be able to point them out to you.

Whether choosing wine or menu items, people prefer to select what is familiar and of proven value to them. Thus some wines should be of a recognized brand, such as Almaden, Inglenook, Paul Masson, Great Western, Taylor, etc. These wineries and labels are continually promoted and advertised and are very popular because of this exposure.

In addition to offering bottled wines, most restaurants sell also a house or bulk wine, usually Chablis, Rosé and/or Burgundy. Bulk wine may be purchased very inexpensively in gallon jugs or five-gallon casks. The wine is then portioned into and served from carafes. All the major California wineries produce a bulk wine. Because the wine is produced by a well-known winery, and the price is often the lowest on the list, bulk wine tends to be a very popular item.

ORDERING WINE

The procedures for ordering wine are identical to those used in purchasing liquor. These orders may be prepared at the same time, since the liquor distributor will probably also carry most of the wines desired. As previously described for the food and liquor items, enter each wine on the Liquor Order and Liquor Inventory Forms.

The computation of the wine beginning inventory is also identical to that of liquor and food. To reiterate, the beginning inventory is the total dollar amount of the item prior to opening day. Based on this starting figure you will then be able to project monthly wine costs. The beginning inventory is covered in Chapters 4 and 5.

PRICING WINE

The procedure for accessing the selling price of wines is similar to the one used in determining bar and menu prices. The first step is to compute a total portion cost for each item. Since wine is sold in the same unit as it is purchased, the total cost is the wholesale price at which each bottle was purchased. Although there are many other costs involved in serving wine—such as labor, wine books, glasses, corkscrews, carafes, decanters, utilities and so forth—the only direct cost is the price of the bottle of wine. To compute the portion cost of bulk wine, simply multiply the cost per ounce by the portion size: glass or carafe.

A fair and customary markup for the wine is approximately 1.5–2.5 times the bottle cost or, on average, 40 percent of cost of sales. Price out each bottle using the formula.

When pricing bottles that are commonly purchased at the local liquor store or supermarket, keep in mind that many of your customers will be fully aware of their retail selling price in these establishments. The markup described may cause customers not to only resist the wine purchase but also to examine your other prices with the same doubt. Unfortunately, 99 percent of your clientele are unaware of the operating costs of a restaurant and will not be able to see the justification for such a markup. In order to avoid this stigma of being overpriced, lower the prices on these bottles and make up the difference on some others and on bulk wine, which is an excellent low-cost item.

Careful examination of market trends and conditions will enable you to purchase wine at substantial discounts. You can then pass on these discounts to your customers while still maintaining the desired profit margin.

But why, the hapless diner asks, does the 1999 California chardonnay from the liquor store cost $15; from your restaurant, $32; at ABC restaurant down the street, $38; and at a large chain, $24? Many diners assume that the price of the wine they order in restaurants has been outrageously inflated, and they're sometimes correct. One of the issues in pricing wine is that the customer knows the retail price. If the perception is that your wine pricing is too high, customers may view all of your prices in that manner.

Wine is a good profit item; it will average approximately the same cost of sales as food, but the labor and operating costs needed to present it are substantially less. This is why a good representative wine list, and a big effort on management's part to promote it, is advocated.

The "Promoting Wine Sales" section of this chapter describes some simple and inexpensive ways to effectively increase wine sales.

SERVING PROCEDURES

Wine is a delicate substance. It must be cared for and served properly in order for it to taste the way it should. Each delivery must be properly received and stored away from light, heat sources and vibrations. Wine must be stored on its side or at enough of an angle to keep the cork moist. Should the bottle be stored upright the cork will soon dry out and allow air to seep into the bottle and spoil the taste of the wine.

The most important consideration in serving wine is to make certain it is at the proper temperature. Much of the wine's flavor, bouquet and body will be lost if it is served too cold or too warm. Most people know that red wines should be served at room temperature, but this is a confusing statement. "Room temperature" in Europe is 10 to 15 degrees cooler than in North America. For clarification, the list below gives the commonly accepted serving temperatures for each wine. However, these are not steadfast rules, as taste is an individual experience, and individuals have different preferences. Always serve wine in the manner the customer wishes.

White and Rosé ....46–50° F

Red Wines ....62–68° F

Champagne and Sparkling...42–48° F
(Serve in an ice bucket with water.)

Always ask the customer when he or she would like the wine to be served or with which course. Red wines should be opened as soon as possible and placed on the table so that they may "breathe." This allows air to enter the bottle, which is supposed to release the wine's flavor and bouquet. Many experts will argue that this step is unnecessary because of the minimal amount of air actually exposed to the wine at the neck of the bottle. Whether or not it is effective, it should always be done for appearance's sake. White wines and champagnes may need to be cooled prior to serving, so take the wine order as soon as possible.

STEPS IN THE PROPER WINE SERVICE

1. Always place a napkin behind the bottle.

2. Display the bottle to the person who ordered it (usually the host). Give him plenty of time to examine the label: he will want to make sure it is the wine and vintage desired.

3. The wine opener used should be the waitperson's folding pocketknife with the open spiral corkscrew and smooth edges.

4. With the knife blade, remove the capsule and foil.

5. Clean the neck and bottle with the napkin.

6. Hold the bottle firmly, and slowly insert the corkscrew into the center of the cork. Stop about two-thirds of the way through the cork. Don't go all the way, as this may result in putting a few pieces of the cork into the wine.

7. With the bottle on the table, pull straight up steadily. Do not jerk out the cork.

8. After opening, check the cork for dryness, and place it end up on the table so that the host may examine it.

9. When the host is satisfied, pour about an ounce into his glass. He must approve of the wine before the other people in the party are served.

   The customer has the prerogative to reject a bottle of wine at any stage of the service. However, once the bottle is opened, his reasoning for rejection must be due to there being something wrong with the wine itself, not because he doesn't like it. If a bottle is rejected, it should be removed from the table and brought to the kitchen where the manager may examine it and act accordingly. Some distributors may issue a credit for damaged bottles, however there is usually no obligation to do so, particularly with older, more expensive bottles.

10. It is customary to pour all the women's glasses first and the host's last. When you are finished pouring a glass, give the bottle a slight twist: this will prevent any dripping. Always pour wine with the label facing you.

OPENING SPARKLING WINE AND CHAMPAGNE

1. Always use a napkin behind the bottle to stop drips, and although it rarely happens, it is possible that the bottle may split from the internal pressure.

2. Remove the foil and wire muzzle.

3. Remove the cork by turning the bottle, NOT the cork. Always point the bottle away from people. The cork should be removed slowly and carefully, it should never explode open with a gush of champagne.

4. Special champagne glasses may be used, however it is perfectly acceptable to serve champagne in tulip-shaped wineglasses.

5. A stuck cork may be removed by placing the neck of the bottle under a stream of hot water for a few seconds. The heat will build up pressure on the inside of the bottle making it easier to extract the cork.

WINE-BY-THE-GLASS PROGRAM

Selling wine by the glass can be an important marketing tool for a restaurant. These days, people who order wine by the glass are likely to be fairly regular wine drinkers and may make a special effort to dine at your restaurant because of your program. A savvy restaurant owner knows that a strong wine-by-the-glass program attracts customers who are willing to spend more for wine. Wine profits can more than double—with profit margins as high as 300 percent, premium wine by-the-glass can be as profitable as specialty drinks!

Some restaurants offer a wine-by-the-glass suggestion for certain appetizers and for each and every entree. Don't rely on the waitstaff to recite the wine-by-the-glass list. Use an attractive table tent or smaller menu design; use notes or individual signs on the dinner menus; and print the list on a blackboard or sign that can be read from several areas of the dining room and bar. Restaurateurs are discovering that they sell more champagne when it's listed as one of the by-the-glass selections, or when the server specifically suggests a glass as a starter. Few people will order a whole bottle, but a lot of guests will start with a glass.

How many wines by-the-glass should your restaurant pour? Depending upon your client base and your beverage-marketing program, you might have as few as 3 wines or as many as 15 or 20. Few operators pour more than 20 wines by-the-glass because of potential losses from wine spoilage. Yet the average number of by-the-glass offerings in restaurants has grown steadily. Many restaurants now pour at least 30 percent more wine than they did five years ago, and their sales have benefited to a great extent. There are various wine-by-the-glass dispensing systems available today that can assist with your wine by-the-glass program. These systems will keep wine as fresh as the moment they were uncorked for up to six weeks, eliminating spoilage and waste. They are all temperature-controlled and use a nitrogen gas replacement system. The nitrogen gas instantly replaces the oxygen in a freshly opened bottle of wine with pure, odorless, tasteless nitrogen gas, thereby stopping the oxidation process that damages wine. There are a variety of manufacturers that now make these systems.

HALF BOTTLES

Half bottles add more options for wine-by-the-glass offerings without waste from full bottles. They're handy for solo diners and couples. There is demand from a niche of customers for half bottles, especially from those who want a specific vintage, freshness and/or ritual without waste. Storage requires creativity, since most cellars are designed for 750-ml bottles. One good way to store them is to remove the case's carton top and turn the box on its side to use it as a bin.

DECANTING

Older wines (aged for more than ten years) should be decanted prior to serving. Decanting means pouring the wine into another container—a decanter or carafe—leaving the sediment behind.

1.   Place a candle on the table alongside the bottle and decanter.

2.   As you pour, watch through the lit bottle for sediment to appear in the neck; when it does, stop pouring. The remainder of the wine may be discarded or strained through cheese cloth in the kitchen.

GLASSWARE

Choosing the wine glass is an important consideration. The wineglass you use will have an apparent effect upon the taste of the wine. Should you doubt this, compare the same wine in a fine crystal glass and then again in a cheap glass; you should notice a difference. This is not to say you should use crystal wine glasses, but purchase the best ones affordable.

Many restaurants use a separate glass for reds, whites and champagnes. This is generally unnecessary. A 10-ounce tulip-shaped glass would be quite suitable for any wine. However, it is a nice touch to have separate champagne glasses.

Don't buy glasses you can't afford to break. Buy simple, clear glasses that are not cut, faceted, etched or colored. You want to be able to see the wine; part of its beauty is how it looks in the glass. Choose glasses with generous bowls. One way of maximizing a wine's flavor is by swirling it in the glass to aerate it; if the glass is too small you cannot. Opt for a thin rim because the wine will flow more easily and evenly over a thin rim than a thick, heavy, rolled one. Be sure the rim of the glass tapers slightly inward. A tapered rim allows the wine's aroma to rise up so you can smell and taste the wine better. Avoid small-footed glasses. The foot, or base, of the glass should be wide enough to keep the glass from tottering when it's filled with wine. There are few things worse for the restaurateur to hear in a restaurant than the sound of breaking wine glasses.

PROMOTING WINE SALES

As stated previously, wine is a very profitable item that requires little preparation, little handling and little additional cost to present. Thus, the sale of wine should be energetically promoted. Described in this section are some simple, inexpensive and yet very effective, ways to increase wine sales—and the restaurants bottom line.

A wine list is a great advertisement for wine. It should be professionally prepared, laid out and printed. There are special wine books that may be purchased to house the wine list. They are impressive to look at and practical. The bindings are of loose-leaf style so that they may be updated as needed. A good wine book lists the price and, if possible, exhibits the label. Labels are available from your distributor or directly from the winery. Just write a brief note on your restaurant's stationery requesting some for a wine list. Wine lists may be a part of the table setting, which will almost guarantee that they will be looked at. Unfortunately, they are also collector's items that many customers admire. You can alleviate this problem by giving each member of the waitstaff one list that can be brought around to each table at the appropriate time. This will also tend to remind the waitperson to suggest a bottle of wine to his or her customers.

Wineglasses should be set on every table, as they are an inducement to order a bottle of wine. Sometimes just suggesting a bottle will get the customer interested when he or she wouldn't have thought of it. The glasses should be removed if no wine is ordered. Whenever touching a wineglass remember to hold it by the stem, otherwise you will leave fingerprints and smudges on it.

Some restaurateurs suggestively set their tables with a bottle of wine and a small tent card to explain the wine and list the price.

The waitstaff must be thoroughly trained and knowledgeable about the wine list. They should know which wines may be served with which foods and the correct procedures for presenting and opening the bottle. Invest in some cheap bottles so that each waitperson may practice opening one. Your wine merchant or wine salesperson will often be glad to set up a meeting in the restaurant with your staff. These people are very knowledgeable about wine and can be great aids in training employees. Remember, it is in their own best interest for you to sell more wine. Once your waitstaff learns how to correctly pronounce each wine and serve it, they will know more than 75 percent of customers do.

Get your employees interested in wine. The best way to accomplish this is to have a wine tasting where they all can try the different types. The cost of this event will be easily substantiated by the increase in wine sales and employee morale. Often your wine merchant will be interested in subsidizing one of these events.

Show your waitstaff that it is in their own best interest to sell more wine. The larger the dinner checks, the larger the tips they will receive. Set up a wine contest: the waitstaff member who sells the most wine in a month might receive some sort of bonus—perhaps a bottle of very expensive wine. If two or more guests are considering wine by the glass, that's a server's cue to suggest sharing a bottle. Upgrading the order saves time. Don't forget the final time to suggest and sell wine: at the end of the meal. Ports, for example, complement desserts. Champagnes and sparkling wines go well with fresh fruit; cabernet, with chocolate.

Many of the more elegant restaurants have wine sommeliers or stewards. These individuals are experts on wine. Their only job is to help the customer with a wine selection and then to open and serve the bottle of wine. They are often paid a small salary and either a percentage of the wine sales or a percentage of each waitperson's tip. This is a very effective way to sell wine, but your restaurant must have the proper atmosphere and clientele in order for it to work.

CONTROLLING WINE

Wine is easy to control and account for, as each bottle purchased is also the serving and portion size. All of the procedures for receiving liquor also apply to wine. The manager must be present when a delivery is received to ensure it is accurate and accounted for. Wine may be stored in the same room as liquor if the physical conditions are suitable. Regardless of where it is stored, it must be put away immediately after delivery and locked securely. The manager must be the only person with the key to the storage area.

Wine should be issued by the bartender and restocked by the manager. Chilled wines may be stored in a cooler set at the proper temperature. Reds may be stored in a locked cabinet under the bar. Each serving area should be stocked with three of each type of white chilled wine and two types of each red. This will be more than sufficient for most restaurants.

When an order for wine is taken, the waiter goes to the bar and requests the bottle from the bartender. The bartender retrieves the bottle while the waiter fills out the ticket (which may be the same kind as used in the bar). The ticket should contain the following information: date, wine's name, table number and the waitperson's name. The bartender must check to make sure the information and price are correct before issuing the wine. The hard paper part of the ticket remains with the bartender, and will be used to verify the issuance. The carbon copy is attached to the customer's bill to ensure that the wine will be charged for. If for some reason the waitperson does not enter the amount on the customer's check, there will be a record of the bottle ordered from the bar.

The cashier will total the bill, ensuring that the price entered is correct. At the end of his or her shift the bartender will deposit the ticket receipts, with the Liquor Breakage Form, in a place designated by the manager.

The following morning the bookkeeper will prepare and present to the manager an itemized list of the bottles sold and verified by the cashier. (Details of these procedures will be outlined in Chapter 16, "Internal Bookkeeping".) This list must match the receipts left by the bartender.

As the liquor is being restocked the manager should also restock the wine used. After restocking is completed there must be three chilled whites and two reds for every type.

Should this count not reconcile, recheck the itemization and the bartender's receipts. If everything reconciles, consider the possibility of theft.

Bulk wine may be issued by the gallon and portioned into carafes. The bartender will list the number of carafes prepared at the beginning of the shift and the number left at the end. This information may be recorded on the Liquor Used and Restocked Form, an example of which may be found at the end of Chapter 8. The carafes may then be treated as though they were full bottles.

WINE INVENTORY FORM

ITEM	SIZE	QUANTITY				TOTAL	COST	EXTENSION

WINE ORDER FORM

ITEM	BUILD TO AMT.	DATE									

❦

SUCCESSFUL MANAGEMENT OF OPERATIONAL COSTS & SUPPLIES

INTRODUCTION

The preceding chapters have described in detail only the costs that pertain directly to the product being sold. In computing the cost of menu items, only food costs were analyzed. When projecting the average cost of each cocktail, only the cost of the liquor poured and the miscellaneous expense was considered. The total wine cost was the wholesale price at which the bottle was purchased. Obviously, there are many other costs involved in presenting food, liquor and wine products to the public. These additional costs are called operational costs. Operational costs are all of the non-food, non-liquor and non wine supplies that are used in preparing these items.

Labor and the cost of equipment are not considered direct operational expenses under this scenario. Labor is computed as a separate cost. Equipment is a capital expenditure and may be depreciated over several years. The operational supplies and costs considered here are only those products that must be continuously renewed each month as they are used up, lost or broken.

Operational supplies and cost are divided into separate categories so that each may be broken down and analyzed. As with food, liquor and wine, a cost for each operational category will be projected at the end of each month. Setting up each category accurately is crucial, as this information will be used later on in projecting budgets and profit and loss statements.

OPERATIONAL CATEGORIES

The following pages list each operational category and some examples of the type of supplies that belong to each. Based on the examples given, list on the **Operational Order Form** and the **Operational Inventory Form** all of the operational supplies the restaurant will need. An example of each form can be found at the end of this chapter. Separate each page by category and clearly label it in the space provided on the form. Always keep the order and inventory forms up to date. Whenever a new product is ordered, enter the new item on both forms. When it comes time to do the weekly order and monthly inventory you will not miss or forget anything, as all the items will be listed. Certain items may fit into two categories because they are used in several areas of the restaurant. Place the item in the category where it is used the most. This will not affect the cost projection as long as the item is listed in only one category.

CHINA AND UTENSILS

All plates, coffee cups, saucers, silverware, etc.

GLASSWARE

All bar glasses, wineglasses, water glasses, carafes, decanters, etc.

KITCHEN SUPPLIES

All of the non-food materials used in preparing food items, such as: kitchen utensils, spatulas, scales, trays, measuring cups, skewers, foil, plastic wrap, fry-o-lator filter paper, etc.

BAR SUPPLIES

All of the miscellaneous supplies used at the bar, such as: mixing spoons, straws, swords, napkins, pour spouts, corkscrews, etc.

DINING ROOM SUPPLIES

All of the miscellaneous supplies used in the dining room, such as: candles, matches, menus, salt and pepper shakers, sugar bowls, tent-card holders, coffeepots, creamers, flower vases, etc.

CLEANING SUPPLIES

All of the miscellaneous cleaning supplies used by both the staff and the maintenance company, such as: soap, paper towels, chemicals, vacuum bags, garbage bags, etc.

OFFICE SUPPLIES

All of the supplies used in the offices, such as: tape, rubber bands, paper, stationery, etc.

UNIFORMS

Encompasses the cost of purchasing employee uniforms, such as: aprons, smocks, hats, pants, dresses, etc.

LAUNDRY AND LINEN

Covers all napkins, tablecloths, kitchen towels, bar towels and soap purchased by the restaurant from a laundry service or for an in-house system. Does not include the cost of services of a laundry company, as this is computed separately.

ORDERING OPERATIONAL SUPPLIES

All of the procedures for storing, ordering and receiving food, liquor and wine also apply to operational supplies. Ordering operational supplies must be carefully thought out. Too large of an inventory (back-stock) will tie up capital at expensive interest rates. However, one careless bus person or waiter who drops a tray of glasses can destroy what little reserve you have, so there must be a large enough inventory to cover the unexpected. One to two cases of each item in the storeroom should suffice. Portion control items such as scales, scoops and ladles are often difficult to obtain; when you find a supplier that has the size and type you desire, order several and keep them in reserve. A common, but poor, excuse for not portion-controlling products is that the employee does not have access to the right type of utensil. Management's responsibility is to provide the employees with proper tools so they can do their jobs.

Allow a lead time of several weeks when ordering china. Your distributor probably doesn't stock all the different types of china and must purchase specially from the manufacturer. Insufficient quantities of place settings will result in extra work, slow service and, hence, a slow turnover in the dining room. Always maintain an adequate supply of stock out of, as well as in, the storeroom. The storeroom should be a separate room or closet, and as mentioned before, the manager must be the only person who has the key. Don't create a situation where it is easier for an employee to run to the storeroom for a new case of water glasses than to help the dishwasher catch up.

BEGINNING INVENTORY

Computing this figure is similar to computing the beginning amount for food, liquor and wine. However, there is one difference. The beginning inventory amount for each operational category is the dollar amount that is in storage when the restaurant is totally set up. This means that all the tables are set and there is plenty of stock in the kitchen and bar. The reason for this is that operational supplies are projected for each month. When you first open, the cost of setting up the restaurant is considered a one-time start-up cost. Operational costs are thus a measure of how well you controlled these costs following start-up. Separating this start-up cost may have some additional tax advantages. Your accountant will be able to advise you on this possibility.

OPERATIONAL ORDER FORM

ITEM	BUILD TO AMT.	DATE											

OPERATIONAL INVENTORY FORM

ITEM	SIZE	QUANTITY				TOTAL	COST	EXTENSION

11

COMPUTERS & YOUR FOOD-SERVICE OPERATION—HOW TO USE THEM & PROFIT FROM THEM

INTRODUCTION

Computers are here, and integrated into every facet of the food-service industry. The main use of computers in the food-service industry can be summarized as a key system that will help operations track sales and purchases, keep track of inventory, compare prices, maintain ledger and payroll, develop menus and minimize food waste.

According to a study commissioned by 13 U.S. and Canadian food-related associations, implementation of an efficient computer-based food-service response program could trim an estimated $14.3 billion in costs annually from the food-service industry in the two countries alone.

The resulting program, Efficient Foodservice Response creates a paperless kitchen, linking buyers to distributors via the Internet. Food and supplies are ordered on-line and paid for by electronic transfer. Participating vendors tag goods with bar codes that are read by laser scanner. At the food-service operation, information is immediately stored in an in-house computer, and the computer's inventory database is instantly updated.

Benefits are across the board: precise inventory management, timely deliveries, reduced warehouse levels and increased kitchen work space.

Let's take a closer look at how computer hardware and software will serve and benefit the food-service industry, and glance at what options and features you might have.

WHAT IS A PC?

The official definition of "PC" from *http://www.pcwebopedia.com:*
1. Short for personal computer or IBM PC. The first personal computer produced by IBM was called the PC, and increasingly the term PC came to mean IBM or IBM-compatible personal computers, to the exclusion of other types of personal computers, such as Macintoshes.

In recent years, the term PC has become more and more difficult to pin down. In general it applies to any personal computer based on an Intel microprocessor or on an Intel-compatible microprocessor. For nearly every other component, including the operating system, there are several options, all of which fall under the rubric "PC".

Common questions are: What kind of computer should I get? How much RAM? How fast should the CPU be? Should I get Pentium or Athlon? What brand and what size monitor? What type of video card? Should I get a dial-up connection, DSL or cable modem? What are the best accounting packages for the computer?

These are difficult questions, and today's answer will be out of date in six months. The best advice on what type of computer system to purchase for your restaurant is, simply, to get the most powerful computer system within your budget. Here are some considerations:

- **CPU speed.** The CPU is the engine of your computer. In general, the faster the engine, the greater its performance. I recommend a processor built for future growth capacity. Therefore, the fastest in your budget is recommended.

- **RAM.** RAM is the temporary storage place for all information on your computer. The fastest RAM is the best to get, and I recommend nothing less than 128 Megabytes (MB) on each computer; at least 256 MB RAM per workstation is preferable.

- **Operating system.** I recommend Microsoft Windows XP Professional Edition or Microsoft Windows 2000. These systems provide stable operating platforms and superior networking capabilities.

- **Monitor.** I recommend 17" or bigger. (19" is my preferred standard.) You have lots of choices in brands, as well as flatscreen and LCD-screen varieties. I prefer 19" flatscreen or 17"-or-larger LCD monitors.

- **Graphics card.** For business applications I recommend a graphics accelerator card with a minimum of 32 MB of RAM. There are dozens to choose from depending on the application, with chipsets from various manufacturers. My favorite for its great business and gaming performance is any card based on the Geforce Chipset.

- **Athlon vs. Pentium.** Both are world-class processors. There are die-hard fans of each.

- **Dial-up, DSL or cable.** If you need high-speed connections, you want DSL or cable (if they are available in your area). Dial-up is the least costly but slowest type of connection. For the average Web browser, dial-up is usually sufficient. For power users, I recommend DSL or cable. Note: If you use a broadband connection, invest in a DSL/cable router or a good firewall software application.

- **Networking.** If you have more than one computer you will want to network your computers. This will allow you to share programs, files, printers, Internet connections and more. There are dozens of networking systems available, including standard wired networking, phone-line networks and wireless networks. There are advantages to each:

- **Standard wired networking** is the fastest, but requires extensive cable installation in your building.

- **Phone-line networks** offer good performance, low cost and use the existing phone lines in your restaurant to make network connections. Note: You can still talk on your phone while your network is being used.

- **Wireless networking** is the most costly, but it's highly versatile, requires no cable installation and is very effective. One major advantage of wireless is you are not limited by phone lines or network cable. You can take your wireless laptop anywhere in your restaurant and maintain your network connection.

- **Platform.** This is essentially Windows vs. Macintosh. A few years ago DOS-based systems would have been in the mix, also, but those software applications are antiquated by current industry standards. The choice is yours to make. Obviously, your hardware preference will select your software platform. In my opinion the Windows-based operating systems and Windows' overall available software packages and long-term industry support make Windows-based platforms the best choice.

FRONT-OF-THE-HOUSE COMPUTER SYSTEMS

POINT-OF-SALE SYSTEMS

The most widely used technology in the food-service industry is the touch-screen, or POS (point-of-sale), system. The POS system is basically an offshoot of the electronic cash register. touch screen POS systems were introduced to the food-service industry in the mid-1980s and have penetrated 90 percent of restaurants nationwide. From fine-dining establishments to fast-food, the touch screen is effortless. In fact, a child could be trained to use it in a few minutes. Such systems will pay for themselves. According to information published by the National Restaurant Association, a restaurant averaging $1,000,000 in food-and-beverage sales can expect to see an estimated savings of $30,000 per year. Understanding the numbers collected by a POS system will give the operator more control over inventory, bar revenues, labor scheduling, overtime, customer traffic and service. Understanding POS ultimately clarifies the bottom line, knocking guesswork out of the equation.

A point-of-sale system is comprised of two parts: the hardware, or equipment, and the software—the computer program that runs the system. This system allows waitstaff to key in their orders as soon as the customers give them. Additional keys are available for particular options and specifications, such as "rare," "medium-rare" and "well-done." Some systems prompt the waitstaff to ask additional questions when the item is ordered, such as, "Would you like butter, sour cream or chives with the baked potato?" Some will suggest a side dish or a compatible wine.

The order is sent through a cable to printers located throughout the restaurant: at the bar and in the kitchen and office. All orders must be printed before they are prepared, thus ensuring good control. When a server has completed the ordering, a guest check can be printed and later presented. Most POS systems allow certain discounts and require manager control over others. Charge cards, cash and checks can be processed separately, and then reports can be generated by payment type.

Some benefits of using a POS system:

- Increases sales and accounting information.

- Custom tracking.

- Reports waitstaff's sales and performance.

- Reports menu-item performance.

- Reports inventory usage.

- Credit-card purchases.

- Accurate addition on guest checks.

- Prevents incorrect items from being ordered.

- Prevents confusion in the kitchen.

- Reports possible theft of money and inventory.

- Records employee timekeeping.

- Reports menu-sales breakdown for preparation and menu forecasting.

- Reduces time spent walking to kitchen and bar.

As the labor market continues to diminish, touch screens with POS systems will become necessary. It has been predicted that in the next few years customers may even place their own orders. Terminals will be simply turned around. During peak seasonal periods, ordering food may be like pumping your own gas; customers will key in their own selections, then slide their credit cards through to pay.

Many POS systems have been greatly enhanced to include comprehensive home delivery, guest books, on-line reservations, frequent-diner modules and fully integrated systems with real-time inventory, integrated caller ID, accounting, labor scheduling, payroll, menu analysis, purchasing and receiving, cash management and reports. Up-and-coming enhancements and add-ons include improved functionality across the Internet, centralized functionality enabling "alerts" to be issued to managers and voice-recognition POS technology.

STAND-ALONE SOFTWARE APPLICATIONS

While there are literally dozens of software packages available to assist the restaurant manager, this discussion will concentrate on what I consider to be the current market leaders. It will provide some insight as to how they work, what they can do for your restaurant, and what benefits you will realize if you include them in your restaurant-management practices. These systems are what we refer to as "stand alone," as they are not part of a POS system:

CHEFTEC

ChefTec is an integrated software program with recipe and menu costing, inventory control and nutritional analysis.

- **Recipe and menu costing.** Store, scale and size an unlimited number of recipes. Write recipe procedures with culinary spell-checker. Instantly analyze recipe and menu costs by portion or yield. Update prices and change ingredients in every recipe with the touch of a button. Cost out bids for catering functions. Attach photos, diagrams and videos to bids, or add pictures of plate layout to recipes for consistency.

- **Nutritional analysis.** Preloaded with USDA information. Add your own items. Calculate nutritional value for recipes and menus. Provide accurate, legal information on "low-fat", "low-salt," etc. Print out "Nutrition Facts" labels. The nutritional-analysis module will get a quick and accurate analysis of nutritional values for up to 5,000 most-commonly-used ingredients. Allows you to add your own specialty items. Calculate nutritional values for your recipes and menu items. See at a glance which menu items are low-fat, low-calorie, etc.

- **Inventory control.** Preloaded inventory list of 1,900 commonly used ingredients with unlimited capacity for adding additional ingredients. Import purchases from on-line vendors' ordering systems. Track fluctuating food costs. Compare vendor pricing. See impact of price increases on recipes. Automate ordering with par values. Use handheld devices for inventory. Generate custom reports. The inventory control module allows you to track rising food costs automatically. Compare vendor pricing at the touch of a button, from purchases or bids. Enter invoices quickly using the "Auto-Populate" feature. Generate customized reports on purchases, price variances, bids and credits, physical inventory, and ordering and maintenance of par levels. Lists ingredients in different languages (Spanish, French, German and others).

ChefTec PDA is also available. ChefTec is available from Atlantic Publishing Company (*http://www.atlantic-pub.com* or 800-541-1336): Item CTC-CS.

NUTRACOSTER

NutraCoster calculates the product cost (including labor, packaging and overhead) and nutritional content for any size batch of food. Ingredient database with nutritional information for approximately 6,000 ingredients (USDA Handbook 8). Include unlimited number of ingredients and process stats. Print camera-ready "Nutrition Facts" labels that comply with the requirements of the Nutrition Labeling and Education Act (NLEA). The "Overhead Calculator" allows you to factor overhead costs into your product cost. No more "rules of thumb" or "fudge factors." Nutritional analysis now accounts for nutrient changes during processing, such as water lost during baking, water gained during boiling, fat lost during broiling, fat gained during frying, or other changes in nutritional value. Print multiple "Nutrition Facts" labels per page. Include ingredient listings with Nutrition Facts. Supports unlimited simultaneous users.

NutraCoster also offers additional libraries with nutritional information for specific brand-name ingredients. NutraCoster is available from Atlantic Publishing Company (*http://www.atlantic-pub.com* or 800-541-1336: Item NUT-CS.

MENUPRO

MenuPro allows you to quickly create your own professional menus at a fraction of the cost of print-shop menus. Whether you need "Daily Specials" or an elaborate dining room menu, MenuPro gives you quick, top-quality designs and artwork without the expense or hassle of using a graphic artist or desktop publisher. MenuPro is available from Atlantic Publishing Company (*http://www.atlantic-pub.com* or 800-541-1336): Item MNP-CS.

EMPLOYEE SCHEDULE PARTNER

Employee Schedule Partner is a complete software package for employee scheduling. Point and click: make a schedule without touching the keyboard. Click a button and the software will fill your schedule with employees automatically. Click a button to replace absent employees, and a list of available employees with phone numbers will appear. The on-line coach will give helpful hints to new users. Accommodates an unlimited number of employees and positions. You can manually override selections at any time and track employees' availability restrictions. Schedule employees to work multiple shifts per day. Track payroll and hourly schedule totals for easy budget management. Schedules can begin on any day of the week. Track stations as well as positions. Specify maximum hours per day, days per week and shifts per day for each employee. Lock any employee into a scheduled shift so the program will not move them when juggling the schedule. Save old schedules for reference when needed.

The software is even password protected to prevent unauthorized use. Employee Schedule Partner is available from Atlantic Publishing Company (800-541-1336 or *http://www.atlantic-pub.com*): Item ESP-CS.

EMPLOYEE TIME CLOCK PARTNER

Our hands-down favorite time clock software is Employee Time Clock. This is a complete employee time clock software package. It is very powerful yet simple to use. Automatically clock in and out (just enter your employee number. Employees can view their time cards to verify information. Password protected so only management may edit time card information. Even calculates overtime both daily and weekly. Management can assign Employee ID number or PIN (personal identification number). Employee Time Clock Partner is available from Atlantic Publishing Company (*http://www.atlantic-pub.com* or 800-541-1336): Item # ETC-CS.

ONLINE RESERVATION SYSTEMS

An online reservation system can be incredibly simple or advanced and complex. Would you believe that a fully functional on-line reservation system can be free? It is true. All you need is an active Web site and a reservation form. Your site visitor fills out the form requesting a reservation. You set up an auto-responder to respond to the site visitor stating that she will be confirmed within a reasonable amount of time, say two hours. You receive the reservation request by e-mail, confirm that you can accommodate the request and then reply back to the person by e-mail or phone. Total cost: zero. Customer satisfaction: superior. That is the basic, no cost approach. There are dozens of reputable software packages and companies that can provide your online reservation system. These FRS (Foodline Reservations Systems) enable you to do the following:

- Accept reservations anytime—day or night.

- Track guests' preferences in order to provide enhanced customer service.

- Use the power of direct marketing to build guest traffic and offer premium services to your most frequent customers.

- Check reservation status from any Internet-connected computer.

- Network all computers and reservation systems in a restaurant group.

- Choose to manage all of your reservations or to put just a few of your tables online.

A search through Google.com will yield dozens of software packages and consultants who can assist you find the right one for your on-line reservation system.

QUICKBOOKS

My favorite accounting package, without a doubt, is the veteran QuickBooks by Intuit. The QuickBooks's 2002 version is rich in features, including built-in remote-access capabilities and Web interfaces. QuickBooks is available at *http://www.quickbooks.com*. Another popular account package is Peachtree, available at *http://www.peachtree.com*.

DESKTOP PUBLISHING APPLICATIONS AND IDEAS

There are hundreds of reasons to own and utilize a computer in your work as a food-service manager. The computer, if utilized effectively, will save you enormous amount of time and money.

Desktop publishing applications will allow you to print your own customer and/or employee newsletters, table tents, menus, business cards, employee-of-the-month certificates, customer gift certificates, advertising posters, employee manuals, wine lists, catering and banquet menus, office stationery and newsletters.

THE FUTURE OF COMPUTERS IN FOOD SERVICE

The food-service operation of the future will most likely resemble what it does today—with integrated software and hardware solutions to increase productivity, eliminate waste and increase profits!

The point-of-sale computer that will allow operators to more closely monitor inventory and costs. Web-site reservations, marketing and e-commerce will increase the return on investment in a Web presence, bringing in more guests than ever imaginable. Diners may enter their own menu selections into laptop POS systems right from their tables. Patrons will be able to pull up a screen showing all menu items, then select dishes with a push of a button. Consumers will also be able to customize meals and beverages—single malt scotch or blended, margarine or butter, salted or unsalted, medium-rare or well-done, spicy or mild. Ultimately, the restaurant will be a paperless operation.

THE EFFECTIVE USE OF E-MAIL

E-mail, short for electronic mail, is a system that enables a computer user to exchange messages with other computer users within a communications network (Internet). To use e-mail, you must have access to a computer that is linked to the Internet via a modem and phone line, cable modem, DSL connection or other network connection. E-mail services are typically provided at no cost from your Internet service provider, and they come with any domain names you purchase for Web sites. Careful consideration should be given to your choice of domain names and/or e-mail addresses, as these represent your company. For example, The Silvermine Tavern, a New England country inn and restaurant in Norwalk, Connecticut, purchased the domain name http://www.silverminetavern.com. Purchasing a domain name that directly represents your restaurant is an outstanding opportunity to gain the use of the corresponding e-mail addresses. In the case of The SilvermineTavern, innkeeper@silverminetavern.com is one of their primary e-mail addresses. This clearly states to the casual observer that any e-mail sent to this address will be directed to the innkeeper of The Silvermine Tavern. We will discuss Web sites and why a Web site is critical to every restaurant later in this chapter.

WHY TO USE E-MAIL INSTEAD OF THE POST OFFICE OR THE TELEPHONE

There are two reasons:

- **Convenience.** One advantage of using e-mail that you send your message when it's convenient for you, even if that's four o'clock in the morning. Your recipient responds at his convenience as well.

- **Cost.** No more toll telephone calls! No more "telephone tag"! You can send dozens of e-mails throughout the world, simultaneously; they will be delivered in mere seconds; and it costs NOTHING. Communicate with all your purveyors or employees with one written message, for free.

Sending e-mail is similar to sending mail through the U.S. Postal Service, but there are several important differences:

1. E-mail is faster
2. E-mail is free.
3. E-mail is simple to use.
4. E-mail requires you to use a password and is private. (Note: We highly recommend utilizing a virus-scanning program for all incoming and outgoing e-mails)
5. E-mail is very fast, very permanent, and very unforgiving. In other words, make sure you said what you wanted to say BEFORE you hit the send button. Once sent, it is too late to get it back.
6. E-mail can be sent to many people at the same time.
7. E-mail often contains typos and misspellings because it is so easy to produce and send. (Most e-mail programs contain a spell-checker—use it!)

To receive e-mail, as with postal letters, you must have an address (sales@atlantic-pub.com, for example).

PROPER E-MAIL ETIQUETTE

1. **Avoid flaming.** A flame is a nasty, personal attack on somebody for something he or she has written, said or done.
2. **Be unambiguous.** If you are responding to a message, include only the relevant

part of the original message. Make sure you clearly refer to the original message's contents. Always include a descriptive subject line for your message. If responding, your subject line should be the same as the original's, preceded by "RE:".

3. **Write clearly and carefully.** Your words may come back to haunt you. Read carefully what you receive to make sure that you are not misunderstanding the message. Read carefully what you send, to make sure that your message will not be misunderstood. **Avoid cluttering your messages with excessive emphasis.** DO NOT USE ALL CAPS.

COMMON E-MAIL MISTAKES

- Typing the message in the subject line instead of in the body of the message.

- Forgetting that what you write, thinking it's funny or harmless, can be misinterpreted at the other end.

- Not signing off before leaving the computer (allowing others to send e-mail from your e-mail address).

- Not checking e-mail often, thus missing something important.

- Forgetting your password.

- Sending a message to the wrong e-mail address.

THE INTERNET AND THE WORLD WIDE WEB

The Internet is a global network of networks enabling computers of all kinds to directly and transparently communicate and share services throughout much of the world. Because the Internet is an enormously valuable, enabling capability for so many people and organizations, it also constitutes a shared global resource of information and knowledge and a means of collaboration and cooperation among countless diverse communities.

The Internet is a worldwide system of computer networks—a network of networks by which users at any one computer can get information from any other computer, talk to other computer users, share information, buy products and services and advertise products and services for sale. The Internet was originally conceived by the Advanced Research Projects Agency (ARPA) of the U.S. government in 1969 and was first known as the ARPANET. The original aim was to create a network that would allow users of a research computer at one university to be able to "talk to" research computers at other universities. A side benefit of ARPANET's design was that, because messages could be routed or rerouted in more than one direction, the network could continue to function even if parts of it were to be destroyed in the event of a military attack or other disaster.

Today, the Internet is a public, cooperative and self-sustaining facility accessible to hundreds of millions of people worldwide. Physically, the Internet uses a portion of the total resources of the currently existing public telecommunication networks. Technically, what distinguishes the Internet is its use of a set of protocols for the transmission of data.

For even the most novice Web users, electronic mail has practically replaced the Postal Service as the primary means of communication between coworkers, family, friends and business acquaintances. Electronic mail is the most widely used application on the Net. You can also "stream" live video feeds from practically any computer with a Web cam, as well as utilize "Instant Messenger" and "chat" services. E-mail use is critical in the restaurant and hospitality industry. It is second only to the telephone as a means of communication between you and your potential customers and clients. We will talk later in the chapter about naming conventions in e-mail and the benefits of maintaining an active Web site to promote your business.

The most widely used part of the Internet is the World Wide Web. The unique underlying language of the World Wide Web is Hypertext, which is the language a Web browser reads and interprets into what you see in your browser window when you view a Web page. On most Web sites, certain words or phrases appear in text of a different color than the rest; often this text is also underlined. These are known as Hyperlinks, or links. When you click on one of these words or phrases, you will be transferred to the site or page that is relevant to this word or phrase. Sometimes there are buttons, images or portions of images that are "clickable." If you move the pointer over a spot on a Web site and the pointer changes into a hand, this indicates that you can click and be transferred to another site. This is known as a "hot spot." Using the Web, you have access to millions of pages of information. Web site viewing is done with a Web browser, the most popular of which are Microsoft Internet Explorer and Netscape Navigator.

DO I NEED A WEB SITE?

In a word, YES!

If your restaurant already has a Web site, you're already reaping the benefits of being on-line. Each day, the Internet reaches millions of people who use it for work, play and research. The Web is the best marketing tool in the world; it allows your restaurant to be visible anywhere in the world. New services, such as digital cities, on-line city restaurant guides and other food-service sites, will increase your Web-site and restaurant visibility to levels unheard of. The Atlantic Publishing Company's Top 50 Restaurant Web Sites Contest promotes creativity and design in the restaurant Web-site business. At the same time, it serves as a free source of Web-site promotion and of key summaries of the restaurants themselves. This is the type of free marketing promotions available to Web-savvy restaurateurs. The Internet is a powerful tool, one that can be put to work for your restaurant.

Use the following checklist of potential advantages and see for yourself whether a Web site is right for you. Place a checkmark next to each ability that would serve your business:

- ☐ Additional, global, sales and marketing tool.

- ☐ Gather marketing information.

- ☐ Analyze and evaluate marketing information.

- ☐ Lower your phone expenses.

- ☐ Establish more frequent communications with customers.

- ☐ Establish more meaningful communications with customers.

- ☐ Reduce FAX costs.

- ☐ Reduce courier costs.

- ☐ Deliver electronically encoded resources around the world.

- ☐ Supplement employee training through electronic updates and bulletins.

- ☐ Broadcast press releases.

- ☐ Communicate to people who are presently not available.

- ☐ Submit invoices and expenses more quickly.

- ☐ Reduce international communications costs and improve response time.

- ☐ Ease of collaboration with colleagues.

- ☐ Establish contact with potential "strategic partners" worldwide.

- ☐ Identify and solicit prospective employees.

- ☐ Provide immediate access to your catalog.

- ☐ Permit customers to place orders electronically.

- ☐ Reduce costs of goods sold through reduced personnel.

The Web is everywhere. You see Web sites promoted in the mass media—on commercials, on billboards and in magazines. You even hear them on the radio. Web site addresses are the wave of the future—today. The Web is the most economical way to communicate with a worldwide audience. Can you think of ANY other tool which lets you advertise or sell products to a worldwide market, 24 hours a day, for a minimal monetary investment? The possibilities are endless—the return on investment, enormous. Here is a brief list of reasons you need to have a presence on the World Wide Web:

A. **It's the worlds largest communications medium.** The World Wide Web provides maximum exposure and maximum potential to communicate with a worldwide audience, 24 hours a day. Following are some Web usage statistics:

   - There are an estimated 285 million people on-line, from nearly every country.

   - 48 percent of users use the Net one to four times a day; 39 percent use it more.

- One-in-five Web users use their browsers more than 35 hours a week.

B. **Instantaneous access to information.** A Web site can be browsed at any time—day or night. Information can be downloaded, e-mails transmitted, supplies and services bought and sold.

C. **Virtually unlimited potential.** There are no time, physical or geographical limits in Cyberspace, and over 62 percent of Web users have bought something on-line.

D. **The user is in control.** Web users may choose where they want to "go," when they want to go there and stay for as little or as long as they choose.

E. **Visual marketing.** Technology provides incredible ways to convey information about your business, products and services.

WHAT TO PUT ON YOUR WEB SITE

The Silvermine Tavern (*http://www.silverminetavern.com*) had a Web site developed by Gizmo Graphics Web Design (*http://www.gizwebs.com*). The Silvermine went from no Web presence to a lively, active Web presence. What kind of information can a Restaurant put on the Web? Here is a brief list of what the Silvermine Tavern has used their Web site for:

- **A picture is truly worth a thousand words.** The Silvermine Tavern has carefully selected high-quality images and photos to truly "sell" the beauty of their inn and restaurant.

- **News, events and specials.** The opportunities are endless. The Silvermine Tavern promotes weekly jazz events, monthly Wine Dinners and holiday dining specials. They have even developed Web-based distribution lists from their long list of loyal customers and use e-mail to promote the monthly and weekly events.

- **Menus.** These aren't just basic menus, but menus with full-color photographs of each entree!

- **Directions.** They have a link into Mapquest.com right on their site. You enter your address, and you get door-to-door directions from your home to The Silvermine Tavern.

- **Products for sale.** The Silvermine Tavern operates a unique country store. They could sell products from that store over the Web for a minimal investment and open up their store to millions more potential customers, who visit the store "virtually" through the World Wide Web.

- **History.** Every restaurant has a history. Sometimes a history is truly unique—a story worth telling. Your Web site can do this for you. The Silvermine Tavern has gone a step further by not only giving you a rich history, but also a virtual walking tour through historic Norwalk, Connecticut.

- **Area attractions.** Sell your restaurant and your local community to the Web site visitor.

The opportunities are endless. Be imaginative!

HOW TO GET AN EFFECTIVE WEB SITE

The choice is entirely yours. There are thousands of Web development companies throughout the world. Consider companies specializing in the food-service and hospitality industries. I recommend Gizmo Graphics Web Design of Land O' Lakes, Florida (*http://www.gizwebs.com*). They have put together a solid, high-quality, low-cost package exclusively for restaurants. It offers a comprehensive cradle-to-grave cost approach, which includes all annual hosting fees, domain registrations and annual support.

Some words of caution:

- Don't overlook the little details.

- A Web site can be a significant investment. Hire a professional if you want professional results.

- Keep in mind the "hidden costs." Most developers don't include Web site hosting, domain-name registration and renewal, support and continued development services after site completion. (Note: The restaurant development package at Gizmo Graphics Web Design is all-inclusive.)

- Make sure you promote your site. A site is worthless if no one knows it exists. Search-engine registration is a critical part of a successful Web site. My favorite search engine is Google.com. If you navigate to Google.com and type in "Restaurants, Norwalk, CT"—guess what the first listing is—the Silvermine Tavern! While they are certainly not the only restaurant in Norwalk, Connecticut, they have used search-engine ranking and effective Web-development services to promote themselves.

A Web site is an investment, not an expense. In the current marketplace, every restaurant MUST have a Web presence, or it is missing the boat!

12

MANAGING THE DINING ROOM & WAITSTAFF PERSONNEL FOR MAXIMUM SERVICE & PRODUCTIVITY

INTRODUCTION

In many countries, waiting on tables is considered an honorable profession and a very respectable way to earn a living. There are even schools to educate people on how to become "professional" servers. In the United States for the most part, this is not the case. In many instances you will be interviewing a student, working mother or someone else looking for part-time employment or even in-between employment. Investing in training and education can reduce turnover and increase productivity. Technology is important in training, but getting through to your employees is even more important. The layout of the dining room and the type of food service affect the duties assigned to waiters and waitresses and the exact manner in which these duties are performed. However, certain fundamental duties that pertain to the serving of food are common to all food operations.

The precise dining-room procedures may differ somewhat between one food-service unit and another. A waitperson's efficiency is measured by the carefulness and completeness with which his or her duties are performed—before the meal service, before the customer's order is taken, after the meal service and after the customer has left the table.

PRE-SERVICE DUTIES

Generally each member of the waitstaff is assigned to a group of tables. These sections are known as "stations." A waitperson may keep a reserve supply of silver, glasses, china and linen at a side table and serve from it. Reserve supplies of condiments, ice, water and butter are often kept on the table, also, as well as a thermos of hot coffee. There is space for the serving tray either on the serving table or on a separate tray rack.

The waitperson should provide tables that are properly set before service is given—with clean linen, polished silver, shining glassware and spotless china. Tables should be promptly cleared after service and reset as needed. When a side table is used, the wait-person is responsible for having there a supply of extra serving equipment and the required foods and stock supplies, arranged in an orderly manner on a clean surface.

The housekeeping duties of the waitperson at the serving station include dusting and cleaning chairs, tables and window ledges, as well as cleaning the floor of spilled food and debris. In many establishments a bus person helps to keep the station in order and the side table supplied. The waitstaff member should notify the bus person when sup-plies are needed and when his or her services are required.

SETTING THE TABLE

THE COVER

This is the space—about 24 inches by 15 inches—within which one place is set with china, silver, linen and glass. An imaginary line may be drawn defining this area to assist in laying the cover (see FIGURE 1).

LINEN

A silence pad, if used, should be placed evenly on the table so that the edges do not hang down below the tablecloth. The tablecloth is laid over the silence pad or undercover or directly over the table, with the center fold up and equidistant from the edges of the table. All four corners should fall an even distance from the floor. The cloth should be free from wrinkles, holes and stains.

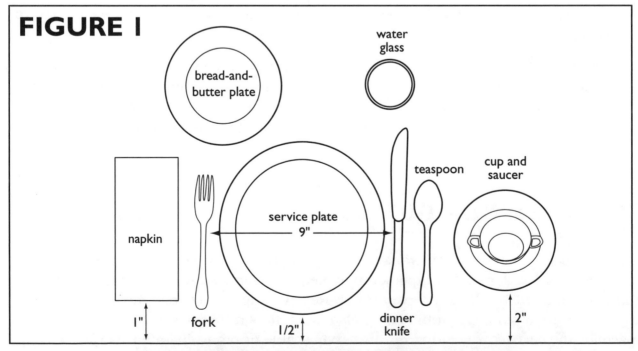

FIGURE I

water glass

bread-and-butter plate

service plate 9"

napkin

fork

teaspoon

cup and saucer

1"

1/2"

dinner knife

2"

"Table Cover Setup" using 16" x 12" doily and showing space allowance for a 24" cover arrangement.

When doily service is used, the doilies should be laid in the center of the cover, about 1 inch from the edge of the table. Silverware is placed on the doily.

The folded napkin is placed, with open corners at the lower right, at the left of the fork and about 1 inch from the front edge of the table. For formal dinners when a service plate is used, the napkin may be folded and placed on the service plate.

SILVER

Knives and forks should be laid about 9 inches apart, so that a dinner plate may be easily placed between them. The balance of the silverware is then placed to the right of the knife and to the left of the fork in the order in which it is to be used (placing the first-used at the outside and proceeding toward the plate). The handles of all silver should be perpendicular to the table edge and about an inch from it. Forks are placed at the left side of the cover, tines pointed up. Knives are placed at the right side of the cover with the cutting edge turned toward the plate.

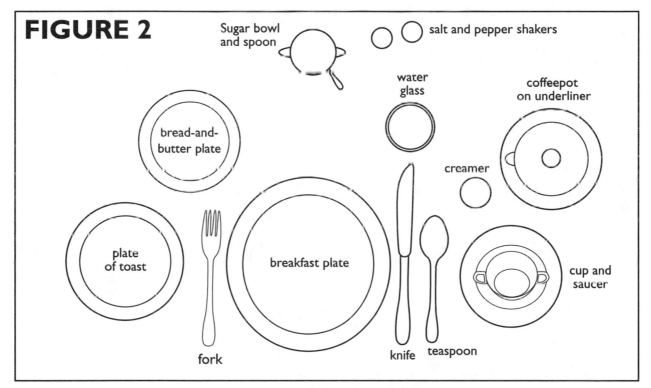

FIGURE 2

Sugar bowl and spoon

salt and pepper shakers

water glass

coffeepot on underliner

bread-and-butter plate

creamer

plate of toast

breakfast plate

cup and saucer

fork

knife   teaspoon

Cover arrangement for main breakfast course.

Spoons are laid, bowls up, at the right of the knives. The butter spreader is placed across the top edge or on the right side of the bread-and-butter plate, with the handle either perpendicular or parallel to the edge of the table, the cutting edge turned toward the butter plate. The butter spreader is properly used only when butter is served and a bread-and-butter plate is provided. Sometimes when a sharp steel-bladed knife is used for the meat course, a small, straight knife for butter is laid at the right of the meat knife.

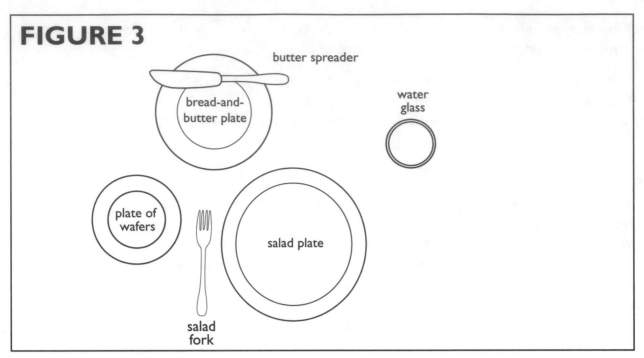

Cover arrangement when a dinner salad is served as separate course.

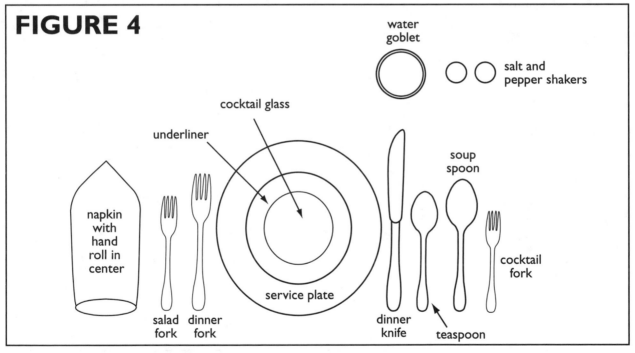

Cover arrangement for appetizer course of a formal dinner.

Oyster and cocktail forks are placed at the extreme right of the cover beyond the teaspoons or laid across the right side of the service plate underlying the cocktail glass or the oyster service.

Silver for dessert service—the iced teaspoon and the parfait, or sundae, spoon—are placed just before the respective course at the right side of the cover. The dessert fork is laid at the right side of the cover if it is placed just before the dessert is served.

Breakfast or luncheon forks, salad forks and dessert forks are placed next to the plate in

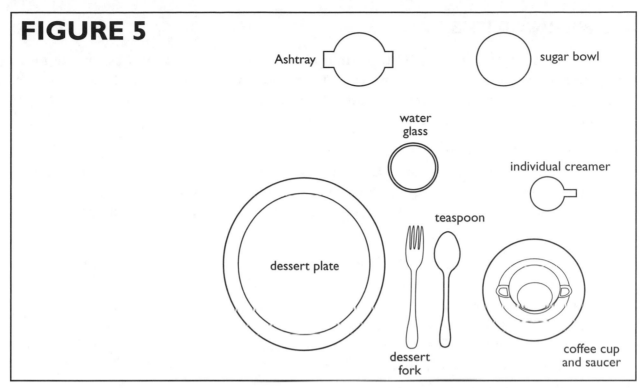

FIGURE 5

Cover arrangement for dessert course for luncheon or dinner.

order of use; the spoons are arranged to the right of the forks, in order of use, beginning in each instance with the first course (on the outside) and working toward the center of the cover. When knives are not used in the cover, both the forks and spoons are placed to the right of the cover.

CHINA AND GLASSWARE

The bread-and-butter plate is placed at the left of the cover, directly above the tines of the meat fork. The water glass is placed at the right of the cover, immediately above the point of the dinner knife.

Wine, liquor and beer glasses, if applicable, are placed to the right of the water glass. When a butter chip is used, it is placed to the left and on a line with the water glass, toward the center or left side of the cover.

Sugar bowls and salt and pepper shakers are generally placed in the center of small tables. When wall tables for two are set, the sugar bowl and shakers usually are placed on the side nearest the wall or the side nearest the room rather than in the center of the table. When an open-topped sugar bowl is used, a clean sugar spoon is laid to the right of the bowl.

When a large table is being set up and several sets of sugars and creamers are needed, the cream pitchers and sugar bowls may be placed at equal distances down the center of the table. Guests can more conveniently handle them if the handles are turned toward the cover. When several sets of salt and pepper shakers are used on a large table, they may be placed between the covers on a line parallel with the bases of the water glasses.

SIDE-WORK DUTIES

Duties performed by the waitstaff other than those related to the actual serving of food are commonly called "side work." This work takes considerable time and is scheduled so that each person is assigned certain duties. Side work is usually done during slack periods, before and after serving hours.

Sugar bowls should be kept spotlessly clean: emptied, washed, thoroughly dried and refilled as often as necessary. Care should be taken to keep the sugar free from lumps and foreign material. If shaker-type containers are used, the screw tops should be securely fastened and the spout examined to see if it is clean and that the sugar flows freely.

Salt and pepper shakers should be washed with a bottlebrush. A piece of wire or a toothpick may be used to unclog the holes in the lids before they are washed. Shakers should not be filled after washing until they are thoroughly dry. An empty saltbox with a spout may be refilled with pepper and used for filling pepper shakers. There is a great invention for filling salt and pepper shakers called a "Posi-Fill Dispenser," which is about $20 and can be found at *http://www.atlantic-pub.com,* or by calling 800-541-1336 (Item PSF-03).

Syrup jugs and oil and vinegar containers should always be clean. The outside should be wiped carefully with a damp cloth after filling, to remove any stickiness.

Condiment bottles should be wiped with a clean, damp cloth. The top and inside of the cap may be wiped with a paper napkin to clean off gummy material. Mustard pots and condiment jars should be emptied and washed frequently. Clean paddles should be provided often.

Napkins should be folded carefully according to the style of the restaurant, with folds straight and edges even.

Menus always must be replaced with new ones if they become soiled and torn.

Flowers should be arranged in containers appropriate in color, size and shape.

Individual creamers should be washed and thoroughly cooled before being filled with cream. A container with a slender spout is used for filling if a cream dispenser is not available. Care should be taken not to fill creamers too full.

Ashtrays should be collected and cleaned frequently, especially during the serving period; a clean one should be provided each time newly arrived guests are seated at the table.

Serving trays should be kept clean and dry, to protect both the waitperson's uniform and the serving-table surface. The top of the tray should be wiped clean before it is loaded, to prevent the bottoms of the dishes from being soiled.

Ice cubes or cracked ice should be clean and free of foreign matter; ice cubes should be handled with tongs and cracked ice with a special scoop or serving spoon. Ice should be transported in containers dedicated for ice only. Ice should be considered a food item.

Butter pots need to be chilled and a pan of ice made ready before serving.

Chairs should have crumbs dusted off after each guest has left. Backs, rounds and legs of chairs should be carefully dusted every day.

Silver or stainless should be cleaned according to the special directions of the restaurant. When a cream polish is used, it should be rubbed with a soft cloth or a small brush over the surface and well into the embossed pattern of the silverware. Then the silver should be thoroughly washed, rinsed and polished with a dry cloth to remove all traces of the silver cream.

CLOSING DUTIES

A waitperson should never go off-duty while guests are still seated at her station. When the serving period is over, tables should be stripped, soiled linen removed, and the tables reset for the next meal. If the tables are not to be reset, all unused tablecloths and napkins should be carefully folded and put in their proper places. Clean dishes and clean silver should be returned to their shelves, trays or drawers; sugar bowls and salt and pepper shakers collected on trays for cleaning and refilling; and supplies, such as condiments, butter and ice, stored in the proper places. The top of the side table should be first washed clean and then wiped down with a dry cloth. Before the waitperson leaves her station, everything should be in order.

SERVICE DUTIES

HOSTING

Every employee in a restaurant is a host; the customer is your guest. Generally the host or hostess greets the customers as they enter the dining room and ushers them to tables. However, when the host is busy or the establishment does not have a host, it becomes the waitstaff's responsibility to meet and seat customers. Whether guests receive a favorable or an unfavorable impression of the restaurant depends to a considerable degree upon the manner in which this service is performed.

Should there be a wait before a party's table is ready, there should be a system in place to monitor waiting times and tables. Electronic wait systems have become popular in recent years. This system consists of logging diners in and then issuing them a lighted coaster or vibrating pager. When their table is ready, the unit lights up or vibrates. At a recent restaurant show I saw a demonstration of a Web-enabled handheld device that allows customers to preview the menu, view promotions, check e-mail and surf the Net. Another innovative system prints out for guests tickets with estimated wait times based upon preprogrammed averages. The system also enables employees who seat guests to notify the front desk immediately if they view a party leaving a table or a bus person about to finish resetting a table. The wait and kitchen staff also use many of these pager systems to communicate any problems or, for instance, that food is ready to be delivered.

If a customer asks for information about the menu or suggestions about the food selection before deciding on his order, a well-informed and intelligent member of the waitstaff can be of real service to the guest and, at the same time, merchandise food effectively for the restaurant. She has an opportunity to be more than an order-taker and server; she can be a successful salesperson as well.

TAKING THE ORDER

Customers usually like to have time to study the menu without feeling that their waitperson is waiting impatiently to take the order. The waiter should be ready to give prompt attention as soon as the guest has decided on her order. He stands at the left of the customer, close enough to hear her easily and to answer her questions distinctly. If the customer makes out a written order, the waiter should read it back to her and ask for any special instructions that may apply. When the waiter writes the order, his writing should be legible, the abbreviations correct and the number of guests and table number indicated.

When a group of people is being served, the waiter should try to discover whether there is a host or hostesses for the group to whom he may go for instructions. While taking the order, he should ask for all the information he needs to serve the meal satisfactorily. For example:

1. The food choices for each course.

2. How, for instance, the eggs are to be cooked.

3. Whether toast is to be dry or buttered.

4. Whether meat is preferred rare, medium or well-done.

5. Whether a sandwich is to be served plain or toasted.

6. What kind of dressing is preferred for the salad.

7. Whether coffee is to be served with the main course or with the dessert.

8. Whether coffee is preferred hot or iced.

9. Whether black or green tea is desired.

10. Whether lemon or cream is preferred with tea.

Printed order forms, usually called "checks," are available in book form, numbered consecutively. When issued a book of checks, each member of the waitstaff is responsible for the numbers he or she receives. Spoiled checks therefore must not be destroyed; corrections should be made by drawing a line through the incorrect item—never by erasing it. The manager should approve these corrections. The check is issued as a means of recording the order, as the customer's bill, and as a source of information about the sale. Duplicate checks are used in filling orders in the kitchen.

MANUALLY GIVING AND COLLECTING ORDERS

The procedures used for giving and collecting orders in the kitchen vary somewhat with the organization, layout and regulations of the restaurant. However, certain general methods are applicable anywhere and help to determine the speed of the service as well as the condition and appearance of the food when it is placed before the customer. When the waiter is courteous and considerate in giving and assembling his order, he helps to maintain harmonious relations between the kitchen and dining room personnel.

The layout of the kitchen and the number of service stations will determine the routing the waitperson must follow in assembling an order. One new to the establishment must learn as quickly as possible the functions of each unit and exactly what foods and supplies are available at each.

The waitperson gives an order by placing a written order on a spindle provided for the purpose, or by giving it to the expediter to "call." Orders may also be sent to the kitchen from a point-of-sale system or "Wireless Waiter," as described below. When a written order is used, the waitperson uses his or her initials or number to identify it.

The waitstaff should not make a habit of saying they are "in a hurry" for their orders; the cooks are probably doing their best to fill orders quickly and in rotation. When extra-fast service is really necessary, a waitperson may be justified in asking to be served rapidly or even out of turn.

TIMING THE ORDER
The waitperson should know when he or she will need a course and the time the meal will take to prepare in the kitchen, especially when foods are cooked to order.

ASSEMBLING THE ORDER
Food requiring the longest time to prepare should be ordered first. The waitperson should plan the assembling of the order so that she can pick up each item as soon as possible after it has been dished. This will ensure food is served when it is at the correct temperature and will prevent it from crowding the serving counters. The following general sequence is recommended:

1. When the order is being filled, collect all the needed serving equipment and cold accompaniments such as bread, crackers, relishes, butter and cream.

2. Pick up cold foods next, taking care to keep them away from hot food on the tray.

3. The hot food should be picked up last. Cover soup to retain the heat. Cover the dinner plate with a hot cover when one is available.

4. If hot breads are served, pick them up last to serve them in their best condition.

5. When bowl or platter service is used, provide heated plates for hot foods and chilled plates for salads and other cold foods.

6. Rinse tea and coffee pots with hot water before filling them with hot beverages. Never pour iced drinks into warm glasses or place butter on a warm plate.

7. Remember that the appearance and temperature of food that is perfectly prepared when it leaves the kitchen can be spoiled in the service by a waitperson who is thoughtless, slow or careless.

LOADING THE TRAY

When a waitperson loads his tray he puts the larger, heavier dinner plates and dishes in the center and the lighter pieces toward the edges. Cups are not placed on saucers. Hot and cold dishes do not touch. Tea and coffee pots are not filled so full that liquid will leak from the spouts. Pot spouts are turned in and away from plates or food. A tray should be loaded so that it will be evenly balanced and the objects on it will neither slip nor spill while it is being carried. Among the precautions to take in loading a tray are the following:

1. Be sure the tray is clean.

2. Before leaving a serving station, check the order to see that it is correct, complete, properly cooked, the right quantity for serving, properly garnished and attractively served, with no spilled food on the edges of dishes.

3. Before leaving the kitchen check to see that all food and the necessary serving equipment for the course are on the tray.

ELECTRONIC ORDERING SYSTEMS

In recent years many restaurants have switched to an "Electronic Guest Check System" or "Wireless Waiter." These systems use a mobile computer. The waitperson carries the mobile computer pad and places the order on the touch-screen display. As each dish is entered this information is transferred in real time to the kitchen, where the order is printed out. The drink order is taken first and sent to the bar. The mobile computer, which the waitperson carries, is then notified by a beep or vibration when the order is ready for pickup, or a "runner" delivers the meal.

Using a "Wireless Waiter" the waitstaff can place multiple orders without ever walking into the kitchen or bar to check for previously placed orders or to pick up prepared orders. The waitstaff in the dining area of the restaurant never leave the sight of their customers. The bill is calculated automatically, removing the risk of human error. Most systems have an optional snap-on credit-card reader, which can be attached to the bottom of the handheld device. Customer credit cards are swiped through the handheld unit and processed. Under this system customers can feel confident that their credit cards are safe, as they are never out of sight. Because waitstaff will always be visible in the dining area customers will be able to get their waitperson's attention easily. In addition, servers will be able to wait on six or seven tables at a time—twice as many as before. If more tables are waited on, more tables can be turned, providing the opportunity to increase sales volume. Utilizing this system you might need fewer waitpersons, since each one will be able to handle more customers. This would, of course, result in a reduction of labor costs.

TABLE SERVICE

The table service adopted by any one food-service unit is developed to provide for the particular conditions in that establishment. Several methods of table service are considered acceptable and may be used appropriately. Restaurant managers strive to give commendable service to their guests. Good food service is achieved by adopting a suitable method of service; by training the sales force in it; and by requiring each waitstaff member to follow the specified procedure. This policy will result in a uniform standard of service.

AMERICAN SERVICE

American table service is "combination" service, which is a compromise among the two or more traditional forms of service that originated in other countries. If, for instance, the soup course is served in a tureen and dipped into the soup plates at the table in the "English" fashion; the main course served on dinner plates from the kitchen or serving pantry in the "Russian" manner; and the salad course offered from a large bowl and served by the waitperson in the "French" style, three forms of service are combined in a single meal. The traditional forms of table service most commonly used in catering to the public are named for the countries in which the services originated: France, Russia and England. Because these traditional methods have been adapted to American usage, it is interesting to consider briefly how they affect modern table service in the United States.

FRENCH SERVICE

The most elaborate form of table service is the "French" service used in some exclusive clubs, hotels and restaurants. In the French service, the waitperson usually serves the guests from a food wagon or a side table. Attractive, tastefully arranged dishes of food are always presented to the guest for inspection before serving. The waiter then serves the individual plates from the platter, serving bowl or chafing dish, as the case may be.

In a modification of French service called "platter service," the food is arranged attractively on serving dishes supplied with silver and offered to the guest so that he may serve himself. A single dish or the entire main course may be served in this way. In some restaurants, serving dishes of fresh-cooked vegetables of a fine quality are thus offered to each guest for selection; others serve attractive compartment trays of assorted relishes. Trays of assorted small cakes are sometimes offered after frozen desserts have been placed. French pastries frequently are offered to customers on a tray.

Another variation of the French service is the salad cart now popular in some restaurants and tearooms. Salads are placed on the cart and wheeled to tables so that the guests may make their selections. The waitperson arranges the individual servings at the cart and places them at each guest's cover. Another variation of French service is the custom practiced in some restaurants of having the waitperson bring to the guest trays of assorted individual salads or assorted desserts from which to make a selection.

ENGLISH SERVICE

The "English" style of service is sometimes called "host service." When this service is used, the platters and serving dishes are placed before the host or hostess, who serves the individual plates. The waiter stands at the right of the host, receives the served plate from him and places it before each guest. Female guests are sometimes served first, then men; however, the usual procedure is to serve each guest in turn, beginning with the person seated to the right of the server. Commercial food-service units do not use English service for the main course of the meal except upon request in connection with private parties. A patron may ask for this type of service on some special occasion, such as a family dinner party or Thanksgiving Day, when, for instance, the host wishes to carve the turkey at the table and to serve the individual plates himself.

Occasionally the English style of service is used in serving the beverage course, perhaps at the tea hours. A tray containing the tea or after-dinner coffee service is placed before the hostess in order that the hostess may serve her guests.

Special desserts and forms of ice cream are sometimes served with host service. During the Christmas season a traditional "blazing plum pudding" may be brought to the table for guests to have the pleasure of watching the flames and seeing it served. A birthday cake may be set before the guest of honor, who is expected to "make a wish and blow out the candles" and cut the first slice or serve all of the guests. In each of these cases a particularly attractive dish is served at the table as an expression of hospitality on the part of the host or hostess. Variations of English service are frequently used in noncommercial operations, such as college dining halls.

RUSSIAN SERVICE

When the "Russian" form of service is followed, individual portions of food are placed on the plates in the kitchen or serving pantry, garnished and ready to serve. The Russian method is used by most restaurants for serving meals as well as banquets.

BUFFET SERVICE

Buffets are used by some establishments for serving appetizer and salad courses. Occasionally an entire meal is served in buffet fashion. For buffet service a table is attractively set with a variety of foods; each guest is given a large service plate, sometimes chilled or heated, and walks along the table, helping herself.

Under the usual procedure for restaurant buffet service, the waitperson serves breads, beverages and desserts at each table. When hot foods are included, a cook or server carves the roast, and helpers serve vegetables and other foods from casseroles, chafing dishes and bowls.

The **SMORGASBORD**, used in many Swedish restaurants, is a form of buffet service. A large variety of typical Swedish appetizers, relishes, smoked meats, pickled fish and salads are arranged on the table. The guest passes by this extensive array, helping himself. Usually the main and dessert courses are served later at the individual tables, but the buffet may be cleared and reset for the dessert and beverage service.

GENERAL RULES FOR TABLE SERVICE

Since there are several methods of table service, each food-service unit must follow the method appropriate to its particular conditions, and each member of the waitstaff must learn to follow the serving directions exactly so that service will be uniform throughout the unit. The following rules are approved by social custom:

1. Place and remove all food from the left side of the guest.

2. Place and remove all beverages, including water, from the right of the guest.

3. Use the left hand to place and remove dishes when working at the left side of the guest, and the right hand when working at the right side of the guest. This provides free arm action for the server and avoids the danger of bumping against the guest's arm.

4. Place each dish on the table, the four fingers of your left hand under the lower edge, and your thumb on the upper edge, of the plate.

5. Never reach in front of the guest, nor across one person in order to serve another.

6. Present serving dishes from the left side, in a position so that the guest can serve himself. Place serving silver on the right side of the dish, with the handles turned toward the guest so that he may reach and handle them easily.

7. Do not place soiled, chipped or cracked glassware and china or bent or tarnished silverware before a guest.

8. Hold silverware by the handles when it is laid in place. Be sure it is clean and spotless.

9. Handle tumblers by their bases and goblets by their stems.

10. Do not lift water glasses from the table to fill or refill; when they cannot be reached conveniently, draw them to a more convenient position.

11. Set fruit-juice and cocktail glasses, cereal dishes, soup bowls and dessert dishes on small plates before placing them in the center of the cover, between the knife and the fork.

12. When it accompanies the main course, place the salad plate at the left of the forks, about 2 inches from the edge of the table. When the salad is served as a separate course, place it directly in front of the guest.

13. Place individual serving trays or bread and rolls above and to the left of the forks. Place a tray or basket of bread for the use of several guests toward the center of the table.

14. Place the cup and saucer at the right of the spoons, about 2 inches from the edge of the table. Turn the handle of the cup to the right, either parallel to the edge of the table or at a slight angle toward the guest.

15. Set tea and coffee pots on small plates and place above and slightly to the right of the beverage cup. Set iced beverage glasses on coasters or small plates to protect tabletops and linen.

16. Place individual creamers, syrup pitchers and small lemon plates above and a little to the right of the cup and saucer.

17. Place a milk glass at the right of and below the water glass.

18. Serve butter, cheese and cut lemon with a fork. Serve relishes, pickles and olives with a fork or spoon, not with the fingers.

More and more, food-service operations are using booth- or banquet-type seating. It is extremely difficult to carry out proper table service in these situations. The general rules for booth service are:

• Serve everything with the hand farthest from the guest; use right hand to serve a guest at your left and your left hand to serve your guest to your right.

• Remove soiled plates with the hand nearest your guest while substituting the next course with the hand farthest from your guest.

BREAKFAST SERVICE

Good breakfast service is important because many customers are in a hurry; some have little appetite; and others are "out of sorts" until they have had their coffee. A cheerful attitude on the part of the waitstaff and prompt and efficient service, therefore, may help customers "start the day right."

Foods served for breakfast are most palatable when they are freshly prepared and when they are served at the correct temperature. The waitperson, therefore, should serve breakfast in courses unless the customer especially requests that the whole order be served at once. Cooked foods and hot beverages should be brought to the customer directly from the serving station and under no circumstances allowed to remain on the serving stand to cool while the customer finishes a preceding course.

Order of service for breakfast:

1. When fresh fruit or fruit juice is ordered, it is desirable to serve it first; then remove the soiled dishes before placing the toast and coffee.

2. When customers order a combination of cooked fruit, toast and coffee, they may ask to have the whole order served at once. Place the fruit dish, set on an underliner, in the center of the cover, the plate of toast at the left of the forks and the coffee at the right of the teaspoons.

3. When the breakfast order includes a cereal and a hot dish, the service procedure may be as follows:

    A. Place the fruit course in the center of the cover.

    B. Remove the fruit service.

    C. Place the cereal bowl, set on an underliner, in the center of the cover. Cut individual boxes of cereal partway through the side near the top so the guest may open them easily.

    D. Remove the cereal service.

    E. Place the breakfast plate of eggs, meat or other hot food in the center of the cover. Place the plate of toast at the left of the forks. Place the coffee service at the right of the spoons.

    F. Remove the breakfast plate and the bread plate.

    G. Place the finger bowl, filled one-third full of warm water. At times the finger bowl is placed after the fruit course when fruits that may soil the fingers have been served.

    H. Place the sales check, face down, at the right of the cover or present it on a clean change tray.

LUNCHEON SERVICE

Luncheon customers usually can be classified in two groups: business people who have a short lunch period and want quick service, and casual diners who want more leisurely service. The duty of the waitperson is to avoid keeping customers in the first group waiting for service, and to avoid making those in the second group feel they are being rushed.

Order of service for luncheon:

1. Fill the water glasses three-fourths full of ice water.

2. Place chilled butter on a cold bread-and-butter plate.

3. Place the appetizer in the center of the cover.

4. Remove the appetizer when the guest has finished.

5. Place the soup service in center of cover.

6. Remove the soup service.

7. Place entree plate in center of cover.

8. Place individual vegetable dishes (if used) above the cover.

9. If salad is served with main course, place salad at the left of the forks, about 2 inches from edge of table.

10. Place tray or basket of bread and rolls at left of salad plate.

11. Place hot beverages above and a little to the right of cup and saucer, with individual creamer above the cup.

12. Place an iced beverage or milk at the right and a little below the water glass.

13. Remove the main-course dishes.

14. Remove any extra silver not used for the main course.

15. Crumb the table, if necessary.

16. Place desert silver to the right of the cover, with fork nearest the dessert plate if fork and teaspoon are used. When several teaspoons are placed, the dessert fork may be laid on the left side, to "balance the cover."

17. Place the dessert service in center of the cover.

18. Serve hot coffee if requested.

19. Remove dessert dishes and silver.

20. Place the fingerbowl on the underliner (when one is used) in the center of the cover.

21. Present the check, face down.

THE RESTAURANT MANAGER'S HANDBOOK

DINNER SERVICE

Because dinner guests are seldom in a hurry, their waitperson is able to give them a more fastidious and leisurely type of service than is possible at breakfast or luncheon. Although the guest should be allowed plenty of time to complete each course, long waits between courses should be avoided. The waitperson should watchfully observe the guests during the meal in order to serve the next course promptly and to comply with any requests made by the guests for special service.

Order of service for dinner:

1. From the left, place the appetizer or hors d'oeuvres service in the center of the cover. A tray of canapés and hors d'oeuvres is often offered to the guest. In this case, an empty plate should first be placed before the guest and the tray of hors d'oeuvres then offered to him.

2. Remove the first-course dishes.

3. Place the soup service in the center of the cover.

4. Remove the soup service.

5. When the entree is served on a platter, place it directly above the cover. Lay the serving silver at the right of the platter. Place the warm dinner plate in the center of the cover.

6. When plate, or "Russian," service is used, place the dinner plate in the center of the cover.

7. Place salad at the left of the forks when it is served with the main course.

8. Place beverages to the right of teaspoons.

9. Offer rolls or place them to the left of the salad plate.

10. Remove the main-course dishes when the guest has finished.

11. When salad is served as a separate course following the main course, place the salad fork at the left and the salad plate in the center of the cover.

12. Remove the salad service.

13. Crumb the table if necessary.

14. Place silver for the dessert course.

15. Place the dessert service in the center of the cover.

16. Serve hot coffee or place the demitasse.

Special attentions to observe when serving:

1. Serve hot food hot, on heated dishes.

2. Serve cold food chilled, on cold dishes.

3. Inquire how food is to be cooked:

    A. Eggs: fried or boiled; how many minutes.

    B. Steak: rare, medium or well-done.

    C. Toast: buttered or dry.

4. Refill water glasses whenever necessary during the meal.

5. Serve extra butter when needed.

6. Refill coffee on request and according to management policies. Bring more cream if necessary.

7. Serve granulated sugar with fresh fruit and unsweetened iced drinks.

8. Place silver necessary for a course just prior to serving.

    A. Soupspoons on extreme right of teaspoons.

    B. Cocktail fork to right of soupspoon.

9. Offer crackers, melba toast and other accompaniments or relishes with appetizer and soup courses, according to policies of management.

10. Provide iced teaspoons for ice drinks and place parfait spoons when a parfait is served. Place soda spoons and straws with malted milks, milkshakes and ice-cream sodas.

CLEARING THE TABLE

The following are standard procedures for clearing the table:

1. After any course, dishes should be removed from the left side, except the beverage service, which should be removed from the right.

2. Platters and other serving dishes should be removed first when clearing the table, or they may be removed as soon as empty.

3. The main-course plate should be removed first, the salad plate next, followed by the bread-and-butter plate.

4. The empty milk or beverage glass is removed from the right after the main course.

5. The table should be crumbed by using a small plate and a clean, folded napkin. This is especially important when hard rolls or crusty breads are served.

6. Hot tea and coffee service should be left on the table until the completion of the dessert course.

7. The water glass should remain on the table and be kept refilled as long as the guest is seated.

8. Replace soiled ashtrays with clean ones as often as necessary throughout the meal.

9. When a guest is seated at a table and it is necessary to change a soiled table-cloth, turn the soiled cloth halfway back, lay the clean cloth half open in front of the guest, and transfer the tableware to the clean cloth. The soiled cloth may then be drawn from the table and the clean one pulled smoothly into place. If this exchange of linen is accomplished skillfully, the guest need not be disturbed unduly during the procedure. Soiled linen should be properly disposed of immediately after it is removed from the table.

PRESENTING THE CHECK

The guest should not be kept waiting for her sales check. It should be presented either immediately after the last course has been served or as soon as she has finished eating. The check should be accurately totaled and laid face down on the table, to the right of the cover, on a small change tray. When a group of several persons has been served, the check should be placed by the host's cover; if the host is not known, and the order has been written on one check, the check should be placed toward the center of the table. When a man and woman are dining together, the check should generally be presented near to the man, unless separate orders have been written. This is a judgment call, however; if in doubt, place the check in the middle of the table.

It is a courteous practice to ask if any other service is desired before presenting the sales check and to thank the customer as the check is laid on the table. When a bill is received in payment, the waitperson should mention the denomination of the bill. When a credit card is presented, be sure to include a pen and the appropriate instruction, such as, "The top white copy is your copy and the bottom yellow copy is for the establishment." When tipping is sanctioned, the waitperson should leave the appropriate change. This will enable the customer to leave a gratuity, should she wish to do so.

Change should be placed on a change tray or tip tray provided for that purpose, not on a china plate, as coins make unnecessary noise when handled on china. Also, once the money is removed the plate will appear clean, and it might later be used for food without being washed. It is incorrect for the waitperson to indicate in any way that a tip is expected or that any certain amount is anticipated. It is also discourteous to show disappointment because the tip was less than is customarily received. When a guest leaves a gratuity, she indicates her desire to reward the waitperson for services rendered.

COURTESY TO DEPARTING CUSTOMERS

Guests should be shown small courtesies when departing. For example, a waiter might draw out a woman's chair and assist with her wraps and packages. The waitperson should endeavor to say goodbye to all customers and to express the hope that they have enjoyed the meal or that they will come again. This sort of courtesy makes customers feel that they have been truly welcome guests.

SUPERVISING THE SERVICE

The primary function of the food-service host or hostess is to dispense hospitality as a representative of the management. When receiving customers, the host should greet them graciously and try to make them feel that they are welcome and will receive good service. A pleasant reception, careful service throughout the meal and courteous treatment as they leave will impress customers with the excellence of the service—and make them feel that their patronage is appreciated. It is the feeling of being a valued patron that converts occasional customers into regular guests.

Food service is one of mankind's oldest forms of hospitality and is associated in one's mind with courtesy, cheerfulness and goodwill. The host should realize that goodwill toward the establishment is created by courteous and interested service, just as it is lost by unwilling and indifferent service.

The host has working relations with all the individuals concerned with sales and service: the manager, the waitstaff and the guests. He must interpret management's policies and standards to the customers. He must convey the wishes of both the management and the guests to the sales staff. The skill with which he conducts himself in this pivotal position will determine to a considerable extent the efficiency of the service and the satisfaction of the guests.

NATURE OF HOST WORK

The food-service host represents the management to the customer; he conveys the wishes of both the management and the customer to the sales staff and kitchen force; he reports to the management recommendations, suggestions and complaints from both the customers and employees. Good judgment and tact on his part, therefore, are essential. When the restaurant is large and there are several dining rooms, more than one host will be necessary to receive guests and supervise service. In large food-service operations, therefore, the host usually has assistant hosts, captains or head waitpersons who are responsible for supervising a section of the dining room or for the execution of specific duties involved in serving guests. It should be understood that the "duties of the host" discussed in this unit include all duties that may be executed by the host or by any of his or her assistants.

INSPECTING THE DINING ROOM

The host is responsible for the appearance, cleanliness and order of the dining room during the service period. Before the meal service begins he should check to be sure that:

1. The main dining room, private rooms, booths and counters are clean and in good order. Any disorder should be reported to the proper authority and remedied before the meal service begins.

2. Window curtains, venetian blinds and window roller-shades are adjusted to furnish satisfactory light.

3. The temperature and ventilation of the dining room are properly adjusted.

4. Tables are arranged properly and completely equipped.

5. Serving stands and side tables are properly arranged and have adequate supplies.

6. There are enough menu cards, and they are distributed properly.

7. Order forms and sharpened pencils are provided.

8. Table reservations and "reserved" signs have been placed.

9. The tables arranged for special parties are ready, and flowers, candles and other decorations provided.

10. Flowers are fresh and attractively arranged. Plants should be inspected for proper care, pruning and watering.

11. There is an adequate supply of tablecloths, table pads, doilies, napkins and serving towels.

12. Necessary repairs have been made to furnishings and fixtures.

RECEIVING CUSTOMERS

The host should receive customers in a gracious yet dignified manner. He should endeavor to make the guests feel welcome and assured that they will receive satisfactory service. With this in mind he may:

1. Stand near the entrance to the dining room in order to greet customers as they arrive and seat them promptly. This responsibility is often assigned to an assistant host when the host is charged with supervisory or service duties.

2. Greet the customers with a pleasant smile and nod, using the appropriate greeting—"Good morning," "Good afternoon," or "Good evening"—and greeting customers by name whenever possible.

3. When a checkroom is located near the entrance, suggest that guests check hats, wraps, umbrellas and packages.

4. Ask how many are in each group and seat the group at a suitable table. Avoid

the use of a table for four to seat one or two persons unless no smaller tables are available.

5. Ask the customers' preferences with regard to table location when the dining room is not too crowded.

6. Walk slightly ahead of the customers when escorting them to a table.

7. Seat couples at small tables or in booths. Place lame and elderly persons near the entrance so they will not be required to walk far. Seat men or women who come alone at small tables, but avoid placing them behind a post, near the entrance doorway or in the direct path to the kitchen doors.

8. Ask permission before seating strangers together, doing so only when the dining room is so crowded that this procedure is unavoidable. First explain the probable length of time the guest will have to wait for a private table, and then ask if she would mind sharing a table with someone else. Avoid seating a man with a woman who is dining alone, or taking a woman to a table where a man is already seated unless they are acquaintances and are willing to share a table.

9. Apportion the seating of customers to the several serving stations in order that no one section of the dining room will be overcrowded.

10. When customers must wait for tables, seat them where they are available, or indicate a place to stand that is out of the way of traffic.

11. Have the table cleared of soiled dishes and reset before customers are seated.

12. Pull out the chair for a woman guest and help her arrange her wraps and packages.

13. Indicate a rack where a man may hang his hat and overcoat, if no checkroom is provided.

14. Provide a junior chair for small children and a highchair for infants in arms. Offer to help seat the child and arrange the napkin or bib if the mother wishes this service.

15. Place the opened menu before each guest, from the left side, or instruct the captain or waitperson to do so.

16. Fill the water glasses or instruct the bus person or waitperson to do so promptly.

HANDLING CUSTOMER COMPLAINTS

One of the most difficult duties of the restaurant host is to receive complaints from customers and make satisfactory adjustments. When complaints are properly handled, the customer leaves the restaurant with a feeling of friendliness rather than animosity toward the management. Customer complaints are an opportunity to turn the situation around and make a lifelong customer. Complaints that are improperly handled make the customer disgruntled and may lead to the loss of her patronage and unfavorable advertising for the restaurant.

In adjusting complaints the host should:

1. Approach the customer in a friendly spirit and not allow her to be put on the defensive.

2. Listen attentively to the complaint and try to get the entire story.

3. Restate the gist of the complaint and have the customer confirm this summarized statement.

4. Express sincere regret for the occurrence.

5. Offer to exchange or substitute food that is unsatisfactory.

6. Cite the restaurant's policies when relevant.

7. When the refusal of a request is necessary, explain the reason clearly and tactfully.

8. When the restaurant is at fault, apologize and promise that an effort will be made to prevent a recurrence the situation.

9. Thank the customer for making the complaint, saying, "I am glad you told me," or "Thank you for bringing this to my attention."

10. When the customer makes a return visit, see that the service is faultless and that she has no further cause for complaint.

11. Refer difficult and unreasonable complaints to the manager for settlement.

12. Report all serious complaints and those involving business policy and regulations to the management.

DEALING WITH DIFFICULT CUSTOMERS

Some customers are difficult to deal with because of their attitudes or special needs; they should be handled with intelligence, tact and good judgment. Different types require different methods of treatment; here are some examples:

1. **The early customer.** Receive him courteously and explain when service will begin. Offer him a comfortable seat, possibly in the lounge, and give him a newspaper or magazine.

2. **The late customer.** Make her feel welcome. If the food selection is limited, explain that it's near closing time. Endeavor to provide good service without making her feel that she is being hurried.

3. **The hurried customer.** Recommend counter service when this is available. Tell him in advance approximately how long the service will take. Give the best service possible under the circumstances.

4. **The overfamiliar customer.** Be courteous but dignified with her. Avoid long conversations. Stay away from the table except when actual service is needed.

5. **The grouchy customer.** Meet him cheerfully and see that his waitperson treats him pleasantly. Do not argue with him. Listen to his complaints courteously, but do not encourage him. Do not be distressed by unreasonable complaints.

6. **The angry customer.** Listen to her, express regret at the occurrence that prompted her complaint, thank her for calling it to your attention and try to rectify the error.

7. **The troublemaker.** Be courteous and do not be drawn into arguments. Neither participate in criticisms of the management, nor make statements that may be construed as complaints about the restaurant. Warn other salespersons serving the troublemaker type to avoid antagonizing him.

8. **The tired customer.** Seat her at a quiet table. Assist her with wraps and packages. In cold weather, suggest a hot soup, a hot drink and some particularly appetizing light food. On a hot day, suggest a chilled salad or a frosted drink and some cold food.

MAKING ARRANGEMENTS FOR SPECIAL PARTIES

Unless there is a supervisor in charge of catering, the host generally takes reservations for special parties. He may improve his ability to handle this business by following the regulations of the management concerning maximum and minimum size for special groups, minimum charges, number of courses, food choices allowed at a given price, time and guarantee of number—and by obtaining the necessary information from the person making the reservation, including:

- Name, address and telephone number of the person calling.

- The name of the organization, if one is involved.

- Day, date and hour of reservation.

- Occasion.

- Probable number in the group, and number of guests guaranteed.

- Preferences as to table location and dining room (main or private).

- Price or price range.

- Whether sample menus are to be mailed.

- Arrangements for flowers and decorations.

- Arrangements for payment of the sales check. Is the check to be paid in one amount or is the money to be collected individually?

When a table reservation is made, obtain the following information:

- Name of person reserving it.

- Number of persons included in reservation.

- Date and time.

- Preference of table location.

- Arrangements for flowers.

- Whether a special menu is desired or guests will make their selections from the regular menu.

SERVING SPECIAL PARTIES

The general responsibilities of the host for the service of a special party include such duties as:

1. Securing and assigning the extra waitstaff and bus persons needed or service.

2. Rearranging the serving schedule to allow use of regular waitstaff employees.

3. Making out the orders for liners and dishes.

4. Giving instructions for setting tables.

5. Checking set tables for completeness, arrangement and appearance.

6. Checking to be sure that the correct number of places has been set.

7. Giving the necessary general instructions to individual servers.

8. Giving specific instructions to individual servers.

9. Notifying the kitchen staff of the time when the service will be required.

10. Notifying the kitchen staff when they should begin serving each course.

11. Signaling the head waitperson when it is time to begin placing each course.

12. Signaling the head waitperson when it is time to begin removing the dishes from each course.

13. Approving and supplying special services that may be requested by customers, such as tea instead of coffee, fish instead of meat, bread instead of rolls, and special foods for persons on special diets.

14. Providing supplies that may be requested, such as a pitcher of water for the speaker's place, a change tray for the person collecting the money at the table, change for the person selling tickets at the door, or an easel or blackboard for the speaker. Anticipate these requests in advance of the meal service, so far as possible, in order that the proper provisions may be made. Otherwise, satisfy such requests to your best ability when they are made.

PERFORMING CLERICAL WORK

Some clerical duties are usually assigned to the host. The amount of these for which he is responsible depends upon the organization of the restaurant, the size of the supervisory staff and the number of office employees. From among the clerical duties, the host may:

- Before the service period, check printed menus with the kitchen menu to discover omissions, inaccuracies or corrections. Change menus accordingly.

- Make out storeroom requisitions for supplies such as matches, paper doilies, paper inserts for metal dishes, candles, nuts and condiments.

- Record reservations for tables and special parties; include all necessary information on a reservation form.

- Record the service hours of dining room employees on the daily time sheet, if a time clock is not used.

- Make out the linen report.

- Make out or assist with the sales analysis for the meal.

- Report to the manager, in writing, any important suggestions, serious complaints or compliments from customers.

INFORMATION NEEDED BY THE HOST

The host needs both good background knowledge of correct procedures for serving food and a working knowledge of psychology. He or she should also be familiar with the policies and regulations of the business. Until the host has mastered this information he or she will not be thoroughly effective in supervising the service, dealing with customers and assisting management to execute the business policies.

In their daily work the hosts and hostesses should be familiar with the management's policy concerning the seating of customers, serving, filling orders in the kitchen and party service. They should have answers to the following questions:

POLICY CONCERNING SEATING

- Is the customer permitted to designate that a particular waitperson shall serve him?

- Does the policy of the restaurant approve seating strangers at the same table?

- During what hours are reservations permitted? How long should tables be held?

POLICY CONCERNING SERVING

- What is the prescribed method for a table setup?

- What specific method of service is used for:

  Table d'hôte meals?

  A la carte orders?

  Special parties?

- What is the division of work between the waitstaff and bus persons? What duties are each expected to perform independently? What duties are performed jointly?

- Are extra servings of hot bread offered? Are second cups of coffee allowed without extra charge?

- When and under what conditions may substitutions be made on a menu? Is there an extra charge when a guest requests a substitution?

POLICY CONCERNING FILLING ORDERS IN THE KITCHEN

- What foods does each kitchen station serve?

- What is the best routine for a waitperson to use in filling an order?

- To whom at each serving station should the waitperson give the order?

- Where are supplies of dishes, glassware, silver and linen kept?

- Where may extra supplies of butter, cream, ice, crackers and condiments be found?

- Are waitstaff required to dish their own orders of desserts and ice cream?

- Are waitstaff expected to make tea and coffee and fill orders for other beverages? Exactly what directions should be followed?

- Are "outs" and substitutions on the menu posted on a board in the kitchen? Should the menu cards be changed accordingly?

POLICY CONCERNING LARGE PARTY SERVICE

- What special rooms and dining room spaces may be reserved?

- What is the largest number of persons that can be accommodated? What is the smallest number for which any one room may be reserved?

- Is any leeway allowed on the guaranteed number of guests? What are the specific regulations concerning this matter?

- At what hours is party service provided? How late may a group remain?

- What is the minimum price for which a special group may be served? What is the usual price?

- What provisions are made for flowers and decorations?

- Is a portable stage available for the speaker's table and for entertainers?

- Are there an electrical connection, an extension cord and a screen available to use for the slide projector or video equipment?

- What is the policy with respect to gratuities?

- Is a special crew provided for party service? How are the members of these crews secured?

GENERAL POLICY

- Are guests permitted to use the dining-room or office telephones?

- Are menus provided as souvenirs without charge?

- Are pies, cakes and rolls made to order? Other foods?

- Are lunches packed to order?

- Are tray meals sent out?

The service in your restaurant can make or break your operation. Numerous industry surveys show that waitstaff service is often the deciding factor in returning to a restaurant or going to a competitor instead. Offering great food is not enough to stay competitive. It is up to you, the manager, to train, motivate and supervise the staff to ensure your success and to keep customers coming back and spreading the word about your establishment.

13

SUCCESSFUL EMPLOYEE RELATIONS & LABOR COST CONTROLS

THE LABOR PROBLEM IN THE FOOD-SERVICE INDUSTRY

According to the National Restaurant Association, the restaurant industry is the nation's largest private-sector employer, providing jobs for 11.6 million individuals. One-third of all adults in the United States have worked in the restaurant industry at some time in their lives. The food-service industry, the fourth largest industry in America, has nearly the highest employee turnover rate (exceeding 100 percent in one year in many units) and one of the lowest average dollar-sales per employee of any industry. The reasons for these statistics are many and varied. However, they can be boiled down to the fact that the industry, in general, has done little in the past fifteen years to alleviate its poor working environment. Unfortunately, low pay, few benefits, long hours that include night, weekend and holiday shifts, hard physical work (mostly while standing) and little interest on management's part in addressing these issues are the rule rather than the exception in most restaurants. Because of the currently low unemployment rate, luring workers into food service is not easy—nor is retaining them.

Employees directly control food quality and presentation. It is a fact that a disgruntled employee will not produce or perform as well as a satisfied one. Yet it is bewildering to note that few operators strive to make the employee's job any easier or more enjoyable through the use of modern training procedures.

Management must make every conceivable effort to relieve employees of toilsome work and make their jobs more rewarding—the results can only be positive! Unfortunately, most operators cannot substantiate or rationalize any investment in an employee's comfort or training because they feel the employee will probably quit in a month or two; they think, "Why bother?" Of course, this starts the cycle all over again.

Management must take the initiative to resolve the problem, because management is where the fault lies. Even simple accommodations—such as separate employee lockers, restrooms and break rooms—are a rarity. Air-conditioning in the hot kitchens is virtually nonexistent. Light and noise levels are usually inappropriate, causing fatigue, inefficiency and accidents. All of these poor physical conditions have been resolved in the manufacturing industry, where the turnover rate is around 8 percent and employees remain for several years or, as in Japan, where employees are virtually guaranteed economic security for their entire lifetimes.

Employees are one of the greatest resources a restaurant has, but this resource will be wasted if management does not first recognize it, and then supply the proper incentive and motivation necessary to harvest it. Management must provide employees with: higher salaries, better training, insurance programs, flexible scheduling, shorter workweeks, childcare and transportation vouchers, incentive plans, safe, clean working conditions, proper training, tools, evaluations, financial security if possible, adequate benefit packages and the opportunity for advancement, as well as an amicable, structured and just working environment. The cost of providing these basic necessities, which have eluded the industry for so long, can be easily substantiated when compared to the ramifications of losing—and the cost of replacing—a discontented skilled employee.

First, consider the indirect cost to the restaurant when an unmotivated and unhappy employee prepares a food item or provides poor service to a regular customer. Just as word-of-mouth advertising can be great publicity, it can also cause the restaurant to come crumbling to the ground from comments like "The food was not as good as it usually is," or "The food was all right but our waitress was slow and unconcerned, the entree was cold and the ice cream half melted. I can get the same thing down the road for much less." Discontented employees will not be concerned about looking out for the restaurant's interests. Dishes will get broken or carelessly thrown away. Food costs will rise and work areas will be left unorganized and dirty. Why should employees care about the restaurant's profits when they barely make enough to survive?

Consider the direct cost of replacing an employee: recruiting expense, interviewer's salary and time, administrative cost, training expense, medical exams, the loss of sales and the cost of materials due to training mistakes, the labor cost paid before the employee's full productivity is reached, and the trainer's and supervisor's salaries. Consider the cost of termination: paperwork, exit interviewing and, possibly, unemployment compensation. According to the American Management Association, the cost to replace an employee who leaves is, conservatively, 30 percent of his or her annual salary. For those with skills in high demand, the cost can rise to a frightening 1.5 times the annual salary. Your ability to retain the kind of workers you want and need has a direct impact on the profitability and effectiveness of your organization.

Restaurant operators must recognize the importance of employees to their success and take the necessary steps to ensure their physical comfort and economic security. Employee relations are an area where corners cannot be cut; the long-term results will outweigh the initial cost. Competent skilled labor is a finite resource that is highly competed for. Skilled labor will work only for organizations that appreciate their skills and can provide them with the proper compensation for their efforts. The industry as a whole should bring its labor policies and procedures up to date before it loses its personnel to other industries or is forced to change by union organization. The following sections will describe in detail, from the initial interview through to the employee's termination, how to set up and administer admirable manager/employee relations for the mutual benefit of each party.

HIRING RESTAURANT EMPLOYEES

The key to hiring good, competent employees is to put aside personal prejudices and select one applicant over another only because you feel he or she will have a better chance of being successful at the job. What a potential employee is qualified and capable of doing is often quite different than what he or she actually will do. The purpose of this section is to provide the interviewer with the information necessary to determine if the applicant has the qualities needed.

THE FOOD-SERVICE LABOR SHORTAGE

According to government statistics, the food-service industry employs 10.4 million people today, which represents 8 percent of the total workforce. The problem is that these numbers show a current deficit of about one million workers. By the year 2005, it is projected, the food-service industry will be short about 2.5 million workers. Many national chains' growth has been stymied by this labor crisis.

The shortage of workers is not unique to the labor side of the equation; good management is also hard to find. The turnover in the population of senior food service managers and directors isn't likely to slow down any time soon. In fact, as the members of the Baby Boom generation start retiring in 2011, the U.S. Department of Labor predicts, the situation will worsen, as these 76 million people exit the nation's labor pool.

The country's tight labor conditions are forcing food-service companies to seek out new sources of labor: minority groups, welfare recipients, senior citizens and the physically handicapped. As a result, the workforce is becoming more diverse. In addition, restaurateurs are extending their recruiting efforts beyond traditional methods, such as newspaper ads or signs posted in the restaurant, to high schools, college campuses, retirement communities, state agencies and the Internet.

KEY POINTS FOR CONDUCTING EMPLOYMENT INTERVIEWS

A. Treat all applicants considerately and show a genuine interest in them, even if they have little or no chance of obtaining the job. Every applicant should be treated as a potential customer, because she is.

B. Make certain that you are on time and ready to receive the applicant. Arriving late or changing appointment dates at the last minute will give the applicant the impression that you are disorganized and that the restaurant is run in the same manner.

C. Know the job being offered thoroughly. You cannot possibly match someone's abilities with a job you do not know or understand completely.

D. All interviews must be conducted in privacy, preferably in the interviewer's office. Interruptions must be kept to a minimum.

E. Make the applicant feel at ease. Have comfortable chairs, ashtrays and, possibly, beverages available. Speak in a conversational, interested tone.

F. Applicants will be full of questions about the job, its duties, the salary, etc. Newspaper advertisements tell only a little about the job and your company, so allow plenty of time for this important discussion.

G. Whenever possible let the applicants speak. You can learn a great deal about them by the way they talk about themselves, past jobs, former supervisors and school experiences. Watch for contradictions, excuses and, especially, the applicant being on the defensive or speaking in a negative manner. Avoiding subjects is an obvious indication that there was some sort of problem there in the past; be persistent about getting the whole story, but don't be overbearing. Come back to it later if necessary.

H. Never reveal that you may disapprove of something an applicant has done or said; always appear open-minded. On the other hand, don't condone or approve of anything that is obviously in error.

I. Always ask a few questions they don't expect and aren't prepared for: What do you do to relax? What are your hobbies? What is the last book you read? Try to understand their attitudes, personalities and energy levels.

J. Perhaps one of the most useful things you can ask when interviewing prospective employees is: What were your favorite parts of your previous job? Look to see if the things they liked to do with previous employers fit with the things you'll be asking them to do for you. This is important; it is important to cross-train employees to do as many jobs as possible, and it helps us to know which of those jobs will be a good fit.

    Often in interviewing prospective food-service employees you'll get two types of applicants—those who say they prefer the "people part" of the job (talking to patients, serving customers, running the cash register) and those who like the "food part" of the job (chef, salad prep, line cook). Most applicants will be fairly honest about what they like to do.

K. Be sure to ask at least one behavior-based question; this will be very useful in getting at how an applicant responds in real-life work situations and how well he or she is able to handle them. For example: What would you do if a customer complained that the "soup just doesn't taste right"? Or, what would you do if your seemingly happy patron did not leave any tip at all?

UNLAWFUL PRE-EMPLOYMENT QUESTIONS

This section is not intended to serve on behalf of, or as a substitute for, legal counsel, or even as an interpretation of the various federal and state laws regarding equal and fair employment practices. The purpose of this section is only to act as a guide to the type of questions that may and may not be legally asked of a potential employee.

A thorough discussion of this subject with both the state and federal labor offices and with your lawyer would be in order. Standard employment applications may be purchased at your office-supply store. Before you use these forms, let your lawyer examine one to make certain that it doesn't contain or insinuate any questions that might be considered illegal.

The Federal Civil Rights Act of 1964 and other state and federal laws ensure that a job applicant will be treated fairly and on an equal basis, regardless of race, color, religious creed, age, sex or national origin.

In order to support these regulations, you cannot ask certain questions of applicants in regard to the aforementioned categories. There is a fine line between what may and may not be asked of applicants. Use basic common sense with regard to the type of questions you ask. Any illegal question would have no bearing on the outcome of the interview anyway, so avoid questions that are related to, or might evoke an answer that infringes upon, the applicant's civil rights.

Age/date of birth. Age is an area of great concern for establishments with liquor, wine or beer licenses. Age is a sensitive pre-employment question, because the Age Discrimination in Employment Act *(http://www.eeoc.gov/laws/adea.html)* protects employees 40 years old and above. It is permissible to ask an applicant to state his or her age if it is fewer than 18 years. If you need the date of birth for internal reasons (e.g., computations with respect to a pension or profit-sharing plan) this information can be obtained after the person is hired.

Drugs, smoking. It is permissible to ask an applicant if he or she uses drugs or smokes. The application also affords an employer the opportunity to obtain the applicant's agreement to be bound by the employer's drug and smoking policies. The application also affords an employer an opportunity to obtain the applicant's agreement to submit to drug testing.

Other problem areas. Questions concerning whether an applicant has friends or relatives working for the employer may be improper if the employer gives a preference to such applicants. Questions concerning credit rating or credit references have been ruled discriminatory against minorities and women. Questions concerning whether an applicant owns a home have been held to be discriminatory against minority members, since a greater number of minority members do not own their own homes. While questions about military experience or training are permissible, questions concerning the type of discharge received by an applicant have been held to be improper. The Americans with Disabilities Act prohibits general inquiries about disabilities, health problems and medical conditions.

Some prohibited questions:

- How tall are you, anyway?

- What color are your eyes?

- Do you work out at the gym regularly?

- Do you or anyone you know have the HIV?

- Did you get any workers' comp from your last employer?

- How old are you, anyway?

- Have you been in prison?

- Are you really a man?

- Do you rent or own your home?

- Have you ever declared bankruptcy?

- What part of the world are your parents from?

- Are you a minority?

- Is English your first language?

- I can't tell if you're Japanese or Chinese. Which is it?

- So which church do you go to?

- Who will take care of the kids if you get this job?

- Is this your second marriage, then?

- Just curious: Are you gay?

- Are you in a committed relationship right now?

- How does your boyfriend feel about you working here?

SCREENING POTENTIAL EMPLOYEES

Screening job applicants will enable you to reject those candidates who are obviously unsuitable before they are referred to a lengthy interview. This saves both the restaurant and the applicants time and money. The preliminary screening can be done by an assistant manager or someone knowledgeable about the restaurant's employment needs and practices. Potential job candidates may then be referred to the manager for intensive interviews. All applicants should leave feeling they have been treated fairly and had an equal opportunity to present their case for getting the job. As previously stated, this is an important part of public relations. Who knows—the applicant that just left may be your next customer.

CRITERIA
Base your preliminary screening on the following criteria:

1. **Experience.** Is the applicant qualified to do the job? Examine past job experience. Check all references.

2. **Appearance.** Is the applicant neatly dressed? Remember she will be dealing with the public; the way the applicant is dressed now is probably better than the way she will come to work.

3. **Personality.** Does the applicant have a personality that will compliment the other employees' and impress customers? Is he outgoing but not overbearing?

4. **Legality.** Does the applicant meet the legal requirements?

5. **Availability.** Can the applicant work the hours needed? Commute easily?

6. **Health and physical ability.** Is the applicant capable of doing the physical work required? All employees hired should be subject to approval only after a complete physical examination by a mutually approved doctor.

Make certain the application is signed and dated.

APPLICANT CATEGORIES

All applicants at this point should be divided into one of the three following categories:

1. **Refer Applicant.** Refer applicant to manager for interview and, if feasible, to the department head where the job is open.

2. **Reject.** Describe the reasons for rejection and place the application on file for future reference.

3. **Prospective File.** Any applicant who is not qualified for this position but may be considered for other areas of the restaurant should be placed in a "prospective applicant" file.

WHAT TO LOOK FOR IN POTENTIAL RESTAURANT EMPLOYEES

1. **Stability.** You don't want employees to leave in two months. Look at "past employment sheet" records. Stability also refers to the applicant's emotional makeup.

2. **Leadership qualities.** Employees must be those who are achievers and doers, not individuals who have to be led around by the hand. Look at past employment positions and growth rate.

3. **Motivation.** Why is the applicant applying to this restaurant? Why the restaurant industry in general? Is the decision career-related or temporary? Does the applicant appear to receive her motivation from within or by a domineering other, such as a spouse or parent?

4. **Independence.** Is the applicant on his own? Does he appear to be financially secure? At what age did he leave home? And for what reasons?

5. **Maturity.** Is the individual mentally mature enough to work in a stressful environment? Will she be able to relate and communicate with other employees and customers who may be much older than her?

6. **Determination.** Does the applicant seem to always finish what he starts? Does he seem to look for, or retreat from, challenges? Examine time at school and at last job.

7. **Work habits.** Is the applicant aware of the physical work involved in restaurant employment? Has the applicant done similar work? Does the applicant appear neat and organized? Look over the application: Is it filled out per the instructions? Neatly? In ink? Examine past jobs for number and rate of promotions and raises.

THE FINAL SELECTION AND DECISION

Reaching the final selection, to whom to offer the position, is often a difficult choice. You may have many applicants who are qualified and would probably become excellent employees, but which one do you decide upon? Always base your choice on the total picture the applicants have painted of themselves through the interviews, resumes and applications. Gather advice from those who interviewed or had contact with the individuals. Not only will this help you reach the correct decision but it will also make the rest of your staff feel a part of the management decision-making team. Whomever you select, he or she must be someone you feel good about having around, someone you hopefully will enjoy working with and who you feel will have a very good chance of being successful at the job.

When you offer him or her the job, make certain the applicant fully understands the following items before accepting it:

1. **Salary.** Starting pay, salary range, expected growth rate, the day payroll is issued, company benefits, vacations, insurance, etc.

2. **Job description.** List of job duties, hours, expectations, etc.

3. **Work details.** Date of first day of work, time to arrive, and to whom to report.

REJECTING APPLICANTS

Rejecting applicants is always an unpleasant and difficult task. The majority of the applications will be rejected almost immediately. Some applicants will ask the reason for rejection. Always be honest, but use tact in explaining the reasoning behind the decision. Avoid a confrontation, explaining only what is necessary to settle the applicant's questions. Usually it will be sufficient to say, "We accepted an applicant who was more experienced," or "…who is better qualified."

As mentioned before, some applications may be transferred into a "prospective file" for later reference. Inform the applicant of this action, but don't give the impression that he or she has a good chance of being hired, nor state a specific date when you will be looking for new employees.

EMPLOYEE HANDBOOK/PERSONNEL POLICY MANUAL

Federal law mandates that all employers, regardless of size, have written policy guidelines. Employee handbooks/policy manuals are used to familiarize new employees with company policies and procedures. They also serve as guides to management personnel. Formally writing down your policies could keep you out of court; prevent problems and misunderstandings; save time spent answering common questions; and look more professional to your employees. Explaining and documenting company policy to your employees has been proven to increase productivity, compliance and retention. Detailed in the chart below are some common areas to be covered.

Lack of communication, along with inadequate policies and guidelines, have been cited as major factors in workplace legal disputes. Failure to inform or notify employees of standard policies has resulted in the loss of millions of dollars in legal judgments. Simply not being aware that their actions violated company policy has been an effective defense for many terminated employees. Most important is to have the employee sign a document stating he or she has received, reviewed, understands and intends to comply with all policies in the manual.

If you have ever written a policy document before, you know how time-consuming it can be. Even if you were a lawyer, it would likely take you 40 hours to research and write a comprehensive employee manual. To pay someone to draw one up for you can cost thousands of dollars. Atlantic Publishing has put together a standard employee handbook guide for the food-service industry. All you have to do is edit the information. The template contains all of the most important company handbook sections, and it's written in Microsoft Word so that customizing and printing your manual will be as easy as possible. The program currently sells for around $70 and is available at *http://www.atlantic-pub.com* and 800-541-1336 (Item EHB-CS). There is also an order form at the back of this book.

TOPICS TO BE COVERED IN EMPLOYEE HANDBOOK

Standards of Conduct	Employee Conduct	Bonus Plan
Absenteeism and Punctuality	Work Performance	Performance Reviews
Neatness of Work Area	Availability for Work	Benefits Program
Personal Telephone Calls	Personal Mail	Benefits Eligibility
Mandatory Meetings	Communications	Insurance
Employee Relations	Problem Resolution	Insurance Continuation
Use of Company Vehicles	Disciplinary Guidelines	Personal Appearance
Safety	Conflicts of Interest	Affidavit of Receipt
Violence and Weapons Policy	Workplace Monitoring	Holidays
Severe Weather	Suggestions	Vacation
Orientation	Termination Procedures	Bereavement Leave
Harassment	Criminal Convictions	Social Security
Personnel Files	Employment References	Pre-Tax Deductions
Employment of Relatives	Outside Employment	Military Leave
Rehiring Former Employees	Searches	Medical Leave of Absence
Substance Abuse	Solicitations and Contributions	Family Leave of Absence
Company Property	Office Equipment	Employee Discounts
Tools and Equipment	Employment Classification	Workers' Compensation
Hours of Work	Break Policy	Jury Duty
Recording Time	Unemployment Compensation	Overtime
Salary and Wage Increases	Payroll	Educational Assistance
Travel Expenses	Reimbursable Expenses	Job Abandonment
Voluntary Resignation	Performance-Based Release	Acts of Misconduct
Equal Employment Opportunity	Other Forms of Separation	Confidentiality of Company Information

PERSONNEL FILE

Once the applicant is hired, an individual personnel file should be set up immediately. It should contain the following information:

1. Application.

2. Form W-4 and Social Security number.

3. Name, address and phone number.

4. Emergency phone number.

5. Employment date.

6. Job title and pay rate.

7. Past performance evaluations.

8. Signed form indicating receipt and acceptance of Employee Handbook/Personnel Policy Manual

9. Termination date, if applicable, and a detailed account of the reasons for termination.

TRAINING

The most serious problem facing labor relations in the restaurant industry today is the lack of trained personnel and structured, industrywide training programs. The manufacturing industry realized the importance of training programs and implemented them decades ago. New restaurant employees are often thrown into jobs, with little or no formal training. While on the job they must gather whatever information and skills—whether correct or not—they can. Blame for this situation lies with management. Managers regard training as a problem that must be dealt with—quickly and all at once—so that the new trainee can be brought up to full productivity as soon as possible.

Getting employees to do things right means taking the time to train them properly from the start so that they understand what needs to be done, how to do it and why it should be done that way. Effective training, however, involves more than simply providing information. Training is not a problem, and it cannot be "solved" and then forgotten. Managers and supervisors at every level must soon realize that training is a continual process, as is learning: it must never stop.

The most effective training technique is interactivity. Get people to stand up and do things. Show them how to set a table, look for lipstick on a glass, wash their hands properly, use a thermometer, wash a dish, make a martini, garnish a plate. Let the employees participate.

Most managers and supervisors think of training as teaching new employees skills, such as dishwashing or bartending. Training needs to be far more than that; management must look beyond its own interests. As mentioned before, we must start to consider the employee's interests, goals, needs and desires, if we are to become successful.

The employee must know not only her job and how to perform it, but how her performance affects others in their jobs in other parts of the restaurant. She must visualize her position as an integral part of an efficient machine, not as a separate, meaningless function. For an example take the plight of the dishwasher in most restaurants. Dishwashers are vitality important to the success of any restaurant, and yet few managers, and virtually no other employees, are consciously aware of their importance. Rather than being treated with dignity and respect, they are considered, in most establishments, insignificant menial laborers. They are often paid minimum wage with little—usually no—benefits, expected to do all the dirty work—cleaning up after others and working in poor conditions—while all the other employees shout orders and instructions. The only time they are really communicated with is when they do something wrong, when someone needs something done or when a mess needs to be cleaned up. Is there really any wonder why an entirely new crew will have to be trained in two weeks? Many managers themselves don't fully realize the importance of this function, or that it is far harder to find a good dishwasher than it is a good waitperson. I have always mandated that every new hire perform at least one shift in this position to fully understand its importance. Try giving the dishwashing staff an hour-long break one night and see the resulting chaos.

Telling an employee that his position and performance is crucial to the restaurant's success and showing him the reasons why are two entirely different things. The importance of performing his job in the manner in which he was trained must by physically demonstrated to the employee, as well as the ramifications of varying from these procedures. Using the example of the frustrated dishwasher, let's apply this philosophy with some practical, hands-on management.

Start the training program by having all of the dishwashers come into the restaurant for dinner, lunch or a pre-shift meal with you. While the waitperson is performing her service, point out the importance of having clean, grease free dishes, and explain why silverware and wineglasses must be checked for spots. Show them why the waitstaff need their stock rapidly and what happens if they don't get it.

Type out a list describing the cost of each plate, glass and so forth in the restaurant. This is the most effective way to show why they must be so concerned and careful about breakage. List the cost of the other articles that pertain to their job, such as the dishwashing machine, chemicals, soaps, pots, pans and knives.

Show them that you are concerned with both them and their performance. Pay more than the other restaurants in the area so that you will attract the best people. Set up some small benefits such as a free meal and free soda per shift. A financial incentive is the most effective type of motivating force. Establish bonuses for the dishwashers, such as giving them 3 to 5 cents extra for each cover served that night. The small cost of these little extras will be substantiated with lower turnover rates and higher production.

Apply this principle of demonstrating rather than lecturing to illustrate your points with all of your employees, and you will have the basis for a good training program and good employee relations.

ORIENTATION AND INSTRUCTION

A complete orientation of the trainee to his or her new job and new company is an intricate part of the training process. The entire orientation will take less than thirty minutes; unfortunately, however, it is rarely done. There is no excuse for not giving the new employee a good introduction before he or she starts the actual training.

Described below are some basic orientation practices:

1. Introduce the new employee to yourself and the company.

2. Introduce the new employee to all of the other employees.

3. Introduce the new employee to HER trainer and supervisor.

4. Explain the company's employee and personnel policies. Present the Employee Handbook/Personnel Policy Manual.

5. Outline the objectives and goals of the training program:
   A. Describe the training, where and how it will take place.
   B. Describe the information that will be learned.
   C. Describe the skills and attitudes that will be developed.

6. Set up a schedule for the employee. It should include:
   A. The date, day and time to report to work during training.
   B. Who will be doing the training and who the supervisor is.
   C. What should be learned and accomplished each day.
   D. The date when the training should be completed.

At this point the trainee may be presented to the trainer. Ideally, the employee's regular supervisor does all of the training. The trainer must be a model employee who is thoroughly knowledgeable about and experienced in the job. He must be able to communicate clearly and have a great deal of patience and understanding.

The trainee must be taught the how, why, when and where of the job. This is best accomplished by following the trainer's example and methods. After confidence is built, the employee may attempt to repeat the procedure under the watchful eye of the trainer.

The trainer must gauge how fast the trainee is learning and absorbing the material against the time schedule set up by the manager. Daily written or oral reports should be presented to the manager on the trainee's progress and needs and placed in her employee file. Compare the trainee's production to that of an experienced worker. Written and practical tests can be given to evaluate how much material is being absorbed and utilized. Add new material when the old material has been assimilated. Relate the old material to the new as you continue to build towards training the employee.

Once the employee has completed the training, the trainer or supervisor should prepare a final written report and evaluation. This report should describe the strengths and weaknesses of the trainee, her knowledge of the job, quality of work and attitude and a general appraisal of the employee. After the manager reviews this report all three parties should meet to discuss the training period. The employee should be congratulated on successfully completing the training program. A review of the final report would be in order and then filed in the employee's personnel file for future reference. Ask the employee her opinion of the training program; she may have some thoughts on improving it. This same question should be presented to the employee after two weeks of work. Find out if the training program adequately prepared the trainee for the actual job.

OUTSIDE HELP IN TRAINING

When training sessions involve several people or even the entire staff, it is a good idea to bring in outside help for your meetings. These people are experts in their fields. Often just a phone call is enough inducement. Reward these people for their time and effort with a complimentary gift certificate.

There are great resources for outside-training information available to assist in your training programs: videos, posters, books, software, etc. One great source for all these products is Atlantic Publishing (*http://www.atlantic-pub.com* and 800-541-1336).

OUTSIDE HELP: SPEAKERS AND SUBJECTS

State Liquor Agent: Liquor laws, compliance, etc.

Health Department Inspector: Health and sanitation practices/requirements.

Wine Distributors: Wine tasting, promotion, etc.

Dishwasher Chemical Company Salesperson: Proper use of machine and chemicals.

Beer Distributor: Presenting and promoting beer.

Red Cross Instructor: Basic first aid, the Heimlich maneuver to stop choking and CPR procedures.

EVALUATING PERFORMANCE

Evaluating each employee's job performance is a crucial element in developing a structured work environment and sound employee relations. Every employee must be aware of his or her strengths and which areas of his or her job performance need improvement. Quarterly or periodic one-on-one evaluations help break down the communication barriers between management and employees. Many of an employee's work-related problems, thoughts and ideas can be revealed in the evaluation session. However, remember to keep in mind that evaluations are only a part of the communication process and should not be considered as a substitute for daily communication. Management must always be available to listen. Communication is an ongoing and continual process. See an example of the **Employee Performance Evaluation Form** at the end of this chapter.

Consider these points prior to filling out the evaluation forms:

1. Know the employee's job description thoroughly. You are evaluating how well the employee meets the job requirements; you are not comparing against other employees nor evaluating the employee according to what you see as his or her potential.

2. Always conduct the evaluation in private, with no interruptions. Schedule each evaluation far enough apart so that there is plenty of time to discuss everything in one sitting.

3. Don't let just one incident or trait—positive or negative—dominate the evaluation. Look at the whole picture over the entire time since the last evaluation.

4. Evaluations should balance positive and negative attributes, never be one-sided. A totally negative evaluation will almost never motivate a poor employee. Bring out some of his or her positive contributions, and in detail describe what changes are needed. A completely negative evaluation will only scare the employee. Should a totally negative evaluation be warranted, it is probable that the employee should have been terminated long ago.

5. Review past evaluations, but don't dwell on them. Look for areas where improvement or a decline in performance has taken place.

6. Always back up your thoughts and appraisals with specific examples. Allow plenty of time for the employee's comments: remember, you could be wrong. If examples or circumstances that were never mentioned before come out in the evaluation, you are guilty of allowing the communication process to deteriorate.

7. Don't cover too much material or expect the employee to make a drastic change overnight. An evaluation is only part in a series of continuous steps to direct the employee.

8. Begin the evaluation with the employee's positive points and then direct the discussion to areas that need improvement.

9. Certain personality traits and deficiencies may not always be changeable. Don't overemphasize them, but show how they might affect the employee's job performance and the performance of others.

10. Finish the evaluation on a positive note. The employee should leave with a good feeling about his positive contributions to the restaurant and know precisely what and how to improve on his weaknesses.

11. After the evaluation make certain that you follow up on the thoughts, ideas and recommendations that were brought out during the evaluation. Without a follow-up the evaluation is of little value.

12. Evaluations are confidential. File them in the employee's personnel file only if no one else has access to them there.

SCHEDULING

The overall objective in scheduling is to place the most efficient employee at the job and shift where he or she will achieve maximum productivity at minimum expense. The greatest tool management has in controlling labor cost is scheduling, and yet scheduling is most often so poorly done that it becomes more a part of the problem than of the solution. In many cases the employee's schedule is scribbled on a piece of paper or, worse, verbally communicated with little thought as to what is actually needed.

Properly preparing the weekly schedule for a restaurant of fifteen employees may take between one and two hours to complete. The individual preparing the schedule has to take into account many different factors, such as:

1. The number of covers and large parties expected each day.

2. At what time maximum production must be reached.

3. The skill and productivity of each employee.

4. Each employee's desired schedule: days off, hours, etc.

Only after several months of operation will you be able to accurately assess your precise labor needs. During the first couple of months be sure you have plenty of employees available should it become suddenly busy. Many customers will understand that you have just opened and don't have all the bugs quite worked out yet, but they are still paying full price for everything. Don't get caught short on trained personnel. The food service on opening day should be consistent with that of several months later.

Schedule employees throughout the night to meet anticipated needs. Don't schedule all six waiters and waitresses and both cooks at 5:00, when you won't need all of them until the big rush at 7:15. Schedule your best employees to open the restaurant, then schedule the other employees in sequence at the time you need them most.

Full-time employees should be cross-trained to perform two or more jobs, such as waiting tables and bartending. There are many beneficial results from this situation. Scheduling will become a lot easier, as the flexible employee can be shifted around to meet your needs. Employees who call in sick or leave without notice can be replaced easily and without disrupting the entire schedule.

Many employees will enjoy performing two jobs, as they will not become as easily bored and will tend to feel like an integral part of the restaurant. An employee who is involved, interested and concerned about the restaurant will always be a better performer than one who is detached. The only possible disadvantage to this cross-training arrangement is that, when the employee does leave, he or she will be harder and more expensive to replace. Perhaps this thinking is a great part of the labor problem the food-service industry faces today. If you never give the employee the opportunity to develop and prove herself because you are afraid she'll leave in a few months, undoubtedly she will. Every employee should be given the opportunity for more and more responsibility.

Should overscheduling occur, employees can be set at tasks that will produce future labor savings, such as preparing nonperishable food items or cleaning and organizing work areas. Additional unneeded employees can be sent home. Check with your Labor Board regarding these regulations. Under most state rulings, the employee who is scheduled to work and then is not needed must be compensated in some manner; usually he is paid a minimum of three hours' wages.

The restaurant's sales history is another important tool in scheduling for productivity. Don't forget special events. For example, large parties, holidays, sporting events and convention traffic are as important to anticipate as business downturns.

In recent years computer software has helped management enormously in scheduling employees. This software simplifies the time-consuming, labor-intensive manual processes involved in scheduling employees, maximizing resources, controlling labor costs and retaining a qualified staff. Most software systems enable the manager to quickly determine the right employee for each position and shift. Most of the software is easily integrated, with time, attendance and payroll systems. All of these systems will save money and enhance employee satisfaction and retention. The software will range in price from a few hundred dollars to several thousand dollars. One good scheduling system with the option of an employee time clock is available from Atlantic Publishing and costs less than $300 (*http://www.atlantic-pub.com* and 800-541-1336): Item ESP-CS.

LABOR COST CONTROL CONCEPTS

So often in the food industry the solution to a high labor cost is to lay off employees, to lower wages or to cut back on hours and/or benefits. These shortsighted measures will initially cut the labor cost, but over a period of time they will result in lower overall productivity, a decrease in the quality and service, low morale and a high turnover rate. Occasionally some employees may have to be laid off due to a drastic decrease in sales or to initial overhiring, but this should occur only rarely. Controlling the restaurant's labor cost takes daily management involvement. It cannot be accomplished with one swift action at the end of each month. Described below are some practical suggestions that may be used to streamline your operation so that it may run more efficiently, effectively and profitably.

PREPARED FOODS

Prepared, frozen, portioned and, even, fresh vegetables, salads, etc., that are ready to use can save a substantial number of preparation and cooking hours and, thus, a lot of labor costs. Prior to committing yourself to using any of these products, inspect a sample to ensure that the product will equal or exceed the desired quality level. Examine the additional food cost of the item: Could you produce the same product with less overall cost? Remember to consider the additional cost of labor, equipment, utilities and so forth in your projection. Most often, the manufactured product is considerably cheaper, as it was prepared in large quantities using commercial equipment and procedures. Prepared foods will also contribute to your overall consistency, as the processed product is always consistently produced.

Restaurants in the years ahead will be moving away from in-house food production and instead will concentrate on marketing and selling food items. The cost of maintaining a big staff of highly trained chefs, butchers, bakers and so forth is simply becoming far too high. Specialization is the key to the future. Why produce a product when someone else can produce it better, more consistently, considerably cheaper and with less administrative work, for you?

The barrier to such modernization in the food-service industry is only psychological resistance to using these products. All restaurateurs and managers would agree that restaurants should serve only the finest quality of food possible, but is it really justifiable to serve a two-day-old steak over a frozen one simply because one is frozen and one is not? Some examples of good-quality prepared items are: frozen dessert products; canned or dried packaged soup and sauce bases; bottled dressings, dips, marinades and demi-glace sauce bases; boneless, marinated chicken breasts; divided, cooked and frozen shrimp; marinated meats; prestuffed chicken breasts; chefs'-name-brand products; washed and prepped greens; precut vegetables; frozen vegetable mixes; garlic puree; IQF (individual quick frozen) vegetables and potatoes that have been pre–flame-roasted; frozen bread dough; chocolate cups/containers; phyllo cups; ready-to-pipe dessert toppings; frozen puff pastry; stuffed appetizers; and premade hors d'oeuvres.

KITCHEN DESIGN AND EQUIPMENT

An efficiently designed kitchen with laborsaving equipment is by far the most effective way to reduce labor costs. After several months of operation, examine the kitchen in action. Look at each employee: What are his or her motions and movements? How many steps must be taken to reach food items and more stock? Look at the position and lay-out of the equipment: Is it set up the most efficient way possible? Ask the employees how they would like their work areas set up, and how work areas could be made more efficient. They are the real experts—they work the same job every day. Look at the wait-staff's work areas: Could they be made more efficient? These investigations and their results will create faster and better service.

A restaurant designer or consultant may be brought in to analyze your setup. In order to design the most efficient systems possible, this person will need to know everything about your equipment, staff, menu, preparation procedures and sales. This is why it might be advantageous to contact one of these individuals after you have been operating for a while and have made all necessary changes. However, a designer certainly would be valuable in the initial planning stage. The savings derived from the increase in productivity and in employee morale created by your new setup will offset the cost of this consultant.

Every year new pieces of equipment, large and small, expensive and inexpensive, are introduced that will save time, labor and energy. Gone forever are the days when cheap labor will replace the need for new modern equipment. Food-service workers, through the use of modernized machines, practical, efficient layout and processed foods, will be producing more and more, in fewer numbers. Aside from saving on labor costs, new mechanization will reduce product handling, eliminate work drudgery and make each task—as well as the overall job more enjoyable for the employee.

The large initial capital expenditure for new equipment can usually be financed over several years through either the manufacturer or distributor. The total cost may be depreci-ated over several years and written off as a business tax-deductible expense.

Restaurant shows and food-service magazines are the best places to look for the announcement and review of new equipment. The appendix in the back of this book con-tains a list of all the trade publications that announce the upcoming shows.

ELECTRONIC ORDERING SYSTEMS

In the previous chapter we discussed the "Electronic Guest Check System" or "Wireless Waiter." These systems use a mobile computer. The waitperson carries the mobile com-puter pad and places the order on the touch-screen display. As each dish is entered, this information is transferred in real-time to the kitchen where the order is printed out. These systems, as they become widespread, will have a dramatic effect on the labor cost in the industry.

THE DECISION TO TERMINATE AN EMPLOYEE

There comes a time when an unsatisfactorily performing employee, after being evaluated and given a fair opportunity to correct his or her deficiencies, must be terminated. Discharging an employee is always a difficult and unpleasant task, but it must be done for the good of the restaurant. Although it may be an unpleasant experience it is far worse to let the employee stay on. Before long the entire staff's morale will drop, causing a decrease in productivity.

The decision as to whether an employee should be terminated or retrained is difficult and often prejudiced by your inability to examine the entire picture of the employee's performance. The final decision to discharge an employee should be reached after carefully weighing the pros and cons—never in anger or when tired or under stress. Ask the employee's supervisor or department head for an evaluation of the situation and the employee. Examine the employee's training, supervision and past evaluations. Make certain the employee has been given a fair opportunity to prove himself. Also be certain that neither you nor any member of your management staff has in any way contributed to, caused or perpetuated the problem.

Immediately after reaching your decision to terminate the employee, set up a meeting with him. Don't let more than twenty-four hours go by; you don't want this information to leak out.

The employee's supervisor or department head should be present during the exit interview. She will be able to add support and witness the action. This is important, as the employee may use some legal means to gain a settlement. Conduct the exit interview in a private room with no interruptions. Should the employee disagree with your reasoning or points, give him the opportunity to discuss them, but make sure you back up everything you say with proven facts and statements. Remain seated and calm during the proceedings; don't get up quickly or move suddenly. Absolutely never touch the employee, except when shaking hands. These actions may be misinterpreted and lead to a confrontation.

Fill out a report on the termination proceedings, and file it in the employee's personnel file. This report will be important should the employee decide to challenge the action. Develop a plan to fill the vacancy as soon as possible. Keep in mind that it will take several months before a new employee can be brought up to full productivity and that, after training, he or she may not work out at all.

Although nothing can fully prevent a former employee from filing a lawsuit, there are ways to decrease the likelihood of litigation: Be honest with the employee about his or her performance and the reason for the termination. Treat employees consistently; aggressively investigate claims of discrimination. Above all, document the chances you've given employees to improve prior to your decision to terminate them. If a termination is challenged, and there are no records of the problems cited as reasons for termination and indicating opportunities given to correct these problems, there could be a problem. Keep in mind your notes don't have to be very detailed, but a dated description of a problem or of the employee's progress that is slipped into a personnel file helps dramatically.

The other employees always perceive the termination of an employee as a threat to their security. You may even be looked upon as unfair or exceedingly harsh. Sometimes an explanation is needed to soothe the other employees; in most cases, though, the reasons will be obvious to them and they will be on your side. Still, and again, document everything.

EMPLOYEE PERFORMANCE EVALUATION FORM

NAME: _____ POSITION: _____

INTERVIEWER: _____ DATE: _____

LAST EVALUATION DATE: _____ SALARY: _____

For each of the following categories grade the employee's performance on a sliding scale of 1 to 10 (see scale below). The overall grade is the average of all scores plus the interviewer's comments.

| 1-2 poor | 3-4 below average | 5 average | 6-7 above average | 8-9 very good | 10 exceptional |

KNOWLEDGE OF JOB
procedures, paperwork, skill, function

RATING: _____

Comments: _____
_____
_____

QUALITY
up to specification, accuracy, consistency

RATING: _____

Comments: _____
_____
_____

ATTITUDE
towards work, management, other employees, customers

RATING: _____

Comments: _____
_____
_____

LEADERSHIP
ability to give direction

RATING: _____

Comments: _____
_____
_____

RELIABILITY
dependable, on time, follows through on assignments

RATING: _____

Comments: _____
_____
_____

PRODUCTIVITY
volume, utilization of time

RATING: _____

Comments: _____
_____
_____

APPEARANCE
uniform, neat

RATING: _____

Comments: _____
_____
_____

SERVICE
alert, fast

RATING: _____

Comments: _____
_____
_____

OVERALL RATING: _____

SALARY ADJUSTED: ❑ YES ❑ NO

NEW SALARY: _____

Recommendations: _____
_____
_____

Items to be followed up on: _____
_____
_____
_____
_____

PUBLIC RELATIONS FOR YOUR RESTAURANT—HOW TO GET CUSTOMERS IN THE DOOR WITH LITTLE OR NO COST

WHAT IS PUBLIC RELATIONS

Public relations is really the sum of its many definitions. It's the message a person, company or organization sends to the public. It's a planned effort to build positive opinions about your business through actions, and communications about those actions. In short, it's any contact your organization has with another human being, and the resulting opinion. This opinion may or may not be accurate, but it comes from everything the public reads, sees, hears and thinks about you. Effective PR has been described as becoming a positive member of your community (and getting credit for it). Basically, good PR sends a positive message to the public about your establishment.

PR should be part of your overall marketing communications program. This includes advertising, internal communications and sales promotion. Speeches, contests, promotions, personal appearances and publicity are parts of PR, but really, the results generated from all of these parts—including acquiring unpaid-for media space and time—are PR. It's who the public thinks you are and the nurturing of that opinion in a positive way.

WHAT PR DOES (AND DOESN'T DO) FOR YOU

If done well, PR distinguishes you from the pack in the eyes of your customers. It leaves them with a favorable impression of you and great tidbits of information to pass on to their friends about your establishment. It makes you newsworthy in a great way and can help save your reputation and standing in your community during an emergency.

Good PR improves sales by creating an environment in which people choose to spend their time and money. As said before, PR is getting credit for being an upstanding member of your community. If you are not, PR can't make you look like you are. PR accentuates the positive and creates lasting value by highlighting what makes your establishment special. PR cannot create lasting value if none is there to begin with. What it can do is communicate existing value effectively, so it lives in your customer's minds.

Good PR can make a good story great, and a bad story less bad. But PR is not just the public's opinion of your business; it's also the physical state of your establishment. People aren't just interacting with your staff; they're interacting with your facility. If the media are reporting on something wonderful that happened at your restaurant, but the place is in a state of disrepair, what are you communicating about your establishment?

The key to implementing an effective PR campaign is determining what your business's image is; what you want it to be; and how best you can create that image in the eyes of the public. You need to clearly define your objectives and create a plan that will implement them. PR is not a way to gloss over a tarnished image or to keep the press at a safe distance; it's an organized and ongoing campaign to accentuate the positives of who you truly are.

THE MARRIAGE OF PR AND MARKETING

Public relations is one of marketing's tools. As a result, most restaurants keep these two departments, or functions, close together. This is because PR is one of the crucial aspects of a successful marketing plan. In fact, in many instances, the two have been combined, and are referred to as marketing public relations, corporate public relations, relationship marketing or mega-marketing. All of these terms reflect the symbiotic relationship between PR and marketing.

On a practical level, this close relationship obtains and retains customers, which is the obvious goal of any marketing plan. When management is communicating effectively with guests, employees and community leaders, it is implementing an effective marketing plan.

Fundamentally, all marketing is integrated. Consumers don't distinguish between one message from your business and another—all the messages are yours. In that light, since it's your job to communicate as well as possible, understanding that all your marketing is integrated allows you to focus on an overall approach to building good PR.

HOW TO APPLY YOUR PR PLAN

Once you have established the objectives of your PR campaign and integrated them into your marketing plan, it is time to execute. These questions can help you do just that:

• What's the right medium for this strategy?

- Who are the key contacts?

- How strong are the necessary personal relationships required for this plan? Do any need to be established or reestablished?

- Is this plan thorough? Have we considered all the downside risks?

- Are we prepared to deliver a package to the media?

This delivery package is an essential part of your plan. It contains descriptions, plots, contacts, phone numbers—all the pertinent information that will inform the media and direct them to you. The press may not use one word of your materials, but there is a much greater likelihood they'll describe you the way you want them to if you've given them the resources to do just that. Following is a list of practical factors that will help you gain recognition:

- **Be honest.** The media want credible, honest material and relationships. Your message should be genuine and factual. This doesn't mean you have to reveal confidential data; it just means that your materials should be thorough and truthful.

- **Respond.** Don't lie, dodge or cover up. If you don't have every answer to a question—and you might not—don't say "no comment," or "that information is unavailable." Simply respond that you don't have that information, but will provide it as soon as humanly possible. Then provide it as soon as humanly possible.

- **Give the facts, and follow up.** If you supply the media with a printed handout of key facts, it greatly lessens the chances of your getting misquoted. Make a concentrated effort to follow up and go over information with the media. Again, if you don't have a requested piece of information, get it and follow up with a note and/or call to make sure the correct data reaches the media.

- **Be concise.** Usually, the media will burn you for what you say, not what you don't. Be deliberate about providing the facts without editorializing, exaggerating or pulling things out of thin air.

- **Nurture relationships.** If you follow the above steps you're on your way to building a strong and lasting relationship with the press. These relationships can sour instantly if you are reactionary, hostile, aloof, hypersensitive or argumentative in any way. No matter what you think of an interviewer, treat him or her with respect, courtesy and professionalism. Causing negative reactions from the press will deny you print space and airtime.

How you interact with the press is crucial, but it's only half the process. The content of what you communicate to them—having a clear and deliberate focus about how you are going to tell your story—is the other side of press relations. The following list will help you identify your purpose and communicate it effectively to the press:

- **Identify your purpose.** Why do you want public exposure? What are you specifically trying to draw attention to? Are you selling your hotel's new lobby renovation? Then don't go on about its famous rose garden. Be sure you are conveying your purpose.

- **Identify your target.** Who are you targeting? Prospective customers? Your employees? The local business community? Civic leaders? Lay out whom you want to reach, and then determine who in the media will speak to them most effectively.

- **Think as they're thinking.** Why would this be interesting to the media? Figure out how your interests can be packaged in a way that directly matches the interests of the press. Make your story one they want to print—i.e., one that will help them sell papers, gain listeners, etc.

- **Customize your materials.** Once you have identified your purpose, who your target is and the media's angle, tailor your materials to include all three. Give the press everything they need to tell the story—photos, copy, etc.—and be sure it's in exactly the style and mediums they're using.

- **Know where to send your materials.** Is your story a news story or a feature story? Do you know the difference? A news story goes to a newspaper's city desk. Feature stories go to the appropriate editor: travel, lifestyle, etc. It's a very good idea to cultivate relationships with these editors beforehand so that when the time arises, they are thinking well of you and would like to help.

- **Make their job easy.** Do not ask the media for the ground rules for getting press and building relationships—learn these on your own and then meet them. Spending valuable time and resources building a relationship with a reporter, only to then submit materials at the last minute or give them insufficient or inaccurate information, burns bridges quickly. Do as much of their work for them as possible: give them something that is ready to go, answers all their questions and is interesting. This is the difference between staying in the middle and rising to the top of a busy person's in-box. Also, be available immediately to answer questions. If a reporter calls and you aren't there or don't return the call immediately, your great story—prepared at considerable expense—may end up in the trash.

BUILDING AND SUPPORTING STRONG MEDIA RELATIONS

Media relations are one of the most important aspects of PR, because effective media relations generate publicity. Effective media relations open the channels for your public to receive the messages you want them to receive. Media relations are how you build your relationships with the press, and this determines how they respond when you want them to report on a story.

The first goal in building strong media relations is to determine who your target media are. The audiences they reach should classify news media and the means they use to carry their messages. Your target media will change according to the type of message you wish to send and the type of audience you wish to reach. Your advertising agency can supply you with contact information for the newspapers, radio and television stations in your area. In addition, you may want to target national media, as well as specialized trade and business publications.

It may be a good idea to hire a part-time PR consultant, former reporter or editor who can help you present your materials to the press. If this is beyond your budgetary limits, the following is a list of essentials for building a good relationship with the press:

FACT SHEET—One of the most helpful items of media information, the fact sheet does most of the reporter's research for her. It also shortens the length of interviews by answering questions in advance. It should describe your property and what you are trying to get press for. At a glance it tells where you are located, when you opened, your architectural style, capacity and number of employees. It should also specify the types of facilities you have and what kind of food you serve.

STAFF BIOGRAPHIES—You will need to write biographies for all of your key executives. These list work experience, education, professional memberships, honors and awards.

GOOD PHOTOGRAPHY—Do not take chances with an amateur photographer. Space is very limited in the print media, and editors go through thousands of photographs to choose just a few. This is true even for local editors. Don't give them any reason to ignore your pictures. Have them taken by a pro. Ask for references and check them thoroughly. When the photos are done, write an explanatory caption for each picture in your collection. This gives editors an easy understanding of what they're looking at. Then, before sending photos to the media, be sure you find out whether they prefer black and white, slides, transparencies, etc., and send them in the desired format.

PRESS KIT FOLDER—Put all of these materials into a single folder with your property's name and logo on the cover. You might also include brochures, rate cards, package flyers, a brief on your involvement with local charities, etc. Don't overstuff it, but give the press a solid idea of what distinguishes you from the competition.

Before you begin your media campaign, you should get to know the media as much as possible. This may mean inviting them—one at a time—to have a brief tour or visit of your establishment and, perhaps, lunch. This gives them a sense of you and your business and begins to build a relationship. These visits are NOT the time to sell them on doing a story on you. It's a time for you to get to know each other and to build a relationship. If the reporters trust you, they will help you, and vice versa. They need article ideas as much as you need press, and getting to know them will give you insight into how you can help them do their job.

Once you've built this relationship, and your friends in the media trust you won't be barraging them with endless story ideas, you can begin your media campaign. It is important to remember that having a positive rapport with a reporter doesn't mean he'll do a story on you. Your relationship with the reporter will help get a newsworthy story printed, but you won't get a boring story to press just because the reporter likes you. Your story needs to be newsworthy on its own. Also, reporters are always working against time. The more you can give them pertinent, accurate, concise information, the better your chances of getting their attention.

If you've built a respectful relationship with the media, a reporter who gets a story from an interview or news conference at your establishment will mention your place in her story. These are the "freebies" that come from developing strong relationships with the media and learning to think in their terms.

Many businesses go one step further and give their media contacts that are written in journalistic style. A news release describes the newsworthy development in your restaurant in a ready-to-print article. Editors can then change it or print it as is. These can be immensely valuable for getting your message out there.

If writing journalistic articles is beyond your reach or budget, **tip sheets** can be very effective in getting your story across. A tip sheet gets the message to the media by simply outlining the who, what, when, where, why and how of your story. It's basically an outline of the story the reporter will then write. Tip sheets give the spine of the story and, because they are so concise, often get more attention from busy editors.

Here are a few more tips on how to work effectively with the media:

- Earn a reputation for dealing with the facts and nothing else.

- Never ask to review a reporter's article before publication.

- Never ask after a visit or an interview if an article will appear.

- Follow up by phone to see if your fact sheet or press release has arrived, if the reporter is interested and if she needs anything else.

- Provide requested information—photos, plans, etc.—ASAP.

WHAT'S NEWS

Once you have identified your target media and begun your media relations program, you need to learn what makes news. To do this, pick up the paper, and turn on the TV. The media is looking for the strange, volatile, controversial and unusual. It's not newsworthy that you run a nice restaurant that provides great food at a reasonable price. It's newsworthy when a customer gets food poisoning at your restaurant, or when a group's convention reservations get cancelled. This is not the type of news you want to make, but it's news. Obviously, you want to be making great news. One of the foundations of this is taking steps to avoid negative articles: making sure your reservations system works, your staff treats guests courteously, etc.

Once you've taken these steps, you are ready to generate positive stories in the media. How? Well, what do editors find newsworthy? Here is a list of basic newsworthiness criteria:

A. Is it local?

B. Is it timely?

C. Is it unique, unusual, strange?

D. Does it involve and affect people?

E. Will it provoke human emotion?

Think in terms of what it is that sets your establishment apart from the competition and what is newsworthy about those qualities. When this is done, again, target your media. When you've got a story, be smart about who would be interested in writing about it and whose audience would love to read about it. Here is a short list of possibly newsworthy ideas:

- A new manager or chef.

- Visits by well-known politicians, entertainers, authors or local heroes.

- Private parties, conventions or meetings of unique organizations: antique car enthusiasts, baseball card collectors, scientific organizations, etc.

- A new menu.

- Hosting a charitable event.

- Reduced rates, special menus, promotions, weekend specials.

- Personal stories about the staff: the waiter who returned a doctor's medical bag, helped a patron stop choking, returned a tip that was too big, etc.

PR IS DIFFERENT FROM ADVERTISING

PR is not advertising; PR uses advertising as one of its tools. A good PR campaign is almost always coordinated with advertising, but PR is not paid-for time and space. In advertising, clients pay the media to carry a message, and the client has complete control over this message. With PR, the media receives no money. Because of this, your story about the medical dinner meeting with a noted speaker at your restaurant may end up on the five o'clock news, in the paper or nowhere at all. The success of a PR story often depends on how timely it is or whether a newspaper editor feels it's worth reporting on. Furthermore, only a portion of your intended message may be used. The media may not even use your restaurant's name. Because they are choosing to write about your topic, and you've basically given them only a potential idea for a story, the story could end up in a very different form than you initially presented or hoped.

Basically, with PR you have none of the control that you do with advertising in terms of the message being delivered. But when done well, PR garners positive attention for your establishment, is hugely cost-effective and is more credible than advertising. This is because the public is getting its information from a third party—not directly from a business. Customers assume advertising to be self-serving but a positive message delivered by a third party to be authentic and trustworthy. Therefore, third-party messages are infinitely more persuasive than advertising.

Seeing the differences between PR and advertising, one sees differences both in guarantees of space and in the effectiveness of the different types of media. The enormous value of securing unpaid media space through your PR campaign becomes clear.

LAUNCHING A CAMPAIGN

In a small restaurant the manager may be solely responsible for public relations. In a larger establishment the director of marketing or sales often plays this role. Regardless of who gets the job, ultimately the PR-buck stops with the general manager. Whoever it is that takes on your PR function, he or she should be your liaison with the media. Having a single person designated as media liaison makes it simple for the press to get their questions answered and makes it much easier for you to control the flow of information to them. This back-and-forth is a critical element in your PR campaign. Once this liaison is determined, notify your staff. Advise them not to talk with the press, but to refer all media inquiries to the liaison.

In launching your campaign it's important to remember that you will be competing with professionals for a very limited amount of airtime and/or editorial space. Reading newspapers and trying to determine which pieces were inspired by PR people—and what about them made editors choose them—is a good discipline. Also, many colleges offer courses in public relations. However it is that you gain your knowledge, the more expertise you have, the more effective your campaign will be.

If your establishment is part of a chain, PR assistance may be available from the headquarters. If you manage an independent property, PR help may be available from your local Chamber of Commerce or Convention/Visitors' Bureau. Chambers of Commerce often have PR departments that will offer advice on how to launch your program.

When contacting the media it is important to determine who will be the most useful to you. What type of customer are you seeking to attract? What's the size of your market area? Are you contacting the media who cater to those demographics? Your advertising agency can be helpful with statistical data and the interpretation of it.

Once you know who your target is, you begin building media lists. These include names of appropriate editors, reporters, news directors, assignment editors, media outlets, addresses and contact numbers. From this list you call, visit or otherwise contact the media who are crucial to your campaign. If you want to mail fact sheets, press releases, press kits, etc., you can hire a company that sells media mailing lists, and you can pay them or another firm to do your mailing for you. If that is beyond your budget, calling the editorial department of a newspaper or a newsroom will get you the contact numbers of the people you seek to reach, and you can put your mailing together yourself. During your campaign, it's also important that you search for allies. Allies are businesses and organizations that have similar goals to yours. Your state's Tourism/Travel Promotion Office can be a great resource for this. This office is working year-round to bring business and leisure guests to your state. These, of course, are your prospective customers. Your state's travel promotion officials will be happy to give you advice on how to tie in with their advertising, PR and other promotional programs.

Most states also have a Business/Economic Development Department that will be happy to help you, since their goal is to create new business in your state. Their mailing list will keep you informed of planned promotions. When meeting with state officials it's a good idea to volunteer to assist their promotional and PR programs. Doing this gets you "in the loop" and, often, ahead of your competition, because you'll know about the programs your state is developing. Hotel and restaurant associations can also prove to be valuable allies, since they either have PR people on staff or use national PR agencies.

There are a number of national travel industry organizations that work privately to generate travel in the United States. They couldn't be more natural allies. Locally, your Chamber of Commerce may organize familiarization (fam) trips to your area. These are trips for travel writers and travel agents that showcase the attributes of your area. Let the organization arranging the "fam" trip know that you're willing to offer free accommodations or meals to the visiting journalists and travel agents. If you are selected, make sure time is allotted for a guided tour of your property, led by your most knowledgeable manager or salesperson. Present each guest with a press kit. Also mail press kits to the agents after the tour, since most of them prefer to travel light but accumulate tons of literature and souvenirs on their trips. Making a good impression with travel agents and writers is great for you because their third-party endorsement is the best kind of advertising.

When these agents and writers do visit, make sure that your establishment is in tip-top shape. Your visitors will probably be visiting numerous other hotels and restaurants, and you want to stand out in every (positive) way. Only the most memorable hotels and restaurants will be on their "recommend" list, and you want to be one of them.

Suppliers can also be a huge ally, because the more business you do, the more orders you send them for their products or services. Airlines, tourist attractions, liquor distributors, wholesalers, etc., can all be incredible allies. They often offer attractive packages of lower room rates, food costs, car rentals, etc. Prices are usually deeply discounted to draw customers who would otherwise not use one of the packaged services. These packages are a great promotion and often garner notice from travel publications and consumer sections of newspapers eager to report a great deal. Also, airlines, car rental companies, cruise lines, etc., have PR departments that can help design and implement your PR program.

SPECIAL EVENTS

Special events can be very effective in generating publicity and community interest. You may be opening a new property or celebrating a renovation or an anniversary. Any such occasions are opportunities to plan a special event that will support or improve your PR program. There are usually two kinds of special events: one-time and ongoing. Obviously you're not going to have a groundbreaking ceremony annually, but you might have a famous Fourth of July party every year.

The key question to ask when designing a special event is "Why?" Clearly defining your objectives before you start is crucial. Is your goal to improve community opinion of your business? to present yourself as a good employer? to show off a renovation? Once these needs have been clearly defined, a timetable and schedule of events can be made. Ample time is necessary, since contractors, inspection agencies and civil officials may be involved. If you are planning an anniversary celebration, research what events were going on in your community when you opened: Was there a huge fire? Had the civil war just ended? Did Dwight Eisenhower speak at the local college? Once you have this information, send it to the press. They will see your event as part of the historical landscape—as opposed to a commercial endeavor that benefits only you—and they'll appreciate your community focus.

Special events require preparation to ensure everything is ready when the spotlight of attention is turned on you. Be certain the day you have chosen does not conflict with another, potentially competing, event or fall on an inappropriate holiday. With a groundbreaking or opening of a new property, you should invite the developer, architect, interior designer, civic officials—all the pertinent folks—and the media. You should prepare brief remarks and ask the architect to comment on the property. In your remarks, remind your listeners that the addition of your business does not boost school taxes or increase the need for police and fire protection; it adds new jobs and new tax revenues.

If you are celebrating an opening, tours of the property are a must and should be led by your most personable employees. Refreshments should be served, and in many cases, lunch or dinner is provided. Whatever your occasion, you should provide press kits to the attending media and mail them to all media that were invited. Souvenirs are a good idea—they can be simple or elaborate, but should always be creative, fun and useful to your guests.

COMMUNICATING TO YOUR GUESTS—AND THE VALUE OF—LOYALTY

We all know first impressions last. If your guests arrive after heavy traffic or unpleasant waits, your first impression on them is that much more important. It's an opportunity to let them know they're welcome and that they'll be taken care of. Many restaurants offer a note welcoming their guests, fresh fruit or coffee—something to make them feel at home.

Obviously how you relate to your guests affects their opinion of you. That opinion then translates into potential loyalty, and loyalty boosts your bottom line. In fact, a 5-percent improvement in customer retention translates into a 15 to 50 percent boost in profits. Those are serious numbers. In common terms, that simply means getting your regular customers to return one more time per month. Furthermore, it costs about five times as much to attract a new customer as it does to retain an existing one. This is another huge benefit of loyalty to your bottom line, and it comes through the overall commitment your establishment makes to its repeat customers. Focusing on your repeat customers—your most profitable clients—allows you to keep them coming back. Two things to focus on for retaining clients:

1. Pay attention to your most profitable clients. Listen. Keep in touch. Find out what they want and need and why they've chosen you.

2. If they go to the competition, find out why.

Brief, succinct comment cards where guests rate your service, facilities, etc., can be a great way to find out what they think of you. You can offer discounts or promotional items for the return of these cards. If you do use a comment card, the one question that must be there is "Would you return to have dinner with us again?" If you get "no's", take immediate action to determine why and then fix the situation.

If your restaurant is located in a hotel, there are infinite ways for you to make your guests' stay more enjoyable and to show you appreciate them. Pamphlets describing local attractions in your community help guests plan their activities (and may entice them to extend their stay). First-aid kits, warm towels, water bottles with your logo on them—anything that makes things more convenient and enjoyable—will distinguish you from the competition. On a larger scale, whenever possible, provide upgrades; let customers know you appreciate them; inform them of services that may be useful to them; and go above and beyond what they expect from you. By doing this, you not only increase the chances of their returning, you increase the chances of them telling their friends about how well they were treated. This will bring in new and, if treated well, soon-to-be-loyal customers.

Many hotels and restaurants have established frequent-stay/diner plans that are similar to airline frequent-flyer plans. Customers accrue "points" or "dollars" towards food, merchandise, upgrades or free rooms. Many hotels even have tie-ins with airlines that allow guests to earn frequent-flyer miles through their stay. These are great customer loyalty plans but are out of reach for many smaller operations. There are, however, many things smaller organizations can do to build loyalty. Here are a few:

*   Build a database (or at least a mailing list) of your customers.

*   Track purchases and behavior: food preferences, table preferences, entertainment needs and special needs.

*   Constantly update your information based on interactions with your customers.

- Recognize birthdays, anniversaries and special occasions.

- Show your appreciation through holiday greetings, special discounts and other forms of recognition.

- Thank your customers for their business.

- Whenever you can, individualize your communications.

- Listen to and act on customer suggestions.

- Inform guests on new or improved services.

- Tell guests of potential inconveniences like renovations, and stress their future benefits.

- Answer every inquiry, including complaints.

- Accommodate all reasonable requests for meal substitutions, table changes, etc.

- Empower employees to solve problems.

- Talk to your customers and employees so you can let them know you're listening and find out what's going on.

This last point—the back and forth between guests and employees and you—is enormously important. Just as you need to focus on getting your message to your guests, you also need to focus on getting their messages to you. If they think their opinions are important to you, they'll think they're important to you—and they'll come back. People have more choices than ever about where to spend their money. If they know their individual needs will be met and that they'll be taken care of, their choice will be to spend it with you.

EMPLOYEE RELATIONS IS ALSO PUBLIC RELATIONS

You cannot succeed in the hospitality industry if your employees don't deliver excellent service. They have the most daily contact with your customers, and are therefore responsible for the opinion—positive or negative—people have of your establishment. Therefore, one of the most important "publics" that your public relations program should focus on is your staff.

Customers want to be taken care of, and they judge a business as much on the quality of the service as the product. Basically, if a member of your waitstaff is grumpy or tired, that's bad PR. Therefore; employee relations should be a main focus of your PR campaign. In order to do this you must have well-trained staff that understand the technical ins and outs of their jobs and also believe in your organization's mission. Your employees need to know the high level of service your customers expect, and they need to be empowered to deliver it. A staff that does this on an ongoing basis is one that generates repeat business through word-of-mouth referrals. And that's good PR.

Keeping your employees informed is a key way of making them feel involved and building positive feelings between staff and management. The following is a list of things to communicate to your staff:

1. How your business is doing, and what you're planning.

2. How the competition is doing, and what you're planning.

3. What community issues you're concerned about and taking a role in.

4. Recent personnel changes.

5. Who's booked in the future: private parties, conventions, social events, etc.

6. Available training and job openings.

7. Staff weddings, birthdays, significant accomplishments or happenings.

Communicating this information gives employees the sense that you care and creates a unified work atmosphere where great service becomes a group responsibility. It also shows that you recognize the difference they make to your bottom line and that you're paying attention to them.

Opening the lines of communication between management and staff is the next step. No one knows the intimate ins and outs of your business like your staff. If they care about your business and know your ears are open, they can be your biggest resource in suggesting improvements and letting you know what's really going on. One-on-one meetings with supervisors, group meetings, employee newsletters, orientation/review sessions and training meetings are all effective ways to open the channels of conversation between you and your employees. These sessions let them know you care and encourage them make the biggest difference they can.

An ongoing employee appreciation program is a good idea. Create a structure that is a part of your daily operation: a large bulletin board in a high-traffic area or a monthly party where awards and prizes are given (cash, great parking spaces, etc.). Give employees something to wear (e.g., a recognition pin) that signifies acknowledgement of the services they provide. Be creative, and find something that effectively and continuously supports the goals of both your employee relations program and your overall PR plan.

TALKING TO YOUR COMMUNITY

All business is local. This is especially true in the restaurant business. While you could make the argument that a large portion of your business comes from out of town, it's still your local community that needs to believe in the value of your business. Restaurants that are not accepted by their local communities disappear. It's as simple as that. Also, you won't find a prosperous restaurant in a depressed area. Your community and you are one and the same, and it's crucial to remember this as you design your PR program.

Restaurants are often considered hubs of their communities. They offer facilities for meetings, banquets, conventions and other important social/economic functions. Many decisions that affect the future of local economies take place in these facilities, so it's easy to see how and why a hotel or restaurant can't be successful unless the local community accepts it.

So, what does that mean to the restaurant GM? It doesn't simply mean that you should help support good causes. It means your business needs to be a leader in its community. In practice this means building bridges between your company and your community to maintain and foster your environment in a way that benefits both you and the community. Basically, your goal is to make your immediate world a better place in which everybody can thrive. The following are a few ideas that can be part of an effective community relations program:

- Fill a community need—create something that wasn't there before.

- Remove something that causes a community problem.

- Include "have-nots" in something that usually excludes them.

- Share your space, equipment or expertise.

- Offer tutoring, or otherwise mobilize your workforce as a helping hand.

- Promote your community elsewhere.

Being a good citizen is, of course, crucial, but you also need to convince your community of the value of your business as a business. Most businesses provide jobs and pay taxes in their communities. Restaurants do these in spades because, despite technological advances, they're still labor-intensive businesses. Per dollar of income, they probably provide employment for more residents of your community than any other business. Also—and remind your community of this—hotels and restaurants not only attract visitors from all over the country and, perhaps, the world, but most hotel income is from money earned outside your community and is spent in it.

These are real benefits, and they should be integrated into the message you send by being a good citizen. Designing this message is a straightforward but remarkably effective process:

1.	**List the things your establishment brings to the community:** jobs, taxes, well-maintained architecture, etc.

2.	**List what your business receives from its community:** employees, fire and police protection, trash removal, utilities, etc.

3.	**List your business's complaints about your community:** high taxes, air pollution, noise pollution, narrow roads, etc.

Once you have outlined these items, look for ways your business can lead the way in improving what doesn't work. As you do this, consult with your local Chamber of Commerce or Visitors' Bureau. They may be able to integrate you into existing community betterment programs aimed at your objectives.

If done well, your community relations program will create positive opinions in your community. In turn, this will cause local residents to recommend you as the place to eat when asked by tourists; it will encourage people to apply for jobs, and may encourage suppliers to seek to do business with you. Also, if there is an emergency at your establishment, having a positive standing in the community will enable your property to be treated fairly.

An effective community relations program is a win-win situation because it gives you the opportunity to be a deep and abiding member of your community—improving the quality of life and opportunities around you—and, at the same time, contributes significantly to your bottom line.

PLANNING FOR THE UNFORESEEN

Emergencies make bad news stories. Bad news stories are bad PR, and they can destroy the image you've worked so hard to build. They can wipe away years of hard-won customer relations. There are numerous kinds of emergencies—earthquakes, fires, floods, political protests, crime and more—and any of these events, if not managed properly, can destroy your public image. The law insists you have fire prevention programs and insurance, but there is no one forcing you to create a crisis–public relations program in case of emergency.

In order to meet a PR emergency, you must prepare now. If you have a strategy developed in advance, then when something bad does happen, you assure the most accurate, objective media coverage of the event. It's important that all your employees are aware of this plan and that they are reminded of it regularly. Since your employees generate a huge amount of your PR, it's crucial for them to know how to act and what to say—and not say—during a crisis. This simple detail can make all the difference in the world. Here are three basic aspects to an emergency press relation's plan:

1. Your general manager or owner should be the only spokesperson during the time of the emergency. Make sure your employees know not to talk to the press and to refer all inquiries to the general manager or publicity coordinator. Make sure the GM is available at all times, day or night.

2. Know the facts of the situation before answering questions from the media.

3. Initiate contact. Once the story is out, don't wait for the media to call you. This way you will ensure that they get accurate information. Plus, the media will appreciate your forthcoming attitude, and your cooperation will reflect in their reporting.

The media will always ask the same who, what, when, where and how questions. Knowing this and being prepared to anticipate their questions, you should be able to answer accurately. If you don't know the answer to a question, don't say, "No comment." Explain why you can't comment: the police are investigating, for example, and you don't have enough information to answer now but you'll try to find the answer and get back to them. Make a point to do as promised.

In times of crisis it's crucial to put a positive slant on the news. Try to focus press attention on the diligent efforts of management to handle the emergency, or on employees whose compassion and assistance made a difference. If something happens in your establishment that is not your fault and your establishment handles it well, it's an opportunity to showcase your heart and responsiveness.

The importance of a crisis-PR plan cannot be overstated. When an employee is injured or killed in your establishment, or a guest suffers from food poisoning, the public assumes you're guilty. Whether or not you're even mildly at fault, people assume you are. Therefore, how you handle public relations during this time means the difference between a temporary loss of public support, or the permanent loss of a great deal of your business.

One always hopes that a crisis-PR plan remains unnecessary. Unfortunately, given the amount of hotel and restaurant accidents, mishaps and disasters every year, being prepared for the worst is the best policy. Furthermore, while the entire establishment suffers during an emergency, the general manager who was caught unprepared suffers the most. Therefore, after calling the police, fire department, etc., it is the GM's job to immediately find out what happened and take corrective actions. If the event warrants it, you should set up a room with a phone as a command post, then communicate to all your employees what you want them to do and not do. As part of your plan, your employees should know where flashlights are in case evacuation is necessary, and they should be ready to guide guests to the nearest exits.

Next, the media must be contacted and the story disclosed, put into context and told from your side. If the media gets all the information they need from you quickly, this increases the chances of the incident appearing as one story and not showing up again. If it is difficult for reporters to gather information and they need to seek other sources, the story may be spaced out over time, which will increase people's chances of seeing it. This is obviously not what you want.

Having built strong media relations pays off during an emergency. A reporter you have a good relationship with may report an incident at a "local restaurant," while one less acquainted with you—or downright hostile—will mention you specifically and push for the story to be on the front page. This is a crucial difference. It means that the person who will be the media liaison during an emergency should be building and nurturing good media relations now, in case anything does happen. And what have you got to lose? Strong media relations benefit you all the time.

All this is to say that if you don't guide the flow of information around your news event, somebody else will misguide it for you. With proper PR, a story that appears to the public, like a seafood restaurant that didn't have any fresh seafood, can be authentically retold to show how the restaurant was the victim of a vendor's warehouse fire. You can shift the public from viewing you as incompetent to having more faith than ever in your establishment. Public opinion depends on how effectively you manage information and how well you get your story across.

15

INTERNAL RESTAURANT MARKETING— HOW TO KEEP CUSTOMERS COMING BACK TO YOUR ESTABLISHMENT

INTRODUCTION

Profitability is what's going to keep you in business, obviously. How and where you focus to become and stay profitable is the key. Are you crunching numbers and pushing your servers to raise their check averages, or are you creating an environment that leaves patrons feeling served and eager to come back? Are you holding staff meetings that leave your crew energized or deflated? Are management, kitchen and wait staffs working independently or as a complete whole towards a common goal? This chapter will give you invaluable insights into how and where you can make these changes in your business and how you can boost your sales volume 15 to 50 percent in the process.

CUSTOMERS FOR LIFE

Take care of your guests, and your sales will take care of themselves. "Customers for life" means that once guests come to your restaurant, they'll never be satisfied with your competitors. Simple, right? It also means that the real work of building sales doesn't happen with your advertising schedule or marketing plan, but on the floor, with your customers.

The key to building restaurant sales is to increase volume from your existing customer base. Think about it: if your customers were to return just one more time per month, that would be an increase in sales volume of between 15 and 50 percent! These are people who already know about you, live within an acceptable travel distance and will recommend you to their friends if you make them happy. These are the people you want to target in order to build a regular, loyal customer base that shares the pleasures of your establishment with friends.

So how do you do this? Work on building loyalty, not the check average!

It's true: a bigger check is a bigger sale. However, selling techniques designed to boost check averages can be dangerous to the survival of your business. Your income comes from serving people, not food. Focusing only on the bottom line puts your customers second at best. If everyone who ever ate at your restaurant were so pleased that he couldn't wait to come back with his friends, what would your sales be like? If eating with you didn't thrill your customers, if they felt pressured to order something expensive, what difference does it make how big their check was—when they won't be coming back?

This isn't to say that suggestive selling can't work. If it's done well it can be very effective. The problem is it's almost never done well, and you run the risk of your guests thinking they come in a distant second to their money. The safest way to achieve sales growth is to have your guests return more often. Focusing on this is a win-win. Your goal is to delight them, win their loyalty and put them first, first, first! If you're a restaurant patron—and you are—what will have you coming back for another meal: your waiter focusing on getting you to spend more money or on treating you like royalty?

PUT YOUR ATTENTION ON DELIGHTING YOUR GUESTS

EXPECTATIONS

Satisfaction isn't even close to good enough. It's an improvement on dissatisfaction, of course, but in today's market, it won't keep people coming back. There is just too much competition. You need to exceed your guests' expectations, every time. The food-service business is built on personal connections. You serve one person at a time, and the more personal that interaction, the more you'll exceed her expectations—and the happier she'll be.

Here is a list of basic guest expectations and some hints on how to meet and/or exceed them:

- **Guests expect hot food hot, and cold food cold.** Serve cold food on a chilled—not frozen—plate. Try removing your heat lamps altogether: they don't keep food hot, and they can cause your staff to delay in getting food to your guests.

- **From order to delivery, guests expect their drinks within 2 minutes, appetizers in 5–10, entrees in 15–25, and dessert in 3–5 minutes.** Check turnaround should take no more than 2 minutes. At the beginning and end of a meal guests are the least tolerant of delays. Make sure your staff does not keep customers waiting after they've been seated or when they're ready to leave.

- **Guests expect their servers to know the menu and how dishes are prepared and to be able to answer questions about the wine list.**

- **Guests expect restaurant staff to care.**

Do you know what your customers expect when they come through the door? Are you out to exceed those expectations and give each guest a memorable and delightful meal every time?

WAYS TO DELIGHT

Customers are delighted when you care—it's as simple as that. Doing things that demonstrate how much you care will make a difference. Part of the trick here, however, is that there is no trick. You've got to be sincere. People know when they're being treated with sincerity or with a mechanical technique. Sincerity works. Here is a list of practices that, when done with sincerity, can give guests a feeling of being taken care of, given real value or simply delighted. These touches may appear to guests to be extraordinary or creative—things that they never would have thought of themselves:

- **Umbrellas when it rains.** Is it possible that, given the weather patterns in your area, your guests could arrive without an umbrella, only to find it raining as they're leaving? Offer them umbrellas to help them get to their cars or offices. This could be a great incentive to have them come back at a later date to return the umbrella. Put your name and logo on the umbrella, and maybe it's not the worst thing if they forget to bring it back.

- **Free stuff while they wait.** People mind a wait a lot less when they've got a complimentary glass of wine or warm cider to keep them toasty, or the local paper or a magazine to read. They will appreciate you going the extra mile. It's something that distinguishes you from the competition and gives them something to talk about.

- **Free local calls—with a portable phone.** This can be a huge convenience to guests, allowing them to change travel plans, contact friends and handle nagging details—at almost no cost to you. Let customers know it's a service you offer, and it will create another great point of difference between you and the competition.

- **Owner or manager on the floor.** People like to meet the person in charge. They appreciate that someone important is checking in on them.

- **Give people something for nothing.** Got some new menu items coming up next week? Why not give away free samples today to whet people's appetites? There's nothing customers like more than something for nothing, and it's another great way to distinguish you from the competition.

- **Books, magazines, newspapers for single diners.** If you draw or want to draw single diners, have reading materials available—and a staff that knows how to offer them politely.

- **Free postcards and postage.** Do a lot of tourist business? If your guests are waiting—or even if they aren't—why not give them stamped postcards (depicting your restaurant, of course) for sending their "Wish you were here" messages?

It's a very low price to pay for giving your guests something they'll appreciate and enabling them to send your advertising all over the world.

- **Fax directions to guests.** Have a great, clear map on hand, and when guests ask for directions to your restaurant, offer to fax it to them. If they don't have a fax, make sure you can give them clear, explicit directions over the phone. Have the directions on your Web site, also. (Don't have a Web site? Get one today!) You don't want them frazzled when they get to you, and you certainly don't want them unable to make it at all!

- **House camera.** If guests are celebrating but forgot a camera, have an instant camera on hand, and snap a few shots for them to take home.

- **Armchairs for the elderly.** It's harder for the elderly to get in and out of their chairs. If you serve a lot of elderly customers, or even a few, have chairs with arms to make it easier for them to get in and out. Let them know you did it just for them. They will certainly appreciate it.

- **Guest book.** Make sure your guests fill in the guest book: you need a mailing list of your patrons for sending them promotional material. Try to collect birth dates and anniversaries for your database, as well.

WORD OF MOUTH

Positive word of mouth is the best advertising there is, without question. But does it just come by accident or only from serving great food? Yes and no. Great word of mouth comes from guests having something great to talk about and their sharing it effectively. Do you have a deliberate, creative and authentic plan in place to create great word of mouth? You can and should have everything to do with whether your guests have something to say and whether or not they're saying it.

Guests don't talk about you unless they're thinking about you. You want them thinking about you in the right way, which means you have to educate your guests on why they come to you. To do this, you must create points of difference between you and your competitors. Then people can tell their friends about why they eat at your restaurant.

An effective word-of-mouth program has five main goals:

1. Inform and educate your patrons.

2. Make the guest a salesperson for your restaurant.

3. Give guests reasons to return.

4. Make your service unique and personal.

5.   Distinguish your business from the competition.

CREATING POINTS OF DIFFERENCE

If you want your guests to return one extra time a month and tell their friends and family about you, you first need to distinguish yourself from the competition. You do this by creating "points of difference." What is different about your establishment? your concept? your type of food? your combination of dishes? Do you guarantee your service? Give free wine to waiting customers? Have an organic vegetable garden in the back? Do you put ice in your urinals and the sports page above them? What makes your place memorable and different from the competition? Here is a partial list of things that every restaurant offers and a few suggestions on how you can create points of difference with them:

- **Water.** Serve local spring water or imported bottled water, or simply filter your tap water so it tastes good. Put a lemon slice or flower petal in the glass or carafe.

- **Soft drinks.** Serve bottled drinks instead of post mix. Have an extensive selection, and offer free refills.

- **Salad.** Have unusual, local and/or organic ingredients and dressings. Serve them in unique or oversized bowls. Serve chilled salads on chilled plates with chilled forks.

- **Restrooms.** Have twice as many restrooms for women. It tends to take them longer; why should they have to wait?

- **Beer.** Have a large microbrew menu, an extensive beer list and/or local brews. Serve beer in exotic glassware, personalized mugs or numerous bottles in a bucket of ice.

Certainly not all of these are appropriate for every restaurant, but finding a great way to distinguish yourself—often through a mishap or brilliantly ridiculous staff idea—is a great way to give your place a real identity and give your customers something to talk about.

EDUCATING GUESTS ON THE DIFFERENCES

Having a great idea in place isn't enough, though; you've got to inform your customers about it, and give them the words they can then pass on. A customer telling his friends he had a great time is great. A customer telling his friends he had the best salad ever because you have an organic garden in the back, and the lettuce was picked five minutes before his salad was prepared, is worth his weight in gold. Details differentiate your product and make yours the place to go for something extraordinary.

How do you get this information across? Arm your staff with words they can comfortably work into a conversation. Do you offer a full menu until midnight? When guests call and ask how late you're open, say, "Dave's Cafe serves a full menu until midnight. We're the only place in town that does that." If a guest comes in at 11:00 P.M. wondering if you're still open, say, "Not only are we open, we serve a full menu until closing at midnight." Over time your customers will be saying "Dave's serves a full menu until midnight—let's go there."

An effective word-of-mouth program not only creates points of difference between you and the competition; it educates your guests on those distinctions. If you give your customers a great experience, and the words to describe it, they'll talk about it to their friends.

INCENTIVES

Incentives work because people do what they are rewarded for doing. It is as simple as that. Reward customers for coming back, and they will.

There are three basic ways to do this:

1. Discounts.

2. Promotions.

3. Customer loyalty programs.

DISCOUNTS

An effective deal actually gives your guests a discount and generates more profit for you. How? By making a sale you wouldn't have made otherwise. Is a customer buying a discounted lobster dinner that, even with the discount, has a 40 percent profit margin, instead of the salmon that she would have ordered and that has a 30 percent profit margin? Then she's getting a deal and you're making more money. Are your business card drawings giving customers a chance to buy drinks at half price, but bringing in more than twice the business, or bringing people in right after work when they're hungry, too, or making your bar the first place people think of to go for a drink after work?

Internal coupons can be a great way to increase repeat business. Three of the most widely used are:

1. **Courtesy coupons.** These are wallet-sized coupons that your staff carries. They can be issued to guests and used on return visits. They are great if a guest has a complaint or is put out somehow, or they can be used to reward customers for their ongoing patronage.

2. **Cross-marketing coupons.** If you have very fast and very slow meal periods, why not offer a discount to customers if they return during the slower time? If you do a great lunch business, for instance, give people a free dessert if they come for dinner on a Tuesday.

3. **Companion coupons.** Encourage your regulars to bring a friend. You can offer a special group of dishes to be shared among four people, a free bottle of wine or free appetizers for two or more.

PROMOTIONS

Five great promotional opportunities are:

1. Birthdays

2. Anniversaries

3. Holidays

4. Special events

5. Festivals

Birthdays and Anniversaries

Do you have an irresistible offer for patrons who celebrate their birthdays or anniversaries with you? You can get the dates of their special occasions when they sign up for your Frequent Diner Plan. (Hint: Let them know when they sign up that you're asking about these dates in order to offer them specials on their birthdays and anniversaries; otherwise they could feel their privacy is being invaded.) With this information you can invite them to celebrate with you. Also, make sure your offer is valid for more than just the actual date being celebrated—within the month is effective—because people need some flexibility in planning their special events.

Holidays

The beauty of the holidays is that someone else advertises them. You don't have to tell your guests Thanksgiving is coming, but you could put a flyer in with their check that lets them know how fun it will be—and what a great deal they'll get—if they spend it with you.

Special Events

Special events can be a great way to promote business and goodwill. Have you thought of hosting a cigar dinner, a winemaker dinner or a charity fundraiser? If a cigar event would fit your restaurant, it's a great way to combine high-priced cigars with fine wine and spirits. Hold a wine tasting early in the evening on a slow night of the week. You can showcase the knowledge of your sommelier or wine steward, and afterwards guests can stay for dinner.

A **charity fundraiser** can be a way to gain exposure for your restaurant that pays off for everyone. It will improve your image and distinguish you from competitors. It doesn't have to be a breakeven venture either, because you only give a portion of the proceeds to the cause. Spirits distributors and other suppliers often give free or discounted product for such events, which could lower your costs and even bring heavy marketing muscle to your event. The charity will also promote you to its supporters, which can bring new people through your door who want to support your business.

Festivals

Festivals are great reasons to invite guests to come back, and they're great things for guests to talk about. They highlight specific cuisines or products and can be a great way to stir things up for staff and customers alike. You can run a festival on a specific night or for a specific time period—usually a week or two. Make sure however, that the festival you hold is right for your establishment, and that it is run frequently enough to break up your routine, but infrequently enough to remain special. Do a memorable job, and build a strong foundation for future events.

Highlighting regional cuisines is a great idea, with foods, wines and recipes from another culture, as well as music, decorations, costumes, posters—you name it. You could have a guest chef from the celebrated country during your festival. Contact the country's embassy for ideas.

Product festivals usually coincide with seasonal items—raspberries, corn, etc.—when the items are abundant and cheaper. Off-season festivals can be great for word of mouth—if you can find the product. People would love a fresh strawberry festival in January. Regional food items like ribs, oysters and lobster work great with various appetizers, salads and soups and can make a dynamite festival.

CUSTOMER LOYALTY PROGRAMS, OR FREQUENT DINER PROGRAMS

These can be a huge benefit to your business, just as they have been for airline companies. Rewarding your customers for continued loyalty gives them an added incentive to choose you over the competition and will help bring them back that extra time per month. They usually come in variations on three basic forms:

1. **Punch cards.** An inexpensive card that is typically issued for free and is punched every time the guest purchases a product. When they have purchased a certain number of items they receive something for free. The biggest plus of punch cards is their ease to produce. The biggest negative is the ease with which they can be altered. Keeping the guests' cards, or duplicate cards, on premises can help counter this.

2. **Point systems.** These are often dollar-for-point systems, in which a customer accrues points towards free food or merchandise. This can be a great way for guests to "eat their way" towards a free bicycle or dinner for four. A point system is considerably more complicated to implement than a punch card system, often including outside vendors.

3. **Percentage-of-purchase programs.** This is the closest type to the airline programs, with guests paying full price for items while accruing dollar credits for

future meals. This gets people in the habit of thinking of their purchases as having a larger than normal value, and keeps them coming to you.

Punch cards, point systems and percentage-of-purchase programs are all ways to monitor your guests' patronage, reward them for coming back, and increase your opportunities to delight them with your food and service. Take some time to figure out which is right for you.

PEOPLE, PEOPLE, PEOPLE

PRESENCE

The food-service business is about personal connection. Of course, it's about food, too, but if you can establish a connection with your customers, you will exist in their minds as a welcoming friend of the family, not just a place to eat. People want to be treated as individuals, and they will repeatedly do business in a place that does this.

So how do you connect? You get present. You get physically and mentally "there" with your guests.

We have wrongly accepted the idea that doing many things at once, "multitasking," is effective. If you're taking a phone reservation, putting tonight's specials on the board and talking to your new waiter, how much real attention will any of those tasks get? Do you think the potential guest on the phone, or your waiter, will feel well treated? Will you have time to check the spelling on the specials board?

The truth is that we really can focus on only one thing at a time. So when you talk to your staff or your guests, really talk to them: Listen, say what needs to be said, and move on. It's the same with the specials board. Drop distractions, handle each item individually and then move on to the next. Presence is simply a lack of distraction. If you act distracted with your staff, they will keep asking the same questions or coming to you with the same problems. If you are distracted around your guests, they won't come back at all. Pay attention. People will notice, and you will too. Be a great listener.

APPRECIATION

What do you do to let your guests know that you appreciate them? If you recognize them and make them feel important, it will draw them closer to your restaurant and further differentiate you in their eyes. The following list touches on a few tried-and-true examples. Many can be done at little or no cost.

- Put them in your newsletter (You can have either a print or an e-mail version).

- Put them on a Wall of Fame or "Outstanding Customer" plaques.

- Give your regulars awards, and/or honor people in your community who make a difference through charitable work.

- Name menu items after guests. Customers LOVE this, and who knows what soon-to-be famous dishes are cooking in their minds?

- Personalize booths or seats.

- Put guests' names up on your bulletin board.

GETTING TO KNOW YOUR GUESTS

In a business that lives and dies on personal connection, getting to know your guests is crucial. Go beyond the procedures of service, and start thinking of your guests as individuals. There is a difference between serving 200 dinners and serving Steve and Mary Carson on their 30th wedding anniversary or a doing fundraiser for the Friends of the Museum of Science.

Numbers are important, but your relationship to your customers drives your business. Furthermore, the two easiest things to learn about your customers are also the most useful: who they are and what they like.

People love it when you remember who they are. It instantly makes them feel like they're insiders and makes them feel important in the eyes of their friends. Remember "Norm!" in Cheers? Norm felt pretty comfortable, and he definitely came back. As a manager you probably know your regulars by name, but do you have a system in place that teaches your new staff who these important folks are? If you were a regular customer at a restaurant and a waitress you had never seen came up and greeted you by name, wouldn't you feel like a celebrity?

You can train your servers to write the guest's name on the back of the check so they can refer to it through the meal, or you can have your greeter put guests' names on their checks when they arrive. However you do it, keeping servers using guests' names will help them remember the names in the future. It will continually remind waitstaff that they are serving people, people, people—not anonymous mouths. Using guests' names is another win-win proposition, because the more you use their names, the easier they will be to remember and the easier it will be to treat them as individuals...which brings you to the next step.

Now that you are talking to customers as individuals, the next step is to find out what they want as individuals. How? You must ask, but you also must remember—not only what you've been told, but also what you've observed. If you were allergic to a certain ingredient, wouldn't it be incredible if the next time you came ate at a restaurant they offered to make you a dish that wasn't on the menu? If you loved the food but were seated too close to the air conditioner, wouldn't it be great if you were seated away from it next time?

Small note cards kept about regular guests can make this possible. The cards hold information about customers' likes and dislikes, patterns and desires—all the information necessary to treat them like royalty. You can even reward your servers for adding to the cards each time a guest dines. Throughout this process it's VERY important never to pry: respect your customer's privacy. If a customer were reticent to share about his life, a savvy server would note on the biography card not to ask too many questions. In this case, you're serving your customer's preferences simply by leaving him alone. Either way, you're finding out what your guests want and giving it to them.

CLUBS

Clubs can be a great way of treating your regulars like individuals and giving them privileges or paraphernalia other customers don't have. If you sell draft beer, here are a few ideas for having a great and effective Mug Club:

1. Keep the mugs or glasses on display, so "Mug Clubbers" have to come in to use them.

2. Have the mugs be so distinctive that other customers ask about them and the people with the mugs feel special.

3. Put customers' names on their mugs.

4. Give them a deal: cheaper product, more for the same price, or another incentive.

Do you sell oysters, ribs or wings? Do you sell anything else could be a club that people would join and, through it, accrue points towards a prize? They could get a discount on appetizers and a free golf cap after they've eaten, say, 300 ribs. Clubs can be a great way to distinguish your products, distinguish your guests and give your guests a sense of belonging. The results will benefit your bottom line.

 **STAFF**

Your restaurant is made up of two things in the eyes of your customers: the food and the staff. The quality of service your customers receive will determine their opinion of your restaurant. Your staff are the ones who delight your guests—or don't—who give them things to talk about and who provide the crucial personal connection. Staff will: execute most of your sales promotions and programs; educate your customers about what makes your rib joint better than the one down the street; and give your guests information they can pass on to their friends.

It's in your waitstaff's best interests to connect with customers, because it's through that connection that their tip averages will go up. But—here's the thing—your staff will treat your guests the same way you treat your staff. If you want your staff to be gracious, to listen and to delight your guests, you've got to do the same for them.

If you take the pressure off your staff to get the check averages up, and instead encourage them to treat their customers in a way that will bring them in one more time per month, then your waitstaff can increase their income in tips by 50 percent. This is just through being nice, and committed to serving your patrons' needs. Also, guests who know their waitpersons usually leave higher tips. As your waitstaff get to know their customers, they're not just increasing the possibility of greater revenue through repeat business, they're also increasing the chance that they'll get a bigger tip this time—just by making a personal connection. Here is a partial list of basic things your waitstaff can do to make a more personal connection and, therefore, up their tip averages:

- **Greet guests within a minute.** Don't leave them waiting. Waiting will negatively affect a customer's mood, and her mood is going to directly affect the tip.

- **Make eye contact.** Don't stare at the table, the floor or the artwork on the wall. Clear your head, smile and pay attention. Make sure you're at the table when you're talking. Don't talk to your guests as you're flying by. It makes people feel unimportant, and no one likes that feeling.

- **Don't ever think about the tip.** Focus your energy on taking care of your guests, making them happy, doing little things that exceed their expectations and generally making their meals as enjoyable as possible. That's how you will consistently get great tips.

- **Encourage your guests' food choices.** People can be strange about making decisions. The simple act on your part of telling them that you've had what they're ordering and it's great can take away any anxiety they have about making a bad choice.

- **Tell the cooks good news.** Just as you need to be sensitive to the mood of your guests, be sensitive to the mood of the kitchen crew. The cooks don't want only to hear about things when they're wrong. Pass along good news to them, and they will probably make it easier for you to take great care of your guests.

- **Notice lefties.** It's a small thing, but if your guest has moved his water glass and/or silverware to the other side of his plate, serve his drinks from there. He'll appreciate it.

- **Make your movements invisible.** That means move with the speed of the room. Good service is invisible: food and drinks simply arrive without a thought on the customer's part. If the room is quiet, don't buzz around in it. If it's more upbeat, move a little quicker. You'll find fitting in seamlessly with the atmosphere will increase your guest's enjoyment, and it's a great way to stay focused.

- **Ask before refilling coffee.** Coffee drinkers can be very particular about the amount of cream and sugar they have in their coffee. Temperature also matters. Don't top off a cup they may have spent considerable time getting just right.

- **Tell guests about specific events at your restaurant, and invite them.** This is a more effective way to let them know you would love for them to come back and to build a personal connection. It can be much more effective to invite guests to return for your rib special on Tuesdays than just to say "Thanks. Come again." While you're at it, invite them to sit at your station. You'll be more likely to remember their names and what they like.

- **Show gratitude.** People are dealing with a lot in their lives, and you have a chance to "make their day." Express gratitude in the tone of your voice when you thank them for their patronage or invite them to come back. Making them feel appreciated will make them remember you—as they leave the tip and the next time they're deciding where to eat.

- **Make personal recommendations.** Tell your guests what you like. This is not suggestive selling, because it's sincere and therefore won't alienate your guests. Your enthusiasm will be infectious, even if guests don't order what you recommend. It won't bother them that you're excited about what's on the menu.

- **Remember: guests leave good tips because they want to leave good tips.**

How as a manager can you make it easiest for your servers to do these things? For one, waitstaff have to have tasted everything on the menu. Ideally, they should know how every item is made so they can speak knowledgeably about it. Even better, as part of their training they could work in the preparation area for a day or two. If you want them to be able to recommend wines with dishes, they should have tasted the wines as well. If your staff have not sampled together all your foods and wines—maybe you could throw a tasting party where everyone gets to know each other and gets an education—then they will be able to make educated and sincere recommendations. Nothing is more persuasive than a waitperson who knows what he is talking about!

Also, let them use their own words to convey their enthusiasm. It's hard to make a personal recommendation using someone else's words. You want them sharing their enthusiasm, not a canned version of yours. Your crew will find their own way of expressing their enthusiasm. Letting them in on what you sell is the best way to give them something to be enthusiastic about!

A TRULY EFFECTIVE STAFF MEETING

How are you going to impart all this newfound wisdom and good spirit to your staff, and how are you going to get them excited about delighting your customers? You need a great, truly effective staff meeting.

Most staff meetings are far from invigorating. In fact, they usually result in a drop in energy and a staff that feels like they are on management's bad side. An effective staff meeting is not just a gathering of bodies with one person giving out information; it's primarily a meeting that generates positive feeling in the entire group. An effective staff meeting has three main goals:

1. Generating positive group feeling.

2. Starting a dialogue.

3. Training.

Positive Group Feeling

This will help your staff discover what it has in common and think in terms of working together, as opposed to strictly as individuals. Share good news in order to build good feeling. Staff meetings are not a good time to address individual or group shortcomings. Find the positive—even if you need to hunt for it—and talk about it. This is how you will build a supportive feeling and get people talking.

Dialogue

A good dialogue is a comfortable back-and-forth of ideas that gets people connected and leaves your staff feeling that they're a truly creative part of your restaurant. You learn from the staff, and they learn from you. Allowing this flow of ideas reduces or eliminates the "Us vs. Them" mentality in your staff and puts everybody on the same team. If everybody is on the same team, service improves, and productivity and profits go up.

Training

Good staff meetings are places to pass on ideas for better performance. If you don't do this, you are passing on the message that things are as good as they could possibly be, or that any fool can wait on a table. Of course, neither is true, and this is your chance not only to effectively pass along tips to your staff, but also to have them learn from each other. Your staff are intelligent people, and they instinctively know what works. Encouraging them to share thoughts about work will turn staff meetings into a forum for discussing ideas. This atmosphere will increase their learning curve dramatically.

Ideally, you should hold a staff meeting before every shift every day. If you frequently cancel staff meetings it sends the message that they are not important and that the staff's opinions are equally unimportant. An effective pre-shift meeting should last no longer than 15 minutes. If it's longer, you may lose people's attention—shorter, you won't get enough said. Pick a length, and start and finish on time. Include the kitchen staff, as well. This may be a good time to let servers taste today's specials and have the kitchen staff tell the waitstaff about them. Also, waitstaff are getting paid for this time, but not tipped, so be sure to not to take advantage of their time.

POSSIBLE FORMAT FOR A 10-TO-15-MINUTE PRE-SHIFT MEETING

Before you start, remember that the thing that most determines how your meeting will go is your own state of mind. Are you looking at your staff as a group of dedicated people committed to doing a great job, or a bunch of layabouts looking to milk the system? Are you a coach on the playing field seeking to facilitate and encourage people's best performances, or a judge looking to identify and punish people's mistakes? Rest assured that whichever it is, your staff feel it, and it will affect the work they do. Get committed to building on people's strengths and holding energizing staff meetings.

- **Good news (1–2 minutes).** Acknowledge what works and create a good mood. Find something about the business that shows people doing a good job and making guests happy. Acknowledge the doer or bearer of the news with sincerity.

- **Daily news (2–3 minutes).** Outline today's specials and upcoming events.

- **Ask your staff (5 minutes).** This is the most important part of the meeting. This is your opportunity to find out what's really going on in your restaurant and what people are thinking about. Listen. Don't interrupt with your own thoughts, and don't judge people's comments. Let them share, and know you are being given a gift. Create a safe space for people to sincerely share what's on their minds and to learn from each other. How well you listen directly affects how much they're willing to say. Since they are the restaurant, as well as your access to the nitty-gritty, get them talking. If they're shy, ask them questions: What's working for you guys? What's making things tough? Where have things broken down? What questions from customers have you been unable to answer? Once you get the ball rolling you may find it hard to stop! Good: That means people have things to say, and you'll benefit. Asking the rest of the staff if they feel the same way as the speaker is a great way to see if there is a group sentiment and to gauge the size of the issue being presented.

- **Training: the latest news (3–5 minutes).** If staff comments run over, let it cut into this time. It's important that your staff learn from you, but it's more important for you to learn from them. Plus they will be open to learning from you if they know you're listening to them. Use this time to talk about a single point you want your staff to focus on during this shift, to give out specific knowledge about a product or to train in another targeted way. Focus is important. If you tell people how long the meeting will last and hold to that, they will give you their attention. If you go over, you'll lose their attention and their trust. Get to the point and trust that they got it.

Becoming good at running staff meetings will translate into a feeling of camaraderie among your staff. They won't just be giving you the true insights into how your business is being run; they will be caring about how to improve it, because they know their suggestions count. You will be more effective, because your staff will take weight off your shoulders, helping your restaurant run better and making your job a lot more fun.

CONCLUSION: FOCUS ON MAKING YOUR GUESTS HAPPY

The food-service business is about personal connection. Getting connected is the way to delight guests and bring them back. Bringing guests back just one time per month will give you a 15-to-50-percent increase in sales volume. If you dedicate your energies towards building an establishment where your servers are treated with respect and gratitude, they will treat you and your customers in the same way. Focus on building an environment that is friendly, helpful, informed and welcoming, and people will come back again and again. This can happen by taking the weight of sales off your staff's shoulders. Everybody—especially customers—should feel they are on the same page. People will give if they are given to and taken care of, and they will never come back if they feel taken advantage of. Your job is to create a place that people think of first when deciding where to eat and that they tell their friends about. You don't want them wondering why they eat at your place; you want them telling their friends why they eat there and getting hungry for your specials in the process. Again:

- Concentrate on building loyalty, not a higher check average. A higher check average will come naturally when the customer has your loyalty. Dedicate your business to delighting your guests.

- Give your guests something to tell their friends about.

- Give customers incentives to return.

- Get connected. Your staff is your restaurant. Get connected with your staff and get them connecting with your guests.

16

INTERNAL BOOKKEEPING—
ACCOUNTING FOR SALES & COSTS—
WHERE DID IT ALL GO?

INTRODUCTION

Internal bookkeeping is the area that ties all departments of the restaurant together into one efficient, airtight operation. Internal bookkeeping is the keystone from which all financial transactions may be monitored, analyzed and reconciled. Management involvement in this department can never be enough.

The preceding chapters have introduced various means of controlling and securing specific areas of the operation. This chapter will cover:

1. The owner/manager's role in these controls systems;

2. Basic principles of accounting; and

3. A system of checks and balances to ensure maximum efficiency and profit.

The internal bookkeeping procedures described in this chapter are simple. However, to ensure complete accuracy, a couple of hours of each day must be devoted to them. It is recommended that a part-time bookkeeper be employed. The bookkeeper need not be highly trained or experienced but must be very accurate and thorough.

A bookkeeper must be willing to follow his or her work through and dig into the facts and figures that are submitted. Since your bookkeeper will only be required for a few hours each morning, he must be well compensated for his efforts. The ideal candidate for this position might be a stay-at-home father or mother wishing to work a few hours each morning while children are at school or daycare. Additional hours may be supplemented if the bookkeeper is able to assist with basic office and administrative functions such as taking reservations, booking private parties or typing. The bookkeeper should not be employed in active floor shifts such as waiting on tables, preparation, or cooking.

A distinction must be made between the bookkeeper and an outside public accountant. The bookkeeper's primary responsibility is to ensure that all sales and products are accurately recorded and balanced. An outside public accountant should be used from time to time to audit the records, prepare financial and tax statements and lend management advisory services.

It is recommended that the bookkeeper not be used in any other capacity in the restaurant (other than office administrative duties), as he will be auditing the money and work of the other employees. The bookkeeper must understand and appreciate the confidential nature and importance of the work he is doing. It may be difficult finding a person suitable for this job. Do not settle for just anyone in this crucial position. Once a competent person is located, make every effort to compensate and satisfy him for his work, and he will be one of your most valuable employees.

This chapter on internal bookkeeping is divided into three separate sections. The first section, Accounts Payable, outlines a unique system for paying and accounting for purchases. The second section, Revenue Accounts and Reconciliation, explains in detail how to account for and reconcile the sales and products from the previous day. The third section describes the steps and procedures used in preparing the payroll.

ACCOUNTING SOFTWARE

As I described in previous chapters, I highly recommend the use of a basic accounting program, such as QuickBooks (*http://www.quickbooks.com*) or Peachtree (*http://www.peachtree.com*). These programs are inexpensive and easy to use and will save time, money and countless errors. The procedures detailed below are for a manual system, but they can be easily (and wisely) brought into a computerized environment. Please note that the use of a POS (point-of-sale) system may also make some of these activities obsolete.

If you are just setting up your accounting program and decide to use QuickBooks, I recommend an add-on product called "The Tasty Profits Guide to QuickBooks Software for Restaurants." This helpful guide to QuickBooks enables you to save thousands of dollars doing your own accounting with its proven, easy-to-use system. Simply install the floppy disc that is included with the "Tasty Profits Guide" directly into your computer. You'll download the pre-configured restaurant accounts, and you are ready to go. You will have instant access to all your financial data; calculate accurate food and bar costs with ease; reconcile bank and credit-card statements; track and pay tips that are charged to credit cards; and calculate sales tax automatically. The program costs about $70 and is available at *http://www.atlantic-pub.com* and 800-541-1336: Item TP-01. If you use QuickBooks in your restaurant, I highly recommend this program.

SECTION 1 ACCOUNTS PAYABLE

Accounts payable represents the money the restaurant owes the purveyors from which it has purchased goods, material or services. Although there are various ways to record the restaurant's transactions, the procedures and systems described here will become an integral part of the restaurant's budgeting, controls and financial management. Therefore, the adoption and use of these procedures is highly recommended.

INVOICES

The start of the accounts payable process begins when the invoices are brought to the manager's office at the end of each day. As I mentioned before, the employees handling the invoices must do so with the utmost of care and concern. Should an invoice become lost or mutilated, it will throw a "monkey wrench" into the bookkeeping records. Ideally, all invoices should be processed on a daily basis so that the transactions are still fresh in everyone's mind and can be easily referred back to. The following are the suggested steps for invoice processing:

1. Make certain the invoice is actually addressed to the restaurant. Although this may sound like an improbable mistake, an invoice may be addressed to the business next door or inadvertently left in the wrong invoice box by the delivery person or in the wrong mailbox by the postperson.

2. Make certain the invoice is signed by one of your employees. This will ensure that the items were, in fact, received intact and accounted for.

3. Verify the delivery date.

4. Check the price and quantity to make certain the amount delivered was the amount ordered and at the price quoted.

5. Check the extensions on the invoice total for accuracy.

6. If everything appears to be in order, stamp the invoice "Approved." This will signify that the invoice should be paid. Should any part of the invoice be in question, take the time to call the company, talk to the employee who received the order and go to the storeroom to check the delivery yourself. A little effort now will save time, money and many headaches later.

CODING THE INVOICE

Every cost the restaurant incurs is assigned a code number. Coding each invoice is an integral part in setting up and establishing bookkeeping and budgeting procedures. Breaking down each invoice and cost into separate categories helps to analyze cost problems later and aids in preparing tax and financial statements.

The following is a standard Chart of Accounts for restaurants, provided by the National Restaurant Association, of every expenditure the restaurant will normally incur during monthly operations:

BALANCE SHEET OF ACCOUNTS

ASSETS

Current Assets
Cash on Hand
Cash in Bank - General Checking
Cash in Bank - High-Yield Checking
Accounts Receivable - Trade
Accounts Receivable - Owner/Employee
Accounts Receivable - Credit Cards
Food Inventory
Beverage Inventory
Prepaid Taxes
Prepaid Insurance
Prepaid Miscellaneous Expenses
Note Receivable - Current Portion

Fixed Assets
Leasehold Improvements
Accumulated Amortization - L/H Imp
Furniture, Fixtures & Equipment
Accumulated Depreciation - FF&E
China, Glass, Flatware Par
Small Equipment Par

Other Assets
Deposits Paid
Liquor License
Organizational Expenses
Logo/Artwork
Note Receivable - Long Term Portion

LIABILITIES & EQUITY

Current Liabilities
Accounts Payable - Trade
Accounts Payable - Other
Gift Certificates Outstanding
Deposits Held
Sales Tax Payable
Payroll Taxes Payable
Other Taxes Payable
Accrued Insurance
Accrued Payroll
Accrued Rent
Accrued Miscellaneous Expenses
Note/Loan Payable - Current Portion
Note/Loan Payable - Current Portion

Long Term Liabilities
Note/Loan Payable - Long Term Portion
Note/Loan Payable - Long Term Portion

Other Liabilities
Other Notes
Shareholder Notes

Shareholders' Equity
Capital Stock
Retained Earnings - Prior Years
Current Profit/Loss(-)

INCOME AND EXPENSE ACCOUNTS

Revenue
Food Sales
Liquor/Beer /Misc. Bar Sales
Wine Sales

Cost of Sales
Food Cost
Liquor/Beer /Misc. Bar Cost
Wine Cost

Salaries & Wages
Administrative Wages
Bar Wages
Kitchen Wages
Restaurant Wages
Bonuses & Incentives
Vacation Pay

Employee Benefits
Employer Payroll Tax Expense
Workers' Compensation Insurance
Medical & Dental Insurance
Employee Meals (cost)
Miscellaneous Employee Benefits

Direct Operating Expenses
Auto/Gas Expense - Operations
China/Glass/Flatware Replacement
Contract Cleaning/Janitorial Service
Decorations
Laundry/Linen
Licenses/Permits
Menus and Wine Lists
Supplies - Banquet/Catering
Supplies - Bar
Supplies - Cleaning/Janitorial
Supplies - Kitchen
Supplies - Restaurant
Uniforms

Music & Entertainment
(see detail list)

Marketing
Complimentary Food & Beverage (cost)
Donations/Charities
Media Advertising
Other Promotional Expenses
Postage/Delivery (promo)
Photo/Printing/Graphics
Programs & Directories
Restaurant Research & Development
Signature Souvenirs
Telephone (promo)

Utility Services
Electricity
Natural Gas/Fuel
Scavenger/Waste Removal
Water & Sewage

Occupancy Costs
Rent/Lease (Premises)
Equipment Lease
Property Taxes
Insurance - Property
Other Taxes

Repairs & Maintenance
Grounds/Gardening
Maintenance Contracts-Equipment
Repairs & Maintenance-Equipment
Repairs & Maintenance-Premises
Miscellaneous Repairs & Maintenance

Depreciation & Amortization
Depreciation Expense
Amortization Expense

Other (Income)/Expense
Interest Income
Room Rental Fees
Gifts/Novelties Sales
Gifts/Novelties Costs
Telephone Coin Box Commissions
Discounts Taken
Miscellaneous Income

Administrative & General
Auto/Mileage Allowance
Bad Debt Expense
Bank Charges
Cash Over/Short
Computer Supplies
Credit Card Discounts
Dues and Subscriptions
Educational Materials
Entertainment (Business Operation)
Forms/Paper Products/Printing (A&G)
Insurance-Liability/Umbrella
Insurance-Miscellaneous
Legal/Accounting Professional Services
Management Fees
Miscellaneous Expenses
Office Supplies
Outside Services
Personnel Expenses
Postage/Delivery (A&G)
Security/Alarm
Seminars/Conventions
Telephone/Communications
Travel Expenses

Interest & Non-Operating Exp.
Interest Expense
Officers' Salaries & Benefits
Corporate Office Expenses

Income Taxes
State Income Tax
Federal Income Tax

BALANCE SHEET FORMAT

ASSETS	
Current Assets	
Cash on Hand	XXX
Cash in Bank - General Checking	XXX
Cash in Bank - High-Yield Checking	XXX
Accounts Receivable - Trade	XXX
Accounts Receivable - Owner/Employee	XXX
Accounts Receivable - Credit Cards	XXX
Food Inventory	XXX
Beverage Inventory	XXX
Prepaid Taxes	XXX
Prepaid Insurance	XXX
Prepaid Miscellaneous Expenses	XXX
Note Receivable - Current Portion	XXX
Total Current Assets	XXX
Fixed Assets	
Leasehold Improvements	XXX
Accumulated Amortization - L/H Imp.	XXX
Furniture Fixtures & Equipment	XXX
Accumulated Depreciation - FF&E	XXX
China, Glass, Flatware Par	XXX
Small Equipment Par	XXX
Total Fixed Assets	XXX
Other Assets	
Deposits Paid	XXX
Liquor License	XXX
Organizational Expenses	XXX
Logo/Artwork	XXX
Note Receivable - Long Term Portion	XXX
Total Other Assets	XXX
Total Assets	**XXX**

LIABILITIES & EQUITY	
Current Liabilities	
Accounts Payable - Trade	XXX
Accounts Payable - Other	XXX
Gift Certificates Outstanding	XXX
Deposits Held	XXX
Sales Tax Payable	XXX
Payroll Taxes Payable	XXX
Accrued Insurance	XXX
Accrued Payroll	XXX
Accrued Rent	XXX
Accrued Miscellaneous Expenses	XXX
Note/Loan Payable - Current Portion	XXX
Note/Loan Payable - Current Portion	XXX
Total Current Liabilities	XXX
Long Term Liabilities	
Note/Loan Payable - Long Term Portion	XXX
Note/Loan Payable - Long Term Portion	XXX
Total Long Term Liabilities	XXX
Other Notes/Loans Payable	XXX
Total Liabilities	XXX
Shareholders' Equity	
Capital Stock	XXX
Retained Earnings - Prior Years	XXX
Current Profit / Loss (-)	XXX
Total Shareholders' Equity	XXX
Total Liabilities and Shareholders' Equity	**XXX**

SUMMARY INCOME STATEMENT FORMAT

	Current Period	% of Sales		Year-To-Date	% of Sales
Revenue					
Food Sales	XXX	XX		XXX	XX
Beverage Sales	XXX	XX		XXX	XX
Total Revenue	XXX	XX		XXX	XX
Cost of Sales					
Food Cost	XXX	XX		XXX	XX
Beverage Cost	XXX	XX		XXX	XX
Total Cost of Sales	XXX	XX		XXX	XX
Gross Profit	XXX	XX		XXX	XX
Operating Expenses					
Salaries & Wages	XXX	XX		XXX	XX
Employee Benefits	XXX	XX		XXX	XX
Direct Operating Expenses	XXX	XX		XXX	XX
Music & Entertainment	XXX	XX		XXX	XX
Marketing	XXX	XX		XXX	XX
Utility Services	XXX	XX		XXX	XX
Occupancy Costs	XXX	XX		XXX	XX
Repairs & Maintenance	XXX	XX		XXX	XX
Depreciation & Amortization	XXX	XX		XXX	XX
Other (Income)/Expense	XXX	XX		XXX	XX
General & Administrative	XXX	XX		XXX	XX
Total Operating Expenses	XXX	XX		XXX	XX
Income Before Interest & Non-Operating Expenses	XXX	XX		XXX	XX
Interest					
Interest Expense	XXX	XX		XXX	XX
Other Expenses	XXX	XX		XXX	XX
Total Interest & Non-Op Expenses	XXX	XX		XXX	XX
Income Before Income Taxes	XXX	XX		XXX	XX
Income Taxes	XXX	XX		XXX	XX
Net Profit or (Loss)	**XXX**	**XX**		**XXX**	**XX**

After approving each invoice, code the invoice to its appropriate category. A rubber stamp for processing invoices may be prepared at most office-supply stores. It should contain a space for the following information:

1. Date

2. Code

3. Amount due

4. Bookkeeper's initials

After stamping the invoice, simply fill in the appropriate blank with the required data. Some invoices may list purchases or costs that must be entered into the expenditure ledger under different codes. For example, a food purveyor's invoice might list 50 pounds of flour and one case of pineapple juice. The cost of the flour would be coded to the cost of food and the cost of the pineapple juice would be coded to the cost of liquor. If you ask them, most purveyors that deliver products for more than one code will be glad to make out a separate invoice for each code.

Every invoice must be copied and filed according to its respective code number and purveyor's company name. Invoices containing two or more codes should have two or more copies prepared, one for each appropriate file. The original invoices should also be filed by code numbers and by the month in which the transaction occurred. Store the originals in a fireproof cabinet.

Most purveyors will issue a monthly statement itemizing all the invoices and the total amount due. Payment may then be made once a month on the total amount rather than with a separate check for each invoice received. Paying purveyors on a monthly-statement basis is advantageous. The restaurant's cash flow will be utilized more effectively, and there will be less administrative work. Prior to issuing the check, be certain that the monthly statement is accurate by cross-checking the statement against the invoices in the file. Staple the received invoices to the monthly statement for future reference.

Accounts must be closed out on the last day of each month in order to accurately compute monthly profits and costs. Most monthly statements will not arrive until the fourth or fifth day of the following month. Thus, the bookkeeper must realize that, even though some bills may be paid in the following month, the cost of the goods and services will be applied to the month they were delivered to the restaurant. This will be a crucial point in the following two chapters when profits and costs will be computed.

In order to accurately record purchases delivered to the restaurant, you must record these expenditures in a separate ledger, called a Purchase Ledger. An example of a **Purchase Ledger** can be found at the end of this chapter. Use a loose-leaf binder to store all the Purchase Ledger pages. Separate Purchase Ledger pages are required for each of the following categories:

1. Food Costs

2. Liquor Costs

3. Wine Costs

4. Each operational category: Services, Utilities, etc.

5. Other Expenses

All invoices must be recorded in the Purchase Ledger under the date the items were delivered to the restaurant. (This is a hard-and-fast rule, regardless of whether goods and services are paid for in cash or by credit or other terms.) This pertains to all expenses, regardless of whether or not you intend to use the items during that particular month. For example, expenses, such as the telephone bill, that may not arrive until the following month must be recorded under the month during which they were incurred.

In summation, this system will provide a record of expenses when they are paid. The Purchase Ledgers will record all invoices when they are received. The ending inventories, discussed in the following chapters, will make the necessary adjustments to determine the actual amount used over the month. This is necessary so that actual costs may be accurately projected. The crucial consideration now is to record every invoice in the Purchase Ledger under the correct expense category. This must be done on the date the material was received to ensure the cost projections calculated at the end of the month will be accurate.

To post the Purchase Ledger, simply determine which type of expense account it should be credited to and enter the invoice amount on the appropriate ledger page. Record the invoice number, amount and the date received under the purveyor's column. "Paid Outs" are recorded as cash purchases even if recorded on the Cashier's or Bartender's Report. Determine which expense account the Paid Out should be credited to and record the transaction in the "Paid Out" column on the proper page.

TOTAL MONTHLY PURCHASES

To compute the total expenditure for each code over the month, simply add each expenditure column then each page total on the Purchase Ledger. Credits are subtracted out of the restaurant's total purchases on the monthly statement.

The cut-off time for each month is the close of business on the last day of the month. Transactions after midnight on the last day of the month are still to be included in the month's totals, as they are a part of the business for that previous month. (The measure of one day, for our purposes, is one complete business day or cycle.) To reiterate an important concept from the last section, costs are to be applied to the month the products were received at the restaurant, regardless of when they were paid for or used.

Some hints on preparing the Purchase Ledger:

- Enter all figures in pencil.

- Enter all credits in red and in parentheses.

- Have purveyors that deliver products for more than one code make out a separate invoice for each code.

MANAGING THE RESTAURANT'S CASH FLOW

Daily involvement and analyses of your financial records are necessary if the restaurant is to take full advantage of the credit terms and discounts offered by suppliers. Simply managing the restaurant's cash flow and utilizing its enormous purchasing power can acquire substantial savings.

After you've been operating for a few months, most purveyors will extend "30-day net" terms if you request them. This is an advantageous situation; through proper management, the restaurant's inventory may be turned over as many as five or six times in a 30-day period. In effect, the purveyors will be financing your operations. Few businesses can turn their inventories over this quickly, so they are forced to pay interest or finance charges. Quick turnover is one of the blessings of the restaurant business. Careful planning and synchronization between the purchasing and bookkeeping departments is needed to obtain maximum utilization of the cash flow. The savings are well worth the additional effort.

SECTION 2 | REVENUE ACCOUNTS AND RECONCILIATION

Revenue is the sales received for the restaurant's products: primarily food and beverages. The procedures in this section for setting up revenue accounts are the basis of the restaurant's controls. Every transaction will be checked and balanced. When the procedures are completed, there will be no margin for error, and no loss of revenue.

PREPARING AND AUDITING SALES REPORTS

The procedures for preparing and auditing sales reports are listed below in numerical order. This is the order in which the bookkeeper should begin to record and reconcile the previous day's transactions. It would be advisable to have the bookkeeper review the other control sections in the restaurant so that he or she will become familiar with how the controls fit together and how they work.

1. Remove the cash drawer, tickets, charge forms, Cook's Forms and reports from the safe, where the manager placed them at the close of the previous business day.

2. Separate the cashier and bartender drawers, tickets and forms into their respective piles. Work in a closed, locked office while the cash is out of the safe.

3. Begin by verifying the Cashier's and Bartender's Reports. Count out and separate the cash by denomination. The total amount taken in must equal the difference between the new and old cash-register readings. These figures should all be in order, as the manager checked and verified the sales of the previous day with the cashier and bartender. Any discrepancies should be immediately brought to the manager's attention.

4. Using new Cashier's and Bartender's Report forms, enter the new register readings in the space provided on the reports.

5. Make up new cash drawers for each register. Enter the total and itemized amounts on the reports in the "Cash In" sections. Sign the reports and place them in the cash drawers. Place the drawers back into the safe. Return to the safe the remaining cash, charges and checks. Later on you will need all these items to make up the daily deposit.

6. Using the Ticket Issuance Form and the bottom part of the Bartender's Report, verify that all tickets have been turned in. The total number issued must equal the amount used and returned. Should there be any tickets missing, determine which ticket number is missing, and using these two forms, you can determine which employee was issued the missing ticket. Notify the manager immediately. The manager should have verified that all tickets were turned in the previous day. This, again, is a double check.

7. From the unused tickets issue new cocktail and bar tickets. Issue the same number of tickets to each employee. Thirty is an average number for each shift. Using the employee schedule, write on the appropriate forms the name of each waitperson and bartender working. Write in the total number of tickets issued and the number sequences of each employee's tickets. Place a rubber band around each pile of tickets. On the top ticket write in the employee's name so that the manager knows to whom they should be issued. When this is completed, place everything in the safe.

8. Take the used tickets from the previous business day and separate waitstaff and bar tickets. Starting with the waitstaff tickets, check each for accuracy. Make certain that:

   A. The correct price was charged. (This is a double check on the cashier.)

   B. The ticket was added correctly, and sales tax was computed and entered correctly. Waitstaff and cashiers may be charged for these mistakes in some states. Regardless of the legality, they must be notified of their errors and correct them in the future. Write up all mistakes and post the sheet on the bulletin board at the completion of each day. Mistakes in writing tickets are caused by careless employees and can be a great expense to the restaurant. Management should use whatever action is necessary to resolve and limit the problem.

9. On the **Food Itemization Form** at the end of this chapter, place an "X" in the appropriate column for each menu item sold. Using the **Wine Itemization Form**, itemize any wine sold from the tickets. List any housed, managerial or complimentary product in the itemization, but also list them separately on the back of the form in their respective categories; this information will be used later.

10. Check the waitstaff, bar and, if utilized, cocktail tickets for accuracy. Any wine or food item listed on these tickets must also be added to the Food and Wine Itemization Forms. Cocktails and liquor are not itemized.

11. Take the credit-card sales drafts and separate them into piles by company. Each employee is responsible for his or her own credit-card charges, but they should be double-checked by the cashier. Verify the accuracy of each charge:

    A. Make sure the charge slip is signed.

    B. If the card was imprinted manually, make sure:

    - the slip was imprinted clearly;

    - the right charge form was used;

    - the expiration date is good;

    - the slip is dated correctly; and

    - the total amount was added correctly.

    C. If the tip was charged, a "Cash Paid Out" from the cashier or bartender should have been given to the employee. The Cash Paid Out is not a purchase, because when the charge goes through, the restaurant will be reimbursed. Set up a cash reserve or special account and reimburse the cash drawer for this Cash Paid Out. When the check or electronic deposit from the credit-card company comes in, put the Paid Out amount back into the reserve or special account.

    D. Be sure an approval code is on the charge, in case the floor limit of the charge card was exceeded.

12. Separate and examine for accuracy any checks received. The manager should have approved personal checks. The customer's driver's license number and telephone number should be listed on the back. Also, only the manager should approve traveler's checks. The manager must witness the second signature and compare it to the first.

13. Total and verify all the charge and check amounts on both reports.

14. Total the Food and Wine Itemization Forms. Multiply the total number sold by the selling price (without sales tax).

15. Compare the itemized number of menu items sold against the daily Cook's

Form and the Ticket Itemization Form. This will ensure that every food item is now accounted and paid for. Should there be a discrepancy, recheck both your figures and the cook's calculations. If everything still appears to be in order, refigure the Cook's Form using the carbon-copy tickets. It is possible a ticket may have been changed after the carbon copy was given to the cook.

16. Total the food sales on the Food Itemization Form. This figure must match the total food sales entered on the Cashier's and Bartender's Reports.

17. Total the wine sales on the Wine Itemization Form. This figure must match the total wine sales entered on the Bartender's and Cashier's Reports.

18. Add the itemized wine and food sales together.

19. The difference between the total itemized food and wine sales and the total sales taken in must equal the liquor sales.

20. The total sales multiplied by the percentage of sales tax must equal the total sales tax taken in. After this step, all sales will be completely checked and balanced by three different individuals and against every other transaction that occurred in the restaurant. There is no possible way items or money could be stolen, undetected, unless every single employee—including the manager—was in collusion.

21. Send the Wine Itemization Form to the manager so that he or she may reconcile and restock the wine for the next day.

22. Make up the daily deposit. Use indelible ink, and prepare two copies of the deposit form. Stamp all checks with the restaurant's account number and "For Deposit Only." Put the appropriate employee's name on the back of each check so that, if it is returned, the manager can go back to the employee who accepted it.

23. Sort the bills and wrap as much of the coins possible. Charge-card sales receipts can usually be deposited along with your cash deposit or electronically, direct from the terminal. If your bank does not offer this service, you will have to mail the receipts directly to the credit-card company. The manager should personally bring the deposit to the bank every day. Change or small bills needed for the following day should be picked up at this time.

24. Never let two days' worth of receipts sit in the safe. Make certain the deposit receipt is returned and filed in a fireproof box. Check the duplicate deposit stub against the deposit receipt to make sure the correct amount was deposited. Enter the deposit amount, date and source onto the check register. Enter the verified figures for the day on the **Daily Sales Report Form** (see example at the end of this chapter).

To compute individual category percentages, divide the category sales by the total daily sales. "Actual Month-to-Date Sales" is a tally of the daily sales. The budget sections will be explained in detail in the next chapter. "Dinner Count" refers to the number of daily customers served. "Cash, Over/Short" refers to any mistakes made at the register. Complimentary, house and manager figures are recorded from when you itemized the food and bar tickets in step 9. Break down the food, liquor and wine sales for each category and enter at full price.

This concludes the reconciliation part of the revenue accounts. Every item and sale is accounted for and reconciled against every other transaction in the restaurant. Keep all of these forms for at least five years in a fireproof storage file. All forms used during the month may be kept in loose-leaf binders in the bookkeeper's office.

The Daily Sales Report should be left at the manager's desk at the end of the day. Remember that all this information is strictly confidential and should never be the subject of idle conversation.

SECTION 3 PAYROLL

As stated in Chapter 1, preparing the payroll is best left to a computerized payroll program, such as QuickBooks® or Peachtree®, or to a payroll service. Please review the section on payroll in Chapter 1.

TAXES AND TIPS

One of the biggest challenges facing restaurant owners and managers in regard to payroll is getting employees to report and pay taxes on their tips, as required by the IRS. Complying with the intricacies of the tip reporting and allocation rules can be difficult and confusing. Tip tax laws are constantly changing. There are at least five legal suits involving tip regulations that are currently pending. You must use extreme caution in this area; get assistance from your accountant, attorney, state restaurant association or the National Restaurant Association (*http://www.restaurant.org*).

U.S. SUPREME COURT DECIDES TIP-REPORTING CASE

United States vs. Fior d'Italia Inc., 01-463

The Internal Revenue Service can use estimates to make sure it is collecting enough taxes on cash restaurant tips, the Supreme Court said Monday, June 17, 2002. The ruling is a defeat for the estimated 350,000 restaurants with tipped workers. The court said the IRS can estimate the amount of cash tips given to employees based on tips shown on credit card receipts. The estimate is used to determine taxes. This case pitted one of the nation's oldest Italian restaurants against U.S. tax collectors. The restaurant contends the IRS formula does not take into account stingy cash tips, take-out meals or tip-sharing among hostesses and other staff.

Justice Stephen Breyer, writing for the 6-3 court, said, while the practice is not illegal, "we recognize that Fior d'Italia remains free to make its policy-related arguments to Congress." The ruling is a follow-up to the Supreme Court's 1973 decision that the IRS can make an educated guess about employees' tip taxes when records are inadequate. Fior d'Italia, operating in San Francisco for 116 years, had challenged an extra $22,000+ bill that was calculated with estimates. Using credit card receipts, the IRS had calculated that workers were tipped about 14 percent on meals. The San Francisco-based 9th U.S. Circuit Court of Appeals said the IRS could not prove that people who paid with cash tipped 14 percent, and that the IRS therefore should stop using the estimates.

OTHER TIP TAX CASES

Since the IRS first began pursuing employer-only and employer-first restaurant audits in the mid-1990s to collect taxes from employers on tips employees allegedly failed to report, the restaurant industry has mounted several major court challenges. Several of these challenges have made it to the federal appeals court level. In the Fior d'Italia case, the 9th Circuit (San Francisco) ruled in the restaurant's favor. Three other federal appeals courts have sided with the IRS.

Get more details on all the rulings:

9th Circuit (California), in Fior d'Italia, Inc. v. United States (March 2001);

11th Circuit (Florida), in Quietwater Entertainment, Inc. v. United States (June 2000; no published opinion);

11th Circuit (Alabama), in Morrison Restaurants, Inc. v. United States of America (August 1997); and

Federal Circuit (Washington, DC): Bubble Room, Inc. v. United States (Pending).

TIPPED EMPLOYEES

The supreme court ruling of June 25, 2002, states that the Internal Revenue Service can use aggregate tip estimates to ensure that the employer is paying enough FICA taxes on allegedly unreported tips. This essentially means the IRS can look at the restaurant's records, come up with a total amount of tips it thinks employees should have reported, and bill the restaurant business for the employer's share of FICA taxes (currently 7.65%) on any allegedly unreported tips. Under the new ruling, the IRS does not need to examine individual employees' records or credit employer FICA tax payments to individual employees' Social Security accounts. It is permissible for the IRS to estimate the amount of cash tips given to employees based on tips included on credit-card receipts. Potentially, a restaurant could face a tax bill for FICA taxes on allegedly unreported tips going as far back as 1988, when Congress first began requiring employees to pay FICA taxes on all tips. As an employer of tipped employees you are essentially being forced to protect yourself from IRS audits and aggregate FICA tax assessments.

So what is the restaurant owner to do? In 2000, the IRS announced it was lifting a five-year moratorium on its employer-only audits. We recommend restaurant owners at least consider signing the Tip Reporting Alternative Commitment (TRAC) with the IRS. Through the TRAC (under a more customized employer-created approach, EmTRAC), a restaurant business agrees to assume greater responsibility for training, educating and getting employees to report their tips. In exchange, the IRS agrees that it will not bill the restaurant for FICA taxes on allegedly unreported tips unless it has first examined which employees had not reported tips accurately. The TRAC program essentially allows you a release from employer-only assessments if you comply with the program. This is the only remedy, albeit a partial one, unless Congress acts on the subject. The National Restaurant Association as well as other trade group associations have vowed to take the fight over tip reporting to Congress. In the meantime, you must govern yourself accordingly, and seek the advice of your CPA.

THE TIP RATE DETERMINATION AND EDUCATION PROGRAM

The Tip Rate Determination and Education Program was developed by the Internal Revenue Service in 1993 to address the concern of widespread underreporting of tip income in the food-and-beverage industry. The goal was to involve employers in monitoring their employees' tip-reporting practices.

There are two different IRS programs available: the Tip Rate Determination Agreement (TRDA) and the Tip Reporting Alternative Commitment (TRAC). Participation in one of these programs is voluntary, and the restaurant may only enter into one of the agreements at a time. *Please note that 1998 tax legislation specifies that IRS agents can't threaten to audit you in order to convince you to sign a TRAC or TRDA agreement.*

The big benefit for you as an employer is that you will not be subject to unplanned tax liabilities. Those who sign a TRAC or TRDA agreement receive a commitment from the IRS that the agency will not examine the owner's books to search for underwithheld or underpaid payroll taxes on tip income. There are benefits to employees, also, including increases in their Social Security, unemployment compensation, retirement plan and workers' compensation benefits.

Under TRDA, the IRS works with you to arrive at a tip rate for your employees. Then, at least 75 percent of your tipped workers must agree in writing to report tips at the agreed-upon rate. If they fail to do so, you are required to turn them in to the IRS. If you do not comply, the agreement is terminated and your business becomes subject to IRS auditing.

The TRAC is less strict but requires more work on your part. There is no established tip rate, but you are required to work with employees to make sure they understand their tip-reporting obligations. You must set up a process to receive employees' cash tip reports, and they must be informed of the tips you are recording from credit-card receipts.

TIP CREDITS FOR EMPLOYERS ARE POSSIBLE

As an employer, you may also be eligible for credit for taxes paid on certain employee tips (IRS Form 8846). The credit is generally equal to the employer's portion of Social Security and Medicare taxes paid on tips received by employees. You will not get credit for your part of Social Security and Medicare taxes on those tips that are used to meet the federal minimum wage rate applicable to the employee under the Fair Labor Standards Act (as detailed later in this chapter). This is also subject to state laws. You must also increase the amount of your taxable income by the amount of the tip credit. Note the following changes to this credit:

1. The credit is effective for your part of Social Security and Medicare taxes paid after 1993, regardless of whether your employees reported the tips to you or when your employees performed the services.

2. Effective for services performed after 1996, the credit applies to the taxes on tips your employees receive from customers in connection with providing, delivering or serving food or beverages, regardless of whether the customers consume the food or beverages on your business premises.

EMPLOYEE TIP REPORTING "FREQUENTLY ASKED QUESTIONS"

Because you're an employee, the tip income you receive—whether it's cash or included in a charge—is taxable income. As income, these tips are subject to federal income tax and Social Security and Medicare taxes, and may be subject to state income tax as well.

What tips do I have to report? If you received $20 or more in tips in any one month you should report all your tips to your employer so that federal income tax, Social Security and Medicare taxes—maybe state income tax, too—can be withheld.

Do I have to report all my tips on my tax return? Yes. All tips are income and should be reported on your tax return.

Is it true that only 8 percent of my total sales must be reported as tips? No. You must report to your employer all (100 percent) of your tips except for the tips totaling less than $20 in any month. The 8-percent rule applies to employers.

Do I need to report tips from other employees? Yes. Employees who are indirectly tipped by other employees are required to report "tip-outs." This could apply to bus persons, for instance.

Do I have to report tip-outs that I pay to indirectly tipped employees? If you are a directly tipped employee, you should report to your employer only the amount of tips you retain. Maintain records of tip-outs with your other tip income (cash tips, charged tips, split tips, tip pool).

What records do I need to keep? You must keep a running daily log of all your tip income.

What can happen if I don't keep a record of my tips? Underreporting could result in you owing substantial taxes, penalties, and interest to the IRS and, possibly, other agencies.

If I report all my tips to my employer, do I still have to keep records? Yes. You should keep a daily log of your tips so that, in case of an examination, you can substantiate the actual amount of tips received.

Why should I report my tips to my employer? When you report your tip income to your employer, the employer is required to withhold federal income tax, Social Security and Medicare taxes, and, maybe, state income tax. Tip reporting may increase your Social Security credits, resulting in greater Social Security benefits when you retire. Tip reporting may also increase other benefits to which you may become entitled, such as unemployment or retirement benefits. Additionally, a greater income may improve financing approval for mortgages, car loans and other loans.

I forgot to report my tip income to my employer, but I remembered to record it on my federal income tax return. Will that present a problem? If you do not report your tip income to your employer, but you do report the tip income on your federal income tax return, you may owe a 50 percent Social Security and Medicare tax penalty and be subject to a negligence penalty and, possibly, an estimated tax penalty.

If I report all my tips, but my taxes on the tips are greater than my pay from my employer, how do I pay the remaining taxes? You can either pay the tax when you file your federal income tax return or you can reach into your tip money and give some to your employer to be applied to those owed taxes.

What can happen if I don't report my tips to the IRS? If the IRS determines through an examination that you underreported your tips, you could be subject to additional federal income tax, Social Security and Medicare taxes and, possibly, state income tax. You will also be charged a penalty of 50 percent of the additional Social Security and Medicare taxes and a negligence penalty of 20 percent of the additional income tax, plus any interest that may apply.

What is my responsibility as an employee under the Tip Rate Determination Agreement (TRDA)? You are required to file your federal tax returns. You must sign a Tipped Employee Participation Agreement proclaiming that you are participating in the program. To stay a participating employee, you must report tips at or above the tip rate determined by the agreement.

What is my responsibility as an employee under the Tip Reporting Alternative Commitment (TRAC)? Directly tipped employee: Your employer will furnish you a written statement (at least monthly) reflecting your charged tips:

1.   You are to verify or correct this statement.

2.   You are to indicate the amount of cash tips received.

3.   When reporting your cash tips, keep in mind that there is a correlation between charged tips and cash tips.

4. You may be asked to provide the name and amount of any tip-outs you've given to indirectly tipped employees.

What about indirectly tipped employees? You are required to report all your tips to your employer.

EMPLOYER'S TIP RECORDS

It is in your company's best interest to insist that all employees accurately report their income from tips. The IRS will hold you responsible. Establishments that do not comply are subject to IRS audit and possible tax liabilities, penalties and interest payments. As a precaution, if you have any employees who customarily receive tips from customers, patrons or other third parties, we recommend you keep the following additional information about tipped employees:

1. Indicate on the pay records—by a symbol, letter or other notation placed next to his or her name—each tipped employee.

2. Weekly or monthly amount of tips reported by each employee.

3. The amount by which the wages of each tipped employee have been increased by tips.

4. The hours worked each workday in any occupation in which the employee does not receive tips, and the total daily or weekly earnings for those times.

5. The hours worked each workday in any occupation in which the employee receives tips, and the total daily or weekly straight-time earnings for those times.

Large Food or Beverage Establishments Need to File Form 8027 with the IRS

You may meet the definition of a "large food or beverage establishment" if you employ more than 10 employees. If you do, the law requires that you file Form 8027, Employer's Annual Information Return of Tip Income and Allocated Tips, with the IRS.

If you meet the definition, the law requires that you report certain tip information to the IRS on an annual basis. You should use Form 8027 to report information such as total charged tips, charged receipts, total reported tips by employees and gross receipts from food-and-beverage operations. Also, employers must allocate tips to certain directly tipped employees and include the allocation on their employees' W-2 forms when the total of reported tips is less than 8 percent.

The IRS offers a program that business owners can enter into to help them educate their employees about tip reporting and tax obligations. This is the "Tip Rate Determination and Education Program." There are two arrangements under the program that a food-and-beverage employer can enter into: TRDA, the Tip Rate Determination Agreement, or TRAC, Tip Reporting Alternative Commitment.

To find out more about these programs and about whether you should be filing Form

8027, contact the Tip Coordinator of your local IRS office. Check your telephone directory for the IRS office in your area. They can provide the mailing address and phone number for the Tip Coordinator.

You can get a copy of Form 8027 and its instructions by calling 800-TAX-FORM (800-829-3676). You can also get copies of most forms by dialing 703-368-9694 from your fax machine.

FOR MORE INFORMATION ON TIP REPORTING

The following IRS forms and publications relating to tip income reporting can be downloaded directly from the government Web site: *http://www.irs.gov/forms_pubs/index.html.* Look under the heading "Forms and Publications by Number."

Pub 505—*Tax Withholding and Estimated Tax*

Pub 531—*Reporting Tip Income*

Form 941—*Employer's Quarterly Federal Tax Return*

Form 4137—*Social Security and Medicare Tax on Unreported Tip Income*

Form 8027—*Employer's Annual Information on Tip Income and Allocated Tips*

"THE IRS TIP AGREEMENTS REALLY HELP EMPLOYERS AND WORKERS" – FROM THE IRS

The IRS is continuing its emphasis on a multiyear strategy to increase tax compliance by tipped employees. Originally developed for the Food and Beverage industry, this program has now been extended to the Gaming (casino) and Hairstyling industries.

There are two arrangements under this program that, depending on their business, employers in specific industries can agree to enter into: The Tip Rate Determination Agreement (TRDA) is available to the Gaming and the Food and Beverage industries and the Tip Reporting Alternative Commitment (TRAC) is available to the Food and Beverage and the Hairstyling industries.

First introduced in 1993, the TRDA set the stage for a new way of doing business at the IRS. This arrangement emphasizes future compliance by tipped employees in the Food and Beverage industry by utilizing the tip rates individually calculated for each restaurant. In addition, as long as the participants comply with the terms of the agreement and accurately report their tip income, the IRS agrees not to initiate any examinations during the period the TRDA is in effect. When TRDA was first introduced in 1993, initial response from the industry was mixed. Today the TRDA is a viable option for many restaurants.

The second arrangement, TRAC, grew out of a collaborative effort between the IRS and a coalition of restaurant industry representatives. It was first introduced in June 1995.

TRAC emphasizes educating both employers and employees to ensure compliance with the tax laws relating to tip income reporting. Employees are provided tip reports detailing the correlation that exists between an employee's charged tip rate and the cash tip rate. In general, the District Director will not initiate any examinations on either the employer or employees while the agreement is in effect if participants comply with the provisions of the agreement.

The overall response to TRDA and TRAC has been very positive among employers who seek to foster compliance by their employees in a manner that is relatively simple and that makes good business sense. In addition, there are benefits for both the employer and the employees.

Employer Benefits—After Congress passed a law in 1988 requiring employers to match and pay assessments made against employees, the IRS performed significant amounts of tip audits. The IRS expended a significant amount of resources to conduct these examinations. Some employers found themselves in a financial crisis, having to come up with the tax being assessed against them when there had not been any financial planning for this. Employees were being hit just as hard. Under the Tip Rate Determination Agreement TRDA, the IRS agrees not to perform any tip audits while either a Tip Rate Determination Agreement or a Tip Reporting Alternative Commitment is in effect. The employer is granted a credit allowance (Code Section 45B) for Social Security taxes paid on tips in excess of minimum wage reported by employees. The employer is then in compliance with the law.

Employee Benefits—The employee receives several benefits. Greater Social Security benefits accrue based on the tip earnings reported. Increased tip earnings translates to increased proof of income when applying for mortgage, car and other loans. There is an increase in unemployment benefits, retirement plan contributions (if applicable), and to workers' compensation. There will not be any subsequent tip examinations of the employee's tax returns as long as the terms of the arrangement have been met and all tips have been reported.

As of June 30, 1998, the IRS has received more than 8,000 TRAC agreements representing over 25,000 establishments nationwide. The number of TRDAs is nearly 1,100, representing over 2,400 establishments. Please note many of the agreements encompass multiple unit locations. The IRS is continuing its efforts to raise the compliance level in this industry and to promote consistency across the country. IRS employees have been receiving updated training in this area.

As part of an outreach effort, IRS employees will be making field calls to businesses where tipping is customary, explaining both arrangements and providing business owners with copies of written material to aid them in educating themselves and their workers. But you don't have to wait for an IRS representative to visit you to get more information about TRDA or TRAC. Information is available through the Tip Coordinator at your local IRS office and the IRS's "Tips on Tips" brochures (employer and employee versions). These and other publications relating to tip income can be ordered by calling the IRS at 800-829-3676.

PAYROLL ACCOUNTING

Although you may decide to use an outside payroll service or a software program, your bookkeeper must still be involved in the computation of the daily labor costs. After each pay period, the bookkeeper will need to compute each employee's time card and call the information to the payroll service company or key the information into the accounting software. There are time clocks now available that can link employee scheduling, time clock administration and accounting all into one foolproof system. Described in this section are the procedures used to compute and analyze by manual system daily and monthly labor costs.

On a daily basis the bookkeeper should:

1. Gather all of the employees' time cards.

2. Using the posted schedule, ensure that each employee punched in at the scheduled time.

3. Compute the number and fraction of hours worked.

4. Enter hours worked on the time card and on the **Daily Payroll Form**. An example of this form can be found at the end of this chapter. Any overtime should be written in red on a separate line. Notify the manager of any overtime or of any employee who is approaching overtime status. She may be able to rearrange the schedule to avoid paying overtime.

5.   Fill in the hourly rate of pay. If the employee performs more than one job, make sure the rate of pay corresponds to the job performed.

6.   Extend the gross amount to be paid.

7   Divide each salaried employee's total monthly salary by the number of days in the month. Enter this figure in the "Gross Paid" column for each day. Although the employee will be paid the same each week, the salary is broken down this way so that labor may be analyzed and budgeted accurately.

8.   The manager and owner's salaries should be listed separately at the bottom of the Daily Payroll Form. These costs are separated, as they will be budgeted differently in an upcoming chapter. Also, by separating them out you may get some additional tax advantages.

9.   Total the gross amount payable for each day at the bottom of the form. When the week is completed (seven days) total each employee's hours worked and total gross pay. Check your calculations by cross-checking all of the figures against each other.

10.   Enter the daily sales and labor costs on the **Labor Analysis Form**. An example of this form can be found at the end of this chapter. Remember that manager and owner salaries are computed separately and are not in the total labor cost computations. The Labor Analysis Form is divided into two sections: the daily payroll and the month-to-date payroll. These are computed by adding each day's transactions to the previous day's balance. Budget figures will be explained in the next chapter.

The month-to-date payroll percentage is computed by dividing month-to-date sales by the month-to-date actual payroll costs. The budget figures are the budgeted total labor costs divided by the number of days in the month. The month-to-date payroll column is the prorated budgeted amount.

ADDITIONAL PAYROLL AND TIP TAX INFORMATION: EXCERPT FROM IRS PUBLICATION #334

The following pages contain various excerpts pertaining to withholding procedures for restaurants, courtesy of the Internal Revenue Service and the U.S. Department of Labor:

TIPPED EMPLOYEES UNDER THE FAIR LABOR STANDARDS ACT (FLSA)

This fact sheet provides general information concerning the application of the FLSA to employees who receive tips. *Use caution: This document was last revised in November 2001; unless otherwise stated, the information reflects requirements that were in effect, or would take effect, as of January 1, 2002.*

CHARACTERISTICS

Tipped employees are those who customarily and regularly receive more than $30 a month in tips. Tips actually received by tipped employees may be counted as wages for purposes of the FLSA, but the employer must pay not less than $2.13 an hour in direct wages.

REQUIREMENTS

If an employer elects to use the tip credit provision the employer must:

1. Inform each tipped employee about the tip credit allowance (including amount to be credited) before the credit is utilized.

2. Be able to show that the employee receives at least the minimum wage when direct wages and the tip credit allowance are combined.

3. Allow the tipped employee to retain all tips, whether or not the employer elects to take a tip credit for tips received, except to the extent the employee participates in a valid tip pooling arrangement.

If an employee's tips combined with the employer's direct wages of at least $2.13 an hour do not equal the minimum hourly wage—$4.75 an hour effective 10/1/96; $5.15 an hour effective 9/1/97—the employer must make up the difference.

Youth Minimum Wage: The 1996 Amendments to the FLSA allow employers to pay a youth minimum wage of not less that $4.25 an hour to employees who are under 20 years of age during the first 90 consecutive calendar days after initial employment by their employer. The law contains certain protections for employees that prohibit employers from displacing any employee in order to hire someone at the youth minimum wage.

Dual Jobs: When an employee is employed concurrently in both a tipped and a non-tipped occupation, the tip credit is available only for the hours spent in the tipped occupation. The Act permits an employer to take the tip credit for time spent in duties related to the tipped occupation, even though such duties are not by themselves directed toward producing tips, provided such duties are incidental to the regular duties and are generally assigned to such occupations. Where tipped employees are routinely assigned to maintenance, or where tipped employees spend a substantial amount of time (in excess of 20 percent) performing general preparation work or maintenance, no tip credit may be taken for the time spent in such duties.

Retention of Tips: The law forbids any arrangement between the employer and the tipped employee whereby any part of the tip received becomes the property of the employer. A tip is the sole property of the tipped employee. Where an employer does not strictly observe the tip credit provisions of the Act, no tip credit may be claimed and the employees are entitled to receive the full cash minimum wage, in addition to retaining tips they may\should have received.

Service Charges: A compulsory charge for service, for example, 15 percent of the bill, is not a tip. Such charges are part of the employer's gross receipts. Where service charges are imposed and the employee receives no tips, the employer must pay the entire minimum wage and overtime required by the Act.

Tip Pooling: The requirement that an employee must retain all tips does not preclude tip splitting or pooling arrangements among employees who customarily and regularly receive tips, such as waiters, waitresses, bellhops, counter personnel (who serve customers), busboys/girls and service bartenders. Tipped employees may not be required to share their tips with employees who have not customarily and regularly participated in tip pooling arrangements, such as dishwashers, cooks, chefs, and janitors. Only those tips that are in excess of tips used for the tip credit may be taken for a pool. Tipped employees cannot be required to contribute a greater percentage of their tips than is customary and reasonable.

Credit Cards: Where tips are charged on a credit card and the employer must pay the credit card company a percentage on each sale, then the employer may pay the employee the tip, less that percentage. This charge on the tip may not reduce the employee's wage below the required minimum wage. The amount due the employee must be paid no later than the regular payday and may not be held while the employer is awaiting reimbursement from the credit card company.

TYPICAL PROBLEMS

Minimum Wage Problems: Employee does not qualify as a "tipped employee"; tips are not sufficient to make up difference between employer's direct wage obligation and the minimum wage; employee receives tips only—so the full minimum wage is owed; illegal deductions for walk-outs, breakages and cash register shortages; and invalid tip pools.

Overtime Problems: Failure to pay overtime on the full minimum wage; failure to pay overtime on the regular rate including all service charges, commissions, bonuses and other remuneration.

WHERE TO OBTAIN ADDITIONAL INFORMATION

This publication is for general information and is not to be considered in the same light as official statements of position contained in the regulations. Copies of Wage and Hour publications may be obtained by contacting the nearest office of the Wage and Hour Division listed in most telephone directories under U.S. Government, Department of Labor Employment Standards Administration/Wage and Hour Division.

MINIMUM HOURLY CASH WAGES FOR TIPPED EMPLOYEES UNDER MINIMUM WAGE LAWS

The Department of Labor is providing this information as a public service to enhance public access to information relating to state wage and hour laws that supplement the federal wage and hour laws administered by the Department of Labor. This is a service that is continually under development. The user should be aware that, while we try to keep the information timely and accurate, there might be a delay between the date when a change in state law takes place and the modification of these pages to reflect the change. Therefore, we make no express or implied guarantees. We will make every effort to correct errors brought to our attention.

The statutes, regulations, and court and administrative decisions of each of the states should be relied upon as the official statement of a state's law. In some instances, county or municipal law also may affect wage and hour standards applicable to employers, employees and other persons.

Some documents on the Department's website contain hypertext pointers to information created and maintained by other public and private organizations. Please be aware that we do not control or guarantee the accuracy, relevance, timeliness or completeness of this outside information. Further, the inclusion of pointers to particular items in hypertext is not intended to reflect their importance, nor is it intended to endorse any views expressed or products or services offered by the author of the reference to the organization operating the server on which the reference is maintained.

This document was last revised in November 2001; unless otherwise stated, the information reflects requirements that were in effect, or would take effect, as of January 1, 2002.

Use Caution: Regulations and Laws on Tips and Tip Reporting Are Constantly Changing.

DAILY PAYROLL FORM

DATE _____ MONTH _____ YEAR _____

H = HOURS   G = GROSS

EMPLOYEE	RATE	H	G	H	G	H	G	H	G	H	G	H	G	H	G	H	G	TOTAL

TOTAL [ ]

DAILY SALES REPORT FORM

	DAY	DATE	FOOD SALES		LIQUOR SALES		WINE SALES		TOTAL SALES	MONTH-TO-DATE	
			AMT $	INV #	AMT $	INV #	AMT $	INV #		ACTUAL	BUDGET
1											
2											
3											
4											
5											
6											
7											
7 DAY TOTAL											
8											
9											
10											
11											
12											
13											
14											
14 DAY TOTAL											
15											
16											
17											
18											
19											
20											
21											
21 DAY TOTAL											
22											
23											
24											
25											
26											
27											
28											
28 DAY TOTAL											
29											
30											
31											
TOTAL											

DAILY SALES REPORT FORM (CONTINUED)

OVER UNDER	# DINERS	PER HEAD	CASH OV/U	MANAGERIAL			HOUSED			COMPLIMENTARY		
				FOOD	LIQR	WINE	FOOD	LIQR	WINE	FOOD	LIQR	WINE

LABOR ANALYSIS FORM

	DAY	DATE	DAILY SALES	DAILY PAYROLL BUDGET	DAILY PAYROLL ACT	DAILY PAYROLL OV/UND	%	MONTH TO DATE	MONTH-TO-DATE PAYROLL BUDGET	MONTH-TO-DATE PAYROLL ACT	MONTH-TO-DATE PAYROLL OV/UND	%
1												
2												
3												
4												
5												
6												
7												
7 DAY TOTAL												
8												
9												
10												
11												
12												
13												
14												
14 DAY TOTAL												
15												
16												
17												
18												
19												
20												
21												
21 DAY TOTAL												
22												
23												
24												
25												
26												
27												
28												
28 DAY TOTAL												
29												
30												
31												
TOTAL												

WINE ITEMIZATION FORM

ITEM	USE A ✔ MARK TO DESIGNATE ONE SOLD	TOTALS
	TOTAL	

FOOD ITEMIZATION FORM

ITEM	USE A ✔ MARK TO DESIGNATE ONE SOLD	TOTALS
	TOTAL	

PURCHASE LEDGER

COMPANY _____ MONTH _____

DATE	INV #	AMT $	INV #	AMT $	INV #	AMT $	PAID OUTS
GRAND TOTAL							
						PAGE TOTAL	

**Department of the Treasury
Internal Revenue Service**

Publication 1244
(Rev. June 1999)

Employee's Daily
Record of Tips
and
Report to Employer

This publication contains:

Form 4070A, Employee's Daily Record of Tips

Form 4070, Employee's Report of Tips to Employer

For the period

beginning .... , ... and

ending .... , ...

Name and address of employee

Publication 1244 (Rev. 6-99)   Cat. No. 44472W

Instructions
You must keep sufficient proof to show the amount of your tip income for the year. A daily record of your tip income is considered sufficient proof. Keep a daily record for each workday showing the amount of cash and credit card tips received directly from customers or other employees. Also keep a record of the amount of tips, if any, you paid to other employees through tip sharing, tip pooling or other arrangements, and the names of employees to whom you paid tips. Show the date that each entry is made. This date should be on or near the date you received the tip income. You may use Form 4070A, Employee's Daily Record of Tips, or any other daily record to record your tips.

Reporting Tips to Your Employer. If you receive tips that total $20 or more for any month while working for one employer, you must report the tips to your employer. Tips include cash left by customers, tips customers add to credit card charges, and tips you receive from other employees. You must report your tips for any one month by the 10th of the month after the month you receive the tips. If the 10th day falls on a Saturday, Sunday, or legal holiday, you may give the report to your employer on the next business day that is not a Saturday, Sunday, or legal holiday.

You must report tips that total $20 or more every month regardless of your total wages and tips for the year. You may use Form 4070, Employee's Report of Tips to Employer, to report your tips to your employer. See the instructions on the back of Form 4070.

You must include all tips, including tips not reported to your employer, as wages on your income tax return. You may use the last page of this publication to total your tips for the year.

Your employer must withhold income, social security, and Medicare (or railroad retirement) taxes on tips you report. Your employer usually deducts the withholding due on tips from your regular wages.

(continued on inside of back cover)

Form **4070A** (Rev. June 1999) Department of the Treasury Internal Revenue Service	Employee's Daily Record of Tips This is a voluntary form provided for your convenience. See instructions for records you must keep.		OMB No. 1545-0065
Employee's name and address	Employer's name		Month and year
	Establishment name (if different)		

Date tips rec'd.	Date of entry	a. Tips received directly from customers and other employees	b. Credit card tips received	c. Tips paid out to other employees	d. Names of employees to whom you paid tips
1					
2					
3					
4					
5					
Subtotals					

For Paperwork Reduction Act Notice, see Instructions on the back of Form 4070.   Page 1

Date tips rec'd.	Date of entry	a. Tips received directly from customers and other employees	b. Credit card tips received	c. Tips paid out to other employees	d. Names of employees to whom you paid tips
6					
7					
8					
9					
10					
11					
12					
13					
14					
15					
Subtotals					

Page 2

Date tips rec'd.	Date of entry	a. Tips received directly from customers and other employees	b. Credit card tips received	c. Tips paid out to other employees	d. Names of employees to whom you paid tips
16					
17					
18					
19					
20					
21					
22					
23					
24					
25					
Subtotals					

Date tips rec'd.	Date of entry	a. Tips received directly from customers and other employees	b. Credit card tips received	c. Tips paid out to other employees	d. Names of employees to whom you paid tips
26					
27					
28					
29					
30					
31					
Subtotals from pages 1, 2, and 3					
Totals					

1. Report total cash tips (col. a) on Form 4070, line 1.
2. Report total credit card tips (col. b) on Form 4070, line 2.
3. Report total tips paid out (col. c) on Form 4070, line 3.

Page 4

Form 4070
(Rev. June 1999)
Department of the Treasury
Internal Revenue Service

Employee's Report
of Tips to Employer

▶ For Paperwork Reduction Act Notice, see back of form.

OMB No. 1545-0065

Employee's name and address	Social security number
Employer's name and address (include establishment name, if different)	1 Cash tips received
	2 Credit card tips received
	3 Tips paid out
Month or shorter period in which tips were received from _____ , _____ , to _____ , _____	4 Net tips (lines 1 + 2 - 3)
Signature	Date

Purpose. Use this form to report tips you receive to your employer. This includes cash tips, tips you receive from other employees, and credit card tips. You must report tips every month regardless of your total wages and tips for the year. However, you do not have to report tips to your employer for any month you received less than $20 in tips while working for that employer.

Report tips by the 10th day of the month following the month that you receive them. If the 10th day is a Saturday, Sunday, or legal holiday, report tips by the next day that is not a Saturday, Sunday, or legal holiday.

See Pub. 531, Reporting Tip Income, for more details.

You can get additional copies of Pub. 1244, Employee's Daily Record of Tips and Report to Employer, which contains both Forms 4070A and 4070, by calling 1-800-TAX-FORM (1-800-829-3676).

Paperwork Reduction Act Notice. We ask for the information on these forms to carry out the Internal Revenue laws of the United States. You are required to give us the information. We need it to ensure that you are complying with these laws and to allow us to figure and collect the right amount of tax.

You are not required to provide the information requested on a form that is subject to the Paperwork Reduction Act unless the form displays a valid OMB control number. Books or records relating to a form or its instructions must be retained as long as their contents may become material in the administration of any Internal Revenue law. Generally, tax returns and return information are confidential, as required by Code section 6103.

The time needed to complete Forms 4070 and 4070A will vary depending on individual circumstances. The estimated average times are: Recordkeeping—Form 4070, 7 min.; Form 4070A, 3 hr. and 23 min.; Learning about the law—each form, 2 min.; Preparing Form 4070, 13 min.; Form 4070A, 55 min.; and Copying and providing Form 4070, 10 min.; Form 4070A, 28 min.

If you have comments concerning the accuracy of these time estimates or suggestions for making these forms simpler, we would be happy to hear from you. You can write to the Tax Forms Committee, Western Area Distribution Center, Rancho Cordova, CA 95743-0001.

Instructions (continued)

Unreported Tips. If you received tips of $20 or more for any month while working for one employer but did not report them to your employer, you must figure and pay social security and Medicare taxes on the unreported tips when you file your tax return. If you have unreported tips, you must use Form 1040 and Form 4137, Social Security and Medicare Tax on Unreported Tip Income, to report them. You may not use Form 1040A or 1040EZ. Employees subject to the Railroad Retirement Tax Act cannot use Form 4137 to pay railroad retirement tax on unreported tips. To get railroad retirement credit, you must report tips to your employer.

If you do not report tips to your employer as required, you may be charged a penalty of 50% of the social security and Medicare taxes (or railroad retirement tax) due on the unreported tips unless there was reasonable cause for not reporting them.

Additional Information. Get Pub. 531, Reporting Tip Income, and Form 4137 for more information on tips. If you are an employee of certain large food or beverage establishments, see Pub. 531 for tip allocation rules.

Recordkeeping. If you do not keep a daily record of tips, you must keep other reliable proof of the tip income you received. This proof includes copies of restaurant bills and credit card charges that show amounts customers added as tips.

Keep your tip income records for as long as the information on them may be needed in the administration of any Internal Revenue law.

Instructions (continued)

Use this space to total your tips for the year

Form **8027**

Department of the Treasury
Internal Revenue Service

Employer's Annual Information Return of Tip Income and Allocated Tips

▶ See separate instructions.

OMB No. 1545-0714

2001

Use IRS label. Make any necessary changes. Otherwise, please type or print.

Name of establishment

Number and street (see instructions)

City or town, state, and ZIP code

Employer identification number

Type of establishment (mark only one checkbox)

☐ 1 Evening meals only

☐ 2 Evening and other meals

☐ 3 Meals other than evening meals

☐ 4 Alcoholic beverages

Employer's name (same name as on Form 941)

Establishment number (see instructions)

Number and street (P.O. box, if applicable)

Apt. or suite no.

City, state, and ZIP code (if a foreign address, see instructions)

Does this establishment accept credit cards or other charges? Yes ☐ No ☐ (lines 1 and 2 must be completed)

Mark if: Amended Return ☐
Final Return ☐

1	Total charged tips for calendar year 2001	1
2	Total charge receipts showing charged tips (see instructions)	2
3	Total amount of service charges of less than 10% paid as wages to employees	3
4a	Total tips reported by indirectly tipped employees	4a
b	Total tips reported by directly tipped employees	4b

Note: Complete the Employer's Optional Worksheet for Tipped Employees on page 4 of the instructions to determine potential unreported tips of your employees.

c	Total tips reported (add lines 4a and 4b)	4c
5	Gross receipts from food or beverage operations (see instructions)	5

6 Multiply line 5 by 8% (.08) or the lower rate shown here ▶ _____ granted by the IRS. (Attach a copy of the IRS determination letter to this return.) **6**

Note: If you have allocated tips using other than the calendar year (semimonthly, biweekly, quarterly, etc.), mark an "X" on line 6 and enter the amount of allocated tips from your records on line 7.

7 Allocation of tips. If line 6 is more than line 4c, enter the excess here **7**

▶ This amount must be allocated as tips to tipped employees working in this establishment. Mark the checkbox below that shows the method used for the allocation. (Show the portion, if any, attributable to each employee in box 8 of the employee's Form W-2.)

a Allocation based on hours-worked method (see instructions for restriction). . . . ☐

Note: If you marked the checkbox in line 7a, enter the average number of employee hours worked per business day during the payroll period. (see instructions) _____

b Allocation based on gross receipts method . . . . ☐

c Allocation based on good-faith agreement (Attach a copy of the agreement.) . . . ☐

8 Enter the total number of directly tipped employees at this establishment during 2001 ▶

Under penalties of perjury, I declare that I have examined this return, including accompanying schedules and statements, and to the best of my knowledge and belief, it is true, correct, and complete.

Signature ▶ _____ Title ▶ _____ Date ▶ _____

For Privacy Act and Paperwork Reduction Act Notice, see page 4 of the separate instructions.   Cat. No. 49989U   Form **8027** (2001)

SUCCESSFUL BUDGETING & PROFIT PLANNING—FOR MAXIMUM RESULTS

INTRODUCTION

All restaurants are in business to make a profit. In order to plan financially you must first set up a long-range plan detailing how much money you want the restaurant to return and when. This financial plan is the restaurant's budget. This chapter will detail the steps for setting up a budget. The following chapter will describe the procedures for projecting actual operating costs, as well as how to recognize, analyze and resolve cost problems.

Aside from being the restaurant's financial plan, the budget is also used to control costs and account for sales and products. Budgeting is an accounting record and a tool used to evaluate how effectively the restaurant, management and employees operated during the month. Based on this information, management can then recognize cost problem areas and act accordingly to correct them. Although many businesses maintain a yearly or quarterly budget, restaurants, because of their fluctuating operating performances, should use a monthly budget. The annual budget and profit and loss statement can then be easily computed by totaling all 12 monthly budgets. Monthly budgeting is the system described in this book. Once set up and operating, about four hours each month is all that will be required to compute the old budget and project a new one. Although the restaurant may be only in the pre-opening stage, it is imperative that you start to develop an operating budget now. As soon as the budget is prepared, you will possess the control for guiding the business towards your financial goal.

Initially the proposed budget may be under- or overinflated. You may have overruns, but at least you will be starting to gain control over the organization, rather than the organization controlling you. After a few months you will have past operating budgets to guide you in projecting new ones. The budgeting process will become easier and more accurate as time goes by.

There are many other benefits to preparing and adhering to a monthly operational budget. Supervisors and key employees will develop increased awareness and concern about the restaurant and controlling its costs. This involvement will invariably rub off on the other employees. A well-structured, defined budget and orderly financial records will aid you greatly in obtaining loans and will develop an important store of information should you decide to expand or sell in the future. Cost problems can be easily pinpointed once the expense categories are broken down. Last—but not least—you will become a better manager. Your financial decisions and forecasts will become increasingly consistent and accurate, as more information will be available to you. Financial problems may be seen approaching down the road rather than suddenly cropping up and forcing you to act quickly and when you are uninformed. Management all too often reacts to a problem's symptoms, instead of curing the disease. Budgeting will give you the tool for an accurate diagnosis

PROJECTING THE OPERATIONAL BUDGET

This section describes in detail all of the operational costs listed on the **Operational Budget** (which can be found at the end of this chapter) as well as how to accurately project each expenditure and revenue for the following month.

TOTAL SALES

Projecting total sales is the most crucial and difficult aspect of budgeting. The fact that it is impossible to know how business will be from day to day makes budgeting total sales a perplexing task. Most costs are either variable or semi variable, which means they will fluctuate directly in relation to the total monthly sales. Thus accurately projecting these costs depends largely upon using an accurate total sales figure. Projecting total sales, at first, will be difficult—and most likely inaccurate—but after several months of operation, your projections will be right on target. You will be surprised at how consistent sales and customer counts are and how easy it will be to consistently budget accurately.

The initial budgets may be unrealistic expectations. Sales will probably be low, as you will not have been able to build a substantial clientele or reputation. Operating costs will be higher than normal. It will take a couple of months to streamline and build an efficient restaurant even with the best-laid plans. Labor and material costs will be extremely high, as there will be a lot of training, low productivity and housed food, liquor and wine. All of these costs are normal and should be anticipated. Profit margins will be small and possibly even nonexistent.

This period of time (4–12 weeks) should be used to ensure that your product is perfected and all the bugs are worked out of the systems. This is no time to cut back on costs. Your intention is to be in business for a long time. Allocate sufficient funds now to make sure the business gets off on the right foot and profits will be guaranteed for many years. Schedule a full staff every night to make certain all details will be covered. Discontinue those items that are passable but not of the quality level desired. Slow, clumsy service and only average food will never build sales. Strive for A-1 quality products and service. Constantly reiterate to employees this primary concern, and before long they will self-monitor the quality. Once you develop a clientele and a solid reputation for serving consistent, quality products, the budget and profits will fall into place.

There are eight basic steps for projecting total sales:

1. If possible, use last year's customer count. This information can be found in last year's Daily Sales Report Form. Projections for the first year can be based upon prior months' reports and educated estimates.

2. Using the **Sales Projection Form** (which can be found at the end of this chapter) and a calendar, calculate the number of days in the month. Enter this figure in the first column. From the information in #1, calculate the average number of covers served each day. Enter this figure in the second column. Compute the average number of covers served on any holidays that may be in the month; include scheduled functions, banquets and large parties in this total.

3. Multiply the number of days in the month by the average number of covers served for that day; enter the result in the "Subtotal" column. Add the eight "Subtotal" columns to arrive at the grand total.

4. Review and analyze the growth in customer counts during the past year, current year and current month. Based upon past customer counts determine the percentage of growth or decline in growth anticipated in the coming month. Percentage of growth or decline can be computed by subtracting the most recent period of customer counts by the past period of customer counts. The difference is then divided by the actual number of dinners served during the past period of time. A negative percentage figure shows a drop in customer counts. A positive figure indicates the percentage of increase.

When computing and analyzing these computations, keep in mind that each period of time must have the same number and type of days. In other words, you can only accurately compare months that have the same number of Mondays, Tuesdays and so forth, since sales are different for each day; otherwise the results and analysis would be inaccurate. The most accurate way to analyze the percentage of growth or loss is to compare the previous month to the same month last year and then compare the percentage to the current month. Remember to only examine actual cover counts as indicators of growth; changes in sales may be the result of a price change.

5. Multiply the percentage of gross or loss by the grand total. Add the result to the grand total to compute the projected volume, or number of dinners. Subtract this figure instead if you are multiplying by a negative percentage figure that indicates a loss in customer counts.

6. Multiply the projected volume by the average check of the past month. The average check amount may be located on the Daily Sales Report Form. Adjust this figure if a price increase will be occurring during the month. Breakfast,

lunch and dinner sales may all be projected together unless the percentage of growth or loss is suspected in one area and not in the other two. A separate chart for each category should then be used to project each sales amount; simply add all three figures together to compute grand total of sales.

7. Compute individual food, liquor and wine sales by simply dividing total sales by the average percentage of sales on last month's Daily Sales Report Form. For example, a restaurant budgeted at $25,000 in sales that has a division of sales at 70 percent food, 20 percent liquor and 10 percent wine would have a breakdown of $17,500 food, $5,000 liquor and $2,500 wine sales.

8. The final step in budgeting sales is to enter the budgeted amount for each day on the Daily Sales Report Form. To compute the budgeted amount for each day, divide the total projected sales by the number of days in the month. This amount is the budgeted sales for one day. Enter this figure on line 1 of the first day of the month. Add this same amount to itself to compute the budgeted sales for day two, and continue adding this same amount to itself until you have computed the sales for each day. Double-check your calculations by running a tape on the sales. The total must equal the total budgeted sales projections. Breaking down sales this way will enable the manager to see exactly where actual sales are in relation to budgeted sales. On a daily basis, enter the amount over or under budget in sales in the appropriate column (Use parentheses and/or a red pencil to enter sales that are under budget).

MATERIAL COSTS

Material costs will fluctuate directly with the sales variance. More food, liquor or wine sales will result in higher material costs. In budgeting material costs, the important figure to analyze is not the actual cost but the percentage of cost, or the cost-of-sales percentage, as it is more commonly known. Compute the cost-of-sales percentage by dividing the actual cost of the category by the category's total sales. The result will be a percentage figure. This formula will present an accurate indication of the category's costs, as the cost of sales are proportionate to each other.

The cost-of-sales percentages for each category—food, liquor and wine—were projected in the previous chapters when determining the selling price of each item. Food cost was projected at between 35 and 40 percent, liquor, 18 to 25 percent, and wine, approximately 40 percent, cost of sales. Enter the percentage figure used in the previous sections in the "Budgeting Percentage" column. This percentage figure can be used initially in order to project the first month's budget. After several months of operation, the actual figure can be substituted.

Multiply the individual material costs by each respective budgeted percentage; the results are the budgeted cost amounts. For example: if food sales were budgeted at $100,000, and the food cost percentage was estimated at 40 percent, the budgeted food cost would be $40,000. Increases in product costs will raise the actual cost-of-sales amount; adjust the budgeted amount accordingly. However, be certain that if an increase is anticipated, the increase will affect the following month, which is what is being budgeted. Items purchased at a higher price and then stored in inventory will have no effect upon the following month's actual cost of sales, as the product will not have been used. Add all three budgeted costs to compute the total budgeted material costs. Subtract the total gross costs from the total sales to compute the gross profit dollar amount. Divide gross profit by total sales to calculate the gross profit percentage.

LABOR

MANAGER SALARY

Manager salaries should be a fixed monthly cost. Total all the manager salaries for one year; divide this figure by the number of days in the year (usually 365), and multiply this cost by the number of days in one month. Salary changes during the year will require adjustments. When owners take an active part in the management of the restaurant, or when the company is incorporated, the owners should have their salary amount included in this category.

EMPLOYEE SALARY

The employee salary expense is a semi variable cost that will fluctuate directly with total sales. Employee labor costs have a breakeven point, the point where the labor cost is covered by the profit from sales. As this point is reached and total sales increase, the labor cost percentage will decrease, increasing net profit. Thus, the cost of labor is determined by its efficiency and by the volume of sales it produces. Multiply the projected total sales by the average labor cost percentage to arrive at the anticipated labor cost dollar amount. Adjust this figure in relation to the amount of employee training anticipated for the month.

OVERTIME

Overtime should be nonexistent—or at least kept to an absolute minimum. No amount should be budgeted for overtime. Money spent on overtime usually indicates poor management and inefficiency. Bookkeepers should be on the lookout for employees approaching 40 hours of work near the end of the week. Carefully prepared schedules will eliminate 98 percent of all overtime work and pay. Employees who wish to switch their schedules around should only be allowed to do so after approval from the manager.

CONTROLLABLE OPERATIONAL COSTS

SUPPLIES

China and Utensils

Cost of china and utensils bought should be a consistent amount and percentage of sales for each month. Review Chapter 10, "Successful Management of Operational Costs and Supplies."

Glassware
Same as china and utensils.

Kitchen Supplies
Same as china and utensils. Capital expenditures for equipment with utility for more than one year generally must be depreciated over the item's anticipated life span.

Bar Supplies
Same as china and utensils.

Dining Room Supplies
Same as china and utensils.

Office Supplies
Cost of office supplies should be a fixed dollar amount each month. Capital expenditures must be depreciated.

Uniforms
The uniform expense will depend upon the state in which the restaurant is located and individual management policies. Some states allow the company to charge the employees for uniforms; others do not. Many restaurants that do charge employees for uniforms do so at cost, which, if done correctly, should cost the restaurant nothing but administrative time.

Laundry and Linen
Laundry and linen buying should be a consistent monthly expenditure, as laundry and linen is usually purchased once or twice a year, in bulk. This expenditure column is for the purchase price only; cleaning is computed in a separate column, under "Services".

SERVICES

Laundry cleaning
Cleaning of laundry is variable expense directly related to total sales. Multiply last month's percentage of cost by budgeted sales. Adjust the figure for price increases.

Protection
Protection should be a consistent, fixed monthly expenditure. Service-call charges should be coded to "Equipment Repairs" under "General Operating Costs".

Freight
This expense may not be applicable to all restaurants. Freight is the expense incurred shipping material via rail, truck or other method to the restaurant for exclusive use in the restaurant. Freight charges are usually incurred only by businesses in remote areas, or when the restaurant purchases a product and then has an independent company deliver it.

Legal

Legal services are a variable expense that can fluctuate greatly. Estimates for most legal work can be obtained, but it's best to budget a little each month to cover periodically large legal fees.

Accounting

A semi fixed expense depending upon the amount and the type of accounting services used. Once set up and operating, the accounting expense should be a consistent monthly charge except for an annual tax-preparation and year-end audit fee.

Maintenance

Maintenance should be a fixed monthly expenditure if you're using a maintenance service company with contract service.

Payroll

A semi fixed expense fluctuating directly with the number of employees on the payroll. Restaurants not utilizing a computerized payroll service will not have a payroll preparation expense. The wages paid to the bookkeeper are included in the employee labor expenditure.

UTILITIES

Telephone

Telephone service should be a relatively consistent monthly expense. All long-distance phone calls should be recorded in a notebook (Your local office-supply store has a specially designed book for this purpose). The itemized phone bill should be compared against the recorded phone calls to justify each one.

Water

Water should be a semi variable expense.

Gas

Gas may be a variable or semi variable expense depending upon the type of equipment it operates. Gas used in heating will be a variable expense, because more will be used during the winter months than in the summer.

Electricity

Electricity may be a variable or semi variable expense depending upon the type of equipment it operates. Electricity bills are normally higher during the summer months, as this is when the air-conditioning units are used.

Heat

Heat includes the cost of any heating material used but not listed above, such as coal, wood, oil, etc.

FIXED OPERATING COSTS

RENT

This should be the monthly amount of rent or, if the building is leased, the monthly lease. Certain business-rental and lease agreements also include payment of a percentage of the total sales or per-tax profit amount. Should this be the situation, use the budgeted total sales figure and project the anticipated amount due. Enter this amount and the total rent amount in the "Budgeted" column.

INSURANCE

Total all insurance premium amounts (fire, theft, liability, workers' compensation, etc.) and divide by 12. This figure will equal the average monthly insurance expense.

PROPERTY TAXES

If applicable, divide the annual property tax amount by 12. This figure will equal the average monthly property tax amount.

DEPRECIATION

Depreciation will be discussed in detail in the following section.

GENERAL OPERATING COSTS

TAXES

Payroll and Labor Taxes

This is the tax amount the employer is required to contribute to the state and federal government. A separate tax account should be set up with your bank to keep all the tax money separate. Labor taxes include: Social Security, Medicare tax, federal unemployment tax and state unemployment tax.

Other Taxes

This includes all miscellaneous taxes, such as local taxes, sales tax paid on purchases, etc. This column is for any tax the restaurant pays for goods and services. It is not for sales tax or other taxes the restaurant collects, as they are not expenditures. Federal income tax is not a deductible expenditure and should not be listed here, either.

REPAIRS AND MAINTENANCE: EQUIPMENT

This includes the cost of scheduled and emergency repairs and maintenance to all equipment. Always budget a base amount for normal service. Adjust this figure if major repairs or overhauls are anticipated.

BUILDING

This includes the cost of minor scheduled and emergency repairs and maintenance to the building. Always budget a base amount for normal repairs and maintenance. Large remodeling or rebuilding projects should be budgeted as a separate expenditure and depreciated.

ENTERTAINMENT

Entertainment includes bands, music, entertainers and so forth.

ADVERTISING

Advertising includes all the costs of advertising the restaurant, including television, radio, mailing circulars, newspapers, etc.

PROMOTIONAL EXPENSE

This is the expense of promotional items: key chains, calendars, pens, free dinners, T-shirts, sponsorship of sporting events, etc.

EQUIPMENT RENTAL

This cost is the expense of either short- or long-term renting of pieces of equipment or machinery.

MISCELLANEOUS

Postage
This is postage paid for business purposes.

Contributions
These are all contributions paid to recognized charitable organizations.

Trade Dues, Etc.
This includes dues paid to professional organizations such as the National Restaurant Association. Trade magazine subscriptions should also be entered in this category. This expense should be divided by 12 to apportion the cost from the month in which it occurs.

Licenses
This is the expense of all business and government licenses: operating licenses, a health permit, liquor licenses, etc. This expense should also be divided by 12 to apportion the cost from the month in which it occurs.

Credit Card Expense
Credit card expense can be computed by multiplying the service-charge cost-of-sales percentage by the total projected credit-card sales volume.

Travel

Travel includes the expense of ordinary and necessary travel for business purposes for yourself and your employees.

Bad Debt

This expense should be nonexistent if the proper procedures for handling credit cards and checks are enforced. Normally, the full amount of a bad debt is a tax-deductible expense. However, you must prove the debt is worthless and uncollectable. In some states, the employee who handled the transaction may be legally held liable for the unpaid amount.

TOTAL EXPENDITURES

Add the total budgeted expenditures from both pages and enter the figure in this column.

TOTAL NET PROFIT

Subtract Total Budgeted Expenditures from Total Sales. The result is the total net profit (or loss). Divide the Total Net Projected Profit by projected Total Sales to compute the projected Pre-Tax Net Profit Percentage. Total projected sales minus total material costs will equal the gross profit amount.

DEPRECIATION

Depreciation may be defined as the expense derived from the expiration of a capital asset's quantity of usefulness over the life of the property. Capital assets are those assets that have utility or usefulness of more than one year. Since a capital asset will provide utility over several years, the deductible cost of the asset must be spread out over its useful life—over a specified recovery period. Each year a portion of the asset's cost may be deducted as an expense.

Some examples of depreciable items commonly found in a restaurant include: office equipment, kitchen and dining room equipment, the building (if owned), machinery, display cases and any intangible property which has a useful life of more than one year. Thus, items such as light bulbs, china, stationery and merchandise inventories may not be depreciated. The cost of franchise rights is usually a depreciable expense.

The **Depreciation Worksheet and Record** on the following page will be a great aid in computing depreciation amounts, regardless of the methods used. Record the purchase of all depreciable items right away and you'll keep on top of this complex and time-consuming area.

The IRS publishes guidelines for the number of years to be used for computing an asset's useful life.

DEPRECIATION WORKSHEET AND RECORD

DATE	DESCRIPTION	METH	LIFE	NEW/ USED	AC RS%	COST		SALVAGE	ADDIT. 1st YEAR

DEPRECIATION WORKSHEET AND RECORD (CONTINUED)

BALANCE	DEPREC 20	BALANCE	DEPREC 20	BALANCE

OPERATIONAL BUDGET

ITEM	BUDGETED	%	ACTUAL	%
SALES				
Food				
Liquor				
Wine				
TOTAL SALES				
MATERIALS				
Food Costs				
Liquor Costs				
Wine Costs				
TOTAL COSTS				
GROSS PROFIT				
LABOR				
Manager Salary				
Employee				
Overtime				
TOTAL LABOR COSTS				
Controller Oper. Costs				
China & Utensils				
Glassware				
Kitchen Supplies				
Bar Supplies				
Dining Room Supplies				
Uniforms				
Laundry/Linen				
Services				
Trash Pick-Up				
Laundry Cleaning				
Protection				
Freight				
Accounting				
Maintenance				
Payroll				
TOTAL THIS PAGE				

OPERATIONAL BUDGET (CONTINUED)

ITEM	BUDGETED	%	ACTUAL	%
Utilities				
Phone				
Water				
Gas				
Electricity				
Heat				
Fixed Operating Costs				
Rent				
Insurance				
Property Taxes				
Depreciation				
General Operating Costs				
Labor Taxes				
Other Taxes				
Repairs—Equipment				
Repairs—Building				
Entertainment				
Advertising				
Promotion				
Equipment Rental				
Postage				
Contributions				
Trade Dues, ect.				
Licenses				
Credit Card Expense				
Travel				
Bad Debt				
TOTAL THIS PAGE				
TOTAL EXPENDITURES				
TOTAL NET PROFIT				

SALES PROJECTION FORM

DATE	# OF EACH	AVG # DINNERS	SUB-TOTAL
MONDAY			
TUESDAY			
WEDNESDAY			
THURSDAY			
FRIDAY			
SATURDAY			
SUNDAY			
HOLIDAYS			

BREAKFAST TOTAL _____

LUNCH TOTAL _____

DINNER TOTAL _____

GRAND TOTAL _____

Grand Total x % Growth/Loss = Projected Volume x Check Avg. = Projected Sales

DIVISION OF SALES

	TOTAL PROJECTED SALES x	% SALES DIVISION	= SALES DIVISION
FOOD			
LIQUOR			
WINE			

HOLIDAYS THAT MUST BE CONSIDERED:

- Washington's Birthday
- Easter
- Mother's Day
- Memorial Day
- Fourth of July

- Labor Day
- Thanksgiving
- Christmas Eve
- Christmas
- New's Year's Eve

- New Year's
- Halloween
- Valentine's Day
- Graduation Day

Depreciation Worksheet (keep for your records.)

Description of Property	Date Placed in Service	Cost or Other Basis	Business/ Investment Use %	Section 179 Deduction and Special Allowance	Depreciation Prior Years	Basis for Depreciation	Method/ Convention	Recovery Period	Rate or Table %	Depreciation Deduction

Depreciation and Amortization
(Including Information on Listed Property)

▶ See separate instructions.   ▶ Attach to your tax return.

OMB No. 1545-0172

2001

Attachment
Sequence No. 67

Name(s) shown on return	Business or activity to which this form relates	Identifying number

Part I   Election To Expense Certain Tangible Property Under Section 179
Note: If you have any listed property, complete Part V before you complete Part I.

1	Maximum amount. See page 2 of the instructions for a higher limit for certain businesses	1	$24,000
2	Total cost of section 179 property placed in service (see page 3 of the instructions)	2	
3	Threshold cost of section 179 property before reduction in limitation	3	$200,000
4	Reduction in limitation. Subtract line 3 from line 2. If zero or less, enter -0-	4	
5	Dollar limitation for tax year. Subtract line 4 from line 1. If zero or less, enter -0-. If married filing separately, see page 3 of the instructions	5	

(a) Description of property	(b) Cost (business use only)	(c) Elected cost	
6			

7	Listed property. Enter the amount from line 29 7		
8	Total elected cost of section 179 property. Add amounts in column (c), lines 6 and 7	8	
9	Tentative deduction. Enter the smaller of line 5 or line 8	9	
10	Carryover of disallowed deduction from line 13 of your 2000 Form 4562	10	
11	Business income limitation. Enter the smaller of business income (not less than zero) or line 5 (see instructions)	11	
12	Section 179 expense deduction. Add lines 9 and 10, but do not enter more than line 11	12	
13	Carryover of disallowed deduction to 2002. Add lines 9 and 10, less line 12 ▶ 13		

Note: Do not use Part II or Part III below for listed property. Instead, use Part V.

Part II   Special Depreciation Allowance and Other Depreciation (Do not include listed property.)

14	Special depreciation allowance for certain property (other than listed property) acquired after September 10, 2001 (see page 3 of the instructions)	14	
15	Property subject to section 168(f)(1) election (see page 4 of the instructions)	15	
16	Other depreciation (including ACRS) (see page 4 of the instructions)	16	

Part III   MACRS Depreciation (Do not include listed property.) (See page 4 of the instructions.)

Section A

17	MACRS deductions for assets placed in service in tax years beginning before 2001	17	
18	If you are electing under section 168(i)(4) to group any assets placed in service during the tax year into one or more general asset accounts, check here . . . . ▶ ☐		

Section B—Assets Placed in Service During 2001 Tax Year Using the General Depreciation System

(a) Classification of property	(b) Month and year placed in service	(c) Basis for depreciation (business/investment use only—see instructions)	(d) Recovery period	(e) Convention	(f) Method	(g) Depreciation deduction
19a 3-year property						
b 5-year property						
c 7-year property						
d 10-year property						
e 15-year property						
f 20-year property						
g 25-year property			25 yrs.		S/L	
h Residential rental property			27.5 yrs.	MM	S/L	
			27.5 yrs.	MM	S/L	
i Nonresidential real property			39 yrs.	MM	S/L	
				MM	S/L	

Section C—Assets Placed in Service During 2001 Tax Year Using the Alternative Depreciation System

20a Class life					S/L	
b 12-year			12 yrs.		S/L	
c 40-year			40 yrs.	MM	S/L	

Part IV   Summary (See page 6 of the instructions.)

21	Listed property. Enter amount from line 28.	21	
22	Total. Add amounts from line 12, lines 14 through 17, lines 19 and 20 in column (g), and line 21. Enter here and on the appropriate lines of your return. Partnerships and S corporations—see instr.	22	
23	For assets shown above and placed in service during the current year, enter the portion of the basis attributable to section 263A costs . . . 23		

For Paperwork Reduction Act Notice, see separate instructions.   Cat. No. 12906N   Form **4562** (2001) (Rev. 3-2002)

Part V Listed Property (Include automobiles, certain other vehicles, cellular telephones, certain computers, and property used for entertainment, recreation, or amusement.)

Note: For any vehicle for which you are using the standard mileage rate or deducting lease expense, complete only 24a, 24b, columns (a) through (c) of Section A, all of Section B, and Section C if applicable.

Section A—Depreciation and Other Information (Caution: See page 8 of the instructions for limits for passenger automobiles.)

24a Do you have evidence to support the business/investment use claimed? ☐ Yes ☐ No   24b If "Yes," is the evidence written? ☐ Yes ☐ No

(a) Type of property (list vehicles first)	(b) Date placed in service	(c) Business/ investment use percentage	(d) Cost or other basis	(e) Basis for depreciation (business/investment use only)	(f) Recovery period	(g) Method/ Convention	(h) Depreciation deduction	(i) Elected section 179 cost
25 Special depreciation allowance for listed property acquired after September 10, 2001, and used more than 50% in a qualified business use (see page 7 of the instructions)				25				
26 Property used more than 50% in a qualified business use (see page 7 of the instructions):								
		%						
		%						
		%						
27 Property used 50% or less in a qualified business use (see page 7 of the instructions):								
		%				S/L –		
		%				S/L –		
		%				S/L –		

28 Add amounts in column (h), lines 25 through 27. Enter here and on line 21, page 1. | 28 |

29 Add amounts in column (i), line 26. Enter here and on line 7, page 1. | 29 |

Section B—Information on Use of Vehicles

Complete this section for vehicles used by a sole proprietor, partner, or other "more than 5% owner," or related person.

If you provided vehicles to your employees, first answer the questions in Section C to see if you meet an exception to completing this section for those vehicles.

		(a) Vehicle 1		(b) Vehicle 2		(c) Vehicle 3		(d) Vehicle 4		(e) Vehicle 5		(f) Vehicle 6	
30	Total business/investment miles driven during the year (do not include commuting miles— see page 2 of the instructions)												
31	Total commuting miles driven during the year												
32	Total other personal (noncommuting) miles driven												
33	Total miles driven during the year. Add lines 30 through 32.												
		Yes	No	Yes	No	Yes	No	Yes	No	Yes	No	Yes	No
34	Was the vehicle available for personal use during off-duty hours?												
35	Was the vehicle used primarily by a more than 5% owner or related person?												
36	Is another vehicle available for personal use?												

Section C—Questions for Employers Who Provide Vehicles for Use by Their Employees

Answer these questions to determine if you meet an exception to completing Section B for vehicles used by employees who are not more than 5% owners or related persons (see page 8 of the instructions).

		Yes	No
37	Do you maintain a written policy statement that prohibits all personal use of vehicles, including commuting, by your employees?		
38	Do you maintain a written policy statement that prohibits personal use of vehicles, except commuting, by your employees? See page 8 of the instructions for vehicles used by corporate officers, directors, or 1% or more owners		
39	Do you treat all use of vehicles by employees as personal use?		
40	Do you provide more than five vehicles to your employees, obtain information from your employees about the use of the vehicles, and retain the information received?		
41	Do you meet the requirements concerning qualified automobile demonstration use? (See page 9 of the instructions).		

Note: If your answer to 37, 38, 39, 40, or 41 is "Yes," do not complete Section B for the covered vehicles.

Part VI Amortization

(a) Description of costs	(b) Date amortization begins	(c) Amortizable amount	(d) Code section	(e) Amortization period or percentage	(f) Amortization for this year
42 Amortization of costs that begins during your 2001 tax year (see page 9 of the instructions):					

43 Amortization of costs that began before your 2001 tax year. | 43 |

44 Total. Add amounts in column (f). See page 9 of the instructions for where to report | 44 |

Form **4562** (2001) (Rev. 3-2002)

HOW TO PREPARE THE MONTHLY AUDIT & COST PROJECTIONS— PUTTING IT ALL TOGETHER

INTRODUCTION

The following sections will prepare the restaurant manager for closing, projecting and analyzing the expenditure and sales records established during the month. The preceding chapters have described in detail how to set up, operate and manage a profitable restaurant. This chapter will go through the procedures for projecting the actual costs for each category so that the budget may be completed and analyzed for possible cost problem areas. The completed budget and abbreviated profit and loss statement will be a measure of how effectively management operated the restaurant during the month.

The procedures described in the following sections are fundamental accounting procedures. However, it must be noted that although the procedures are fundamental in nature, great care must be taken when compiling and processing the information to ensure complete accuracy. Management will be basing its decisions upon the statistics provided in these reports. Inaccurate information will ultimately result in faulty decisions.

The individuals collecting and utilizing the various data should be familiar with the restaurant's operations and the various internal control systems. All calculations should be double-checked by another employee prior to being used in the cost projections. Calculators with printed tapes should always be used so that column totals may be verified.

The general manager must take an active part in the end-of-the-month closeout. This will serve two purposes:

1.   It will ensure that the closeout procedures are correctly carried out; and

2.   The computations will be much easier for the manager to recall and hold more meaning in the day-to-day operations.

The most common error made in the end-of-month closeout is carelessness. Attention to detail and proper management involvement will eliminate most errors. Countless hours of extra work for the internal bookkeeper, manager and public accountant could easily be avoided simply by taking a little more time to ensure all business and accounting papers are handled correctly.

For the purposes described in this book, the accounting period, or cycle, begins on the first day of each month and ends on the last day, regardless of the actual number of days in the month. At the end of the month all the sales and expense accounts will be closed out and balanced. The ending inventory, the computation of which will be described in an upcoming section, will be taken on the last day of the month after the close of business. This month's ending inventory will be the new beginning inventory for next month.

DEFINING THE ACCOUNTING PERIOD

As noted in Chapter 16, "Internal Bookkeeping," it is imperative that all expenses be entered into the Purchase Ledger for the month in which they were received. The expenses must be entered in this manner regardless of when the restaurant was billed for the items, when they are actually paid for or when the items are actually used. Adjustments will be necessary to accurately record prepaid accounts—such as insurances and magazine subscriptions—to ensure the expense is entered into the budget during the month the expense is incurred. Most of these adjustments may be computed during the budgeting process.

Certain expenditures—such as the telephone and utilities bills—might not be received until five to six working days after the end of the month. Since the bank statement and suppliers' monthly statements will arrive during the first week of the month, it is recommended that the final profit and loss statement not be prepared until the 7th or 15th of the following month. This will allow time for the bank statement to be reconciled, unrecorded expenses to be entered into the Purchase Ledger and any necessary final adjustments to be included. Although the profit and loss statement will not be published until the middle of the next month, the ending inventories and most costs will be projected on the first of the month, prior to opening.

MONTHLY AUDIT PROCEDURES

On the last day of the month:

1. Gather the completed inventory forms for food, liquor, wine and operational supplies.

2. Using current invoices and past inventories, cost out the Inventory Form. The

unit cost (or price) entered on the Inventory Form must correspond to the item and unit in the actual inventory. Correct prices are ensured by continual evaluation of invoices and/or contact with the suppliers. Review the section on the beginning inventory in Chapter 5, "Profitable Menu Planning."

3. Ensure that the employees organize and clean the storage areas and walk-ins, so that the ending inventory may easily be taken the following morning. Combine all containers and bottles. Organize and label all shelves.

4. Schedule the bookkeeper and the employees involved in taking the physical inventory—the assistant manager, kitchen director, bar manager and general manager—to arrive early in the morning prior to the start of business on the first of the month.

5. Schedule the preparation cooks to arrive an hour after the inventory crew so that you may inventory the food areas without disturbing them.

On the following morning, the first of the month:

6. The bookkeeper should arrive as early as possible in order to complete all of his or her work prior to management's completion of the inventory:

A. Reconcile and record all the transactions from the previous day, as usual.

B. Enter the information on the Daily Sales Report Form. Total, double-check and verify all the columns.

C. From the employee time cards complete, total, double-check and verify the Labor Analysis Form.

D. Ensure that all purchases are recorded in the Purchase Ledger. Complete, total, double-check and verify the Purchase Ledger for each company. Total the purchases in each expenditure category: food, liquor, wine and each individual operational category.

Ensure that all paid-outs entered on the Cashier's and Bartender's Reports have been posted into the appropriate Purchase Ledger categories. Total the cash paid-outs. Add this figure into the purchase total for each expense category.

COMPUTING THE ENDING INVENTORY

PURPOSE

An ending inventory is taken for a complete and accurate count of the stock and materials on hand for each cost category (food, liquor, wine and operational supplies) so that the unused amount may be used in projecting the total cost for each category.

PROCEDURE

1. Use pencils, scales, scratch pads and a clipboard, and be accurate. Liquor should be weighed on a liquor scale.

2. Two people should take the inventory. One will count while the other writes. The person counting states each item, its unit and its total amount. The other employee enters the figure on the inventory sheet on the correct line. If there is only a part of the item, estimate how much on a scale from 0.1 to 0.9 (0.5 being half of a container). Make sure there is a figure on either side of the decimal point (e.g., 0.5, 3.0).

3. Count shelves all the way across. Do not jump around.

4. Put a zero (0) in columns where there is no item to be counted.

5. Convert all items that are in prepared form into pound and unit costs. Example: 15 fish dinners at 12.5 oz. = 11.72 lbs.

6. For multiple weights or numbers of items, use a separate pad and double-check the entries.

7. Make sure there is an entry for every item.

8. Complete each area before moving on to a new one. Check for blanks and possible misentries.

9. When estimates must be made, they should be made with sound reasoning, not idle guessing.

EXTENDING THE INVENTORY

1. Add the amount of each item counted and enter the figure in the "Total" column.

2. Multiply each item total by the unit price to compute the extended total. Double-check the figures. Add the total amount of the extended column to compute the page total. Double-check every figure.

3. Add the page totals to compute the total for each category. Exchange papers with each other to double-check all figures again. Save the calculator tapes and staple them onto the front of the inventories.

4. All extension columns should have a figure or a zero to ensure the item was considered.

PROJECTING COSTS

From the previous sections you will need:

A.   The completed Daily Sales Reports.

B.   The completed Purchase Ledgers.

C.   The beginning inventory amounts.

D.   From the inventory just completed, the total ending inventory amounts.

E.   The Operational Supplies Cost Projection Forms on the following pages.

Step 1. From the Daily Sales Report:

1.   Enter total food sales less tax on the "Food Sales" line of the Materials Cost Projection Form.

2.   Enter total wine sales less tax on the "Wine Sales" line of the Materials Cost Projection Form.

3.   Enter total liquor sales less tax on the "Liquor Sales" line of the Materials Cost Projection Form.

4.   Enter total sales (food plus liquor plus wine sales less tax) on each sales line of the Operational Supplies Cost Projection Form.

5.   Double-check the complimentary and manager charge columns for food, liquor and wine. Multiply the food total by .50 and place this figure on the "Food Comp/Manager" line on the Materials Cost Projection Form.

6.   Multiply the wine comp/manager total by .40 and place this figure on the "Wine Comp/Manager" line on the Materials Cost Projection Form.

7.   Multiply the liquor comp/manager total by .25 and place this figure on the "Liquor Comp/Manager" line on the Materials Cost Projection Form.

In essence, through these actions (5, 6 and 7) you are taking a credit in the cost projections for products from which you have received no revenue, even though the items were perfectly acceptable to be sold. The products were given away to promote business or as a benefit to the manager and owners. Multiplying the total comp/manager sales recorded by the estimated cost percentage results in an estimated cost for these benefits. This will more than cover the costs if the food cost averages 40 percent; wine, 33 percent; and liquor, 22 percent. There is no credit taken for housed products—items that were improperly handled and, therefore, had to be discarded.

Step 2. From the Purchase Ledger:

Enter the total purchases including cash paid-outs for each category on the Materials Cost Projection Form. Enter the purchases for each operational supply category in the appropriate "Projection" column on the Operational Supplies Cost Projection Form. Keep in mind that each expense category must be projected separately. In order for each operational supply category to have a separate "Projection" column, additional Operational Supplies Cost Projection Forms will need to be copied. There is a space provided above each projection for the category's name and code number.

Step 3.

Enter the beginning inventory dollar amount (last month's ending inventory) for each category on the appropriate line of the cost projection sheets. For new restaurants, the first month's beginning inventory amounts would have been computed when the inventory sheets were initially set up. Once the original beginning inventory is computed, it need not be calculated again since the previous month's ending inventory amount will be the following month's beginning inventory amount.

Step 4.

Enter the ending inventory amount (just computed by taking the inventory) for each category on the "Ending Inventory Amount" line on both cost projection forms.

COMPUTING THE COST AND PERCENTAGE FIGURE FOR EACH CATEGORY

Add: beginning inventory (+) purchases and paid-outs (+)
Subtract: comp/manager (–) ending inventory (–)

This will equal the **cost of sales** for each category.

Cost of sales, divided by sales, equals the **percentage of cost**.

If the figure seems incorrect:

- Check mathematics on projection sheet.

- Check ending inventory for mistakes (counting, extending).

- Check all mathematics from the beginning.

If costs seem too high:

- Go over Purchase Ledger, sales, invoices, credits and totals.

- Check purchases recorded but not inventoried.

- Check for incorrect beginning inventory.

If costs seem too low:

- Check items inventoried but not on the Purchase Ledger.

- Check for incorrect beginning inventory.

COMPLETING THE BUDGET.

Once the cost projections are computed, the operating budget may be completed and the net pre-tax profit calculated.

1. Enter the total sales and sales breakdown in the "Actual" column of the operating budget.

2. From the cost projection forms, enter the actual cost of each category onto the budget.

3. Subtract the total material costs from the total sales to determine gross profit.

4. From the Labor Analysis Form, enter the total labor costs and cost breakdowns.

5. Office supplies may be actually projected, but as this will require a lengthy inventory, an estimate may be used.

6. The uniform expense will vary depending upon the state in which you reside. Some states require the restaurant to provide uniforms, where as others allow the restaurant to charge the employees for them.

7. "Service Expenses" is the total amount recorded in the Purchase Ledger plus any additional invoices.

8. The fixed operating expenses should remain constant. The monthly accumulated depreciation may vary when new assets are purchased during the month and the depreciation expense is prorated.

9. General operating costs. Labor taxes may be computed by multiplying the total labor cost for the month by the sum of:

    A. The current employer's Social Security contribution, plus

    B. The state unemployment compensation rate, plus

    C. The federal unemployment compensation rate, plus

    D. Any miscellaneous payroll taxes.

    Sales tax collected is not an expense and should not appear on the budget. In essence, the proprietor is acting as an agent for the state—providing a collection service.

10. Other general operating expenses may be computed by totaling the Purchase Ledger for each category plus any additional invoices.

11. Total all expenses and enter this figure in the "Total Expenditure" column. The total net pre-tax profit is computed by subtracting total expenditures from total sales.

ANALYZING THE COMPLETED BUDGET

A comparison analysis of the current budget against past operating budgets is perhaps the best way to identify cost problem areas. The goal of management is for the restaurant to operate in all ways consistently: consistent food products, consistent service and consistent cost percentages and net profits. Thus, when striving to identify cost overruns, examine the operating budget's costs against those of previous months and past years of the same month. The important figure to regard when computing the budgets is not the actual dollar amount at cost, but the percentage of cost in relation to sales.

Examine budgeted and actual sales closely. Is the sales level as high as anticipated and needed? Are customer counts increasing or decreasing when compared to previous months and last year? Why? Without a sufficient level of sales, the restaurant will ultimately fail, as sales will eventually not be able to meet the fixed costs necessary to maintain the operation.

Concentrate all efforts on increasing sales. Advertise, develop promotional programs, make menu changes, do whatever is required to locate the problem, resolve it and increase sales. However, before looking to the outside for answers to this problem, take a good, hard look at the entire operation. Make certain all areas of the restaurant are operating properly, and that all internal controls previously described throughout this book are in force, being adhered to and working.

VARIATIONS IN GROSS PROFIT

Changes in gross profit from month to month may be due to any one, or a combination, of the following variables:

- Changes in sales caused by a change in selling price.

- Changes in cost of goods sold caused by changes in materials costs and/or changes in volume of goods sold.

- Sales volume changes, which may be further analyzed into a change in the final sales volume. For an illustration of this point, consider the following example:

Assume a restaurant serves only two products:

1. Shrimp, with a total food cost of $5 and a selling price of $10.

2. Chicken breast, with a total food cost of $2.50 and a selling price of $8.50.

MONTH 1 (1,000 Entrees Sold)
  900 Shrimp Dinners
  Sales (900 X $10)   = $9,000
  Cost of Sales (900 X $5)   = $4,500

  100 Chicken Breasts
  Sales (100 X $8.50)   = $850
  Cost of Sales (100 X $2.50)   = $250

  Total Items Sold   = 1,000
  Total Sales   = $9,850
  Total Cost of Sales   = $4,750
  $4,750 ÷ $9,850 X 100   **= 48% Food Cost**

Now examine the second month with the reverse sales mix:

MONTH 2 (1,000 Entrees Sold)
  900 Chicken Breasts
  Sales (900 X $8.50)   = $7,650
  Cost of Sales (900 X $2.50)   = $2,250

  100 Shrimp Dinners
  Sales (100 X $10)   = $1,000
  Cost of Sales (100 X $5)   = $500

  Total Items Sold   = 1,000
  Total Sales   = $8,650
  Total Cost of Sales   = $2,750
  $2,750 ÷ $8,650 X 100   **= 32% Food Cost**

Thus, in this simplified example, you can clearly see the effect the weighted average sales has on food cost percentages. This example will also apply to liquor and wine cost percentages under similar circumstances.

POSSIBLE FOOD COST PROBLEM AREAS

1. No balance of high- and low-cost items on the menu.

2. No consideration of locally obtainable products.

3. No competitive purchasing plan.

4. Theft in any form.

5. Purchasing more than needed (spoilage).

6. No daily check of invoices, quality and prices.

7. Improper rotation procedures.

8. No perpetual inventory.

9. No controls on issuing items from storage areas.

10. Low yields on products.

11. Over-preparing (waste, spoilage).

12. Not using or following exact recipes.

13. Not following exact portion sizes.

14. Improper handling (wrapping, rotating, storing).

15. No reconciliation of dinners sold versus dinners consumed.

16. Employee theft.

COMPUTING THE ACTUAL YIELD OVER A SPECIFIED PERIOD OF TIME

Add: beginning inventory (lbs.) (+) purchases for period (lbs.) (+)

Subtract: ending inventory (lbs.) (−)

Multiply the total by 16. This is the total ounces used.

From the itemized cooks sheets, compute the number of dinners sold using this particular product.

Multiply the number of dinners sold by portion size to compute ounces sold.

Divide ounces used by ounces sold. This is the actual yield percentage. It is a check of the yields projected by the kitchen director and shows the actual yield percentage of raw products sold.

FOOD COST PERCENTAGE

This basic ratio is often misinterpreted because it is often calculated in so many different ways. It is food cost divided by food sales. However, whether your food cost is determined by food sold or consumed is a crucial difference. Also, for your food cost percentage to be accurate, a month-end inventory must be taken. Without this figure, your food cost statement is inaccurate and, therefore, basically useless. This is because your inventory will vary month-to-month—even in the most stable environment.

Food cost of sales calculation

Beginning inventory +	$5,000.00
Purchases +	$100,000.00
Total =	$105,000.00
Ending Inventory –	$35,000.00
Food used =	$70,000.00
*Employee meals, comp. food, manager –	$3,000.00
Cost of Food Sold	**$67,000.00**

Divide the cost of food by the Food Sales

Food Sales	**$175,000.00**
Food Cost Percentage	**38.28%**

* *Employee meals, complimentary food, and manager-consumed food are removed from the food cost equation as these costs should be reclassified on the P&L. Employee meals are an employee benefit, complimentary meals are considered promotional costs, and manager meals are a management benefit.*

Distinguishing between food sold and consumed is important. This is because all food consumed is not sold. Food consumed includes all food used, sold, wasted, stolen or given away to customers and employees. Food sold is determined by subtracting all food bought (at full price) from the total food consumed. See the above example.

WEIGHTED FOOD COST PERCENTAGE

What must be determined once your food cost is calculated is a weighted food cost percentage. A weighted food cost percentage will tell you what your food cost should have been had all procedures and controls in place operated at 100% efficiency.

On the following page, we have summarized sales information from the restaurant's point of sales (POS) system, or from other bookkeeping records. Basically, what you are doing is recreating the food cost for each item based on the standard recipe costs to determine what your food cost and, thus, food cost percentage should have been. For this example we will assume that only four menu items are served in this restaurant. From this example you can see that $7,000.00 in food costs have slipped away (assuming all calculations are accurate). The restaurant should have actually had a 34.28%.

MENU ITEM	COST PER MEAL	NUMBER OF MEALS SERVED	COST PER MENU ITEM
Chicken Kiev	$5.00	2,000	$10,000.00
Steak Oscar	$8.00	4,000	$32,000.00
Stuffed Flounder	$9.00	1,000	$9,000.00
Hamburger Platter	$3.00	3,000	$9,000.00

Weighted Total Cost...$60,000.00

Actual Sales...$175,000.00

Weighted Food Cost Percentage 34.28%

Variation Over Actual Food Cost Percentage........................4% (or $7,000.00)

DAILY FOOD COST ANALYSIS

Traditionally the food cost of sales amount is calculated once a month. There is no reason, however, why you cannot compute a daily food cost and a daily weighted food cost to analyze problem areas. Much of the inventory counting can be eliminated by moving only the products used for production into the kitchen at the beginning of the shift. This way, you can pinpoint problem areas or possibly problem employees or shifts. You can also calculate a separate food cost for breakfast or lunch.

BUDGETING & PROFIT PLANNING

BREAK-EVEN ANALYSIS

Break-even analysis is a simple, yet very important and useful accounting tool for the restaurant manager. An understanding of break-even analysis will aid the restaurant manager in budgeting, profit planning, expansion decisions and pricing decisions.

Break-even analysis is concerned with the break-even point which may be defined as the point or level of operations where neither a profit nor loss is incurred. The break-even point then is the point where total sales minus total costs equal zero. Total sales may also be regarded as the customer count times the average check amount.

All costs may be broken down into three major categories:

1. **Fixed Costs.** The costs which remain the same regardless of a change in sales or production. Fixed costs remain constant at all possible levels of sales.

Examples of fixed costs are: depreciation, insurance, and property taxes.

2. **Variable Costs.** The costs which change in direct proportion to a change in the level of sales or production. Example of variable costs are: food, liquor, and wine material costs.

3. **Semi-variable costs.** The costs which contain both properties of fixed and variable costs. A good example of a semi-variable cost would be the telephone expense. A fixed monthly service charge will be billed to the restaurant regardless of use. When sales are increased, more long distance phone calls will be made to suppliers. This additional use of the telephone for toll charges is the variable cost.

The first step in computing the break-even point is to separate the semi-variable cost into its two components; fixed and variable expenses. Using the **Breakeven Cost Analysis Form** and the completed budget, break up each semi variable cost into its variable and fixed amounts (many costs will be either fixed or variable). Enter the full amounts of each of these expenditures in the appropriate column. Some semi-variable costs may be difficult to precisely break down into either a fixed or variable amount. Should this be the case, estimate the figures. Although, the total expense must remain the same. Using the previous example of the telephone expenditure, the monthly service charge would be entered in the fixed column, toll charges would be entered in the variable column. The total bill remains the same. In order to better visualize the concept of break-even analysis, view the graph at the end of this chapter. Note that the fixed costs are $40,000 total sales are $100,000 and the variable cost per customer is $7.20. The break-even point occurs at $8,333. The average sale per customer is $12.

$$\$100,000 - \$40,000 = \$60,000 / \$7.20 = \$8,333$$

Total sales - Fixed costs = Variable costs divided by the variable cost per customer.
Total sales = customer count x average per head sales.

Note that as sales increase, the profit margin percentage will substantially increase once the break-even point or margin is realized. The restaurant manager should also note that once sales fall below the break-even point, losses will be incurred proportionately. Once the graph is set up and drawn, it is interesting to note how changes in the level of sales effect the profit margin. The profit or loss at any customer count level may be easily determined by the difference between the total sales line and cost line.

For example, suppose sales were increased to $120,000, or in other words approximately 10,000 additional customers were served. At this level of sales, total costs are $112,000. $40,000 fixed costs + ($7.20 variable cost per customer x 10,000 the number of customers served), which shows a profit of $8,000 or a 40% profit on the additional $20,000 in total sales. Thus, once the break-even point is reached, it would be accurate to assume that each additional dollar in sales will result in 40% profit.

Thoroughly understanding break-even analysis will aid the restaurant manager in the following situations:

1. When determining how many customers must be served in a specific time period (usually one month) before a profit is realized.

2. When analyzing remodeling or rebuilding plans to see how long the cost of the project can be recovered and how many additional customers must be served in order to make the project profitable.

3. When evaluating menu prices and net pre-tax profit margins, and what additional profits could be realized from a menu price increase.

All of these situations are common problems faced by the restaurant manager, and all could be easily solved through the understanding and application of break-even analysis and one of the formulas used to compute the break-even point. The three situations just described will be resolved using break-even analysis. For ease in understanding the major concepts, the information used in the graphic representation will remain the same in the following problems.

Situation 1

Situation number one is really only presenting the problem of calculating the breakeven point in other terms, which is the number of customers that must be served to reach the breakeven point rather than the level of total sales. The following formula will resolve this problem:

The breakeven point = Fixed Costs
The average check amount   **Variable cost per customer**
$40,000 = $40,000   **= 8,333 customers**
$12.00 - $7.20 = $4.80

Situation 2

Situation number two requires some additional information before the problem may be solved. The cost of the remodeling or rebuilding is required and the recovery time,(the period in which you will want the construction repaid by the additional customers it serves) is also needed. For example, we shall estimate the renovation amount at $50,000 which the owner wants to recover in two years. Thus, what is being stated is that over the average of both years, $25,000 in additional profits must be recovered each year. The following formula will resolve this problem:

The number of additional customers needed per year = The increase in Fixed Costs
The average check amount   **Variable cost per customer**
$25,000 = $25,000   **= 5,208 additional customers**
$12.00 - $7.20 = $4.80

Situation 3

Situation number three requires an additional assumption. The desired additional monthly pre-tax profit of $5,000. The following formula will resolve this problem: The variable cost per customer + (fixed costs + the desired additional profit/customer count). Computations surrounded by parentheses must be calculated first.

$7.20 + ($40,000 + $5,000 / 10,000) = $7.20 + $4.50 = $11.70

This formula will also be helpful in determining the prices which must be charged in order to reach the break-even point. Assume a particular number of customers sold and a constant cost structure in these calculations. Whenever computing a break-even formula it is always a good idea to check your answers.

Check: Sales - fixed costs - variable costs = 0

Using the above situation, the check is computed below:

Sales $11.70 x 10,000 customers = $117,000

Variable costs $7.20 x 10,000 customers = 72,000 fixed costs = $40,000
Desired additional profit $5,000

There are certain assumptions made in projecting break-even analysis which may not always hold true, and should be pointed out. The most common assumption is that the menu or selling price and costs will remain constant over a long period of time. This of course may not be the case, as no one can accurately foresee the future. A change in the product mix (the portion of each individual menu item to the total number of menu items sold), may drastically change, thus effecting the break-even point.

Break-even analysis will provide the restaurant manager with a valuable tool in analyzing the relationships between volume, selling prices and expenses. Furthermore, break-even analysis will enable the restaurant manager to effectively prepare long range budgets and provide essential information relating to price levels, expansion possibilities and past operational performances. The graphic representation of this data provides an easy-to-read-and-interpret report containing information from several financial statements, from which the restaurant manager may then make decisions based upon accurate relevant information.

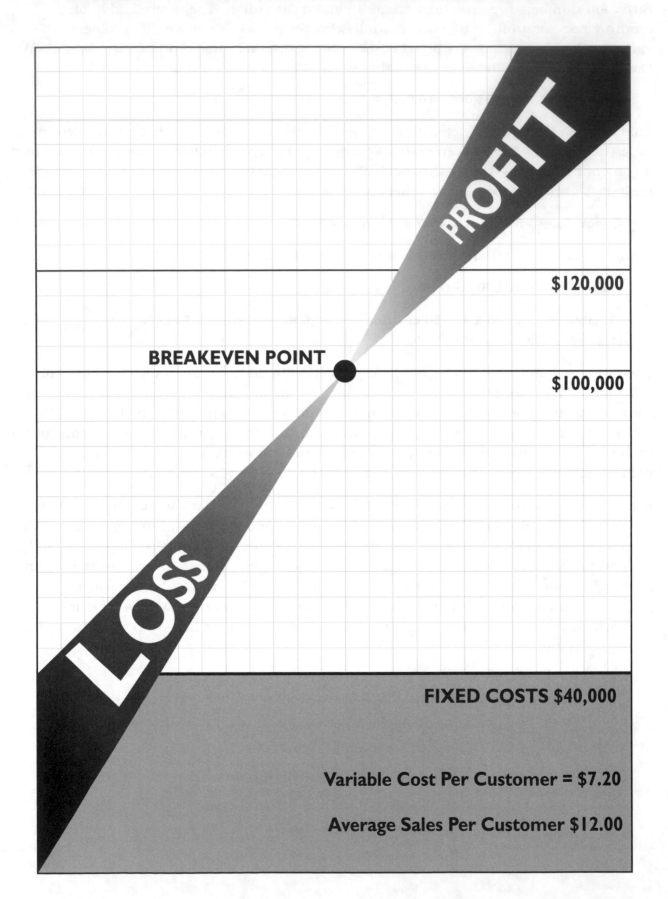

BREAKEVEN COST ANALYSIS

COST	TYPE	FIXED	VARIABLE	TOTAL

MATERIALS COST PROJECTION FORM

MONTH _____

FOOD

Beginning Inventory _____

Purchases _____

Comp/Manager _____

Ending Inventory _____

Cost _____

Sales _____

TOTAL FOOD COST PERCENTAGE _____

WINE

Beginning Inventory _____

Purchases _____

Comp/Manager _____

Ending Inventory _____

Cost _____

Sales _____

TOTAL WINE COST PERCENTAGE _____

LIQUOR

Beginning Inventory _____

Purchases _____

Comp/Manager _____

Ending Inventory _____

Cost _____

Sales _____

TOTAL LIQUOR COST PERCENTAGE _____

OPERATIONAL SUPPLIES COST PROJECTION FORM

PAGE _____ MONTH _____

CATEGORY _____ # _____

Beginning Inventory _____

Purchases _____

Ending Inventory _____

Cost _____

Sales _____

TOTAL COST PERCENTAGE _____

CATEGORY _____ # _____

Beginning Inventory _____

Purchases _____

Ending Inventory _____

Cost _____

Sales _____

TOTAL COST PERCENTAGE _____

CATEGORY _____ # _____

Beginning Inventory _____

Purchases _____

Ending Inventory _____

Cost _____

Sales _____

TOTAL COST PERCENTAGE _____

CATEGORY _____ # _____

Beginning Inventory _____

Purchases _____

Ending Inventory _____

Cost _____

Sales _____

TOTAL COST PERCENTAGE _____

HOW TO PERFORM AN INTERNAL AUDIT ON A RESTAURANT/BAR OPERATION— LOCATE & FIX PROFIT-LEAKING AREAS

INTRODUCTION

The purpose of this chapter is to demonstrate methods of auditing your restaurant and/or bar operation or any such operation. These methods are helpful in attempting to locate and understand cost control problems. In addition, these methods of investigation are very useful if you are considering purchasing a restaurant operation. Many of these methods are utilized by IRS examiners as well as national restaurant chains. The cost of good audit procedures for this chapter utilize liquor costs and liquor sales. These procedures will also apply to food and wine.

PRE-AUDIT PLAN

As with any pre-audit plan, an analysis of the tax return should be conducted to determine potential issues. One form of analytical review, comparing balance sheets and income statements, will give meaning to the changes that took place between the years, the individual figures of which are relatively meaningless. Large percentage changes or percentages that are not standard for the industry can be highlighted as potential issues and areas where the initial interview should focus. An important ratio that can be computed on the comparative income statement is the gross profit ratio. It is computed from the following:

gross sales − cost of goods sold = gross profit

GROSS SALES RATIO

This ratio tells us approximately how much of an item's sale price represents gross profit and how much is a recovery of the cost of the item. During the initial interview, the manager/owner should be asked the markup percentage on the goods sold. The percentage obtained from the interview can be compared to the computed ratio to see if it is similar. If not, this could be a possible indication that cost of goods may be overstated, or revenues, understated. An analysis of these accounts should be performed to determine if this is the case.

THIRD-PARTY SOURCES OF INFORMATION

The following represent possible third-party sources of information that can aid you in examining your bar and/or restaurant. The information may not be organized in the same way in your state; also, additional information may be available in your state. You should research your state to obtain the needed information.

- **Alcohol Beverage Control.** Demands that holders of on-premises licenses maintain available records of all purchases for three years.

- **State Liquor Dispensary.** Maintains records of all purchases by liquor license number. Does not maintain the details of the purchases. Maintains records of the liquor costs for most periods of time.

- **Local beer/wine distributor.** Maintains records of purchases made by customers. Maintains the records of the costs of the products. Permits required by the state.

- **Building permits.** Give cost of building. Also may contain blueprints of the building.

- **Health Department Permit.**

- **Bank statement.**

- **Bank reconciliation.**

- **Paid-out recaps** (by account classification).

- **Unpaid bills recap** (vendor and account classification).

- **Equipment purchases** (include copy of invoice).

- **Payroll summary.**

- **Accrued payroll.**

- **Monthly and/or quarterly tax returns.**

- **Copies of daily and weekly profit and loss statements.**

QUESTIONS PREPARED FOR THE INTERVIEW OF THE OWNER

1. Who runs the business? Is it family-operated or management-operated?

2. What are the duties of those who run the business?

3. What amount of time does each individual spend at the business?

4. What types of reports (e.g. tip reports, daily sales reports, etc.) are prepared for the business, and who prepares them?

5. How much of the bookkeeping is done and/or kept at the business site?

6. Does the owner have an accountant or bookkeeper who maintains his or her own bookkeeping system?

7. Who else has managerial control over the employees at the restaurant?

8. Does the management have any prior experience in the industry?

9. What are the days and hours of normal business operations?

10. What type of restaurant is it?

11. What type of clientele frequents the restaurant?

12. What is the customer capacity of the restaurant?

13. What are the average number of dinners sold on the weekdays and weekends?

14. What type of payment is accepted (cash only, credit cards, checks)?

15. What is the average cost of a meal?

16. Who determines the price of the meal?

17. What type of entertainment, if any, is offered?

18. Is there a cover charge for the bar or any entertainment at some time during the evening?

19. How are the entertainers paid?

20. Are banquet facilities available?

21. Is there a set fee for banquets or is the charge determined on an individual basis?

22. Is there a "Happy Hour" (i.e., a time period when alcoholic drinks are sold at a discount)?

23. Are food specials offered daily?

24. What is the average number of employees on the payroll?

25. How many people are working on day, afternoon or night shifts for the various areas of the restaurant?

26. What type of shifts do the employees work (day, afternoon, evening, etc.)?

27. How are employees paid: weekly, biweekly or monthly?

28. Are any individuals working at the restaurant considered independent contractors?

29. How is time kept for the employees: sign-in or time clock?

30. What type of side duties, if any, do the employees have on a daily, weekly or monthly basis?

31. Who calculates tips for each server?

INTERVIEW QUESTIONS

MANAGEMENT AND/OR OWNER INTERVIEW

1. On what days is the restaurant open?

2. What are the restaurant's hours of operation?

3. How many shifts are there?

4. What's the average number of employees on each shift?
   A. Captains?
   B. Waitpersons?
   C. Bus persons?
   D. Others?

5. Does an employee work the same shift on a regular basis?

6. If not, how are shifts rotated? How are different shifts recorded?

7. Who sets up the room?

8. What is the average set-up time?

9. How is set-up time rotated?

10. If stations are not rotated, how are they assigned?

11. What is the seating capacity of the restaurant?

12. Are tips pooled and split among waitpersons?

13. How are tips split?

14. If tips are not split, who gets tipped out, and what percent of the tips do they get?

15. Where do customers pay for their meals? That is, do they pay the waitperson or a cashier on the way out?

16. How do the employees receive their charge tips?

17. Do you have the following types of sales?
Charge sales?
Banquets?
Complimentary sales?
Ticket/Tour sales?
    A. Approximately what percentage of sales does each of these types bring in?
    B. How do the employees receive any non-cash tips for these types of sales?

18. Are waitpersons required to pay for customers who leave without paying?

19. Does the average cash customer tip better or worse than the average charge customer? If so, by how much?

19. Do customers tip differently according to the time they eat?

20. Are there any unusual factors that affect tipping in your establishment?

21. Other Comments:

EMPLOYEE INTERVIEW

1. Who is your manager?

2. How many shifts are there that you might be scheduled for in a given day?

3. How many hours are there in each shift?

4. Do all waitpersons work set-up and breakdown?

5. If not, who does, and how long does it take?

6. Do you have a steady schedule?

7. Are shifts rotated?

8. How are they rotated?

9. How are stations assigned?

10. Are stations rotated?

11. How are they rotated?

12. What is the average number of tables per station?

13. What is the average number of chairs per station?

14. How many tables, on the average, do you serve per shift?

15. How many checks, on the average, do you write per shift?

16. Who assigns workstations?

17. Who assigns work shifts?

18. Does the average cash customer tip better or worse than the average charge customer? By how much?

19. Do you have to pay for walkouts? If yes, how often does this happen?

20. What is your position?

21. What are your duties?

22. How long have to you worked at this establishment?

23. Have you worked in any other position at this establishment?

24. As a food server, do you consider yourself above average, average or below average?

25. Is there a reason why a determination of average sales and tips would be unfair to you?

26. Other Comments:

INTERNAL CONTROLS: QUESTIONS FOR THE OWNER AND/OR MANAGER—INVENTORY

1. Who are the primary suppliers of the business? What do they supply?

2. When are the purchases recorded (daily, weekly, etc.)?

3. Who is responsible for making the purchases?

4. Are the purchases recorded from checks or invoices?

5. What types of records are available for purchases? For example, is there a purchase journal?

6. Are there any records available for the number and size of bottles of alcohol purchased?

7. Are purchase discounts available? Were they taken?

8. Do the suppliers offer kickbacks or rebates? How are they recorded?

9. How many ounces of liquor are in each mixed drink? What are the prices of the mixed drinks?

10. Is the inventory of alcohol and food stored in a locked storeroom?

11. Who has access to the storeroom?

12. Who restocks the bar from the storeroom inventory, and at what intervals?

13. What type of record is maintained of stock being removed from the storeroom?

14. Does the bartender have to turn in an empty bottle before he or she can receive a new bottle?

15. Who checks in incoming merchandise to the storeroom?

16. Are the contents of incoming cases verified?

17. Are automatic liquor-dispensing devices used?

18. What is the price per beer for imported beer? Domestic?

19. If draft beer is available, how many ounces are in a glass? A pitcher?

20. Is there a price list of drinks available?
    A. Do you have wine for sale? By the glass and/or bottle?
    B. How many ounces are in a glass? Carafe?
    C. What are their prices?

21. What is the price of the wine coolers sold?

22. How many glasses of wine are served from each bottle?

23. What is the normal markup on mixed drinks? Beer? Wine? Wine coolers?

24. Do you compute spillage?

25. At what intervals are physical inventories of merchandise taken, and who is responsible for it?

26. Is beginning bar inventory plus storeroom withdrawals less ending inventory periodically extended to retail prices and compared to receipts?

27. Who checks incoming inventory for the kitchen?

28. Are incoming shipments weighed?

29. Once the incoming inventory has been accounted for, what happens to the receiving document?

30. Do the employees eat on the premises? Are they given the meals at a discount?

31. Are written records maintained for complimentary and employee-consumed meals and drinks?

1. How are sales by the waitstaff controlled?

2. Are prenumbered meal tickets used for each customer and/or table? If so, how are they issued to each server?

3. How is each server responsible for his or her numbered meal tickets?

4. What happens to voided meal tickets?

5. Does someone in management verify voided tickets?

6. Are cash registers used for the restaurant and/or bar?
   A. Where are they maintained?
   B. Are they preset for the individual menu or drink items?

7. Who has access to the cash registers?

8. Are cash-register drawers closed after each sale?

9. Do the cash registers print sales tickets?

10. How are over-rings handled?

11. Are sales tickets given to the customers?

12. Is access to the register tapes restricted? To whom?

13. Are the registers closed out at the end of each shift? By whom?

14. Are beginning and ending cash-register transaction numbers compared?

15. If two or more bartenders and/or hosts, etc., work simultaneously, do they use the same or different cash registers?

16. Are cash-register readings taken during each cashier's shift?

17. Is the cash reconciled to the register tapes and deposited in the bank intact? If so, at what intervals and by whom?

18. How are expenses for the business paid?

19. Are any expenses paid in cash? If so, are these amounts accounted for?

20. What types of controls are placed on the cash?

21. Who has access to the cash receipts?

Other Information

1. Who determines the prices of the meals offered?

2. How are portions controlled?

3. Do you have valet parking?

---

4. What happens to the money received for valet parking?

5. What type of advertising is used?

6. Are there any promotions used?

7. What happens to the used grease?

8. Are there any coin-operated machines in the restaurant/bar?

9. What is the age and condition of the equipment?

10. What is the employee turnover?

BALANCE SHEET EXAMINATION

An examination of the balance sheet can be advantageous for detecting certain items that might not be detected through examination of the income statement only. This section provides a correlation between the balance sheet and the income statement. By proper planning of an examination, one can eliminate a duplication of effort and conduct a more thorough examination.

The following information can be used to conduct the examination.

- A detailed examination of accounts receivable can eliminate the sales cutoff procedures of the income statement.

- An analysis of the bad-debt reserves on the balance sheet will determine if the provision to the bad-debt reserve is reasonable.

- An analysis of the debits of the prepaid assets will verify what items are being amortized or expensed.

- A detailed examination of the fixed assets and the accumulated depreciation would eliminate the need to verify depreciation expense.

- Examining accounts payable can basically eliminate the need to audit the accrued amounts that were expensed on the income statement. Similarly, examining loans payable will eliminate the need to verify interest expense.

The first step in examining the balance sheet is to prepare a comparative balance-sheet analysis. Generally, a minimum of three years will be involved: the assigned year and the prior and subsequent years. These three years will provide four years of "end-of-year" balances.

The primary emphasis in this examination of the balance sheet is placed on the last year because it eliminates the duplication of efforts for each year examined because of "rollovers." Rollovers are items that would affect the subsequent years if they were adjusted. It is at the agent's discretion whether prior years' balances are to be adjusted just for the interest due to the government.

Cash in the bank should be reconciled between book balances and the bank statements. Generally the taxpayer's accountant will have bank reconciliations available to inspect or examine. The bank reconciliation(s) should then be reconciled to the tax return.

UNREPORTED INCOME

Normal audit procedures such as tracing gross receipts to bank deposits, doing a bank deposit analysis on the business bank accounts, etc., should be performed. However, it is important to remember that these types of establishments are cash driven, and cash can be hard to tie down in a bank deposit analysis if the cash is not being deposited into the bank accounts. Therefore, it is important to tie down the cash that is collected as gross receipts from every source and cash that is paid out as expenditures. In the income statement section an indirect method is presented on how to audit the gross receipts from a bar and/or restaurant; however, consider the following techniques in auditing the cash on the balance sheet.

INTERNAL AUDIT TECHNIQUES

- Obtain the year-end reconciliation and compare it to the books. Old outstanding checks should be considered for possible inclusion in income.

- Likewise, the most recently issued outstanding checks should be examined to determine if the taxpayer engages in the practice of drawing checks but not issuing them promptly. This practice is usually applicable to cash-basis taxpayers. If you believe this practice exists, observe the dates checks were paid, as stamped (by the bank) on the cancelled checks. Another way is to look for a credit balance in the cash account indicating checks drawn but not issued until later.

- Using cancelled checks, test one month's returned checks in the following manner: Compare the name of the payee with that of the endorser. If they do not agree, or if the name of any officer, partner, shareholder, etc., appears as secondary endorser, determine why. The cash disbursement book should be open to the appropriate month while this is being done. If the payees of any checks are the officers, etc., or if the checks are drawn to "bearer" or "cash," look at the cashbook to see if the payee described therein is the same one named on the check itself.

- Review the cash disbursements journal for a selected period. Note any missing check numbers and large or unusual items. Determine the propriety of these items by comparing with vouchers and other records.

- Determine if voided checks have been properly handled.

- Review the cash receipts journal for items identified as ordinary business sales, and be alert for items such as sale of an asset or prepaid income.

- Review entries in the general ledger under "Cash Accounts," for unusual items which do not originate from the cash receipts or disbursements journal. These entries may indicate unauthorized withdrawals or expenditures, sales of capital assets, or omitted income.

- Determine whether the taxpayer has included interest income from time deposit accounts.

- Verify that any method of inventory valuation conforms:
  A. Compare inventory balances in the return with the balances for the prior and subsequent years' returns, and verify.
  B. Check for unauthorized changes from cost to cost or market.
  C. Check for gross profit percentage variations.
  D. Determine meaning and significance of any notes or qualifying statements on financial reports prepared by independent accounting firms.
  E. Determine that all direct and indirect overhead and burden expenses are in the overhead pool that is used in the computation of overhead rates where applicable.
  F. Analyze unusual entries to cost of sales account for labor, material and burden charges not directly related to sales or transfers of finished goods, if applicable.
  G. Confirm that year-end purchases were included in closing inventory.
  H. Determine whether there have been write-downs for "excess" inventory at below cost. Verify the method of inventory valuation for "excess" inventory.

DISCRETIONARY AUDIT PROCEDURES

1. Compare prior year's closing inventory with current year's opening inventory.

2. Determine whether a consistent and acceptable pricing method has been used.

3. Review manner in which overhead has been applied to inventories.

4. Review all inventory adjustments to ensure that no premature write-downs or reserve of anticipated losses have been included therein.

5. Where obsolescence adjustments have been made, review usage for prior, current and subsequent years.

6. Where a standard cost system is used, review the factors composing the standard frequency of updating and disposition of variances.

7. Test end-of-year purchases and accruals to ensure inclusion of these items in inventory.

LOANS TO SHAREHOLDERS—AUDIT TECHNIQUES

Most bar and restaurant corporate returns will be organized as closely held corporations. Many of these will have loans to the shareholders. The following information will provide the general audit techniques to use when addressing this issue.

Obtain copies of any notes or evidence of indebtedness. Test them to see if the terms of the note are being followed. For example, is interest (if any) being accrued as income? Does the loan call for monthly payments, or is it payable on demand? Does the note have a fixed maturity date? Does it have an interest rate? Is the interest rate near market? The absence of one or all of the above may indicate the loan was made at less than an arm's length transaction or below the prevailing market rate and may be construed as a constructive dividend (or, in an alternative position, interest income).

DISCRETIONARY AUDIT PROCEDURES

1. Analyze the composition of the account balance.

2. Trace the source of repayments.

3. Determine whether or not a bona fide debtor-creditor relationship exists.

4. Ascertain whether the current year's increase represents dividends.

5. Confirm that interest income has been properly recorded.

FIXED ASSETS

The initial investment for starting a restaurant and/or bar is quite high. Capital is required for the purchase of the property, leasehold improvements, equipment and furnishings, possible franchise fees, licenses, permits, taxes, liquor licenses, utilities, insurance, food inventory, advertising and payroll. The basic fixed assets that will be found in any bar and/or restaurant are as follows:

A. **Kitchen equipment.** Stove, grill, fryer, walk-in freezers, walk-in refrigerators, ovens, dishwashers and storage equipment.

B. **Office equipment.** Desk, computer and telephone.

C. **Property.** Fencing, building and outside seating.

D. **Dining room.** Tables, chairs, music (stereo/speakers), jukebox, cash register, floor coverings, salad bar, coffee makers, soda fountains, silverware, glassware and dishes.

E. **Bar.** Refrigerators, cash register, sinks, bar, glassware, ice machine, ice bin, draft beer dispensers, alcohol dispensers, telephone and coin-operated machines.

AUDIT PROCEDURES

1. Review the acquisitions to confirm that they have been properly recorded.

2. Where the acquisition consideration is other than cash, fully review the manner of arriving at basis.

3. Does the basis include all expenditures required to place the asset in readiness for operating use?

4. Allocations should be reviewed where a lump-sum purchase price is involved.

5. If there is an allocation in the contract between buyer and seller, verify that the allocation is consistent with the agreement. Also, verify that the allocation reflects economic reality.

PROFIT AND LOSS STATEMENT EXAMINATION

Examining the profit and loss statement may be the quickest and easiest way to perform an audit on a bar and/or restaurant. This approach is limited, however, when examining the gross receipts of the establishment. Since these establishments deal largely in cash, you will need to determine if the internal controls in place are adequate to ensure that the cash is being deposited into the bank accounts. Because of this uncertainty, an indirect method—besides a bank deposit analysis—may be warranted.

AUDIT TECHNIQUE

The first step in examining the profit or loss statement is to prepare a comparative analysis. Generally, a minimum of two years will be involved: the assigned year and the subsequent year. Based on the analysis, unusual or significant fluctuations in account balances can be selected for a more detailed examination.

The primary emphasis of an examination of the profit or loss statement is placed on "permanent" types of issues. Permanent types of issues are contrary to the "rollover" types of issues and do not affect the subsequent year: e.g., travel and entertainment, political contributions, investment tax credit and investment tax credit recapture.

NOTE: Not all classifications of income or expenses are included in this package, which does not imply that the other items are correct or should not be audited.

SALES

The sales generated by a bar and/or restaurant can be generated from the following sources: receipts from the sale of food, receipts from the sale of beverages (alcoholic and nonalcoholic) and receipts from coin-operated machines. The sales generated from these sources are hard to trace, since income is being generated by every customer. Also, the level of sophistication of the books may be poor. To gauge the daily, weekly or monthly performance of sales, you will have to rely heavily on the information obtained in the initial interview, such as the number of meals sold in a typical day, average price of a meal, markup percentages on food and alcohol, etc.

If you can obtain accurate information in these areas, you will be able to accurately estimate what the sales should have been for a specific period. This estimate will enable you to determine if unreported sales are possible. If it is discovered that underreporting exists, further detailed analysis of the information gathered will ensure that the underreporting can be adjusted in the examiner's report.

Since the bar/restaurant business is largely a cash-basis one, the use of the indirect methods discussed in this section may only uncover that an understatement of income exists; it may be difficult or impossible to detect how the understatement came about. For example, the taxpayer may be only reporting income from one cash register when two are used. The only possible way to uncover this is to ask a lot of questions and keep your eyes open on the tour of the business. Another helpful technique would be to visit the operation during its normal business hours and observe how the transactions are handled, or send in a secret shopping service.

INCOME FROM THE SALE OF FOOD

The formula below can provide a reasonable estimation of annual sales for you to compare to figures on the tax return. The numbers used should be derived from the initial interview. Any large discrepancy between the income derived from these numbers and those reported on the tax return may indicate unreported income or inflated expenses. You should then look closely at the pertinent accounts (such as food/beverage purchases, monthly sales, etc.) in the books and records.

possible daily volume x average check per seat = daily sales

The possible daily volume would be the number of seats in the establishment multiplied by how many times in a day they are occupied. The possible daily volume can be broken down into time periods—breakfast, lunch or dinner—to get a more accurate tally.

The average check per seat can be obtained from the initial interview or past records.

The daily sales can be extended to weekly and yearly sales based on the days open in a week and the weeks open in a year.

daily sales x days open in a week = weekly sales
weekly sales x weeks open in a year = yearly sales

These estimates can be accurate if consideration is made for vacant seats and people who walk out before paying their bills. During the initial interview ask enough pertinent questions to determine if these or any other situations should be considered.

Normal audit procedures, such as tracing gross receipts to bank deposits, doing a bank deposit analysis of all business and (owner/manager) personal accounts, etc., should be performed. Consider the interview responses received concerning internal controls. Does the same person who counts the daily receipts also make the bank deposit? Are the meal orders taken on numbered tickets, or would it be easy to simply not ring up a sale on the cash register for some orders? Look closely at the supervision habits in the restaurant to evaluate how sales might be understated or how easily theft may occur and by whom.

Another account to examine to test the accuracy of income reported is advertising. Are specials advertised? How often? Specials may refer to certain menu items or discounted prices, or both. Are the times during which specials are offered (such as Happy Hour, breakfast hours, etc.) reflected in the daily receipts ledger?

CASH TRANSACTION ANALYSIS, NET WORTH AND OTHER INDIRECT METHODS

A cash transaction analysis, net worth or other indirect method may be used to determine an understatement. One way to further support your suspicions of an understatement is this indirect method: Inspect the supply invoices to find the name of the printer of the guest checks. This printer can provide the number of guest checks purchased by the restaurant in a year. A projected income can then be determined from the average guest-check dollar amount multiplied by the number of checks. If these indirect methods are used in combination, they strengthen the case.

In the case of bars, it happens that even in states where the distribution of liquor is carefully regulated, the bar owner may remove cash from his or her drawer; purchase liquor off the shelf at a store; sell the drinks in his or her establishment; and return the amount of cash to the drawer, while pocketing the profits. In such a case there usually will be no indication in the books that anything is wrong, as neither the invoice or the income touches the books. An indirect method may uncover this.

INCOME FROM THE BAR

As in any audit, the auditing techniques used depend on the quality and quantity of the books and records maintained by the taxpayer. If the examination consists of a larger bar—where there are inventory records maintained which detail the daily and/or monthly purchases and quantities sold—then the liquor cost percentage can be computed and applied to total purchases to determine the gross receipts and gross profit of the taxpayer. If the examination is of a smaller, "Mom and Pop," bar chances are it is going to be time consuming and possibly difficult to determine the purchases for one day or one month. In this situation it might be better to rely partly on third-party information to verify purchases and compute the markup on cost. The markup can then be applied to total purchases to determine the gross receipts and gross profit.

USING THE LIQUOR COST PERCENTAGE TO COMPUTE GROSS RECEIPTS

To compute gross receipts using the liquor cost percentage, the following steps should be followed:

1. Determine the cost of some of the more popular brands of liquor.

2. Determine the sales value of the bottles if all liquor out of these bottles were sold.

3. Divide the sales value into the cost to get the potential pouring cost.

Example 1

1. **Determine the cost of liquor.**
   Verify from third-party sources that the cost per quart (bottle) is, in fact, $4.48.

2. **Determine the sales value of the bottle.**
   A quart has 32 ounces in it. If there are 1 $\frac{1}{4}$ ounces per drink, there are 25.60 drinks per bottle. (32 ÷ 1.25 = 25.60)

   If drinks go for $1.10, then the sales value per bottle—less sales tax of $1.97— would be $26.19. (25.60 X $1.10 = $28.16 – $1.97 = $26.19)

3. **Compute the liquor cost percentage.** Divide the sales value into the cost. This gives you the potential pouring cost.

   The sales value per bottle is 26.19, and the cost is $4.48, so the liquor cost percentage would be 17.1 percent. **$4.48 ÷ $26.19 = 17.1%**

Conclusion: 17.1 percent of $26.19 is the cost. The rest is the markup. If this percentage is applied to total purchases of $5,000, the gross receipts should be $29,239.77. ($5,000 ÷ 17.1% = $29,239.77)

Gross receipts (100%)	**29,239.77**
Less: purchases (17.1%)	**–$5,000.00**
Equals: gross profit (82.9%)	**$24,239.77**

The computations done with the formula discussed above could be used to calculate the total sales value of all bottles sold in a week, a month or a year.

USING THE MARKUP ON COST TO COMPUTE GROSS RECEIPTS

If it is difficult to determine daily and/or monthly purchases by an establishment, the markup on cost might be used to compute gross receipts and gross profit. This method works closely with the liquor cost percentage method; however, different percentages will be determined.

As with the cost percentage method, the cost and sales value of the various items need to be computed. Then the markup on cost can be computed. Markup on cost is the amount of the sales price over the cost of an item.

Example 2 (simplified)

price ($10) – cost ($5) = gross profit ($5)

sales price ($10) ÷ cost ($5) = percentage markup (200%)

The following steps should be followed to compute gross receipts based on markup on cost:

1. **Determine the markup of the various alcoholic items sold.**

   The markup should be determined, if possible, in the initial interview. If the manager/owner does not know the markup of the bar items, you must compute it based on the sales price of drinks and the cost of the drinks.

2. **Determine the purchases made.**

   You can get this information off the invoices provided, if available and accurate. If accurate records are not available, you should request in the initial interview the names of all the vendors used. Send letters to the vendors requesting records of all purchases made.

3. **Apply the markup to the purchases of the various types of alcohol.**

   Using the figures from Example 2:

   purchases and total costs ($5) X markup (200%)
   = projected sales ($10.00)

The steps discussed above do not take into account amounts for spillage, Happy Hour prices, etc. This information must be determined in the initial interview so that these amounts can be adjusted in determining the correct gross receipts.

OTHER INCOME

INCOME FROM COIN-OPERATED ACTIVITIES

Another important area of income to audit is the receipts generated by the coin-operated machines located in a bar. Coin-operated machines may include jukeboxes, cigarette machines, pool tables, dartboards, etc. These machines can be owned or leased from another party. If the machines are leased, the general rule is that the income generated from the machines is split based on some percentage determined by the owner of the machine. Income generated from coin-operated activities is very difficult to determine accurately. Therefore, it is important to ask a lot of pertinent questions in the initial interview regarding the operation of and income generated from these machines.

OTHER ACTIVITIES

Other areas of producing possible income in a bar/restaurant are the sale of lottery tickets, check-cashing, cover charges and gaming pools. Again, close scrutiny must be made concerning these areas in the initial interview. Ask pertinent questions to determine if the business engages in these areas and how the cash is handled and reported on the tax return.

COST OF GOODS SOLD

The cost of goods sold can be one of the largest expenses on the return. You should be aware that the purchase figure reported might be a "plug" figure in order to balance the cost-of-goods-sold computation.

PURCHASES

1. Review the cutoff date. Confirm that year-end purchases were recorded in the proper accounting period.

2. Determine whether the owners consume or withdraw merchandise for personal use, such as food, liquor, appliances, etc. If so, proper reductions should be made to purchases or cost of sales.

3. Scan "Purchases" column in the cash disbursements journal, voucher register, etc., and look for items unusual in amount, and to payee or vendors not generally associated with the products or services utilized.

4. Review entries in the general ledger control account. Note and verify entries that originate from other than usual sources (general journal entries, debit and credit memos, etc.).

5. Test check the recorded purchases for a representative period with vendor's invoices and cancelled checks, etc. Be alert to such items as personal expenditures and capital expenditures.

6. If purchases are made from related or controlled foreign entities, review a representative number of such transactions to determine if the
    following are present:
    A. Prices in excess of fair market value.
    B. Excessive rebates and allowances.
    C. Goods or services not received.

7. Ascertain if merchandise, prizes, trips, etc., were received from suppliers as a result of volume purchases.

UNIT BREAKDOWN OF LIQUOR

The following items are unit breakdowns of liquor that are useful in computing liquor cost percentages or markup percentages:

Keg of beer 15 $\frac{1}{2}$ gallons

Keg of beer	1,984 ounces
1 gallon	128 ounces
1 fifth	750 milliliters
1 fifth	approx. 21.8 ounces
1 liter	approx. 33.8 ounces
$\frac{1}{2}$ gallon	64 ounces
$\frac{1}{2}$ gallon	1.9 liter
1 quart	32 ounces
1 quart	approx. 0.95 liters
1 pint	approx. 475 milliliters
1 pound	16 ounces
Miniature	50 milliliters
Miniature	1.6 ounces

METRIC SIZE—FLUID OZ.	NUMBER OF DRINKS SIZED IN OUNCES				
	$1\frac{3}{4}$ oz.	1 oz.	$1\frac{1}{8}$ oz.	$1\frac{1}{4}$ oz.	$1\frac{1}{2}$ oz.
1.75 Liter—59.2	78.9	59.2	52.6	47.4	39.5
1 Liter—33.8	45.1	33.8	30.0	27.0	22.5
750 Milliliters—25.4	33.9	25.4	22.6	20.3	16.9
500 Milliliters—16.9	22.5	16.9	15.0	13.5	11.3
200 Milliliters—6.8	9.1	6.8	6.0	5.4	4.5

SAMPLE MONTH LIQUOR PURCHASES BY BOTTLE

BRAND	COST	# PURCHASED	TOTAL COST	$ PER DRINK	# OF DRINKS EA	SALES BOTTLE VALUE/ SALES TOTAL VALUE
FRANGELICO	17.50	3	52.50	3.00	22.5	67.50 / 202.50
GALLIANO	12.55	1	12.55	2.50	22.5	56.25 / 56.25
BLUE CURACO	6.20	1	6.20	3.25	22.5	73.13 / 73.13
C BROS BRANDY	8.05	7	56.35	2.25	22.5	50.63 / 354.38
BL BER BRANDY	7.10	2	14.20	2.25	22.5	50.63 / 101.25
CHERRY BRANDY	7.10	1	7.10	2.25	22.5	50.63 / 50.63
CR DE CACAO DK	7.05	3	21.15	2.50	22.5	56.25 / 168.75
CR DE CACAO LT	7.05	1	7.05	2.50	22.5	56.25 / 56.25
TANQUERAY	13.80	10	138.00	3.00	22.5	67.50 / 675.00
BOMBAY SAPHIR	14.80	2	29.60	3.00	22.5	67.50 / 135.00
BEEFEATER	13.85	11	152.35	3.00	22.5	67.50 / 742.50
ABSOLUT	13.15	3	39.45	3.00	22.5	67.50 / 202.50
STOLICHNAYA	12.70	10	127.00	3.00	22.5	67.50 / 675.00
SO COMFORT	7.90	3	23.70	2.50	22.5	56.25 / 168.75
AMARETTO	8.65	5	43.25	2.75	22.5	61.88 / 309.38
VERMOUTH	6.20	1	6.20	2.25	22.5	50.63 / 50.63
BUSHMILLS	14.90	10	149.00	3.00	22.5	67.50 / 675.00
KAHLUA	14.75	22	324.50	2.75	22.5	61.88 / 1361.25
BAILEYS	17.85	13	232.05	3.25	22.5	73.13 / 950.63
PEACH SCHNPS	6.35	8	50.80	2.25	22.5	50.63 / 405.00
RASPBERRY	5.70	1	5.70	2.25	22.5	50.63 / 50.63
CROWN ROYAL	5.75	6	94.50	3.00	22.5	67.50 / 405.00
MALIBU	8.65	20	173.00	2.75	22.5	61.88 / 1237.50
QUERVO GOLD	10.70	13	139.10	2.75	22.5	61.88 / 804.38
CUTTY SARK	5.70	7	109.90	3.00	22.5	67.50 / 472.50
DEWARS WHITE	15.50	7	108.50	3.00	22.5	67.50 / 472.50
RED LABEL	5.05	1	5.05	3.00	22.5	67.50 / 67.50
BACARDI LT	8.00	6	48.00	2.75	22.5	61.88 / 371.25
BARCARDI DK	8.00	3	24.00	2.75	22.5	61.88 / 185.63
MYERS DK	10.95	5	54.75	2.75	22.5	61.88 / 309.38
YUKON JACK	10.30	4	41.20	2.75	22.5	61.88 / 247.50
RUMPLE MINZE	12.90	5	64.50	3.00	22.5	67.50 / 337.50
WILD TURKEY	13.50	1	13.50	3.00	22.5	67.50 / 67.50
JIM BEAM	7.35	1	7.35	2.50	22.5	56.25 / 56.25
EARLY TINES	7.05	1	7.05	2.50	22.5	56.25 / 56.25
JACK DANIELS	10.95	27	295.65	2.75	22.5	61.88 / 1670.63
CANADIAN CLUB	10.25	2	20.50	2.75	22.5	61.88 / 123.75
SEAGRAMS 7	7.75	3	23.25	2.75	22.5	61.88 / 185.63
SEAGRAMS VO	10.25	18	184.50	2.75	22.5	61.88 / 1113.75
CANADIAN MIST	7.25	9	65.25	2.75	22.5	61.88 / 556.88
MACNAUGHTON	6.75	11	74.25	2.75	22.5	61.88 / 680.63
BLACK VELVET	7.10	23	163.30	2.75	22.5	61.88 / 1423.13
RICH & RARE	7.05	3	21.15	3.75	22.5	84.38 / 253.13
GILBYS	6.25	51	318.75	2.25	22.5	50.63 / 2581.88
MONTEGO BAY	5.75	56	322.00	3.25	22.5	73.13 / 4095.00
KANCHATKA	5.10	143	729.30	2.50	22.5	56.25 / 8043.75
TRIPLE SEC	5.65	14	79.10	3.25	22.5	73.13 / 1023.75
ARANDAS	6.65	20	133.00	3.25	22.5	73.13 / 1462.50
USHERS	9.70	30	291.00	3.75	22.5	84.38 / 2531.25
CANAD'N HUNTER	6.70	40	268.06	3.75	22.5	84.38 / 3375.00
ARANDAS GAL	14.65	4	58.60	3.25	52.6	170.95 / 683.80
PEPPERMINT	6.10	6	36.60	2.25	22.5	50.63 / 303.75
GLENLVT SCOTCH	23.75	2	47.50	3.00	22.5	67.50 / 135.00
APR TRIPLE SEC	6.10	8	48.80	3.25	22.5	73.13 / 585.00
FLSMN ROYAL	5.10	13	66.30	2.50	22.5	56.25 / 731.25
ARR TRPE SF	3.70	4	14.80	3.25	22.5	73.13 / 292.50
CAN LTD	6.25	2	12.50	3.00	22.5	67.50 / 135.00

TOTALS 5,673.20 / 44,541.93

MARKUP FOR SAMPLE MONTH
SALES PRICE: $44,541.93
COST MARKUP: $5,673.20

THE RESTAURANT MANAGER'S HANDBOOK

COMPUTATION OF KEY PERCENTAGES

bar supplies ÷ bar sales = bar supplies cost percentage

beer cost ÷ beer sales = beer cost percentage

food cost ÷ food sales = food cost percentage

labor ÷ total sales = labor cost percentage

liquor cost ÷ liquor sales = liquor cost percentage

paper cost ÷ food sales = paper cost percentage

other ÷ total sales = other cost percentage

wine cost ÷ wine sales = wine cost percentage

ONCLUSION

As stated in the introduction of this book, more restaurants are opened, and fail, each year than most other businesses in America today. We sincerely feel we have remedied this problem with the release of *THE RESTAURANT MANAGER'S HANDBOOK.* You now have the basis for setting up, operating and managing a profitable restaurant. As this volume will be continuously updated, we would greatly appreciate hearing your comments, suggestions and thoughts for improvement in any area.

ATLANTIC PUBLISHING GROUP, INC.
1210 SW 23rd PLACE
OCALA, FLORIDA 34474-7014

800-541-1336
800-555-4037

Your complete resource for books, videos, training materials, tools, and software for the foodservice, restaurant, and hospitality industry professional:

http://www.atlantic-pub.com • E-mail: *sales@atlantic-pub.com*

GLOSSARY OF TERMS

80/20 RULE Eighty percent of the value is from 20 percent of the resources.

A

A LA CARTE Items are prepared to order and each one is priced separately.

AP WEIGHT As-purchased weight.

ACCOUNTANT A person skilled in keeping and adjusting financial records.

ACCOUNTS PAYABLE Money owed for purchases.

ACCOUNTS RECEIVABLE Money owed by the customers.

ACTUAL PRICING METHOD All costs plus the desired profits are included to determine a menu selling price.

ADVERSE IMPACT Impact of employer practices that result in higher percentages of employees from minorities and other protected groups.

ADVERTISING Purchase of space, time or printed matter for the purpose of increasing sales.

AFFIRMATIVE ACTION Steps to eliminate the present effects of past discrimination.

AGE DISCRIMINATION IN EMPLOYMENT ACT OF 1967 Protects individuals over 40 years old.

AMBIANCE Sounds, sights, smells and attitude of an operation.

AMERICANS WITH DISABILITIES ACT (ADA) Prohibits discrimination against disabled persons.

ANNUAL Happening once in 12 months.

ANNUAL BONUS Monetary incentive tied to company profitability and designed to encourage continuous improvement in employee performance.

ANNUITY Promise of a definite payment for a specific period.

APPLICATION FORM A form that, when filled out by a potential employee, gives information on education, prior work record and skills.

ARBITRATION Third-party intervention, in which the arbitrator has the power to determine and dictate the terms.

AS PURCHASED (AP) Item as purchased or received from the supplier.

AS SERVED (AS) Weight, size or condition of a product as served or sold after processing or cooking.

ASSESSOR Someone who estimates the value of property for the purpose of taxation.

ASSETS Anything of value; all property of a person, company or estate that can be used to pay debts.

AUTOMATION Automatic control of production by electronic devices.

B

BALANCE The amount that represents the difference between debit and credit sides of an account.

BALANCE SHEET Written statement that shows the financial condition of a person or business. Exhibits assets, liabilities or debts, profit and loss, and net worth.

BANK NOTE A note issued by a bank that must be paid back upon demand. Used as money.

BASELINE BUDGET Based on a past budget and adjusted for current conditions.

BASIC MARKETING MOVES Basic moves that an operation should use to increase its sales volume.

BATCH PREP RECIPE Lists prices per ingredient for a detailed recipe for the purpose of obtaining a total cost for one batch of a meal.

BATCHING Adjusting recipes for equipment or recipe size constraints.

BEGINNING INVENTORY The quantity and value of beverage and food products or operational supplies in stock at the beginning of an accounting period.

BEHAVIOR MODELING A training technique. Trainees are shown good management techniques by role-play or viewing a film. Trainees are then asked to play roles in a simulated situation, and supervisors give feedback.

BEHAVIORISTIC APPROACH TO CONTROL Control through workers' desire to perform for the best interests of the organization.

BENCHMARK JOB The job that is used to secure the employer's pay scale and around which other jobs are systematized in order of relative worth.

BENCHMARKING Analyzing operation features in comparison to the best of its competitors in the industry.

BENEFITS Indirect payments given to employees. These may include paid vacation time, pension, health and life insurance, education plans and/or rebates on company products.

BID SHEET A sheet that is used in comparing item prices from different vendors.

BLIND RECEIVING When there are no quantities or weights printed on packages. The receiver must count or weigh items.

BLOCK SCHEDULING Workers begin and end work at the same time on a specified shift.

BONA FIDE OCCUPATIONAL QUALIFICATION (BFOQ) Requirement that an employee be of a certain religion, sex or national origin where this is reasonably necessary to the organization's normal operation. Specified by the 1964 Civil Rights Act.

BOTTLE MARK A label or ink stamp with information that identifies bottled products as company property.

BOTTOM UP BUDGET Secondary employees prepare a budget and then send it to upper management for approval and combining.

BOUNCEBACK CERTIFICATE OR COUPON A coupon good for a product upon a return visit. The customer is "bounced back" to the business.

BREADING The process of placing an item in flour, egg wash (egg and milk), then bread crumbs before frying or baking.

BREAKEVEN ANALYSIS A computative method used to find the sales amount needed for a food-service operation to break even.

BREAKEVEN CHART A chart that shows the relationship between the volume of business and the sales income, expenditures and profits or losses.

BREAKEVEN POINT The association between the amount of business and the resulting sales income, expenditures and profits or losses. When income and costs are equal.

BUDGET A plan for a specific period that estimates activity and income and determines expenses and other adjustments of funds. Planning the company's expenditures of money, time, etc.

BUDGET CALENDAR The dates/time that a budget should be finished.

BURGLARY Unlawful entry.

BURNOUT Depletion of physical and mental capabilities usually caused by setting and attempting unrealistic goals.

BUSINESS INTERRUPTION INSURANCE Insurance that covers specific costs when a business cannot operate as normal.

BUSINESS PLAN Defines the business image, clarifies goals, calculates markets and competition and determines costs and capital needs.

BUTCHER AND YIELD TESTS Testing of products to determine usable amounts after preparation.

BY-PRODUCT Item or items that are made in the course of producing or preparing other items.

C

CALCULATE Compute or estimate an amount.

CALENDAR YEAR Consisting of 365 days. The period that begins on January 1 and ends on December 31.

CALL BRAND The brand (of a type of liquor) asked for by customers.

CALL DRINK A drink made with brand-name liquor.

CAPACITY The volume limit.

CAPACITY MANAGEMENT The use of an operation's resources to serve the greatest number of guests.

CAPITAL Financial assets.

CAPITAL ACCUMULATION PROGRAMS Long-term incentives. Plans include stock options, stock appreciation rights, performance achievement plans, restricted stock plans, phantom stock plans and book value plans.

CAPITAL BUDGET Equipment, building and other fixed assets.

CARRYOVER Amount left over.

CASE STUDY METHOD Method in which the manager is given a written description of an organizational problem to diagnose and solve.

CASH BUDGET The amount of money received, the amount of money disbursed, and the resulting cash position.

CASH FLOW Profit plus depreciation allowances.

CASH ON DELIVERY (COD) Merchandise must be paid for on delivery or prior to delivery.

CASH OR CASH OUTLAY FOR PROJECT Annual net income (or savings) from project before depreciation but after taxes.

CASHBOOK A book containing records of all income and expenses of a business operation.

CELSIUS A unit used to measure temperature in the metric system, divided into 100 equal parts called degrees; previously called centigrade.

CENTIGRADE See Celsius.

CENTIMETER One hundredth part of a meter.

CENTRAL TENDENCY The disposition to rate all employees the same way, such as rating them all average.

CERTIFICATE Authorizing document issued by a bank indicating that a specific amount of money is set aside and not subject to withdrawal except on surrender of the certificate.

CHAIN OF COMMAND A top authority and a clear line of authority from that top to each person in the organization. Also called the scalar principle.

CIPHER Zero.

CITATIONS SUMMONS Informs employers and employees of regulations and standards that have been violated.

CIVIL RIGHTS ACT Law that makes it illegal to discriminate in employment on the basis of race, color, religion, sex or national origin.

CIVIL RIGHTS ACT OF 1991 (CRA 1991) Places the burden of proof back on employers and permits compensatory and punitive damages.

CLASSES Groupings of jobs based on a set of rules for each grouping. Classes usually contain similar jobs.

CLASSICAL PRINCIPLES (OR THEORY) OF ORGANIZATION Focuses on enterprise structure and work allocation.

CLASSIFICATION (OR GRADING) METHOD Categorizing jobs into groups.

CLASSIFICATION RANKING SYSTEM Constitutes grades and categories to rank various jobs.

COLLECTIVE BARGAINING Representatives of management and the union meet to negotiate the labor agreement.

COMMISSION An individual's pay based on the amount of sales personally derived.

COMMITTED ITEM A product that is scheduled for production between the time it is ordered and the time it is received.

COMMON SIZE ANALYSIS Analysis of financial statements by dividing each item on two or more statements by the total revenue for the period.

COMPARATIVE ANALYSIS Analysis of displaying the difference of line items on financial statements for two or more financial periods or two or more financial dates along with the percentage changes.

COMPENSABLE FACTOR A fundamental, compensable element of a job, such as skills, effort, responsibility and working conditions.

COMPENSATION Something given in return for a service or a value.

COMPETITIVE ADVANTAGE The elements that allow an organization to distinguish its product or service from those of its competitors.

COMPOUND Composed of more than one part.

COMPUTERIZED By means of a computer or computers.

CONFIGURATION An arrangement.

CONFRONTATION MEETINGS The method of explaining and bringing up intergroup misconceptions and problems so that they can be resolved.

CONSIGNMENT PRODUCTS Items provided to a company by a vendor who charges for them after they are used.

CONSUMER ORIENTATION The needs of consumers determine management decisions.

CONTRIBUTION RATE The contribution margin, in dollars, divided by sales.

CONTROL To have charge of.

COOK/CHILL SYSTEM Cooking food item to "almost done" state, packaging it (above pasteurization temperature) and chilling it rapidly.

CO-OP BUYING A group of similar operations working together to secure pricing through mass purchasing at quantity discount prices.

CORPORATION A group of people who obtain a charter giving them (as a group) certain legal rights and privileges distinct from those of the individual members of the group.

COST The amount paid to acquire or produce an item.

COST ALLOCATION The process of distributing costs among departments.

COST CONTROLLER The person or persons whose responsibilities include analyzing expenses, revenues and staffing levels.

COST FACTOR Cost calculated by dividing the cost per servable pound by the purchase price per pound.

COST LEADERSHIP Being the low-cost leader in an industry.

COST OF SALES Food and beverage cost for menu items in relation to the sales attained by these items during a specific period.

COST PER PORTION The cost of one serving calculated by total recipe cost divided by the number of portions.

COST PER SERVABLE POUND The cost calculated by multiplying the purchase price by the cost factor.

COST-BENEFIT ANALYSIS Determining the cost, in monetary terms, of producing a unit within a program.

COST-EFFECTIVENESS ANALYSIS Identifying the cost, in nonmonetary terms, of producing a unit.

COST-PLUS Paying vendors cost plus a percentage.

COUNT The number of units or items.

CPA (CERTIFIED PUBLIC ACCOUNTANT) An accountant who has fulfilled certain requirements and abides to rules and regulations prescribed by the American Institute of Certified Public Accountants.

CPP (COST PER POINT) BUDGETING Method used to obtain an advertising level at a predetermined cost.

CRITERION VALIDITY Validity is based on showing that scores on a test are related to job performance.

CULTURAL CHANGE Changes in a company's shared values and aims.

CURRENT LIABILITY A debt or obligation that will become due within a year.

CURRENT RATIO Current assets divided by current liabilities.

CUTTING LOSS Weight lost from a product during fabrication.

CVP The relationship between cost, volume and profit.

D

DAILY PRODUCTION REPORT A list of items and quantities produced during a specific shift or day.

DEAD STOCK ITEM Item no longer offered.

DEBIT Showing something owed or due.

DECIMAL A system of counting by tens and powers of ten.

DECIMETER Equal to one tenth of a meter.

DEDUCTION A value that may be subtracted from taxable income.

DEFAULT Failure to pay when due.

DEFERRED PROFIT-SHARING PLAN A plan in which a certain amount of profits are credited to an employee's account. May be payable at retirement, termination or death.

DEFINED BENEFIT PENSION PLAN A formula for determining retirement benefits.

DEFINED-CONTRIBUTION PLAN The employer makes specific contributions to an employee's pension but does not guarantee the amount.

DEGREE DAY The difference between outside temperature and 65° F.

DECAMETER Equal to 10 meters.

DELEGATION Distribution of authority and responsibility downward in the chain of command.

DEMOGRAPHIC SEGMENTATION Segmentation based on human population variables such as age, gender and family size.

DENOMINATOR Common trait or standard.

DEPOSIT To put in a place, especially a bank, for safekeeping.

DEPRECIATION Lessening or lowering in value.

DESIGNATE Point out; indicate definitely.

DIFFERENTIAL (BEVERAGE) Difference of the sales value of a drink from the standard sales value of beverages used.

DIFFERENTIATE To distinguish a product or service from similar products or services.

DIFFERENTIATION Trying to be unique within an industry with dimensions that are valued by buyers.

DIRECT COSTS (FOOD) The costs associated with direct purchases.

DIRECT ISSUE Items that are directly delivered and charged to a food-and-beverage outlet—not stored in a central storeroom.

DIRECT LABOR Labor used directly in the preparation of a food item.

DIRECT PURCHASES Food delivered directly into the kitchen and charged as a food cost on that day.

DIRECTING Showing and explaining to others what needs to be done and helping them do it.

DISCIPLINE A correction or action towards a subordinate when a rule or procedure has been violated.

DISMISSAL Involuntary termination of employment.

DIVIDEND An owner's share of the surplus when a company shows a profit at the end of a period.

DIVISOR A number by which another (the dividend) is divided.

DOWNSIZING The process of reducing the size of an operation.

E

EP WEIGHT Edible portion weight. The usable portion after processing.

EARNINGS PER SHARE Earnings of a company divided by the number of its stock shares outstanding.

EARNINGS RATIO The net profit before taxes divided by net sales.

ECONOMIC ORDER QUANTITY (EOQ) Determines a purchase quantity that does the best of minimizing purchases and inventory costs.

ECONOMIC STRIKE A strike resulting from a failure to agree about terms of a contract that involve wages, benefits and other employment conditions.

EDIBLE PORTIONS (EP) The actual yield

available for processing a food item.

ELASTICITY OF DEMAND How demand for a product can fluctuate in response to other factors.

ELASTICITY OF SUPPLY The response of output to changes in price. Quantity supplied divided by the percentage change in the price.

ELECTRONIC DATA INTERCHANGE (EDI) Allows a food-service operator to receive prices electronically and generate an order form to send back.

ELECTRONIC SPREADSHEET Computerized worksheet with vertical and horizontal columns that are easily manipulated.

EMBEZZLEMENT Taking of property by someone to whose care it has been entrusted.

EMPLOYEE ADVOCACY Human Resources takes responsibility for defining how management should treat employees and represent the interests of employees within the framework of its obligation to senior management.

EMPLOYEE ASSISTANCE PROGRAM (EAP) Program employers promote to help employees overcome employee assistance program, usually in regard to alcoholism, drug abuse,

EMPLOYEE COMPENSATION Any form of pay or reward an employee gets from his or her employment.

EMPLOYEE ORIENTATION Introduction of basic company background information to new employees.

EMPLOYEE RETIREMENT INCOME SECURITY ACT (ERISA) The law that provides government protection of pensions for all employees with pension plans.

EMPLOYEE STOCK OWNERSHIP PLAN (ESOP) A company contributes shares of its own stock to a trust to which additional contributions are made annually. Upon retirement or separation from service the trust distributes the stock to employees.

EMPOWERMENT Giving lower-level employees the opportunity, responsibility and authority to solve problems.

ENDING INVENTORY The quantity and value of items on hand at the end of a period.

ENTREE The main dish of a meal.

ENTROPY Lack of useful input causing a system to solidify or run down.

EQUAL EMPLOYMENT OPPORTUNITY COMMISSION (EEOC) The commission, created by Title VII, empowered to investigate job discrimination complaints and sue on behalf of complainants.

EQUAL PAY ACT OF 1963 An amendment to the Fair Labor Standards Act designed to require equal pay for women doing the same work as men.

EQUIPMENT Machines or major tools necessary to complete a given task.

EQUITY FINANCING Financing by owners of the organization or company.

EQUIVALENT Equal in value or power.

ESTIMATE Judgment or guess determining the size, value, etc., of an item.

EVALUATE To find the value or amount of.

EXCEPTION PRINCIPLE Recurring decisions are handled in the normal manner and specific ones are referred upward for appropriate action.

EXPECTANCY CHART Shows the relationship between test scores and job performance.

EXPENDITURE Amount spent.

EXPIRATION The date on which a food or beverage product ceases to be usable.

EXPLODED RECIPE Changing recipe quantities to create the number of portions required.

EXTENSION To equate out, lengthen or widen.

EXTRA INDUSTRY Comparison of your practices with other industries.

F

FABRICATED Made or made up.

FABRICATED PRODUCT The item after trimming, boning, portioning, etc.

FABRICATED YIELD PERCENTAGE The yield, or edible portion, of an item shown as a percentage of the item as purchased.

FACTOR One of two or more quantities, multiplied.

FACTOR SYSTEM Raw food cost is multiplied by a factor to determine a menu selling price.

FAIR LABOR STANDARDS ACT Passed in 1936 to provide for minimum wages, maximum hours, overtime pay and child labor protection.

FINANCES Funds, money or revenue; financial condition.

FINANCIAL POSITION The status of a company's assets, liabilities and equity.

FINANCIAL STATEMENTS Used in a business operation to inform management of its exact financial position.

FINISHED GOODS Menu items that are prepared and ready to serve.

FIRM PRICE The price agreed to by the purchaser and vendor.

FISCAL YEAR The time between one yearly settlement of financial accounts and another.

FIXED BUDGET Budget figures based on a definite level of activity.

FIXED EMPLOYEES Employees who are necessary no matter the volume of business.

FLEX PLAN A plan giving employees choices regarding benefits.

FLEXIBLE BUDGET Projected revenue and expenditures based on production.

FLEXIBLE CAPACITY STRATEGY Handling varying volumes of business without having high overhead costs.

FLEXTIME A system that allows employees build their workdays around a core of midday hours.

FLIGHT The period of an advertiser's campaign.

FLUCTUATE Change continually.

FOOD COST The cost of food items purchased for resale.

FOOD INGREDIENT DATABASE Contains basic information about each food item. Name, cost, purchase units, inventory units, issue units, vendors and conversion factors are included.

FOOD ITEM DATA FILE (FIDF) NUMBER The number assigned to a food item in a database.

FOOD COST PERCENTAGE Cost of food divided by sales from that food.

FORECAST A prediction.

FORECASTING Estimating future revenue and expense.

FORMAT Refers to size, shape and general arrangement of a book, magazine, etc.

FORMULA A recipe or equation.

FOUR Cs OF CREDIT Character, capital, collateral and the capacity to repay.

FOUR-DAY WORKWEEK An arrangement that allows employees to work four ten-hour days instead of the more usual five eight-hour days.

FRACTION One or more of the equal parts of a whole.

FRANCHISE A franchise grants the right to use a name, methods and product in return for franchise fees.

FRANCHISEE The person or organization acquiring the franchise.

FRANCHISOR The person or company selling the franchise.

FREEZER BURN Fat under the surface of food having become rancid and possibly having caused a brown deterioration.

FTE, OR FULL-TIME EQUIVALENT A method of measuring labor costs with use of overtime pay.

FUNDAMENTAL EQUATION ASSETS Liabilities plus equity.

G

GARNISH To decorate.

GELATIN A tasteless, odorless substance that dissolves easily in hot water and is used in making jellied desserts and salads.

GENERAL LEDGER (GL) A ledger containing all financial statement accounts.

GOURMET A lover of fine foods.

GRADUATED Arranged in regular steps, stages or degrees.

GRAM Twenty-eight grams are equal to one ounce.

GRATUITY/TIP A gift or money given in return for a service.

GRAZING When employees consume food, unauthorized.

GRIEVANCE A complaint against the employer that may include factors involving wages, hours or conditions of employment.

GROSS The overall total.

GROSS COST The total cost of food consumed.

GROSS MARGIN Sales minus the cost of food.

GROSS PAY Money earned before deductions are subtracted.

H

HARD WATER Water containing excessive calcium and magnesium.

HEALTH MAINTENANCE ORGANIZATION (HMO) Health-care providers that use their own physicians and facilities.

HECTOMETER Equal to 100 meters.

HEDGING A contract on a future price entered into to secure a fixed price.

HOMOGENEOUS ASSIGNMENT A form of specialization that assigns an employee to one job or limits the employee to a related specific task.

HORIZONTALLY On the same level.

HOST/HOSTESS The person who receives guests.

HOUSE BRAND The brand of liquor normally served by a given bar.

HVAC Heating, ventilation and air-conditioning.

HYPOTHETICAL Assumed or supposed.

I

IMPERIAL SYSTEM A measurement system using pounds and ounces for weights and pints for volume.

INDICATOR That which points out.

INGREDIENT One part of a mixture.

INGREDIENT ROOM Where non-cooking personnel prepare food before it is sent to cooking personnel.

INSTALLMENT Part of a sum of money or debt to be paid at regular times.

INSUBORDINATION Willful disobedience or disregard of a boss's authority.

INSURANCE Trading the possibility of a loss for the certainty of reimbursement. Paid by small premiums.

INTEGRATED BEVERAGE CONTROL SYSTEM An automatic beverage dispensing system integrated with a computer or point-of-sale register.

INTEREST Money paid for the use of borrowed money.

INTERNAL CONTROL The methods and measures within a business to safeguard assets, check the accuracy and reliability of accounting data and promote operational efficiency.

INVENTORY A list of items with their estimated value and the quantity of each.

INVENTORY CONTROL System used for maintaining inventories.

INVENTORY CONTROL METHOD (BEVERAGE) Method in which the beverage amount used is determined from guest checks and then reconciled with replacement requisitions.

INVENTORY TURNOVER The amount of times inventory turns over during a specific period.

INVENTORY VARIANCE ACCOUNTING The amount of sales of an item is compared with the number used from inventory records, and the variance is noted.

INVERT Turn upside down.

INVOICE Shows prices and amounts of goods sent to a purchaser.

ITEMIZE To state by item.

J

JIGGER Used to serve a volume predetermined of a beverage.

JOB ANALYSIS Job description and specifications.

JOB DESCRIPTION A description of tasks and duties required on a job.

JOB SHARING Allowing two or more people to share a single full-time job.

JOB SPECIFICATIONS The qualifications needed to hold a job. Includes educational, physical, mental and age requirements.

K

KILOGRAM Equal to 1,000 grams.

KILOMETER Equal to 1,000 meters.

KLEPTOMANIA The persistent impulse to steal.

L

LAPPING A type of embezzlement when funds are taken from an account then covered with later receipts.

LEAST SQUARES ANALYSIS In-depth method of calculating an average of variable or fixed costs.

LEGUMES Vegetables, especially beans and peas; technically, plants in the pea family, or the fruits and seeds of such plants.

LEVERAGING Using borrowed money to acquire assets to make money.

LIABILITY Being under obligation or debt.

LINE MANAGER The manager who is authorized to direct work and is responsible for accomplishing the company's goals.

LINE OF IMPLEMENTATION Division of planning and organizing activities from "doing" activities.

LIQUIDITY RATIOS Ratios that show the ability to meet short-term obligations.

LIQUOR COST Amount paid for liquor after discounts.

LIQUOR COST PERCENT The portion cost divided by the selling price.

LITER Metric system measure of volume.

LOCKOUT When an employer refuses to provide opportunities to work.

LOGO Trademark.

LONG-TERM DEBT Fixed liabilities.

LOSS CONTROL Attempting to prevent losses.

M

MAITRE D' Person in charge of dining room service.

MANAGEMENT BY OBJECTIVES (MBO) Setting measurable goals with employees and periodically reviewing their progress.

MANAGEMENT PROCESS Five basic functions of planning, organizing, staffing, leading and controlling.

MANAGEMENT PROFICIENCY RATIO Net profit after taxes divided by total assets.

MANUAL Done by hand.

MARGIN The difference between the cost and the selling price.

MARGINAL COST The amount of output by which aggregate costs are changed if the volume of output is increased or decreased by one unit.

MARKET Groups with similar characteristics, wants, needs, buying power and willingness to spend for dining or drinking out.

MARKET PRICE INDEX Used to show the change in the cost of raw foods.

MARKET SHARE The share of a market that a business has for its products or services.

MARKETING Means by which an outlet is exposed to the public.

MARKETING OBJECTIVES Measurable and achievable goals that marketing efforts are intended to accomplish.

MARKETING PERSPECTIVE Consumer satisfaction is placed first in all planning, objectives, policies and operations.

MARKETING POLICY A course of action to be followed as long as conditions exist.

MARKETING SEGMENTATION Dividing the market into smaller submarkets or segments.

MARKETING STRATEGY Overall plan of action that enables the outlet to reach an objective.

MARKUP Amount by which a higher price is set.

MBWA Management by walking around.

MEASURE A lineal measure equal to a thousandth of a meter.

MEAT TAG Used for identification and verification.

MEDIA Various types of advertising, such as television, radio and newspapers.

MEDIATION Intervention using a neutral third party to help reach an agreement.

MEDICARE A federal health insurance program for people 65 or older and certain disabled people.

MENU A list of dishes served at a meal.

MENU ENGINEERING Technique that is used for analyzing menu profitability and popularity.

MENU MIX Menu popularity calculation.

MENU PREFERENCE FORECASTING Predicts how various items will sell when in competition with other items.

MENU PRICE The amount that will be charged for an item.

METRIC Pertains to the meter or to the system of weights and measures based on the meter and the kilogram.

MILL When dealing with monetary numbers, the third place to the right of the decimal.

MILLIGRAM One thousandth part of a gram.

MILLILITER One thousandth part of a liter.

MILLIMETER One thousandth part of a meter.

MISSION STATEMENT A statement giving the reason why the organization exists and what makes it different from other organizations.

MODEM ORGANIZATION THEORY A behavioral approach to organization.

MODULE A discrete and identifiable program.

MONETARY To do with money or coinage.

MOVING AVERAGE The total of demand in previous periods divided by the number of periods.

MUNICIPAL SOLID WASTE (MSW) Waste products that are deposited in landfills.

N

NATIONAL EMERGENCY STRIKES Strikes that might "imperil the national health and safety."

NET The remaining amount after deducting all expenses.

NET PRESENT VALUE (NPV) The present value of future returns discounted at the appropriate cost of capital minus the cost of the investment.

NET PROFIT Profit after all product costs, operating expenses and promotional expenses have been deducted from net sales.

NET PURCHASE PRICE The price paid by the company for one unit.

NET WORTH Excess value of resources over liabilities.

NORRIS-LAGUARDIA ACT This law marked the era of strong encouragement of unions and guaranteed each employee the right to bargain collectively "free from interference, restraint or coercion."

NUMERAL Symbol for a number.

O

OCCUPATIONAL MARKET CONDITIONS Published projections of labor supply and demand for various occupations by the Bureau of Labor Statistics of the U.S. Department of Labor.

OCCUPATIONAL SAFETY AND HEALTH ACT Law passed by Congress in 1970 assuring every working man and woman in the nation safe and healthful working conditions to preserve our human resources.

OCCUPATIONAL SAFETY AND HEALTH ADMINISTRATION (OSHA) The agency created within the Department of Labor to set safety and health standards for all workers in the United States.

ON-THE-JOB TRAINING (OJT) Training to learn a job while working it.

OPEN BAR Practice at banquet functions whereby customers are not charged individually for the drinks they consume. The host pays for banquet-goers' consumption.

OPEN DEPARTMENT REGISTER KEYS Keys that break down sales by categories.

OPEN MARKET BUYING Food purchasing method where competitive bids are secured for various items.

OPERATING BUDGET Detailed revenue and expense plan for a determined period.

OPERATING RATIO Net profit divided by net sales.

ORGANIZATIONAL CHART Shows the relationships of jobs to each other with lines of authority, responsibility and communication.

ORGANIZATIONAL DEVELOPMENT INTERVENTIONS Techniques aimed at changing employees' attitudes, values and behavior.

OUTPUT The end product.

OUTSOURCING Calling upon other companies help supply your products.

OVERHEAD-CONTRIBUTION METHOD All non-food cost percentages are subtracted from 100. The resulting figure is divided into 100 and that figure times the raw food cost equals the menu selling price.

OVERTIME Time exceeding regular hours.

P

P AND L SHEET A profit and loss statement.

PAR STOCK Stock levels established by management for individual inventory items in varying locations.

PARKINSON'S LAW Workers adjust pace to the work available.

PAYBACK PERIOD Period of time required to recover an expenditure.

PAYROLL A list of employees and amounts to pay them, as well as records pertaining to these payments.

PENSION BENEFITS GUARANTEE CORPORATION (PBGC) Established under ERISA to ensure that pensions meet vesting obligations and to insure pensions should a plan terminate without sufficient funds to meet its vested obligation.

PENSION PLANS Plans that provide a fixed sum when employees reach a predetermined retirement age or when they no longer work due to disability.

PERCENTAGE CONTROL SYSTEM Wherein the cost of food or beverage is divided by sales to provide a percentage.

PERCEPTION OF VALUE A consumer's perception of what a product is worth.

PERPETUAL Continuous, endless.

PERPETUAL INVENTORY Accounting for inventory changes. Beginning and ending inventory figures are changed along with any sales or purchases.

PHYSICAL INVENTORY A count of all items on hand.

PIECEWORK The system of pay based on the number of items produced by each individual worker.

POINT-OF-SALE (POS) SYSTEM A sales transaction register and processor.

POPULARITY INDEX Total sales of an item divided by total number of that item sold.

PORTION One serving.

PORTION CONTROL Ensures that the correct amount is being served each time.

PORTION COST The cost of one serving.

PORTION SERVED The amount served to a customer.

PORTION SIZE A specific portion amount.

POSITION REPLACEMENT CARD A card prepared for each position in a company. Shows possible replacement candidates and their qualifications.

POTENTIAL COST Calculating what the expected cost of an item should be.

PPBSE Planning, programming, budgeting, staffing and evaluating.

PRE-CHECKING SYSTEM Independent record of what is ordered from a kitchen.

PRE-COST/PRE-CONTROL Accounting system that determines what the food cost should be, compares it with the actual food cost, and includes sales analysis.

PREFERRED PROVIDER ORGANIZATIONS (PPOS) Groups of health-care providers that contract with employers, insurance companies or third-party payers to provide medical care services at a reduced fee.

PREP YIELD PERCENTAGE The ratio of product yield after preparation to the quantity of product as purchased.

PRICE ELASTICITY The change in the rate of sales due to the change in price.

PRICE INDEXING Measures the effect of product price changes.

PRICE LOOK-UP (PLU) Assigned menu item numbers in POS systems.

PRIMAL CUT Primary division for cutting meat into smaller cuts.

PRIME COST The cost of a product after calculating and adding in labor.

PRINCIPAL Sum of money on which interest is paid.

PRIVILEGE CONTROL SYSTEM A system that permits or denies access to restricted areas.

PRO FORMA Statement prepared on the basis of anticipated results.

PROCEDURE The method of doing a task.

PRODUCT SPECIFICATION A listing of quality and service requirements necessary for each product to be purchased from a vendor.

PRODUCTION SCHEDULE The items and quantities that must be produced for a specific meal, day, etc.

PROFILE Data creating an outline of significant features.

PROFIT Gain.

PROPORTION The relationship between one thing and another with regard to size, number or amount.

PROPRIETORSHIP Ownership.

PSYCHOGRAPHIC SEGMENTATION Segmentation based on lifestyles.

PURCHASE SPECIFICATIONS Standard requirements established for procuring items from suppliers.

PURVEYOR One who supplies provisions or food.

Q

QUALITY CONTROL Assuring the execution of tasks and responsibilities according to established standards.

QUANTITATIVE FORECASTING Forecasting based on past and present numerical data.

QUANTITATIVE METHODS Using numbers to help make decisions.

QUANTITY The amount; how much.

QUICK RATIO Current assets less inventory value divided by current liabilities.

R

RANDOM WALK Assuming a present period of sales will be the same as a past period.

RANKING METHOD Ranks each job relative to all other jobs.

RATIO The ratio between two quantities is the number of times one contains the other.

RATIO ANALYSIS A technique for determining staff needs by using ratios between sales volume and the number of employees needed.

REACH Percentage of people in a target audience who will see or hear a specific advertising message.

RECEIPT A written statement that something has been received.

RECEIVING REPORT A report that indicates the value and quantity of items received.

RECIPE Directions used for preparing a menu item.

RECIPE COST The total cost of all ingredients in a recipe.

RECIPE YIELD The weight, count or volume of food that a recipe will produce.

RECONSTITUTE Put back into original form, especially by rehydration.

RED-LINING Placing a red mark on a guest check so it cannot be used again.

REENGINEERING To change an enterprise to be more customer oriented or more efficient.

REPORT An account of facts used to give or get information.

REQUISITION To apply for something needed.

RESIDUAL INCOME ANALYSIS (RIA) Comparing the return on an investment to the cost of invested capital.

RETURN ON INVESTMENT A ratio found by dividing profit by investment.

REVENUE Income.

REVENUE CENTER Outlet or department that produces revenue.

RFP Request for proposal.

ROI (RETURN ON INVESTMENT) Incremental sales dollars divided by total costs.

ROP (RUN OF PAPER/RUN OF PRESS) Placement of advertisement anywhere within a publication that the publisher elects.

ROTATING MENU A menu that alternates in a series. Usually set up on a yearly basis.

S

SALARY A regular payment for services rendered.

SALES MIX The number of sales of individual menu items.

SALES REVENUE Money from the sale of certain items.

SCATTER PLOT Helps identify the relationship between two variables.

SEAT TURNOVER The number of times a seat is occupied during a meal period. Calculate by dividing the number of guests seated by the number of available seats.

SENSIBLE HEAT Heat measured by a thermometer.

SERVER BANKING When the server or bartender also does the cashier duties.

SHRINKAGE The amount of food lost due to cooking, dehydration or theft.

SHRINKAGE (INVENTORY) The difference between what is on hand and what should be on hand.

SIMPLE RANKING SYSTEM Ranking jobs in order of difficulty or importance.

SIMPLIFY To make easier to understand or carry out.

SMART CARD A credit card with a computer chip that holds data.

SOCIAL APPROACH TO MANAGEMENT Considers management's responsibilities to employees, customers and community as well as to its stockholders.

SOLO INSERT Usually printed on different stock than that used by the publication, this page is printed by the advertiser and inserted into a magazine or newspaper by the publisher.

SOLVENCY RATIOS Ratios that show an organization can meet its long-term debt obligations.

SPECIFICATION A detailed statement of the particulars of an item.

SPILLAGE The alcohol lost during the drink making process.

SPOILAGE Loss due to poor food handling.

STAFF MANAGER The manager who assists and advises line managers.

STAGGERED SCHEDULING Scheduling employees to start and stop at different times according to the work pattern.

STAGGERED STAFFING Employees are staffed according to business volume.

STANDARD HOUR PLAN An employee is paid a basic hourly rate and an extra percentage of his or her base rate for production exceeding the standard.

STANDARD RECIPE Producing a particular food or drink item by a definite formula.

STANDARD-COST METHOD (BEVERAGE) Determines the cost of beverages from the number of each beverage sold then compares it to the cost of beverage requisitions.

STANDARDIZE To make the same in size, shape, weight, quality, quantity, etc.

STANDARDIZED RECIPE Directions describing the way an establishment prepares a particular dish.

STANDARD-SALES METHOD (BEVERAGE) Comparing actual beverage sales with the sales value of the beverage.

STANDING ORDER An order for delivery that is automatic.

STATEMENT OF INCOME Shows whether an operation has made or lost money.

STATIC MENU A menu that rarely changes.

STEPPED COSTS Costs which increase in elongated steps but at regular intervals.

STOCK OPTION The right to purchase a stated number of shares in a company at today's price at a future time.

STOCKHOLDER The owner of stocks or shares in a company.

STOREROOM PURCHASES Items are placed into storage rather than sent to the kitchen.

STORES (FOOD COST) The value of food that is in storage.

STRAIGHT LINE METHOD Used when figuring depreciation on an item.

STRATEGIC CHANGE A change in a company's strategy, mission or vision.

SUMMARIZE Briefly express, stating the main points.

SUNK COSTS Costs already incurred that cannot be recouped.

SYSTEM Components working together in the most efficient way.

T

TABLE D'HOTE A complete meal at a set price.

TARGET FOOD COST The amount a company hopes to spend for a particular menu item.

TENDER KEYS Cash register keys that break down sales by payment method.

THERM 100,000 Btu.

TIE-INS Joint venture promotions involving your company and another.

TIME AND MOTION STUDY A study done to establish a standard time for each job.

TIPPING FEE The cost of disposing of waste at a landfill.

TITLE VII OF THE 1964 CIVIL RIGHTS ACT States that an employer cannot discriminate on the basis of race, color, religion, sex or national origin.

TOP DOWN BUDGET A budget prepared by upper management and "passed on" to operating units.

TOTAL QUALITY MANAGEMENT (TQM) A program aimed at maximizing customer satisfaction through continuous improvements.

TRAINING Teaching new employees the basic skills needed to perform their jobs.

TREND ANALYSIS Study of a company's past employment needs over a time period of years to predict future needs.

TRIM The part or quantity of a product removed during preparation.

TRIPLICATE Three identical copies.

TUMBLE CHILL SYSTEM Pumpable foods prepared with steam kettles and then rapidly chilled.

U

U.S. SYSTEM The system of measurement used in the United States, whereby weight is measured in pounds and ounces, and volume is measured in cups and gallons.

UNIFORM PRODUCT CODE (UPC) A computer readable code on a package.

UNIT Refers to the number or amount in a package.

UNIT COST The purchase price divided by the applicable unit.

USABLE PORTION The part of a fabricated product that has value.

USAGE METHOD (OF FOOD PURCHASING) Purchasing food based on past consumption.

V

VARIABLE COST The production cost that changes in direct proportion to sales volume.

VARIABLE EMPLOYEES Employees whose time requirements change with changes in business volume.

VARIABLE RATE Variable costs divided by sales.

VARIATION The extent to which a thing changes, or the change itself.

VENDOR The person or company who sells.

VERBALLY Expressed in words.

VERSATILE Easily changing or turning from one action to another.

VERTICAL Straight up and down.

VOLUME Calculated as length times width times height.

VOUCHER Evidence of payment in written form such as a receipt.

W

WAGES The amount paid or received for work.

WEIGHT The measurement of mass or heaviness of an item.

WELL DRINK A drink not made with name-brand liquor.

WITHHOLDING TAX The deduction from a person's paycheck for the purpose of paying income taxes.

WORK SAMPLES Job tasks used in testing an applicant's performance.

WORK SIMPLIFICATION Finding the easiest and most productive way to perform a job or task.

WORKING CAPITAL The difference between current assets and current liabilities.

X

X MODE Allows reports to be produced on the POS register without resetting totals.

Y

YIELD The total created or the amount remaining after fabrication. The usable portion of a product.

YIELD CONVERSION FACTORS A factor that when multiplied by the gross weight amount of an item purchased shows how much will be available.

YIELD PERCENTAGE/YIELD FACTOR The ratio of the usable amount to the amount purchased.

Z

Z MODE Produces final reports and clears information from a POS register.

ZERO-BASED BUDGET A budget prepared without previous budget figures.

INDEX

F

G

H

N

O

OSHA, C7-28
overhead, C11-5
overscheduling, C13-17
overtime, C17-5
Owner, C4-5

P

promotion, C1-20, C2-4, C3-2
promotions, C1-6, C15-6
proof, C8-6
property taxes, C17-8
prospective applicant, C13-7
protection, C17-6
public relations, C1-6, C3-6, C14-1
public utilities, C1-23
publicity, C3-2
punch cards, C15-8
purchase agreement, C1-2
purchase ledger, C16-8
purchasing, C4-14, C6-1, C6-7, C7-5
purified water, C8-9
purveyors, C1-28

Q

quality, C8-19
questions, C13-4
quick-chilling, C7-13
Quickbooks accounting software, C1-22, C11-7, C16-2, C16-14

R

radio, C14-5, C17-9
RAM, C11-2
ratio of food to beverage sales, C4-7
rats, C7-23
raw ingredients, C7-2
real estate, C2-1, C2-2
receipt, C6-17
receivables, C2-8
receiving, C4-3, C6-1, C6-8, C7-5
Recipe and Procedure Manual, C5-12
recipes, C8-16, C11-5
records, C4-15
recycling, C1-27
red wine, C9-2
reduction, C4-3
refrigerated storage, C7-7
refrigeration systems, C1-28
register, C6-15

regulations, C12-26
reheating, C7-13
rejecting applicants, C13-8
rejection, C13-7
renovations, C2-12
rent, C17-8
repairs, C17-8
reporter, C14-4
reports, C3-4
repurchase agreement, C2-9
reservations, C12-21, C14-6
restaurant designer, C13-19
restrooms, C7-17, C15-5
return on investment, C11-12
revenue, C16-10
reversion assets, C2-2
right, C12-13
rimmed, C8-7
rinsing, C7-14
rodents, C7-23
rosé, C9-3
rotation procedures, C6-4, C6-9
rough preparation, C4-3
royalty, C3-3
rum, C8-4
rye, C8-2

S

S corporations, C1-11
safe combinations, C1-24
safe cooking, C7-10
salad, C12-16, C15-5
salad preparer, C6-6
salaries, C1-8, C3-8
sales, C15-1
sales check, C12-19
sales contract, C2-22
sales mix, C4-7
sales price, C2-16
sales records, C18-1
sales report, C16-10
sales representative, C1-22

STATE RESTAURANT ASSOCIATIONS

Offices outside of the U.S are located at the end of the list.

ALABAMA

Alabama Restaurant and Foodservice Association
P.O. Box 230207
Montgomery, AL 36123-0207
334-244-1320
FAX: 334-271-4621

Physical Address:
2000 Interstate Park Dr., Suite 402
Montgomery, AL 36109

ALASKA

Alaska Cabaret, Hotel and Restaurant Association
341 East 56th Avenue
Anchorage, AK 99518
901-563-8133
FAX: 907-563-8640

ARIZONA

Arizona Restaurant Association
2701 N 16th Street, Suite 221
Phoenix, AZ 85006
602-234-0701
FAX: 602-266-6043

ARKANSAS

Arkansas Hospitality Association
603 Pulaski Street
P.O. Box 3866
LIttle Rock, AR 72203-3866
501-376-2323
FAX: 501-376-6517

CALIFORNIA

California Restaurant Association
3435 Wilshire Blvd., Suite 2230
Los Angeles, CA 90010
213-384-1200 • 800-794-4272
FAX: 213-384-1623

California Restaurant Association, Government Affairs
980 9th Street, Suite 1480
Sacramento, CA 95814
916-447-5793 • 800-765-4842 (in CA)
FAX: 916-447-6182

Golden Gate Restaurant Association
415-781-5348

State Restaurant Association of California (CALSRA)
P.O. Box 418446
Sacramento, CA 95841
888-994-2257
FAX: 888-993-2922

Western Restaurant Association (CALSRA)
P.O. Box 418446
Sacramento, CA 95841
888-994-2257 • 888-994-2257
FAX: 888-993-2922

American Restaurant Association (CALSRA)
P.O. Box 418446
Sacramento, CA 95841
888-994-2257
FAX: 888-993-2922

COLORADO

Colorado Restaurant Association
899 Logan Street, Suite 300
Denver, CO 80203
303-030-2972
FAX: 303-830-2973

CONNECTICUT

Connecticut Restaurant Association
731 Hebron Avenue
Glastonbury, CT 06033
203-633-5484
FAX: 203-657-8241

DELAWARE

Delaware Restaurant Association
P.O. Box 7838
Newark, DE 19714-7838
302-366-8565
FAX: 302-738-8865

Physical Address:
Five Embry Court
Drummond North
Newark, DE 19711

DISTRICT OF COLUMBIA

Restaurant Association of Metropolitan Washington, Inc.
7926 Jones Branch Dr., Suite 530
McLean, VA 22102-3303
703-356-1315
FAX: 703-893-4926

FLORIDA

Florida Restaurant Association
200 West College Avenue
Tallahassee, FL 32301
904-224-2250
FAX: 904-222-9213

GEORGIA

Georgia Hospitality and Travel Association
600 W Peachtree St., Suite 1500
Atlanta, GA 30308
404-873-4482
FAX: 404-874-5742

HAWAII

Hawaii Restaurant Association
1188 Bishop Street, Suite 1507
Honolulu, HI 96813
808-536-9105
FAX: 808-534-0117

IDAHO

Idaho Hospitality & Travel Association, Inc.
P.O. Box 7587
Boise, ID 83707
208-362-2637 • 800-959-2637 (in ID)
FAX: 208-362-0855

Physical Address
4930 Umarilla • Boise, ID 83709

ILLINOIS

Illinois Restaurant Association
350 W Ontario
Chicago, IL 60610
312-787-4000
FAX: 312-787-4792

INDIANA

Restaurant and Hospitality Association of Indiana
115 W Washington St., Suite 11655
Indianapolis, IN 46204
317-673-4211
FAX: 317-673-4210

IOWA

Iowa Hospitality Association
606 Merle Hay Tower
Des Moines, IA 50310
515-276-1454
FAX: 515-276-3660

KANSAS

Kansas Restaurant and Hospitality Association
359 S Hydraulic
Wichita, KS 67211
316-267-8383
FAX: 316-267-8400

KENTUCKY

Kentucky Restaurant Association
422 Executive Park
Louisville, KY 40207
502-896-0464
FAX: 502-896-0465

LOUISIANA

Louisiana Restaurant Association
2700 N Arnoult
Metairie, LA 70002
504-454-2277
FAX: 504-454-2299

MAINE

Maine Restaurant Association
Five Wade Street
P.O. Box 5060
Augusta, ME 04330-0552
207-623-2178
FAX: 207-623-8377

MARYLAND

Restaurant Association of Maryland, Inc.
7113 Ambassador Road
Baltimore, MD 21244
410-298-0011
FAX: 410-298-0299
www.marylandrestaurants.com

MASSACHUSETTS

Massachusetts Restaurant Association
95-A Turnpike Road
Westborough, MA 01581-9775
508-366-4144 • 800-852-3042 (in MA)
FAX: 508-366-4614

Massachusetts Restaurant Association, Government Affairs
141 Tremont Street, 6th Floor
Boston, MA 02111
617-426-1081
FAX: 617-426-8564

MICHIGAN

Michigan Restaurant Association
225 W Washtenaw Street
Lansing, MI 48933
800-968-9668

MINNESOTA

Minnesota Restaurant Association
871 Jefferson Avenue
Street Paul, MN 55102
612-222-7401
FAX: 612-222-7347

MISSISSIPPI

Mississippi Restaurant Association
P.O. Box 16395
Jackson, MS 39236
601-982-4281
FAX: 601-982-0062

MISSOURI

Missouri Restaurant Association
P.O. Box 10277
Kansas City, MO 64171
816-753-5222
FAX: 816-753-6993

Physical Address:
4049 Pennsylvania Ave., Suite 201
Kansas City, MO 64111

MONTANA

Montana Restaurant Association
1537 Avenue D, Suite 320
Billings, MT 59102
406-256-1105
FAX: 406-256-0785

Physical Address:
3495 W Broadway
Missoula, MT 59802

NEBRASKA

Nebraska Restaurant Association
5625 "O" St. Building, Suite 7
Lincoln, NE 68510
402-483-2630
FAX: 402-483-2746

NEVADA

Nevada Restaurant Association
4820 Alpine Place, Suite B202
Las Vegas, NV 89107
702-878-2313
FAX: 702-878-5009

NEW HAMPSHIRE

New Hampshire Lodging and Restaurant Association
4 Park Street, Suite 413
P.O. Box 1175
Concord, NH 03301
603-228-9585
FAX: 603-226-1829

NEW JERSEY

New Jersey Restaurant Association
One Executive Drive, Suite 100
Somerset, NJ 08873
908-302-1800
FAX: 908-302-1804

NEW MEXICO

New Mexico Restaurant Association
7800 Marble NE, Suite 4
Albuquerque, NM 87110
505-268-2474
FAX: 505-268-5848

NEW YORK

New York State Restaurant Association
505 Eighth Avenue, 7th Floor
New York, NY 10018
212-714-1330
FAX: 212-643-2962

New York State Restaurant Association
455 New Karner Road
Albany, NY 12205
800-452-5212
FAX: 518-452-4497

NORTH CAROLINA

North Carolina Restaurant Association
P.O. Box 6528
Raleigh, NC 27628
919-782-5022
FAX: 919-782-7251

Physical Address:
3105 Charles B. Root Wynd
Raleigh, NC 27612

NORTH DAKOTA

North Dakota State Hospitality Association
P.O. Box 428
Bismarck, ND 58502
701-223-3313
FAX: 701-223-0215

Physical Address:
919 S. 7th Street, Suite 601
Bismarck, ND 58504

OHIO

Ohio Restaurant Association
1525 Bethel Road, Suite 301
Columbus, OH 43215
614-442-3535 • 800-282-9049
FAX: 614-442-3550

OKLAHOMA

Oklahoma Restaurant Association
3800 N Portland
Oklahoma City, OK 73112
405-942-8181
FAX: 405-942-0541

OREGON

Oregon Restaurant Association
8565 SW Salish Lane, Suite 120
Wilsonville, OR 97070
503-682-4422
FAX: 503-682-4455

PENNSYLVANIA

Pennsylvania Restaurant Association
100 State Street
Harrisburg, PA 17101-1024
717-232-4433 • 800-346-7767
FAX: 717-236-1202

RHODE ISLAND

Rhode Island Hospitality Association
P.O. Box 6208
Providence, RI 02940
401-732-4881
FAX: 401-732-4883

Physical Address:
1206 Jefferson Blvd.
Warwick, RI 02886

SOUTH CAROLINA

South Carolina Restaurant Association
Barringer Building, Suite 505
1338 Main Street
Columbia, SC 29201
803-765-9000
FAX: 803-252-7136

SOUTH DAKOTA

South Dakota Restaurant Association
P.O. Box 638
Pierre, SD 57501
605-224-5050

FAX: 605-224-2059

Physical Address:
320 E Capitol
Pierre, SD 57501

TENNESSEE

Tennessee Restaurant Association
P.O. Box 681207
Franklin, TN 37068-1207
615-790-2703
FAX: 615-790-2768

Physical Address:
1224-A Lakeview Drive
Franklin, TN 37064

TEXAS

Texas Restaurant Association
P.O. Box 1429
Austin, TX 78767
512-472-3666
FAX: 512-472-2777

Physical Address
1400 Lavaca
Austin, TX 78701

UTAH

Utah Restaurant Association
1555 E Stratford Street, #100
Salt Lake City, UT 84115
801-487-4821
FAX: 801-467-5170

VERMONT

Vermont Lodging and Restaurant Association
Route 100 N R1, #1522
Waterbury, VT 05676
802-244-1344
FAX: 802-244-1342

VIRGINIA

Virginia Hospitality and Travel Association-Restaurant Division
2101 Libbie Avenue
Richmond, VA 23230
804-288-3065
FAX: 804-285-3093

WASHINGTON

Restaurant Association of the State of Washington, Inc.
2405 Evergreen Park Drive SW
Suite A2
Olympia, WA 98502
360-956-7279
FAX: 360-357-9232

WEST VIRGINIA

West Virginia Hospitality and Travel Association
P.O. Box 2391
Charleston, WV 25328
304-342-6511
FAX: 304-345-1538

Physical Address:
20003 Quarrier Street
Charleston, WV 25311

WISCONSIN

Wisconsin Restaurant Association
2801 Fish Hatchery Road
Madison, WI 53713
608-270-9950 • 800-589-3211
FAX: 608-270-9960
http://www.wirestaurant.org

WYOMING

Wyoming Lodging & Restaurant Association
P.O. Box 1003
Cheyenne, WY 82003-1003
307-634-8816
FAX: 307-632-0249

Physical Address:
211 W 19th, Suite 201
Cheyenne, WY 82001

OUTSIDE OF U.S.

CANADA

Canadian Restaurant & Foodservices Association
316 Bloor Street W
Toronto, Ontario Canada
M5S 1W5
416-923-1450
FAX: 416-923-1450

ONTARIO

Ontario Restaurant Association
121 Richmond Street W
Suite 1201
Toronto, Ontario Canada M6S 2P2
416-359-0533
FAX: 416-359-0531

U.S. VIRGIN ISLANDS

Virgin Islands Restaurant & Bar Association
c/o Virgin Rhythms Public Relations
P.O. Box 12048
St. Thomas, VI 00801
809-777-6161
FAX: 809-777-6036

PUERTO RICO

Puerto Rico Hotel and Tourism Association
954 Ponce de Leon Avenue
Suite 703
San Juan, PR 00907-3605
805-725-2901

Bar & Beverage Business Magazine
Mercury Publications
1839 Inkster Blvd.
Winnipeg, Manitoba R2X 1R3

Bartender Magazine
Foley Publishing Corporation
P.O. Box 158
Liberty Corner, NJ 07938-0158

Beer, Wine & Spirits Beverage
Retailer
Oxford Publishing
307 W Jackson Avenue
Oxford, MS 38655

Beverage & Food Dynamics
Adams Business Media
1180 Avenue of the Americas
11th Floor
New York, NY 10036-8401

Beverage Bulletin
6310 San Vicente Blvd., Suite 530
Los Angeles, CA 90048

Beverage World Periscope
Keller International Publishing
Corporation
150 Great Neck Road
Great Neck, NY 11021

Center of the Plate
American Culinary Foundation
10 San Bartola Drive
St. Augustine, FL 32086-5766

Cheers
Adams Business Media
50 Washington Street, 10th Floor
Norwalk, CT 06854

Chef
Talcott Communication Corp.
20 N Wacker Drive, #1865
Chicago, IL 60606-2905

Coffee & Cuisine
1218 3rd Avenue, #1315
Seattle, WA 98101-3021

Consultant
Foodservice Consultants Society
International
304 W Liberty, Suite 201
Louisville, KY 40202-3011

Cooking For Profit
CP Publishing
P.O. Box 267
Fond du Lac, WI 54936-0267

Correction Foodservice
International Publishing Company
of America
665 La Villa Drive
Miami, FL 33166-6095

Council on Hotel, Restaurant &
Institutional Education Communique
Council on Hotel, Restaurant &
Institutional Education
3205 Skipwith Road
Richmond, VA 23294-3006

Culinary Trends
Culinary Trends Publications
6285 Spring Street, 107
Long Beach, CA 90808-4000

El Restaurante Mexicano
Maiden Name Press
P.O. Box 2249
Oak Park, IL 60303-2249

Fancy Foods & Culinary Products
Talcott Communication
Corporation
20 N Wacker Drive, #1865
Chicago, IL 60606-2905

FEDA News & Views
Foodservice Equipment
Distributors Association
223 W Jackson Blvd., #620
Chicago, IL 60606-6911

Food & Beverage News
886 W Bay Drive, #E6
Largo, FL 33770-3017

Food Arts Magazine
M Shanken Communications
387 Park Avenue S, 8th Floor
New York, NY 10016-8872

Food Businesses: Snack Shops, Speciality
Food Restaurants & Other Ideas
Prosperity & Profits Unlimited
P.O. Box 416
Denver, CO 80201-0416

Food Channel
Noble & Associates
515 N State Street, 29th Floor
Chicago, IL 60610-4325

Food Distribution Research Society
News
Silesia Companies
P.O. Box 441110
Fort Washington, MD 20749-1110

Food Distributors International
201 Park Washington Court
Falls Church, VA 22046-4519

Food Management
Donohue/Meehan Publishing
The Penton Media Building
1300 E 9th Street
Cleveland, OH 44114-1503

Food Service Equipment and Supplies
Specialist
Cahners Business Information
2000 Clearwater Drive
Oak Brook, IL 60523

FoodService and Hospitality
23 Lesmill Road, Suite 101
Toronto, Ontario M3B 3P6

Foodservice Equipment and Supplies
Cahners Business Information
1350 East Touhy Avenue
Des Plaines, IL 60018

FoodTalk
Pike & Fischer
1010 Wayne Avenue, Suite 1400
Silver Springs, MD 20910

Fresh Cup Magazine
P.O. Box 14827
Portland, OR 97293-0827

Frozen Food Executive
National Frozen Food Association
4755 Linglestown Road, Suite 300
Harrisburg, PA 17112-8526

Healthcare Foodservice
International Publishing Company
of America
665 La Villa Drive
Miami, FL 33166-6095

Hotel, Restaurant, Institutional Buyers
Guide
Urner Barry Publications
P.O. Box 389
Toms River, NJ 08754-0389

International Association of Food
Industry Suppliers
1451 Dolly Madison Boulevard
McLean, VA 22101

Journal of Food Protection
International Association for Food
Protection
6200 Aurora Avenue, Suite 200W
Des Moines, IA 50322-2863

Journal of Restaurant and Foodservice
Marketing
Haworth Press
21 E Broad Street
West Hazelton, PA 18201-3809

Midwest Foodservice News
Pinnacle Publishing
2736 Sawbury Blvd.
Columbus, OH 43235

National Association of
Concessionaries
35 E Wacker Drive, Suite 1816
Chicago, IL 60601-2270

National Culinary Review
American Culinary Federation
10 San Bartola Drive
St. Augustine, FL 32086-5766

National Dipper
US Exposition Corp.
1841 Hicks Road, #C
Rolling Meadows, IL 60008-1215

Nation's Restaurant News
Lebhar Friedman
425 Park Avenue
New York, NY 10022-3506

Nightclub & Bar Magazine
Oxford Publishing
307 W Jackson Avenue
Oxford, MS 38655

On Campus Hospitality
Executive Business Media
825 Old Country Road
P.O. Box 1500
Westbury, NY 11590

Onboard Services
International Publishing Company
of America
665 La Villa Drive
Miami, FL 33166-6095

OnSite
Nation's Restaurant News
3922 Coconut Palm Drive
Tampa, FL 33619-8321

Pizza Today
ProTech Publishing &
Communications
P.O. Box 1347
New Albany, IN 47151-1347

Prepared Foods
Cahners Business Information
2000 Clearwater Drive
Oak Brook, IL 60523

Restaurant Business
Bill Communications
353 Park Avenue S
New York, NY 10010-1706

Restaurant Digest
Panagos Publishing
3930 Knowles Avenue, #305
Kensington, MD 20895-2428

Restaurant Hospitality
Penton Media
The Penton Media Building
1300 East 9th Street
Cleveland, OH 44114-1503

Restaurant Management Today
Atcom
1541 Morris Avenue
Bronx, NY 10457-8702

Restaurant Marketing
Oxford Publishing
307 W Jackson Avenue
Oxford, MS 38655

Restaurant Wine
Wine Profits
P.O. Box 222
Napa, CA 94559-0222

Restaurants & Institutions
Cahners Business Information
1350 East Touhy Avenue
Des Plaines, IL 60018

Restaurants USA
National Restaurant Association
1200 17th Street NW
Washington, D.C. 20036-3006

Restaurants, Resorts & Hotels
Publishing Group
P.O. Box 318
Trumbull, CT 06611-0318

Showcase Magazine
National Association for the
Specialty Food Trade
120 Wall Street, 27th Floor
New York, NY 10005-40001

Southern Beverage Journal
14337 SW 119th Avenue
Miami, FL 33186-6006

Wine on Line Food and Wine Review
Enterprise Publishing
138 N 16th Street
Blair, NE 68008

Yankee Food Service
Griffin Publishing Company
616 Main Street
Dennis, MA 02638

Other great books available from Atlantic Publishing:

1-800-541-1336 Call toll-free 24 hours a day, 7 days a week. Or fax completed form to: **1-352-622-5836.** Order Online!
Just go to **www.atlantic-pub.com** for fast, easy, secure ordering.

This new series from the editors of the Food Service Professional Magazine are the best and most-comprehensive books for serious food service operators available today. These step-by-step guides on specific management subjects are easy to read, easy to understand and will take the mystery out of the subject. The information is "boiled down" to the essence. They are filled to the brim with up-to-date and pertinent information. These books cover all the bases, providing clear explanations and helpful, specific information. All titles in the series include the phone numbers and Web sites of all companies discussed.

SOFTWARE GUIDE

SAVE 40%
EMPLOYEE HANDBOOK CREATOR GUIDE
Finally, a cost-effective solution for developing your own employee handbook. Simply review the 100-plus policies already written for you and insert your own information when prompted. Complete with table of contents, introduction and a form for each employee to sign. Use with Windows or any word processor.

Item #EHB-CS ~~$99.95~~ **Sale $59.95**

Qty	Order Code	Book Title	Price	Total
	Item # EHB-CS	Employee Handbook Creator Guide	$59.95	
	Item # FS1-01	Restaurant Site Location	$19.95	
	Item # FS2-01	Buying & Selling A Restaurant Business	$19.95	
	Item # FS3-01	Restaurant Marketing & Advertising	$19.95	
	Item # FS4-01	Restaurant Promotion & Publicity	$19.95	
	Item # FS5-01	Controlling Operating Costs	$19.95	
	Item # FS6-01	Controlling Food Costs	$19.95	
	Item # FS7-01	Controlling Labor Costs	$19.95	
	Item # FS8-01	Controlling Liquor Wine & Beverage Costs	$19.95	
	Item # FS9-01	Building Restaurant Profits	$19.95	
	Item # FS10-01	Waiter & Waitress Training	$19.95	
	Item # FS11-01	Bar & Beverage Operation	$19.95	
	Item # FS12-01	Successful Catering	$19.95	
	Item # FS13-01	Food Service Menus	$19.95	
	Item # FS14-01	Restaurant Design	$19.95	
	Item # FS15-01	Increasing Rest. Sales	$19.95	
	Item # FSALL-01	**Entire 15-Book Series**	**$199.95**	

Best Deal! **SAVE 33%**
15 GUIDE TO SERIES books for $199.95

Subtotal	
Shipping & Handling	
Florida 6% Sales Tax	
TOTAL	

SHIP TO:

Name_____ Phone(_____) _____

Company Name_____

Mailing Address _____

City_____ State _____ Zip _____

FAX _____ E-mail _____

❑ My check or money order is enclosed   ❑ Please send my order COD   ❑ My authorized purchase order is attached

❑ Please charge my: ❑ Mastercard ❑ VISA ❑ American Express ❑ Discover

Card # ☐☐☐☐ – ☐☐☐☐ – ☐☐☐☐ – ☐☐☐☐   Expires ☐☐☐☐

Please make checks payable to: **Atlantic Publishing Company** • 1210 SW 23 Place • Ocala, FL 34474-7014
USPS Shipping/handling: add $5.00 first item, $2.50 each additional or $15.00 for the whole set. Florida residents PLEASE add the appropriate sales tax for your county.

THE FOOD SERVICE PROFESSIONAL'S DIRECTORY OF FOOD-SERVICE SUPPLIERS, MANUFACTURERS & DISTRIBUTORS

Atlantic Publishing has exhaustively searched the food service industry for all companies that provide products and/or services. This is the most comprehensive resource for finding companies and products manufactured in North America. Companies are listed alphabetically. We have provided Web sites and e-mail addresses if available.

Help us help you! If you know some data that has changed or know of a company that should be listed, please use the form below and contact us via our toll free fax at 877-682-7819.

EDIT DIRECTORY OF FOOD-SERVICE SUPPLIERS FORM

❏ Please add a new listing   ❏ Please edit/append my listing on page # _____

Your Name: _____

Organization Name: _____

Address: _____

_____

City: _____ State: _____ Zip: _____

Telephone: _____ Fax: _____

Web site URL: _____

E-mail Address: _____

Comments: _____

_____

_____

_____

Please fax this form to 877-682-7819

$2.95 GUYS
13750 Stowe Dr.
Poway, CA 92064-8828
www.295guys.com
800-536-5959 • Fax 858-513-7018

1ST BANK TRUST
909 Poydras St Ste 100
New Orleans, LA 70112-4020
504-584-5975

20-10
3049 Industrial Way NE
Salem, OR 97303-4289
503-399-2010

3M COMPANY
3M M # 220
Saint Paul, MN 55144-0001
651-733-8581

3M/PACKAGING
3M Center
Saint Paul, MN 55144-1001
651-733-1110

3M COMPANY
3M Center Bldg 223-4N-15
Saint Paul, MN 55144-1000
www.3m.com
800-698-4595 • Fax 800-447-0408

3M COMPANY
223 Building 3N 05 3
Saint Paul, MN 55144-0001
612-736-3836 • Fax 651-733-4012

5TH AVENUE CHOCOLATIERE
27 72nd St
Brooklyn, NY 11209-1801
e-mail: rspay@aol.com
718-921-4770 • Fax 212-563-2749

86.COM
201 N Union St Ste 300
Alexandria, VA 22314-2642
e-mail: arubin@86.com
703-857-0286

A & A GRAPHICS
6940 Aragon Cir
Buena Park, CA 90620-1155
714-521-8784

A & E PRODUCTS CO.
4235 Richmond Ave
Houston, TX 77027-6840
www.aeproducts.com
713-621-0022

A & J CHEESE CO.
1490 Railroad St
Corona, CA 92882-6929
909-735-3321 • Fax 909-735-0311

A & S FROZEN BAKERY PROD.
25 Andrews Dr
Little Falls, NJ, 07424-2607
973-812-9422

A A SPECIALTY ADVERTISING PRODUCTS
PO Box 161821
Altamonte Springs, FL 2716-1821
407-869-4900

A B B LABELS
1010 E 18th St
Los Angeles, CA 90021-3008
www.abblabels.com
213-748-7480 • 213-748-5838

A B C O PRODUCTS
6800 NW 36th Ave
Miami, FL 33147-6504
888-694-2226

A CUSTOMERS CONNECTION
1677 Old Cahaba Ct
Helena, AL 35080-7055
205-621-9866 • Fax 205-621-9866

A D M
4666 E Faries Pkwy
Decatur, IL 62526-5678
217-424-5200

A D M MILLING CO
8000 W 110th St
Overland Park, KS 66210-2312
913-491-9400

A D M NUTRACEUTICAL
PO Box 1470
Decatur, IL 62525-1820
800-510-2178

A E I MUSIC NETWORK
900 E Pine St
Seattle, WA 98122-3844
800-831-8001

A F C SYSTEMS
1902 N 71st St
Tampa, FL 33619-3346
813-622-7834

A I G/AMER INTERNATIONAL GROUP
70 Pine St
New York, NY 10270-0002

A K O RESOURCES INC
1943 Sherwood St Ste A
Clearwater, FL 33765-1933
727-447-0073

A LA CARTE INC
10900 S Commerce Blvd # A
Charlotte, NC 28273-6322
800-762-2278

A LA CARTE INTERNATIONAL
3330 Pacific Avenue, ste 500
Virginia Beach, VA 23451-2997
757-425-6111 • Fax 757-425-8507

A LA MODE DISTRIBUTORS
150 Dempsey Rd,
Madison, WI 53714-3043
608-249-7413 • Fax 608-249-2648

A M F/BAKERY SYSTEMS
2115 W Laburnum Ave
RIchmond, VA 23227-4315
804-355-7961

A P V BAKER INC
1200 W Ash St
Goldsboro, NC 27530-9739
919-735-4570

A T KEARNEY
222 W Adams St. FL 25
Chicago, IL 60606-5239
312-648-0111 • Fax 312-223-6362

A V IMPORTS
6450 Dobbin Rd Ste G
Columbia, MD 21045-5824
800-638-7720

A V OLSSON TRADING CO. INC.
2001 W Main St Ste 21
Stamford, CT 06902-4501
e-mail: terry@avolsson.com
203-969-2090 • Fax 203-969-2098

A Y-SLIP USA CORP
2077 Sunnydale Blvd
Clearwater, FL 33765-1202
727-462-0401 • Fax 727-462-5298

A&D WEIGHING
1555 McCandless Dr
Milpitas, CA 95035-8001
www.andwighing.com
800-726-3364 • Fax 408-263-0119

A&R REPAIRS BAKERS KNEADS
24551 Ryan Rd
Warren, MI 48091-1660
586-758-4440

A.B.S. ATLANTIC ADVANCED BUILD
PO Box 545
Hillburn, NY 10931-0545
845-368-3208 • Fax 845-368-4652

A.C. FURNITURE CO. INC.
PO Box 200
Axton, VA 24054-0200
www.acfurniture.com
276-650-3356 • Fax 276-650-3747

A.C. PAPER & SUPPLY
200 Linus Pauling Dr
Hercules, CA 94547-1823
www.acpaper.com
510-527-0841 • Fax 510-527-0547

A.D.M. INTERNATIONAL INC.
5565 N Elston Ave
Chicago, IL 60630-1314
e-mail: admchigo@aol.com
www.admintl.com
773-774-2400 • Fax 773-774-2099

A.G. PETERSON ALDEN MFG
PO Box 232
Boxford, MA 01921-0232
www.agpeter53@aol.com
978-887-2895 • Fax 978-887-3539

A.J. ANTUNES & COMPANY
PO Box 87700
Carol Stream, IL 60188-7700
www.ajantunes.com
630-784-3413 • Fax 630-784-1652

A.M. MANUFACTURING
14151 Irving Ave
Dolton, IL 60419-1050
www.ammfg.com
708-841-0959 • Fax 708-841-0975

A.R. ALVAREZ ENTERPRISES
8000 W Ih 10 Ste 1150
San Antonio, TX 78230-3885
210-342-1900 • Fax 210-259-0000

A/C SUPPLY, INC
1350 Edwards Ave
New Orleans, LA 70123-2232
504-733-5600

A-1 BUSINESS SUPLIES, INC.
158 W Clinton St Ste BB
Dover, NJ 07801-3411
e-mail: salesa-1@garden.net
www.a1businesssupplies.com
800-631-3421

A-1 EXTERMINATORS
183 Shepard St
Lynn, MA 01902-4597
e-mail: pest@earthlink.net
781-592-2731 • Fax 781-592-7641

A-1 TABLECLOTH
450 Huyler St Ste 102
S Hackensack, NJ 07606-1563
800-727-8987 • Fax 201-525-2084

A-1 TABLECLOTH COMPANY
136 Berry St
Hackensack, NJ 07601-4327
e-mail: a-1@a-1tablecloth.com
201-457-1172 • Fax 201-525-2367

AAA SIGNS, INC.
3200 Cameron St
Lafayette, LA 70506-1525
www.aaasigns.com
337-233-5686 • Fax 337-221-0533

AABURCO INC
13421 Grass Valley Ave
Grass Valley, CA 95945-9516
800-533-7437

AAT SALES
360 Melvin Dr
Northbrook, IL 60062-2025
847-498-3700 • Fax 847-255-9958

AATELL & JONES
1000 Mount Laurel Cir
Shirley, MA 01464-2425
e-mail: papershark@birchpoint.com
800-231-2256 • Fax 888-216-2315

ABACUS 21
2746 Delaware Ave
Buffalo, NY 14217-2702
800-544-7310

ABACUS MARKETING, INC.
PO Box 240440
Milwaukee, WI 53224-9016
414-228-1010 • Fax 414-228-1076

ABALON EXTERMINATING CO.
386 Park Ave S
New York, NY 10016-8804
212-685-0505 • Fax 212-685-8141

ABC PEST & LAWN SERVICES
12460 Northwest Fwy
Houston, TX 77092-3114
713-730-9500 • Fax 713-316-0049

ABCON PRODUCTS
325 Westridge Dr
Watsonville, CA 95076-4169
831-728-7363 • Fax 831-761-0547

A-BEAR REFRIGERATION INC.
5740 Heebe St
New Orleans, LA 70123-5505
504-733-3600

ABFORM WORKWEAR
PO Box 53983
Lafayette, LA 70505-3983
337-261-2440

ABH DESIGN INC.
153 E 61st St
New York, NY 10021-8123
212-688-2764 • Fax 212-593-5441

ABITA BREWING CO., LLC
PO Box 1510
Abita Springs, LA 70420-1510
985-893-3143

ABLE & SCHAEFER
20 Alexander Ct
Ronkonkoma, NY 11779-6573
www.kompletusa.com
800-443-1260

ABLE & SCHAFER, INC.
2963 SW 20th St
Miami, FL 33145-2341
305-445-8557 • Fax 305-445-8557

ABLE BODY TEMPORARY SERVICES
30750 US Highway 19 N
Palm Harbor, FL 34684-4411
e--mail: dpiccini@ablebody.com
727-771-1111

ABLE CARD CORPORATION
11817 Wicks St
Sun Valley, CA 91352-1906
e-mail: sales@ablecardcorp.com
818-771-9033 • Fax 818-771-0809

ABRAMSON & DIBENEDETTO MARKETING
23 Bradford St
Concord, MA 01742-2971
e-mail: dishreps@aol.com
978-287-1400 • Fax 978-287-4619

ABSOLUTE ACTIVEWEAR
4281 Produce Rd
Louisville, KY 40218-3064
www.absolutestore.com
502-964-8912 • Fax 502-964-9267

ABSOLUTE ACTIVEWEAR & UNIFORMS
4217 Produce Rd
Louisville, KY 40218-3064
800-890-7213

ABSOLUTE ESPRESSO
6909 Ashcroft Dr Ste 102
Houston, TX 77081-5817
e-mail: absoluteespresso@mind-spring.com
www.absolute-espresso.com

AC HUMKO
7171 Goodlett Farms Pkwy
Cordova, TN 38016-4909
901-381-3000 • Fax 901-381-3067

ACCARDIS SYSTEMS INC
20061 Doolittle St
Montgomery Village, MD 20886-1313
800-852-1992 • Fax 301-330-9026

ACCENT COMMUNICATIONS
2031 E Calumet St
Appleton, WI 54915-4742
920-993-5370 • Fax 920-993-5371

ACCESS TO MONEY
628 State Route 10 Ste 5
Whippany, NJ 07981-1522
www.accesstomoney.com
973-701-9183 • Fax 973-701-0322

ACCESS TO TRADITION, INC
890 Colusa Ave
Berkeley, CA 94707-1858
www.accesstradition.com
510-525-5377

ACCESS WORLD WIRELESS SERVICES
1801 N Pine Island Rd
Ft Lauderdale, FL 33322-5205
800-840-6051

ACCU CHECK, INC.
PO Box 2864
Tuscaloosa, AL 35403-2864
www.accuchekinc.com
800-759-2034 • Fax 800-934-4923

ACCULINE
8901 NW 38th Dr
Pompano Beach, FL 33065-7806
954-646-2110 • Fax 954-752-7720

ACCU-SCAN INC
PO Box 80037
Conyers, GA 30013-8037
770-922-1220

ACCUSERV
3865 Produce Rd Ste 208
Louisville, KY 40218-6013
e-mail: epierce@accu-serv.com
502-961-0096 • Fax 877-707-7678

ACCUTEMP
9411 Tara Cay Dr
Seminole, FL 33776-1152
e-mail: philgibson@email.com
727-593-2078

ACCUTEMP PRODUCTS INC.
12004 Lincoln Hwy E
New Haven, IN 46774-9378
800-210-5907 • Fax 260-493-0318

ACCUTEMP PRODUCTS, INC.
12005 Lincoln Hwy E
New Haven, IN 46774-9378
800-875-1740 • Fax 260-416-6120

ACE MART RESTAURANT SUPPLY
PO Box 18100
San Antonio, TX 78218-0100
www.acemart.com
210-323-4400 • Fax 210-323-4401

ACE OF HEARTS IMPORTS,
6495 New Hampshire Ave Ste 318
Hyattsville, MD 20783-3286
e-mail: aceofhearts@msn.com
www.ace-of-hearts.net
301-853-8590 • Fax 301-853-8592

ACME AMERICAN REPAIRS
99 Scott Ave
Brooklyn, NY 11237-1329
www.acmegroup.net
718-456-6544 • Fax 718-366-5359

ACME ENGINEERING & MFG
PO Box 978
Muskogee, OK 74402-0978
918-682-7791

ACME REFRIGERATION
11844 S Choctaw Dr
Baton Rouge, LA 70815-2184
225-273-1740

ACME SMOKED FISH CORP.
30 Gem St
Brooklyn, NY 11222-2804
800-697-6828 • Fax 702-869-3508

ACME/MCCLAIN & SEN
4759 Durfee Ave
Pico Rivera, CA 90660-2037
562-699-4542 • Fax 562-692-0026

ACORDIA
311 Park Place Blvd
Clearwater, FL 33759-4904
800-282-3343

ACORTO
1287 120th Ave NE
Bellevue, WA 98005-2121
www.acorto.com
425-453-2800 • Fax 425-453-2167

ACP INTL LIMITED
4000 NW 39th St
Oklahoma City, OK 73112-2964
e-mail: glwolf@sb-okc.com
www.acproommate.com
405-416-3100 • Fax 405-416-3141

ACTION ENTERPRISES
1364 Ferndale Ave
Highland Park, IL 60035-2810
312-791-1969

ACTION LIGHTING
PO Box 6428
Bozeman, MT 59771-6428
406-586-5105

ACTIVE USA, INC
1349 Regal Row Ste 302
Dallas, TX 75247-3615
e-mail: dskomer@activusa.net
www.activusa.net
877-228-4879 • Fax 972-365-5414

ACURID COMMERCIAL SERVICES
3901 Braxton Dr
Houston, TX 77063-6303
www.orkin.com
713-784-2706 • Fax 713-784-2776

ACURID COMMERCIAL SERVICES
3755 68th Ave
Pinellas Park, FL 33781-6110
727-526-9450

AD ART LITHO INC MENU-GRAPHIC
3133 Chester Ave
Cleveland, OH 44114-4818
216-6961-460 • Fax 216-696-1463

ADAMATIC
607 Industrial Way W
Eatontown, NJ 07724-2213
732-544-8400

ADAMATION INC
87 Adams St
Newton, MA 02458-1188
617-244-7500 • Fax 617-244-4609

ADAMS & BROOKS INC
1915 S Hoover St
Los Angeles, CA 90007-1322
213-749-3226

ADAMS BUSINESS FORMS
200 SW Jackson St
Topeka, KS 66603-3336
www.adamsbusinessforms.com
785-233-4101 • Fax 758-232-2709

ADAMS BUSINESS MEDIACHEERS MAGAZINE
364 Wilshire Dr
Bloomfield Hills, MI 48302-1064
248-253-0108 • Fax 248-253-0164

ADAM'S MARK BUFFALO NIAGARA
120 Church St
Buffalo, NY 14202-3911
e-mail: creader@adamsmark.com
www.adamsmark.com
716-845-5100 • Fax 716-845-0310

ADDEN FURNITURE
26 Jackson St
Lowell, MA 01852-2199
978-454-7848 • Fax 978-453-1449

ADL HOSPITALITY GROUP DIV.
276 5th Ave
New York, NY 10001-4509
e-mail: adhosp@banet.net
212-684-7999 • Fax 212-545-7902

ADM COCOA
12500 W Carmen Ave
Milwaukee, WI 53225-6199
www.adamworld.com
414-358-5700 • Fax 414-358-5755

ADM ENVIRONMENTAL GROUP
1370 Coney Island Ave
Brooklyn, NY 11230-4120
e-mail: ademenvironmental@aol.com
718-951-3300 • Fax 718-951-3572

AD-MAT INTL COASTERS
PO Box 3724
Johnson City, TN 37602-3724
e-mail: cs@admat.com
www.admat.com
423-434-2373 • Fax 423-434-2210

ADMIRAL CRAFT
940 S Oyster Bay Rd
Hicksville, NY 11801-3518
800-223-7750 • Fax 516-433-4453

ADMIRAL LINEN
2030 Kipling St
Houston, TX 77098-1599
713-529-2608 • Fax 713-529-3061

ADRIANO RESTAURANT SEATING
1919 Bay S
Los Angeles, CA 90021-1604
213-627-2911 • Fax 213-627-2920

ADVANCE ENERGY TECHNOLOGIES, INC
1 Solar Dr
Clifton Park, NY 12065-3402
e-mail: advanceet@aol.com
www.advanceet.com
518-371-2140 • Fax 518-371-0737

ADVANCE FOOD CO.
3503 NW 63rd St
Oklahoma City, OK 73116-2239
405-840-0964

ADVANCE FOOD COMPANY
13800 Wireless Way
Oklahoma City, OK 73134-2501
405-775-8600 • Fax 405-775-8686

ADVANCE FOOD COMPANY
301 W Broadway Ave
Enid, OK 73701-3837
www.advf.com
580-237-6656 • Fax 580-213-4576

ADVANCE TABCO
200 Heartland Blvd
Brentwood, NY 11717-8379
631-242-4800

ADVANCED AIR SOLUTIONS
7504 Fegenbush Ln # C-1
Louisville, KY 40228-1571
www.advancedairsolutions.com
502-231-4482 • Fax 502-231-1028

ADVANCED EQUIPMENT CORP
2401 W Commonwealth Ave
Fullerton, CA 92833-2999
e-mail: sdickson@accorp.net
www.advancedequipment.com
909-635-5350 • Fax 909-525-6083

ADVANCED INTERACTIVE SYSTEMS
565 Andover Park W Ste 201
Seattle, WA 98188-3345
206-575-9797

ADVANCEME INC
1925 Vaughn Rd NW Ste 205
Kennesaw, GA 30144-4566
www.advanceme.com
888-700-8181

ADVANSTAR EXPOSITIONS
1700 E Dyer Rd
Santa Ana, CA 92705-5704
714-250-8060

ADVANTA BUSINESS SERVICES
1020 Laurel Oak Rd
Voorhees, NJ 08043-3505
800-255-0022

ADVANTAGE FOOD MARKETING CORP.
PO Box 367
Roslyn Heights, NY 11577-0367
516-625-2600 • Fax 516-625-2612

ADVANTAGE INTL. DIST.
4100 NE 2nd Ave Su
Miami, FL 33137-3528
e-mail: hiii@advantage-us-net
305-573-3132 • Fax 305-576-7428

ADVANTAGE PAYROLL SERVICES
747 Main St Ste 222
Concord, MA 01742-3326
e-mail: payrolladv@aol.com
www.advantagepayroll.com
978-318-9990 • Fax 978-318-9979

ADVANTICA
203 E Main St
Spartanburg, SC 29319-0002
864-597-8000

ADVEST
2 Jericho Plz
Jericho, NY 11753-1658
516-733-1282 • Fax 516-933-6643

ADVO SYSTEM
5172 S 13th St
Milwaukee, WI 53221-3663
414-325-2651 • Fax 414-325-2690

AEGEAN CHEESE
2606 W Oakland Ave
Austin, MN 55912-4612
507-433-1292 • Fax 507-433-1909

AEP INDUSTRIES INC
125 Phillips Ave
S Hackensack, NJ 07606-1546
800-782-3456

AERO MANUFACTURING CO
310 Allwood Rd
Clifton, NJ 07012-1786
973-473-5300

AEROBITRON
225 Oser Ave
Hauppauge, NY 11788-3710
631-851-7050

AEROGLIDE CORPORATION
PO Box 29505
Raleigh, NC 27626-0505
919-851-2000

AF ENTERPRISES
502 S Main St
Cochrane, WI 54622-9530
www.afenterprise.com
608-248-2662

AFLAC
11777 Katy Fwy Ste 100
Houston, TX 77079-1705
email: jtwrsctxs@aol.com
281-531-5288 • Fax 281-531-5281

AFLAC
1932 Wynnton Rd
Columbus, GA 31999-0002
706-660-7047

AFNAF PURCHASING OFFICE
9504 N Ih 35 Ste 370
San Antonio, TX 78233-6600
www.afanfpo.com
210-657-5804 • Fax 210-652-6309

AFTER DINNER DIST-DESSERTS ETC
2032 Plainfield Pike
Cranston, RI 02921-2013
401-944-4194

AFTERMARKET SPECIALTIES
980 Cobb Place Blvd NW
Kennesaw, GA 30144-4803
800-438-5931

AG EDWARDS & SONS, INC.
1 N Jefferson Ave
Saint Louis, MO 63103-2205
314-289-5064

AGAR SUPPLY COMPANY, INC.
225 John Hancock Rd
Taunton, MA 02780-7318
508-442-6814 • Fax 508-880-5388

AGORA ARCHITECTS
630 5th St NE
Washington, DC 20002-5202
202-337-7901

AGRIBUYS.COM
3528 Torrance Blvd
Torrance, CA 90503-4827
310-944-9655

AGRILINK FOODS
90 Linden Oaks
Rochester, NY 14625-2808
800-999-5044

AIDELLS SAUSAGE COMPANY
1625 Alvarado St
San Leandro, CA 94577-2636
510-614-5450 • Fax 510-614-2287

AIGION O&A
2538 31st St
Astoria, NY 11102-1749
718-267-8766 • Fax 718-267-8764

AIPT
10400 Little Patuxent Pkwy Ste
Columbia, MD 21044-3518
www.aipt.org
410-997-2200 • Fax 410-992-3924

AIR FRY, INC.
4100 Nine McFarland Dr # A
Alpharetta, GA 30004-3386
678-667-0115

AIR PROCESSING SERVICES
4100 N Powerline Rd
Pompano Beach, FL 33073-3083
e-mail: ftlauderdale@airpro.com
www.airpro.com
954-970-9595

AIR PURIFICATION SERVICES
4014 W Bay Villa Ave
Tampa, FL 33611-1224
e-mail: info@weclearnair.com
www.wecleanair.com
813-835-8087

AIR PURIFIERS, INC.
1086 Shore Rd
Cape Eliz, ME 04107-1921
781-788-4950 • Fax 781-788-4951

AIR QUALITY SPECIALISTS
805 Douglas Ave Ste 161
Altamonte Springs, FL 32714-2008
407-774-5700

AIRE-MASTER OF AMERICA
PO Box 2310
Nixa, MO 65714-2310
417-725-2691

AIRTECH
15400 Knoll Trail Dr
Dallas, TX 75248-3467
www.airtech.com
972-960-9400 • Fax 972-960-9488

AJ ANTUNES & CO/ROUNDUP
PO Box 206
Addison, IL 60101-0206
630-543-8650

AJAVA PINATA
4 Olde Orchard Park Apt 422
South Burlington, VT 05403-6967
802-862-7993 • Fax 802-862-7310

AJAX OF LOUISIANA
4100 Tchoupitoulas St
New Orleans, LA 70115-1435
504-891-8113

AJINOMOTO USA INC.
19675 Mariner Ave
Torrance, CA 90503-1647
310-370-2500

AK STEEL COP
703 Curtis St
Middletown, OH 45043-0001
513-425-2929 • Fax 513-425-2115

AKPHARMA/BEANO
PO Box 111
Pleasantville, NJ 08232-0111
800-257-8650

ALACK REFRIGERATION CO
1010 W Coleman Ave
Hammond, LA 70403-3922
985-345-9476

ALADDIN INDUSTRIES
703 Murfreesboro Rd
Nashville, TN 37210-3526
615-748-3442 • Fax 615-748-3163

ALADDIN SYNERGETICS
555 Marriott Dr Ste 400
Nashville, TN 37214-5066
615-748-3600

ALAIN & MARIE LENOTRE
CULINARY
7070 Allensby St
Houston, TX 77022-4322
www.lenotre-alain-marie.com
713-692-0077 • Fax 713-692-7399

ALASKA FISHERIE DEV FNDTN
900 W 5th Ave Ste 400
Anchorage, AK 99501-2048
907-276-7315

ALASKA SEAFOOD
INTERNATIONAL
6689 Seafood Dr
Anchorage, AK 99518-1578
877-245-8800

ALASKA SEAFOOD MKTG
111 W 8th St Ste 100
Juneau, AK 99801-1606
206-467-9372

ALBA SPEC SEAFOOD CO INC
233 Water St
New York, NY 10038-2016
212-349-5730

ALBUISSON ET MERE
1506 Main St
Port Jefferson, NY 11777-2236
e-mail: EricAlbuisson@aol.com
516-319-9310

ALCAN FOIL PRODUCTS
1513 Redding Dr
Lagrange, GA 30240-5719
www.foil.alcan.com
706-812-2000 • Fax 706-812-2039

ALCOHOL CONTROLS INC
1023 Havenridge Ln NE
Atlanta, GA 30319-2692
800-285-2337

ALDEN MERRILL
4 Graf Rd
Newburyport, MA 01950-4699
www.aldenmerrell.com
978-462-3248 • Fax 978-462-5367

ALECO
PO Box 589
Tuscumbia, AL 35674-0589
256-381-4970

ALESSIS BAKERY
2909 W Cypress St
Tampa, FL 33609-1699
e-mail: gary@alessibaleries.com
813-348-0128 • Fax 813-874-0828

ALEX BROWN & SONS
135 E Baltimore St
Baltimore, MD 21202-1607
410-783-3144

ALEXANDRA SHOWERS
DESIGN
1719 Costa Del Sol
Boca Raton, FL 33432-1746
e-mail: alex@boca.net
www.alexndra-showers.com
561-392-3077 • Fax 561-392-1844

ALEXIS FOODS
215 W Burnside St
Portland, OR 97209-3914
503-224-8577 • Fax 503-224-9354

ALFA INTERNATIONAL CORP.
4 Kaysal Ct
Armonk, NY 10504-1309
914-273-2222

ALGHER FOODS, INC.
4619 San Dario Ave # 382
Laredo, TX 78041-5773
956-727-0099 • Fax 956-727-0213

ALISEO INTERNATIONAL
1831 NE 146th St
Miami, FL 33181-1423
305-895-8845

ALKAR/DEC INTERNATIONAL
105 Spring St
Lodi, WI 53555-1129
608-592-3211

ALL ABOUT HOSPITALITY
65 Columbine Dr
Durango, CO 81301-8703
970-259-1424

ALL AMERICAN CANDELABRAS
18 Market St
Paterson, NJ 07501-1721
201-351-8100 • Fax 973-357-4782

ALL AMERICAN FOOD
EQUIPMENT
3210 Winter Lake Rd
Lakeland, FL 33803-9756
e-mail: hancock42@aol.com
863-665-1472 • Fax 863-667-0551

ALL AMERICAN GATOR
PRODUCTS
1883 SW 31st Ave
Hallandale, FL 33009-2021
954-894-8003

ALL AMERICAN SEASONINGS
1540 Wazee St
Denver, CO 80202-1312
e-mail: spice@qadas.com
303-623-2320 • Fax 303-623-0061

ALL COUNTY TRAPMATE
99 Maple Grange Rd
Vernon, NJ 07462-3206
973-764-6100 • Fax 973-764-9148

ALL DECK
3321 S Susan St
Santa Ana, CA 92704-6858
714-641-1340

ALL KITCHENS OF AMERICA
209 W Main St
Boise, ID 83702-7263
208-336-7003 • Fax 208-338-7180

ALL PHASE VIDEO-SECURITY
70 Cain Dr
Brentwood, NY 11717-1265
800-945-0909

ALL SEASONS UNIFORMS &
TEXTILE
3600 Hacienda Blvd Ste G
Fort Lauderdale, FL 33314-2822
e-mail: allseasons3@aol.com
954-583-5208

ALL SERVICE KITCHEN REPAIR
PO Box 310
New Hyde Park, NY 11040-0251
718-446-7866 • Fax 516-378-1735

ALL STARS CARTS & VEHICLES
1565 5th Industrial Ct
Bay Shore, NY 11706-3434
www.allstarscarts.com
631-666-5252 • Fax 631-666-1319

ALLANN BROS COFFEE CO
501 SW 2nd St
Corvallis, OR 97333-4443
541-754-7166

ALLEGIANT CORP
4191 Fayetteville Rd
Raleigh, NC 27603-3605
919-772-8604

ALLEN & CO, J W
555 Allendale Dr
Wheeling, IL 60090-2638
800-323-8271

ALLEN BROTHERS, INC.
3737 S Halsted St
Chicago, IL 60609-1609
773-890-5100

ALLEN CANNING CO
305 E Main St
Siloam Springs, AR 72761-3200
479-524-6431

ALLEN FOODS
8543 Page Ave
Saint Louis, MO 63114-6096
314-473-3128

ALLIANCE BAKERY
SYSTEMS
130 Northpoint Ct
Blythwood, SC 29016-8875
803-691-9227

ALLIANCE
HEALTHCARE
3500 Parkway Ln Ste 310
Norcross, GA 30092-2883
770-734-9255 • Fax 770-734-9253

ALLIANT
1 Technology Dr
Peabody, MA 01960-7994

ALLIANT FOODSERVICE
1125 Weems St
Pearl, MS 39208-6257
601-939-9433

ALLIANT FOODSERVICE
502 S Carty St
Salem, MO 65560-1805
573-729-6131

ALLIANT FOODSERVICE, INC.
PO Box 324
Deerfield, IL 60015-0324
708-405-8975

ALLIANT FOODSERVICES, INC
7004 E Hanna Ave
Tampa, FL 33610-9527
www.alliantlink.com
813-621-6677

ALLIED BAKERY EQUIP
12015 Slauson Ave
Santa Fe Springs, CA 90670-2607
562-945-6506

ALLIED CAPITAL EXPRESS
1919 Pennsylvania Ave NW
Washington DC 20006-3404
www.alliedcapitalexpress.com
888-657-7755 • Fax 202-659-2053

ALLIED DOMECQ- ALLIANCE
1620 Branchview Ct
Keller, TX 76248-6844
817-498-5847

ALLIED DOMECQ RETAILING
USA
14 Pacella Park Dr
Randolph, MA 02368-1756
800-777-9983

ALLIED DOMECQ SPIRITS USA
355 Riverside Ave
Westport, CT 06880-4810
203-637-6500

ALLIED DOMECQ SPRITS WINE
U S
3000 Town Ctr Ste 31
South Field, MI 48075-1120
248-948-6500 • Fax 248-948-8920

ALLIED DOMECQ WINE US
375 Healdsburg Ave
Healdsburh, CA 95448-4119
707-433-8268

ALLIED DOMEQ-EQUITY
3301 Continental Dr
Kenner, LA 70065-2613
504-463-5953

ALLIED FLOORING
3013 Bank St
Charlotte, NC 28203-5403
e-mail: cworth06162@aol.com
704-522-0597 • 800-767-5754

ALLIED METAL SPINNING
CORP.
1290 Viele Ave
Bronx, NY 10474-7133
718-893-3300 • Fax 718-589-5780

ALLIED SECURITY EQUIPMENT
5901 4th Ave S
Seattle, WA 98108-3209
e-mail: safejim@aol.com
206-777-9107 • Fax 206-767-1069

ALLIED WATER SYSTEM INC.
PO Box 364
Metairie, LA 70004-0364
504-834-1124

ALLMERICA FINANCIAL
203 Carondelet St Ste 410
New Orleans, LA 70130-3030
504-525-3427

ALLTEL
10551 Coursey Blvd
Baton Rouge, LA 70816-4040
225-291-5990 • Fax 225-293-5119

ALL-TEMP REFRIGERATION
271 Highway 1085
Madisonville, LA 70447-9559
985-898-1967

ALLTRISTA INDUSTRIAL PLASTICS
87 S Main St Ste 3
Newtown, CT 06470-2315
e-mail: sbostick@att.net
203-270-7730 • Fax 203-270-7797

ALMOND BOARD OF CA.
1150 9th St Ste 1500
Modest, CA 95354-0845
e-mail: skollmeyer@
almondboard.com
www.almondsarein.com
209-549-8262 • Fax 209-549-8267

ALMOST NEW & NEW INC
2633 Pemberton Dr
Apopka, FL 32703-9451
407-293-2288

ALOHA BY IBERTECH
1320 Tennis Dr
Bedford, TX 76022-6352
www.alohapos.com
972-252-9499 • Fax 972-252-9490

ALOHA P.O.S.
17497 Village Green Dr
Houston, TX 77040-1004
713-896-0187

ALOHA/LOUISIANA P.O.S.
2626 N Arnoult Rd Ste 206
Metairie, LA 70002-5942
504-888-7861 • Fax 504-888-2974

ALPHA BAKING CO
4545 W Lyndale Ave
Chicago, IL 60639-3492
773-489-5400 • Fax 773-489-4144

ALPHA BAKING CO.
5001 W Polk St
Chicago, IL 60644-5244
www.alphabaking.com
773-561-6000 • Fax 773-261-6065

ALPHA BAKING CO. INC
1920 E College Ave
Cudahy, WI 53110-2801
414-571-1240 • Fax 414-571-1241

ALPHA DISTRIBUTORS
4700 N Ronald St
Harwood Heights, IL 60706-3816
312-867-5200 • Fax 312-867-6870

ALPHA FOODS CO., INC.
8209 Dunlap St
Houston, TX 77074-7830
e-mail: alphafoods@hotmail.com
713-778-3019 • Fax 713-778-0122

ALPHA PRODUCTS
500 Interstate West Pkwy
Lithia Springs, GA 30122-3231
800-888-8018

ALPINE INDUSTRIES
4546 American Way
Cottage Grove, WI 53527-9734
608-839-5447 • Fax 608-839-5628

ALPINE LACE
PO Box 64101
Saint Paul, MN 55164-0101
800-328-9680 • Fax 651-481-2969

AL'S FAMOUS FILLED BAGELS
9990 SW 77th Ave Ph 8
Miami, FL 33156-2661
305-271-5865 • Fax 305-270-1674

ALSTON QUALITY INDUSTRIES
1200 Fuller Rd
Linden, NJ 07036-5774
e-mail: aqi1200@aol.com
908-925-2000

ALTA DENA DAIRY
17637 Valley Blvd
La Puente, CA 91744-5796
800-535-1369

ALTO SHAAM, INC.
W164 N9221 Water St # 450
Menomonee Falls, WI 53051-1401
262-251-3800

ALTRO FLOORS
224 Nazareth Pike
Bethlehem, PA 18020-9080
e-mail: krichards@altrofloors.com
610-746-4324 • Fax 610-746-4325

ALUMA SHIELD INDUSTRIES
405 Fentress Blvd
Daytona Beach, FL 32114-1207
386-255-5391

ALUMAWORKS
15731 Chemical Ln
Huntington Beach, CA 92649-1508
800-277-7267

ALUMIN-NU CORPORATION
PO Box 24359
Cleveland, OH 44124-0359
www.aluminnu.com
216-421-2116 • Fax 216-791-8018

ALVEY WASHING EQUIPMENT
11337 Williamson Rd
Cincinnati, OH 45241-2232
e-mail:
alverysales@afindustries.com
513-489-3060 • Fax 513-489-6018

AM G
30 S Wacker Dr Ste 2600
Chicago, IL 60606-7512
312-207-2932 • Fax 312-207-6172

AMANA APPLIANCES
2800 220th Trl
Amana, IA 52204-0011
www.amanacommercial.com
800-843-0304 • Fax 319-622-8589

AMANA HEATING/AIR CONDITIONING
226 Lowell St
Wilmington, MA 01887-3074
800-647-2982 • Fax 978-658-9041

AMANA REFRIGERATION, INC.
Amana, IA 52204-0001
319-622-5511

AMBASSADOR FINE FOODS
16625 Saticoy St
Van Nuys, CA 91406-2837
818-787-2000 • Fax 818-778-6464

AMBASSADOR FINE FOODS
3701 25th Ave
Schiller Park, IL 60176-2147
847-928-2166 • Fax 847-928-0895

AMBASSADOR FINE FOODS
441 Clifton Blvd
Clifton, NJ 07013-1834
973 815 1200 • Fax 973 815 0052

AMBATH CORPORATION
1055 S Country Club Dr
Mesa, AZ 85210-4613
e-mail:dsanders@ambath.com
www.ambath.com
888-826-2284 • Fax 480-844-7544

AMBER MILLING
PO Box 64089
Saint Paul, MN 55164-0089
651-641-6457

AMBOY SPECIALITY FOODS
820 Palmyra St
Dixon, IL 61021-1900
800-292-0400

AMBRETTA FOODS A DIV. OF BOBOL
3247 W March Ln Ste 210
Stockton, CA 95219-2351
209-473-3507 • Fax 209-473-0492

AMC INDUSTRIES, INC
8408 Temple Terrace Hwy
Tampa, FL 33637-5808
e-mail: amcind@tampabay.rr.com
www.amcind.com
813-989-9663

AMCOM CORPORATION
1109 Zane Ave N
Minneapolis, MN 55422-4605
952-949-9400

AMELIA BAY BEVERAGE SYSTEMS
1000 Field Rd NW Ste 130
Atlanta, GA 30318-4426
www.ameliabay.com
678-772-6360 • Fax 678-772-4766

AMENITY SERVICES
1721 1st Ave S
Seattle, WA 98134-1403
800-533-2619

AMER BAKING SYS
3780 4th Ave
Marion, IA 52302-3872
319-373-5006

AMER BEVERAGE CORP/A B C
1 Daily Way
Verona, PA 15147-1135
800-245-2929

AMER COMMERCIAL CAPITAL
5963 La Place Ct Ste 300
Carlsbad, CA 92008-8823
888-272-6333

AMER CULINARY FEDERATION
10 San Bartola Dr # 3466
Saint Augustine, FL 32086-5766
904-8244468

AMER D J SUPPLY INC
4295 Charter St
Los Angeles, CA 90058-2520
323-582-2650

AMER DAIRY ASSOCIATION
10255 W Higgins Rd
Des Plaines, IL 60018-5606
847-803-2000

AMER EAGLE FOOD MACHINERY
3557 S Halsted St
Chicago, IL 60609-1606
773-376-080

AMER EXPRESS COMPANY
American Express Tower
New York, NY 10285-0001
212-640-2000

AMER HEALTH PRODS CORP
500 Park Blvd
Itasca, IL 60143-3121
630-285-9191

AMER INGREDIENT/ MIXATRON
550 S 18th St
Kansas City, KS 66105-1104
800-669-1092

AMER MUSIC ENVIRONMENTS
4198 Orchard Lake Rd
West Bloomfield, MI 48323-1681
248-681-2660

AMER SOCIETY OF BAKING
1200 Central Ave
Wilmette, IL 60091-2683
847-920-9885

AMER SOCIETY TRAVEL AGENT
1101 King St
Alexandria, VA 22314-2944
703-739-2782

AMER YEAST/LALLEMAND
3 A St
Derry, NH 03038-1755
800-432-1090

AMER-A-CAN CONSULTANTS & SUPPLY
5448 Hoffner Ave Ste 201
Orlando, FL 32812-2507
e-mail: americacan@ao.net
www.americacan.com
407-273-4107 • Fax 407-282-0424

AMERADA HESS
1 Hess Plz
Woodbridge, NJ 07095-1229
e-mail: poman@hess.com
www.hess.com
732-750-6611

AMERANTH TECHNOLOGY SYSTEMS
1809 Dawson St
Vienna, VA 22182-2575
703-281-4995

AMERANTH TECHNOLOGY SYSTEMS
12230 El Camino Real Ste 330
San Diego, CA 92130-2090
www.ameranth.com
858-794-8282 • Fax 858-794-8222

AMERI PURE OYSTER CO.
803 Willow St
Franklin, LA 70538-6030
800-328-6729 • Fax 337-413-8003

AMERICA BELARUSIAN IMPORT EXPO
21 Pleasant St Ste 216
Newburyport, MA 01950-2623
e-mail: abiea7@newburyport.net
www.charodei.com
978-499-9797 • Fax 978-462-4545

AMERICA ELECTRIC POWER
PO Box 944
Findlay, OH 45839-0944
419-425-7504

AMERICAN ALMOND
103 Walworth St
Brooklyn, NY 11205-2898
718-875-8310

AMERICAN AMUSEMENT MACHINE
45 E Higgins Rd # 210
Elk Grove Village, IL 60007-1433
www.coin-op.org
847-290-9088 • Fax 847-290-9121

AMERICAN AROMATHERAPY
25 Bennett Ave Apt 7
Long Beach, CA 90803-2923
www.nutraspa.com
562-433-9691 • Fax 562-433-9691

AMERICAN ATELIER, INC.
301 N Front St
Allentown, PA 18102-5309
e-mail: sales@americanatelier.com
www.americanatelier.com
610-439-4040 • Fax 610-439-4141

AMERICAN BEST FURN. MFG
6505 Gayhart St
Los Angeles, CA 90040-2507
323-888-9800

AMERICAN BEVERAGE MARKETERS
6900 College Blvd Ste
Leawood, KS 66211-1547
913-451-8311 • Fax 913-451-8655

AMERICAN BUSINESS FORMS
775 Park Ave Ste 225
Huntington, NY 11743-7582
e-mail: abfbusforms@msn.com
631-423-1777 • Fax: 631-271-2768

AMERICAN COFFEE
800 Magazine St
New Orleans, LA 70130-3692
504-581-7234

AMERICAN CONNECTIONS
110 Crossways Park Dr
Woodbury, NY 11797-2043
e-mail: gschneider@ aconnection-snj.com
631-812-9600 • Fax 516-644-0399

AMERICAN CONNOISSEUR
PO Box 8338
Bloomfield Hills, MI 48302-8338
248-681-820 • Fax 248-683-0470

AMERICAN CULINARY FEDERATION
10 San Bartola Dr
Saint Augustine, FL 32086-5766
904-824-4486 • Fax 904-825-4758

AMERICAN DELPHI, INC.
7110 Fenwick Ln
Westminster, CA 92683-5248
www.americandelphi.com
714-894-0515 • Fax: 714-897-5596

AMERICAN DRYER CORP
88 Currant Rd
Fall River, MA 02720-4781
508-678-9000

AMERICAN EGG BOARD
1460 Renaissance Dr
Park Ridge, IL 60068-1331
www.aeb.org
847-296-7043 • Fax 847-296-7007

AMERICAN EXPREES
13428 Maxella Ave # 283
Marina Del Rey, CA 90292-5620
www.americanexprees.com/restaurant
310-305-9657 • Fax: 310-305-7467

AMERICAN EXPRESS
World Financial Center
New York, NY 10285-0001
www.americanexpress.com/merchant
212-640-5309

AMERICAN EXPRESS
141 Robert E Lee Blvd #
New Orleans, LA 70124-2534
800-710-9832

AMERICAN EXPRESS
13423 Blanco Rd # 289
San Antonio, TX 78216-2192
800-706-9784 • Fax 800-706-9784

AMERICAN EXPRESS
200 Vesey St Fl 45
New York, NY 10285-0002
www.americanexpress.com/lodging
800-528-5200

AMERICAN EXPRESS
200 Vesey St Fl 45
New York, NY 10285-0002
212-640-3529

AMERICAN FINE FOODS, INC.
PO Box 460
Payette, ID 83661-0460
208-642-9061

AMERICAN FLATBREAD
46 Lareau Rd
Waitsfield, VT 05673-6010
www.americanflatbread.com
802-496-8856

AMERICAN FLORESCENT
2345 Ernie Krueger Cir
Waukegan, IL 60087-3264
847-249-5970 • Fax 847-249-2618

AMERICAN FOOD & AG EXPPRT.
PO Box 810391
Boca Raton, FL 33481-0391
561-447-0810 • Fax 561-368-9125

AMERICAN FOODS GROUP
544 Acme St
Green Bay, WI 54302-1807
920-437-6330 • Fax 920-436-6466

AMERICAN GAS ASSOC.
1515 Wilson Blvd
Arlington, VA 22209-2402
703-841-8436

AMERICAN HEALTH DIAGNOSTICS
405 N Meridian Ave
Oklahoma City, OK 73107-6509
e-mail: brussell@jacksmerch.com
405-685-5703

AMERICAN HEALTH PRODUCTS
500 Park Blvd Ste 1260
Itasca, IL 60143-2639
800-828-2964 • Fax 630-285-9289

AMERICAN HOLTZKRAFT, INC.
RR 1 Box 65
Mount Pleasant Mills, PA 17853-9731
e-mail: holtzkraft@alo.com
www.holtzkraft.com
570-539-8945 • Fax 570-539-2592

AMERICAN HOTEL & MOTEL ASSOCIATION
1201 New York Ave NW
Washington DC 20005-3917
e-mail: info@ahma.com
www.ahma.com
202-289-3100 • Fax 202-289-3199

AMERICAN HOTEL REGISTER
100 S Milwaukee Ave
Vernon Hills, IL 60061-4305
e-mail: market@americanhotel.com
www.americanhotel.com
847-743-1000 • Fax 847-743-1092

AMERICAN INFANT CARE PRODUCTS
6352 320th Street Way
Cannon Falls, MN 55009-4073
507-263-5354 • Fax 507-263-5350

AMERICAN INFLATABLES INC.
947 Newhall St
Costa Mesa, CA 92627-4408
www.americaninflatables.com
888-904-9949 • Fax 949-515-9765

AMERICAN INST OF BAKING
1213 Bakers Way
Manhattan, KS 66502-4576
785-537-4750

AMERICAN ISUZU MOTORS
13340 183rd St
Cerritos, CA 90703-8748
e-mail:
eacrainfo@americanisuzu.com
www.isuzucv.com
562-229-5275 • Fax 562-229-5453

AMERICAN LAMB COUNCIL
6911 S Yosemite St
Englewood, CO 80112-1426
303-771-3500

AMERICAN LINEN
505 E South Temple
Salt Lake City, UT 84102-1004
801-320-0112 • Fax 801-363-5680

AMERICAN LINEN & UNIFORM SERVICE
1003 W North Ave
Milwaukee, WI 53205-1332
414-374-5600 • Fax 414-374-3406

AMERICAN LUXURY LIMOU-SINES
PO Box 19878
New Orleans, LA 70179-0878
504-269-5466

AMERICAN MARAZZI TILE
359 Clay Rd
Sunnyvale, TX 75182-9710
214-965-3441 • Fax 972-233-0157

AMERICAN METALCRAFT
2074 George St
Melrose Park, IL 60160-1523
www.amnow.com
708-345-1177 • Fax 708-345-5758

AMERICAN NATIONAL CAN COMPANY
8770 W Bryn Mawr Ave Fl 06B
Chicago, IL 60631-3515
773-399-3000 • Fax 773-399-8090

AMERICAN OF MARTINSVILLE
PO Box 5071
Martinsville, VA 24115-5071
e-mail:
aom@amerofmartinsville.com
www.americanofmartinsville.com
276-634-2990 • Fax 276-632-4707

AMERICAN OSTRICH ASSOCIATION
12180 Clint Parker Rd
Conroe, TX 77303-3112
www.ostriches.org
936-624-3322 • Fax 936-624-2047

AMERICAN PANEL
PO Box 762
Marshfield, MA 02050-0762
e-mail: wyllie@wllie.com
www.wyllie.com
781-834-5250 • Fax 781-834-5601

AMERICAN PANEL CORPORATION
5800 SE 78th St
Ocala, FL 34472-3407
www.americanpanel.com
352-245-7055 • Fax 352-245-0726

AMERICAN PRISM, INC.
1524 Brookhollow Dr Ste A
Santa Ana, CA 92705-5458
714-556-9122

AMERICAN PRODUCTS
10741 Miller Rd
Dallas, TX 75238-1303
e-mail: 6dir693679@aol.com
214-343-4816 • Fax 214-343-9462

AMERICAN RANGE CORP
13592 Desmond St
Pacoima, CA 91331-2315
www.americanrange.com
818-753-9893 • Fax 818-753-0526

AMERICAN RANGE/ HOSHIZAKI
5589 Commonwealth Ave
Jacksonville, FL 32254-1635
904-783-6069

AMERICAN RESORT DEVELOPMENT
1220 L St NW Ste 500
Washington DC 20005-4018
e-mail: ljackson@arda.org
www.arda.org
202-371-6700 • Fax 202-289-8544

AMERICAN ROLAND FOOD CORP.
71 W 23rd St
New York, NY 10010-4102
www.rolandfood.com
212-741-8290 • Fax 212-741-6572

AMERICAN SCHOOL FOOD SERVICE
1600 Duke St
Alexandria, VA 22314-3421
703-739-3900 • Fax 703-739-3915

AMERICAN SECURITY PROD CO
11925 Pacific Ave
Fontana, CA 92337-8205
800-421-6142 • Fax 909-685-8544

AMERICAN SPOON FOODS
PO Box 566
Petoskey, MI 49770-0566
www.spoon.com
800-222-5886 • Fax 800-647-2512

AMERICAN TABLES & SEATING MFG
5025 N Royal Atlanta Dr # C
Tucker, GA 30084-3034
e-mail: sandraxing@aol.com
770-270-1688

AMERICAN TILE
2839 Merrell Rd
Dallas, TX 75229-4700
e-mail: ats.sales@americantilesupply.com
www.americantilesupply.com
972-243-2377 • Fax 972-484-5020

AMERICAN TISSUE CORP.
135 Engineers Rd
Hauppauge, NY 11788-4008
www.americantissue.com
631-435-9000 • Fax 631-435-8980

AMERICAN UNIFORM COMPANY
PO Box 2130
Cleveland, TN 37320-2130
800-251-5862

AMERICAN RED CROSS OF SE LOUISIANA
3224 26th St
Metairie, LA 70002-6006
504-587-1500

AMERICAONE, INC
PO Box 4
Tavares, FL 32778-0004
e-mail: info@theatcompany.com
www.theatcompany.com
352-742-2200

AMERICA'S KITCHEN
2150 Brandon Trl
Alpharetta, GA 30004-8457
www.america'skitchen.com
770-754-0707 • Fax 770-754-0708

AMERICINN INTERNATIONAL
250 Lake Dr
Chanhassen, MN 55317-9364
612-476-9020

AMERICLEAN SYSTEMS CORPORATION
1099 Mount Kemble Ave Ste AB
Morristown, NJ 07960-6642
www.americleansystems.com
973-425-8898 • Fax 973-425-8899

AMERICLEAN SYSTEMS INC
26935 Northwestern Hwy
Southfield, MI 48034-8445
800-626-5015 • Fax 2483043567

AMERICLEAN SYSTEMS, INC.
1 W 4th St Ste 2600
Cincinnati, OH 45202-3608
513-381-1019

AMERICLEAN SYSTEMS-DIVERSEY
13231 Champion Forest Dr # 21
Houston, TX 77069-2600
281-586-8795

AMERICO, INC.
601 E Barton Ave
West Memphis, AR 72301-2011
www.nationalcontrols.com
800-626-2350 • Fax 870-735-4129

AMERICOLD
1515 SW 5th Ave
Portland, OR 97201-5406
503-224-3480

AMERIFax CORPORATION
7709 W 20th Ave
Hialeah, FL 33014-3227
e-mail: mike@faxpaper.com
www.faxpaper.com
305-828-1701

AMERIGAS
2812 Silver Star Rd
Orlando, FL 32808-3995
e-mail: ladner@amerigas.com
www.amerigas.com
407-293-6644

AMERIHOST INN FRANCHISE
2400 E Devon Ave Ste 280
Des Plaines, IL 60018-4617
847-298-4501

AMERIKEM LABORATORIES LTD.
136 Arlington Ave
Bloomfield, NJ 07003-4616
973-748-6500 • Fax 973-748-6776

AMERIKOOLER, INC
575 E 10th Ave
Hialeah, FL 33010-4639
www.amerikooler.com
305-884-8384

AMERIPLAST
6290 NW 27th Way
Ft Lauderdale, FL 33309-1729
954-984-4800

AMERISAFE INDUSTRIES, INC.
6996 NW 82nd Ave
Miami, FL 33166-2765
e-mail: ameribtv@ameriworld.com
www.ameriworld.com
305-477-4222 • Fax 305-477-4050

AMERISUITES
700 Route 46
Fairfield, NJ 07004-1568
888-778-3111 • Fax 973-882-1991

AMERITECH ADVERTISING SERVICES
13600 Bishops Ct
Brookfield, WI 53005-6201
www.yellowpages.net
800-553-9592 • Fax 262-797-2703

AMERIVAP SYSTEMS MERITECH
1292 Logan Cir NW
Atlanta, GA 30318-2857
e-amil: werner.diercks@mind-spring.com
404-350-0239 • Fax 404-350-9214

AMERLCAN EXPRESS
501 N Kingshighway St
Saint Charles, MO 63301-1744
800-609-8301

AMETECK/ NATIONAL CONTROLS CORP.
1725 Western Dr
West Chicago, IL 60185-1880
www.nationalcontrols.com
800-323-2593 • Fax 630-231-1377

AMI CANDLE, INC.
1140 Airport Rd
Fall River, MA 02720-4736
508-678-1945 • Fax 508-678-2920

AMOCO FABRICS & FIBERS CO
550 Interstate North Pkwy SE
Atlanta, GA 30339-5007
770-956-9025

AMRESCO
265 Franklin St
Boston, MA 02110-3113
508(617)350290

AMRESCO
11100 Ash St Ste 104
Leawood, KS 66211-1764
www.amresco.com
913-696-1120 • Fax 913-696-0450

AMRESCO COMMERCIAL FINANCE
142 E Parkcenter Blvd
Boise, ID 83706-3938
www.ameresco.com
208-333-2000 • Fax 208-333-2050

AMRESCO INC.
315 E Eisenhower Pkwy # 9A
Ann Arbor, MI 48108-3350
734-994-8440 • Fax 734-994-8474

AMRESCO, INC
700 N Pearl St Ste 2400
Dallas, TX 75201-2832
e-mail: mfranklin@amresco.com
www.amersco.com
214-953-7738

AMTICO INTERNATIONAL
6480 Roswell Rd NE
Atlanta, GA 30328-3148
404-303-1660

AMUSEMENT SHOWCASE INTERNATIONAL
10729 163rd Pl
Orland Park, IL 60467-8861
708-226-1300

AMY'S KITCHEN
PO Box 449
Petaluma, CA 94953-0449
707-762-6194

ANALYDICAL FOOD LABORATORIES
865 Greenview Dr
Grand Prairie, TX 75050-2439
e-mail: afl@flash.net
www.afltexas..com
972-339-0336 • Fax 972-623-0055

ANALYTIC IMPACT MARKETING INC
560 Oakwood Ave Ste 2
Lake Forest, IL 60045-1972
847-735-9100 • Fax 847-735-9101

ANAMAX
PO Box 10067
Green Bay, WI 54307-0067
920-494-5233

ANCHOR AUDIO INC
3415 Lomita Blvd
Torrance, CA 90505-5010
310-784-2300

ANCHOR BREWING COMPANY
1705 Mariposa St
San Francisco, CA 94107-2334
415-863-8350 • Fax 415-552-7094

ANCHOR FOOD
555 N Hickory Farm Ln
Appleton, WI 54914-3076

www.anchorfoods.com
920-997-2828 • Fax 920-997-7604

ANCHOR FROZEN FOODS
PO Box 887
Westbury, NY 11590-0887
516-333-6344 • Fax 516-687-2977

ANCHOR GLASS CONTAINER CORP.
4343 Anchor Plaza Pkwy
Tampa, FL 33634-7537
813-882-7854

ANCHOR HOCKING
519 N Pierce Ave
Lancaster, OH 43130-2969
www.anchorhocking.com
740-681-6201 • Fax 740-687-2977

ANCHOR HOCKING
509 N Pierce Ave
Lancaster, OH 43130-2927
www.anchorhocking.com
800-848-7200 • Fax 800-848-0082

ANCHOR INDUSTRIES
1100 Burch Dr
Evansville, IN 47725-1700
812-867-2421

ANDERSEN CONSULTING
69 W Washington St
Chicago, IL 60602-3134
312-580-0069

ANDERSON FOODSERVICE DIRECT
1017 N Main Ave Ste 300
San Antonio, TX 78212-4721
210-223-6233 • Fax 210-223-9692

ANDERSON INTERNATIONAL FOODS,
645 S Anderson St
Los Angeles, CA 90023-1105
323 780 1091 • Fax 323-261-0591

ANDIS COMPANY
PO Box 085005
Racine, WI 53408-5005
e-mail: info@andisco.com
www.andis.com
262-884-2600 • Fax 262-884-1100

ANDREW GARY
900 Passaic Ave Bldg 6
Harrison, NJ 07029-2833
973-484-2500 • Fax 973-484-8883

ANDREW YOUNG & CO., INC.
19 Tamarack Rd
Mahopac, NY 10541-1408
914-621-2410

ANDY RUSSO FACTORY AGENTS
3503 Forest City Dr
Humble, TX 77339-2630
800-221-3335 • Fax 281-259-5951

ANDY THORNTON LTD./UK BREWING
1392 Columbia Ave
Lancaster, PA 17603-4743
e-mail: ukb@ukbrewing.com
www.ukbrewing.com
717-293-8111 • Fax 717-293-5789

ANETSBERGER BROTHERS INC
180 Anets Dr
Northbrook, IL 60062-5499
847-272-0770

ANEW, INC.
32 Cunningham Rd
Debary, FL 32713-3168
386-668-7785 • Fax 386-668-1981

ANGEL/RAMCO
222 N Western Ave Unit
Carpentersville, IL 60110-1750
847-836-1434 • Fax 847-836-1861

ANGELICA IMAGE APPAREL
700 Rosedale Ave
Saint Louis, MO 63112-1408
e-mail:
kimnoerteman@worldnet.att.net
www.angelica-corp.com
314-889-1314 • Fax 314-889-1205

ANGOSTURA INTERNATIONAL
PO Box 1387
Auburn, ME 04211-1387
908-272-2200

ANHEUSER-BUSCH
1 Busch Pl
Saint Louis, MO 63118-1852
314-854-3984

ANHEUSER-BUSCH
20325 Bartlett Dr
Brookfield, WI 53045-4169
262-789-5293 • Fax 262-789-5294

ANHEUSER-BUSCH
11814 W 138th St
Overland Park, KS 66221-9396
913-851-4008

ANHEUSER-BUSCH, INC.
1800 West Loop S Ste 1100
Houston, TX 77027-3228
713-622-2400

ANKO
3007 29th Ave E
Bradenton, FL 34208-7422
941-446-2656

ANKO FOOD MACHINE USA CO., LTD
116 Park Blvd
Millbrae, CA 94030-1228
www.ankofood.com
650-624-6038 • Fax 650-624-8039

ANN BOND ASSOCIATES INC
3388 Woods Edge Cir Ste 101
Bonita Spgs, FL 34134-1368
239-280-6002 • Fax 239-280-5442

ANN SACKS, A KOHLER COMPANY
8120 NE 33rd Dr
Portland, OR 97211-2018
www.kohlerco.cm
800-278-TILE

ANNABELLE'S NATURAL ICE CREAM
49 Ceres St
Portsmouth, NH 03801-3738
www.annabellesicecream.com
603-436-3400 • Fax 603-431-7686

ANNA'S UNLIMITED, INC.
PO Box 141154
Austin, TX 78714-1154
e-mail: anasalsa@juno.com
www.annasunlimited.com
512-837-2203 • Fax 512-837-0003

ANNAVISIONS
777 N Michigan Ave Apt 1700
Chicago, IL 60611-6625
312-943-8682 • Fax 312-943-2598

ANNIE GRAY ASSOCIATES, INC.
12400 Olive Blvd Ste 555
Saint Louis, MO 63141-5460
314-275-4405

ANNIE PIE'S BAKERY
1275 Bennett Dr
Longwood, FL 32750-7601
407-831-7288 • Fax 407-831-7065

ANNIE'S FROZEN YOGURT
5251 W 73rd St Ste F
Minneapolis, MN 55439-2221
952-835-2110 • Fax 952-835-2378

ANOVA FOOD
PO Box 272072
Tampa, FL 33688-2072
800-661-0952

ANSELL PROTECTIVE PRODUCTS
1300 Walnut S
Coshocton, OH 43812-2262
740-623-3542 • Fax 740-623-2838

ANSUL
1 Stanton St
Marinette, WI 54143-2597
715-735-7411

ANTHONY & SONS BAKERY
20 Luger Rd
Denville, NJ 07834-2639
973-625-2323

ANTHONY AND SONS BAKERY, INC.
1275 Bloomfield Ave
Fairfield, NJ 07004-2708
973-575-5865 • Fax 973-575-0289

ANVIL AMERICA, INC
3005 SW 2nd Ave Ste 102
Ft Lauderdale, FL 33315-3339
e-mail: anvil@anvilproducts.com
www.anvilproducts.com
954-525-0401

ANZA TENTS
375 Maple Ave
Torrance, CA 90503-2602
888-637-8086

AP PURATOS
3590 NW 60th St
Miami, FL 33142-2027
305-635-0845 • Fax 305-633-3086

APEC DISPLAY
160 Fornelius Ave
Clifton, NJ 07013-1844
e-mail: MikeV@apecdisplay.com
973-458-9400 • Fax 973-458-9444

APEX BAKERY EQUIPMENT
803 Main St
Belmar, NJ 07719-2705
888-571-3599

APEX U.S.A.
PO Box 120
Neodesha, KS 66757-0120
www.powerplumber.com
620-325-3536 • Fax 620-325-3978

APEX-MAGNE SIGN
820 Thompson Ave Apt 37
Glendale, CA 91201-2049
877-624-6374 • Fax 818-241-1576

APFFELS SPECIALTY COFFEE
2115 S Grand Ave
Los Angeles, CA 90007-1439
800-443-2252 • Fax 323-846-5503

APICOLTURA RIGONI USA
PO Box 353
Plantsville, CT 06479-0353
860-276-9675 • Fax 860-620-0793

APILCO/CUTHBERTSON
PO Box 3098
Darien, CT 06820-8098
203 834 0506 • Fax 203-034-0610

APPA FINE FOODS
135 Klug Cir
Corona, CA 92880-5424
909-278-2772 • Fax 909-273-2780

APPEL UNIFORMS
10099 Seminole Blvd
Seminole, FL 33772-2564
800-557-1168

APPLE COOKIE & CHOCOLATE
501 Braddock Ave
Turtle Creek, PA 15145-2066
800-223-9866

APPLEGATE FARMS
10 County Line Rd
Somerville, NJ 08876-6007
e-mail: help@applegatefarms.com
908-725-5800 • Fax 908-725-3383

APPLIED BUSINESS CONCEPT
2829 Virginia St
Kenner, LA 70062-5348
504-467-2679

APPLIED GRAPHICS, INC
1415 3rd St
San Rafael, CA 94901-2826
415-454-7878 • Fax 415-454-1666

APROPOS STUDIOS, INC.
250 3rd Ave N
Minneapolis, MN 55401-1637
www.aproposstudio.com
612-672-077 • Fax 612-673-0411

APW
729 3rd Ave
Dallas, TX 75226-2098
www.apwwyott.com
214-421-7366 • Fax 214-565-0976

AQUA CUISINE, INC.
12554 W Bridger St Su
Boise, ID 83713-1583
e-mail: dsims@aquacuisine.net
208-323-3782 • Fax 208-323-4730

AQUA FOODS
1050 W Laurel Ave
Eunice, LA 70535-3124
337-457-0111

AQUA PRODUCTS
25 Rutgers Ave
Cedar Grove, NJ 07009-1443
e-mail: car9251@aol.com
www.aquaproducts.com
800-221-1750 • Fax 973-857-8981

AQUA-AIR WET/DRY BUILT-IN
542 Confluence Ave
Salt Lake City, UT 84123-1385
www.aquaair-wetdry.com
801-265-9699 • Fax 801-268-3856

AQUAFARMS
INTERNATIONAL
630 Main St
Little Falls, NJ 07424-1020
973-785-1211

AQUATIC INDUSTRIES INC.
PO Box 889
Leander, TX 78646-0889
www.aquaticwhirpools.com
512-259-2255 • Fax 512-259-3633

ARA GROUP
8025 NW 60th St
Miami, FL 33166-3412
305-592-5558 • Fax 305-592-6045

ARABAN COFFEE COMPANY
2 Keith Way
Hingham, MA 02043-4204
617-439-3900 • Fax 617-439-3091

ARACHNID INC
PO Box 2901
Loves Park, IL 61132-2901
815-654-0212

ARAMARK
1107 Market St Fl 29
Philadelphia, PA 19107-2901
e-mail: pillmeier-
susan@aramark.com
www.aramark.com
215-238-6891 • Fax 215-238-8170

ARBOR ACRES FARM INC
439 Marlborough Rd
Glastonbury, CT 06033-2831
860-633-4681 • Fax 860-657-9193

ARBY'S/T.J. CINNAMONS
1000 Corporate Dr
Fort Lauderdale, FL 33334-3655
e-mail: roshins@arbys.com
954-351-5200 • Fax 954-351-5222

ARCADE INDUSTRIES, INC.
PO Box 898
Northborough, MA 01532-0898
508-393-2100 • Fax 508-393-0064

ARC-COM FABRICS, INC.
33 Ramland Rd S
Orangeburg, NY 10962-2618
845-365-1100 • Fax 845-365-3627

ARCH DESIGN GROUP INC
1512 E Broward Blvd # STE.100
Fort Lauderdale FL 33301-2122
954-522-1667

ARCHITECTURAL BRASS CO.
996 Huff Rd NW
Atlanta, GA 30318-4339
404-351-0594

ARCTIC AIR
6440 City West Pkwy
Eden Prairie, MN 55344-3298
www.arcticairco.com
952-941-2270 • Fax 952-941-3066

ARCTIC INDUSTRIES, INC
9731 NW 114th Way
Miami, FL 33178-1178
305-883-5581 • Fax 305-883-4651

ARDCO, INC.
12400 S Laramie Ave
Alsip, IL 60803-3209
708-388-4300 • Fax 708-388-0952

AREA DISTRIBUTORS, INC.
PO Box 1133
Quincy, IL 62306-1133
217-223-3600

ARGENTINE BEEF COMPANY
1901 L St NW # 67
Washington DC 20036-3506
www.argbeef.com
202-393-1891 • Fax 202-628-2921

ARICHELL TECHNOLOGIES
55 Border St
West Newton, MA 02465-2005
617-796-9001

ARIS MFG/LAKESIDE
1951 S Allis St
Milwaukee, WI 53207-1248
800-558-8565

ARIZA CHEESE, INC.
7602 Jackson St
Paramount, CA 90723-4912
e-mail: arizacheez@aol.com
562-630-4144 • Fax 562-630-4174

ARKANSAS BEST HUSHPUPPY
PO Box 146
Eudora, AR 71640-0146
870-355-4551 • Fax 870-355-4192

ARLA FOODS, INC.
2840 Morris Ave
Union, NJ 07083-4851
908-964-4410 • Fax 908-964-2878

ARMANINO FOODS
30588 San Antonio S
Hayward, CA 94544-7102
e-mail: warmanino@aol.com
510-441-9300 • Fax 510-441-0101

ARMBRUSTER
8600 S Old Route 66
Springfield, IL 62707-8699
800-637-4326

ARMCHAIR RACES
1931 Mott Ave
Far Rockaway, NY 11691-4103
718-327-2248

ARNEG. INC.
4243 Lonate Dr
Nazareth, PA 18064-8403
e-mail: arneg@earthlink.net
610-746-9570 • Fax 610-746-9580

AROMONT-USA, INC.
PO Box 821
Diablo, CA 94528-0821
925-314-0435 • Fax 925-838-2552

ARR TECH, INC
PO Box 1432
Yakima, WA 98907-1432
509-452-7143

ART ASAP
415 W 50th St
New York, NY 10019-6526
e-mail: artasap1@aol.com
www.artasap.com
212-956-0805 • Fax 212-956-0796

ART CLASSIC
811 Garonne Dr
Ballwin, MO 63021-5604
e-mail: jbsmith7@swbell.net
www.artclassicsltd.com
636-227-9699 • Fax 636-227-9542

ART COCO CHOCOLATE CO.
2660 Walnut St
Denver, CO 80205-2231
303-634-6627 • Fax 303-634-6636

ART.COM
122 S Michigan Ave Ste 900
Chicago, IL 60603-6117
312-673-3560 • Fax 312-360-1112

ARTE DE MEXICO
1000 Chestnut St
Burbank, CA 91506-1623
www.artedemexico.com
818-753-4559 • Fax 818-563-1015

ARTEC MFG. DIV. OF KIMBALL
INTL
1037 E 15th St
Jasper, IN 47549-1007
www.artec.kimball.com
812-482-8813 • Fax 812-482-8730

ARTEX INTERNATIONAL, INC.
1405 Walnut St
Highland, IL 62249-2009
e-mail: artex@artex-int.com
www.artex-int.com
618-654-2113 • Fax 618-654-0200

ARTHUR ANDERSEN
1150 17th St NW
Washington DC 20036-4603
800-278-4871

ARTHUR ANDERSEN
201 Saint Charles Ave
New Orleans, LA 70170-1000
504-581-5454

ARTHUR AVENUE BAKING CO.
2413 Arthur Ave
Bronx, NY 10458-6076
718-365-8860 • Fax 718-365-8198

ARTHUR D. LITTLE, INC.
25 Acorn Park
Cambridge, MA 02140-2301
617-498-5123

ARTHUR J. GALLAGHER &
COMPANY
2600 McCormick Dr Ste 100
Clearwater, FL 33759-1058
727-799-4190 • Fax 727-791-1613

ARTHUR M. WELLING, LTD.
117 Old Rutherford Rd
Taylors, SC 29687-5736
e-mail: arthurwellingltd@aol.com
www.artwellingltd.com
888-774-7738 • Fax 864-877-7564

ARTIC TEMP INC.
PO Box 637
Meeker, OK 74855-0637
405-279-3592

ARTICHOKES ETC., INC
PO Box 222
Moss Landing, CA 95039-0222
317-224-945 • Fax 831-722-6369

ARTISANS, INC.
716 S River Street Ext
Calhoun, GA 30701-3260
e-mail: thomasc@nwga.com
www.artisansinc.com
706-625-1119 • Fax 706-629-4247

ARTISTIC FRAMING, INC.
860 Chaddick Dr Ste F
Wheeling, IL 60090-6462
847-808-0200 • Fax 847-808-0205

ARTS COUNCIL OF NEW
ORLEANS
225 Baronne St Ste 1712
New Orleans, LA 70112-1768
504-523-1465

ARTUSO PASTRY FOODS CORP.
158 S 12th Ave
Mount Vernon, NY 10550-2915
e-mail: nycannoli@aol.com
914-663-8806 • Fax 914-663-8815

ARY INC.
10301 Hickman Mills Dr Ste 200
Kansas City, MO 64137-1600
816-761-2900 • Fax 816-761-0055

ASCAP
1 Lincoln Plz
New York, NY 10023-7129
212-621-6403

ASDI-AIR SCREEN DESIGN INTL
142 S 15th St
Newark, NJ 07107-1053
800-466-2734 • Fax 973-268-1343

ASE DELI COMPANY
2001 Butterfield Rd Fl 18
Downers Grove, IL 60515-1050
630-512-1775 • Fax 630-512-1115

ASE FOODSERVICE
2001 Butterfield Rd
Downers Grove, IL 60515-1050
630-512-1000 • Fax 630-512-1119

ASI FOOD SAFETY
CONSULTANTS
7625 Page Ave
Saint Louis, MO 63133-1009
800-477-0778

ASI/RESTAURANT
MANAGER
1734 Elton Rd Ste 219
Silver Spring, MD 20903-5719
www.actionsystems.com
301-445-6100 • Fax 301-445-6104

ASK FOODS, INC.
PO Box 388
Palmyra, PA 17078-0388
e-mail: webmaster@askfoods.com
717-838-6356 • Fax 717-838-7458

ASPEN
PRODUCTS
4231 Clary Blvd
Kansas City, MO 64130-2328

ASPENAIR-CERTIFIED
2723 Fulton Dr NW
Canton, OH 44718-3505
330-453-1998 • Fax 330-453-1995

ASPEON
16832 Red Hill Ave
Irvine, CA 92606-4803
www.aspeon.com
949-440-8000 • Fax 949-440-8086

ASSETRADE.COM
7711 Carondelet Ave
Saint Louis, MO 63105-3313
314-725-1355

ASSOCIATED FOOD SERVICE
EQPT.
13769 Airline Hwy
Baton Rouge, LA 70817-5924
800-673-5504

ASSURED
ENVIRONMENTS
360 Lexington Ave Fl 15
New York, NY 10017-6502
e-mail: aklein3@juno.com
212-557-7500 • Fax 212-557-1650

ASTOR CHOCOLATE
CORP.
651 New Hampshire Ave
Lakewood, NJ 08701-5452
e-mail: sales@astorchocolate.com
www.astorchoclate.com
732-901-1000 • Fax 732-901-3610

ASTORIA
350 Morgan Ave
Brooklyn, NY 11211-2794
e-mail: astoria@nac.net
800-879-4004 • Fax 718-963-3043

ASTORIA ESPRESSO
CAPPUCCINO MACHINES
2381 Lafayette Ave
Bronx, NY 10473-1103
718-931-2473 • Fax 718-863-3774

ASTORIA/GENERAL ESPRESSO
EQUIP
7912 Industrial Village Rd
Greensboro, NC 27409-9691
336-393-0224

ASTRA INFORMATION
SYSTEMS
1920 N Commerce Pkwy Ste 2
Fort Lauderdale, FL 33326-3243
800-305-5567

ASTRA MFR.
21520 Blythe St
Canoga Park, CA 91304-499
www.astramfr.com
818-340-1800 • Fax 818-340-5830

AT SYSTEMS
2311 Motor St
Dallas, TX 75235-8005
214-631-5355 • Fax 214-637-4959

AT&T
150 Mount Airy Rd Rm 1N29
Basking Ridge, NJ 07920-2021
908-630-2270

ATALANTA CORPORATION
520 Avenue H E Ste 203
Arlington, TX 76011-3114
817-649-5515 • Fax 817-649-5585

ATEECO INC
PO Box 606
Shenandoah, PA 17976-0606
570-291-7999

ATHENS PASTRIES
13600 Snow Rd
Brookpark, OH 44142-2596
216-676-8500

**ATKINS ELEGANT
DESSERTS**
15510 Stony Creek Way
Noblesville, IN 46060-4385
www.atkinstech.com
800-887-8808 • Fax 317-378-4146

ATKINS TECHNICAL
1855 NE 12th Ave
Gainesville, FL 32641 4611
800-342-7951

ATKINS TECHNICAL
1855 NE 12th Ave Ste A
Gainesville, FL 32641-4611
www.atkinstech.com
352-378-5555 • Fax 352-335-3736

**ATLANTA HOTEL INVEST CON-
FERENCE**
1 Northside 75 N
Atlanta, GA 30310-7715
404 355 0880

**ATLANTA INVITATIONAL CULI-
NARY**
43 Greene St NE
Fairburn, GA 30213-1446
770-969-6315

ATLANTIC ARTS INC.
29 Francis St
Annapolis, MD 21401-1713
410-263-2554 • Fax 410-263-1362

ATLANTIC BAKERY EXPO
PO Box 447
Livingston Manor, NY 12758-0447

ATLANTIC DISTRIBUTORS
4750 Highway Ave
Jacksonville, FL 32254-3790
904-387-1882

ATLANTIC GAME MEATS
PO Box 84
Hampden, ME 04444-0084
207-277-5387 • Fax 207-277-5388

**ATLANTIC LOBSTER
SYSTEMS**
735 E Industrial Park Dr
Manchester, NH 03109-5640
603-669-2728 • Fax 603-669-1691

ATLANTIC MICRO SYSTEMS
8535 Baymeadows Rd Ste 18
Jacksonville, FL 32256-7445
904-519-9500

**ATLANTIC PREMIUM
BRANDS**
16801 Addison Rd Ste 410
Addison, TX 75001-5194
972-267-6363 • Fax 972-267-7279

ATLANTIC PUBLISHING CO.
1210 SW 23rd Pl
Ocala, FL 34474-7014
352-622-6220

**ATLANTIC RUBBER
PRODUCTS, INC.**
3065 Cranberry Hwy
East Wareham, MA 02538-1325
www.atlrubber.com
508-291-1123 • Fax 508-291-1211

**ATLANTIC STORE FIXTURE CO.
INC**
PO Box 2635
Woburn, MA 01888-1135
781-935-4300

ATLANTIS PLASTICS
PO BOX 4309
Mankato, MN 56002-4309
800-686-4420 • Fax 507-388-4420

ATLAS CARPET MILLS, INC
2200 Saybrook Ave
Los Angeles, CA 90040-1720
800-372-6274 • Fax 800-272-8527

ATLAS COLD STORAGE
1731 Morrow St
Green Bay, WI 54302-2607
www.atlascold.com
920-468-8314 • Fax 920-468-0210

ATLAS METAL
1135 NW 159th Dr
Miami, FL 33169-5882
www.atlasfoodserv.com
305-625-2451 • Fax 305-623-0475

ATLAS TECHNOLOGY
201 S Alloy Dr
Fenton, MI 48430-1797
810-629-6663

ATM NETWORK
17420 Minnetonka Blvd
Minnetonka, MN 55345-1005
www.atmnetworkinc.com
800-929-0228 • Fax 800-929-0114

**AT-YOUR-SERVICE
SOFTWARE, INC.**
450 Bronxville Rd
Bronxville, NY 10708-1133
914-337-9030

AUNTIE ANNE'S INC
PO Box 529
Gap, PA 17527-0529
www.auntieannes.com
717-442-4766 • Fax 717-442-1296

**AURORA DESIGN
ASSOCIATES INC.**
1308 S 1700 E Ste 203
Salt Lake City, UT 84108-2273
801-588-0111 • Fax 801-588-0333

AUSTIN NICHOLS & CO
777 Westchester Ave
West Harrison, NY 10604-3520
914-455-9400

AUSTIN QUALITY FOODS INC
1 Quality Ln
Cary, NC 27513-2004
919-677-3400 • Fax 800-334-3532

**AUSTIN-WALSH BEVERAGE
SPECIALITIES**
7218 McNeil Dr Ste 404
Austin, TX 78729-7617
512-219-8666 • Fax 512-219-8667

AUSTRALIAN IMPORTS
PO Box 726
Los Angeles, CA 90078-0726
626-466-7866 • Fax 626-466-5366

**AUSTRIAN TRADE
COMMISSION**
500 N Michigan Ave Ste 1950
Chicago, IL 60611-3722
www.austriandrade.org
312-644-5556 • Fax 312-644-6526

AUTHENTIC MARBLE
670 8th Ct
Vero Beach, FL 32962-1644
772-567-1072

**AUTO-CHLOR
SERVICES INC.**
PO Box 13588
New Orleans, LA 70185-3588
504-482-2169

AUTO-CHLOR SYSTEM
110 1st St # 20
Los Altos, CA 94022-2705
www.autochlorsystems.com
650-949-3383 • Fax 650-949-4185

AUTO-CHLOR SYSTEM
PO Box 171608
Kansas City, KS 66117-0608
913-281-1022

AUTO-CHLOR SYSTEM
7163 123rd Cir
Largo, FL 33773-3037
e-mail: timcarpenter@unjever.com
727-539-1798

AUTO-CHLOR SYSTEM, INC.
1000 Ridgeway Loop Rd Ste 100
Memphis, TN 38120-4037
901-684-0600

AUTOCRAT COFFEE
PO Box 285
Lincoln, RI 02865-0285
e-mail: sales@autocrat.com
www.autocrat.com
401-333-3300 • Fax 401-333-3719

AUTOFRY
6 Huron Dr
Natick, MA 01760-1315
800-348-2976

**AUTOMATED FINANCIAL,
L.L.C.**
145 W Juanita Ave Ste B-15
Mesa, AZ 85210-6128
www.atmconnection.com
100-020-1000 • Fax 480-831-7623

**AUTOMATED MERCHANT
SERVICES, INC**
1999 N University Dr Ste 210
Pompano Beach, FL 33071-6068
e-mail: amsbankcard@aol.com
www.amsbankcard.com
954-752-0999

**AUTOMATIC BAR
CONTROLS, INC.**
790 Eubanks Dr
Vacaville, CA 95688-9470
www.wunderbar.com
707-448-5151 • Fax 707-448-1521

**AUTOMATIC DATA
PROCESSING**
12200 Weber Hill Rd
Saint Louis, MO 63127-1599
314-974-5585

**AUTOMATIC DATA
PROCESSING**
1 ADP Blvd
Roseland, NJ 07068-1786
973-994-5201

**AUTOMATIC FIRE
PROTECTION**
3265 N 126th St
Brookfield, WI 53005-3185
www.autofire.com
262-781-9665 • Fax 262-781-1152

AUTOMATIC JUICER
PO Box 4310
Forest Hills, NY 11375-9310
718-326-1492 • Fax 718-326-3362

AUTOMATIC SWITCH
50-60 Hanover Rd
Florham Park, NJ 07932-1591
973-966-2181

**AUTOMATION
ELECTRONICS, INC.**
6101 Pepsi Way
Windsor, WI 53598-9642
e-mail: aei@inxpress.net
608-846 8285 • Fax 608-846-8287

**AUTON MOTORIZES
SYSTEMS**
PO Box 802320
Santa Clarita, CA 91380-2320
661-257-9282

AVA ADVERTISING INC
100 E Wisconsin Ave Ste
Milwaukee, WI 53202-4107
414-271-2000 • Fax 414-271-0505

AVANTE
70 Washington Rd
Princeton Junction, NJ 08550-1012
609-799-9388

AVANTI PRODUCTS
PO Box 520604
Miami, FL 33152-0604
800-323-5029

AVANTI PRODUCTS
10880 NW 30th St
Miami, FL 33172-2189
www.avantiproducts.com
305-592-7830 • Fax 305-591-3629

AVED ELECTRONICS
59 Technology Dr
Lowell, MA 01851-2729
800-441-2833

AVENUES COFFEE COMPANY
7105 Old Katy Rd
Houston, TX 77024-2111
713-868-8124 • Fax 713-868-8292

AVIKO USA
1251 N Plum Grove Rd
Schaumburg, IL 60173-5600
877-284-5687

AVIKO USA L.L.C.
5855 3rd St SE
Jamestown, ND 58401-6800
www.avikousa.com
701-252-5222 • Fax 701-252-6863

AVIS FURNITURE COMPANY
1410 Union Ave
Kansas City, MO 64101-1331
816-421-5939

AVO-KING INTERNATIONAL
2140 W Chapman Ave Ste 240
Orange, CA 92868-2332
714-937-1551 • Fax 714-937-1974

AVOMEX
8500 Old Denton Rd
Keller, TX 76248-9692
877-428-6639 • Fax 877-437-9308

AVTEC
120 Kendall Point Dr
Oswego, IL 60543-8698
www.avtecind.com
630 851 4800 • Fax 630-851-5777

**AWARD BAKING
INTERNATIONAL**
1101 Stinson Blvd
Minneapolis, MN 55413-1249
www.oblaten.com
612-331-3523 • Fax 612-331-1685

AWESOME APRONS
44 Court St
Milford, CT 06460-5201
e-mail: marilunowe@aol.com
203-783-1033 • Fax 203-783-1033

AWL & ASSOCIATES
23015 N 15th Ave Ste 104
Phoenix, AZ 85027-1323
623-580-1900 • Fax 623-580-1915

AWREY BAKERIES INC
12301 Farmington Road
Livonia, MI 48150-1747
734-522-1100• Fax 734-522-1585

**AXCESS TECHNOLOGY
SOURCE**
2015 Royal Ln # 470
Dallas, TX 75229-3220
www.axcesstechnologysource.com
877-301-3211 • Fax 972-231-3822

**AXWELL PAPER
PRODUCTS**
914 Regal Row
Dallas, TX 75247-4490
www.maxwellpaper.com
214-631-5550 • Fax 214-634-2014

AYRKING CORPORATION
2013 Cobalt Dr
Louisville, KY 40299-2417
www.ayrking.com
502-266-6270 • Fax 502-266-6274

AZ OSTRICH COMPANY, INC.
7120 Memory Ln
Dayton, OH 45414-2066
e-mail: goodnews@azostrich.com
937-454-1889 • Fax 937-264-0019

AZAR NUT CO
1800 Northwestern Dr
El Paso, TX 79912-1125
915-877-4079 • Fax 915-877-2092

AZBAR/CSTECHNOLOGIES
PO Box 9130
Dallas, TX 75209-9130
www.azbamerica.com
214-361-2422 • Fax 214-361-8885

AZTEC TENTS
540 Hawaii Ave
Torrance, CA 90503-5148
310-328-5060

AZTECA MILLING CO
501 W Chapin St
Edinburg, TX 78539-2412
956-383-4911

AZTECAS DESIGN INC.
PO Box 1189
Spring Valley, CA 91979-1189
www.aztecasdesign.com
858-429-5802 • Fax 619-579-3891

B & D DIST. INC
PO Box 3945
Olathe, KS 66063-3945
913-768-8588

B & G FOODS
4 Gatehall Dr Ste 110
Parsippany, NJ 07054-4522
973-401-6500 • Fax 973-401-6526

B & J FOOD SERVICES EQUIP
236 N 7th St
Kansas City, KS 66101-3202
913-621-6165

B & L MARKETING GROUP
PO Box 670958
Dallas, TX 75367-0958
214-373-2492 • Fax 972-891-9758

B C BUNDT
PO Box 271848
Tampa, FL 33688-1848
813-963-2784

B F GOODRICH CO
2550 W Tyvola Rd
Charlotte, NC 28217-4543
330-659-7600

B F GOODRICH PERF MATERIALS
9911 Brecksville Rd
Brecksville, OH 44141-3201
216-447-5000

B W I AIRPORT
PO Box 8766
Baltimore, MD 21240-0766
410-859-7030

B.A. SILVER & COMPANY
205 E 42nd St Ste 132
New York, NY 10017-5706
212-286-9860 • Fax 212-573-9747

B2B GALAXY/FOODGALAXY.COM
400 Lanidex Plz
Parsippany, NJ 07054-2722
888-270-9140

B2BXCHANGE
6462 City West Pkwy
Eden Prairie, MN 55344-7731
www.b2bxchange.com
952-944-7900

BAADER NORTH AMERICA
777 Church St
New Bedford, MA 02745-1445
508-995-5900

BABB'S HEALTHY HEART FARM
PO Box 726
Dalton, GA 30722-0726
706-226-5455

BABCO INTERNATIONAL
911 S Tyndall Ave
Tucson, AZ 85719-6635
520-628-7596 • Fax 520-628-9622

BABE FARMS, INC
PO Box 6539
Santa Maria, CA 93456-6539
www.babyveggies.com
805-925-4144 • Fax 805-922-3950

BABY ACAPULCO & SANCHEZ
1628 Barton Springs Rd
Austin, TX 78704-1035
512-328-5835

BACALL & CONNIFF, P.C.
111 State St
Boston, MA 02109-2905
e-mail: bc111state@aol.com
www.beancounters.com
617-367-3250 • Fax 617-367-2511

BACARDI IMPORTS
2100 Biscayne Blvd
Miami, FL 33137-5088
305-573-8511

BACARDI USA, INC
14643 Dallas Pkwy Ste 620
Dallas, TX 75254-8814
469-385-8700 • Fax 469-385-4539

BACHTELLE AND ASSOCIATES
14841 Yorba St Ste 102
Tustin, CA 92780-2942
714-731-5830 • Fax 714-731-1337

BACI BY REMCRAFT
12870 NW 45th Ave
Opa Locka, FL 33054-5120
305-687-9031

BACKYARD URGERS INC
1657 N Shelby Oaks Dr Ste 105
Memphis, TN 38134-7436
901-367-0888 • Fax 901-367-0999

BACTA-PUR LLC/PROCEPTOR
97 Cove St
New Bedford, MA 02744-2516
www.bactapur.com
877-222-8278 • Fax 819-842-2902

BADGER BOILED HAM CO., INC.
3521 W Lincoln Ave
Milwaukee, WI 53215-2332
414-645-1756 • Fax 414-645-5189

BADGER POPCORN AND CONCESSION
2914 Latham Dr
Madison, WI 53713-3233
800-962-6227 • Fax 608-274-5408

BAGCRAFT
3900 W 43rd St
Chicago, IL 60632-3490
www.bagcraft.com
773-254-8000 • Fax 773-254-8204

BAGEIS BY BELL, LTD.
10013 Foster Ave
Brooklyn, NY 11236-2117
718-272-2780 • Fax 718-272-2789

BAGELMANIA BAGEL BOYS
10057 Sunset Strip
Fort Lauderdale, FL 33322-5303
e-mail: bagelmaniac@aol.com
954-748-5077 • Fax 954-748-4202

BAHAMA QUEST LTD.
8575 Sleepy Hollow Dr
Cincinnati, OH 45243-1180
www.bahama-q.com
877-984-1057 • Fax 513-793-3588

BAIARDI CHAIN FOOD CORP.
PO Box 1568
S Hackensack, NJ 07606-0168
201-440-2200 • Fax 201-440-6608

BAIN PEST CONTROL
1320 Middlesex St
Lowell, MI 01851-1297
e-mail: bbug1320@aol.com
www.bainpestconrtol.baweb.com
800-272-3661 • Fax 978-459-3184

BAKE N JOY
351 Willow St S
North Andover, MA 01845-5973
978-683-1414

BAKER & BAKER
1301 Estes Ave
Elk Grove Village, IL 60007-5403
www.bakerbaker.com
847-593-5700 • Fax 847-593-0749

BAKERS PRIDE
30 Pine St
New Rochelle, NY 10801-6997
www.bakerspride.com
914-576-0200 • Fax 914-576-0605

BAKERY CRAFTS/BERGHAUSEN
PO Box 37
West Chester, OH 45071-0037
800-543-1673

BAKERY INNOVATIVE TECH
139 N Ocean Ave
Patchogue, NY 11772-2018
631-243-5288

BAKING INDUSTRY SANITATION
1400 W Devon Ave
Chicago, IL 60660-1312
773-761-4100

BAKING MACHINERY DESIGN
90 Jacktown Rd
Bangor, PA 18013-9504
610-588-7788

BAKING MACHINES
4577 Las Positas Rd # B
Livermore, CA 94550-9615
925-449-3369

BAKON USA
10117 Sepulveda Blvd
Mission Hills, CA 91345-2600
818-895-7303

BALANCE FOOD BAR INC
114 E Haley St Ste D
Santa Barbara, CA 93101-2347
800-678-4246

BALBOA CAPITAL CORPORATION
2010 Main St Fl 11
Irvine, CA 92614-7203
949-756-0800 • Fax 949-399-3149

BALCHEM CORP
PO Box 175
Slate Hill, NY 10973-0175
845-355-5300

BALDOR
511 Barry St
Bronx, NY 10474-6605
e-mail: baldorman@aol.com
718-456-1300 • Fax 718-456-5400

BALDWIN RICHARDSON FOODS CO.
4440 Lincoln Hwy # STE.205
Matteson, IL 60443-2349
www.brfoods.com
708-283-1820 • Fax 708-283-1822

BALLANTYNE OF OMAHA/FLA-VOR-CRI
4350 McKinley St
Omaha, NE 68112-1643
www.flavor-crisp.com
402-453-4444 • Fax 402-453-7238

BALLY REFRIGERATED BOXES
771 1st Ave
King of Prussia, PA 19406-1401
610-337-8600

BALLY REFRIGERATED BOXES
135 Little 9 Rd
Morehead City, NC 28557-8483
www.ballyreboxes.com
252-240-2829 • Fax 252-240-0384

BALTIC LINEN
250 Waymont Ct Ste 100
Lake Mary, FL 32746-6747
e-mail: zcmz@aol.com
407-330-4989

BALTIC LINEN COMPANY, INC.
PO Box 9017
Valley Stream, NY 11582-9017
516-792-2118 • Fax 516-792-2124

BANA PARTS, INC
1501 Kuebel St
New Orleans, LA 70123-6959
504-734-0076

BANCORP GROUP INC
46719 Hayes Rd
Utica, MI 48315-5507
800-244-3392

BANK OF AMERICA
335 Madison Ave Fl 5
New York, NY 10017-4698
www.bankofamerica.com
212-503-7608 • Fax 516-462-7699

BANK OF AMERICA
1225 North Loop W Ste 750
Houston, TX 77008-1759
713-803-6707 • Fax 713-803-6649

BANK OF AMERICA
6100 N Federal Hwy
Ft Lauderdale, FL 33308-2200
954-493-5288

BANK OF LOUISIANA
3340 Severn Ave Fl 4
Metairie, LA 70002-7407
504-889-9368 • Fax 504-889-9425

BANKERS TRUST
130 Liberty St
New York, NY 10006-1105
212-250-9694

BAN-KOE SYSTEMS/ CASH REGISTER
1300 Grand Ave
Des Moines, IA 50309-2908
515-229-5343

BANKSHOT
809 Veirs Mill Rd
Rockville, MD 20851-1632
301-309-0260

BANO FRESH PRODUCE
6930 S Choctaw Dr
Baton Rouge, LA 70806-1350
225-923-0160

BANTA FOODS INC
1620 N Packer Rd
Springfield, MO 65803-5271
800-492-2682

BANTA HEALTHCARE GROUP FOODCARE
570 Enterprise Dr
Neenah, WI 54956-4865
920-751-4300 • Fax 920-751-4370

BAR BEVERAGE CONTROL SYSTEMS
8621 NW 54th St
Miami, FL 33166-3324
e-mail: barbeverage@ad.com
www.bar-stuff.com
305-592-5255

BAR BOY
250 Merritts Rd
Farmingdale, NY 11735-3292
e-mail: barboyprod@aol.com
516-293-7155 • Fax 516-293-7984

BAR B-Q SYSTEMS, INC
3240 Highway 152
Homer, LA 71040-8498
318-352-2210

BAR CODE DISCOUNT WAREHOUSE
9841 York Alpha Dr
North Royalton, OH 44133-3514
440-582-1144

BAR INVESTMENTGROUP
301 E 7th St
Charlotte, NC 28202-2513
704-358-0008

BAR MAID
2950 NW 22nd Ter
Pompano Beach, FL 33069-1045
800-526-5278

BAR RAGS
133 E Market St
Sandusky, OH 44870-2507
800-707-RAGS

BAR SUPPLIES UNLIMITED
3702 Artdale St
Houston, TX 77063-5244
713-781-0984

BARABOO SYSCO
910 South Blvd
Baraboo, WI 53913-2793
800-733-8217 • Fax 608-942-9417

BARABOO TENT AND AWNING
PO Box 5
Baraboo, WI 53913-0005
www.barabooawning.com
800-332-8303 • Fax 608-356-0140

BARBADOS INVESTMENT & DEVELOPMENT
800 2nd Ave Frnt 2
New York, NY 10017-4709
e-mail: bidc@bidc.com
www.bidc.com
212-867-6420 • Fax 212-682-5496

BARBARA'S BAKERY
3900 Cypress Dr
Petaluma, CA 94954-5694
707-765-2273

BARBER FOODS
PO Box 4821
Portland, ME 04112-4821
207-221-931

BARBER FOODS
46 Jackson Dr
Cranford, NJ 07016-3504
908-497-300 • Fax 908-497-3010

BARBE'S DAIRY
PO Box 186
Westwego, LA 70096-0186
504-340-8425

BARCO
11 N Batavia Ave
Batavia, IL 60510-1961
800-338-2697 • Fax 630-879-1961

BARCO UNIFORMS
350 W Rosecrans Ave
Gardena, CA 90248-1728
310-719-2172 • Fax 310-515-3547

BARDES PLASTICS, INC
PO Box 240167
Milwaukee, WI 53224-9008
Fax 414-354-6331

BARGOS
PO Box 158
Liberty Corner, NJ 07938-0158

BARI ITALIAN FOODS
3875 Bengert St
Orlando, FL 32808-4659
407-298-0560

BARKER METACRAFT, INC.
1701 W Belmont Ave
Chicago, IL 60657-3019
773-248-1115 • Fax 773-929-2281

BARLETT BUSINESS MACHINES
301 North Loop W
Houston, TX 77008-2028
e-mail: barlettbbm@aol.com
713-869-3478 • Fax 713-862-7885

BARLO SIGNS
158 Greeley St
Hudson, NH 03051-3422
www.barlosigns.com
800-227-5674 • Fax 603-882-7680

BARN FURNITURE MART, INC.
6222 1/2 Sepulveda Blvd
Van Nuys, CA 91411-1110
www.barnfurniture.com
310-551-6445 • Fax 818-241-1834

BARNES FOOD
613 Misty Isle Pl
Raleigh, NC 27615-1544
800-579-3324 • Fax 919-844-7816

BARNETT & ASSOCIATES 740
8001 Centerview Pkwy Ste 120
Cordova, TN 38018-4260
901-751-1125

BARNHORST, SCHREINER & GOONAN
550 W C St Ste 1350
San Diego, CA 92101-8545
619-544-0900

BARON INTERNATIONAL
148 S Valley Rd
West Orange, NJ 07052-4324
e-mail: baron5809@aol.com
www.baronInternational@mierodsi.net
973-736-7171 • Fax 973-736-9437

BARON R INC
13805 Magdalene Lake Cv
Tampa, FL 33613-1910
813-265-8224

BAR-PLEX
440 88th St
Brooklyn, NY 11209-5208
718-921-0565 • Fax 718-680-7057

BARRIE HOUSE COFFEE & TEA
945 Nepperhan Av
Yonkers, NY 10703-1727
e-mail: bhcofee@barriehouse.com
www.barriehouse.com
914-423-8499 • Fax 914-423-8499

BARRY CALLEBAUT U.S.A., INC
1500 Suckle Hwy
Pennsauken, NJ 08110-1432
www.barry-callebaut.com
856-663-2260

BAR-S FOOD CO INC
PO Box 29049
Phoenix, AZ 85038-9049

BARTECH SYS CORP
80 Red Schoolhouse Rd
Spring Valley, NY 10977-7053
845-352-2021

BARTON BEERS
699 W 239th St
Bronx, NY 10463-1246
718-884-4875 • Fax 718-796-1173

BARTON BEERS
18330 Patti Ln
Brookfield, WI 53045-3868
262-827-9264 • Fax 262-827-9387

BARTON BEERS LTD.
500 W Cummings Park # STE.135
Woburn, MA 01801-6503
www.stpauligirl.com
781-938-3540 • Fax 781-938-3632

BARTUSH-SCHINITZIUS FOODS
1137 N Kealy St
Lewisville, TX 75057-2662
e-mail: sales@bartushfoods.com
www.bartushfoods.com
972-219-1270 • Fax 972-436-5719

BASIC AMERICAN FOODS
2999 Oak Rd
Walnut Creek, CA 94596-2066
925-472-4000 • Fax 925-472-4450

BASS HOTELS & RESORTS
3 Ravinia Dr Ste 2900
Atlanta, GA 30346-2143

BATHROOM AND TOWEL SYSTEMS
275 W Side Ave
Jersey City, NJ 07305-1130
201-333-3377 • Fax 201-333-9410

BATSCHE DESIGN
1830 Marshall St
Houston, TX 77098-2639
713-527-0074

BATTISTONI-BISON
81 Dingens St
Buffalo, NY 14206-2307
e-mail: battistoni81@cs.com
716-826-2700 • Fax 716-826-0603

BAUMER FOOD
4301 Tulane Ave
New Orleans, LA 70119-6797
504-482-576 • Fax 504-483-2425

BAUSCHER INC
8378 Six Forks Rd
Raleigh, NC 27615-5082
888-840-4333

BAXTER MFG. CO., INC.
19220 State Route 162 E
Orting, WA 98360-9236
www.baxtermfg.com
800-777-2828 • Fax 360-893-6836

BAY BRAND
22 Roache Rd
Freedom, CA 95019-2816
831-786-9540 • Fax 831-688-3912

BAY NETWORKS, INC.
8 Federal St
Billerica, MA 01821-3570
978-436-3669

BAY OVERLAYS, INC.
807 Polaris Cresent Dr
Traverse City, MI 49684-8670
231-933-9913 • Fax 231-941-4233

BAY STATE MILLING COMPANY
100 Congress St
Quincy, MA 02169-0906
800-553-5687

BAY TOWEL LINEN & UNIFORM
PO Box 121
Green Bay, WI 54305-0121
www.baytowel.com
920-490-3354 • Fax 920-497-4866

BAY VIEW COMMERCIAL LEASING
2121 S El Camino Real
San Mateo, CA 94403-1855
650-2946677

BAY WEST PAPER
4153 Heartstone Dr
Grapevine, TX 76051-6547
800-723-0002*815
Fax 817 540 6298

BAYCLIFF COMPANY INC.
242 E 72nd St
New York, NY 10021-4574
212-772-6078 • Fax 561-472-8980

BAYLINE PAPER SUPPLY CO
1600 Atlantic St
Union City, CA 94587-2017
510-429-3800 • Fax 510-475-0118

BAYMONT INN
250 E Wisconsin Ave Ste 17
Milwaukee, WI 53202 4232
414-905-1376

BAYS CORPORATION
PO Box 1455
Chicago, IL 60690-1455
www.bays.com
312-346-5757 • Fax 312-226-3435

BAYSIDE FIRST AID & SAFETY SUPPLIES
2222 Francisco Dr # 510177
El Dorado Hills, CA 95762-3762
e-mail: tmii4life@aol.com
916-939-7927 • Fax 916-939-0134

BAY-TEK
1077 E Glenbrook Dr
Pulask, WI 54162-9765
561-588-5200 • Fax 920-493-2999

BCN RESEARCH LABORATORIES, INC
4009 Henson Rd
Knoxville, TN 37921-5391
800-236-0505

BE SMART WASTE REDUCTION COALITION
2647 N Stowell Ave
Milwaukee, WI 53211-4221
www.enviroweb.org/wastecap-wi
414-961-1100 • Fax 414-961-1105

BEACON FRUIT & PRODUCE
119 New England Produce Ctr
Chelsea, MA 02150-1711
617-889-2011 • Fax 617-889-7242

BEAR CREEK COUNTRY KITCHENS
325 W 600 S
Heber City, UT 84032-2230
435-654-6415 • Fax 435-654-4525

BEARD
1180 McLester St Ste 8
Elizabeth, NJ 07201-2931
www.sambonet.it
908-351-4800 • Fax 908-351-3351

BEARD JAMES FOUNDATION
167 W 12th St
New York, NY 10011-8201
212-675-4984

BEATRICE CHEESE INC
770 N Springdale Rd
Waukesha, WI 53186-1815
262-782-2750 • Fax 262-782-8097

BEATTY, SATCHELL & COMPANY LLP
PO Box 1187
Easton, MD 21601-1187
410-822-6950

BEAUFURN
PO Box 1795
Clemmons, NC 27012-1795
www.beaufurn.com
336-766-7746 • Fax 336-766-2790

BEAULIEU VINEYARD
PO Box 219
Rutherford, CA 94573-0219
707-967-5200

BEAULLIEU REFRIGERATION INC.
200 N Luke St
Lafayette, LA 70506-1987
337-225-9755 • Fax 337-235-7014

BEAVERTON FOODS, INC.
PO Box 687
Beaverton, OR 97075-0687
e-mail:
dombg@beavertonfoods.com
503-646-8138 • Fax 503-644-9204

BECHER & CARLSON COMPANIES
2300 Windy Ridge Pkwy SE Ste 1
Atlanta, GA 30339-5665
770-955-6892

BECKS NORTH AMERICA
1 Station Pl
Stamford, CT 06902-6800
203-388-2325

BECK'S NORTH AMERICA
404 Gordon Ave
New Orleans, LA 70123-3920
504-450-2829

BEDEMCO, INC.
200 Hamilton Ave
White Plains, NY 10601-1812
e-mail: info@bedemco.com
914-683-1119 • Fax 914-683-1482

BEDFORD INDUSTRIES
1659 Rowe Ave
Worthington, MN 56187-8700
507-376-4136

BEE GEE SHRIMP INC.
1600 Kathleen Rd
Lakeland, FL 33805-3435
863-687-4411

BEER ASSOCIATES
96 Atlantic Ave
Lynbrook, NY 11563-3412
516-593-2270

BEHRLE & ASSOC BILL
271 Grove Ave
Verona, NJ 07044-1730
973-239-4900

BEKINS DISTRIBUTION SERVICES
9362 Dielman Industrial Dr
Saint Louis, MO 63132-2205
www.bdscoinc.com
800-325-4074 • Fax 314-817-0055

BEL CANTO FANCY FOODS, LTD.
5701 49th St
Maspeth, NY 11378-2020
718-497-3888 • Fax 718-497-3799

BEL/KAUKAUNA USA
PO Box 1974
Kaukauna, WI 54130-7074
800-588-3500 • Fax 920-788-9725

BELEW AVERITT
700 N Pearl St Ste 2000
Dallas, TX 75201-2867
e-mail: bstallard@belewaveritt.com
www.belewaveritt.com
214-969-7007 • Fax 214-953-0722

BELFONTE ICE CREAM AND DAIRY
1700 Prospect Ave
Kansas City, MO 64127-2544
816-231-2000

BELGIOIOSO CHEESE INC
5810 State Highway 29
Denmark, WI 54208-8830
920-863-2123

BELGIUM COMPANY
825 E Lakeshore Blvd
Kissimmee, FL 34744-5408
407-348-0177 • Fax 407-348-0320

BELL ATLANTIC PUBLIC COMM.
13100 Columbia Pike
Silver Spring, MD 20904-5247
301-282-8994 • Fax 301-236-0074

BELL MARK SHEFFIELD SILVER INC
7642 W Vogel Ave Ste 3
Peoria, AZ 85345-6603
623-412-2112 • Fax 623-412-2116

BELL-CARTER OLIVE COMPANY
3742 Mt Diablo Blvd
Lafayette, CA 94549-3682
e-mail: tmcgrath@bellcarter.com
925-284-5933 • Fax 925-284-1954

BELLISSIMO FOODS
1299 4th St
San Rafael, CA 94901-3040
800-813-2974

BELLISSIMO FOODS
985 Moraga Rd Ste 203
Lafayette, CA 94549-4433
e-mail: info@bellissimo.com
510-721-4850 • Fax 510-721-4905

BELLSOUTH MOBILITY
3900 N Causeway Blvd
Metairie, LA 70002-1746
504-830-1800

BELLWETHER FARMS
9999 Valley Ford Rd
Petaluma, CA 94952-9781
e-mail: bfcheese@pacbell.net
707-763-0993 • Fax 707-763-2443

BELL-WETHER LABORATORIES
7805 83rd St
Ridgewood, NY 11385-7640
718-381-7818 • Fax 732-706-0821

BELSON OUTDOORS
111 N River Rd
North Aurora, IL 60542-1324
www.belson.com
630-897-8489 • Fax 630-897-0573

BEL-TERR CHINA
PO Box 218
New Waterford, OH 44445-0218
330-457-2371 • Fax 330-457-7524

BELVEDERE HERE!
700 W Bittersweet Pl Apt 905
Chicago, IL 60613-2383
773-549-2903

BEN & JERRY'S HOMEMADE
PO Box 240
Waterbury, CT 06720-0240
860-244-5641

BEN & JERRY'S ICE CREAM/DAIRY
30 Community Dr
South Burlington, VT 05403-6809
www.benjerry.com
802-846-1500 • Fax 802-651-9705

BEN E KEITH FOOD
PO Box 901001
Fort Worth, TX 76101-2001
e-mail: dwoatman@becko.com
www.benekeith.com
817-759-6800 • Fax 817-759-6886

BENCHMARK SALES & MARKETING
1400 Providence Hwy
Norwood, MA 02062-5015
www.benchmarksales.com
781-237-0800 • Fax 781-237-8986

BENDER MARKETING SYSTEMS
738 Edinburgh St
San Francisco, CA 94112-3535
877-767-0267

BENETT BROTHERS, INC.
30 E Adams St
Chicago, IL 60603-5610
www.bennettbrothers.com
312-263-4800 • Fax 312-621-1669

BENIER USA INC
1781 Westfork Dr
Lithia Springs, GA 30122-1565
770-739-0700

BENJAMIN WEST LLLP
6420 Gunpark Dr
Boulder, CO 80301-3380
303-530-3885

BERG CO. - DISPENSERS
2001 S Stoughton Rd
Madison, WI 53716-2882
608-221-4281

BERG LIQUOR & DRAFT BEER SYSTEMS
5606 Wimbledon Ct
Mc Farland, WI 53558-8400
608-838-0221 • Fax 608-838-0081

BERKEL INCORPORATED
4406 Technology Dr
South Bend, IN 46628-9700
www.averyberkel.com
219-326-7000 • Fax 219-325-0949

BERKELEY PRODUCTS INC.
18400 Gale Ave
Rowland Heights, CA 91748-1214
www.berkeleyforge.com
626-810-0101 • Fax 626-810-6811

BERKLEY FARMS/DEAN DAIRY
25500 Clawiter Rd
Hayward, CA 94545-2739
510-265-8600

BERKS PACKING CO INC
307 Bingaman St
Reading, PA 19602-2671
610-376-7291

BERMAR AMERICA
42 Lloyd Ave
Malvern, PA 19355-3000
www.leverredevin.com
610-889-4900 • Fax 610-889-0289

BERNADETTE BAKING CORP.
85 Commercial St
Medford, MA 02155-4923
e-mail: bern630@cs.com
www.bernadettebaking.com
781-393-8700 • Fax 781-393-0414

BERNARD PECASO LIGHTING
395 Wythe Ave
Brooklyn, NY 11211-5918
718-599-4579 • Fax 718-963-2868

BERNARDAUD
41 Madison Ave Fl 41
New York, NY 10010-2203
212-696-2433 • Fax 212-532-8284

BERNER AIR DOORS
PO Box 5205
New Castle, PA 16105-0205
e-mail: twhite@berner.com
www.berner.com
724-652-0682 • Fax 724-652-0682

BERNER CHEESE
11824 Main St
Roscoe, IL 61073-9561
815-623-1722

BERNS & KOPPSTEIN
17 Battery Pl
New York, NY 10004-1207
800-221-7143

BERRY PLASTICS CORP
PO Box 959
Evansville, IN 47706-0959
812-424-2904 • Fax 812-463-7735

BER-TER CHINA
3672 Silliman St
New Waterford, OH 44445-9658
800-900-2371 • Fax 800-457-5820

BERTOLINI, INC.
13941 Norton Ave Ste A
Chino, CA 91710-5455
e-mail: Mike@bidirect.com
www.bidirect.com
909-613-1393 • Fax 909-517-3125

BERTOLLI USA INC
1 Harmon Plz
Secaucus, NJ 07094-2803
201-863-2088

BERTRAND'S INC.
2216 Silver St
Houston, TX 77007-2802
e-mail: bertrand@email.msn.com
713-880-0577 • Fax 713-880-4222

BERYL YUHAS ASSOCIATES
121 Paul Dr Ste B
San Rafael, CA 94903-2047
415-499-0348

BES CONSULTANTS INC
1201 S Kansas Ave
Topeka, KS 66612-1330
785-233-3803

BESSAM AIRE
PO Box 391525
Solon, OH 44139-8525
800-321-5992

BEST BRAND FOODS INC
6307 N 53rd St
Tampa, FL 33610-4098
e-mail: curtisg@bestbrands.com
800-282-0565 • Fax 813-626-7897

BEST BRANDS INC
1765 Yankee Doodle Rd
Saint Paul, MN 55121-1691
614-454-5850

BEST CHEESE CORP
40 Radio Circle Dr
Mount Kisco, NY 10549-2624
e-mail: info@parrano.com
914-241-2300 • Fax 914-241-8989

BEST EVENT PRODUCTS
PO Box 772
Lodi, NJ 07644-0772
e-mail: besteventsales@aol.com
973-777-2717 • Fax 800-705-4431

BEST JUICE DISTRIBUTORS
14632 Winslow Dr
Pride, LA 70770-9719
225-261-2017

BEST KOSHER
3944 S Morgan St
Chicago, IL 60609-2511
773-650-5938 • Fax 773-650-5999

BEST MFG/HOSPTLTY SALES
1530 Kell Ln
Griffin, GA 30224-8824
770-227-5561

BEST PROVISION CO.,INC.
14 Avon Ave
Newark, NJ 07108-2802
908-686-3310 • Fax 908-964-5900

BEST VANTAGE, INC.
3175 Commercial Ave Ste 211
Northbrook, IL 60062-1924
847-714-9527

BEST VINYL & FABRICS
12126 Sherman Way
North Hollywood, CA 91605-5501
818-764-6531 • Fax 818-764-6272

BEST WESTERN INTERNATIONAL, INC
6201 N 24th Pkwy
Phoenix, AZ 85016-2023
www.bestwestern.com
602-957-4200 • Fax 602-957-5575

BESTFOODS
9353 Belmont Ave
Franklin Park, IL 60131-2809
www.bestfoods.com
800-342-4634

BESTON WEST
213 E Harris Ave
South San Francisco, CA 94080-6807
www.bestondist.com
650-952-4220 • Fax 650-952-6819

BETA EXPROT, INC.
PO Box 542583
Dallas, TX 75354-2583
e-mail: betaexport@infosel.net.mx
214-821-1702 • Fax 214-821-1752

BETA RESEARCH CORPORATION
6400 Jericho Tpke
Syosset, NY 11791-4497
www.nybeta.com
516-935-3800 • Fax 516-935-4092

BETHUNE COOKMAN COL-LEGE
640 Dr Mary McLeod Bethune Blvd
Daytona Beach, FL 32114-3099
www.bethune.cookman.edu
386-255-1401 • Fax 386-257-5960

BETRAS PLASTICS, INC.
2525 Chesnee Hwy
Spartanburg, SC 29307-4121
864-599-0855 • Fax 864-599-7090

BETTCHER INDUSTRIES, INC.
PO Box 336
Vermilion, OH 44089-0336
www.bettcher.com
800-321-8763 • Fax 440-965-4900

BEVACCESS.COM
90 John St
New York, NY 10038-3202
212-571-3232

BEVACCESS.COM
116 John St
New York, NY 10038-3300
e-mail: info@bevaccess.com
www.bevaccess.com
877-lin-kbev

BEVENCO, INC.
10101 Southwest Fwy Ste 33
Houston, TX 77074-1126
e-mail: bevenco@bevenco.com
www.bevenco.com
713-772-4922 • Fax 713-772-5936

BEVERAGE CONNECTION
5904 Jessamine St Ste A2
Houston, TX 77081-6523
713-838-0641 • Fax 713-838-0645

BEVERAGE EQUIPMENT COMPANY.
9555 S Howell Ave
Oak Creek, WI 53154-5000
414-764-2211 • Fax 414-764-2227

BEVERAGE HOUSE INC. 1525
107 North Ave
Cartersville, GA 30120-2759
770-387-0451

BEVERAGE LAW CONSULTANTS, INC.
4201 Vineland Rd Ste 1-3
Orlando, FL 32811-7486
e-mail: biccorp@aol.com
407-246-6678 • Fax 800-537-9863

BEVERAGE MARKETING ASSOCIATES
1621 Francis Ave
Metairie, LA 70003-4649
504-887-9512

BEVERAGE SPECIALTIES, LTD.
196 John St Fl 21
New York, NY 10038-3513
www.majorpeters.com
716-673-1000 • Fax 716-673-8424

BEVERAGE-AIR
700 Buffington Rd
Spartanburg, SC 29303-4717
800-845-9800

BEVINCO BAR SYSTEMS
PO Box 954
Tyler, TX 75710-0954
e-mail: bevincotx@aol.com
www.bevinco.com
888-610-7768 • Fax 903-597-2893

BEVLES COMPANY, INC
PO Box 965
Chino, CA 91708-0965
www.bevles.com
909-465-6010 • Fax 909-465-6020

BH SERVICES, INC.
HC 82 Box 216
Box Elder, SD 57719-9801
605-923-5031

BIBB HOSPITALITY
1301 Avenue of the Americas
New York, NY 10019-6022
212-554-0327

BIC GRAPHIC USA
PO Box 23088
Tampa, FL 33623-2088
727-538-3483 • Fax 813-661-0498

BICYCLE HEALTH BENEFITS
111 S Calvert St Ste 2800
Baltimore, MD 21202-6100
www.bicyclehealth.com
410-986-2092 • Fax 410-986-2157

BIERY CHEESE
6544 Paris Ave
Louisville, OH 44641-9544
330-875-3381 • Fax 330-875-5896

BIG APPLE EQUIPMENT
PO Box 408
Yonkers, NY 10705-0408
e-mail:
bigappleequipcorp@juno.com
914-376-9300 • Fax 914-376-9375

BIG CHEF, INC.
5830 Funston St
Hollywood, FL 33023-1932
e-mail: bigchef5830@aol.com
Fax 954-965-7860

BIG CHILL MFG INC.
PO Box 322
Caney, KS 67333-0322
620-879-2905 • Fax 620-879-2192

BIG CITY REDS
3174 Doolittle Dr
Northbrook, IL 60062-2409
www.bigcityreds.com
847-714-1640 • Fax 847-714-1647

BIG JOHN GRILLS & ROTISSERIES
PO Box 5
Bellefonte, PA 16823-0005
e-mail: bjgrills@aol.com
www.bigjohngrills.com
814-359-2755 • Fax 814-359-2621

BIG RICK'S LLC
115 N Grove Dr
Wichita, KS 67214-4516
e-mail: bigrick@bigrick.com
800-964-7425 • Fax 316-264-4475

BIG TRAY
290 Division St
San Francisco, CA 94103-4882
www.bigtray.com
415-522-5080 • Fax 415-522-5099

BIG TRAY.COM
111 Gilbert St
San Francisco, CA 94103-4912
800-244-8729

BIG VALLEY MARKETING CORP
PO Box 14175
Fremont, CA 94539 1375
510-651-2270

BIG VALLEY MARKETING, LLC
2301 Armstrong St
Livermore, CA 94550-9348
e-mail: ybrewer@big-valley.com
www.big-valley.com
925-245-3300 • Fax 925-294-8581

BIGA BAKERY
9006 NW 105th Way
Miami, FL 33178-1218
e-mail: Jloos@bigabakery.com
www.bigabakery.com
305-884-2606

BIGELOW TEA LAND O'LAKES
1 Corporate Dr Ste 402
Shelton, CT 06484-6230
e-mail: mscinto@imsfood .com
203-929-2254 • Fax 203-926-0916

BIGTRAY.COM
290 Division St Fl 2
San Francisco, CA 94103-4882
e-mail: info@higtray.com
www.bigtray.com
800-BIG-TRAY

BILDON PARTS & SERVICES, INC.
16910 W 7 Mile Rd
Detroit, MI 48235-3098
313-272-6515

BI-LINE SYSTEMS
PO Box 16009
Winston Salem, NC 27115-6009
e-mail: bi-line@bi-line.net
www.bi-line.net
336-661-1951 • Fax 336-661-0498

BILL BROKAW ADVERTISING INC
425 W Lakeside Ave
Cleveland, OH 44113-1029
216-241-8003 • Fax 216-241-8033

BILL DICKIE ENTERPRISES
420 Ashwood Ln
Mc Kinney, TX 75069-8546
e-mail: docimpgy@aol.com
972-235-9946 • Fax 972-235-7031

BILMAR
8300 96TH AVE
Zeeland, MI 49464-9701
616-875-8131 • Fax 616-875-7565

BINDI DESSERT SERVICE
405 Minnisink Rd
Totowa, NJ 07512-1804
973-812-8118 • Fax 973-256-8828

BINDING-BRAUEREI USA
1621 Red Cedar Dr Apt 18
Fort Myers, FL 33907-7626
e-mail: andybbusa@aol.com
239-229-0111 • Fax 800-831-6417

BINDING-BRAUEREI USA, INC.
194 Main St
Norwalk, CT 06851-3502
203-229-0111

BIND-N-STIX, LLC
316 E Bruneau Ave
Kennewick, WA 99336-3727
e-mail: info@bindnstix.com
www.bindnstix.com
509-586-3236 • Fax 509-582-5845

BINNEY & SMITH INC.
1100 Church Ln
Easton, PA 18040-6638
www.crayola.co
610-253-6271 • Fax 610-250-5862

BINNEY & SMITH, INC.
16619 Harbour Town Dr
Silver Spring, MD 20905-4082
240-461-3445

BIO DYNAMICS INTL.
3308 Darion Ln
Plano, TX 75093-6721
972-758-1395

BIO ORTHOTICS INTERNATIONAL
1111 Jupiter Rd Ste 112A
Plano, TX 75074-7035
972-437-5454 • Fax 972-437-5519

BIO-CIDE INTERNATIONAL
PO Box 722170
Norman, OK 73070-8644
800-323-1398

BIODYNAMICS CORP
4515 Purdue Ave NE
Seattle, WA 98105-2141
206-526-0205

BIOLOGICAL SOLUTIONS CORP
7 Westchester Dr
Rocky Point, NY 11778-8811
888-615-7773

BIOLYNIX.COM
853 Sanders Rd # 101
Northbrook, IL 60062-2901
www.biolynx.com
847-509-0305 • Fax 847-509-0378

BIO SAFE ENTERPRISES, INC.
4120 SE International Way
Portland, OR 97222-6071
503-653-8937

BIOSTIM OF HOUSTON
603 W 17th St
Houston, TX 77008-3633
e-mail: biostim@insync.net
713-868-6246 • Fax 713-868-9346

BIRCHWOOD FOODS
PO Box 639
Kenosha, WI 53141-0639
www.bwfoods.com
262-859-2881 • Fax 262-859-2414

BIRD-B-GONE, INC.
23918 Skyline
Mission Viejo, CA 92692-1872
www.birdbgone.com
800-392-6915 • Fax 949-472-3116

BIRKENSTOCK
8171 Redwood Blvd
Novato, CA 94945-1403
800-487-9255 • Fax 415-899-1323

BIRO MFG CO
1114 W Main St
Lakeside Marblehead, OH 43440-2099
419-798-4451

BISCUIT & CRACKER MFG
1400 L St NW
Washington DC 20005-3509
202-898-1636

BISHOP WINES & SPIRITS
10810 Inland Ave
Mira Loma, CA 91752-3235
www.bishopbrands.com
909-681-8600 • Fax 909-681-8666

BITTNER CASH REG
3705 Main St
Houston, TX 77002-9599
e-mail: bcr@pdq.net
713-523-5531 • Fax 713-523-7633

BIZERBA U S A INC
31 Gordon Rd
Piscataway, NJ 08854-5945
732-819-0121

BKI
PO Box 80400
Simpsonville, SC 29680-0007
www.bki-food-equip.com
864-963-3471 • Fax 864-967-2787

BLACK HAT SPECIALITY FOODS
PO Box 2781
Wimberley, TX 78676-7681
e-mail: blkhatspec@aol.com
888-480-2140 • Fax 330-865-0450

BLACKMAN KALLICK & BARTLESTEIN
300 S Riverside Plz Ste 660
Chicago, IL 60606-6613
312-207-1040

BLACKSTONE
7900 NW 36th St
Miami, FL 33166-6604
305-639-9590

BLADE SPORTWEAR, INC.
4390 Interstate Dr
Macon, GA 31210-6807
www.bladesportswear.com
478-477-9070 • Fax 478-757-0170

BLAKAR, INC
192 Lexington Ave Ste 50
New York, NY 10016-6823
e-mail: rromberg@blakar.com
212-686-0810 • Fax 212-683-7995

BLAKESLEE
1844 S Laramie Ave
Cicero, IL 60804-1944
773-242-2710

BLAKESLEE C/O B.S.E. MARKETING
116 Gazza Blvd
Farmingdale, NY 11735-1420
e-mail: bsemkting@aol.com
631-694-0300 • Fax 631-694-0313

BLAKESLEE DISH MACHINES
13911 N Dale Mabry Hwy
Tampa, FL 33618-2414
813-969-0006

BLANC INDUSTRIES, INC
37 Ironia Rd
Flanders, NJ 07836-9124
e-mail: csmedira@blancind.co
www.blancind.com
973-598-9585 • Fax 973-598-9590

BLATTLERS FINE FOODS
11536 D Ave
Auburn, CA 95603-2710
530-888-7540 • Fax 530-888-0663

BLAZE PRODUCTS/AAPER
11 Isaac Shelby Dr
Shelbyville, KY 40065-9128
502-633-0650

BLENDCO, INC
8 J M Tatum Industrial Dr
Hattiesburg, MS 39401-8341
601-544-9800

BLENDEX
11208 Electron Dr
Louisville, KY 40299-3875
502-267-1003 • Fax 502-267-1024

BLEU FOODS
611 S Congress Ave Ste 515
Austin, TX 78704-1733
512-467-2851 • Fax 512-467-2604

BLICKMAN SUPPLY/ SAQUELLA USA
280 Midland Ave
Saddle Brook, NJ 07663-6404
201-791-2244 • Fax 201-791-2288

BLIMPIE INTERNATIONAL
1775 The Exchange SE
Atlanta, GA 30339-2016
800-447-6256

BLISS BROTHERS DAIRY, INC.
PO Box 2288
Attleboro, MA 02703-0039
508-222-0787 • Fax 508-226-6320

BLOCK AND ASSOCIATES
1001 Bridgeway Ste 638
Sausalito, CA 94965-2158
415-332-2662

BLODGETT COMBI
PO Box 586
Burlington, VT 05402-0586
e-mail: dpacka@maytag.com
www.maytag.com
800-860-3718 • Fax 802-860-3809

BLODGETT OVEN CO, INC.
50 Lakeside Ave
Burlington, VT 05401-5242
802-658-6600

BLOUNT SEAFOOD CORP
383 Water St
Warren, RI 02885-3333
401-245-8800

BLUE BELL CREAMERIES
1101 S Horton St
Brenham, TX 77833-4413
www.bluebell.com
979-836-9777 • Fax 979-830-2198

BLUE BELL CREAMERIES
34623 Grantham College Dr
Slidell, LA 70460-6815
985-847-0594 • Fax 985-847-0598

BLUE BUNNY
1 Blue Bunny Dr SW
Le Mars, IA 51031-2207
www.bluebunny.com
800-942-3800 • Fax 712-548-3114

**BLUE DIAMOND
GROWERS**
1802 C St
Sacramento, CA 95814-1099
www.bluediamondgrowers.com
916-442-0771 • Fax 916-446-8461

**BLUE DOLPHIN
DESIGNS**
8826 Grow Dr
Pensacola, FL 32514-7050
800-523-8833 • Fax 850-478-4343

BLUE POINT
3312 Livonia Ave
Los Angeles, CA 90034-3112
www.foodmachine.com
310-202-7600 • Fax 310-838-9645

BLUE RIDGE FARMS
3301 Atlantic Ave
Brooklyn, NY 11208-1946
718-827-9000 • Fax 718-647-0052

**BLUE RIDGE MOUNTAIN
COOKERY**
PO Box 70
Waynesboro, PA 17268-0070
e-mail:
cookers@classiccookers.com
www.classsiccookers.com
717-762-1211 • Fax 717-762-1966

BLUE RIDGE SIGNS
PO Box 400
Weatherford, TX 76086-0400
817-598-0025

**BLUEWATER
AQUACULTURE**
12600 Fair Lakes Cir
Fairfax, VA 22033-4904
703-995-6500

BO BO BO COMPANY, INC.
260 Secaucus Rd
Secaucus, NJ 07094-2131
201-583-1957 • Fax 201-583-1958

**BOB EVENS FARMS/
G&J MARKETING**
3776 S High St # B
Columbus, OH 43207-4012
e-mail:
bill_meredith@bobevans.com
614-491-2225 • Fax 800-272-7675

BOCA BURGER
910 Mayer Ave
Madison, WI 53704-4256
www.bocaburger.com
608-285-6950 • Fax 608-242-6153

BOCA BURGER
PO Box 157
Techny, IL 60082-0157
www.bocaburger.com
312-201-0300 • Fax 312-201-2305

BOCA BURGER INC
54 E Harbor Dr
Lake Zurich, IL 60047-3076
847-438-4466

BOCA TERRY
6601 Lyons Rd Ste H9
Pompano Beach, FL 33073-3632
e-mail: bocaterry@aol.com
www.bocaterry.com
800-548-3583 • Fax 561-999-4452

BOCAR ENTERPRISES, INC.
1542 E Greyhound Pass
Carmel, IN 46032-1036
317-587-1460

**BOCK ENGINEERED
PRODUCTS INC**
3600 N Summit St
Toledo, OH 43611-3147
www.bockengineered.com
419-726-2645 • Fax 419-726-8583

**BODACIOUS FOOD
COMPANY**
339 Gennett Dr
Jasper, GA 30143-1140
e-mail: cathy@bodaciousfoods.com
800-391-1979 • Fax 706-253-1156

**BODY BALANCE
ORTHOTICS**
6105 NW 31st St
Bethany, OK 73008-4212
405-495-8393 • Fax 580-421-8396

BOELTER
1110 W Silver Spring Dr
Milwaukee, WI 53209-5151
www.boelter.com
414-461-3400 • Fax 414-461-5058

BOGGIATO PRODUCE INC
PO Box 2266
Salinas, CA 93902-2266
831-424-8952 • Fax 831-424-1974

BOGNER INDUSTRIES INC
199 Trade Zone Dr
Ronkonkoma, NY 11779-7362
631-981-5123

BOGNON CANDY CO
2316 Troost Avenue
Kansas City, MO 64108-2835
800-821-6641 • Fax 816-842-0228

BOJANGLES EXPRESS
9432 Southern Pines Blvd
Charlotte, NC 28273-5553
704-527-2675

BOKUM TOOL CO
32301 Dequindre Rd
Madison Hts, MI 48071-1594
248-585-0222

BOLLINGER FOWLER CO
830 Morris Tpke
Shorth Hills, NJ 07078-2625
800-446-5311

BOLTEX TEXTILES
34 Walker St
New York, NY 10013-3514
212-226-8884 • Fax 212-941-1206

**BON APPETIT
INTERNATIONAL INC**
3737 Savannah Loop
Oviedo, FL 32765-9204
407-366-4973

BOND FOOD PRODUCTS
235 Cook Ave
Oconto, WI 54153-1915
www.bondsfoods.com
920-834-4433 • Fax 920-834-2598

BONDUELLE INC.
PO Box 405
Millington, NJ 07946-0405
www.bonduelle.com
908-790-1600 • Fax 908-790-1603

**BONFAIRE FDS. DIST. BY
PLACON**
6096 McKee Rd
Madison, WI 53719-5103
608-271-3952

BONGRAIN-USA, INC.
400 S Custer Ave
New Holland, PA 17557-9220
717-355-8500 • Fax 717-355-8848

BONNIST INTERNATIONAL
382 Route 59 Ste 280
Monsey, NY 10952-3422
www.bonnist.com
845-368-2220 • Fax 845-368-2424

BONVIV, INC.
2068 Walsh Ave # B
Santa Clara, CA 95050-2530
408-986-0216

BOOK OF THE MONTH CLUB
Camp Hill, PA 17012-0001
717-867-4300

BOOKINGCENTER.COM
PO Box 184
Occidental, CA 95465-0184
e-mail: info@bookingcenter.com
www.BookingCenter.com
707-750-0174 • Fax 707-762-4700

BOOS & CO
315 S 1st St
Effingham, IL 62401-3735
217-347-7701

**BORAX PAPER PRODUCTS,
INC.**
1390 Spofford Ave
Bronx, NY 10474-6100
e-mail: boraxpaper@aol.com
718-665-8500 • Fax 718-665-3661

**BORDEN FOODS C/O G.A.
DAVIS FOODS**
20 Crossways Park Dr N
Woodbury, NY 11797-2007
e-mail: adavis@gadavis.com
516-364-0910 • Fax 516-364-0917

**BORDEN FOODSERVICE
GROUP**
180 E Broad St
Columbus, OH 43215-3707
614-672-6274

**BORDEN INC FOODSERVICE
GROUP**
180 E Broad St # BB26
Columbus, OH 43215-3707
614-225-4000 • Fax 614-627-8593

BORDEN MILK PRODUCTS
5327 S Lamar St
Dallas, TX 75215-4972
214-565-0332 • Fax 214-426-5841

BORDEN MILK PRODUCTS
4743 Florida Blvd
Baton Rouge, LA 70806-4026
225-926-7130 • Fax 225-927-9106

BORMIOLI
11440 86th Rd N
West Palm Beach, FL 33412-1331
e-mail: tablesod@aol.com
561-776-0083

BORMIOLI ROCCO HOTEL DIV
14101 Sullyfield Cir Ste 300
Chantilly, VA 20151-1625
800-296-7508

BOSE
The Mountain MS #466
Framingham, MA 01701-8863
www.bose.com
508-766-1679 • Fax 508-766-1800

BOSKOVICH FARMS, INC.
PO Box 1352
Oxnard, CA 93032-1352
www.boskovichfarms.com
805-487-7799 • Fax 805-487-5189

BOSTON BEER
75 Arlington St
Boston, MA 02116-3936
www.samadams.com
617-368-5000

BOSTON BEER CO
31 Germania St
Jamaica Plain, MA 02130-2314

BOSTON BEER COMPANY
6108 Kenwood Ave
Dallas, TX 75214-3014
e-mail: rmicu@msn.com
214-823-9555 • Fax 214-823-9529

**BOSTON CHOWDA
COMPANY**
101 Phoenix Ave
Lowell, MA 01852-4930
978-970-1144 • Fax 978-970-0450

**BOSTON PIZZA
RESTAURANTS INC**
1505 Lyndon B Johnson Fwy
Dallas, TX 75234-6069
972-484-9022

BOUGAINVILLEA INC.
PO Box 20008
Rochester, NY 14602-0008
585-321-1140 • Fax 585-321-1140

**BOULDER CREEK STONE/BRICK
CO.**
8282 Arthur St NE
Minneapolis, MN 55432-2132
www.bouldercreekstone.com
612-786-7138 • Fax 612-786-7276

BOURGEAT
12428 Wycliff Ln
Austin, TX 78727-5238
512-339-2456

**BOWDEN MIDDLETON
CONSULTING**
6238 NW 23rd St
Boca Raton, FL 33434-4330
www.bowden-middleton.com
561-477-3069 • Fax 561-477-1071

**BOWLING GREEN STATE
UNIVERSITY**
Hospitality Mgmt Prg, 242 B A
Bowling Green, OH 43403-0001
e-mail: kcrocke@cba-bgsu.edu
419-372-2025 • Fax 419-372-2875

BOWLIN'S/STUCKEY'S
136 Louisiana Blvd NE
Albuquerque, NM 87108-2055
505-266-5985

**BOWMAN DISPLAYS DIGITAL
IMAGING**
648 Progress Ave
Munster, IN 46321-2872
www.bowphoto.com
219-922-8200 • Fax 574-822-8329

BOXCO INDUSTRIES, INC.
780 International Pkwy
Fort Lauderdale, FL 33325-6219
www.boxcoindustries.com
800-654-2932 • Fax 954-747-8902

BOXERBRAND
5600 Murray St
Little Rock, AR 72209-2539
800-252-2772

BOYD COFFEE COMPANY
PO Box 20547
Portland, OR 97294-0547
503-666-4545

**BOYD COFFEE
COMPANY**
19730 NE Sandy Blvd
Portland, OR 97230-7310
800-341-2242

BOYDS
2009 108th St Ste 902
Grand Prairie, TX 75050-1490
www.boyds.com
972-453-1722

**BRACH BROCK
CONFECTIONS ANDES**
401 N Cicero Ave
Chicago, IL 60644-2000
773-473-2387 • Fax 773-473-2390

**BRAD WALLER &
ASSOCIATES, INC.**
803 Stadium Dr Ste 103
Arlington, TX 76011-6246
817-265-7253 • Fax 817-265-9940

**BRADFORD
ASSOCIATES**
4 Hubbard St
Canton, MA 02021-1114
781-828-0064 • Fax 781-828-9747

BRADLEY'S
32 Cannery Row Ste 1
Monterey, CA 93940-1447
831-655-6799

BRAGARD INC.
215 Park Ave S Ste
New York, NY 10003-1603
212-982-8031 • Fax 212-353-0318

BRAGARDM REPUBLIC UNIFORM
1413 E 20th St
Los Angeles, CA 90011-1301
www.chefappeal.com
213-745-7866 • Fax 213-746-4756

BRAJUHA MANAGEMENT CONSULTING
PO Box 402
Lake Grove, NY 11755-0402
631-471-2302

BRAKEBUSH BROTHERS INC
711 W Jefferson St
Auburn, IL 62615-1339
217-438-6611

BRAMAN CHEMICAL INC
1027 Main St
Worcester, MA 01603-2491
www. Bramanchemical.com
508-755-5410 • Fax 508-798-4741

BRAMSON HOUSE INC
5 Nassau St
Rockville Centre, NY 11570-4715
e-mail:
bramson@bramsonhouse.com
www.bramsonhouse.com
516-764-5006 • Fax 516-764-4539

BRAND BUILDERS INTERNATIONAL
3555 Harbor Gtwy S Ste A
Costa Mesa, CA 92626-1470
714-662-5515 • Fax 714-662-5811

BRASS SMITH
3880 Holly St
Denver, CO 80207-1214
800-662-9595 • Fax 303-331-8444

BRAUN BRUSH
43 Albertson Ave
Albertson, NY 11507-2198
www.brush.com
800-645-4111 • Fax 516-741-6000

BRAUN, G.A. INC.
161 E Brighton Ave
Syracuse, NY 13210-4143
315-475-3123

BRAVE COAST
9383 NW 13th St
Miami, FL 33172-2807
305-599-0440 • Fax 305-599-0670

BRAVO FARMS
34292 Road 124
Visalia, CA 93291-9514
559-627-3525 • Fax 559-625-0490

BRAZIL STONE CORP.
439 State Rt 17
Carlstadt, NJ 07072-1232
201-964-1940 • Fax 201-964-1939

BRAZILIAN GOVERNMENT TRADE BUR
1185 Avenue of the Americas
New York, NY 10036-2601
e-mail: info@brazilny.com
www.brazilny.com
212-827-0976 • Fax 212-827-0225

BREAD ALONE, INC.
PO Box 358
Boiceville, NY 12412-0358
e-mail: brdalone@mhv.net
www.breadalone.com
845-657-3328 • Fax 845-657-3328

BREAKAWAY INTERNATIONAL
803 Stadium Dr
Arlington, TX 76011-6246
800-677-2986

BRENHAM WHOLESALE GROCERY COMPANY
PO Box 584
Brenham, TX 77834-0584
979-836-7925 • Fax 979-830-0346

BREWMATIC COMPANY
20333 Normandie Ave
Torrance, CA 90502-1215
310-787-5444 • Fax 310-787-5412

BREWSTER DAIRY INC
675 Wabash Ave S
Brewster, OH 44613-1302
330-767-3492 • Fax 330-767-3386

BRIDGE MACHINE COMPANY, INC.
PO Box 45
Palmyra, NJ 08065-0045
www.bridgeonline.com
856-829-1800 • Fax 856-786-8147

BRIDGEMAN'S
6201 Brooklyn Blvd
Minneapolis, MN 55429-4035
www. bridgemans.com
612-931-3099 • Fax 612-931-3199

BRIDGFORD FOODS CORP
170 N Green St
Chicago, IL 60607-2313
800-621-4241

BRIDGFORD FOODS CORPORATION
1308 N Patt St
Anaheim, CA 92801-2551
www.bridgford.com
714-526-5533 • Fax 714-526-4360

BRIDGFORD FOODS CORPORATION
2570 Edgewood Ln
York, PA 17403-9541
e-mail: lindatuttle@bridgford.com
www.bridgford.com
800-527-2105 • Fax 717-428-0332

BRIDGFORT FOODS CORPORATION
118 Mathieson Pt
Jasper, GA 30143-2711
888-564-4438 • Fax 706-692-9866

BRIGHAMS
30 Mill St
Arlington, MA 02476-4700
781-648-9000

BRIJON PREMIER CHOCOLATE
115 Commerce Dr
Hauppauge, NY 11788-3901
e-mail: lancobrij@aol.com
631-231-2300 • Fax 631-231-2731

BRILL HYGENIC PRODUCTS INC
2905 S Congress Ave
Delray Beach, FL 33445-7337
800-330-6696 • Fax 561-272-3542

BRINTONS US AXMINSTER INC
PO Box 877
Greenville, MS 38702-0877
662-332-1581

BRISK/RCR COFFEE
507 N 22nd St
Tampa, FL 33605-6084
e-mail: brisk01@spraynet.com
813-248-6264

BRISTOL BENCH COMPANY
4175 Lyndon Way
Louisville, KY 40207-5007
800-390-6883

BRISTOL RETAIL SOLUTIONS/NCR
17062 Murphy Ave
Irvine, CA 92614-5914
949-252-8765 • Fax 949-252-8220

BRISTOL SEAFOOD INC
PO Box 486
Portland, ME 04112-0486
207-774-3177

BRISTOL-MYERS SQUIBB CO
345 Park Ave
New York, NY 10154-0004
212-546-4000

BRITHISH TRADITIONS
12901 2nd St
Grandview, MO 64030-2291
e-mail: sales@britishtraditions.com
www.britishtraditions.com
816-767-1203 • Fax 816-767-8064

BRIZARD MARIE USA
11900 Biscayne Blvd
Miami, FL 33181-2743
305-893-3394

BROADCAST MUSIC, INC. (BMI)
10 Music Sq E
Nashville, TN 37203-4399
615-401-2804

BROADCAST VISION LLC
5126 Clareton Dr
Agoura Hills, CA 91301-4529
800-770-9770

BROADLEAF GAME
3050 E 11th St
Los Angeles, CA 90023-3606
800-336-3844

BROASTER CO
2855 Cranston Rd
Beloit, WI 53511-3997
www.broaster.com
608-365-0193 • Fax 608-365-5158

BROASTER RECIPE FOODS
PO Box 1327
Beloit, WI 53512-1327
608-362-2820 • Fax 608-362-2982

BROASTER/SMOKAROMA
57 Mall Dr # A
Commack, NY 11725-5703
e-mail: efb65@aol.com
www.efdist.com
631-864-9090 • Fax 631-864-9191

BROCAR PRODUCTS INC
4335 River Rd
Cincinnati, OH 45204-1041
www.brcar.com
513-861-671 • Fax 513-861-6773

BROKER'S CHOICE
15 Browning Ct
Mendham, NJ 07945-3301
900-027-0500

BROLITE
2542 N Elston Ave
Chicago, IL 60647-2030
773-384-0210

BROMAK SALES INC.
E9770 7th St
Clintonville, WI 54929-9520
715-823-4429 • Fax 715-823-7493

BROOKLYN UNION A KEYSPAN ENERG
1 Metrotech Ctr
Brooklyn, NY 11201-3831
www.bug.com
800-GAS-2000 •Fax 718-488-1766

BROOKLYN'S BEST
7 Metrotech Ctr Ste 200
Brooklyn, NY 11201-3841
www.brooklynchamber.com
718-875-1000 • Fax 718-237-4274

BROTHERS PRODUCE, INC.
3116 Produce Row
Houston, TX 77023-5814
713-924-4196 • Fax 713-924-5055

BROWN FORMAN BEV. WORLD-WIDE
2200 Powell St Ste 400
Emeryville, CA 94608-1879
510-653-7400

BROWN JORDAN
9860 Gidley St
El Monte, CA 91731-1138
626-443-8971

BROWN JUDD DESIGNS INC.
647 Jefferson Blvd
Warwick, RI 02886-1318
401-738-8624

BROWN-FORMAN BEVERAGES WORLDWIDE
458 Wilcrest Dr
Houston, TX 77042-1074
e-mail: jeff_fullam@b-f.com
281-584-9844 • Fax 281-584-9844

BROWN-FORMAN CORP
850 Dixie Hwy
Louisville, KY 40210-1091
www.jackdaniels.com
502-585-1100 • Fax 502-585-1100

BROWN'S VELVET DAIRY
PO Box 52559
New Orleans, LA 70152-2559
504-529-2221

BROYHILL FURNITURE INDUSTRIES
1 Broyhill Park
Lenoir, NC 28633-0003
828-758-4131 • Fax 704-735-4756

BRUNSWICK
1 N Field Ct
Lake Forest, IL 60045-4811
847-735-4131 • Fax 847-735-4756

BRUSS CO
3548 N Kostner Ave
Chicago, IL 60641-3898
773-282-2900 • Fax 773-282-6966

BRYAN ASHLEY INTERNATIONAL INC
2601 Gateway Dr
Pompano Beach, FL 33069-4321
e-mail:
bryanashley@bryanshley.com
800-331-1225 • Fax 954-351-9922

BT ALEX BROWN INCORPORATED
1 South St
Baltimore, MD 21202-3298
410-895-3344 • Fax 410-895-3200

BUBBIES OF SAN FRANCISCO, INC.
PO Box 7326
Stockton, CA 95267-0326
209-957-9411 • Fax 209-957-9413

BUCKEYE EGG FARMS
PO Box 173
Croton, OH 43013-0173
740-893-7200 • Fax 740-893-2897

BUDGET HOST INTERNATIONAL
PO Box 14341
Arlington, TX 76094-1341
800-283-4678

BUDGET SUITES OF AMERICA
4640 S Eastern Ave
Las Vegas, NV 89119-6135

BUELL DOOR CO
5200 E Grand Ave
Dallas, TX 75223-2233
www.buelldoor.com
214-827-9260 • Fax 214-826-9163

BUFFALO CHINA
500 Bailey Ave
Buffalo, NY 14210-1733
716-361-3000 • Fax 716-361-3290

BUFFETS INC
1460 Buffet Way
Saint Paul, MN 55121-1133
952-942-9760

BUILTRIGHT CHAIR COMPANY
901 Connor St
Statesville, NC 28677-5617
e-mail: builtright@twave.net
704-873-6431 • Fax 704-874-8495

BULBMAN
630 Sunshine Ln
Reno, NV 89502-1555
775-788-5661

BULBRITE INDUSTRIES
145 W Commercial Ave
Moonachie, NJ 07074-1704
e-mail: info@bulbrite.com
www.bulbrite.com
201-531-5900 • Fax 201-531-1271

BULBTRONICS
45 Banfi Plz N
Farmingdale, NY 11735-1539
e-mail: bulb@bulbtronics.com
www.bulbtonics.com
631-249-2272 • Fax 631-249-6066

BULLSEYE, INC.
1014 Fairdell Dr
Hummelstown, PA 17036-8710
www.bullseyeinc.net
717-566-4366 • Fax 717-566-9742

**BUMBLE BEE
SEAFOODS INC**
8899 University Center Ln
San Diego, CA 92122-1013
858-550-4000

BUNGE
885 N Kinzie Ave
Bradley, IL 60915-1230
800-251-7210 • Fax 815-825-8186

BUNGE FOODS
725 N Kinzie Ave
Bradley, IL 60915-1228
815-933-0600

BUNGE FOODS
902 La Cascada
San Antonio, TX 78258-2929
e-mail: bphillips@bunge.com
210-497-1303 • Fax 210-497-1306

BUNKER HILL CHEESE
6005 County Road 77
Millersburg, OH 44654-9045
330-893-2131 • Fax 330-893-2079

BUNN-O-MATIC
1400 Stevenson Dr
Springfield, IL 62703-4291
217-529-6601

BUNZL NEW YORK
300 Duffy Ave
Hicksville, NY 11801-3612
516-937-7400 • Fax 516-937-7419

BUNZL DISTRIBUTION USA
701 Emerson Rd Ste 500
Saint Louis, MO 63141-6754
888-997-4515 • Fax 314-997-0247

BURCH & PARTNERS, INC
12465 2nd St E Apt B105
Saint Petersburg, FL 33706-4962
e-mail: alexd@intellifonegroup.com
727-550-2222

BURFORD CORP
PO Box 748
Maysville, OK 73057-0748
405-867-4467

BURGER KING CORP
17777 Old Cutler Rd
Miami, FL 33157-6347
800-937-1800

BURKE CORPORATION
PO Box 209
Nevada, IA 50201-0209
e-mail: sales_info@burkecorp.com
800-654-1152 • Fax 515-382-2834

BURNS & ASSOCIATES
3303 Harbor Blvd Ste E-
Costa Mesa, CA 92626-1530
e-mail: bandafoodsvc@earthlink.net
714-429-1901 • Fax 714-429-1915

**BURNS CHEMICAL SYSTEMS
INC**
3003 Venture Ct
Export, PA 15632-8950
724-327-7600

**BURRELL LEDER
BELTECH INC**
7501 Saint Louis Ave
Skokie, IL 60076-4033
800-428-7735

BURROWS PAPER
200 Shotwell Dr
Franklin, OH 45005-4656
800-732-1933

BURROWS PAPER CORP.
13805 Mount Anderson St
Reno, NV 89506-1330
e-mail: dfischer@burline.com
775-356-0408 • Fax 775-356-8968

BURSON-MARSTELLER
1 Gateway Ctr Fl 20
Pittsburgh, PA 15222-1435
412-471-9600

BUSH BROS
1016 E Weisgarber Rd Bldg 1
Knoxville, TN 37909-2678
865-588-7685

BUSINESS GRAPHIC INC.
955 Dieckman St
Woodstock, IL 60098-9262
www.businessgraphics.com
800-435-4874 • Fax 815-338-2652

BUSINESS INSURANCE GROUP
3131 W Alabama St Ste 200
Houston, TX 77098-2030
713-541-7272 • Fax 713-772-5224

**BUSINESS SOUND &
COMMUNICATION**
15200 E Hardy Rd Ste 230
Houston, TX 77032-2727
e-mail: bsctx@aol.com
281-590-3400 • Fax 281-590-0383

BUSSETO FOODS
PO Box 12403
Fresno, CA 93777-2403
559-237-9591 • Fax 559-237-5745

**BUTTER BUDS FOOD
SERVICE**
2330 Chicory Rd
Racine, WI 53403-4113
262-637-9288

BUTTERBALL FARMS
1435 Buchanan Ave SW
Grand Rapids, MI 49507-1699
616-243-0105

BUY PRODUCE.COM
15375 Barranca Pkwy
Irvine, CA 92618-2217
800-400-6244

BYRONS
PO BOX 1747
Gallatin, TN 37066-1747
615-452-4892 • Fax 615-451-3428

C & G MANUFACTURING
243 Little Park Rd
Grand Junction, CO 81503-1725
970-241-9206

**C & M BUSINESS MACHINES
INC**
2207 N Belt Hwy
Saint Joseph, MO 64506-2205
816-233-3758

C & M FINE PACK
1048 High Point Loop
Longwood, FL 32750-8401
e-mail: bogorman@moinet.net
407-322-4949 • Fax 407-322-8308

C & M FINE PACK, INC.
4162 Georgia Blv
San Bernardino, CA 92407-1852
www.cmfinepack.com
909-880-1781 • Fax 909-878-805

C & M FINE PACK, INC.
4710 Echo Falls Dr
Humble, TX 77345-4901
281-548-8357 • Fax 281-360-0200

C / S GROUP
PO Box 380
Muncy, PA 17756-0380
570-546-5941

C B RICHARD ELLIS
533 S Fremont Ave
Los Angeles, CA 90071-1712
800-994-0303

C E C ENTERTAINMENT INC
4441 W Airport Fwy
Irving, TX 75062-5834

C F CHEFS INC
4030 Black Gold Dr
Dallas, TX 75247-6304
214-905-1518

C F I/COMBINED FORMS INC
4554 Saint Johns Ave
Jackonsville, FL 32210-1839
904-387-4225

C F SAUER
2000 W Broad St
Richmond, VA 23220-2000
804-359-5786 • Fax 804-359-6942

C H BABB
19 Tech Cir
Natick, MA 01760-1023
508-655-4700

C H H CHESS
PO Box 2429
Charlottesville, VA 22902-2429
434-977-5029

C M F CORPORATION
1524 W 15th St
Long Beach, CA 90813-1207
562-437-2166

**C N L RESTAURANT
GROUP**
450 S Orange Ave
Orlando, FL 32801-3383
407-650-1510

**C P D F C/CALIF PORTABLE
FLOOR**
4600 Calle Quetzal
Camarillo, CA 93012-8558
805-383-6262

C S L INC
10 Commerce Dr
Desti, FL 32541-2359
800-622-6069

C S LIGHTING
9104 Osborne Tpke
Richmond, VA 23231-8115
e-mail: cslighting@erols.com
804-795-1476 • Fax 804-795-2012

C&K MANUFACTURING
28825 Ranney Pkwy
Westlake, OH 44145-1173
440-871-7763

C.C.I INDUSTRIES, INC.
350 Fischer Ave Ste A
Costa Mesa, CA 92626-4508
714-662-3879 • Fax 714-662-0943

C.E.S.I.
2526 50th St
Woodside, NY 11377-7823
e-mail: sales@gesi-usa.com
www.uniqey.com
718-777-5177 • Fax 718-777-3787

**C.J. HIGGINS
ENGINEERING CO.**
PO Box 794
Norwell, MA 02061-0794
781-659-7380 • Fax 781-659-2542

C.R. MFG.
PO Box 428
Mound, MN 55364-0428
www.crmfg.com
952-472-3600 • Fax 952-472-7808

CABOT CREAMERY
PO Box 128
Cabot, VT 05647-0128
800-639-4031

**CABOT CREAMERY
COOP., INC.**
100 Grandview Rd
Braintree, MA 02184-2686
781-356-0991 • Fax 781-356-8502

CAC CHINA, INC.
10 Camptown Rd
Irvington, NJ 07111-1105
www.cacchina.com
973-371-4300 • Fax 973-371-4611

CACHE BOX, INC.
PO Box 17375
Arlington, VA 22216-7375
www.cachebox.net
703-276-2500 • Fax 703-276-2504

CADCO, LIMITED
145 Colebrook River Rd
Winsted, CT 06098-2203
www.cadco-ltd.com
860-496-4925 • Fax 860-496-5677

CADWELL COMPANY
3 Kuniholm Dr
Holliston, MA 01746-1390
e-mail: cadwellco@aol.com
508-429-3100 • Fax 508-429-3284

CAFE BUSTELLO
7970 NW 60th St
Miami, FL 33166-3491
305-305-592-73

CAFE BUSTELLO
7970 NW 60th St # O
Miami, FL 33166-3491
305-592-7302 • Fax 305-592-9471

CAFE LA SEMEUSE
PO Box 429
Brooklyn, NY 11222-0429
800-242-6333

**CAFESTYLE/CAFE MOCHA
BLEND INC**
12559 Lakeshore N
Auburn, CA 95602-8121
e-mail: cmbi@foothill.net
530-806-3838 • Fax 530-268-2604

CAFFE D'AMORE
1107 S Mountain Ave
Monrovia, CA 91016-4258
626-792-9146 • Fax 626-792-4382

CAFFE ITALIA ENTERPRISES
PO Box 41
Waterbury, CT 06720-0041
203-757-5230 • Fax 203-591-9270

**CAFFERATA AND JOHN
DOUGH**
1100 Marina Way S Ste D
Richmond, CA 94804-3727
www.cafferata.com and
jondoghco.com
510-620-1010 • Fax 510-620-1018

CAFTEC, INC
3450 3rd St Ste 4F
San Francisco, CA 94124-1439
800-707-6381

CAFE AU LAIT, INC.
1111 E Watson Center Rd
Carson, CA 90745-4217
310-834-4400 • Fax 310-834-0300

CAIN FOOD IND
PO Box 35066
Dallas, TX 75235-0066
214-630-4511

CAIN'S COFFEE COMPANY
922 W 34th St
Houston, TX 77018-6319
www.cainscoffee.com
713-864-1487 • Fax 713-864-1034

**CAIRE HOTEL
& RESTAURANT SUPPLIES**
433 N Bernadotte St
New Orleans, LA 70119-4311
504-482-0294 • Fax 504-482-1304

CAIS INTERNET
1255 22nd St NW
Washington, DC 20037-1217
www.cais.com
Fax 202-714-1890

CAJUN JERK SEASONING
11814 Coursey Blvd # 181
Baton Rouge, LA 70816-4403
225-753-4338

CAL LIGHTING
13875 Ramona Ave
Chino, CA 91710-5426
e-mail: calighting@dataframe.com
800-321-6677 • Fax 909-590-5955

CALABRO CHEESE CORP.
588 Coe Ave
East Haven, CT 06512-3847
800-969-1311• Fax 203-469-6929

CALAVO GROWERS OF CALIFORNIA
2530 Red Hill Ave
Santa Ana, CA 92705-5542
www.calavo.com
949-833-4253 • Fax 949-223-1114

CALICO INDUSTRIES INC
PO Box 2005
Annapolis Junction, MD 20701-2005
800-638-0828

CALIENTE FOOD CORP
61 7th Ave S
New York, NY 10014-6701
www.calientecab.com
212-243-1633 • Fax 212-243-1252

CALIF AVOCADO COMMISSION
1251 E Dyer Rd
Santa Ana, CA 92705-5639
714-558-6761

CALIF FOOD & VENDING
3000 S Robertson Blvd
Los Angeles, CA 90034-3158
310-233-3131

CALIF MILK ADVISORY BOARD
1090 Adams St
Benicia, CA 94510-2953

CALIF OLIVE INDUSTRY
1903 N Fine Ave Ste 102
Fresno, CA 93727-1510
559-456-9096

CALIF PISTACHIO COMMSN
117 Post St
San Francisco, CA 94108-4701
415-781-2430

CALIF PRUNE BOARD
5990 Stoneridge Dr
Pleasanton, CA 94588-4517
925-734-0150

CALIF RAISIN MKTG BOARD
3445 N 1st St Ste 101
Fresno, CA 93726-6865
559-248-0287

CALIF RESTAURANT ASSOC.
3780 Wilshire Blvd
Los Angeles, CA 90010-2805
213-384-0500

CALIF TREE FRUIT AGRMNT
PO Box 255383
Sacramento, CA 95865-5383

CALIFORNIA BLIMPS
738 W 17th St Ste D
Costa Mesa, C 92627-4340
e-mail: blimps@pacbell.net
949-650-1183 • Fax 949-650-8421

CALIFORNIA CREATIVE FOODS
3245 Production Ave
Oceanside, CA 92054-1309
e-mail: csantry@sbsalsa.com
760-687-1695 • Fax 760-721-2600

CALIFORNIA CULINARY ACADEMY
625 Polk St
San Francisco, CA 94102-3336
www.baychef.com
415-292-8241 • Fax 415-775-5129

CALIFORNIA DATE COMMISSION
45691 Monroe St Ste 5
Indio, CA 92201-3943
e-mail: cadates@aol.com
760-347-4510 • Fax 760-347-6374

CALIFORNIA DAY FRESH-NAKED JUICE
533 W Foothill Blvd
Glendora, CA 91741-2476
e-mail: laduriel@nakedjuice.com
626-852-2500 • Fax 626-852-2560

CALIFORNIA DIETETIC ASSOC.
7740 W Manchester Ave Ste
Playa Del Rey, CA 90293-8408
www.dietitian.org
310-822-0177 • Fax 310-823-0264

CALIFORNIA EGG COMMISSION
1150 N Mountain Ave Ste
Upland, CA 91786-3668
www.eggcom.com
909-981-4923 • Fax 909-946-5563

CALIFORNIA ENVIRONMENTAL HEALTH
980 9th St Ste 1600
Sacramento, CA 95814-2736
www.ceha.org
916-552-2189 • Fax 916-552-2592

CALIFORNIA FIRE ROASTED LLC
PO Box 55187
Stockton, CA 95205-8687
209-931-3484 • Fax 209-931-0286

CALIFORNIA FOODSERVICE SOURCE
6950 SW Hampton St Ste 336
Portland, OR 97223-8332
www.calfood.com
503-598-8500 • Fax 503-598-8551

CALIFORNIA FOUNDATION
660 J St Ste 270
Sacramento, CA 95814-2495
www.cfilc.org
916-325-1690

CALIFORNIA LOTTERY
600 N 10th St
Sacramento, CA 95814-0393
e-mail: dvilardi@calottery.com
916 324 0095 • Fax 916 323 2727

CALIFORNIA STATE POLYTECHNIC U
3801 W Temple Ave
Pomona, CA 91768-2557
909-869-3646 • Fax 909-869-4329

CALIFORNIA STRAWBERRY COMMISSION
PO Box 269
Watsonville, CA 95077-0269
www.calstraberry.com
831-724-1301 • Fax 831-724-5973

CALIPER
741 Mount Lucas Rd
Princeton, NJ 08540-1997
www.caliperonline.com
609-252-8972 • Fax 609-683-8560

CALISE & SONS BAKERY, INC.
2 Quality Dr
Lincoln, RI 02865-4266
www.calisebakery.com
401-943-1111 • Fax 401-943-8230

CAL-JAVA INTERNATIONAL
19521 Business Center Dr
Northridge, CA 91324-3402
800-207-2750

CALL CENTER CONF & EXPO
201 Sandpointe Ave Ste 600
Santa Ana, CA 92707-8700
800-265-5665

CALLAHAN & COMPANY, INC.
1101 Saint Paul St Ste 403
Baltimore, MD 21202-0903
410-366-3841

CALLARD & BOWSER
800 Westchester Ave
Port Chester, NY 10573-1322
914-335-8400

CAL-MIL PLASTIC PRODUCTS
4079 Calle Platino
Oceanside, CA 92056-5805
www.calmil.com
760-630-5100 • Fax 760-630-5010

CAL-TWIG FURNITURE CO
PO Box 1337
Lake Elsinore, CA 92531-1337
800-225-8944 • Fax 909-698-5747

CALZONE & CO., INC.
18080 NE 68th St Ste B140
Redmond, WA 98052-8516
e-mail: m.peters@gte.net
425-869-5353 • Fax 425-861-8430

CAM SPRAY
520 Brooks Rd
Iowa Falls, IA 50126-8005
www.camspray.com
800-648-5011 • Fax 641-648-5013

CAMBRIDGE INC
PO Box 399
Cambridge, MD 21613-0399
800-638-9560

CAMBRO MANUFACTURING COMPANY
5801 Skylab Rd
Huntington Beach, CA 92647-2051
www.cambro.com
800-854-7631 • Fax 714-842-3430

CAMBRO MFG CO
PO Box 2000
Huntington Beach, CA 92647-2000
714-848-1555

CAMERA, INC
1315 Forestedge Blvd
Oldsmar, FL 34677-5135
www.camera-inc.com
727-570-3900 • Fax 727-579-4438

CAMPANIA INTERNATIONAL
401 Fairview Ave
Quakertown, PA 18951-1739
www.campaniainternational.com
215-538-1106 • Fax 215-538-2522

CAMPBELL SOUP
1 Campbell Pl
Camden, NJ 08103-1799
856-342-4800

CAMPUS COLLECTION
PO Box 2904
Tuscaloosa, AL 35403-2904
800-289-8744 • Fax 205-758-0678

CAN CREDIT
122 Woodmill Dr
Cranbury, NJ 08512-2503
www.receivablesprotection.com
732-788-9744 • Fax 732-788-5355

CANADIAN CONSULATE
750 N Saint Paul St Ste 1700
Dallas, TX 75201-3281
e-mail: laura.aune@dfait-maeci.gc.ca
www.canada-dallas.org
214-922-9806 • Fax 214-922-9815

CANAMOULD, A DIVISION OF MAX P
PO Box 400
Birdsboro, PA 19508-0400
e-mail:
cater.benjamin@canamould.usa.ne
www.canamould.com
800-238-2541 • Fax 610-385-8811

CANANDAIGUA BARTON INC
55 E Monroe St
Chicago, IL 60603-5713
312-346-9200 • Fax 312-346-3084

CANANDAIGUA WINE COMPANY
116 Buffalo St
Canandaigua, NY 14424-1086
585-394-7900

CANANDAIGUA WINE COMPANY
23 North St
Canandaigua, NY 14424-1053
813-792-5673 • Fax 813-792-5673

CANCUN CERAMICS WITH PIZAZZ
15 Mockingbird Rd
Covington, LA 70433-4516
800-698-8955

CANDELARI'S SPECIALITY SAUSAGE
2476 Bolsover St Ste 50
Houston, TX 77005-2518
281-568-8078 • Fax 281-568-8098

CANDLE CORPORATION OF AMERICA
999 E Touhy Ave Ste 450
Des Plaines, IL 60018-2748
847-294-1100 • Fax 847-294-0947

CANDLE FUEL CO. INC
135 Townsend St Ste 603
San Francisco, CA 94107-1907
415-270-0420

CANDLE LAMP COMPANY
1799 Rustin Ave
Riverside, CA 92507-2466
www.candlelamp.com
909-682-9600 • Fax 909-784-5801

CANDLEWOOD HOTEL COMPANY
8621 E 21st St N Ste 200
Wichita, KS 67206-2993
e-mail: bgordon@candlewood-suites.com
www.candlewoodsuites.com
316-631-1361 • Fax 316-631-1333

CANFOLD INC
PO Box 551
Choteau, MT 59422-0551
406-466-2342

CANISIUS COLLEGE
2001 Main St
Buffalo, NY 14208-1098
716-888-3270 • Fax 716-888-3211

CANNOLI FACTORY INC. 509
75 Wyandanch Ave
Wyandanch, NY 11798-4441
631-643-2700

CANNON WINES LIMITED
350 Sansome St Ste 1010
San Francisco, CA 94104-1346
e-mail: jwells.cwl@pmg-na.com
415 394 6454 • Fax 415 394 7005

CANTARE FOODS INC
7678 Miramar Rd
San Diego, CA 92126-4202
858-578-8490 • Fax 858-578-8065

CANTRELL INTERNATIONAL
3245 May St # 11216
Fort Worth, TX 76110-4124
817-923-7382

CAPE CANAVERAL SHRIMP CO.
860 N Singleton Ave
Titusville, FL 32796-2311
e-mail: patti@castlegate.net
321-383-7464 • Fax 321-2690-3687

CAPE COD BAY SEAFOOD, INC.
PO Box 2154
Hyannis, MA 02601-7154
www.capecodbayseafood.com
508-420-7111 • Fax 508-420-0156

CAPE COD CHOWDER
141 Falmouth Rd
Hyannis, MA 02601-2755
sale@capecodchowder.com
508-774-5511 • Fax 508-7710883

CAPE HONEY BUSH TEA
34 E 67th St Rm 5R
New York, NY 10021-6119
e-mail: lautriche@aol.com
212-737-1089 • Fax 212-737-1785

CAPITAL BREWERY COMPANY, INC.
7734 Terrace Ave
Middleton, WI 53562-3163
www.capital-brewery.com
608-836-7100 • Fax 608-831-9155

CAPITAL CITY PRODUCTS
PO Box 569
Columbus, OH 43216-0569
800-428-5298

CAPITAL COFFEE
5835 Pinellas Park
Spring, TX 77379-2583
e-mail: info@capitalcoffee.com
www.capitalcoffee.com
281-320-2283 • Fax 281-320-2248

CAPITAL CULINARY INSTITUTE
1700 Halstead Blvd
Tallahassee, FL 32309-3489
e-mail: kevink@keisercollege.co.fl.us
www.keisercollege.cc.fl.us
850-906-9494

CAPITAL THINKING INC
52 Vanderbilt Ave
New York, NY 10017-3808
212-692-4009

CAPITOL AWNING COMPANY SAFETY
10515 180th St
Jamaica, NY 11433-1818
e-mail: capitolawn@aol.com
www.stripdoors.co
718-454-6444 • Fax 718-657-8374

CAPITOL RENOVATION & SUPPLY
110 3rd St Ste 200
New Cumberland, PA 17070-2106
717-770-1640 • Fax 717-770-1642

CAPPUCCINE, INC.
1285 N Valdivia Way
Palm Springs, CA 92262-5428
www.cappuccine.com
760-864-7355 • Fax 760-864-7360

CAPPUCCINO GUY, INC.
8795 W Colfax Ave
Denver, CO 80215-4029
e-mail: cappuccinoguy@uswest.net
303-237-4801 • Fax 303-237-2661

CAPRICCIO ULTIMATE BEVERAGE
10021 1/2 Canoga Ave
Chatsworth, CA 91311-0981
818-718-7620

CAPRINE ESTATES
PO Box 307
Bellbrook, OH 45305-0307
937-848-5740 • Fax 937-848-7437

CAPTAIN KENS
344 Robert St S
Saint Paul, MN 55107-2200
e-mail: jtraxler@captainkens.com
651-298-0071 • Fax 651-298-0849

CAPTIVE AIRE SYSTEMS
3402 Oak Grove Ave Ste 302
Dallas, TX 75204-0353
e-mail: reg45@captivair.com
www.captiveair.com
800-833-3786 • Fax 214-220-0099

CAPTIVE-AIRE SYSTEMS, INC.
112 Wheaton Dr
Youngsville, NC 27596-9414
919-554-2410

CAPWAY SYSTEMS
725 Vogelsong Rd
York, PA 17404-1765
717-843-0003

CARBON CO/JB FINE NFOODS
3300 S 6th St
Lincoln, NE 68502-4303
402-423-2872

CARBON TRI-STATE WAFFLES
PO Box 197
Milford, NH 03055-0197

CARBONE INTERNATIONAL, INC.
306 Bryant St
Palo Alto, CA 94301-1407
650-326-3995

CARBON'S
4101 William Richardson Dr
South Bend, IN 46628-9485
574-247-2270 • Fax 574-247-2280

CARBON'S/WAFFLES OF CALIFORNIA
PO Box 1448
Brea, CA 92822-1448
562-691-0050 • Fax 562-691-5070

CARD CAPTURE SERVICES
7340 SW Hunziker St
Portland, OR 97223-8285
800-783-8366

CARD SERVICE INTERNATIONAL
507 E Hospital St Ste 200
Nacogdoches, TX 75961-5254
e-mail: jgfred@lcc.net
936-552-7170 • Fax 936-559-0015

CARDCOM TECHNOLOGY
6301 Beach Blvd Ste 216
Buena Park, CA 90621-4030
800-476-7811

CARDCOM TECHNOLOGY, INC.
6301 Beach Blvd Ste 21
Buena Park, CA 90621-2840
www.cardcom.com
714-670-6992 • Fax 714-670-7292

CARDINAL INT'L
30 Corporate Dr
Wayne, NJ 07470-3113
www.cardinaglass.com
Fax 973-633-5555

CARDINAL PRODUCTS INC.
PO Box 395
Amityville, NY 11701-0395
e-mail: cpim6@aol.com
631-598-3011 • Fax 516-528-6338

CARDSERVICE INTERNATIONAL
24527 35th Ave S
Kent, WA 98032-4133
253-529-1314

CARDSERVICE INTERNATIONAL
6101 Condor Dr
Moorpark, CA 93021-2602
www.useachargeit.com
800-456-5989 • Fax 805-878-8500

CARDSERVICE INTERNATIONAL
939 W Granada Blvd
Ormond Beach, FL 32174-5908
e-mail: john@csmerchant.com
www.csmerchant.com
386-673-1122

CAREER EXPO
2367 Auburn Ave
Cincinnati, OH 45219-2815
513-721-3030

CAREER FAIR WORLD
8220 Northcreek Dr Ste 220
Cincinnati, OH 45236-2295
513-891-0095

CAREFREE KANOPY
915 Dolphin Dr
Malvern, PA 19355-3143
610-889-3304

CARGILL FOODS
PO Box 9300
Minneapolis, MN 55440-9300
612-742-7575

CARGILL FOODS
PO Box 20788
Waco, TX 76702-0788
www.cargillturkey.com
800-733-0733 • Fax 254-799-1520

CARGILL SALT
PO Box 5621
Minneapolis, MN 55440-5621
952-984-8280 • Fax 952-984-8717

CARIBBEAN ENT/ BARBADOS
1032 River St
Hyde Park, MA 02136-3008
e-mail: caribenter@aol.com
www.caribenter.com
617-364-7543 • Fax 617-361-2084

CARIBBEAN FOOD DELIGHTS
117 Route 303
Tappan, NY 10983-2115
e-mail: cfdny@aol.com
www.caribbeanfooddelights.com
845-398-3000 • Fax 845-398-3001

CARITAS RANCH BBQ
919 State Highway 46 E
Boerne, TX 78006-5758
830-336-2858 • Fax 830-336-2991

CARL BUDDIG & CO.
950 175th St
Homewood, IL 60430-2027
708-798-0900

CARLIN MANUFACTURING, INC
3714 N Valentine Ave
Fresno, CA 93722-4457
www.carlinmfg.com
559-276-0123 • Fax 559-222-1538

CARLISLE FOODSERVICE
W5218 Lakewood Ci
Elkhorn, WI 53121-3109
wwwcarlislefsp.com
262-742-4967 • Fax 262-742-4968

CARLISLE FOODSERVICE PRODUCTS
PO Box 53006
Oklahoma City, OK 73152-3006
www.carlislefsp.com
405-528-3011 • Fax 405-528-6338

CARLISLE SURFACING SYSTEMS
PO Box 1563
Lancaster, PA 17608-1563
800-851-4746

CARLO'S OYSTER LNC.
PO Box 817
Amite, LA 70422-0817
985-748-5493 • Fax 985-748-5044

CARLSON HOSPITALITY GROUP
PO Box 59159
Minneapolis, MN 55459-8200
612-540-5170

CARMUN INTERNATIONAL, INC.
702 San Fernando St
San Antonio, TX 78207-5041
210-224-1781

CARO FOODS, INC.
2324 Bayou Blue Rd
Houma, LA 70364-4301
504-733-4728

CAROLINA MIRROR COMPANY
201 Elkin Hwy
North Wilkesboro, NC 28659-3443
336-838-2151 • Fax 336-838-9734

CAROLINA SOLAR STRUCTURES
8 Loop Rd
Arden, NC 28704-8401
e-mail: btbcss97@aol.com
www.carolinasolar.com
828-684-9900 • Fax 828-684-9977

CAROLINA TURKEYS
PO Box 589
Mount Olive, NC 28365-0589
800-523-4559 • Fax 919-658-5865

CAROUSEL CAKES
5 Seeger Dr
Nanuet, NY 10954-2323
845-627-2323

CAROUSEL GOURMET SODAS
1810 E Northwest Hwy
Arlington Heights, IL 60004-6944
www.carolinaturkeys.com
847-577-9007 • Fax 847-255-7945

CAROZZI NORTH AMERICA
200 Metro Center Blvd
Warwick, RI 02886-1753
401-732-2494 • Fax 401-732-2141

CARPET & RUG SPECIALIST
PO Box 61
Dalton, GA 30722-0061
e-mail: crsi@vol.com
706-277-4712 • Fax 706-226-1022

CARPET CUSHION ASSOCIATES
11841 Preston Trails Ave
Northridge, CA 91326-1447
800-344-6977 • Fax 323-626-5959

CARROLL CO./TRACTION PLUS
2900 W Kingsley Rd
Garland, TX 75041-2378
www.carollco.com
972-278-1304 • Fax 972-840-0678

CARROLL MFG INTERNATIONAL
23 Vreeland Rd
Florham Park, NJ 07932-1510
973-966-0315

CARROUSEL TRADING CO.
PO Box 3128
Lawrence, KS 66046-0128
785-841-4100 • Fax 785-841-5941

CARRY HOT
511 W 33rd St
New York, NY 10001-1320
212-279-0732 • Fax 212-279-0734

CART SYSTEMS, INC.
1316 Webford Ave
Des Plaines, IL 60016-4309
847-803-1875 • Fax 847-803-9027

CARTER & MAYES
PO Box 169
Middlebourne, WV 26149-0169
800-253-9398

CARTER CUSTOM CARPETS
75 Eden Valley Rd SE
Rome, GA 30161-3799
e-mail: carter@catercarpets.com
www.cartercarpets.com
706-235-8657 • Fax 706-378-1001

CARTER HOFFMAN
1551 McCormick Blvd
Mundelein, IL 60060-4491
www.carter-hoffmann.com
847-362-5500 • Fax 847-367-8981

CARTS OF COLORADO INC
501 S Cherry St
Denver, CO 80246-1325
800-227-8634

CARVEL ICE CREAM BAKERY
20 Batterson Park Rd
Farmington, CT 06032-4500
800-322-4848

CARY CUSTOM CATERING
3202 Northwest Hwy
Cary, IL 60013-3507
847-639-1666

CAS CORPORATION
99 Murray Hill Pkwy
East Rutherford, NJ 07073-2148
www.cas-usa.com
201-933-9002 • Fax 201-933-9025

CAS THE SIGN SYSTEMS COMPANY
10280 Glenoaks Blvd
Pacoima, CA 91331-1604
e-mail: info@casigns.com
www.casigns.com
818-899-1888 • Fax 800-636-6696

CASA DE BERTACCHI
1910 Gallagher Dr
Vineland, NJ 08360-1597
e-mail: twest@rich.com
856-696-5600 • Fax 856-696-3341

CASA DILISIO PRODUCTS, INC.
486 Lexington Ave
Mount Kisco, NY 10549-2715
914-666-5021 • Fax 914-666-7209

CASA SANCHEZ FOODS
53 Camellia Ave
San Francisco, CA 94112-1538
415-586-2400 • Fax 415-586-2482

CASCADE GLACIE ICE CREAM CO.
885 Grant St
Eugene, OR 97402-4345
www.cascadeglacier.com
800-828-2202 • Fax 541-482-7653

CASCADIAN FARMS
719 Metcalf St
Sedro Woolley, WA 98284-1456
360-855-2722

CASE SWAYNE COMPANY INC
1930 California Ave
Corona, CA 92881-6491
909-737-4000 • Fax 909-737-1953

CASH CADDY, DIV. OF PLASTICS
1010 San Jose Ave Ste 10
Clovis, CA 93612-2826
e-mail: info@cashcaddy.com
www.cashcaddy.com
559-297-1047 • Fax 559-297-0453

CASH CONVENIENCE INDUSTRIES
PO Box 169
Muskego, WI 53150-0169
262-679-6566 • Fax 262-679-6545

CASH REGISTER SALES
3020 N Arnoult Rd
Metairie, LA 70002-4715
504-888-2090

CASH REGISTER SERVICE
4247 N 35th St
Milwaukee, WI 53216-1795
414-447-6200 • Fax 414-447-0868

CASH REGISTER SPECIALTIES
1316 S West Ave
Waukesha, WI 53186-5944
262-544-2030 • Fax 262-544-5446

CASH REGISTERS PLUS
W227 N2879 Duplainville Rd
Waukesha, WI 53186-1003
262-549-6315 • Fax 262-549-6418

CASIO
570 Mount Pleasant Ave
Dover, NJ 07801-1631
www.casio.com
973-361-5400 • Fax 973-537-8964

CASPER MARKETING GROUP
4464 N Maryland Ave
Milwaukee, WI 53211-1651
414-964-5775 • Fax 414-964-9466

CAST CLASSIC LANDGRAVE
1270 Valley Brook Ave
Lyndhurst, NJ 07071-3510
201-896-1515 • Fax 201-896-1539

CASTALDI HOSPITALITY/ SERVICE
13617 Inwood Rd Ste 220
Dalla, TX 75244-4629
972-726-0300 • Fax 972-726-9779

CASTLEBERRY SNOWS BRANDS
1621 15Th St
Augusta, GA 30901-6999
706-733-7765 • Fax 706-733-5079

CASTRO COVERTIBLES
200 N Berry St
Brea, CA 92821-3903
888-898-3735

CASUAL DINING
W156N11523 Fond Du Lac Ave
Germantown, WI 53022-3386
www.quiz.com
262-250-0173

CASUAL GOURMET FOODS
614 Grand Central St
Clearwater, FL 33756-3410
e-mail: info@cgfoods.com
www.cgfoods.com
727-298-8307 • Fax 727-298-0616

CASUALINE CORPORATION
1065 E Story Rd
Winter Garden, FL 34787-3732
e-mail: casualline@casualine.com
www.caualine.com
800-223-7730 • Fax 407-656-6328

CATALINA LAMPSHADES
9917 Gidley St
El Monte, CA 91731-1111
e-mail: j2360@aol.com
Adnetmk.com/cataline.com
800-447-7611 • Fax 626-448-4791

CATCO MARBLE & GRANITE
200 Markley St
Port Reading, NJ 07064-1820
732-602-9600 • Fax 732-602-0665

CATER PRO
7961 Jefferson Hwy
New Orleans, LA 70123-4625
504-738-3429 • Fax 504-737-6635

CATERAID/ GELATI CELESTI
1167 Fendt Dr
Howell, MI 48843-6501
517-546-8217 • Fax 517-546-8674

CATEREASE SOFTWARE/ HORIZON BUS
1020 Goodlette Rd N
Naples, FL 34102-5449
e-mail: sales@caterease.com
239-261-5828 • Fax 239-261-0061

CATEREASE, CATERING & EVENT S
PO Box 577
Naples, FL 34106-0577
www.caterease.com
800-863-1616 • Fax 239-261-0067

CATERING MAGAZINE
2531 W Dunlap Ave
Phoenix, AZ 85021-2704
www.minico.com
602-870-1711 • Fax 602-861-1094

CATERLINE BY AVON PLASTICS
451 Grand St
Brooklyn, NY 11211-4703
718-384-2952 • Fax 718-486-5608

CATERMATE
311 Nassau Ave
Paulsboro, NJ 08066-1140
e-mail: nissco@errols.com
856-423-9571 • Fax 856-423-1233

CATERMATE CATERING & EVENTS
1844 Century Way Ste 2000
Indianapolis, IN 46260-5558
www.catermate.com
317-876-0242 • Fax 317-876-1608

CATERSOURCE CONF
PO Box 14776
Chicago, IL 60614-0776
800-844-1374

CATUS MAT
4131 Arden Dr
El Monte, CA 91731-1999
www.cactusmat.com
626-443-9369 • Fax 626-401-2003

CAVANNA USA
286 Houses Corner Rd
Sparta, NJ 07871-3462
973-973-383037

CBS PAYROLL
814 N Arrowhead Ave
San Bernardino, CA 92401-1016
909-884-6328 • Fax 909-383-7798

CBS PAYROLL
1215 Country Club Ln # 100
Fort Worth, TX 76112-2304
e-mail: smvaughan@cbspayroll.com
www.cbspayroll.com
817-457-8877 • Fax 817-457-4220

CBS PAYROLL SOLUTION
400 Fuller Wiser Rd Ste 105
Euless, TX 76039-3876
817-571-6290

CBS PROMOTIONS
4301 Westbank Dr Ste B # 3
Austin, TX 78746-6564

CCTV WHOLESALERS.COM
1308 Dealers Ave
New Orleans, LA 70123-2208
504-736-9187

CCR DATA SYSTEMS
128 Airport Rd
Concord, NH 03301-5296
800-633-6500

CCS EXPRESS ATM CARDCAPTURE
13190 SW 68th Pkwy Ste 2
Portland, OR 97223-8368
www.ccsexpress.com
Fax 503-670-0822

CCSEXPRESS ATM NORTHEAST
27 Maynard Rd
Sudbury, MA 01776-1651
e-mail: jpacheco3@cs.com
978-443-5477 • Fax 978-443-2094

CECILWARE CORP
4305 20th Ave
Astoria, NY 11105-1295
800-935-2211

CECILWARE CORPORATION
4305 29th St
Long Island City, NY 11101-3701
www.cecilware.com
718-932-1414 • Fax 718-932-7860

CEDAR CREST ICE CREAM
7369 State Road 60
Cedarburg, WI 53012-9702
262-377-7252 • Fax 262-377-5554

CEDAR GROVE CHEESE
2064 Tiger Links Dr
Henderson, NV 89012-6111
e-mail: cgcheese@execpc.com
608-546-5284 • Fax 608-546-2805

CEDAR KEY AQUACULTURE
PO Box 428
Mango, FL 33550-0428
888-252-6735

CEDARLANE NATURAL FOODS
1135 E Artesia Blvd
Carson, CA 90746-1602
562-745-4255

CEDAR'S MEDITERRANEAN FOODS
PO Box 1037
Plaistow, NH 03865-1037
www.cedarsfoods.com
603-521-9119 • Fax 603-373-2729

CEFAP, CORP
3211 Ponce De Leon Blvd
Miami, FL 33134-7274
www.fripan.com
305-461-2244 • Fax 305-443-3417

CEILPRO TILE CEILING REFINISHING
PO Box 1507
Wakefield, MA 01880-5507
e-mail: ceilpro@aol.com
800-659-5591 • Fax 781-245-1067

CELEBFRAME, INC
36555 Bankside Dr # B
Cathedral City, CA 92234-7602
www.celebframe.com
760-202-8464 • Fax 760-202-2311

CELEBRATION EVENT SUPPLY
2400 Weccacoe Ave
Philidelphia, PA 19148-4222
888-864-3992

CELEBRATOR BEER NEWS
PO Box 375
Hayward, CA 94543-0375
510-670-0121 • Fax 510-670-0639

CELEBRITY ENTERTAINMENT SYSTEM
1120 Calle Cordillera Ste 102
San Clemente, CA 92673-6299
e-mail: cesturkey@aol.com
949-348-8255 • Fax 949-348-8323

CELESTIAL SEASONING
4600 Sleepytime Dr
Boulder, CO 80301-3292
www.celestialseasonings.com
303-581-1484 • Fax 303-581-1294

CELLGATE TECHNOLOGIES
6420 Congress Ave
Boca Raton, FL 33487-2811
561-999-9077

CELLGATE.COM
6420 Congress Ave Ste 2
Boca Raton, FL 33487-2811
www.cellgate.com

CELTIC DISTRIBUTORS
2746 Marietta Ave
Kenner, LA 70062-5212
504-712-9156

CENDANT CORP
6 Sylvan Way
Parsippany, NJ 07054-3826
973-428-9700

CENDANT CORPORATION
2340 S River Rd
Des Plaines, IL 60018-3212
www.cendant.com
847-827-8855 • Fax 847-827-8856

CENDANT CORPORATION
1 Sylvan Way
Parsippany, NJ 07054-3887
e-mail: tom.bernardo@cendant.com
www.cendant.com
973-496-5236 • Fax 973-496-5351

CENTER FOR ADVERSTISING SERICES.
1271 Avenue Of The Americas
New York, NY 10020-1401
212-399-8032

CENTERCORE
201 Industrial St
Marked Tree, AR 72365-2306
e-mail: info@centercore.com
www.centercore.com
870-358-2500 • Fax 870-358-3330

CENTIMARK CORPORATION
12 Grandview Cir
Canonsburg, PA 15317-8533
e-mail: dana.coleman@centimark.com
www.centimark.com
800-558-4100 • Fax 724-743-7780

CENTO FINE FOODS
100 Cento Blvd
Thorofare, NJ 08086-2133
e-mail: sales@cento.com
www.cento.com
856-853-5445 • Fax 856-853-0962

CENTRAL FINE PACK INC
7707 Vicksburg Pike
Fort Wayne, IN 46804-5549
www.cfine.com
260-436-7225 • Fax 260-432-9275

CENTRAL FLORIDA-FIGHT BACK
604 Courtland St Ste 200
Orlando, FL 32804-1343
e-mail: info@csgis.com
www.csgis.com
407-927-9292

CENTRAL HUDSON ENTERPRISE CORP
110 Main St
Poughkeepsie, NY 12601-6707
e-mail: nrgdude@chenergy.com
www.chenergy.com
845-485-5770 • Fax 845-485-5947

CENTRAL MICHIGAN UNIVERSITY
Hospitality Services Admi
Mount Pleasant, MI 48859-0001
e-mail: yvett.green@cmich.edu
www.mkt.cba.cmich.edu
989-774-3701 • Fax 989-774-7406

CENTRAL PLACE REAL ESTATE
8383 Greenway Blvd
Middleton, WI 53562-4626
608-536-9070

CENTRAL POINT TECH INC
500 Fairway Dr
Deerfield Beach, FL 33441-1814
954-698-5151

CENTRAL TEXAS COLLEGE HOSPITAL
PO Box 1800
Killeen, TX 76540-1800
254-526-1523 • Fax 254-526-1170

CENTRAL VALLEY CHEESE
115 S Kilroy Rd
Turlock, CA 95380-9531
209-664-1080 • Fax 209-664-1001

CENTURY MANAGEMENT SYSTEMS
1041 Wyoming Ave Bldg 2
Kingston, PA 18704-4002
570-288-6373

CENTURY SPECIALTIES
2410 W Aero Park Ct
Traverse City, MI 49686-9168
231-946-7500

CEO PARTNERS INC
100 N Waukegan Rd
Lake Bluff, IL 60044-1694
847-615-2595 • Fax 847-615-2640

CERAMIC DE ESPANA
7700 NW 54th St
Miami, FL 33166-4106
www.moniquecde.com
305-597-9161 • Fax 305-591-0989

CERTIFICHECKS.COM
8901 N Dixie Dr
Dayton, OH 45414-1805
www.certifichecks.com
937-264-9809 • Fax 937-264-9828

CERTIFIED AANGUS BEEF, LLC
206 Riffel Rd
Wooster, OH 44691-8588
330-345-2333 • Fax 330-345-0808

CERTISAFE
PO Box 6366
Laguna Niguel, CA 92607-6366
www.safekitchen.com
949-481-2245 • Fax 949-495-9002

CERVITOR KITCHENS, INC
10775 Lower Azusa Rd
El Monte, CA 91731-1351
e-mail: dennis@cervitor.com
www.certivor.com
800-523-2666 • Fax 626-443-0400

CEVERYTHING
233 Broadway Fl 22
New York, NY 10279-2299
e-mail: tlynch@ceverything.com
212-618-1392 • Fax 212-618-1205

CEVERYTHING.COM
270 14th St
San Francisco, CA 94103-2420
www.everything.com
415-882-4001 • Fax 415-252-8459

CGG MARKETING MANAGEMENT, INC.
179 Saw Mill River Rd
Yonkers, NY 10701-6616
914-963-9181 • Fax 914-963-9207

CHAIN ACCOUNT MENU SURVEY
107 N Hale S Ste 212
Wheaton, IL 60187-5117
630-690-8790 • Fax 630-690-8712

CHAIN STORE GUIDE
3922 Coconut Palm Dr
Tampa, FL 33619-1389
www.csgis.com
813-390-6800 • Fax 813-627-6882

CHAIR FACTORY
208 Bowery
New York, NY 10012-4203
212-941-0033

CHAIRCRAFT/CENTURY
3086 Main Ave NW
Hickory, NC 28601-5663
www.centuryfurniture.com
828-495-8291 • Fax 828-495-8661

CHAIRMASTERS INC
200 E 146th St
Bronx, NY 10451-5512
718-292-0600

CHAIRS TO GO
4277 Exchange Ave Ste 6
Naples, FL 34104-7090
239-353-3763 • Fax 239-353-7086

CHALK TALK
17 Corte Montena
Lake Elsinor, CA 92532-0216
e-mail: chalktlk@gte.net
909-841-4411 • Fax 909-841-1099

CHALLENGER LIGHTING CO.
2420 E Oakton St Ste V
Arlington Heights, IL 60005-4827
e-mail:
info@challengerlighting.com
www.challengerlighting.com
847-364-9100 • Fax 847-956-6113

CHALLENGER WALK-INS, INC.
1445 Yates Ave
Beloit, WI 53511-4662
262-697-6031 • Fax 262-697-7313

CHAMBERLIN & COMPANY, PC
7550 W Yale Ave Ste A140
Denver, CO 80227-3470
303-987-1700

CHAMPIGNON NORTH AMER
600 E Palisade Ave
Englewood Cliffs, NJ 07632-1828
201-871-7211

CHAMPION INDUSTRIES, INC.
PO Box 4149
Winston Salem, NC 27115-4149
336-661-1556

CHAMPION SHUFFLEBOAR
7216 Burns St
Fort Worth, TX 76118-6810
800-826-7856

CHANDRE'S CORPORATION
14 Catharine St
Poughkeepsie, NY 12601-3104
www.chandre.com
845-473-8003 • Fax 845-473-8004

CHANNEL FISH PROCESSING
18 Food Mart Rd
Boston, MA 02118-2802
617-445-9070

CHAPMAN & BELL
3703 Taylorsville Rd # 20
Louisville, KY 40220-1354
502-452-1543

CHAP'S PARTY RENTAL SERVICE
1519 Alvar St
New Orleans, LA 70117-5245
504-944-2536 • Fax 504-943-6558

CHAR CRUST
3017 N Lincoln Ave
Chicago, IL 60657-4242
312-528-0600

CHARACTERS UNLIMITED INC
709 Foothill Ct
Boulder City, NV 89005-1847
www.accessnv.com/characters
702-294-0563 • Fax 702-294-2387

CHARCUTERIE TOUR EIFFEL, INC.
PO Box 1644
New York, NY 10276-1644
212-674-8930 • Fax 212-674-5380

CHARLES AND LAUREL DESSERTS
537 Greenwich St
New York, NY 10013-1000
e-mail: dessertsny@aol.com
www.ebrowine.net
212-229-9339 • Fax 212-633-6226

CHARLES CRAFT, INC.
PO Box 1049
Laurinburg, NC 28353-1049
910-844-3521

CHARLES SAMELSON INC.
102 Madison Ave
New York, NY 10016-7417
e-mail: info@samelson.com
www.csamelson
212-686-6829 • Fax 212-213-6459

CHARLEY & SONS
5366 Dixie Industrial
Morro, GA 30260-3559
404-366-4442 • Fax 404-366-8905

CHARLIE FLOYD COMMERCIAL REFRIGERATION
PO Box 551503
Jacksonville, FL 32255-1503
904-724-7486

CHART/MVE, INC.
3505 County Road 42 W
Burnsville, MN 55306-3803
www.mve_inc.com
800-247-4446 • Fax 612-882-5185

CHARTER OF LYCHBURG
PO Box 11988
Lynchbur, VA 24506-1988
e-mail: charterlyby@lynchburg.net
www.chefdirect.com
434-239-2671 • Fax 434-239-0410

CHARTRES CORPORATION
PO Box 23770
New Orleans, LA 70183-0770
504-736-0008 • Fax 504-736-0030

CHASE DOORS
10021 Commerce Park Dr
Cincinnati, OH 45246-1333
www.chasedoors.com
800-543-4455 • Fax 800-626-5684

CHASE MERCHANT SERVICE
265 Broadhollow Road
Melville, NY 11747-4802
natalie.curzio@firstdata.com
www.chase.com/merchantservices
631-843-6931 • Fax 631-843-6828

CHASEN FOOD SPECIALTIES
PO Box 48546
Los Angeles, CA 90048-0546
e-mail: chasens@chasenschili.com
310-271-2168 • Fax 310-271-9583

CHATEAU TARDAIS CORP.
14120 Live Oak Ave Ste A
Baldwin Park, CA 91706-1345
626-813-6198 • Fax 626-813-0039

CHATER FURNITURE CORP.
9401 Whitmore St
El Monte, CA 91731-2821
626-572-7500 • Fax 626-572-7722

CHECK FERNANDO'S
1600 Oklahoma Dr
Buford, GA 30519-5001
www.qayc.com
770-614-6481 • Fax 770-831-6776

CHECKCARE SYSTEMS OF LOUISIANA
2211 Weymouth Dr
Baton Rouge, LA 70809-1486
225-291-8590

CHECKCARE SYSTEMS OF TEXAS
17000 Dallas Pkwy Ste 204
Dallas, TX 75248-1940
e-mail: joe_brown@checkcare.com
www.checkcare.com
972-380-5600 • Fax 972-407-5777

CHEESECAKE MOMMA
200 W Henry St Ste B
Ukiah, CA 95482-4355
www.chefamerica.com
707-462-2236 • Fax 707-790-2589

CHEESEMONGER CO.
31 Riordan Pl
Shrewsbury, NJ 07702-4305
e-mail: naustin534@aol.com
732-282-4485 • Fax 732-527-6624

CHEF AMERICA
9601 Canoga Ave
Chatsworth, CA 91311-4147
818-718-8111

CHEF AMERICA
20 Inverness Pl E
Englewood, CO 80112-5622
www.chefamerica.com
303-705-2236 • Fax 303-790-2589

CHEF DIRECT
1623 Eastern Pkwy
Schenectady, NY 12309-6011
www.chefdirect.com
518-374-5155 • Fax 518-374-4845

CHEF FRANCISCO/H J HEINZ
1062 Progress St
Pittsburgh, PA 15212-5931
412-237-5757

CHEF PAUL PRUDHOMME'S MAGIC
824 Distributors Row # O
New Orleans, LA 70123-3210
www.chefpaul.com
504-731-3590 • Fax 504-731-3576

CHEF REVIVAL USA
2 Industrial Rd
Lodi, NJ 07644-2608
www.chefrevival.com
973-916-2060 • Fax 973-916-6680

CHEF WORKS
8940 Activity Rd Ste G
San Diego, CA 92126-4462
www.chefwork.com
858-549-0632 • Fax 858-549-4609

CHEFMASTER
3701 W Carriage Dr
Santa Ana, CA 92704-6417
800-333-7443

CHEFWARE
3111 N Knox Ave
Chicago, IL 60641-5297
773-427-6700

CHEMLAB PRODUCTS
5160 E Airport Dr
Ontario, CA 91761-7824

CHEMMARK
6531 Petropark Dr
Houston, TX 77041-4900
800-818-5291 • Fax 713-864-1735

CHEM-PLUS SERVICE SYSTEMS, INC
770 Big Tree Dr
Longwood, FL 32750-3540
407-261-9922

CHEN INTERNATIONAL INC.
1160 Chess Dr Ste 7
San Mateo, CA 94404-1142
650-578-9000 • Fax 650-578-8999

CHEP USA
225 E Robinson St
Orlando, FL 32801-4322
800-243-7872 ª Fax 407-422-4614

CHERIE'S BROWNIES, INC.
23679 Calabasas Rd Ste 189
Calabasas, CA 91302-1502
818-222-1542

CHERITH VALLEY GARDENS
PO Box 12040
Fort Worth, TX 76110-8040
817-922-8822 • Fax 817-922-8884

CHER-MAKE SAUSAGE CO./SMOKE VA
2915 Calumet Ave
Manitowoc, WI 54220-5550
e-mail: markm@cher-make.com
800-242-7679 • Fax 920-683-5990

CHERNOFF SALES INC
3308 Park Central Blvd N
Pompano Beach, FL 33064-2212
e-mail: turetzky@chernoffsales.com
800-226-7600

CHERRYSTONE AQUA FARMS
PO Box 347
Cheriton, VA 23316-0347
757-331-1208

CHESTER FRIED OF WIS. INC.
3150 Voyager Dr
Green Bay, WI 54311-8342
920-468-5353 • Fax 920-468-5313

CHESTERFIELD MANUFACTURERS
2630 Nelda Dr # D
Monroe, NC 28110-8498
800-322-1746

CHESTER-JENSEN CO INC
PO Box 908
Chester, PA 19016-0908
800-685-3750

CHESTNUT IDENTITY APPAREL INC.
PO Box 253
Brookdale, CA 95007-0253
www.chicagoartsource.com
831-336-8977 • Fax 831-336-3926

CHEYENNE RIVER
210 29th Ave
San Mateo, CA 94403-2725
e-mail: rkjenney@pacbell.com
650-578-0647 • Fax 650-578-0441

CHF INDUSTRIES
1 Park Ave
New York, NY 10016-5802
e-mail: tmarcus@concentric.net
212-951-7800 • Fax 212-951-8001

CHIANTI CHEESE CO
207 Hanover St
Pemberton, NJ 08068-1004
609-894-0900

CHICAGAO BROTHERS INC
7696 Formula Pl
San Diego, CA 92121-3426

CHICAGO ART SOURCE
1871 N Clybourn Ave
Chicago, IL 60614-4747
www.chicagoartsource.com
773-248-3100 • Fax 773-248-3926

CHICAGO FAUCET CO
2100 Clearwater Dr
Des Plaines, IL 60018-5999

CHICAGO LAMB AND VEAL PROCESSORS
140 S Dearborn St Ste 320
Chicago, IL 60603-5236
312-421-3300 • Fax 312-243-0909

CHICAGO MEAT AUTHORITY, INC.
1120 W 47th Pl
Chicago, IL 60609-4302
www.chicagomeat.com
800-383-3811 • Fax 773-254-5851

CHICAGO STATE UNIV
9501 S King Dr
Chicago, IL 60628-1598
773-995-3968 • Fax 773-995-2269

CHICAGO WICKER AND TRADING COM
1657 N Kilpatrick Ave
Chicago, IL 60639-4606
773-276-5220 • Fax 773-276-5209

CHICK FIL-A
5200 Buffington Rd
Atlanta, GA 30349-2998
404-765-8059

CHICKEN OF THE SEA INTERNATION
4510 Executive Dr
San Diego, CA 92121-3021
619-231-1911

CHICKEN OF THE SEA INTERNATIONAL
221 E Main St
Milford, MA 01757-2825
e-mail: jtanner@cosintl.com
www.chickenofthesea.com
508-634-8011 • Fax 508-634-8014

CHICKEN OF THE SEA INTERNATIONAL
1377 Cowart R
Plant City, FL 33567-3684

e-mail: dlentz@cosintl.com
www.cos.com
813-737-3155

CHICKEN OF THE SEA INTERNATIONAL
4510 Executive Dr Ste 300
San Diego, CA 92121-3029
e-mail: vsabbs@cosintl.com
619-567-4517 • Fax 858-597-4568

CHICOPEE
2351 US Highway 130
Dayton, NJ 08810-1521
800-835-2442

CHIEFTAIN WILD RICE
PO Box 550
Spooner, WI 54801-0550
www.chieftainwildrice.com
800-262-6368 • Fax 715-635-6415

CHILL RITE
14601 McCormick Dr
Tampa, FL 33626-3025
e-mail: tfs-sales@mindspring.com
813-855-4871

CHILLED CONCEPTS LIMITED
7239 4th Ave S
Saint Petersburg, FL 33707-1231
727-430-3526

CHILL-RITE 32/DESCO, INC
PO Box 5566
Slidell, LA 70469-5566
985-641-4865

CHINA MIST TEA COMPANY
7435 E Tierra Buena Ln
Scottsdale, AZ 85260-1608
www.chinamist.com
480-998-8807 • Fax 480-596-0811

CHINESE CONSULATE
3400 Montrose Blvd Ste 700
Houston, TX 77006-4336
e-mail: moftec@wt.net
www.chinahouston.org
713-524-0464 • Fax 713-524-3547

CHINESE RESTAURANT NEWS
1020 Webster St
Oakland, CA 94607-4224
www.c-r-n-.com
501-832-1234 • Fax 510-444-1044

CHIPMAN ADAMS LTD.
1550 N Northwest Hwy
Park Ridge, IL 60068-1411
www.ca-ltd.com
847-298-6900 • Fax 847-298-6966

CHIPPERY
PO Box 18163
Austin, TX 78760-8163
512-385-8822 Fax 512-385-8985

CHIPPERY
10215 Summerlin Way
Fishers, IN 46038-9580
www.thechippery.com
317-577-3669 • Fax 317-578-4269

CHISESI BROTHERS MEAT PACKING
2419 Julia St
New Orleans, LA 70119-7527
504-822-3550 • Fax 504-822-3916

CHOCK FULL O NUTS FOOD-SERVICE
10 Empire Blvd
Moonachie, NJ 07074-1303
201-865-0200 • Fax 201-865-0154

CHOCOLATE SHOPPE ICE CREAM CO.
2221 Daniels St
Madison, WI 53718-6745
608-221-8640 • Fax 608-221-8650

CHOCOLATE-A'LA-CARTE
13190 Telfair Ave
Sylmar, CA 91342-3573
www.chocolate-ala-carte.com
800-818-2462 • Fax 818-364-8303

CHOCOLATES A LA CARTE
28455 Livingston Ave

Valencia, CA 91355-4173
e-mail: LWheeler@candymaker.com
www.chocolatesalacarte.com
661-257-3700 • Fax 661-257-4999

CHOICE HOTELS INTL
10750 Columbia Pike
Silver Spring, MD 20901-4491
franchise_info@choicehotels.com
www.choicehotels.com
301-592-5081 • Fax 301-592-6205

CHOICEHIRE
3111 Stirling Rd
Fort Lauderdale, FL 33312-6566
www.choicehire.com
800-825-0244 • Fax 954-964-9026

CHRIS CONSULTANTS INC
1520 W Airport Fwy
Irving, TX 75062-6130
972-253-3583

CHRIS'S COOKIES
1 Exchange Pl Ste 301
Jersey City, NJ 07302-3919
e-mail: gary@chriscookies.com
www.chriscookies.com
201-451-3500 • Fax 201-432-3627

CHRISTIN LOUDON
11858 Abercorn Ct
Reston, VA 20191-2703
703-715-8471

CHRISTOFLE HOTEL/GUY DEGRENNE
390 George St Ste 403
New Brunswick, NJ 08901-2019
732-565-0820 • Fax 732-565-0828

CHRISTOPHER RANCH
305 Bloomfield Ave
Gilroy, CA 95020-9565
408-847-1100 • Fax 408-847-5488

CHRISTY MACHINE CO
PO Box 32
Fremont, OH 43420-0032
419-332-6451

CHRYSLER KOPPIN CO
7000 Intervale St
Detroit, MI 48238-2498
313-491-7100

CHURCHILL CONTAINER CO.
19919 Shawnee Mission Pkwy
Shawnee, KS 66218-9792
www.churchilcontainer.com
913-422-4790 • Fax 913-422-2077

CHURNY COMPANY INC
2215 Sanders Rd Ste 550
Northbrook, IL 60062-6147
847-400-5504 • Fax 847-480-5591

CIAO BELLA GELATO COMPANY
231 40th St
Irvington, NJ 07111-1154
e-mail: info@ciaobellagelato.com
www.ciaobellagelato.com
973-373-1200 • Fax 973-373-1224

CIAO BELLA GELATO COMPANY
685 Harrison St
San Francisco, CA 94107-1312
ww.ciaobellagelato.com
415-541-4940 • Fax 415-541-4967

CIC APPLICANT BACKGROUND CHECK
12505 Starkey Rd Ste K
Largo, FL 33773-2617
e-mail: cicsales@hirecheck.com
www.hirecheck.com
727-535-4473

CIGAR COMPADRES, LTD.
5000 Harvard Ter
Skokie, IL 60077-2825
e-mail: cigarcompadres@gpg.com
847-568-0950 • Fax 8475680955

CINCINNATI TIME RECORDER
907 Broadway
New York, NY 10010-7107
e-mail: ctrny@flashcom.net
www.ctrny.com

212-777-7311 • Fax 212-260-3852

CINI-LITTLE INTERNATIONAL, INC
2275 Research Blvd Ste 700
Rockville. MD 20850-6203
301-926-2400

CINO INTERNATIONAL INC.
7503 Megan Elissa Ln
Orlando, FL 32819-7766
407-354-3318 • Fax 407-354-3319

CINTAS
6800 Cintas Blvd
Mason, OH 45040-9151
www.cintas-corp.com
513-459-1200 • Fax 513-573-4232

CITADEL COMPUTER CORP
29 Armory Rd
Milford, NH 03055-3456
603-672-5500

CITICORP DINERS CLUB
7958 S Chester St
Englewood, CO 80112-3426
800-525-7376

CITICORP NORTH AMERICA
2600 Michelson Dr Fl 12
Irvine, CA 92612-1550
949-250-6480

CITIZEN-CBM AMERICA CORP
365 Van Ness Way Ste 510
Torrance, CA 90501-6292
www.cbma.com
310-944-1313 • Fax 310-944-6669

CITTERIO USA CORP.
5115 35th St
Long Island City, NY 11101-3256
e-mail: sales@citterio.com
800-435-8888 • Fax 718-937-7138

CITY HARVEST, INC
159 W 25th St
New York, NY 10001-7203
212-463-0456 • Fax 212-727-2439

CITY MARKET PRODUCE CO
1251 Argentine Blvd
Kansas City, KS 66105-1508
913-342-8344

CITY NOVELTY INC/BAR SUPPLIES
13214 S Choctaw Dr
Baton Rouge, LA 70815-2813
225-272-7783

CITY OF HOPE
208 W 8th St
Los Angeles, CA 90014-3208
800-266-7920

CITY OF MILWAUKEE HEALTH DEPARTMENT
841 N Broadway Rm 105
Milwaukee, WI 53202-3613
www.ci.mil.wi.us/health
414-286-2674 • Fax 414-286-5164

CIVITAN INTERNATIONAL
PO Box 130744
Birmingham, AL 35213-0744
e-mail: jcraig@civitan.org
205-591-8910 • Fax 205-592-6307

CJ PRODUCTS
4556 Morro Bay St
Oceanside, CA 92057-4210
858-541-2421 • Fax 858-541-2554

CKC PLANNING & DESIGN CORP.
110 Lafayette St
New York, NY 10013-4116
212-274-0808

CLARITAS STUDIOS
30 Janis Way Ste A
Scotts Valley, CA 95066-3528
www.claritasusa.com
831-438-2777 • Fax 831-438-6106

CLARK PEST CONTROL
PO Box 1480
Lodi, CA 95241-1480
e-mail: j.bowyer@clarkpest.com
800-421-7829 • Fax 209-368-1103

CLARK, MALONE & ASSOCIATES
PO Box 510745
New Berlin, WI 53151-0745
262-796-8661 • Fax 262-796-8662

CLARMIL MANUFACTURING
30865 San Clemente St
Hayward, CA 94544-7136
e-mail: info@clarmilmfg.com
510-476-0700 • Fax 510-476-0707

CLASSIC AMENITIES
1947 N Wood St
Chicago, IL 60622-1139
e-mail:
sandyb@classicamenities.com
www.classicamenities.com
773-862-9728 • Fax 773-227-8305

CLASSIC FOODS
629 W Mony St
Fort Worth, TX 76102-1705
e-mail: sheriffb@cowtown.com
www.sheriffb.com
800-422-4454 • Fax 817-335-2771

CLASSIC WEAVERS
715 Curtis Pkwy SE
Calhoun, GA 30701-3677
706-277-7767

CLASSIC WINES OF CALIFORNIA
6342 Bystrum Rd
Cere, CA 95307-9513
800-692-5780

CLASSICO
801 N Clay St
Peru, IN 46970-1068
765-473-6691

CLASSICO DESSERTS, INC.
430 Ansin Blvd Ste K
Hallandale, FL 33009-3112
e-mail: flandi@classicodesserts.com
954-458-6584 • Fax 954-454-2957

CLASSICO SEATING
PO Box 48
Peru, IN 46970-0048
800-968-6655

CLASSY ART WHOLESALERS
300 N York St
Houston, TX 77003-1747
713-225-0700 • Fax 713-225-2623

CLAUSEN SUPPLY INC/GLOW-ZONE
22630 88th Ave S
Kent, WA 98031-2432
800-257-4055

CLAWSON MACHINE
12 Cork Hill Rd
Franklin, NJ 07416-1304
973-827-8209

CLEAN AIR CONCEPTS/ FLORIDA
3294 Latana Dr
Palm Harbor, FL 34684-3421
e-mail: jusphfl@aol.com
727-772-0068

CLEAN AIR SYSTEMS, INC.
2140 W Pershing St
Appleton, WI 54914-6074
920-731-8504 • Fax 920-731-0502

CLEAN CONTROL CORP
PO Box 7444
Warner Robins, GA 31095-7444
478-922-5340

CLEAR SPRINGS FOODS
PO Box 712
Buhl, ID 83316-0712
www.clearsprings.com
208-543-4316 • Fax 208-543-5603

CLEARMIRROR
425 Weir Dr
Saint Paul, MN 55125-1243
e-mail: sales@clearmirror.com
www.clearmirror.com
877-242-5327 • Fax 651-739-0403

CLEAR-VU INDUSTRIES
200 Homer Ave Bldg 3
Ashland, MA 01721-1717
www.clear-vuindustries.com
508-8819-100 • Fax 508-881-9111

CLEMENS GROUP
13750 W Morningview Ct
New Berlin, WI 53151-6897
262-796-0046 • Fax 262-796-1046

CLEMENTS-STELLA MARKETING
53 Danes St
Patchogue, NY 11772-3834
516-758-5316 • Fax 516-758-5947

CLEVELAND
4350 W Sunrise Blvd
Fort Lauderdale, FL 33313-6775
800-338-2204

CLEVELAND MENU PRINTING
3142 Superior Ave E
Cleveland, OH 44114-4343
216-241-5256

CLEVELAND RANGE
1333 E 179th St
Cleveland, OH 44110-2587
216-481-4900 • Fax 216-481-3782

CLEVER IDEAS INC
180 N Stetson Ave
Chicago, IL 60601-6710
800-411-0705

CLEVER IDEAS, INC.
180 N Stetson Ave Ste 5300
Chicago, IL 60601-6795
312-616-3600 • Fax 312-288-9402

CLIMAX MFG CO
7798 N State St
Lowville, NY 13367-1290
e-mail:
bob.bowman@climaxpkg.com
www.climaxpkg.com
315-376-2034

CLINTON ASSOCIATES, INC.
102 Wilmot Rd Ste 240
Deerfield, IL 60015-5100
847-945-4075

CLIPPER MILL
888 Brannan St Ste 455
San Francisco, CA 94103-5642
www.clippermill.com
415-552-5005 • Fax 415-552-6296

CLOG-MASTER OF SWEDEN INC
440 1/2 N La Cienega Blvd
Los Angeles, CA 90048-1907
310-657-8083 • Fax 310-657-8090

CLOROX - HIDDEN VALLEY
PO Box 24305
Oakland, CA 94623-1305
510-271-7758

CLOTHES CLINIC LINEN & UNI-FORM
PO Box 955
West Bend, WI 53095-0955
www.clothesclinic.com
800-924-6162 • Fax 262-338-5224

CLOTHIER & HEAD PS
1325 4th Ave Ste 1100
Seattle, WA 98101-2520
206-622-1326

CLUB CAR INC
PO Box 204658
Augusta, GA 30917-4658
706-863-3000

CLUB DATA CORPORATION
10125 Crosstown Cir
Eden Prairie, MN 55344-3319
952-941-0855

CLUB INTERNET SERVICES
PO Box 3333
Pinehurst, NC 28374-3333
877-932-5827

CLUB MANAGEMENT MAGAZINE
107 W Pacific Ave
Saint Louis, MO 63119-2323
www.club-mgmt.com
314-961-6644 • Fax 314-961-4809

CLUB MARK CORP
PO Box 670608
Dallas TX 75367-0608
214-357-5787

CLUB TECHNOLOGY CORP
1610 Corporate Ct
Irving, TX 75038-2203
810-800-5506

CLUBCOM INC
6522 Brick Hearth Ct
Alexandria, VA 22306-3313
888-239-6824

CLV MARKETING
77 Broadway
Amityville, NY 11701-2785
www.clvmarketing.com
516-264-5303 • Fax 516-264-5402

C-M EQUIPMENT CO., INC
3690 W Navy Blvd
Pensacola, FL 32507-1216
850-458-3460

CMA DISHMACHINES
12700 Knott St
Garden Grove, CA 92841-3904
714-898-8781 • Fax 714-891-9836

CMA INCORPORATED
11007 Chicago Dr Ste 21
Zeeland, MI 49464-9186
616-772-3672 • Fax 616-772-3671

CNERESTAURANT.COM
633 SE 5th St Ste 200
Stuart, FL 34994-2333
e-mail: lmr@cnerestaurant.com
www.cnerestaurant.com
772-219-3733

CNL INVESTMENT COMPANY
PO Box 4920
Orlando, FL 32802-4920
800-522-3863

CNS/RQA, INC.
7900 S Cass Ave Ste 150
Darien, IL 60561-5073
www.foodsafe.com
630-512-0011 • Fax 630-512-0014

CO OPPORTUNITIES INC
2849 Paces Ferry Rd SE Ste
Atlanta, GA 30339-6201
770-801-3180 • Fax 770-801-3188

COAKLEY & WILLIAMS
7501 Greenway Center Dr Ste 80
Greenbelt, MD 20770-3514
301-474-6200

COAST NOVELTY
4064 Glencoe Ave
Marina Del Rey, CA 90292-5644
310-823-0911

COAST PAPER & RIBBON PRODUCTS,
1100 S Cypress St
La Habra, CA 90631-6870
800-423-3303 • Fax 714-447-8028

COAST TO COAST EXEC. SEARCH
3000 Pearl St Ste 2
Boulder, CO 80301-2438
303-449-5922

COAST TO COAST INCORPORATED
3276 Arbor Oaks Ln
Vero Beach, FL 32960-4965
e-mail: CTC@coastpack.com
www.coastpack.com
772-770-4733

COAST TO COAST SEAFOODS
10613 NE 38th Pl
Kirkland, WA 98033-7927
425-889-2862

COASTAL MARKETING
2 Master Dr
Franklin, MA 02038-3034
e-mail: coastaldig@aol.com
508-520-6699

COASTAL SEAFOODS, INC.
PO Box 455
Ridgefield, CT 06877-0455
203-431-0453 • Fax 203-438-7099

COBATCO INC
1215 NE Adams St
Peoria, IL 61603-4005
309-676-2663 • Fax 309-676-2667

COCA COLA
1 Coca Cola Plz NW
Atlanta, GA 30313-2499
404-676-2121

COCA COLA
11800 W Brown Deer Rd
Milwaukee, WI 53224-1442
414-357-7650 • Fax 414-357-7088

COCA-COLA BOTTLING CO.
9 B St
Needham Heights, MA 02494-2701
781-292-7131 • Fax 781-292-7110

COCA-COLA BOTTLING CO .OF N.Y.
3 Skyline Dr
Hawthorne, NY 10532-2174
914-345-3900. • Fax 914-345-2963

COCA-COLA BOTTLING COMPANY
7400 N Oak Park Ave
Niles, IL 60714-3818
847-647-0607

COCA-COLA CO.
5601 Citrus Blvd
New Orleans, LA 70123-5508
504-818-7300

COCA-COLA FOODS DIVISION
2000 Saint James Pl
Houston, TX 77056-4123
713-888-5000

COCA-COLA FOUNTAIN
3900 Dallas Pkwy Ste 100
Plano, TX 75093-7866
469-467-8820 • Fax 469-467-8825

COCA-COLA USA
PO Box 1734
Atlanta, GA 30301-1734
404-676-5008

COCO COMPANY
363 W Erie St
Chicago, IL 60610-6903
312-915-0043 • Fax 312-915-5933

COCO LOPEZ, USA/ BORDEN
8000 Governors Square Blvd
Hialeah, FL 33016-6201
305-820-9095

COCONUT CODE, INC.
1430 S Federal Hwy Ste 200
Deerfield Beach, FL 33441-7244
954-481-9331

COE & DRU, INC.
14701 Clark Ave
Hacienda Heights, CA 91745-1307
www.coedru.com
626-330-9917 • Fax 626-330-1317

COFFEE INN'S LLC
3617 E La Salle St
Phoenix, AZ 85040-3975
www.coffeeinns.com
602-438-8286 • Fax 602-437-2270

COFFEE BELLA, EURO IMPEX, INC
10840 Missouri Ave
Los Angeles, CA 90025-4657
www.coffeebella.com
310-552-8299 • Fax 310-552-8273

COFFEE DISTRIBUTING CORP.
200 Broadway
New Hyde Park, NY 11040-5329
516-746-7010 • Fax 516-742-7018

COFFEE ENTERPRIESES
286 College St
Burlington, VT 05401-8319
www.coffeeinns.com
802-865-4480 • Fax 802-865-3364

COFFEE FEST
9655 SE 36th St
Mercer Island, WA 98040-3798
206-232-2982

COFFEE INTERNATIONAL OF FLORIDA
6140 Spring Lake Hwy
Brooksville, FL 34601-7910
e-mail: coffee_inter@hotmail.com
352-799-2644 • Fax 352-754-9315

COFFEE ROASTERS OF NEW ORLEANS
1401 S Rendon St
New Orleans, LA 70125-1707
504-827-0878

COFFEE-KING DISTRIBUTOR
3422 35th St
Astoria, NY 11106-1219
www.coffee-king.com
718-706-8921 • Fax 718-937-6270

COGENERATION SYSTEMS
42 George Dr
Mundelein, IL 60060-3015
www.cogensys.com
847-949-9449 • Fax 847-949-9349

COLAGATE-PALMOLIVE COMPANY
PO Box 1928
Morristown, NJ 07962-1928
www.colpalipd.com
973-631-9000 • Fax 973-292-6028

COLBORNE CORP
28495 Ballard Dr
Lake Forest, IL 60045-4510
847-724-5070

COLBURN TREAT LLC
191 Thompson Rd
Shelburne, VT 05482-7378
877-877-3201

COLD TECH
651 W Tower Ave
Alameda, CA 94501-5047
800-314-4477 • Fax 510-337-8787

COLDELITE
PO Box 4069
Winston Salem, NC 27115-4069
800-648-4389 • Fax 336-661-9895

COLDELITE BY CARPIGIANI/MIC
600 Leverkuhn St
Houston, TX 77007-5744
e-mail: sales@machineice.com
www.machineice.com
713-868-1300 • Fax 713-868-4424

COLDTECH-JIMEX CORP
616 McClary Ave
Oakland, CA 94621-1915
www.jimex-coldtech.com
510-632-4200 • Fax 510-632-4298

COLDWATER FISH FARMS
PO Box 1
Lisco, NE 69148-0001
800-658-4450

COLDWATER SEAFOOD CORP
133 Roton Ave
Norwalk, CT 06853-1643
203-852-1600

COLDWATER SEAFOOD CORP.
12555 Wirth St
Brookfield, WI 53005-2417
262-783-7100 • Fax 262-783-5094

COLDZONE
221 S Berry St
Brea, CA 92821-4829
714-529-4461

COLESON FOODS INC
PO Box 30535
Seattle, WA 98103-0535
877-265-3766

COLGATE PALMOLIVE CO. INSTITUTE
930 Shady Meadow Ct
Lewisville, TX 75077-8550
e-mail: tom_faile@colpal.com
940-241-1169 • Fax 940-455-5009

COLGATE-PALMOLIVE CO
300 Park Ave
New York, NY 10022-7402
212-310-2000

COLLECTIVE ARTS OF MEXICO
9136 Fainwood Ln
Austin, TX 78749-4133
512-989-1181

COLLECTIVE ARTS OF MEXICO
8008 Davis Mountain Cv
Austin, TX 78726-4040
www.collectiveartsofmexico.com
800-851-3993

COLLEGE OF DUPAGE
425 22nd St
Glen Ellyn, IL 60137-6784
www.cod.edu
630-942-2315 • Fax 630-858-9399

COLOMBIAN COFFEE
140 E 57th St
New York, NY 10022-2763
212-421-8300

COLONIAL CASTINGS, INC.
15301 NW 34th Ave
Opa Locka, FL 33054-2459
305-688-8901 • Fax 305-688-8932

COLORADO RESTAURANT ASSOCIATION
430 E 7th Ave
Denver, CO 80203-3605
303-830-2972

COLOR-ONS CO.
1700 S Eisenhower Ave
Mason City, IA 50401-1539
www.mach3ww.com/colorons
641-424-1554 • Fax 641-423-7843

COLSON CASTER
3700 Airport Rd
Jonesboro, AR 72401-4463
www.colsoncaster.com
800-643-5515 • Fax 800-356-6708

COLUMBIA GAS
200 Civic Center Dr
Columbus, OH 43215-4157
614-460-6236

COLUMBIA INDUSTRIES
5005 West Ave
San Antonio, TX 78213-2711
210-344-9211

COLUMBIA NAPLES CAPITAL
100 Ring Rd W Unit 214
Garden City, NY 11530-3205
516-349-5566

COLUMBUS SALAME CO
30977 San Antonio St
Hayward, CA 94544-7109
e-mail: llamanna@columco.com
510-921-3442 • Fax 510-921-3581

COMARK INSTRUMENTS
9710 SW Sunshine Ct
Beaverton, OR 97005-4100
800-555-6658

COMBIBLOC
4800 Roberts Rd
Columbus, OH 43228-9699
614-876-3700 • Fax 614-876-8678

COMDIAL
PO Box 7266
Charlottesville, VA 22906-7266
800-347-1432

COMDIAL CORPORATION
1180 Seminole Trl
Charlottesville, VA 22901-2829
e-mail: info@comdial.com

www.comdial.com
434-978-2200 • Fax 434-978-2230

COMED ENERGY SERVICES ORGANIZATION
1919 Swift Dr
Oak Brook, IL 60523-1502
630-684-3347 • Fax 630-684-3729

COMET AMERICAN RICE
PO Box 2587
Houston, TX 77252-2587
e-mail: lmceuen@amrice.com
www.amrice.com
281-272-8800

COMMAND COMMUNICATIONS, INC.
10800 E Bethany Dr
Aurora, CO 80014-2687
www.command-comm.com
303-751-7000 • Fax 303-750-6437

COMMAND PACKAGING
3840 E 26th St
Los Angeles, CA 90023-4507
www.commandpackaging
323-260-4800 • Fax 323-260-7047

COMMEG SYSTEMS, INC.
4300 Lincoln Ave Ste J
Rolling Meadows, IL 60008-1157
www.commeg.com
847-359-2800 • Fax 847-359-3892

COMMERCIAL APPLIANCE SERVICE
8416 Laurel Fair Cir Ste 114
Tampa, FL 33610-7360
813-879-2461

COMMERCIAL BUSINESS CREDIT
2727 Ulmerton Rd Ste 350
Clearwater, FL 33762-3374
727-573-9400 • Fax 727-573-9100

COMMERCIAL CARPETS OF AMERICA
430 S Pickett St
Alexandria, VA 22304-4706
e-mail: comcarpets@aol.com
703-212-6372 • Fax 703-823-8355

COMMERCIAL COFFEE EQUIP.
7150 Lockwood Rd
Lake Worth, FL 33467-7817
800-973-3352

COMMERCIAL COFFEE EQUIP.
2930 Commerce Park Dr
Boynton Beach, FL 33426-0727
e-mail: ccer@mindspring.com
800-873-3352 • Fax 561-585-3237

COMMERCIAL FOOD EQUIPMENT SRVICES
9247 N Meridian St
Indianapolis, IN 46260-1879
317-844-4700

COMMERCIAL LAMINATIONS
2801 Murfreesboro Rd
Antioch, TN 37013-2011
615-361-0000

COMMERCIAL-MONEY.COM
2665 S Bayshore Dr Ste
Miami, FL 33133-5448
e-mail: info@commercial-money.com
866-266-6663 • Fax 305-854-2418

COMMERICAL KITCHEN
1377 N Brazos St
San Antonio, TX 78207-1271
www.commercialkitchen.com
210-735-2811 • Fax 210-735-7421

COMMISSARY SUPPLY/D.&D. EQUIPMENT
4386 Independence Ct
Sarasota, FL 34234-4711
941-359-2448

COMMKITCHEN.COM
999 18th St
Denver, CO 80202-2499
303-302-7211

COMMKITCHEN.COM
1900 Wazee St Ste 250
Denver, CO 80202-1180
www.commkitchen.com
303-308-9109 • Fax 303-382-1455

COMMON WEALTH FINANCIAL GROUP
3 Bethesda Metro Ctr Ste 300
Bethesda, MD 20814-5360
301-951-5339

COMM-TRANS
792 S Cooper St
Memphis TN 38104-5406
901-726-9394

COMMUNITY COFFEE CO., LLC
5913 Blessey St
New Orleans, LA 70123-5504
504-733-3649

COMMUNITY COFFEE CO.
447 W 38th St
Houston, TX 77018-6603
713-691-4422 • Fax 713-691-7035

COMMUNITY, A DIVISION OF JASPER
932 Mill St
Jasper, IN 47546-2821
e-mail: glenn@jasperseating.com
www.jasperseating.com
800-622-5661 • Fax 812-482-1548

COMOBAR 2000, INC.
174 NE 24th St
Miami, FL 33137-4831
786-623-0868 • Fax 786-623-0284

COMPANYFLOORS.COM
1954 Airport Rd
Atlanta, GA 30341-4956
800-474-1178

COMPASS FLOORING SOLUTIONS
44 Concord St
Wilmington, MA 01887-2126
978-694-0433

COMPASS FOODS C/O SOUTHLAND CO
PO Box 711
Dallas, TX 75221-0711
800-869-1991

COMPASS GROUP NORTH AMERICA
2400 Yorkmont Rd
Charlotte, NC 28217-4511
compass-usa.com
www.compass-usa.com
704-329-1192 • Fax 704-329-7985

COMPLIANCE ASSOCIATES
316 Wildwood Rd
Council Bluffs, IA 51503-5363
712-325-6888

COMPLIANCE CONTROL INC
1355 Piccard Dr Ste 460
Rockville, MD 20850-4338
800-810-4000

COMPLIMINTS
1616 Walnut St Ste 1912
Philadelphia, PA 19103-5319
215-732-2400 • Fax 215-732-4040

COMPRIS TECHNOLOGIES
1000 Cobb Place Blvd NW Ste 30
Kennesaw, GA 30144-3682
770-795-3319

COMPUREGISTER BY NEWBOLD CORP
450 Weaver St
Rocky Mount, VA 24151-2200
www.compuregister.com
800-552-3282 • Fax 540-489-2381

COMPUTEL
2300 NW Corporate Blvd
Boca Raton, FL 33431-7374
954-944-5577

COMPUTER GOLF SOFTWARE
1700 SW 12th Ave
Boca Raton, FL 33486-6699
800-327-9465

COMPUTER RESOURCE GROUP
8403 Kingston Pike
Knoxville, TN 37919-5352
e-mail:
sales@computerresourcegroup.co
865-690-4585 • Fax 865-690-8734

**COMPUTER SERVICES
OF FLORIDA**
8302 Regina Pl
Tampa, FL 33615-1713
813-243-1025

COMPUTER WORLD, INC.
111 Gill Dr
Lafayette, LA 70507-5401
337-234-3071

COMPUTRITION INC
PO Box 4689
Chatsworth, CA 91313-4689
800-222-4488

COMPUTRITION, INC
19808 Nordhoff Pl
Chatsworth, CA 91311-6607
www.computrition.com
818-701-5544 • Fax 818-701-1702

COMSTOCK-CASTLE STOVE
119 Washington St
Quincy, IL 62301-3860
217-223-5070

COMTELCO
4360 Chamblee Dunwoody Rd
Atlanta, GA 30341-1049
770-234-0008

COMTROL CORPORATION
900 Long Lake Rd
Saint Paul, MN 55112-6428
800-926-6876

**COMUS RESTAURANT
SYSTEMS**
2502 Urbana Pike
Ijamsville, MD 21754-8624
www.comus.com
301-874-2900 • Fax 301-874-2994

**COMUS RESTAURANT
SYSTEMS**
27591 S Dixie Hwy
Homestead, FL 33032-8225
305-248-0959

CONAGRA
6 Conagra Dr
Omaha, NE 68102-5006
402-595-7719 • Fax 402-595-6964

CONAGRA FLOUR MILL
1 Conagra Dr # G-L180
Omaha, NE 68102-5003
888-442-5848

**CONAGRA FLOUR
MILLING CO**
PO Box 3500
Omaha, NE 68103-0500
800-537-4795

CONAGRA FOODSERVICE
6225 N Meeker Pl Ste 200
Boise, ID 83713-1590
208-658-5020 • Fax 208-658-2202

**CONAGRA
FROZEN FOODS**
5 Conagra Dr
Omaha, NE 68102-5005
402-595-6000

**CONAGRA POULTRY
COMPANY**
PO Box 1389
Duluth, GA 30096-1389
770-232-4227

**CONAGRA POULTRY
FOODSERVICE**
2475 Meadowbrook Pkwy Ste A
Duluth, GA 30096-2366
800-782-9824 • Fax 770-232-4419

**CONAGRA SIGNATURE MEATS
GROUP**
1930 Aa St
Greeley, CO 80631-9663
970-353-2311 • Fax 970-395-8701

CONCA D'ORO IMPORTERS
7202 51st Ave
Woodside, NY 11377-7611
718-446-0800 • Fax 718-424-3300

**CONCENTRA MEDICAL
CENTERS**
800 E Commerce Rd Ste 302
New Orleans, LA 70123-3428
504-733-7313

**CONCENTRA MEDICAL
CENTERS**
9321 Kirby Dr
Houston, TX 77054-2516
www.concentramc.com
713-797-9696 • Fax 713-797-6134

CONCEPT 2 BAKERS
7350 Commerce Ln NE
Minneapolis, MN 55432-3113
www.c2b.com
800-266-2782 • Fax 763-574-2210

**CONCEPT EQUIPMENT
CORP.**
57 Bay State Rd
Cambridge, MA 02138-1203
617-868-1147 • Fax 617-868-2716

**CONCEPT HOSPITALITY
GROUP**
401 S El Cielo Rd Apt 84
Palm Springs, CA 92262-7923
760-492-8875

CONCEPTS INTERNATIONAL
5315 Tremont Ave
Davenport, IA 52807-2640
563-386-6620 • Fax 563-3861-352

CONCIERGE COMMERCIAL
5509 Lacy Rd
Madison, WI 53711-5317
800-227-9066

CONCINNITY
40 Melville Park Rd
Melville, NY 11747-3147
www.concinnityusa.com
631-293-7272 • Fax 631-777-4629

CONCO FOOD SERVICE
918 Edwards Ave
New Orleans, LA 70123-3188
504-733-5200

CONCORD E F S
2525 Horizon Lake Dr Ste 120
Memphis, TN 38133-8119
800-238-7675

CONCORD FOODA INC
10 Minuteman Way
Brockton, MA 02301-7508
508-580-1700

CONEDISON SOLUTION
701 Westchester Avenue
West Harrison, NY 10604-3002
e-mail: peartd@conedsolutions.com
914-286-7083 • Fax 914-448-0057

CONGRESS FINANCIAL
1 Post Office Sq
Boston, MA 02109-2106
617-338-1998

CONNECTIVITY INC
240 Commercial Blvd
Fort Lauderdale, FL 33308-4444
954-776-9542

CONNELLY ASSOCIATES
2180 Noblestown Rd
Pittsburgh, PA 15205-3938
412-920-4100

**CONNEXXION MULTIMEDIA
TECHNOLOGY**
12277 SW 55th Street, Ste 901
Fort Lauderdale, FL 33330-3311
e-mail:
ahernadez@cybertotems.com
954-252-5728 • Fax 954-252-5786

CONNOVER PACKAGING INC.
111 Parce Ave
Fairport, NY 14450-1467
www.connoverpacking.com
585-377-2510 • Fax 585-377-2604

**CONRAD & COMPANY TABLE-
TOP, INC**
1212 Laclair St
Pittsburgh, PA 15218-1206
412-244-0865 • Fax 412-244-0169

CONROY FOODS
906 Old Freeport Rd
Pittsburgh, PA 15238-3124
e-mail: beanos@conroyfoods.com
412-967-0554 • Fax 412-967-0558

**CONSOLIDATED COMMERCIAL
CONTROL**
8130 River Dr
Morton Grove, IL 60053-2637
847-966-9700 • Fax 847-966-9701

**CONSOLIDATED
DISTRIBUTORS**
4712 SW 74th Ave
Miami, FL 33155-4417
www.beef-natural.com
305-265-9994 • Fax 305-265-4494

**CONSOLIDATED
INTERNATIONAL CORP**
333 Main St
East Greenwich, RI 02818-3660
401-884-0160

**CONSTELLATION
BRANDS**
300 Willowbrook Office Park
Fairport, NY 14450-4222
888-724-2169

CONSULATE OF GERMANY
1330 Post Oak Blvd
Houston, TX 77056-3031
713-627-7770 • Fax 713-627-0506

CONSUMER APTITUDES, INC.
1309 W Borders Dr
Palatine, IL 60067-6605
www.conapt.com
847-991-1806 • Fax 847-835-9516

CONSUMERS CHOICE COFFEE
4271 Produce Rd
Louisville, KY 40218-6012
502-968-4151

**CONSUMERS FLAVORING
EXTRACT**
921 McDonald Ave
Brooklyn, NY 11218-5600
718-435-0201

CONTEMPO COLOURS
1 Paper Pl
Kalamazoo, MI 49001-4646
616-349-2626 • Fax 616-349-6412

CONTENTARTS.COM
45 E 20TH ST
New York, NY 10003-1308
212-358-1088 • Fax 914-732-8720

**CONTINENTAL COFFEE
PRODUCTS**
235 N Norwood St
Houston, TX 77011-2311
713-928-6281

**CONTINENTAL
DELI FOODS**
2601 NW Expressway St Ste 1000
Oklahoma City, OK 73112-7272
800-926-3354

CONTINENTAL GIRBAU, INC.
2500 State Road 44
Oshkosh, WI 54904-8914
www.cont-girbau.com
920-231-8222 • Fax 920-231-4666

**CONTINENTAL
MANUFACTURING**
123 Byassee Dr
Hazelwood, MO 63042-3177
314-731-0402

**CONTINENTAL
MANUFACTURING CO**
13330 Lakefront Dr
Earth City, MO 63045-1513
314-770-9949 • Fax 314-770-9938

**CONTINENTAL
MANUFACTURING CO**

809 Genoa Red Bluff Rd
Pasadena, TX 77504-4006
281-991-0804 • Fax 281-991-0820

CONTINENTAL REFRIGERATOR
539 Dunksferry Rd
Bensalem, PA 19020-5908
www.continental-refrig.com
215-244-1400 • Fax 215-244-9579

CONTINENTAL WINGATE MFG
75 Central St
Boston, MA 02109-3411
617-574-9000

CONTRACT & LEISURE
150 W 22nd St
New York, NY 10011-2421
212-206-6337 • Fax 212-633-8218

**CONTRACT CONNECTION,
INC**
PO Box 848254
Hollywood, FL 33084-0254
www.contractcon.com
954-925-2800

**CONTRACT DESIGNS
OF AMERICA**
37 Lady Godiva Way
New City, NY 10956-6349
845-634-0600 • Fax 845-634-4325

**CONTRACT FURNITURE
SHOWROOM**
4645 Gun Club Rd
West Palm Beach, FL 33415-2859
e-mail: forchair@aol.com
561-686-9522 • Fax 561-686-9523

CONTRACT MARKETING
9325 Progress Pkwy
Mentor, OH 44060-1855
440-639-9100

**CONTRACT SEATING
SOLUTIONS**
PO Box 360
Walls, MS 38680-0360
662-781-0300 • Fax 662-781-0309

CONTROL PRODUCTS, INC
1724 Lake Dr W
Chanhassen, MN 55317-8580
www.controlproductsinc.com
952-448-2217 • Fax 952-448-1606

CONWAY IMPORT CO.
11050 Addison Ave
Franklin Park, IL 60131-1402
e-mail:
conwaydressings@mindspring.com
847-455-5600 • Fax 847-455-5630

CONWAY IMPORTS CO INC
11051 Addison Ave
Franklin Park, IL 60131-1496
800-323-8801 • Fax 800-304-4021

COOK FAMILY FOOD LTD
200 S 2nd St
Lincoln, NE 68508-2499
402-475-6700

COOKIES AND MORE INC
3670 Dodd Rd
Saint Paul, MN 55123-1326
e-mail: cookiesandmore@msn.com
651-406-9600 • Fax 651-406-8220

COOKIES FOOD PRODUCTS
PO Box 458
Wall Lake, IA 51466-0458
www.cookiesbbq.com
800-331-4995 • Fax 712-664-2675

COOKIETREE BAKERIES
PO Box 57888
Salt Lake City, UT 84157-0888
801-268-2253 • Fax 801-265-2727

COOKSHACK INC
2304 N Ash St
Ponca City, OK 74601-1100
www.cookshack.com
580-765-3669 • Fax 580-765-2223

COOKTEK
954 W Washington Blvd Ste 37
Chicago, IL 60607-2224
312-563-9600

COOL SCHOOL INCENTIVES
PO Box 47430
Minneapolis, MN 55447-0430
800-468-3287

COOL TUBE, INC
760 E Parkridge Ave
Corona, CA 92879-1042
www.cooltube.com
909-278-4280 • Fax 909-278-9727

COOPER INSTRUMENT CORP.
33 Reeds Gap Rd
Middlefield, CT 06455-1138
800-835-5011

COORS BREWING COMPANY
240 Treakle Dr
Jackson, LA 70748-4341
225-658-6211

COORS BREWING COMPANY
909 Hidden Rdg Ste 550
Irving, TX 75038-3824
800-936-5259

COPELAND CORP
1675 W Campbell Rd
Sidney, OH 45365-2493
www.copeland-corp.com
937-498-3011 • Fax 937-498-3334

COPESAN-SPECIALISTS IN PESTS
3490 N 127th St
Brookfield, WI 53005-3118
www.copesan.com
262-783-6261 • Fax 262-783-6267

COPLEY UPHOLSTERING
120 Linda St
Abington, MA 02351-2379
781-566-1000 • Fax 339-469-4212

COPUNET EBUSINESS GROUP
15235 Alton Pkwy Ste 100
Irvine, CA 92618-2616
www.compuwave.net
949-585-9500 • Fax 949-585-9510

CORA ITALIAN SPECIALITIES
9630 Joliet Rd
La Grange, IL 60525-4138
708-482-4660 • Fax 708-482-4663

CORBETT LIGHTING
2816 Commodore Dr
Carrollton, TX 75007-4612
www.corbettlighting.com
972-512-8800 • Fax 972-512-8999

CORBIN FOODS EDIBOWLS
PO Box 28139
Santa Ana, CA 92799-8139
714-966-6695 • Fax 714-966-0382

CORBY HALL INC
3 Emery Ave
Randolph, NJ 07869-1308
973-625-5770

CORE COMMUNICATIONS
100 Greyrock Rd S
Port Chester, NY 10573-5320
e-mail: pgottwald@core.net
914-937-4688 • Fax 914-937-8047

CORE EMPOLOYER SERVICES, INC
12600 Belcher Rd S Ste 104.
Largo, FL 33773-1656
e-mail: corempsrv@msn.com
www.corempsrv.org
727-535-2673

CORE SYSTEMS
2027 Park St
Houston, TX 77019-6117
800-324-2673

CO-RECT PRODUCTS
7105 Medicine Lake Rd
Minneapolis, MN 55427-3675
www.co-rectproducts.com
612-542-9200 • Fax 612-542-9205

CORMAN & ASSOCIATES, INC.
881 Floyd Dr
Lexington, KY 40505-3694
www.cormans.com
859-233-0544 • Fax 859-253-0119

CORN PRODUCTS INTL
6500 S Archer Rd
Summit Arg, IL 60501-1933
708-563-2400

CORNELIUS
30 Pine St
Pittsburgh, PA 15223-1995
e-mail: capisales@aol.com
412-781-9003 • Fax 412-781-7840

CORNING FOODSERVICE CO.
55 Shuman Blvd Ste 705
Naperville, IL 60563-8488
630-637-1041 • Fax 630-637-1047

CORONA BEER
8004 West Ave
San Antonio, TX 78213-1870
www.corono.com
210-341-2172 • Fax 210-341-1960

CORONA HOTELWARE CORP.
PO Box 2766
Orlando, FL 32802-2766
407-566-0786 • Fax 407-566-9121

CORONET FOODS
25 Southwood Dr
Southborough, MA 01772-1979
508-485-9858 • Fax 508-485-7566

CORONET LIGHTING
16210 S Avalon Blvd
Gardena, CA 90248-2908
e-mail: jb-coronet@usa.net
www.coronetlighting.com
310-327-6700 • Fax 310-532-8092

CORPORATE ART GROUP, INC
25 Western Industrial Dr
Cranston, RI 02921-3406
e-mail:
corporateartgroup@prodigy.net
www.corporateart.baweb.com
401-946-7200 • Fax 401-946-7207

CORPORATE DINING PARTNERS
265 Park Pl
Chagrin Falls, OH 44022-4456
440-247-8679

CORPORATE SAFE
14800 McKinley Ave
Posen, IL 60469-1525
www.corporatesafes.com
708-371-4200 • Fax 708-371-3326

CORRUGATED PACKAGING COUNCIL
2850 Golf Rd
Rolling Meadows, IL 60008-4050
847-364-9600

CORTINA LEATHERS
15 W 20th St
New York, NY 10011-3708
e-mail: info@cortinaleathers.com
www.cortinaleathers.com
212-463-0645 • Fax 212-463-0725

COSCO INC
2525 State St
Columbus, IN 47201-7443
www.coscoinc.com
812-372-4200 • Fax 812-372-0911

COSMIC CO.
151 Haskins Way # A
South San Francisco, CA 94080-6213
e-mail: clearpak@aol.com
650-742-0888 • Fax 650-742-6777

COSTA MACARONI MFG. CO
4790 Valley Blvd
Los Angeles, CA 90032-3834
www.pastabycosta.com
800-433-7785 • Fax 323-225-1667

COSTCO WHOLESALE
46000 Manekin Plz
Sterling, VA 20166-6513
e-mail: Bobokyle@emril.msn.com
www.costco.com
703-406-6955 • Fax 703-406-6984

COSTUME SPECIALISTS
211 N 5th St
Columbus, OH 43215-2603
614-464-2115 • Fax 614-464-2114

COUNCIL HOTEL & REST TRAINERS
741 Carleton Rd
Westfield, NJ 07090-2505
800-463-5918

COUNTRY CASUAL
9085 Comprint Ct # 7909
Gaithersburg, MD 20877-1306
800-284-8325

COUNTRY CELLAR
514 S Main St
Westby, WI 54667-1314
608-634-2468 • Fax 608-634-2400

COUNTRY FAIR FOOD PRODUCTS CO.
307 N Union St
Stockton, CA 95205-4555
e-mail: ctay@jps.net
916-771-8642 • Fax 916-771-8643

COUNTRY HOME BKRY
720 Metropolitan Pkwy SW
Atlanta, GA 30310-2093
404-758-5581

COUNTRY MUFFIN AND CAKE COMPANY
1500 Front St
Yorktown Heights, NY 10598-4638
914-245-9319 • Fax 914-245-9327

COUNTRY PURE FOODS INC
681 W Waterloo Rd
Akron, OH 44314-1547
330-753-2293 • Fax 330-745-7838

COUNTRYSIDE BAKING CO, INC
1711 Kettering
Irvine, CA 92614-5615
949-851-9654

COUNTRYSIDE PRODUCTS
PO Box 1417
Pataskala, OH 43062-1417
www.countrysideproducts.com
614-861-6116 • Fax 614-864-0888

COUNTY DRAPERIES, INC
105 Sprague Ave
Middletown, NY 10940-5301
e-mail: info@drape.com
www.drape.com
845-342-9009 • Fax 845-342-1530

COURISTAN INC
919 3rd Ave
New York, NY 10022-3902
212-371-4200

COURTYARD COLLECTIONS
210 Folkstone Circle
Augusta, GA 30907-3773
e-mail:
courtyardcoll@mindspring.com
706-854-9133 • Fax 706-854-9765

COVENT GARDEN
1600 Union St
San Francisco, CA 94123-4507
415-536-0227 • Fax 415-536-0222

COVERALL
50 Suffolk St
Worcester, MA 01604-3719
800-356-2961

COVERINGS ETC INC
89 NE 40th St
Miami, FL 33137-3509
e-mail: offer@coveringsetc.com
www.coveringsetc.com
305-572-1080 • Fax 305-572-1070

COVINGTON INDUSTRIES CONTRACT
15 E 26th St
New York, NY 10010-1505
212-592-8562 • Fax 212-576-1167

COWAN, THOMPSON & ROHDE INSURANCE
1001 Fourier Dr
Madison, WI 53717-1958
608-831-9660 • Fax 608-831-9661

COX BUSINESS SERVICES
1250 Poydras St Ste 1050
New Orleans, LA 70113-1876
504-304-1700 • Fax 504-681-1708

COYNE & DELANY CO
PO Box 411
Charlottesville, VA 22902-0411
434-296-0166

COZZINI INC
4300 W Bryn Mawr Ave
Chicago, IL 60646-5943
773-478-9700 • Fax 773-478-8689

COZZINI INC
1919 Premier Row
Orlando, FL 32809-6205
e-mail: rfernandez@cozzini.com
800-648-2242

CP GLOBAL EQUIP & SERV NET
9 Chesley Dr
Barrington, NH 03825-3906
603-664-6852

CPFILMS INC.
PO Box 5068
Martinsville, VA 24115-5068
e-mail: llumar@cpfilms.com
www.llumar.com
800-255-8627 • Fax 276-627-7022

CRA EDUCATION FOUNDATION
1011 10th St
Sacramento, CA 95814-3501
www.calrest.org
916-447-5793 • Fax 916-447-6182

CRAFT BREWERS GUILD
5 Mear Rd
Holbrook, MA 02343-1338
781-767-9600 • Fax 781-767-5811

CRAIG MANUFACTURING
30 Loretto St
Irvington, NJ 07111-4710
e-mail: buycraig@aol.com
www.craigmfg.com
973-923-3211 • Fax 973-923-1767

CRAM-A-LOT/J.V. MANUFACTURING
701 Butterfield Coach Rd
Springdale, AR 72764-0224
e-mail: sales@jv.com
www.cram-a-lot.com
800-678-7320

CRANE PEST CONTROL
2700 Geary Blvd
San Francisco, CA 94118-3498
www.cranepestcontrol.com
415-922-1666 • Fax 650-415-9217

CREAMISER PRODUCTS
6122 N 7th St
Phoenix, AZ 85014-1823
602-274-3600

CREATIONS GALORE
118 Sierra St
Metairie, LA 70001-5326
504-834-4777 • Fax 504-834-4708

CREATIVE BATH
250 Creative Dr
Central Islip, NY 11722-4414
e-mail: cbathmkt@aol.com
www.creativebath.com
631-582-8000 • Fax 631-582-6194

CREATIVE BEDDING TECH
300 Exchange Dr Ste A
Crystal Lake, IL 60014-6290
800-526-2158

CREATIVE CANDLES
PO Box 412514
Kansas City, MO 64141-2514
816-474-9711

CREATIVE CONSUMER CONCEPTS
10955 Granada Ln
Leawood, KS 66211-1401
913-491-6444

CREATIVE CONTROL DESIGNS
7017 Americana Parkway Dr
Reynoldsburg, OH 43068-4118
www.creativecontrol.com
614-751-3000 • Fax 614-751-3002

CREATIVE ESSENTIALS
600 Johnson Ave
Bohemia, NY 11716-2614
www.menusasap.com
631-467-8370 • Fax 631-467-4255

CREATIVE GRAPHICS
107 W Ohio Ave
Mount Vernon, OH 43050-2441
www.cgkidspress.com
740-392-4327 • Fax 740-392-2317

CREATIVE IMPRESSIONS INC.
7697 9th St
Buena Park, CA 90621-2898
www.creativeimpressioninc.com
800-524-5278 • Fax 714-522-2733

CREATIVE IMPRESSIONS USA
1 Wiltshire Dr
Englishtown, NJ 07726-3570
e-mail:
sales@creativeimpressionsusa.com
www.creativeimpressionsusa.com
732-792-9977 • Fax 732-792-2442

CREATIVE INDUSTRIES, INC.
9911 Brook Rd
Glen Allen, VA 23059-6502
804-266-0204

CREATIVE MENUS
7530 S Madison St Ste
Willowbrook, IL 60527-8434
630-734-3244 • Fax 630-734-3274

CREATIVE PLASTICS
254 Rano St
Buffalo, NY 14207-2105
www.creativecases.com
716-873-4166 • Fax 716-873-4575

CREATIVE PRODUCT INTERNATIONAL
PO Box 781073
San Antonio, TX 78278-1073
800-368-3882

CREATIVE PURCHASING.COM
PO Box 220247
Chicago, IL 60622-0247
www.mirapoix.com

CREATIVE SALES & MARKETING
145 US Highway 46
Wayne, NJ 07470-6830
973-890-1333 • Fax 973-890-1020

CREATIVE SEATING & FIXTURES
1141 Texas Ave
Baxter Springs, KS 66713-1423
620-856-5468

CREATIVE SHADES/ KITOV LAMP CO.
76 N 4th St
Brooklyn, NY 11211-3106
e-mal: info@creativei-kitov.com
718-486-8700 • Fax 718-486-8915

CREATURE COMFORTS TOYS
908 Niagara Falls Blvd
North Tonawanda, NY 14120-2019
888-228-5001 • Fax 888-228-4888

CREDIT CARD CENTER
4850 Rhawn St
Philadelphia, PA 19136-2935
215-335-2773 • Fax 215-624-2196

CREDIT CARD CENTER
4850 Rhawn St Ste 200
Philadelphia, PA 19136-2935
e-mail: johnfdeal@aol.com
www.usfindit.com/ccc
888-760-8601 • Fax 775-833-1093

CREEGAN COMPANY INC
510 Washington St
Steubenville, OH 43952-2140
www.weir.net/creegans
740-283-3708 • Fax 740-283-4117

CREMES UNLIMITED INC
600 Holiday Plaza Dr
Matteson, IL 60443-2241
708-748-1336

CRES COR/COASTAL MARKETING
12825 Taft Ave
Cleveland, OH 44108-1635
216-851-9734

CRESCENT BUSINESS MACHINES
1605 Airline Dr
Metairie, LA 70001-5991
504-831-3751 • Fax 504-834-2845

CRESCENT CITY CANDLE
PO Box 820402
Memphis, TN 38182-0402
901-454-1997

CRESCENT CITY CANDLE
225 River Rd
New Orleans, LA 70121-4216
504-606-5200

CRESCENT DUCK FARM
PO Box 500
Aquebogue, NY 11931-0500
e-mail: doug@crescentduck.com
631-722-8000 • Fax 631-722-5324

CRES-COR
5925 Heisley Rd
Mentor, OH 44060-1833
www.crescor.com
440-350-1100 • Fax 440-350-7267

CRESS INSURANCE CONSULTANTS
6101 Moon St NE
Albuquerque, NM 87111-1131

CREST ELECTRONICS INC. - VIDEO
3706 Alliance Dr
Greensboro, NC 27407-2016
e-mail:
custserv@crestelectronics.com
www.crestelectronics.com
800-873-2121

CREST MEAT CO., LNC.
PO Box 1208
Hammond, LA 70404-1208
985-345-6845 • Fax 985-345-6866

CRESTAR FOOD PRODUCTS INC
750 Old Hickory Blvd
Brentwood, TN 37027-4528
615-377-4400 • Fax 615-377-4411

CRESTMARK INTERNATIONAL
275 Market St Ste 423
Minneapolis, MN 55405-1625
www.crestmarkinternational.com
612-343-5567 • Fax 612-343-5568

CRESTWARE
520 N Redwood Rd
North Salt Lake, UT 84054-2747
www.crestware.com
801-292-0656 • Fax 801-295-5732

CRESTWARE
PO Box 540210
N Salt Lake, UT 84054-0210
www.crestware.com
800-345-0513

CRETEL FOOD EQUIPMENT
PO Box 5717
Wakefield, RI 02880-5717
401-789-0900

CRIMSCO INC.
500 E 59th St
Kansas City, MO 64110-3004
800-821-3912 • Fax 816-444-2199

CRIS SYSTEMS INC.
1295 S Emerson St
Denver, CO 80210-1621
303-758-5171 • Fax 303-758-5246

CROCKER, LINDSLEY & ASSOC.
1899 Porter Lake Dr Ste 1
Sarasota, FL 34240-7894

e-mail: rolindsley@msn.com
941-343-0209 • Fax 941-343-0347

CROOKES & HANSEN
PO Box 201818
Cleveland, OH 44120-8113.
216-292-9600 • Fax 216-292-0076

CROOKES & HANSON
23900 Mercantile Rd
Beachwood, OH 44122-5910
800-999-0263

CROWLEY MARKETING ASSOCIATES
350 Park St Ste 106
North Reading, MA 01864-2162
www.cmarep.com
978-664-6606 • Fax 978-664-2254

CROWN BAKERY
4484 Whittier Blvd
Los Angeles, CA 90022-1534
e-mail: crownbakery@aol.com
323-981-0079 • Fax 323-269-0543

CROWN INDUSTRIES
155 N Park St
East Orange, NJ 07017-1790
973-672-2277

CROWN LINEN SERVICES
39 Damrell St
Boston, MA 02127-2702
e-mail:
lflanders@crownuniform.com
www.crownuniform.com

CROWN PLAZA RESORT
130 Shipyard Dr # J
Hilton Head, SC 29928-4932
843-341-1833 • Fax 843-785-4879

CRS INC.
2909 Anthony Ln
Minneapolis, MN 55418-3238
www.crs-usa.com
612-781-3474 • Fax 612-781-9418

CRS TEXAS
8303 Westglen Dr
Houston, TX 77063-6309
e-mail: dlarock@crstexas.com
www.crstexas.com
713-785-4646 • Fax 713-785-5237

CRUNCHTIME INFO SYSTEMS
86 Condor St
Boston, MA 02128-1306
617-567-5228

CRUVINET BEVERAGE SYSTEMS, INC
PO Box 10304
Reno, NV 89510-0304
www.cruvinetsys.com
775-827-4044 • Fax 775-827-0432

CRYOVAC NORTH AMERICA
PO BOX 464
Duncan, SC 29334-0464
864-433-2000 • Fax 864-433-3180

CRYSTAL CLEAR LIGHTING
300 Industrial Ave
Ridgefield Park, NJ 07660-1346
e-mail: serxner@ccilighting.com
201-229-0200 • Fax 201-229-1623

CRYSTAL SPIRITS
10810 72nd St Ste 206
Seminole, FL 33777-1524
e-mail: denise@kosher-vodka.com
727-548-8390 • Fax 727-548-8390

CSA INTERNATIONAL
8501 E Pleasant Valley Rd
Independence, OH 44131-5516
www.csa-international.org
216-524-4990 • Fax 216-328-8138

CSC
5885 Landerbrook Dr Ste 3
Cleveland, OH 44124-4031
440-449-3600 • Fax 440-442-3071

CSI BATH FURNISHINGS-DIVISION
25300 Al Moen Dr
North Olmsted, OH 44070-5619
800-882-0116 • Fax 800-848-6636

CUCINA CLASSICA ITALIANA
1835 Swarthmore Ave
Lakewood, NJ 08701-4533
732-363-3800 • Fax 732-363-1019

CUDAHY INC PATRICK
PO Box 8905
Cudahy, WI 53110-8905
414-744-2000

CUISINE SOLUTIONS
85 S Bragg St
Alexandria, VA 22312-2793
888-285-4679

CUISINEDUJOUR.COM
439 Steele Blvd
Baton Rouge, LA 70806-5137
225-931-3343 • Fax 225-267-5070

CULI- SERVICES OF CENTRAL CAL
1830 S Mooney Blvd
Visalia, CA 93277-4484
www.culi-service.com
888-577-7417 • Fax 559-741-1315

CULINARY ARCHIVES & MUSEUM
315 Harborside Blvd
Providence, RI 02905-5202
401-598-1471

CULINARY ARTS INSTITUTE OF HUDSON
162 Sip Ave
Jersey City, NJ 07306-3009
201-714-2127 • Fax 201-714-2136

CULINARY ARTS INSTITUTE OF HUDSON
161 Newark Ave
Jersey City, NJ 07302-2811
e-mail: baumeyer@email.njin.net
www.hudson.cc.nj.us
201-714-2193 • Fax 201-656-1522

CULINARY CLASSICS
1628 S Prairie Ave
Chicago, IL 60616-1317
www.culinaryclassics.com
800-373-2963 • Fax 312-427-9668

CULINARY CONCEPTS GROUP
2000 N Racine Ave Ste 2160
Chicago, IL 60614-4045
773-871-6792

CULINARY CONCEPTS CHEF CREATIONS
408 Virginia Dr
Orlando, FL 32803-1800
e-mail: darrell@culinaryconceptsinc.com
407-228-0069

CULINARY EDUCATION CENTER
101 Drury Ln
Asbury Park, NJ 07712-5037
732-988-3299

CULINARY FOODS, INC.
4201 S Ashland Ave
Chicago, IL 60609-2305
312-650-4000

CULINARY INSTITUTE
1946 Campus Dr
Hyde Park, NY 12538-1499
www.ciachef.edu
845-452-9430 • Fax 845-451-1067

CULINARY SAFARI
339 W Melody Ln # 1810
Casselberry, FL 32707-3256
407-830-1112 • Fax 407-8301-959

CULINARY SOFTWARE SERVICES INC
1630 30th St Ste 300
Boulder, CO 80301-1014
www.culinarysoftware.com
800-447-1466 • Fax 303-786-9776

CULINARY SOURCE, INC
3800 Commerce Loop
Orlando, FL 32808-3818
407-481-2526

CULINARY TRENDS
6285 E Spring St Pmb 107
Long Beach, CA 90808-4000
www.culinarytrends.com
562-826-9188 • Fax 562-826-0332

CULI-SERVICES
1 Grove St
San Francisco, CA 94102-4702
www.culi-services.com
415-431-2885 • Fax 415-431-1580

CULI-SERVICES OF SOUTHERN CA
20490 Via Castile
Yorba Linda, CA 92886-4564
www.culi-services.com
714-695-0630 • Fax 714-695-0352

CULI-SERVICES, INC
104 E 40th St Ste 90
New York, NY 10016-1801
e-mail: culiofNYC@aol.com
www.culi-services.com
631-941-0104 • Fax 631-941-0475

CULLIGAN INTERNATIONAL
1 Culligan Pkwy
Northbrook, IL 60062-6287
www.culligan.com
847-205-6000 • Fax 8472056030

CUMMINS-ALLISON CORP
091 Techniville Dr
Mount Prospect, IL 60056-6098
www.cumminsallison.com
847-299-9550 • Fax 847-299-4939

CUNO
400 Research Pkwy
Meriden, CT 06450-7161
203-237-5541

CURLY'S FOODS
11753 NW 28th St
Pompano Beach, FL 33065-3312
954-340-1222

CURTON PRODUCTS
5350 Campbells Run Rd
Pittsburgh, PA 15205-9738
www.tmi-pvc.com
412-7879-750 • Fax 412-7873-665

CURTRON INDUSTRIES, INC.
337 Mt Merino Rd
Hudson, NY 12534-4119
518-943-6931

CUSIMANO PRODUCE CO., INC.
1001 S Dupre St
New Orleans, LA 70125-1303
504-822-7726 • Fax 504-827-0904

CUSTOM BIOLOGICALS, INC
902 Clint Moore Rd Ste 208
Boca Raton, FL 33487-2846
e-mail: buybugs@custombio.com
www.custombio.com
561-998-1699

CUSTOM BUSINESS SOLUTIONS
1312 S State College Pkwy
Anaheim, CA 92806-5241
www.cbs-posi.com
800-551-7674 • Fax 714-827-0325

CUSTOM CANDLE SALES
86 Wolfe St
Bay Saint Louis, MS 39520-8923
228-466-4512 • Fax 228-463-915

CUSTOM CONTRACT FURNISHINGS
PO Box 7
High Point, NC 27261-0007
e-mail: sales@customcontract.com
www.customcontract.com
800-882-8565 • Fax 336-885-9174

CUSTOM CUTS INC
2842 S 5Th Ct
Milwaukee, WI 53207-1472
414-483-0491 • Fax 414-483-4244

CUSTOM DECO
1343 Miami St
Toledo, OH 43605-3338
419-698-2900

CUSTOM FOOD PRODUCTS
5145 W 123rd St
Alsip, IL 60803-3105
708-388-8883 • Fax 708-388-8910

CUSTOM LOOMS RUG MILLS
275 Warner Ave
Roslyn Heights, NY 11577-1057
516-484-0522

CUSTOM SYNDICATED RESEARCH INC
900 Skokie Blvd Ste 107
Northbrook, IL 60062-4014
847-714-0714 • Fax 847-714-9900

CUSTOM TELEPHONE PRINTING
1002 McHenry Ave
Woodstock, IL 60098-3036
e-mail: ctp@mc.net
www.customtel.com
815-338-0000 • Fax 815-338-0009

CUTLER INDUSTRIES
8300 Austin Ave
Morton Grove, IL 60053-3209
847-965-3700

CVI BRANDS
1025 Tanklage Rd Ste F
San Carlos, CA 94070-3230
650-595-1768 • Fax 650-595-8147

CVR & ASSOCIATES, INC.
4455 Dardanelle Dr Ste D
Orlando, FL 32808-3850
e-mail: lory@cvcorlando.com
407-299-7619 • Fax 800-940-7619

CVS PURCELL
206 E St NE
Washington, DC 20002-4923
202-546-8300 • Fax 202-546-9099

CYBERNET BUSINESS DEVELOPMENT
PO Box 781
Huntington Beach, CA 92648-0781
714-969-1752

CYBERPIXIE
68 E Wacker Pl Ste 600
Chicago, IL 60601-7207
e-mail:
hiroko_osaka@cyberpixie.com
www.cyberpixie.com
312-379-3200 • Fax 312-379-2350

CYBERPLATE LLC
20 W 20th St Ste 406
New York, NY 10011-9258
212-366-0439

CYBORG EQUIPMENT CORP.
300 Tosca Dr
Stoughton, MA 02072-1516
e-mail: cec-bz@cyborgeq.com
781-297-0110 • Fax 781-297-0097

CYBUS CAPITAL MARKETS LLC
520 Walnut St Ste 500
Des Moines, IA 50309-4106
515-246-8558 • Fax 515-246-0129

CYCLAMAN COLLECTION
2140 Livingston St
Oakland, CA 94606-5219
510-597-3640 • Fax 510-597-3644

CYNTERGY CORPORATION
656 Quince Orchard Rd Fl 7
Gaithersburg, MD 20878-1409
301-926-3400

CYPRESS BATHROBES - HOTEL DIVISION
1 Charlton Ct Ste 101
San Francisco, CA 94123-4219
www.cypressbathrobes.com
888-757-7623 • Fax 415-440-1035

CYPRESS HILL
1520 Kuebel St
New Orleans, LA 70123-6972
504-734-8424

CYRIL'S FINEST
1301 NW 89th Ct Ste 206
Miami, FL 33172-3006

e-mail: adam@cyrils.com
www.cyrils.com
800-929-7457

CYRIL'S FINEST
1301 NW 89th Ct
Miami, FL 33172-3034
e-mail: adam@cyrils.com
305-592-9858 • Fax 305-592-9856

D & F INTERNATIONAL
PO Box 1229
Bonita, CA 91908-1229
888-206-3215 • Fax 619-472-9295

D & J SALES AND SERVICE
6815 Fresh Meadow Ln
Fresh Meadows, NY 11365-3420
718-463-0298 • Fax 718-961-0769

D & L INDUSTRIES
PO Box 292
St Petersburg, FL 33731-0292
800-550-4230 • Fax 727-323-9161

D & N ASSOCIATES
1340 Park Dr
Azle, TX 76020-3734
800-976-6694

D C I MARKETING
2727 W Good Hope Rd
Milwaukee, WI 53209-2048
414-228-4314

D E R SALES, LLC
PO Box 365
Norwalk, CT 06852-0365
203-846-4062

D FW CONSULTING
7319 Williamswood Dr
Dallas, TX 75252-6335
972-733-4188 • 972-732-6898

D J POWER INTL LLC
501 Deodara Dr
Los Altos, CA 94024-7140
650-964-5339

D KANOPY, INC
PO Box 963
Elfers, FL 34680-0963
e-mail: shade@writeme.com
www.kdkanopy.com
800-460-8006

D M INDUSTRIES
2320 NW 147th St
Opa Locka, FL 33054-3190
305-685-5739 • Fax 305-688-9415

D N E WORLD FRUIT SALES
1900 N Old Dixie Hwy
Fort Pierce, FL 34946-1423
800-327-6676

D T N TRAVEL CENTER
9110 W Dodge Rd
Omaha, NE 68114-3306
800-610-0777

D&W FINE FURNITURE MFG
2 Mill St
Cornwall, NY 12518-1266
845-534-7576 • Fax 845-534-7568

D.W. HABER & SON INC.
825 E 140th St
Bronx, NY 10454-1903
www.habersilver.com
718-993-6405 • Fax 718-585-0726

DA'BANANA-FROZEN CHOCO-LATE BAN
1242 E Piedmont Rd
Marietta, GA 30062-2819
800-719-9017

DADE ENGINEERING
558 W 18th St
Hialeah, FL 33010-2482
e-mail: daeco@webtv.net
www.daeco.net
305-885-2766

DAHLGREN DUCK & ASSOC.
2554 Tarpley Rd Ste 110
Carrollton, TX 75006-2385
www.dahlgrenduck.com
972-478-5991 • 972-478-5996

DAILY FOODS
3535 S 500 W
Salt Lake City, UT 84115-4205
801-269-1998 • Fax 801-269-1409

DAIN RAUSCHER WESSELS
60 S 6th St
Minneapolis, MN 55402-4400
612-371-2800

DAINES ASSOCIATES
265 E 100 S Ste 265
Salt Lake City, UT 84111-1609
801-363-3400

DAIRY SOURCE INC
PO Box 903
Delavan, WI 53115-0903
262-728-8023

DAIRYLAND, THE CHEF'S WAREHOUSE
1300 Viele Ave
Bronx, NY 10474-7134
www.thechefswarehouse.com
718-842-8700 • Fax 718-378-2234

DAISY BRAND INC.
12750 Merit Dr Ste 600-158
Dallas, TX 75251-1206
www.daisybrand.com
972-726-0800 • Fax 972-726-0115

DAISY BRAND, INC
12750 Merit Dr Ste 600-LB
Dallas, TX 75251-1206
www.dartcontainer.com
972-671-3800

DAKOTA GROWERS PASTA CO
1 Pasta Ave
Carrington, ND 58421-2500
701-652-2855

DALLAS DRAPERY
1000 W Crosby Rd Ste 120
Carrollton, TX 75006-6924
888-431-8913

DALLAS FOOD GROUP
15226 Moonlit Grv
San Antonio, TX 78247-2941
210-496-6477

DALLIS BROS COFFEE
10030 Atlantic Ave
Ozone Park, NY 11416-1795
www.Dallisbros.com
718-845-3010 • Fax 718-843-0178

DAMASCUS
56 Gold St
Brooklyn, NY 11201-1297
www.damascusbakery.com
718-855-1456 • Fax 718-403-0948

D'AMICO & PARTNERS, INC.
2210 Hennepin Ave
Minneapolis, MN 55405-2737
612-374-1776

DAMON INDUSTRIES FRUITFUL CORP
10334 Osprey Trce
West Palm Beach, FL 33412-1543
e-mail: ragreatjuice@aol.com
561-386-9419 • Fax 561-799-6019

DAMONS INTERNATIONAL
4645 Executive Dr
Columbus, OH 43220-3601
614-442-7900

DAN CARTER INC
PO Box 106
Mayville, WI 53050-0106
e-mail: ihook@dancarterinc.com
920-387-5740 • Fax 920-387-2194

DANESI CAFFE USA, INC.
575 Lexington Ave
New Yor, NY 10022-6102
www.danesi-coffee.com
212-527-7515 • Fax 212-527-7516

DANIELS EQUIPMENT CO. INC.
45 Priscilla Ln
Auburn, NH 03032-3724
e-mail: sales@decequip.com
www.decequip.com
603-641-9487 • Fax 603-641-8492

DANISCO-CULTOR INGREDIENTS
PO Box 2
New Century, KS 66031-0026
800-255-6837

DANISH FOOD EQUIPMENT
1633 E Madison S
Petaluma, CA 94954-2320
707-763-0110

DANONE-EVIAN SPRING WATER
208 Harbor Dr Fl
Stamford, CT 06902-7467
203-425-1022

DANSKO
8 Federal Rd
West Grove, PA 19390-9182
800-326-7564

D'ARBO, INC. BY GOURMAND FINE
2869 Towerview Rd
Herndon, VA 20171-3205
800-627-7272 • Fax 703-708-9393

DARDEN RESTAURANTS
5900 Lake Ellenor Dr
Orlando, FL 32809-4634
407-245-4000

DARIA GROUP
PO Box 10722
Rockville, MD 20849-0722
301-258-0813

DARLING INTERNATIONAL
251 O Connor Ridge Blvd Ste 30
Irving, TX 75038-6538
972-281-4425

DARLING RESTAURANT SERVICES
700 NW 57th St
Fort Lauderdale, FL 33309-2825
e-mail: ssouthard@darlingii.com
954-351-9474 • Fax 954-351-9479

DART CONTAINER
500 Hogsback Rd
Mason, MI 48854-9547
www.darcontainer.com
800-248-5960 • Fax 517-676-3883

DATA COLLECTIONS UNLIMITED
1095 Powers Pl
Alpharetta, GA 30004-8358
770-442-8892

DATAHOST CORPORATION
PO Box 3155
Englewood, CO 80155-3155
303-220-7733

DATAPROFIT CONSULTING CORP.
330 Whitney Ave Ste 600
Holyoke, MA 01040-2754
e-mail: kmruk@dataprofit.com
www.dataprofit.com
413-536-269 • Fax 413-536-3354

DATAWORKS DOCUMENT SUPPORT.COM
4550 S Windermere St
Englewood, CO 80110-5541
www.documentsupport.com
303-7616-975 • Fax 303-761-6985

DATEK
70 Hudson St
Jersey City, NJ 07302-4599
201-744-9150

DAVE'S GOURMENT, INC.
2000 McKinnon Ave Bldg 4
San Francisco, CA 94124-1621
www.davesgourment.com
415-401-9100 • Fax 415-401-9107

DAVID & GOLIATH COMM MARKETING
215 Broadway St NE
Minneapolis, MN 55413-1970
612-379-7661

DAVID BERG
2501 N Damen Ave

Chicago, IL 60647-2101
773-278-5195 • Fax 773-278-4759

DAVID DEE & COMPANY
8033 Biscayne Blvd
Miami, FL 33138-4620
305-754-4411

DAVID SHERMAN CORP
5050 Kemper Ave
Saint Louis, MO 63139-1185
314-772-2626

DAVID'S COOKIES
12 Commerce Rd
Fairfield, NJ 07004-1637
973-227-2800 • Fax 973-882-6998

DAVIDSON HOTEL CO
1755 Lynnfield Rd
Memphis, TN 38119-7243
901-761-4664

DAVIS & ASSOCIATES
W184 S8372 Challenger Dr
Muskego, WI 53150-8747
262-679-9510 • Fax 262-679-5441

DAVIS PLAYING CARD DIST.
2400 W 84th St
Hialeah, FL 33016-5707
305-558-1161

DAVISBALDWIN INSURANCE & RISK
4600 W Cypress St
Tampa, FL 33607-4032
e-mail: measton@davisbaldwin.com
www.davisbaldwin.com
813-287-1936

DAWN ENTERPRIESES
712 Bread And Milk St
Coventry, CT 06238-1093
www.trashcans.com
860-742-5990 • Fax 860-742-6268

DAWN FOOD PRODUCTS, INC.
1980 Afton St
Houston, TX 77055-2204
www.dawnfoods.com
713-683-0300 • Fax 713-688-8501

DAY LEE FOODS
13055 Molette St
Santa Fe Springs, CA 90670-5593
562-329-5331 • Fax 562-926-8630

DAYLIGHT SOFTWARE INC
100 Main St
Dover, NH 03820-3835
603-743-6677

DAYMARK FOOD SAFETY SYSTEMS
12836 S Dixie Hwy
Bowling Green, OH 43402-9697
www.dissolveaway.com
800-847-0101 • Fax 419-354-0514

DAYSTAR DESSERTS
437 Railroad Ave
Westbury, NY 11590-4314
e-mail: info@daystardesserts.com
www.daystardesserts.com
516-255-5253 • Fax 516-255-5254

DAYVA INTERNATIONAL
7642 Windfield D
Huntington Beach, CA 92647-7139
714-842-9697

DCI FOOD EQUIPMENT
5350 E Davison St
Hamtramck, MI 48212-1233
313-369-1666

DCS
5800 Skylab Rd
Huntington Beach, CA 92647-2054
www.dcsappliances.com
714-372-7000 • Fax 714-372-7001

DE BOER FOOD IMPORTERS
101 Coastline Rd
Sanford, FL 32771-6629
407-322-2499 • Fax 407-322-1815

DE CECCO PRODITTI MEDITER-RAEN
712 5th Ave
New York, NY 10019-4108

212-582-6500 • Fax 212-582-4914

DE CHOIX SPECIALTY FOODS
5825 52nd Ave
Woodside, NY 11377-7402
e-mail: dechoix@dechoix.com
718-507-8080 • Fax 718-335-9150

DE LORIS FROZEN DOUGH
624 Elizabeth St
Utica, NY 13501-2413
e-mail: delorios@prodigy.net
800-649-7612 • Fax 315-732-7621

DE O'MALLEY INC.
12540 S Holiday Dr Unit A
Alsip, IL 60803-3234
708-371-3550

DEAL-MEX INTERNATIONAL
AV Agustin Yanez NO 1920 2DO
Cleveland, OH 44190-0001
e-mail: dealmex@prodigy.net.mx
440-810-8201 • Fax 440-810-1542

DEAN & DELUCA INC
560 Broadway
New York, NY 10012-3938
212-431-1691

DEAN DISTRIBUTORS, INC
1350 Bayshore Hwy Ste 400
Burlingame, CA 94010-1813
800-792-0816 • Fax 650-401-3752

DEAN INDUSTRIES
14501 S Broadway St
Gardena, CA 90248-1809
800-995-1210 • Fax 310-324-2697

DEBRAGGA AND SPILTER
826D Washington St
New York, NY 10014-1479
e-mail: debragga@aol.com
212-924-1311 • Fax 212-206-8437

DECO TRADE INT
2223 N Cicero Ave
Chicago, IL 60639-3327
773-889-0000 • Fax 773-889-5978

DECOPAC
5736 Main St NE
Minneapolis, MN 55432-5437
612-934-0838

DECOTY COFFEE CO.
1920 Austin St
San Angelo, TX 76903-8704
e-mail: bbaker@decotycoffee.com
www.decotycoffee.com
800-588-8001 • Fax 915-655-6837

DEEP FOODS INC
1090 Springfield Rd
Union, NJ 07083-8119
908-810-7500

DEEP SOUTH BLENDERS, INC
720 Saint George Ave
New Orleans, LA 70121-1119
504-733-3751

DEER PARK RAVIOLI
1882 Deer Park Ave
Deer Park, NY 11729-4318
e-mail: slitrel@aol.com
www.deerparkravioli.com
631-667-4644 • Fax 631-667-3565

DEGRENNE, GUY-TABLE FRNCE
373 Park Ave S # FL.4
New York, NY 10016-8805
212-725-3461

DEISS SEAFOOD
130 S Chaparral Ct # 2
Anaheim, CA 92808-2238
e-mail: deisseafood@earthlink.net
714-974-9513 • Fax 714-974-8136

DEITZ(M) & SONS
490 Hillside Ave
Hillside, NJ 07205-1119
908-686-8800

DEL BAJIO JALAPENOS & SAUCES
9330 Corporate Dr Ste 511
Schertz, TX 78154-1255
210-651-6067 • Fax 210-651-5595

DEL MAR COLLEGE
101 Baldwin Blvd

Corpus Christi, TX 78404-3894
e-mail: bard@delmar.edu
361-698-1734 • Fax 361-698-1829

DEL MONTE CORPORATION
PO Box 193575
San Francisco, CA 94119-3575
415-247-3000 • Fax 415-247-3683

DEL SOL FOOD COMPANY, INC
PO Box 2243
Brenham, TX 77834-2243
979-836-597 • Fax 979-836-6953

DELCO TABLEWARE INTL
19 Harbor Park Dr
Port Washington, NY 11050-4657
www.delcotableware.com
516-625-0808 • Fax 516-625-0859

DELFIELD
980 S Isabella Rd
Mount Pleasant, MI 48858-9200
989-773-7981

DELFIELD WALK-INS
3201 NE Loop 820 Ste 150
Fort Worth, TX 76137-2447
800-318-6802 • Fax 817-306-1502

DELGADO COMMUNITY COLLEGE
615 City Park Ave
New Orleans, LA 70119-4399
504-483-420

DELICATO VINEYARDS
12001 S Highway 99
Manteca, CA 95336-8499
209-239-1215

DELIVERY CONCEPTS EAST
351 Dogwood Ln
Hampstead, NC 28443-2026
e-mail: dceast@bellsouth.net
910-270-2090 • Fax 910-270-2091

DELIZIA OLIVE OIL CO
1991 Dennison St
Oakland, CA 94606-5225
www.evoliveoil.com
510-535-6833 • Fax 510-532-2837

DELMARVA POWER
PO Box 6066
Newark, DE 19714-6066
302-452-6273

DELOITTE & TOUCHE
2 World Financial Ctr
New York, NY 10281-1008
212-436-3868

DELTA EQUIPMENT CO.
223 Highpoint Dr
Ridgeland, MS 39157-6018
800-423-2164 • Fax 601-957-3939

DELTA FAUCET CO
55 E 111th St
Indianapolis, IN 46280-1071
317-848-1812

DELTA HOSPITAL SUPPLY
31 Astor Ave
Norwood, MA 02062-5016
www.deltagloves.com
781-551-0051 • Fax 781-769-6515

DELTA PRIDE CATFISH, INC.
PO Box 850
Indianola, MS 38751-0850
e-mail: walterh@deltapride.com
www.deltapride.com
662-887-5401 • Fax 662-887-5950

DELTATRACK SCIENTIFIC
5653 Stoneridge Dr Ste 120
Pleasanton, CA 94588-8503
www.deltatrak.com
925-467-5940 • Fax 925-467-5949

DELUXE BUILDING SYS
499 W 3rd St
Berwick, PA 18603-2936
570-752-5914

DELUXE EQUIPMENT CO.
4414 28th St W
Bradenton, FL 34207-1107
e-mail: deluxe@gte.net
941-753-4184 • Fax 941-753-4529

DELVERDE USA
1901 Research Blvd Ste 160
Rockville, MD 20850-6122
www.delverde.com
301-838-7013 • Fax 301-838-7010

DEMMA FRUIT COMPANY
11404 W Dodge Rd Ste 500
Omaha, NE 68154-2584
402-592-7285

DEPETRO BROTHERS
1 Riverview Blvd
Methuen, MA 01844-6026
877-264-7627

DESIGN FORUM
7575 Paragon Rd
Dayton, OH 45459-5316
937-439-4400 • Fax 937-439-4340

DESIGN FURNISHING, INC
2500 Dinneen Ave Ste B
Orlando, FL 32804-4204
407-294-0507

DESIGN MAJIK
4770 NE 12th Ave
Fort Lauderdale, FL 33334-4802
954-489-7661

DESIGNER PREVIEWS
36 Gramercy Park E
New York, NY 10003-1741
e-mail. decorpro@aol.com
www.designerpreviews.com
212-777-2966 • Fax 212-420-1736

DESIGNLINE CONSTRUCTION SERVICES
442 State Route 35 S Bldg A
Eatontown, NJ 07724-2200
732-935-1440 • Fax 732-935-1481

DESIGNTEX FABRICS
200 Varick St Fl 8
New York, NY 10014-7433
212-886-8100

DESTINY PLASTICS
57 Bell Canyon Dr
Trabuco Canyon, CA 92679-3807
e-mail: destinyplastic@home.com
949-709-1985 • Fax 949-709-2683

DETECTO SCALE COMPANY
PO Box 151
Webb City, MO 64870-0151
e-mail: ssinne@aol.com
www.cardet.com
417-673-4631 • Fax 417-673-5001

DEUTSCHE & SONS
1 Byram Brook Pl
Armonk, NY 10504-2319
914-251-9463

DEUTSCHE BANK
31 W 52nd St
New York, NY 10019-6118
212-469-5100

DEVINE PEARSON INC
300 Congress St
Quincy, MA 02169-0907
617-472-2700 • Fax 617-472-8880

DEXTER CO THE
2211 W Grimes Ave
Fairfield, IA 52556-2681
641-472-5131

DFG FOODS
550 W 14th Pl
Chicago, IL 60607-5126
312-279-1327 • Fax 888-678-7344

DH SALES-SUREFLOW
402 SE 31st Ave
Portland, OR 97214-1929
e-mail: dhsales.com
503-236-9263 • Fax 503-236-9264

DI LEONARDO INTERNATIONAL
2346 Post Rd
Warwick, RI 02886-2207
401-732-2900

DI LUIGI'S
PO Box 248
Revere, MA 02151-0008
617-561-6030 • Fax 617-561-0334

DIABLO PRODUCTS
3139 5th Ave S
Fort Dodge, IA 50501-2913
www.diablo-products.com
515-5766-4948 • Fax 515-955-4206

DIAMOND CRYSTOL SPECIALTY FOOD
10 Burlington Ave
Wilmington, MA 01887-3924
800-225-0592 • Fax 978-658-4760

DIAMOND WALNUT GROWERS
1050 Diamond St
Stockton, CA 95205-7087
209-467-6000

DIAMOND WIPES INTL INC.
320 Clary Ave
San Gabriel, CA 91776-1306
www.diamondwipes.com
626-454-1012 • Fax 626-454-1014

DIANNE'S GOURMET DESSERTS
410 W Industrial St
Le Center, MN 56057-1200
www.diannesdesserts.com
507-357-4161 • Fax 507-357-4162

DIAZ CASH REGISTERS
715 Aurora Ave
Metairie, LA 70005-2692
504 834 148

DICARLO DISTRIBUTORS
1630 N Ocean Ave
Holtsville, NY 11742-1838
www.dicarlofood.com
631-758-6000 • Fax 631-758-6096

DICKS COFFEE
2750 Fort Royal Dr Ste A
Houston, TX 77038-3399
e-mail: amolloy@dickscoffee.com
www.dickscoffee.com
281 999 9929 • Fax 201-999-2240

DIEBOLD, INCORPORATED
5995 Mayfair Rd
Canton, OH 44720-1550
www.diebold.com
330-490-6262 • Fax 330-490-4460

DIEDRICH COFFEE
2144 Michelson Dr
Irvine, CA 92612-1304
www.diedrich.com
949-260-1600 • Fax 949-553-1165

DIEDRICH COFFEE ROASTERS
PO Box 1708
Sandpoint, ID 83864-0901
e-mail: roasters@micron.net
208-263-1276 • Fax 208-265-4584

DIEHL MILK PRODUCTS CO
24 N Clinton St
Defiance, OH 43512-1800
800-251-3033

DIETZ & WATSON MEAT CO.
5701 Tacony St
Philadelphia, PA 19135-4311
215-831-9000 • Fax 215-831-1044

DIGITAL GLOBAL INTERNET-ROOMHOST
1 E Chase St Ste 207
Baltimore, MD 21202-7402
e-mail: info@roomhost.com
www.roomhost.com
410-244-1600 • Fax 410-752-0880

DIGITAL GRAPHICS, INC
73 2nd Ave
Burlington, MA 01803-4413
e-mail: customerservice@dgiusa.com
www.dgiusa.com
781-270-3670 • Fax 81-270-3663

DIGITAL JAVA INC.
370 Knollwood St Ste 500
Winston Salem, NC 27103-1880
www.digitaljava.net
888-200-5282 • Fax 630-894-0847

DIME GROUP INTL, INC.
100 N Fairway Dr Ste 126

Vernon Hills, IL 60061-1859
847-573-0009 • Fax 847-573-0008

DIMITRIA DELIGHTS
81 Creeper Hill Rd
North Grafton, MA 01536-1421
800-763-1113 • Fax 508-839-1685

DINATOUCH
25800 Industrial Blvd Apt 1202
Hayward, CA 94545-5213
www.dinatouch.com
510-347-3588 • Fax 510-347-3349

DINE MOR FOODS INC
PO Box 170971
Birmingham, AL 35217-0971
2053438080 • Fax 205-343-0357

DINE-A-MATE, INC.
455 Court St
Binghamton, NY 13904-1650
607-772-1134

DINEONLINE, INC.
PO Box 950
Germantow, MD 20875-0950
www.dineoline.com
888-990-4200 • Fax 301-353-1848

DINERS CLUB INTERNATIONAL
8430 W Bryn Mawr Ave
Chicago, IL 60631-3473
www.dinersclubus.com
773-380 5129

DINING A LA CARD (SIGNAT GRP)
200 N Martingale Rd
Schaumburg, IL 60173-2040
312-615-3119

DINING RESOURCES
408 Westheimer Rd
Houston, TX 77006-3030
e-mail: diningre@flash.net
877-809-9980 • Fax 713-529-6688

DIP AWAY DISTRIBUTORS
508 Division St
Jeannette, PA 15644-2333
724-527-3035

DIRECT WAITSTAFF APPAREL
615 W Roosevelt Rd
Chicago, IL 60607-4911
800-343-0003

DIRECTIONS RESEARCH
401 E Court St Ste 500
Cincinnati, OH 45202-1332
513-651-2990

DIRECTSOURCE GLOBAL PURCHASING
13222 SE 30th Street
Bellevue, WA 98005-4459
e-mail: customerservice@directsource.com
www.directsource.com
425-378-1864 • Fax 425-378-1325

DIRECTV
2230 E Imperial Hwy # N35
El Segundo, CA 90245-3531
310-535-5095 • Fax 310-535-5225

DIRECTV INC
2230 E Imperial Hwy
El Segundo, CA 90245-3531
310-535-5000

DISC MARKETING
510 S Marengo Ave
Pasadena, CA 91101-3115
e-mail: info@discmarketing.com
www.discmarketing.com
626-795-0432 • Fax 626-405-2370

DISCOVER
12160 Abrams Rd Ste 501
Dallas, TX 75243-4586
972-680-8804

DISCOVER BUSINESS SERVICES
2500 Lake Cook Rd
Deerfield, IL 60015-3851
www.discoverbiz.com
800-347-6673 • Fax 847-405-3523

DISCOVER BUSINESS SERVICES
10 New King St
West Harrison, NY 10604-1205
www.discoverbiz.com
914-437-6393 • Fax 845-339-8875

DISCOVER-NOVUS NETWORK
10 New King St Ste 207
West Harrison, NY 10604-1211
www.novusnet.com
914-747-5000 • Fax 914-747-5130

DISCOVER-NOVUS NETWORK
100 River Ridge Dr Ste 110
Norwood, MA 02062-5041
781-551-9400 • Fax 781-769-2356

DISCOVERY PRODUCTS CORP
4917 Evergreen Way # 9
Everett, WA 98203-2828
www.discoveryproducts.com
425-267-9577 • Fax 425-267-9156

DISPENSER JUICE INC.
2090 Farallon Dr
San Leandro, CA 94577-6602
e-mail: dji@pacbell.net
510-346-2200 • Fax 510-357-9500

DISPENSER SERVICES, INC.
117 Beaver Dr Ste A1
Waltham, MA 02452-8400
781-891-8595 • Fax 781-891-7576

DISPLAY PRODUCTS INC.
800 Fabric Xpress Way
Dallas, TX 75234-7260
www.dproducts.com
800-322-7429 • Fax 888-322-7429

DISTRIBUTOR MARKETING ALLIANCE
1515 E Woodfield Rd Ste 8
Schaumburg, IL 60173-6046
847-413-0082 • Fax 847-413-0089

DISUSA IMPORTS CO
5858 Laurel Hill Blvd
Woodside, NY 11377-7414
718-651-9800

DITO DEAN
4231 Pacific St
Rocklin, CA 95677-2135
www.ditodean.com
800-331-7958 • Fax 916-652-4154

DITTA MEAT CO
4924 Oak Ave
Pasadena, TX 77503-3796
281-487-2010 • Fax 281-487-8956

DIV HOTEL & REST-HOSPITALITY
1940 N Monroe St
Tallahassee, FL 32399-6506
850-644-8247

DIV. OF ALCOHOLIC BEVER-AGES
400 W Robinson St Ste N709
Orlando, FL 32801-1700
407-245-0780

DIVA-USA INC.
142 Knollwood Ct
Aston, PA 19014-1260
e-mail: rmagello@cs.com
610-358-1605 • Fax 610-358-3557

DIVERSEY LEVER, SUPERMARKET
11899 Edgewood Rd Ste O
Auburn, CA 95603-3440
e-mail: karen.huso@diverseylever.com
530-888-8140 • Fax 530-823-0919

DIVERSEYLEVER
7758 W 78th St
Minneapolis, MN 55439-2520
www.americleansystems.com
952-942-8581 • Fax 952-942-9803

DIVERSEYLEVER CORPORATION
255 E 5th St
Cincinnati, OH 45202-4700
513-762-6000

DIVERSIFIED EXPOSITIONS
121 Free St
Portland, ME 04101-3919
207-772-3005

DIVERSIFIELD METAL PRODUCTS
2205 Carlson Dr
Northbrook, IL 60062-6705
www.dispense-rite.com
847-753-9595 • Fax 847-753-9648

DIXIE CRYSTAL BRANDS
PO Box 9177
Savannah, GA 31412-9177
912-651-5112

DIXIE FOODSERVICE
1214 Forest Hills Dr
Southlake, TX 76092-7802
e-mail:
brenda.pelton@fortjamesmail.com
817-416-9402 • Fax 817-416-9210

DIXIE FOODSERVICE
PO Box 6000
Norwalk, CT 06856-6000
www.fortjames.com
203-854-2339 • Fax 203-854-2616

DIXIE FOODSERVICE FORT JAMES
2410 Northampton St
Easton, PA 18042-3822
610-250-7426 • Fax 610-250-7410

DIXIE-NARCO
PO Box 719
Williston, SC 29853-0719
www.dixienarco.com
800-688-9090 • Fax 803-266-5150

DIXON, ODOM & CO., LLP
PO Box 2646
High Point, NC 27261-2646
336-889-5156

DMX MUSIC
11400 W Olympic Blvd
Los Angeles, CA 90064-1550
www.dmxmusic.com
310-444-1744 • Fax 310-444-1760

DMX MUSIC
770 N Jefferson St
Milwaukee, WI 53202-3701
414-271-3070 • Fax 414-271-0115

DMX MUSIC
4085 Nelson Ave Ste A
Concord, CA 94520-1257
www.dmxmusic.com
800-748-6309 • Fax 925-436-8318

DMX MUSIC SOUND & MEDIA
300 W Main St
Northborough, MA 01532-2132
www.dmxmusic.com
508-393-2591 • Fax 508-393-5137

DMX, LLC
2155 Stonington Ave Ste 112
Schaumburg, IL 60195-2057
www.dmxmusic.com
847-839-7890 • Fax 847-839-9481

DOBOY PACKAGING MACHINERY
869 S Knowles Ave
New Richmond, WI 54017-1745
715-246-6511

DODGE-REGUPOL INC
715 Fountain Ave
Lancaster, PA 17601-4547
888-383-7655

DODSON GROUP
9201 State Line Rd
Kansas City, MO 64114-3234
www.dodsongroup.com
800-825-3760 • Fax 800-825-6035

DOERLE FOOD SERVICES, INC.
401 W Admiral Doyle Dr
New Iberia, LA 70560-6515
337-367-8551

DOHLER AMERICA
45 Stouts Ln Ste 10

Monmouth Junction, NJ 08852-1914
www.dohlerusa.com
732-438-0430 • Fax 732-438-0453

DOLE & BAILEY
16 Conn St
Woburn, MA 01801-5664
e-mail: iluvcab@ix.netcom.com
www.doleandbailey.com
781-935-1234 • Fax 781-935-9085

DOLE FOOD COMPANY
1 Dole Dr
Thousand Oaks, CA 91362-7300
818-879-6600

DOLE FRESH FRUIT & VEGETABLE CO
545 Columbia Dr Ste 2003
Lawrence, KS 66049-2363
785-832-2500 • Fax 785-832-2800

DOLE FRESH VEGETABLES CO
PO Box 1759
Salinas, CA 93902-1759
800-333-5454

DOLE PACKAGE FOODS
93 Farley Rd
Nashua, NH 03063-5901
603-881-5877

DOLE PACKAGED FOOD CO
PO Box 5500
Westlake Village, CA 91359-5500
800-325-7102

DOLEFAM CORPORATION
1322 E Best Dr
Arlington Heights, IL 60004-1617
847-392-1152

DOLLY MADISON ICE CREAM
888 Jamaica Ave
Brooklyn, NY 11208-1525
718-235-3000 • Fax 718-647-1430

DOLORES CANNING CO. INC.
1020 N Eastern Ave
Los Angeles, CA 90063-3214
e-mail: chilibrick@earthlink.net
323-263-9155 • Fax 323-269-4876

DOMANI FOODS- G & L INTERNATIONAL
1175 NE 125th St
Miami, FL 33161-5015
e-mail: gltrade@bellsouth.net
305-893-2020 • Fax 305-893-2048

DOMETIC
PO Box 490
Elkhart, IN 46515-0490
e-mail: lodging@dometic.com
www.minibar.com
574-294-8665 • Fax 574-294-3369

DOMINEX THE EGGPLANT PEOPLE
PO Box 5069
Saint Augustine, FL 32085-5069
904-692-1348 • Fax 904-692-2348

DOMINO SPECIALTY INGREDIENTS
1100 E Key Hwy
Baltimore, MD 21230-5123
410-752-6150

DOMINO SUGAR CORPORATION
301 State Rt 1
Rutherford, NJ 07070-2575
212-789-9700

DON & CO EDWARD
2500 Harlem Ave
Riverside, IL 60546-1415
708-442-9400

DON FRANCISCO CHEESE
PO Box 1247
Riverbank, CA 95367-1247
209-869-5232 • Fax 209-869-5234

DON MIGUEL MEXICAN FOODS
2125 E Orangewood Ave

Anaheim, CA 92806-6109
714-634-8441

DONATOS PIZZA INC
935 Taylor Station Rd
Columbus, OH 43230-6657

DONGHIA
485 Broadway
New York, NY 10013-5998
212-925-2777

DONNELY HAMCO
1050 Hercules Ave
Houston, TX 77058-2722
e-mail: dhamco@aol.com
281-488-3127 • Fax 281-488-4329

DOODCONNEX
11865 Edgewood Rd
Auburn, CA 95603-3407
www.ammg.com
530-887-2191 • Fax 530-887-3225

DOPACO
100 Arrandale Blvd
Exton, PA 19341-2544
610-269-1776 • Fax 610-269-8349

DORAN SCALES
1315 Paramount Pkwy
Batavia, IL 60510-1460
www.doranscales.com
800-262-6844 • 630-879-0073

DORMONT MFG. COMPANY
6015 Enterprise Dr
Export, PA 15632-8969
www.dormont.com
724-733-4800

DORNBRACHT USA INC
1750 Breckinridge Pkwy
Duluth, GA 30096-7615

DOSKOCIL FOOD SERVICE CO.
PO Box 1570
Hutchinson, KS 67504-1570
620-669-2932 • Fax 620-669-2902

DOT FOODS INC.
PO Box 192
Mount Sterling, IL 62353-0192
217-773-4411

DOT-IT FOOD SAFETY PRODUCTS
602 Magic Mile St
Arlington, TX 76011-5108
www.magicmile.com
800-642-3687 • Fax 800-320-3687

DOUBLE RAINBOW GOURMET ICE CREAM
275 S Van Ness Ave
San Francisco, CA 94103-3733
e-mail: doublerian@alo.con
www.doublerainbow.com
415-861-5858 • Fax 415-861-5872

DOUBLE-WRAP CUP & CONTAINER
PO Box 008459
Chicago, IL 60608-0459
www.comforgripwrap.com
312-382-1537 • Fax 312-466-0139

DOUBLEDAVES PIZZAWORKS SYSTEMS
3563 Far West Blvd Ste 104
Austin, TX 78731-3029
www.doubledaves.com
512-343-0330 • Fax 512-343-0248

DOUCE FRANCE BAKERY INC
4085 L B McLeod Rd Ste G
Orlando, FL 32811-5659
407-849-0123

DOUGH-TO-GO, INC
480 Perry Ct
Santa Clara, CA 95054-2624
www.dough-to-go.com
408-727-4049 • Fax 408-727-4095

DOUGLAS MACHINES CORP
2101 Calumet St
Clearwater, FL 33765-1310
727-461-3477

DOUGLASS INDUSTRIES, INC.
PO Box 70

Egg Harbor City, NJ 08215-0070
e-mail: info@dougind.com
www.dougind.com
609-965-6030 • Fax 609-965-7271

DOUWE EGBEARTS
700 Hilltop Dr
Itasca, IL 60143-1326
630-238-1414 • Fax 360-238-7211

DOW COVER
373 Lexington Ave
New Haven, CT 06513-4061
e-mail: sam@dowcover.com
www.dowcover.com
800-735-8877 • Fax 203-469-0742

DOWN INC
1071 Avenue Of The Americas
New York, NY 10018-3704
e-mail: tamdown.inc@aol.com
www.downinc.com
800-369-3642 • Fax 212-575-5092

DOWN LIFE INTERNATIONAL
8153 Duke Blvd
Mason, OH 45040-8104
513-677-3696 • Fax 513-677-3812

DOYAN
237 E Bayridge Dr
Fort Lauderdale, FL 33326-3531
e-mail: doyan@doyan.qc.ca
800-463-4273

DR PEPPER SEVEN UP COMPANY
PO Box 869077
Plano, TX 75086-9077
214-360-7000 • Fax 214-360-7843

DR PEPPER-SEVEN UP, INC.
5301 Legacy Dr
Plano, TX 75024-3109
972-673-7780 • Fax 972-673-7115

DR. MARTENS COMMERCIAL AND IND
1251 1st Ave
Chippewa Falls, WI 54774-9998
800-962-0166 • Fax 800-446-2329

DR. SMOOTHIE ENTERPRISES
10532 Walker St Ste D
Cypress, CA 90630-4740
e-mail: info@drsmoothie.com
714-826-7875 • Fax 714-826-4214

DRACKETT PROFESSINAL
1525 Howe St
Racine, WI 53403-2237
800-645-8888

DRACKETT PROFESSIONAL
8600 Governors Hill Drive, Ste 3
Cincinnati, OH 45249-1360
513-583-3923 • Fax 513-583-3928

DRAIN WORKS
100 Stromquist Ave
Lowell, MA 01852-5307
e-mail: drainworks@msn.com
www.drainworks.baweb.com
978-459-2080 • Fax 888-237-2467

DRAPES 4 SHOW, INC
5171 Douglas Fir Rd Ste 2
Calabasas, CA 91302-2578
www.drapes.com
818-591-1777 • Fax 818-222-7469

DRAYTON FOODS, LLC
PO Box 9018
Fargo, ND 58106-9018
701-277-9947

DREAM TREE INC.
1010 W Green Dr
High Point, NC 27260-734
www.dreamtreeinc.com
336-889-4058 • Fax 336-889-5817

DREAMMAKER BATH & KITCHEN
1020 N University Parks Dr
Waco, TX 76707-3858
e-mail: dminjoedwyergroup.com
www.dreammaker-remodel.com
800-583-2133 • Fax 254-745-5095

DREYERS ICE CREAM
5929 College Ave
Oakland, CA 94618-1391
800-888-3442 • Fax 510-450-4625

DRI-DEK CORP
PO Box 8839
Naples, FL 34101-8839
800-348-2398

DRINKWORKS
425 30th St Ste 2
Newport Beach, CA 92663-3733
www.drinkworks.com
949-675-7702 • Fax 949-675-7797

**DRISCOLL
STRAWBERRY ASSC.**
PO Box 50045
Watsonville, CA 95077-5045
831-761-5995

**DRYDEN &
PALMER CO**
16 Business Park Dr
Branford, CT 06405-2964
203-481-3725

DSG ASSOCIATES, INC.
2110 E 1st St Ste 106
Santa Ana, CA 92705-4019
714-835-3020

DSR MKTG
100 Wilmot Rd Ste 243
Deerfield, IL 60015-5137
847-940-8200

**DUAL-DRYER
CORPORATION**
1334 Timberlane Rd
Tallahassee, FL 32312-1766
e-mail: info@dual-dryer.com
www.dual-dryer.com
888-DUA-LDRY

**DUCK TRAP RIVER
FISH FARM**
57 Little River Dr
Belfast, ME 04915-6036
www.ducktrap.com
207-388-6280 • Fax 207-388-6288

DUCKLING COUNCIL
PO Box 641433
Chicago, IL 60664-1433
800-571-3466

DUDA & SONS INC
PO Box 620257
Ovledo, FL 32762-0257
407-365-2111

DUDSON USA, INC
5604 Departure Dr
Raleigh, NC 27616-1841
www.dudson.co.uk
919-877-0200 • Fax 919-877-0300

**DUFOUR PASTRY
KITCHENS, INC**
25 9th Ave
New York, NY 10014-1209
212-929-2800 • Fax 212-645-8460

**DUKANE PATTERNED
CARPET**
PO Box 339
Dalton, GA 30722-0339
800-833-6950

**DUKE MANUFACTURING
COMPANY**
2035 N Broadway
Saint Louis, MO 63102-1303
314-231-1130 • Fax 314-231-5074

DULUDE COMPANY
3030 Cayente Way
Shingle Springs, CA 95682-8879
530-676-0655 • Fax 530-676-0655

DUNBAR
50 Schilling Rd
Hunt Valley, MD 21031-1424
410-527-7108 • Fax 410-527-7109

DUNBAR SYSTEMS INC
1186 Walter St
Lemont, IL 60439-3993
630-257-2900

DUNI CORP
W165 N5830 Ridgewood Dr
Menomonee Falls, WI 53051-5655
800-242-3864

DUNM ROCK SPECIALTY CO.
PO Box 7001
Warwick, RI 02887-7001
www.drumrockproducts.com
401-737-5165 • Fax 401-737-5060

DUPONT-FIBERS-SONTARA
1007 Market St
Wilmington, DE 19898-0001
302-774-1000

DURABLE PACKAGING
933 Remington Rd
Schaumburg, IL 60173-4515

DURACOLD
3050 Fite Cir Ste 210
Sacramento, CA 95827-1807
916-361-9500 • Fax 916-361-4500

DUR-A-FLEX, INC.
95 Goodwin St
East Hartford, CT 06108-1146
800-253-3539 • Fax 860-528-2802

DURAFRAME BY KWALU, INC
PO Box 1870
146 Woodlawn St
Ridgeland, SC 29936-1870
e-mail: kscoggins@duraframe.com
www.duraframe.com
800-405-3441 • Fax 843-726-9230

DURALEE FABRICS LTD
150 W 25th St
New York, NY 10001-7404
212-807-7266

DURKAN PATTERNED CARPET
405 Virgil Dr
Dalton, GA 30721-4844
www.durkan.com
706-278-7037 • Fax 706-226-0360

DUSCHQUEEN INC.
461 W Main St
Wyckoff, NJ 07481-1419
e-mail: info@duschqueeninc
www.duschqueeninc.com
800-348-8080 • Fax 800-348-8458

DUTCHESS-BAKERS MACHINERY
1101 John Ave
Superior, WI 54880-1640
800-223-2774

DWL LNDUSTRIES
161 Coolidge Ave
Englewood, NJ 07631-4523
e-mail: pding@dwlintl.com
201-568-9500 • Fax 201-568-6665

DYNAFOAM INTERNATIONAL
853 Valley Rd
Lancaster, PA 17601-4838
e-mail: dynafoam@earthlink.net
717-569-3040 • Fax 717-569-8115

DYNAMIC
PO Box 3322
Champlain, NY 12919-3322
514-956-0127 • Fax 514-956-8983

DYNAMIC DESIGN INC.
1940 Hazen St
East Elmhurst, NY 11370-1211
e-mail: mgerlett@planter.com
www.plantar.com
718-204-0100 • Fax 718-274-7075

DYNAMIC EXPRESSIONS
PO Box 430
Tomball, TX 77377-0430
e-mail: joanie2047@yahoo.com
281-356-1424 • Fax 281-356-1424

DYNAMICS AMERICA, INC.
1 E Delaware Pl Apt 25A
Chicago, IL 60611-4983
312-988-7199

DYNYNSTYL, INC.
1902 7th Ct N # B
Lake Worth, FL 33461-3302
e-mail: dstl@bellsouth.net
561-547-5585 • Fax 561-547-0993

**E & A RESTAURANT SUPPLY &
EQUIPMENT**
140 E 5th St
Plainfield, NJ 07060-1704
e-mail: easupply@aol.com
908-755-9333 • Fax 908-755-1668

E & J GALLO WINERY
PO Box 1130
600 Yosemite Blvd
Modesto, CA 95353-1130
209-579-4224

E & W FOODS
3209 Willis St
Gautier, MS 39553-5735
228-522-0105

E H THOMPSON
937 N Main St
Jacksonville, FL 32202-3092
www.ehthompson.com
800-780-1555

E P C INTERNATIONAL
17300 Red Hill Ave
Irvine, CA 92614-5643
949-660-9252

E P S MOLDERS ASSOC
1926 Waukegan Rd
Glenview, IL 60025-1790
800-607-3772

E R B INDUSTRIES INC
1 Safety Way
Woodstock, GA 30188-1677
800-800-6522

E R C DATAPLUS INC
24 Belden Ave
Norwalk, CT 06850-3314
203-846-4455

E TV NETWORK
111 N Buena Vista St
Burbank, CA 91505-3663
818-842-0004

E W GROBBEL SONS, INC
PO Box 07580
Detroit, MI 48207-0580
e-mail: ewgrobbel@aol.com
313-567-8000 • Fax 313-567-3324

EL DU PONT DE NEMOURS & CO.
1002 Industrial Rd
Old Hickory, TN 37138-3693
888-476-6827

**E.PROVISIONS.COM-GLOBAL
EXPRESS**
90 Safe Trek Pl
Bozeman, MT 59718-7534
www.e.provisions.com
406-587-5571 • Fax 406-582-0614

E.W. HELMICK GROUP
22201 Amberwood Ct
Tehachapi, CA 93561-8530
805-687-1317

EA TOSI & SONS CO., INC.
PO Box 850915
Braintree, MA 02185-0915
781-848-1040

EAGLE CHAIR, INC
9419 Clay Rd
Houston, TX 77080-1445
e-mail: info@eaglechair.com
www.eaglechair.com
713-690-1161 • Fax 713-690-7661

**EAGLE FAMILY
FOODS, INC**
735 Taylor Rd
Columbus, OH 43230-6274
www.eaglegrp.com
614-631-3100 • Fax 614-631-4006

EAGLE GROUP
100 Industrial Blvd
Clayton, DE 19938-8903
www.eaglegrp.com
800-441-8440 • Fax 302-653-2065

EAGLE SCOREBOARDS
PO Box 21327
Reno, NV 89515-1327
800-524-2228

EAGLEWOOD MFG
3001 NE 12th Ter
Fort Lauderdale, FL 33334-4402
954-565-9005 • Fax 954-764-1873

EARTH AMERICA
17283 Davenport Rd
Winter Garden, FL 34787-9106
www.earthcareusa.com
407-948-6869 • Fax 407-654-7542

EARTH TONES
2013 Avery Rd
Canton, GA 30115-9192
770-720-2825

EARTHAMERICA
11145 Morrison Ln
Dallas, TX 75229-5608
www.RestaurantCare.com
800-583-3784 • Fax 214-358-4101

EARTHCARE USA
PO Box 421
Bellaire, TX 77402-0421
e-mail: info@earthcareusa.com
www.earthcareusa.com
800-750-7584 • Fax 713-747-4616

**EARTHSTONE WOOD FIRED
OVEN**
1233 N Highland Ave
Los Angeles, CA 90038-1208
www.earthstoneovens.com
800-840-4915 • Fax 323-962-6408

EAST BAY REST. SUPPLY
49 4th St
Oakland, CA 94607-4690
e-mail: jimt@ebrs.net
510-627-0234 • Fax 510-465-2138

EAST COAST OLIVE CORP.
66 Bridge Ave.
Red Bank, NJ 07701-1160
www.easternchai.com
732-741-9229 • Fax 732-741-7547

EASTERN BAG & PAPER
200 Research Dr
Milford, CT 06460-2880
800-972-9622 • Fax 203-877-9482

EASTERN BUTCHER BLOCK
25 Eagle St
Providence, RI 02908-5622
e-mail: Gary@butcherblock.com
www.butcherblock.com
401-274-1811 • Fax 401-274-1811

EASTERN CAROLINAS MGMNT.
4702 Oleander Dr Ste 300
Myrtle Beach, SC 29577-5744
843-449-8834

EASTERN CASUALTY INS.
325 Donald Lynch Blvd
Marlborough, MA 01752-4729
800-462-1206 • Fax 508-303-1030

EASTERN CHAI
23 Emmons St
Long Branch, NJ 07740-6004
e-mail: chai@danroc.com
www.easternchai.com
732-571-9005 • Fax 732-571-8095

**EASTERN CHAI C-O ICE &
BEVERAGE**
PO Box 20369
Bradenton, FL 34204-0369
e-mail: bfreeland@icebevdepot.com
www.info@icebevdepot.com
941-756-3800

EASTERN FISHERIES INC
14 Hervey Tichon Ave
New Bedford, MA 02740-7348
508-993-5300

**EASTERN FROSTED FOOD
ASSOCIATION**
109 Skyline Dr Ste 2
Ringwood, NJ 07456-2013
973-835-3345

EASTERN TABLETOP MFG. CO
445 Park Ave
Brooklyn, NY 11205-2735
www.easterntabletop.com
718-522-4142 • Fax 718-522-4155

EASYBAR BEVERAGE MGMNT.
PO Box 2156
Lake Oswego, OR 97035-0648
www.teleport.com-~easybar
503-624-6744 • Fax 503-624-6741

EASYBAR OF MINNESOTA
2525 Nevada Ave N
Minneapolis, MN 55427-3662
612-545-7599

EATEC
2904 San Pablo Ave
Berkeley, CA 94702-2426
510-548-1810

EATEC CORPORATION
1350 Ocean Ave
Emeryville, CA 94608-1129
www.eatec.com
510-594-9011 • Fax 510-549-9091

**EATEM FOODS
COMPANY**
1829 Gallagher Dr
Vineland, NJ 08360-1548
856-692-1663 • Fax 856-692-0847

EATIN ISLAND LTD.
PO Box 50057
Indianapolis, IN 46250-0057
317-849-9555

**EBSCO CONSUMER
MAGAZINE SERVICE**
2517 Highway 35 Ste N101
Manasquan, NJ 08736-1991
www.ebscoind.com
732-223-7177 • Fax 732-223-7178

ECARRYOUT.COM
10801 Wayzata Blvd
Hopkins, MN 55305-5510
www.ecarryout.com
612-595-8282 • Fax 612-595-8666

ECCE PANIS, INC.
447 Gotham Pkwy
Carlstadt, NJ 07072-2409
201-939-1616 • Fax 201-438-7088

**ECHOSTAR
COMMUNICATION**
5701 S Santa Fe Dr
Littleton, CO 80120-1813
www.dishnet.com
303-723-2841 • Fax 303-723-3888

ECKSID ENTERPRISES INC
PO Box 370395
Brooklyn, NY 11237-0395
718-497-7143 • Fax 718-497-1613

**ECLECTIC CONTRACT
FURNITURE**
5941 Rink Dam Rd
Taylorsville, NC 28681-8217
888-311-6272 • Fax 888-311-2539

ECOLAB INC
370 Wabasha St N
Saint Paul, MN 55102-1349
651-293-2149

ECOLAB PEST ELIMINATION
2748 Metairie Lawn Dr # B
Metairie, LA 70002-6109
985-966-0250

**ECOLOGICAL GLASS, TERRA
COTTA**
2530 Superior Ave E Flr 6
Cleveland, OH 44114-4230
www.siuegatep.com
216-241-3259 • Fax 216-241-3609

ECOLOGY GROUP INC
2939 Kenny Rd
Columbus, OH 43221-2406
877-424-3927

ECOMPARTS.COM
1150 Applewood Dr
Papillio, NE 68046-5786
402-597-0808

**ECONOMICS RESEARCH ASSO-
CIATES**
1101 Connecticut Ave NW Ste 75
Washington DC 20036-4303
202-496-9870

**ECONOMY MAINTENANCE
SUPPLY**
11 Acacia Ln
Sterling, VA 20166-9307
e-mail: emsi@ems-corp.com
www.ems-corp.com
703-404-7700 • Fax 571-323-9276

**ECO-PURE WASTE WATER
SYSTEM**
12455 Summerwood Dr
Fort Myers, FL 33908-6801
e-mail:
purescents@ecoquestintt.com
www.ecoquestintt.com-puresce
888-999-0936

ECO-QUEST
10751 S Ocean Dr Lot A8
Jensen Beach, FL 34957-2630
e-mail:
purescents@ecoquestintl.com
www.ecoquestintl.com-puresce
772-229-1986

**ECO-QUEST
INTERNATIONAL**
2281 Citrus Ct
Clearwater, FL 33763-4307
e-mail: ipagani1@tampabay.rr.com
727-797-5136 • Fax 727-797-5136

ECREVISSE ACADIENNE
228 Saint Charles Ave
New Orleans, LA 70130-2601
504-524-3660

ED CAREY DESIGN, INC
3200 S Congress Ave
Boynton Beach, FL 33426-9041
561-737-0340

ED CAREY DESIGN, INC.
2600 High Ridge Rd
Boynton Beach, FL 33426-8763
561-585-9700 • Fax 561-585-9734

ED NOONAN ASSOCIATES
155 Boston Rd
Southborough, M 01772-1650
508-460-0508 • Fax 508-460-9091

ED O'CONNOR ASSOCIATES
12026 81st Ave
Seminole, FL 33772-4503
e-mail: edjudyoc@gateway.net
727-398-2895

EDEN STAFFING SERVICES
280 Madison Ave
New York, NY 10016-0801
212-685-0055 • Fax 212-545-8037

EDGE RESOURCES, INC
PO Box 257
Hopedale, MA 01747-0257
www.edgeresources.com
888-849-0998

EDGECRAFT CORPORATION
825 Southwood Rd
Avondale, PA 19311-9765
www.egecraft.com
610-268-0500 • Fax 610-268-3545

EDHARD CORP
279 Blau Rd
Hackettstown, NJ 07840-5221
908-850-8444

**EDISON LIQUOR-ALLIED
DOMECQ**
21125 Enterprise Ave
Brookfield, WI 53045-5229
262-821-0600 • Fax 262-8210-363

**EDITIONS LIMITED
GALLERIES, INC**
4090 Halleck St
Emeryville, CA 94608-3532
415-695-2375 • Fax 415-695-2370

EDLUND
159 Industrial Pkwy
Burlington, VT 05401-5494
802-862-9661

EDRA-CHAPMAN COMPANY
197 S Main St
Natick, MA 01760-4935
508-655-0380 • Fax 508-651-0995

EDUCATION MGMT SYSTEMS
1638 Military Cutoff Rd
Wilmington, NC 28403-5716
800-541-8999

EDUCATIONAL INST-AH&MA
800 N Magnolia Ave
Orlando, FL 32803-3252
407-999-8100

**EDWARD B. WARD & CO
SOUTHERN**
337 Roebling Rd
South San Francisco, CA 94080-4814
650-873-1660 • Fax 650-873-6829

EDWARD DON & COMPANY
2200 SW 45th St
Fort Lauderdale, FL 33312-5740
954-378-7110

EDWARD DON AND CO.
2005 McDaniel Dr
Carrollton, TX 75006-8302
972-484-2300 • Fax 972-969-6926

EDWARD WHITE CO
21700 Oxnard St Ste 400
Woodland Hills, CA 91367-3692
818-716-1120

EDWARDS BAKING CO.
1 Lemon Ln NE
Atlanta, GA 30307-2860
800-241-0559

**EDWARDS TECHNOLOGIES,
INC.**
139 Maryland St
El Segundo, CA 90245-4116
800-662-4577

**EDY'S GRAND
ICE CREAM**
3255 Meridian Pkwy
Fort Lauderdale, FL 33331-3503
954-384-6141

EFCO PRODUCTS INC
130 Smith St
Poughkeepsie, NY 12601-2109
845-452-4715

**EI DORADO MEXICAN FOOD
PRODUCT**
2928 N Main St
Los Angeles, CA 90031-3325
323-225-1737 • Fax 323-225-0075

EI MATADOR FOODS, INC.
7529 Bayway Dr
Baytown, TX 77520-1309
281-424-4555

EI RESTAURANTE MEXICANO
804 Harrison St Ste E2
Oak Park, IL 60304-1149
708-445-9454 • Fax 708-445-9477

EICHENAUER SERVICES
130 S Oakland Ave
Decatur, IL 62522-2997
217-429-4229

EIRE PARTNERS
230 W Superior St Ste 600
Chicago, IL 60610-3585
312-335-4366

EIU
600 Lincoln Ave
Charleston, IL 61920-3099
www.eiu .edu-~famsci
217-581-6680 • Fax 217-581-6090

E-J INDUSTRIES, INC.
1275 S Campbell Ave
Chicago, IL 60608-1013
312-226-5023 • Fax 312-226-5976

**EKIOSK.COM
CORPORATION**
114 Church St Ste 101B
New Lenox, IL 60451-1881
e-mail: info@ekioskdotcm.com
www.ekioskdotcm.com
815-485-1492 • Fax 815-485-0886

**EL BURRITO FOODS
PRODUCTS INC**
PO Box 90125
City Of Industry, CA 91715-0125

e-mail: markroth@elburrito.com
800-933-7828 • Fax 626-369-6972

EL MILGRO, INC.
3120 W 36th St
Chicago, IL 60632-2304
773-650-4682 • Fax 773-523-1009

ELAN FINANCIAL SERVICES
PO Box 2066
Milwaukee, WI 53201-2066
800-523-5354 • Fax 414-765-4451

ELASTIC NETWORKS
1121 Alderman Dr
Alpharetta, GA 30005-4102
e-mail: dmoore@elastic.com
678-297-3100

ELEANOR M. ROSS & ASSOC.
5210 Island Dr
Stone Mountain, GA 30087-4268
800-781-7077

ELECTOFREEZE
PO Box 303
Easton, MA 02334-0303
www.skaleast.com
508-238-0106 • Fax 508-238-5273

ELECTRIC MIRROR
4014 170th St SW
Lynnwood, WA 98037-6956
e-mail: sales@eletricmirror.com
www.electricmirror.com
425-787-0140 • Fax 425-787-1143

ELECTRO FREEZE
2116 8th Ave
East Moline, IL 61244-1823
309-755-4553 • Fax 309-755-9858

ELECTRO FREEZE
435 W Fork Dr
Arlington, TX 76012-3450
e-mail: efreeze@flash.net
817-469-7491 • Fax 817-861-4342

**ELECTRONIC BUSINESS
SOLUTIONS**
200 NW Business Park Ln
Riverside, MO 64150-9696
816-551-900

ELECTRONIC PROCESSING
PO Box 88
Fanwood, NJ 07023-0088
908-322-0477 • Fax 908-322-7999

ELEGANT DESSERTS
275 Warren St
Lyndhurst, NJ 07071-2017
www.elegantdesserts.com
201-933-0770 • Fax 201-933-7309

**ELEGANT LINENS & TABLE
SKIRTING**
5712 Granger St
Corona, NY 11368-3932
718-760-9401 • Fax 718-760-9461

ELEMENTS BY GRAPEVINE INC
PO Box 1458
Lockeford, CA 95237-1458
e-mail: elementsgv@aol.com
www.elementsbygrapevine.com
209-727-3711 • Fax 209-727-3716

ELGIN AREA CHAMBER
32 S Grove Ave
Elgin, IL 60120-6404
e-mail: elginchamber.com
847-741-5660 • Fax 847-741-5677

ELGIN DAIRY FOODS
3707 W Harrison St
Chicago, IL 60624-3622
773-722-7100

ELIASON CORPORATION
PO Box 2128
Kalamazoo, MI 49003-2128
e-mail: doors@eliasoncorp.com
www.eliasoncorp.com
616-327-7003 • 800-828-3577

ELIASON CORPORATION
PO Box 1026
Woodland, CA 95776-1026
www.eliasoncorp.com
530-662-5494 • Fax 530-662-5192

ELI'S BREAD
403 E 91st St
New York, NY 10128-6800
212-831-4800 • Fax 212-423-9078

ELITE COMPANIES
11445 Moog Dr
Saint Louis, MO 63146-3560
314-941-9500

ELITE PROMOTIONAL MARKETING
55 Northern Blvd Ste 001
Great Neck, NY 11021-4058
www.elite-us.com
516-829-9022

ELLIOT SOLUTIONS
104 S Broadway
Tarrytown, NY 10591-4006
www.onetouchtraining.com
914-332-9555 • Fax 914-332-4711

ELLIOTT-WILLIAMS CO INC
3500 E 20th St
Indianapolis, IN 46218-4485
www.elliot-williams.com
317-545-2295 • Fax 317-545-1977

ELLIS (CALL, INC.)
3520 N University Ave
Provo, UT 84604-6648
ww.ellisworld.com
810-374-3424

ELLISON BAKERY
4108 W Ferguson Rd
Fort Wayne, IN 46809-3141
800-711-8091

ELMECO USA - KANAWATI ENTERPRISES
160 Johnson Ave
Hackensack, NJ 07601-4901
e-mail: elmeco1st@aol.com
201-265-9569 • Fax 201-265-4432

ELSAFE INC.
4303 Vineland R
Orlando, FL 32811-7176
407-423-7233

ELTRAX HOSP. GROUP
400 Galleria Pkwy SE Ste 300
Atlanta, GA 30339-3182
770-612-3500

ELTRAX SYSTEMS INC
6825 Jimmy Carter Blvd
Norcross, GA 30071-1228
770-447-5000

EMBASSY OF THE REPUBLIC OF POLAND
201 E 42nd St Rm 675
New York, NY 10017-5704
e-mail: brhusa@ix.netcom.com
www.home.netcom.com-~brhusa-
212-370-5300 • Fax 212-818-9623

EMBER FARMS
2200 Rivers Edge Dr
New Kensington, PA 15068-4540
e-mail:
betsy.thomas@northsidefoods.com
www.emberfarms.com
724-335-5800

EMBER-GLO, DIV OF MIDCO INTL
4140 W Victoria St
Chicago, IL 60646-6727
www.emberglo.com
773-604-8700 • Fax 773-604-4070

EMBERS
1664 University Ave W
Saint Pau, MN 55104-3794
www.embersamerica.com
651-645-6473 • Fax 651-645-6866

EMERY THOMPSON MACHINE & SUPPLY
1349 Inwood Ave
Bronx, NY 10452-3222
www.emerythompson.com
718-588-7300 • Fax 718-588-7911

EMERY WORLDWIDE
10881 Lowell Ave

Overland Park, KS 66210-1653
800-443-6379

EMESS CONTRACT LIGHTING
1 Early St
Ellwood City, PA 16117-2255
800-688-2579

EMET PREVISIONS, INC.
2689 S Park Rd
Hallandale, FL 33009-3815
954-962-7542 • Fax 954-981-4424

EMIL'S-E.G. EMIL & SON, INC.
1345 Germantown Ave
Philadelphia, PA 19122-4407
800-228-3645 • Fax 215-763-9755

EMJAC-KOOLCO INDUSTRIES
1075 Hialeah Dr
Hialeah, FL 33010-5551
800-767-8339

EMKAY CANDLE CO.
PO Box 4969
Syracuse, NY 13221-4969
e-mail: rdvore@emkaycandle.com
315-471-4515 • Fax 315-471-4581

EMLIN COSMETICS
290 Beeline Dr
Bensenville, IL 60106-1600
630-860-5773 • Fax 630-616-0237

EMMPARK FOODS, INC.
1515 W W Canal St
Milwaukee, WI 53233-2617
414-645-6500 • Fax 414-645-4816

EMPIRE RESTAURANT SUPPLY
114 Bowery
New York, NY 10013-4727
212-226-4447 • Fax 212-226-4463

EMPLOYER SOLUTIONS
215 Ann Arbor Rd W Ste 301
Plymouth, MI 48170-2251
734-451-7650

EMPLOYER'S ALLIANCE, INC
702 Tillman Pl
Plant City, FL 33566-7169
e-mail: eaigarcia@aol.com
813-707-8652

EMPLOYERSLINK OF FLORIDA
5951 Cattleridge Blvd
Sarasota, FL 34232-6040
e-mail:
tstevens@unisourceadmin.com
www.employerslink.com
888-881-6628

EMPRESS INTERNATIONAL
10 Harbor Park Dr
Port Washington, NY 11050-4681
516-621-5900 • Fax 516-621-8318

EMR SERVICE
700 E 25th St
Baltimore, MD 21218-5436
410-467-8080

EMTROL INC
3050 Hempland Rd
Lancaster, PA 17601-1310
800-634-4927

EMU AMERICAS LLC
360 Fairfield Ave Ste 30
Bridgeport, CT 06604-6007
e-mail: cbruno@emuamericas.com
www.emuamericas.com
800-970-7708

EMU-BRIXEY
30414 Ganado Dr Ste A
Rancho Palos Verdes, CA 90275-6221
www.emuamericas.com
310-544-6098 • Fax 310-544-4316

ENACA INTERNATIONAL
3900 NW 79th Ave
Miami, FL 33166-6556
305-599-8877

ENCORE PAPER COMPANY
1 River St
South Glens Falls, NY 12803-4790
518-793-5684

ENCORE PLASTICS
5642 Research Dr

Huntington Beach, CA 92649-1615
www.encoreplastics.com
714-893-7889 • Fax 714-897-7968

END HUNGER NETWORK
2323 S Voss Rd Ste 370
Houston, TX 77057-3820
713-693-0099 • Fax 713-963-0199

ENERGY MICRO SYSTEMS
PO Box 1259
Geneva, FL 32732-1259
e-mail: energymicro@netscape.net
407-349-3205 • Fax 407-349-3170

ENERSYST DEELOPMENT CENTER INC
2051 Valley View Ln
Dallas, TX 75234-8920
972-247-9624 • Fax 972-247-9738

ENGAGE TECHNOLOGIES
100 Brickstone Sq
Andover, MA 01810-1428
978-684-3884

ENGLAND LOGISTICS
4701 W 2100 S
Salt Lake City, UT 84120-1223
800-887-0764

ENGLANDER SLEEP PRODUCTS
2055 Corvair Ave
Columbus, OH 43207-1719
www.englandersleep.com
800-449-0037 • Fax 614-449-4375

ENGLEHARD
PO Box 6
Hiram, OH 44234-0006
330-569-3245 • Fax 330-569-3276

ENGLISH BAY BATTER, INC.
4491 Dunleary Dr
Dublin, OH 43017-8442
e-mail: morrpj@mindspring.com
614-760-9921

ENGLISH BAY BATTER, INC.
837 Green Crest Dr
Westerville, OH 43081-2838
614-890-9994 • Fax 614-890-9992

ENGLUND ENTERPRISES, INC.
6860 Shingle Creek Pkwy Ste 10
Minneapolis, MN 55430-1411
612-560-7862

ENGTECH & EQUIPMENT INTL
16 Berkshire Ct
Streamwood, IL 60107-2182
630-736-9871 • Fax 630-736-9871

ENHANCED PERFORMANCE MGMT
3225 S Garrison St
Denver, CO 80227-4650
303-763-9300

ENMIRON CORPORATION
408 Silver Hill Rd
Cherry Hill, NJ 08002-1641
856-321-1322 • Fax 856-321-0871

ENRON CAPITOL & TRADE RESOURCE
400 Metro Pl N
Dublin, OH 43017-3378

ENSIGN RIBBON BURNERS
PO Box 9
Pelham, NY 10803-0009
914-738-0600

ENSPOT.COM
1250 E Hallandale Beach Blvd
Hallandale, FL 33009-4634
305-643-6776 • Fax 305-675-0946

ENTERGY TEXAS
9425 Pinecroft Dr
Spring, TX 77380-3224
e-mail: chatche@entergy.com
www.entergy.com-retserv-econ-tx-
936-760-7069 • Fax 936-760-7037

ENTERTAINMENT PUBLICATIONS
550 Cochituate Rd

Framingham, MA 01701-4654
508-620-5600 • Fax 508-620-6550

ENTERTAINMENT PUBLICATIONS
25 Walker Way
Albany, NY 12205-4963
518-785-6232 • Fax 518-785-0363

ENTERTAINMENT PUBLICATIONS
4531 Deleon St Ste 201
Fort Myers, FL 33907-1280
239-274-6900

ENTERTAINMENT PUBLICATIONS
1022 Wirt Rd Ste 304
Houston, TX 77055-6858
www.entertainment.com
713-688-6532 • Fax 713-688-6425

ENTERTAINMENT PUBLICATIONS
707 Summer St
Stamford, CT 06901-1026
203-637-8457

ENTERTAINMENT PUBLICATIONS
2125 Butterfield Dr
Troy, MI 48084-3423
248-637-8400 • Fax 248-637-9777

ENTOLETER
251 Welton St
Hamden, CT 06517-3944
800-729-3575

ENTRANCE INC.
2651 Leisczs Bridge Rd
Leesport, PA 19533-9333
610-926-1229

ENTREE MAGAZINE AND TV
1120 Springfield Ave
Mountainside, NJ 07092-2906
www.entreeonline.com
908-232-0583 • Fax 908-232-5605

ENVIROMATIC CORP. OF AMERICA
5936 Pillsbury Ave
Minneapolis, MN 55419-2327
800-325-8476

ENVIRONMENTAL BIOTECH
1717 Solano Way # STE.33
Concord, CA 94520-5453
925-671-917 • Fax 925-671-9171

ENVIRONMENTAL BIOTECH
1915 Peters Rd Ste 311
Irving, TX 75061-3246
e-mail: ebdallas@prodigy.net
www.envbiotech.com
972-554-7675 • Fax 972-554-7780

ENVIRONMENTAL BIOTECH
7224 Sandscove Ct Ste 4
Winter Park, FL 32792-6903
407-678-9228

ENVIRONMENTAL BIOTECH
1701 Biotech Way
Sarasota, FL 34243-3982
941-358-9112

ENVIRONMENTAL POOL SYSTEMS
7820 E Evans Rd
Scottsdale, AZ 85260-6978
480-596-0404

ENVIRONMENTS BIOTECH
3991 N W St Ste 8
Pensacola, FL 32505-4007
850-438-5500

EPA ENERGY STAR SMALL BUSINESS
1200 Pennsylvania Avenue
Washington DC 20460-0001
www.epa.gov.-smallbiz
888-STAR-YES • Fax 301-977-8474

EPI MERCHANT SERVICES
11327 W Lincoln Ave
Milwaukee, WI 53227-1037
www.entertainment.com
414-543-3565 • Fax 414-543-5996

EPIC INDUSTRIES
1007 Jersey Ave
New Brunswick, NJ 08901-3626
www.epicindustries.com
732-249-6867 • Fax 732-249-7683

EPK & ASSOCIATES, INC.
PO Box 2940
Windermere, FL 34786-2940
407-896-6300

EPL FOOD PRODUCTS
PO Box 1108
Somis, CA 93066-1108
805-386-3931 • Fax 805-386-3901

EPRESSOPODS.COM
116 W 20th St
Norfolk, VA 23517-2221
www.espressopods.com
877-G04-PODS • Fax 757-497-6908

EPSON AMERICA INC
PO Box 93012
Long Beach, CA 90809-3012
310-782-0770

EQUIP FOR COFFEE
8 Adrian Ct
Burlingame, CA 94010-2101
e-mail: info@equipforcoffee.com
650-259-7801 • Fax 650-259-7803

EQUIPEX, LTD
765 Westminster St
Providence, RI 02903-4018
401-273-3300 • Fax 401-273-3328

EQUIPMENT CONCEPTS, INC.
1011 Live Oak Loop
Mandeville, LA 70448-6380
504-835-4254

EQUIPMENT PREFERENCE
1711 S Interstate 35e Ste 100
Carrollton, TX 75006-7417
972-242-8986 • Fax 972-242-3682

EQUITABLE SECURITIES CORP.
511 Union St Ste 800
Nashville, TN 37219-1743
615-780-9352

ERC WIPING PRODUCTS INC
19 Bennett St
Lynn, MA 01905-3001
e-mail: erc@ercwipe.com
www.ercwipe.com
800-225-9473 • Fax 781-593-4020

ERICKSEN, KRENTEL, CANTON & LA
4227 Canal St
New Orleans, LA 70119-5996
504-486-7275

ERIKA RECORD INC
7 Just Rd
Fairfield, NJ 07004-3407
973-882-1008

ERIKA RECORD LLC
20 Vanderhoof Ave
Rockaway, NJ 07866-3138
www.erikarecord.com
973-664-1750 • Fax 973-664-1752

ERNET STOCKLIN INTL
135 Fort Lee Rd
Leonia, NJ 07605-2247
201-585-9420 • Fax 201-592-6860

EROOMSYSTEM TECHNOLOGIES
390 N 3050 E
Saint George, UT 84790-9000
e-mail: evp@eroomsystem.com
www.eroomsystem.com
435-628-8500 • Fax 435-628-8611

ERVIN PAPER PRODUCTS INC
PO Box 13006
Green Bay, WI 54307-3006
800-444-0212 • Fax 920-337-0223

ERWYN PRODUCTS
200 Campus Dr Ste C
Morganville, NJ 07751-2101
e-mail: stacey@erwyn.com
www.erwyn.com
800-331-9208 • Fax 800-972-1263

ESA DIRECT MARKETING SERVICES
1900 E Military Ave Ste 216
Fremont, NE 68025-5433
216-881-8909 • Fax 216-881-1208

ESCALON PACKERS
PO Box 8
Escalon, CA 95320-0008
209-838-7341

ESCALON PREMIER BRANDS
7015 Old York Rd
Mc Kinney, TX 75070-5716
e-mail: chris.craig@husa.com
972-562-0911 • Fax 972-540-6690

ESKIMO PANELS INC.
2545 W 80th St
Hialeah, FL 33016-2740
305-550-6116 • Fax 305-556-5736

ESKIMO PIE CORPORATION
4175 Veterans Memorial Hwy
Ronkonkoma, NY 11779-7639
516-560-8400 • Fax 516-330-3911

ESKYE.COM
733 S West St
Indianapolis, IN 46225-1253
www.eskye.com
317-632-3870 • Fax 317-632-6430

E-SOURCE, INC.
13744 Omega Dr
Dallas, TX 75244-4516
972-788-0411 • Fax 972-788-0449

ESP 2000, INC
4108 W Magnolia Blvd
Burbank, CA 91505-2741
818-722-6115 • Fax 818-722-6723

ESPN INC
ESPN Plz
Bristol, CT 06010-1099
860-585-2000

ESPRESSO BY THE CUP
74 Green St
Hackensack, NJ 07601-4004
201-342-6322 • Fax 201-342-3692

ESPRESSO SPECIALISTS, INC.
4544 Leary Way NW
Seattle, WA 98107-4541
www.esi-online.com
206-784-9563 • Fax 206-784-9582

ESPRESSO SYSTEMS-EMPORIUM
65 Commerce St
Brooklyn, NY 11231-1642
718-384-8724 • Fax 718-834-9022

ESROCK
14550 S 94th Ave
Orland Park, IL 60462-6211
708-349-8400 • Fax 708-349-8471

ESSEN NUTRITION
1414 Sherman Rd
Romeoville, IL 60446-4046
630-739-6700 • Fax 630-739-6464

ESSENTIAL AMENITIES
9 Law Dr
Fairfield, NJ 07004-3233
973-882-8441

ESSENTIAL COMMUNICATIONS
124 W 30th St Ste 31
New York, NY 10001-4013
212-239-7200 • Fax 212-268-3266

ETEEGOLF.COM
107 Royal St SW
Leesburg, VA 20175-2913
888-293-4600

ETREC.COM
72470 Varner Rd
Thousand Palms, CA 92276-3429
760-343-2001 • Fax 760-343-1096

EUREKA TENTS
1326 Willow Rd
Sturtevant, WI 53177-1917
800-572-8822

EURO-AMERICA EXPORT
2 Penn Plz Rm 1500
New York, NY 10121-1590
212-953-2616 • Fax 212-953-4301

EUROBAR
525 N Barry Ave
Mamaroneck, NY 10543-1656
914-381-5175 • Fax 914-381-5425

EUROCAFE LLC
PO Box 98
Barnard, VT 05031-0098
802-775-8108 • Fax 802-234-9011

EUROPAEUS U.S.A., INC.
8 John Walsh Blvd
Peekskill, NY 10566-5330
e-mail: europaeus@earthlink.net
www.europaeus.co
914-739-1900 • Fax 914-739-5229

EUROPEAN IMPORTS LTD
2475 N Elston Ave
Chicago, IL 60647-2033
800-323-3464

EUROPEAN PRETZEL
5410 Tonnelle Ave
North Bergen, NJ 07047-3038
201-867-6117 • Fax 201-867-5310

EUROSTEAM NATIONAL HEADQUARTERS
110 S Hampton Rd
Crowley, TX 76036-3210
e-mail: johnw@eurosteam.com
800-613-3874

EUROSTEAM SYSTEMS
20 Todds Mill Cir
Madison, CT 06443-3455
203-318-0134 • Fax 203-668-2002

EVCO WHOLESALE FOOD CORP
309 Merchant St
Emporia, KS 66801-7207
620-343-7000

EVE SALES CORPORATION
945 Close Ave
Bronx, NY 10473-4906
e-mail: escny@juno.com
718-589-6800 • Fax 718-617-6717

EVENT EQUIPMENT SALES
51 E Plainfield Rd
La Grange, IL 60525-2912
www.eventeqptsales.com
708-352-0662 • Fax 708-352-8267

EVENT SOLUTIONS
PO Box 40079
Phoenix, AZ 85067-0079
e-mail: bargona@vpico.com
www.event-solutions.com
520-990-1101 • Fax 520-990-0819

EVERGREEN PAINTING STUDIO
450 W 31st St Fl 7
New York, NY 10001-4608
212-244-2800 • Fax 212-244-6204

EVERBRITE, INC.
PO Box 2002
Milwaukee, WI 53220-0020
414-529-3500

EVEREST BROADBAND NETWORKS
1 Executive Dr
Fort Lee, NJ 07024-3309
888-686-9779

EVERGREEN MFG.
6159 28th St SE, ste.9
Grand Rapids, MI 49546-6968
www.napkinbands.com
800-968-2243 • Fax 616-977-0878

EVERLASTING IMAGES
PO Box 830
Cape Neddick, ME 03902-0830
www.everlastingimages.com
207-351-3277 • Fax 207-351-3281

EVERPURE INC
2375 Sanders Rd
Northbrook, IL 60062-6108
www.everpure.com
847-654-4000 • Fax 847-654-1115

EVERPURE-FILTER PURE SYSTEMS,
5405 Boran Dr
Tampa, FL 33610-2012
e-mail: rusty@filterpure.com
813-626-9600

EVERSON SPICE CO.
2667 Gundry Ave
Long Beach, CA 90806-1808
562-988-1223 • Fax 562-988-0219

EVERWOOD TEAK FURNITURE
4 Parks Dr
Sherborn, MA 01770-1228
888-288-9191

EVOLUTIF FURNITURE
12200 Herbert Wayne Ct Ste 180
Huntersville, NC 28078-6396
www.evolutiffurniture.com
704-948-0440 • Fax 704-948-0190

EXCEL DESIGN
267 Commonwealth Dr
Carol Stream, IL 60188-2450
630-681-1122 • Fax 630-681-0066

EXCEL TERRY
180 Madison Ave Ste 2305
New York, NY 10016-5267
e-mail: excelterry@aol.com
www.excelterry.com
212-532-8082 • Fax 212-532-8136

EXCELL METAL PRODUCTS INS.
11240 Melrose Ave
Franklin Park, IL 60131-1332
847-451-0451 • Fax 847-451-0458

EXCELLENT BAKERY EQUIP
315 Fairfield Rd
Fairfield, NJ 07004-1930
973-244-1664

EXECULTECHS SQUIRREL
8 Pequot Way
Canton, MA 02021-2306
800-879-3932 • Fax 781-821-8143

EXECUTIVE APPAREL INC.
13430 Damar Dr
Philadelphia, PA 19116-1810
e-mail: mara@executiveapparel.com
www.executiveapparel.com
215-464-5400 • Fax 215-464-7330

EXECUTIVE REFERRAL SERVICES
8770 W Bryn Mawr Ave Ste 110
Chicago, IL 60631-3515
www.ers-online.com
773-693-6622 • Fax 773-693-8466

EXIT INFORMATION GUIDE
4205 NW 6th St
Gainesville, FL 32609-1798
352-371-3948 • Fax 352-377-4129

EXOTICA OILS, INC.
838 Eastlake Club Dr
Oldsmar, FL 34677-2464
e-mail: kouhirra@exoticaoils.com
727-786-6213 • Fax 727-786-7103

EXPACK SEAFOOD, INC
1 Woodbridge Center
Woodbridge, NJ 07095-1150
www.expack.com
732-621-3030 • Fax 732-621-3047

EXPANETS
1111 Freeport Pkwy
Coppell, TX 75019-4451
e-mail: roy_james@yahoo.com
www.expanets.com
972-745-5773 • Fax 972-745-5830

EXPEDIA.COM
13810 SE Eastgate Way Ste 4
Bellevue, WA 98005-4417
e-mail: travsup@expedia.com
www.expedia.com
877-EXPEDIA • Fax 206-374-2940

EXPO ARCHITECTS
18040 Chalet Dr Apt 201
Germantown, MD 20874-5881
301-972-5404

EXPRESS PROMOTIONS
231 E Chicago St
Milwaukee, WI 53202-5705
www.expresspromotions.com
414-220-4689 • Fax 414-220-4688

EXPRESS TECHNOLOGIES
114 Glenmore Rd
Apex, NC 27502-6151
www.express-techonologies.com
919-312-1647 • Fax 919-387-1359

EXTREME FOODS-JET TEA-MIND BLA
6320 McLeod Dr Ste 3
Las Vegas, NV 89120-4427
888-676-3832 • Fax 760-416-2255

EZ 2 GET
PO Box 740068
Dallas, TX 75374-0068
www.ez2get.com
214-931-8622 • Fax 214-931-2168

E-Z CASH ATM, INC
9614 3rd Ave
Brooklyn, NY 11209-7708
718-680-1515 • Fax 718-680-5589

F & A CHEESE CO
436 N Mountain Ave
Upland, CA 91786-5117
80-634-4109

F A B INC
1225 Old Alpharetta Rd Ste 235
Alpharetta, GA 30005-2903
770-449-1333 • Fax 800 328-3261

F AND S ENGRAVING INC
1620 W Central Rd
Mt. Prospect, IL 60056-2269
847-870-8400

F CHRISTIANA CO
7251 River Rd
Marrero, LA 70072-1145
504-348-3391

F M A C
3 American Ln
Greenwich, CT 06831-2551
800-884-3622

F M C FOOD TECH
57 Cooper Ave
Homer City, PA 15748-1361
724-479-4500

F M P-FRANKLIN MACH. PROD
3 E Stow Rd
Marlton, NJ 08053-3118
800-257-7737

F S - TEC
425 Park Ave
New York, NY 10022-3506
212-756-5245

F & H GROUP INC (SAFARI SAUCE)
1172 Hillsboro Mile
Pompano Beach, FL 33062-1620
e-mail: feaman@safarisauce.com
954-428-0210 • Fax 954-428-0210

F. RAY MOORE OIL COMPANY
PO Box 36
Washington, DC 27889-0367
252-946-9061

F.E.S. MARKETERS-JACK STRAWTHE
2156 W Northwest Hwy Ste 3
Dallas, TX 75220-4221
972-401-1885 • Fax 972-401-1886

F.G. PUBLICOVER & ASSOCIATES
158 Pantry Rd
Sudbury, MA 01776-1137
978-443-8628 • Fax 978-443-2438

FABCO SYSTEMS
3531 E Miraloma Ave
Anaheim, CA 92806-2104
e-mail: sales@fabcosystems.com
www.fabcosystems.com
714-579-3555 • Fax 714-993-1067

FABRICATION SPECIALISTS
1600 Industrial Park Cir

Mobile, AL 36693-5648
800-426-6473 • Fax 251-660-0647

FABRICUT
9303 E 46th St
Tulsa, OK 74145-4895
e-mail: contract@fabricut.com
www.fabricut.com
918-622-7700 • Fax 918-665-1177

FABTEX, INC.
111 Woodbine Ln
Danville, PA 17821-9118
e-mail: info@fabtex.com
www.fabtex.com
800-772-2791 • Fax 800-532-2839

FAB-X METALS INC
PO Box 7127
Rocky Mount, NC 27804-0127
800-677--3229

FACILITEC CORP
180 Corporate Dr
Elgin, IL 60123-9354
800-284-8273

FACTORY RESOURCE LLC
909 Warren Xing
Coppell, TX 75019-3198
972-471-0642

FAEMA CORP OF AMERICA
1375 Kings Hwy
Fairfield, CT 06430-3318
203-334-7100

FAHNESTOCK & COMPANY
110 Wall St
New York, NY 10005-3801
212-668-8028

FAIR OAKS FARMS
7600 95th St
Pleasant Prairie, WI 53158-2713
262-947-0320 • Fax 262-947-0340

FAIRCHILD PUBICATIONS
7 W 34Th St
New York, NY 10001-8100
212-630-4750 • Fax 212-630-4760

FAIREST FOODS, INC.
PO Box 618
Baldwin, WI 54002-0618
952-933-6939 • Fax 952-933-6968

FALCON BELL ENTERPRISES
1236 Clough Pike
Batavia, OH 45103-2502
888-873-6326 • Fax 513-752-1891

FALCON PRODUCTS, INC
9387 Dielman Industrial Dr
Saint Louis, MO 63132-2214
e-mail: falcon@falconproducts.com
www.falconproducts.com
800-873-3252 • Fax 314-918-328

FAMA SALES CO.
450 W 44th St
New York, NY 10036-5205
e-mail: famasales@aol.com
212-757-9433 • Fax 212-765-4193

FAMILY TRADITION FOODS-GATEWAY
1240 Muirwood Ct
Rochester, MI 48306-3789
e-mail: john@gatewayfood.com
248-377-9032

FAMOUS FOOTWEAR
7010 Mineral Point Rd
Madison, WI 53717-1701
www.famousfootwear.com
608-827-3715 Fax 608-827-3675

FAMOUS SPECIALTIES CO
55B Saratoga Blvd
Island Park, NY 11558-1117
516-889-9099

FANTASIA FRESH JUICE CO.
5617 Pearl St
Des Plaines, IL 60018-5112
www.fantasiafresh.com
847-671-3900 • Fax 847-671-4384

FANTASTIC PLASTICS, INC.
34465 US Highway 285

Pine, CO 80470-9551
800-748-2035 • Fax 303-816-0865

FANTINI BAKERY
375 Washington St
Haverhill, MA 01832-5398
978-373-1273 • Fax 978-373-6252

FARBERWARE, INC.
1500 Bassett Ave
Bronx, NY 10461-2306
718-863-8000

FARBERWARE-FCI CORP
130 Marlborough St
Boston, MA 02116-1954
617-267-5427 • Fax 617-267-6622

FARMER BROS. CO
9844 Kitty Ln
Oakland, CA 94603-1070
510-569-1685 • Fax 510-569-1941

FARMER BROS. COFFEE
W182 S8335 Racine Ave
Muskego, WI 53150-9046
262-679-5120 • Fax 262-679-2201

FARMER BROTHERS COFFEE
744 Avenue H E
Arlington, TX 76011-3187
817-640-8111 • Fax 817-652-0451

FARMER BROTHERS COFFEE
8250 NE Underground Dr # 144A
Kansas City, MO 64161-9734
816-455-5877

FARMER FRESH PRODUCE
13000 Carrere Ct
New Orleans, LA 70129-2235
504-254-3544 • Fax 504-254-3545

FARMERS INSURANCE GROUP
4700 Wilshire Blvd
Los Angeles, CA 90010-3853
800-321-1255

FARMINGTON FRESH
PO Box 30667
Stockton, CA 95213-0667
209-926-3518 • Fax 209-926-3528

FARMLAND FOODS INC
PO Box 7527
Kansas City, MO 64116-0227
800-843-6603 • Fax 816-891-2638

FARMSO FOODS
777 Dedham S
Canton, MA 02021-1402
e-mail: nick@famosofoods.com
www.famosofoods.com
781-575-9592 • Fax 781-575-9338

FASHION SEAL UNIFORMS
PO Box 4002
Seminole, FL 33775-4002
727-397-9611

FAST-FOODSERVICE ADV SCI & TEC
2331 Bush St
San Francisco, CA 94115-3123
415-931-2910

FASTRANS LOGISTICS INC.
4618 World Parkway Cir
Saint Louis, MO 63134-3114
800-844-8044 • Fax 314-426-3434

FASTSIGNS
2550 Midway Rd Ste 150
Carrollton, TX 75006-2372
www.fastsigns.com
800-827-7461 • Fax 972-250-6807

FATHER SAM'S BAKERY
105 Msgr Valente Dr
Buffalo, NY 14206-1815
716-853-1071 • Fax 716-853-1062

FAUX PAS PRINTS
620 Papworth Ave
Metairie, LA 70005-3113
504-834-8342

Fax FOODS INC
1392 Poinsettia Ave Ste A
Vista, CA 92083-8507
www.faxfoods.com
760-599-6030 • Fax 760-599-6040

FB JOHNSTON GROUP
300 E Boundary St
Chapin, SC 29036-9416
www.fbjohnston.com
803-345-5484 • Fax 803-345-5512

FBSTAR.COM
277 E Mitchell Ave
Santa Rosa Beach, FL 32459-5621
www.fbstar.com
850-585-6453 • Fax 850-231-4568

FCD TABLETOPS
1 Roscoe Ct
Greenvale, NY 11548-1143
800-822-5399

FDA
9200 Corporate Blvd
Rockville, MD 20850-3223
888-332-4543

FDC RESTAURANT SYSTEMS
4800 Hampden Ln
Bethesda, MD 20814-2930
301-961-0500

FDSE INC.
85 Lexington Ln
Wayne, NJ 07470-6332
e-mail: matzav@erols.com
973-616-6685 • Fax 973-616-7055

FEARING'S SATELLITE & SOUND
2088 Village Rd
Portage, WI 53901-1121
608-742-2099 • Fax 608-742-8040

FEDCO SYSTEMS CO
1920 Gunn Hwy
Odessa, FL 33556-3524
813-920-6641

FEDERAL SIGN
4602 North Ave
Oceanside, CA 92056-3509
760-361-6600

FEDERATED LINEN & UNIFORM SERVICE
11620 Wilshire Blvd Ste 440
Los Angeles, CA 90025-1779
310-473-4833

FEEDBACK PLUS, INC.
5580 Peterson Ln Ste 120
Dallas, TX 75240-5157
www.gofeedback.com
800-882-7467 • Fax 972-661-5414

FEIN BROS
2007 N Dr Martin Luther King D
Milwaukee, WI 53212-3192
www.feinbrothers.com
414-562-0220 • Fax 414-562-3346

FERKO MEAT COMPANY, INC.
PO Box 170966
Milwaukee, WI 53217-8086
414-967-5500 • Fax 414-967-5515

FERNANDO'S FOODS
5601 E E Slauson Ave Ste 11
Los Angeles, CA 90040-2926
323-890-1300 • Fax 323-890-4564

FERNANDOS FOODS CORP
6 Centerpointe Dr Ste 35
La Palma, CA 90623-2503
714-228-3500 • Fax 714-228-9061

FERNQVIST LABELING SOLUTIONS
1245 Space Park Way Ste C
Mountain View, CA 94043-1433
www.fernqvist.com
800-426-8215 • Fax 650-428-1615

FERRARA BAKERY & CAFE
195 Grand St
New York, NY 10013-3795
e-mail: Ferrara1892@aol.com
www.ferraracafe.com
212-226-6150 • Fax 212-226-0667

FERRY HAYES DESIGNER
1100 Spring St NW
Atlanta, GA 30309-2846
404-874-4411

FESSEL INTERNATIONAL
3505 Cadillac Ave Ste F1
Costa Mesa, C 92626-1431
949-756-1166

FETCO
640 Heathrow Dr
Lincolnshire, IL 60069-4205
www.fetco.com
847-821-1177 • Fax 847-821-1178

FETCO CORP
PO Box 0199
Lincolnshire, IL 60069-0199
800-338-2699

FEW-FOOD WARMING EQUIPMENT CO.
PO Box 1001
Crystal Lake, IL 60039-1001
www.fewco.com
815-459-7500 • Fax 815-459-7989

FF&E INSTALLATIONS INC
979 Doral Dr
Bartlett, IL 60103-3030
e-mail: ffeinstalle@yahoo.com
630-830-7700 • Fax 630-830-7800

FIBER DOES, INC
1470 N 4th St
San Jose, CA 95112-4715
www.fiberdoes.com
408-453-5533 • Fax 408-453-9303

FIBER LITE
950 SE M Sreet
Grants Pass, OR 97526-3201
www. Fiberoptic-lighting
541-476-6900 • Fax 541-476-0796

FIBRED GROUP, THE
PO Box 3349
Cumberland, MD 21504-3349
800-598-8894

FIELD CONTAINER CO L P
1500 Nicholas Blvd
Elk Grove Village, IL 60007-5516
847-437-1700 • Fax 847-952-2409

FIELDBROOK FARMS
1 Ice Cream Dr
Dunkirk, NY 14048-3300
800-333-0805

FIESTA PACIFIC PRODUCTS
2855 A Ave
National City, CA 91950-7334
619-477-8004 • Fax 619-477-8081

FIFTH THIRD BANK MERCHANT SERV
38 Fountain Square Plz
Cincinnati, OH 45263-0001
www.53.com
800-731-3777 • Fax 513-744-8540

FIGRCERTIFICATES.COM
11510 Blondo St Ste 103
Omaha, NE 68164-3846
www.giftcertificates.com
402-951-4149 • Fax 402-445-2300

FIJI NATURAL ARTESIAN WATER
630 Delaware Dr
Claremont, CA 91711-3457
www.fijiwater.com
909-624-5925 • Fax 909-624-6216

FIJI NATURAL ARTESIAN WATER
30 Jelliff Ln Ste 205
Southport, CT 06490-1482
www.fijiwater.com
203-256-8462 • Fax 203-256-1584

FILTAFRY OF FLORIDA
600 N Thacker Ave
Kissimmee, FL 34741-4892
e-mail: admin@filtafryusa.com
407-518-5599 • Fax 407-518-6610

FILTER EXPRESS DIV. OF PROCAM
2605 Technology Dr
Plano, TX 75074-7496
www.filterxpress.com
972-881-9797 • Fax 972-442-6262

FILTERCORP
9805 NE 116th St Ste A200
Kirkland, WA 98034-4248
425-487-0101

FILTERCROP
9805 NE 116th St # A-200
Kirkland, WA 98034-4248
www.fitercrop.com
425-820-4889 • Fax 425-820-2816

FINANCIAL INDEPENDENCE CO
21300 Victory Blvd
Woodland Hills, CA 91367-2525
800-677-2209

FINANCIAL TIMES
1330 Avenue Of The Americas
New York, NY 10019-5400
212-641-6500

FINCASTLE COUNTY CHRWRK
2821 S English Station Rd
Louisville, KY 40299-4851
502-635-3565

FINDAHALL.COM
PO Box 761
Maywood, NJ 07607-0761
201-221-8096 • Fax 201-221-8096

FINE ART LAMPS
5770 Miami Lakes Dr E
Hialeah, FL 33014-2418
305-821-3850 • Fax 305-821-8114

FINE FOODS R C
PO Box 236
Belle Mead, NJ 08502-0236
908-359-5500

FINK BAKERY
535 54th Ave
Long Island City, NY 11101-5991
e-mail: sales@finkbaking.com
www.finkbaking.com
718-392-8300 • Fax 718-729-1303

FINN MARKET GROUP, INC
701 Enterprise Rd E Ste 605
Safety Harbor, FL 34695-5342
e-mail: email@finnmarketing.com
www.finnmarketing.com
727-791-3388

FINOVA GROUP INC
4800 N Scottsdale Rd
Scottsdale, AZ 85251-7630
800-734-6682

FIORUCCI FOODS
1800 Ruffin Mill Rd
Colonial Heights, VA 23834-5910
804-520-7775 • Fax 804-520-2681

FIREMANS FUND INSURANCE
NCCIC Product Management 777 S
Novato, CA 94998-0001
415-899-2670

FIRESIDE COFFEE CO
3239 Elms Rd
Swartz Creek, MI 48473-7928
810-635-7527

FIRST AMERICAN PAYMENT SYSTEM
611 SW Federal Hwy Ste A
Stuart, FL 34994-2925
e-mail: usmerch@onerrow.net
www.first-american.net
772-220-7515

FIRST BANK CARD SYSTEMS, INC.
4335 Big Barn Dr
Little River, SC 29566-6802
e-mail: fbs@sccoast.net
www.firstbankcardsystems.com
843-399-0518 • Fax 843-399-0530

FIRST CARDINAL CORPORATION
210 Washington Ave
Albany, NY 12210-1312
e-mail: tbishop@firstcardinal.com
www.firstcardinal.com
518-456-6144 • Fax 518-456-6978

FIRST DATA COR
3975 NW 120th Ave
Pompano Beach, FL 33065-7632
954-845-4514

FIRST DATABANK
1111 Bayhill Dr
San Bruno, CA 94066-3027
650-588-5454

FIRST ENERGY
395 Ghent Road, rm.412
Akron, OH 44333-2695
www.firstenergyservices.com
330-315-6781 • Fax 330-315-6784

FIRST MARKETING
3300 Gateway Dr
Pompano Beach, FL 33069-4883
800-641-9251

FIRST SCIENTIFIC CORP.
1877 W 2800 S STE 200
Ogden, UT 84401-3282
e-mail: mflore@firstscientific.com
801-393-5781

FIRST UNION CORP
301 S Tryon Street
Charlotte, NC 28288-0001
704-374-6161

FISCHER BEVERAGES INTERNATIONAL
6465 Pacific Ave # 134
Stockton, CA 95207-3715
e-mail: pnlenz@aol.com
209-957-4852 • Fax 209-957-4852

FISH & SCHULKAMP INSURANCE AGE
2117 Sherman Ave
Madison, WI 53704-5936
608-244-3576 • Fax 608-244-9117

FISHER MFG. CO
PO Box 60
Tulare, CA 93275-0060
www.fisher-mfg.com
800-421-6162 • Fax 800-832-8238

FISHER MILLS INC
3235 16th Ave SW
Seattle, WA 98134-1023
206-622-4430

FISHERY PRODUCTS
18 Electronics Ave
Danvers, MA 01923-1086
978-777-2660

FISHKING-UNISEA FOODS
1320 Newton St
Los Angeles, CA 90021-2724
213-763-0275 • Fax 213-749-3160

FISHMONGER.COM
12220 113th Ave NE
Kirkland, WA 98034-6915
877-467-9100

FISHTAIL MANAGEMENT SERVICES
919 Tanager Way
Grants Pas., OR 97527-6194
www.fishtailmanagment.bigstep.com
541-839-2785 • Fax 541-839-3682

FITZ BOTTLING COMPANY
6605 Delmar Blvd
Saint Louis, MO 63130-4504
314-726-9555

FIVE STAR ESTORATIONS
4690 Settles Point Rd
Suwanee, GA 30024-1987
800-613-7827

FIXTURES-R-US
17300 El Camino Real
Houston, TX 77058-2715
877-734-9787

FIZZYFRUIT
PO Box 1478
Galveston, TX 77553-1478
e-mail: gdk@fizzyfruit.com
www.fizzyfruit.com
409-763-0506 • Fax 409-747-1633

FLA CITRUS COMMISSION
115 E Memorial Blvd
Lakeland, FL 33801-1762
863-499-2500

FLA RESTAURANT ASSOCIATION
230 S Adams St
Tallahassee, FL 32301-1729
850-224-2250

FLAIR FLEXIBLE PACKAGING, USA
PO Box 537
Southampton, MA 01073-0537
e-mail: ted@flairpackaging.com
413-376-9044 • Fax 413-376-3432

FLAME GARD, INC.
6627 E Washington Blvd
Los Angeles, CA 90040-1813
www.flamegard.com
323-888-8707 • Fax 323-888-9395

FLAT ROCK FURNITURE, INC
PO Box 65
Waldron, IN 46182-0065
wwwflatrockhickory.com
765-525-5265 • Fax 765-525-5296

FLAVOR RIGHT FOODS
PO Box 16835
Columbus, OH 43216-6835
800-544-9447

FLAVOR RIGHT FOODS
PO Box 2186
Glen Ellyn, IL 60138-2186
630-858-0402 • Fax 630-858-0702

FLAVOR SHAKES-BORA INT.
845 Bluestem Dr
Bolingbrook, IL 60440-4209
www.flavorshakes.com
815-783-085 • Fax 815-783-0856

FLAVOR WEAR DIV
28425 Cole Grade Rd
Valley Center, CA 92082-6572
www.flavorwear.com
760-749-1332 • Fax 760-749-6164

FLAVORITE LABORATORIES
PO Box 1315
Memphis, TN 38101-1315
601-393-3610 • Fax 601-280-5208

FLEET CENTER
50 Kennedy Plz
Providence, RI 02903-2393
800-238-3737

FLEET FINANCIAL GROUP INC
1 Federal St
Boston, MA 02110-2012
617-346-4000

FLEETWOOD EQUIPMENT
71 Bloomfield Ave
Newark, NJ 07104-1914
973-482-5070

FLETCHER'S FINE FOODS
502 Boundary Blvd
Auburn, WA 98001-6503
253-735-0800 • Fax 253-929-8024

FLEUR'S ALLUMAGE
PO Box 670
Mount Kisco, NY 10549-0670
914-242-8900 • Fax 914-242-1138

FLEXION CASTERS & MATERIAL HAN
PO Box 70318
Houston, TX 77270-0318
e-mail: flexionhouston@aol.com
713-861-0400 • Fax 713-861-0508

FLEXTEEL INDUSTRIES, INC.
212 Industrial Park Rd
Starkville, MS 39759-3990
www.flexsteel.com
662-323-548 • Fax 800-444-5481

FLINT HILLS FOODS
PO Box 2256
Wichita, KS 67201-2256
800-325-6164 • Fax 316-828-7846

FLITZ
821 Mohr Ave
Waterford, WI 53185-4257
262-534-5898

FLO-COLD INC
PO Box 930317
Wixom, MI 48393-0317
248-348-6666

FLOJET CORPORATION
20 Icon
Foothill Ranch, CA 92610-3000
www.flojet.com
949-859-4945 • Fax 949-859-1153

FLORA FOOD DISTRIBUTORS
1371 SW 8th St
Pompano Beach, FL 33069-4524
e-mail: flora@florafoods.com
800-697-3567 • Fax 954-785-2353

FLORIDA COCA-COLA BOTTLING COM
100 Tampa Oaks Blvd
Tampa, FL 33637-1920
813-664-4900

FLORIDA DEPARTMENT OF CITRUS
1115 E Memorial Blvd
Lakeland, FL 33801-2021
www.floridajuice.com
863-499-2459 • Fax 863-499-2374

FLORIDA FOOD SERVICE EQUIPMENT
10400 Griffin Rd Ste 109
Fort Lauderdale, FL 33328-3320
954-252-6000

FLORIDA GOURMET FOODS
1838 Patterson Ave
Deland, FL 32724-1923
e-mail: flgroumet@fbs.net
www.islandgrove.com
386-734-3029

FLORIDA INTL UNIV
3000 NE 151st St
Miami, FL 33181-3000
www.fiu.edu-~hospman
305-919-4515 • Fax 305-919-4555

FLORIDA POULTRY FEDERATION
4508 Oak Fair Blvd
Tampa, FL 33610-7330
e-mail: fpf290@aol.com
813-628-4551

FLORIDA SEATING
4205 116th Ter N
Clearwater, FL 33762-4972
727-540-9802

FLORIDA'S NATURAL GROWERS
650 N US Highway 27
Lake Wales, FL 33853-3025
e-mail: dshepard@citrusworld.com
863-676-1411

FLORIDE AGENTS
2160 Tanglewood Way NE
St Petersburg, FL 33702-4754
www.flagents.com
800-683-5606

FLOWER FRAMERS
671 Wilmer Ave
Cincinnati, OH 45226-1814
800-315-1805

FLOWERS FOREVER
311 E 61st St Apt 17
New York, NY 10021-8248
www.floralsculptures.com
212-826-9162 • Fax 212-308-3736

FLYNN BURNER CORP
425 Fifth Ave
Pelham, NY 10803-1253
914-636-1320

FLYTECH TECHNOLOGY (USA)
1931 Hartog Dr
San Jose, CA 95131-2213
www.flytech.com.tw
408-573-9113 • Fax 408-573-9509

FMG TECHNLOGIES
583 Shoemaker Rd
King of Prussia, PA 19406-4201
e-mail:
sheri.kearney@demgroup.com
610-992-0889 • Fax 610-992-0169

FMLTD SALES
PO Box 28
Hobart, IN 46342-0028
219-947-4283 • Fax 219-947-7143

FOAM ENTERPRISES
13630 Water Tower Cir
Minneapolis, MN 55441-3785
800-888-3342

FOLEY & WALACE
13 Robbie Rd
Avon, MA 02322-1132
e-mail:
foley.eallace@worldnet.att.net
508-583-6900 • Fax 508-583-9970

FOLEY ENTERPRISES
11500 Manchaca Rd
Austin, TX 78748-2712
512-282-3237 • Fax 512-282-0958

FOLLETT COPORATION
801 Church Ln
Easton, PA 18040-6637
800-523-9361 • Fax 610-250-0696

FONTANINI ITALIAN MEATS
911 W 37th Pl
Chicago, IL 60609-1412
www.fontanini.com
773-890-0600 • Fax 773-890-1680

FONTINA FOODS INC
485 NW Enterprise Dr
Port Saint Lucie, FL 34986-2202
772-878-1400 • Fax 772-878-8196

FOOD & BEVERAGE INVESTIGATION
277 San Marin Dr Ste 111
Novato, CA 94945-1250
415-892-1027

FOOD & BEVERAGE NEWS
PO Box 14428
Bradenton, FL 34280-4428
e-mail: fbn@aol.com
www.fbnews.com
941-585-7745

FOOD ARTS-WINE SPECTATOR
387 Park Ave S
New York, NY 10016-8810
212-684-4224 • Fax 212-481-1523

FOOD AUTHORITY
3400 Lawson Blvd
Oceanside, NY 11572-3708
516-887-0500 • Fax 516-887-0573

FOOD AUTOMATION SERVICES
905 Honeyspot Rd
Stratford, CT 06615-7147
203-377-4414 • Fax 203-377-8187

FOOD CHAIN
116 S Michigan Ave
Chicago, IL 60603-6016
800-845-3008

FOOD CONSULTANTS, INC.
PO Box 718
Carnegie, PA 15106-0718
412-276-0908

FOOD EQUIPMENT SALES & MARKETING
512 1st Ave SW
Largo, FL 33770-3408
e-mail: fesma@att.net
727-545-9997

FOOD INDUSTRY PRODUCTIVITY
PO Box 992
Falls Church, VA 22040-0992
703-532-9400

FOOD MACHINERY OF AMERICA-OMC

4600 Witmer Industrial Est
Niagara Falls, NY 14305-1364
www.omcan.com
800-465-0234 • Fax 905-832-8272

FOOD MACHINER SALES
PO Box 1549
Athens, GA 30603-1549
706-549-220

FOOD MARKETING COORDINATORS
800 Hingham St Ste 101
Rockland, MA 02370-1067
781-982-1880

FOOD MARKETING INSTITUTE
1750 K St NW
Washington DC 20006-2305
202-452-8444

FOOD MASTERS INC.
1442 Aaron Ct Ste F
Jefferson City, MO 65101-2868
573-635-4711 • Fax 573-635-4604

FOOD MASTERS, INC
10421 Skycrest Dr
Boise, ID 83704-1960
e-mail: okupet69@aol.com
208-658-5206 • Fax 208-658-5142

FOOD MASTERS, INC
300 W Broad St
Griffin, GA 30223-290
e-mail: masterfood@aol.com
www.foodmaster.com
770-227-0330

FOOD SAFETY CONSULTING SERVICES INC
222 Utah St
Morgan City, LA 70380-2648
905-385-0498

FOOD SAFETY TECHNOLOGY COUNCIL
524 Broadway Fl 3
New York, NY 10012-4408
212-941-6252 • Fax 212-334-2131

FOOD SERVICE HOLDINGS
1222 Ozark St
Kansas City, MO 64116-4314
816-221-7300

FOOD SERVICE PARTS & SMALLWARE
PO Box 58626
Los Angeles, CA 90058-0626
www.fspusa.com
323-581-7166 • Fax 323-583-4012

FOOD SERVICE SALES
936 N Amelia Ave
San Dimas, CA 91773-1401
www.mssc.com
909-282-8355

FOOD SERVICE SOLUTION
2870 SW 36th Ave
Miami, FL 33133-3420
www.foodservsol.com
305-441-7941 • Fax 305-648-3498

FOOD SERVICE TECHNOLOGY CENTER
12949 Alcosta Blvd
San Ramon, CA 94583-1323
www.pge.com-fste
925-866-2844 • Fax 925-866-2864

FOOD SERVICES OF AMERICA
PO Box 84628
Seattle, WA 98124-5928
206-933-5000 • Fax 206-933-5283

FOOD TEAM INC
55 W Monroe St Ste 1050
Chicago, IL 60603-5135
312-372-7620

FOOD-TRAK SOFTWARE
15900 N 78th St
Scottsdale, AZ 85260-1215
www.foodtrack.com
480-951-8011 • Fax 480-951-2807

FOOD.COM
200 W Thomas St
Seattle, WA 98119-4216
888-246-9669

FOOD.COM
690 Bermuda Dr
Toms River, NJ 08753-4709
e-mail: jpadovano@food.com
732-270-2242 • Fax 732-270-9594

FOOD.COM
22 4th St Fl 10
San Francisco, CA 94103-3148
www.food.com
415-403-5200 • Fax 415-981-4801

FOODBUY.COM
50 Mansell Ct
Roswell, GA 30076-4807
800-896-4442

FOODCOMM
100 Avenue Of The Americas
New York, NY 10013-1689
212-925-7011 • Fax 212-966-5546

FOODCOMM INTERNATIONAL
4260 El Camino Real
Palo Alt, CA 94306-4404
www.foodcomm.com
650-813-1300 • Fax 650-813-1500

FOODCRAFTERS, INC.
5985 Clerkenwell Ct
Burke, VA 22015-3261
703-764-3080

FOODEDGE.COM NORTHEAST FOODTEC
1140 Post Rd
Fairfield, CT 06430-6020
e-mail: info@foodedge.com
www.foodedge.com
203-319-0036

FOODHANDLE
514 Grand Blvd
Westbury, NY 11590-4712
www.foodhandler.com
800-338-4433 • Fax 516-338-5486

FOODLINE .COM
135 5th Ave Fl 10
New York, NY 10010-7101
www.foodline.com
212-420-7080 • Fax 212-420-9963

FOODLINE.COM
209 Richland Dr E
Mandeville, LA 70448-6330
985-674-6887

FOODLINE.COM
105 South St
Boston, MA 02111-2802
e-mail: jgrimaldi@ foolinr.com
www.foodline.com
617-695-3600 • Fax 617-695-3668

FOODLINES
209 S 9th St
Lincoln, NE 68508-2214
402-475-1787

FOODS & BEVERAGE JOURNAL
835 Piner Rd Ste A
Santa Rosa, CA 95403-2063
www.fbworld.com
707-568-5960 • Fax 707-568-5980

FOODS FROM SPAIN
405 Lexington Ave
New York, NY 10174-0002
212-661-2787 • Fax 212-972-2494

FOODSAFE SOLUTION
455 Fairway Dr Ste 10
Deerfield Bch, FL 33441-1804
e-mail: zshever@worldnet.att.net
www.foodsafessolutions.om
954-678-9136

FOODSERVICE CONSULTANTS SOCIETY
304 W Liberty St Ste 201
Louisville, KY 40202-3011
www.fcsi.org
502-583-3783 • Fax 502-589-3602

FOODSERVICE DATABASE CO
5724 W Diversey Ave
Chicag, IL 60639-1233
www.foodservice-database.com
773-745-9400 • Fax 773-745-7432

FOODSERVICE EAST
294 Washington St Ste 1032
Boston, MA 02108-4615
e-mail: fdsvceast@aol.com
617-695-9080 • Fax 617-695-9083

FOODSERVICE EAST
220 Commercial St # 1A
Boston, MA 02109-1309
e-mail: fdsvceast@aol.com
617-673-9080 • Fax 617-742-5938

FOODSERVICE EQUIPMENT REPORTS
8001 Lincoln Ave Ste 400
Skokie, IL 60077-3657
www.fermag.com
847-332-1647 • Fax 847-332-1648

FOODSERVICE GRAPHIC SYSTEMS
500 10th Ave
New York, NY 10018-1180
www.vgs-inc.com
800-203-0301 • Fax 212-563-9334

FOODSERVICE RESOURCE GROUP INC
PO Box 637
Downers Grove, IL 60515-0637
630-960-0759

FOODSERVICE RESOURCES
PO Box 41099
Fredericksburg, VA 22404-1099
540-786-3663

FOODSERVICE.COM
134 W 26th St Fl 9
New York, NY 10001-6803
e-mail: sales@foodservie.com
www.foodservice.com
212-645-2804 • Fax 212-645-2804

FOODSERVICEDIRECT.COM
905 G St
Hampton, VA 23661-1717

FOODSERVICEDIRECT.COM
27 Forest Ave
Locust Valley, NY 11560-1723
www.foodservicedirect.ocm
516-759-9000 • Fax 516-759-5782

FOODSERVICES CENRAL.COM
700 Dresher Rd Ste 100
Horsham, PA 19044-2265
www.foodservicecentral.com
215-328-6100 • Fax 215-784-1967

FOODSERVICES EDUCATORS NETWORK
959 Melvin Rd
Annapolis, MD 21403-1315
410-268-5542

FOODSERVICE EQUIP DIST ASSOCIATION
332 S Michigan Av
Chicago, IL 60604-4434
312-427-9605

FOODTOOLS INC
315 Laguna St
Santa Barbara. CA 93101-1716
805-962-8383

FOODTRADER.COM
3191 Coral Way
Miami, FL 33145-3213
305-461-2939

FOODTRAK
405 Tarrytown Rd Ste 433
White Plains, NY 10607-1313
e-mail: jdunbar401@aol.com
www.members.aol,com-jdunbar-401
914-793-5068 • Fax 914-793-5091

FOODUSA.COM
505 S Rosa Rd
Madison, WI 53719-1262
800-800-6732

FOORMA-KOOL MFG., INC.
46880 Continental Dr
New Baltimore, MI 48047-5269
586-949-4813 • Fax 586-949-9286

FOOTMARKETPLACE.COM
24992 Normans Way
Calabasas, CA 91302-3089
www.foodmarketplace.com
818-716-9441 • Fax 818-716-9469

FORAN & SCHULTZ
125 S Wacker Dr Ste 1700
Chicago, IL 60606-4478
312-368-8330

FORBES INDUSTRIES
1933 E Locust St
Ontario, CA 91761-7608
www.forbesindustries.com
909-923-4559 • Fax 909-923-1969

FORE SUPPLY CO
PO Box 341
Addison, IL 60101-0341
630-543-4422

FOREIGN AFFAIRS
417 McDonough Pkwy
McDonough, GA 30253-6597
e-mail: foreignaffairs@bellsouth.net
www.foreignaffairsinc.com
770-957-9224 • Fax 770-957-3369

FOREMOST
19211 144th Ave NE
Woodinville, WA 98072-6455
425-483-9090

FOREST CITY RATNER CO
1 Metrotech Ctr N
Brooklyn, NY 11201-3870
718-923-8400

FOREST GROUP USA
PO Box 1281
Cartersville, GA 30120-1281
e-mail:
forestgroup@mindspring.com
www.kssystem.com
770-966-9900 • Fax 770-966-0015

FORLENZA & ASSOCIATES
3450 Edenbridge Rd
York, PA 17402-4217
e-mail: forlenzaallie@aol.com
717-840-1175 • Fax 717-840-1824

FORMERS BY ERNIE INC
7905 Almeda Genoa Rd
Houston, TX 77075-2059
713-991-3455

FORMERS OF HOUSTON INC
3533 Preston Ave
Pasadena, TX 77505-2008
281-998-9570

FORREST FOODS, INC.
1050 Thorndale Av
Bensenville, IL 60106-1142
630-766-0400

FORT JAMES CORPORATION
1919 S Broadway
Green Bay, WI 54304-4905
e-mail:
nathaniel.hedtke@fortjamesmail.com
920-236-6086 • Fax 920-236-6462

FOSSIL FARMS OSTRICH, LLC
244 Concord Dr
Paramus, NJ 07652-4544
e-mail: fossilfarm@aol.com
www.fossilfarmostrich.com
201-261-9000 • Fax 201-634-1150

FOSTER FARMS
PO Box 457
Livingston, CA 95334-0457
www.fosterfarms.com
209-394-7901 • Fax 209-394-6366

FOSTER REFRIGERATOR CORP.
88 Milo St
Hudson, NY 12534-2741
518-828-3311

FOSTER-MILLER, INC.
195 Bear Hill Rd
Waltham, MA 02451-1003

www.foster-miller.com
781-684-4172 • Fax 781-290-0693

FOSTORIA INDUSTRIES INC
1200 N Main St
Fostoria, OH 44830-1911
419-435-9205

FOUNTAIN PRODUCTS, INC.
1066 N Garfield St
Lombard, IL 60148-1336
630-620-1899

FOUNTAIN SERVICE, INC.
PO Box 1098
Boylston, MA 01505-1698
508-869-3390 • Fax 508-757-1355

FOURSTATES WHOLESALE DIST.
PO Box 2916
Longview, TX 75606-2916
903-758-3500

FOX SPORTS DIRECT
100 E Royal Ln Ste 250
Irving, TX 75039-4213
972-868-1400

FOXTAIL FOODS
6075 Poplar Ave Ste 80
Memphis. TN 38119-4740
800-487-2253 • Fax 901-881-7910

FPL ENERGY SERVICES
700 Universe Blvd
North Palm Beach, FL 33408-2657
561-694-4000

FPNDAL HOFFMASTER
2013 NW 4th Ave
Delray Beach, FL 33444-3114
e-mail: paulhollis@earthlink.net
561-265-0345

FRAME ART
943 Oak St Ofc BO
Eatonton, GA 31024-6748
706-484-0944 • Fax 706-484-1594

FRAN DOCS
81904 Overseas Hwy
Islamorada, FL 33036-3605
305-517-9751 • Fax 305-517-9752

FRANCHISE FINANCE CORP OF AMERICA
17207 N Perimeter Dr
Scottsdale, AZ 85255-5401
480-585-4500

FRANCHISE TIMES
2500 Cleveland Ave N
Saint Paul, MN 55113-2728
651-631-4995 • Fax 651-633-8749

FRANCORP, INC
20200 Governors Dr
Olympia Fields, IL 60461-1087
www.francrop.cpm
708-481-2900 • Fax 708481-5885

FRANCO'S COCKTAIL MIXES
121 SW 5th Ct
Pompano Beaach, FL 33060-7909
954-782-7491

FRANK SIDNEY IMPORTING CO
20 Cedar St
New Rochell, NY 10801-5247
914-633-5630

FRANKE COMMERCIAL SYSTEMS
310 Tech Park Dr
La Vergne, TN 37086-3618
615-793-4530 • Fax 615-793-4450

FRANKEL & COMPANY
111 E Wacker Dr
Chicago, IL 60601-3713
312-938-1900

FRANKLIN BRASS MFG. CO.
PO Box 4887
Carson, CA 90749-4887
e-mail: davida@franklinbrass.com
www.franklinbrass.com
310-885-3200 • Fax 310-885-5739

FRANKLIN FOODS
PO Box 486
Enosburg Falls, VT 05450-0486
e-mail: fcc@sover.net

www.franklinfoods.com
802-933-4338 • Fax 802-933-2300

FRANMARA INC
PO Box 2139
Salinas, CA 93902-2139
831-422-4000

FRAZIER'S MUSHROOM FARM
1487 NE 63rd Ct
Fort Lauderdale, FL 33334-5121

FRDERAL INDUSTRIES
215 Federal Ave
Belleville, WI 53508-9201
608-424-3331 • Fax 608-424-3234

FRED TIBBITTS ASSOCIATES INC
303 Lexington Ave
New York, NY 10016-3165
212-684-0214 • Fax 212-447-0937

FREDERICKSBURG HERB FARM
407 Whitney St
Fredericksburg, TX 78624-3600
830-997-8615 • Fax 830-997-5069

FREE STATE SIGN & NEON
RR 5 Box 15
Canton, TX 75103-9610
903-567-5604

FREEDMAN FOOD SERVICE
2901 Polk St
Houston, TX 77003-4633
713-229-8000

FREEDOM BEVERAGE SYSTEMS
1200 N State Pkwy
Chicago, IL 60610-2219
312-587-7300

FREEDOM BEVERAGE SYSTEMS
8 W Division St
Chicago, IL 60610-2272
www.freedombeverage.com
312-587-3000 • Fax 312-642-3332

FREEDOM SECURITY SYSTEMS
195 Armstrong Rd
New Hyde Park, NY 11040-5346
www.freedomsystems.com
516-741-6500 • Fax 516-739-1674

FRENCH CULINARY INSTITUTE
462 Broadway
New York, NY 10013-2618
212-219-8890

FRENCH GOURMET
500 Kuwili St
Honolulu, HI 96817-5363
e-mail: chef@frenchgourmet.com
808-524-4000 • Fax 808-528-0329

FRENCH MEADOW BAKERY
2610 Lyndale Ave S
Minneapolis, MN 55408-1321
e-mail: bread@frenchmeadow.com
612-870-4740 • Fax 952-457-0907

FRENCH PASTRY SCHOOL INC
226 W Jackson Blvd
Chicago, IL 60606-6959
312-726-2419

FREQUENCEY MARKETING
6101 Meijer Dr
Milford, OH 45150-2190
513-248-2882

FRESH & FANCY FOODS
669 Elmwood Ave
Providence, RI 02907-3362
e-mail: Freshfancy@mindspring.com
401-467-3777 • Fax 401-467-3787

FRESH ADVANTAGE
1142 Avenue S
Grand Prairie, TX 75050-1252
972-988-8553

FRESH AND WILD, INC.
PO Box 2981
Vancouver, WA 98668-2981
360-737-3652

FRESH MARK, INC.
PO Box 8440
Canton, OH 44711-8440
e-mail: mslaughter@freshmark.com
800-860-6777 • Fax 330-430-5656

FRESH MARKETING
2491 W Shaw Ave Ste 101
Fresno, CA 93711-3306
559-229-5998

FRESH PRODUCTS
4010 South Ave
Toledo, OH 43615-6292
888-373-7436

FRESH SAMANTHA. INC.
86 Industrial Park
Saco, ME 04072-1840
www.freshsamantha.com
800-658-4635 • Fax 207-929-8263

FRESH SAMANTHA. INC.
41 Spring Hill Rd
Saco, ME 04072-9650
www.freshsamantha.com
207-248-0011 • Fax 207-284-8331

**FRESH START FRUIT &
PRODUCE CO**
165 Market St
Everett, MA 02149-5801
www.fresh.produce.com
617-389-3889 • Fax 617-289-7362

FRESHNEX.COM
PO Box 1102
New Haven, CT 06504-1102
www.freshnex.com
800-801-5119 • Fax 203-499-2624

FRIAR TUX UNIFORMS
18889 Beach Blvd
Huntington Beach, CA 92647-4809
800-232-4477

FRIEDR DICK CORPORATION
33 Allen Blvd
Farmingdale, NY 11735-5611
516-454-6955 • Fax 516-454-6184

FRIEDRICH AIR CONDITIONING
4200 N Pan Am Expy
San Antonio, TX 78218-5260
210-357-4400

FRIELING USA INC.
1920 Center Park Dr
Charlotte, NC 28217-2901
www.frieling.com
704-329-5100 • Fax 704-329-5151

FRIGIDAIRE COMMERCIAL
707 Robins St
Conway, AR 72034-6565
www.frigicomm.com
501-327-8945 • Fax 501-450-3793

FRIONE MARKETING
17 Gabriel St
New Haven, CT 06513-2708
203-467-3369 • Fax 203-468-2542

FRIONOR USA
PO Box 2087
New Bedford, MA 02741-2087
800-343-8046

FRITO LAY
7701 Legacy Dr
Plano, TX 75024-4099
972-334-7000

FRITO LAY INC
PO Box 660634
Dallas, TX 75266-0634
214-334-7000 • Fax 214-334-5280

FRITSCH U S A INC
1000 Central Pkwy N
San Antonio, TX 78232-5050
210-491-9309

FRITZ INDUSTRIES, LLC
3345 Rawson St
Idaho Falls, ID 83406-7712
e-mail: sportsblaster@ida.net
www.sportsblast.com
208-529-8169 • Fax 208-529-8190

**FRITZ'S SUPERIOR
SAUSAGE COMPANY**
10326 State Line Rd
Leawood, KS 66206-2658
913-381-9694

FROMARTHARIE
1 Crown Dr

Warren, NJ 07059-5111
908-647-6485 • Fax 908-647-6590

FRONTLINE SYSTEMS
21601 N 21st Ave
Phoenix, AZ 85027-2602
www.frontlinesystems.com
623-581-5188 • Fax 623-581-5285

**FROSTY FACTORY OF
AMERICAN INC**
2301 S Farmerville St
Ruston, LA 71270-9042
www.frostyfactory.com
800-544-4071 • Fax 318-255-1170

FRUIT & VEGETABLE CARVING
7800 SW 24th Ave
Gainesville, FL 32607-4722
352-335-1204

FRYMASTER
8700 Line Ave
Shreveport, LA 71106-6800
318-865-1711 • Fax 318-868-5987

FSBUY.COM
1000 S Anaheim Blvd
Anaheim, CA 92805-5801
714-491-1112 • Fax 714-491-1106

FUJITSU AMERICA
3055 Orchard Dr
San Jose, CA 95134-2022
800-915-9950

**FULLERTON BUILDING
SYSTEMS, INC**
34620 250th St
Worthington, MN 56187-9515
www.fullertonbldg.com
800-450-9782 • Fax 507-376-9530

FUN E-BUSINESS
140 Marine View Ave Ste 210
Solana Beach, CA 92075-2123
www.fun-business.com
858-259-7016 • Fax 858-259-7015

FUN EXPRESS
5455 S 90th St
Omaha, NE 68127-3501
www.funexpress.com
800-228-9959 • Fax 800-228-1002

FUQUA FRIEDOW INC
14180 Dallas Pkwy Ste 2
Dallas, TX 75254-4341
972-233-3991 • Fax 972-233-3497

FURMAN FOODS INC
PO Box 500
Northumberland, PA 17857-0500
www.furmanos.com
570-473-3516 • Fax 570-473-7367

FURNITURE DESIGN STUDIOS
PO Box 90
Woodbury, NY 11797-0090
e-mail:
jill-signaturehospitality@msn.com
516-364-6479 • Fax 516-364-7274

FURNITURE.COM INC
18033 Rhumba Way
Boca Raton, FL 33496-4116
800-442-3525

**FURTHER MANAGEMENT
GROUP**
4938 Hampden Ln Ste 163
Bethesda, MD 20814-2914
301-907-7334

FUTURE LMAGE LNC.
1401 27th St
Kenner, LA 70062-5307
504-464-9824 • Fax 504-464-9825

FUTURES INC
55 Old Bedford Rd
Lincoln, MA 01773-1125
781-259-4500 • Fax 781-259-4508

G & F SYSTEMS
208 Babylon Tpke
Roosevelt, NY 11575-2146
516-868-4923

G & J MARKETING
1261 E Sample Rd
Pompano Beach, FL 33064-6277

e-mail: kated@gandj.com
954-781-4600 • Fax 954-781-8600

G & K SERVICES
5995 Opus Pkw
Hopkins, MN 55343-9058
952-912-5500 • Fax 952-912-5975

G A LOTZ
540 N Cortez St
New Orleans, LA 70119-4897
504-486-6076

GAR PRODUCTS
170 Lehigh Ave
Lakewood, NJ 08701-4526
732-364-2100

G C S SERVICE, INC.
9 Hunts Lane
Chappaqua, NY 10514-2631
914-238-3501

GET ENTERPRISES INC
1515 W Sam Houston Pkwy N
Houston, TX 77043-3112
713-467-9394

GFA BRANDS
211 Knickerbocker Rd
Cresskill, NJ 07626-1830
201-568-9300

GSD PACKAGING LLC
33 Powel Dr
Hazleton, PA 18201-7360
800-486-0490

GYYR INC
1515 S Manchester Ave
Anaheim, CA 92802-2907
714-772-1000

**G. MORGAN INSURANCE
AGENCY**
10777 Northwest Fwy Ste 460
Houston, TX 77092-7313
e-mail: reginawitter@hotmail.com
713-681-8282 • Fax 713-681-9727

G.A.F. SEELIG, INC.
5905 52nd Ave
Woodside, NY 11377-7480
718-899-5000 • Fax 718-803-1198

G.E.C. CONSULTANTS
4604 Birchwood Ave
Skokie, IL 60076-3835
847-671-6310

G.L.MEZZETTA, INC.
2752 Dos Rios Dr
San Ramon, CA 94583-2037
e-mail: thrcopco@aol.com
925-820-1919 • Fax 925-743-0685

G.S. DISTRIBUTORS
9 Newman Ave
Rumford, RI 02916-1939
401-438-9111 • Fax 401-438-7910

G.S. GELATO & DESSERTS, INC.
236 Miracle Strip Pkwy SE
Fort Walton Beach, FL 32548-5854
850-243-5455

GABILA
120 S 8th St
Brooklyn, NY 11211-6099
718-387-0750 • Fax 718-384-8621

GAINEY CERAMICS
1200 Arrow Hwy
La Verne, CA 91750-5293
e-mail:
gaineyceramics@worldnet.att.net
www.gaineyceramics.com
909-593-3533 • Fax 909-596-9337

GAINT ADVERTISING INC.
20 Mason
Irvine, CA 92618-2706
www.giantad.com
949-891-5928 • Fax 949-891-5958

GAIS BAKERY
2006 S Weller St
Seattle, WA 98144-2294
206-726-7528 • Fax 206-726-7533

GALAXY DESSERTS
40 Golden Gate Dr
San Rafael, CA 94901-5407

www.galaxydesserts.com
415-459-3537 • Fax 415-457-7929

GALAXY FOODS
2441 Viscount Row
Orlando, FL 32809-6250
www.galaxyfoods.com
407-855-5500 • Fax 407-855-7485

GALAXY TEA CORPORATION
13571 Larwin Cir
Santa Fe Springs, CA 90670-5032
e-mail: rogerwheeloc@earthlink.net
www.shangrilaicedtea.com
562-926-2211

GALILEAN SEAFOOD INC.
16 Broadcommon Rd
Bristol, RI 02809-2722
401-253-3030 • Fax 401-253-9207

GALLAGHER & CO., ARTHUR J
2 Pierce Pl
Itasca, IL 60143-1203
708-773-3800

GALLARD-SCHLESINGER INC
777 Zeckendorf Blvd
Garden City, NY 11530-2126
516-333-5600

**GALLIMORE
NDUSTRIES INC**
200 Park Ave
Lake Villay., IL 60046-8915
847-356-3331

GALLO SALAME
2411 Baumann Ave
San Lorenzo, CA 94580-1801
510-276-1300 • Fax 510-278-8497

**GALVESTON COLLEGE
CULINARY ART**
4015 Avenue O
Galveston, TX 77550-6647
e-mail: chef@gc.edu
www.gc.edu-chef
409-763-6551 • Fax 409-762-0973

GAMBINO'S BAKERIES
2308 Piedmont St
Kenner, LA 70062-7960
985 727-1408

GAMBRINUS IMPORTING CO
14800 San Pedro Ave
San Antonio, TX 78232-3733
210-940-9182

GAMCO INC
PO Box 272
Niles, MI 49120-0272
e-mail: gamcoinc@cadillnk.net
616-683-4280 • Fax 616-683-4339

**GAME SALES
INTERNATIONAL**
PO Box 5314
Loveland, CO 80538-0513
970-667-4090

**GARDEN
COMPLEMENTS INC.**
920 Cable Rd
Kansas City, MO 64116-4244
816-421-1090

GARDEN ROW FOODS-IL PRIMO
411 Stone Dr
Saint Charles, IL 60174-3301
630-455-2200 • Fax 630-455-9100

GARDENBURGER INC
2422 SE Hawthorne Blvd
Portland, OR 97214-3925
503-205-1500

**GARGIULO FOODS, LLC THU-
MANN'S**
2412 Sand Lake Rd
Orlando, FL 32809-7642
e-mail:
thedelibest@mymailstation.com
888-969-4269 • Fax 407-251-1759

**GARLAND-A WELBILT
COMPANY**
185 South St
Freeland, PA 18224-1916
570-636-1000 • Fax 570-636-3903

GARLIC SURVIVAL
1094 Revere Ave Ste A1
San Francisco, CA 94124-3442
e-mail: garlicsurv@aol.com
800-342-7542 • Fax 415-822-6224

GARMENT MACHINERY
51 Moulton St
Cambridge, MA 02138-1176
e-mail: garment98@aol.com
617-868-6930 • 800-238-6930

GARNAND MARKETING, INC.
129 Eastland Dr
Twin Falls, ID 83301-7436
208-734-5744

GARON INDUSTRIES
PO Box 339
Mosinee, WI 54455-0339
715-693-1593

**GAS FOODSERVICE
EQUIPMENT NETW**
400 N Capitol St NW
Washington, DC 20001-1511
www.gfen.org
202-824-7000 • Fax 202-824-7088

GASSER CHAIR CO INC
4136 Logan Way
Youngstown, OH 44505-1797
www.gasserchair.com
330-759-2234 • Fax 330-759-9844

GASTRO-GNOMES INC
22 Brightview Dr
West Hartford, CT 06117-2001
860-236-0225

GATCO, INC.
1550 Factor Ave
San Leandro, CA 94577-5616
e-mail: hardware@gatco-inc.com
www.gatco-inco.com
510-352-8770 • Fax 510-895-5676

**GATEWAY MARKETING
CONCEPT**
9360 Activity Rd Ste G
San Diego, CA 92126-4410
www.gatewaymc.com
800-981-8517 • Fax 858-689-8332

GATTO FURNITURE
2240 SW 34th St
Fort Lauderdale, FL 33312-5049
e-mail: gattofurn@aol.com
954-584-6400 • Fax 954-321-0369

GAVINA & SONS
2369 E 51st St
Los Angeles, CA 90058-2893
www.gavina.com
323-582-0671 • Fax 323-581-1127

GAYCHROME
220 Exchange Dr Ste D
Crystal Lake, IL 60014-6282
e-mail: gaychrome@csltd.com
815-459-6000 • Fax 815-459-6562

GAYLORD INDUSTRIES
10900 SW Avery St
Tualatin, OR 97062-8578
503-691-2010 • Fax 503-692-6048

GAZELLE SYSTEMS INC
381 Elliot St
Newton Upper Falls, MA 02464-1157
617-630-8600

GE APPLIANCES
Appliance Park, Bldg 3
Louisville, KY 40225-0001
www.ge.com/appliances
502-452-3466 • Fax 502-452-0401

GE SPACENET
1750 Old Meadow Rd
Mc Lean, VA 22102-4327
703-848-1000

GEAC
175 Ledge St
Nashua, NH 03060-3107
www.gelbergsigns.com
603-889-5152 • Fax 603-889-7538

GEAC COMPUTER, INC.
15621 Red Hill Ave

Tustin, CA 92780-7322
www.hospitality.com
714-258-5861 • Fax 714-258-5880

**GEHL'S GUERNSEY
FARMS, INC**
PO Box 1004
Germantown, WI 53022-8204
e-mail: kstclair@gehls.com
262-251-8572

GEM INSURANCE
3355 W Alabama St Ste 850
Houston, TX 77098-1799
e-mail: sweil@gemins.com
www.casualty.com
713-622-2330 • Fax 713-622-2053

GEMINI BAKERY
9990 Gantry Rd
Philadelphia, PA 19115-1092
800-468-9046 • Fax 215-673-3944

GEMINI DATA SYSTEMS
1876 N University Dr
Fort Lauderdale, FL 33322-4130
954-370-6070

**GEMINI FOOD
INDUSTRIES INC**
258 Main St
Sturbridge, MA 01566-1540
508-347-2800 • Fax 508-347-1945

**GEMINI SOUND
PRODUCTS**
120 Clover Pl
Edison, NJ 08837-3735
732-969-9000

**GENERAL DYNAMICS
INTERACTIVE**
77 A Street
Needham Heights, MA 02494-2806
781-455-4020

GENERAL ELECTRIC LIGHTING
1975 Noble Rd Bldg.307-E
Cleveland, OH 44112-1719
216-266-6958 • Fax 216-266-3510

GENERAL ELECTRIC SUPPLY
2 Corporate Dr # F
Shelton, CT 06484-6238
e-mail:
gaetano-esposito@gesupply.com
203-944-3000 • Fax 203-944-3049

**GENERAL ELECTRIC-APPLI-
ANCE**
Appliance Park
Louisville, KY 40225-0001
502-452-4311

**GENERAL HOTEL &
RESTAURANT SUPPLIES**
7300 NW 77th St
Miami, FL 33166-2289
www.generalhotel.com
800-330-5900

GENERAL MILLS
1 GeneralL Mills Blvd
Minneapolis, MN 55426-1348
612-540-2311 • Fax 612-540-7779

**GENERAL MOTORS
ACCEPT CRP**
3044 W Grand Blvd
Detroit, MI 48202-3037
313-556-1508

**GENERAL MOTORS-FLEET AND
COMMERCIAL**
100 Renaissance, Ctr , Mailcod
Detroit, MI 48265-0001
313-667-1136 • Fax 313-667-8166

**GENERAL PERSONNEL
MANAGEMENT**
9449 Balboa Ave Ste 310
San Diego, CA 92123-4370
www.gpmworks.com
858-637-7237 • Fax 582-793-528

GENERAL POLYMERS
145 Caldwell Dr
Cincinnati, OH 45216-1505
www.generalpolymers.com
513-761-0011

GENERAL SERVICES, INC.
PO Box 60
Medford, MA 02155-000
www.gsisharp.com
781-396-1022 • Fax 781-396-6633

GENERAL SLICING-RED GOAT
1152 Park Ave
Murfreesboro, TN 37129-4912
615-893-4820

**GENEVA BUS RES-BUS
INFO SERVICE**
5 Park Plz
Irvine, CA 92614-5995
949-756-2200

GENISOY PRODUCTS CO
2351 N Watney Way
Fairfield, CA 94533-6746
888-848-2343

GENON WALLCOVERING
175 Ghent Rd
Akron, OH 44333-333
e-mail: ted.torres@omnova.com
www.cw.gencorp.com
330-276-7440 • Fax 330-276-7469

GENO'S ALL IN ONE SAUCE
9908 Prospect Ave
Santee, CA 92071-4317
800-934-3667 • Fax 619-444-4363

GENPAK CORP
68 Warren St
Glens Falls, NY 12801-4530
518-798-9511

GENT-YOUNG & ASSOCIATES
N54 W30904 Windwood Dr
Hartland, WI 53029-1040
www.gentyoung.com
262-376-8542 • Fax 262-367-8543

**GEOCHILLER APPLIED
SCIENTIFIC**
7009 W 86th Pl
Crown Point, IN 46307-4964
219-776-4623 • Fax 219-365-8951

**GEOGRAPHIC DATA
TECHNOLOGY INC**
11 Lafayette St
Lebanon, NH 03766-1445
www.geopraphyic.com
800-331-7881 • Fax 603-448-2715

GEOMERX
41 Pine St
Rockaway, NJ 07866-3139
www.geomerx.com
973-586-4242 • Fax 201-486-4244

GEORGE E. DELALLO CO. INC.
101 Lincoln Hwy E
Jeannette, PA 15644-3143
724-523-5000 • Fax 724-529-1504

GEORGE GOLF DESIGN INC
609 Twinridge Ln
Richmond, VA 23235-5268
804-272-4700

GEORGE K. BAUM & CO.
120 W 12th St
Kansas City, MO 64105-1918
816-283-5129

GEORGE MOUK & ASSOCIATES
315 N 5th St
Monroe, LA 71201-6831
318-322-0588

GEORGE S MAY INTL CO
303 S Northwest Hwy
Park Ridge, IL 60068-4255
847-825-8806

**GEORGE WASHINGTON
UNIVERSITY**
Dept of Tourism & Mgmt, School
Washington, DC 20052-0001
202-994-6281 • Fax 202-994-1630

GEORGETOWN FARM
RR 1 Box 14W
Madison, VA 22727-9759
e-mail: buffalo@monumental.com
www.ealtean.com
540-948-4209 • Fax 540-948-4279

GEORGIA PACIFIC CORP.
PO BOX 740075
Atlanta, GA 30374-0075
404-652-4000 • Fax 404-588-5236

GEORGIA-PACIFIC CORP.
233 Peachtree St NE Ste 1800
Atlanta, GA 30303-1504
404-652-2496

GEORGIA STATE UNIVERSITY
35 Broad St # 1215
Atlanta, GA 30303-2302
e-mail: hrtal@angate.gsu.edu
www.cba.gus.edu
404-651-3512 • Fax 404-651-3670

GERBER PRODUCTS
445 State St
Fremont, MI 49413-0001
231-928-2000

GERRY LANE ENTERPRISES
6505 Florida Blvd
Baton Rouge, LA 70806-4464
225-926-4600

GESSNER PRODUCTS CO INC.
241 N Main St
Ambler, PA 19002-4224
215-646-7667 • Fax 215-646-6222

GETWAY GROUP, THE
3040 N 44th St
Phoenix, AZ 85018-7225
e-mail: mark@gwgroup.com
www.gwgroup.com
602-224-9944 • Fax 602-224-9499

GHIRADELLI CHOCOLATES
2000 Van Ness Ave Ste 708
San Francisco, CA 94109-3015
415-345-0007 • Fax 415-345-6222

GHIRARDELLI CHOCOLATES
1111 139th Ave
San Leandro, CA 94578-2671
www.ghirardelli.com
510-483-6970 • Fax 510-297-2649

GIACONA CONTAINER
121 Industrial Ave
New Orleans, LA 70121-2908
www.giacona.com
800-299-4332 • Fax 504-835-5581

GIATI DESIGN, INC.
614 Santa Barbara St
Santa Barbara, CA 93101-1638
e-mail: info@giati.com
www.giati.com
805-965-6535 • Fax 805-965-6295

GIESSER USA
6119 Adams St
West New York, NJ 07093-1505
201-453-1460 • Fax 201-453-9255

GIFT CARD SERVICES, INC.
8138 E 63rd St
Tulsa, OK 74133-1917
www.giftcardservices.com
918-663-1610 • Fax 918-663-9099

GIFTS & DECORATIVE
345 Hudson St, Fl 4
New York, NY 10014-4587
e-mail: lrotond@cahners.com
www.giftsanddec.com
212-519-7200 • Fax 212-519-7431

GILBERT INDUSTRIES
5611 Krueger Dr
Jonesboro, AR 72401-6818
870-932-6070

GILCHRIST & SOAMES
PO Box 33806
Indianapolis, IN 46203-0806
800-592-8862

GILES ENTERPRISES INC
PO Box 210247
Montgomery, AL 36121-0247
334-272-3528

GILES FOODSERVICE-CHESTER
2750 Gunter Park Dr W
Montgomery, AL 36109-1016
www.gilesent.com
800-288-1555 • Fax 334-272-3561

GILL MARKETING COMPANY
2128 Espey Ct Ste 7
Crofton, MD 21114-2445
www.gillmarketing.com
Fax 410-451-8520

GILROY FOODS
PO Box 1088
Gilroy, CA 95021-1088
408-847-1418 • Fax 408-847-3758

GINA MARIE REFRIGERATION EQUIP
910 Wellwood Ave
Lindenhurst, NY 11757-1226
631-789-1757 • Fax 631-789-2163

GINERIS, INC.
1488 Aberdeen St
Chicago Heights, IL 60411-3413
708-754-4587

GINKGO INTL. LTD.
5107 Chase Ave
Downers Grove, IL 60515-4012
www.ginkgoint.com
630-852-6960 • Fax 630-852-8418

GINO'S FOODS
200 E Grand Ave
Des Moines, IA 50309-1856
515-242-4731

GIORGIO FOODS, INC.
PO Box 96
Temple, PA 19560-0096
610-926-2139 • Fax 610-926-7012

GIRARD'S SALAD DRESSING
5442 Jillson St
Los Angeles, CA 90040-2118
www.girardsdressing.com
323-742-2519 • Fax 323-726-0934

GIRARD'S SALAD DRESSINGS
1202 N Fountain Green Rd
Bel Air, MD 21015-2504
www.girardsdressings.com
410-836-6662 • Fax 410-803-8935

GIUFFRIDA ASSOCIATES INC
204 E St NE
Washington, DC 20002-4923
202-547-6340 • Fax 202 547-6348

GIULIANOS' SPECIALITY FOODS
12132 Knott St
Garden Grove, CA 92041-2801
e-mail: brian@giulianopeppers.com
714-895-9661 • Fax 714-373-6872

GIVAUDAN ROURE FLAVORS
1199 Edison Dr
Cincinnati, OH 45216-2265
513-948-8000 • Fax 513-948-3558

GIVAUDAN-ROURE CORP.
300 Waterloo Valley Rd
Budd Lake, NJ 07828-1384
973-365-8359

GLACIER BAY BEVERAGES
199 E Linda Mesa Ave
Danville, CA 94526-3339
www.glacierbaybeverages.com
925-314-9125 • Fax 925-314-9143

GLACIER FISH CO
1200 Westlake Ave N
Seattle, WA 98109-3543
206-298-3131

GLACIER ISLAND INC
165 Chilian Ave
Palm Beach, FL 33480-4436
e-mail: glacierisland@aol.com
561-655-4408

GLADDER'S GOURMET COOKIES
PO Box 1228
Lockhart, TX 78644-1228
512-398-4523 • Fax 512-398-6323

GLAMI U.S.A.
22030 Peterhill Ct
Waukesha, WI 53186-5388
414-342-8989 • Fax 414-342-8997

GLARO, INC.
PO Box 12245
Hauppauge, NY 11788-0870

e-mail: info@glaro.com
www.glaro.com
631-234-1717 • Fax 631-234-9510

GLASS EMPORIUM INC
5603 Hollywood Blvd
Hollywood, FL 33021-6325
e-mail: acndle@bellsouth.net
www.restaurantcandles.com
954-963-2000

GLASS PRO INC.
511 Jennings Dr
Lake in the Hills, IL 60156-1676
www.glass-pro@immaxx.ocm
815-477-7230 • Fax 815-477-7262

GLASS SENTINAL
925 Sunshine Lane Ste 1020
Altamonte Springs, FL 32714-3825
e-mail:
k.w.kitchen@worldnet.att.net
www.glastender.com
407-774-1214

GLASS UNICORN, THE
1230 N Jefferson St
Anaheim, CA 92807-1631
714-666-2231

GLASTENDER INC
1455 Agricola Dr
Saginaw, MI 48604-9700
www.glastender.com
000-740-0423 • Fax 989-752-4444

GLASTENDER INC.
799 Broadway Ste 310
New York, NY 10003-6811
e-mail: yutermarketing@juno.com
212-777-4422 • Fax 212-777-4835

GLAZER COMPANIES OF LOUISIANA
111 Riverbend Dr
Saint Rose, LA 70087-3318
504-443-8600

GLAZER'S MIDWEST
5800 Stilwell St
Kansas City, MO 64120-1238
816-421-1145

GLAZER'S WHOLESALE DISTRIBUTOR
14860 Landmark Blvd
Dallas, TX 75254-6701
972 702 0900 • Fax 972-702-8508

GLEDHILL COMPANIES
PO Box 493
Onset, MA 02558-0493
e-mail:
glennandpaige@mediaone.net
508-291-4338 • Fax 508-291-8036

GLENMARK
1225 Corporate Blvd Ste 300
Aurora, IL 60504-6416
630-978-3840

GLENMARK INDUSTRIES LTD
4545 S Racine Ave
Chicago, IL 60609-3371
773-927-4800 • Fax 773-847-2946

GLIT-DISCO, INC.
1895 Brannan Rd
McDonough, GA 30253-4303
770-474-7575 • Fax 770-474-9464

GLOBAL BILLIARD MFG
1141 Sandhill Ave
Carson, CA 90746-1314
310-764-5000

GLOBAL ENTERPRISE TECHNOLOGY
7500 N Dreamy Draw Dr Ste 120
Phoenix, AZ 85020-4668
480-831-1000

GLOBAL FOOD & BEVERAGE CO.
4100 N Powerline Rd Ste U1
Pompano Beach, FL 33073-3051
www.iceecappuccion.com
954-957-7780 • Fax 954-957-7779

GLOBAL FOODSERVICE PUBLICATION
150 Great Neck Rd

Great Neck, NY 11021-3309
www.golbalfoodservices.com
516-829-9210 • Fax 516-829-5414

GLOBAL HOSPITALITY SOLUTIONS
15721 N Greenway Hayden Loop
Scottsdale, AZ 85260-1650
480-596-5156

GLOBAL ODOR CONTROL TECH.
PO Box 51005
New Bedford, MA 02745-0034
e-mail: info@ecolo.com
508-991-3939 • Fax 508-993-5090

GLOBAL PAYMENTS
3433 Highway 190 PMB 247
Mandeville, LA 70471-3101
985-892-0539 • Fax 985-892-6248

GLOBAL RESTAURANT EQUIPMENT SU
650 NW 123rd St
Miami, FL 33168-2608
305-688-8700

GLOBAL SEAFOOD EXCHANGE
430 10th St NW
Atlanta, GA 30318-5768
404-872-4489

GLOBAL STONE COMPANY
3120 46th Ave N
St Petersburg, FL 33714-3818
www.globalstone.net
727-450-0678 • Fax 727-450-0679

GLOBE FOOD
695 Belmont St
Belmont, MA 02478-4458
e-mail: edss@gis.net
www.globefoodservice.com
617-923-1274 • Fax 617-489-5550

GLOBE FOOD EQUIPMENT
2268 N Moraine Dr
Dayton, OH 45439-1508
www.globeslicers.com
937-299-5493 • Fax 937-299-4147

GLOBE FOOD EQUIPMENT CO
3033 Kettering Blvd
Dayton, OH 45439-1962
800-347-5423

GLOBETRENDS INC
PO Box 461
Chatham, NJ 07928-0461
800-416-8327

GLOLITE
2200 E Devon Ave
Des Plaines, IL 60018-4503
www.nudell.com
847-803-4500 • Fax 847-803-4584

GLORIA KAY UNIFORMS
4040 N 128th St
Brookfield, WI 53005-1813
www.gloriakay.com
800-242-7454 • Fax 262-790-0077

GLORY FOODS, INC.
901 Oak St
Columbus, OH 43205-1204
614-252-2042

GLOSTER FURNITURE, INC.
PO Box 1067
South Boston, VA 24592-1067
e-mail: ginger@gloster.com
www.gloster.com
434-575-1003 • Fax 4345-751-503

GLOVE CLEANERS & SAFETY
278 Union St
East Walpole, MA 02032-1037
508-668-0632 • Fax 508-668-8907

GLOWMASTER CORPORATION
535 Midland Ave
Garfield, NJ 07026-1658
www.glomaster.com
973-772-1111 • Fax 973-772-4040

GM IMPORT EXPORTS CORP.
315 E Redondo Beach Blvd
Gardena, CA 90248-2343

www.gmimportexport.com
310-643-6010 • Fax 310-643-6012

GMR MARKETING
16535 W Bluemound Rd Ste 230
Brookfield, WI 53005-5906
262-786-5600

GNL TECHNOLOGIES INC
374 E Ridgewood Dr
Independence, OH 44131-2829
e-mail:
geore-gnltech@buckeyeweb.com
440-736-9349

GO CO-OP
696 N Maitland Ave
Maitland, FL 32751-4423
407-628-3636

GO2COMPASS.COM
PO Box 5108
Winter Park, FL 32793-5108
e-mail: cline@go2compass.com
www.go2compass.com
407-971-2061

GOCO-OP, INC.
631 N Wymore Rd
Maitland, FL 32751-4246
e-mail: jsorrentino@goco-op.com
www.goco-op.com
407-691-5000 • Fax 107-622-4756

GODIVA CHOCOLATIER
614 E 3rd St # 3
Boston, MA 02127-2319
www.godiva.com
617-269-0441 • Fax 617-269-0448

GOELITZ
1501 Morrow Ave
North Chicago, IL 60064-3200
www.jellybelly.com
847-599-3540 • Fax 847-599-3586

GOFISH.COM
PO Box 15340
Portland, ME 04112-5340
800-777-3533

GOGLANIAN BAKERIES, INC
3401 W Segerstrom Ave
Santa Ana, CA 92704-6404
714-444-3500 • Fax 714-444-3800

GOJO INDUSTRIES
PO Box 991
Akron, OH 44309-0991
800-321-9647

GOL PAK CORPORATION
214 Overlook Ct Ste 215
Brentwood, TN 37027-3215
615-376-8820 • Fax 615-376-8824

GOLBON
877 W Main St
Boise, ID 83702-5883
800-657-6395

GOLD BAND OYSTERS
1039 Toulouse St
New Orleans, LA 70112-3425
504-523-2651 • Fax 504-522-4960

GOLD COAST INGREDIENTS
2429 Yates Ave
Los Angeles, CA 90040-1917
323-724-8935

GOLD LEAF DESIGN GROUP
337 N Oakley Blvd
Chicago, IL 60612-2215
www.goldleafdesigngroup.com
312-738-1790 • Fax 312-738-1795

GOLD MEDAL PRODUCTS CO.
10700 Medallion Dr
Cincinnati, OH 45241-4807
www.gmpopcorn.com
513-769-7676 • Fax 513-769-8500

GOLD PROMOTIONS, INC.
1999 Westbelt Dr
Columbus, OH 43228-3815
e-mail:
billwood@goldpromotions.com
www.goldpromotions.com
614-876-7354 • Fax 614-876-9847

GOLD STAR COFFEE
51 Bridge St # A
Salem, MA 01970-4198
978-744-2672 • Fax 978-744-8238

GOLDEN CHEESE COMPANY OF CALIFORNIA
1123 W Rincon St
Corona, CA 92880-9696
e-mail: gccc@compuserve.com
909-493-4700 • Fax 909-493-4701

GOLDEN DIPT
100 E Grand Ave
Beloit, WI 53511-6255
e-mail: bkiefer@kerrygroup.com
608-363-1650 • Fax 608-363-1659

GOLDEN LYNX
20423 State Road 7
Boca Raton, FL 33498-6797
www.davina18@aol.com
561-487-2150 • Fax 561-479-2531

GOLDEN WEST EQUIPMENT
1000 S Euclid St
La Habra, CA 90631-6806
714-879-3850 • Fax 714-879-4071

GOLDEN WEST SALES
15391 Electronic Ln
Huntington Beach, CA 92649-1331
800-827-6175

GOLDMAN DESIGN GROUP
360 W Putnam Ave
Greenwich, CT 06830-5245
e-mail:
contactus@goldmandesigngroup.com
www.goldmandesigngroup.com
203-618-1280 • Fax 203-618-1823

GOLDMAN'S GOURMENT, INC
619 N Grand Ave E
Springfield, IL 62702-3989
www.goldmansgourmet.com
217-523-0885 • Fax 217-523-0676

GOLDMAX INDUSTRIES, INC.
1030 Lawson St
Rowland Heights, CA 91748-1107
www.goldmax.com
626-964-8820 • Fax 626-964-6629

GOLIGER LEATHER CO INC
1580 Saratoga Ave
Ventura, CA 93003-7381
800-423-2329

GONNELLA BAKING CO
2002 W Erie St
Chicago, IL 60612-1397
312-733-2020 • Fax 312-733-7670

GOOD FOOD SERVICE, INC.
2209 Varnum St
Mount Rainier, MD 20712-1457
301-864-1780

GOOD HEALTH NATURAL FOOD, INC.
81 Scudder Ave
Northport, NY 11768-2966
www.E-goodhealth.com
631-261-2111 • Fax 631-261-2167

GOOD HUMOR-BREYERS ICE CREAM
PO Box 19007
Green Bay, WI 54307-9007
920-499-5151

GOOD HUMOR-BREYERS ICE CREAM
PO Box 242
Garwood, NJ 07027-0242
e-mail:
rich.mckenney@unilever.com
908-272-8746 • Fax 908-276-0705

GOOD OLD DAYS FOODS
PO Box 269
Springdale, AR 72765-0269
479-756-2230 • Fax 501-759-9598

GOOD STUFF FOOD CO., INC.
1771 Blake Ave
Los Angeles, CA 90031-1006
323-913-7240

GOOD WIVES, INC.
86 Sanderson Ave
Lynn, MA 01902-1937
781-596-0070 • Fax 781-596-1331

GOODHEART SPECIALTY MEATS
11122 Nacogdoches Rd
San Antonio, TX 78217-2314
210-637-1963

GOODWAY INDUSTRIES
54 Davis Ln
Easton, MD 21601-4000
410-567-2929

GORDON FOOD SERVICE INC
PO Box 1787
Grand Rapids, MI 49501-1787
616-530-7000 • Fax 616-249-4165

GORDON HANRAHAN INC
180 N Michigan Ave Ste 4
Chicago, IL 60601-7401
312-372-0935 • Fax 312-372-1409

GORMLEY'S ORCHARD
99 West Rd
Pittsford, VT 05763-9691
802-483-2400 • Fax 802-483-2698

GORTON'S OF GLOUCESTER
128 Rogers St
Gloucester, MA 01930-5005
978-283-3000

GOTAJOB.COM
6312 S Fiddlers Green Cir
Englewood, CO 80111-4943
e-mail: help@gotajob.com
www.gotajob.com
303-220-7501 • Fax 303-220-9946

GOTHAM PASTRY, INC.
4344 21st St
Long Island City, NY 11101-5002
e-mail: gothampastry@aol.com
718-392-7744 • Fax 718-472-0385

GOTRADESEAFOOD.COM
PO Box 025216
Miami, FL 33102-5216
305-249-0160

GOURMAND FINE FOOD
3051 La Cienega Blvd
Culver City, CA 90232-7314
800-839-7272 • Fax 310-839-9155

GOURMENT TABLESKIRTS
1323 N 1st St
Bellaire, TX 77401-6001
www.gourmet-table-skirts.com
713-666-0602 • Fax 713-666-0623

GOURMET BISON COMPANY
16435 Peck St
Ashton, SD 57424-6002
e-mail: gourmetbison@nuc.net
www.gourmetbison.com
605-472-2281 • Fax 605-472-2306

GOURMET BOUTIQUE
16535 145th Dr
Jamaica, NY 11434-5108
718-995-5169 • Fax 718-656-7544

GOURMET DISPLAY
309 S Cloverdale St
Seattle, WA 98108-4568
206-767-4711

GOURMET EXPRESS
18945 Fm 2252
San Antonio, TX 78266-2562
888-599-8230

GOURMET FOOD MARKETING
410 Ocean Ave
Lynbrook, NY 11563-3833
516-596-2502 • Fax 516-593-3884

GOURMET FUSIONS
1104 Kenilworth Dr
Wheeling, IL 60090-3920
800-200-2725 • Fax 847-357-9444

GOURMET GEAR INC.
2320 Abbot Kinney Blvd
Venice, CA 90291-4727
www.gourmetgear.com
310-301-4111 • Fax 310-301-4115

GOURMET HOMEMADE
1515 N Federal Hwy
Boca Raton, FL 33432-1911
e-mail: seafood@gate.net
954-992-4600 • Fax 561-276-7068

GOURMET HOTELIER COMPANY
7032 NW 1st St
Pompano Beach, FL 33063-4911
954-984-1740 • Fax 954-984-1748

GOURMET SORBET INC. 1404
1507 Demosthenes St
Metairie, LA 70005-2701
504-828-1400

GOURMET TECHNOLOGIES
51 Trade Zone Dr
Ronkonkoma, NY 11779-7343
631-981-2100 • Fax 631-981-3509

GOW & HANNA HOSP SVC
2000 West Loop S
Houston, TX 77027-3513
713-621-7439

GRA LAB INSTRUMENTAL DIVISION
8200 S Suburban Rd
Dayton, OH 45458-2710
e-mail: sales@dimco-gray.com
800-876-8353 • Fax 937-433-0520

GRAEBEL COMPANIES, INC
16346 Airport Cir
Aurora, CO 80011-1558
800-373-1970

GRAHAM BROS. ENTERTNMT
6201 Andrews Hwy
Odessa, TX 79762-3649
915-362-0401

GRAND DECOR
510 W Carob St
Compton, CA 90220-5215
www.granddecor.com
310-900-0280 • Fax 310-900-0289

GRAND HOTEL EQUIPMENT CO.
8350 Burnet Ave Unit 013
North Hills, CA 91343-6648
e-mail: cattle-44hotmail.com
www.shanghaigrand.com
818-894-8864 • Fax 818-891-2053

GRAND RAPIDS CHAIR CO.
433 Century Ave SW
Grand Rapids, MI 49503-4902
www.grandrapidschair.com
616-774-0561 • Fax 616-774-0563

GRAND SILVER
289 Morris Ave
Bronx, NY 10451-6198
e-mail: grandsilver@aol.com
718-585-1930 • Fax 718-402-4724

GRANDE BAKERY
671 N Poplar St
Orange, CA 92868-1085
714-971-0061

GRANDMA'S BAKE SHOP
PO Box 457
Beatrice, NE 68310-0457
e-mail: roy@metzbaking.com
402-223-4465 • Fax 402-223-4465

GRANELLI
22122 20th Ave SE#159
Bothell, WA 98021-4433
www.granelli.com
425-487-6824 • Fax 425-487-6826

GRANNYS KITCHEN LTD
10 Industrial Park Dr
Frankfort, NY 13340-4798
315-735-5000

GRANT FRUIT PROCESSING
8484 Highway 165
Pollock, LA 71467-3004
318-765-2230

GRANT THORNTON LLP
2700 S Commerce Pkwy Ste 300

Fort Lauderdale, FL 33331-3630
954-768-9900

GRANT WM & SONS INC
130 Fieldcrest Ave
Edison, NJ 08837-3620
732-225-9000

GRAPHIC CONTROLS CORP.
PO Box 1271
Buffalo, NY 14240-1271
e-mail: deberhardt@ludlaugh.com
www.graphiccontrols.com
716-853-7500 • Fax 877-268-0877

GRAPHIC PACKAGING CORP
2183 Hawkins St
Charlotte, NC 28203-4901
704-377-2691

GRAPHICS SYSTEMS
313 Ida St
Wichita, KS 67211-1588
www.gsi-graphics .com
316-267-4171 • Fax 620-348-6174

GRAPHICS TYPE & COLOR
6993 NW 82nd Ave
Miami, FL 33166-2782
305-591-7600

GRATE SIGNS
4044 McDonough St
Joliet, IL 60431-8816
815-729-9700

GREAT AMERICAN BARBECUE COMPANY
PO Box 868
Weimar, TX 78962-0868
e-mail: skloesel@gabbq.com
888-909-7427 • Fax 979-725-8521

GREAT AMERICAN INSURANCE
580 Walnut St Ste 11
Cincinnati, OH 45202-3110
513-369-5021

GREAT AMERICAN STOCK
5200 Pasadena NE Unit C
Albuquerque, NM 87113-2208
505-892-7747

GREAT CHINA
1232 Factory Pl
Los Angeles, CA 90013-2231
e-mail: greatchina@greatchina.com
213-622-3594 • Fax 213-622-3585

GREAT CRESCENT INTL. INC.
17 Clear Vista Dr
Palos Verdes Peninsula, CA 90274-5433
310-377-9415

GREAT DISCOVERY'S CIGARS
5401 Mitchelldale St Ste A-TX
Houston, TX 77092-7232
713-680-3215 • Fax 713-680-3251

GREAT FISH CO
800 Vinial St # B-308
Pittsburgh, PA 15212-5128
412-321-8501

GREAT LAKES CHEESE COMPANY INC.
17825 Great Lakes Pkwy
Hiram, OH 44234-9677
440-834-2500 • Fax 440-834-1002

GREAT SOUTHERN GREASE STOPPER
4305 Boggy Creek Rd
Kissimmee, FL 34744-9107
407-348-2989

GREAT SOUTHERN WINE & SPIRITS
809 Jefferson Hwy
New Orleans, LA 70121-2522
504-849-6273

GREAT SPIRITS
1331 Lamar St Ste 900
Houston, TX 77010-3025
713-750-0033 • Fax 713-756-6150

GREAT WESTERN MFG CO
PO Box 149
Leavenworth, KS 66048-0149
913-682-2291

GREAT WESTERN TOY CO., LLC
12220 Parkway Centre Dr
Poway, CA 92064-6867
800-466-4192 • Fax 858-679-3943

GREATER LOUISIANA ICE MACHINE
4 Knox Rd
New Orleans, LA 70121-2906
504-833-3734

GREATER INSURANCE SERVICE CORP
414 Atlas Ave
Madison, WI 53714-3106
www.greater-ins.com
608-221-3996 • Fax 608-221-0868

GREATER MILWAUKEE CONVENTION & VISITORS' BUREAU
510 W Kilbourn Ave
Milwaukee, WI 53203-1400
www.milwaukee.org
414-287-4238 • Fax 414-273-5596

GREATER TEXAS ICE
6350 Alder Dr
Houston, TX 77081-4404
e-mail: sales@greatertexasice.com
713-661-6321 • Fax 713-661-8460

GRECI C-O I.Q.S.
111 John St Rm 1720
New York, NY 10038-3114
212-791-2187 • Fax 212-791-2196

GRECIAN DELIGHT FOODS
1201 Tonne Rd
Elk Grovevillage, IL 60007-4925
800-621-4387 • Fax 847-364-1077

GREEK GOURMET LTD.
5 Pond Park R
Hingham, MA 02043-4365
e-mail: greekgourmet@yahoo.com
781-749-1866 • Fax 781-740-2005

GREEN & ASSOCIATES MYSTERY SHOPPERS
PO Box 9869
College Statio, TX 77842-7869
800-677-2264

GREEN COUNTRY FOODS, INC
1112 7th Ave
Monroe, WI 53566-1364
800-233-3564 • Fax 608-328-8648

GREEN GARDEN PACKAGING CO
133 Produce Row
Houston, TX 77023-5813
e-mail: lfaour@aol.com
713-926-5042 • Fax 713-926-8571

GREEN MOUNTAIN COFFEE ROASTERS
33 Coffee Ln
Waterbury, VT 05676-8900
www.gmcr.com
802-244-5621 • Fax 802-244-6565

GREEN SUITES INTERNATIONAL
1551 W 13th St
Upland, CA 91786-2900
909-920-1277

GREEN THOMAS, L & CO INC
7802 Moller Rd
Indianapolis, IN 46268-2117
317-263-6935

GREENBAUM BROS. INC.
1655 Union Ave
Chicago Heights, IL 60411-3502
www.greenbaumbrothers.com
800-755-8779 • Fax 708-756-3525

GREENFIELD WORLD TRADE
4901 NW 17th Way
Fort Lauderdale, FL 33309-3780
954-202-7336

GREENHECK FAN COMPANY
PO Box 410
Schofield, WI 54476-0410
715-359-6171

GREGOR JONSSON ASSOCIATES
1520 Berkeley Rd
Highland Park, IL 60035-2799
847-831-2030

GREIF & CO
633 W 5th St
Los Angeles, CA 90071-2005
213-346-9250

GREYSTONE BAKERY
114 Woodworth Ave
Yonkers, NY 10701-2500
e-mail: marshallp@greystone.com
914-375-1510 • Fax 914-375-1514

GRIFFIN INDUSTRIES
408 W Landstreet Rd
Orlando, FL 32824-7805
407-857-5474

GRIFFIN PUBLISHING CO.
100 Weymouth St Ste D2
Rockland, MA 02370-1145
e-mail: griffinpub@aol.com
781-878-5300 • Fax 781-8714721

GRIFFITH LABORATORIES
1 Griffith Ctr
Alsip, IL 60803-4702
708-371-0900 • Fax 708-597-3294

GRILLS TO GO, LLC
37140 Marciel Ave
Madera, CA 93636-0636
www.grillstogo.com
559-645-8089 • Fax 559-645-8088

GRIMASTER CORPORATION
4003 Collins Ln
Louisville, KY 40245-1643
www.grimaster.com
502-425-4776 • Fax 502-425-4662

GRIME REAPER
2451 N McMullen Booth Rd Ste 2
Clearwater, FL 33759-1352
e-mail: celticsys@aol.com
800-952-4857

GRINGO TRANSLATION
1410 W North Loop Blvd Apt 201
Austin, TX 78756-2142
e-mail: donadelmar@aol.com
512 554-7067 • Fax 512-266-0150

GRINNELL FIRE PROTECTION
7604 Kempwood Dr
Houston, TX 77055-1322
www.grinfire.com
713-644-8872 • Fax 713-644-9469

GRINNELL FIRE PROTECTION
835 Sharon Dr
Westlake, OH 44145-1522
e-mail: priegler@tycoint.com
440-899-5407 • Fax 440-871-2301

GROEN
1055 Mendell Davis Dr
Byram, MS 39272-9788
www.groen.com
888-676-9040 • Fax 888-371-6049

GROEN JOYLIN FOOD EQUIPMENT CO
1900 Pratt Blvd
Elk Grove Village, IL 60007-5906
e-mail: info@groen.com
www.grown.com
601-372-3903 • Fax 888-864-7636

GROHE AMERICA INC
900 Lively Blvd
Wood Dale, IL 60191-1204
708-350-2600

GROSFILLEX
230 Old West Penn Ave
Robesonia, PA 19551-8904
610-693-5835 • Fax 610-693-8254

GROSFILLEX FURNITURE
2300 Via Carrillo
Palos Verdes Peninsula, CA 90274-2717
e-mail: grosfillex@aol.com
310-791-9979 • Fax 310-791-9989

GROTE & WEIGEL
76 Granby St
Bloomfield, CT 06002-3512
860-242-8528 • Fax 860-242-4162

GROUP ONE COMMUNICATIONS
1221 Nicollet Ave
Minneapolis, MN 55403-2420
612-334-8100 • Fax 612-334-8102

GROVE MEAT COMPANY LAMB & VEAL
2222 Grove St
Blue Island, IL 60406-2555
800-356-0426

GROW A DOT, INC.
600 S Barracks St
Pensacola, FL 32501-6000
850-444-9330 • Fax 850-444-9331

GROW WITH ME, INC.
2401 W 208th St Unit C6
Torrance, CA 90501-6212
e-mail: growwme@zunzu.com
www.zunzu.com
310-320-9811 • Fax 310-320-9812

GROW-M-TALL OSTRICH RANCH
HC 1 Box 73
Hermitage, MO 65668-9610
417-745-2616

GRUBB & ELLIS
1100 Glendon Ave
Los Angeles, CA 90024-3503
310-235-2933

GRUENEWALD MANUFACTURING
100 Ferncroft Rd
Danvers, MA 01923-4027
800-229-9447

GSA, FEDERAL SUPPLY SERVICE
819 Taylor St
Fort Worth, TX 76102-6114
e-mail: alan.searsy@gsa.gov
www.gsa.gov-regions-7fss-7-fx-
817-978-8370 • Fax 817-978-2776

GSB VENTURES
PO Box 148331
Chicago, IL 60614-8331
312-702-5421

GSD PACKAGING
6 Tomkins Ridge Rd
Tomkins Cove, NY 10986-1408
845-429-5226

GSD PACKAGING-FOLD-PAK
1854 E Home Ave
Fresno, CA 93703-3636
559-441-1181 • Fax 559-441-0190

G-TEL ENTERPRISES INC
16840 Clay Rd
Houston, TX 77084-4067
800-804-4835

GUENTHER & SON INC
129 E Guenther
San Antonio, TX 78204-1402
888-215-9795

GUEST ACCESS INTL
2080 Commerce Dr
Midland, TX 79703-7502
e-mail: joy@guestaccess.com
www.guestaccess.com
888-483-7822 • Fax 888-539-5945

GUEST AMENITIES
388 Market St
San Francisco, CA 94111-5311
415-981-7627

GUEST AMENITIES GROUP
5149 S 94th East Ave
Tulsa, OK 74145-8179
e-mail: jpmtgag@aol.com
www.theguestamenitiesgroup.com
918-622-2666 • Fax 918-622-3054

GUEST CHOICE INC
3815 E Grove St
Phoenix, AZ 85040-9002
800-483-7836

GUEST CHOICE NETWORK
1775 Pennsylvania Ave NW
Washington, DC 20006-4605
202-463-7112

GUEST HOSPITALITY SERVICES INC
132 S Pelham Dr
Dayton, OH 45429-1564
937-299-6682

GUEST SUPPLY, INC.
PO Box 902
Monmouth Junction, NJ 08852-0902
e-mail: info@guestsupply.com
www.guestsupply.com
609-514-9696 • Fax 609-514-2692

GUESTHOUSE INNS-HOTELS
1501 N University Ave
Little Rock, AR 72207-5242
501-663-6606

GUESTSPECS
441 Warwick Rd
Deerfield, IL 60015-3333
www.guestspecs.com
847-374-1740 • Fax 847-374-1732

GUIDA MILK & ICE CREAM CO.
PO Box 2110
New Britain, CT 06050-2110
www.supercow.com
860-224-2404 • Fax 860-225-0035

GUINNESS IMPORT CO
6 Landmark Sq
Stamford, CT 06901-2704
203-323-3311

GUITTARD CHOCOLATE CO
10 Guittard Rd
Burlingame, CA 94010-2203
www.guittard.com
650-697-4427 • Fax 650-692-2761

GULF ICE SYSTEM
7790 Sears Blvd
Pensacola, FL 32514-4542
850-474-1784

GUMBO SHOP
5900 S Front St
New Orleans, LA 70115-2152
504-899-2460 • Fax 504-897-3454

GUST JOHN FOODS & PRODUCTS
1350 Paramount Pkwy
Batavia, IL 60510-1461
630-879-8700

GUSTAVE A. LARSON CO.
W233 N2869 Roundy Cir W
Pewaukee, WI 53072-5794
www.galarson.com
262-542-0200 • Fax 262-542-2405

GW ASSOCIATES
305 Oakwood Cir
Martinez, CA 94553-3565
e-mail: gildaw@ik.netcom.com
510-420-7014 • Fax 510-420-1408

GWALTNEY OF SMITHFIELD
601 N Church St
Smithfield, VA 23430-1221
757-357-3131 • Fax 757-357-1529

H & H BAGEL
639 W 46th St
New York, NY 10036-1916
www.hhbagels.com
212-595-8000 • Fax 212-765-7391

H & M FOOD, INC.
239 E Depot St
Antioch, IL 60002-1860
www.bandito.com
800-880-5938 • Fax 847-838-4392

H & N FISH CO
2390 Jerrold Ave
San Francisco, CA 94124-1081
415-821-6637

H C RHODES
BAKERY EQUIPMENT
400 NE 11th Ave
Portland, OR 97232-2791
503-232-9101

H M FOOD SYSTEMS
COMPANY
6350 Browning Ct
N Richland Hills, TX 76180-6013
817-831-0981 • Fax 817-838-4468

H S INC
501 SW 9th St
Oklahoma City, OK 73109-1301
405-239-6864

H S S LTD
1711 Amuskai Rd
Parkville, MD 21234-3714
410-882-7864

H.C. BRILL CO., INC.
1912 Montreal Rd
Tucker, GA 30084-5238
800-241-8526 • Fax 770-723-3453

H.F. COORS CHINA
COMPANY-MASON
8729 Aviation Blvd
Inglewood, CA 90301-2003
www.coorschina.com
310-338-8921 • Fax 310-641-9429

H.H. BROWN
124 W Putnam Ave
Greenwich, CT 06830-5317
e-mail: sessal@hhbrown.com
203-661-1818

H.P. HOOD, INC.
90 Everett Ave Ste 200
Chelsea, MA 02150-2337
617-887-3000 • Fax 617-887-8314

H.P.HOOD INC.
34 Harrison Ave
Braintree, MA 02184-4912
888-356-8980 • Fax 888-356-8981

H.T. PATRICK INC.
2275 Warwick Ave
Warwick, RI 02889-4272
401-737-5141 • Fax 401-738-6078

H.W. BAKER LINEN CO., INC.
PO Box 544
Mahwah, NJ 07430-0544
e-mail: srichey@bakerlinen.com
201-825-2000 • Fax 201-825-0649

HAAGEN DAZ INC
701 Zerega Ave
Bronx, NY 10473-1183
www.haagen-dazs.com
718-518-8700 • Fax 718-518-8904

HAAGEN-DAZS
1601 N 50th St
Tampa, FL 33619-3221
e-mail: gmartin@pillsbury.com
www.haagen-dazs.com
813-267-5095

HAAGEN-DAZS
1938 Taylor Ln
Tampa, FL 33618-1514
813-969-3198 • Fax 813-391-3513

HAAGEN-DAZS COMPANY INC
300 Frank W Burr Blvd
Teaneck, N 07666-6704

HAAGEN-DAZS ICE CREAM
2000 Afton St
Houston, TX 77055-2206
www.haagen.dazs.com
713-956-4875

HAAKE INSURANCE
3103 Broadway St Ste 650
Kansas City, MO 64111-2405
816-753-1999

HAAS MACHINERY AMER
FRANZ
6207 Settler Rd
Richmond, VA 23231-6044
804-222-6022

HABAGALLO FOODS, INC
2931 N Gulley Rd

Fayetteville, AR 72703-9018
e-mail: monenterprises@msn.com
www.habagallo.com
479-443-0636

HABAGALLO FOODS, INC.
2101 N 23rd St
McAllen, TX 78501-6127
e-mail: habagell@swbell.net
www.habagall.com
956-682-1524 • Fax 956-682-7561

HABAR CORPORATION
PO Box 1763
Jamaica Plain, MA 02130-0015
617-524-6107 • Fax 617-524-4826

HADELER WHITE PUBLIC
RELATIONS
5430 Lyndon B Johnson Fwy
Dallas, TX 75240-2601
972-776-8020

HAFELE AMERICA CO
3901 Cheyenne Dr
High Point, NC 27263-3157
336-889-2322

HAIER AMERICA TRADING LLC
45 W 36th St Fl 4
New York, NY 10018-7637
e-mail: skan@haieramerica.com
www.haieramerica.com
212-594-3330 • Fax 212-594-3311

HAIFA CHEMICALS
6800 Jericho Tpke
Syosset, NY 11791-4436
516-921-0044

HAIN FOOD GROUP
PO Box 48006
Gardena, CA 90248-0806
626-334-3241

HAKUSAN SAKE, KOHANAN
1 Executive Way
Napa, CA 94558-6271
e-mail: gambrow@pacbell.net
949-369-779 • Fax 925-369-0679

HALIFax GROUP
3264 McCall Dr
Atlanta, GA 30340-3306
800-878-7808

HALL HENRY
DESIGNS
297 Kansas St
San Francisco, CA 94103-5127
800-367-9150

HALLMARK BUILDING
SUPPLIES
6060 N 77th St
Milwaukee, WI 53218-1241
www.hllmark.com
800-274-7842 • Fax 800-688-7842

HALLMARK LIGHTING
9631 De Soto Ave # O
Chatsworth, CA 91311-5013
e-mail: marca@hallmarklighting.com
www.hallmarklighting.com
818-885-5010 • Fax 818-885-5013

HALSTEAD ASSOCIATES PK
6900 E Camelback Rd Ste 500
Scottsdale, AZ 85251-8052
480-994-0014

HALTON CO
101 Industrial Dr
Scottsville, KY 42164-7932
800-442-5866

HAM I AM!
320 Woodlake Dr
Plano, TX 75094-3430
e-mail: sharon@hamian.com
972-424-0127 • Fax 972-424-0147

HAMCO NEW ORLEANS
PO Box 23824
New Orleans, LA 70183-0824
504-734-7513

HAMILTON BEACH
263 Yadkin Rd
Southern Pines, NC 28387-3415
800-572-3331

HAMILTON BEACH
COMMERCIAL
4421 Waterfront Dr
Glen Allen, VA 23060-3375
804-527-7355 • Fax 804-527-7174

HAMMETT PACKAGING
13700 Cimarron Ave
Gardena, CA 90249-2462
e-mail:
mmccarthy@hammettpkg.com
310-324-3224 • Fax 310-324-3359

HAMPSTEAD LIGHTING
4505 Peachtree Industrial Blvd
Norcross, GA 30092-3000
770-447-1700

HANCO SYSTEMS INC
401 W Park Ct # 100
Peachtree City, GA 30269-1456
770-487-3733

HANDGARDS, INC.
901 Hawkins Blvd
El Paso, TX 79915-1202
www.handgards.com
800-351-8161 • Fax 915-564-5917

HANDY WACKS CORP
PO Box 26
Sparta, MI 49345-0026
800-445-4434

HANDYSITT ADT MARKETING
4 Lindley Ave
Tenafly, NJ 07670-2817
e-mail: mazori@carroll.com
201-871-8508 • Fax 201-894-8581

HANNA INSTRUMENTS
584 Park East Dr
Woonsocket, RI 02895-6177
www.hannainst.com
401-765-7500 • Fax 401-765-7575

HANNA INSTRUMENTS
4852 NW 76th Rd
Gainesville, FL 32653-1171
www.hannainst.com
352-271-3009

HANSEN CAVIAR
COMPANY
93 S Railroad Ave Ste D
Bergenfield, NJ 07621-2352
e-mail: hcaviar@aol.com
201-385-6221 • Fax 201-385-9882

HANSEN TECHNOLOGIES
6827 High Grove Blvd
Willowbrook, IL 60527-7579
630-325-1565

HANSGROHE
1490 Bluegrass Lakes Pkwy
Alpharetta, GA 30004-7710
e-mail: info@hansgrohe.com
www.hansgrohe-usa.com
678-360-9880 • Fax 678-360-9887

HANSGROHE INC
1465 Ventura Dr
Cumming, GA 30040-4501
770-844-7414

HANSON BRASS
7530 San Fernando Rd
Sun Valley, CA 91352-4344
e-mail: info@hansonbrass.com
818-767-3501 • Fax 818-767-7891

HAPER ASSOCIATES
29870 Middlebelt Rd
Farmington, MI 48334-2316
248-932-1170

HARBOR EMBROIDERY
PO Box 446
Boothbay Harbor, ME 04538-0446
e-mail:
terry@harborembroidery.com
207-633-0601 • Fax 207-633-4438

HARBOUR HOUSE BAR
CRAFTING
737 Canal St Ste 16
Stamford, CT 06902-5930
www.harnourhouse.com
203-348-6906 • Fax 203-348-6190

HARDIS
1424 Parker St
Dallas, TX 75215-1282
e-mail: rpuckett@hardies.com
www.hardies.com
214-426-5666 • Fax 214-421-2222

HARFORD DURACOOL LLC
PO Box 700
Aberdeen, MD 21001-0700
410-272-9999

HARFORD DURACOOL, LLC
PO Box 1026
Aberdeen, MD 21001-6026
800-638-7620 • Fax 410-272-8508

HARKER'S DISTRIBUTION
801 6th St SW
Le Mars, IA 51031-1817
www.harkers.com
712-546-8171 • Fax 712-546-3106

HARMONY CREEK
SEAFOOD
3233 SW 33rd Rd
Ocala, FL 34474-8470
e-mail:
sales@harmonycreekseafood.com
352-237-6145 • Fax 352-237-0944

HARNEY & SONS
FINE TEAS
PO Box 665
Salisbury, CT 06068-0665
www.harney.com
860-435-5050 • Fax 860-435-5044

HAROLD LEONARD & CO
2835 E Ana St
Compton, CA 90221-5626
310-604-0404 • Fax 310-604-1748

HAROLD LEONARD & CO INC
600 Green Ln
Union, NJ 07083-8074
www.halco.com
908-289-1000 • Fax 908-289-3186

HARPOON BREWERY
306 Northern Ave
Boston, MA 02210-2324
e-mail:
mnorbis@harpoonbrewery.com
www.harpoonbrewery.com
217-574-9551 • Fax 617-482-9361

HARRAH HOTEL COLLEGE-
UNLV
4505 S Maryland Pkwy # 4560
Las Vegas, NV 89154-9900
www.unlv.edu
702-895-3161 • Fax 702-895-4109

HARRIS TEA COMPANY INC
344 New Albany Rd
Moorestown, NJ 08057-1167
856-662-6430 • Fax 856-486-9311

HARRY C. DANCIGER &
ASSOCIATES
3427 Park Ave
Memphis, TN 38111-4148
901-323-1005

HARRY WILS & COMPANY
PO Box 2549
Secaucus, NJ 07096-2549
212-431-9731 • Fax 212-431-3620

HARRY'S FRESH FOOD
11735 NE Sumner St
Portland, OR 97220-1057
800-307-7687 • Fax 503-257-7363

HARTFORD PROVISION CO.
205 Enterprise Dr
Bristol, CT 06010-8402
860-583-3908

HARVEST BROKERS
1025 S Jefferson Davis Pkwy
New Orleans, LA 70125-1218
504-304-3370 • Fax 504-304-3371

HARVEST STATES
COOPERATiVE
5500 Cenex Dr
Inver Grove, MN 55077-1733
651-646-9433

HARVESTERS
1811 N Topping Ave
Kansas City, MO 64120-1258
816-231-3173

HARVICO
5535 Gross Ct
Orlando, FL 32810-4506
e-mail: sales@harvico.com
407-538-2337 • Fax 407-295-0018

HATCH-JENNINGS
PO Box 744
Harvard, MA 01451-0744
www.hatch-jennings.com
978-456-8702 • Fax 978-456-8067

HATCO CORPORATION
PO Box 340500
Milwaukee, WI 53234-0500
www.hatcocorp.com
414-615-2223 • 800-968-1158

HATFIELD QUALITY MEAT
2700 Funks Rd
Hatfield, PA 19440-2847
215-368-2500 • Fax 215-368-9462

HATTERAS HAMMOCKS INC
PO Box 1602
Greenville, NC 27835-1602
800-643-3522

HAUG INTERNATIONAL
400 El Bosque
Laguna Beach, CA 92651-2533
949-484-1207

HAUSER ENTERPRISES
46 Washington Dr
Sudbury, MA 01776-2936
978-443-3438

HAUSER PRINTING CO., INC
5720 Heebe St
New Orleans, LA 70123-5505
504-733-2022

HAVEN HOMES, INC.
PO Box 178
Beech Creek, PA 16822-0178
e-mail: info@havenhomes.com
www.haven.com
570-962-2111 • Fax 570-962-3181

HAWAIIAN NATURAL WATER CO.
98-746 Kuahao Pl
Pearl City, HI 96782-3125
e-mail: rrhispring@aol.com
808-483-0526 • Fax 808-483-0536

HAWKEYE FOOD SYSTEMS
PO Box 1820
Iowa City, IA 52244-1820
319-645-2193

HAWKINS INC MICHAEL
1615 W Colonial Pkwy
Palatine, IL 60067-4732
847-705-5400

HAYMAN SYSTEMS
15 Arlive Ct
Potomac, MD 20854-2978
301-470-2111

HAZELNUT COUNCIL
PO Box 545
Matawan, NJ 07747-0545
888-335-4744

HAZELNUT GOURMET COFFEE'S
PO Box 544
La Feria, TX 78559-0544
956-797-9319 • Fax 956-565-0718

HAZELWOOD FARM BAKERIES
8840 Pershall Rd
Hazelwood, MO 63042-2916
314-595-4150 • Fax 314-595-4116

HBG INTERNATIONAL, INC
5600 Roswell Rd NE Ste E300
Atlanta, GA 30342-1131
e-mail: info@hbgintl.com
www.hbgintl.com
404-943-0944 • Fax 404-847-0571

HEALTH COMMUNICATIONS

1101 Wilson Blvd Ste 1700
Arlington, VA 22209-2266
703-524-1200

HEALTH REGULATION COMP.
1 Green St
Langhorne, PA 19047-5541
215-750-3184

HEALTH TEC
18401 N 25th Ave Ste B
Phoenix, AZ 85023-1208
www.health-tec.com
480-429-0525 • Fax 480-970-1362

HEALTHETECH
433 Park Point Dr
Golden, CO 80401-5752
303-526-5085

HEARTHWARE HOME PRODUCTS
302 Terrace Dr
Mundelein, IL 60060-3836
888-287-0763

HEARTLAND FOOD PRODUCTS
4930 13th Ave N
St Petersburg, FL 33710-6015
727-321-3066

HEARTLAND PAYMENT SYSTEMS
1600 Golf Rd Ste 1200
Rolling Meadows, IL 60008-4229
847-981-5105 • Fax 847-981-5106

HEARTLAND PAYMENT SYSTEMS
616 Woodbine Dr
Papillion, NE 68046-6038
402-597-2339

HEARTLAND PAYMENT SYSTEMS
9495 E San Salvador Dr Ste 20
Scottsdale, AZ 85258-5539
www.heartlandpaymentsystem.com
888-472-0065 • Fax 480-451-6020

HEAT AND CONTROL INC
225 Shaw Rd
S. San Francisco, CA 94080-6684
650-871-9234

HEAT CRAFT
315 Murfreesboro St
Murfreesboro, TN 37127-4799
www. Infernopizzapak.com
615-907-7501 • Fax 615-907-7571

HEAT RECOVERY TECHNOLOGY
3491 Industrial Hwy
York, PA 17402-9051
800-959-7725

HEATH DESIGN GROUP
316 N Charles St
Baltimore, MD 21201-4302
e-mail:
dasgerholm@heathdesigngroup.com
410-752-2700 • Fax 410-752-2752

HEAVEN HILL DISTILLERIES
PO Box 729
Bardstow, KY 40004-0729
502-348-3921

HECHO A MANO LTD.
PO Box 1304
Wainscott, NY 11975-1304
e-mail: cbarrett@madebyhand.com
www.madebyhand.com
877-429-4263 • Fax 631-283-5018

HEGA FOOD PRODUCTS
238 Saint Nicholas Ave
South Plainfield, NJ 07080-1810
908-753-9100 • Fax 908-753-9635

HEIDI'S GOURMET DESSERTS
1651 Montreal Cir
Tucker, GA 30084-6917
770-491-2100 • Fax 770-491-2112

HEIDI'S GOURMET DESSERTS
6875 Jimmy Carter Blvd
Norcross, GA 30071-1237
770-449-4900

HEINEKEN USA
360 Hamilton Ave
White Plains, NY 10601-1811
914-681-4100 • Fax 914-681-1900

HELLAS INTERNATIONAL INC
35 Congress St
Salem, MA 01970-5529
800-274-1233

HELO SAUNA & STEAM
575 Cokato St E
Cokato, MN 55321-4247
e-mail: helo@saunatec.com
www.helosaunas.com
320-286-6304 • Fax 320-286-2224

HENA LAMPS
8400 Alban Rd
Springfield, VA 22150-2304
703-533-3333

HENKEL'S FOOD CORPORATION
419 Rose Ln
Rockville Center, NY 11570-1429
e-mail: henkels@earthlink.net
www.henkelscaesar.com
516-766-7605 • Fax 516-766-3325

HENNY PENNY
200 Rittenhouse Cir Ste 5
Bristol, PA 19007-1619
215-785-3250 • Fax 215-785-1340

HENNY PENNY CORPORATION
1501 College Ave
South Houston, TX 77587-5407
713-946-6608 • Fax 713-941-0969

HENNY PENNY CORPORATION
1219 Us Route 35 W
Eaton, OH 45320-8671
www.hennypenny.com
937-456-8400 • Fax 937-456-8402

HENRY & HENRY INC
3765 Walden Ave
Lancaster, NY 14086-1494
800 820-7130

HENRY J. EASY PAK MEATS
1160 W Armitage Ave
Chicago, IL 60614-4104
773-227-5400 • Fax 773-227-0414

HENRY HANGER
3101 S Hill St
Los Angeles, CA 90007-3884
213 747-6141 • Fax 213-747-6953

HENRY LEE-SMART & FINAL
3301 NW 125th St
Miami, FL 33167-2409
e-mail: oanne.evans@henrylee.com
305-507-2851

HERITAGE FOOD SVC. EQUIP
5130 Executive Blvd
Fort Wayne, IN 46808-1149
www.hfse.com
260-482-1444 • 800-800-4981

HERLOCHER FOODS INC
415 E Calder Way
State College, PA 16801-5663
e-mail: herlochem@aol.com
814-237-0134 • Fax 814-237-1893

HERMAN-STEWART CONST & DEV INC
7611 S Osborne Rd Ste 205
Upper Marlboro, MD 20772-4200
301-952-8505

HERR FOODS, INC.
PO Box 300
Nottingham, PA 19362-0300
www.herrs.com
610-932-6471 • Fax 610-932-6746

HERSEYS FOODSERVICE
PO Box 0810
100 Crystal A Dr
Hershey, PA 17033-9524
717-534-6584 • Fax 717-534-4395

HEUBLEIN INC

16 Munson Rd
Farmington, CT 06032-2013
860-231-5000

HEWLETT PACKARD
3000 Hanover St
Palo Alto, CA 94304-1181
800-752-0900

HEWLETT PACKARD
19091 Pruneridge Ave
Cupertino, CA 95014-0794
www.resourcelink.org
408-447-0714 • Fax 408-447-2262

HGLOBE.COM
19762 Macarthur Blvd
Irvine, CA 92612-2404
949-553-9664

HIALEAH PRODUCTS-OH NUTS
2207 Hayes St
Hollywood, FL 33020-3437
e-mail: richnuts@aol.com
954-923-3379 • Fax 954-923-4010

HICKORY INDUSTRIES
4900 W Side Ave
North Bergen, NJ 07047-6411
201-223-0050

HICKORY SPECIALTIES
3776 S High St
Columbus, OH 43207-4012
800 251-2076

HICKORY SPRINGS MANUFACTURING
45 Brookside Dr
Roselle, IL 60172-1917
630-235-3162 • Fax 630-582-3868

HIDE-AWAY IRONING BOARDS
PO Box 702624
Tulsa, OK 74170-2624
800-759-4766

HIFFMAN SHAFFER -HSA
180 N Wacker Dr Ste 500
Chicago, IL 60606-1618
312-332-3555

HIGDON FURNITURE
130 N Virginia St
Quincy, FL 32351-1951
850-627-7564

HIGH ENERGY DANCE LIGHTING
2499 Lynnville Hwy
Cornersville, TN 37047-5124
800-880-0883

HIGH TECH PLUMBING
PO Box 890807
Houston, TX 77289-0807
713-488-1510

HIGHEND SYSTEMS
2217 W Braker Ln
Austin, TX 78758-4090
512-836-2242

HILDEN AMERICA, INC.
PO Box 1
South Boston, VA 24592-0001
800-431-2514 • Fax 434-572-4781

HILL & ASSOCIATES-KOPER ENTERPRISES
6304 Windcrest Dr Apt 413
Plano, TX 75024-3019
e-mail: gkoper@aol.com
www.koperenterprises.com
972-378-3686 • Fax 972-378-4036

HILLARY'S SWEET TEMPTATIONS
2677 Forest Ln
Garland, TX 75042-6546
e-mail: baker@hillaryscookies.com
www.hillaryscookies.com
972-485-1005 • Fax 972-485-8866

HILLBILLY JOE
PO Box 91
Van Buren, MO 63965-0091
573-323-5040

HILLI DUNLAP ENTERPRISES, INC.
5301 Laurel Canyon Blvd Ste 25
Valley Village, CA 91607-2736
818-760-7688

HILLSHIRE FARM AND KAHNS COMPANY
3241 Spring Grove Ave
Cincinnati, OH 45225-1329
513-541-4000 • Fax 513-853-1360

HILLSIDE METALWARE CO.
1060 Commerce Ave
Union, NJ 07083-5089
908-964-3080 • Fax 908-964-3082

HILO FISH CO
55 Holomua St
Hilo, HI 96720-5101
808-961-0877

HILTON
6850 N Central Park Ave
Lincolnwood, IL 60712-2703
www.hiltoncorporatecasuals.com
800-323-5590 • Fax 800-441-1044

HILTON HEAD COOKIE COMPANY
PO Box 7994
Hilton Head, SC 29938-7994
e-mail: marcyelam@yahoo.com
843-987-0880 • Fax 843-987-0881

HILTON HOTEL CORPORATION
9336 Civic Center Dr
Beverly Hills, CA 90210-3698
800-321-3232

HILTON TRADING CORP.
7104 NW 50th St
Miami, FL 33166-5636
e-mail:
marketing@hiltontradingcorp.com
www.hiltontradingcorp.com
305-594-0950 • Fax 305-594-0953

HINDS-BOCK CORPORATION
14690 NE 95th St
Redmond, WA 98052-1014
425-885-1183

HIS
6405 Congress Ave Ste 120
Boca Raton, FL 33487-2861
www.his-solution.com
561-241-9998 • Fax 516-241-8457

HIS
3701 Fau Blvd Ste 200
Boca Raton, FL 33431-6491
e-mail: info@his-solutions.com
www.his-solutions.com
877-HIS-9900

HIS
9977 N 90th St Ste 150
Scottsdale, AZ 85258-4426
e-mail: info@his-solutions.com
www.his-solutions.com
877-474-9900 • Fax 480-707-6223

HITACHI-AMERICA
3617 Parkway Ln
Norcross, GA 30092-2836
www.hitel.com
770-446-8821 • Fax 770-242-2555

HITEC GROUP INTERNATIONAL
8160 S Madison St
Willowbrook, IL 60527-5854
630-654-9200

HL&A CONTRACT LIGHTING MAGAZINE
1011 Clifton Ave
Clifton, NJ 07013-3518
e-mail: contract@hoelighting.com
973-779-1600 • Fax 973-779-3242

HM ELECTRONICS
6675 Mesa Ridge Rd
San Diego, CA 92121-3996
www.hme.com
800-848-4468 • Fax 858-552-0139

HMS GROUP, THE
195 McGregor St Ste 322
Manchester, NH 03102-3749
e-mail: shenry@thehmsgroup.com
603-644-5565 • Fax 603-644-4863

HMS POSCHANNEL
111 8th Ave
New York, NY 10011-5201
e-mail: sales@hms-inc.com
www.poschannel.com
212-647-0091 • Fax 212-647-0392

HMS REMACS
PO Box 365
Merrimack, NH 03054-036
e-mail: remacs@nehms.com
www.nehms.com
603-429-0150 • Fax 603-429-0712

HOBART
5424 W Waters Ave
Tampa, FL 33634-1294
e-mail: bryanaj@pmi.feg.com
813-884-3466 • Fax 813-887-3553

HOBART CORP
16860 W Victor Rd
New Berlin, WI 53151-4133
262-782-0100 • Fax 262-782-6801

HOBART CORP.
75 Stergis Way
Dedham, MA 02026-2637
781-329-3340 • Fax 718-329-3482

HOBART CORPORATION
701 S Ridge Ave
Troy, OH 45374-0001
www.hobartcorp.com
937-332-3000 • Fax 937-332-2585

HOBART CORPORATION
1000 Riverbend Dr Ste H
Saint Rose, LA 70087-3024
504-465-0490

HOBART CORPORATION.
8120 Jetstar Dr Ste 100
Irving, TX 75063-2800
e-mail: kauffmp@pmi.com
972-915-6831 • Fax 972-915-6830

HOCKENBERGS
7002 F St
Omaha, NE 68117-1013
402-339-8900

HODELL INTERNATIONAL
1750 N University Dr Ste 230
Pompano Beach, FL 33071-8900
954-752-0010 • Fax 954-752-0080

HODGES COMPANY
4645 W Walton St
Chicago, IL 60651-3341
800-444-0011

HODGES WARD ELLIOT
3399 Peachtree Rd NE
Atlanta, GA 30326-1120
404-233-6000

HOECHST-TREVIRA
PO Box 87
Shelby, NC 28151-0087

HOECKER INC
11595 Kelly Rd # 115
Fort Meyers, FL 33908-2539
800-482-9505

HOFFMASTER
PO Box 2038
Oshkosh, WI 54903-2038
800-558-9300

HOGATEC
150 N Michigan Ave
Chicago, IL 60601-7553
312-781-5180

HOLDSTICK, LTD.
6065 Roswell Rd NE Ste 420
Atlanta, GA 30328-4014
404-257-1400 • Fax 404-847-0491

HOLIDAY FOODS
2050 McKinley St
Hollywood, FL 33020-3119
www.holidayfoods.com
954-921-7786

HOLIDAY INN WORLDWIDE
3 Ravinia Dr
Atlanta, GA 30346-2118
770-604-2104

HOLLERAN CONSULTING
2901 Whiteford Rd
York, PA 17402-8976
717-757-2802 • Fax 717-755-7661

HOLLMAN INC
1825 W Walnut Hill Ln Ste 110
Irving, TX 75038-4453
972-313-1121

HOLLOWICK
316 Fayette St
Manlius, NY 13104-1699
www.hollowick.com
315-682-2163 • Fax 315-682-6948

HOLLY INTL MEDI-RUB M
240 Calle Pintoresco
San Clemente, CA 92672-7504
e-mail: medirub1@aol.com
949-369-6900 • Fax 949-366-6363

HOLLY INTMEDI-RULE MASSAGERS
PO Box 265
Lake Elsinore, CA 92531-0265
909-678-8386 • Fax 909-678-7856

HOLLY RIDGE FOODS
PO Box 116
Holly Ridge, NC 28445-0116
910-329-9061 • Fax 910-329-1999

HOLLYMATIC CORP
600 E Plainfield Rd
La Grange, IL 60525-6900
708-579-3700

HOLLYWOOD GOURMET COFFEE
2238 Hayes St
Hollywood, FL 33020-3438
www.sangiorgiocoffee.com
954-927-6278

HOLMAN COOKING EQUIPMENT
PO Box 880
Saco, ME 04072-0880
207-282-1589

HOLMES ASSOC BRUCE
4900 Richmond Sq Ste 104
Oklahoma City, OK 73118-2042
580-496-8686

HOLSTEIN MANUFACTURING, INC.
5368 110th St
Holstein, IA 51025-8131
www.barbequeholstein.com
712-368-4342 • Fax 712-368-2351

HOLSUM FOODS
500 S Prairie Ave
Waukesha, WI 53186-5955
800-558-2007

HOLT HUGHES STAMELL
50 Monument Sq
Portland, ME 04101-4039
207-871-1310 • Fax 207-775-1714

HOLTEN MEAT, INC.
1682 Sauget Business Blvd
East Saint Louis, IL 62206-1454
e-mail: egonzalez@holtenment.com
www.holtenmeat.com
618-337-8400 • Fax 618-337-7266

HOME BOX OFFICE INC
1100 Avenue Of The Americas
New York, NY 10036-6712
212-512-1000

HOME ECONOMICS CAREER - PREP
5100 Maple St # 1
Bellaire, TX 77401-4936
713-295-3736 • Fax 713-295-3763

HOME MADE BRAND FOODS
2 Opportunity Way
Newburyport, MA 01950-4043
e-mail: donna.alderette@hmbf.com
978-462-3663 • Fax 978-462-7117

HOME MARKET FOODS
507 Circle Dr
Burlington, NC 27215-5011
336-436-0009 • Fax 336-436-0009

HOME RUN INN FROZEN FOODS
1300 Internationale Pkwy
Woodridge, IL 60517-4928
630-783-9696 • Fax 630-783-0069

HONEYWELL
5353 W Bell Rd
Glendale, AZ 85308-3900
602-436-4466

HONEYWELL COMMERCIAL AIR PRODUCTS
4524 E Highway 20
Niceville, FL 32578-9755
800-997-1919 • Fax 800-221-3248

HONEYWELL INC
1985 Douglas Dr N
Minneapolis, MN 55422-3992
763-954-6945

HONEYWELL POWER SYSTEMS
8725 Pan American Fwy NE
Albuquerque, NM 87113-1938
e-mail:
greg.gonzalez@honeywell.com
www.Parallon75.com
505-798-6406 • Fax 505-798-6070

HOOVER CO
101 E Maple St
Canton, OH 44720-2597
www.hoover.com
330-499-9200 • Fax 330-497-5808

HOPE HEALTH DEPOT, INC
4205 Brooktree Ln
Dallas, TX 75287-6721
www.hopehealthdepot.com
972-407-9129 • Fax 972-407-9687

HORIZON ORGANIC DAIRY
PO Box 17577
Boulder, CO 80308-0577
800-237-2711

HORMEL FOODS
1 Hormel Pl
Austin, MN 55912-3680
507-437-5611 • Fax 507-437-5158

HORNELL BREWING
1191 Morris Ave
Union, NJ 07083-3378
908-687-9102 • Fax 908-687-9436

HORWATH INTERNATIONAL
415 Madison Ave
New York, NY 10017-1111
212-838-5566

HOSEMASTER
1233 E 222nd St
Euclid, OH 44117-1121
216-481-2020

HOSHIZAKI
618 Highway 74 S
Peachtree City, GA 30269-3016
www.hoshizaki .com
770-487-2331 • Fax 770-487-1325

HOSHIZAKI
14829 Trinity Blvd
Fort Worth, TX 76155-2683
e-mail: jrwilkins@hoshizaki.com
www.hoshizaki.com
817-540-4665 • Fax 817-283-8562

HOSHIZAKI NORTHEASTERN
20 Drexel Dr
Bay Shore, NY 11706-2202
www.hoshizaki.com

HOSNET INTERNATIONAL,
PO Box 22867
Orlando, FL 32830-2867
321-396-1313

HOSPITAL SPECIALTY CO
7501 Carnegie Ave
Cleveland, OH 44103-4896
800-323-2443

HOSPITALITY & GAMING RISK MGMT
3335 Wynn Rd
Las Vegas, NV 89102-8218
702-871-6780

HOSPITALITY CONCEPTS-ONEIDA
5854 San Felipe St Ste 6
Houston, TX 77057-3079
713-984-1985 • Fax 713-984-1984

HOSPITALITY DESIGN EXPO
PO Box 17413
Washigton, DC 20041-0413
800-785-7815

HOSPITALITY FIN TECH PROF
11709 Boulder Ln
Austin, TX 78726-1833
512-249-5333

HOSPITALITY INTERNATIONAL INC
1726 Montreal Cir
Tucker, GA 30084-6819
800-247-4677

HOSPITALITY MARKETING GROUP
292 Sugarberry Cir
Houston, TX 77024-7248
713-789-9215

HOSPITALITY MINT
213 Candy Ln
Boone, NC 28607-6713
www.hospitalitymints.com
828-264-3040 • Fax 704-364-6933

HOSPITALITY MINTS
PO Box 780076
Maspeth, NY 11378-0076
718-476-3663 • Fax 718-476-9004

HOSPITALITY MINTS
PO Box 3140
Boone, NC 28607-3140
e-mail: mints@boone.net
www.hospitalitymints.com
828-264-3045 • Fax 828-264-6933

HOSPITALITY NET
11200 Rockville Pike
Rockville, MD 20852-3154
301-468-4984

HOSPITALITY PROFILES
30 Technology Pkwy S
Norcross, GA 30092-2912
e-mail: drrick.fyffe@cmdg.com
www.hponl.com
800-259-1654 • Fax 770-209-3669

HOSPITALITY SAFE CORP.
10214 NW 47th St
Fort Lauderdale, FL 33351-7980
e-mail: 740962@prodigy.net
800-545-4947 • Fax 877-897-3234

HOSPITALITY SALES WRKSHP
810 University City Blvd
Blacksburg, VA 24060-3825
540-231-5182

HOSPITALITY SOFNET, INC.
60 State St Ste 700
Boston, MA 02109-1803
e-mail:
Lrichards@hospitalitysoftnet.com
www.hospitalitysoftnet.com
617-854-6554 • Fax 617-731-1602

HOSPITALITY SOLUTIONS
4 Morgan Rd
Beverly, MA 01915-4708
www.h-soulutions.co
978-921-1133

HOSPITALITY SOLUTIONS INTERNATIONAL
6405 Congress Ave
Boca Raton, FL 33487-2844
954-596-5451

HOSPITALITY SYSTEMS INTEGRATION SOLUTIONS
PO Box 770294
Pompano Beach, FL 33077-0294
954-830-9159

HOSPITALITY TECHNOLOGY
10 W Hanover Ave
Randolph, NJ 07869-4221
www.htmagazine.com
973-895-3300 • Fax 973-895-7711

HOSPITALITY TECHNOLOGY-EDGELL
4 Middlebury Blvd
Randolph, NJ 07869-1111
e-mail: lhausman@edgellmail.com
www.htmagazine.com
973-252-0100 • Fax 973-252-9020

HOSPITALITY UPGRADE, THE TECHNOLOGY
3200 Windy Hill Rd SE Ste 40
Atlanta, GA 30339-5640
e-mail: resiegal@hospitalityupgrade.com
770-953-2300 • Fax 770-953-2309

HOSPITALITY WORKS
3924 W Devon Ave
Lincolnwood, IL 60712-1043

HOSPITALITYPRODUCTS.COM
15350 Barranca Pkwy
Irvine, CA 92618-2215
e-mail:
Patrick@HospitalityProducts.com
www.HospitalityProducts.com
949-789-5359 • Fax 949-789-9038

HOSPITALITYZONE.COM
331 Montvale Ave Ste 3
Woburn, MA 01801-4670
www.hospitalityzone.com
781-935-2227 • Fax 781-939-5899

HOSTAR INTERNATIONAL
18845 NE 49th Pl
Sammamish, WA 98074-3200
e-mail: hostar@hostar.com
www.hostar.com
425-868-0400 • Fax 425 868 2220

HOSTMARK HOSPITALITY GROUP
1111 N Plaza Dr
Schaumburg, IL 60173-6021
847-517-9100

HOT FOOD BOXES INC.
4109 W Lake St
Chicago, IL 60624-1719
www.hotfoodboxes.com
773-553-5912 • Fax 773-533-5475

HOT SAUCE HARRY
10606 Shady Trl Ste 20
Dallas, TX 75220-2524
e-mail: bob@hotsauceharry.com
214-902-8522 • Fax 214-956-9885

HOTEL & MOTEL MANAGEMENT MAGAZINE
7500 Old Oak Blvd
Cleveland, OH 44130-3343
e-mail: hnm@advanstar.com
www.hmmonline.com
440-891-3105 • Fax 440-891-3120

HOTEL & REST. DEPT. CITY
50 Phelan Ave
San Francisco, CA 94112-1821
www.ccsf.org-hotelandrestaurant
415-239-3455 • Fax 415-239-3913

HOTEL ASSOCIATION OF NY
437 Madison Ave Fl 36
New York, NY 10022-7001
e-mail: hotel@hancy.org
www.hancy.org
212-754-9300 • Fax 212-754-0243

HOTEL BROKER ONE
4900 Richmond Sq
Oklahoma City, OK 73118-2028
405-810-1414

HOTEL BUSINESS
45 Research Way Ste 106
East Setauket, NY 11733-6401
www.hotelbusiness.com
631-246-9300 • Fax 631-246-9696

HOTEL CONCEPTS USA, LLC
325 Chestnut St Ste 400
Philadelphia, PA 19106-2604

e-mail: info@hotelconcepts.com
www.hotelconcepts.com
215-928-9370 • Fax 215-928-9366

HOTEL INFORMATION SYSTEMS
9601 Jeronimo Rd
Irvine, CA 92618-2025
e-mail: sales@hotelinfosys.com
www.hotelinfosys.com
800-497-0532 • Fax 949-598-6324

HOTEL INTERACTIVE
160 E Main St
Huntington, NY 11743-2948
e-mail: jallen@hotelinteractive.com
www.hotelinteractive.com
631-424-7755 • Fax 631-424-8797

HOTEL INTERNET TECHNOLOGY
5610 NW 12th Ave Ste 209
Fort Lauderdale, FL 33309-6608
e-mail: info@hotelinternettech.com
www.hotelinternettech.com
954-491-0867 • Fax 954-491-2608

HOTEL-MOTEL ASSOCIATION OF ILLINOIS
27 E Monroe St Ste 1200
Chicago, IL 60603-5672
www.hmai.com
312-346-3135 • Fax 312-346-6036

HOTEL MOTEL REST SUPPLY
PO Box 332
Myrtle Beach, SC 29578-0332
800-261-8991

HOTEL TECHNOLOGY BUYERS CLUB
1 Beach St
Narragansett, RI 02882-3356
877-436-3331

HOTELNET.COM
1100 Sherm St Ste 1400
Denver, CO 80204-2049
www.hotelnet.com
303-623-8880 • Fax 303-623-8881

HOTELS MAGAZINE
1350 E Touhy Ave
Des Plaines, IL 60018-3303
www.hotelsmag.com
847-635-8800 • Fax 847-635-6856

HOTELSUPPLIES.COM
1265 N Manassero St
Anaheim, CA 92807-1973
800-728-6869

HOTELTOOLS
300 Galleria Pkwy SE Ste 12
Atlanta, GA 30339-3153
404-799-5380 • Fax 770-951-1021

HOTELTOOLS INC
100 Galleria Pkwy SE
Atlanta, GA 30339-3179
770-956-4080

HOTELWORKS.COM
201 Alhambra Cir
Miami, FL 33134-5107
305-774-3000

HOTSHOT BY DELIVERY CONCEPTS
155 Covington Dr
Bloomingdale, IL 60108-310
www.deliverconveryconcepts.com
630-924-8817 • Fax 630-924-8819

HOUSE OF RAEFORD FARMS
520 E Central Ave
Raeford, NC 28376-3020
www.houseofraeford.com
910-875-5161 • Fax 910-875-8300

HOUSE OF TROY
902 Silver Ridge Rd
Hyde Park, VT 05655-9396
www.houseoftroy.com
800-585-1145 • Fax 802-373-1569

HOUSE OF WEBSTER
1013 N 2nd St
Rogers, AR 72756-2898
479-636-4640 • Fax 479-636-2974

HOUSTON CHRONICLE-GUSTO OFFICE
2211 Norfolk St Ste 1060
Houston, TX 77098-4056
713-524-5535 • Fax 713-524-5545

HOUSTON COMMUNITY COLLEGE
1300 Holman St Rm 30
Houston, TX 77004-3898
e-mail: moradi_e@hccs.cc.tx.us
www.hccs.cc.tx.us
713-718-6072 • Fax 713-718-6073

HOUSTON LINEN SERVICE
347 Delz St
Houston, T 77018-1615
e-mail: houlinen@aol.com
713-691-5511 • Fax 713-691-5693

HOUSTON MACK-ISUZU
5216 N McCarty St
Houston, TX 77013-2504
e-mail: sales@houstonmack.com
www.houstonmack.com
713-673-1444 • Fax 713-673-7354

HOWARD MILLER (HEKMAN AND WOOD)
860 E Main Ave
Zeeland, MI 49464-1365
e-mail: johnera@howardmiller.com
www.howardmiller.com
616-772-9131 • Fax 616-772-5897

HOWARD-MCCRAY REFRIGERTATOR
2501 Grant Ave
Philadelphia, PA 19114-2307
215-464-6800 • Fax 215-969-4890

HOWW MFG
PO Box 276
Barrington, IL 60011-0276
800-223-4649

HR NICHOLSON CO
6320 Oakleaf Ave
Baltimore, MD 21215-2288
410-764-2323 • Fax 410-764-9125

HRM CONSULTING LLC
1000 W Nifong Blvd Ste 300-1
Columbia, MO 65203-5661
573-256-8888

HRT, INC. POOL PARK
PO Box 3452
York, PA 17402-0452
e-mail: info@hrt-inc.com
www.hrt-inc.com
717-757-2648 • Fax 717-757-5085

HSMAI HOSPITALITY SALES & MARKETING
1300 L St NW
Washington DC 20005-4107
e-mail: bgilbert@hsmai.org
www.hsmai.org
202-789-0089 • Fax 202-789-1725

HSS—HOTEL SOFTWARE SYSTEMS
9320 SW Barbur Blvd # T
Portland, OR 97219-5437
e-mail: kfuller2@juno.com3
503-768-9100 • Fax 503-768-9200

HUB GRINDING SERVICE
10 Hartshorn Rd
Walpole, MA 02081-3504
508-668-9344 • Fax 508-660-8804

HUBBARRDTON FORGE
PO Box 827
Castleton, VT 05735-0827
e-mail: info@vtforge.com
www.vtforge.com
800-826-4766 • Fax 802-468-3284

HUBER & ASSOCIATES
6116 Fox Valley Dr
Prospect, KY 40059-8603
502-228-8098

HUBERT
9555 Dry Fork Rd
Harrison, OH 45030-1994
800-543-7374

HUDDLE HOUSE RESTAURANTS
365 E Winthrope Ave
Millen, GA 30442-1640
478-982-2222

HUDSON AWNING & SIGN-HUDSON ST
27 Cottage St
Bayonne, NJ 07002-4334
800-624-1012 • Fax 201-339-9858

HUFCOR, INC.
PO Box 591
Janesville, WI 53547-0591
e-mail: hufcor@hufcor.com
www.hufcor.com
800-542-2371 • Fax 608-758-8253

HUISKEN MEATS
1911 W 57th St
Sioux Falls, SD 57108-2875
800-852-1863

HULMAN & CO. MFG
900 Wabash Ave
Terre Haute, IN 47807-3208
812-232-9446

HUMICON CIGARS & HUMIDORS
639A Old Willets Path
Hauppauge, NY 11788-4105
e-mail: sales@humicon.com
www.humicon.com
631-582-8850 • Fax 631-582-9302

HUNT WESSON FOODSERVICE
200 Boysenberry Lane
Placentia, CA 92870-6413
714-680-1000 • Fax 714-578-6040

HUNT WESSON INC
1645 W Valencia Dr # M
Fullerton, CA 92833-3860
714-578-6286 • Fax 714-578-6122

HUNTER CO, R.F.
113 Crosby Rd
Dover, NH 03820-4370
603-742-9565

HUNTER FAN
2500 Frisco Ave
Memphis, TN 38114-4889
e-mail: rross@hunterfan.com
901-248-2235 • Fax 901-248-2265

HUNTER GROUP
480 Central Ave
Winnetka, IL 60093-3016
847-441-6500

HUNT-WESSON FOODS
7217 W Morgan Ave
Milwaukee, WI 53220-1123
414-327-5111 • Fax 414-327-6085

HUSSMANN CORP
12999 Saint Charles Rock Rd
Bridgeton, MO 63044-2483
www.Hussmann.com
314-291-2000

HV COVILLO & CO., INC.
1777 S Harrison St
Denver, CO 80210-3925
303-759-9875

HVS TECHNOLOGY STRATEGIES
2229 Broadway St
Boulder, CO 80302-4824
e-mail: ghartmann@hvsit.com
www.hvsit.com
303-443-3933 • Fax 303-443-4186

HY TEST SAFETY FOOTWEAR
9341 Courtland Dr
Rockford, MI 49351-0001
www.hytest.com
800-635-4536 • Fax 616-866-7617

HYATT HOTELS & RESORTS
200 W Madison S
Chicago, IL 60606-3414
www.hyatt.com
312-750-1234 • Fax 312-920-2350

HYCO RESTAURANT SUPPLY DIVISION
967 E 149th St
Bronx, NY 10455-5021
718-292-6800 • Fax 718-292-8171

HYDROGIENE CORPORATION
11870 Caminito Ronaldo Apt 139
San Diego, CA 92128-4820
858-675-0857 • Fax 858-675-8070

HYDROPEDES
108 Carolwood Blvd
Casselberry, FL 32730-2908
321-447-9223 • Fax 321-438-0671

HYDROPEDE
PO Box 61404
Fort Myers, FL 33906-1404
239-939-7150 • Fax 239-939-7150

HYDROPEDES INSOLES
554 Rosa Ave
Metairie, LA 70005-2811

HYDROPURE SYSTEM, INC.
7804 Anderson Rd
Tampa, FL 33634-3006
www.hydropure.ebb.net
888-880-1829 • Fax 813-885-2316

HYGRADE PRODUCTS
1718 Bean Oller Rd
Delaware, OH 43015-7804
www.hygradeproducts.com
614-759-6168

HYPERMEALS.COM
5934 N Northwest Hwy
Chicago, IL 60631-2643
www.hypermeals.com
773-775-6850 • Fax 773-467-1760

I B M CORP
1 N Castle Dr
Armonk, NY 10504-1725
845-465-1900

I F C O UNITED STATES
5401 W Kennedy Blvd Ste 711
Tampa, FL 33609-2447
800-444-4274

I G M-INTERNATIONAL GOLF MANAGEMENT
331 S Florida Ave
Lakeland, FL 33801-4626
863-686-2376

I H M SYSTEMS
518 Johnson Ave
Bohemia, NY 11716-2639
800-446-5463

I P I X
1009 Commerce Park Dr Ste 400
Oak Ridge, TN 37830-8008
888-909-4749

I S I NORTH AMERICA INC
PO Box 11316
Fairfield, NJ 07004-7316
973-227-2426

I.N.S. OFFICE OF BUSINESS LIAISONS
425 I St # 3034
Washington DC 20536-0001
e-mail:
Crystal.A.Coulson@usdoj.gov
202-305-2462 • Fax 202-305-2462

IAP-INTERNATIONAL ART PROPERTIES
101 Henry Adams St Ste 380
San Francisco, CA 94103-5223
e-mail: iap@hooked.net
www.iapsf.com
415-863-3406 • Fax 415-863-3530

IB ROOF SYSTEMS
2877 Chad Dr
Eugene, OR 97408-7396
www.ibroof.com
800-426-162 • Fax 877-741-1160

IBC (INTL BEDDING CORP.)
701 W Landstreet Rd
Orlando. FL 32824-8022
e-mail: roy@bcgroup.com
407-851-8169 • Fax 407-857-1564

IBERTECH-ALOHA
235 NE Loop 820
Hurst, TX 76053-7328
817-284-2488

IBM CORP-IBM FOOD CONS. GRP.
PO Box 12195
Durham, NC 27709-2195
919-301-5809

IBP INC
PO Box 515
Dakota City, NE 68731-0515
402-241-2820 • Fax 402-241-3121

ICE CREAM PARTNERS, USA
12647 Alcosta Blvd
San Ramon, CA 94583-4439
925-327-8130 • Fax 925-328-1004

ICEBERG CORPORATION OF AMERICA
252 Park Ave
Allendale, NJ 07401-2105
e-mail: Iceberg@idt.net
www.borealisice.com
201-760-0198 • Fax 201-760-0198

ICEE COMPANY
10232B Rahning Rd
Saint Louis, MO 63127-1707
314-842-7003

ICELAND SEAFOOD CORP.
190 Enterprise Dr
Newport News, VA 23603-1368
757-820-4000 • Fax 757-888-6250

ICE-O-MATIC (A WELBILT COMPANY)
11100 E 45th Ave
Denver, CO 80239-3006
303-371-3737 • Fax 303-371-6296

ICOM AMERICA INC
2380 116th Ave NE
Bellevue, WA 98004-3036
425-454-8155

ICS
1610 Saint Charles Ave
New Orleans, LA 70130-4436
504-587-9170 • Fax 504-587-9167

ID MAGAZINE
355 Park Ave S
New York, NY 10010-1706
www.foodservicetoday.com
212-592-6500 • Fax 212-592-6613

IDAHO PACIFIC CORP
PO Box 478
Ririe, ID 83443-0478
208-538-6971

IDAHO POTATO COMMISSION
599 W Bannock St
Boise, ID 83702-5917
www.idahopotato.com
208-334-2350 • Fax 208-334-2274

IDAHO-OREGON ONION
PO Box 909
Parma, ID 83660-0909
208-722-5111

IDEA ART
PO Box 291505
Nashville, TN 37229-1505
800-433-2278

IDEAL FIRE CONTROL, INC.
132 Metropolitan Ave
Brooklyn, NY 11211-3921
www.idealfire.com
718-384-1215 • Fax 718-782-3190

IDEAL PRODS INC
1625 Fremont Ct
Ontario, CA 91761-8309
909-923-3311

IDENTISCAN CO
420 Somers Rd
Ellington, CT 06029-2629
860-871-7540

IDV-HEUBLEIN, INC.
PO Box 778
Hartford, CT 06142-0778
860-702-4585

IGEMAR
4550 N Pershing Ave
Stockton, CA 95207-6745
209-472-7078

IGLOO PRODUCTS CORP.
1001 W Sam Houston Pkwy N
Houston, TX 77043-5011
www.igloocommercial.com
713-461-5955 • Fax 713-935-7763

IGUANA TOM'S INC
PO Box 473431
Charlotte, NC 28247-3431
e-mail: info@iguanatoms.com
704-847-4857

IHF FOODSERVICE
1633 Littleton Rd
Parsippany, NJ 07054-3808
973-254-5471 • Fax 973-254-5474

IHW, INC.
170 53rd St
Brooklyn, NY 11232-4319
info@ihwusa.net
718-492-8400 • Fax 71-849-23878

ILCO UNICAN
2941 Indiana Ave
Winston Salem, NC 27105-4425
336-725-1331

ILLINOIS RANGE COMPANY
708 W Central Rd
Mount Prospect, IL 60056-2339
847-253-4950

ILLINOIS RESTAURANT ASSOC.
200 N La Salle St Ste 880
Chicago, IL 60601-1030
312-787-4000 • Fax 312-787-4792

ILLUMINATING EXPERIENCE
233 Cleveland Ave
Highland Park, NJ 08904-1841
732-745-5858

ILLY ESPRESSO
200 Clearbrook Rd
Elmsford, NY 10523-1314
www.illy.com
800-455-969 • Fax 914-784-0580

ILLY ESPRESSO OF AMERICA
15455 N Greenway Hayden Loop
Scottsdale, AZ 85260-1611
800-8722-4559

IMAGE DIFFERENTIATORS INC
PO Box 11277
Springfield, MO 65808-1277
417-887-6086 • Fax 417-882-1636

IMAGE TIME, INC.
2519 Pittsburgh Rd
Perryopolis, PA 15473-1011
www.neonclock.com
724-736-8200 • Fax 724-736-8082

IMAGE WORKS, INC.
PO Box 20379
Atlanta, GA 30325-0379
404-350-2100

IMC-TEDDY
50 Ranick Dr E
Amityville, NY 11701-2822
800-221-5644 • Fax 631-789-3633

IMEX ENTERPRISES, INC.
110 Gerstley Rd
Hatboro, PA 19040-1911
e-mail: imexenter@aol.com
215-672-2887 • Fax 215-672-9552

IMI CORNELIUS
1 Cornelius Pl
Anok, MN 55303-6234
www.cornelius.com
800-238-360 • Fax 763-422-3255

IMI CORNELIUS INC.
10400 E Hillery Dr
Scottsdale, AZ 85259-8565
602-421-6120 • Fax 602-422-3255

IMPACT GROUP
6550 S Pecos Rd
Las Vegas, NV 89120-2828
www.impactgrouplv.com
702-450-4133 • Fax 702-547-9533

IMPACT GROUP
122 Old Route 202
Pomona, NY 10970-2823
e-mail: infor@impaccgroupay.com
845-354-3133

IMPACT SIGN & DESIGN, INC
10360 72nd St Ste 804
Seminole, FL 33777-1545
e-mail:
impactsigns@mindspring.com
www.impactsignanddesign.com
727-541-3730

IMPACT USA, LP
117 S Morgan St Ste 100
Chicago, IL 60607-2669
www.eimpactusa.com
312-491-0701 • Fax 312-491-0710

IMPASTI MIXERS
2365 Hammond Dr
Schaumburg, IL 60173-3815
e-mail: info@impastimixers.com
847-397-6981 • Fax 847-397-6817

IMPERATIVES
2818 Curry Rd
Schenectady, NY 12303-3463
e-mail: jill@imperatives.com
www.imperatives.com
518-356-5160 • Fax 518-356-5161

IMPERIAL COMMERCIAL COOKING
1560 Flower Ave
Duarte, CA 91010-2925
e-mail: impsls@imperialrange.com
626-357-7411 • Fax 626-359-4983

IMPERIAL ESPRESSO COMPANY
3582 Rocking J Rd
Round Rock, TX 78664-9494
e-mail:
imperialespresso@mail.ev1.net
512-255-0079 • Fax 512-255-0476

IMPERIAL MARBLE
327 E Lasalle St # O
Somonauk, IL 60552-9561
815-498-2303 • Fax 815-498-3732

IMPERIAL TRADING COMPANY
701 Edwards Ave
New Orleans, LA 70123-3157
www.ecigar.com
504-733-1400 • Fax 504-736-4158

IMPERIAL-DIAMOND CRYSTEL
PO Box 9
Sugar Land, TX 77487-0009
e-mail: tspears@imperialsugar.com
800-727-8427 • Fax 281-490-9584

IMPEX DEVELOPMENT LLC
2203 1st Ave S
Seattle, WA 98134-1446
e-mail:
hjo@impexdevelopment.com
206-46-71972 • Fax 206-467-1896

IMPORTED RESTAURANT SPECIALTIES
331 Curie Dr
Alpharetta, GA 30005-2264
404-325-0585 • Fax 404-325-0342

IMPROVEMYRESTAURANT.COM
1201 3rd Ave
Seattle, WA 98101-3029
www.improvemyrestaurant.com
206-903-6300 • Fax 206-903-6671

IMR CORPORATION
639 Manhattan Blvd
Harvey, LA 70058-4420
504-362-9888

IN -BOARDS, BY TED'S SIGNS
1417 Alexander St
Statesville, NC 28677-3868
704-872-0038

IN VISION CONSULTING
2 5th Ave Apt 7Q
New York, NY 10011-8836
e-mail: glecooy@aol.com
www.invision
212-475-7759 • Fax 212-473-9768

IN-BOARDS, INDOOR MOTION BILLBOARDS
305 Seaboard Ln Ste 304
Franklin, TN 37067-8288
www.in-boards.com
615-331-1654

INCA SPIRITS, INC.
PO Box 5742
Atlanta, GA 31107-0742
e-mail: wabauer69@yahoo.com
404-876-6727

INCHCAPE TESTING SERVICES
1 Tech Dr
Andover, MA 01810-2452
978-689-9353

INCREDIBLE TECHNOLOGIES
1600 Hicks Rd
Rolling Meadows, IL 60008-1231
800-262-0323 • Fax 847-870-0120

INCRETE SYSTEMS
PO Box 151103
Tampa, FL 33684-1103
e-mail: marketing@increte.com
www.increte.com
813-886-8811 • Fax 813-886-0188

INDEL B-BARTECH
1 Sharps Rock Dr
Hopatcong, NJ 07843-1623
miveron@minibar sales.com
www.indelb.it
888-517-8924 • Fax 800-858-0721

INDEL FOODS
11415 Cedar Oak Dr
El Paso, TX 79936-6009
915-590-5914 • Fax 915-590-5916

INDEPENDENT CAN COMPANY
4500 Wharf Point Ct
Belcamp, MD 21017-1212
e-mail:
salesdept@independentcan.com
410-272-0090 • Fax 410-273-7500

INDEPENDENT INSURANCE ASSOCIATION
710 Baronne St
New Orleans, LA 70113-1062
504-586-1000

INDEPENDENT RESTAURANT ASSOCIATION
PO Box 3445
Lawrence, KS 66046-0445
www.kitchenmanager.com
785-841-3656 • Fax 785-841-6671

INDEX SENSORS & CONTROLS, INC.
7112 265th St NW
Stanwood, WA 98292-6293
www.indexsensors.com
360-821-6400 • Fax 360-821-4112

INDIAN HARVEST SPECIALTY FOODS
PO Box 428
Bemidji, MN 56619-0428
916-458-8512

INDIAN ROCK PRODUCE
530 California Rd
Quakertown, PA 18951-2409
800-882-0512 • Fax 215-529-9447

INDIANA CARTON CO. INC.
1721 W Bike St # B
Bremen, IN 46506-2123
e-mail:
feedback@indianacarton.com
574-546-384 • Fax 574-546-5953

INDIANA GLASS LANCASTER COLONE
PO Box 630
Columbus, OH 43216-0630
www.iccpinc.com
614-263-2850 • Fax 614-263-2857

INDO CLEANING CONCEPTS
5203 Leesburg Pike Ste 907
Falls Church, VA 22041-3468
703-718-9238 • Fax 703-718-0329

INDON INTERNATIONAL
PO Box 103
West Point, MS 39773-0103
662-494-6474 • Fax 662-494-0992

INDOOR AIR—QUALITY CONTROL
907 Twinbrooke Dr
Houston, TX 77088-2012
281-445-0736

INDOORABLE, INC.
295 Madison Ave Fl 45
New York, NY 10017-6304
e-mail: LeoHubermann@aol.com
212-271-0403 • Fax 212-271-0404

INDUSTRIAL ENVIRONMENTAL
127 Bruckner Blvd
Bronx, NY 10454-4698
e-mail: foamatic@cs.com
718-585-2410 • Fax 718-292-8353

INDUSTROZONE TECH
1601 W Marion Ave
Punta Gorda, FL 33950-3202
800-736-1351

INDUSTROZONE TECHNOLOGIES
1601 W Marion Ave Ste 1
Punta Gorda, FL 33950-3202
e-mail: industrozone@snl.net
www.industrozone.com
941-575-980 • Fax 941-575-7571

INETHOTEL BY SENTR@NET
4801 W 81st St Ste 112
Minneapolis, MN 55437-1111
e-mail: ebergerson@sentranet.com
www.centranet.com
952-841-7490 • Fax 952-841-7497

INFANTI INTERNATIONAL INC.
PO Box 4
Middletown, NJ 07748-0004
e-mail: infantiinernational.com
718-447-5632 • Fax 718-447-5667

INFEPRO, INC.
9 Allen Pl
Bronxville, NY 10708-4501
e-mail: Christobe@worldnet.att.net
866-846-3377 • Fax 914-738-5732

INFINITY A.V.L.
2525 Royal Ln Ste 316
Dallas, TX 75229-3429
972-247-9993

INFOFISH
PO Box 462
Fair Oaks, CA 95628-0462
916-967-3502

INFOGENESIS
1351 Holiday Hill Rd
Golet, CA 93117-1815
e-mail: posinfo@infogenesis.com
www.infogenesis.com
805-681-8600 • Fax 805-681-8609

INFORMATION ACCESS INC
8801 E Pleasant Valley Rd
Independence, OH 44131-5510
216-328-0100 • Fax 216-328-0913

INFORMATION RETRIEVAL METHODS
1525 N Interstate 35E
Carrolito, TX 75006-3890
972-389-3100 • Fax 972-323-1805

INFOTRONICS
23370 Commerce Dr
Farmington, MI 48335-2726
800-423-0418

INFOUSA
3921 S Bristol St
Santa Ana, CA 92704-7427
www.infousa.com
714-432-6700 • Fax 714-432-6701

INGREDIENTS CORP. OF AMERICA
676 Huron Ave
Memphis, TN 38107-1511
901-525-4422

INLAND SEAFOOD
2527 Perdido St
New Orleans, LA 70119-7434
504-821-4500

INLAND SEAFOOD
1222 Menlo Dr NW
Atlanta, GA 30318-4163
800-882-3474

INLINE PLASTICS
42 Canal St
Shelton, CT 06484-3265
800-826-5567

INN TECHNOLOGY
201 S Brand Blvd
Glendale, CA 91204-1309
e-mail: randy@inntechnology.com
www.inntechnology.com
818-552-2251 • Fax 818-249-7534

INNAVISION GLOBAL MKTG. CONS.
1615 Count Turf Ln
Racine, W 53402-2058
262-639-3657

INN-CLIENT SERVER SYSTEMS
45 River Rd Ste 301
Flemington, NJ 08822-6026
e-mail: dmrgrath@inn client.com
www.inn-client.com
732-729-8000 • Fax 732-729-6909

INNCOM INTERNATIONAL
PO Box 1060
Old Lyme, CT 06371-0998
e-mail: sales@inncom.com
www.inncom.com
860-434-7777 • Fax 860-434-8005

INNOVATION VOICE TECH
1841 Bourbon Rd
Cross Plains, WI 53528-9436
800-424-6757

INNOVATIONS IN WAL COVERINGS
150 Varick St
New York, NY 10013-1218
e-mail: innovawal@aol.com
www.innovationsusa.com
212-807-6300 • Fax 212-807-1944

INNOVATIVE CONCEPTS ONE
5460 33rd St SE
Grand Rapids, MI 49512-2074
800-352-6275

INNOVATIVE TRAVEL MKTG
322 US Highway 46
Parsippany, NJ 07054-2352
212-557-5005

INNOVATIVE VOICE TECHNOLOGIES
PO Box 183
Cross Plains, WI 53528-0183
401-454-8111 • Fax 401-454-8777

INN-ROOM SYSTEMS, INC.
747 Glenn Ave
Wheeling, IL 60090-6019
www.innroom.org
847-808-0380 • Fax 847-808-0384

INNVEST
1600 Broadway
New York, NY 10019-7413
212-541-4545

INNOVATIVE CONSTRUCTION
608 Bougainvillea Ct
Naples, FL 34110-6318
239-597-2542

IN-PHASE
PO Box 600
Harris, NY 12742-0600
845-794-2222 • Fax 845-794-1211

INPRO CORPORATION
PO Box 406
Muskego, WI 53150-0406
e-mail: service@inprocorp.com
www.inprocorp.com
262-679-9010 • Fax 262-679-5407

INSIDE DESIGNER-LEATHER
43 State Plz Fl 8
New York, NY 10004-1407
212-645-0518 • Fax 212-645-4168

INSIGNIA ESG HOTEL PARTNERS
200 Park Ave
New York, NY 10166-0005
212-984-8216

INSINGER MACHINE COMPANY
6245 State Rd
Philadelphia, PA 19135-2996
800-344-4802 • Fax 215-624-6966

INSINKERATOR
4700 21st St
Racine, WI 53406-5093
www.insinkeator.com
800-558-5712 • Fax 262-554-3639

INSPARATION INC.
11950 Hertz Ave
Moorpark, CA 93021-7145
e-mail: inspas@jetlink.net
www.insaparation.com
805-553-0820 • Fax 850-553-0826

INSTANT WHIP
|1031 Hot Wells Blvd
San Antonio, TX 78223-2797
e-mail: lindalh@flash.net
www.instantwhip.com
210-333-2771 • Fax 210-333-0717

INSTILL CORPORATION
330 Twin Dolphin Dr
Redwood City, CA 94065-1408
www.instill.com
650-551-5600 • Fax 650-551-5601

INSTITUTE FOR BREWING STUDIES
PO Box 1679
Boulder, CO 80306-1679
www.beertown.org
303-447-0816 • Fax 303-447-2825

INSTITUTIONAL & SERVICE TEXTILES
1609 Connecticut Ave NW Ste
Washington DC 20009-1034
202-986-0105 • Fax 202-986-0448

INSTITUTIONAL SALES
PO Box 1627
West Chester, PA 19380-0051
610-725-0906 • Fax 610-647-3478

INSULAIR INC
529 Commercial St Ste 200
San Francisco, CA 94111-3005
www.insulair.com
415-989-2877 • Fax 415-781-2877

INTEGRATED BUILDING SYS.
14512 Pebble Hill Ln
Gaithersburg, MD 20878-2473
301-762-2576

INTEGRATED POS, INC
PO Box 127
Winnebago, IL 61088-0127
877-442-4757 • Fax 815-355-3062

INTEGRATED RESTAURANT SOFTWARE
1402 Bergen Blvd
Fort Lee, NJ 07024-2116
www.rmstouch.com
201-461-9096 • Fax 201-947-3870

INTELEX
1001 3rd Ave SW
Carmel, IN 46032-7568
e-mail: sales@ntlx.com
www.ntlx.com
800-876-0922 • Fax 317-815-1514

INTELLI-CHECK INC
246 Crossways Park Dr W
Woodbury, NY 11797-2031
800-444-9542

INTERA COMMUNICATIONS
155 5th Ave
Minneapolis, MN 55401-2540
612-573-1805 • Fax 612-573-1802

INTERACTIVE ENTER. SYSTEMS
PO Box 1565
Norman, OK 73070-1565
405-321-8818

INTERBIO
PO Box 130549
Spring, TX 77393-0549
713-293-2033

INTERCON MARKETING. INC.
1540 Northgate Blvd
Sarasota, FL 34234-4759
e-mail: icmmktg@get.net
www.interconmktg.com
941-355-4488 • Fax 941-355-1558

INTERMEDIA COMMUNICATIONS
1100 Poydras St Ste 1100
New Orleans, LA 70163-1200
504-599-8600

INTERMETRO INDUSTRIES
651 N Washington St
Wilkes Barre, PA 18705-1799
www.metro.com
570-825-2741 • Fax 570-824-2705

INTERNAL REVENUE SERVICE
310 W Wisconsin Ave Stop
Milwaukee, WI 53203-2213
414-297-3302 • Fax 414-297-1600

INTERNAL REVENUE SERVICE
600 S Maestri Pl Stop 21
New Orleans, LA 70130-3414
504-558-3005 • Fax 504-558-3061

INTERNATIONAL AIR FILTRATION
413 W University Dr
Arlington Heights, IL 60004-1813
847-797-1000

INTERNATIONAL ASSOC CULINARY
203 W Adams St
Phoenix, AZ 85003-1602

INTERNATIONAL ASSOC. REFR.
7315 Wisconsin Ave
Bethesda, MD 20814-3202
301-652-5674

INTERNATIONAL BAKERS
1902 N Sheridan St
South Bend, IN 46628-1592
800-345-7175

INTERNATIONAL BAKING INDUSTRY
401 N Michigan Ave
Chicago, IL 60611-4255
312-789-1121

INTERNATIONAL BUSINESS TRADE
4624 W Esplanade Ave
Metairie, LA 70006-2700
504-457-2047 • Fax 504-457-2049

INTERNATIONAL CELLULOSE
12315 Robin Blvd
Houston, TX 77045-4820
e-mail: icc@spray-on.com
www.spary-on.com
713-433-6701

INTERNATIONAL COLD STORAGE
PO Box 425
Andover, KS 67002-0425
316-733-1385

INTERNATIONAL COLD STOR-AGE CO.
6250 Harbin Dr
Alexandria, VA 22310-2505
800-470-0001 • Fax 703-921-1502

INTERNATIONAL COMMERCIAL SUPPLIES
569 Bantam Rd
Litchfield, CT 06759-3203
860-657-4558 • Fax 860-567-3706

INTERNATIONAL CONVERTER
17153 County Road 57
Caldwell, OH 43724-9779
740-732-5665 • Fax 740-732-7515

INTERNATIONAL COUNCIL OF CUISINE
2111 Wilson Blvd
Arlington, VA 22201-3001
e-mail: kshore@iccl.org
www.iccl.org
703-522-8463

INTERNATIONAL CULINARY
PO Box 2202
Long Branch, NJ 07740-2202
www.chefharvey.com
732-229-0008

INTERNATIONAL DAIRY DELI BAKERY
PO Box 5528
Madison, WI 53705-0528
608-238-7908

INTERNATIONAL DEHYDRATED FOODS
PO Box 10347
Springfield, MO 65808-0347
417-881-7820 • Fax 417-881-7274

INTERNATIONAL EVENT PRODUCTS
2029 83rd St
North Bergen, NJ 07047-4710
e-mail: inteventproducts@aol.com
201-453-2600 • Fax 201-453-2605

INTERNATIONAL EVENT PRODUCTS
115 Graham Ln
Lodi, NJ 07644-1622
973-777-9277

INTERNATIONAL FOAM SOLUTIONS
PO Box 218
Delray Beach, FL 33447-0218
800-856-3626

INTERNATIONAL FOOD SAFETY COUNCIL
250 S Wacker Dr Ste 1400
Chicago, IL 60606-5851
800-456-0111

INTERNATIONAL HOME FOODS
25 Marr St
Milton, PA 17847-1520
570-742-7621

INTERNATIONAL HOTEL-MOTEL & REST.
2 Park Ave Rm 1100
New York, NY 10016-5702

INTERNATIONAL MARKETING SYSTEM
2022 Hobbyhorse Ave
Henderson, NV 89012-2225
702-260-6797

INTERNATIONAL MERCHANT SERVICE
1331 Airport Fwy # A
Euless, TX 76040-4153
817-868-1810

INTERNATIONAL PAPER
6400 Poplar Ave
Memphis, TN 38197-0198
901-763-6000 • Fax 901-763-7463

INTERNATIONAL PAPER FOOD-SERVICE
3 Paragon Dr
Montvale, NJ 07645-1725
201-291-1776 • Fax 201-307-6125

INTERNATIONAL PAPER
8339 Telegraph Rd
Odenton, MD 21113-1322
443-569-5000

INTERNATIONAL PATTERNS
50 Inez Drive
Bay Shore, NY 11706-2238
www.internationalpatterns.com
631-952-2000 • Fax 631-952-7602

INTERNATIONAL PATTERNS
4801 Keller Springs Rd
Addiso, TX 75001-5912
e-mail: cgmgdallas@aol.com
www.claesandgreenoe.com
972-733-1724 • Fax 972-733-1726

INTERNATIONAL PROMOTIONAL IDEA
8129 Austin Ave
Morton Grove, IL 60053-3204
847-966-9120 • Fax 847-966-9228

INTERNATIONAL SHOP ZONE
3165 29th St Apt F5
Astoria, NY 11106-3337
www.internationalshopzone.com
718-274-5306 • Fax 718-204-1711

INTERNATIONAL SILVER CO.-FOODS
PO Box 175
Boston, MA 02128-0009
617-568-1501 • Fax 617-568-9185

INTERNATIONAL SMOKING SYSTEMS
PO Box 480
Ashburnham, MA 01430-0480
978-827-3160

INTERNATIONAL STORAGE
11230 Harland Dr NE
Covington, GA 30014-6438
800-874-0375 • Fax 800-577-2210

INTERNATIONAL TRADING COMPANY
3100 Canal St
Houston, TX 77003-1698
713-546-1461 • Fax 713-546-1480

INTERNATIONAL TRAVEL CARD
489 W Fullerton Ave
Elmhurst, IL 60126-1404
312-764-8210

INTERNET MEDIA GROUP
77 Alexander Rd
Billerica, MA 01821-5065
e-mail: mail@imgkiosk.com
www.imgkiosk.com
978-262-0809

INTERNATIONAL FOOD SAFE-TY ASSOCIATION
PO Box 2000
Layton, UT 84041-7000
801-771-2000

INTERPLAN PRACTICE
933 Lee Rd Ste 120
Orlando, FL 32810-5543
407-645-9124

INTERSTAR SYSTEMS, INC.
3741 Mangum Rd
Houston, TX 77092-5407
e-mail: kim@interstarsystems.com
www.interstarsystems.com
713-957-0411 • Fax 713-957-8003

INTERSTATE AMERICA-A B A
5715 Oakbrook Pkwy
Norcross, GA 30093-1808
800-683-3948

INTERTRADE SYSTEMS CORPORATION
100 E Hamilton Ave
Campbell, CA 95008-0245
408-871-8010 • Fax 408-871-8020

INTERVAL NTERNATIONAL
6262 Sunset Dr
Miami, FL 33143-4843
305-666-1861

INTIRION-MICROFRIDGE
12219 S Debkay Ct
Monrovia, MD 21770-9325
e-mail: prestonintirion@psinet.com
301-798-0030 • Fax 301-798-0031

INTL SELLING PROFESSIONALS
820 E 47th St Ste B2
Tucson, AZ 85713-5074
520-322-8953 • Fax 520-322-0604

INTL. FOODSERVICE EXECS. ASSOC
PO Box 191
Tryon, NC 28782-0191
828-863-4613

INT'L. KIT. EXHAUST CLNG. ASSOCIATION
1518 K St NW Ste 503
Washington, DC 20005-1203
202-638-2031

INTRALIGHT, LLC
1443 S 550 E
Orem, UT 84097-7719
www.intralight.com
801-227-7173 • Fax 425-928-9421

INTRALOX INC
201 Laitram Ln
New Orleans, LA 70123-5395
800-535-8848

INTREX-ASI
40 Park St
Brooklyn, NY 11206-4541
e-mail: info@intrexfurniture.com
www.intrex-asi.com
718-455-5042 • Fax 718-919-5202

INTROSUL
103 Industrial Park Dr
Perry, GA 31069-2404
478-987-3185

INVENTORY CONTROL SYS.
PO Box 1272
Minot, ND 58702-1272
800-910-4642

IOWA ROTOCAST PLASTICS
PO Box 336
Decorah, IA 52101-0336
563-382-9636

IPHFHA, INC.
PO Box 782710
Wichita, KS 67278-2710
316-685-1208

IPROMOTEU.COM
23 Strathmore Rd
Natick, MA 01760-2442
e-mail: cherzog@ipromoteu.com
www.ipromoteu.com
508-655-5700 • Fax 508-655-5704

IPSO, USA
99 Aberdeen Loop
Panama City, FL 32405-6463
e-mail: sales@ipsousa.com
www.ipsousa.com
800-872-4776 • Fax 850-281-5901

IQ-INTELLIGENT MKTG SERV
7900 Xerxes Ave S Ste 2400
Minneapolis, MN 55431-1152
952-897-7300

IRESERVE.COM
27 W 24th St Ste 200
New York, NY 10010-3204
www.ireserve.com
212-727-9090 • Fax 212-658-9596

IRISH DAIRY BOARD
825 Green Bay Rd
Wilmette, IL 60091-2597
e-mail: cntact@idbusa.com
847-256-8289 • Fax 847-256-8299

IRPINIA IMPORTS CORPORA-TION
10219 General Dr Ste 4
Orlando, FL 32824-8529
www.irpiniaimports.com
407-240-1227

ISA S.P.A
PO Box 503
East Granby, CT 06026-0503
e-mail: heiner@maierstoreinteriors.com
860-653-9595 • Fax 860-653-0008

ISEATZ.COM ONLINE RESTAURANT
650 Poydras St Ste 1530
New Orleans, LA 70130-6107
504-586-1234

ISHIDA CORP OF AMERICA
4600 N Royal Atlanta Dr Ste 60
Tucker, GA 30084-3828
800-969-7260

ISI COMMERCIAL REFRIGERATION ,
640 W 6th St
Houston, TX 77007-2422
e-mail: sales@isi-texas.com
www.isi-texas.com
800-777-0314 • Fax 713-861-3759

ISLAND OASIS
PO Box 769
Walpole, MA 02081-0769
800-777-4752

ISLAND OASIS FROZEN BEVERAGE
1419 N Highway 190 Ste 204
Covington, LA 70433-8966
985-893-6763

ISLAND REFRIGERATION AND FOOD
1811 Newbridge Rd
Bellmore, NY 11710-1633
516-826-5048

ISLAND SORBET
18395 Gulf Blvd Ste 10
Indian Rocks Bch, FL 33785-2083
727-391-4052 • Fax 727-398-1649

ISN WIRELESS COMMUNICATIONS
3723 Southside Blvd
Jacksonville, FL 32216-4685
e-mail: chris.stood@isnwireless.com
904-641-7878 • Fax 904-641-7801

ISO PANEL
8085 W 26th Ct
Hialeah, FL 33016-2731
e-mail: isopanel@cybergate.net
www.isopanel.com
305-828-4147 • Fax 305-828-0977

ITALGI USA INC
PO Box 89
Westwood, NJ 07675-0089
201-666-2378

ITALIAN TRADE COMMISSION
401 N Michigan Ave Ste 303
Chicago, IL 60611-4255
www.italtrade.com
312-670-4360 • Fax 312-670-5147

ITALIAN TRADE COMMISSION
499 Park Ave
New York, NY 10022-1240
e-mail: newyork@italtrade.com
212-980-1500 • Fax 212-758-1050

ITALIAN VILLAGE RAV-PASTA
575 Windsor Dr
Secaucus, NJ 07094-2708
201-601-0800

ITALY AMERICA CHAMBER OF COMMERCE
4605 Post Oak Place Dr
Houston, TX 77027-9729
713-626-9303 • Fax 713-626-9306

ITC DELTA COM
4092 Memorial Pkwy SW
Huntsville, AL 35802-4343
256-382-3998 • Fax 256-382-3997

ITHACA PERIPHERALS
20 Bomax Dr
Ithaca, NY 14850-1200
www.transact-tech.com
607-257-8901 • Fax 607-257-3868

ITO CARIANI SAUSAGE COMPANY
3190 Corporate Pl
Hayward, CA 94545-3916
510-887-0882 • Fax 510-887-8323

ITO PACKING CO
PO Box 707
Reedley, CA 93654-0707
559-638-6802

IVAR'S
500 Terry Ave N
Seattle, WA 98109-4328
206-682-5333 • Fax 206-682-7282

IWASAKI IMAGES
20460 Gramercy Pl
Torrance, CA 90501-1507
www.iwaski-images.com
310-328-7121 • Fax 310-618-0876

IWATANI INTERNATIONAL CORP.
2050 Center Ave
Fort Lee, NJ 07024-4996
201-585-2442

IWATANI INTERNATIONAL CORP.
385 Van Ness Ave Ste 110
Torrance, CA 90501-6299
www.iwatani.com
310-324-9174 • Fax 310-324-9177

IXFOODSERVICE.COM
PO Box 968
Traverse City, MI 49685-0968
877-493-3778

IZABEL LAM NEW YORK
204 Van Dyke St
Brooklyn, NY 11231-1034
718-797-3983 • Fax 718-797-0030

J & D INTERNATIONAL
250 44th St Fl 3
Brooklyn, NY 11232-2816
www.tapestrywarehouse.com
718-492-4107 • Fax 718-492-6276

J & J SNACK FOOD CORP
955 Hamilton Ct
Palm Harbor, FL 34683-6334
e-mail: rsage@jjsnack.com
www.jjsnack.com
727-771-6663

J & J SNACK FOODS INC
6000 Central Hwy
Merchantville, NJ 08109 4607
856-665-9533

J & J SNACK FOOD
5353 S Downey Rd
Los Angeles, CA 90058-3756
323-581-0171 • Fax 323-581-1681

J & K INGREDIENTS
PO Box 8600
Saddle Brook, NJ 07663-8600
973-942-1498

J & M DISTRIBUTORS
247 Little Farms Ave
New Orleans, LA 70123-1305
504-738-0483

J & R MANUFACTURING INC
820 W Kearney St Ste B
Mesquite, TX 75149-8804
www.jrmanufacturing.com
972-205-4855 • Fax 972-288-9488

J & S FOOD BROKERAGE
120 Campus Dr
Edison, NJ 08837-3936
732-225-4770 • Fax 732-225-4730

J C ENTERTAINMENT
7421 Bentley Station Pl
Reynoldsburg, OH 43068-5263
614-501-7229

J HORNY'S LEGENDRY PIES & DESSERTS
400 W 48th Ave
Denver, CO 80216-1806
e-mail: james.donegon@vicorpinc.com
800-820-1074 • Fax 303-672-2674

J S FIBER CO
290 Marble Rd
Statesville, NC 28625-2351
800-782-0558

JT MEGA MARKETING COMMUNICATIONS
4020 Minnetonka Blvd
Minneapolis, MN 55416-4100
612-929-1370 • Fax 612-929-5417

J. HARRIS & SONS
22 Makefield Turn
Morrisville, PA 19067-5010
215-428-3951 • Fax 215-293-5704

J. LOHR WINERY-ARIEL VIN-YARDS
1000 Lenzen Ave
San Jose, CA 95126-2739
www.jlohr.com
408-288-5057 • Fax 408-993-2276

J. POCKER & SON, INC.
135 E 63rd St
New York, NY 10021-7333
212-838-5488 • Fax 212-752-2172

J.G.VAN HOLTEN & SON, INC.
703 W Madison St
Waterloo, WI 53594-1365
920-478-2144 • Fax 920-478-2316

J. J. MATTHEW LLC
100 Oakland Ave
Closter, NJ 07624-2609
e-mail: jjmatthew1@aol.com
201-750-1800 • Fax 201-750-7933

J. KINGS FOODSERVICE PROFESSION
700 Furrows Rd
Holtsville, NY 11742-2001
e-mail: info@jkings.com
www.jkings.com
631-289-8401 • Fax 631-758-0187

J.L. DEGRAFFENREID & SONS
2848 N Le Compte Rd
Springfield, MO 65803-5729
417-862-9411 • Fax 417-862-8615

J.L. FOODS, INC
1498 S Broadway
Camden, NJ 08104-1344
www.jlfoods.com
800-881-3250 • Fax 856-964-8775

J.L.KAHN CARL KAUFMANN ASSOCIATION
2087 Newbridge Rd
Bellmore, NY 11710-2226
e-mail: sales@kahnkaufmann.com
www.kahnkaufmann.com
516-783-8200 • Fax 516-783-8079

J.M. SMAK INC.
1424 S Mason St
Appleton, WI 54914-5541
920-954-8287 • Fax 920-954-1290

J.P.'S SHELLFISH
PO Box 278
Kittery, ME 03904-0278
207-439-6018

J.R. SIMPLOT COMPANY
6360 S Federal Way
Boise, ID 83716-9617
www.simplotfoods.com
208-384-8261 • Fax 208-384-8022

J.T. BINSTEAD
217 Lantwyn Ln
Narberth, PA 19072-2005
610-667-2383

J.V. TRADING GLENDALE LTD.
6575 Traffic Ave
Ridgewood, NY 11385-3328
www.janlibo.com
888-369-8688 • Fax 718-326-4019

JAC PAC FOODS LTD
PO Box 5220
Manchester, NH 03108-5220
800-522-7220

JACCARD CORPORATION
3421 N Benzing Rd
Orchard Park, NY 14127-1592
716-825-3814 • Fax 716-825-5319

JACK THE RIPPER TABLESKIRTING
11246 S Post Oak Rd Ste 420
Houston, TX 77035-5743
www.tableskirting.com
713-661-4700 • Fax 713-723-8627

JACKNABITT.COM
22605 SE 56th St Ste 250
Issaquah, WA 98029-5297
www.jacknabbit.com
425-557-8955 • Fax 425-557-8576

JACK'S CUSTOM WOODWORKING
3 Aberjona Dr
Woburn, MA 01801-2043
e-mail: jcw@tlc.net
www.jcwcountertops.com
781-935-1907 • Fax 781-935-8645

JACKSON MACHINE SALES
801 Airpark Center Dr
Nashville, TN 37217-2942
800-736-8144

JACKSON-LLOYD INSURANCE MANAGA
PO Box 187
Longview, TX 75606-0187
800-657-5242 • Fax 800-933-8662

JACKSON'S GREASE TRAP SERVICE
PO Box 1007
Kenner, LA 70063-1007
504-466-5995

JACLO INDUSTRIES
1115 Globe Ave
Mountainside, NJ 07092-2903
e-mail: showerall@jaclo.com
www.jaclo.com
908-789-7006 • Fax 908-789-3336

JACOB TUBING LP
3948 Willow Lake Blvd
Memphis, TN 38118-7040
901-566-1110

JACQUES VIEAU, INC.
1354 Martha Washington Dr
Milwaukee, WI 53213-2944
414-454-0377 • Fax 414-454-0747

JACQUIN CHARLES
2633 Trenton Ave
Philadelphia, PA 19125-1896
215-425-9300

JADE RANGE
7355 E Slauson Ave
Los Angeles, CA 90040-3660
323-728-5700

JADEN FABRICS
2625 Brenner Dr
Dallas, TX 75220-1319
214-357-2888 • Fax 214-352-5646

JADO BATHROOM & HARDWARE MFG.
7845 E Paradise Ln
Scottsdale, AZ 85260-1797
800-227-2734 • Fax 800-552-5236

JAGUAR COFFEE COMPANY
13719 Linden Dr
Spring Hill, FL 34609-5023
e-mail: coffee@jaguarcoffee.com
www.jaguarcoffee.com
352-688-3468

JAKE'S INC.
PO Box 70467
Houston, TX 77270-0467
e-mail: info@jakesfinerfoods.com
www.jakesfinerfoods.com
713-868-1301 • Fax 713-868-4326

JALAPENO FOODS COMPANY
1450 Lake Robbins Dr Ste 350
Spring, TX 77380-3252
e-mail: sales@jalapenofoods.com
www.jalapenofoods.com
281-363-4585 • Fax 281-364-8452

JALAPENO KETCHUP CO.
PO Box 852742
Richardson, TX 75085-2742
e-mail: bean@spiceitup.com
www.spiceitup.com
972-414-2182 • Fax 972-414-9966

JAMES ARNOLD CO.
1405 Walnut St # 309
Highland, IL 62249-2009
618-984-3465 • Fax 618-654-7672

JAMES G HARDY & CO
1501 Lancer Dr
Moorestown, NJ 08057-4254
www.hardylinen.com
856-222-1111 • Fax 856-222-1010

JAMES J HILL REFERENCE LIBRARY
80 4Th St W
Saint Paul, MN 55102-1605
651-227-9531 • Fax 651-222-4139

JAMES M. DEGEN & CO., INC.
PO Box 377
Cayucos, CA 93430-0377
805-995-0900

JAMES VARLEY & SONS, LTD.
1200 Switzer Ave
Saint Louis, MO 63147-1840
e-mail: jvsinc@aol.com
www.jamesvarley.com
800-325-3303 • Fax 314-383-4379

JAMISON BEDDING, INC.
PO Box 681948
Franklin, TN 37068-1948
e-mail: jb@jamisonbedding.com
800-255-1883 • Fax 800-794-2254

JANI KING
16885 Dallas Pkwy
Addison, TX 75001-5202
800-552-5264

JANUS-MORROW TECHNOLOGIES
2300 Tall Pines Dr
Largo, FL 33771-5342
www.janusdisplay.com
727-531-4000 • Fax 727-531-3531

JARD MARKETING CORP
PO Box 288
Lawrence, MA 01842-0588
978-681-8900 • Fax 978-975-7800

JARRATT ASSOCIATES, INC.
5263 Plymouth Rd
Ann Arbor, MI 48105-9520
888-527-7288

JASPER WYMAN SON
22 S Main St
Topsfiled, MA 01983-1835
978-887-7472 • Fax 978-887-6881

JAVA CUP GRAPHICS
44247 260th St
Canistota, SD 57012-6012
www.javacupgraphics.com
605-296-3634 • Fax 605-296-3634

JAVA JACKET, INC.
5712 NE Hassalo St
Portland, OR 97213-3642
www.javajacket.com
800-208-4128 • Fax 503-281-6462

JAVA TRADING CO.
14032 Kostner Ave Ste D
Midlothian, IL 60445-2287
877-402-2739 • Fax 708-687-7082

JAY R. SMITH MFG. CO.
PO Box 3237
Montgomery, AL 36109-0237
www.jrsmith.com
334-277-8520 • Fax 334-272-7396

JAY SANDERS, INC.
2 Kiel Ave
Butler, NJ 07405-2572
973-492-8800 • Fax 973-492-8812

JAZZY JUICES LNC.
500 Hagan Ave
New Orleans, LA 70119-4911
504-913-8599

JBS PACKING CO., INC
101 Houston Ave # O
Port Arthur, TX 77640-6413
409-982-3216 • Fax 409-982-3549

JBS PACKING COMPANY, INC.
PO Box 399
Port Arthur, TX 77641-0399
409-982-5766 • Fax 409-982-2480

JC BRADFORD
3100 W End Ave Ste 110
Nashville, TN 37203-5812
615-748-9443

JD GILBERT & COMPANY
600 W Hillsboro Blvd Ste 510
Deerfield Beach, FL 33441-1611
954-419-1000

JDL LEVANTIS & ASSOCIATES
2818 Ditmars Blvd
Astoria, NY 11105-2716
718-626-5900

JEC CONSULTING & TRADING
165 Sabal Palm Dr Ste 103
Longwood, FL 32779-2591
e-mail: cav0l@sprynet.com
407-869-9609

JEECO LABS-SMS TECHNOLOGIES
2650 W Bradley Pl # B
Chicago, IL 60618-4717
773-654-4900

JEFFER MANGLES BUTLER
2121 Avenue of the Stars
Los Angeles, CA 90067-5010
310-201-3591

JEFFERIE'S & COMPANY
11100 Santa Monica Blvd
Los Angeles, CA 90025-3384
310-575-5278

JEFF'S GOURMET PIES
6704 Parke East Blvd
Tampa, FL 33610-4145
813-622-7437

JEM ASSOC. LINWOOD COMMONS
2106 New Rd Ste B2
Linwood, NJ 08221-1048
609-927-4747

JENNIE-O FOODS
20609 Via Azul
Yorba Linda, CA 92886-3110
714-871-1660 • Fax 714-952-3294

JENNIE-O FOODS, INC.
PO Box 778
Willmar, MN 56201-0778
e-mail: mcase@jennie-o.com
www.jennie-o.com
800-328-1756 • Fax 320-231-7100

JERDON PRODUCTS
PO Box 851978
Richardson, TX 75085-1978
800-223-3571

JEROME FOODS, INC.
34 N 7th St
Barron, WI 54812-1231
715-537-3131

JEWELS OF JAVA
106 Adams Ave
Endicott, NY 13760-5504
www.jewelsofjava.cc
877-560-TEAK • Fax 607-797-1947

JIFFY MIXER CO INC
4120 Tigris Way
Riverside, CA 92503-4843
909-272-0838

JIFFYVAPOR CLEAN
900 S Meadows Pkwy Apt 1521
Reno, NV 89511-5965
800-369-8458

JIM BEAM BRANDS COMPANY
510 Lake Cook Rd
Deerfield, IL 60015-5610
www.jimbeam.com
847-948-8888

JIM BRADY ENTERPRISES, INC.
2715 Springrock Hill Trl
Lawrenceville, GA 30043-7612
770-271-2343

JIM HAUGH ASSOCIATES
PO Box 293
Andover, MA 01810-0005
978-474-1988 • Fax 978-474-6244

JIMMY DEAN FOODS
8000 Centerview Pkwy
Cordova, TN 38018-4227
901-753-1600 • Fax 901-758-6707

JINRO AMERICA, INC.
3470 Wilshire Blvd Ste 1024
Los Angeles, CA 90010-3910
www.jinro.com
213-637-1500 • Fax 213-637-1501

JKL SPECIALTY FOOD, INC.
1002 Hope St Ste 150
Stamford, CT 06907-2104
e-mail: jklfoods@aol.com
203-348-8862 • Fax 203-325-3148

JM SMUCKER CO.
1 Strawberry Ln
Orrville, OH 44667-1241
330-682-3000

JOHN BOOS & COMPANY
PO Box 609
Effingham, IL 62401-0609
888-431-2667

JOHN CALARESE & CO.
12 Regent Cir
Franklin, MA 02038-2703
e-mail:
jcalareseco@norfolk-county.com
508-528-7801 • Fax 508-520-3509

JOHN DEERE & CO
1 John Deere Pl
Moline, IL 61265-8098
309-765-8000

JOHN F. DAVIS & ASSOC.
15500 Wayzata Blvd
Wayzata, MN 55391-1435
612-475-2513 • Fax 612-476-9077

JOHN KEELER CO., INC.
3770 NW 80th St
Miami, FL 33147-4443
www.onecrab.com
305-836-6858 • Fax 305-836-6859

JOHN MORRELL & CO. KRETSCHMER
805 E Kemper Rd
Cincinnati, OH 45246-2515
e-mail: rbrandon@johnmorrell.com
800-818-9587 • Fax 513-346-7551

JOHN MORRELL CO
8000 W 78Th St Ste 120
Minneapolis, MN 55439-2535
952-943-0111 • Fax 952-943-1124

JOHN RICHARDS CO.
11171 Venture Dr
Mira Loma, CA 91752-3200
e-mail: nrichards796@cs.com
www.johnrichardsco.com
909-360-7534 • Fax 909-360-7535

JOHN RITZENHALER CO
40 Portland Rd
Conshohocken, PA 19428-2714
610-825-9321 • Fax 610-834-8617

JOHN WILLARD'S SEASONINGS CO.
229 Spring Ave
Glen Ellyn, IL 60137-4823
www.johnwillards.com
630-469-4524 • Fax 630-469-5047

JOHN WM. MACY'S CHEESE STICKS
80 Kipp Ave
Elmwood Park, NJ 07407-1011
e-mail: tmacy@earthlink.com
www.cheesesticks.com
201-791-8036 • Fax 201-797-5068

JOHNSON & WALES UNIVERSITY
8 Abbott Park Pl
Providence, RI 02903-3775
www.jwu.edu
401-598-2345 • Fax 401-598-1835

JOHNSON & WALES UNIVERSITY
701 E Bay St
Charleston, SC 29403-5033
843-727-3014

JOHNSON & WALES UNIVERSITY
7150 Montview Blvd
Denver, CO 80220-1866
www.jwu.edu
303-256-9308 • Fax 303-256-9333

JOHNSON & WALES UNIVERSITY
8 Abbott St
Providence, RI 02906-1817
www.jwu.edu
401-598-1000 • Fax 401-598-2948

JOHNSON PLASTICS
16910 Munn Rd
Chagrin Falls, OH 44023-5493
e-mail: info@johnsonite.com
www.johnsonite.com
440-543-8916 • Fax 440-543-5774

JOHNSON SALES COMPANY
PO Box 221370
Hollywood, FL 33022-1370
e-mail:
johnsonsales@worldnet.att.net.com
954-927-3900

JOHNSON WAX PROFESSIONAL
8310 16th St
Sturtevan, WI 53177-1964
262-631-4001 • Fax 262-631-4056

JOHNSON-RICE COMPANY
639 Loyola Ave Ste 2775
New Orleans, LA 70113-3143
504-525-3795

JOHNSONVILLE FOODS INC
PO Box 786
Sheboygan, WI 53082-0786
800-733-7432 • Fax 920-459-7824

JOLIET JUNIOR COLLEGE
1215 Houbolt Rd
Joliet, IL 60431-8800
e-mail: jjc.cc.il.us
815 200-2039 • Fax 815-280-2696

JON DONAIRE DESSERTS
9511 Ann St
Santa Fe Springs, CA 90670-2615
www.jondonaire.net
562-946-6396 • Fax 562-946-3781

JON DONAIRE DESSERTS
5001 Forest Lawn Dr
Mc Kinney, TX 75071-6467
e-mail: dadkins@rich.com
www.jondonaire.com
972-562-5699 • Fax 972-562-7180

JORDAN'S MEATS
PO Box 588
Portland, ME 04112-0588
207-772-5411

JORDON REFRIGERATION
5400 Eadom St
Philadelphia, PA 19137-1303
800-523-0171 • Fax 215-289-1597

JOSE CUERVO INTERNATIONAL
16414 San Pedro Ave
San Antonio, TX 78232-2277
210-495-2295

JOSEPH CAMPIONE INC.
2210 W South Branch Blvd
Oak Creek, WI 53154-4907
414-761-8944 • Fax 414-761-2005

JOSEPH FARMS CHEESE
PO Box 775
Atwater, CA 95301-0775
209-394-7984 • Fax 209-394-4988

JOSEPH SCHMIDT CONFECTIONS
2000 Folsom St
San Francisco, CA 94110-1318
415-626-7900 • Fax 415-626-7991

JOSEPH'S LITTLE COOKIES
3700 J St SE
Deming, NM 88030-7106
e-mail: joseph@zianet.com
505-546-2839 • Fax 505-546-6951

JOSEPHS PASTA CO
133 Hale St
Haverhill, MA 01830-3969
888-327-2782

JOYLIN FOOD EQUIPMENT CORP.
120 Fulton Ave
New Hyde Park, NY 11040-5325
e-mail: joylin1961@aol.com
516-742-1800 • Fax 516-742-2123

JP MC HALE PES MANAGEMENT
241 Bleakley Ave
Buchanan, NY 10511-1001
www.nopest.com
914-739-6762

JSL FOODS, INC.
3550 Pasadena Ave
Los Angeles, CA 90031-1946
323-223-2484 • Fax 323-223-9882

JTECH COMMUNICATIONS
6413 Congress Ave Ste 150
Boca Raton, FL 33487-2839
www.jtechinc.com
800-321-6221 • Fax 561-997-0773

JTM FOOD GROUP
200 Sales Ave
Harrison, OH 45030-1485
800-626-2308 • Fax 513-367-132

JUBILATIONS CHEESECAKES
1536 Gardner Blvd Bldg 7
Columbus, MS 39702-2813
662-328-9210

JUDEL PRODUCTS CORP.
45 Knollwood Rd
Elmsford, NY 10523-2815
914-592-6200 • Fax 914-592-1216

JUDY HAVELKA ENTERPRISES
5008 Stanley Keller Rd
Haltom City, TX 76117-1250
e-mail: jheltd@swbell.net
www.havelka.com
817-222-1142 • Fax 817-222-1966

JUICE TYME INC
4401 S Oakley Ave
Chicago, IL 60609-3020
www.juicetyme.com
773-579-1291 • Fax 773-579-1251

JUMBO JACK'S COOKBOOKS
301 Broadway St
Audubon, IA 50025-1101
800-798-2635 • Fax 712-563-3118

JUMEX NECTARS - VILORE FOODS C
PO Box 1560
Laredo, TX 78042-1560
956-726-3633 • Fax 956-727-1499

JUMO PROCESS CONTROL
885 Fox Chase
Coatesville, PA 19320-5811
e-mail: info@jumousa.com
www.jumousa.com
610-380-8002

JUMP INTERNATIONAL
3364 Eastwoodlands Trl
Hilliard, OH 43026-9340
888-400-5586

JUMPWARE, INC.
11806 Nene Dr
Austin, TX 78750-2130
www.jumpware.com
877-586-7927

JUS-MADE1610
10310 Zodiac Ln
Dallas, TX 75229-4725
800-969-3746 • Fax 972-241-5544

JUST BAGELS
2366 Waterbury Ave
Bronx, NY 10462-5017
e-mail: cliff@justbagels.com
www.justbagel.com
718-892-8898 • Fax 718-904-9215

JUST FRESH AIR
10924 Grant Rd
Houston, TX 77070-4445
800-525-1866 • Fax 281-469-4676

JUST GODIRECT.COM
4851 S Overland Dr
Tucson, AZ 85714-3436
www.enuts.com
877-368-8772 • Fax 520-748-9166

K & H PACFIC
2632 Kilihau St # B

Honolulu, HI 96819-2020
808-836-8855 • Fax 808-836-8887

K & J PACKAGING
PO Box 69
River Edge, NJ 07661-0069
201-907-0517 • Fax 201-262-1014

K & L INTERNATIONAL PRODUCT
20470 Yellow Brick Rd # 5B
Walnut, CA 91789-2927
www.knl-international .com
909-598-5588 • Fax 909-598-3380

K B FOODS
6315 John J Pershing Dr
Omaha, NE 68110-1176
402-457-5700

K P M G PEAT MARWICK INTL
767 5th Ave Fl 4
New York, NY 10153-0023
212-307-7761

K S F-QUILLEN LLC
PO Box 296
Lowell, AR 72745-0296
800-640-0131

K V P SYSTEMS INC
11255 Pyrites Way
Rancho Cordova, CA 95670-4481
916-635-5151

K.I.I. MANAGEMENTS, INC.
8700 W Bryn Mawr Ave Ste 800
Chicago, IL 60631-3512
773-741-5148 • Fax 312-362-1986

KABOBS, THE HORS D'OEUVRE SPEC
5423 N Lake Dr
Morrow, GA 30260-3534
e-mail: mpergolini@kabobs.com
www.kabobos.com
404-361-6281 • Fax 404 361-0008

KAGOME U S A INC
268 Harbor Blvd
Belmont, CA 94002-4017
650-349-2271 • Fax 650-349-6570

KAHIKI FOODS
3004 E 14th Ave # 3004
Columbus, OH 43219-2355
e-mail: kahiki@kahiki.com
888-436-2500 • Fax 614-253-8581

KAHN & ASSOCIATES
614 S Carrollton Ave
New Orleans, LA 70118-1008
504-822-2700

KAIN-MCARTHUR INC
2000 E Prairie Cir
Olathe, KS 66062 1268
913-829-3700

KAIRAK, INC.
23955 President Ave
Harbor City, CA 90710-1333
310-530-1766 • Fax 310-539-2341

KALLAS COMPANY
645 Griswold St Ste 1500
Detroit, MI 48226-4103
313-962-6000

KALLISTA PLUMBING A KOHLER COMPANY
2446 Verna Ct
San Leandro, CA 94577-4223
www.kohlerco.com
888-4KALLIS

KAMCO SUPPLY CORP.
PO Box 2489
Woburn, MA 01888-0989
e-mail:
mwillaims@kamcoboston.com
781-938-0909 • Fax 781-935-1696

KANSAS CITY HEALTH DEPART.
2400 Troost Ave Ste 3000
Kansas City, MO 64108-2860
816-513-6315

KANSAS CITY STEAK
100 Osage Ave
Kansas City, KS 66105-1415
913-371-1107 • Fax 913-281-4399

KANSAS STATE UNIVERSITY
103 Justin Hall
Manhattan, KS 66506-1400
785-532-2210 • Fax 785-532-5522

KAREN'S FABULOUS BISCOTTI-FOOD
50 Main St
White Plains, NY 10606-1901
www.foodltd.com
914-681-0773 • Fax 914-328-4276

KARL'S PARTY RENTAL
7000 S 10th St
Oak Creek, WI 53154-1421
www.karls.com
414-831-7022 • Fax 414-831-7080

KARLSBURGER FOODS
12450 Fernbrook Ln N
Dayton, MN 55327-9765
763-421-5481

KARMA INC.
500 Milford St
Watertown, WI 53094-6032
www.karma-inc.com
800-558-9565 • Fax 920-261-3302

KAROUN DIARIES INC.
5117 Santa Monica Blvd
Los Angeles, CA 90029-2413
e-mail: karoundairies@earthlink.net
323-666-6222 • Fax 323-666-1501

KARP'S
93 Heath Pl
Hastings on Hudson, NY 10706-3618
e-mail: pfaraone@bakerbaker.com
914-478-3472 • Fax 914-478-4459

KARP'S BAKER & BAKER
6 Martel Way
Georgetown, MA 01033-2223
e-mail: pbrown@bakerbaker.com
www.karps.com
800-373-5277

KARTRI SALES CO., INC.
PO Box 126
Forest City, PA 18421-0126
e-mail: kartri@nep.net
570-785-3365 • Fax 570-785-9094

KASHWERE LLC
7855 Gross Point Rd Ste J
Skokie, IL 60077-2646
e-mail: kashwere@aol.com
847-677-6344 • Fax 847-677-6341

KASON WESTERN
3883 Via Pescador Ste C
Camarillo, CA 93012-5053
800-935 2766 • Fax 805-987-4080

KATCHALL INDUSTRIES
5400 Creek Rd
Cincinnati, OH 45242-4002
www.katchall.com
704-987-9951 • Fax 704-987-9685

KATCHALL INDUSTRIES INTL
5800 Creek Rd
Cincinnati, OH 45242-4010
www.katchall.com
513-793-5366 • Fax 513-792-4230

KATIC OF NY
107 Northern Blvd
Great Neck, NY 11021-4309
516-829-1633

KAUFMAN ROSSIN & CO.
2699 S Bayshore Dr
Miami, FL 33133-5408
305-858-5600

KAUFMANN ASSOCIATES
2201 Cross Country Blvd
Baltimore, MD 21209-4223
e-mail: billk@contraq.com
www.contraq.com
800-229-9737 • Fax 800-229-9329

KAUFMANN-KWALE MARKETING
145 Dixon Ave
Amityville, NY 11701-2811
e-mail: kaufmannkwale@aol
631-226-2222 • Fax 631-226-2291

KAVEN COMPANY, INC.
787 Brannan St
San Francisco, CA 94103-4921
415-552-5544 • Fax 415-552-6987

KAY CHEMICAL COMPANY
8300 Capital Dr
Greensboro, NC 27409-9790
e-mail: al.music@ecolab.com
800-333-4300 • Fax 800-770-9763

KAYEM FOODS, INC.
PO Box 505728
Chelsea, MA 02150-5728
e-mail: kim.puleo@kayem.com
www.kayem.com
617-889-1600 • Fax 617-889-5478

KD KANOPY, INC.
3755 W 69th Pl
Westminster, CO 80030-6008
www.kdkanopy.com
800-432-4435 • Fax 303-650-5093

KD KANOPY,INC.
PO Box 203281
Austin, TX 78720-3281
800-383-6498

KEATING OF CHICAGO INC
715 25th Ave
Bellwood, IL 60104-1997
www.keatingofchicago.com
708-544-6500 • Fax 708-544-6505

KEEBLER COMPANY
1 Hollow Tree Ln
Elmhurst, IL 60126-1501
630-833-2900 • Fax 630-617-5350

KEEBLER FOOD SERVICE
2003 Mountain View Rd
Austin, TX 78703-2203
www.keebler.com
512-478-1004 • Fax 512-478-2590

KEELER & CO JOHN
370 NW 80th St
Miami, FL 33150-2945
888-663-2722

KELEIDOSCOPE KITCHENS
5674 Stoneridge Dr
Pleasanton, CA 94588-8500
925-734-1595 • Fax 925-734-1599

KELLAY GOURMET FOODS
2095 Jerrold Ave Ste 218
San Francisco, CA 94124-1628
415-648-9200 • Fax 415-648-6164

KELLER'S CRAMERY
832 Harleysville Pike
Harleysville, PA 19438-1039
www.kellercreamery.com
215-256-3193 • Fax 215-256-9015

KELLEY-CLARKE FOOD BROKERS
6300 Dumbarton Cir
Fremont, CA 94555-3644
510-790-6300

KELLOGG'S
1 Kellogg Sq
Battle Creek, MI 49017-3534
616-961-6617 • Fax 616-961-3487

KELMAX EQUIPMENT CO.
814 Jordan Ln
Decatur, GA 30033-5711
404-296-9080 • Fax 404-296-3040

KEMLITE CO.
PO Box 2429
Joliet, IL 60434-2429
www.Kemlite.com
815-467-8600 • Fax 815-467-8666

KEMP LOUIS SEAFOOD CO
PO Box 85362
San Diego, CA 92186-5362
800-422-1421

KEMPCO
525 Park East Blvd Ste 4
New Albany, IN 47150-7259
812-948-7800 • Fax 812-948-7882

KEMPER BAKERY SYSTEMS
PO Box 188
Madison, CT 06443-0188
800-244-9819

KEN COAT, INC.
210 Kane Ave
Leitchfield, KY 42754-1314
www.kencoat.com
270-259-5798 • Fax 270-259-9858

KEN LOYD
406 Brooks Ave
Venice, CA 90291-3038
800-536-5693

KEN WHITE CONSULTANTS
7 James St
Westwood, NJ 07675-2916
201-664-5664

KENDALL COLLEGE
2408 Orrington Ave
Evanston, IL 60201-2899
www.kendall.edu
847-866-1300

KENERSON ASSOCIATES
461 Boston St Unit 2
Topsfield, MA 01983-1234
e-mail: kenerson@kenerson.com
978-887-2727 • Fax 978-887-1918

KEN'S CASUAL, INC.
1352 Combermere Dr
Troy, MI 48083-4803
248-585-6629

**KEN'S STEAKHOUSE
DRESSING & SALAD**
20711 Vista Del Norte
Yorba Linda, CA 92886-3121
714-701-9400 • Fax 714-701-9400

KENT SEATECH CORP
11125 Flintkote Ave
San Diego, CA 92121-1213
858-452-5765

KENT STATE UNIVERSITY
100 Nixson Hall
Kent, OH 44242-0001
330-672-2197 • Fax 330-672-2194

**KENTUCKY RESTAURANT
ASSOCIATION**
422 Executive Park
Louisville, KY 40207-4204
502-896-0464

KENYON INTERNATIONAL
8 Heritage Park Rd
Clinton, CT 06413-1836
www.kenyoncustom.com
860-664-4906 • Fax 860-664-4907

**KEREKES BAKERY AND
RESTAURANT**
6103 15th Ave
Brooklyn, NY 11219-5402
e-mail: kerekeseqp@aol.com
www.kerekesequip.com
718-232-7044 • Fax 718-232-4416

KERIAN MACHINES INC
PO Box 311
Grafton, ND 58237-0311
701-352-0480

KESSENICHS
131 S Fair Oaks Ave
Madison, WI 53704-5897
608-249-5391 • Fax 608-249-1628

KETCHUP WORLD
315 Baird Rd
Merion Station, PA 19066-1414
e-mail: bailis@ketchupworld.com
610-667-0769 • Fax 610-667-2751

KETTLE COOKED FOODS
7401 Will Rogers Blvd
Fort Worth, TX 76140-6019
817-568-9000

KETTLE CUISINE
270 2nd St
Chelsea, MA 02150-1802
www.kettlecuisine.com
617-884-1131 • Fax 617-884-1041

KETTLE FOODS
3944 NE Hoyt St
Portland, OR 97232-3330
www.kettlefoods.com
503-232-7426 • Fax 503-230-9471

KETTLE FOODS, INC.
PO Box 664
Salem, OR 97308-0664
503-364-0399 • Fax 503-371-1447

KETTLE KING COMPANY
630 S Main St
Rice Lake, WI 54868-2578
800-399-8288 • Fax 253-891-3071

KEVRY CORPORATION
16133 W 45th Dr
Golden, CO 80403-1791
www.kevry.com
303-271-9300 • Fax 303-271-3645

**KEW FOREST MAINTENANCE
SUPPLY**
6890 Austin St
Forest Hills, NY 11375-4242
718-268-0040 • Fax 718-263-5508

KEY LINEN RENTAL
411 Hames Ave
Orlando, FL 32805-1512
www.kirbytent.com
407-422-1001

KEYFARMS
PO Box 2158
Gadsden, AL 35903-0158
256-492-4050

KG ASSOCIATES
237 Pembroke Ave
Wayne, PA 19087-4836
610-687-6490 • Fax 610-687-9505

KICHLER LIGHTING
7711 E Pleasant Valley Rd # R
Independence, OH 44131-5552
e-mail: mgardiner@kichler.com
www.kickler.com
216-573-1005 • Fax 216-573-1003

KID STUFF
PO Box 19235
Topeka, KS 66619-0235
www.kidstuffnet.com
800-667-4712 • Fax 785-862-0070

KIDDE FIRE SYSTEMS
400 Main St
Ashland, MA 01721-2150
800-872-6527

KIDZFIT INTERNATIONAL
2015 Birdcreek Ter Ste 106
Temple, TX 76502-8006
888-497-1300

KIGSTON MCKNIGH
877 Malcolm Rd
Burlingame, CA 94010-1406
www.kigstonmckinght
650-259-6400 • Fax 650-259-6406

KIKO FOODS, INC.
2628 Lexington Ave
Kenner, LA 70062-5369
504-466-2090

KILLER SALSA PICANTE
PO Box 943
Minden, NV 89423-0943
775-782-0048 • Fax 775-783-9922

**KIM & SCOTT'S GOURMET
PRETZELS**
2107 W Carroll Ave
Chicago, IL 60612-1603
312-243-9971 • Fax 312-243-9972

KIMBALL & YOUNG INC.
2142 Rheem Dr Ste D
Pleasanton, CA 94588-5600
e-mail: kimballyou@aol.com
www.kimballyoung.com
800-639-6864 • Fax 925-426-1685

**KIMBALL INTERNATIONAL
MFG.**
1710 Kimball Blvd
Jasper, IN 47549-1006
www.kimball.com
812-634-3382 • Fax 812-634-3149

KIMBALL L ROBERT & ASSOC
615 W Highland Ave
Ebensburg, PA 15931-1048
814-472-7700

KIMBALL LODGING GROUP
1180 E 16th St
Jasper, IN 47549-1009
www.kimball.com
800-451-8090 • Fax 812-482-8188

KIMBERLY-CLARK CORP
1400 Holcomb Bridge Rd
Roswell, GA 30076-2190
770-587-8909

KING ARTHUR
PO Box 6029
Statesville, NC 28687-6029
800-257-7244 • Fax 704-872-4194

KING ARTHUR FLOUR
PO Box 876
Norwich, VT 05055-0876
800-777-4434

KING CHESSECAKE CO, INC.
150 Lockhaven Dr
Houston, TX 77073-5500
281-209-1511 • Fax 281-209-1611

KING COMMERCIAL
10024 Office Center Ave # 1
Saint Louis, MO 63128-1381
314-842-7000

KING MENUS
124 NW 10th St Ste 104
Meridian, ID 83642-3726
208-888-4688

KING PLASTICS INC
840 N Elm St
Orange, CA 92867-7908
714-997-7540

**KING SAILFISH
MOUNTS, INC.**
PO Box 2962
Pompano Beach, FL 33072-2962
www.kingsailfish.com
954-784-8373 • Fax 954-784-8453

KING TRUCKS GM - ISUZU
1406 Sand Lake Rd
Orlando, FL 32809-7054
800-444-8701 • Fax 407-851-6618

KINGS CANYON CORRIN LLC
1750 S Buttonwillow Ave
Reedley, CA 93654-4400
559-638-3571

KING'S COMMAND FOODS
7622 S 188th St
Kent, WA 98032-1021
www.kingscommand.com
425-251-6788 • Fax 425-251-0523

KINGS FOODSERVICE, INC.
824 Meadowbrook Dr
Lexington, KY 40503-3724
859-254-6475

KING'S HAWAIIAN BREAD
406 Amapola Ave
Torrance, CA 90501-6217
310-533-3250 • Fax 310-533-8352

KIP INCORPORATED
72 Spring Ln
Farmington, CT 06032-3140
www.kipinc.com
860-677-0272 • Fax 860-677-4999

KITCHEN - TEK SOUTH
4750 N Dixie Hwy
Fort Lauderdale, FL 33334-3948
954-771-7970 • Fax 954-771-1887

KITCHENS OF THE OCEANS
4400 N Federal Hwy Ste 410
Boca Raton, FL 33431-5180
www. Kotoshrimp.com
954-421-2192 • Fax 954-421-5207

KITCHEN-TEK
3202 Greenpoint Ave
Long Island City, NY 11101-2010
e-mail: kitchentek@aol.com
www.kitchen-tek.com
718-937-2993

KIYBELE CREATIONS
PO Box 428
Armonk, NY 10504-0428
914-273-6659 • Fax 914-273-4336

KLEIN BROS LTD
1515 S Fresno Ave
Stockton, CA 95206-1179

KLEMENTS SAUAGE CO
207 E Lincoln Ave
Milwaukee, WI 53207-1593
414-481-4840

KLINEDINST FLIEHMAN MCKILLOP
501 W Broadway Ste 600
San Diego, CA 92101-3584
619-239-8131

KLNB, INC.
4061 Powder Mill Rd
Beltsville, MD 20705-3149
301-937-5151

KLOCKE OF AMERICA
14201 Jetport Loop
Fort Myers, FL 33913-7713
e-mail:
packaging@klockeamerica.com
www.klockeamerica.com
239-561-5800 • Fax 239-561-5811

KLOGS-USA
400 Ramsey Dr
Sullivan, MO 63080-1458
www.klogs.com
573-468-5564 • Fax 573-468-5560

KLOPPENBURG & CO
2627 W Oxford Ave
Englewood, CO 80110-4391
800-346-3246

KNAPP SHOES, INC.
1 Knapp Ctr
Brockton, MA 02301-5575
800-869-9306

KNF FLEXPAK CORPORATION
RR 3 Box 6B
Tamaqua, PA 18252-9433
e-mail: sales@knfcorporation.com
www.knfcorporation.com
570-386-3550 • Fax 570-386-3703

KNIGHT DISTRIBUTING CO.
2150 Boggs Rd Ste 370
Duluth, GA 30096-8695
e-mail: knightdist@juno.com
770-623-2650 • Fax 770-623-2663

KNIGHT EQUIPMENT INTL
2945 Airway Ave
Costa Mesa, CA 92626-6007
714-557-5400

KNOOP & ASSOCIATES, INC.
2212 Mahan Dr
Louisville, KY 40299-1700
502-244-2035

KOALA CORPORATION
11600 E 53rd Ave Unit D
Denver, CO 80239-2329
303-574-1000

KOALA TEE, INC
2160 17th St
Sarasota, FL 34234-7654
e-mail: dakoalaman@aol.com
941-954-7700

KOBLENZ-THRONE ELECTRIC
610 Lanark Dr Ste 205
San Antonio, TX 78218-1844
e-mail: info@koblenz-electric.com
www.koblenz-electric.com
210-590-1226 • Fax 210-590-1258

KOBRAND
134 E 40th St
New York, NY 10016-1796
212-692-4702 • Fax 212-983-0774

KOBRAND CORPORATION
440 NW 113th Ave
Pompano Beach, FL 33071-7970
e-mail: lnocera@kobrand.com
954-345-3967 • Fax 954-345-1967

KOCH SUPPLIES
1411 W 29th St
Kansas City, MO 64108-3681
816-753-2150

KOERNER COMPANY
4820 Jefferson Hwy
New Orleans, LA 70121-3127
504-734-1100

KOHLER COMPANY
444 Highland Dr # 19
Kohler, WI 53044-1541
www.kohlerco.com
920-457-4441 • Fax 920-459-1747

KOHLER MIX SPECIALITIES
4900 Constellation Dr
Saint Paul, MN 55127-2218
651-765-6200 • Fax 651-765-6290

KOLD-DRAFT
1525 E Lake Rd
Erie, PA 16511-1088
814-453-6761

KOLDMASTER
2920 NW 109th Ave
Miami, FL 33172-5005
305-357-0280 • Fax 305-492-2240

KOLPAK
244 W 7th St
Parsons, TN 38363-4661
www.kolpak.com
800-826-7036 • Fax 731-847-5264

KONAMI AMUSEMENT OF AMERICA
900 Deerfield Pkwy
Buffalo Grove, IL 60089-4510
847-215-5100

KONTOS FOODS, INC.
PO Box 628
Paterson, NJ 07544-0628
973-278-2800 • Fax 973-278-7943

KOOL STAR
15001 S Broadway St
Gardena, CA 90248-1819
310-851-6060 • Fax 310 715-1110

KOPYKAKE
3699 W 240th St
Torrance, CA 90505-6002
310-373-8906

KORIN TRADING
57 Warren St
New York, NY 10007-1018
212-587-7021 • Fax 212-587-7027

KOSA-AVORA
198 Hosch Dr
Shelby, NC 28152-2720
704-480-4844

KOSTA FURNITURE
825 Brickell Bay Dr Ste 1
Miami, FL 33131-2936
e-mail: sales@kostafurniture.com
www.kostafurniture.com
305-577-3785 • Fax 305-577-3783

KOZA'S, INC.
2910 S Main St
Pearland, TX 77581-4710
e-mail: jmk@kozas.com
www.kozas.com
281-485-1462 • Fax 281-485-8000

KOZY SHACK INC
83 Ludy St
Hicksville, NY 11801-5114
800-938-1233

KPMG PEAT MARWICK LLP
90 S 7th St
Minneapolis, MN 55402-3903
612-305-5411 • Fax 612-305-5041

KRAFT FOOD INC.
5142 Franklin Dr
Pleasanton, CA 94588-3355
925-416-4351 • Fax 925-416-4395

KRAFT FOOD SERVICE
7656 Executive Dr
Eden Prairie, MN 55344-3677
www.kraftfoods.com
952-949-8056 • Fax 952-949-9082

KRAFT FOOD SERVICE
9645 Legler Rd
Lenexa, KS 66219-1292
913-752-1859

KRAFT FOOD SERVICES
3110 Cherry Palm Dr
Tampa, FL 33619-8304
www.kraftfoods.com
813-744-2671

KRAFT FOODS
3 Lakes Dr
Winnetka, IL 60093-2754
847-646-2000

KRAFT FOODS
8150 Springwood Dr
Irving, TX 75063-3119
e-mail: kfhsgoo@msx.kraft.geis.com
www.kraftfoods.com
972-307-4641 • Fax 972-367-6080

KRAVET
225 Central Ave S
Bethpage, NY 11714-4990
e-mail: Contract@kfi.net
888-891-4112 • Fax 516-293-9358

KREATIVE FOODS
1112 Industrial Pkwy
Brick, NJ 08724-2508
732-840-1670 • Fax 732-840-1608

KROEGER ASSOCIATES
1259 S Cedar Crest Blvd
Allentown, PA 18103-6206
610-821-1299

KRONOS PRODUCTS, INC
501 W 42nd Pl
Chicago, IL 60632-3925
773-847-2250 • Fax 773-847-2492

KROST BAUMGARTEN KNISS & GUERR
719 E Union St
Pasadena, CA 91101-1821
626-449-4225

KROWNE METAL CROP
257 Verona Ave
Newark, NJ 07104-2454
973-485-2611 • Fax 973-485-1424

KRUGER PICKLES
22958 Saklan Rd
Hayward, CA 94545-1404
www.krugerfoods.com
510-782-2636 • Fax 510-782-8130

KRUSE-LALLY-ROLFES ASSOC.
4739 Delhi Ave
Cincinnati, OH 45238-5405
513-244-2250

KRYSTAL BLDG
1 Union Sq
Chattanooga, TN 37402-2505
800-458-5912

KS FERGUSON CO INC
15146 Beech Dr
Lowell, AR 72745-9224
479-751-1155 • Fax 479-927-0534

K-TEC
1206 S 1680 W
Orem, UT 84058-4938
800-748-5400

KULLMAN INDUSTRIES, INC
1 Kullman Corporate Campus Dr
Lebanon, NJ 08833-2163
www.kullman .com
888-882-CART • Fax 908-236-8467

K-WAY PRODUCTS, INC.
PO Box 7
Mount Carroll, IL 61053-0007
815-244-2800

KWC FAUCETS, INC
1770 Corporate Dr Ste 580
Norcross, GA 30093-2945
www.kwcfaucets.com
770-248-1600 • Fax 770-248-1608

KWIK LOK CORP
PO Box 9548
Yakima, WA 98909-0548
800-688-5945

KWV INTERNATIONAL-57 MAIN STRE
585 Stewart Ave Ste 544
Garden City, NY 11530-4785
e-mail: ralovettny@aol.com
www.kwv.co.za
516-357-2070 • Fax 516-357-8799

KYRUS CORP
113 Regional Park Dr
Kingsport, TN 37660-7455
800-932-6737

KYSOR-WARREN
1600 Industrial Blvd NW
Conyers, GA 30012-3936
770-483-5600 • Fax 770-929-4364

L & C MEAT INC
1136 S Vista Ave
Independence, MO 64056-2342
816-796-6100

L A VEN SALES
PO Box 1349
Simi Valley, CA 93062-1349
805-579-0220

L C GROUP
100 Walnut St
Champlain, NY 12919-5322
518-298-2929

L G C WIRELESS
2540 Junction Ave
San Jose, CA 95134-1902
408-952-2400

L & B EMPIRE
193 Route 303
Valley Cottage, NY 10989-2017
845-268-0082 • Fax 845-268-0323

L & B CONTRACT INDUSTRIES, INC.
PO Box 405
Haverstraw, NY 10927-0405
845-429-5700

L.A. BABY
2050 E 49th St
Los Angeles, CA 90058-2802
e-mail: lababyco@aol.com
www.photopoint.com
323-584-5198 • Fax 323-584-4819

L.A.M. ENTERPRISES, INC.
19 Trescott St
Huntington Station, NY 11746-7147
e-mail: anapoli@lam_solutions.com
www.lam.solutions.com
631-254-6600 • Fax 631-254-4014

L.F.I. INCORPORATED
271 US Highway 46 Ste C101
Fairfield, NJ 07004-2458
e-mail: ifiinc@aol.com
973-882-0550 • Fax 973-882-0554

L.R.ENTERPRISES
1022 Oak Grove Rd
Breezewood, PA 15533-8711
800-932-3942 • Fax 814-735-2055

LA BREA BAKERY
15963 Strathern St
Van Nuys, CA 91406-1313
818-742-4242 • Fax 818-373-5164

LA CANASTA MJEXICAN FOOD PRODUCTS
3101 W Jackson St
Phoenix, AZ 85009-4833
www.La-Canasta.com
602-269-7721 • Fax 602-269-7725

LA CROSSE COOLER CO.
W6636 L B White Rd
Onalaska, WI 54650-9082
608-783-2800 • Fax 608-783-6115

LA DESIGN & MARKETING
11100 Cumpston St Ste 41
North Hollywood, CA 91601-2713
e-mail: ladandmkt@aol.com
818-769-9314 • Fax 818-769-8891

LA ESPIGA DE ORO
1202 W 15th St
Houston, T 77008-3816
713-861-4200 • Fax 713-861-3923

LA FAMIGLIA, INC.
PO Box 841731
Houston, TX 77284-1731
e-mail: lafamigliainc@mciworld.com
www.lafamigliacucina.com
713-345-4575 • Fax 713-550-5549

LA FE FOODS
230 Moonachie Ave
Moonachie, NJ 07074-1805
201-867-3141

LA MEXICANA
2703 S Kedzie Ave
Chicago, IL 60623-4735
e-mail: LAMEX@enteract.com
773-247-5443 • Fax 773-247-9004

LA MOUSSE
11162 La Grange Ave
Los Angeles, CA 90025-5632
www.lamoussedesserts.com
310-478-6051 • Fax 310-477-2415

LA NOVA WINGS INC
371 W Ferry St
Buffalo, NY 14213-1947
716-881-3355

LA PREFERIDA
3400 W 35th St
Chicago, IL 60632-3399
www.lapref.com
773-254-7200 • Fax 773-254-8546

LA ROMAGNOLA
2215 Tradeport Dr
Orlando, FL 32824-7005
407-856-4343

LA ROSA
19191 Filer St
Detroit, MI 48234-2883
800-527-6723

LA TOPATIA TORTILLERIA, INC
104 E Belmont Ave
Fresno, CA 93701-1403
559-441-1030 • Fax 559-441-1712

LA. DEPT. OF AGRICULTURE
122 Saint John St Rm 231
Monroe, LA 71201-7373
318-362-3185

LA. DEPT. OF HEALTH & HOSPITAL
6867 Bluebonnet Blvd
Baton Rouge, LA 70810-1635
225-763-5553

LABATT USA
PO Box 5075
Norwalk, CT 06856-5075
800-769-5337 • Fax 203-750-6699

LABRAZEL, LLC
PO Box 4357
Hamden, CT 06514-0357
203-281-3888 • Fax 203-281-5873

LACTALIS USA
950 3rd Ave
New York, NY 10022-2705
212-758-6666

LACUS COFFEE COMPANY
7950 National Hwy
Pennsauken, NJ 08110-1412
856-910-8663 • Fax 856-910-8671

LADDER WORKS
1125 E Saint Charles Rd
Lombard, IL 60148-2090
www.uncommonusainc.com
630-268-9672 • Fax 630-268-9655

LADY BALTIMORE FOODS INC
1601 Fairfax Trfy
Kansas City, KS 66115-1407
913-279-6538

LAFFERTY AND COMPANY
PO Box 588
Grandview, MO 64030-0588
816-765-2710

LAFRANCAIS
111 Northwest Ave

Melrose Park, IL 60164-1683
800-654-7220 • Fax 708-562-0373

LAGUNA LIGHTING
13280 Amar Rd
La Puente, CA 91746-1202
626-912-6844

LAITRAM MACHINERY INC
PO Box 50699
New Orleans, LA 70150-0699
504-733-6000

LAKE CHAMPLAIN CHOCOLATES
750 Pine St
Burlington, VT 05401-4923
www.lakechamplainchocolate.com
802-864-1808 • Fax 802-864-1806

LAKE INDUSTRIES CO
715 Arrow Grand Cir
Covina, CA 91722-2148
800-261-4501

LAKESIDE MFG INC
1977 S Allis St
Milwaukee, WI 53207-1248
414-481-3900

LAM LEE GROUP
488 S Royal Ln
Coppell, TX 75019-3820
972-957-0434 • Fax 972-957-6523

LAMAR ADVERTISING
8510 Breen Dr
Houston, TX 77064-8407
e-mail: ofmg223@lamarhg.com
www.lamar.com
281-896-0447 • Fax 281-896-9246

LAMB WESTON INC
PO Box 1900
Pasco, WA 99302-1900
509-735-4651 • Fax 509-736-0345

LAMB WESTON, INC.
8701 W Gage Blvd
Kennewick, WA 99336-1034
509-943-3552 • Fax 509-943-5218

LAMBERT FURNITURE
1301 New York Ave
Trenton, NJ 08638-3398
e-mail: sales@lambertfurniture.com
609-394-7000 • Fax 609-396-9781

LAMBERTSON
490 S Rock Blvd
Reno, NV 89502-4111
www.lambertson.net
775-857-1100 • Fax 775-857-3289

LAMB-WESTON, INC.
8701 W Gage Blvd # C
Kennewick, WA 99336-1034
509-736-0482

LAMD WESTON, INC
913 W River St Ste 300
Boise, ID 83702-7080
www.lambweston.com
208-388-4287 • Fax 208-422-2111

LAMONIA ASSOCIATES
9812 Falls Rd StE 114
Potomac, MD 20854-3963
301-365-4996 • Fax 301-365-4997

LANCASTER PRODUCTS, INC.
1731 Midway Rd
Odenton, MD 21113-1127
410-519-0190

LANCE, INC.
636 Gause Blvd Ste 202
Slidell, LA 70458-2038
985-641-1690

LANCE, INC.
PO Box 32368
Charlotte, NC 28232-2368
e-mail: bboley@lance.com
704-554-1421 • Fax 704-556-5638

LANCER
6655 Lancer Blvd
San Antonio, TX 78219-4735
210-310-7000 • Fax 210-310-7250

LAND O' LAKES
4001 Lexington Ave N

Saint Paul, MN 55126-2998
651-481-2222

LANDAU IDENTITY APPAREL
8410 W Sandidge Rd
Olive Branch, MS 38654-3412
662-895-7200

LANDAUER REALTY ADVISERS, INC.
225 W Wacker Dr Ste 2300
Chicago, IL 60606-1236
312-372-3133

LANDAUER REALTY ADVISORS, INC.
1 State St Fl 6
Boston, MA 02109-3507
617-720-0515

LANDGRAFF, MILBRETT & CO. LTD.
PO Box 87
Mankato, MN 56002-0087
507-625-2526

LANDOLL, INC.
1250 George Rd
Ashland, OH 44805-8916
www.landoll-inc.com
419-281-1100 • Fax 419-282-4145

LANE CONTRACT
701 5th St
Altavista, VA 24517-1719
e-mail: jconrad@lanefurn.com
www.lanecontract.com
434-369-3719 • Fax 434-369-3669

LANG MANUFACTURING CO.
6500 Merrill Creek Pkwy
Everett, WA 98203-5860
www.langworld.com
425-349-2400 • Fax 425-349-2733

LANIKAI INTERNATIONAL
1950 Radcliff Dr
Cincinnati, OH 45204-1823
513-244-6800

LAQUINTA INNS, INC
909 Hidden Rdg Ste 600
Irving, TX 75038-3822
www.laquinta.com
214-492-6712

LARANCHERA FOOD PROD. INC.
503 Berry Rd
Houston, TX 77022-3213
713-699-4400 • Fax 713-699-4343

LARIEN PRODUCTS
351 Pleasant St
Northampton, MA 01060-3900
800-462-9237

LAROCHE FILTER SYSTEMS, INC.
1100 Johnson Ferry Rd NE
Atlanta, GA 30342-1709
404-851-0616

LARONGA BAKERY
599 Somerville Ave
Somerville, MA 02143-3296
617-625-8600 • Fax 617-625-1853

LARSON-KRAMER-KJELSTROM
701 N York Rd
Hinsdale, IL 60521-2400
630-325-0384

LARSON-BINKLEY ASSOCIATES, INC
8900 State Line Rd Ste 150
Leawood, KS 66206-1940
913-383-2621

LASK SEATING-GRAND SEATING
2414 W 21st St
Chicago, IL 60608-2413
www.stoolsandchairs.com
773-254-3448 • Fax 773-254-1373

LAST SIGNATURE PRODUCTS
4751 Gulf Shore Blvd N
Naples, FL 34103-2638
877-943-7100 • Fax 877-880-1754

LAU INDUSTRIES INC

435 E Lincoln St
Banning, CA 92220-6061
909-849-6778

LAUIRE GATES DESIGNS
1936 Pontius Ave
Los Angeles, CA 90025-5612
310-575-1418 • Fax 310-575-1419

LAURA LEE DESIGN INC.
57 E Palm Ave
Burbank, CA 91502-1832
www.lauraleedesign.com
818-842-5300 • Fax 818-842-5730

LAVAZZA PREMIUM COFFEES
3 Park Avenue
New York, NY 10016-5902
www.lavazzausa.com
212-725-8800 • Fax 212-725-9475

LAVI INDUSTRIES
27810 Avenue Hopkins
Valencia, CA 91355-3409
800-624-6622

LAVI INDUSTRIES
2 Geneva Rd
Brewster, NY 10509-2340
e-mail: paulk@lavi.com
www.lavi.com
845-278-1766 • Fax 845-278-1765

LAWLER FOODS, INC.
PO Box 2558
Humble, TX 77347-2558
281-446-0059 • Fax 281-446-3806

LAWRENCE ESSENTIALS & NESTINGS
260 5th Ave Ste 417
New York, NY 10001-6408
e-mail: lawrence.e1@att.net
917-480-0042 • Fax 212-481-4078

LAWRENCE GLASER ASSOCIATES INC
505 S Lenola Rd
Moorestown, NJ 08057-1549
856-778-9500 • Fax 856-778-4390

LAWRENCE METALS
260 Spur Dr S
Bay Shore, NY 11706-3900
www.lawrencemetal.com
800-441-0019

LAWRENCE METALS
260 S Spur Dr # O
Bay Shore, NY 11706-3900
e-mail: service@lawrencemetal.com
www.lawrencemetal.com
631-666-0300 • Fax 631-666-0336

LAWRENCE'S DELIGHTS
2080 Peachtree Industrial Ct
Atlanta, GA 30341-2246
770-451-7774 • Fax 770-451-7623

LAWRYS FOODS INC
222 E Huntington Dr
Monrovia, CA 91016-3524
323-225-2491

LAWSON MARDON THERMAPLATE CORP
3033 E 16th St
Russellville, AR 72802-9435
732-469-6300 • Fax 732-469-0167

LAWSON SOFTWARE
380 Saint Peter St
Saint Paul, MN 55102-1313
800-477-1357

LAZAR INDUSTRIES
620 E Slauson Ave
Los Angeles, CA 90011-5234
www.lazarcontract.com
323-232-7170 • Fax 323-232-6366

LAZER-TRON
201 Lindbergh Ave
Livermore, CA 94550-7667
925-460-0873 • Fax 925-460-0365

LBP MUNUFACTURING
1325 S Cicero Ave
Cicero, IL 60804-1404
800-545-6200 • Fax 708-625-5537

LE BISTRO COFFEE & TEA
PO Box 1224
Bellmore, NY 11710-0717
516-902-5586

LE CHEF BAKERY
1221 Date St
Montebello, CA 90640-6318
323-888-2929

LE GOUR MATES BY MOSSHAIM INNO
772 Busch Ct
Columbus, OH 43229-1704
www.legourmates.com
888-995-7775 • Fax 888-995-7776

LE- JO ENTERPRISES, INC.
2 Lee Blvd
Malvern, PA 19355-1246
www.lejo.com
610-296-2800 • Fax 610-296-7993

LE NATURES
11 Lloyd Ave
Latrobe, PA 15650-1711
724-532-0600

LEA & PERRINS
15-01 Pollitt Dr
Fair Lawn, NJ 07410-2795
201-791-1600

LEADERSHIP NETWORK CORPORATION
1400 E Southern Ave Ste 405
Tempe, AZ 05282-5693
480-905-0907 • Fax 480-905 1224

LEADING EDGE—A DIVISION OF MARLEY
470 Beauty Spot Rd E
Bennettsville, SC 29512-2770
www.marleymeh.com
843-479-4006 • Fax 843-479-8912

LEADING HOTELS OF THE WORLD
747 3rd Ave
New York, NY 10017-2803
212-838-3110

LEATHER CENTER
2724 Realty Dr
Carrollton, TX 75006-5421
e-mail: lccommercial@leather-center.com
www.leathercenter.com
972-417-2282 • Fax 972-416-3022

LEAVES-PURE TEAS
1392 Lowrie Ave
South San Francisco, CA 94080-6402
www.leaves.com
650-583-1157 • Fax 650-583-1163

LEAVITT COMMUNICATIONS
PO Box 579
Lincolnshire, IL 60069-0579
www. leavittcom.com
800-870-3686 • Fax 630-676-8744

LEBOEUF & ASSOCIATES
PO Box 932
N Falmouth, MA 02556-0932
e-mail: leboeuf@aol.com
508-884-5666 • Fax 508-884-2040

LECOQ CUISINE CORPORATION
430 Fairfield Ave
Stamford, CT 06902-7522
203-359-1571 • Fax 203-359-1572

LEE KUM KEE (USA) INC.
304 S Date Ave
Alhambra, CA 91803-1404
www.lkk.com
626-282-0337 • Fax 626-282-3425

LEE TENNIS PRODUCTS
999 Grove St
Charlottesville, VA 22903-3400
800-327-8379

LEES COMMERCIAL CARPETS
3330 W Friendly Ave
Greensboro, NC 27410-4806
336-379-2000

LEESTEMAKER FINE ARTS
13158 Chandler Blvd
Van Nuys, CA 91401-6051
e-mail: luc@lucleestemaker.com
www.lucleestemaker.com
818-461-1385 • Fax 818-461-1385

LEGEL AGE SYSTEMS, INC
5135 Adanson St Ste 200
Orlando, FL 32804-1353
407-628-2700

LEGGETT & PLATT INC
7250 Santa Fe Dr
La Grange, IL 60525-5017
708-579-8900

LEGGETT AND PLATT
1 Leggett Rd
Carthage, MO 64836-9649
www.leggett.com
417-358-8131 • Fax 417-542-7155

LEGION INDUSTRIES
PO Box F
Dallas, PA 18612-0108
800-833-9803

LEGITO, INC.
950 Longfellow Ave
Bronx, NY 10474-4809
718-617-6832 • Fax 718-542-6012

LEGO & SONS DAIRY, INC.
212 Pembroke St
Concord, NH 03301-5760
603-224-1942 • Fax 603-224-9558

LEHIGH SAFETY SHOE COMPANY
120 Plaza Dr Ste A
Vestal, NY 13850-3640
www.lehighsafetyshoes.com
607-757-4364 • Fax 607-757-4070

LEHMAN BROTHERS
3 World Financial Ctr
New York, NY 10285-0001
www.lehman.com
212-526-5849 • Fax 212-526-0035

LEIFHEIT INTERNATIONAL USA
510 Broadhollow Rd
Melville, NY 11747-3671
516-501-1054

LEKTRON INC
1319 Wabash Ave
Terre Haute, IN 47807-3313
888-335-8894

LELAND LIMITED, INC.
PO Box 466
South Plainfield, NJ 07080-0466
www.lelandltd.com
908-668-1008 • Fax 908-668-7716

LEMAITRE & ASSOCIATES
3534 E Corona Ave
Phoenix, AZ 85040-2842
602-243-1918

LEMON-X CORP.
PO Box 20800
Huntington Sta, NY 11746-0863
www.lemon-x.com
516-997-3334 • Fax 516-997-2519

LEN TEX
1 Len-Tex Ln
North Walpole, NH 03609-1140
603-445-2342

LENOX BRANDS
100 Lenox Dr
Trenton, NJ 08648-2309
609-844-1490

LENOX MARTEL, INC.
89 Heath St
Jamaica Plain, MA 02130-1402
617-442-7777 • Fax 617-522-9455

LEON BERKOWITZ ASSOCIATES, INC
111 Washington Ave
Dumont, NJ 07628-3067
e-mail: fdsvcpdlr@aol.com
www.lberkowitz.com
201-387-9555 • Fax 201-387-9595

LEON'S TEXAS CUISINE
PO Box 1850
Mc Kinney, TX 75070-1850
www.texascuisine.com
972-529-5050 • Fax 972-529-2244

LEPRINO FOODS CO
1830 W 38th Ave
Denver, CO 80211-2200
800-537-7466

LES CHATEAUX DE FRANCE
1 Craft Ave
Inwood, NY 11096-1609
e-mail: lcdf@compuserve.com
516-239-6795 • Fax 516-239-6215

LES TROIS PETITS COCHONS
453 Greenwich St
New York, NY 10013-1757
e-mail: info@3pigs.com
212-941-9726

LESTER LANIN ORCHESTRAS
157 W 57th St
New York, NY 10019-2210
212-265-5208

LEUCOS USA INC
70 Campus Dr
Edison, NJ 08837-3911
732-225-0010

LEVENSON, KATZIN
3001 Hollywood Blvd # A
Hollywood, FL 33021-6758
954-961-7940

LEVONIAN BROTHERS INC.
27 River St
Troy, NY 12180-4449
518-274-3610 • Fax 518-274-0098

LEVTOV INTERNATIONAL
4023 18th Ave
Brooklyn, NY 11218-5707
e-mail: lexmark_cpt@hotmail.com
800-871-3211 • Fax 347-277-6236

LEWIS PARTNERS INC
433 California St
San Francisco, CA 94104-2016
415-362-7511 • Fax 415-362-7518

LEXINGTON SERVICES CORP
150 Independence Dr
Dallas, TX 75237-2911
972-714-0585

LIBBEY GLASS, INC.
5 Fencourt Rd
Canton, MA 02021-3211
e-mail: mccardp@libbey.com
www.libbey.com
781-830 0247 • Fax 781-830-0249

LIBBEY, INC.
300 Madison Ave
Toledo, OH 43604-1561
www.libbey.com
419-325-2288 • Fax 419-325-2367

LIBBEY, INC.
PO Box 10060
Toledo, OH 43699-0060
419-727-2504

LIBBEY, INC.
3793 Charleston Loop
Oviedo, FL 32765-9202
e-mail: martinjp@libbey.com
407-977-3044 • Fax 407-977-3051

LIBERTY BELL STEAK CO. INC.
3457 Janney St
Philadelphia, PA 19134-2607
800-496-6868 • Fax 215-537-1256

LIBERTY FRUIT CO INC
1247 Argentine Blvd
Kansas City, KS 66105-1508
913-281-5200

LIBERTY PAPER & JANITORIAL SUPPLIES
180 W 52nd St
Bayonne, NJ 07002-2111
e-mail: libpaper@ix-netcom.com
201-823-1100 • Fax 201-823-1156

LIBERTY SYSTEMS INTERNATIONAL INC
2171 W Park Ct Ste E
Stone Mountain, GA 30087-3556
770-469-0333

LIBERTY TEXTILE CO
5600 S Marginal Rd
Cleveland, OH 44103-1077
800-881-5994

LIBERTY WOODCRAFTS INC
3300 N Benzing Rd
Orchard Park, NY 14127-1538
e-mail: libertywoodcrafts.com
www.libertywoodcrafts.com
716-824-6067 • Fax 716-824-6075

LIFE GUARD SUPPLY, INC.
18400 San Jose Ave
Rowland Heights, CA 91748-1254
www.lifeguardgloves.com
626-965-1588 • Fax 626-965-3599

LIFEDANCE DISTRIBUTION
3479 NW Yeon Ave
Portland, OR 97210-1535
503-228-9430 • Fax 503-228-5039

LIFELINE FOODS CO INC
426 Orange Ave
Seaside, CA 93955-3517
831-899-5040 • Fax 831-899-0285

LIFETIME
PO Box 160010
Clearfield, UT 84016-0010
www.lifetime.com
801-776-1532 • Fax 801-776-4397

LIGHT WAVES
1 Bond St Apt 2C
New York, NY 10012-2307
212-677-5267 • Fax 914-212-6945

LIGHT VISION CONFECTIONS
1776 Mentor Ave
Cincinnati, OH 45212-3554
www.lightvision.com
513-351-9441 • Fax 513-981-0758

LIGHTHOUSE MEDIA, INC.
1050 Broadway Ste 17
Chesterton, IN 46304-2173
219-921-0993

LIGHTINGUNIVERSE.COM
12804 NE 125th Way
Kirkland, WA 98034-7718
888-404-2744

LIGHTS OF DISTINCTION-CRYSTORA
95 Cantiague Rock Rd
Westbury, NY 11590-2826
516-931-9090 • Fax 516-931-1254

LIK-NU
179 Woodbury Rd
Hicksville, NY 11801-3039
516-781-5542 • Fax 516-933-8380

LI'L GUY FOODS
1717 N Topping Ave
Kansas City, MO 64120-1225
816-241-2000

LIL' ORBITS, INC.
2850 Vicksburg Ln N
Minneapolis, MN 55447-1878
www.lilorbits.com
763-559-7505 • Fax 763-559-7545

LILY FOODS, INC.
1836 S Canal St
Chicago, IL 60616-1502
312-733-1688 • Fax 312-733-7917

LIME BOMBER
445 Village Grn Unit 203
Lincolnshire, IL 60069-3092
e-mail: limebombwe1@aol.com
847-955-9889 • Fax 847-955-9890

LIMPERT BROTHERS, INC.
PO Box 520
Vineland, NJ 08362-0520
856-794-8968

LINCOLN FOODSERVICE PROD.
PO Box 122
Fort Wayne, IN 46801-0122
e-mail: jjohnson@lincolnFP.com
www.lincolnFP.com
260-459-8200 • Fax 260-436-0735

LINCOLN FOODSERVICE PRODUCTS-WELBILT
PO Box 1229
Fort Wayne, IN 46801-1229
260-432-9511

LINENS OF THE WEEK
713 Lamont St NW
Washington, DC 20010-1526
www.linensoftheweek.com
202-291-9200

LINK'S SNACKS INC
PO Box 397
Minong, WI 54859-0397
715-466-2234

LINKSOURCE CORP
8912 E Pinnacle Peak Rd
Scottsdale, AZ 85255-3659
800-546-5768

LINPAC MATERIALS HANDLNG
3626 N Hall St Ste 729
Dallas, TX 75219-5127
214-599-9023

LINVILLE ARCHITECTS
408 E Wilson St
Madison, WI 53703-3429
608-251-6696

LION APPAREL-AARON UNIFORM
6450 Poe Ave # 14576
Dayton, OH 45414-2600
937-898-1949

LIONI LATTICINI MOZZERELLA
555 Lehigh Ave
Union, NJ 07083-7976
e-mail: jeffsilver@worldnet.att.net
800-528-3252 • Fax 908-241-4981

LIPPINCOTT WILLIAMS & WILKINS
351 W Camden St
Baltimore, MD 21201-7912
800-486-5643

LIPTEN & COMPANY
4376 L B McLeod Rd
Orlando, FL 32811-5619
407-425-2651

LIPTON
800 Sylvan Ave
Englewood Cliffs, NJ 07632-3201
201-567-8000

LIQUID ASSETS
5904 Jessamine St Ste A1
Houston, TX 77081-6523
e-mail: assets@liuid-assets.com
www.liquid-assets.com
713-838-065 • Fax 713-836-0645

LIQUID DISTRIBUTORS, INC.
13439 NE 17th Ave
Miami, FL 33181-1716
e-mail:
liquid_distributors@yahoo.com
305-892-1188 • Fax 305-892-1255

LIQUID ICE
29 Oxford Rd
Natick, MA 01760-1432
508-651-2563 • Fax 508-651-2182

LIQUOR LICENSE SPECIALISTS-ABC
10350 Santa Monica Blvd
Los Angeles, CA 90025-5055
www.liquorlicense.com
310-553-6363 • Fax 310-553-3996

LITE ANTIQUE HARDWARE
453 S La Brea Ave
Los Angeles, CA 90036-3523
e-mail: shop@lahardware.com
www.lahardware.com
323-939-4403 • Fax 323-939-4387

LITEHOUSE DRESSINGS, DIPS, & SALADS
PO Box 1969
Sandpoint, ID 83864-0910
www.litehousefoods.com
208-669-3169 • Fax 208-263-7821

LITERATURE DISPLAY PROD.
PO Box 501790
Indianapolis, IN 46250-6790
800-669-4399 • Fax 317-841-4391

LITTLE LADY FOODS, INC.
2323 Pratt Blvd
Elk Grove Village, IL 60007-5918
www.littleladyfoods.com
847-806-1440 • Fax 847-806-0026

LITTLE TIKES COMMERCIAL PLAY
1 Iron Mountain Rd
Farmington, MO 63640-9103
e-mail: lcdesign3@aol.com
800-325-8863 • Fax 573-760-7453

LITTLER MENDELSON
885 3rd Ave Fl 14
New York, NY 10022-4834
212-308-1900

LO DUCA BROTHERS, INC.
400 N Broadway
Milwaukee, WI 53202-5510
800-569-6848 • Fax 414-347-1232

LOBSTER TRAP CO
290 Shore Rd
Buzzards Bay, MA 02532-4104
508-759-4928

LOCAL INVESTMENT COMMIS-SION
417 Walker Ave
Kansas City, KS 66101-2339
913-371-7904

LOCKTECH, INC.
214 E Lea Blvd
Wilmington, DE 19802-2301
e-mail: itikeycard@aol.com
www.hotelkeycard.com
800-365-0004 • Fax 302-765-3761

LOCKWOOD MANUFACTURING
31251 Industrial Rd
Livonia, MI 48150-2099
800-521-0238 • Fax 734-427-5650

LODGCON
102 Pilgrim Village Dr
Cumming, GA 30040-2577
770-887-2949

LODGENET ENTERTAINMENT
808 N West Ave
Sioux Falls, SD 57104-5720
605-330-1330

LODGING CONCEPTS, INC.
203 Berg St
Algonquin, IL 60102-3537
e-mail: sales@lodgingconcepts.com
www.lodgingconcepts.com
800-330-5983 • Fax 847-854-8874

LODGING CONFERENCE
150 E 58th St
New York, NY 10155-0002
80-338-3004

LODGING KIT COMPANY
13492 State Route 12
Boonville, NY 13309-3531
e-mail: Lkc@borg.com
www.lodgingkit.com
315-942-4246 • Fax 315-942-5622

LODGING MANAGEMENT SYS.
578 Old Norcross Rd
Lawrenceville, GA 30045-4314
800-241-8768 • Fax 770-962-3231

LODGING TECHNOLOGY CORP.
PO Box 7919
Roanoke, VA 24019-0919
540-362-7500 • Fax 540-366-3521

LODGISTIX-HMS
2150 E Highland Ave
Phoenix, AZ 85016-4718
602-952-7240

LOFFREDO FRESH PRODUCE CO. INC
4001 SW 63rd St
Des Moines, IA 50321-1607
515-285-3367

LOFTHOUSE FOODS
PO Box 160460
Clearfield, UT 84016-0460
801-776-3500 • Fax 801-776-3700

LOGISTICS CONSULTANTS OF AMERICA
2635 Victoria Park Dr
Riverside, CA 92506-3341
909-784-6255 • Fax 909-788-1655

LOGIX COMPANIES, THE
2101 Ken Pratt Blvd
Longmont, CO 80501-6567
e-mail: dmitry.rozendorf@logixco.com
303-757-0064 • Fax 303-757-0104

LOGO FLOOR MATS
PO Box 230
Forest City, IA 50436-0230
888-628-5646

LOGOIZE
3001 Cherry St
Kansas City, MO 64108-3124
816-931-4477 • Fax 816-931-0504

LOGRET IMPORT & EXPORT CO.
150 Willow Ave
La Puente, CA 91746-2038
e-mail: admin@logret.com
626-961-9800

LOMBARDI BROTHERS MEATS
7501 Commerce Ln NE
Minneapolis, MN 55432-3123
763-571-6760 • Fax 763-571-9335

LOMBARDIS SEAFOOD
7491 Brokerage Dr
Orlando, FL 32809-5633
e-mail: terri@lombardis.com
www.lombardis.com
407-859-1015

LONE PALM INC.
8 Rosemary Ln
Clarksville, AR 72830-9186
e-mail: david@swabi.com
800-840-2499 • Fax 479-754-5233

LONE STAR CONSOLIDATED FOODS
1727 N Beckley Ave
Dallas, TX 75203-1077
214-946-2185 • Fax 214-946-2286

LONG RANGE SYSTEMS
9855 Chartwell Dr
Dallas, TX 75243-8303
www.pager.net
214-553-5308 • Fax 214-221-0160

LONGMONT FOODS COMPANY
PO Box 1479
Longmont, CO 80502-1479
303-776-6611

LOOMIS, FARGO & CO.
3030 Lyndon B Johnson Fwy
Dallas, TX 75234-7781
www.loomisfargo.com
972-241-9876 • Fax 972-241-4642

LOOP LINEN & UNIFORM SERVICE
463 Avenue A
Westwego, LA 70094-3644
504-341-3401

LOREN COOK CO.
2015 E Dale St
Springfield, MO 65803-4637
www.lorencook.com
417-869-6474 • Fax 417-862-0968

LORINA SUPREME FOODS, INC.
20 Oser Ave
Hauppauge, NY 11788-3825
631-231-7940

LOUBAT EQUIPMENT CO., INC
4141 Bienville St
New Orleans, LA 70119-5149
504-482-2554

LOUIS WOHL & SONS, INC
11101 N 46th St
Tampa, FL 33617-2009
www.louiswohl.com
800-226-9645

LOUISIANA BEEF INDUSTRY COUNCIL
4921 Frontage Rd
Port Allen, LA 70767-4195
225-343-3491

LOUISIANA COOKIN' MAGA-ZINE
129 S Cortez St
New Orleans, LA 70119-6118
504-482-3914

LOUISIANA DEPT. OF WILDLIFE
2415 Darnell Rd
New Iberia, LA 70560-9622
337-373-0032

LOUISIANA FISH FRY PRODUCTS
5267 Plank Rd
Baton Rouge, LA 70805-2730
800-356-2905

LOUISIANA GAS ASSOCIATION
2500 Highway 14
New Iberia, LA 70560-9614
225-354-3024

LOUISIANA OFFICE OF TOURISM
PO Box 94291
Baton Rouge, LA 70804-9291
225-342-8100

LOUISIANA OYSTER TASK FORCE
1600 Canal St Ste 210
New Orleans, LA 70112-2839
504-568-5693

LOUISIANA SEAFOOD EXCHANGE
428 Jefferson Hwy
New Orleans, LA 70121-2515
504-834-9393

LOUISIANA SPECIALTY DRINKS
1603 S Gayoso St
New Orleans, LA 70125-2931
504-482-1189

LOUISIANA VIDEO
803 W University Ave
Lafayette, LA 70506-3553
337-235-6404 • Fax 337-235-0760

LOVE AND QUICHES
178 Hanse Ave
Freeport, NY 11520-4698
www.loveandquiches.com
800-525-5251 • FA 516-623-8817

LOW TEMP-COLORPOINT INDUSTRIES
PO Box 795
Jonesboro, GA 30237-0795
770-478-8803 • Fax 770-471-3715

IOWA STATE UNIVERSITY HRIM DEP
11 Mackay Hall
Ames, IA 50011-0001
515-294-1730 • Fax 515-294-8551

LOWE REFRIGERATION, INC.
105 Cecil Ct
Fayetteville, GA 30214-7906
770-461-9001 • Fax 770-461-8020

LOWELL PRODUCTS DVLPMNT-LPD
PO Box 446
Marysville, WA 98270-0446
360-743-2993

LSI INDUSTRIES
PO Box 42728
Cincinnati, OH 45242-0728
513-793-3200

LSU AGRICULTURAL CENTER
6640 Riverside Dr Ste 100
Metairie, LA 70003-7110
504-838-1170

LUCASEY MFG CORP
2744 E 11th St
Oakland, CA 94601-1429
510-534-1435

LUCENT TECHNOLOGIES
600 Mountain Ave
New Providence, NJ 07974-2008
888-458-2368

LUCKS FOOD DECORATING CO
3003 S Pine St
Tacoma, WA 98409-4793
800-426-9778

LUCKS FOOD EQUIPMENT CO
21112 72nd Ave S
Kent, WA 98032-1339
253-872-2180

LUCKY COIN
1525 Airline Dr
Metairie, LA 70001-5986
504-835-3232

LUCKY SUNSHINE ENTERPRISES
PO Box 640003
Oakland Gardens, NY 11364-0003
800-770-8890

LUDLOW CASH REGISTER
122 Sewall St
Ludlow, MA 01056-2764
413-589-1190 • Fax 413-583-7804

LUFTRON ELECTRONICS CO., INC.
7200 Suter Rd
Coopersburg, PA 18036-1249
www.lutron.com
610-282-3800 • Fax 610-282-3044

LUGANO IMPORTS, INC
580 Irwin St Ste 7
San Rafael, CA 94901-3968
e-mail: marchisef@aolcom
41-545-91547 • Fax 415-453-7007

LUIGINOS INC
525 S Lake Ave
Duluth, MN 55802-2300
218-723-5555

LUMSDEN CORPORATION
PO Box 4647
Lancaster, PA 17604-4647
717-394-8871

LUNCHBYTE SYSTEMS
136 Harding Rd
Rochester, NY 14612-5718
585-621-8448

LUNCHSTOP INC.
16170 Vineyard Blvd
Morgan Hill, CA 95037-5498
www.lunchstop1@aol.com
408-779-3434 • Fax 408-779-6226

LUXEL TECHNOLOGIES
PO Box 23825
Chagrin Falls, OH 44023-0825
www.thelightshop.com
216-361-4355 • Fax 216-361-1822

LUXURY BATH SYSTEMS
1958 Brandon Ct
Glendale Heights, IL 60139-2086
800-758-7771

LUXURY COMMERCIAL BATH SYSTEMS
5050 Newport Dr Ste 5
Rolling Meadows, IL 60008-3824
e-mail: luxcom1@aol.com
847-394-8060 • Fax 847-394-4270

LYNN UNIVERSITY
3601 N Military Trl
Boca Raton, FL 33431-5598
www.lynn.edu
561-237-7000 • Fax 561-237-7862

LYONS MAGNUS
1636 S 2nd St
Fresno, CA 93702-4143
www.lyonsmagnus.com
559-268-5966 • Fax 559-233-8249

M & E MFG CO INC
PO Box 1548
Kingston, NY 12402-1548
845-331-2111

M & M ENGINEERING & CONSTRUCTION
3 Sanborn Rd Ste 4A
Londonderry, NH 03053-2362
www.ccmandm.com
603-434-8684 • Fax 603-434-1532

M & N INTERNATIONAL
13860 W Laurel Dr
Lake Forest, IL 60045-4531
847-680-4700

M & Q PACKAGING
PO Box 180
Schuylkill Haven, PA 17972-0180
800-600-3068

M & Q PLASTIC PRODUCTS
1364 Welsh Rd Ste A-1
North Wales, PA 19454-1913
www.mqplasticproducts.com
877-PAN-SAVR • Fax 267-641-4572

M D M COMMERCIAL
2320 3rd St S
Jacksonville Beach, FL 32250-4058
904-247-7735

M K COMMERCIAL KITCHENS
5302 Texoma Pkwy
Sherman, TX 75090-2112
www.yahoocake.com-wholesale
903-893-8151 • Fax 903-893-5036

M T J WOODSMITHS INC
W67 N222 Evergreen Blvd Ste 115
Cedarburg, WI 53012-2650
262-377-9185

M WINDOWS—MINDY GREENBERG
25126 71st Rd
Bellerose, NY 11426-2726
e-mail: mindy@mwindows.com
718-470-9530 • Fax 718-470-9500

M & M TRADING
1901 Vallejo St Apt 7
San Francisco, CA 94123-4945
415-264-5979 • Fax 415-351-2856

M & N INTERNATIONAL
4937 Otter Lake Rd
Saint Paul, MN 55110-6603
800-479-2043 • Fax 800-727-8966

M. TUCKER CO., INC.
900 S 2nd St
Harrison, NJ 07029-2323
e-mail: info@mtucker.com
www.mtucker.com
973-484-1200 • Fax 973-484-8112

M.A.B. PAINTS
600 Reed Rd
Broomall, PA 19008-3505
e-mail: cbruder@mabpaints.com
www.mabpaints.com
610-353-3939 • Fax 610-353-8189

M.G. WALDBAUM CO.
5353 Wayzata Blvd
Minneapolis, MN 55416-1340
612-595-4700 • Fax 612-595-4710

M.J.'S
1513 Metairie Rd
Metairie, LA 70005-3938
504-835-6099

MA BAENSCH
1025 E Locust St
Milwaukee, WI 53212-2695
www.mabaensch.com
414-562-4643 • Fax 414-562-5525

MAC GRAY
10 Walpole Park S
Walpole, MA 02081-2523
800-994-0165

MACHALEK COMMUNICATIONS INC
432 Gateway Blvd
Burnsville, MN 55337-2559
800-846-5520

MACKNIGHT SMOKED FOODS
15 Britain Dr
Doylestown, PA 18901-5186
800-572-5666

MACRO MANAGEMENT SERVICES, INC
800 Navarro St Ste 260
San Antonio, TX 78205-1742
210-226-1047

MACRO PLASTICS INC
2250 Huntington Dr
Fairfield, CA 94533-9732
800-845-6555

MADERA CANYON CHILE & SPICE CO
PO Box 2600
Tempe, AZ 85280-2600
www.chilepowder.com
888-442-0628 • Fax 888-837-9072

MAGIC GLO INC
1 Chestnut Ridge Rd # A
Montvale, NJ 07645-1842
800-524-0848

MAGIC ICE PRODUCTS
1015 E Oak St
Stockton, CA 95205-4420
e-mail: magiciceproducts@attglob-al.com
209-464-8032 Fax 209-464-0750

MAGIC SEASONING BLENDS
824 Distributors Row
New Orleans, LA 70123-3210
e-mail: info@chefpaul.com
www.chefpaul.com
504-731-3579

MAGIKITCH'N
PO Box 501
Concord, NH 03302-0501
800-441-1492

MAGLINER INC
503 S Mercer St
Pinconning, MI 48650-9310
800-624-5463

MAGNET STREET
1749 S Naperville Rd Ste 2
Wheaton, IL 60187-8192
www.magnetstreet.com
630-653-5525 • Fax 630 653 5125

MAGNIFICENT PEWTER
4011 Harding Pl
Nashville, TN 37215-4034
www.mpewter.com
615-665-0123 • Fax 615-665-1341

MAGNUSON INDUSTRIES INC
3005 Kishwaukee St
Rockford, IL 61109-2061
www.posi-pour.com
800-435-2816 • Fax 815-229-2978

MAHONEY ENVIRONMENTAL
1819 Moen Ave
Joliet, IL 60436-9323
www.mahoneyenvironmental.com
815-730-2080 • Fax 815-730-2087

MAIER MARKETING SYNERGY INC
121 Cheshire Ln Ste 500
Hopkins, MN 55305-1070
612-404-5800 • Fax 612-404-5848

MAIL I WANT.COM
207 1-2 E Superior St
Duluth, MN 55802-2100
www.mailiwant.com
218-727-5343 • Fax 218-727-7847

MAIL.COM
399 Thornall St
Edison, NJ 08837-2236
e-mail: jherold@staff.mail.com
www.mail.com
732-906-2000 • Fax 732-352-6567

MAILERS SOFTWARE
22382 Avenida Empresa
Rancho Santa Margarita, CA 92688-2112
949-589-5200

MAIN STREET GOURMET
170 Muffin Ln
Cuyahoga Falls, OH 44223-3358
www.mainstreetmuffins.com
800-678-6246 • Fax 330-920-8329

MAINE BEEF INDUSTRY COUNCIL
149 Clark Ln
Whitefield, ME 04353-3223
e-mail: mbic@mint.net
www.mainebeef.org
207-549-5972 • Fax 207-549-4602

MAINE DEPARTMENT OF AGRICULTURE
28 State House
Augusta, ME 04333-0028
e-mail: maine.food@state.me.us
www.mainefoodandfarms.com
207-287-7558 • Fax 207-287-5576

MAINE FRESH POTATOES
721 Bay Rd
Duxbury, MA 02332-5219
e-mail: opnes@aol.com
781-934-3200 • Fax 781-934-3222

MAINE LOBSTER PROMOTION
PO Box 7505
Portland, ME 04112-7505
207-773-2800

MAINE POTATO BOARD
744 Main St
Presque Isle, ME 04769-2271
e-mail: mainepotatoes@mainepotatoes.com
207-769-5061 • Fax 207-764-4148

MAINSTREET MENU SYSTEM
1375 N Barker Rd
Brookfield, WI 53045-5215
www.mainstreetmenus.com
800-782-6222 • Fax 262-782-6515

MAINSTREET MENU SYSTEMS
PO Box 0748
Brookfield, WI 53008-0748
262-782-6006

MAINTENANCE USA
3333 Lenox Ave
Jacksonville, FL 32254-4225
www.musa.com
904-384-6530 • Fax 904-388-2723

MAINTENANCE WAREHOUSE
10641 Scripps Summit Ct
San Diego, CA 92131-3961
858-552-6200

MAISON & OBJET
1611 N Kent St Ste 903
Arlington, VA 22209-2111
703-522-5000

MAJESTIC INDUSTRIES
9 Nursery Ln
Westport, CT 06880-2163
203-226-9976 • Fax 203-227-3213

MAJESTIC INDUSTRIES, INC.
225 Passaic St
Passaic, NJ 07055-6414
973-473-3434

MAJESTIC MIRROR
7765 W 20th Ave
Hialeah, FL 33014-3227
305-827-7661 • Fax 305-827-2663

MAJESTIC SOFTWARE INC
7710 Balboa Ave Ste 317
San Diego, CA 92111-2254
888-662-4767

MAJOR PETERS
3375 N Arlington Heights Rd
Arlington Heights, IL 60004-7701

MAKER'S MARK
9003 Covent Garden St
Houston, TX 77031-3015
713-777-6275 • Fax 713-777-6276

MAKKOS OF BROOKLYN LTD.
200 Moore St
Brooklyn, NY 11206-3708
718-366-9800 • Fax 718-821-4544

MALLARDS FOOD PRODUCTS
708 L Street
Modesto, CA 95354-2240
209-522-1018 • Fax 209-577-8364

MALLOYS CASH REGISTER CO
2101 Polk St
Houston, TX 77003-4395
www.malloys.com
703-224-9528 • Fax 713-224-4915

MALONEY VEITCH & ASSOCIATES
2090 Weaver Park Dr
Clearwater, FL 33765-2130
www.mvassoc.com
727-442-3038

MALT-O-MEAL COMPANY
80 S 8th St Ste 2600
Minneapolis, MN 55402-2100
612-338-8551 • Fax 612-373-2516

MALT-O-MEAL CORP
30 8th Ave NE
Minneapolis, MN 55413-1806
800-328-4452

MAMMA BELLA-AUSMAC INC
5100 Rivergrade Rd
Baldwin Park, CA 91706-1406
626-338-3000

MAMMA SAYS
49 Lincoln Rd
Butler, NJ 07405-1801
www.mammasays.com
973-283-9220 • Fax 973-283-2799

MANAGEMENT INSIGHT REST. CONS.
96 Arlington Rd
Buffalo, NY 14221-7066
716-631-3319

MANAGEMENT TECHNOLOGIES
14380 SW 139th Ct
Miami, FL 33186-5557
e-mail: sales@m-tech.com
www.m-tech.com
305-256-0429 • Fax 305-254-5900

MANAGEMENT TIME SYSTEMS
PO Box 20249
Floral Park, NY 11002-0249
e-mail:
jmaggio@management-time.com
www.management-time.com
516-488-1116 • Fax 516-758-0773

MANCHESTER FARMS, INC
PO Box 97
Dalzell, SC 29040-0097
e-mail:
rmontbach@mindspring.com
www.manchesterfarms.com
800-845-0421

MANDA FINE MEATS
PO Box 3374
Baton Rouge, LA 70821-3374
225-334-7636 • Fax 225-334-7647

MANE-SEAFLA INC
999 Tech Dr
Milford, OH 45150-9535
513-248-9876

MANHATTAN BEER COORS BREWING CO.
400 Rose Feiss Blvd
Bronx, NY 10454-2018
718-292-9300 • Fax 718-292-4319

MANHATTAN EAST SUITE HOTELS
500 W 37th St
New York, NY 10018-1118
e-mail: hresources@mesuite.com
www.mesuite.com
212-465-3700 • Fax 212-465-3511

MANHATTAN SOUP MAN WORLD GOURMET
567 Fashion Ave
New York, NY 10018-1804
www.soupman.net
212-221-9898 • Fax 212-221-9721

MANHATTAN SPECIAL BOTTLING
342 Manhattan Ave
Brooklyn, NY 11211-2404
www.manhattanspecial.com
718-388-4144 • Fax 718-384-0244

MANION MUSIC
1171 Morgan Ford Rd
Front Royal, VA 22630-9362
540-635-9166

MANITOWOC
299 Main St
North Reading, MA 01864-1327
978-664-3501 • Fax 978-664-2407

MANITOWOC ICE INC
12723 Grant St
Overland Park, KS 66213-3032
913-897-0515

MANITOWOC ICE, INC.
2110 S 26th St
Manitowoc, WI 54220-6321
www.manitowocice.com
920-682-0161 • Fax 920-683-7589

MANNEKEN-BRUSSEL IMPORTS,
PO Box 6026
Austin, TX 78762-6026
www.mbibeer.com
512-385-2188 • Fax 512-385-2122

MANNHART, INC
651 Industrial Blvd
Grapevine, TX 76051-3915
817-421-0100 • Fax 817-421-0246

MANNING & SMITH INSURANCE
9340 E Central Ave
Wichita, KS 67206-2555
800-984-1201

MANNS MEAT
9097 F St
Omaha, NE 68127-1398
402-339-7000 • Fax 402-339-1579

MANNYS
4866 Tchoupitoulas St
New Orleans, LA 70115-1698
504-899-2358

MANOR ENTERPRISES
6116 Mulford Village Dr
Rockford, IL 61107-6657
815-398-5551

MANSFIELD PAPER COMPANY
380 Union St
West Springfield, MA 01089-4123
e-mail: info@mansfieldpaper.com
www.mansfieldpaper.com;
413-781-2000

MANTROSSE—HAEUSER CO.
1175 Post Rd E
Westport, CT 06880-5431
www.mbzgroup.com
203-454-1800 • Fax 203-227-0558

MANUFACTURERS AGENT'S FOOD SVC
2402 Mount Vernon Rd
Atlanta, GA 30338-3095
770-698-8994

MAPLE LEAF BAKERY
1011 E Touhy Ave Ste 500
Des Plaines, IL 60018-5829
847-451-8100 • Fax 847-451-2274

MAPLE LEAF FARMS
PO Box 308
Pierceton, IN 46562-0308
574-658-4121

MAPLE LEAF FARMS
PO Box 308
Milford, IN 46542-0308
e-mail: eessig@earthlink.net
www.mapleleaffarms.com
800-348-2812 • Fax 574-658-2233

MAPLEHURST BAKERIES
50 Maplehurst Dr
Brownsburg, IN 46112-9085
317-858-9000 • Fax 317-858-0499

MAQUIPAN INTERNATIONAL, INC.
7326 NW 46th St
Miami, FL 33166-6425
e-mail: maquipanint@msn.com
305-406-9662 • Fax 305-406-9664

MARC REFRIGERATION MANUFACTURING
7453 NW 32nd Ave
Miami, FL 33147-5877
e-mail: info@marcrefrigeration.com
www.marcrefrigeration.com
305-691-0500 • Fax 305-691-1212

MARCEL ET HENRY CHARCUTERIE FR
415 Browning Way
South San Francisco, CA 94080-6301
650-871-4230 • Fax 650-871-5948

MARCH PUMPS
1819 Pickwick Ln
Glenview, IL 60025-5793
www.marchpump.com
847-729-5300 • Fax 847-729-7062

MARCO FINE ARTS
201 Nevada St
El Segundo, CA 90245-4211
www.marcofinearts.com
310-615-1818 • Fax 310-615-1850

MARCONI ITALIAN SPECIALTIES
710 W Grand Ave
Chicago, IL 60610-3908
www.marconi-foods.com
312-421-0485 • Fax 312-421-1286

MARCUS & MILLICHAP
3281 E Guasti Rd
Ontario, CA 91761-7622
909-605-1800

MARCUS DRAKE CONSULTANTS
2 Dena Ct
Park Ridge, NJ 07656-1803
201-505-9122 • Fax 201-930-0629

MARDER
22 S Water St
New Bedford, MA 02740-7286
508-991-3200

MARIE'S QUALITY FOODS
1244 E Beamer St
Woodland, CA 95776-6002
530-662-9538

MARIETTA CORP
PO Box 5250
Cortland, NY 13045-5250
607-753-6746

MARIETTA CORP
37 Huntington St
Cortland, NY 13045-3098
e-mail: mmktg@mariettacorp.com
www.mariettacorp.com
800-950-7772 • Fax 800-756-0658

MARIETTA DRAPE & WNDW COV
PO Box 569
Marietta, GA 30061-0569
800-634-3713

MARIGOLD FOODS, INC.
118 Village St Ste B
Slidell, LA 70458-5302
985-726-0405

MARIGOLD FOODS
2929 University Ave SE
Minneapolis, MN 55414-3221
800-322-9566

MARINE PROD EXPORT DEV
17 Battery Pl # 3227
New York, NY 10004-1207
212-425-9437

MARINER BISCUIT
1245 Federal Ave E
Seattle, WA 98102-4329
e-mail: marinerb@aol.com
206-325-5450 • Fax 206-325-5828

MARK DAVID, INC.
621 Southwest St
High Point, NC 27260-8108
e-mail: sales@markdavid.net
www.markdavid.net
336-821-2250 • Fax 336-883-2961

MARK III INDUSTRIES
PO Box 2525
Ocala, FL 34478-2525
e-mail: patmaloy2markiii.com
www.markiii.com
800-359-6275 • Fax 352-351-8129

MARKET DIRECTION
200 Walnut St Ste 100
Kansas City, MO 64106-1028
816-842-0020

MARKET FORGE CO
35 Garvey St
Everett, MA 02149-4403
617-387-4100

MARKET METRIX
1299 4th St Ste 402
San Rafael, CA 94901-3030
e-mail: jbarsky@marketmetrix.net
www.hotelimprovement.com
415-721-1300 • Fax 415-721-1314

MARKET TOOLS INC-ZOOMERANG
2330 Marinship Way
Sausalito, CA 94965-2800
415-289-0238

MARKET VISION
91 Clinton Rd Ste 2A
Fairfield, NJ 07004-2913
973-882-9888

MARKETING AGENTS SOUTH
848 Centre St
Ridgeland, MS 39157-4501
800-647-7786 • Fax 601-956-4726

MARKETING CONCEPTS INC
2060 Glacier Cir
Cross Plains, WI 53528-9119
608-798-1444 • Fax 608-798-1464

MARKETWORKS INC
12 Courtney Rd
Walpole, MA 02081-2255
508-668-4036 • Fax 508-668-4060

MARKO INTERNATIONAL
1050 W Hubbard St
Chicago, IL 60622-6528
www.marko.com
800-435-0857 • Fax 800-321-0857

MAR-LEEA SEAFOOD, INC.
110 Herman Melville Blvd
New Bedford, MA 02740-7344
508-991-6026 • Fax 508-990-3468

MARLO MFG CO INC
140 5th Ave
Hawthorne, NJ 07506-2134
973-423-0226

MARQUE'S FOOD DIST.
2401 8th St
Harvey, LA 70058-4011
504-366-3745

MARQUEZ BROTHER
5807 Rue Ferrari
San Jose, CA 95138-1857
408-960-2700 • Fax 408-960-3213

MARRINER MARKETING COMMUNICATIONS
10221 Wincopin Cir
Columbia, MD 21044-3423
410-715-1500 • Fax 410-995-3609

MARRIOTT INTERNATIONAL
1 Marriott Dr
Washington, DC 20058-0001
www.marriott.com
202-380-1365 • Fax 202-380-6699

MARS AIR PRODUCTS
14716 S Broadway St
Gardena, CA 90248-1814
e-mail: danaa@marsair.com
www.marsair.com
310-532-1555 • Fax 310-324-3030

MARS INCORPORATED
6885 Elm St
Mc Lean, VA 22101-3810
703-821-4900

MARSAL
181 E Hoffman Ave
Lindenhurst, NY 11757-5090
631-226-6688

MARSH INDUSTRIES, INC.
1117 Bowers Ave NW
New Philadelphia, OH 44663-4129
e-mail: wdsinghaus@marsh-ind.com
www.marsh-ind.com
330-343-8825 • Fax 330-343-9515

MARSHALL AIR SYSTEMS
419 Peachtree Dr S
Charlotte, NC 28217-2098
704-525-6230 • Fax 704-525-6229

MARSHALL DURBIN PREPARED FOODS
PO Box 59748
Birmingham, AL 35259-9748
205-870-5800 • Fax 205-414-3251

MARSHALL PRODUCTIONS
415 W Huron St
Chicago, IL 60610-3401
312-944-0720 • Fax 312-944-0721

MARSI SYSTEMS.
6003 Randolph Blvd
San Antonio, TX 78233-5719
e-mail: john@marsi.com
www.marsi.com
210-690-9505 • Fax 210-690-9733

MARSTON MFG.-CAST IRON PRODUCT
PO Box 24407
Richmond, VA 23224-0407
www.marstonmfg.com
804-233-0020 • Fax 804-232-4950

MARTA'S VINEYARDS, INC.
9660 Rush St
South El Monte, CA 91733-1779
e-mail:
leonard@wiesfromdownunder.com
626-575-0537 • Fax 626-575-0360

MARTHA GREGORY & ASSOC., INC.
4124 Taylorsville Rd
Louisville, KY 40220-1537
502-452-1500

MARTIN LINEN SUPPLY COMPANY
421 Roosevelt Ave
San Antonio, TX 78210-2799
210-533-9111 • Fax 210-533-6649

MARTIN PREFERRED FOODS
2011 Silver St
Houston, TX 77007-2801
e-mail: samh@martinpreferred-foods.com
www.martinpreferredfoods.com
713-869-6191 • Fax 713-863-4999

MARTIN PROFESSIONAL INC
700 Sawgrass Corporate Pkwy
Fort Lauderdale, FL 33325-6260
954-927-3003

MARTINELLI'S
PO Box 1868
Watsonville, CA 95077-1868
www.martinellis.com
831-724-1126 • Fax 831-742-2910

MARUKA LIME-PIT USA
1472 Country Vistas Ln
Bonita, CA 91902-4274
www.marukalime.com
619-421-8317 • Fax 619-421-5134

MARVIL ICE MARKETING
2824 Roehampton Close
Tarpon Springs, FL 34688-8424
e-mail: astapp@hotmail.com
727-945-7880 • Fax 727-934-5562

MARWOOD CHEESE SALES
6400 Glenwood St
Mission, KS 66202-4016

e-mail: mwood55982@aol.com
913-722-1534 • Fax 913-262-9132

MARYLAND DEPARTMENT OF AGRICULTURE
50 Harry S Truman Parkway
Annapolis, MD 21411-0001
410-841-5820

MARYLAND MATCH CORP
605 Alluvion St
Baltimore, MD 21230-2039
www.marylandmatch.com
800-423-0013 • Fax 410-752-3441

MARZIPAN SPECIALTIES, INC.
1513 Meridian St # O
Nashville, TN 37207-5061
e-mail: marzipan@iscln.net
615-226-4800 • Fax 615-226-4882

MASECA-AZTECA MILLING L.P.
3960 Prospect Ave Ste K
Yorba Linda, CA 92886-1753
888-462-7322 • Fax 888-627-3221

MAS-HAMILTON GROUP
749 W Short St
Lexington, KY 40508-1200
859-253-4744

MASON CONTRACT PRODUCTS, LLC
8000 Cooper Ave Ste 28
Ridgewood, NY 11385-7734
e-mail: chuck@masoncontract.com
718-326-3100 • Fax 718-326-3244

MASS CASH REGISTER
6 Greenwood St
Wakefield, MA 01880-4008
781-245-6644

MASS. DEPT. OF AGRICULTURE
100 Cambridge St
Boston, MA 02202-0044
e-mail: aginfo@statema.us
www.massgrown.org
617-626-1754 • Fax 617-626-1850

MASSACHUSETTS RESTAURANT ASSOC
95A Turnpike Rd
Westborough, MA 01581-2835
508-366-4144 • Fax 508-366-4614

MASSEY SERVICES, INC
610 N Wymore Rd
Maitland, FL 32751-4216
www.masseyservices.com
407-645-2500

MASSON CHEESE
6180 Alcoa Ave
Los Angeles, CA 90058-3974
e-mail: messana@earthlink.net
323-583-1251 • Fax 323-585-8765

MASTER -BILT PRODUCTS
908 State Highway 15 N
New Albany, MS 38652-9507
www.master-bilt.com
662-534-9061 • Fax 662-534-6049

MASTER-BILT PRODUCTS
PO Box 59
New Albany, MS 38652-0059
800-647-1284

MASTER DISPOSERS INC
1701 Dana Ave
Cincinnati, OH 45207-1111
513-631-4242

MASTER FOOD SERVICES-UNCLE BEN
5721 Harvey Wilson Dr
Houston, TX 77020-8025
www.masterfoodservices.com
713-674-9484 • Fax 713-670-2254

MASTER GRADE
1611 Greg St
Sparks, NV 89431-5916
e-mail: mastergrade@yahoo.com
775-356-1156 • Fax 775-355-9688

MASTER PIECE CRYSTAL
PO Box 848
Jane Lew, WV 26378-0848
304-884-7841 • Fax 304-884-7842

MASTERCARD INTERNATIONAL
2000 Purchase St
Purchase, NY 10577-2509
914-649-5518

MASTERCRAFT
234 W Northland Ave
Appleton, WI 54911-2017
920-739-7682 • Fax 920-739-3208

MATADOR PROCESSORS, LNC.
PO Box 2200
Blanchard, OK 73010-2200
405-485-3567 • Fax 405-485-2597

MATFER, INC.
16300 Stagg St
Van Nuys, CA 91406-1717
818-782-0792

MATHES FARM LLC
PO Box 6
Sharon Springs, KS 67758-0006
785-852-4203

MATHEW LAMPSHADE
2932 Fulton St
Brooklyn, NY 11207-2710
800-437-5272 • Fax 718-647-3726

MATLAWS
135 Front Ave
West Haven, CT 06516-2837
e-mail: tbenevelli@matlaws.com
800-934-8266 • Fax 203-933-8506

MATRIX ENGINEERING
3434 Industrial 33rd St
Fort Pierce, FL 34946-8680
www.griprock.com
772-461-2156 • Fax 772-461-7185

MATSUKAS FOOD CO., INC.
PO Box 1944
Buellton, CA 93427-1944
e-mail: info@santabarbarabay.com
805-688-5248 • Fax 805-688-3688

MATTSON & COMPANY
383D Vintage Park Dr
San Mateo, CA 94404-1135
650-574-8824

MATUSALEM & CO.
1205 SW 37th Ave # 300
Miami, FL 33135-4226
www.matusalem.com
305-448-8255 • Fax 305-445-1835

MAUI FRUIT BLENDS
10 Summer St
Manchester, MA 01944-1579
e-mail: al@mauifrozendrinks.com
www.mauifrozendrinks.com
978-526-0082 • Fax 978-526-0084

MAUI PINEAPPLE CO
PO Box 4003
Concord, CA 94524-4003

MAVERICK MENUS
34 E Main St Ste 322
Smithtown, NY 11787-2804
e-mail: info@maverickmenus.com
www.maverickmenus.com
516-842-2191

MAVERICK XCHANGE
424 W End Ave Apt 3D
New York, NY 10024-5765
212-787-4418 • Fax 212-787-4483

MAX PACKAGING
109 6th Ave NW
Attalla, AL 35954-2016
800-543-5369 • Fax 256-538-1929

MAX PRATT COMPANY
3118 Holly Green Dr
Humble, TX 77339-1369
281-360-5493 • Fax 281-360-0852

MAXHAM & SONS INC
3261 SW 44th St
Fort Lauderdale, FL 33312-6930
e-mail: beersystem@aol.com
954-964-5301

MAXLITE SK AMERICA INC
60E Commerce Way
Totowa, NJ 07512-1156

e-mail: info@maxlite.com
www.maxlite.com
973-256-3330 • Fax 973-256-9444

MAYTAG
403 W 4th St N
Newton, IA 50208-3034
e-mail: dpacka@maytag.com
www.maytag.com
641-787-7000 • Fax 641-787-8115

MAYTAG INC
1 Dependability Sq
Newton, IA 50208-9239
641-792-8000

MAZZETTA CO.
1990 Saint Johns Ave
Highland Park, IL 60035-3103
847-433-1150

MBE BUSINESS EXPRESS JV
200 Plant Ave
Wayne, PA 19087-3520
e-mail: mbroadwell@usatech.com
www.usatech.com
610-989-0340 • Fax 610-989-0344

MBI ENTERPRISES, INC.
2 New Rd Ste 134
Aston, PA 19014-1038
610-459-4543 • Fax 610-388-2745

MBNA, INC.
10267 E Caribbean Ln
Scottsdale, AZ 85259-8553
480-837-2080

MC CAIN FOODS
2905 Butterfield Rd
Oak Brook, IL 60523-1102
www.mccain.com
800-938-7799 • Fax 630-472-1633

MC ILHENNY COMPANY TABASCO
305 Dove Creek Ln
Danville, CA 94506-1360
925-736-5426 • Fax 925-736-5826

MCALISTER'S DELI
731 S Pear Orchard Rd
Ridgeland, MS 39157-4800
888-855-3354

MCBRIDE ELECTRIC
1229 W 34th St
Houston, TX 77018-6207
e-mail:
rblodgett@mcbrideelectric.com
www.mcbrideelectric.com
713-864-7800 • Fax 713-864-7776

MCCALL REFRIGERATION
81 W Holley St
Parsons, TN 38363-4807
www.4mccall.com
731-847-5570 • Fax 731-847-9012

MCCANN'S ENGINEERING - ICEFLOW
PO Box 119
West Bloomfield, NY 14585-0119
e-mail: icepuff@aol.com
www.mccannsenq.com
585-582-9867 • Fax 585-582-1987

MCCANN'S ENGINEERING & MFG. CO
4570 Colorado Blvd
Los Angeles, CA 90039-1198
www.mccannseng.com
818-637-7200 • Fax 818-637-7222

MCCLANCY SEASONINGS
1 Spice Rd
Fort Mill, SC 29715-9501
803-548-2366

MCCONCEPTS - HEAVY WEIGHT
PO Box 5098
Houston, TX 77262-5098
832-781-7699

MCCORMICK & CO
226 Schilling Cir
Hunt Valley, MD 21031-8668
e-mail: larry_vitor@mccormick.com
410-771-7751 • Fax 410-771-7512

MCCORMICK DISTILLING CO
6129 Mission Rd
Mission, KS 66205-3252
913-384-1569

MCCORMICK DISTILLING CO.
1 Mc Cormick Ln
Weston, MO 64098-9558
816-640-2276 • Fax 816-640-5405

MCE SYSTEMS CORP.
PO Box 40466
Houston, TX 77240-0466
832-462-6231

MCFALL ASSOCIATES
201 Riverview Ter
Benicia, CA 94510-2753
925-435-3316

MCGANN SOFTWARE SYSTEMS
651 Taft St NE
Minneapolis, MN 55413-2814
e-mail: larry@mcgannsoft.com
612-331-2020 • Fax 612-331-5187

MCGLAUGHLIN OIL CO
3750 E Livingston Ave
Columbus, OH 43227-2246
614-231-2518

MCGUIRE FURNITURE CO
151 Vermont St
San Francisco, CA 94103-5039
415-626-1414

MCGUIRE FURNITURE, A KOHLER CO
1201 Bryant St
San Francisco, CA 94103-4306
www.kohlerco.com
800-662-4847

MCGUNN SAFE COMPANY L.L.C
2001 W 21st St
Broadview, IL 60155-4631
www.mcgunnsafes.com
773-884-3560 • Fax 773-884-6560

MCKINSEY & CO.
133 Peachtree St NE Ste 2300
Atlanta, GA 30303-1816
404-525-9900

MCKINSEY & COMPANY
55 Park Avenue Plz Fl
New York, NY 10055-0002
212-446-8924

MCLLHENNY CO.—TABASCO
601 Poydras St Ste 1815
New Orleans, LA 70130-6028
www.tabasco.com
504-523-7370 • Fax 504-596-6444

MCMOHAN WELLS ASSOCIATES
770 New Haven Rd
Durham, CT 06422-2408
e-mail: allswells@worldnet.att.net
800-799-0068 • Fax 860-349-0893

MCNAIRN PACKAGING
6 Elise St
Westfield, MA 01085-1414
www.mcnairnpackaging.com
800-867-1898 • Fax 413-562-1903

MEAD JOHNSON & CO
2400 W Loyd Expy
Evansville, IN 47721-0001

MEADOWCRAFT
1401 Meadowcraft Rd
Birmingham, AL 35215-4143
205-853-9898

MEAT & LIVESTOCK AUSTRALIA LTD
750 Lexington Ave Fl 17
New York, NY 10022-1200
212-486-2405

MEAT PROCESSING CONCEPTS AMERICA
700 Prospect St SW
Le Mars, IA 51031-3030
www.mpcainc.com
712-546-4070 • Fax 712-546-5502

MECHOSHADE SYSTEMS, INC.
4203 35th St
Long Island City, NY 11101-2301
877-774-2572

MEDAL OF HONOR PARK
PO Box 508
Belle Chasse, LA 70037-0508
504-394-2892

MEDALLION LABS
9000 Plymouth Ave N
Minneapolis, MN 55427-3870
800-245-5615

MEDALLION MIRROR
2223 Plantside Dr
Louisville, KY 40299-1929
502-671-7203 • Fax 502-671-7204

MEDINA CIGARS, INC.
3855 SW 137th Ave # U
Miami, FL 33175-8820
e-mail: medinacigar@att.net
305-223-9511 • Fax 305-598-2807

MEDI-RUB ENTERPRISES
PO Box 434
North Easton, MA 02356-0434
e-mail: medirub@earthlink.net
www.medi-rub.com
508-230-9707 • Fax 508-230-8098

MEDI-RUB MASSAGERS
PO Box 691735
Houston, TX 77269-1735
e-mail: sales@medirub.com
www.medirub.com
713-880-5100 • Fax 713-880-5256

MED-MART
6002 Jet Port Industrial Blvd
Tampa, FL 33634-5160
800-654-8944 • Fax 813-960-2040

MELISSA LIBBY & ASSOCIATES
6 Piedmont Ctr NE Ste 230
Atlanta, GA 30305-1542
404-816-3068

MELITTA INC
1401 Berlin Rd
Cherry Hill, NJ 08034-1402
856-428-7202

MELLO SMELLO
5100 Highway 169 N
Minneapolis, MN 55428-4028
888-394-1406

MELO-TONE
130 Broadway
Somerville, MA 02145-3299
617-666-4900 • Fax 617-666-4906

MEMBRANE STRUCTURE SOLUTION
11 Wolfe Run Ct
Long Valley, NJ 07853-3083
908-876-0146

MENDOCINO BREWING CO.
PO Box 400
Hopland, CA 95449-0400
www.mendobrew.com
707-744-1015 • Fax 707-744-1910

MENDOCINO MUSTARD, INC.
1260 N Main St Ste 11
Fort Bragg, CA 95437-4099
707-964-2250 • Fax 707-964-0525

MENDON TRUCK LEASING & RENTAL
362 Kingsland Ave
Brooklyn, NY 11222-1905
e-mail: info@mendonleasing.com
www.mendonleasing.com
718-391-5300 • Fax 718-349-2514

MENU ANYWHERE.COM
738 Armstrong Ave Ste 200
Kansas City, KS 66101-2702
www.menuanywhere.com
913-832-9669 • Fax 419-858-3722

MENU CONCEPTS
PO Box 1123
Eastland, TX 76448-1123
800-414-6368

MENU MASTERS
12579 W Custer Ave
Butler, WI 53007-1108
262-542-6368 • Fax 262-521-3232

MENU ME
5201 Kingston Pike Ste 6196
Knoxville, TN 37919-5026
865-637-8065

MENU MEN, INC
1301 NW 27th Ave
Miami, FL 33125-2509
e-mail: menumeninc@aol.com
305-374-6119

MENU WORKS
101 W Park Ave
Greenville, SC 29601-1513
e-mail: menuworks@aol.com
864-233-6368 • Fax 864-233-6365

MENUANYWHERE MEAT & QUALITY FOODS
3737 N Broadway
Saint Louis, MO 63147-3418
314-241-4800

MENUCART.COM ONLINE MENU SERVICE
11 Sunflower Rd Apt A
Maple Shade, NJ 08052-8432
e-mail: info@menucart.com
www.menucart.com
856-321-9036 • Fax 856-321-9036

MENUCLUB, INC
3566 S Higuera St Ste 103
San Luis Obispo, CA 93401-7348
e-mail: sales@menuclub.com
888-636-8252 • Fax 805-543-8174

MENUCO CORPORATION
350 5th Ave Ste 7509
New York, NY 10118-7509
e-mail: rlang@menuco.com
212-736-1039 • Fax 212-736-0340

MENULINK
7777 Center Ave Ste 600
Huntington Beach, CA 92647-3099
www.menulink.com
714-934-6368

MENUMARK SYSTEMS
5700 W Bender Ct
Milwaukee, WI 53218-1608
www.dcimarketing.com
877-636-8627 • Fax 414-228-4373

MENU-QUIK C-O SIGNETS, INC.
7280 Industrial Park Blvd
Mentor, OH 44060-5326
800-775-6368 • Fax 440-946-4646

MENUS
PO Box 9059
Spring, TX 77387-9059
281-364-7714

MENUS ETC., INC.
PO Box 1677
Boca Raton, FL 33429-1677
561-638-7659

MENUS FOR PROFIT
100 W Harrison St Ste 530
Seattle, WA 98119-4116
206-284-5413

MENUS.COM
10780 Santa Monica Blvd Ste 33
Los Angeles, CA 90025-4749
www.menus.com
310-234-2440 • Fax 310-234-9730

MENUSOFT SYSTEMS CORP.
7370 Steele Mill Dr
Springfield, VA 22150-3600
703-912-3000

MENUUSA.COM
1018 Webster St
Oakland, CA 94607-4224
www.menuusa.com
510-839-1234 • Fax 510-834-3333

MEPCO-LID-OFF
15321 Connector Ln
Huntington Beach, CA 92649-1119
714-898-1884

MERCHANT BANKCARD NETWORK
2380 Sunset Point Rd
Clearwater, FL 33765-1430
727-726-3021 • Fax 727-726-6132

MERCHANT DUVIN CORP
2503 3rd Ave # 324
Seattle, WA 98121-1444
206-448-1228

MERCHANT'S CHOICE CARD SERVICES
16211 Park Ten Pl
Houston, TX 77084-5113
www.mccs-corp.com
281-579-4481 • Fax 281-579-3581

MERCHANT'S CHOICE CARD SERVICES
2141 NW 85th Way
Pompano Beach, FL 33071-6202
e-mail: biwapa@aol.com
954-753-1900

MERCO SAVORY-WELBILT
1111 N Hadley Rd
Fort Wayne, IN 46804-5540
800-547-2513

MERCYHURST COLLEGE
501 E 38th St
Erie, PA 16546-0001
814-824-2512 • Fax 814-824-2107

MERIDIAN BEVERAGES
5675 Oakbrook Pkwy Ste A
Norcross, GA 30093-1878
800-728-1481

MERIDIAN MERCANTILE COMPANY
505 Beachland Blvd
Vero Beach, FL 32963-1710
e-mail: mmc@meridianmmc.com
772-231-7751 • Fax 772-231-7065

MERISTAR CO
1010 Wisconsin Ave NW
Washington, DC 20007-3603
202-295-1000

MERIT INDUSTRIES
PO Box 1006
Dalton, GA 30722-1006
800-241-4032 • Fax 706-279-8332

MERIT INDUSTRIES INC
2525 State Rd
Bensalem, PA 19020-7311
800-523-2760

MERITECH, INC.
8250 S Akron St Ste 201
Englewood, CO 80112-3506
www.meritech.com
800-932-7707 • Fax 303-790-4859

MERITT, WELLER & WELLER
14411 Commerce Way Ste 400
Hialeah, FL 33016-1600
e-mail: mnarine@trainx.com
305-822-8010 • Fax 305-822-8033

MERIWETHER-GODSEY, INC.
4944 Old Boonsboro Rd
Lynchburg, VA 24503-1828
434-384-3663

MESA INTERNATIONAL
169 Kearsarge Mountain Rd
Warner, NH 03278-4037
603-456-2002 • Fax 603-456-2112

METALKRAFT SYSTEMS
6020 Crane Rd
Edinboro, PA 16412-3906
www.metalkraft.com
814-734-4131 • Fax 814-734-1111

METRO FACTORS
PO Box 38604
Dallas, TX 75238-0604
800-288-0600

METRO WAL COVERINGS LTD
230 E Ohio St Ste 30
Chicago, IL 60611-3265
e-mail: metroch@msn.com
312-943-9633 • Fax 312-943-1287

METRO, METRO & ASSOCIATES
11810 Parklawn Dr Ste 260
Rockville, MD 20852-2551
301-468-1047

METROMEDIA REST GROUP
6500 International Pkwy
Plano, TX 75093-8222
800-543-9670

METROMEDIA SOFTWARE
1 Meadowlands Plz
E Rutherford, NJ 07073-2150
201-373-4520

METROPOLIS TECHNOLOGIES
5580 La Jolla Blvd
La Jolla, CA 92037-7651
858-488-4600

METROPOLIS TECHNOLOGIES, INC.
5580 La Jolla Blvd Ste 8
La Jolla, CA 92037-7651
e-mail: info@metropolis-tech.com
800-973-556 • Fax 858-488-4699

METROTOUCH
2 Executive Dr
Fort Lee, NJ 07024-3308
e-mail: metrot523@aol.com
www.metrot.com
201-944-4700 • Fax 201-944-8092

METTLER TOLEDO
1900 Polaris Pkwy
Columbus, OH 43240-4035
e-mail: leads@mt.com
800-786-0038 • Fax 614-438-4900

METZ BAKING CO.
918 W Somers St
Milwaukee, WI 53205-2339
414-263-1700 • Fax 414-263-8019

MEXCOR INC
2250 Dartmouth St Apt 411
College Sta, TX 77840-4691
713-399-2299

MEYENBERG GOAT MILK
PO Box 5425
Santa Barbara, CA 93150-5425
805-565-1538 • Fax 805-565-3083

MEYER JABARA HOTELS
1601 Belvedere Rd
West Palm Beach, FL 33406-1541
561-689-6602

MGM GRAND HOTEL & CASINO
3799 Las Vegas Blvd S
Las Vegas, NV 89109-4319
702-891-3370 • Fax 702-891-1001

MGM SERVICES, INC.
12770 Coit Rd Ste 919
Dallas, TX 75251-1306
800-683-9200

MI T-M
PO Box 50
Peosta, IA 52068-0050
800-367-6486

MIC FOODS
12123 SW 131st Ave
Miami, FL 33186-6474
305-254-4697 • Fax 305-254-5679

MICA-CASE INC
PO Box 4385
Tampa, FL 33677-4385
e-mail: mcigroup@msn.com
800-782-2897 • Fax 813-247-2315

MICELI DAIRY
2721 E 90th St
Cleveland, OH 44104-3396
e-mail: ejpleszko@miceli-dairy.com
216-791-6222 • Fax 216-231-2504

MICELI'S SPECIALITY FOODS CO.
PO Box 1261
Danbury, CT 06813-1261
e-mail: micelis@aol.com
203-797-9714 • Fax 203-743-1420

MICHAEL ANGELOS GOURMET
200 Michael Angelo Way
Austin, TX 78728-1200
800-526-4918

MICHAEL FOODS INC
5353 Wayzata Blvd Ste304
Minneapolis, MN 55416-1317
612-546-1500 • Fax 612-546-1500

MICHAEL FOODS—PAPETTI'S EGG
100 Trumbull St
Elizabeth, NJ 07206-2105
908-351-0477

MICHAEL TOSHIO CUISINE
1415 Rollins Rd Ste 210
Burlingame, CA 94010-2300
www.michaelttoshio.com
650-348-6140 • Fax 650-348-6149

MICHAEL WAINWRIGHT POTTERY
475 Dean St
Brooklyn, NY 11217-2114
vmwain@msn.com
718-789-8911 • Fax 718-789-9104

MICHAELO ESPRESSO INC
3801 Stone Way N
Seattle, WA 98103-8005
www.michaelo.com
206-695-4950 • Fax 206-695-4951

MICHEL'S MAGNIFIQUE
35 E 9th St Apt 4
New York, NY 10003-6351
212-431-1070 • Fax 212-219-3173

MICHI DESIGNS
20671 High Desert Ct
Bend, OR 97701-8654
650-637-1889

MICHIGAN STATE UNIVERSITY
232 Eppley Ctr
East Lansing, MI 48824-1121
www.bus.msu.edu-shb-
517-353-9211 • Fax 517-432-1170

MICKEY'S BREAD
2145 Viscount Row
Orlando, FL 32809-6223
e-mail: bakebiz1@aol.com
407-859-4456

MICKEY'S LINEN & TOWEL SUPPLY
7400 W Douglas Ave
Milwaukee, WI 53218-1215
414-438-4800 • Fax 414-438-4818

MICRO MATIC
321 Marianne St
Brooksville, FL 34601-3412
888-233-7827

MICRO PACK CORPORATION
5 Commonwealth Rd Ste 3A
Natick, MA 01760-1530
508-647-1090 • Fax 508-647-1092

MICRO TOUCH SOLUTIONS
3399 NW 72nd Ave
Miami, FL 33122-1349
e-mail: touchpos@fdn.com
305-597-0008 • Fax 305-599-0877

MICROBAN PRODS CO
11515 Vanstory Dr
Huntersville, NC 28078-6309
704-875-0806

MICROFLEX CORP
PO Box 32000
Reno, NV 89533-2000
www.microflex.com
775-746-6600 • Fax 775-787-4615

MICROS FIDELIO DIRECT
632 S Military Trl
Deerfield Beach, FL 33442-3023
e-mail: info@microspos.com
www.microspos.com
954-421-3184

MICROS OF CENTRAL FLORIDA
270 W Marvin Ave
Longwood, FL 32750-5473

e-mail: microsorl@aol.com
407-767-6441

MICROS SYSTEMS
7031 Columbia Gateway Dr
Columbia, MD 21046-2289
www.micros.com
443-285-6000 • Fax 443-285-0380

MICROS SYSTEMS, INC.
1850 Crown Dr Ste 1107
Dallas, TX 75234-9414
e-mail: ewoods@micros.com
www.micros.com
972-831-8250 • Fax 972-831-0519

MICROSOFT CORP
1 Microsoft Way
Redmond, WA 98052-8300
425-882-8080

MICRO-SURFACE FINISHING PRODUCTS
PO Box 70
Wilton, IA 52778-0002
e-mail: salems@netins.net
www.micro-surface.com
563-732-3240 • Fax 563-732-3390

MICROVIEW SECURITY SYSTEMS
1414 W Sam Houston Pkwy N
Houston, TX 77043-3186
e-mail: microview@pdq.net
www.mviewsystems.com
713-465-1013 • Fax 713-465-7790

MID-ALANTIC FOODS, INC
PO Box 367
Pocomoke City, MD 21851-0367
e-mail: info@mafi.com
410-957-4100 • Fax 410-957-1303

MID-AMER PURCHASING GROUP
PO Box 43728
Cleveland, OH 44143-0728

MID-AMERICA REST SHOW
29 Oakridge Rd
Wellesley Hills, MA 02481-2503
800-909-7469

MID-ATLANTIC EXPO
6301 Hillside Ct
Columbia, MD 21046-1048
410-290-6800

MIDDLEBY MARSHALL, INC
1400 Toastmaster Dr
Elgin, IL 60120-9272
www.middleby.com
847-741-3300 • Fax 847-741-0015

MEDITERRANEAN VENTURES
3984 S Michael Rd
Ann Arbor, MI 48103-9345
734-662-1740 • Fax 734-662-6038

MIDLANDS BUSINESS EQUIP
5602 Gateway Dr
Grimes, IA 50111-6596
515-986-9601

MID-PACIFIC SEA FOODS
5970 Alcoa Ave
Los Angeles, CA 90058-3942
www.midpacific.com
323-588-9933 • Fax 323-588-9935

MIDTOWN CELLULAR
251 W 95th St
New York, NY 10025-6313
e-mail: midtown_cellular@msn.com
212-666-2600 • Fax 212-666-2900

MIDTOWN CELLULAR ASSOCIATES
22 E 36th St
New York, NY 10016-3419
e-mail: midtown_cellular@msn.com
212-448-9800 • Fax 212-448-9870

MIDWAY GAMES, INC.
3401 N California Ave
Chicago, IL 60618-5853
773-961-1000 • Fax 773-961-1060

MIDWEST FOLDING
1414 S Western Ave
Chicago, IL 60608-1893
800-621-4716 • Fax 312-666-2606

MIDWEST FOLDING PRODUCTS
1411 S Western Ave
Chicago, IL 60608-1801
312-666-3366

MIDWEST GRAIN
1300 Main St
Atchison, KS 66002-2697
913-367-1480

MIDWEST PHOTO CO
4900 G St
Omaha, NE 68117-1400
402-734-7200

MIDWEST PROCESSING & PACKAGING
1081 Sesame St
Franklin Park, IL 60131-1316
630-595-8284

MIDWEST PROFESSIONAL REPS
1266 Southwest Blvd # 216
Kansas City, KS 66103-1902
913-677-4994

MIES PRODUCTS INC
505 Commerce St
West Bend, WI 53090-1698
262-338-0676 • Fax 262-338-1244

MIFFAT INC.
PO Box 4129
Winston Salem, NC 27115-4129
www.miffat.com
210-590-9381 • Fax 210-590-9479

MIGALI IND
1475 S 6th St
Camden, NJ 08104-1105
856-963-3600

MIKASA
1 Mikasa Dr
Secaucus, NJ 07094-2501
201-867-9210 • Fax 210-876-5642

MILANO'S PASTA FACTORY
2129 W Alabama St
Houston, TX 77098-2401
e-mail: milanos@milanospasta.com
www.milanopasta.com
713-528-1329 • Fax 713-528-1338

MILDARA BLASS WINES
655 Airpark Rd
Napa, CA 94558-6272
707-846-5800

MILEA TRUCK SALES
885 E 149th St
Bronx, NY 10455-5088
www.mileatruck.com
718-292-6200 • Fax 718-292-7972

MILK PRODUCTS - BORDEN DAIRY
2410 Gordon Ave
Monroe, LA 71202-3104
318-322-4491

MILLARD REFRIGERATED SVC
4715 S 132nd St
Omaha, NE 68137-1701
402-896-6600

MILLENIA TABLEWARE
328 Thomas St
Newark, NJ 07114-2811
e-mail: johandrewgordon@aol.com
973-274-9190 • Fax 973-274-9191

MILLENIUM BROADWAY
145 W 44th St
New York, NY 10036-4012
e-mail:
mitchell.gottleman@mill-corp.cm
www.milleniumbroadway.com
212-789-7589 • Fax 212-789-7694

MILLENNIUM IMPORT CO
25 Main St SE
Minneapolis, MN 55414-1024
612-331-6230

MILLENNIUM SIGNS
22 Natmark Ct
Woodcliff Lake, NJ 07677-8029
e-mail: info@millenniumsigns.com
www.millenniumsigns.com
201-391-0225 • Fax 201-307-1399

MILLER & ASSOCIATES
2920 Merrell Rd
Dallas, TX 75229-4904
e-mail: sales@millerequip.com
www.millerequip.com
214-353-0498 • Fax 214-353-0451

MILLER BREWING
3939 W Highland Blvd
Milwaukee, WI 53208-2866
www.mbc.com
414-931-2000 • Fax 414-931-6893

MILLER BREWING CO
3850 N Causeway Blvd Ste 1325
Metairie, LA 70002-1766
504-832-3126

MILLER BREWING CO
16052 Swingley Ridge Rd
Chesterfield, MO 63017-2079
636-532-6403

MILLER BREWING CO.
20975 Swenson Dr
Waukesha, WI 53186-2034
www.millerbrewing.com
262-798-1380 • Fax 262-798-1431

MILLER BREWING COMPANY
1000 Main St Ste 405
Voorhees, NJ 08043-4633
609-750-3870 • Fax 609-750-3509

MILLER BREWING COMPANY
616 Fm 1960 Rd W Ste 450
Houston, TX 77090-3040
e-mail:
brown.cirstopher@mbcom.com
281-872-2907 • Fax 281-872-8332

MILLER MEESTER ADVERTISING
17 Washington Ave N
Minneapolis, MN 55401-2604
612-337-6600 • Fax 612-337-9100

MILLIKEN
920 Milliken Rd
Spartanburg, SC 29303-4995
864-503-1751 • Fax 864-503-1716

MILLIKEN CARPET
201 Lukken Industrial Dr W
Lagrange, GA 30240-5913
e-mail: dean.gaffney@milliken.com
www.millikencarpet.com-hospitali-ty-
706-880-5154 • Fax 706-880-5888

MILLIKEN PACKAGING
PO Box 736
White Stone, SC 29386-0736
864-474-2224

MILLING MFG. INC
PO Box 70
Labadieville, LA 70372-0070
985-369-3440 • Fax 985-369-3441

MILLS, INC.
PO Box 3070
Salinas, CA 93912-3070
e-mail: info@millsdc.com
831-757-3061 • Fax 831-424-9475

MILOS INC. DBCA MILOS FARMS
81 E College Ave
Johnstown, OH 43031-1203
740-967-9811 • Fax 740-967-0766

MILWAUKEE AREA TECHNICAL COLLEGE
700 W State St
Milwaukee, WI 53233-1419
414-2976-834

MILWAUKEE BUCKS
1001 N 4th St
Milwaukee, WI 53203-1314
414-227-0535 • Fax 414-227-0840

MILWAUKEE FIRE DEPART-MENT
6680 N Teutonia Ave
Milwaukee, WI 53209-3117
414-286-5287 • Fax 414-286-5270

MILWAUKEE JOURNAL SENTINEL
333 W State St
Milwaukee, WI 53203-1309

www.jsonline.com
414-224-2222

MIMS MEAT CO
12634 East Fwy
Houston, TX 77015-5698
713-453-0151 • Fax 713-451-7820

MINCEY MARBLE MFG
3421 Browns Bridge Rd
Gainesville, GA 30504-5438
e-mail:
tmorgan@minceymarble.com
www.minceymarble.com
770-532-0451 • Fax 770-531-0935

MINDLE & ASSOC.
870 Napa Valley Corporate Way
Napa, CA 94558-6263
707-255-8990

MINERAL SPRINGS BOTTLED WATER
PO Box 370
Petersburg, PA 16669-0370
e-mail: john@mineralsprings.com
www.mineralsprings.com
814-669-4203 • Fax 814-669-1922

MINGLEWOOD FARMS
44 Wood St
Hopkinton, MA 01748-1106
e-mail: yogice@aol.com
508-435-2264 • Fax 508-497-0792

MINH FOOD CORPORATION
612 Georgia Ave
Deer Park, TX 77536-2512
281-479-5588 • Fax 713-740-7299

MINIAT INC
16250 Vincennes Ave
South Holland, IL 60473-1260
773-927-9200 • Fax 708-331-8413

MINIBAR SYSTEMS
7340 Westmore Rd
Rockville, MD 20850-1260
800-365-6227

MINNEGASCO, INC.
800 Lasalle Ave Fl 11
Minneapolis, MN 55402-2006
612-321-4472

MINNERS DESIGNS
641 Lexington Ave
New York, NY 10022-4503
www.minners.com
212-688-7441 • Fax 212-980-6309

MINSA CORP
RR 1 Box 111A
Red Oak, IA 51566-9643
800-701-5892

MINTERBROOK OYSTER CO
PO Box 432
Gig Harbor, WA 98335-0432
253-857-5253

MIONETTO USA INC.
282 W 25th St
New York, NY 10001-7304
e-mail: info@mionettousa.com
www.mionettousa.com
212-414-5961 • Fax 212-414-5970

MIRACLE EXCLUSIVE, INC.
64 Seaview Blvd
Port Washington, NY 11050-4618
e-mail: miracle-exc@juno.com
www.miracleexclusives.com
516-621-3333 • Fax 516-621-1997

MIRACLE RECREATION
PO Box 420
Monett, MO 65708-0420
www.miracle-recreation.com
800-523-4202 • Fax 417-235-1713

MIRKOVICH AND ASSOCIATES
1064 N Garfield St
Lombard, IL 60148-1336

MIROIL
602 Tacoma St
Allentown, PA 18109-8103
www.miroil.com
610-437-4618 • Fax 610-437-3377

MIROIR BROT-FRENCH REFLEC
820 S Robertson Blvd
Los Angeles, CA 90035-1601
310-659-3800

MIRUS
9821 Katy Fwy
Houston, TX 77024-1206
713-468-7300

MISISSIPPI RESTAURANT ASSOC.
7 Lakeland Cir Ste 300
Jackson, MS 39216-5022
888-981-4464

MISS MERINGUE
1709 La Costa Meadows Dr
San Marcos, CA 92069-5105
www.missmeringue.com
800-561-6516 • Fax 760-471-4938

MISSION CRANE SERVICE, INC.
5190 Via Margarita
Yorba Linda, CA 92886-4531
714-456-0550

MISSION FOODS
1159 Cottonwood Ln
Irving, TX 75038-6106
www.missionfoodsfsc.com
214-232-5000 • Fax 214-232-5280

MISSION FOODS
225 John B Brooks Rd
Pendergrass, GA 30567-4614
800-240-2447

MISSION FOODS CORPORATION
5750 Grace Pl Ste A
Los Angeles, CA 90022-4121
www.missionfoods.com
323-887-6600 • Fax 323-727-5021

MISSISSION LINEN & UNIFORM SERVICE
2936 De La Vina St
Santa Barbara, CA 93105-3310
www.mission-linen.com
805-730-3620 • Fax 805-687-2684

MISSISSIPPI RESTAURANT ASSOC.
PO Box 16395
Jackson, MS 39236-6395
800-898-0343

MISSOURI BEEF INDUSTRY COUNCIL
2306 Bluff Creek Dr # 220
Columbia, MO 65201-3552
573-817-0899

MISSOURI DEPT. OF AGRLCUL-TURE
PO Box 630
Jefferson City, MO 65102-0630
573-751-6808

MIST INC .
547 Amherst St Fl 2
Nashua, NH 03063-4000
www.mistwireless.com
603-886-8620 • Fax 603-886-5516

MITCHELL DESIGN GROUP
2075 Maryland Dr
Irving, TX 75061-3329
972-986-8355

MITSUBISHI ELECTRONICS-GA
3100 Avalon Ridge Pl
Norcross, GA 30071-1582
770-613-5840

MITSUBISHI ELECTRIC & ELECTRONICS
5665 Plaza Dr
Cypress, CA 90630-5023
www.mitsubishi.ids.com
714-220-2500 • Fax 714-236-6434

MITSUBISHI FUSO TRUCK OF AMERICA
PO Box 100
Bridgeport, NJ 08014-0100
www.mitfuso.com
856-467-4500 • Fax 856-467-2781

MITSUI FOODS INC.
35 Maple St
Norwood, NJ 07648-2003
e-mail: paull@mustsui.foods.com
201-750-0500 • Fax 201-750-0148

MITY LITE
1301 W 400 N
Orem, UT 84057-4442
www.mitylite.com
801-224-0589 • Fax 801-224-6191

MIVILA
226 Getty Ave
Paterson, NJ 07503-2690
973-278-4148 • Fax 973-278-9332

MLP SEATING CORP
2125 Lively Blvd
Elk Grove Village, IL 60007-5207
www.mlpseating.com
800-723-3030 • Fax 847-956-1776

MNAZO FOOD SALES
10815 NW 33rd St
Miami, FL 33172-2188
305-596-5399

MOBILESTAR NETWORK
1601 N Glenville Dr
Richardson, TX 75081-7209
972-994-4900

MOBOLAZER & CO
790 Hampshire Rd Ste D
Westlake Village, CA 91361-5934
805-230-2166

MODERN BAKED PRODUCTS
301 Locust Ave
Oakdale, NY 11769-1652
e-mail:
sales@modernbakedprod.com
www.modernbakedprod.com
631-589-7300

MODERN CASH REG. CO. INC.
8023 W National Ave
Milwaukee, WI 53214-4507
414-257-2007 • Fax 414-257-1978

MODERN CASH REGISTER SYSTEMS
2222 American Dr
Neenah, WI 54956-1006
920-725-2007 • Fax 920-725-1088

MODERN FOOD SERVICE
1 University Plz Ste 200
Hackensack, NJ 07601-6206
201-488-1800 • Fax 201-488-7357

MODERN PEST SERVICES
14 Maine St
Brunswick, ME 04011-2026
e-mail:
sstevenson@modernpest.com
www.modernpest.com
207-938-7378 • Fax 207-933-9080

MODERN POSTCARD
1657 Faraday Ave
Carlsbad, CA 92008-7314
www.modernpostcard.com
800-959-8365 • Fax 760-431-1939

MODERN ROCK MUSIC
6014 Stoddard Ct
Alexandria, VA 22315-5656
800-373-7625

MODERN STOOL MFG CO INC
6320 E Lafayette St
Detroit, MI 48207-4334
313-567-5955

MODERNFOLD, INC
PO Box 310
New Castle, IN 47362-0310
e-mail: marketing@modernfold.com
www.modernfold.com
765-593-6431 • Fax 765-521-6204

MOD-PAC CORP
1801 Elmwood Ave
Buffalo, NY 14207-2409
800-666-3722 • Fax 800-873-1269

MOEN INC-MASTERBRAND IND
377 Woodland Ave
Elyria, OH 44035-3217
440-962-2000

MOKA
845 Grand St
Brooklyn, NY 11211-5099
718-387-2373 • Fax 718-387-1563

MOKAROW FINANCIAL
15923 76th Ave
Tinley Park, IL 60477-1302

MOLINARO KOGER
1676 International Dr
Mc Lean, VA 22102-4832
703-760-9600

MOLINE MACHINERY LTD
114 S Central Ave # 6308
Duluth, MN 55807-2302
218-624-5734

**MONADNOCK MOUNTAIN
SPRING WATE**
134 Penn St
Quincy, MA 02169-7508
e-mail: monadnockwater@juno.com
617-472-4200 • Fax 617-770-2720

**MONARCH MARKING
SYSTEMS, INC.**
170 Monarch Ln
Miamisburg, OH 45342-3638
www.monarch.com
937-865-2369 • Fax 937-865-8024

MONASTERY HILL BINDERY
1751 W Belmont Ave
Chicago, IL 60657-3019
773-525-4126 • Fax 773-525-4820

MONEY TREE ATM, LLC.
PO Box 5468
Destin, FL 32540-5468
www.moneytreeatm.com
850-837-3123 • Fax 850-837-8355

MONEYS MUSHROOMS
PO Box 169
Blandon, PA 19510-0169
800-661-8623

**MONEYTREE ATM
MANUFACTURING**
11 Eglin Pkwy SE
Fort Walton Beach, FL 32548-5426
e-mail: moneytree@destin.net
850-244-5543 • Fax 850-664-0457

MONFREY & ASSOCIATES
4803 Mill Creek Pl
Dallas, TX 75244-6913
e-mail: monfrey@earthlink.net
972-387-4531

MONIN, INC.
2100 Range Rd
Clearwater, FL 33765-2125
727-461-3033 • Fax 727-461-3305

**MONOGRAMME
CONFECTIONS**
74 Millwell Dr
Maryland Heights, MO 63043-2515
800-645-2007

MONROE CO, THE
316 N Walnut St
Colfax, IA 50054-1042
800-247-2488

MONSANTO CO
800 N Lindbergh Blvd
Saint Louis, MO 63167-0001
314-694-1000

**MONT BLANC
CHOCOLATIER**
425 S Cherry St
Denver, CO 80246-1226
800-877-3811

MONT BLANC GOURMET
425 S Cherry St Ste 630
Denver, CO 80246-1233
www.montblancgourmet.com
303-399-1616 • Fax 303-399-2323

MONT GRANITE
4817 E 355th St

Willoughby, OH 44094-4633
800-831-8232

MONTANA KNIFE WORKS
23 Pleasant St
Riverside, CT 06878-1706
www.montanaknifeworks.com
203-637-2886 • Fax 203-698-0400

MONTAUK GOURMET FOODS
25 Wits End
Spring Valley, NY 10977-1720
845-354-8510 • Fax 914-794-0897

MONTEREY MUSHROOMS INC
260 Westgate Dr
Watsonville, CA 95076-2452
831-763-5300 • Fax 831-763-0100

MONTEREY MUSHROOMS, INC
5816 Highway 75 S
Madisonville, TX 77864-7112
936-348-3511

MONTEREY PASTA COMPANY
1528 Moffett St
Salinas, CA 93905-3342
e-mail: info@montereypasta.com
831-753-6262 • Fax 831-753-6255

**MONTROSE HANGER
COMPANY**
PO Box 1149
Wilson, NC 27894-1149
www.montrosehanger.com
252-237-8038 • Fax 252-243-0470

MOODY DUNBAR
PO Box 68
Limestone, TN 37681-0068
800-251-8202

MOODY, CAVANAUGH AND CO.
793 Turnpike St
North Andover, MA 01845-6120
978-688-2081

**MOONEY FARMS SUN DRIED
TOMATOES**
1220 Fortress St
Chico, CA 95973-9029
e-mail: mooneyfarm@aol.com
530-899-2661 • Fax 530-899-7746

MOORE BUSINESS PRODUCTS
701 Woodlands Pkwy
Vernon Hills, IL 60061-3101
800-647-0400

MOORE IDEAS, INC.
1012 Creek Crossing
Coppell, TX 75019-6377
972-393-3526

MORE THAN GOURMET
929 Home Ave
Akron, OH 44310-4107
330-762-6652 • Fax 330-762-4832

MORGAN & CO.
27995 Greenfield Dr Ste D
Laguna Niguel, CA 92677-4432
949-448-5774 • Fax 949-448-9995

MORGAN STANLEY
1585 Broadway Frnt 2
New York, NY 10036-8200
212-761-1598

**MORGAN STANLEY
DEAN WITTER**
1 Pickwick Plz
Greenwich, CT 06830-5551
e-mail: daulat_dipshan@msdw.com
www.msdw.com
203-625-4600 • Fax 203-625-4667

MORNINGSTAR FARMS
900 Proprietors Rd
Columbus, OH 43085-3152
800-243-1810

MORNINGSTAR FOODS INC
5956 Sherry Ln
Dallas, TX 75225-6531
214-360-4700 • Fax 214-360-9100

MORRELL, JOHN AND COMPANY
250 E 5th St
Cincinnati, OH 45202-4119
513-852-3500

MORRISON MANAGEMENT

SPECIALIST
1955 Lake Park Dr SE
Smyrna, GA 30080-7649
800-686-6323

MORRISON MILLING CO.
PO Box 719
Denton, TX 76202-0719
800-580-5487 • Fax 940-566-5992

MORRISONS PASTRY CORP.
4901 Maspeth Ave
Maspeth, NY 11378-2219
718-937-7515 • Fax 718-937-5391

MORTIMER SCHWARTZ
1200 California St # 60
San Francisco, CA 94109-0001
415-346-7491

MORTON INTERNATIONAL
123 N Wacker Dr
Chicago, IL 60606-1743
312-807-2000 • Fax 312-807-2899

MOTEL 6
14651 Dallas Pkwy Ste 500
Dallas, TX 75254-8897
800-440-6000

MOTHER MURPHY
2826 S Elm St
Greensboro, NC 27406-4435
336-273-1737 • Fax 336-273-2615

MOTHER'S KITCHEN
499 Veterans Dr
Burlington, NJ 08016-1269
800-566-8437 • Fax 609-386-5329

MOTOROLA
1125 Satellite Blvd NW
Suwanee, GA 30024-4629
678-584-2927 • Fax 678-584-2969

MOTOROLA ACS
12013 Goddard Ave
Overland Park, KS 66213-1905
913-851-2999

MOTOROLA TWO-WAY RADIOS
647 Blackhawk Dr
Westmont, IL 60559-1115
800-240-5391 • Fax 800-939-5391

**MOTOROLA-ASTRA
COMMUNICATIONS**
12045 Magnolia Blvd
Valley Village, CA 91607-2740
www.astracomm.com
800-422-7133 • Fax 800-422-7119

MOTOROLA-PAGING
1500 Gateway Blvd
Boynton Beach, FL 33426-8221
800-382-9336

MOTTS U.S.A.
6 High Ridge Park
Stamford, CT 06905-1327
203-968-7500

MOULI MANUFACTURING
1 Montgomery St
Belleville, NJ 07109-1305
973-751-6900 • Fax 973-751-0345

**MOUNTAIN LAKE FISHERIES
CAVIOR**
PO Box 1067
Columbia Falls, MT 59912-1067
e-mail:
mtkfish@whitefishcavior.com
Fax 406-892-2077

**MOUNTAIN-SERVICE
DISTRIBUTORS**
12B Seabro Ave
Amityville, NY 11701-1202
516-997-2688 • Fax 516-997-2691

**MOUNTAIRE FARMS OF
DELMARVA**
PO Box 710
Selbyville, DE 19975-0710
800-441-8263

MOVING TARGETS
812 W Chestnut St
Perkasie, PA 18944-1332
www.movingtargets.com
800-926-2451 • Fax 215-257-1570

MOYER DIEBEL
PO Box 4183
Winston Salem, NC 27115-4183
www.moyerusa.com
336-661-1992 • Fax 336-661-1979

MOZZARELLA COMPANY
2944 Elm St
Dallas, TX 75226-1509
www.mozzco.com
214-741-4072

MOZZARELLA FRESCA INC.
538 Stone Rd
Benicia, CA 94510-1174
www.italcheese.com
707-746-6818 • Fax 707-746-6829

MP3. COM
4790 Eastgate Mall
San Diego, CA 92121-1970
www.mp3.com-retail
858-623-7000 • Fax 858-623-7323

MPBS INDUSTRIES
2820 E Washington Blvd
Los Angeles, CA 90023-4217
e-mail: info@mpbs.com
323-268-8514 • Fax 323-268-6305

MR. BAR-B-Q, INC.
445 Winding Rd
Old Bethpage, NY 11804-1311
www.mrbarbq.com
516-752-0670 • Fax 516-752-0683

MR. COFFEE CONCEPTS, INC
6901 Northpark Blvd
Charlotte, NC 28216-2388
www.mrcoffeeconcepts.com
704-596-3661 • Fax 704-569-3112

MR. ESPRESSO
696 3rd St
Oakland, CA 94607-3560
510-287-5200 • Fax 510-287-5204

MR. ROOTER PLUMBING
1010 N University Parks Dr
Waco, TX 76707-3854
www.mrrooter.com
800-503-8003 • Fax 254-745-2501

MRS CLARK'S FOODS
740 SE Dalbey Dr
Ankeny, IA 50021-3908
www.mrsclarks.com
515-964-8100 • Fax 515-964-8397

MRS SMITHS BAKERIES INC
2855 Rolling Pin Ln
Suwanee, GA 30024-7218
800-245-8963

MRS SMITHS BAKERIES INC
145 N Jonathon Blvd
Chaska, MN 55318-2342
952-448-4493 • Fax 952-448-4095

MRS TRADING, INC.
8516 Old Winter Garden Rd
Orlando, FL 32835-4410
e-mail: mrstrad@bellsouth.net
407-296-9113 • Fax 407-296-9143

MRS. BAIRD'S BAKERIES-BBU
7301 South Fwy
Fort Worth, TX 76134-4004
817-615-3135

MRS. CROCKETT'S KITCHENS
1523 High Bluff Dr
Diamond Bar, CA 91765-2631
909-861-8522

MRS. CROCKETT'S KITCHENS
8821 Forum Way
Fort Worth, TX 76140-5009
800-527-2523

MRS. D'S GOURMET COOKIES
3657 NW 124th Ave
Pompano Beach, FL 33065-2445
e-mail: cookiedr44@aol.com
954-344-5102

MRS. LEEPER'S PASTA
12455 Kerran St Ste 200
Poway, CA 92064-8834
e-mail: mlpinc@pacbell.net
858-486-1101 • Fax 858-486-1770

MRS. STRATTON'S SALADS
PO Box 190187
Birmingham, AL 35219-0187
205-940-9640 • Fax 205-940-9658

MRS.T'S PIEROGIES ATEECO
PO Box 600
Shenandoah, PA 17976-0600
e-mail: ateeco@ptd.net
www.pierogy.com
570-462-2745 • Fax 570-462-1392

MS. DESSERTS, INC.
2275 Rolling Run Dr
Windsor Mill, MD 21244-1848
800-876-6554

MASTER PURVEYORS
452 W 13th St
New York, NY 10014-1105
212-929-7883 • Fax 212-727-8381

MT.VIKOS
4 Calypso Ln
Marshfield, MA 02050-3601
e-mail: mtvikos@worldnet.att.net
781-834-0828 • Fax 781-837-8403

MTI WHIRLPOOLS
670 N Price Rd
Buford, GA 30518-4722
e-mail: thecleanone@msn.com
www.mtiwhirlpool.com
800-783-8827 • Fax 770-271-8254

MTS SEATING
7100 Industrial Dr
Temperance, MI 48182-9105
877-847-3875

MU-H
121 E 24th St Fl 4R
New York, NY 10010-2912
e-mail: cseebach@mu-h.com
www.mu-h.com
212-228-7779 • Fax 212-228-7779

MUCKLER INDUSTRIES, INC
9962 Lin Ferry Dr Ste 206
Saint Louis, MO 63123-6961
800-444-0283

MUELLER CO PAUL
PO Box 828
Springfield, MO 65801-0828
800-683-5537

MULITFOODS
111 Cheshire Ln
Hopkins, MN 55305-1060
612-404-7500 • Fax 612-404-7650

MULTI GRAINS, INC.
PO Box 8195
Haverhill, MA 01835-0695
978-374-8288 • Fax 978-374-8470

MULTI-UNIT FOODSERVICE MARKETING
5120 Ranchita Canyon Rd
San Miguel, CA 93451-9548
805-467-3896 • Fax 805-467-3020

MULTICULTURAL FOODSERVICE
PO Box 1113
Minneapolis, MN 55440-1113
612-540-3267 • Fax 612-540-4794

MULTIFOODS DISTRIBUTION GROUP
1700 Avenue B
Kissimmee, FL 34758-2015
e-mail: richard_schon@mfdg.com
www.mfdg.com
407-870-9900

MULTIFOODS DISTRIBUTIONS
6855 Business Park Dr
Houston, TX 77041-4034
713-896-4200 • Fax 713-896-4212

MULTIFOODS TOWER
33 S 6th St
Minneapolis, MN 55402-3601
612-340-3300

MULTIMEDIA COMMUNICATIONS
60 E Hanover Ave # B-4
Morris Plains, NJ 07950-2457

e-mail: gc@mulmcom.net
www.mulmcom.net
973-285-1020 • Fax 973-285-1030

MULTIMEDIA, INC.
3300 Monier Cir Ste 150
Rancho Cordova, CA 95742-6866
www.multimedialed.com
916-852-4220 • Fax 916-852-8325

MULTIPLEX COMPANY INC
250 Old Ballwin Rd
Ballwin, MO 63021-4800
www.multiplex-beverage.com
636-256-7777 • Fax 636-527-4313

MULTI-SYSTEMS INC.
1825 E Northern Ave
Phoenix, AZ 85020-3940
e-mail: info@msisolution.com
www.msisolutions.com
602-870-4200 • Fax 602-861-3711

MULTIVAC INC
11021 N Pomona Ave
Kansas City, MO 64153-2035
816-891-0555 • Fax 816-891-0622

MUNDIAL INC
50 Kerry Pl
Norwood, MA 02062-4709
781-762-8310

MUNLEY ASSOCIATES
PO Box 297
Needham Heights, MA 02494-0002
e-mail: j4pun@aol.com
781-433-0130 • Fax 781-444-8917

MUNN MARKETING GROUP
4845 Keller Springs Rd
Addison, TX 75001-5912
e-mail: sales@munn-mktg.com
www.munn-mktg.com
972-732-0057 • Fax 972-248-2161

MUNTERS CORP
16900 Jordan
Schertz, TX 78154-1272
210-737-5197

MUNTERS ZEOL
79 Monroe St
Amesbury, MA 01913-3204

MURASPEC N.A.
67 Pacella Park Dr
Randolph, MA 02368-1755
e-mail: helop@muraspecna.com
www.murapecna.com
800-679-5120 • Fax 781-963-4975

MURRAY ENTERPRISES
102 N George Mason Dr
Arlington, VA 22203-2900
703-528-4564

MURRAY FEISS LIGHTING
125 Rose Feiss Blvd
Bronx, NY 10454-3624
e-mail: rdillion@feiss.com
www.feiss.com
718-292-2024 • Fax 718-292-0083

MURRAY'S CHICKENS
28 Lady Godiva Way
New City, NY 10956-6350
e-mail: omfp@murrayschicken.com
845-639-3154 • Fax 845-639-9272

MUSCO OLIVE PRODUCTS
17950 Via Nicolo
Tracy, CA 95377-9767
e-mail: sales@muscoolive.com
800-523-9828 • Fax 209-836-0518

MUSHROOM CANNING CO
401 Birch St
Kennett Square, PA 19348-3609
www.mushroomcanning.com
610-444-6654 • Fax 610-444-9457

MUSICMUSICMUSIC INC.
580 Broadway Rm 306
New York, NY 10012-3223
www.musicmusicmusic.com
877-874-0911 • Fax 646-613-0079

MUSSO'S GOURMET BAKERY, INC
PO Box 1858

Union City, CA 94587-6858
e-mail: elissbb@earthlink.com
510-441-0311 • Fax 510-441-0315

MUTUAL WHOLESALES LIQUOR, INC
4510 S Boyle Ave
Los Angeles, CA 90058-2418
323-587-7641 • Fax 323-587-0820

MUZAK
1020 James Dr Ste A
Hartland, WI 53029-8305
www.muzak.com
262-369-9300 • Fax 262-369-9400

MUZAK
4300 W Royal Ln
Irving, TX 75063-2227
www.muzak.com
972-929-9808 • Fax 972-929-9530

MUZAK, FLORIDA GROUP
5750 S Semoran Blvd
Orlando, FL 32822-4814
www.muzak.com
407-281-6311

MUZAK, L.L.C.
4517 Fairfield St
Metairie, LA 70006-2848
504-455-9899

MUZAK, L.L.C.
20 Plover St
New Orleans, LA 70124-4408
504-283-3440 • Fax 504-286-5852

MUZAK L.L.C
1626 Broadway St
Kansas City, MO 64108-1208
816-221-1515

MVNEIL SPECIALTY PRODUCTS
501 George St
New Brunswick, NJ 08901-1161
www.splenda.com
732-524-1900 • Fax 732-524-1807

MY BROTHER BOBBY'S SALSA
PO Box 3659
Poughkeepsie, NY 12603-0659
e-mail: mbbsalsa@aol.com
Fax 845-462-1667

MY STYLE
614 N West St
Raleigh, NC 27603-1310
e-mail: mystyle@bigplanet.com
919-832-2526 • Fax 919-832-1546

MYERS CONSULTING
5000 Lansing Ave
Jackson, MI 49201-8137
517-789-7775

N E C
8 Corporate Center Dr
Melville, NY 11747-3112
516-753-7000

N F B FOODWORKS
530 Clubhouse Rd
Woodmere, NY 11598-1902
516-295-9191

N K I LEASING
143 Lake St N
Forest Lake, MN 55025-2531
800-506-8908

N L P INDUSTRIES
280 Trousdale Dr # E
Chula Vista, CA 91910-1014
619-474-8807

N S M AMERICA INC
1158 Tower Ln
Bensenville, IL 60106-1028
630-860-5100

N.Y. BEEF INDUSTRY COUNCIL
PO Box 250
Westmoreland, NY 13490-0250
www.nybic.org
315-339-6922 • Fax 315-339-6931

N.Y.CASH REGISTER CO.,INC.

2010 Coney Island Ave
Brooklyn, NY 11223-2329
e-mail: nycr001@aol.com
www.newyorkcash.com
718-998-1914 • Fax 718-998-8012

NABISCO FOODS GROUP F S DIV
PO Box 311
Parsippany, NJ 07054-0311
973-682-5000

NAKANO FOODS INC
55 E Euclid Ave Ste 300
Mt Prospect, IL 60056-1286
847-290-0730 • Fax 847-290-9861

NALLEYS FINE FOODS
3303 S 35th St
Tacoma, WA 98409-4701
253-383-1621 • Fax 253-272-2730

NAMCO AMERICA, INC.
877 Supreme Dr
Bensenville, IL 60106-1106
630-238-2248 • Fax 630-238-9333

NANCY CALHOUN, INC
PO Box 130
Corona, CA 92878-0130
e-mail: nancycalhoun@surfside.net
909-272-0041 • Fax 909-272-0069

NANTUCKET NECTARS
45 Dunster St
Cambridge, MA 02138-5900
617-868-3600

NAP - NEW AGE PRODUCTS, INC
4779 Woodlane Cir
Tallahassee, FL 32303-6844
e-mail: nap@chop-chop.com
www.chop-chop.com
800-886-2467 • Fax 888-886-0380

NAPA VALLEY VINTNERS ASSOCIATION
PO Box 141
Saint Helena, CA 94574-0141
707-942-9775

NASCO
901 Janesville Ave
Fort Atkinson, WI 53538-2497
920-563-2446

NASS PARTS & SERVICE, INC
1108 Woods Ave
Orlando, FL 32805-3857
e-mail: nass@nassparts.com
407-425-2681

NATARE CORP
5905 W 74th St
Indianapolis, IN 46278-1786
317-872-8828

NATCO FOOD SERVICE MERCHANTS
1341 Magazine St
New Orleans, LA 70130-4221
504-525-7224

NATION PIZZA PRODUCTS
2491 N Milwaukee Ave
Chicago, IL 60647-2661
www.nationpizza.com
773-782-3300 • Fax 773-782-3400

NATIONWIDE MARKETING GROUP
RR 1 Box 93
Trenton, TX 75490-9801
800-496-4376

NATIONAL CHECKING CO.
899 Montreal Way
Saint Paul, MN 55102-4245
www.nationalchecking.com
800-328-6508

NATIONAL ASSOCIATION CATERING
250 Wilshire Blvd Ste 17
Casselberry, FL 32707-5377
e-mail:
nacc@rainbowassoc-meeting.com
www.orlandoacc.net
407-831-7825

NATIONAL BARBECUE ASSOCIATION
723 S Sharon Amity Rd Ste 214
Charlotte, NC 28211-2835
704-365-3622

NATIONAL CATERERS' ASSOCIATION
860 Bay St
Staten Island, NY 10304-3717
www.ncacarter.org
800-NCA-0029 • Fax 718-448-5961

NATIONAL CATTLEMEN S BEEF ASSOCIATION
444 N Michigan Ave
Chicago, IL 60611-3903
312-467-5520 • Fax 312-467-9767

NATIONAL CHEF SUPPLY WAREHOUSE
3601 N Dixie Hwy
Boca Raton, FL 33431-5929
www.nationalchefsupply.com
888-330-6279

NATIONAL DATA CORP.
14502 N Dale Mabry Hwy
Tampa, FL 33618-2075
e-mail:
tampa.ndcorp@minosorind.com
www.ndcecommerce.com
813-963-5516

NATIONAL DISTRIBUTING CO.
4901 Savarese Cir
Tampa, FL 33634-2413
e-mail: shai.froelich@natdistco.com
813-885-3200 • Fax 813-884-6063

NATIONAL DISTRIBUTING COMPANY
PO Box 44127
Atlanta, GA 30336-1127
e-mail: fred.brown@natdistco.com

NATIONAL ENVIRONMEMTAL GROUP
PO Box 385
Cedarhurst, NY 11516-0385
e-mail: rne@mail.idt.net
516-569-5211 • Fax 516-569-5737

NATIONAL FOODSERVICE PANEL INC
318 Main St
West Newbury, MA 01985-1420
978-363-2144 • Fax 978-363-1179

NATIONAL FRANCHISE SALES
1520 Brookhollow Dr Ste 45
Santa Ana, CA 92705-5422
www.nationalfranchisesales.com
714-434-9400 • Fax 714-434-9401

NATIONAL FRUIT FLAVOR CO
935 Edwards Ave
New Orleans, LA 70123-3124
www.nationalfruitflavor.com
504-733-6757 • Fax 504-736-0168

NATIONAL FRUIT PRODUCT COMPANY
PO Box 2040
Winchester, VA 22604-1240
540-662-3401 • Fax 540-665-4670

NATIONAL LINEN SERVICE
1420 Peachtree St NE # 551
Atlanta, GA 30309-3002
404-853-6000 • Fax 404-853-6002

NATIONAL LITHOGRAPHICS, INC.
1173 Broadway
Hewlett, NY 11557-2323
516-374-0700

NATIONAL LOOSE LEAF
15505 Cornet St
Santa Fe Springs, CA 90670-5511
www.thenationalcompanies.com
562-926-4511 • Fax 562-926-0222

NATIONAL MARKETING ASSOCIATES
1664 US Highway 395 N Ste 104
Minden, NV 89423-4322
www.nma-creditservices.com
775-782-7589 • Fax 775-782-7572

NATIONAL MENUBOARD INC.
4302 B St NW Ste D
Auburn, WA 98001-1722
www.nationalmenuboard.com
800-800-5237 • Fax 253-859-8412

NATIONAL PIZZA PRODUCTS
601 E Algonquin Rd
Schaumburg, IL 60173-3803
e-mail: stornerj@nationpizza.com
630-782-3333 • Fax 847-348-5496

NATIONAL PORK PRODUCERS
1776 NW 114th St
Clive, IA 50325-7000
515-223-2600

NATIONAL PROCESSING CO
1231 Durrett Ln
Louisville, KY 40213-2008
800-255-1157 • Fax 502-315-3535

NATIONAL REGISTRY OF FOOD SAFE
1200 Hillcrest St Ste 303
Orlando, FL 32803-4737
e-mail: lviau@nrfsp.com
www.nrfsp.com
407-228-0909

NATIONAL RESTAURANT ASSOCIATION
1200 17th St NW
Washington, DC 20036-3006
www.restaurant.org
800-424-5156 • Fax 202-331-5946

NATIONAL SANITIZER, INC.
2120 Metro Cir SW
Huntsville, AL 35801-5344
256-880-9998

NATIONAL STEAK AND POUL-TRY
301 E 5th Ave
Owasso, OK 74055-3450
918-274-8787 • Fax 918-274-0046

NATIONAL TOWELETTE CO
1400 Taylors Ln
Riverton, NJ 08077-2512
www.towelettes.com
856-786-7300 • Fax 856-786-7304

NATIONWIDE HOTEL SUPPLY
625 N Michigan Ave Ste 1910
Chicago, IL 60611-3178
800-222-9947

NATIONWIDE SALES AND SER-VICE
55 Lamar St
West Babylon, NY 11704-1301
www.shopnss.com
631-491-6625 • Fax 631-491-6634

NATL ASSOC MARGARINE MFG
5775 Peachtree Dunwoody Rd NE
Atlanta, GA 30342-1556
404-252-3663

NATL AUTOMATIC MERCHANDISING
20 N Wacker Dr
Chicago, IL 60606-2806
312-346-0370

NATL BAKING CENTER
818 Dunwoody Blvd
Minneapolis, MN 55403-1141
612-374-3303

NATL CASH SYSTEMS
12 Mauchly Ste O
Irvine, CA 92618-6308
888-642-2274

NATL CATTLEMENS BEEF ASSC
9110 E Nichols Ave
Englewood, CO 80112-3450
303-694-0305

NATL COMPUTER CORP
211 Century Dr Ste 100B
Greenville, SC 29607-1594
www.nccusa.com
864-233-8824 • Fax 864-235-7688

NATL CONFECTIONERS ASSOCIATION
7900 Westpark Dr
Mc Lean, VA 22102-4242
703-790-5750

NATL CONTENT LIQUIDATORS
2090 Hewitt Ave
Dayton, OH 45440-4238
937-435-2340

NATL COTTONSEED PRODUCTS ASSOCIATION
PO Box 172267
Memphis, TN 38187-2267
901-682-0800

NATL FISH & SEAFOOD INC
11-15 Parker St
Gloucester, MA 01930-3017
978-283-8907

NATL FISHERIES INST
1525 Wilson Blvd Ste 50
Arlington, VA 22209-2411
703-524-8881

NATL FROZEN FOOD ASSOCIATION
4755 Linglestown Rd Ste 30
Harrisburg, PA 17112-8508
717 657 0601

NATL FROZEN FOOD CORP
PO Box 9366
Seattle, WA 98109-0366
206-322-8900

NATL REST ASSOCIATION - EDUCATION FUND
250 S Wacker Dr
Chicago, IL 60606-6301
800-765-2122

NATL TICKET CO
PO Box 547
Shamokin, PA 17872-0547
800-829-0829

NATL TURKEY FEDERATION
1225 New York Ave NW
Washington, DC 20005-6156
202-898-0110

NATN'L ASSOC OF MEAT PUR-VEYORS
1920 Association Dr Ste 400
Reston, VA 20191-1545
703-758-1900

NATURAL BRANDS FRESH JUICES
9191 Garland Rd Apt 511
Dallas, TX 75218-3985
e-mail: duchesnea@aol.com
www.naturalbrands.com
214-319-0784 • Fax 214-319-0622

NATURAL LIFE
14108 Lake Street Ext
Minnetonka, MN 55345-3019
e-mail: naturalife@earthlink.net
www.paincarestore.com
952-930-0971

NATURAL SELECTION FOODS
1721 San Juan Hwy
San Juan Bautista, CA 95045-9780
831-623-7888

NATURALLY FRESH FOODS
1000 Naturally Fresh Blvd
Atlanta, GA 30349-2909
404-765-9000 • Fax 404-765-9016

NATURE'S CATCH INC
1090 Willis Rd
Clarksdale, MS 38614-9292
662-627-1482

NATURE'S CHOICE FOODS
3300 NW 112th St
Miami, FL 33167-3313
e-mail: wgreen@natchoice.com
www.natchoice.com
305-953-9933

NATURE'S WORLD, INC.
119 Garden Hill Dr

Calhoun, GA 30701-2029
e-mail: sales@aviariums.com
706-625-8220 • Fax 706-629-2587

NAUTICALSUPPLYSHOP.COM
4600 Cecile Dr
Kissimmee, FL 34746-5701
e-mail:
customerservice@shellworld.com
www.nauticalsupplyshop.com
407-787-3362

NCR
2651 Satellite Blvd
Duluth, GA 30096-5810
770-623-7232

NCR CORPORATION
9095 Washington Church Rd
Miamisburg, OH 45342-4496
937-297-5700

NCR-VAR-CRYAN & ASSOCIATES
63 River St
South Yarmouth, MA 02664-6051
e-mail: dcryan2000@aol.com
www.ncr.com
508-398-7780 • Fax 508-394-5043

NDC ECOMMERCE
5000 W Esplanade Ave
Metairie, LA 70006 2551
504-469-6054

NDC ECOMMERCE
6215 W Howard St
Niles, IL 60714-3403
www.ndcecommerce.com
800-638-4600 • Fax 847-647-6832

NEARMEALTIME.COM
32 Offutt Rd
Hanscom AFB, MA 01731-2608
781-274-0187

NEBS INC
500 Main St
Groton, MA 01471-0001
800-367-6327

NE-BUD SERVICES GROUP OF FLORIDA
1234 S John Young Pkwy
Kissimmee, FL 34741-6388
407-944-9401 • Fax 407-944-9412

NED KELLY'S RESTAURANT MGMNT
13451 McGregor Blvd Ste 34
Fort Myers, FL 33919-5942
239-433-4477

NEEDWAITSTAFF.COM
2269 Chestnut St Ste 96
San Francisco, CA 94123-2600
e-mail: info@needwaitstaff.com
www.needwaitstaff.com
415-750-0882

NEESVIG PURVEYORS
PO Box 288
Windsor, WI 53598-0288
608-846-1150 • Fax 608-846-1155

NEIGHBORHOOD MKTG INST
44 Cocoanut Row
Palm Beach, FL 33480-4069
800-235-9647

NEIL ALLEN-THE STONE RESOURCE
2101 E Kivett Dr
High Point, NC 27260-5819
e-mail: neilallen@aol.com
www.neilallenindustries.com
336-887-6500 • Fax 336-887-7402

NEIL FISHMAN & ASSOCIATES
8457 SW 132nd St
Miami, FL 33156-6505
e-mail: neilfish@bellsouth.net
305-378-0378 • Fax 305-378-8545

NEMCO FOODS EQUIPMENT
301 Meuse Argonne St
Hicksville, OH 43526-1143
419-542-7751 • Fax 419-542-6690

NE-MO'S BAKERY, INC
416 N Hale Ave
Escondido, CA 92029-1420
e-mail:
salesadmin@nemossales.com
760-741-5725 • Fax 760-741-0659

NESCAFE - NESTLE FOODSERVICES
8720 SW 175th St
Miami, FL 33157-5839
e-mail:
vinnie.merida@us.nestle.com
305-256-8035 • Fax 305-971-4695

NESS PLASTICS
8555 Tonnelle Ave Ste 21
North Bergen, NJ 07047-4732
201-869-0088

NESTLE BRANDS FOODSERVICE
PO Box 29059
Glendale, CA 91209-9059
323-932-6000

NESTLE BRANDS FOODSERVICE COMP
800 N Brand Blvd
Glendale, CA 91203-1245
818-549-6000 • Fax 818-549-6952

NESTLE FOODSERVICE - FROZEN FOOD
5750 Harper Rd
Solon, OH 44139-1831
440-498-7797

NESTLE NESPRESSO
214 E 52nd St
New York, NY 10022-6207
e-mail:
greggory.kronhaus@nespresso.com
212-755-0585 • Fax 212-755-0043

NESTLES
30003 Bainbridge Rd
Solon, OH 44139-2290
440-248-3600 • Fax 440-498-1754

NET-TECH INTERNATIONAL
1 W Front St Fl 3
Red Bank, NJ 07701-1623
732-845-0600

NET2000 COMMUNICATIONS
1775 Wiehle Ave Ste 400
Reston, VA 20190-5159
703-654-2543 • Fax 703-654-2025

NETHERLANDS MINISTRY OF AGRICULTURE
4200 Linnean Ave NW
Washington DC 20008-3809
www.netherlands-embassy.org-fn_econ
202-274-2716 • Fax 202-244-3325

NETWORLD EXCHANGE
5256 S Mission Rd
Bonsall, CA 92003-3614
www.networldexchange.com
760-639-4900 • Fax 760-639-4909

NETZOW'S PIANOS & ORGANS
8837 W North Ave
Milwaukee, WI 53226-2725
414-476-9985 • Fax 414-476-9044

NEUMAN BAKERY SPECIALITIES
1405 Jeffrey Dr
Addison, IL 60101-4331
e-mail: neuman546@aol.com
630-916-8909 • Fax 630-916-8919

NEW & BETTER WAYS
2605 51st Ave SE
Olympia, WA 98501-4905
www.new&betterways.com
360-561-8655 • Fax 360-456-2924

NEW AGE INDUSTRIAL
PO Box 520
Norton, KS 67654-0520
www.newageindustrial.com
785-877-5121 • Fax 785-877-2616

NEW AMERICAN FOODS
1407 N Mohawk St
Chicago, IL 60610-5503
312-951-9339

NEW BELGUIM BREWING CO
500 Linden St
Fort Collins, CO 80524-2457
www.newbelgium.com
970-221-0524 • Fax 970-221-0535

NEW CHEF FASHIONS
910 S Los Angeles St
Los Angeles, CA 90015-1726
800-626-2433

NEW ENGLAND COFFEE CO
100 Charles St
Malden, MA 02148-6704
800-225-3537

NEW ENGLAND COIN-OP DIST.
232 Vanderbilt Ave
Norwood, MA 02062-5039
781-769-9760 • Fax 781-762-8225

NEW ENGLAND CULINARY INSTITUTE
250 Main St
Montpelier, VT 05602-4201
802-223-6324 • Fax 802-223-0634

NEW ENGLAND ICE CREAM
250 Belmont St
Brockton, MA 02301-5150
508-580-6100 • Fax 508-580-5959

NEW ERA OF NETWORKS INC
99 Rosewood Dr
Danvers, MA 01923-1300
800-495-7500

NEW FRENCH BAKERY
2609 26th Ave S
Minneapolis, MN 55406-1501
www.newfrenchbakery.com
612-728-0193 • Fax 612-728-9278

NEW HAMPSHIRE COLLEGE
2500 N River Rd
Hooksett, NH 03106-1045
e-mail: poznanbr@nhc.edu
www.nhc.edu
603-645-9611 • Fax 603-645-9693

NEW HAVEN MANUFACTURING CORPORATION
446 Blake St
New Haven, CT 06515-1286
203-387-2572

NEW HAVEN MOVING EQUIPMENT
1111 E 16th St
Los Angeles, CA 90021-2605
www.newhaven-usa.com
800-421-8700 • Fax 213-749-8171

NEW JERSEY RESTAURANT ASSOCIATION
1 Executive Dr Ste 100
Somerset, NJ 08873-4002
e-mail: njrest@ix.netcom.com
www.njra.org
800-848-6368 • Fax 732-302-1804

NEW MEXICO STATE UNIV
PO Box 30003
Las Cruces, NM 88003-8003
e-mail: mcerlett@nmsu.edu
www.nmsu.edu--hrtm
505-646-5995 • Fax 505-646-8100

NEW ORLEANS EAST BUSINESS ASSOCIATION
7045 Read Blvd Ste 10
New Orleans, LA 70127-7617
504-241-7800 • Fax 504-242-8059

NEW ORLEANS ESPRESSO CO
805 Howard Ave
New Orleans, LA 70113-1107
504-522-3871

NEW ORLEANS FISH HOUSE
921 S Dupre St
New Orleans, LA 70125-1343
504-821-9700 • Fax 504-821-9011

NEW ORLEANS HOSPITALITY COALITION
PO Box 52886
New Orleans, LA 70152-2886
504-556-5821 • Fax 504-566-5067

NEW ORLEANS MISSION
PO Box 56565
New Orleans, LA 70156-6565
504-523-2116

NEW ORLEANS SAINTS
5800 Airline Dr
Metairie, LA 70003-3876
504-731-1770

NEW RA MARKETING, INC.
PO Box 1349
Waukesha, WI 53187-1349
262-524-8788 • Fax 262-524-1666

NEW YORK CITY OFF TRACK BETTING
1501 Broadway
New York, NY 10036-5601
212-704-5118 • Fax 212-704-5186

NEW YORK DEPARTMENT OF AGRICULTURE
1 Winners Circle
Albany, NY 12235-0001
www.agmkt.state.ny.us
518-457-7076 • Fax 518-457-2716

NEW YORK INTERNATIONAL BREAD
1500 W Church St
Orlando, FL 32805-2408
407-843-9744

NEW YORK STATE HOSPITALITY
11 N Pearl St Fl 11
Albany, NY 12207-2786
e-mail: info@nyshta.org
www.nyshta.org
518-465-2300 • Fax 518-465-4025

NEW YORK STATE LIQUOR AUTHORITY
84 Holland Ave
Albany, NY 12208-3435
e-mail: mhart@abc.state.ny.us
518-486-4767 • Fax 518-402-4015

NEW YORK STATE LOTTERY
PO Box 7500
Schenectady, NY 12301-7500
518-388-3405 • Fax 518-388-3403

NEW YORK STATE RESTAURANT ASSOCIATION
505 8th Ave Rm 700
New York, NY 10018-6570
e-mail: commwiz@albany.net
www.nysra.org
212-714-1330 • Fax 212-643-2962

NEW YORK UNIVERSITY
7 E 12th St Fl 11
New York, NY 10003-4475
212-998-9100

NEW ZEALAND LAMB CO INC
8000 Towers Crescent Dr
Vienna, VA 22182-2700
703-347-5488

NEW ZEALAND AUSTRALIAN LAMB CO
106 Corporate Park Dr # 11
West Harrison, NY 10604-3806
914-253-4020 • Fax 914-253-8155

NEWBOLD CORPORATION
510 Weaver St
Rocky Mount, VA 24151-2280
540-489-4400

NEWBURY JR COLLEGE
129 Fisher Ave
Brookline, MA 02445-5796
www.newbury.edu
617-730-7007 • Fax 617-730-7290

NEWCO ENTERPRISES INC
1735 S River Rd
Saint Charles, MO 63303-4159
www.newcocoffee.com
800-325-7867 • Fax 636-925-0029

NEWLYWEDS FOODS
4140 W Fullerton Ave
Chicago, IL 60639-2198
773-489-7000 • Fax 773-489-2799

NEWMARKET INTERNATIONAL
135 Commerce Way
Portsmouth, NH 03801-3200
603-436-7500

NEWPORT CREAMERY
124 Washington St Ste 101
Foxboro, MA 02035-1368
www.newportcreamery.com

NEWSPAPERDIRECT
230 Park Ave
New York, NY 10169-0005
212-808-3031

NEWSPAPERDIRECT INC.
135 Park Ave
New York, NY 10017-5518
e-mail: hospitality@newspaperdirect.com
www.newspaperdirect.com
212-869-3909 • Fax 604-278-4684

NEXEL INDUSTRIES
22 Harbor Park Dr
Port Washington, NY 11050-4650
800-245-6682

NEXT DAY GOURMET - US FOODSERVICE
9755 Patuxent Woods Dr
Columbia, MD 21046-2286
410-312-7100

NEXT DIMENSION STUDIOS
2552 American Ct
Ft Mitchell, KY 41017-1548
e-mail:
decollins@nextdimensionstudios.com
888-346-3674 • Fax 859-426-9922

NEXT GENERATION MARKETING
1295 Northern Blvd
Manhasset, NY 11030-3002
e-mail: jlshea@att.net
www.twodogs.com
917-689-6568 • Fax 516-869-6228

NEXTEL COMMUNICATIONS
300 Park Blvd Ste 100
Itasca, IL 60143-2604
www.nextel.com
630-875-5000 • Fax 630-875-5091

NEXTEL COMMUNICATIONS
7007 College Blvd Ste 50
Leawood, KS 66211-1558
913-663-7018

NFB FOODWORKS DBA BOC-CONCINO
140 W Commercial Ave
Moonachie, NJ 07074-1703
e-mail: nfbfoodworks@aol.com
201-933-7474 • Fax 201-933-1530

NFL
280 Park Ave
New York, NY 10017-1216
www.nflsundayticket.com
212-450-2172 • Fax 212-681-7584

NICE PAK PRODUCTS
2 Nice Pak Park
Orangeburg, NY 10962-1376
845-365-1700

NICHE W. & S.
60 E Hanover Ave
Morris Plains, NJ 07950-2457
973-993-8450

NICHIREI FOODS AMERICA
1124 54th Ave E
Tacoma, WA 98424-2702
253-922-5577 • Fax 253-922-3807

NICHOLLS STATE UNIVERSITY CHEF
PO Box 2099
Thibodaux, LA 70310-0001
www.nich.edu-jfolse
985-449-7091 • Fax 985-449-7089

NICHOLS FOODSERVICE, INC.
PO Box 729
Wallace, NC 28466-0729
910-285-3197

NICOLA INTERNATIONAL, INC.
4561 Colorado Blvd
Los Angeles, CA 90039-1103
818-545-1515 • Fax 818-247-8585

NIECO CORPORATION
15 Guittard Rd
Burlingame, CA 94010-2203
www.nieco.com
650-697-7335 • Fax 650-697-3014

NIETO REFRIGERATION SA. DE C.V
808 Berkley Dr
Cleburne, TX 76033-6160
817-556-2195 • Fax 817-641-6056

NIGHTCLUBITEMS.COM LLC
3808 E Monterosa St
Phoenix, AZ 85018-4819
480-636-1420

NIKKO CERAMICS, INC
114 Seaview Dr
Secaucus, NJ 07094-1800
e-mail: nikkousa@l-2000.com
201-863-5200 • Fax 201-866-6216

NILFISK ADVANCE AMERICA
14600 21st Ave N
Minneapolis, MN 55447-4648

NILSSON SWEDEN
5715 Wild Olive Ln
Crystal Lake, IL 60012-1267
e-mail. info@nilssonusa.com
www.nilssonsweden.com
815-444-6872 • Fax 815-444-7244

NIPSCO
801 E 86th Ave
Merrillville, IN 46410-6272
219-647-5480

NISONGER ASSOCIATES, INC.
PO Box 201
Terrace Park, OH 45174-0201
513-248-1441

NISSAN DIESEL AMERICA INC
PO Box 152034
Irving, TX 75015-2034
972-756-5500

NISSCO, INC.
45600 Terminal Dr Ste 200
Sterling, VA 20166-4302
703-592-9340

NITTA CASINGS, INC.
PO Box 858
Somerville, NJ 08876-0858
908-218-4424

NO BARRIERS INTERFACE SOLUTIONS
8 Central St
Salem, MA 01970-3703
www.nobarriersinterfaces.com
978-741-1805 • Fax 978-744-1588

NOBLE ASSOCIATES
2155 W Chesterfield Blvd
Springfield, MO 65807-8650
417-831-3663 • Fax 417-831-8282

NOBLE ASSOCIATES
515 N State St
Chicago, IL 60610-4325
312-644-4600 • Fax 312-644-0493

NODINE'S SMOKEHOUSE
PO Box 1787
Torrington, CT 06790-1787
860-489-3213 • Fax 860-496-9787

NOLET SPIRITS
30 Journey
Aliso Viejo, CA 92656-3317
800-243-3618

NOLU PLASTICS, INC.
PO Box 2120
Aston, PA 19014-0120
www.nolu.com
610-358-1770 • Fax 610-358-9480

NOMADIX
31355 Agoura Rd
Westlake Village, CA 91361-4610
e-mail: jreihm@nomadix.com
818-575-2453 • Fax 818-597-1502

NORBEST INC.
PO Box 1000
Midvale, UT 84047-1000
www.norbest.com
801-566-5656 • Fax 801-255-2307

NORDIC GROUP INC
286 Congress St
Boston, MA 02210-1038
800-486-4002 • Fax 617-423-2057

NORDIC GROUP INC
1 Fish Pier
Boston, MA 02210-2054
617-423-5770

NOREX ENTERPRISES, INC.
PO Box 281
Blauvelt, NY 10913-0281
845-353-2121

NOR-LAKE, INC.
727 2nd St
Hudson, WI 54016-1515
www.norlake.com
800-955-5253 • Fax 715-386-6149

NORMA ORIGINALS
6033 N Sheridan Rd Apt 21G
Chicago, IL 60660-3040
773-275-1442 • Fax 773-275-0894

NORPAC
4350 Galewood St
Lake Oswego, OR 97035-2499
800-547-6716

NORRIS LINEN SERVICE
2255 S 170th St
New Berlin, WI 53151-2293
262-786-7660 • Fax 262-786-7503

NORSUN FOOD GROUP
PO Box 1760
West Chester, OH 45071-1760
513-777-0964

NORTH AMERICAN ENTERPRISES
4330 N Campbell Ave Ste 256
Tucson, AZ 85718-5467
520-885-0110 • Fax 520-298-9733

NORTH AMERICAN ENTERPRISES
5050 Pear Ridge Dr
Dallas, TX 75287-3147
972-732-0898 • Fax 972-3841-0221

NORTH AMERICA PROVISIONER
PO Box 672
New Rockford, ND 58356-0672
800-630-7363

NORTH AMERICAN PROVISIONER
PO Box 498
Martinsburg, WV 25402-0498
www.buffalo-nickel.com
304-264-4864 • Fax 304-264-4084

NORTH AMERICAN PROVISIONER, INC
1658 Highway 281
New Rockford, ND 58356-8765
www.buffalo-nickel.com
701-947-2505 • Fax 701-947-2105

NORTH AMERICAN PROVISIONER
PO Box 1077
Hillsboro, OR 97123-1077
www.buffalo-nickel.com
503-640-4589 • Fax 503-648-2326

NORTH AMERICAN PROVISIONER
13724 Industrial Rd Ste 10
Omaha, NE 68137-1151
e-mail: naprovisioner@alltell.net
www.buffalo-nickel.com
402-392-2756 • Fax 402-392-2899

NORTH CAROLINA DEPART-MENT OF AGRICULTURE
PO Box 2066
Elizabeth City, NC 27906-2066
252-331-4773

NORTH COUNTRY BUSINESS PRODUCT
3557 E Washington Ave
Madison, WI 53704-4154
608-241-1800 • Fax 608-241-2203

NORTH DAKOTA MILL
PO Box 13078
Grand Forks, ND 58208-3078
800-538-7721

NORTH STAR ICE EQUIPMENT
PO Box 80227
Seattle, WA 98108-0227
206-763-7300

NORTH STAR RENTAL SYSTEMS
37 Fremont St
Somerville, MA 02145-1416
617-623-1200 • Fax 617-623-5625

NORTHEAST FOODERVICE & LODGING
383 Main Ave
Norwalk, CT 06851-1543
800-840-5612

NORTHEAST PIZZA SHOW
PO Box 1403
New Albany, IN 47151-1403
800-746-1122

NORTHEAST REGION SOYBEAN BOARD
118 Kings Hwy
Swedesboro, NJ 08085-5040
856-467-5189 • Fax 856-467-2293

NORTHEAST TEXTILES, INC
759 E Lincoln Ave
Rahway, NJ 07065-5713
e-mail: jsteffens@netextile.com
732-815-9795 • Fax 732-815-1918

NORTHERN ILLINOIS GAS
PO Box 190
Aurora, IL 60507-0190
630-983-8676 • Fax 630-983-9183

NORTHERN STAR CO
3171 5th St SE
Minneapolis, MN 55414-3374
612-339-8981 • Fax 612-331-3434

NORTHERN WISCONSIN
PO Box 126
Manitowoc, WI 54221-0126
920-684-4461 • Fax 920-684-4471

NORTHLAND CRANBERRIES, INC.
PO Box 8020
Wisconsin Rapids, WI 54495-8020
www.northlandcran.com
715-424-4444 • Fax 715-422-6903

NORTHWEST CARPETS INC
3358 Carpet Capital Dr SW
Dalton, GA 30720-4900
706-259-9486

NORTHWEST CARPETS INC.
PO Box 1844
Dalton, GA 30722-1844
e-mail: nwestcpts@hotmail.com
www.nwcarpets.com
800-367-2508 • Fax 706-259-9014

NORTHWEST CASCADE
PO Box 73399
Puyallup, WA 98373-0399
253-848-2371

NORTHWEST ENTERPRISES
900 Lunt Ave
Elk Grove Village, IL 60007-5020
847-806-0034 • Fax 847-806-0577

NORTHWEST INTERNATIONAL CORP.
2105 McKinney St
Houston, TX 77003-3530
713-224-8287 • Fax 713-224-6488

NORTHWEST PACKING COMPANY
PO Box 30
Vancouver, WA 98666-0030
360-696-4356 • Fax 360-693-3411

NORTHWEST RESTURANT SUPPLY, INC
6955 W 43rd St
Houston, TX 77092-4447
www.nwrsi.com
713-690-8815 • Fax 713-690-8876

NORTHWESTERN CASH REGIS-TER, INC
463B N Washburn St
Oshkosh, WI 54904-7812
920-233-5023 • Fax 920-233-4244

NORTHWESTERN MICHIGAN COLLEGE
1701 E Front St
Traverse City, MI 49686-3061
231-922-1195 • Fax 231-922-1134

NORTHWOOD UNIVERSITY
3225 Cook Rd
Midland, MI 48640-2311
989-837-4257 • Fax 989-837-4331

NORWALK COMMUNITY COLLEGE
188 Richards Ave
Norwalk, CT 06854-1655
e-mail: nk_connolly@commnet.edu
203-857-7355 • Fax 203-857-3327

NORWEGIAN SEA. EXP COUN-CIL INC
2300 Clarendon Blvd Ste 1010
Arlington, VA 22201-3382
703-527-4414

NOVA CORP.
Concourse Pkwy NE Ste 1745
Atlanta, GA 30328-5379
770-522-1787 • Fax 770-522-1615

NOVA INFORMATION SYSTEMS, INC.
5 Concourse Pkwy NE Ste 700
Atlanta, GA 30328-6154
800-725-1243

NOVAMEX
8365 Gregory Way
Beverly Hills, CA 90211-3418
www.novamex.com
323-951-0964 • Fax 323-951-0345

NOVARTIS NUTRITION CORP
5320 W 23rd St
Minneapolis, MN 55416-1657
612-593-2163

NOVATEL WIRELESS, INC.
9360 Towne Center Dr Ste 110
San Diego, CA 92121-3030
www.novatelwireless.com
858-320-8800 • Fax 858-812-2000

NOVELTY CRYSTAL CORP
7955 Albion Ave
Elmhurst, NY 11373-3724
e-mail: novcryscrp@aol.com
718-458-6700 • Fax 718-458-9408

NOVELTY CRYSTAL CORP
21005 Obrien Rd
Groveland, FL 34736-9590
352-429-9036 • Fax 352-429-9039

NOVON COMPANY, INC.
PO Box 1690
Pleasanton, CA 94566-0168
925-417-0617

NPD FOODSERVICE INFORMATION
9399 W Higgins Rd Ste
Des Plaines, IL 60018-6900
847-692-6700 • Fax 847-692-2812

NSF INTERNATIONAL
789 N Dixboro Rd
Ann Arbor, MI 48105-9723
www.nsf.org
800-NSF-MARK • Fax 734-769-0109

NSTC
1916 Doolittle Dr
San Leandro, CA 94577-3235
e-mail: nstc@aol.com
510-483-7394 • Fax 510-483-5080

NTN COMMUNICATIONS, INC.
5966 La Place Ct Ste 100
Carlsbad, CA 92008-8830
www.ntn.com
760-438-7400 • Fax 760-438-3505

NUCO2 INC.
2800 SE Market Pl
Stuart, FL 34997-4965
www.nuco2.com
772-781-3500 • Fax 772-781-3527

NUESKE HILLCREST FARM MEATS
RR 2 Box D
Wittenberg, WI 54499-9802
www.nueske.com
715-253-2226 • Fax 715-253-2021

NUGGET DISTRIBUTORS COOPERATIVE
4226 Coronado Ave
Stockton, CA 95204-2328
209-948-8122 • Fax 209-546-7406

NULAID FOODS
200 W 5th St
Ripon, CA 95366-2793
209-599-2121 • Fax 209-599-5220

NULCO LIGHTING
30 Beecher St
Pawtucket, RI 02860-1805
401-728-5200 • Fax 401-728-8210

NU-INTERNATIONAL RESTAURANT SUPPLY
11609 Myrtle Ave
Richmond Hill, NY 11418-1749
e-mail: chris@nu-international.com
www.nu-international.com
718-849-1829 • Fax 718-849-1863

NUOVA SIMONELLI
6940 Salashan Pkwy
Ferndale, WA 98248-8314
www.nuovasimonelli.it
360-366-2226 • Fax 360-366-4015

NUOVO PASTA PRODUCTIONS, LTD.
35 Brentwood Ave
Fairfield, CT 06432-5451
e-mail: nuovopasta@epos.com
203-331-0033 • Fax 203-336-0656

NUTERIORS
12 Tulip Ave
Floral Park, NY 11001-1901
e-mail: nuteriors12@cs.com
www.nuteriors.com
516-616-1000 • Fax 718-661-6116

NUTRASWEET COMPANY
1751 Lake Cook Rd
Deerfield, IL 60015-5615
847-940-9800

NUTRIFASTER, INC
209 S Bennett St
Seattle, WA 98108-2226
www.nutrifaster.com
206-767-5054 • Fax 206-762-2209

NU-VU FOOD SERVICE SYSTEMS
PO Box 35
Menominee, MI 49858-0035
www.nu-vu.com
800-338-9886 • Fax 906-863-5889

NY WINE & GRAPe FOUNDATION
350 Elm St
Penn Yan, NY 14527-1499
e-mail: uncork@nywine.com
www.uncorknewyork.com
315-536-7442 • Fax 315-536-0719

NYCK. INC
344 W 38th St
New York, NY 10018-2995
e-mail: knyny@aol.com
212-967-9117 • Fax 212-967-9009

NYS INSTITUTE FOR ENTREPRENEURS
41 State St Ste M110
Albany, NY 12207-2831
518-443-5614 • Fax 518-443-5610

O B I CLUB SOFTWARE
PO Box 9194
Bend, OR 97708-9194
800-982-9151

O K FOODS INC
PO Box 1787
Fort Smith, AR 72902-1787
479-783-0244 • Fax 479-784-1100

O K INTERNATIONAL CORP
73 Bartlett St
Marblorough, MA 01752-3071
508-303-8286

O O C L (USA) INC.
PO Box 8175
Pleasanton, CA 94588-8775
925-460-4800

OAK FARMS DAIRY
PO Box 1270
Houston, TX 77251-1270
e-mail: ofsale@apl.com
www.oakfarmsdairy.com
713-547-7185 • Fax 713-223-1384

OAKBLUFF VENTURES
8036 Aviation Pl Ste 11
Dallas, TX 75235-2824
214-357-8400

OAKES CORP. E.T.
686 Old Willets Path
Hauppauge, NY 11788-4102
631-232-0002

OAKHURST DAIRY
364 Forest Ave
Portland, ME 04101-2092
207-772-7468 • Fax 207-874-0714

OAKLEAF WASTE MANAGEMENT
19 Thomas St
East Hartford, CT 06108-2043
888-625-5323

OASIS OUTSOURCING INC
800 Corporate Dr Ste 602
Fort Lauderdale, FL 33334-3621
e-mail:
dtyson@wackenhutresources.com
www.oasisoutsourcing.com
954-772-0525

OCEAN BEAUTY INTL INC
1100 W Ewing St
Seattle, WA 98119-1321
206-285-6800

OCEAN FRESH SEAFOOD, INC.
473 E Washington St
North Attleboro, MA 02760-2310
e-mail: wholesale@oceanfresh.com
www.oceanfresh.com
508-695-7087 • Fax 508-699-6970

OCEAN GARDEN PRODUCTS
PO Box 85527
San Diego, CA 92186-5527
619-571-5002

OCEAN SPRAY
1 Ocean Spray Dr
Middleboro, MA 02349-0001

OCEAN TO OCEAN SEAFOOD
PO Box 8067
Virginia Beach, VA 23450-8067
757-496-6600

OCEANLINK USA
6310 Queens Blvd
Woodside, NY 11377-5760
718-651-1800 • Fax 718-651-0007

O-CEDAR BRANDS, INC.
PO Box 1606
Springfield, OH 45501-1606
www.ocedar.com
937-324-5596 • Fax 937-328-6313

O'CONNELL-MARTINO
254 Franklin St
Buffalo, NY 14202-1902
716-842-2244

ODD BALLS
1004 S Main St
Pine Bluff, AR 71601-4910
870-541-0173 • Fax 870-535-4313

ODIN FOODS, INC.
1900 S Puget Dr Ste 202
Renton, WA 98055-4418
425-228-0632

OEM AMERICA
13615 S Dixie Hwy
Miami, FL 33176-7254
e-mail: mazi@oemamerica.net
305-869-9991 • Fax 305-869-9323

OFFICIAL AIRLINE GUIDE
2000 Clearwater Dr
Oak Brook, IL 60523-1955
630-574-6735

OKI DATA
3 Joseph Cir
Franklin, MA 02038-2670
508-533-4073 • Fax 508-533-4291

OKIDATA GROUP
532 Fellowship Rd
Mount Laurel, NJ 08054-3405
856-235-2600

OKLAHOMA DEPT OF AGRICULTURE
PO Box 528804
Oklahoma City, OK 73152-8804
405-522-5560 • Fax 405-522-4855

OKLAHOMA RESTAURANT ASSOC
3800 N Portland Ave
Oklahoma City, OK 73112-2948
405-942-8181

OKLAHOMA STATE UNIVERSITY - HR
210 HES
Stillwater, OK 74078-6120
www.osuhrad.com
405-744-6713 • Fax 405-744-6299

OLD CHATHAM SHEEPHERDING COMPANY
155 Shaker Museum Rd
Old Chatham, NY 12136-2603
e-mail:
wische@blacksheepcheese.com
518-794-7733 • Fax 518-794-7641

OLD COUNTRY BAKERY
456 W Maude Ave
Sunnyvale, CA 94085-3516
408-522-9952 • Fax 408-732-0391

OLD DOMINION BOX CO.
PO Box 680
Lynchburg, VA 24505-0680
www.olddominionbox.com
804-782-1105 • Fax 804-782-1188

OLD EUROPE CHEESE INC - RENYPICO
1330 E Empire Ave
Benton Harbor, MI 49022-2018
616-925-5003 • Fax 616-925-9560

OLD FASHIONED KITCHEN
1045 Towbin Ave
Lakewood, NJ 08701-5931
732-364-4100 • Fax 732-905-7352

OLD HICKORY FURNITURE CO.
403 S Noble St
Shelbyville, IN 46176-2166
e-mail: mail@oldhickory.com
www.oldhickory.com
800-232-2275 • Fax 317-398-2275

OLD WORLD SPICES & SEASONINGS
4601 Van Brunt Blvd
Kansas City, MO 64130-2366
816-861-0400

OLDCASTLE PRECAST MODULAR GROUP
PO Box 210
Telford, PA 18969-0210
e-mail: info@oldcastleprecast.com
www.oldcastleprecast.com
215-257-8081 • Fax 215-453-5813

OLDE COUNTRY REPRODUCTIONS
PO Box 2617
York, PA 17405-2617
www.users.aol.com-pewtarex-
717-848-1859 • Fax 717-845-7129

OLDE WESTPORT SPICE
PO Box 12525
Overland Park, KS 66282-2525
913-541-0179

OLE HICKORY PITS
333 N Main St
Cape Girardeau, MO 63701-7205
www.olehickorypits.com
573-3347-3377 • Fax 573-334-6512

OLE HICKORY PITS
630 Hawthorne N
Brandon, MS 39047-8676
601-664-0808

OLE MEXICAN FOODS, INC
6585 Crescent Dr
Norcross, GA 30071-2901
e-mail: omfatl@msn.com
www.olemexicanfoods.com
770-582-9200

OLIVEO LLC
1717 Rice St
Rosenberg, TX 77471-5858
281-633-9335 • Fax 281-232-9169

OLIVIA GARDEN INTL.
1021 Shary Ct # A
Concord, CA 94518-2409
e-mail: prennette@oliviagarden.com
www.formiausa.com
925-686-9916 • Fax 925-686-9919

OLSON COMMUNICATIONS
445 W Erie St Ste 109
Chicago, IL 60610-6924
312-280-4573 • Fax 312-280-9203

OLYMPIC TENT
9150 SW Pioneer Ct
Wilsonville, OR 97070-9621
800-621-2495

OLYMPUS
9000 W Heather Ave
Milwaukee, WI 53224-2410
www.olympus-flag.com
414-355-2010 • Fax 414-355-1931

OMAHA STEAKS
11030 O ST
Omaha, NE 68137-2346
800-228-9521

OMEGA FOODS
PO Box 21256
Eugene, OR 97402-0402
541-349-0731 • Fax 541-349-0435

OMEGA PATTERN WORKS
PO Box 875
Calhoun, GA 30703-0875
800-241-4908

OMEGA PRODUCTS INC.
6291 Lyters Ln
Harrisburg, PA 17111-4622
717-561-1105 • Fax 717-561-1298

OMNI GLOW CORP
96 Windsor St
West Springfield, MA 01089-3528
800-762-7548

OMRON SYSTEMS, INC.
55 Commerce Dr
Schaumburg, IL 60173-5302
847-843-0515

ON COMMAND CORP
6331 San Ignacio Ave
San Jose, CA 95119-1202
800-842-2961

ONE PATH NETWORKS
600 College Rd E Ste 3
Princeton, NJ 08540-6636
e-mail: mhorwitz@onepathnet.com
www.onepathnet.com
609-514-1800 • Fax 609-514-1881

ONE SYSTEM
1187 Coast Village Rd
Santa Barbara, CA 93108-2737
805-965-7007

ONOX INC
43132 Christy St
Fremont, CA 94538-3168
510-226-1400

ON-SITE LANGUAGE
9 Vernon Pl
Mount Vernon, NY 10552-2325
914-668-2252

ONTHERAIL.COM
1011 23rd St
San Francisco, CA 94107-3472
415-285-4917

OPENAIRE INC
PO Box 376
Cedarburg, WI 53012-0376
800-267-4877

OPENPOINT SYSTEMS
4030 W Vickery Blvd
Fort Worth, TX 76107-6433
e-mail:
traceyekkensmith@hotmail.com
817-732-2896 • Fax 817-731-0939

OPENTABLE.COM
2111 Mission St Ste 402
San Francisco, CA 94110-1276
www.opentable.com
415-551-1510 • Fax 415-551-1441

ORANFRESH U.S. WEST
PO Box 21845
Los Angeles, CA 90021-0845
e-mail: oranfresh@hotmail.com
213-312-1380 • Fax 213-312-1384

**ORCHID ISLAND JUICE
COMPANY**
330 N US Highway 1
Fort Pierce, FL 34950-4207
e-mail: jijc@gate.net
www.oijc.com
772-465-1122 • Fax 772-465-4303

**ORDER-MATIC
CORPORATION**
320 Bryant Pl
Oklahoma City, OK 73115-1004
www.ordermatic.com
800-767-6733 • Fax 405-672-5349

ORDERTAKEOUT.COM
PO Box 82618
Baton Rouge, LA 70884-2618
e-mail: mail@ordertakeout.com
www.ordertakeout.com
888-WEB-MEAL • Fax 225-346-0805

ORE CAL
634 Crocker St
Los Angeles, CA 90021-1085
213-680-9540

ORECK COMMERCIAL SALES
100 Corporate Park Dr
Pembroke, MA 02359-1910
781-826-1112 • Fax 781-826-1584

OREGON CHAI
1745 NW Marshall St
Portland, OR 97209-2420
www.oregonchai.com-wholesale
503-221-2424 • Fax 503-796-0980

OREGON CHAI TEA
725 SE 9th Ave Ste T
Portland, OR 97214-2208
888-874-2424

**OREGON DUNGENESS CRAB.
COM**
PO Box 1160
Coos Bay, OR 97420-0301
541-267-5810

ORGANIC VALLEY
507 W Main St
La Farge, WI 54639-8601
608-625-2602

ORGANICLEAN
270N N Canon Dr
Beverly Hills, CA 90210-5302

ORIENTAL ACCENT INC.
13405 N Stemmons Fwy
Dallas, TX 75234-5767
972-488-4663 • Fax 972-488-4664

ORIENTAL TRADING CO
426 S 108th Ave
Omaha, NE 68154-2626
800-228-0096

ORIENTAL TRADING COMPANY
PO Box 2319
Omaha, NE 68103-2319
402-596-1200

ORIGINAL BAGEL CO
2 Fairfield Cres
Caldwell, NJ 07006-6205
973-227-5777

**ORIGINAL BEVERAGE
CORPORATION**
13000 S Spring St
Los Angeles, CA 90061-1634
www.reedsgingerbrew.com
323-589-5590 • Fax 323-589-5006

ORIGINAL CRISPY PIZZA CO.
PO Box 304
Lincoln, RI 02865-0304
401-333-9558 • Fax 401-333-4785

**ORIGINAL JACK'S BAKING
COMPANY**
3465 San Gabriel River Pkwy
Pico Rivera, CA 90660-1450
888-252-8274 • Fax 562-699-5899

ORIGINALS IN WOOD
423 S 8th St
La Porte, TX 77571-4947
e-mail: alain@originalsinwood.com
www.milworkoriginals.com
281-470-8666 • Fax 281-470-8694

ORION FOOD SYSTEMS
PO Box 780
Sioux Falls, SD 57101-0780
e-mail:
james.perry@orionfoodsys.com
www.orionfoodsys.com
605-336-6961 • Fax 605-336-0141

ORKIN EXT. CO
6208 Grandview St
Mission, KS 66202-2836
913-831-0633

ORKIN PEST CONTROL
2170 Piedmont Rd NE
Atlanta, GA 30324-4135
www.orkin.com
404-888-2000 • Fax 404-888-2012

ORLANDI STATUARY
1801 N Central Park Ave
Chicago, IL 60647-4703
www.statue.com
773-489-0303 • Fax 773-489-2159

ORLANDO BAKERY
7777 Grand Ave
Cleveland, OH 44104-3099
e-mail:
norlando@orlandobaking.com
800-345-5504 • Fax 216-391-3469

ORVAL KENT FOOD CO
120 W Palatine Rd
Wheeling, IL 60090-5880
847-459-9000 • Fax 847-459-6284

ORWAK USA INC.
10820 Normandale Blvd
Minneapolis, MN 55437-3112
www.orwak.com
800-747-0449 • Fax 952-881-8578

OSCEOLA FOODS INC
PO Box 368
Osceola, AR 72370-0368
870-563-2601 • Fax 870-563-2223

OSCODA PLASTICS, INC.
PO Box 189
Oscoda, MI 48750-0189
www.oscodaplastics.com
800-544-9538 • Fax 800-548-7678

OSEM USA, INC.
333 Sylvan Ave
Englewood Cliffs, NJ 07632-2724
210-871-4433 • Fax 201-871-8726

OSHA
9100 Bluebonnet Blvd
Baton Rouge, LA 70810-2809
225-389-0474 • Fax 225-389-0463

OSHIKIRI CORP OF AMERICA
10425 Drummond Rd

Philadelphia, PA 19154-3898
215-637-6005

OSTERBY & WILLIAMSON
5 Janet Ct
Miller Place, NY 11764-2613
e-mail: osterwill@aol.com
www.williamsongroup.net
631-821-0678 • Fax 631-821-0658

OSWALT MENU COMPANY
PO Box 447
Hartford City, IN 47348-0447
www.mugjoint.com-oswalt
800-822-6368 • Fax 765-348-3137

OTAFUKU USA., INC.
377 Van Ness Ave Ste 120
Torrance, CA 90501-1461
www.otafuku.co.jp
310-787-8000 • Fax 310-787-0900

O'TASTY FOODS, INC.
9587 W Olympic Blvd
Beverly Hills, CA 90212-4243
310-553-7005

OTIS SPUNKMEYER
9009 Pinehill Ln Ste 204
Houston, TX 77041-9339
e-mail:
bgetschman@spunkmeyer.com
www.spunkmeyer.com
800-683-8474 • Fax 713 095-0358

OTIS SPUNKMEYER COOKIES
527 Springfield Rd # R
Kenilworth, NJ 07033-1020
908-563-2727 • Fax 908-563-9086

OTIS SPUNKMEYER INC.
14490 Catalina St
San Leandro, CA 94577-5516
www.spunkmeyer.com
800-938-1900 • Fax 510-352-5680

OTTENBERG BAKERY
655 Taylor St NE
Washington, DC 20017-2098
800-334-7264

OTTER CREEK BREWING
793 Exchange St
Middlebury, VT 05753-1193
e-mail: ottcreek@souer.ent
www.ottercreekbrewing.com
802-388-0727 • Fax 802-388-1654

OUTBOUND SERVICES INC
23521 Paseo De Valencia
Laguna Hills, CA 92653-3107
949-597-3100

OUTDOOR LIVING DESIGNS
PO Box 1618
Pawtucket, RI 02862-1618
e-mail: outdoorliv@aol.com
www.outdoorfurniture.qpg.com
401-726-2201 • Fax 401-725-3277

OVEN ARTS, INC.
455 W 16th St
New York, NY 10011-5892
www.ovenart.com
212-627-1111 • Fax 212-627-9822

OVEN POPPERS
405 Spruce St
Manchester, NH 03103-4223
800-451-7259

OVEN READY FOODS
22000 Industrial Blvd
Rogers, MN 55374-2108
612-708-2299 • Fax 612-708-2299

OVERHILL FARMS INC
5730 Uplander Way Ste 201
Culver City, CA 90230-6631
310-641-3680 • Fax 310-645-3914

OWENS
PO Box 830249
Richardson, TX 75083-0249
972-235-7118

**OWENS INFORMATION
SERVICES INC**
277 E High St
Lexington, KY 40507-1421
800-477-6858 • Fax 859-225-8742

OZARK SALAD CO.
PO Box 30
Baxter Springs, KS 66713-0030
800-231-7013 • Fax 620-856-5697

P & K PRODUCTS COMPANY
2000 Fox Ln
Elgin, IL 60123-7814
www.pkproducts.com
800-624-5353 • Fax 847-695-3494

P & L SYSTEMS, LLC
1050 Triad Ct
Marietta, GA 30062-2259
678-464-0991

**P C S REVENUE CONTROL
SYSTEMS**
560 Sylvan Ave
Englewood Cliffs, NJ 07632-3119
800-247-3061

P D Q RESTAURANT SYSTEMS
1265 W 86th St
Indianapolis, IN 46260-2281
317-255-1006

P I C S RETAIL NETWORK
PO Box 26312
San Francisco, CA 94126-6312

P M A A
1901 Fort Myer Dr
Arlington, VA 22209-1604

P S G CONTROLS, INC
1225 Tunnel Rd
Perkasie, PA 18944-2131
215-257-3621

P T'S COFFEE COMPANY
5660 SW 29th St Ste B
Topeka, KS 66614-2443
785-862-5282

**P & H COMPANY, INC.
FLEX-A-LITE**
1440 N Federal Hwy
Delray Beach, FL 33483-5922
www.flexaliteinc.com
561-330-8660 • Fax 561-330-8665

P.A. MENARD, INC
PO Box 50158
New Orleans, LA 70150-0158
504-523-6882

P.E.M. SAFETY FLOORING
12890 Haster St
Garden Grove, CA 92840-6515
888-588-4846 • Fax 949-455-9284

P. KAUFMANN
153 E 53rd St
New York, NY 10022-4611
212-292-2200 • Fax 212-292-2285

P. PASCAL COFFEE ROASTERS
960 Nepperhan Ave
Yonkers, NY 10703-1726
e-mail: pascalcoffee.com
www.pascalcoffee.com
914-9639-7933 • Fax 914-969-8248

PAASCHE AIRBRUSH CO
7440 W Lawrence Ave
Harwood Heights, IL 60706-3412
800-621-1907

PACA FOODS INC
5212 Cone Rd
Tampa, FL 33610-5302
813-628-8228 • Fax 813-628-8426

PACE FOODS
PO Box 12636
San Antonio, TX 78212-0636
210-224-2211

PACIFIC BEVERAGE
6216 Seabrook Rd # D
Lanham, MD 20706-4037
www.pacificchai.com
888-882-4248 • Fax 301-429-9442

**PACIFIC COAST CONTRACT
LIGHTING**
20238 Plummer St
Chatsworth, CA 91311-5449
e-mail: comfort@pcf.com
www.pacificcoast.com
800-903-7225 • Fax 818-772-1656

PACIFIC COAST PRODUCERS
PO Box 1600
Lodi, CA 95241-1600
209-367-8800 • Fax 209-339-8816

PACIFIC CORAL SEAFOOD
2240 NE 2nd Ave
Miami FL 33137-4806
800-827-9707

PACIFIC DIRECT
92 Gray Rd
Ithaca, NY 14850-8762
607-273-1984

PACIFIC GRAIN PRODUCTS
351 Hanson Way
Woddland, CA 95776-6224
800-747-0161

PACIFIC INTERTRADE CO.
1640 E Edinger Ave Ste G
Santa Ana, CA 92705-5023
714-571-0588 • Fax 714-571-0685

PACIFIC NORTHWEST CANNED PEAR
105 S 18Th St
Yakima, WA 98901-2175
509-453-4880 • Fax 509-453-4837

PACIFIC STEAMEX, INC.
2259 S Sheridan Dr
Muskegon, MI 49442-6252
www.pacificsteamex.com
231-773-1330 • Fax 231-773-1642

PACIFIC SUN
340 E Menlo Ave
Hemet, CA 92543-1424
www.pacsunfurniture.com
800-624-4385

PACIFIC WEST INTERNATIONAL
3868 W Carson St Ste 214
Torrance, CA 90503-6714
310-515-3800

PACIFIC WEST MARKETING
20 Anacapri
Laguna Niguel, CA 92677-8629
www.pacificwestmarketing.com
949-363-9129 • Fax 949-363-8429

PACIFICORP
201 South Main # 2200
Salt Lake City, UT 84140-0001
801-220-2959

PACKAGING PROGRESSIONS
102 G P Clement Dr
Collegeville, PA 19426-2044
610-489-8601

PACKAGING SPECIALTIES
3 Opportunity Way
Newburyport, MA 01950-4044
www.pack-spec.com
978-462-1300 • Fax 978-462-5596

PACKARD PAPER
124 Turnpike St
West Bridgewater, MA 02379-1046
e-mail: sales@packardpaper.com
www.packardpaper.com
800-289-9696

PACKAGE MATERIALS
8 Tanner St
Haddonfield, NJ 08033-2404
e-mail: gordonpmc@aol.caom
856-428-7190 • Fax 856-429-2737

PACS INSTERNATIONAL
1305 W Belt Line Rd Ste 3
Carrollton, TX 75006-6925
e-mail: pacs@diw.net
www.pacsinternational.com
972-242-9191 • Fax 972-245-3085

PAELLADOR USA, INC.
445 Park Ave Fl
New York, NY 10022-2606
e-mail: paellador@aol.com
212-755-8845 • Fax 212-755-8863

PAETEC COMMUNICATIONS
460 Totten Pond Rd
Waltham, MA 02451-1991
marlene.marshalleck@paetec.com

www.paetec.com
781-419-7237 • Fax 781-895-9869

PAIN D'AVIGNON
192 Airport Rd
Hyannis, MA 02601-1804
508-771-9771 • Fax 508-778-6778

PAINTED PIECES, LTD.
2 Cooper Ave
Huntington Station, NY 11746-3506
631-385-7200 • Fax 516-351-0207

PAK-MAN PACKAGING & SUPPLY CO.
3939 Hillcroft St Ste 180
Houston, TX 77057-7741
e-mail: sales@pak-man.com
www.pak-man.com
713-977-6811 • Fax 713-977-0292

PAK-SHER
2500 N Longview St
Kilgore, TX 75662-6840
www.paksher.com
903-984-8596 • Fax 903-984-1524

PALATINIT OF AMERICA INC
101 Gibraltar Dr
Morris Plains, NJ 07950-1287
973-539-6644

PALM BAY IMPORTS INC
100 SE 5th Ave
Boca Raton, FL 33432-5071
561-362-9642

PALM MANAGEMENT CORP.
1730 Rhode Island Ave NW Ste 9
Washington, DC 20036-3101
202-775-7256

PALMBAY LIMITED
3739 58th St
Woodside, NY 11377-2408
e-mail: info@palmbayltd.com
www.palmbayltd.com
800-556-6089 • Fax 718-396-4488

PALMER & PALMER
1060 W 106th St
Carmel, IN 46032-9603
317-843-1613

PALMER SNYDER
400 N Executive Dr Ste 200
Brookfield, WI 53005-6029
262-780-8780

PAN READY FOODS, INC.
150 Airport Blvd
South San Francisco, CA 94080-4739
www.panreadyfoods.com
650-583-7920 • Fax 650-583-9416

PANASONIC
1 Panasonic Way # 4A-4
Secaucus, NJ 07094-2999
201-392-5304 • Fax 201-392-6779

PANASONIC COMM & SYSTEMS CO
1707 N Randall Rd
Elgin, IL 60123-7820
847-468-4600

PANAZ USA INC.
220 Park Ave Ste 1
Laguna Beach, CA 92651-2101
949-376-3361 • Fax 949-376-3461

PANFISH SALES INC
201 Queen Anne Ave N
Seattle, WA 98109-4835
206-674-9584

PAPER PLUS, INC
600 Federal Blvd
Carteret, NJ 07008-1007
732-750-1900 • Fax 732-750-2824

PAPERCON CORPORATION
2700 Apple Valley Rd NE
Atlanta, GA 30319-3139
800-241-0619 • Fax 404-237-6778

PAPETTI'S EGG PRODUCTS
1 Papetti Plz
Elizabeth, NJ 07206-1421
800-447-3447

PAP-R PRODUCTS CO., INC.
PO Box N
Martinsville, IL 62442-0169
800-547-3708

PAP'S LOUISINAN CUISINE, INC.
16322 Highway 929
Prairieville, LA 70769-5328
225-622-3262 • Fax 225-622-3588

PAR T GOLF MARKETING CO
7310 Smoke Ranch Rd
Las Vegas, NV 89128-0258
702-243-6811

PARACLIPSE
2271 E 29th Ave
Columbus, NE 68601-3166
402-563-3625

PARADIGM ENTERPRISES
11583 Maple Ridge Rd
Reston, VA 20190-3605
703-471-1714 • Fax 703-471-2285

PARADISE TOMATO KITCHEN INC
1500 S Brook St
Louisville, KY 40208-1950
502-637-1700

PARAMOUNT CAPITAL CORPORATION
19325 Aqua Springs Dr
Lutz, FL 33558-9709
813-265-1070

PARAMOUNT FARMS
11444 W Olympic Blvd
Los Angeles, CA 90064-1549
310-393-5121

PARAMOUNT RESTAURANT SUP. CORP
333 Harborside Blvd
Providence, RI 02905-5202
401-461-3000

PARAMOUNT RESTAURANT SUPPLY
PO Box 388
Warren, RI 02885-0388
401-432-0500 • Fax 401-432-0545

PARCO FOODS INC
2200 138th St
Blue Island, IL 60406-3209
708-371-9200 • Fax 708-371-5301

PARDEE FREEMAN, INC.
221 Washington St
Gloucester, MA 01930-2642
e-mail: pfreps@aol.com
978-281-2700 • Fax 978-281-2987

PARIS GOURMET PATISFRANCE
145 Grand St
Carlstadt, NJ 07072-2106
800-727-8791

PARISI-ROYAL STORE FIXTURES
3031 Red Lion Rd
Philadelphia, PA 19114-1123
215-632-4495 • Fax 215-632-1660

PARK CHEESE CO. INC
PO Box 1499
Fond du Lac, WI 54936-1499
920-923-8484 • Fax920-923-8485

PARK FOODS L P
511 Lake Zurich Rd
Barrington, IL 60010-3178
847-381-8550 • Fax 847-381-8599

PARKSITE INC
1563 Hubbard Ave
Batavia, IL 60510-4405
630-774-8539 • Fax 630-761-6820

PARRISH'S CAKE DECOR SUPLY
225 W 146th St
Gardena, CA 90248-1803
310-324-2253

PARROT-ICE-N.E.
42 Mid Tech Dr
West Yarmouth, MA 02673-2560
508-771-3764 • Fax 508-775-6044

PARTI LINE
362 Memorial Dr
Cambridge, MA 02139-4304
617-225-7214

PARTNERS & SIRNY ARCHITECTS
100 Union Plz
Minneapolis, MN 55401-8888
612-341-1070 • Fax 612-341-2124

PARTS COMPANY OF AMERICA
1657 Shermer Rd
Northbrook, IL 60062-5362
847-498-5900 • Fax 847-498-3402

PARTY CLOTHS
2426 Linden Ln
Silver Spring, MD 20910-1201
301-608-3600

PARTY PERFECT CATERING SOFT WARE
3030 Dudley St
Houston, TX 77021-2111
www.partyperfect.net
713-522-3932 • Fax 713-522-1746

PARTY YARDS INC
159 Dalton Dr
Oviedo, FL 32765-6252
407-696-9440

PAR-WAY-TRYSON
107 Bolte Ln
Saint Clair, MO 63077-3219
636-629-4545 • Fax 573-324-8277

PASCAGOULA ICE & FREEZER
PO Box 1090
Pascagoula, MS 39568-1090
228-762-2541

PASCO BRANDS
PO Box 97
Dade City, FL 33526-0097
800-874-9061

PASQUINI
1501 W Olympic Blvd
Los Angeles, CA 90015-3803
e-mail: pasquini@pasquini.com
213-739-0480 • Fax 213-385-8774

PASTA FACTORY
11225 W Grand Ave
Melrose Park, IL 60164-1036
www.pastafactoryusa.com
800-615-6951 • Fax 847-451-6563

PASTA MIA
15554 Producer Ln
Huntington Beach, CA 92649-1308
www.pastamiacorp.com
714-903-3211 • Fax 714-903-3221

PATCRAFT COMMERCIAL CARPET
2305 Lakeland Rd SE
Dalton, GA 30721-5018
800-241-4014

PATERNO IMPORTS
900 Armour Dr
Lake Bluff, IL 60044-1926
847-604-8900

PATERNO IMPORTS
2701 S Western Ave
Chicago, IL 60608-5290
312-247-7070

PATIO ENCLOSURES
720 Highland Rd E
Macedonia, OH 44056-2188
www.patioenclosuresinc.com
800-468-0720 • Fax 330-467-4297

PATRICK HENRY PROMOS
11104 W Airport Blvd Ste 155
Stafford, TX 77477-3033
281-983-5500

PATTERSON'S CALIFORNIA BEVERAGE
4910 W San Fernando Rd
Los Angeles, CA 90039-1131
www.beveragelink.com
818-291-1171 • Fax 818-547-4607

PATTY'S PRESTO PIZZA, INC
13381 Beach Ave
Marina Del Rey, CA 90292-5621
www.pattyspizza.com
310-821-6150 • Fax 323-456-8859

PAUL B. ABRAMS
5600 Wisconsin Ave Apt 19A
Chevy Chase, MD 20815-4414
301-652-3313

PAUL RICO STUDIO
1533 Melpomene St
New Orleans, LA 70130-4411
504-529-2966 • Fax 504-529-7600

PAUL W. MARKS CO., INC
PO Box 6300
Chelsea, MA 02150-0011
617-389-4121 • Fax 617-389-1206

PAULANER NORTH AMERICA CORP
8100 S Akron St Ste 313
Englewood, CO 80112-3508
303-792-3242

PAVAILLER INC
232 Pegasus Ave
Northvale, NJ 07647-1904
201-767-0766

PAVILLION-SUNBURST FURNITURE
16200 NW 49th Ave
Hialeah, FL 33014-6315
www.pavillionfurniture.com
305-823-3480 • Fax 305-823-7785

PAVONI ITALIA SPA
Via Enrico Fermi Sn
Roanoke, VA 24040-0001
www.pavonitalia.com

PAXTON CORP
897 Bridgeport Ave
Shelton, CT 06484-4621
203-925-8720

PAY SYSTEMS OF AMERICA
2325 Crestmoor Rd Ste 200
Nashville, TN 37215-2027
615-292-0000

PAY USA, INC.
2001 W Main St Ste 160
Stamford, CT 06902-4547
203-363-5252

PAYBACK TRAINING SYSTEMS
14 Ridgedale Ave
Cedar Knolls, NJ 07927-1106
888-541-3099

PAYBACK TRAINING SYSTEMS
14 Ridgedale Ave Ste 20
Cedar Knolls, NJ 07927-1106
www.paybacktraining.com
973-326-8989 • Fax 973-326-8997

PAYCHEX
911 Panorama Trl S
Rochester, NY 14625-2396
www.paychex.com
800-867-3869

PAYCHEX, INC.
33 Dodge Rd Ste 110
Getzville, NY 14068-1540
800-828-4411 • Fax 585-383-3869

PAYMENTECH
1601 Elm St Ste 700
Dallas, TX 75201-7286
www.paymentech.com
800-824-4313

PAYMENTECH
1000 Johnson Ferry Rd
Marietta, GA 30068-2114
e-mail: dwhite123@hushmail.com
770-321-0908 • Fax 770-321-8784

PAYPHONESDIRECT
503 E Pierce Ave
Fairfield, IA 52556-3857
641-469-5847

PAYPOINT ELECTRONIC PAYMENT SYSTEM
221 S Figueroa St
Los Angeles, CA 90012-2552

www.paypointeps.com
213-486-0707 • Fax 213-486-3840

PAYROLL COMPUTING SERVICES
79 Mill Rd
Freeport, NY 11520-4639

PAYSMART AMERICA-T S I COMM
1500 W Cypress Creek Rd
Ft. Lauderdale, FL 33309-1833
954-928-1850

PEACH STATE ROOFING, INC
1655 Spectrum Dr # A
Lawrenceville, GA 30043-5743
e-mail: jonte@mindspring.com
770-962-7885 • Fax 770-962-7809

PEAK LIGHTING GROUP INC
150 E Meda Ave Ste 230
Glendora, CA 91741-2607
www.peaklighting.com
626-852-0802 • Fax 626-852-0862

PEARL MEAT PACKAGING CO
196 Quincy St
Boston, MA 02121-1919
617-445-6020 • Fax 617-445-4174

PECHTER'S BAKING GROUP
840 Jersey St
Harrison, NJ 07029-2056
973-483-3374 • Fax 973-481-2319

PECINKA-DUMBACH-FERRI ASSOC.
328 Willis Ave # M
Mineola, NY 11501-1513
e-mail: sales@pecinkadumbachferri.com
www.pecinkadumbachferri.com
516-742-2113 • Fax 516-742-2337

PEER FOOD
1400 W 46th St
Chicago, IL 60609-3294
312-927-1440

PEER FOODS INC
4631 S McDowell Ave
Chicago, IL 60609 3211
773-927-1440 • Fax 773-927-9859

PEERLESS COFFEE
260 Oak St
Oakland, CA 94607-4587
www.peerlesscoffee.com
510-763-1763 • Fax 510-763-5026

PEERLESS MACHINERY CORP
500 S Vandemark Rd
Sidney, OH 45365-8986
937-492-4158

PEG-PARK ARCHITECTS
30 Glenn St
White Plains, NY 10603-3254
e-mail: info@pegpark.com
914-949-6505 • Fax 914-949-1694

PEGASUS
1111 Mateo St
Los Angeles, CA 90021-1717
www.astrochef.com
213-627-9860 • Fax 213-627-9870

PEI PREFERRED EUQIPMENT, INC.
10 Jewel Dr
Wilmington, MA 01887-3350
978-657-8640 • Fax 978-657-0280

PELICAN PRODUCTS CO., INC.
1049 Lowell St
Bronx, NY 10459-2608
e-mail: pelicanproducts@prodigy.net
www.pelicanproducts.com
718-860-3220 • Fax 718-860-4415

PELLERIN MILNOR CORPORATION
700 Jackson St
Kenner, LA 70062-7774
www.milnor.com
504-467-9591 • Fax 504-468-3094

PELOUZE SCALE
7400 W 100th Pl

Bridgeview, IL 60455-2438
800-654-8330 • Fax 800-654-7330

PENCOM INTERNATIONAL
1630 Welton St Ste 415
Denver, CO 80202-4239
303-595-3991

PENN REFRIGERATION
PO Box 1261
Wilkes Barre, PA 18703-1261
800-233-8354 • Fax 570-825-5705

PENN STATE TEXTILE
PO Box 140995
Nashville, TN 37214-0995
888-TEAMPST

PENN STATE UNIVERSITY
PO Box 850
Hershey, PA 17033-0850
800-252-3592

PENNANT FOODS
2200 Cabot Dr Ste 100
Lisle, IL 60532-0913
800-877-1157

PENNSYLVANIA CULINARY
717 Liberty Ave
Pittsburgh, PA 15222-3511
www.paculinary.com
800-432-2433 • Fax 412-566-2434

PENNSYLVANIA DEPT OF AGRICULTURE
2301 N Cameron St Rm 310
Harrisburg, PA 17110-9405
www.pda.state.pa.us.gov
717-783-3181 • Fax 717-787-1858

PENNSYLVANIA DUTCH CANDIES
PO Box 3411
Camp Hill, PA 17011-3411
717-486-3496

PENNVALLEY FARMS
6807 W Irving Park Rd
Chicago, IL 60634-2305
773-685-9929 • Fax 773-685-8084

PENTON FOODSERVICE NETWORK
1100 Superior Ave E
Cleveland, OH 44114-2531
www.penton.com
216-696-7000 • Fax 216-696-0836

PEOPLE MISTERS
4255 Frontage Rd N
Lakeland, FL 33810-2855
e-mail: info@peoplemisters.com
863-686-4558 • Fax 863-606-4668

PEPINO FOODS, INC
3201 44th Ave N
Saint Petersburg, FL 33714-3809
727-525-6660

PEPPERMILLS SUPREME
PO Box 646
Fort Jones, CA 96032-0646
www.peppermills.com
530-468-5305

PEPSI
7380 W Sand Lake Rd
Orlando, FL 32819-5248
407-354-5840

PEPSI COLA
5500 N Lovers Lane Rd
Milwaukee, WI 53225-3038
414-438-2305 • Fax 414-438-2337

PEPSI COLA
1800 Preston Park Blvd
Plano, TX 75093-5188
972-599-5000

PEPSI COLA COMPANY
1 Pepsi Way
Somers, NY 10589-2212
914-767-6000 • Fax 914-767-7761

PEPSI-7UP BEVERAGE GROUP OF LOUISIANA
5733 Citrus Blvd
New Orleans, LA 70123-1662
504-734-2811

PEPSI-COLA GENERAL BOTTLERS
1772 E Kansas City Rd
Olathe, KS 66061-3004
913-791-3054

PEPSI-COLA NORTH AMERICA
700 Anderson Hill Rd
Purchase, NY 10577-1401
914-253-2000 • Fax 914-253-8096

PERDUE FARMS INC
PO Box 1537
Salisbury, MD 21802-1537
410-543-3000

PERDUE FARMS INC.
PO Box 537
Salisbury, MD 21803-0537
www.perdue.com
800-774-4734 • Fax 410-543-3267

PERFECT COLOR, LLC
599 Valley Health Plz
Paramus, NJ 07652-3616
e-mail: PerfectCol@aol.com
www.parchtek.com
201-262-8204 • Fax 201-262-1272

PERFECT PUREE
151 Kalmus Dr Ste C160
Costa Mesa, CA 92626-7961
900 556 3707

PERFECTION EQUIPMENT INC
4259 Lee Ave
Gurnee, IL 60031-2175
847-244-7200 • Fax 847-244-7205

PERFORMANCE REVIEW
201 W 70th St Apt 42H
New York, NY 10023-4358
212-447-7252

PERKINS FOODS
108 Henning Ct
Los Gatos, CA 95032-1372
408-378-5557 • Fax 408-378-4797

PERKYS FOODSERVICE CONCEPTS
5402 E Hanna Ave
Tampa, FL 33610-4033
813-626-6675

PERLICK CORP.
8300 W Good Hope Rd
Milwaukee, WI 53223-4524
www.perlick.com
414-353-7060 • Fax 414-353-7069

PERMA-VAULT SAFE CORPORATION
3015 Philmont Ave
Huntingdon Valley, PA 19006-4212
www.perma-vault.com
215-938-4300 • Fax 215-938-4310

PERONA FARMS FOOD SPECIALTIES
350 Andover Sparta Rd
Andover, NJ 07821-5016
973-729-7878 • Fax 973-729-4424

PERRIER-F.S. SALES
777 W Putnam Ave
Greenwich, CT 06830-5091
203-531-4100

PERRONE & SONS
4512 Zenith St
Metairie, LA 70001-1209
504-455-3663

PERSECO
701 Harger Rd
Oak Brook, IL 60523-1489
630-575-4400

PERSPECTIVES THE CONSULTING
11030 Santa Monica Blvd # 30
Los Angeles, CA 90025-7514
310-477-8877 • Fax 310-479-8448

PEST MANAGEMENT SYSTEM INC.
93 Whittemore St
Fitchburg, MA 01420-1901
800-442-9988

PETER GOOD SEMINARS
45 N Madison Ave
La Grange, IL 60525-2018
708-352-2901

PETER PAN SEAFOODS INC
2200 6th Ave Ste 1000
Seattle, WA 98121-1821
www.ppsf.com
206-727-7225 • Fax 206-728-1855

PETER RABBIT FARMS
85810 Grapefruit Blvd
Coachella, CA 92236-1831
760-398-0136

PETERS MACHINE
4700 N Ravenswood Ave
Chicago, IL 60640-4493
312-561-9000

PETERSEN SUPPLY
421 Wheeler Ave # O
Fredonia, WI 53021-9307
www.petersen.com
262-692-2416 • Fax 262-692-2418

PETERSON CORPORATION
PO Box 664
Denison, IA 51442-0664
e-mail: pmc@pionet.net
www.petersonmfg.com
712-263-2442 • Fax 712-263-5090

PETERSON GREASEPROOF
3 Manhattanville Rd
Purchase, NY 10577-2116
914-696-9350

PETERSON PACK SYSTEMS INC
1201 Andover Park E Ste 102
Seattle, WA 98188-3912
425-282-2601

PETES BREWING COMPANY
514 High St
Palo Alto, CA 94301-1623
650-328-7383 • Fax 650-327-3675

PETITES CHOSES
1528 W Adams St
Chicago, IL 60607-2410
312-733-9476 • Fax 312-733-9482

PETRINI FOODS INTERNATIONAL
543 Valley Rd
Montclair, NJ 07043-1881
973-746-9488

PFEIL & HOLING
5815 Northern Blvd
Woodside, NY 11377-2297
800-247-7955

PFENING CO.
1075 W 5th Ave
Columbus, OH 43212-2629
614-294-5361

PFIZER
235 Rosa Ave
Metairie, LA 70005-3415
504-458-4284

PHASE II PASTA MACHINES INC
55 Verdi St
Farmingdale, NY 11735-6316
www.pastamachines.net
516-293-4259 • Fax 516-293-4572

PHI ENTERPRISES, INC.
12832 Garden Grove Blvd
Garden Grove, CA 92843-2002
714-537-7858 • Fax 714-537-8228

PHIL BRANT FACTORY AGENTS
2362 Emerson St
Jacksonville, FL 32207-6742
e-mail: jennifer@philbrant.com
www.philbrant.com
904-399-2001

PHILADELPHIA CHEESESTEAK
520 E Hunting Park Ave
Philadelphia, PA 19124-6009
www.phillycheesesteak.com
215-423-3333 • Fax 215-423-3131

PHILADELPHIA FURNITURE
100 Rochester St
Salamanca, NY 14779-1509
716-945-5500 • Fax 716-945-5658

PHILIP MORRIS COMPANIES INC.
120 Park Ave
New York, NY 10017-5577
917-663-3469 • Fax 917-663-5475

PHILIPS CONSUMER ELECTRONICS CO
1 Philips Dr # 14810
Knoxville, TN 37914-9608
800-531-0039

PHILIPS CONSUMER ELECTRONICS
64 Perimeter Ctr E
Atlanta, GA 30346-2295
www.philipsusa.com
770-821-2244 • Fax 770-821-3126

PHILIPS SECURITY INTERNATIONAL
3165 N 37th Ave
Hollywood, FL 33021-1347
e-mail: phillipsintl@msn.com
954-965-9636 • Fax 954-965-0815

PHILLIP FOODS & SEAFOOD
137 S Warwick Ave
Baltimore, MD 21223-2143
www.phillipsfoods.com
410-947-0780 • Fax 410-233-5628

PHILLIPS FOODS INC
2004 N Philadelphia Ave
Ocean City, MD 21842-3560
410-289-6821

PHILLIPS FOODS INC.
1011 Kaolin Rd
Kennett Square, PA 19348-2605
610-925-0520 • Fax 610-925-0527

PHILLIPS FOODS, INC
21250 Box Springs Rd Ste 2
Moreno Valley, CA 92557-8705
909-784-7282 • Fax 909-784-7281

PHOENIX DOWN CORPORATION
85 US Highway 46
Totowa, NJ 07512-2301
e-mail: phod@phoenixdown.com
973-812-8100 • Fax 973-812-9077

PHOENIX GROUP
7501 Currency Dr
Orlando, FL 32809-6922
e-mail:
LC@phoenixgroupflorida.com
407-240-0699 • Fax 407-240-2665

PIANODISC
4111 N Freeway Blvd
Sacramento, CA 95834-1209
www.pianodisc.com
916-567-9999 • Fax 916-567-1941

PIANTEDOS BAKERY
240 Commercial St
Malden, MA 02148-6780
781-321-3400 • Fax 781-324-5647

PIC A CARD
95 Reeve Ave
Bloomingdale, NJ 07403-1539
e-mail: picacard@aol.com
www.picacard.com
973-838-1806 • Fax 973-838-8771

PICKARD INCORPORATED
782 Pickard Ave
Antioch, IL 60002-1574
www.pickardchina.com
847-395-3800 • Fax 847-395-3827

PICTURES & MIRRORS INTL
4356 SW 34th St
Orlando, FL 32811-6414
407-423-7011 • Fax 407-423-5889

PIDY, GOURMET PASTRY SHELLS
58 Chris Ct
Dayton, NJ 08810-1536
732-274-2828

PIEDMONT NATURAL GAS CO
PO Box 33068
Charlotte, NC 28233-3068
704-364-3120

PIEMONTE FOODS INC
PO Box 9239
Greenville, SC 29604-9239
864-242-0424 • Fax 864-235-0239

PIERCE FOODS
149 Creekside Ln
Winchester, VA 22602-2447
540-667-7710 • Fax 540-723-6520

PIERI CREATIONS
100 W Oxford St
Philadelphia, PA 19122-3996
e-mail: pieri@erols.com
www.piericreations.com
215-634-0700 • Fax 215-634-5525

PIGHETTI'S ESPRESSO EQUIPMENT
2934 Forsyth Rd
Winter Park, FL 32792-6612
e-mail: don@ourespresso.com
www.ourespresso.com
407-673-2441

PILGRIMS PRIDE
2011 S Good Latimer Expy
Dallas, TX 75226-2297
214-421-7611

PILGRIMS PRIDE CORPORATION
2777 N Stemmons Fwy
Dallas, TX 75207-2277
972-920-2200 • Fax 972-920-2396

PINAHS CO INC
N8 W22100 Johnson Dr
Waukesha, WI 53186-1866
262-547-2447

PINE ISLAND CLAMS
2657 8th Ave
Saint James City, FL 33956-2181
239-282-5576

PINKERTON FIELD RESEARCH SERVICES
400 Chastain Center Blvd NW
Kennesaw, GA 30144-5558
www.pinkertons.com
800-540-6077 • Fax 800-278-5228

PINNACLE
1651 Sherman Ave
Pennsauken, NJ 08110-2624
856-665-3040

PINNACLE FOOD BROKERS
99 S Bedford St Ste 5
Burlington, MA 01803-5153
781-229-2277 • Fax 781-229-5757

PINNACLE FURNISHINGS, INC.
7401 NW 32nd Ave
Miami, FL 33147-5803
305-696-3266

PINNACLE HOSPITALITY SYSTEM
2001 W Cypress Creek Rd
Fort Lauderdale, FL 33309-1865
e-mail: don@pinnaclehs.com
www.pinnaclehs.com
954-938-8870

PINNACLE HOSPITALITY SYSTEMS
3102 Cherry Palm Dr Ste 1
Tampa, FL 33619-8314
813-626-3131 • Fax 813-626-2998

PIONEER
2265 E 220th St
Long Beach, CA 90810-1643
800-782-7210

PIONEER BALLOON CO
5000 E 29th St N
Wichita, KS 67220-2111
www.promostore.com-pioneer
316-685-2266 • Fax 316-685-2409

PIONEER MARKETING ASSOCIATES
3432 Dundee Ln
Jackson, MS 39212-3809
601-372-1033

PIONEER MAT COMPANY
PO Box 5757
Chattanooga, TN 37406-0757
www.pioneermat.com
800-333-8516 • Fax 423-622-7787

PIONEER SALES CO., INC
PO Box 1103
Saugus, MA 01906-0303
e-mail: sales@pioneersalesco.com
781-233-8174 • Fax 781-233-8549

PIONEER VALLEY REFRIGERATED
149 Plainfield St
Chicopee, MA 01013-1522
413-736-1976

PIPER JAFFRAY, INC.
800 Nicollet Mall Ste 800
Minneapolis, MN 55402-7020
612-342-6344

PITCO FOODS-PGI FOODS
255 Channel St
San Francisco, CA 94107-1533
415-865-0404

PIZZA & RESTAURANT PROMOTIONS
26111 Brush Ave Ste 314
Euclid, OH 44132-3236
www.pizzapromotions. com
800-277-2564 • Fax 216-289-1890

PIZZA CRISP INTERNATIONAL
1510 Old Deerfield Rd
Highland Park, IL 60035-3068
800-344-0077

PIZZA EXPO-INFO
1641 W Carroll Ave
Chicago, IL 60612-2501
800-937-4464

PIZZA HUT SCHOOL
14841 Dallas Pkwy
Dallas, TX 75254-7552
972-338-7700

PIZZA MARKETING QUARTERLY
605 Edison St
Oxford, MS 38655-2901
www.pmq.com
662-234-5481 • Fax 662-234-0665

PIZZA TODAY
137 E Market St
New Albany, IN 47150-3432
www.pizzatoday.com
812-949-0909 • Fax 812-941-9711

PIZZAMATIC
130 E 168th St
South Holland, IL 60473-2836
www.pizzamaticusa.com
708-331-0660 • Fax 708-331-0663

PKF CONSULTING
5 Post Oak Park Ste 1940
Houston, TX 77027-3409
713-621-5252

PKF CONSULTING, INC.
425 California St Ste 1650
San Francisco, CA 94104-2102
415-421-5378

PLANETBISTRO.COM
9404 W 150th Ter
Overland Park, KS 66221-2503
www.planetbistro.com
913-685-0190 • Fax 913-684-0425

PLANSOFT
8285 Darrow Rd
Twinsburg, OH 44087-2307
330-405-5555

PLASTIC CARD SERVICES
201 Boston Post Rd W
Marlborough, MA 01752-4667
508-229-2470

PLASTIC CORPORATION OF AMERICA
5333 S Downey Rd
Los Angeles, CA 90058-3725
323-277-3700 • Fax 323-277-3737

PLASTILINE
623 E Emory Rd
Powell, TN 37849-3558
www.plasti-line.com
865-947-8421 • Fax 865-947-8445

PLASTI-LINE, INC
PO Box 59043
Knoxville, TN 37950-9043
www.plasti-line.com
865-938-1511 • Fax 865-947-8534

PLAZA SWEETS
521 Waverly Ave
Mamaroneck, NY 10543-2235
914-698-0233 • Fax 914-698-3712

PLEET DISPENSING SYSTEMS
6400 S Lewis Ave Ste 1000
Tulsa, OK 74136-1046
www.exactamate.com
918-746-7000 • Fax 918-746-7010

PLEE-ZING INC
1640 Pleasant Ln
Glenview, IL 60025-1847
847-998-0200

PLOTKINS BARMEDIA ROBERT
PO Box 14486A
Tucson, AZ 85732-4486
800-421-7179

PLUMROSE INC
PO Box 160
Elkhart, IN 46515-0160
574-295-8190

PLUMROSE USA
PO Box 1066
East Brunswick, NJ 08816-1066
www.plumroseusa.com
732-651-3355 • Fax 732-257-4601

PLYMOLD
615 Centennial Dr
Kanyon, MN 55946-1252
www.plymold.com
800-759-6653 • Fax 800-544-0480

PM COMPANY
1500 Kemper Meadow Dr
Cincinnati, OH 45240-1638
www.pmcompany.com
800-327-4359-\ • Fax 800-626-2140

PENNSYLVANIA COLLEGE OF TECHNOLOGY
1 College Ave
Williamsport, PA 17701-5778
e-mail: fbecker@pct.edu
www.pct.edu
570-326-3761

POCAHONTAS FOODS U S A
PO Box 9729
Richmond, VA 23228-0729
804-262-8614

POCASSET SEAFOODS OF LA-GUMBO
1582 Grand Anse Hwy
Breaux Bridge, LA 70517-7106
877-584-8626

POCINO FOODS COMPANY
14250 Lomitas Ave
La Puente, CA 91746-3014
626-968-8000 • Fax 626-968-0196

POKANOKET OSTRICH FARM
177 Gulf Rd
South Dartmouth, MA 02748-1514
e-mail: pokanoket@aol.com
www.pokanoket.com
508-992-6188 • Fax 508-993-5356

POLAR HOSPITALITY PRODUCTS
2046 Castor Ave
Philadelphia, PA 19134-2132
www.the-polar.com
800-831-7823 • Fax 215-535-6971

POLAR TAP, INC.
10 Merrimack River Rd
Groveland, MA 01834-1424
e-mail: polartap@aol.com
978-372-8124 • Fax 978-372-8462

POLAR TECH
415 E Railroad Ave
Genoa, IL 60135-1200
www.polar-tech.com
815-784-9000 • Fax 815-784-9009

POLAR WARE COMPANY
PO Box 211
Sheboygan, WI 53082-0211
920-458-3561

POLAROID DIGITAL SOLUTIONS
1101 Broad St
Saint Joseph, MI 49085-1790
e-mail: etaylor@polaroidforms.com
www.polaroidforms.com
800-234-8727 • Fax 616-982-0077

POLDER INC.
8 Slater St
Port Chester, NY 10573-4984
e-mail: joans@polder.com
www.polderinc.com
914-937-8200 • Fax 914-937-8297

POLISH CONSULATE -COMM DIV.
333 E Ontario St Ste 3906
Chicago, IL 60611-4856
www.homepage.interaccess.com
312-642-4102 • Fax 312-642-8829

POLLUTION RESEARCH
931 John Stark Hwy
Newport, NH 03773-2614
www.pollutionresearch.com
800-426-2611 • Fax 603-863-7590

POLY-TAK PROTECTION SYSTEMS
5731 McFadden Ave
Huntington Beach, CA 92649-1321
www.polytak.com
800-899-0871 • Fax 714-842-7128

POLYWOOD WHOLESALE SHUTTER CO.
11445 E Via Linda Ste 2 PMB-61
Scottsdale, AZ 85259-2654
602-312-7205 • Fax 602-314-0158

POMPEII CONTRACT FURNITURE
255 NW 25th St
Miami, FL 33127-4329
e-mail: Pompeii@worldnet.att.net
www.pompeiifurniture.com
305-576-3600 • Fax 305-576-2339

POP N GO INC.
12429 Putnam St
Whittier, CA 90602-1023
www.popngo.com
888-476-7646 • Fax 562-945-6341

POPPI AL'S FROZEN FOODS
7750 Allentown Blvd
Harrisburg, PA 17112-3703
717-652-6263 • Fax 717-652-7108

POPPIE'S DOUGH
2411 S Wallace St
Chicago, IL 60616-1855
www.poppiesdough.com
312-640-0404 • Fax 312-640-0450

PORT- A-COOL-DIV. OF GEN SHELT
709 Southview Cir
Center, TX 75935-4341
936-598-5651 • Fax 936-598-5057

PORT-A-COOL
PO Box 2108
Center, TX 75935-2108
e-mail: cmaguire@sat.net
936-598-5651 • Fax 936-598-5057

PORTION PAC INC
7325 Snider Rd
Mason, OH 45040-9193
513-398-0400

PORTLAND BREWING COMPANY
2730 NW 31st Ave
Portland, OR 97210-1718
www.portlandbrew.com
877-429-2739 • Fax 503-226-2702

POS SPECIALISTS
401 Sunset Dr Ste E
Antioch, CA 94509-2824
www.posspecialists.com
925-417-2163 • Fax 925-417-2168

POS SUPPLIES, INC.
241 Ipswich Rd
Boxford, MA 01921-1620
e-mail: possupplies@juno.com
978-887-1465 • Fax 978-887-0699

POS SYSTEMS INC-RESTAURANT MAN
7620 Gunn Hwy Ste 120
Tampa, FL 33625-3144
e-mail: possystem@worldnet.att.net
813-968-8754

POSIFLEX BUSINESS MACHINES
29460 Union City Blvd
Union City, CA 94587-1239
www.posiflexusa.com
510-429-7097 • Fax 501-475-0982

POSITION, INC
PO Box 24877
New Orleans, LA 70184-4877
504-482-7094

POSITOUCH
491 Kilvert St
Warwick, RI 02886-1344
www.positouch.com
401-732 5700 • Fax 401-732-8550

POSITOUCH
300 Observer Hwy Ste 6
Hoboken, NJ 07030-2412
201-418-0600 • Fax 201-418-0022

POSONE
6400 Westpark Dr Ste 238
Houston, TX 77057-7215
e-mail: gregb@posone.com
www.posone.com
713-972-0039 • Fax 713-972-1099

POSTER MONTAGE, L.C.
1640 Seminole Rd SE
Grand Rapids, MI 49506-6533
e-mail: bafery@ibm.net
616-245-7731 • Fax 616-241-4373

POSTERLOID
4862 36th St
Long Island City, NY 11101-1918
800-651-5000 • Fax 718-786-9310

POSTERNAK BAUER ASSOC.
479 White Plains Rd
Eastchester, NY 10709-5516
914-793-9000 • Fax 914-793-9209

POTATO PRODUCTS OF IDAHO
PO Box 617
Rigby, ID 83442-0617
www.minutebaker.com
208-522-4424 • Fax 208-529-5750

POWELL INSURANCE
131 Airline Dr Ste 300
Metairie, LA 70001-6274
504-835-5000

POWER SOAK-METCRAFT
13910 Kessler Dr
Grandview, MO 64030-2810
816-761-3250 • Fax 816-761-0544

POWERVAR INC.
28457 Ballard Dr Ste C
Lake Forest, IL 60045-4545
www.powervar.com
847-816-8585 • Fax 847-816-8988

POWER-FLITE
3101 Wichita Ct
Fort Worth, TX 76140-1755
800-880-2913

PRACTICAL BAKER EQUIP CO
1001 W Diggins St
Harvard, IL 60033-2386
815-943-6040

PRACTICAL EMPLOYEE SOLUTIONS
12770 Merit Dr Ste 700
Dallas, TX 75251-1213
972-778-9627 • Fax 972-239-8767

PRAENDEX PACIFIC INC.
206 E Forest Ave
Arcadia, CA 91006-2511
626-359-8422 • Fax 626-256-9129

PRAIRIE CITY BAKERY
PO Box 6979
Libertyville, IL 60048-6979
www.pcbakery.com
847-573-9640 • Fax 847-573-9643

PRAIRIE VIEW INDUSTRIES, INC.
PO Box 575
Fairbury, NE 68352-0575
www.pviramps.com
402-729-4055 • Fax 402-729-4258

PRATO, LANE & HEUMANN ARCH
412 Osceola Ave
Jacksonville Beach, FL 32250-4077
904-249-5688

PRATT LAUNDRY ASSOC
530 S Jefferson Davis Pkwy
New Orleans, LA 70119-7193
504-827-3600

PRE PAID LEGEL SERVICE, INC
45 Savoie Dr
Mandeville, LA 70448-3461
800-264-7564

PREFERRED SOURCE, INC.
4900 Laurel St
Bellaire, TX 77401-4427
713-667-0383 • Fax 713-667-2258

PRECISION DYNAMICS
13880 Del Sur St
San Fernando, CA 91340-3490
888-432-2657

PRECISION FOODS INC
11457 Olde Cabin Rd Ste 100
Saint Louis, MO 63141-7139
314-216-0704

PRECISION FOODS, INC
11457 Olde Cabin Rd
Saint Louis, MO 63141 7139
314-567-7400 • Fax 314-567-5402

PRECISION FURNITURE CORP.
1838 Adee Ave
Bronx, NY 10469-3298
e-mail: prefurn@aol.com
www.precisionfurniture.com
718-379-5200 • Fax 718-320-1270

PRECISION POURS INC.
9977 Valley View Rd
Eden Prairie, MN 55344-3586
800-549-4491

PRECISION PRESS
2030 Lookout Dr
Mankato, MN 56003-1713
507-625-7155 • Fax 507-625-2594

PRECISION TEMP INC.
1006 Kieley Pl
Cincinnati, OH 45217-1118
www.precisiontemp.com
800-934-9690 • Fax 513-641-0733

PRECOR INCORPORATED
20001 N Creek Pkwy # O
Bothell, WA 98011-8218
e-mail: elton@precor.com
www.precor.com
877-842-0639 • Fax 425-240-5505

PREFERRED CAPITAL, INC.
6860 W Snowville Rd # 110
Brecksville, OH 44141-3214
440-546-7400 • Fax 440-546-7406

PREFERRED CLUB PROGRAM
1301 Wrights Ln E
West Chester, PA 19380-3413
610-692-0953

PREFERRED MARKETING AGENTS
1001 E Sample Rd Ste 7
Pompano Beach, FL 33064-5161
e-mail: pma1662@aol.com
954-943-1661

PREFERRED PRINTING
10393 Boca Springs Dr
Boca Raton, FL 33428-4228
561-218-0408

PREMIER BEVERAGE CO.
2400 Sand Lake Rd Ste 600
Orlando, FL 32809-9109
407-240-4631

PREMIER BRASS
255 Ottley Dr NE
Atlanta, GA 30324-3926
www.premierbrass.com
800-251-5800 • Fax 800-251-2515

PREMIER DATA SOLUTIONS
PO Box 1865
Kankakee, IL 60901-1865
www.premierdata.net
815-937-1811 • Fax 815-939-7788

PREMIER FOOD SERVICES SALES
1021 W Harimaw Ct
Metairie, LA 70001-6231
504-833-4605

PREMIER LABEL WATER CO.
1110 S Robertson Blvd
Los Angeles, CA 90035-1420
310-859-1322 • Fax 310-859-1906

PREMIER PARTY SERVERS, INC.
295 Madison Ave Rm 1805
New York, NY 10017-6366
e-mail: waiterkng@aol.com
212-499-0886 • Fax 212-499-0884

PREMIER SKIRTING PRODUCTS INC.
241 Mill St
Lawrence, NY 11559-1209
www.premierskirting.com
516-239-6581 • Fax 516-239-6810

PREMIERE SAFETY PRODUCTS, INC.
4301 N Greats Rd
Sand Springs, OK 74063-5813
e-mail: premiere@safefloors.com
www.safefloors.com
800-752-1425 • Fax 918-245-6854

PREMIUM BLEND COCKTAILS A.M.N
2661 W 81st St
Hialeah, FL 33016-2756
e-mail: pb@premiumblend.com
305-557-1464 • Fax 305-557-8454

PRENTICE HALL
1 Lake St
Saddle River, NJ 07458-1813
201-236-7283 • Fax 201-236-7210

PREPCHEK FOOD SAFETY SERVICE
6712 Washington Ave Ste 103
Egg Harbor Townshi, NJ 08234-1999
800-800-8140

PRESSTO VALET
8825 Woodman Way
Sacramento, CA 95826-2157
800-913-5555

PRESSTO VALET IRONING CENTERS
4880 San Juan Ave # 33
Fair Oaks, CA 95628-4719
e-mail: jim@presstovalet.com
www.presstovalet.com
916-338-9333 • Fax 916-338-9339

PRESSURE KING, INC.
231 Herbert Ave
Closter, NJ 07624-1332
201-768-1911 • Fax 201-768-1911

PRESSURE ZONE, INC
2813 Richland Ave Ste A
Metairie, LA 70002-6815
504-888-9166

PRESTIGE BAKING CO.
580 55th St
West New York, NJ 07093-4626
e-mail: prestigger@aol.com
201-422-7900 • Fax 201-422-0199

PRESTO FOOD PRODUCTS
16975 Mariah Ct
Yorba Linda, CA 92886-1537
714-854-7610

PRICE CHOPPER INC
2721 Forsyth Rd
Winter Park, FL 32792-8220
888-695-6220

PRICE PURCHASING, INC.
10001 Wayzata Blvd Ste 110
Hopkins, MN 55305-1591
612-525-1992

PRICE WATERHOUSE LLP
200 E Randolph St
Chicago, IL 60601-6436
312-540-1500 • Fax 312-565-2193

PRICE WOODS INC
2610 E University Dr Ste 102
Mesa, AZ 85213-8473
www.pricewood.com
480-948-9451 • Fax 480-948-8608

PRICEWATERHOUSE COOPERS LLC
100 N Torrence St Ste 5400
Charlotte, NC 28204-2517
704-424-4738

PRIDE BEVERAGES
1887 McFarland Rd
Alpharetta, GA 30005-8341
www.pridebeverages.com
770-663-0990 • Fax 770-663-0091

PRIDE MKTG & PROCUREMENT
509 N Carrollton Ave
New Orleans, LA 70119-4704
800-466-9088

PRIDHAM ELECTRONICS
2902 Perry St
Madison, WI 53713-3237
608-273-3676 • Fax 608-273-3420

PRIMARILY SEATING INC.
475 Park Ave # 3A
New York, NY 10022-1945
www.primarilyseating.com
212-838-2588 • Fax 212-838-2588

PRIMAVERA PUBLIC RELATIONS INC
2718 Hickory St
Yorktown Heights, NY 10598-2728
914-245-5390

PRIME ADVANTAGE CORP
980 N Michigan Ave
Chicago, IL 60611-4501
312-573-1111

PRIME FOOD PROCESSING CORP.
236 N 10th St
Brooklyn, NY 11211-2132
e-mail: primefood@earthlink.net
888-639-2323 • Fax 718-963-3256

PRIME TIME COMMUNICATIONS
10160 SW Nimbus Ave
Portland, OR 97223-4338
www.mellennia.com
503-598-9867 • Fax 503-620-7804

PRINCE CASTLE INC
355 Kehoe Blvd
Carol Stream, IL 60188-1833
www.princecastle.com
630-462-8800 • Fax 630-462-1460

PRINCE CASTLE
21063 Network Pl
Chicago, IL 60673-1210
800-722-7853 • Fax 312-462-1460

PRINCE SEATING
1355 Atlantic Ave
Brooklyn, NY 11216-2810
e-mail: info@princeseating.com
718-363-2300 • Fax 718-363-9880

PRINCIPAL RESOURCE INC PREVIEW
3407 Halifax St
Dallas, TX 75247-5903
800-422-4862 • Fax 214-951-9438

PRINTPACK INC
PO Box 43687
Atlanta, GA 30336-0687
800-241-9984

PRIORITY LEASING SERVICES
6670 Villa Sonrisa Dr Apt 211
Boca Raton, FL 33433-4017
e-mail: leases@bellsouth.net
www.priorityleases.com
561-394-0950

PRISM SANITATION MANAGEMENT
N532 Williams Rd
Genoa City, WI 53128-1922
262-279-8900 • Fax 262-279-8901

PRISTINEOYSTER.COM
PO Box 638
Apalachicola, FL 32329-0638
www.pristineoyster.com
850-697-8691

PRIVATE LABEL MFG ASSOCIATION
369 Lexington Ave
New York, NY 10017-6506
212-972-3577

PRIVATE LABEL PREMIUM CIGAR
4135 Lavista Rd
Tucker, GA 30084-5314
770-496-5562

PRIVID-EYE SYSTEM, INC
4061 SW 47th Ave
Fort Lauderdale, FL 33314-4023
e-mail: mspring@privid-eye.com
954-581-1756

PRIZE POSSESSIONS
203 Carnegie Row
Norwood, MA 02062-5000
800-283-1166

PRO DESIGN & VENDING TECH
68 Route 125
Kingston, NH 03848-3562
www.bulkvending.com
603-642-9290

PRO MOTION SLIDES, INC. CINEMA
1 International Blvd Ste 510
Mahwah, NJ 07495-0084
e-mail: kromano@cinemaads.com
www.cinemaads.com
201-684-2600 • Fax 201-684-2617

PRO TECH COMMUNICATIONS, INC.
4492 Okeechobee Rd
Fort Pierce, FL 34947-5405
e-mail: dlloyd@protechcom.com
www.protechcom.com
772-464-5100 • Fax 772-464-6644

PROCON
910 Ridgely Rd
Murfreesboro, TN 37129-2790
615-890-5710 • Fax 615-896-7729

PROCTER & GAMBLE
104 Barbann Cir
Slidell, LA 70461-3013
985-649-7050

PROCTER & GAMBLE FOOD-FOOD SVC
PO Box 599
Cincinnati, OH 45201-0599
513-562-1100

PROCTOR AND GAMBLE
217 10th St Apt A
Hoboken, NJ 07030-4379
201-386-5223 • Fax 201-386-5223

PRODUCE MARKETING ASSOC
1500 Casho Mill Rd
Newark, DE 19711-3598
www.pma .com
302-738-7100 • Fax 302-731-2409

PRODUCE ONLINE.COM
117 E Colorado Blvd
Pasadena, CA 91105-1938
888-528-3823

PRODUCERS RICE MILL, INC.
523 Louisiana St Ste 925
Little Rock, AR 72201-5709
www.producersricemill.com
501-374-9100 • Fax 501-374-8758

PRODUCT GROUP INC.
4870 Frank Rd NW
Canton, OH 44720-7426
330-497-5283 • Fax 330-497-1807

PRODUCT INNOVATION VALUE, INC
PO Box 607190
Orlando, FL 32860-7190
e-mail: booblysugar@prodigy.net
www.pivsugar.com
407-851-1009

PRODUCT MAINTENANCE REPAIR
371 Buckalew Rd
Freehold, NJ 07728-8408
732-780-1316 • Fax 732-303-0319

PRODUCTS BY TEXANN
800 N Pacific St
Conroe, TX 77301-2517
vtexann@lcc.net
www.texann.com
936-273-0030 • Fax 936-273-0530

PROFESSIONAL CONNECTIONS
4133 Edinburgh Dr
Virginia Bch, VA 23452-2543
757-495-8708

PROFESSIONAL EMPLOYEE MANAGEMENT
1819 Main St Fl 8
Sarasota, FL 34236-5951
e-mail: jcox@pempo.com
www.pempo.com
800-392-7823

PROFESSIONAL SALON, SPA & RESORT
3375 Motor Ave
Los Angeles, CA 90034-3711
e-mail: lisa@prosalon.com
www.prosalon.com
310-837-2091 • Fax 310-837-2414

PROFESSIONAL WAITERS SCHOOL
17732 Duncan St
Encino, CA 91316-6403
818-996-0404 • Fax 818-996-0404

PROFILE MARKETING RESEARCH
4020 S 57th Ave Ste 101
Lake Worth, FL 33463-4399
561-965-8300

PROFILES INTERNATIONAL
10707 Corporate Dr, Ste.104
Stafford, TX 77477-4095
e-mail: bjsingl@msn.com
www.profilestexas.com
281-240-5524 • Fax 281-240-0913

PROFITS RESTAURANT SYSTEMS INC
PO Box 841798
Houston, TX 77284-1798
713-752-7700

PROFITS RESTAURANT SYSTEMS, INC
12012 Wickchester Ln Ste 200
Houston, TX 77079-1295
vinfo@profitsrs.com
www.profitsrs.com
877-448-5300 • Fax 281-799-1100

PROGRESS LIGHTING
101 Corporate Dr Ste L
Spartanburg, SC 29303-5043
vtregan@progresslighting.com
www.progresslighting.com
864-599-6024 • Fax 864-599-6159

PROGRESSIVE PRO ENTERPRISES
PO Box 125
North Oxford, MA 01537-0125
508-892-9618 • Fax 508-892-9745

PROGRESSIVE SOFTWARE, INC.
2301 Crown Center Dr
Charlotte, NC 28227-7705
704-849-6400

PROGRESSIVE SPECIALTY GLASS
PO Box 636
Southington, CT 06489-0636
e-mail: funfoam@aol.com
www.longshutz.com
860-620-5090

PROHOST
2414 Arbuckle Ct
Dallas, TX 75229-4506
972-241-9607 • Fax 972-241-0714

PROJECT PLANET CORP
PO Box 888
Dawsonville, GA 30534-0019
800-527-1195

PRO-LITE, INC.
3505 Cadillac Ave Ste D
Costa Mesa, CA 92626-1464
e-mail: chrish@pro-lite.com
www.pro-lite.com
714-668-9988 • Fax 714-668-9980

PROLON, DIV OF NATL PLASTICS
PO Box 568
Port Gibson, MS 39150-0568
601 137-4211

PROMAXIMA FITNESS MFG.
5325 Ashbrook Dr
Houston, TX 77081-4101
www.promaximamfg.com
800-231-6652 • Fax 713-667-9941

PROMO ONLY
257 S Lake Destiny Rd
Orlando, FL 32810-6254
407-331-3600

PROMOTE FOR LESS
10708 Wingate Dr
Tampa, FL 33624-5228
813-962-8882

PROMOTEFOOD.COM
6333 E Mockingbird Ln
Dallas, TX 75214-2692
469-335-9466

PRONTO PRODUCTS CO.
11765 Goldring Rd
Arcadia, CA 91006-5894
www.prontoproducts.com
626-358-5718 • Fax 626-358-9194

PROPAC IMAGES INC
PO Box 1969
Albertville, AL 35950-0032
800-977-6722

PROPAC IMAGES INC
1292 Wagner Dr
Albertville, AL 35950-8551
256-593-1505 • Fax 256-593-0506

PROPER FOODS INC,
1319 E Pine St
Deming, NM 88030-7065
www.properfoods.com
505-546-4442 • Fax 505-546-4449

PROPROCESS CROP-DOUGH-PRO
7328 Madison St
Paramount, CA 90723-4030
www.doughpro.com
562-531-0305 • Fax 562-869-7715

PROTEAM ENTERPRISES
208 E 13800 S
Draper, UT 84020-9290
801-523-9566

PRO-TEAM, INC.
5118 N Sawyer Ave
Garden City, ID 83714-1489
www.pro-team.com
208-377-9555 • Fax 208-377-8444

PROTEIN SPECIALISTS INC.
40949 N Courage Trl
Phoenix, AZ 85086-2537
602-451-030 • Fax 602-513-2845

PROTEIN TECHNOLOGIES INTL
Checkerboard Square-14T
Saint Louis, MO 63164-0001
314-982-2380

PROTEIN TECHNOLOGIES INTL
PO Box 1606
Saint Louis, MO 63188-1606
800-344-6937

PROTEIN TECHNOLOGIES INTL
901 Chouteau Ave # 5C
Saint Louis, MO 63102-1009
314-982-1000 • Fax 314-982-5894

PROVIMI VEAL
W2103 County Road V
Seymour, WI 54165-9174
800-833-8325

PROVIMI VEAL CORP
20800 Swenson Dr
Waukesha, WI 53186-2058
262-784-8520

PROVINTECH INTERNATIONAL
6620 Southwest Fwy # 244
Houston, TX 77074-2210
e-mail: provintech@provintech.com
www.provintech.com
713-270-1712 • Fax 713-270-6143

PROWARE SYSTEMS
24 Faucett St
Stamford, CT 06906-2008
www.proware.com
203-329-1255 • Fax 203-461-9505

PRUDENTIAL
2500 Citywest Blvd
Houston, TX 77042-3000
e-mail:
richard-bunch@prudential.com
www.prudential.com
713-783-1622 • Fax 713-266-3325

PRUDHOMME, CHEF PAUL
406 Chartres St
New Orleans, LA 70130-2100
800-654-6017

PS CHEZ
1036 Saint Rita Hwy
Saint Martinville, LA 70582-6315
337-394-8118

PUBLIC IMAGERY - ART MART
8120 Anderson Rd
Tampa, FL 33634-2318
813-884-5554 • Fax 813-885-3227

PUBLIC SERVICE MUTUAL INS.
132 W 31st St
New York, NY 10001-3406
212-560-5267

PUBLIC SERVICES
1 Penn Plz Fl 8
New York, NY 10119-0800
212-290-4327 • Fax 212-290-4457

PULVER GENAU, INC.
4140 Industrial Way
Tracy, CA 95304-1611
209-835-5190

PUMPSKINS RESURFACING SYSTEMS
4901 Center St
Tacoma, WA 98409-2321
253-564-4600

PURATOS CORP
1941 Old Cuthbert Rd
Cherry Hill, NJ 08034-1417
856-428-4300

PURCELL & MADDEN ASSOCIATES
93 Schumacher Dr
New Hyde Park, NY 11040-3644
e-mail: purmadinec@aol.com
516-873-1749 • Fax 516-873-6256

PURCHASE PRO, INC.
3291 N Buffalo Dr
Las Vegas, NV 89129-7437
e-mail: sales@purchasepro.com
www.purchasepro.com
702-316-7000 • Fax 702-316-7001

PURCHASE PRO.COM
3291 N Buffalo Dr Ste 1
Las Vegas, NV 89129-7437
www.purchasepro.com
888-830-4600 • Fax 702-316-7031

PURCHASINGFIRST.COM
5080 Tuttle Crossing Blvd
Dublin, OH 43016-3540
www.purchasingfirst.com
614-760-9280 • Fax 614-760-9285

PURDUE UNIVERSITY RHIT DEPT.
1266 Stone Hall
West Lafayette, IN 47907-1266
www.cfs. Purdue.edu-RHIT
765-494-4643 • Fax 765-494-0327

PURE MIST SYSTEMS
183 Discovery Dr
Colmar, PA 18915-9759
www.puremistsystems.com
888-221-3555 • Fax 215-822-8612

PURITY GROUP INC SUNNYSIDE FOOD
PO Box 213
Minotola, NJ 08341-0213
800-220-5150 • Fax 856-794-9332

PUTTING GREENS INTERNATIONAL
7320 E 86th St Ste 400
Indianapolis, IN 46256-1250
e-mail: pgi@putting.com
www.putting.com
317-842-9430 • Fax 317-578-1871

PYA MONARCH
2850 Selma Hwy
Montgomery, AL 36108-5068
334-288-3111 • Fax 334-286-5276

PYA MONARCH INC
PO Box 1328
Greenville, SC 29602-1328
864-676-8600 • Fax 864-676-8756

PYCO INDUSTRIES, INC.
2901 Avenue A
Lubbock, TX 79404-2231
e-mail:
nwaston@pycoindustries.com
www.pycoindustries.com
806-747-3434 • Fax 806-744-3221

PYRAMID BREWERIES
91 S Royal Broughamway
Seattle, WA 98134-1219
www.pyramidbrew.com
206-682-8322

PYRAMID SALES INC
120 E La Habra Blvd
La Habra, CA 90631-5475
562-690-2208

Q A PRODUCTS INC
1301 Mark St
Elk Grove Village, IL 60007-6711
847-595-2390

QDEBIT INNOVATIVE PAYMENT SOLUTIONS
2814 Dogwood Pl
Nashville, TN 37204-3106
877-767-2647

QINDUSTRIES FOODS EQUIP-MENT COMPANY
2230 Elmhurst Rd
Elk Grove Village, IL 60007-6309
www.q-maticovens.com
847-427-0127 • Fax 847-427-0132

Q-SALES & LEASING
16720 Mozart Ave
Hazel Crest, IL 60429-1061
708-331-0094 • Fax 708-331-0096

QSR MAGAZINE
4905 Pine Cone Dr # 2
Durham, NC 27707-5258
800-662-4834 • Fax 919-489-4767

QTECH BUSINESS PRODUCTS
PO Box 100
Jewett, NY 12444-0100
518-734-6514

QUADRA-TECH
864 E Jenkins Ave
Columbus, OH 43207-1317
614-443-0630 • Fax 614-443-2024

QUAKE CITY-CAPSTONE
1800 S Flower St
Los Angeles, CA 90015-3424
213-746-0540

QUAKER MAID MEATS
PO Box 350
Reading, PA 19607-0350
610-376-1500

QUALITY BAKERY PRODUCTS
14330 Interdrive W
Houston, TX 77032-3316
e-mail: qbphou@aol.com
281-449-4977 • Fax 281-449-7820

QUALITY CHEKD DAIRIES
1733 Park St
Naperville, IL 60563-8478
630-717-1110

QUALITY FOOD-HEINZ USA
628 Shrewsbury Ave
Red Bank, NJ 07701-4912
732-530-7757 • Fax 732-530-5257

QUALITY FOODS-CFP GROUP
1117 W Olympic Blvd
Montebello, CA 90640-5123
e-mail: sawoodard@aol.com
www.phillysteaks.com
800-275-8902 • Fax 626-288-5804

QUALITY REFERIGARATION INC
2937 Terrace St
Kansas City, MO 64108-3619
816-756-5959

QUALITY SYSTEMS SOLUTIONS
40 Lydecker St
Nyack, NY 10960-2104
845-353-5010 • Fax 845-353-5013

QUALITY TABLEGAMES, INC.
PO Box 8650
Aspen, CO 81612-8650
e-mail:
qualitytablegames@compuserve.com
970-704-1122 • Fax 970-704-1121

QUANTUM CORPORATE FUNDING
1140 Avenue Of The Americas Fl
New York, NY 10036-5803
212-768-1200

QUANTUM FOODS, INC
750 S Schmidt Rd
Bolingbrook, IL 60440-4813
www.quantumfoods.com
815-679-2300 • Fax 815-679-1257

QUANTUM MULTIMEDIA TECH
11693 San Vicente Blvd
Los Angeles, CA 90049-5105
800-277-7607

QUANTUM TECHNICAL SERVICES
9524 Gulfstream Rd
Frankfort., IL 60423-2520
www.q-t-s.com
815-464-1540 • Fax 815-464-1541

QUEST INTERNATIONAL
5115 Sedge Blvd
Schaumburg, IL 60192-3708
847-645-7000 • Fax 847-645-7052

QUICK N' CRISPY
12021 Plano Rd
Dallas, TX 75243-5455
972-669-8993

QUICKBEAM SYSTEMS INC
4201 Yale Blvd NE Ste A
Albuquerque, NM 87107-4152
505-345-9230

QUIGLEY, SARAH
6770 Brown Rd
Parma, MI 49269-9684
517-531-4656

QUIKSERV BY M.C.E.
SYSTEMS CORP
11441 Brittmoore Park Dr
Houston, TX 77041-6919
www.quickserv.com
281-849-5882 • Fax 281-849-5708

QUIK-TO-FIX FOODS
9441 Lyndon B Johnson Fwy
Dallas, TX 75243-4545
972-690-7675

QUILL CORPORATION
100 Schelter Rd
Lincolnshire, IL 60069-3621
www.quillcorp.com
800-789-1331 • Fax 800-789-8955

QUINZANI BAKERS
380 Harrison Ave
Boston, MA 02118-2281
www.quinzanisbakery.com
617-426-2114 • Fax 617-451-8075

QUOIZEL, INC
590 Old Willets Path
Hauppauge, NY 11788-4106
631-273-2700 • Fax 631-231-7102

QUEST COMMUNICATIONS
555 17th St
Denver, CO 80202-3950
e-mail: jill.imwalle@quest.com
303-992-5956 • Fax 303-992-1015

R & R INDUSTRIES INC
1000 Calle Cordillera
San Clemente, CA 92673-6235
800-234-5611 • Fax 949-361-2731

R E L PRODUCTS
517 S 28th St
Van Buren, AR 72956-6119
479-474-3450

R S GLOBAL INC
1225 W College Ave
Carrollton, TX 75006-3682
800-451-6762

R S M MCGLADREY INC
100 NE 3rd Ave
Fort Lauderdale, FL 33301-1176
954-462-6300

R T D BEVERAGE
1201 Placetas Ave
Miami, FL 33146-3242
877-783-2383

R&D GROUP
INTERNATIONAL
11505 Pyramid Dr
Odessa, FL 33556-3457
e-mail: rdvdl@worldnet.att.net
www.berghoff-cookware.com
727-375-7523 • Fax 727-375-5424

R&M SPECIALTY SALES INC.
704 Ginesi Dr Ste 30
Morganville, NJ 07751-1235
800-976-7732 • Fax 732-972-4803

R.A.O. CONTRACT SALES
392 Atwood Pl
Wyckoff, NJ 07481-2322
e-mail: brian@rao.com
www.rao.thomasregister.com
201-652-1500 • Fax 973-279-6448

R.F. TECHNOLOGIES INC.
542 S Prairie St
Bethalto, IL 62010-1818
www.rfechno.com
618-377-2654 • Fax 618-377-1320

R.H.FORSHNER
1 Research Dr
Shelton, CT 06484-6223
www.swissarmy.com
800-243-4032 • Fax 800-243-4006

R.J.F. INTERNATIONAL
3875 Embassy Pkwy
Akron, OH 44333-8330
3306-687-600 • Fax 330-668-7703

R.L. SCHREIBER, INC.
1741 NW 33rd St
Pompano Beach, FL 33064-1327
954-972-7102 • Fax 954-972-1016

R.W. BEATY RESTAURANT
EQUIPMENT
4322 NW 13th St
Gainesville, FL 32609-1803
e-mail: beatyequip@aol.com
www.rwbeaty.com
352-376-5939

RABURN PRODUCTS
1060 Thorndale Ave
Elk Grove Village, IL 60007-6796
847-350-2229 • Fax 847-350-2657

RADEMAKER USA
PO Box 416
Hudson, OH 44236-0416
330-650-2345

RADER FOODS, INC
2900 NW 75th St Ste C200
Miami, FL 33147-5927
e-mail: sales@raderfoods.com
www.raderfoods.com
305-836-1711

RAFFIA
55 Myrtle St
Manhasset, NY 11030-2249
e-mail: raffiany@aol.com
516-869-3580 • Fax 516-869-3581

RAILEX
8902 Atlantic Ave
Ozone Park, NY 11416-1497
e-mail: railex@railexcorp.com
www.railexcorp.com
718-845-5454 • Fax 718-738-1020

RAINBOW SEAFOODS INC
PO Box 1345
Gloucester, MA 01931-1345
978-283-5103

RAINBOW SIGNS-SIGNS NOW
337 Highway 80 W
Jackson, MS 39201-6328
601-353-7711

RAINER NATURAL FOODS
38629 Auburn Enumclaw Rd SE
Auburn, WA 98092-9347
e-mail: bakery@Zipcon.net
253-833-4369 • Fax 253-833-5398

RAINSAFE
PO Box 154
Harrington Pk, NJ 07640-0154
e-mail: johnkim33@hotmail.com
www.rainsafe.com
201-944-5355 • Fax 201-944-9077

RALPH MARLIN & COMPANY
1050 Walnut Ridge Dr
Hartland, WI 53029-8303
www.ralphmarlin.com
262-369-8800 • Fax 262-369-8810

RAM CENTER-AUTOMATED
EQUIPMENT
5128 Moundview Dr
Red Wing, MN 55066-1100
www.ram-aeg.com
651-385-2273 • Fax 651-385-2166

RAMCO INC.
81 Henry St Unit C
East Stroudsburg, PA 18301-2406
570-476-8006 • Fax 570-476-9943

RAMESYS (HOSPITALITY) INC
10 Parsonage Rd
Edison, NJ 08837-2429
e-mail: enquiry@us.ramesys.com
www.us.ramesys.com
800RAMESYS • Fax 732-321-4149

RANDALLOS INC.
PO Box 9766
Ft. Lauderdale, FL 33310-9766
954-524-0425 • Fax 954-467-5862

RANDELL MFG INC
520 S Coldwater Rd
Weidman, MI 48893-9683
www.randell.com
989-644-3331 • Fax 989-644-3186

RANDOLPH ROSE
COLLECTION
500 Nepperhan Ave
Yonkers, NY 10701-6602

e-mail: nybronze@aol.com
914-423-2047 • Fax 914-423-2095

RANDY OUZTS
GARDEN SENSE INC
1034 Marys Grove Rd
Cherryville, NC 28021-9613
704-435-4836 • Fax 704-435-4400

RANGE PACKING COMPANY
2255 Aberdeen St
Kenner, LA 70062-7911
504-469-2333

RANKIN-DELUX, INC.
PO Box 4488
Whittier, CA 90607-4488
562-944-7076

RAPID FIRE SOLUTIONS
5529 NW Five Oaks Dr
Hillsboro, OR 97124-9340
503-645-0300

RAPIDPAY CORPORATION
370 Lexington Ave
New York, NY 10017-6503
e-mail: azar54@aol.com
www.rapidpays.com
212-697-4441 • Fax 212-69-71611

RAPP COLLINS
COMMUNICATIONS
901 Marquette Ave # 1
Minneapolis, MN 55402-3205
612-373-3000 • Fax 612-373-3063

RASPBERRY ON-LINE FOOD
MENUS
3166 N Lincoln Ave Ste 314
Chicago, IL 60657-3119
773-929-8663

RATIONAL COOKING SYSTEMS
455 E State Pkwy Ste 101
Schaumburg, IL 60173-4575
e-mail: edianea@rationalusa.com
www.rationalusa.com
847-273-2904

RATIONAL COOKING SYSTEMS
455 E State Pkwy Ste 201
Schaumburg, IL 60173-4579
www.rationalusa.com
847-273-2900 • Fax 847-755-9584

RATIONAL COOKING SYSTEMS
455 E State Pkwy
Schaumburg, IL 60173-4561
www.rationalusa.com
847-884-9950 • Fax 847-755-9583

RAYMOND CORP THE
PO Box 130
Greene, NY 13778-0130
800-235-7200

RAYMOND JAMES &
ASSOCIATES
991 US Highway 22 Ste 200
Bridgewater, NJ 08807-2957
908-704-1060

RAYS ICE CREAM
4233 Coolidge Hwy
Royal Oak, MI 48073-1696
248-549-5256

RAYTEK
1201 Shaffer Rd
Santa Cruz, CA 95060-5761
www.raytek.com
831-458-1175 • Fax 831-425-4561

RB INDUSTRIES
9919 Prospect Ave
Santee, CA 92071-4318
www.rbindustries.com
619-448-3930 • Fax 619-449-7124

RBB ASSOCIATES
20408 Altavista Way
Ashburn, VA 20147-3301
703-729-0606

RBS COMPUTER CORP.
7 Short Hills Ave
Short Hills, NJ 07078-2504
e-mail: sales@rbscc.com
www.rbscc.com
973-379-3957 • Fax 973-379-6957

RCI, INC.
510 Douglas Ave Ste 101
Altamonte Springs, FL 32714-2530
407-389-1802 • Fax 407-389-1802

RDS OF FLORIDA
380 S North Lake Blvd
Altamonte Springs, FL 32701-5260
e-mail: marketing@rdsflorida.com
www.rdsflorida.com
407-831-2011

READI-BAKE INC
301 28th St SE
Grand Rapids, MI 49548-1107
616-975-1540

READI-BAKE, INC.
2660 Horizon Dr SE Ste A
Grand Rapids, MI 49546-7933
616-246-1540

READING PRETZEL
380 Old West Penn Ave
Robesonia, PA 19551-8949
610-693-5816

READY ACCESS
1815 Arthur Rd
West Chicago, IL 60185-1601
630-778-3700

READY ACCESS, INC.
1845 Arthur Rd
West Chicago, IL 60185-1601
www.ready-access.com
630-876-7766 • Fax 630-876-7767

READY CARE INDUSTRIES
6870 Broadway
Denver, CO 80221-2867
303-427-4566

READY PAC
4401 Foxdale St
Baldwin Park, CA 91706-2196
626-261-3422

REAL SAUSAGE CO.
2710 S Poplar Ave
Chicago, IL 60608-5909
312-842-5330 • Fax 312-842-5414

REAL TIME COMPUTER CORP.
225 Santa Monica Blvd Ste 1208
Santa Monica, CA 90401-2217
310-393-3767

RECKITT & COLMAN FS FOODS
901 E Saint Louis St Fl 1800
Springfield, MO 65806-2548
41-837-1800

RECKITT BENCKISER
FS FOODS
1655 Valley Rd
Wayne, NJ 07470-2044
973-633-3600

RECOGNITION CONCEPTS
13985 Diplomat Dr
Dallas, TX 75234-8805
www.rcipromotions.com
972-241-8333 • Fax 972-241-5302

RECRUIT AMERICA
PERSONNEL SERVICES
9525 Katy Fwy Ste 203
Houston, TX 77024-1414
713-973-2525 • Fax 713-973-8989

RED ARMY VODKA-HPG,INC
8380 Miramar Mall Ste 226
San Diego, CA 92121-2550
www.redarmy.com
858-677-9374 • Fax 619-667-9385

RED BARONS ANTIQUES
6320 Roswell Rd NE
Atlanta, GA 30328-3210
404-252-3770

RED BULL ENERGY DRINK
5048 Addison Cir
Addison, TX 75001-3332
972-661-2855 • Fax 972-661-2151

RED BULL NORTH AMERICA
1453 3rd Street Promenade
Santa Monica, CA 90401-2397
www.redbull.com
310-393-4647 • Fax 310-230-2361

RED BULL NORTH AMERICA
550 Elmwood Park Blvd Ste B
New Orleans, LA 70123-6800
504-734-3883 • Fax 504-734-3884

RED BULL NORTH AMERICA
1818 Weber St
Orlando, FL 32803-3368
e-mail: dallas.mcrae@redbull-us.com
407-896-8286 • Fax 407-896-9041

RED KAP IMAGE APPAREL
545 Marriott Dr
Nashville, TN 37214-5011
www.redkap.com
615-391-1200 • Fax 615-882-2364

RED KOALA CEILING RESTORATION
544 E Ogden Ave Ste 70
Milwaukee, WI 53202-2698
www.redkoala.com
414-406-7335

RED LION HOTELS
201 NE Park Plaza Dr
Vancouver, WA 98684-5808
360-696-0001

RED LOBSTER RESTAURANTS
PO Box 593330
Orlando, FL 32859-3330
e-mail: careers@redlobster.com
www.redlobster.com
407-245-6082 • Fax 407-245-6037

RED PARROT
PO Box 425
Lyons, IL 60534-0425
708-442-2007 • Fax 708-447-0188

RED ROBIN INTERNATIONAL
5575 Dtc Pkwy Ste 110
Englewood, CO 80111-3012
e-mail: rfix@redrobin.com
303-331-2519 • Fax 303-331-2558

RED ROOF INN
121 E Nationwide Blvd
Columbus, OH 43215-2500
614-850-7777

RED ROSE SALES & MARKETING
PO Box 888
Zebulon, NC 27597-0888
919-269-6060 • Fax 919-269-7739

RED WING SHOE COMPANY
314 Main St
Red Wing, MN 55066-2300
www.redwingshoes.com
651-388-8211 • Fax 651-385-0897

REDBOW INDUSTRIES LLC
PO Box 775
Redmond, WA 98073-0775
425-376-2827

REDD PEST CONTROL INC.
3740 Florida Ave Ste 3
Kenner, LA 70065-3032
504-464-0073

REDHOOK BREWERY
35 Corporate Dr
Portsmouth, NH 03801-7852
www.redhook.com
603-430-8600 • Fax 603-430-6011

REDI-CUT FOODS KC - KANSAS CITY
3951 NE Kimball Dr
Kansas City, MO 64161-9480
816-371-4466

REDI-CUT FOODS, INC.
9501 Nevada Ave
Franklin Park, IL 60131-3331
847-288-2200 • Fax 847-288-2205

REED & BARTON
144 W Britannia St
Taunton, MA 02780-1643
508-824-6611

REEL SMOKERS CIGAR DISTRIBUTOR
504 S Federal Hwy
Deerfield Beach, FL 33441-4112
954-429-1335

REESE HENRY & COMPANY, INC.
400 E Main St
Aspen, CO 81611-2943
970-925-3771

REEVES
51 Newcomb St
Attleboro, MA 02703-1420
508-222-2877

REFCON
118 Railroad Ave
West Haverstraw, NY 10993-1416
e-mail: sales@refconcase.com
www.refconcase.com
845-786-5500 • Fax 845-786-0076

REFINISHING TOUCH
9350 Industrial Ter
Alpharetta, GA 30004-3383
800-523-9448

REFRIGERATED CONSTRUCTION SERVICE
9637 Palm River Rd
Tampa, FL 33619-4433
813-663-9500

REFRIGERATED WAREHOUSE MARKETING
1652 Sumner Ave
Claremont, CA 91711-3036
909-625-4512 • Fax 909-625-4612

REGAL CUSTOM FIXTURE CO
PO Box 446
Mount Holly, NJ 08060-0446
609-261-3323 • Fax 609-261-4929

REGAL INTERNATIONAL
3101 S Harbor Blvd
Santa Ana, CA 92704-6826
www.regalinternational.com
714-424-6320 • Fax 714-424-6322

REGAL SPRINGS TRADING CO.
PO Box 392
Bradenton, FL 34206-0392
941-729-3059

REGAL WARE , INC.
1675 Reigle Dr
Kewaskum, WI 53040-8923
www.regalware.com
262-626-8503 • Fax 262-626-8532

REGENCY WRAPS, INC.
10734 N Stemmons Fwy
Dallas, TX 75220-2420
www.regencywraps.com
214-357-0099 • Fax 214-352-1029

REGION BANK NOVA
9590 Florida Blvd
Baton Rouge, LA 70815-1125
225-922-8009

REGIONS BANK-NOVA
5353 Essen Ln Ste 500
Baton Rouge, LA 70809-0504
225-767-9359 • Fax 225-767-9317

REGO CORPORATION
200 Broadhollow Rd Ste 400
Melville, NY 11747-4806
516-753-3700

REIGN DOWN BREAD SPREAD, INC
PO Box 671
Blessing, TX 77419-0671
361-588-6514

REILLY DAIRY & FOOD COMPANY
PO Box 19217
Tampa, FL 33686-9217
813-839-8458

REIMBURSEMENT CONSULTANTS
433 Metairie Rd Ste 403
Metairie, LA 70005-4343
504-835-4240

REINHART FOODSERVICE
9950 S Reinhart Dr
Oak Creek, WI 53154-4949
www.reinhartfoodservice.com
414-761-5000 • Fax 414-761-4780

REISER ROBERT & CO
725 Dedham St
Canton, MA 02021-1402
781-821-1290

REMCO SOFTWARE INC
30 S State Ave
Dickinson, ND 58601-5594
701-225-8336

REMCO SOFTWARE INC.
38 S State Ave
Dickinson, ND 58601-5594
e-mail: remco@remcosoftware.com
www.remcosoftware.com
701-225-4033 • Fax 701-225-2433

REMY AMERIQUE
1350 Avenue Of The Americas
New York, NY 10019-4702
212-399-4200

RENATO SPECIALTY PRODUCTS, INC
2775 W Kingsley Rd
Garland, TX 75041-2406
www.renatos.com
972-864-8800 • Fax 972-864-8900

RENDER
1800 Elmwood Ave
Buffalo, NY 14207-2410
e-mail: cheryl@render1800.com
www.render1800.com
716-447-1010 • Fax 716-447-8918

RENTALS UNLIMITED
31 Tosca Dr
Stoughton, MA 02072-1507
781-341-1600 • Fax 781-341-8840

RENTOKIL PEST CONTROL
4067 Industrial Park Dr
Norcross, GA 30071-1638
e-mail: chm@rentokilusa.com
www.rentokilusa.com
800-732-3716

REPUBLIC BEVERAGE COMPANY
9835 Genard Rd
Houston, TX 77041-7623
www.republicbeverage.com
713-690-8888 • Fax 713-690-1169

REQUEST FOODS
PO Box 2577
Holland, MI 49422-2577
616-786-0900 • Fax 616-786-9180

RESERS
15570 SW Jenkins Rd
Beaverton, OR 97006-6099
800-333-6431 • Fax 503-646-9233

RESERS FINE FOODS
PO Box 8
Beaverton, OR 97075-0008
503-643-6431

RESER'S FINE FOODS
624 Brownwood Ave SE
Atlanta, GA 30316-3804
e-mail: kassler@mindspring.com
404-627-8877 • Fax 404-622-1398

RESERVATION SOURCE
50 Briar Hollow Ln Ste 490W
Houston, TX 77027-9322
www.reservationsource.com
713-751-7503 • Fax 713-751-7580

RESERVE INTERACTIVE BY EFFICIENT FRONTIERS
2664 Crescent Ct
Livermore, CA 94550-6843
www.efficient-frontiers.com
925-606-7597 • Fax 925-443-9641

RESORT CONDOMINIUMS INTERNATIONAL
PO Box 2070
Carmel, IN 46082-2070
317-871-9644

RESOURCES IN FOOD - FOOD TEAM
3901 Main St Ste 200
Kansas City, MO 64111-1927
816-756-3233

RESPONSIBLE VENDORS, INC.
1111 Park Center Blvd
Miami, FL 33169-5365
305-628-2428 • Fax 305-628-2515

REST SUP SERV FIN SERV-MEDIA
800 N Clark St Ste 311
Chicago, IL 60610-3262
312-573-0102

REST. & CAFE. CONSULTANTS, INC
144 Railroad Ave Ste 220
Edmonds, WA 98020-4121
206-283-4993

RESTAR INC.
160 Oak St # 1
Glastonbury, CT 06033-2399
www.restar.com
860-657-3099 • Fax 860-657-3662

RESTAURANT ADVISORY SERVICES
1265 Drummers Ln Ste 300
Wayne, PA 19087-1570
610-254-8999

RESTAURANTBUILDER.COM
8955 S Ridgeline Blvd Ste
Littleton, CO 80129-2362
www.restaurantbuilder.com
303-346-1444 • Fax 303-346-1434

RESTAURANT BUSINESS MAGAZINE
770 Broadway
New York, NY 10003-9522
www.foodservicetoday.com
212-645-4500

RESTAURANT CONSULTANT
360 W 5th Ave
Columbus, OH 43201-3163
800 859-7201

RESTAURANT CONSULTANTS INC
360 N 5th St
Columbus, OH 43215-2103
vrestcon@earthlink.net
www.guestrak.com
614-421-1441

RESTAURANT CONSULTANTS, INC.
216 Foxcroft Rd
Broomall, PA 19008-2039
610-325-3663

RESTAURANT CONSULTING GROUP
9801 Westheimer Rd Ste 302
Houston, TX 77042-3955
713-783-6171

RESTAURANT CONSULTING GROUP
8930 Gross Point Rd
Skokie, IL 60077-1854
847-965-0303

RESTAURANT DATABASE SERVICES
125 NW 43rd St
Boca Raton, FL 33431-4254
e-mail:
info@restaurantdbservices.com
561-367-9432 • Fax 561-995-0820

RESTAURANT DEPORT
105 Embarcadero
Oakland, CA 94606-5138
510-628-0600 • Fax 510-496-9760

RESTAURANT DEPOT
1030 W Division St
Chicago, IL 60622-4205
312-255-9800 • Fax 312-255-1530

RESTAURANT DEPOT
1524 132nd St
College Point, NY 11356-2440
718-939-0510 • Fax 718-939-2680

RESTAURANT DEPOT
5250 S 6th St
Milwaukee, WI 53221-3664
www.restaurantdepot.com
414-483-1800 • Fax 414-483-2996

RESTAURANT DEPOT
253 Williams St
Chelsea, MA 02150-3806
617-889-2244

RESTAURANT DEV. SERVICES
2434 S Walter Reed Dr Apt A
Arlington, VA 22206-1181
703-671-7639

RESTAURANT EFFCIENCIES
903 Ashbury St Apt 3
San Francisco, CA 94117-4427
www.ordersmart.com
415-504-6500 • Fax 415-680-1605

RESTAURANT EQUIP. & SUPP.
PO Box 783
Mishawaka, IN 46546-0783
574-258-5785

RESTAURANT FORUM MAGAZINE
PO Box 195504
Winter Springs, FL 32719-5504
e-mail: restr4um@aol.com
www.restaurantforum.com
407-699-8275

RESTAURANT MAGIC
1323 W Fletcher Ave
Tampa, FL 33612-3310
e-mail: lutz@rmagic.com
www.restaurantmagic.com
813-269-8222

RESTAURANT MAGIC
5301 W Cypress St Ste 1
Tampa, FL 33607-1727
e-mail: abeckett@rmagic.com
813-288-2633 • Fax 813-288-2623

RESTAURANT MANAGEMENT COMPANY
3020 N Cypress Dr Ste 100
Wichita, KS 67226-4010
316-684-5119

RESTAURANT MANAGEMENT SERVICES
28364 S Western Ave # 314
Rancho Palos Verdes, CA 90275-1434
310-831-5985

RESTAURANT MARKET.COM
495 Broadway
New York, NY 10012-4457
212-274-0442 • Fax 212-274-0302

RESTAURANT PARTNERS, INC.
112 E Concord St
Orlando, FL 32801-1308
407-839-5070

RESTAURANT REPORT
811 N Fairway Rd
Glenside, PA 19038-1406
e-mail: rbickell@restaurant.com
www.restaurant.com
215-884-2686 • Fax 215-884-2509

RESTAURANT RESULTS
4521 Pga Blvd Ste 326
West Palm Beach, FL 33418-3997
561-625-3215

RESTAURANT TECHNOLOGIES INC
940 Apollo Rd # 110
Saint Paul, MN 55121-2203
e-mail: salesinfo@rti-inc.com
www.rti.inc.com
877-833-8048

RESTAURANT TECHNOLOGIES, INC.
1039 Miller Dr
Altamonte Springs, FL 32701-2067
407-834-2680 • Fax 407-834-4008

RESTAURANT WINE
PO Box 222
Napa, CA 94559-0222
800-243-8847

RESTAURANT.COM, INC
304 Park Ave S
New York, NY 10010-5339
212-512-0570 • Fax 212-512-0572

RESTAURANTMARKET.COM
3842 N Old Dixie Hwy
Delray Beach, FL 33483-6322

RESTAURANTPRO.COM
150 California St
San Francisco, CA 94111-4500
415-277-0150

RESTAURANTSURVEYS.COM
412 W Broadway
Glendale, CA 91204-4117
www.resturantsurveys.com
888-364-7464 • Fax 818-242-3975

RESTONIC MATTRESS CORP
9450 Bryn Mawr Ave
Des Plaines, IL 60018-5248
708-671-1616

RESTONIC MATTRESS CORP.
9450 Bryn Mawr Ave Ste 640
Des Plaines, IL 60018-5276
e-mail: restonicrf@aol.com
www.restonic.com
847-671-1616 • Fax 847-671-1676

RETAIL & REST. GROWTH CAPITAL
10000 N Central Expy Ste 1060
Dallas, TX 75231-2323
214-750-0065

RETAIL AUTOMATION PRODUCTS
45 W 38th St
New York, NY 10018-5511
vrappos@aol.com
212-391-6500 • Fax 212-391-0575

RETAIL CONTROL SOLUTIONS
1300 Mark St
Bensenville, IL 60106-1044
www.rcs-usa.com
630-521-9900 • Fax 630-521-1994

RETAIL CONTROL SOLUTIONS
460 Hillside Ave
Needham Heights, MA 02494-1279
e-mail: info@wefixmicros.com
www.wefixmicros.com
781-444-7300 • Fax 781-444-7882

RETAIL CONTROL SOLUTIONS INC
9 Junction Dr W Ste 7
Glen Carbon, IL 62034-2931
800-767-2212

RETAIL DATA
106 Greystone Ave
Kansas City, KS 66103-1394
913-281-1333

RETAIL DATA SYSTEMS OF CHICAGO
421 Eisenhower Ln S
Lombard, IL 60148-5706
847-495-4100

RETAIL DATA SYSTEMS OF WISCONSIN
1900 Pewaukee Rd Ste M
Waukesha, WI 53188-2447
262-896-2600 • Fax 262-896-2605

RETAIL ENTERPRISE
3925 Brookside Pkwy
Alpharetta, GA 30022-4429
www.retailenterprise.com
770-576-6000 • Fax 678-360-7320

RETAIL HOSPITALITY SYSTEMS, INC
725 River Rd Ste 104
Edgewater, NJ 07020-1170
e-mail: billytouch@aol.com
201-945-6677 • Fax 201-945-7186

RETAIL REAL ESTATE CONSULTANTS
7731 Tuckerman Ln Ste 195
Potomac, MD 20854-3266
301-762-4067

RETAILER'S BAKERY ASSOC.
14239 Park Center Dr
Laurel, MD 20707-5261

RETRIEVER
PO Box 24034
New Orleans, LA 70184-4034
504-282-8494 • Fax 504-282-8493

RETROAIRE
5780 Success Dr
Rome, NY 13440-1743
315-336-3716

REVENT INC
12 Worlds Fair Dr Ste L
Somerset, NJ 08873-1348
www.revent.com
732-356-6177 • Fax 732-356-7557

REVOLUTION TEA
204 S River Dr
Tempe, AZ 85281-3056
www.revolutiontea.com
480-731-9555 • Fax 480-731-9661

REXCRAFT FINE CHAFERS
4139 38th St
Long Island City, NY 11101-1708
718-361-3052 • Fax 718-361-3054

REYNOLDS METALS
6603 W Broad St
Richmond, VA 23230-1701
www.rmc.com-foodservice
804-281-3369 • Fax 804-281-3289

REYNOLDS METALS CO
6601 W Broad St
Richmond, VA 23230-1723
804-281-2000

REYNOLD'S MEXICAN FOOD COMPANY
4911 Mason St
South Gate, CA 90280-3518
323-560-8420 • Fax 323-567-0997

RGE DISTRIBUTING CO, INC.
PO Box 68
Oldsmar, FL 34677-0068
e-mail: rgewafffles@aol.com
www.rgewaffles.com
800-814-0606

RHEEM NATIONAL ACCOUNTS
5887 Glenridge Dr NE Ste 400
Atlanta, GA 30328-5577
770-256-5321

RHEON
9490 Toledo Way
Irvine, CA 92618-1804
949-768-1900 • Fax 949-855-19991

RHEON USA
13400 Reese Blvd W
Huntersville, NC 28078-7925
704-875-9191 • Fax 704-875-9595

RHODES INTERNATIONAL INC
PO Box 25487
Salt Lake City, UT 84125-0487
801-972-0122

RIB CRIB
4271 W Albany St
Broken Arrow, OK 74012-1233
e-mail: cabney@ribcrib.com
Fax 918-459-0699

RIBA FOODS, INC.
3735 Arc St
Houston, TX 77063-5235
www.ribafoods.com
713-975-7001 • Fax 713-975-7036

RICH PRODUCTS
1150 Niagara St
Buffalo, NY 14213-1797
716-878-8000

RICH PRODUCTS
PO Box 511
Brookfield, WI 53008-0511
262-784-8426 • Fax 2627-840-571

RICHARD COOPER
1800 S Ocean Blvd
Boca Raton, FL 33432-8534
561-395-3965

RICHARD DANIELS ASSOCIATES
60 Revere Dr Ste 800
Northbrook, IL 60062-1580
847-433-0900 • Fax 847-433-7873

RICHARD'S RESTAURANT SUPPLY
PO Box 4035
Houma, LA 70361-4035
985-868-9240 • Fax 985-872-9160

RICHARDSON BRANDS CO.
6330 Manor Ln Ste 200
Miami, FL 33143-4953
305-667-3291 • Fax 305-667-5180

RICHARDSON SEATING CORPORATION
2545 W Arthington St
Chicago, IL 60612-4107
www.richardsonseating.com
312-829-4040 • Fax 312-829-8337

RICHELIEU FOODS, INC.
2215 Sanders Rd
Northbrook, IL 60062-6126
847-480-2900 • Fax 847-480-2914

RICHLOOM CONTRACT FIBERS
261 5th Ave
New York, NY 10016-7701
212-685-2187

RICHMAN, INC.
1941 Lakewind Dr
Bloomfield Hills, MI 48302-0156
248-335-0916

RICHMOND TEXTILES INC
900 N Franklin St
Chicago, IL 60610-8100
312-944-8787 • Fax 312-944-8910

RICHWOOD IMPORTS, INC.
1510 E Cedar St
Ontario, CA 91761-5761
909-930-6677 • Fax 909-930-9927

RICOH TECHNOLOGIES INC.
1022 Santerre St
Grand Prairie, TX 75050-1937
www.aquaprofryer.com
972-602-1155 • Fax 972-602-3126

RIEDEL CRYSTAL OF AMERICA
24 Aero Rd
Bohemia, NY 11716-2902
631-567-7515 • Fax 631-567-7039

RIEGEL TABLE LINES - MOUNT VERN
51 Riegel Rd
Johnston, SC 29832-2715
www.riegellinen.com
800-845-2232 • Fax 803-275-2219

RIGO INDUSTRIES
50 California Ave
Paterson, NJ 07503-2518
973-881-1780 • Fax 973-881-0906

RIMANN & ASSOCIATES
1722 Westwood Blvd Ste 201
Los Angeles, CA 90024-5610
e-mail: rimann@world.att.net
www.rimann.com
310-441-7333 • Fax 310-441-7336

RINGLEIN CONSULTING (F&B RES.)
263 Ohina Pl
Kihei, HI 96753-8503

RINO GNESI COMPANY, INC.
410 Riverside Ave
Medford, MA 02155-4949
www.rinognesico.com
781-395-8821 • Fax 781-395-9399

RISING SUN FARMS
5126 S Pacific Hwy
Phoenix, OR 97535-6606
www.risingsunfarms.com
514-535-8331 • Fax 541-535-8350

RISVOLDS
1234 W El Segundo Blvd
Gardena, CA 90247-1593
risvolds@aol.com
323-770-2674 • Fax 323-770-0800

RITCHIE ASSOCIATES
1025 Crest Valley Dr NW
Atlanta, GA 30327-4669
404-847-0359

RITCHIE ASSOCIATES INC
1073 Huff Rd NW # C
Atlanta, GA 30318-4129
404-888-9951 • Fax 404-888-0925

RITE HITE - TRAXXELL
8900 N Arbon Dr
Milwaukee, WI 53223-2472
800-456-0600

RITE WAY SALES & MARKETING
PO Box 24539
Lakeland, FL 33802-4539
e-mail: dsweat@ritewayfoods.com
863-646-4319 • Fax 863-648-1406

RIVELLA (USA) INC.
3100 NW Boca Raton Blvd
Boca Raton, FL 33431-6650
www.rivella-usa.com
561-417-5810 • Fax 561-417-5811

RIVER INC DAN
2291 Memorial Dr
Danville, VA 24541-4741
434-799-7000

RIVER RANCH FRESH FOODS
1156 Abbott St
Salinas, CA 93901-4503
800-538-5868 • Fax 831-755-8281

RIVERSIDE SEA FOODS
2520 Wilson St
Two Rivers, WI 54241-2397
920-793-4511 • Fax 920-794-7332

RIVIANA FOODS INC.
2777 Allen Pkwy
Houston, TX 77019-2141
713-525-9543 • Fax 713-529-1661

RIXIE PAPER PRODUCTS
10 Quinter St
Pottstown, PA 19464-6514
610-323-9200

RIXIE PAPER PRODUCTS
4016 Blue Ridge Industrial Pkw
Norcross, GA 30071-1601

RJ REYNOLDS TOBACCO CO.
401 N Main St
Winston Salem, NC 27101-3804
336-741-2418

RMS TOUCH
2350 Westminster Ter
Ovied, FL 32765-7500
e-mail:
computerassistance@efl.rr.com
www.hospitalityspecialits.com
407-365-1991

ROBAR INTERNATIONAL INC.
3013 N 114th St
Milwaukee, WI 53222-4208
414-259-1104 • Fax 414-259-0842

ROBERN MIRRORED CABINETS
701 N Wilson Ave
Bristol, PA 19007-4517
www.kohlerco.com
215-826-9800

ROBERT ALLEN CONTRACT FABRICS
79 Madison Ave Fl 11
New York, NY 10016-7896
212-696-0535 • Fax 212-779-0241

ROBERT E. SPENCE CO.
34 Central Ave
Needham Heights, MA 02494-2914
e-mail: bspenceo@aol.com
781-449-1040 • Fax 781-455-8592

ROBERT E. KARDOS ASSOCIATES
52 Chenango Dr
Jericho, NY 11753-1523
mike@nytabletop.com
www.nytabletop.com
516-681-6670 • Fax 516-935-6739

ROBERT H. KAISER ASSOCIATES, INC.
159C Heritage Hls
Somers, NY 10589-1115
914-271-5525

ROBERT HALF-ACCOUNT TEMPS
3117 22nd St Ste 1
Metairie, LA 70002-4988
504-835-4296

ROBERT KAUFMAN PHOTOGRAPHY
PO Box 610415
Newton Highlands, MA 02461-0415
e-mail: silver@silvervisions.com
www.silvervisions.com
617-244-9504 • Fax 617-964-4081

ROBERT WAGNER, CPA
400 Colony Sq NE Ste 540
Atlanta, GA 30361-6314
404-874-7000

ROBERTS DAIRY
3805 Van Brunt Blvd
Kansas City, MO 64128-2356
816-921-7370

ROBERTSON
720 Elberton St
Toccoa, GA 30577-3649
Fax 706-281-2967

ROBERTSON STEPHENS & CO.
555 California St Ste 2600
San Francisco, CA 94104-1502
415-693-3426

ROBIN'S FOOD DISTRIBUTION INC
PO Box 617637
Chicago, IL 60661-7637
312-243-8800 • Fax 312-243-9495

ROBINSON C H CO
8100 Mitchell Rd Ste 200
Eden Prairie, MN 55344-2178
952-937-7854

ROBINSON DAIRY, INC.
646 Bryant St
Denver, CO 80204-4122
303-825-2990

ROBOT COUPE USA INC.
PO Box 16625
Jackson, MS 39236-6625
www.robotcoupeusa.com
601-824-1646 • Fax 601-898-8411

ROBOT COUPE USA, INC.
280 S Perkins St # 16625
Ridgeland, MS 39157-2719
800-824-1646 • Fax 601-898-9134

ROCCO, INC.
PO Box 549
Harrisonburg, VA 22801-0549
800-336-4003 • Fax 540-568-1401

ROCHE
150 Clove Rd
Little Falls, NJ 07424-2138
973-235-5000

ROCHE DIAGNOSTICS
1080 US Highway 202 S
Somerville, NJ 08876-3771
908-253-7200

ROCHELLE GROUP LIMITED
164 N Route 303 Unit 3
Congers, NY 10920-1761
845-634-8302

ROCHESTER INSTITUTE OF TECHNOLOGY
14 Lomb Memorial Dr
Rochester, NY 14623-5604
www.rit.edu
585-475-2608 • Fax 585-475-5099

ROCHESTER MEATS
1825 7th St NW
Rochester, MN 55901-0288
507-289-0701 • Fax 507-289-1864

ROCK SYSTEMS
11551 Forest Central Dr Ste 32
Dallas, TX 75243-3920
214-340-4080

ROCKLAND TECHNOLOGY CORP
921 N Mill St
Lewisville, TX 75057-3172
972-221-6190

ROCKLAND TECHNOLOGY CORP
817 S Mill St Ste 104
Lewisville, TX 75057-4637
www.rocklandtech.com
972-221-6190 • Fax 972-420-0055

ROCK-OLA
2335 W 208th St
Torrance, CA 90501-6209
310-328-1306 • Fax 310-328-3736

RODER USA
1954 N 30th Rd
Hollywood, FL 33021-4401
800-432-5091

RODS FOOD
17380 Railroad St
Rowland Heights, CA 91748-1091
626-912-1671 • Fax 626-964-5447

ROGER & SONS, INC.
268 Bowery
New York, NY 10012-3501
e-mail: rogerandsons@ aol.com
212-226-0721 • Fax 212-226-7103

ROLAND INDUSTRIES
2280 Chaffee Dr
Saint Louis, MO 63146-3304
800-325-1183

ROLAND SAFE & LOCK
1926 Airline Dr
Metairie, LA 70001-5983
504-835-7233

ROLLFIX USA
7540 W 160th St
Stilwell, KS 66085-8100
913-764-0622

ROLLHAUS SEATING PRODUCTS
134 Grand St
New York, NY 10013-3104
www.rolhaus-seating.com
212-334-1111 • Fax 212-941-8193

ROMANCING PROVENCE LTD.
225 5th Ave Ste 502
New York, NY 10010-8266
e-mail:
sales@romancingprovence.com
www.romancingprovence.com
212-481-9879 • Fax 212-481-9875

ROMERO'S FOOD PRODUCTS
15155 Valley View Ave
Santa Fe Springs, CA 90670-5323
562-802-1858 • Fax 562-921-7240

RON HYMAN & ASSOCIATES
201 Bienville Dr
Waveland, MS 39576-4307
228-467-0039

RONDO INC
75 Atlantic St
Hackensack, NJ 07601-4132
201-488-0121

RONNOCO COFFEE COMPANY
4241 Sarpy Ave
Saint Louis, MO 63110-1704
314-371-5050

RON'S LIGHTING, INC.
11659 W 29th St
Zion, IL 60099-9761
www.ronslighting.com
800-359-4569 • Fax 847-872-8550

ROOSEVELT UNIVERSITY
430 S Michigan Ave
Chicago, IL 60605-1313
www.roosevelt.edu
312-341-4321 • Fax 312-341-2417

ROSE PACKING CO
65 S Barrington Rd
Barrington, IL 60010-9589
www.rosepacking.com
847-381-5700 • Fax 847-381-9436

ROSEN PRODUCTS
1020 Owen Loop N
Eugene, OR 97402-9173
e-mail: info@rosenproducts.com
www.rosenproducts.com
541-994-4422 • Fax 541-342-4912

ROSENTHAL USA LTD
355 Michele Pl
Carlstadt, NJ 07072-2304
201-804-8000

ROSINA FOOD PRODUCTS
6633 N Mesa St
El Paso, TX 79912-4427
888-767-4621

ROSINA FOOD PRODUCTS
75 Industrial Pkwy
Buffalo, NY 14227-2777
e-mail: jchesier@rosina.com
www.rosina.com
716-668-0123 • Fax 716-668-1132

ROSITA BISANI IMPORTS
940 S La Brea Ave
Los Angeles, CA 90036-4808
www.rosito-bisani.com
323-397-1888 • Fax 323-938-0728

ROSITO BISANI EAST, INC.
1402 Fall River Ave
Seekonk, MA 02771-3711
508-336-2100 • Fax 508-336-2727

ROSEMARIE CARROLL
2 Bratenahl Pl Apt 1F
Cleveland, OH 44108-1187
216-691-3800

ROSMARINO FOODS
16216 Turnbury Oak Dr
Odessa, FL 33556-2870
e-mail: roger@rosmarinofoods.com
www.rosmarinofoods.com
813-926-9053

ROSS LABORATORY
625 Cleveland Ave
Columbus, OH 43215-1724
614-624-7677

ROSSBACH INTERNATIONAL TRADING
47 Portland Pl
Staten Island, NY 10301-2806
e-mail: ritcny@aol.com
www.fancyfoods.com
718-816-0423 • Fax 718-816-4513

ROTH KASE USA LTD.
PO Box 319
Monroe, WI 53566-0319
608-328-2122 • Fax 608-328-2120

ROTISOL-FRANCE INC
237 S La Brea Ave
Los Angeles, CA 90036-3022
323-933-7232

ROTO-GRAPHIC PRINTING CO.
PO Box 1495
Fond du Lac, WI 54936-1495
920-921-7150 • Fax 920-921-7209

ROUND TABLE OWNERS ASSOCIATION
422 Larkfield Ctr Ste 266
Santa Rosa, CA 95403-1408
707-823-0574

ROUSE COMPANY
10275 Little Patuxent Pkwy
Columbia, MD 21044-3455
410-992-6342

ROUTIN AMERICA INC.
PO Box 460003
Denver, CO 80246-0003
www.routin.com
303-300-0400 • Fax 303-300-0500

ROYAL FOODS, INC.
8900 SW 117th Ave
Miami, FL 33186-2175
305-271-2007 • Fax 305-271-2016

ROVERGARDEN USA
154 Tices Ln
East Brunswick, NJ 08816-2015
732-254-9167

ROWLAND DESIGN INC
701 E New York St
Indianapolis, IN 46202-3708
317-636-3980

ROY WALTERS PROVISION CO
3925 Burgundy St
New Orleans, LA 70117-5419
504-944-4110

ROYAL BALTIC
9829 Ditmas Ave
Brooklyn, NY 11236-1925
718-385-8300 • Fax 718-385-4757

ROYAL CROWN COLA
441 Route 202
Towaco, NJ 07082-1298
973-334-2617

ROYAL CUP COFFEE
2112 E Randol Mill Rd
Arlington, TX 76011-8217
817-661-7527

ROYAL CUP DINE MOR
160 Cleage Dr
Birmingham, AL 35217-1461
800-366-5836 • Fax 205-271-6016

ROYAL DOULTON
701 Cottontail Ln
Somerset, NJ 08873-1273
732-356-7880

ROYAL ENTERPRISES, INC.
170 Ludlow St
Yonkers, NY 10705-1746
www.urnex.com
914-963-2042 • Fax 914-963-2145

ROYAL HAEGER LAMP CO.
1300 W Piper St
Macomb, IL 61455-2741
309-837-9966 • Fax 309-837-5267

ROYAL INDUSTRIES
538 N Milwaukee Ave
Chicago, IL 60622-5963
312-733-4920 • Fax 312-733-9774

ROYAL INDUSTRIES, INC.
1768 W 1st St
Azusa, CA 91702-3259
626-812-4434 • Fax 626-812-4437

**ROYAL PACIFIC FOODS
(THE GINGER PEOPLE)**
2700 Garden Rd # G
Monterey, CA 93940-5337
www.gingerpeople.com
831-645-1090 • Fax 831-645-1094

ROYAL SCANDINAVIA
140 Bradford Dr
West Berlin, NJ 08091-9268
856-985-8740 • Fax 856-985-8749

ROYALE CHEF, INC.
2440 Railroad St
Corona, CA 92880-5418
www.prochef2000.com
877-459-6200 • Fax 909-549-9139

**ROYALTON FOODSERVICE
EQUIPMENT**
9981 York Theta Dr
North Royalton, OH 44133-3512
800-662-8765 • Fax 440-237-1694

ROYER CORPORATION
805 East St
Madison, IN 47250-3210
www.royercorp.com
800-457-8997 • Fax 812-265-3207

ROYSONS CORPORATION
40 Vanderhoof Ave
Rockaway, NJ 07866-3138
973-625-5570 • Fax 973-625-5917

RSI SERVICES
76 Midland Pl
Tuckahoe, NY 10707-4204
914-771-8000 • Fax 914-771-8009

RSVP UNIFORMS
4116 Progress Ave
Naples, FL 34104-7041
800-375-7787

RUBBAIR DOOR
100 Groton Shirley Rd
Ayer, MA 01432-1050
e-mail: rubbair@shore.net
www.rubbair.net
978-772-0480 • Fax 978-772-7114

RUBBERMAID
3124 Valley Ave
Winchester, VA 22601-2695
540-667-8700 • Fax 540-542-8838

**RUBBERMAID COMMERCIAL
PRODUCTS**
14531 Chimneywood Dr
Baton Rouge, LA 70816-2810
225-751-7339

**RUBBERMAID COMMERCIAL
PRODUCTS**
11 Bay St
Tilton, NH 03276-1602
e-mail: balove@msn.com
603-286-3021 • Fax 603-286-7091

RUBSCHLAGER BAKING
3220 W Grand Ave
Chicago, IL 60651-4180
312-826-1245

RUBY MFG. INCORPORATED
9853 Alpaca St
South El Monte, CA 91733-3101
626-443-1171 • Fax 626-443-0028

RUDI'S BAKERY, INC.
3640 Walnut St Ste B
Boulder, CO 80301-2500
vjjez@rudisbakery.com
303-447-0495 • Fax 303-447-0516

RUDY'S TORTILLAS
535 Regal Row
Dallas, TX 75247-5207
e-mail: national@rudystortillas.com
www.rudystortillas.com

RUG DOCTOR
4701 Old Shepard Pl
Plano, TX 75093-5218
www.rugdoctor.com
972-673-1492 • Fax 972-673-1403

RUGGIERO SEAFOOD, INC.
117 Avenue L
Newark, NJ 07105-3809
e-mail: steve@ruggieroseafood.com
www.ruggieroseafood.com
973-589-0524 • Fax 973-589-5690

RUIZ FOOD PRODUCTS
501 S Alta Ave
Dinuba, CA 93618-2100
559-591-1969

RUIZ FOOD PRUDUCTS
PO Box 37
Dinuba, CA 93618-0037
559-591-5510 • Fax 559-591-1968

RUMMEL ASSOCIATES
1561 Palisades Dr
Pacific Palisades, CA 90272-2104
310-573-9385 • Fax 310-573-9465

RUPRECHT
370 N Carpenter St
Chicago, IL 60607-1227
312-829-4100 • Fax 312-850-2875

RURAL INSURANCE COMPANIES
PO Box 5555
Madison, WI 53705-0555
www.ruralins.com
608-836-5525 • Fax 608-828-5442

RUSSELL HARRINGTON CO.
44 River St
Southbridge, MA 01550-1834
508-765-0201

RUSSELL HARRINGTON CUTLERY
615 N Riverside Dr Ste 20
Pompano Beach, FL 33062-4743
954-784-1494

RUSSER FOODS
665 Perry St
Buffalo, NY 14210-1384
800-828-7021 • Fax 716-826-5138

**RX AIR DIV OF CLEAN AIR
RESEARCH**
13711 Omega Dr
Dallas, TX 75244-4517
e-mail: sales@rxair.com
www.rxair.com
972-233-2777 • Fax 972-233-0533

RYAN MILK - DEAN DAIRY
100 Chestnut St
Murray, KY 42071-2100
800-626-3932

RYAN TECHNOLOGY
2705 SE 39th Loop
Hillsboro, OR 97123-8415
800-277-2290

RYDER SYSTEM INC
3600 NW 82nd Ave
Miami, FL 33166-6623
305-500-3726

RZ REGISTER RESALE
2020 Silver Bell Rd
Saint Paul, MN 55122-1050
612-454-0383

S & G PACKAGING
205 N Michigan Ave
Chicago, IL 60601-5927
www.sgpack.com
312-565-1200 • Fax 312-856-8180

S & H UNIFORM CORP.
200 William St
Port Chester, NY 10573-4620
www.s-huniform.com
800-210-5295 • Fax 914-937-0741

S & S BUSINESS SYSTEMS, LNC.
12323 S Choctaw Dr
Baton Rouge, LA 70815-2122
225-275-2795 • Fax 225-275-2887

**S & S CONTRACT
FURNITURE INC.**
1025 Miller Dr
Altamonte Springs, FL 32701-2082
www.ssfurniture.com
407-767-6515 • Fax 407-767-8389

S & V RESTAURANT EQUIP
4320 Park Ave
Bronx, NY 10457-2442
718-220-1140 • Fax 718-364-1764

**S & W INTERNATIONAL FOOD
SPECIALTIES**
PO Box 787
Forest Park, GA 30298-0787
404-363-1199 • Fax 404-363-1427

S A F PRODUCTS
400 S 4th St
Minneapolis, MN 55415-1411
800-641-4615

S A S I B
7515 Linder Ave
Skokie, IL 60077-3223
847-677-7800

S C A PROMOTIONS
8300 Douglas Ave
Dallas, TX 75225-5603
972-860-3717

**S C S SUPPLY CHAIN
SOLUTIONS**
502 10th Ave N
Auburn, WA 98001-6551
253-833-7233

S C SYSTEM
1 Columbus Pl
New York, NY 10019-8200
212-765-7690

S F GLASSWORKS
7117 Atwell Dr
Houston, TX 77081-6007
713-665-1784

S I G PACK SYSTEMS
2401 Brentwood Rd
Raleigh, NC 27604-3686
919-877-0886

S K G
200 N Central Ave
Hartsdale, NY 10530-1991
e-mail: efusxo@skginsurance.com
www.skginsurance.com
914-761-9000 • Fax 914-761-3749

S L D LIGHTING
318 W 47th St
New York, NY 10036-3101
212-245-4155

SPI POLYOLS INC
321 Cherry Ln
New Castle, DE 19720-2780
302-576-8545

SRS HOTELS
152 W 57th St
New York, NY 10019-3310
212-956-0200

STS HOTEL NET
383 Corona St
Denver, CO 80218-3939
303-292-6396

S&J LABORATORIES, INC.
2948 Business One Dr
Kalamazoo, MI 49048-8719
616-349-0662

**S.Y. MARBEL & GRANITE
IMPORTERS**
670 Morgan Ave
Brooklyn, NY 11222-3710
718-384-1180 • Fax 718-384-7930

S.A.F.E. SYSTEMS, INC.
901 N Batavia Ave Ste
Batavia, IL 60510-1278
www.e-cache.com
800-366-8244 • Fax 630-761-9324

S.WALLACE EDWARDS & SONS
PO Box 25
Surry, VA 23883-0025
800-200-4267 • Fax 757-294-5378

SAAG MEAT SPECIALTIES
1799 Factor Ave
San Leandro, CA 94577-5617
510-352-8000 • Fax 510-352-4100

SABERT CORP
879 Main St
Sayreville, NJ 08872-1463
www.sabert.com
732-721-5544 • Fax 732-721-8443

SABLE TECHNOLOGIES INC
21216 Cabot Blvd
Hayward, CA 94545-1647
925-358-9041

SABLE TECHNOLOGIES, INC
6250 N Military Trl
West Palm Beach, FL 33407-1407
e-mail: bmiref@bellsouth.net
www.sabletechnologies.com
561-842-4450

**SABRETT HOTDOGS &
HOTDOG CARTS**
1807 W Harris Rd
Arlington, TX 76001-6749
e-mail: sabrett@home.com
www.sabretts.com
817-467-5590 • Fax 817-465-8525

SABROSO COMPANY
690 S Grape St
Medford, OR 97501-3626
www.sabroso. Com
541-772-5653 • Fax 541-779-3572

**SADLER'S BAR-B-QUE
SALES**
PO Box 1088
Henderson, TX 75653-1088
e-mail: colleen@sadlersbbq.com
www.sadlersbbq.com
903-657-5581 • Fax 903-655-8404

SAECO USA INC.
451 Defense Hwy # A1
Annapolis, MD 21401-8956
www.saeco-usa.com
410-573-0562 • Fax 410-573-0657

SAFARI TECHNOLOGIES, INC
406 Liberty Park Ct
Flowood, MS 39232-8642
601-992-1322

SAFE FOOD SYSTEMS, INC
2448 NE 13th Ave
Ft Lauderdale, FL 33305-1304
e-mail:
buffet@safefoodsystems.com
www.saintleouniv.edu
954-564-8993

SAFE -STRIDE OF THE OZARKS
619 E Lindberg St
Springfield, MO 65807-2817
www.aimsintl.org-saf.htm
800-879-7528 • Fax 417-889-1108

SAFE WHEN WET
1933 Keystone Dr
Plano, TX 75075-6750
e-mail: info@safewhenwet.com
www.safewhenwet.com
972-423-2083

SAFECO SELECT MARKETS
1200 Ashwood Pkwy Ste 23
Atlanta, GA 30338-4767
770-395-1199 • Fax 770-512-4366

SAFEMARK SYSTEMS
6355 Metrowest Blvd
Orlando, FL 32835-6433
407-299-0044

SAFE-STRAP CO., INC.
30 Centre Rd
Somersworth, NH 03878-2900
603-692-6796

SAFETY FLOOR INC.
23 Meador Dr
Tuscaloosa, AL 35401-2042
800-732-7547

SAFETY NET ACCESS
83 E Water St
Rockland, MA 02370-1834
781-871-9126 • Fax 617-480-4551

SAFETY WALKWAYS
PO Box 52801
Lafayette, LA 70505-2801
888-419-2238

SAFETY-FIRE-SECURITY
6226 Jefferson Hwy Ste A
New Orleans, LA 70123-5188
504-737-7171

SAFLOK
1020 W 17th St
Costa Mesa, CA 92627-4503
e-mail: info@cssmain.com
www.saflok.com
949-722-5400 • Fax 949-722-0129

SAINT PAUL COMPANIES
385 Washington St
Saint Paul, MN 55102-1396
651-310-7911

SALES PARTNER SYSTEM, INC.
757 S Nova Rd
Ormond Beach, FL 32174-7332
386-672-8434 • Fax 386-673-4730

SALES USA
220 Salado Creek Rd
Salado, TX 76571-5706
254-947-3838

SALES WEST PARTNERS
526 McCormick St
San Leandro, CA 94577-1108
www.saleswestpartners.com
510-567-1000 • Fax 510-567-1005

SALEWATCH INC
580 Thames St
Newport, RI 02840-6741
888-847-0431

SALLY SHERMAN
300 N Macquesten Pkwy
Mount Vernon, NY 10550-1093
914-664-6262 • Fax 914-664-2846

SALVAJOR
4530 E 75th Ter
Kansas City, MO 64132-2081
www.salvajor.com
800-821-3136 • Fax 800-832-9373

SAM FAZIO'S STEAM CLEANING SERVICE
7301 W Judge Perez Dr # 413
Arabi, LA 70032-1629
504-283-3000

SAM HAUSMAN MEAT PACKER, INC.
PO Box 2422
Corpus Christi, TX 78403-2422
e-mail: info@samhausmen.com
www.samhausmen.com
361-883-5521 • Fax 361-883-1003

SAM TELL & SON, INC.
5851 Maspeth Ave
Maspeth, NY 11378-2700
718-386-0707 • Fax 718-497-6513

SAMBONET USA INC
1180 McLester St
Elizabeth, NJ 07201-2948
800-887-4863

SAMPSON & ASSOCIATES
6065 Roswell Rd NE Ste 632
Atlanta, GA 30328-4011
770-256-7456

SAM'S CLUB
608 SW 8th St
Bentonville, AR 72712-6207
479-277-7035 • Fax 479-277-7849

SAM'S CLUB
608 Southwest 8th Street
Bentonville, AR 72716-0001
e-mail: dejohnson@samsclub.com
www.samsclub.com
479-277-7384 • Fax 479-277-7479

SAM'S HOMEMADE CHEESECAKE INC.
7666 Miramar Rd
San Diego, CA 92126-4202
858-578-3460 • Fax 858-578-3346

SAMSON TECHNOLOGIES
575 Underhill Blvd
Syosset, NY 11791-3426
e-mail: fgiovanelli@samsonclub.com
www.samsontech.com
516-364-2244 • Fax 516-364-3888

SAMSUNG ELECTRONICS AMERICA
105 Challenger Rd
Ridgefield Park, NJ 07660-2106
www.sosimple.com
210-229-4138 • Fax 201-229-4029

SAMSUNG TELE-COMMUNICATONG AMERICA
2700 NW 87th Ave
Miami, FL 33172-1607
800-876-4782

SAMUEL I BAILIN INC
644 N Country Club Dr
Mesa, AZ 85201-4983
602-820-8333 • Fax 480-839-5212

SAN AIRE INDUSTRIES
101 W Felix St
Fort Worth, TX 76115-3531
817-924-7189

SAN FRANCISCO FRENCH BREAD CO.
580 Julie Ann Way
Oakland, CA 94621-4034
e-mail: sffb@1x.netcom.com
800-223-6645 • Fax 510-636-9628

SAN FRANCISCO STATE
1600 Holloway Ave
San Francisco, CA 94132-1740
415-338-7010 • Fax 415-338-0997

SAN JACINTO COLLEGE
8060 Spencer Hwy
Pasadena, TX 77505-5998
e-mail: lpring@central.sjco.cc.tx.us
281-542-2099 • Fax 281-478-2790

SAN JAMAR
969 Koopman Ln
Elkhorn, WI 53121-2045
262-495-2991

SAN JAMAR
555 Koopman Ln
Elkhorn, WI 53121-2012
www.sanjamar.com
800-248-9826 • Fax 262-723-4204

SAN PELLEGRINO U.S.A.
13 Sprain Pl
Yonkers, NY 10701-5425
914-966-3350 • Fax 914-966-0462

SANDELMAN & ASSOCIATES, INC.
19075 Ridgeview Rd
Villa Park, CA 92861-1307
714-993-7116

SANDERS MARKETING GROUP
PO Box 970250
Pompano Beach, FL 33097-0250
e-mail: jm4smg@aol.com
954-345-5205

SANDERSON'S FARMS
PO Box 988
Laurel, MS 39441-0988
601-649-4030

SANDLER SEATING
5 Piedmont Ctr NE Ste 505
Atlanta, GA 30305-1509
www.sandlerseating.com
404-982-9000 • Fax 404-321-2882

SANDRIDGE FOOD CORPORATION
133 Commerce Dr
Medina, OH 44256-1333
330-725-2348 • Fax 330-772-3998

SANDUSKY PLASTICS INC
400 Broadway St
Sandusky, OH 44870-2006
419-626-8980 • Fax 419-626-1803

SANDVIK PROCESS SYSTEMS I
21 Campus Rd
Totowa, NJ 07512-1211
973-790-1600

SANIJET CORP
1461 S Belt Line Rd Ste 100
Coppell, TX 75019-4938
877-934-0477

SANISAFE & ASSOCIATES
954 W Washington Blvd
Chicago, IL 60607-2224
312-432-0703

SANISAFE-KEY TECH
327 Doyle Rd
Osteen, FL 32764-9598
407-492-8173

SANISERV MFG CO
PO Box 1089
Mooresville, IN 46158-5089
800-733-8073

SANITECH CORP
6901 Old Keene Mill Rd Ste G4
Springfield, VA 22150-2802
www.sanitechcorp.com
703-569-8174 • Fax 703-569-2635

SANITECH CORP.
4166 N 126th St
Brookfield, WI 53005-1804
262-783-1777 • Fax 262-783-4560

SAN-J INTERNATIONAL INC
2880 Sprouse Dr
Richmond, VA 23231-6072
e-mail: sales@san-j.com
804-226-8331 • Fax 804-226-8383

SANOLITE CORPORATION
26 Papetti Plz
Elizabeth, NJ 07206-1421
908-353-8500 • Fax 908-353-6752

SANRIA TIE'S
661 Jepson Ln
Middletown, RI 02842-4607
401-849-3267

SANTA BARBARA OLIVE CO
PO Box 1570
Santa Ynez, CA 93460-1570
805-688-9917 • Fax 805-686-1659

SANTA BARBARA OLIVE CO
12477 Calle Real
Goleta, CA 93117-9766
e-mail: sbolive@thegrid.net
805-562-1456 • Fax 805-562-1464

SANTA FE NATURAL TOBACCO
PO Box 25140
Santa Fe, NM 87504-5140
800-332-5595

SANTE MAGAZINE
100 South St
Bennington, VT 05201-2244
www.santemagazine.com
802-442-6771 • Fax 802-442-6859

SANTEE DAIRIES, INC.
17851 Railroad St
Rowland Heights, CA 91748-1118
e-mail: sales@santeedairies.com
626-923-3271 • Fax 626-923-3038

SANYO FISHER COMPANY
21605 Plummer St
Chatsworth, CA 91311-4131
e-mail: tdunn@sanyo.com
www.sanyohvac.com
888-653-6173 • Fax 818-350-3193

SANYO SALES & SUPPLY CORP
900 N Arlington Heights Rd
Itasca, IL 60143-2867
630-875-3512

SAPPORO USA BREWERIES LTD.
5105 Mayspring
San Antonio, TX 78217-6403
www.sapporobeer.com
210-525-9612 • Fax 210-525-9643

SAPUTO CHEESE USA INC.
25 Tri State Intl
Lincolnshire, IL 60069-4452
847-444-4539 • Fax 847-267-0224

SARA LEE COFFEE AND TEA
7101 Tpc Dr Ste 130
Orlando, FL 32822-5137
e-mail: tdrescher@saraleecoffee.com
800-831-6465 • Fax 407-251-8150

SARA LEE REFRIGERATED FOODS
900 N North Branch St
Chicago, IL 60622-4278
312-274-8200 • Fax 312-274-8241

SARA LEE REFRIGERATED FOODS
5359 Robinwood Rd
Bonita, CA 91902-2147
619-470-1648 • Fax 619-267-7454

SARABETH'S BAKERY
75 9th Ave
New York, NY 10011-7006
212-989-2424 • Fax 212-989-1171

SARATOGA WATER
11 Geyser Rd
Saratoga Springs, NY 12866-9048
518-584-6363 • Fax 518-584-0380

SARFINO & RHOADES CPA
11921 Rockville Pike Ste 501
Rockville, MD 20852-2794
301-770-5500

SARGENTO CHEESE
1 Persnickety Pl
Plymouth, WI 53073-3547
920-893-0851 • Fax 920-892-6822

SARGENTO FOOD SERVICE CO
PO Box 380
Plymouth, WI 53073-0380
920-893-8484

SARTAIN FISCHBEIN
3010 S Harvard Ave Ste 400
Tulsa, OK 74114-6193
918-749-6601

SARTORI FOOD CORPORATION
107 Pleasant View Rd
Plymouth, WI 53073-4948
e-mail: info@sartorifoods.com
920-893-6061 • Fax 920-893-2732

SASSINORO-EXPRESSO & CAPPUCCINO
PO Box 1685
White Plains, NY 10602-1685
e-mail: sassinoro@palm.net
888-235-3565 • Fax 914-686-2295

SATISFACTION GUARANTEED
419 Occidental Ave S Ste 207
Seattle, WA 98104-2877
206-625-0598

SAUVAGE COSMETIQE INC.
730 5th Ave Fl 9
New York, NY 10019-4105
212-333-8685 • Fax 212-333-8645

SAYERS BROOK BISON RANCH
PO Box 10
Potosi, MO 63664-0010
e-mail: art@sayersbrook.com
573-518-1665 • Fax 573-518-1669

SAZERAC CO
803 Jefferson Hwy
New Orleans, LA 70121-2584
504-841-3431

SCAFATI & COMPANY
20 W Lincoln Ave
Atlantic Highlands, NJ 07716-1127
732-291-9325 • Fax 732-291-2099

SCALA HOSPITALITY
1787 Sentry Pkwy W Ste 18
Blue Bell, PA 19422-2200
484-327-5742

SCALAMONDRE
300 Trade Zone Dr
Ronkonkoma, NY 11779-7381
631-467-8800

SCEPTRE HOSPITALITY RESOURCES
5775 Dtc Blvd Ste 300
Englewood, CO 80111-3209
e-mail: idangelo@richfield.com
303-220-2054 • Fax 303-220-2047

SCES
PO Box 73
Upland, CA 91785-0073
626-338-6963

SCHAERER USA CORPORATION
2900 Orange Ave Ste 102
Long Beach, CA 90806-1821
www.schaererusa.com
562-989-3004 • Fax 562-989-3075

SCHAFER CONDON CARTER
116 W Illinois St
Chicago, IL 60610-4532
312-464-1666 • Fax 312-464-0628

SCHANTINI & ASSOCIATES
1158 Oak Gate Cir
Altamonte Spring, FL 32714-1834
407-774-3333

SCHARFFEN BERGER CHOCOLATE
914 Heinz Ave
Berkeley, CA 94710-2717
888-206-4619

SCHAUMBURG SPECIALTIES CO
9230 Chestnut Ave
Franklin Park, IL 60131-3014
847-451-0070

SCHEIBE, R.R.
88 Lincoln St
Brockton, MA 02302-3113
508-584-4900

SCHEPPS DAIRY
PO Box 55567
Houston, TX 77255-5567
713-688-5511 • Fax 713-688-5747

SCHIEFFELIN & SOMERSET COMPANY
2 Park Ave
New York, NY 10016-5675
212-251-8235

SCHILLER INTERNATIONAL UNIVERSITY
453 Edgewater Dr
Dunedin, FL 34698-7532
e-mail: schiller.edu-isthm
727-736-5082 • Fax 727-736-6263

SCHLANSER DESIGN STUDIO
91 N San Gabriel Blvd
Pasadena, CA 91107-3749
e-mail: schalanserd@aol.com
www.schlanserdesign.com
626-793-1759 • Fax 626-793-3918

SCHLOTZSKYS DELI
203 Colorado St
Austin, TX 78701-3922
512-236-3631

SCHMIDT PROGRESSIVE LLC
PO Box 380
Lebanon, OH 45036-0380
e-mail: spsales@schmidtprogres-sive.com
www.schmidtprogressive.com
513-934-2600 • Fax 513-932-8768

SCHNEIDER PAPER PRODUCTS
2839 N Robertson St
New Orleans, LA 70117-7134
504-943-3301

SCHOENMANN PRODUCE CO.
6950 Neuhaus St
Houston, TX 77061-4607
e-mail: kfaour@mtnking.com
713-923-2728 • Fax 713-923-5897

SCHOKINAG CHOCOLATE NORTH AMERICA
5301 Office Park Dr Ste 200
Bakersfield, CA 93309-0652
www.schokinagna.com
800-807-2465 • Fax 661-322-1156

SCHONBEK WORLDWIDE LIGHT
61 Industrial Blvd
Plattsburgh, NY 12901-1998
518-563-7500

SCHOOLCRAFT COLLEGE
18600 Haggerty Rd
Livonia, MI 48152-2696

SCHOOLHOUSE SOFTWARE
3017 Douglas Blvd # 260
Roseville, CA 95661-3848
800-350-4600

SCHOUTEN USA INC
3300 Edinborough Way
Minneapolis, MN 55435-5923
952-920-7700

SCHREIBER FOODS INTL
PO Box 299
Ramsey, NJ 07446-0299
www.ambrosia-foods.com
201-327-3535 • Fax 201-327-2812

SCHREIBER FOODS, INC.
PO Box 19010
Green Bay, WI 54307-9010
920-437-7601

SCHREIBER FOODS, INC.
1028 Mulberry St
Lake Mills, WI 53551-1303
920-648-3486 • Fax 920-648-5241

SCHROEDER MILK CO
2080 Rice St
Saint Paul, MN 55113-6892
www.schroedermilk.com
651-487-1471 • Fax 651-487-1476

SCHULSTAD USA INC
5007 Lincoln Ave
Lisle, IL 60532-4187
630-963-4781

SCHULTZ RICHARD
805 Gravel Pike
Palm, PA 18070-1114
215-679-2222

SCHUMACHER CONTRACT
79 Madison Ave
New York, NY 10016-7802
e-mail: maryb@isco.com
www.fschumacher.com
212-213-7840 • Fax 212-213-7734

SCHUYLKILL DESIGN & PRINT
215 E Church St
Orwigsburg, PA 17961-1900

e-mail: kadams@sdnp.com
www.sdnp.com
570-366-7343 • Fax 570-366-7317

SCHWANS
600 Michigan Rd
Marshall, MN 56258-2740
e-mail: bart.tracy@schwanstech.com
813-716-2406 • Fax 507-647-4108

SCHWAN'S FOOD
115 W College Dr
Marshall, MN 56258-1747
e-mail: Lisa.VanVickle@schwans.com
800-533-5290 • Fax 507-537-8376

SCHWARTZ PICKLE COMPANY
4401 W 44th Pl
Chicago, IL 60632-4305
800-621-4273 • Fax 773-927-3750

SCHWEITZER KARON BREMER
121 S 8th St Ste 1400
Minneapolis, MN 55402-2856
612-339-7811

SCHY-TOWN INC.
PO Box 2424
Northbrook, IL 60065-2424
www.ketchapeno.com
847-498-2667 • Fax 847-498-2667

SCIEFFELIN & SOMERSET
6363 N State Highway 161
Irving, TX 75038-2215
972-343-7060

SCIENTIFIC FIRE PREVENTION
PO Box 119060
Brooklyn, NY 11211-9060
718-486-9600 • Fax 718-486-0618

SCIMECA'S ITALIAN SAUSAGE
3116 E Truman Rd
Kansas City, MO 64127-2131
816-483-7444

SCITEC INC
1212E E University Ave
Urbana, IL 61802-2011
217-384-6041

SCORE
310 W Wisconsin Ave # 420
Milwaukee, WI 53203-2213
414-291-3942

SCORPIO APPAREL, INC.
3328 Commercial Ave
Northbrook, IL 60062-1909
www.scorpioapparel.com
847-559-3100 • Fax 847-559-3103

SCOTSMAN BEVERAGE SYSTEMS- BOOTH INC.
2007 Royal Ln
Dallas, TX 75229-3263
www.BoothInc.com
800-497-2958 • Fax 888-441-9576

SCOTSMAN ICE SYSTEM
775 Corporate Woods Pkwy
Vernon Hills, IL 60061-3151
www.scotsman-ice.com
847-215-4500 • Fax 847-913-9844

SCOTT ADVERTISING INC
1031 N Astor St
Milwaukee, WI 53202-3399
414-276-1080 • Fax 414-276-3327

SCOTT R. LOEB - RESTAURANT CONSULTANTS
414 Strathmore Rd
Havertown, PA 19083-3736
610-853-2829

SCOTT'S OF WISCONSIN
301 Broadway Dr
Sun Prairie, WI 53590-1742
e-mail: rkrause@scottsofwi.com
800-365-2100 • Fax 608-837-0736

SCREENFLEX PORTABLE PARTITIONS
585 Capital Dr
Lake Zurich, IL 60047-6712
www.screenflex.com
847-726-2900 • Fax 847-726-2990

SDH ENTERPRISES
495 Edison Ct Ste C
Suisun City, CA 94585-1683
e-mail: sdhenti@aol.com
707-864-8075 • Fax 707-864-6832

SE DBTAC
490 10th St NW
Atlanta, GA 30318-5754
e-mail: lfedor@ucpanj.org
888-322-1918 • Fax 404-392-3505

SEA GULL LIGHTING PRODUCTS
PO Box 329
Riverside, NJ 08075-0329
e-mail: rdecola@seagulllighting.com
www.seagulllighting.com
856-764-0500 • Fax 856-764-0813

SEA PORT PRODUCTS CORP
15 10th Ave
San Mateo, CA 94401-4304
650-340-9900

SEA STAR SEAFOOD CO.
5 Kuniholm Dr
Holliston, MA 01746-1354
800-223-1338

SEA WATCH INTL LTD
8978 Glebe Park Dr
Easton, MD 21601-7004
410-820-7848 • Fax 410-822-1266

SEABROOK WALLCOVERINGS, INC.
1325 Farmville Rd
Memphis, TN 38122-1002
800-707-3259 • Fax 901-861-4045

SEABURY & SMITH
1255 23rd St NW
Washington, DC 20037-1125
800-323-2106

SEACO INSURANCE
PO Box 9165
Framingham, MA 01701-9165
800-557-1117 • Fax 508-424-3247

SEAFOOD SALES & SERVICES
6708 La Loma Dr
Jacksonville, FL 32217-2610
e-mail: sales@bielski-seafood.com
904-739-1894 • Fax 904-731-4531

SEAFOOD SUPPLIERS
299 Lawrence Ave
South San Francisco, CA 94080-6818
650-988-5800

SEAFOOD WHOLESALERS, INC
PO Box 571196
Houston, TX 77257-1196
e-mail: peterg@agemgroup.com
800-521-1561 • Fax 281-695-5668

SEAGA MANUFACTURING, INC.
700 Seaga Dr
Freeport, IL 61032-9644
www.seagamfg.com
815-297-9500 • Fax 815-297-1700

SEAGRAM & SONS, JOSEPH
375 Park Ave
New York, NY 10152-0002
212-572-7000

SEAGRAM AMERICAS
800 3Rd Ave FL 10
New York, NY 10022-7604
212-572-7879 • Fax 212-572-1359

SEAL TEX
8908 Chancellor Row
Dallas, TX 75247-5312
214-688-7770 • Fax 214-688-7710

SEAL-A-FRIDGE
1455 Semoran Blvd Ste 14
Casselberry, FL 32707-6522
e-mail: sealfridge@hotmail.com
www.seal-a-fridge.com
407-252-7855

SEALY INC - MATTRESS
1228 Euclid Ave
Cleveland, OH 44115-1834
216-522-1310

SEAPAC OF IDAHO
PO Box 546
Buhl, ID 83316-0546
208-326-3100

SEATING INTERNATIONAL
4770 E 50th St
Los Angeles, CA 90058-2708
800-352-3334

SEATRADE INTERNATIONAL
105 Bartlett St
Portsmouth, NH 03801-3672
603-431-5184

SEATTLE MENU
5150 Russell Ave NW
Seattle, WA 98107-3913
www.seattlemenu.com
206-984-2340 • Fax 206-782-7778

SEATTLE'S BEST COFFEE
413 Pine St Ste 500
Seattle, WA 98101-3669
www.seabest.com
206-442-0227 • Fax 206-682-3143

SEATTLE'S BEST COFFEE
1138 Palms Blvd
Venice, CA 90291-3525
310-306-6162

SEBASTIANI
389 4th St E
Sonoma, CA 95476-5790
707-938-5532

SECO SYSTEMS, A WELBILT CO.
1124 Menzler Rd
Nashville, TN 37210-4700
www.secosystems.com
800-544-5727 • Fax 615-256-8811

SECOND HARVEST FOOD BANK
2008 Brengle Ave
Orlando, FL 32808-5604
e-mail: rweeks@secondharvest.org
407-295-1066

SECOND HARVEST FOOD BANK OF WISCONSIN
1700 W Fond Du Lac Ave
Milwaukee, WI 53205-1261
414-931-7400 • Fax 414-931-1996

SECURE ID, LLC
1780 S Bellaire St Ste 306
Denver, CO 80222-4319
303-450-7354

SECURE LOX INC
5755 Bonhomme Rd Ste 414
Houston, TX 77036-2013
713-266-0065

SECURITY INNOVATIONS INC
18528 S Dominguez Hills Dr
Compton, CA 90220-6415
310-638-0400

SECURITY LABS, INC.
15540 Herriman Blvd
Noblesville, IN 46060-4217
www.spycorder.com
317-773-0284 • Fax 317-773-8057

SECURITYCAMERAS.COM
3 Musick
Irvine, CA 92618-1638
714-438-1570

SEE-A-CAKE
PO Box 2540
Paso Robles, CA 93447-2540
800-854-1920

SEEDS OF CHANGE
PO Box 15700
Santa Fe, NM 87592-5700
505-586-3455

SEGAFREDO ZANETTI USA
1920 Rankin Rd Ste 140
Houston, TX 77073-5113
281-821-3717 • Fax 281-821-3730

SEI INFORMATION TECHNOLOGY
2811 S Fairfield Ave
Lombard, IL 60148-1359
708-515-3600

SELBY-UCRETE FLOORING DIVISION
23700 Chagrin Blvd
Beachwood, OH 44122-5506
216-831-5500

SELBYSOFT INC
8326 Woodland Ave E
Puyallup, WA 98371-5535
800-454-4434

SELECT AMENITIES, LTD.
359 Mockingbird Hill Rd
Hockessin, DE 19707-9723
e-mail: vince@selectamenities.com
www.selectamenities.com
800-234-9294 • Fax 302-234-1805

SELECT SEATING GROUP
2300 Lockbourne Rd
Columbus, OH 43207-2167
614-228-5550 • Fax 614-443-6499

SELECTO SCIENTIFIC, INC.
3980 Lakefield Ct
Suwanee, GA 30024-1256
www.selectoinc.com
678-475-0799 • Fax 678-475-9655

SELMA'S COOKIES
2230 E Semoran Blvd
Apopka, FL 32703-5724
www.selmas.com
407-884-9433 • Fax 407-884-6121

SELTMANN USA INC.
919 Sherwood Dr
Lake Bluff, IL 60044-2203
847-564-2433 • Fax 847-564-2791

SELTMANN WEIDEN
3450 Commercial Ave
Northbrook, IL 60062-1819
708-546-2433

SEMCO INC
1800 E Pointe Dr
Columbia, MO 65201-3508
www.semcoinc.com
573-443-1481 • Fax 573-886-5408

SENERCOMM INC
3930 Rca Blvd
West Palm Beach, FL 33410-4214
800-839-0027

SENN-DELANEY-UNIT OF ART ANDER
33 W Monroe St Fl 27
Chicago, IL 60603-5300
312-931-1122

SENSITECH INC
800 Cummings Ctr Ste 258X
Beverly, MA 01915-6197
www.sensitech.com
978-927-7033 • Fax 978-921-2112

SENTRANET
4801 W 81st St
Minneapolis, MN 55437-1111
888-852-2590

SEQUOIA SPECIALITY CHEESE CO.
PO Box 1207
Tipton, CA 93272-1207
e-mail: seqswis@inreach.com
559-752-4106 • Fax 559-752-4108

SERBEC MASLER
625 Robert Fulton Hwy
Quarryville, PA 17566-1400
717-786-5331

SERENDIPITEA
3229 Greenpoint Ave
Long Island City, NY 11101-2005
e-mail: tea@serendipitea.com
www.serendipitea.com
203-894-9650 • Fax 203-894-9649

SERTA
325 Spring Lake Dr
Itasca, IL 60143-2073
e-mail: fred.gibson@serta.com
www.serta.com
630-285-9350 • Fax 630-285-9330

SERVE PROGRAM
PO Box 15730

Fort Lauderdale, FL 33318-5730
e-mail: serveprogram@hotmail.com
www.server-program.com
954-321-0886

SERVEND INTERNATIONAL INC
2100 Future Dr
Sellersburg, IN 47172-1868
www.servend.com
812-246-7000 • Fax 812-246-7020

SERVER PRODUCTS, INC.
PO Box 530
Menomonee Falls, WI 53052-0530
www.server-products.com
800-558-8722 • Fax 262-251-2688

SERVICE IDEAS, INC.
2354 Ventura Dr
Saint Paul, MN 55125-3929
www.serviceideas.com
651-730-8800 • Fax 651-730-8880

SERVICE MANUFACTURING
1601 Mountain St
Aurora, IL 60505-2402
www.servicemfg.com
630-898-6800 • Fax 630-898-7800

SERVICE READY
3092 Aloma Ave
Winter Park, FL 32792-3723
407-601-9950 • Fax 407-681-9948

SERVICE WITH STYLE
PO Box 2132
Brandon, FL 33509-2132
e-mail: servstyle@prodigy.net
813-661-1149 • Fax 813-661-1110

SERVICEMASTER INDUSTRIES
1 Servicemaster Way
Downers Grove, IL 60515-1700

SERVOLIFT-EASTERN
266 Hancock St
Boston, MA 02125-2149
617-825-9000

SFP FOOD PRODUCTS
PO Box 1617
Conway, AR 72033-1617
501-327-0744

SGS (SOCIETE GENERALE DE SUNVE
291 Fairfield Ave
Fairfield, NJ 07004-3833
973-575-5252 • Fax 973-575-1193

SHADE SOLUTIONS
3466 N Miami Ave
Miami, FL 33127-3534
www.shadesolutions.com
305-856-9928 • Fax 305-856-3314

SHAFTER COMMERCIAL SEATING
4101 E 48th Ave
Denver, CO 80216-3206
e-mail: sales@shafer.com
www.shafter.com
303-322-7792 • Fax 303-393-1836

SHAMROCK SEAFOOD CO INC
2832 NW 72nd Ave
Miami, FL 33122-1310
305-499-9080

SHANGRI-LA ICED TEA CO.
1260 Suffield St
Agawam, MA 01001-2933
413-786-8610 • Fax 413-789-9685

SHANKER INDUSTRIES
3435 Lawson Blvd
Oceanside, NY 11572-4903
516-766-4477 • Fax 516-766-6655

SHARE CORP
PO Box 245013
Milwaukee, WI 53224-9513
800-776-7192

SHARE OUR STRENGTH
733 15th St NW Ste 640
Washington, DC 20005-6030
800-969-4767

SHARP ELECTRONIC CORPORATION
5700 NW Pacific Rim Blvd

Camas, WA 98607-9489
360-834-2500

SHARP ELECTRONICS CORPORATION
1 Sharp Plz # 24
Mahwah, NJ 07430-1123
201-529-8708

SHARPER FINISH
4500 W Augusta Blvd
Chicago, IL 60651-9800
e-mail: finish@attmail.com
www.sharpfinish.com
773-276-4800 • Fax 773-276-6868

SHASTA SALES INC
1343 Garner Ln
Columbia, SC 29210-8360
803-750-9244

SHASTA SALES INC
26901 Industrial Blvd
Hayward, CA 94545-3346
510-783-3200 • Fax 510-785-3228

SHAT-R-SHIELD
116 Ryan Patrick Dr
Salisbury, NC 28147-5624
800-223-0853

SHAVER SPECIALTY CO
20608 Earl St
Torrance, CA 90503-3009
www.shaverkeenkutter.com
310-370-6941 • Fax 310-370-3851

SHAW HOSPITALITY
PO Box 2128
Dalton, GA 30722-2128
e-mail: kevin_sanders@shawinc.com
www.shavinc.com
706-278-3812 • Fax 706-275-2639

SHAW-ROSS INTERNATIONAL IMPORT
15960 NW 15th Ave
Miami, FL 33169-5608
305-625-6561

SHEFFIELD PLATERS
9850 Waples St
San Diego, CA 92121-2921
www.sheffieldplaters.com
858-546-8484 • Fax 858-546-7653

SHELBY WILLIAMS INDUSTRIES, INC
150 Shelby Williams Dr
Morristown, TN 37813-1138
www.shelbywilliams.com
423-586-7000 • Fax 423-587-4839

SHELTON CORPORATION
PO Box 4087
Deltona, FL 32725-0087
407-324-3101

SHERMAN SPECIALTIES
114 Church St
Freeport, NY 11520-3887
www.shermannet.com
516-546-7400 • Fax 516-546-2979

SHICK TUBE VEYOR
4346 Clary Blvd
Kansas City, MO 64130-2386
816-861-7224

SHILD CO
1425 37th St
Brooklyn, NY 11218-3755
e-mail: shild1@aol.com
718-686-3852 • Fax 212-779-2837

SHILOH FOODS, INC.
PO Box 1000
Savannah, TN 38372-1000
800-795-2550 • Fax 731-925-1855

SHIRTS UNLIMITED
5553 Kearny Villa Rd
San Diego, CA 92123-1107
858-278-3322 • Fax 858-278-4242

SHOCKIM ENTERPRISE LTD.
2500 Wilshire Blvd
Los Angeles, CA 90057-4303
e-mail:
shockimenterprises@usa.com
213-365-2279 • Fax 213-365-2278

SHOES FOR CREWS INC
1400 Centrepark Blvd
West Palm Beach, FL 33401-7402
800-218-4770

SHOES FOR CREWS, INC.
1400 Centrepark Blvd # 31
West Palm Beach, FL 33401-7402
www.shoesforcrews.com
561-683-5090 • Fax 772-227-0740

SHOFAR KOSHER FOODS
1251 E Linden Ave
Linden, NJ 07036-1501
908-925-6000 • Fax 908-925-5960

SHOLODGE FRANCHISE SYSTEMS
217 W Main St
Gallatin, TN 37066-3245
800-552-4667

SHONNA'S GOURMET GOODIES
320 W Center St
West Bridgewater, MA 02379-1626
508-580-2033 • Fax 508-580-2044

SHOOK DESIGN GROUP INC.
2000 South Blvd Ste 510
Charlotte, NC 28203-5047
www.shookdesign.com
704-377-0661 • Fax 704-377-0953

SHOPCO USA INC
7171 W Sam Houston Pkwy N
Houston, TX 77040-3155
713-683-0033

SHORE DISTRIBUTION RESOURCES
18 Manitoba Way
Marlboro, NJ 07746-1219
e-mail: shordist@aol.com
732-972-1711 • Fax 732-972-7669

SHORELINES
13311 Oleander Dr
Panama City Beach, FL 32407-3304
850-234-2332

SHORT MILLING CO
500 W Madison St
Chicago, IL 60661-4544
800-544-8734

SHOT STEWARD
1933 S Broadway Ste 1251
Los Angeles, CA 90007-4503
www.shotsteward.com
213-747-2771 • Fax 213-748-1334

SHOW DIGITAL, INC
21 Penn Plz
New York, NY 10001-2727
e-mail: sales@showdigital.com
www.showdigital.com
212-246-2600 • Fax 212-246-9456

SHOWER TOWER INC
1191 Taylor Ave
Dunedin, FL 34698-2118
800-330-9073

SHOWTENDERS
7502 S Orange Blossom Trl
Orlando, FL 32809-6989
www.showtender.com
407-851-9500 • Fax 407-851-9998

SHOWTIME NETWORKS INC
1633 Broadway
New York, NY 10019-6708
212-708-1600

SHURFLO
12650 Westminster Ave
Santa Ana, CA 92706-2100
www.shurflo.com
714-554-7709 • Fax 714-554-5668

SIBBALD ASSOCIATES INC, JOHN
7733 Forsyth Blvd
Saint Louis, MO 63105-1817
314-727-0227

SICO
7525 Cahill Rd
Minneapolis, MN 55439-2745
952-941-1700

SICOM SYSTEMS, INC.
4140 Skyron Dr
Doylestown, PA 18901-1124
e-mail:
wkemmerer@sicom-sys.com
www.sicom-systems.com
800-547-4266 • Fax 215-489-2769

SID WAINER & SON SPECIALTY PRO
2301 Purchase St
New Bedford, MA 02746-1686
www.sidwainer.com
800-423-8333 • Fax 508-999-6795

SIERRA CONVERTING CORP.
1400 Kleppe Ln
Sparks, NV 89431-6426
775-331-8221

SIERRA MILLS
2375 Lincoln Ave
Hayward, CA 94545-1117
www.sierramills.com
800-670-3050 • Fax 510-781-3906

SIERRA NATIONAL CORP.
13000 Danielson St Ste Q
Poway, CA 92064-6827
www.sierranational.com
858-391-5500 • Fax 858-391-5523

SIERRA NEVADA BREWING CO.
1075 E 20th St
Chico, CA 95928-6722
530-893-3520 • Fax 530-893-1275

SIFA SINTHESI
3282 N 29th Ct
Hollywood, FL 33020-1320
e-mail: sifasin@cs.com
www.sifasinthesi.com
954-925-8050

SIGLA FURNITURE
711 E Rosecrans Ave
Los Angeles, CA 90059-3508
310-715-6593 • Fax 310-715-6439

SIGN BUILDERS OF AMERICA
4125 Todd Ln
Austin, TX 78744-1151
vmike@sboa.com
www.sboa.com
512-447-3147 • Fax 512-443-8828

SIGNATURE BUTTER FARMS
11596 Pierson Rd Bldg M
West Palm Beach, FL 33414-8770
e-mail: sales@signaturebutter.com
561-841-1881 • Fax 561-841-7171

SIGNATURE HOSPITALITY CARPETS
396 Cross St
Dalton, GA 30721-6453
800-809-7086

SIGNATURE LEGENDARY SALES
3770 Ridge Mill Dr
Hilliard, OH 43026-9231
e-mail: amyklies@legendary.net
www.legendary.net
614-766-5101 • Fax 614-718-5371

SIGNOLOGIES, INC.
95 Plaistow Rd
Plaistow, NH 03865-2827
www.signologies.com
603-469-1998 • Fax 603-374-0077

SIGNOLOGIES A DIVISION OF HYSEN
1725 Mendon Rd Unit 204
Cumberland, RI 02864-4340
401-334-7777 • Fax 401-334-7775

SIGNOLOGIES DIVISION OF HYSEN
1725 Mendon Rd
Cumberland, RI 02864-4337
www.signologies.com
www.hysen.com
401-382-0099 • Fax 401-382-0077

SIGNS & SHAPES INTL, INC.
9988 F St
Omaha, NE 68127-1103
www.signsandshapes.com
402-331-3181 • Fax 402-331-2729

SIGNS NOW CORPORATION
4900 Manatee Ave W
Bradenton, FL 34209-3859
www.signsnow.com
941-747-7747 • Fax 941-750-8604

SIGNSTAR
7720 Highway 301 N
Tampa, FL 33637-6763
800-486-3660 • Fax 813-980-6857

SILESIA GRILL MACHINES, INC.
4770 County Road 16
Saint Petersburg, FL 33709-3130
www.silesia.ltd.uk
727-544-1340 • Fax 727-544-2821

SILIKAL RESIN SYSTEMS
173 Interstate Ln
Waterbury, CT 06705-2640
e-mail:
information@silikalresins.com
www.silikaresins.com
800-477-4545 • Fax 203-754-8791

SILVA SAUSAGE COMPANY
1266 E Julian St
San Jose, CA 95116-1009
800-745-8288 • Fax 408-293-5766

SILVER KING
1600 Xenium Ln N
Minneapolis, MN 55441-3706
www.silverking.com
763-553-1881 • Fax 763-553-1209

SILVER KING
3401 Enterprise Ave
Hayward, CA 94545-3201
510-786-1144

SILVER SERVICE
1638 Lakeside Dr
Jackson, MS 39216-4809
www.trainreaction.com
601-362-0048 • Fax 601-362-5122

SILVERLAND DESSERTS
439 Des Plaines Ave
Forest Park, IL 60130-1763
www.silverlanddesserts.com
800-737-3636 • Fax 708-488-0894

SIMMONS CO
1 Concourse Pkwy NE
Atlanta, GA 30328-5564
770-512-7700

SIMMONS COMPANY
6428 Warren Dr
Norcross, GA 30093-1113
e-mail:
simmonscontract@mindspring.com
www.simmons.com
770-613-5544 • Fax 770-613-5559

SIMMONS FOODS INC
PO Box 430
Siloam Springs, AR 72761-0430
479-524-8151 • Fax 479-524-6562

SIMON DISTRIBUTING
5423 Fargo Ave
Skokie, IL 60077-3211
773-274-2977

SIMON PROPERTY GROUP
PO Box 7033
Indianapolis, IN 46207-7033
317-263-7011

SIMPLY DELICIOUS DISTRIBUTORS
W232 N6633 Waukesha Ave
Sussex, WI 53089-3242
262-246-6321 • Fax 262-246-4577

SINGLETON SEAFOOD CO
PO Box 2819
Tampa, FL 33601-2819
813-241-1500

SIR AUBREY'S TEA COMPANY LTD
7825 E Evans Rd Ste 500
Scottsdale, AZ 85260-6927
e-mail: pfisher@siraubrey.com
www.siraubery.com
480-607-5300

SISSON IMPORTS
50 37th St NE
Auburn, WA 98002-1753
253-939-1520 • Fax 253-939-1099

SITRAM COOKWARE
156 Halsey Rd
Parsippany, NJ 07054-5202
973-515-3500 • Fax 973-515-3467

SJS SPECIALTY COMPANY
73 Brunswick Woods Dr
East Brunswick, NJ 08816-5601
732-613-0303 • Fax 732-613-8080

SKORR PRODUCTS INC.
90 George St
Paterson, NJ 07503-2319
www.skorrproducts.com
973-523-2606 • Fax 973-523-3009

SKY RANCH FOUNDATION
PO Box 8420
Fredericksburg, VA 22404-8420
504-891-7201

SKYE LARKE JEWELRY
3231 E 29th St
Bryan, TX 77802-2706
979-823-2125

SLICECHIEF CO INC
3333 Maple St
Toledo, OH 43608-1155
419-241-7647

SLIP-FREE SYSTEMS, INC.
15502 Highway 3 Ste 407
Webster, TX 77598-2123
e-mail: slipfree@slipfreesystems.com
www.slipfreesystems.com
281-280-0656 • Fax 281-280-0096

SLOAN VALVE CO
10500 Seymour Ave
Franklin Park, IL 60131-1259
847-671-4300 • Fax 847-671-6944

SLUSH PUPPIE
13955 Murphy Rd Ste 224
Stafford, TX 77477-4916
281-499-5843 • Fax 281-499-8014

SLUSH PUPPIE CORPORATION
1131 Victory Pl
Hebron, KY 41048-8293
800-543-0860

SM AUTOMATIC
10301 Jefferson Blvd
Culver City, CA 90232-3511
800-533-3040

SM FRANCE - USA
86 Walker Ln
Newtown, PA 18940-1888
www.sm.-france.com
267-757-0870 • Fax 267-757-0879

SMART & FINAL
600 Citadel Dr
Los Angeles, CA 90040-1562
www.smartandfinal.com
323-869-7896 • Fax 323-869-7865

SMART PUBLISHING
4648 N University Dr
Fort Lauderdale, FL 33351-4516
e-mail: smartpubl@aol.com
954-746-5750 • Fax 954-746-9106

SMA-THE ISLANDS
2901 S Highland Dr Ste 13C
Las Vegas, NV 89109-1054
702-894-9340 • Fax 702-894-9886

SMD TRADING CO., LLC
33 Timberline
Irvine, CA 92604-3033
www.smdtrading.com
949-552-0405 • Fax 949-552-0406

SMG, INC.
2890 Chancellor Dr Ste 2
Ft Mitchell, KY 41017-2153
859-344-3700 • Fax 859-344-3737

SMITH FILTER CORPORATION
5000 41st Street
Moline, IL 61265-7583
www.smithfilter.com
309-764-8324 • Fax 309-764-6816

SMITHFIELD PACKING COMPANY
501 N Church St
Smithfield, VA 23430-1214
e-mail:
paulowen@smithfieldpacking.com
757-357-1312 • Fax 757-357-1331

SMITHKLINE BEECHAM PHARMACEUTICAL
200 N 16th St Lbby 1
Philadelphia, PA 19102-1201
215-751-4000 • Fax 215-751-5050

SMOKE RINGS-A-FUENTE COFFEE
2419 Smallman St
Pittsburgh, PA 15222-4609
www.fuentecoffee.com
412-261-0160 • Fax 412-261-0898

SMOKEY DENMARK SAUSAGE COMPANY
3505 E 5th St
Austin, TX 78702-4913
e-mail:
jonathan@smokeydenmark.com
www.smokeydenmark.com
512-385-0718 • Fax 512-385-4843

SMURFIT - STONE CONTAINER
1952 Cherrylawn Dr
Toledo, OH 43614-3507
419-385-4189 • Fax 419-385-5465

SMURFIT-STONE CONTAINER
105 Summer St
Torrington, CT 06790-6333
860-482-7657 • Fax 860-482-5974

SMURFIT-STONE CONTAINER CORP
1133 Culpepper Dr SW
Conyers, GA 30094-5997
877-684-9296

SMUTTY NOSE BREWING
225 Heritage Ave
Portsmouth, NH 03801-5610
603-436-4026 • Fax 603-431-6768

SMYTH SYSTEMS INC
PO Box 8800
Canton, OH 44711-8800
330-499-6392

SNAP DRAPE
2045 Westgate Dr Ste 100
Carrollton, TX 75006-9478
800-527-5147

SNAP LOCK INDUSTRIES
2102 E 3300 S
Salt Lake City, UT 84109-2633
800-457-0174

SNAP SYSTEMS, INC.
PO Box 2410
Santa Monica, CA 90407-2410
800-423-2113

SNAP-DRAPE COMPANY
2045 Westgate Dr
Carrollton, TX 75006-6478
972-466-1030

SNEEZEGUARD SOLUTIONS INC
1123 Wilkes Blvd Ste 2A
Columbia, MO 65201-4774
www.sneezeguard-solutions.com
573-443-5756 • Fax 573-449-7126

SNOKIST GROWERS
PO Box 1587
Yakima, WA 98907-1587
509-453-5631

SNOW BALL FOODS, INC
1051 Sykes Ln
Williamstown, NJ 08094-3522
800-360-7669

SOBE BEVERAGE CO
PO Box 3165
Wallingford, CT 06494-3165

SOBE BEVERAGE COMPANY
108 Winthrop Rd Apt 5
Brookline, MA 02445-4585
617-264-4984 • Fax 617-264-4984

SOCIETY INSURANCE
150 Camelot Dr
Fond du Lac, WI 54935-8030
888-576-2438

SODEXHO MARRIOTT SERVICES
4425 W Airport Fwy
Irving, TX 75062-5822
972-594-6600 • Fax 972-594-8700

SODEXHO MARRIOTT SERVICES
3923 Coconut Palm Dr
Tampa, FL 33619-1356
e-mail:
cortiz@sodexhomarriott.com
813-621-2558 • Fax 813-621-0536

SODEXHO MARRIOTT SERVICES
10400 Fernwood Rd
Bethesda, MD 20817-1109
800-763-3946

SODEXHO MARROTT SERVICES
200 Continental Dr Ste 4
Newark, DE 19713-4334
www.sodexhomarriott.com
302-738-9500 • Fax 302-738-5218

SOLE LTALIAN SPRING WATER
477 Beardsley Ave
Bloomfield, NJ 07003-5661
www.solewater.com
973-429-2538 • Fax 973-429-2503

SOLE NATURAL ITALIAN SPRING WATER
17941 Sky Park Cir Ste H
Irvine, CA 92614-4373
e-mail: sole@earthlink.net
949-222-9026 • Fax 949-222-9057

SOLID SURFACE ACRYLICS
800 Walck Rd
North Tonawanda, NY 14120-3500
www.solidsurface.buffnet.net
716-743-1870 • Fax 716-743-0475

SOLO CUP
1700 Old Deerfield Rd
Highland Park, IL 60035-3792
www.solocup.com
847-831-4800 • Fax 847-831-4358

SOMAT CORPORATION
555 Fox Chase Ste 107
Coatesville, PA 19320-1885
www.somatcorp.com
610-384-7000 • Fax 610-380-8500

SOMERSET INDUSTRIES
1 Esquire Rd
North Billerica, MA 01862-2501
978-667-3355

SOMETHING DIFFERENT LINEN
474 Getty Ave
Clifton, NJ 07011-2149
800-422-2180

SOMETHING DIFFERENT LINEN
2057 SW Heronwood Rd
Palm City, FL 34990-4620
www.tableclothsonline.com
800-886-1947 • Fax 616-353-8266

SONA & HOLLEN FOODS
3712 Cerritos Ave
Los Alamitos, CA 90720-2487
562-431-1379 • Fax 562-598-6207

SONIC CORPORATION
101 Park Ave Ste 1400
Oklahoma City, OK 73102-7216
405-280-7508

SONOCO PRODUCTS COMPANY
101 E Carolina Ave
Hartsville, SC 29550-4213
843-383-3344

SONOCO - RIXIE-STANCAP DIVISION
4061 Blue Ridge Industrial Pkw
Norcross, GA 30071-1605
www.sonoco.com
770-623-5723 • Fax 770-623-4745

SONOCO -STANCAP-RIXIE
3150 Clinton Ct
Norcross, GA 30071-1643
e-mail: stancap@sonoco.com
www.stancaps.com
404-505-5900 • Fax 404-505-5926

SONOMA CHEESE FACTORY
2 E Spain St
Sonoma, CA 95476-5777
707-996-1000 • Fax 707-935-3535

SONOMA CIDER MILL
25 Healdsburg Ave
Healdsburg, CA 95448-4003
www.sonomacider.com
707-431-8938 • Fax 707-431-8414

SONOMA SALSA
322 Bellevue Ave
Santa Rosa, CA 95407-7711
707-765-1643 • Fax 707-765-2043

SONY ELECTRONICS INC
16450 W Bernardo Dr
San Diego, CA 92127-1804
877-822-8703

SOOFER CO., INC.
2828 S Alameda St
Los Angeles, CA 90058-1347
e-mail: info@sadaf.com
323-231-6666 • Fax 323-231-2117

SOPAKCO FOODS
215 S Mullins St
Mullins, SC 29574-3207
843-464-0121 • Fax 843-464-2178

SOPRANO SPECIALTY FOOD
26064 75th Ave
Glen Oaks, NY 11004-1119
e-mail: sopranofood@aol.com
718-831-9000 • Fax 718-831-9000

SOSKI PIROEFF INC
335 Lancaster Ave
Malvern, PA 19355-1854
e-mail: sales@specequip.com
610-648-0100

SOULES FOODS INC JOHN
PO Box 4579
Tyler, TX 75712-4579
800-338-4588

SOUND PRODUCTS
14849 W 95th St
Lenexa, KS 66215-5220
913-599-3666

SOURCE ATLANTIQUE INC
140 Sylvan Ave
Englewood Cliffs, NJ 07632-2514
201-947-1000

SOUTH CORP. WINES
60 Garden Ct Ste 200
Monterey, CA 93940-5341

SOUTHBEND - A MIDDLEBY CO.
1100 Old Honeycutt Rd
Fuquay Varina, NC 27526-9312
www.southbendnc.com
919-762-1000 • Fax 919-552-9798

SOUTHCORP WINES USA
60 Garden Ct
Monterey, CA 93940-5362
831-655-4848

SOUTHEAST WHOLESALE EQPT.
2830 Piedmont St
Kenner, LA 70062-4950
504-888-2700

SOUTHEASTERN FISHERIES
312 E Georgia St
Tallahassee, FL 32301-1250
850-224-0612

SOUTHERN ALUMINUM MFG
PO Box 884
Magnolia, AR 71754-0884
www.southernaluminum.com
870-234-8660 • Fax 870-234-2823

SOUTHERN BEAR
1950 Hayes St
Hollywood, FL 33020-3550
954-923-0977

SOUTHERN CALIF EDISON
2244 Walnut Grove Ave
Rosemead, CA 91770-3714
800-336-2822

SOUTHERN CHAMPION TRAY, LP
220 Compress St
Chattanooga, TN 37405-3724
423-756-5121 • Fax 427-560-223

SOUTHERN COMMERCIAL PRODUCTS
5820 River Oaks Rd S
New Orleans, LA 70123-2155
504-733-2547

SOUTHERN ILLINOIS UNIVERSITY
1205 Lincoln Dr
Carbondale, IL 62901-4304
www.siu.edu
618-453-2329 • Fax 618-453-5231

SOUTHERN OFFICE EQUIPMENT
PO Box 1166
Hammond, LA 70404-1166
985-345-0856

SOUTHERN PRIDE
2102 E Main St
Marion, IL 62959-5002
www.southern-pride.com
618-997-9348 • Fax 618-993-5960

SOUTHERN PRIDE
122 White Oak Trl
Centerville, MA 02632-1642
508-775-1920 • Fax 508-778-0784

SOUTHERN PRIDE
902 W 23rd St
Houston, TX 77008-1810
e-mail: fjamar@aol.com
800-491-1136 • Fax 713-864-5073

SOUTHERN PRIDE CATFISH
PO Box 436
Greensboro, AL 36744-0436
334-624-4021

SOUTHERN SIGNATURE, INC.
PO Box 3456
Fayetteville, AR 72702-3456
479-621-5686

SOUTHERN STORE FIXTURES, INC.
275 Drexel Rd SE
Bessemer, AL 35022-6416
800-552-6283 • Fax 205-428-2552

SOUTHWEST DISPOSABLE CONCEPTS
4393 Sunbelt Dr # 300
Addison, TX 75001-5134
e-mail: brendab@swdc.com
972-407-1888 • Fax 972-407-1812

SOUTHWEST DECOR
3645 Fredericksburg Rd
San Antonio, TX 78201-3842
e-mail: southwestdecor@msn.com
210-496-5701 • Fax 210-496-5704

SOUTHWEST FOOD SERVICE NEWS
4011 W Plano Pkwy Ste 121
Plano, TX 75093-5620
e-mail: sabllard@sfsn.com
www.sfsn.com
972-943-1254 • Fax 972-943-1258

SOUTHWEST FOODSERVICE EXPO
1400 Lavaca St
Austin, TX 78701-1635
800-395-2872

SOUTHWEST NEON SIGNS
7208 S Ww White Rd
San Antonio, TX 78222-5204
www.swnsigns.com
210-648-3221 • Fax 210-648-4709

SOUTHWOOD FURNITURE
PO Box 2245
Hickory, NC 28603-2245
828-465-1776

SOUTHWORD CROSS, INC.
42 Park Plz Fl
Morristown, NJ 07960-4268
e-mail: SouthwordC@aol.com
973-539-5666 • Fax 973-539-5446

SPARKLING WATER DIST.
PO Box 695
Merrick, NY 11566-0695
516-867-8291 • Fax 516-377-1228

SPARKLING WATER DIST.
1638 Meadowbrook Rd
Merrick, NY 11566-2555
e-mail: waterpower@aol.com
516-867-8291

SPARKLING SPRING WATER CO.
700 N Deerpath Dr
Vernon Hills, IL 60061-1802
847-247-5350

SPARRER SAUSAGE CO., INC.
4325 W Ogden Ave
Chicago, IL 60623-2925
800-666-3287 • Fax 773-521-9368

SPARTA FOODS
1565 1st Ave NW
Saint Paul, MN 55112-1988
651-697-5500 • Fax 6516-970-600

SPARTAN BAKERY EQUIP USA
3501 Vernon Blvd
Astoria, NY 11106-5122
877-637-8622

SPARTAN CHEMICAL CO INC
PO Box 1030
Maumee, OH 43537-8030
800-537-8990

SPARTAN FOODS OF AMERICA
4250 Orchard Park Blvd
Spartanburg, SC 29303-4400
www.mamamarys.com
864-595-6262

SPARTAN SHOWCASE
PO Box 470
Union, MO 63084-0470
800-325-0775

SPEAKMAN COMPANY
PO Box 191
Wilmington, DE 19899-0191
www.speakmancompany.com
302-765-0307 • Fax 800-977-2747

SPEAR SAFER HARMON & CO.
10820 SW 138th St
Miami, FL 33176-6560
305-591-8850

SPECIAL EVENTS MAGAZINE
23815 Stuart Ranch Rd
Malibu, CA 90265-4861
www.specialevents.com
310-317-4522 • Fax 310-317-9644

SPECIAL HANDS, INC.
163 Mulberry St
New York, NY 10013-6101
e-mail: info@specialhand.com
646-210-5555 • Fax 212-941-9962

SPECIALTY BRANDS INC
2030 Iowa Ave
Riverside, CA 92507-2435
800-548-6363

SPECIALTY BRANDS INC.
2030 Iowa Ave Bldg C-100
Riverside, CA 92507-2435
909-774-4020 • Fax 909-774-4303

SPECIALTY EQUIPMENT
1245 Corporate Blvd
Aurora, IL 60504-6407
www.specialty-equipment.com
630-585-5111 • Fax 630-585-9450

SPECIALTY IMPORTS
2901 26th St W Apt 512
Bradenton, FL 34205-3760
e-mail: torchlighter@hotmail.com
941-748-5122 • Fax 941-708-9209

SPECIALTY PACKAGING, INC.
3250 W Seminary Dr Unit A
Fort Worth, TX 76133-1157
817-922-9727 • Fax 800-284-7788

SPECIALTY ROLL PRODUCTS
601 25th Ave
Meridian, MS 39301-4918
800-647-6267 • Fax 601-693-6211

SPECIALTY WORLD FOODS
84 Montgomery St
Albany, NY 12207-2344
e-mail: swfoods@worldnet.att.net
518-436-7603 • Fax 518-436-9035

SPECTECH SYSTEMS CORP
4695 18th St E
Bradenton, FL 34203-3786

SPECTRA INTELLIGENT MRKTG
200 W Jackson Blvd
Chicago, IL 60606-6910
312-583-5100

SPECTRUM PLASTICS
14700 Marquardt Ave
Santa Fe Springs, CA 90670-5125
www.ipspi.com
562-926-4256 • Fax 562-926-4356

SPEED OF LIGHT
35325 Date Palm Dr Ste 157
Cathedral City, CA 92234-7008
www.speedelink.com
760-672-2774 • Fax 760-626-2715

SPEEDLINE SOLUTIONS
525 W Southern Ave
Mesa, AZ 85210-5009
888-400-9185

SPELLBOUND DEV GROUP
3419 Via Lido
Newport Beach, CA 92663-3908
949-474-8577

SPERO LIGHTING
1705 Noble Rd
Cleveland, OH 44112-1633
216-851-3300 • Fax 216-581-0300

SPICE WORLD INC
8101 Presidents Dr
Orlando, FL 32809-9113
www.spiceworldinc.com
407-851-9432 • Fax 407-857-7171

SPIR-IT INC.-ZOO PIKS
11 Lake St
Wakefield, MA 01880-3194
www.zoopiks.com
800-343-0996 • Fax 718-245-7976

SPONGE-CUSHION, INC
902 Armstrong St # O
Morris, IL 60450-1921
e-mail: info@sponge-cushion.com
www.sponge-cushion.com
800-435-4062 • Fax 800-423-3557

SPORTS SOLUTIONS
2855 Dairy Milk Ln
Dallas, TX 75229-4704
972-406-9955

SPORTSERVICE
401 Channelside Dr
Tampa, FL 33602-5400
813-301-6909

SPORTSMASTER BY STANDARD MFG.
750 2nd Ave
Troy, NY 12182-2205
518-235-2200 • Fax 518-235-2668

SPORTZBARZ.COM
12322 Saint Simon Dr
Boca Raton, FL 33428-4647
561-414-3397

SPRAY MASTER TECH (SMT)
115 E Linden St
Rogers, AR 72756-6035
479-636-5776

SPRING AIR COMPANY
2980 S River Rd
Des Plaines, IL 60018-4203
e-mail: dpffitz@aol.com
www.springcontract.com
847-297-5577 • Fax 847-299-0196

SPRING GROUP, INC.
832 Lexington Ave
Brooklyn, NY 11221-2912
e-mail: springgroup68@hotmail.com
718-602-2720 • Fax 718-602-2763

SPRING INDUSTRIES
205 N White St
Fort Mill, SC 29715-1654

SPRING SWITZERLAND USA
1701 Quincy Ave
Naperville, IL 60540-3955
630-434-0700

SPRING SWITZERLAND USA
1701 Quincy Ave Ste 28
Naperville, IL 60540-6684
www.springusa.com
630-517-8600 • Fax 630-527-8677

SPRING WATER FARMS
3155 S Highway 65
Eudora, AR 71640-9781
800-264-2594 • Fax 870-355-4024

SPRINGER-MILLER SYSTEMS
782 Mountain Rd # 1547
Stowe, VT 05672-4629
802-253-7377

SPRINGFIELD FOOD COMPANY
PO Box 3024
Springfield, MA 01101-3024
413-733-3053, 800
Fax 413-737-1663

SPRINGPRINT MEDALLION DIVISION
1431 Marvin Griffin Rd
Augusta, GA 30906-3882
www.marcalpaper.com
706-793-2832 • Fax 800-982-6434

SPRINGS INDUSTRIES INC
104 W 40th St
New York, NY 10018-3617
212-556-6278

SPULBOY-THE BONDEE GROUP
PO Box 23011
Chagrin Falls, OH 44023-0011
440-708-0971 • Fax 440-708-0972

SPUNKMEYER COOKIES, OTIS
14390 Catalina St
San Leandro, CA 94577-5514
800-245-3456

SPY TEK 2000
1545 Lapalco Blvd
Harvey, LA 70058-3378
504-371-4000

SPYWARE
227 York Rd
Warminster, PA 18974-4515
215-444-0405

SQUIRREL COMPANIES INC.
1550 Bryant St Ste 830
San Francisco, CA 94103-4878
415-255-0119

SSI CUSTOM DATA CARDS
1027 Waterwood Pkwy
Edmond, OK 73034-5324
www.ssicards.com
405-359-6000 • Fax 405-359-6528

SSP, INC
421 N Freya St
Spokane, WA 99202-4606
800-726-0553

ST JAMES CHINA, INC.
2140 W Olympic Blvd Ste 142
Los Angeles, CA 90006-2275
213-368-4242 • Fax 213-368-4240

ST LOUIS STAINLESS
1736 Rudder Industrial Park Dr
Fenton, MO 63026-2019
www.stlouisstainless.com
888-507-1578

ST PHILLIPS COLLEGE
1801 Martin Luther King Dr
San Antonio, TX 78203-2098
e-mail: cberkely@accd.edu
www.accd.edu-spc
210-531-3315 • Fax 210-531-3351

ST. JOHN'S UNIVERSITY
Hospitality Management, 8000 U
Jamaica, NY 11439-0001
718-990-6137 • Fax 718-990-1898

STA ENTERPRISE
3359 Farrington St
Flushing, NY 11354-2820
718-353-0805 • Fax 718-353-6350

STACEY'S FOODS, INC.
10334 N Taryne St
Hayden, ID 83835-9807
www.staceyscrabcakes.com
800-782-2395

STAFF LEASING
24850 Old 41 Rd Ste 22
Bonita Springs, FL 34135-7024
888-302-4446

STAMPEDE MEAT INC
4551 S Racine Ave
Chicago, IL 60609-3371
773-376-4300 • Fax 773-376-9349

STAND EASY PRODUCTS
1100 Cleveland St Ste 1
Clearwater, FL 33755-4840
727-442-9222 • Fax 727-442-8799

STANDARD COFFEE SERVICE CO
640 Magazine St
New Orleans, LA 70130-3406
504-524-6131

STANGANELLI'S ITALIAN FOODS
602 E 25th St
Erie, PA 16503-2114
814-456-0965 • Fax 814-456-7897

STANISLAUS FOOD PRODUCTS CO
1202 D St
Modesto, CA 95354-2407
209-522-7201

STAP & COMPANY, INC.
224 E Michigan Ave
Kalamazoo, MI 49007-3910
616-344-1412

STAR MFG INTL INC.
10 Sunnen Dr
Saint Louis, MO 63143-3800
www.star-mfg.com
800-264-7827 • Fax 800-264-6666

STAR SERVICE OF NEW ORLEANS
3117 26th St
Metairie, LA 70002-6003
504-833-7637 • Fax 504-833-7654

STAR SERVICES, LLC
333 Scott St Ste 300
Covington, KY 41011-1556
www.starservices.net
859-655-8873 • Fax 859-655-7073

STAR TRAC UNISEN INC
14410 Myford Rd
Irvine, CA 92606-1001
714-669-1660

STARBUCKS COFFEE COMPANY
PO Box 34067
Seattle, WA 98124-1067
206-447-1575 • Fax 206-623-8050

STARCHEFS.COM
270 Lafayette St Ste 205
New York, NY 10012-3327
www.starchefs.com
212-966-3775 • Fax 212-966-6644

STARFISH INC
707 N 35th St
Seattle, WA 98103-8802
206-547-3000

STARGATE
PO Box 17221
San Diego, CA 92177-7221
858-483-8206

STARLITE CUISINE
1429 Virginia Ave Ste F
Baldwin Park, CA 91706-5869
www.starlitecuisine.com
626-338-8233 • Fax 626-338-8408

STARPORT FOODS
PO Box 323
San Carlos, CA 94070-0323
650-592-6052

STASERO INTERNATIONAL
2001 S Plum St
Seattle, WA 98144-4536
www.stasero.com
206-328-0690 • Fax 206-324-4586

STASH TEA CO.
1420 18th Ave Apt 38
Belmar, NJ 07719-3760
e-mail: bheight1@aol.com
www.stashtea.com
732-280-5583 • Fax 732-280-5593

STATE FAIR FOODS
3900 Meacham Blvd
Haltom City, TX 76117-1603
www.statefairfoods.com
817-427-7700 • Fax 817-427-7777

STATE FAIR FOODS, INC
4547 Westgrove Dr
Addison, TX 75001-3215
800-874-0453

STATE HOTEL SUPPLY
125 Newark St
Newark, NJ 07103-3197
973-621-7766 • Fax 973-621-1661

STAVIS SEAFOODS INC
7 Channel St
Boston, MA 02210-2385
617-482-6349

STAWSKI DISTRIBUTING CO.
1521 W Haddon Ave
Chicago, IL 60622-3961
www.stawskidistributing.com
773-278-4848 • Fax 773-278-5206

STEARNS & LEHMAN, INC.
30 Paragon Pkwy
Mansfield, OH 44903-8074
www.stearns-lehman.com
419-522-2722 • Fax 419-522-1152

STEEL XTREME
15844 Briarwood Dr
Redding, CA 96001-9784
e-mail:
b@restaurantaccessories.com
415-495-3424 • Fax 415-546-6664

STEELITE INTERNATIONAL USA
4041 Hadley Rd Ste A
South Plainfield, NJ 07080-1111
800-367-3493

STEFANO FOODS, INC.
5230 Terminal St
Charlotte, NC 28208-1250
www.stefanofoods.com
704-399-3935 • Fax 704-399-3930

STEFANO'S PROVISIONS, INC
PO Box 650
Huntington, NY 11743-0650
516-942-0147

STELLAR GROUP
2900 Hartley Rd
Jacksonville, FL 32257-8221
904-260-2900

STEP FORWARD COMPANY
15406 SE 280th St
Kent, WA 98042-4345
www.stepforward.com
253-631-0683 • Fax 253-631-6135

STEPHAN AND BRADY
1850 Hoffman St
Madison, WI 53704-2594
608-241-4141

STEPHAN BRADY ADVERTISING
333 Waukegan Rd
Glenview, IL 60025-5122
847-486-8400 • Fax 847-486-8840

STEPHAN MACHINERY CORPORATION
7200 Alum Creek Dr Ste 1
Columbus, OH 43217-1349
www.stephan-usa.com
614-497-8951

STERIL-SIL COMPANY
150 Causeway St
Boston, MA 02114-1301
617-742-2710

STERLING & STERLING, INC.
PO Box 161
Great Neck, NY 11022-0161
516-773-8692 • Fax 516-487-0372

STERLING CHINA
511 12th St
Wellsville, OH 43968-1399
www.sterlingchina.com
330-532-1544 • Fax 330-532-4587

STERLING FOODS, INC.
1075 Arion Pkwy
San Antonio, TX 78216-2883
www.sterlingfoodsusa.com
210-490-1669 • Fax 210-490-7964

STERLING SAFE COMPANY
10122 Long Point Rd Ste 103
Houston, TX 77043-4319
e-mail: stercy@cs.com
713-935-0087 • Fax 713-935-0049

STERLING-RICE GROUP, INC.
1035 Pearl St Ste 300
Boulder, CO 80302-5157
303-444-6311

STERN PINBALL
2070 Janice Ave
Melrose Park, IL 60160-1011
708-345-7700 • Fax 708-345-7813

STEVE CONNOLLY SEAFOOD
34 Newmarket Sq
Boston, MA 02118-2601
617-427-7700

STEVE'S MOM, INC.
113 16th St
Brooklyn, NY 11215-4710
e-mail: ruggiebake@aol.com
718-832-6300 • Fax 718-832-6302

STEVEN L. MOONEY, P.C.
315 Commercial Dr Ste D3
Savannah, GA 31406-3645
912-354-6322

STEVENS & ASSOCIATES MARKETING
15B Enterprise Ln Ste B
Smithfield, RI 02917-2424
e-mail:
saoffice@steven-associates.com
401-231-0604 • Fax 401-231-4419

STEWART SUTHERLAND
PO Box 162
Vicksburg, MI 49097-0162
800-253-1034 • Fax 616-649-3961

STEWARTS PRIVATE BLEND
4110 W Wrightwood Ave
Chicago, IL 60639-2172
773-489-2500

STICK PACK USA
134 W 32nd St Ste 605
New York, NY 10001-3201
e-mail: stickpack@aol.com
www.sonnenco.com
212-695-3333 • Fax 212-695-7368

STICK PACK USA
226 S Jackson St
Denver, CO 80209-3128
e-mail: stickpack@aol.com
wwwsonnenco.com
720-982-6937 • Fax 720-941-5796

STIGLMEIR SAUSAGE COMP
619 Chaddick Dr
Wheeling, IL 60090-6037
e-mail:
Stiglmeier@compuserve.com
800-451-8199 • Fax 847-537-1367

STIMSON LANE VINEYARDS
1 Stimson Ln
Woodinville, WA 98072-6982
425-488-1133

STO CORPORATION
3800 Camp Creek Pkwy SW
Atlanta, GA 30331-6247

e-mail: clazowsk@stocorp.com
www.stocorp.com
404-541-0441 • Fax 404-541-1322

STO FINISH SYSTEM
6175 Riverside Dr SW
Atlanta, GA 30331-8039
440-346-3666

STOCK POT
1820 Hypoluxo Rd Ste C-1
Lake Worth, FL 33462-4056
e-mail: kcress@bellsouth.net
561-547-3987

STOCKPOT INC.
22505 State Route 9 SE
Woodinville, WA 98072-6010
www.stockpot.com
425-415-2000 • Fax 425-415-2006

STOCKPOT SOUPS
18211 NE 68th St
Redmond, WA 98052-6732
425-885-0779

STOELTING INC
502 Highway 67
Kiel, WI 53042-1600
www.stoelting.com
920-894-2293 • Fax 920-894-7029

STOELZLE-OBERGLAS USA
7385 Industry Dr
North Charleston, SC 29418-8428
www.stoelzle-oberglas-usa.com
877-786-5953 • Fax 843-767-5557

STOFFEL SEALS
400 High Ave
Nyack, NY 10960-2475
www.stoffel.com
800-345-3503 • Fax 800-566-5855

STOKELY USA INC
PO Box 248
Oconomowoc, WI 53066-0248
262-569-1800 • Fax 262-569-3796

STOLT SEA FARM INC
9149 E Levee Rd
Elverta, CA 95626-9559
916-991-4420

STONE AGE ARTISTRY
PO Box 103
Orlando, FL 32802-0103
e-mail:
ttuscher@stoneageartistry.com
407-876-3660 • Fax 407-876-3660

STONE CARLIE & COMPANY
7710 Carondelet Ave Ste 200
Saint Louis, MO 63105-3317
314 721 5800

STONE HILL WINERY AND RESTAURANT
1110 Stone Hill Hwy
Hermann, MO 65041-1280
573-486-2120

STONE SILO FOODS
PO Box 77
South Sterling, PA 18460-0077
570-676-0809 • Fax 570-676-4031

STONEBRIDGE BUSINESS PART-NERS
135 Corporate Woods Ste 300
Rochester, NY 14623-1459
www.stonebridgebp.com
888-247-9764 • Fax 585-427-8948

STONEGRILL AMERICA, INC.
12810 NE 178th St
Woodinville, WA 98072-5768
e-mail: info@stonegrillamerica.com
425-482-0270 • Fax 425-482-9152

STONELIGHT
5805 Glencove Dr Apt 705
Naples, FL 34108-3144
e-mail: stonelight@worldnet.att.net
www.stonelight.com
239-514-3272 • Fax 239-594-7778

STONEVILLE FURNITURE CO.
PO Box 15
Stoneville, NC 27048-0015
336-573-3751 • Fax 336-573-2773

STONYFIELD FARM YOGURT
10 Burton Dr
Londonderry, NH 03053-7436
603-437-4040

STOOL PLACE
6227 W National Ave
Milwaukee, WI 53214-5049
414-258-2095 • Fax 414-258-0845

STORY & CLARK PIANOS
269 Quaker Dr
Seneca, PA 16346-2419
814-676-6683 • Fax 814-676-9340

STOVE PARTS SUPPLY CO., INC.
PO Box 14009
Haltom City, TX 76117-0009
e-mail: bud@stoveparts.com
www.stoveparts.com
800-433-1804 • Fax 800-272-7358

STRATTON PICTURE CO.
2575 S Park Rd
Hallandale, FL 33009-3813
e-mail: artwork@hotelartwork.com
www.hotelartwork.com
954-966-7078 • Fax 954-966-7795

STRATTON-CROOKE
PO Box 215H
Scarsdale, NY 10583-8715
914-725-5166

STRAUSS FAMILY CREAMERY
PO Box 768
Marshall, CA 94940-0768
e-mail: family@strausmilk.com
415-663-5464 • Fax 415-663-5465

STROEHMANN BAKERIES INC
3996 Paxton St
Harrisburg, PA 17111-1423
717-564-1891 • Fax 717-564-9231

STROMBERG ARCHITECTURAL PRODUC
4400 Oneal St
Greenville, TX 75401-7018
www.strombergarchitectural.com
903-454-8682 • Fax 903-454-3642

STRONGWELL
400 Commonwealth Ave
Bristol, VA 24201-3800
e-mail: webmaster@strongwell.com
www.strongwell.com
276-645-8000 • Fax 276-645-8132

STRUCTURAL CONCEPTS CO
888 Porter Rd
Muskegon, MI 49441-5895
www.sudwerk.com
231-798-6232 • Fax 231-798-0590

STRUCTURES UNLIMITED INC
PO Box 4105
Manchester, NH 03108-4105
800-225-3895

STSN
7090 Union Park Ctr
Midvale, UT 84047-4156
e-mail: llitton@stsn.com
www.stsn.com
801-265-2202 • Fax 801-265-2212

STUART FEIGENBAUM ASSOCIATES
4602 Wimbleton Way
Kalamazoo, MI 49009-2411
616-342-0363

STUART'S BEVERAGES
112 W Trillium Cir
Spring, TX 77381-6006
936-273-6800 • Fax 936-273-6864

STUDENTS IN FREE ENT
1959 E Kerr St
Springfield, MO 65803-4775
800-677-7433

STYLELINE DOORS
6200 Porter Rd
Sarasota, FL 34240-9696
www.styleline.com
800-237-3940

STYLES MANUFACTURING CORPORATION
3571 Hargale Ct
Oceanside, NY 11572-5821
e-mail: irenes@erols.com
www.hotelhangers.com
800-393-7230 • Fax 347-234-2272

SUBURBAN LODGES OF AMERICA
1000 Parkwood Cir SE
Atlanta, GA 30339-2131
770-951-9511

SUBWAY FRANCHISES
325 Bic Dr
Milford, CT 06460-3059
203-877-4281

SUBZONE CORPORATION
9238 Madison Blvd Ste 1500
Madison, AL 35758-9103
256-772-7299

SUCCESS CREATIONS
700 Vassar Ave
Lakewood, NJ 08701-6907
732-364-4357

SUDEK INTERNATIONAL
402 Springhouse Dr
Whitehouse Station, NJ 08889-3217
www.sudekinternational.com
908-534-9242 • Fax 908-534-0808

SUDWERK
2001 2nd St
Davis, CA 95616-5474
www.sudwerk.com
530-758-8700 • Fax 530-753-0590

SUGAR ASSOCIATION
1101 15th St NW
Washington, DC 20005-5002
202-785-1122

SUGAR CREEK PACKING CO
2101 Kenskill Ave
Washington Crt House, OH 43160-9404
740-355-3586 • Fax 740-333-3962

SUGAR FLOWERS PLUS
601 Vine St
Glendale, CA 91204-1417
www.sugarflowers.com
818-545-3592 • Fax 818-545-7459

SUGAR FOODS CORP
950 3rd Ave Fl 21
New York, NY 10022-2786
800-832-4968

SUGAR STIX INC
9550 Satellite Blvd
Orlando, FL 32837-8468
e-mail: stewcfc@gte.net
www.sugarstixflorida.com
407-816-8110

SUGAREX-CONSORCIO SAN MIGUEL
515 S Fry Rd # 132
Katy, TX 77450-9101
e-mail: sugara1999@aol.com
713-850-9232 • Fax 281-693-1508

SUGARLOAF CREATIONS
5650 Central Ave
Boulder, CO 80301-2821
303-444-2559 • Fax 303-247-0479

SUGATSUNE AMERICA, INC.
221 Selandia Ln
Carson, CA 90746-1414
www.sugatsune.com
310-329-6373 • Fax 310-329-0819

SUGO MUSIC & DESIGN
77 Federal St Fl 2
San Francisco, CA 94107-1414
415-278-1330 • Fax 415-278-1303

SULLIVAN COLLEGE'S NATIONAL
3101 Bardstown Rd
Louisville, KY 40205-3013
www.sullivan.edu
502-456-6505 • Fax 502-456-0040

SULLIVAN CONSULTING JIM
694 S Keller Park Dr
Appleton, WI 54914-8545
920-830-3915

SUMIKIN BUSSAN INTERNATIONAL CORP
1305 Wiley Rd Ste 130
Schaumburg, IL 60173-4354
e-mail: tsuchi@sbicc.com
847-882-6700 • Fax 847-882-3725

SUMMA CORPORATE IMAGE
1412 Broadway Rm 706
New York, NY 10018-3325
e-mail: ny02@brigatta.com
800-655-5572 • Fax 212-997-7530

SUMMIT BANK
301 Carnegie Ctr
Princeton, NJ 08540-6227
www.summitbank.com

SUMMIT BREWING COMPANY
910 Montreal Cir
Saint Paul, MN 55102-4246
651-256-7800 • Fax 651-265-7801

SUMMIT CATALOG CO
7006 S Alton Way Ste D
Englewood, CO 80112-2019
800-378-6648

SUMMIT COMMERCIAL DIVISION
1435 Watson Ave
Bronx, NY 10472-5303
www.summitcommercial.com
718-893-3900 • Fax 718-842-3093

SUMMIT CONSULTING, INC
2310 Az Park Rd
Lakeland, FL 33801-6880
863-665-6060

SUMMIT RESTAURANT REPAIRS
272 Elmont Rd
Elmont, NY 11003-1600
516-326-7900 • Fax 516-326-8021

SUN BELT EQUIPMENT SALES
5018 24th Ave S
Tampa, FL 33619-5340
813-247-1220

SUN COAST INDUSTRIES
2700 S Westmoreland Rd
Dallas, TX 75233-1312
214-330-8671

SUN COM
1555 Poydras St Ste 2200
New Orleans, LA 70112-3726
504-525-1112

SUN MARKETING AGENTS, INC
3609 Parkway Blvd
Leesburg, FL 34748-9662
e-mail: sunmarketing@aol.com
352-365-2781

SUN ORCHARDS
1198 W Fairmont Dr
Tempe, AZ 85282-3437
www.sunorchard.com
480-966-1770 • Fax 480-921-1426

SUN ORCHARDS, INC.
1200 S 30th St
Haines City, FL 33844-9099
e-mail: lrhoden@sunorchard.com
863-422-5062 • Fax 863-422-5176

SUN RAY SEAFOOD INC.
15223 NW 60th Ave
Hialeah, FL 33014-2410
e-mail: pmcapp@mindspring.com
305-216-8670 • Fax 305-819-8172

SUN RICH FRESH FOODS, INC.
515 E Rincon St
Corona, CA 92879-1353
e-mail: johnk@sun-rich.com
909-735-3800 • Fax 909-735-3322

SUN TELECOM INTERNATIONAL
11321 Decimal Dr
Louisville, KY 40299-2445
www.suntelnt.com
502-240-0255 • Fax 502-261-9234

SUNBEAM COMMERCIAL PRODUCTS
2381 NW Executive Center Dr
Boca Raton, FL 33431-7321
e-mail: tarquim@sunbeam.com
www.sunbeamcommercial.com
561-912-4606 • Fax 561-912-4313

SUNBEAM PRODUCTS
PO Box 247
Laurel, MS 39441-0247
888-891-5696

SUNBELT FLOORING INC
3340 Riverside Dr Ste A
Chino, CA 91710-2980
909-628-1090 • Fax 909-628-1280

SUNBELT FOODSERVICE
517 Green St NW
Gainesville, GA 30501-3313
e-mail: shelbypub@aol.com
770-534-8380 • Fax 770-535-0110

SUNBELT IMPORTS
1639 Bissonnet St
Houston, TX 77005-1815
e-mail: salvatore@sunbeltimports.com
www.sunbeltimports.com
713-942-9585 • Fax 713-942-9587

SUNBELT — UBL BUSINESS BROKERS
3200 Ridgelake Dr Ste 400
Metairie, LA 70002-4961
504-828-1515 • Fax 504-828-1599

SUNBERRIES DISTRIBUTOR, INC
2875 Palm Beach Blvd
Fort Myers, FL 33916-1573
e-mail: dfrench4@juno.com
www.sunberries.com
239-337-4293

SUNBURST TRADING COMPANY, INC.
PO Box 630934
Houston, TX 77263-0934
e-mail: suntrade1@cs.com
281-796-9500 • Fax 281-796-8825

SUNCOAST FURNITURE
6291 Thomas Rd
Fort Myers, FL 33912-2269
e-mail: sales@suncoastfurniture.com
www.suncoastfurniture.com
239-267-8300 • Fax 239-267-3010

SUNDANCE AWNING SYSTEMS
515 Ferguson Dr Ste A
Orlando, FL 32805-1040
321-297-1337

SUNDIAL TOWELS INC
4730 Bradley Blvd Apt 105
Chevy Chase, MD 20815-6331
301-869-0055 • Fax 301-760-9494

SUNDOWNER, INC
8550 Laureldale Dr
Laurel, MD 20724-2008
e-mail: jim@sundwnr.com
www.sundwnr.com
410-880-6318

SUNDRELLA CASUAL FURNITURE
8849 W Clarendon Ave
Phoenix, AZ 85037-2655
602-966-9521

SUNKIST
14130 Riverside Dr
Sherman Oaks, CA 91423-2392
818-986-4800 • Fax 818-379-7141

SUNKIST GROWERS
PO Box 3720
Ontario, CA 91761-0993
800-383-7141

SUNKIST GROWERS, INC.
PO Box 7888
Van Nuys, CA 91409-7888
818-379-7181

SUNKIST GROWERS, INC.
720 E Sunkist St # O

Ontario, CA 91761-1861
e-mail: dtitlton@sunkistgrowers.com
909-933-2160 • Fax 909-933-2169

SUNLIGHT FOODS, INC
3550 NW 112th St
Miami, FL 33167-3317
www.sunlightfoods.com
305-688-5400

SUNLITE CASUAL FURNITURE
1600 Jones Rd
Paragould, AR 72450-8866
800-652-5638 • Fax 615-365-6098

SUN-MAID GROWERS OF CALIF
13525 S Bethel Ave
Kingsburg, CA 93631-9232
559-896-8000

SUNMET
5286 S Del Rey Ave
Del Rey, CA 93616-9700
800-821-5134

SUNNY AVOCADO, LTD.
2605 Camino Del Rio S # 22
San Diego, CA 92108-3706
www.sunny-avocado.com
619-297-3573 • Fax 619-297-2960

SUNNY DELL FOODS, INC.
214 S Mill Rd
Kennett Square, PA 19348-3260
www.sunnydell.com
610-444-5820 • Fax 610-444-8477

SUNNY FRESH
206 W 4th St
Monticello, MN 55362-8421
763-271-5600

SUNNYLAND MILLS
4469 E Annadale Ave
Fresno, CA 93725-2221
e-mail: info@sunnylandmills.com
559-223-4983 • Fax 559-233-6431

SUNNYLAND REFINING CO
3330 Richard Arrington Jr Blvd
Birmingham, AL 35234-2304
205-254-0206

SUNSHINE BISCUITS, INC.
100 Woodbridge Center Dr
Woodbridge, NJ 07095-1162
732-855-4000

SUNSWEET GROWERS
901 N Walton Ave
Yuba City, CA 95993-9370
530-674-5010

SUNTORY INTERNATIONAL
515 S Figueroa St Ste 1030
Los Angeles, CA 90071-3390

SUNTRUST MERCHANT SERVICES
7455 Chancellor Dr
Orlando, FL 32809-6213
e-mail: denise.white@suntrust.com
www.suntrust.com
407-858-7440

SUPER CHEM, INC.
1801 N East Ave
Sarasota, FL 34234-7669
941-366-1663

SUPERIOR COFFEE
250 Carol Pl
Moonachie, NJ 07074-1315
e-mail: staceywynn@aol.com
201-393-7470 • Fax 201-939-7569

SUPERIOR COFFEE
1201 Edwards Ave
New Orleans, LA 70123-2229
504-736-9678

SUPERIOR COFFEE
200 W Boden St
Milwaukee, WI 53207-6272
800-686-2326 • Fax 414-483-8593

SUPERIOR COFFEE
23541 Eichler St
Hayward, CA 94545-2742
www.superiorcoffee.com
510-785-8600 • Fax 510-785-1218

SUPERIOR COFFEE
PO Box 535488
Grand Prairie, TX 75053-5488
e-mail: jjones@superiorcoffee.com
www.superiorcoffee.com
800-511-5464 • Fax 214-882-8557

SUPERIOR COFFEE
208 NW Business Park Ln
Riverside, MO 64150-9696
800-798-7987

SUPERIOR COFFEE
5105 S Lois Ave
Tampa, FL 33611-3444
www.superiorcoffee.com
813-837-5513

SUPERIOR DRAPERY
385 Prospect Ave
Hackensack, NJ 07601-2570
e-mail: supdrape@aol.com
201-343-3300 • Fax 201-343-0602

SUPERIOR FARMS
1477 Drew Ave
Davis, CA 95616-4881
800-228-5262

SUPERIOR FARMS
1477 Drew Ave Ste 101
Davis, CA 95616-4881
www.superiorfarms.com
530-758-3091 • Fax 530-758-3152

SUPERIOR KITCHEN SERVICE
399 Ferry St
Everett, MA 02149-5617
e-mail: sksboston@aol.com
www.superiorkitchen.com
617-389-1899 • Fax 617-389-1996

SUPERIOR PRODUCTS
165 Dexter Ave
Watertown, MA 02472-4228
www.superprod.com
617-926-0999 • Fax 617-926-7339

SUPERIOR PRODUCTS MFG. CO
2223 Lombardy Ln
Dallas, TX 75220-2319
www.superprod.com
972-556-1515 • Fax 972-869-4025

SUPERIOR PRODUCTS - NEXT DAY GOURMET
730 The Alameda
San Jose, CA 95126-3154
www.superprod.com
408-293-3123 • Fax 408-293-3198

SUPERIOR PRODUCTS - NEXT DAY GOURMET
2301 Premier Row
Orlando, FL 32809-5602
407-859-7300

SUPERIOR QUALITY FOOD
2355 E Francis St
Ontario, CA 91761-7727
www.superiortouch.com
909-923-4733

SUPERIOR QUALITY PRODUCTS
602 Potential Pkwy
Schenectady, NY 12302-1041

SUPERIOR TEA & COFFEE CO
990 Supreme Dr
Bensenville, IL 60106-1184
www.superiorcoffee.com
630-860-1400 • Fax 630-787-0243

SUPERSERV TECHNOLOGIES
1501 NE Deer Ct
Lees Summit, MO 64086-5965
www.superserv.com
816-525-6800 • Fax 816-525-6886

SUPERVISION INTERNATIONAL
8210 Presidents Dr
Orlando, FL 32809-7623
e-mail: rheiner@svision.com
407-857-9900 • Fax 407-857-0050

SUPHERB FARMS
PO Box 610
Turlock, CA 95381-0610
www.supherbfarms.com
209-633-3600 • Fax 209-633-3644

SUPPLY SIDE INC
2465 Maple St
Atlanta, GA 30344-2429
800-768-0078

SUPREME CORPORATION
PO Box 463
Goshen, IN 46527-0463
574-642-4888

SUPREME METAL
3125 Trotters Pkwy
Alpharetta, GA 30004-7746
www.supremetal.com
Fax 678-740-6010

SUPREME MFG. CO. INC.
5 Connerty Ct
East Brunswick, NJ 08816-1633
732-254-0087 • Fax 732-254-5736

SURAM TRADING
2655 S Le Jeune Rd
Miami, FL 33134-5832
305-488-7165

SUREBEAM CORP
3033 Science Park Rd
San Diego, CA 92121-1101
858-552-9480

SUREFISH QUALITY SPEC.
9600 Stone Ave N
Seattle, WA 98103-2802
206-525-3680

SURFACE SYSTEMS, INC
2121 Chartres St
New Orleans, LA 70116-2029
504-947-7825

SURVEY EXPRESS
5850 Oberlin Dr
San Diego, CA 92121-4719
858-755-4307

SUSHI HOUSE
3720 22nd St
Long Island City, NY 11101-3505
e-mail: sushihouse@yahoo.com
www.sushihouse.com
718-937-2120 • Fax 718-937-2328

SUTER COMPANY, INC.
PO Box 188
Sycamore, IL 60178-0188
815-895-9186

SUTTER HOME WINERY
PO Box 248
Saint Helena, CA 94574-0248
707-963-3104

SWAVELLE-MILLCREEK
295 5th Ave
New York, NY 10016-7103
212-532-8670 • Fax 212-213-0518

SWEDISH SPRING WATER, INC
303 Anastasia Blvd # B
Saint Augustine, FL 32080-4506
e-mail: harryspost@aol.com
904-347-4850

SWEET ART
10576 Lackman Rd
Lenexa, KS 66219-1224
913-495-9825

SWEET BABY RAY'S INC.
3919 Wesley Ter
Schiller Park, IL 60176-2172
www.sweetbabyrays.com
847-928-9300 • Fax 847-928-9341

SWEET HEART CUP CO
4444 W Ledbetter Dr
Dallas, TX 75236-1696
www.sweetheart.com
214-339-3131

SWEET ILLUSIONS ENTERTAINMENT
4110 Sunrise Hwy
Oakdale, NY 11769-1013
631-244-3555

SWEET LIFE ENTERPRISES, INC.
2350 Pullman St
Santa Ana, CA 92705-5507
e-mail: katack@sweetlifeinc.com
949-261-7400 • Fax 949-261-7470

SWEET SAME BAKING CO.
1049 Zerega Ave
Bronx, NY 10462-5401
718-822-0599 • Fax 718-409-0309

SWEET STREET DESSERTS
722 Hiesters Ln
Reading, PA 19605-3095
www.sweetstreet.com
610-921-8113 • Fax 610-921-1465

SWIFTSURE SEAFOOD, INC.
2875 Roeder Ave
Bellingham, WA 98225-2063
e-mail: swiftsure@telcompus.net
www.swiftsureseafoods.com
360-734-8330 • Fax 360-734-6092

SWISHER HYGIENE
6849 Fairview Rd
Charlotte, NC 28210-3363
www.swisheronline.com
800-444-4138 • Fax 800-444-4565

SWISHER HYGIENE
2269 Chestnut St Ste 181
San Francisco, CA 94123-2600
www.swisheronline.com
415-453-0880 • Fax 415-453-8310

SWISHER HYGIENE
PO Box 263
Humble, TX 77347-0263
www.swisheronline.com
281-441-6336 • Fax 281-441-6211

SWISS CHALET FINE FOODS
9455 NW 40th Street Rd
Miami, FL 33178-2941
305-592-0008

SWISS-AMERICAN, INC.
4245 Papin St
Saint Louis, MO 63110-1735
e-mail: kvarrone@swissamerican
800-325-8150 • Fax 314-533-0765

SWITZERLAND CHEESE MKTG
704 Executive Blvd
Valley Cottage, NY 10989-2010
e-mail: rosemari@switzcheese.com
845-268-2460 • Fax 845-268-2480

SYD & DIANE'S
120 W Indiana Ave
Perrysburg, OH 43551-1577
e-mail: sydanddi@primenet.com
419-874-8012 • Fax 419-874-4064

SYLVEST FARMS, INC.
5550 Mallory Rd
Atlanta, GA 30349-2740
800-525-6911 • Fax 404-768-2971

SYMBOL MATTRESS
PO Box 6689
Richmond, VA 23230-0689
e-mail: akirtland@worldnet.att.net
www.symbolmattress.com
800-446-2791 • Fax 800-353-8762

SYMBOL TECHNOLOGIES
116 Wilbur Pl
Bohemia, NY 11716-2427
631-563-2400

SYMPHONY PASTRIES INC.
114 Wyllis Ave
Everett, MA 02149-1142
800-224-7630

SYNXIS
7926 Jones Branch Dr
Mc Lean, VA 22102-3303
e-mail: clevitt@synxis.com
703-448-2530 • Fax 703-448-2570

SYRACUSE CHINA CORP
PO Box 4820
Syracuse, NY 13221-4820
315-455-5671

SYRACUSE SAUSAGE CO.
PO Box 118
Ponder, TX 76259-0118
940-479-2700 • Fax 940-479-2715

SYROCO
7528 State Fair Blvd
Baldwinsville, NY 13027-9158
315-635-9911 • Fax 315-635-1089

SYSCO
PO Box 15316
Houston, TX 77220-5316
713-679-5204 • Fax 713-679-5227

SYSCO
200 W Story Rd # 200
Ocoee, FL 34761-3004
e-mail: kermmoade.don.r022@sysco.com
407-877-1476

SYSCO CORPORATION
1390 Enclave Pkwy
Houston, TX 77077-2099
www.sysco.com
281-584-1390 • Fax 281-584-4070

SYSCO FOOD SERVICE OF EASTERN WISCONSIN
1 Sysco Dr
Jackson, WI 53037-9226
262-677-6363 • Fax 262-677-6392

SYSCO FOOD SERVICE OF NEW ORLEANS
1451 River Oaks Rd W
New Orleans, LA 70123-2176
504-731-3226

SYSCO FOOD SERVICES
3000 69th St E
Palmetto, FL 34221-8440
941-721-1406 • Fax 941-721-1588

SYSCO FOOD SERVICES OF SAN FRANCISCO
5900 Stewart Ave
Fremont, CA 94538-3134
510-226-3000 • Fax 510-226-3481

SYSCO FOOD SERVICES OF KANSAS
1915 E Kansas City Rd
Olathe, KS 66061-5858
913-780-8377

SYSTEM IV
6641 W Frye Rd
Chandler, AZ 85226-3322
www.systemsiv.com
480-961-1225

SYSTEMS3 POS
166 Sunflower Rd
Opelousas, LA 70570-1709
337-543-6389

TEC AMERICA
4401 Bankers Cir # A
Atlanta, GA 30360-2787
www.tecamerica.com
770-449-3040 • Fax 770-449-1152

TNA NORTH AMER
PO Box 35
Williamsport, PA 17703-0035
570-326-1300

T & L CREATIVE SALADS
8802 Foster Ave
Brooklyn, NY 11236-3211
e-mail: tnlsalads@netscape.net
718-272-6400 • Fax 718-272-0035

T & S BRASS & BRONZE WORKS
PO Box 1088
Travelers Rest, SC 29690-1088
www.tsbrass.com
864-834-4102 • Fax 864-834-3518

T. LYNN ASSOCIATES
5772 Northpointe Ln
Boynton Beach, FL 33437-2018
561-733-0723

T.A. DOWD & CO., INC
5625 Crawford St
New Orleans, LA 70123-5515
504-733-5047

T.C. MILLWORK, INC
PO Box 826
Bensalem, PA 19020-0826
www.spectrimmoldings.com
215-245-4210 • Fax 215-216-1051

T.G. LEE DAIRY
315 N Bumby Ave
Orlando, FL 32803-6088
407-894-4941

T.G.I.F
429 Islamorada Blvd
Punta Gorda, FL 33955-1889
941-505-2447

T. MARZETTI COMPANY
PO Box 29163
Columbus, OH 43229-0163
614-846-2232 • Fax 614-828-8330

TABLE DECOR INTERNATIONAL
PO Box 71872
Marietta, GA 30007-1872
www.tabledecor.com
770-432-1156 • Fax 770-436-9463

TABLE TOP RESOURCES, INC
7703 Kings Passage Ave
Orlando, FL 32835-5952
e-mail: tabletops@aol.com
407-292-2654

TABLE TOPPINGS INC
3651 NW 81st St
Miami, FL 33147-4444
305-836-8807

TABLECHECK TECHNOLOGIES, INC.
13276 N Highway 183 Ste 103
Austin, TX 78750-3225
www.tablecheck.com
800-522-1347 • Fax 512-219-6964

TABLECLOTH CO INC
514 Totowa Ave
Paterson, NJ 07522-1541
973-942-1555

TABLECRAFT PRODUCTS CO
801 Lakeside Dr
Gurnee, IL 60031-2489
www.tablecraft.com
847-855-9000 • Fax 847-855-9012

TABLEMATE PRODUCTS
2150 Oxford Rd
Des Plaines, IL 60018-1920
847-827-5600 • Fax 847-827-4949

TACO BELL
17901 Von Karman Ave
Irvine, CA 92614-6221
800-487-8226

TACONIC
PO Box 69
Petersburg, NY 12138-0069
518-658-3202

TAFCO
PO Box 269
Hyde, PA 16843-0269
e-mail: tafcob@aol.com
814-765-9615

TAI FOONG USA, INC
6542 US Highway 41 N
Apollo Beach, FL 33572-1710
e-mail: bo-cannon@mindspring.com
www.northernchef.com
813-641-0491

TAICO USA
3451 S Main St
Los Angeles, CA 90007-4413
e-mail: leo@taikousa.com
www.taikousa.com
800-874-7822 • Fax 323-232-8318

TAIKO ENTERPRISES CORP.
1467 W 178th St
Gardena, CA 90248-3227
310-715-1888 • Fax 310-324-1115

TAKE-A-BYTE
PO Box 3649
Gardena, CA 90247-7349
e-mail:
rweinberg@compuserve.com
310-559-5300 • Fax 310-559-0355

TAMPA MAID FOODS INC
PO Box 3709
Lakeland, FL 33802-3709
800-237-7637

TANDEM STAFFING - HOSPITALITY SE
1600 W Sam Houston Pkwy N

Houston, TX 77043-3115
e-mail: len@tandemhouston.com
www.tandemhouston.com
713-722-0220 • Fax 713-722-0285

TANDY SIGN SYSTEM
1908 Peyco Dr S
Arlington, TX 76001-6714
e-mail: cwilli4@tandy.com
817-419-4300 • Fax 817-419-4391

TANGO SHATTERPROOF DRINKWARE
141 Norfolk St
Walpole, MA 02081-1703
888-898-2646

TANIMURA & ANTLE INC
PO Box 4070
Salinas, CA 93912-4070
831-455-2950

TANITA CORPORATION OF AMERICA
2625 S Clearbrook Dr
Arlington Heights, IL 60005-4625
www.tanita.com
847-640-9251 • Fax 847-640-9261

TAPAS INTERNATIONAL, INC
1201 E Landstreet Rd
Orlando, FL 32824-7924
www.tapasfoods.com
407-857-6699

TAPATIO
4685 District Blvd
Los Angeles, CA 90058-2731
e-mail: tapatiohotsauce@earthlink.net
www.tapatiohotsauce.com
323-587-8933 • Fax 323-587-5266

TARA FOOD SYSTEMS - SIEGMASTER SALES
1407 Chestnut Ave
Hillside, NJ 07205-1124
973-923-6978

TARA LINENS
2621 Lee Ave
Sanford, NC 27332-5916
919-774-1300

TARGET DATA SYSTEMS INC
5 Shaws Cv
New London, CT 06320-4974
860-701-3736

TARGET MARKETING
11404 Cronridge Dr
Owings Mills, MD 21117-2217
410-560-1505

TARIFOLD
1930 Raymond Dr
Northbrook, IL 60062-6715
800-594-9170

TAS MANAGEMENT GROUP
7835 Hyacinth Dr
Orlando, FL 32835-5321
407-257-3039

TASK FORCE STAFFING SERVICES INC.
1605 Airline Dr Ste 106
Metairie, LA 70001-5991
504-821-0772

TASSEY'S PIER, INC.
618 Herb River Dr
Savannah, GA 31406-3217
912-355-8654

TASTE IT PRESENTS INC.
200 Sumner Ave
Kenilworth, NJ 07033-1319
908-241-9191 • Fax 908-241-9410

TAXI'S RESTURANTS INTERNATIONAL
1840 San Miguel Dr Ste 206
Walnut Creek, CA 94596-4912
www.taxishamburgers.com
877-448-TAXI • Fax 925-937-7227

TAYLOR CO
750 N Blackhawk Blvd
Rockton, IL 61072-2199
www.taylor-company.com
815-624-5267 • Fax 815-624-8000

TAYLOR DISTRIBUTORS, INC.
873 Cambridge Dr
Elk Grove Village, IL 60007-2436
708-678-0820

TAYLOR ENT. OF WI INC
N8108 Maple St
Ixonia, WI 53036-9403
262-567-7286 • Fax 262-567-7201

TAYLOR ENVIRONMENTAL INSTR.
280 Cane Creek Rd
Fletcher, NC 28732-7402
828-684-5178

TAYLOR FARMS
911 Blanco Cir
Salinas, CA 93901-4449

TAYLOR FARMS FLORIDA, INC
7492 Chancellor Dr
Orlando, FL 32809-6242
407-859-3373

TAYLOR FREEZER OF NEW ENGLAND
1030 University Ave
Norwood, MA 02062-2644
800-245-4002

TAYLOR PRECISION PRODUCTS
2311 W 22nd St
Oak Brook, IL 60523-1225
www.taylorusa.com
630-954-1250 • Fax 630-954-1275

TAYLOR PRECISION PRODUCTS
PO Box 2829
Las Cruces, NM 88004-2829
800-289-0944 • Fax 505-526-4347

TAYLOR PRODUCTS
1328 Southfield Dr SE
Decatur, AL 35603-1439
800-314-7177

TAYLOR PRODUCTS, INC.
255 Raritan Center Pkwy
Edison, NJ 08837-3613
732-225-4620 • Fax 732-225-4630

TAYLOR SHELLFISH FARMS
130 SE Lynch Rd
Shelton, WA 98584-8615
360-426-6178

TAYLOR U.S.
1780 N Commerce Pkwy
Fort Lauderdale, FL 33326-3204
e-mail: salestusco@aol.com
954-217-9100

TAYLOR - FORTUNE DISTRIBUTORS
4137 Washington Ave
New Orleans, LA 70125-1941
504-822-7587

TAYLOR-WHARTON
4075 Hamilton Blvd
Theodore, AL 36582-8575
www.taylor-wharton.com
800-898-2657 • Fax 251-443-2209

TAYMAR INDUSTRIES INC.
PO Box 561
Hayward, CA 94543-0561
800-388-9887 • Fax 800-288-8133

TAZO
301 SE 2nd Ave
Portland, OR 97214-1028
www.tazo.com
800-299-9445 • Fax 503-231-8801

TAZO
1128 Morgan Ave
Drexel Hill, PA 19026-3329
e-mail: bgithens2tazo.com
610-924-0406 • Fax 610-924-0407

TBWA CHIAT DAY, INC.
5353 Grosvenor Blvd
Los Angeles, CA 90066-6913
310-314-5995

TCBY TOWER
425 W Capitol Ave Fl 12
Little Rock, AR 72201-3479
e-mail: modom@tcby.com
501-688-8201 • Fax 501-688-8549

TCS SYSTEMS
217 Route 303
Valley Cottage, NY 10989-2533
845-268-0475

TD ROWE AMUSEMENTS
3 Riverway, Ste 1150
Houston, TX 77056-1948
e-mail: ccotie@tdrowe.com
713-961-2922 • Fax 713-961-3248

TEAM ITALIA
3429 Galt Ocean Dr
Fort Lauderdale, FL 33308-7003
954-563-7575 • Fax 954-563-6465

TECHKNOW
393 Mayfield Rd
Duncan, SC 29334-9755
www.gotechknow.com
864-381-1027 • Fax 864-281-1028

TECHNIBILT - CARI-FLEX
PO Box 309
Newton, NC 28658-0309
800-223-3972

TECHNICAL CONCEPTS
1301 Allanson Rd
Mundelein, IL 60060-3835
e-mail:
jnickel@technicalconcepts.com
www.technicalconcepts.com
847-837-4100 • Fax 847-837-4110

TECHNICAL CONSUMER PRODUCTS
300 Lena Dr
Aurora, OH 44202-8098
www.springlamp.com
440-542-5151 • Fax 440-542-5160

TECHNIUM SPECIALIZED EQUIPMENT
68 Stacy Haines Rd
Medford, NJ 08055-4106
www.techjuice.com
856-702-5910 • Fax 856-702-5915

TECHNOBAKE SYSTEMS, INC
18 Featherbed Ln
Hopewell, NJ 08525-1002
609-466-4502

TECHNOMATIC USA CORP.
1301 W Copans Rd Ste D1.
Pompano Beach, FL 33064-2228
www.techno-coffee.com
800-575-1445 • Fax 954-917-5633

TECMARK LLC
2060 Centre Pointe Blvd
Saint Paul, MN 55120-1269
www.loyaltymarketing.com
651-452-9551 • Fax 651-452-9196

TECO ENERGY
3650 Spectrum Blvd Ste 1
Tampa, FL 33612-9446
e-mail:nbstreetman@tecoenergy.com
www.etrc.com
813-202-1774

TECO PARTNERS
702 N Franklin St
Tampa, FL 33602-4429
e-mail: mtucker@tecopartners.com
813-228-4373 • Fax 813-228-1527

TEECO PRODUCTS, INC
16881 Armstrong Ave
Irvine, CA 92606-4913
www.grandhall.com
949-261-6295 • Fax 949-474-8863

TEEROO'S PRIVATE LABEL BEV-ERAGE
PO Box 2197
Sugar Land, TX 77487-2197
281-242-6444 • Fax 281-242-6444

TEINS DECORATIVES
3 North Ave
Garden City, NY 11530-2125
516-227-1184 • Fax 516-227-1183

TEKNOR APEX
505 Central Ave
Pawtucket, RI 02861-1900
800-556-3864 • Fax 401-725-8000

TELEDYNE WATER PIK
1730 E Prospect Rd
Fort Collins, CO 80525-1310
970-484-1352

TELEMATRIX INC.
5025 Galley Rd
Colorado Springs, CO 80915-2374
e-mail: sales@telematrixusa.com
www.telematrixusa.com
719-638-8821 • Fax 719-638-8815

TELEPHONE TECHNOLOGIES
PO Box 475
Jericho, NY 11753-0475
e-mail: sblidner@ttitel.com
www.ttitel.com
516-433-5962 • Fax 516-433-8342

TELESCOPE CASUAL FURNITURE, INC
PO Box 299
Granville, NY 12832-0299
e-mail:
henryv@telescopecasual.com
www.telescopecasual.com
518-642-1100 • Fax 518-642-2536

TELESCREEN, INC.
PO Box 831
Athens, AL 35612-0831
256-771-7510

TELEDEX LLC
6311 San Ignacio Ave
San Jose, CA 95119-1239
e-mail: sales@teledex.com
www.teledex.com
800-786-8353 • Fax 408-363-3136

TELLER (NEW YORK METRO TELLERM)
321 Grove St
Montclal, NJ 07042-4223
e-mail: oliver@tellermate-us.com
www.tellermate-us.com
973-746-8755 • Fax 973-744-6474

TELLER WEST, INC.
PO Box 50448
Santa Barbara, CA 93150-0448
805-969-6150

TELLERMATE
4016 Flowers Rd Ste 460
Atlanta, GA 30360-3203
800-835-6283

TEMPBADGE PLUS-TEMTEC INC
100 Route 59
Suffern, NY 10901-4927
800-628-0022

TEMPLETON CARPET MILLS
1900 Willowdale Rd NW
Dalton, GA 30720-7107
706-275-8665 • Fax 706-226-4732

TENNEK INC
972 Tapadero Rd
Bailey, CO 80421-1037
303-838-0922

TENNESSEE INSURANC SERVICES INC.
PO Box 10328
Knoxville, TN 37939-0328
865-691-4847

TENNESSEE MAT COMPANY
1414 4th Ave S
Nashville, TN 37210-4123
www.wearwell.com
615-254-8381 • Fax 800-874-4551

TENTE CASTERS, INC
2266 S Park Dr
Hebron, KY 41048-9537
www.tente.com
859-586-5558 • Fax 859-586-5859

TEPPER, WHITMILL & ASSOCIATES
5330 Central Ave
Saint Petersburg, FL 33707-6130
e-mail:
rtepper@tepperwhitmill.com
www.tepperwhitmill.com
727-322-1212

TERMINIX
84 Cummings Park
Woburn, MA 01801-2125
781-932-9244 • Fax 781-935-4787

TERMINIX INTERNATIONAL
655 W Grand Ave Ste 150
Elmhurst, IL 60126-1035
800-432-6084 • Fax 630-369-2027

TERMINIX INTERNATIONAL
938 Linden Ave
South San Francisco, CA 94080-1754
650-225-0131 • Fax 650-225-0365

TERMINIX INTERNATIONAL
PO Box 17167
Memphis, TN 38187-0167
901-537-1762

TERRAPIN RIDGE
120 E Clark St
Freeport, IL 61032-3328
e-mail: lora.morrow@mcness.com
800-999-4052 • Fax 815-232-9768

TERRSOL
254 5th Ave
New York, NY 10001-6406
e-mail: tsolve@aol.com
212-684-1006 • Fax 212-684-4346

TERRYBERRY JEWELRY
2033 Oak Industrial Dr NE
Grand Rapids, MI 49505-6076
800-253-0882

TESA ENTRY SYSTEMS, INC
2100 Nancy Hanks Dr Ste A
Norcross, GA 30071-2922
e-mail: moreinfo@tesalocks.com
www.tesalocks.com
700-447-4105 • Fax 770-448-9429

TETLEY TEA
100 Commerce Dr
Shelton, CT 06484-6204
203-929-9295

TETRA PAK INC
333 W Wacker Dr Fl 15
Chicago, IL 60606-1220
312-553-9200

TEXACO STAR MART
10445 Westoffice Dr
Houston, TX 77042-5308
888-629-6919

TEXAS AGRICULTURAL EXTENSION
2 Abercrombie St
Houston, TX 77084-4233
281-855-5600 • Fax 281-855-5638

TEXAS BEEF COUNCIL
8708 Ranch Road 620 N
Austin, TX 78726-3503
e-mail: beef@txbeef.org
www.txbeef.org
512-335-2333 • Fax 512-335-0582

TEXAS BY-PRODUCTS
515 Pontiac Ave
Dallas, TX 75203-2114
877-943-6300 • Fax 214-946-4917

TEXAS CHEFS ASSOCIATION
1011 Dandelion Dr
Mesquite, TX 75149-2651
972-285-3252 • Fax 972-285-8966

TEXAS CHILL COMPANY
PO Box 4281
Fort Worth, TX 76164-0281
817-626-0983 • Fax 817-626-9105

TEXAS CULINARY ACADEMY
6020 Dillard Cir
Austin, TX 78752-4415
e-mail: lechef@onr.com
www.txca.com
512-323-2511 • Fax 512-323-2126

TEXAS DEPT. OF AGRICULTURE
PO Box 12847
Austin, TX 78711-2847

e-mail: jjones@state.tx.us
www.agr.state.tx.us
512-463-7563 • Fax 512-463-9968

TEXAS FOOD RESEARCH
3202 W Anderson Ln Ste 203
Austin, TX 78757-1022
www.sataysua.com
512-467-9008 • Fax 512-467-0347

TEXAS LEASING COMPNAY
2855 Mangum Rd Ste 403
Houston, TX 77092-7484
e-mail: jljones@texasleasing.com
www.texasleasing.com
713-686-7765 • Fax 713-686-7875

TEXAS OSTRICH ASSOCIATION
2006 Westmoor Pl
Arlington, TX 76015-1149
www.mindspring.com\txostrich\index
817-377-6233

TEXAS RESTAURANT INSURANCE SOLUTIONS
PO Box 26610
Austin, TX 78755-0610
888-874-1584 • Fax 512-346-0518

TEXAS TECH UNIVERSITY
PO Box 41162
Lubbock, TX 79409-1162
806-742-3068 • Fax 806-742-3042

TEXAS WOMEN'S UNIVERSITY
PO Box 425888
Denton, TX 76204-5888
e-mail: nutrfdsci@twu.edu
www.twu.edu-hs-nfs
940-898-2636 • Fax 940-898-2534

TEXASWEET CITRUS MARKETING, INC
901 Business Park Dr
Mission, TX 78572-6048
e-mail: bob@texasweet.com
www.texasweet.com
956-580-8004 • Fax 956-580-1843

TEXTRON INC-EZ-GO DIVISION
1451 Marvin Griffin Rd
Augusta, GA 30906-3852
800-231-7087

TFIS
2108 Walnut Creek Dr
League City, TX 77573-6408
281-538-4556 • Fax 281-538-6452

THAI KITCHEN
2121 Peralta St Ste 114
Oakland, C 94607-1619
www.thaikitchen.com
510-268-0209 • Fax 510-834-3102

THAYER EGG COMPANY
962 87th Ave
Oakland, CA 94621-1646
e-mail: jbenson@jswest.com
510-569-7943 • Fax 510-569-0352

THE ALLIED GROUP OF COMPANIES
20 Commerce Dr
Cranford, NJ 07016-3612
e-mail: bfiorito@alliedna.com
908-709-2075 • Fax 908-709-3720

THE AMERICAN CHEESE SOCIETY
PO Box 303
Delavan, WI 53115-0303
e-mail: ljwelch@elknet.net
262-728-4458 • Fax 262-728-1658

THE AMERICAN INSTITUTE OF WINE
445 E Illinois St Ste 450
Chicago, IL 60611-5306
312-329-1280 • Fax 312-329-1281

THE AMERICAN WATER BROOM COMPANY
3565 McCall Pl
Atlanta, GA 30340-2801
800-241-6565 • Fax 770-455-4478

THE ANTIGO CHEESE COMPANY
PO Box 503

Antigo, WI 54409-0503
800-356-5655 • Fax 715-623-4501

THE ART INSTITUTE OF HOUSTON
1900 Yorktown St
Houston, TX 77056-4113
e-mail: neidigkb@aii.edu
www.aih.aii.edu
713-623-2040 • Fax 713-966-2797

THE ART INSTITUTES — CULINARY
675 S Broadway
Denver, CO 80209
www.aii.edu
303-778-8300 • Fax 303-778-8312

THE BAKER AGENCY
14850 Montfort Dr Ste 197
Dallas, TX 75254-6724
214-661-1186

THE BAXTER GROUP
225 C St SE
Washington, DC 20003-1910
202-544-3313

THE BLUE FISH FURNITURE CO.
1722 Jefferson Ave
Saint Paul, MN 55105-2052
www.bluefishfurniture.com
651-698-8188 • Fax 651-698-8188

THE BOG BAMBOO LAMP CO
514 14th St
West Palm Beach, FL 33401-2608
e-mail: booklamps@msn.com
561-659-1723 • Fax 561-659-5009

THE BREAD DIP COMPANY
378 Terrace Dr
Friday Harbor, WA 98250-8931
e-mail: breaddip@interisland.net
360-378-6070 • Fax 360-378-5346

THE BUCKHEAD BEEF CO.
2194 Marietta Blvd NW
Atlanta, GA 30318-2136
www.buckheadbeef.com
800-888-5578 • Fax 404-355-4541

THE BUNTIN GROUP
1001 Hawkins St
Nashville, TN 37203-4758
615-244-5720

THE BYTE DOCTOR
534 Durie Ave
Closter, NJ 07624-2008
e-mail: robert@thebytedoctor.com
Fax 201-541-1195

THE CAPPUCCINO COMPANY IMPORTS
205 Colony Center Dr
Woodstock, GA 30188-6204
www.cappuccinocompany.com
770-649-8541 • Fax 770-649-9444

THE CAPPUCCINO ESPRESSO CO.
1798 Grant St
De Pere, WI 54115-9486
920-983-2324 • Fax 920-983-2325

THE CAWLEY COMPANY
1544 N 8th St
Manitowoc, WI 54220-1902
www.namebadges.com
920-682-7754 • Fax 920-682-5520

THE CHEESECAKE FACTORY PRODUCTS
26950 Agoura Rd
Agoura Hills, CA 91301-5335
818-871-3000 • Fax 818-871-3106

THE CHEF'S SOURCE, INC.
138 Noanett Rd
Needham Heights, MA 02494-2442
781-444-5176 • Fax 781-444-2982

THE CHICAGO CORPORATION
208 S La Salle St
Chicago, IL 60604-1000
312-855-8790

THE CHILE GUY
PO Box 1839
Bernalillo, NM 87004-1839
vchile489@aol.com
www.chileguy.com
800-869-9218 • Fax 505-867-4252

THE CHINET COMPANY
PO Box 228
Dennis, TX 76439-0228
972-724-1148 • Fax 972-724-1297

THE CHINET COMPANY
242 College Ave
Waterville, ME 04901-6226
207-873-3351 • Fax 207-877-6254

THE CHOCOLATE.COM
16 Colonel Robert Magaw Pl
New York, NY 10033-5232
212-781-9980 • Fax 212-781-9997

THE CLARK COMPANY
822 Perdido St Ste 105
New Orleans, LA 70112-4035
504-524-0788

THE CLARK GROUP LTD
715 Cedar Creek Rd
Grafton, WI 53024-1197
262-375-3129 • Fax 262-375-1041

THE CLOROX COMPANY
1221 Broadway
Oakland, CA 94612-1837
510-271-7000 • Fax 510-271-7758

**THE COASTAL
GROUP - REDSCOPE**
149 5th Ave Fl 4
New York, NY 10010-6828
e-mail: dweiss@thcoastalgroup.com
www.thecoastalgroup.com
212-505-6000 • Fax 212-505-6996

THE COBORD GROUP, INC.
61 Brown Rd
Ithaca, NY 14850-1247
www.cbord.com
607-257-2410 • Fax 607-257-1902

**THE COOKING AND
HOSPITALITY INC**
361 W Chestnut St
Chicago, IL 60610-3050
www.chicnet.org
312-944-0882 • Fax 312-944-8557

THE COVEWORKD
PO Box 297
Chatsworth, GA 30705-0297
706-517-5170 • Fax 706-517-9483

**THE CULINARY INSTITUE OF
AMERICA**
433 Albany Post Rd
Hyde Park, NY 12538-1405
845-452-9600 • Fax 845-451-1068

THE CUSTOMER CONNECTION
621 S Andreasen Dr Ste B
Escondido, CA 92029-1904
760-489-8339

**THE DALLAS GROUP OF
AMERICA INC**
PO Box 489
Whitehouse, NJ 08888-0489
www.dallasgroupofamerica.com
908-534-7800 • Fax 908-534-0084

THE DANNON COMPANY
120 White Plains Rd
Tarrytown, NY 10591-5526
914-366-9700 • Fax 914-366-2805

THE DESIGNER'S TOUCH
200 Opatrny Dr
Fox River Grove, IL 60021-1020
www.frescoplaster.com
847-639-1484 • Fax 847-639-1485

THE DIAL CORPORATION
15501 N Dial Blvd
Scottsdale, AZ 85260-1619
800-253-DIAL • Fax 800-599-7606

THE DODDS COMPANY
1661 Botelho Dr
Walnut Creek, CA 94596-5038
800-963-6337 • Fax 925-943-2084

THE EATHGRAINS CO.
8400 Maryland Ave
Saint Louis, MO 63105-3668
314-259-7000 • Fax 314-259-7281

THE ECOFLAME COMPANY
7066 NW 50th St
Miami, FL 33166-5634
e-mail: ecoflame@ecoflame.com
305-470-6595 • Fax 305-470-8046

THE ELEK GROUP LTD.
919 Wilhelm St
Pittsburgh, PA 15220-5726
412-434-6275

**THE ELI'S CHEESECAKE
COMPANY**
6701 W Forest Preserve Ave
Chicago, IL 60634-1470
www.eliasoncorp.com
773-736-3417 • Fax 773-205-3801

THE ELVASTON GROUP
559 E 82nd St
Brooklyn, NY 11236-3118
718-531-1311

THE EMPIRE CO
6500 NE Halsey St
Portland, OR 97213-4968
www.empireco.com
503-227-6433 • Fax 503-227-4187

THE EUREKA COMPANY
1201 E Bell St
Bloomington, IL 61701-6902
309-288-5512 • Fax 309-823-5335

**THE FMP DIRECT
MARKETING GROUP**
1019 W Park Ave
Libertyville, IL 60048-2550
www.accessfmp.com
847-816-1919 • Fax 847-816-1969

THE FOOD EXCHANGE
5610 W Bloomingdale Ave
Chicago, IL 60639-4110
773-745-5900 • 800-283-1990

THE FOOD GROUP
60 Madison Ave # F
New York, NY 10010-1600
212-725-5766 • Fax 212-686-2901

THE FORESIGHT GROUP
153 Windham Ct
Newtown, PA 18940-1751
215-579-8469

THE FREEMAN COMPANIES
5040 W Roosevelt Rd
Chicago, IL 60644-1436
773-379-0600

THE FRENCH PATISSERIE, INC.
1080 Palmetto Ave
Pacifica, CA 94044-2216
www.frenchpatisserie.com
650-738-4990 • Fax 650-738-4995

THE FRESH FISH COMPANY
1621 Locust St
Kansas City, MO 64108-1417
816-221-2464

THE GAMBRINUS CO.
4512 Henican Pl
Metairie, LA 70003-1204
504-454-8308

THE GAMBRINUS CO.
14100 San Pedro Ave
San Antonio, TX 78232-4361
210-424-1434 • Fax 210424-1434

THE GAMBRINUS COMPANY
379 Thornall St Ste 6
Edison, NJ 08837-2226
732-439-7799 • Fax 732-439-8811

THE GELATO FACTORY CO.
13331 Garden Grove Blvd #
Garden Grove, CA 92843-2254
www.thegelatofactory.com
714-750-5000 • Fax 714-750-5005

THE GIFT MENU
800 Main St
Antioch, IL 60002-1542
847-838-5238

THE GROUNDWORK GROUP
719 S 17th St
Philadelphia, PA 19146-2015
215-790-0144 • Fax 2155-455-643

THE H CHAMBERS CO
1010 N Charles St
Baltimore, MD 21201-5492
410-727-4535

THE HAIN FOOD GROUP
50 Charles Lindbergh Blvd
Uniondale, NY 11553-3626
516-237-6200 • Fax 516-237-6242

THE HALE GROUP
8 Cherry St
Danvers, MA 01923-2893
978-777-9077 • Fax 978-774-7883

THE HALL CHINA COMPANY
1 Anna St # 989
East Liverpool, OH 43920-3675
www.hallchina.com
330-385-2900 • Fax 330-385-6185

THE HAPPY CHEF UNIFORMS
22 Park Pl
Butler, NJ 07405-1377
www.happychefuniformas.com
973-492-2525 • Fax 973-492-0303

THE HARLOFF COMPANY INC.
650 Ford St
Colorado Springs, CO 80915-3712
e-mail: exezsets@harloff.com
www.harloff.com
800-433-4064 • Fax 719-597-8273

THE HAYNES GROUP
15235 Alton Pkwy Ste 200
Irvine, CA 92618-2617
949-250-8630 • Fax 949-250-8836

THE HENRY C. ADAMS CORP.
PO Box 707
Mattapoisett, MA 02739-0707
e-mail: bogbeans@ultranet.com
508-758-2726 • Fax 508-758-6064

THE HYSEN GROUP
41740 6 Mile Rd Ste 103
Northville, MI 48167-4383
248-347-0700

THE IRONEES CO
101 E Venango St
Philadelphia, PA 19134-1097
e-mail: Ironees@fast.net
215-634-4474 • Fax 215-634-8678

THE LAUX AGENCY INC
400B City Center
Oshkosh WI 54901-4828
920-231-0090 • Fax 920-231-4313

**THE LESTER E. KABACOFF
SCHOOL**
Lakefront
New Orleans, LA 70148-0001
e-mail: www.uno.edu-~hrt
504-280-6385 • Fax 504-280-3189

THE LOBSTER ZONE BY WIRED
43 Maple Valley Rd
Lynn, MA 01904-1121
781-596-1379 • Fax 781-596-1327

THE MAIN EVENT
15730 Cindy Ct
Fort Myers, FL 33908-4132
239-481-5357 • Fax 239-481-9905

**THE MARKETING
DISTINCTION**
44151 S El Macero Dr
El Macero, CA 95618-1025
530-757-2869 • Fax 530-756-7385

**THE MAYA ROMANOFF
CORPORATION**
1730 W Greenleaf Ave
Chicago, IL 60626-2412
www.mayaromanoff.com
773-465-6909 • Fax 773-465-7089

THE METROPOLITAN TEA CO.
1010 Niagara St
Buffalo, NY 14213-2007
www.metrotea.com
800-388-0351 • Fax 800-319-8327

THE MONARCH COMPANY
1100 Johnson Ferry Rd NE Ste 4
Atlanta, GA 30342-1709
404-252-4511

THE MONTAGUE COMPANY
1830 Stearman Ave
Hayward, CA 94545-1018
510-785-8822 • Fax 510-785-3342

THE MPH GROUP INC.
80 Cedar St
Canton, MA 02021-4218
781-575-9020 • Fax 781-575-9164

THE NETWORK CONNECTION
1811 Chestnut St Ste 11
Philadelphia, PA 19103-3721
e-mail: jcohil@tncx.com
www.tncx.com
215-832-1046 • Fax 215-832-1055

THE NETWORK CONNECTION
806 S Lafayette Ave
Royal Oak, MI 48067-3125
www.tnex.xom
248-541-3113 • Fax 248-541-0066

THE NORTON GROUP
919 Foxborrough Ln Ste 100
Missouri City, TX 77489-3249
281-835-0300

THE NYMAN GROUP LTD.
13942 N 97th Way Ste 100
Scottsdale, AZ 85260-3873
602-488-3666

**THE OLD FASHIONED SYRUP
CO.**
3350 NW Boca Raton Blvd Ste A2
Boca Raton, FL 33431-6653
e-mail: syrup2u@aol.com
561-417-6800 • Fax 561-417-6888

**THE ORIGINAL MANAGER
MEDIC**
7149 Woodmont Way
Fort Lauderdale, FL 33321-2640
www.oriontrading.com
954-718-9275 • Fax 305-884-0891

THE ORTH COMPANY
7350 S 10th Street
Oak Creek, WI 53154-1934
414-764-5500 • Fax 414-764-6739

THE PEPSI BOTTLING GROUP
5000 Hopyard Rd Ste 270
Pleasanton, CA 94588-3319
925-416-2551 • Fax 925-416-2600

**THE PERFECT PUREE OF NAPA
VALLEY**
975 Vintage Ave Ste B
Saint Helena, CA 94574-1400
www.perfectpuree.com
707-967-8700 • Fax 707-967-8799

THE PERLICK CO.
153 South St
East Bridgewater, MA 02333-2303
508-378-2744 • Fax 508-378-1330

THE PERRY GROUP
595 Market St Ste 2500
San Francisco, CA 94105-2838
415-434-0135

THE PIPIA GROUP
2421 N Mayfair Rd Ste 17
Milwaukee, WI 53226-1407
www.pipia.com
414-456-9550 • Fax 414-456-9551

**THE PLATINUM BEEF &
SEAFOOD**
29 W School St
Bonne Terre, MO 63628-1509
573-358-8850

THE PLITT CO
1455 W Willow St
Chicago, IL 60622-1552
773-276-2200 • Fax 773-276-3350

**THE PROMOTION IN MOTION
CO INC**
1410 N Main St Ste D
Salisbury, NC 28144-3722
704-637-7966

THE PRO-QUIP CORPORATION
44 Gretna Blvd
Gretna, LA 70053-4950
504-367-8774

THE QUAKER OATS COMPANY
321 N Clark Street
Chicago, IL 60610-4714
312-222-7111 • Fax 312-222-8305

THE RAMSEY COMPANY
67 Forest St
Marlborough, MA 01752-3088
e-mail:
akaczmar@ramseycompany.com
508-787-2075 • Fax 508-485-9998

THE REDCO GROUP
11905 W Dearbourn Ave
Milwaukee, WI 53226-3912
800-722-5460 • Fax 414-774-2410

THE RESCO COMPANY
1450 Heggen St
Hudson, WI 54016-2284
715-386-8832 • Fax 715-386-6731

THE RESTAURANT CONNECTION
7527 E 1st St
Scottsdale, AZ 85251-4501
602-957-0570

THE RESTAURANT SCHOOL
4207 Walnut St
Philadelphia, PA 19104-5296
e-mail:
kbecker@therestaurantschool.com
www.therestaurantschool.com
215-222-4200 • Fax 215-222-4219

THE ROASTERIE DESSERTS
69 Empire Dr
Saint Paul, MN 55103-1856
651-312-0912

THE ROBEWORKS, INC
2485 Hunter St
Los Angeles, CA 90021-2519
www.robeworks.com
213-687-1177 • Fax 213-687-3314

THE ROBOT FACTORY, INC.
3740 Interpark Dr
Colorado Springs, CO 80907-5058
www.robotfactory.com
719-447-0331 • Fax 719-447-0332

THE ROOF DOCTORS, INC
229 Hambrick Rd
Houston, TX 77060-5729
e-mail: texflexrf@ev1.net
800-426-9002 • Fax 281-448-5864

THE RYAN GROUP DATACENTER
1521 S Lake Shore Drive
Sarasota, FL 34231-3405
941-922-4723 • Fax 941-922-6037

THE SAUCE.COM
1 Parkway N
Deerfield, IL 60015-2532
www.thesause.com
877-92-SAUCE • Fax 847-529-6730

THE SILVERTO RIDGE FARMS CO.
9229 S Baltimore Ave
Chicago, IL 60617-4626
773-374-5600 • Fax 773-374-9954

THE SIMONSON GROUP
35 Washington St
Winchester, MA 01890-2927
781-729-8906

THE SMART COOKIE, LLC
1350 Manufacturing St Ste 209
Dallas, TX 75207-6591
e-mail: dichoman@onramp.net
www.thesmartcookie.com
214-939-2401 • Fax 214-745-1978

THE SNYDER CONSULTING GROUP
PO Box 10588
Pittsburgh, PA 15235-0588
724-281-4802

THE STELWORTH GROUP, LLC
1315 Brookside Dr
Hurst, TX 76053-3942
e-mail: Ct711@yahoo.com
817-282-3508 • Fax 817-282-3579

THE STERITECH GROUP, INC
3760 N John Young Pkwy Ste 1
Orlando, FL 32804-3220
e-mail: dmackenzie@steritech.com
www.steritech.com
407-578-8172

THE STERO COMPANY
3200 Lakeville Hwy
Petaluma, CA 94954-5675
www.stero.com
800-762-7600 • Fax 707-762-5036

THE STERO COMPANY
35 Forest Ln
Hopkinton, MA 01748-3201
508-435-9889 • Fax 508-435-9779

THE SUTER CO INC
258 May St
Sycamore, IL 60178-1395
800-435-6942 • Fax 815-895-4814

THE SWAN CORPORATION
1 City Ctr Ste 2300
Saint Louis, MO 63101-1874
www.theswancorp.com
314-231-8148 • Fax 314-231-8165

THE SYSTEMS CONSULTING GROUP
790 NW 107th Ave Ste 105
Miami, FL 33172-3100
305-225-3325

THE TEE-ZEL COMPANY INC.
172 Spanish Point Dr
Beaufort, SC 29902-6141
e-mail: lnjl32@aol.com
Fax 843-525-6442

THE THERMOS COMPANY
300 N Martingale Rd Ste 250
Schaumburg, IL 60173-2098
www.thermos.com
888-226-7130 • Fax 847-240-3224

THE TOASTSWELL COMPANY
640 Tower Grove Ave
Saint Louis, MO 63110-1638
314-371-2732

THE TRENWITH GROUP
3200 Bristol St Ste 400
Costa Mesa, CA 92626-1800
949-729-3200

THE UNEMPLOYMENT SERVICE CO.
1119 North Blvd
Baton Rouge, LA 70802-4794
225-292-1602 • Fax 225-344-3919

THE VICTOR COFFEE COMPANY
120 Shawmut Rd
Canton, MA 02021-1414
617-268-6280 • Fax 617-268-8058

THE VOLLRATH COMPANY LLC
1236 N 18th St
Sheboygan, WI 53081-3201
www.vollrathco.com
920-457-4851 • Fax 920-459-6570

THE WARDEN COMPANY
940 S Orange Ave Ste 101
Orlando, FL 32806-1242
www.cwardencompany.com
407-877-0555

THE WHEEL TOUGH COMPANY
1597 E Industrial Dr
Terre Haute, IN 47802-9280
www.wheeltough.com
888-765-8833 • Fax 812-298-1166

THE WINNIE GROUP INC
1636 S Glenstone Ave
Springfield, MO 65804-1506
417-882-1512 • Fax 417-882-7141

THE WORNICK COMPANY
10825 Kenwood Rd
Cincinnati, OH 45242-2811
513-794-9800 • Fax 513-794-0107

THE ZINGS COMPANY
250 Adams Blvd
Farmingdale, NY 11735-6615
631-454-0339 • Fax 631-694-2326

THERMACO INC
646 Greensboro St
Asheboro, NC 27203-4739
800-633-4204

THERMA-KLEEN, INC
8821 Ramm Dr Ste 4
Naperville, IL 60564-3606
e-mail: steamtk@aol.com
www.therma-kleen.com
630-820-6700

THERMAL BAGS BY INGRID INC.
131 Sola Dr
Gilberts, IL 60136-9748
www.thermalbags.com
847-836-4400 • Fax 847-836-4408

THERMAL ENGINEERING (TEC)
PO Box 868
Columbia, SC 29202-0868
800-331-0097 • Fax 888-581-0286

THERMO SOLUTIONS INC.
6311 Cambridge St
Minneapolis, MN 55416-2418
www.thermosolutions.com
612-920-1340 • Fax 612-915-0620

THERMODYNE
4424 New Haven Ave
Fort Wayne, IN 46803-1650
e-mail: kmarkham@uptag.com
www.polarking.com
260-422-1941

THERMODYNE FOODSERVICE
2300 Meyer Rd
Fort Wayne, IN 46803-2910
www.tdyne.com
800-526-9182 • Fax 260-426-0427

THERMOHAUSER
529 Ashland Ave
Southbridge, MA 01550-3149
www.thermohauser.com
508-756-0200 • Fax 508-756-5580

THERMO-KOOL
PO Box 989
Laurel, MS 39441-0989
800-647-7074

THERMO-KOOL MID SOUTH INDUSTRIES
723 E 21st St
Laurel, MS 39440-2457
e-mail: thermo@c-gate.net
610-649-4600 • Fax 601-649-0558

THERMO-SERV, INC.
3901 Pipestone Rd
Dallas, TX 75212-6017
www.thermoserv.com
214-631-0307 • Fax 214-631-0566

THESAUCE.COM
1800 W Larchmont Ave
Chicago, IL 60613-2414
877-927-2823

THE VOLLRATH COMPANY, LLC
PO Box 611
Sheboygan, WI 53082-0611
800-624-2051

THINKDIRECTMARKETING .COM
400 Lashley St Ste D1
Longmont, CO 80501-7612
www.thinkdirectmarketing.com
303-651-6778 • Fax 303-651-6835

THIRD COAST PRODUCE
3145 Produce Row
Houston, TX 77023-5813
e-mail:
gfinch@thirdcoastproduce.com
www.thirdcoastproduce.com
713-924-4020 • Fax 713-924-6992

THOMAS FOOD INDUSTRY REGISTER
5 Penn Plz
New York, NY 10001-1810
www.tfir.com
212-290-7341 • Fax 212-290-8749

THOMAS LEON IMPORTS
1203 5th Ave
Rock Island, IL 61201-8540
309-788-0135 • Fax 309-788-0148

THOMAS SIGN & AWNING
4590 118th Ave N
Clearwater, FL 33762-4405
e-mail: info@thomas-sign.com
727-573-7757 • Fax 727-573-0328

THOMASVILLE FURNITURE INDUSTRIES
PO Box 339
Thomasville, NC 27361-0339
e-mail: csnider@thomasville.com
www.thomasville.com
336-476-2175 • Fax 336-472-4057

THOMPSON PACKERS, INC.
PO Box 6150
Slidell, LA 70469-6150
985-641-6640

THOMPSON ASSOCIATES
4444 US Highway 98 N Lot 312
Lakeland, FL 33809-0128
863-653-2003

THOMSON CONSUMER ELECT
10330 N Meridian St
Indianapolis, IN 46290-1088
317-587-3000

THORMAN ASSOCIATES
950 Watertown St Ste 12
West Newton, MA 02465-2103
e-mail: mikethor@1x.netcom.com
617-332-0918 • Fax 617-965-7169

THOROGOOD DIVISION WEIN-BRENNER
108 S Polk St
Merrill, WI 54452-2348
715-536-5521 • Fax 715-536-1172

THOUGHT FOR FOOD
3114 Eoff St
Wheeling, WV 26003-4116
304-232-7970

THREE COINS IMPORT INC
PO Box 1178
Palmetto, GA 30268-7178
e-mail: threecoins@mindspring.com
www.threecoins.com
770-253-0078 • Fax 770-253-0555

THREE SISTERS FARMSTEAD CHEESE
17456 Avenue 232
Lindsay, CA 93247-9767
559-562-2132 • Fax 559-562-9596

THUNDER GROUP (TAR-HONG)
5717 Ferguson Dr
Los Angeles, CA 90022-5101
www.tarhong.com
800-844-1828 • Fax 323-869-9881

THUNDERBIRD FOOD MACHINERY
PO Box 3258
Blaine, WA 98231-3258
360-366-9328

TIBERSOFT CORPORATION
1 Research Dr
Westborough, MA 01581-3922
www.tibersoft.com
508-898-9555 • Fax 508-898-1820

TIEFENTHALER MACHINERY
450 N Sunny Slope Rd Ste 2
Brookfield, WI 53005-4860
262-789-0300

TIGER CORPORATION - I-WARD USA
15531 Carmenita Rd
Santa Fe Springs, CA 90670-5609
562-926-7171 • Fax 562-926-3383

TIGER REF
6 Ashland St
Everett, MA 02149-3396
617-389-2900 • Fax 617-387-1448

TIGER REWARD SYSTEMS, INC.
PO Box 210
Edgewater, NJ 07020-0210
e-mail:
sales@tigerrewardsystems.com
www.tigerrewardsystems.com
201-224-8820 • Fax 201-224-3263

TILLAMOOK FOOD SALES
PO Box 230667
Portland, OR 97281-0667
503-639-5512 • Fax 503-639-7037

TIME MANAGEMENT CORP.
9979 Valley View Rd
Eden Prairie, MN 55344-3596
www.timemgmt.com
952-943-9077 • Fax 952-943-4860

TIMECORP SYSTEMS
8800 Roswell Rd
Atlanta, GA 30350-1826
770-552-1167

TIMELESS HOSPITALITY
317 Madison Ave Rm 1122
New York, NY 10017-5240
e-mail: david@bookonlinenow.com
www.bookonline.com
212-581-5226 • Fax 212-898-1145

TIMELOX INC
500 N Rainbow Blvd
Las Vegas, NV 89107-1082
702-221-2099

TIMELY DOOR SYSTEMS
10241 Norris Ave
Pacoima, CA 91331-2218
818-896-3094

TIMEPAY$
11 Hillside St
Milton, MA 02186-5217
617-698-6414 • Fax 617-698-6825

TLC NOVELTY COMPANY INC.
8488 Highway 23
Belle Chasse, LA 70037-2528
800-943-0800

TLC SERVICES,INC
1226 Montegut St
New Orleans, LA 70117-7237
504-945-1148

TM PRATT & COMPANY
100 NE 38th St Ste 5
Miami, FL 33137-3654
e-mail: info@permitex.com
www.permitex.com
305-576-3316 • Fax 305-576-8416

TNT CRUST
1438 Cedar St
Green Bay, WI 54302-1859
920-431-7240 • Fax 920-431-7249

TNT SHIRT CO.
2400 Taft St
Houston, TX 77006-3110
www.tntshirts.com
713-522-0986

TODAY'S RESTAURANT NEWS
PO Box 970182
Boca Raton, FL 33497-0182
e-mail: trn1997@aol.com
www.trnusa.com
561-470-7679

TODDS ENTERPRISES
2450 White Rd
Irvine, CA 92614-6250
800-568-6337 • Fax 949-724-1338

TODDY PRODUCTS
1206 Brooks St
Houston, TX 77009-8809
www.toddyproducts.com
713-225-2066 • Fax 713-225-2110

TODHUNTER IMPORTS
222 Lakeview Ave
West Palm Beach, FL 33401-6145
561-655-8977

TOM ATSIDE'S RESTAURANT EQUIPMENT
3102 W Silver Springs Blvd
Ocala, FL 34475-5648
352-622-5532

TOM CAT BAKERY
4305 10th St
Long Island City, NY 11101-6829
718-786-7659 • Fax 718-472-0510

TOMCO SERVICES, INC.
4756 S Buckner Blvd
Dallas, TX 75227-2301
e-mail: sales@tomcotexas.com
www.tomcotexas.com
214-381-3000 • Fax 214-275-6206

TOMLINSON INDUSTRIES
13700 Broadway Ave
Cleveland, OH 44125-1945
e-mail: jengle@ameritech.net
www.tomlinsonind.com
216-587-3400 • Fax 216-587-0733

TOMY CORPORATION
4695 Macarthur Ct Ste 130
Newport Beach, CA 92660-8846
www.tomy.com
949-955-1030

TONE BROTHER'S INC.
2301 SE Tones Dr
Ankeny, IA 50021-8790
www.spiceadvice.com
515-965-2711 • Fax 515-965-2802

TONY CHACHERE'S INC.
PO Box 1639
Opelousas, LA 70571-1639
800-551-9066

TONY'S BAR SUPPLY CO., INC.
5201 S Wayside Dr
Houston, TX 77087-2000
713-641-2277 • Fax 713-641-2298

TOO COOL, INC
411 Lake Tree Dr
Fort Lauderdale, FL 33326-1706
954-385-5640

TOOTERS PROMOTIONS
767 Clearlake Rd
Cocoa, FL 32922-5208
321-631-1005

TOP BRASS
3502 Parkdale Ave
Baltimore, MD 21211-1430
e-mail: klaug45871@aol.com
410-523-5591 • Fax 410-523-5590

TOPPO MANFACTURING CORPORATION
5655 Riggins Ct Ste 20
Reno, NV 89502-6554
www.toppo.com
775-331-0183 • Fax 775-331-2730

TOPS, INC.
PO Box 99
Burleson, TX 76097-0099
817-447-1275

TOP-SHELF MARKETING
2495 Main St Ste 402
Buffalo, NY 14214-2154
716-871-5931

TORANI ITALIAN SYRUPS
2545 Westglen Farms Dr
Ballwin, MO 63011-1930
636-273-6069

TORANI SPECIALTY SYRUPS
233 E Harris Ave
South San Francisco, CA 94080-6807
www.torani.com
650-875-1200 • Fax 650-635-1169

TORKE COFFEE ROASTING CO.
3455 Paine Ave
Sheboygan, WI 53081-8457
800-242-7671 • Fax 920-458-0488

TORREY USA
13003 Murphy Rd
Stafford, TX 77477-3956
281-564-3150

TORTILLA INDUSTRY ASSOC.
16000 Ventura Blvd
Encino, CA 91436-2744
818-981-2547

TORVAC
3000 Wireton Rd
Blue Island, IL 60406-1861
708-388-3223

TOTAL BALANCE ORTHOTICS
PO Box 612
Branson, MO 65615-0612
417-335-8979 • Fax 417-335-8979

TOTAL BALANCE ORTHOTICS
2206 W 76 Country Blvd
Branson, MO 65616-2180
417-355-8979 • Fax 417-338-0800

TOTAL EMPLOYMENT CO.
5050 W Lemon St
Tampa, FL 33609-1104
e-mail:
cdodson@totalemployment.net
www.totalemployment.com
813-289-5566

TOTAL FOOD SERVICE
282 Railroad Ave
Greenwich, CT 06830-6375
e-mail: p-klashmams3@yahoo.com
www.totalfood.com
203-661-9090 • Fax 203-661-9325

TOTAL LOGISTIC CONTROL
8300 Logistics Dr
Zeeland, MI 49464-9379
616-772-9009

TOTAL MANAGEMENT SOLUTIONS INC
6555 Powerline Rd
Fort Lauderdale, FL 33309-2067
954-229-0505

TOTAL ULTIMATE FOODS
683 Manor Park Dr
Columbus, OH 43228-9369
614-870-0732

TOTAL ULTIMATE FOODS - TUF
5134 La Posita St
San Antonio, TX 78233-5843
e-mail: wwestaway@aol.com
210-655-7958 • Fax 210-655-7985

TOTO KIKI USA INC
1155 Southern Rd
Morrow, GA 30260-2917
770-282-8686

TOTO USA
21 Mercer St Fl 4
New York, NY 10013-5812
www.totousa.com
212-752-0008 • Fax 212-751-0121

TOUCH 2000
20 Moody Ave
Fairfield, CT 06432-1925
203-366-8673 • Fax 203-366-8673

TOUCH MENUS, INC.
PO Box 3067
Redmond, WA 98073-3067
www.touchmenus.com
800-688-6368 • Fax 425-867-9735

TOUCH POLL INC.
1870 Aloma Ave Ste 260
Winter Park, FL 32789-4049
e-mail: altoncl@earthlink.net
407-647-7655 • Fax 407-629-7655

TOUCHTUNES DIGITAL JUKEBOX
1110 W Lake Cook Rd
Buffalo Grove, IL 60089-1944
847-419-3300

TOUFAYAN BAKERIES
175 Railroad Ave
Ridgefield, NJ 07657-2312
e-mail: msteve@toufayan.com
800-328-7482 • Fax 201-861-0392

TOUFAYAN BAKERY
9255 Kennedy Blvd
North Bergen, NJ 07047-5395
201-861-4131

TOUFAYAN BAKERY OF FLORIDA
3826 Bryn Mawr St
Orlando, FL 32808-4669
www.toufayan.com
407-295-2257

TOWNSEND CULINARY INC
PO Box 468
Millsboro, DE 19966-0468
302-497-6900 • Fax 302-497-6927

TPA IMPEX USA INC
5261 SW 10th Ct
Fort Lauderdale, FL 33317-4729
954-373-3836 • Fax 954-433-06640

TRAC DOG.COM
PO Box 174
Petersburg, IN 47567-0174
www.tracdog.com
812-789-3702 • Fax 646-924-8563

TRACKIT L.L.C.
3147 N Highway 89
Ogden, UT 84404-1213
e-mail: ksmith@trackit.cc
www.trackit.cc
801-782-0101 • Fax 801-782-3317

TRACOMAN INC
3000 SW 42nd St
Ft Lauderdale, FL 33312-6809
954-929-8999

TRACTION PLUS FOOTWEAR
4920 Jefferson Hwy
New Orleans, LA 70121-3101
www.strengthsystems.com
504-818-1270 • Fax 504-818-1273

TRACTION PLUS, INC.
2350 Airport Fwy Ste 222
Bedford, TX 76022-4010
817-685-7184

TRACY LOCKE ADVERTISING
200 Crescent Ct Ste 900
Dallas, TX 75201-1895
214-969-9000

TRADEZONE
3645 San Fernando Rd
Glendale, CA 91204-2916
818-265-2888

TRADINGMEAT.COM
2600 Kitty Hawk Rd
Livermore, CA 94550-7618
888-709-2522

TRAEGER INDUSTRIES - CRAWFORD
PO Box 363
Plainville, KS 67663-0363
785-434-4631

TRAEX CORPORATION
PO Box 217
Dane, WI 53529-0217
800-356-8006

TRAINA DRIED FRUIT
337 Lemon Ave
Patterson, CA 95363-9634
209-892-5472 • Fax 209-892-6231

TRAININ WHEELS
666 Lovett Ave SE
Grand Rapids, MI 49506-3030
e-mail: doug@traininwheels.com
www.traininwheels.com
616-977-6107 • Fax 616-776-9026

TRAINING ACHIEVEMENT PROGRAM
171 E Thousand Oaks Blvd
Thousand Oaks, CA 91360-5712
www.tapseries.com
818-880-5058 • Fax 818-880-9557

TRAINING SOLUTIONS INTERACTIVE
3440 Oakcliff Rd Ste 104
Atlanta, GA 30340-3006
770-220-2500

TRAK-AIR
555 Quivas St
Denver, CO 80204-4915
303-779-9888 • Fax 303-694-3575

TRAMONTINA USA, INC.
12955 W Airport Blvd
Sugar Land, TX 77478-6119
281-340-8400 • Fax 281-340-8410

TRANS OCEAN PRODUCTS
350 W Orchard Dr
Bellingham, WA 98225-1769
360-671-6886 • Fax 360-671-0354

TRANSACT COMMUNICATIONS INC
8423 Mukilteo Speedway
Mukilteo, WA 98275-3237
425-348-5000

TRANSMEDIA RESTAURANT CO., INC
750 Lexington Ave
New York, NY 10022-1200
212-308-7676

TRAP-ZAP ENVIRONMENTAL SYSTEMS
255 Braen Ave
Wyckoff, NJ 07481-2903
201-791-9690 • Fax 201-791-7175

TRAULSEN & CO., INC.
4401 Blue Mound Rd
Fort Worth, TX 76106-1928
www.traulsen.com
800-825-8220 • Fax 817-624-4302

TRAULSEN & COMPANY, INC.
PO Box 560169
College Point, NY 11356-0169
800-937-0013

TRAVELOPS.COM
6833 Vista Pkwy N
West Palm Beach, FL 33411-2710
561-478-8484

TRAVELSCAPE.COM
8951 W Sahara Ave Ste 100
Las Vegas, NV 89117-5826
888-335-0101

TRAVERS COLLINS PARTNERS
120 Delaware Ave
Buffalo, NY 14202-2707
716-842-2222 • Fax 716-842-6424

TRAYCON MANUFACTURING
555 Barell Ave
Carlstadt, NJ 07072-2891
201-939-5555

TREASURE ISLAND CONTRACT DIVISION
31 McKee Dr
Mahwah, NJ 07430-2123
800-291-4666 • Fax 201-529-8090

TREBON EUROPEAN SPECIALTIES
210 Green St
South Hackensack, NJ 07606-1301
201-343-5161 • Fax 201-343-5102

TREE TOP INC
PO Box 248
Selah, WA 98942-0248
509-697-7251

TREESCAPES INTERNATIONAL
4039 Avenida De La Plata
Oceanside, CA 92056-5802
760-631-6789

TREIF USA
464 Westport Ave
Norwalk, CT 06851-4424
203-847-9699 • Fax 203-849-8517

TRENDLINES INC
15506 College Blvd
Lenexa, KS 66219-1350
913-362-0070

TRENTON BRIDGE LOBSTER
RR 3
Ellsworth, ME 04605-9803
207-667-2977

TRI VALLEY GROWERS
12667 Alcosta Blvd
San Ramon, CA 94583-4424
925-327-6400 • Fax 925-327-6976

TRIAC BEVERAGE GROUP
709 Westchester Ave
West Harrison, NY 10604-3103
www.snapple.com
914-397-9200 • Fax 914-286-4648

TRIANGLE FOOD SERVICE
13601 Preston Rd Ste 1050W
Dallas, TX 75240-4901
214-553-7703

TRIANGLE HEALTHCARE INC.-EAST
76 National Rd
Edison, NJ 08817-2809
e-mail: eatco@aol.com
732-287-6100 • Fax 732-287-9292

TRIANGLE METAL & MFG. CO.
11600 Big John St # 38271
Houston, TX 77038-3302
e-mail: triangle@netropolis.net
www.members.tripod.com
281-445-4251 • Fax 281-445-4276

TRIAR SEAFOOD CO.
2046 McKinley St
Hollywood, FL 33020-3165
954-921-1113

TRIARC BEVERAGE
0 Crystal Ln
North Easton, MA 02356-2568
e-mail: snapplepc@aol.com
508-238-2847 • Fax 508-238-2847

TRIARCH INDUSTRIES
4816 Campbell Rd
Houston, TX 77041-9111
713-690-9977

TRIBECA OVEN, INC.
55 Roebling St
Brooklyn, NY 11211-2126
718-300-0000 • Fax 718-782-7961

TRI-C CLB SPPLY INC
6661 Chase Rd
Dearborn, MI 48126-1746
800-274-8742

TRICON FOODSERVICE CONSULTANTS
115 Beulah Rd NE # 2005E
Vienna, VA 22180-4749
703-242-7020

TRIDENT SEAFOODS
5303 Shilshole Ave NW
Seattle, WA 98107-4000
206-783-9817 • Fax 206-782-7246

TRI-MED ENVIRONMENTAL RESEARCH
PO Box 1444
Noblesville, IN 46061-1444
317-776-9942 • Fax 317-773-3612

TRINITY LIGHTING, INC.
PO Box 14
Jonesboro, AR 72403-0014
e-mail: jnlampman@aol.com
www.trinitylighting.com
870-971-1177 • Fax 870-972-6381

TRION INDUSTRIES INC
297 Laird St
Wilkes Barre, PA 18702-6997
570-824-1000

TRISOME FOODS INC
72 Portsmouth Ave
Stratham, NH 03885-2566
877-874-7663

TRITON COLLEGE
2000 5th Ave
River Grove, IL 60171-1995
708-456-0300

TRITON SYSTEMS INC
522 E Railroad St
Long Beach, MS 39560-4933
228-868-1317

TROJAN, INC.
PO Box 850
Mt Sterling, KY 40353-0850
www.trojaninc.com
859-498-0526 • Fax 859-498-0528

TROON GOLF
955 W Vistoso Highlands Dr
Tucson, AZ 85737-5867
520-797-9900

TROPIC CRAFT FURNITURE
4251 S Pine Ave
Ocala, FL 34480-8826
800-327-1541

TROPIC ICE INC
2805 N Commerce Pkwy
Hollywood, FL 33025-3956
954-441-9990

TROPIC STAR SEAFOOD, INC
3620 Ventura Dr E
Lakeland, FL 33811-1229
863-619-2278

TROPICAL AQUACULTURE PROD
128 Merchants Row
Rutland, VT 05701-5909
802-747-6311

TROPICAL CHEESE INDUSTRIES
450 Fayette St
Perth Amboy, NJ 08861-3805
e-mail: tc_sales@tropicalcheese.com
732-442-4898 • Fax 732-442-8227

TROPICAL FRUIT GROWERS OF SOUTHERN FLORIDA
18710 SW 288th St
Homestead, FL 33030-2309
305-248-3311

TROPICAL ILLUSIONS INC
1436 Lulu St
Trenton, MO 64683-1819
660-359-5422

TROPICAL NUT & FRUIT
3368 Bartlett Blvd
Orlando, FL 32811-6482
e-mail: nutsnorl@aol.com
www.tropicalnutandfruit.com
407-843-8141

TROPICANA
1001 13Th Ave E
Bradenton, FL 34208-2699
941-747-4461 • Fax 941-742-3512

TROPICS FROZEN COCKTAILS
920 N Ridge Ave Ste C2
Lombard, IL 60148-1226
630-691-1200 • Fax 630-691-1200

TROPITONE FURNITURE
5 Marconi
Irvine, CA 92618-2594
e-mail: micfel@tropitone.com
www.tropitone.com
949-595-2089 • Fax 949-951-0716

TRUE & ASSOCIATES
PO Box 638
Westfield, NJ 07091-0638
908-232-0760 • Fax 908-232-9271

TRUE FITNESS TECH INC
865 Hoff Rd
O Fallon, MO 63366-1900
800-426-6570

TRUE FOOD SERVICE EQUIPMENT
PO Box 970
O Fallon, MO 63366-0970
www.truemfg.com
Fax 636-272-2408

TRUE TO FORM
250 Crawford St
Fall River, MA 02724-2302
508-324-9090

TRUEGREEN CHEMLAWN
860 Ridge Lake Blvd
Memphis, TN 38120-9421
800-374-8888 • Fax 901-681-1966

TRUESOUPS
26401 79th Ave S
Kent, WA 98032-7321
253-872-0403 • Fax 253-872-0552

TRUFRESH, LLC
334 Ella Grasso Tpke
Windsor Locks, CT 06096-1042
jcgok@aol.com
www.trufresh.com
800-894-1167

TRUSCELLO FOODS
7880 NW 62nd Street
Miami, FL 33166-3539
pappas@truscellofoods.com
305-592-5070

TRY FOODS INTERNATIONAL
207 Semoran Commerce Place
Apopka, FL 32703-4670
800-421-8871 • Fax 407-884-0809

TUBE WORKS, INC
5173 Douglas Fir Rd Ste 1
Calabasas, CA 91302-2582
www.tubeworks.com
818-879-2386 • Fax 818-879-2388

TUBULAR ENGINEERING
71 Merchants Park Drive
Hoschton, GA 30548-2383
rsj1tes@aol.com
www.tubularengineering.com
800-466-6066 • Fax 770-448-7805

TUCKER INDUSTIRES INC
2835 Janitell Road
Colorado Springs, CO 80906-4104
www.burnguard.com
800-786-7287 • Fax 719-527-1499

TUFCO TECHNOLOGIES
4800 Simonton Road
Dallas, TX 75244-5317
800-438-9588

TULKOFF FOOD PRODUCTS
1101 S Conkling Street
Baltimore, MD 21224-5209
410-327-6585 • Fax 410-327-7033

TULSACK
5400 S Garnett Road
Tulsa, OK 74146-590
www.tulsack.com
800-228-1936 • Fax 888-473-3224

TUMARO'S GOURMET TORTILLAS
5300 Santa Monica Blvd # 3
Los Angeles, CA 90029-1131
www.tumaros.com
323-464-6317 • Fax 323-464-6299

TURANO BAKING CO
6501 Roosevelt Road
Berwyn, IL 60402-0718
www.turanobakery.com
708-788-9220 • Fax 708-788-3075

TURANO BAKING CO.
334 S Curtis Road
Milwaukee, WI 53214-1015
414-778-0807 • Fax 414-778-1810

TURBO AIR, INC.
3088 Walnut Avenue
Long Beach, CA 90807-5222
www.turboairinc.com
310-632-3233 • Fax 310-632-1559

TURBO REFRIGERATING
1815 Shady Oaks Drive
Denton, TX 76205-7963
www.turboice.com
940-387-4301 • Fax 940-382-0364

TURBO SYSTEMS INC
700 Pennsylvania Drive
Exton, PA 19341-1129
610-321-1100

TURKISH CONSULATE GENERAL
1990 Post Oak Blvd Ste 1
Houston, TX 77056-3818
713-622-5849 • Fax 713-623-6639

TURNER BROADCASTING SYSTEMS
1 CNN Center NW
Atlanta, GA 30303-2762
404-827-1700

TURTLE ISLAND FOODS
P.O. Box 176
Hood River, OR 97031-0006
seth@tofurky.com
541-386-7766 • Fax 541-386-7754

TUXTON CHINA LLC.
21011 Commerce Point Drive
Walnut, CA 91789-3052
www.tuxton.com
909-595-7700 • Fax 909-595-5353

TWANG, INC
800 Buena Vista Street, Bldg 2
San Antonio, TX 78207-4448
info@twang.com • www.twang.com
210-226-7008 • Fax 210-226-4040

TWIN MARQUIS INC.
328 Johnson Avenue
Brooklyn, NY 11206-2802
www.twinmarquis.com
718-386-6868 • Fax 718-417-0049

TWININGS FOODSERVICE
777 Passaic Avenue
Clifton, NJ 07012-1804
frank@winzig.com
201-342-5765 • Fax 973-650-3063

TWIST & TURNS
625 Campbell Ave SW
Roanoke, VA 24016-3531
540-985-9513 • Fax 540-985-9526

TWO CHEFS ON A ROLL INC
22625 S Western Avenue
Torrance, CA 90501-4950
310-533-0190 • Fax 310-533-5909

TX HOSPITALITY COALITION
P.O. Box 11507
Austin, TX 78711-1507
www.clearingtheair.org
800-965-4689 • Fax 512-708-8699

TXU ELCTRIC & GAS
1601 Bryan Street
Dallas, TX 75201-3401
energyassist@txu.com
www.txu.com
877-290-3722 • Fax 800-253-9602

TY, TY & TY
8225 NW 68th Street
Miami, FL 33166-2760
info@tytyty.com
www.tyrobes.com
305-594-4989 • Fax 305-594-3044

TYFIELD IMPORTERS INC
1410 Allen Drive
Troy, MI 48083-4013
248-589-8282

TYLER REFRIGERATION CO
1329 Lake Street
Niles, MI 9120-1297
800-992-3744

TYMYL CORPORATION
9978 Merito Drive, Apt A
Saint Louis, MO 63128-1745
www.tymyl.com
314-966-5755 • Fax 314-955-8728

TY'S SPICES
3035 Bonney Briar Drive
Missouri City, TX 77459-3110
800-461-0608 • Fax 281-438-2756

TYSON FOODS, INC
P.O. Box 2020
Springdale, AR 72765-2020
www.tyson.com
479-290-4000 • Fax 479-290-4603

TYSON MEXICAN ORIGINAL
4601 Curtiss Drive
Virginia Beach, VA 23455-4319
gordong@tyson.com
757-464-9136 • Fax 757-460-6782

UCLA EXTENSION
10995 Le Conte Avenue, Rm 51
Los Angeles, CA 90095-3001
818-784-7006

USA PEARS
4382 SE International Way
Portland, OR 97222-4635

USA RICE COUNCIL
P.O. Box 740121
Houston, TX 77274-0121
281-270-6699

USA TODAY
1000 Wilson Blvd
Arlington, VA 22209-3901
703-276-5385

US COLD STORAGE INC
100 Dobbs Lane
Cherry Hill, NJ 08034-1436
856-354-8181

US COOLER
325 Payson Avenue
Quincy, IL 62301-4805
217-228-2421

US FRANCHISE SYSTEMS
13 Corporate Sq NE
Atlanta, GA 30329-1906
404-321-4045

US MINT
1111 20th St NW
Washington, DC 20526-0001
202-622-2000

US NONWOVENS CORP
100 Emjay Blvd
Brentwood, NY 11717-3322
631-952-0100

U S P T A/U S PROF TENNIS ASSOCIATION
3535 Briarpark Drive, Ste 1
Houston, TX 77042-5245
800-877-8248

US POTATO BOARD
7555 E Hampden Avenue
Denver, CO 80231-4830
303-369-7718

US PRO TENNIS ASSOC
302 Casey Lane
Dalton, GA 30721-8249
800-438-7782

UTA BUSINESS SYSTEMS
950 N Glebe Road
Arlington, VA 22203-1824
800-282-8909

U V/F X SCENIC PRODUCTIONS
171 Pier Avenue
Santa Monica, CA 90405-5363
310-392-6817

U.A.S., INC
700 Abbott Drive
Broomall, PA 19008-4323
www.uas.com
800-421-6661 • 610-328-2000

U.C. CHAIR COMPANY
23420 Lakeland Blvd
Euclid, OH 44132-2612
800-822-4247

U.S. ACRYLIC, INC.
99 Bond Street
Lincolnshire, IL 60069-4226
847-564-2600 • Fax 847-564-0003

U.S. BEVERAGE
P.O. Box 231224
Montgomery, AL 36123-1224
334-280-1116

U.S. FOODSERVICE
1 Sexton Dr
Glendale Height, IL 60139-1965
630-980-3000 • Fax 630-980-3659

U.S. FOODSERVICE
P.O. Box 14698
Oklahoma City, OK 73113-0698
405-475-4655

U.S. FOODSERVICE
1899 N US Highway 1
Ormond Beach, FL 32174-2579
scottr@datona.usfood.com
386-677-2240

U.S. FOODSERVICE
201 Beacham Street
Everett, MA 02149-5518
617-389-3300 • Fax 617-381-6929

U.S. INTERACTIVE
6955 Portwest Drive, Ste 160
Houston, TX 77024-8018
troy@takehome.com
www.takehome.com
888-520-5133 • Fax 915-520-5120

U.S. LIQUIDS OF DALLAS
4960 Singleton Blvd
Dallas, TX 75212-3337
214-252-5000 • Fax 214-252-5099

U.S. VINYL MANUFACTURING
1766 Broomtown Road
La Fayette, GA 30728-3409
706-638-8400 • Fax 706-638-0137

U.S. FOODSERVICE HAAR DIVISION
849 Newark Tpke
Kearny, NJ 07032-4308
201-955-2100 • Fax 201-246-9318

U.S. SEATING PRODUCTS INC.
1715 S Orange Blossom Trail
Apopka, FL 32703-7746
www.usseating.com
800-476-7328 • 407-884-0911

UBS PAINE WEBBER
P.O. Box 3906
Tampa, FL 33601-3906
michael.bruno@ubspainewebber.com
813-227-2841 • Fax 813-227-2878

UCI, INC
205 Berg Street
Algonquin, IL 60102-3537
847-854-7292 • Fax 847-854-1296

ULTIMATE PROMOTION GROUP
P.O. Box 289
Liberty Corner, NJ 07938-0289
908-580-6667 • Fax 908-580-6668

ULTIMATE TEXTILE
522 E 22nd Street
Paterson, NJ 07514-2616
800-567-4451

ULTIMATE UMBRELLA CO.
69 SW 7th Street
Miami, FL 33130-3009
305-373-7723 • Fax 305-372-9170

ULTRA THIN READY-TO-BAKE PIZZA
82 S Bayles Avenue
Port Washington, NY 11050-3729
ultrathinp@aol.com
516-797-3349 • Fax 516-767-9260

ULTRAFRYER SYSTEMS
P.O. Box 5369
San Antonio, TX 78201-0369
www.ultrafryer.com
800-545-9189 • Fax 210-737-5748

ULTRAGLAS INC.
9200 Gazette Avenue
Chatsworth, CA 91311-5919
sales@ultraglas.com
www.ultraglass.com
818-772-7744 • Fax 818-772-8231

UMANOFF & PARSONS INC
467 Greenwich Street
New York, NY 10013-1762
212-219-2240

UNCLE WALLY'S
41 Natcon Drive
Shirley, NY 11967-4700
631-342-9636

UNDERWRITERS LABORATORIES
333 Pfingsten Road
Northbrook, IL 60062-2096
www.ul.com
847-272-8800 • Fax 847-509-6219

UNGER BAKERY/DELI PKGS
12401 Berea Road
Cleveland, OH 44111-1617
800-321-1418

UNIFIED MERCHANT SERVICES
3023 Highway K, Ste 536
Saint Charles, MO 63304-8696
636-541-0526

UNIFIED MERCHANT SERVICES
672 N Semoran Blvd., Ste 203
Orlando, FL 32807-3372
www.umsestore.com
407-207-6155

UNIFIED PRODUCTS
20001 S Western Avenue
Torrance, CA 90501-1306
310-381-0500 • Fax 310-381-0549

UNIFOCUS
1330 Capital Pkwy
Carrollton, TX 75006-3647
800-352-9740

UNIFORM SOURCE, INC
1100 24th Street
Kenner, LA 70062-5290
504-469-0985

UNIFORM WIZARD
715 Twining Rd Ste 109
Dresher, PA 19025-1832
robert@uniformwizard.com
www.uniformwizard.com
215-886-7336 • Fax 215-886-7608

UNIFORMANIA
3302 Maggie Blvd
Orlando, FL 32811-6607
sschaeffer@uniformania.com
407-999-9750 • Fax 407-999-2661

UNIFORMS TO YOU
5600 W 73rd Street
Chicago, IL 60638-6273
www.uty.com
708-563-2626 • 800-864-3888

UNIMAR/UNIVERSAL MARKETING INC
35 River Street
New Rochelle, NY 10801-4351
www.unimar-ny.com
914-576-5383 • Fax 914-576-1711

UNION BRANDS
1066 Bayswater Drive
Union, KY 41091-8652
www.unionbrand.com
859-384-1497 • Fax 859-384-9254

UNIPRO FOODSERVICE INC
280 Interstate North Pkwy SE
Atlanta, GA 30339-2411
770-952-0871

UNIQUE HARDWARE INDUS-TRIES
906 Murray Road
East Hanover, NJ 07936-2200
973-428-0400

UNIQUE MANUFACTURING
831 W Center Avenue
Visalia, CA 93291-6013
559-739-1007 • Fax 559-739-7725

UNIQUE PRODUCTS
15894 Brothers Ct
Fort Myers, FL 33912-2277
239-267-5588 • Fax 239-267-9422

UNISOURCE MARKETING GROUP
7712 Weeping Willow Circle
Sarasota, FL 34241-6429
usmg@aol.com
941-923-5888

UNISYS CORPORATION
Township Line & Union Mt
Blue Bell, PA 19424-0001
215-986-4011

UNITED AIR SPECIAL
4440 Creek Road
Cincinnati, OH 45242-2832
513-891-0455 • Fax 513-891-4171

UNITED BAKERY EQUIP.
15815 W 110th Street
Lenexa, KS 66219-1397
913-541-8700

UNITED BEVERAGE GROUP
P.O. Box 2985
Davenport, FL 33836-2985
burtsookram@cs.com
863-420-2823 • Fax 863-420-4084

UNITED CITRUS PRODUCTS
244 Vanderbilt Avenue
Norwood, MA 02062-5046
781-769-7300 • Fax 781-769-9492

UNITED INSULATED STRUCTURES
5430 Saint Charles Rd
Berkley, IL 60163-1291
708-544-8200

UNITED INTERTRADE CORP.
P.O. Box 821192
Houston, TX 77282-1192
unico@unicocoffee.com
www.unicocoffee.com
281-827-7799 • Fax 281-827-7881

UNITED PARCEL SERVICE
55 Glenlake Pkwy NE
Atlanta, GA 30328-3498
770-828-6000

UNITED PURCHASING, INC
240 E Lake Street, Ste 301C
Addison, IL 60101-2874

UNITED RECEPTACLE INC.
P.O. Box 870
Pottsville, PA 17901-0870
www.unitedrecept.com
570-622-7715 • Fax 570-622-3817

UNITED RENTALS SPECIAL EVENTS
130 Skipjack Road
Prince Frederick, MD 20678-3408
unitedrentals.com
800-852-9441 • Fax 410-414-2146

UNITED SHOW CASE CO INC
P.O. Box 145
Wood Ridge, NJ 07075-0145
201-438-4100

UNITED SIGNATURE FOODS
6500 Overlake Place
Newark, CA 94560-1083
510-786-1415 • Fax 510-786-5009

UNITED SUGARS CORP
7801 E Bush Lake Road
Minneapolis, MN 55439-3120
800-227-2973

UNIV. SOUTHERN MISS./CULINARY
730 E Beach Blvd
Long Beach, MS 39560-6259
228-867-8783

UNIVERSAL FLAVORS
5600 W Raymond Street
Indianapolis, IN 46241-4366
800-445-0073 • Fax 317-240-1524

UNIVERSAL FOODS CORP
777 E Wisconsin Avenue, Ste 1100
Milwaukee, WI 53202-5305
414-347-3891

UNIVERSAL NOLIN
P.O. Box 4000
Conway, AR 72033-2202
501-327-8745 • Fax 501-327-0663

UNIVERSAL PAYMENT PROCESSING
745 N 4th Street
Milwaukee, WI 53203-2101
www.usb.com
414-297-4812 • Fax 414-297-4871

UNIVERSAL TRAINING
255 Revere Drive
Northbrook, IL 60062-1564
847-498-7466

UNIVERSITY LOFT COMPANY 433 E
Washington Street
Indianapolis, IN 46204-2629
tfernkas@universityloft.com
www.universityloft.com
800-423-5638 • Fax 317-631-1516

UNIVERSITY OF CENTRAL FLORIDA
P.O. Box 161400
Orlando, FL 32816-1400
407-823-2188 • Fax 407-823-5696

UNIVERSITY OF DELAWARE
321 S College Avenue
Newark, DE 19716-3366
www.udel.edu/HRIM
302-831-6077 • Fax 302-831-6395

UNIVERSITY OF DENVER
2030 East Evans Avenue
Denver, CO 80208-0001
www.du.edu
303-871-4270 • Fax 303-871-4260

UNIVERSITY OF HOUSTON-CONRAD
4800 Calhoun
Houston, TX 77204-0001
bshrm@uh.edu
www.hrm.uh.edu
713-743-2446 • Fax 713-743-2581

UNIVERSITY OF NORTH TEXAS
P.O. Box 311100
Denton, TX 76203-1100
tas@smhm.cmm.unt.edu
940-565-3438 • Fax 940-565-4348

UNIVERSITY OF PHOENIX
2290 Lucien Way, Ste 400
Maitland, FL 32751-7058
jennifer.mattison@apollogrp.edu
http://www.uophx.com
407-667-0555

UNIVERSITY OF SOUTH CAROLINA
Columbia, SC 29208-0001
www.aps.sc.edu/hrta.html
803-777-6665 • Fax 803-777-1224

UNIVEX
3 Old Rockingham Road
Salem, NH 03079-2140
603-893-6191

UNI-WORLD FISHERIES INC
438 E Katella Avenue
Orange, CA 92867-4839
714-538-2900

UPDATE INTERNATIONAL
5801 S Boyle Avenue
Los Angeles, CA 90058-3926
323-585-0616 • Fax 323-585-0939

UPG VENDING & AMUSEMENT
P.O. Box 240
Jefferson Valley, NY 10535-0240
upgvending@worldnet.att.net
www.upgvending.com
914-245-0367

UPPER CRUST BAKING CO
2121 2nd St # 2126
Davis, CA 95616-5472
530-758-1522

URBAN ARTIFACTS
867 Valley Road
Menasha, WI 54952-1119
920-380-4149 • Fax 920-380-4184

URNER BARRY PUBLISHERS
P.O. Box 389
Toms River, NJ 08754-0389
800-932-0617

URSCHEL LABORATORIES
P.O. Box 2200
Valparaiso, IN 46384-2200
219-464-4811

US COLD STORAGE
33400 Dowe Avenue
Union City, CA 94587-2038
www.uscoldstorage.com
510-471-1703

US FOODSERVICE
5330 Fleming Ct
Austin, TX 78744-1127
jrgarcia@austin.usfood.com
www.usfoodservice.com
512-447-4121 • Fax 512-440-4340

US FOODSERVICE CONTRACT DESIGN
9910 Horn Road Ste 1
Sacramento, CA 95827-1959
888-949-9060 • Fax 916-697-9800

US LIQUIDS INC./CALDWELL
55 Messina Drive
Braintree, MA 02184-6783
781-848-0358 • Fax 508-846-5185

US TOY COMPANY
1227 E 119th Street
Grandview, MO 64030-1117
816-761-9000

US XCHANGE
5305 Buttonwood Drive
Madison, WI 53718-2110
www.usxchange.com
608-268-7200 • Fax 888-676-0063

USA DISPLAY/DIV. OF LEISURE
P.O. Box 1700
Hendersonville, NC 28793-1700
www.usadisplay.com
828-693-8241 • Fax 828-693-1803

USDC/SEAFOOD INSPECTION PROGRAM
1315 E West Hwy
Silver Spring, MD 20910-6233
www.seafood.nmfs.gov
301-713-2355 • Fax 301-713-1081

USTER IMPORTS INC, ALBERT
9211 Gaither Road
Gaithersburg, MD 20877-1419
301-258-7350

UTELL INTERNATIONAL
810 N 96th Street
Omaha, NE 68114-2594
402-398-3200

UTENSIL-REST COMPANY
P.O. Box 87
Exeter, NH 03833-0087
603-772-0188 • Fax 603-772-0188

UTILIMASTER
P.O. Box 58
Wakarusa, IN 46573-0058
574-862-4561

UTTERMOST COMPANY
P.O. Box 558
Rocky Mount, VA 24151-0558
dbarker@uttermost.com
800-678-5486 • Fax 540-489-0954

U-TURN
1460 Commerce Way
Idaho Falls, ID 83401-1233
www.usvendtech.com
208-524-4969 • Fax 208-529-4417

UWINK.COM INC
5443 Beethoven Street
Los Aangeles, CA 90066-7016
310-827-6900

VGM GOLF INC
1111 W San Marnan Drive
Waterloo, IA 50701-9007
319-232-5480

VACATION ADVENTURES INTL
P.O. Box 4354
North Myrtle Beach, SC 29597-4354
843-280-2000

VACU VIN USA, INC
P.O. Box 5489
Novato, CA 94948-5489
www.vacuvin.com
415-382-1241 • Fax 415-382-2063

VALENCIA COMMUNITY COLLEGE
P.O. Box 3028
Orlando, FL 32802-3028
www.valencia.cc.fl.us
407-299-5000

VALENTINE RADFORD, INC
P.O. Box 13407
Kansas City, MO 64199-3407
816-842-5021

VALLEY FORGE FABRICS INC
2981 Gateway Drive
Pompano Beach, FL 33069-4326
800-223-7979

VALLEY FRESH, INC.
9701 Commons East Drive, Apt E
Charlotte, NC 28277-1718

jfhvalfrsh@aol.com
704-543-6393 • Fax 704-543-7194

VALLEY INNOVATIVE SERVICES
4400 Mangum Drive
Flowood, MS 39232-2113
601-664-3100

VALLEY LAHVOSH BAKING
2120 Calumet Street
Clearwater, FL 33765-1309
888-524-8674

VALLEY LAHVOSH BAKING
502 M Street
Fresno, CA 93721-3013
www.valleylahvosh.com
559-485-2700 • Fax 559-485-0173

VALLEY POPCORN CO.
6172 Dixie Road
Neenah, WI 54956-9787
www.valleypopcorn.com
920-722-2676 • Fax 920-232-1630

VALLEY SUN OF CALIFORNIA
P.O. Box 549
Newman, CA 95360-0549
209-862-1200 • Fax 209-862-1100

VALLEY-DYNAMO LP
2525 Handley Ederville Road
Fort Worth, TX 76118-6910
817-299-3070

VALLEYVIEW
13834 Kostner Avenue
Midlothian, IL 60445-1997
valleyview@valleyviewindustries.com
www.valleyviewind.com
800-323-3262

VAL-PAK DIRECT MARKETING SYSTEM
8575 Largo Lakes Drive
Largo, FL 3773-4909
800-889-1145

VAL-PAK OF GREATER HOUSTON
13101 Northwest Fwy
Houston, TX 77040-6309
www.valpak.com
713-462-0706 • Fax 713-939-7809

VALUE LINE COMPANY
1205 N 10th Street
Arkadelphia, AR 71923-2701
www.value-line.com
870-246-6387 • Fax 870-246-0631

VALUEMONICS RESEARCH
10090 Pasadena Avenue, Ste A2
Cupertino, CA 95014-5939
408-257-8521

VAN SAN CORP
16735 E Johnson Drive
Hacienda Heights, CA 91745-2469
www.vansan.com
626-961-7211 • Fax 626-369-9510

VAN TEAL
7240 NE 4th Avenue
Miami, FL 33138-5316
sales@vanteal.com
www.vanteal.com
305-751-6767 • Fax 305-756-0631

VANGUARD TECHNOLOGY
29495 Airport Road
Eugene, OR 97402-9524
vangardtechnologyinc@aol.com
541-461-6020 • Fax 541-461-6023

VAN-LANG FOOD PRODUCTS
88 Eisenhower Lane N
Lombard, IL 60148-5414
www.van-lang.com
630-268-1953 • Fax 630-268-1954

VANTAGE
1061 S 800 E
Orem, UT 84097-7228
www.vantageinc.com
801-229-2800 • Fax 801-224-0355

VATEL DISTRIBUTORS
1245 S Cleveland Massillon Road
Akron, OH 44321-1657
330-666-5713 • Fax 330-668-2002

VAVRICKA JUNTTI & CO.
430 1st Ave N, Ste 270
Minneapolis, MN 55401-1741
612-335-8865

VCI BEVERAGE CENTER
6050 E Hanna Avenue
Indianapolis, IN 46203-6125
www.sergio.com
317-791-1900 • Fax 317-791-0522

VCOM.COM, INC
210 E 49th St
New York, NY 10017-1502
212-758-2087

VCS MARKETING/EUROSTEAM
209 Trellis Walk
Centerville, GA 31028-8511
478-953-5189

VEAL COMMITTEE OF THE WI BEEF COUNCIL
630 Grand Canyon Drive
Madison, WI 53719-1044
www.beeftips.com
608-833-7177 • Fax 608-833-4725

VECTRON SYSTEMS USA
2045 N Forbes Blvd
Tucson, AZ 85745-1444
520-617-0030

VEGGIELAND
222 New Road
Parsippany, NJ 07054-4269
973-808-1540 • Fax 973-882-3030

VEGTA MEALS
1225 Corporate Blvd
Aurora, IL 60504-6408
630-851-6600 • Fax 630-851-9778

VELDA FARMS
402 S Kentucky Avenue
Lakeland, FL 33801-5367
grace.corbino@veldafarms.com

VENDINGAUCTION.COM
6299 Nall Avenue Ste 100
Mission, KS 66202-3547
877-932-8363

VENICE MAID FOODS INC
P.O. Box 1505
Vineland, NJ 08362-1505
800-257-7070 • Fax 856-696-1295

VENISON WORLD, INC.
P.O. Box 100
Eden, TX 76837-0100
fred@venisonworld.com
www.venisonworld.com
915-869-5220 • Fax 915-869-7220

VENTURA FOODS
1100 Defiel Road
Fort Worth, TX 76179-5699
817-345-6408

VENTURA FOODS
14233 Westgate Street
Overland Park, KS 66221-2877
816-746-1550

VENTURA FOODS, LLC
14840 Don Julian Road
La Puente, CA 91746-3109
626-855-2258 • Fax 626-934-1496

VENTURE MARKETING
P.O. Box 957
Menomonee Falls, WI 53052-0957
262-255-1033

VENUS WAFERS, INC
70 Research Road
Hingham, MA 02043-4341
781-749-9553 • Fax 781-749-7195

VENUSO ASSOCIATES INC
415 N La Salle Drive, Ste 4
Chicago, IL 60610-4540
312-321-8690 • Fax 312-321-8693

VERE NICOLL & ASSOCIATES
P.O. Box 617
Middleburg, VA 20118-0617
540-687-3033

VERIDIAN CORPORATION
2875 McI Drive
Pinellas Park, FL 33782-6105

info@veridien.com
727-576-1600 • Fax 727-576-1611

VERIMAR COMMUNICATIONS
13396 Contour Drive
Sherman Oaks, CA 91423-4802
gsbern1@earthlink.net
www.verimar.com
818-501-7457 • Fax 818-501-7452

VERMAX INC.
P.O. Box 6
Salt Lake City, UT 84110-0006
www.vermax.com
801-973-7770 • Fax 801-973-7077

VERMONT BEEF INDUSTRY COUNCIL
P.O. Box 2029
Colchester, VT 05449-2029
vtbic@aol.com
802-872-8385 • Fax 802-872-8385

VERMONT ISLANDS
279 River Road S
Putney, VT 05346-8710
vtisland@sover.net
802-387-4541 • Fax 802-387-5736

VERN'S CHEESE, INC
312 W Main Street
Chilton, WI 53014-1312
920-849-7717 • Fax 920-849-7883

VERSAILLES LIGHTING INC.
242 W 30th Strett
New York, NY 10001-4903
versaltg@aol.com
www.versailleslighting.com
212-564-0240 • Fax 212-595-1993

VERSARE
P.O. Box 24319
Minneapolis, MN 55424-0319
800-833-7570 • Fax 800-833-8032

VERSATECH INDUSTRIES
1356 NW Boca Raton Blvd
Boca Raton, FL 33432-1609
877-873-8377

VERTEX CHINA
20947 Currier Road
Walnut, CA 91789-3046
800-879-9889

VERTEX CHINA
131 Brea Canyon Road
Walnut, CA 91789-3029
800-483-7839

VERTICAL MOBILITY, LLC
3949 Dayton Park Drive, Ste J
Dayton, OH 45414-1400
937-236-2888

VERTICALNET
700 Dresher Road
Horsham, PA 19044-2206
pschmidt@verticalnet.com
www.verticalnet.com
215-315-3701 • Fax 2156581870

VERYFINE PRODUCTS INC
P.O. Box 670
Westford, MA 01886-0670
978-692-0030

VESID STATE EDUCATION DEPT.
116 W 32nd Street
New York, NY 10001-3212
lvarela@mail.nysed.gov
www.nysed.gov/vesid/
212-630-2309 • Fax 212-695-1691

VESUVIO FOODS COMPANY
141 Fieldcrest Avenue
Edison, NJ 08837-3622
732-346-0600 • Fax 732-346-0882

VIA ITALIA
47 Grand Street
Albany, NY 12207-1409
jimrua@aol.com
www.viaitalia.net
518-465-6822

VICINITY CORP
370 San Aleso Avenue
Sunnyvale, CA 94085-1410
650-237-0300

VICTOR CORNELIUS MENUS
400 W Main Street
Eastland, TX 76448-2650
www.vcmenus.com
800-826-3687 • Fax 254-629-1134

VICTORIA L'ORIGINALE
212 N Federal Hwy
Dania, FL 33004-2850
www.vlo.com
954-922-2512

VICTORIA PORCELAIN CO.
7790 NW 67th Street
Miami, FL 33166-2702
www.victory-refring.com
305-428-4200 • Fax 305-428-7299

VICTORY JOYLIN FOOD EQUIP.
P.O. Box 507
Cherry Hill, NJ 08003-0507
www.victoryrref.com
856-428-4200 • Fax 856-428-7299

VIDEOTEK
2835 Hollywood Blvd
Hollywood, FL 33020-4235
954-925-4778

VIDEOYELLOWPAGES.COM
5711 S 86th Circle
Omaha, NE 68127-4146
www.vyp.com
402-537-7726 • Fax 402-537-7736

VIE DE FRANCE CORP
2070 Chain Bridge Road
Vienna, VA 22182-2536
703-442-9205

VIE DE FRANCE CORP.
85 S Bragg St Ste 600
Alexandria, VA 22312-2793
703-750-9600 • Fax 703-750-1158

VIEWINNUSA
1339 Cherokee Trail
Lawrenceville, GA 30043-5805
dave@viewinnusa.com
www.viewinn.com
800-483-9974 • Fax 678-376-9998

VIKING FISH
50 Crystal Street
Malden, MA 02148-5993
781-322-2000 • Fax 781-397-0527

VIKING RANGE CORP.
111 W Front Street
Greenwood, MS 38930-4442
vikingrange.com
www.vikingrange.com
662-455-1200 • Fax 662-453-7939

VILLEROY & BOCH
106 N Waterview Drive
Richardson, TX 75080-4842
972-231-4060 • Fax 972-238-5002

VILLEROY & BOCH TABLE-WARE, LTD
5 Vaughn Dr Ste 1180
Princeton, NJ 08540-6313
800-223-1762 • Fax 732-641-9902

VILORE FOODS CO., INC.
8303 Southwest Fwy, Ste 105
Houston, TX 77074-1606
viloreho@icsi.net •
www.vilore.com
713-779-0100 • Fax 713-779-0123

VINCENT GLORDANO CORP.
2600 Washington Avenue
Philadelphia, PA 19146-3834
215-467-6629 • Fax 215-467-6339

VINTAGE POSTERS INTL LTD.
1551 N Wells Street
Chicago, IL 60610-1334
312-951-6681 • Fax 312-951-6565

VINTAGE VERANDAH
P.O. Box 29
Marion, AR 72364-0029
800-249-3357 • Fax 870-732-3017

VIOLA MARKETING GROUP
P.O. Box 1130
Madison, CT 06443-1130
203-245-0711 • Fax 203-245-8974

VIRCO MANUFACTURING
201 Highway 65 N
Conway, AR 72032-3500
510-329-2901

VIRCO MFG. CORPORATION
2027 Harpers Way
Torrance, CA 90501-1524
310-533-0474 • Fax 310-328-0292

VIRGA'S PIZZA CRUST OF VIR-GINIA
4005 Victory Blvd
Portsmouth, VA 23701-2816
757-488-4493

VIRGINIA MARINE PRODUCTS BOARD
554 Denbigh Blvd
Newport News, VA 23608-4240
757-874-3474

VIRTUALINC
2425 N Central Expy
Richardson, TX 75080-2756
877-876-5462

VISA USA
3155 Clearview Way
San Mateo, CA 94402-3700
650-570-3200

VISA USA, INC
P.O. Box 8999
San Francisco, CA 94128-8999
650-432-2410

VISION MARKETING
215 N Jefferson Davis Pkwy
New Orleans, LA 70119-5309
504-482-4500

VISIT FLORIDA - FLAUSA
661 E Jefferson Street, Ste 300
Tallahassee, FL 32301-2788
www.flausa.com
813-805-2500

VISKSE CORPORATION
625 Willowbrook Center Pkwy
Willowbrook, IL 60527-7969
708-496-4200 • Fax 708-496-4412

VISUAL ONE SYSTEMS CORP
7361 Calhoun Place, Ste 301
Derwood, MD 20855-2777
301-926-2500

VITALITY FOODSERVICE
400 N Tampa Street, Ste 1700
Tampa, FL 33602-4716
www.vitalityfoodservice.com
813-301-4600

VITA-MIX CORPORATION
8615 Usher Road
Olmsted Falls, OH 44138-2199
440-235-4840

VITASOY USA INC
99 Park Lane
Brisbane, CA 94005-1309
800-848-2769

VLASIC FOODS INTL
38777 6 Mile Road
Livonia, MI 48152-2694
734-542-4400

VODAVI TECHNOLOGY
8300 E Raintree Drive
Scottsdale, AZ 85260-2598
800-207-9944

VOGT MACHINE COMPANY   1000 W
Ormsby Avenue
Louisville, KY 40210-1810
502-634-1511

VOILA BAKERY
65 Porter Avenue
Brooklyn, NY 11237-1415
www.voilabakery.com
718-366-1100 • Fax 718-366-5088

VOLPI ITALIAN MEATS
5254 Daggett Avenue
Saint Louis, MO 63110-3026
billh@volpifoods.com
314-772-8550 • Fax 314-772-0411

VOLUNTEERS OF AMERICA
1660 Duke St
Alexandria, VA 22314-3427
800-899-0089

VOS INDUSTRIES LIMITED
P.O. Box 2275
Waterloo, IA 50704-2275
319-233-6363

VULCAN HART CORP
2006 N Western Pkwy
Louisville, KY 40203-1054
502-778-2795

VYNATEX, INC
7 Carey Pl
Port Washington, NY 11050-2421
vynatex@aol.com
www.vynatex.com
516-944-6130 • Fax 516-767-7056

W & B SERVICE CO., INC
3228 Bennington Street
Houston, TX 77093-9222
wbhou@aol.com
www.wbservice.com
713-224-4200 • Fax 713-224-4333

W & W DISTRIBUTING CO
5105 McClanahan Drive, Ste J8
North Little Rock, AR 72116-7001
800-528-8341

WA BROWN
2001 S Main Street
Salisbury, NC 28144-6885
wabrown.com
http://www.wabrown.com
704-636-5131

WH REYNOLDS DIST
4824 N Renellie Dr
Tampa, FL 33614-6200
ekozlowski@whreynolds.com
813-873-2402

WJ PENCE CO
W227N880 Westmound Drive
Waukesha, WI 53186-1691
262-524-6300

WRG SERVICES INC
37500 N Industrial Pkwy
Willoughby, OH 44094-6214
216-531-1222

W.T.D. ASSOCIATES
325 N 18th Avenue
Laurel, MS 39440-3860
601-426-6325

**WABASH VALLEY
MANUFACTURING**
505 E Main Street
Silver Lake, IN 46982-8943
800-253-8619 • Fax 260-352-2160

**WACHOVIA/ DAVIS
BALDWIN**
4600 W Cypress St # B
Tampa, FL 33607-4032
measton@davisbaldwin.com
813-349-5462 • Fax 813-207-2086

WADDINGTON NORTH AMERICA
6 Stuart Rd
Chelmsford, MA 01824-4108
Fax 978-256-1614

**WAFFLES OF LOUISIANA/
CARBON'S**
17914 Prestwick Ave
Baton Rouge, LA 70810-7915
800-772-3111

**WAILAN
COMMUNICATIONS**
2040 Ringwood Ave
San Jose, CA 95131-1728
bhertz@wailan.com
www.wailan.com
408-435-7511 • Fax 408-435-7512

WALCO STAINLESS
820 Noyes Street
Utica, NY 13502-5053
sales@walcostainless.com
www.walcostainless.com
315-733-6602

WALK THE WALK
15032 7th Avenue NW
Andover, MN 55304-2849
763-422-6886 • Fax 763-422-9524

WALKER & ASSOCIATES
1011 N Orange Drive
Los Angeles, CA 90038-2317
323-874-2441

WALKER FOOD
506 E 12th Avenue
Kansas City, MO 64116-4100
salads2@aol.com
816-472-8121 • Fax 816-421-7273

WALKER FOODS
66 Fadem Road
Springfield, NJ 07081-3178
www.walkerfoods.com
973-467-9400 • Fax 908-487-6752

WALKER ZANGER
8901 Bradley Avenue
Sun Valley, CA 91352-2602
818-394-3083 • Fax 818-394-3076

WALKER, NORTH AMERICA
4304 Airport Fwy
Haltom City, TX 76117-6218
800-928-9995

WALKERS SHORTBREAD INC.
170 Commerce Drive
Hauppauge, NY 11788-3944
cs@walkersshortbread.com
800-521-0141 • Fax 631-273-0438

WALL BED SYSTEMS INC.
P.O. Box 20
Wapakoneta, OH 45895-0020
wallbeds@bright.net
www.wallbedsystems.com
419-730-5207 • Fax 419 738 5209

WALLACE & HINZ INC
1065 K Street
Arcata, CA 95521-5544
www.whbars.com
707-826-1729 • Fax 707-826-0224

WALLACE PARTNERS
703 Pier Ave, Ste B-208
Hermosa Beach, CA 90254-3943
310-546-9430

WAL-MART REALTY CO
2001 SE 10th Street
Bentonville, AR 72712-6489
479-273-4535

WALNUT MARKETING BOARD
865 Woodside Way
San Mateo, CA 94401-1611
650-340-8311

WALTERS WICKER, INC
979 3rd Avenue, Ste 538
New York, NY 10022-1234
Paul@walterwicker.com
www.walterwicker.com
212-758-0472 • Fax 212-826-6775

WALTHAM SERVICES INC
817 Moody St
Waltham, MA 02453-5024
800-562-9287

WAMPLER FOODS - FOODSERVICE
800 Coop Drive
Timberville, VA 22853-9574
800-388-2128

WAMPLER FOODS INC
P.O. Box 7275
Broadway, VA 22815-7275
www.wampler.com
540-896-7000 • Fax 540-896-0978

WANCHESE FISH CO
48 Water St
Hampton, VA 23663-1718
wanchese.com
www.fresh@wanchese.com
757-722-1443

WANCHESE FISH CO.
102 N Mallory St
Hampton, VA 23663-1742
fresh@wanchese.com
757-723-2069 • Fax 757-728-0607

WANT CORPORATION
1484 Lake Dr W
Chanhassen, MN 55317-8518
brucep@wandcorp.com
www.wandcorp.com
952-361-6200 • Fax 952-361-6211

WARDEN COMPANY, THE
940 S Orange Avenue
Orlando, FL 32806-1248
hospitality@wardencompany.com
407-650-0333 • Fax 407-650-9984

WARDS ICE CREAM
93 Sherwood Avenue
Paterson, NJ 07502-1818
973-595-8100 • Fax 973-595-7828

**WARING PROD. DIV
CUISINART**
1 Cummings Point Rd
Stamford, CT 06902-7901
800-726-6247

**WARING PRODUCTS
DIVISION**
314 Ella Grasso Avenue
Torrington, CT 06790-2345
860-379-0731 • Fax 860-738-0249

**WARREN FREEDENFELD &
ASSOCIATES**
39 Church St
Boston, MA 02116-5311
info@freedenfeld.com
617-338-0050 • Fax 617-426-2557

WARREN FROZEN FOODS
803 8th St SW
Altoona, IA 50009-2306
jlarson@auntvi.com
515-967-4245 • Fax 515-967-4147

WARSTEINER IMPORTS
9359 Allen Rd
West Chester, OH 45069-3846
513-261-9901

WARWICK INDUSTRIES
230 5th Avenue, Ste 1601
New York, NY 10001-7704
212-725-3278 • Fax 212-725-3285

WASCOMAT
461 Doughty Blvd
Inwood, NY 11096-1384
salesdept@wascomat.com
www.wascomat.com
516-371-4400 • Fax 516-371-4204

WASHIGTON STATE UNIV.
P.O. Box 644742
Pullman, WA 99164-4742
www.cbe.wsu.edu/hra
509-335-5766 • Fax 509-335-3857

**WASHINGTON APPLE
COMMISION**
1704 Skyline Dr
Wenatchee, WA 98801-3238
www.bestapples.com
509-665-7008 • Fax 509-665-3669

**WASHINGTON APPLE
COMMISSION**
P.O. Box 18
Wenatchee, WA 98807-0018
509-663-9600

**WASHINGTON STATE POTATO
COMMISSION**
108 S Interlake Rd
Moses Lake, WA 98837-2950
www.potatoes.com
509-765-8845 • Fax 509-765-4853

WASHINGTON STATE UNIV
208 Van Doren Hall
Pullman, WA 99164-0001
509-335-3530

WASSERSTROM CO
477 S Front Street
Columbus, OH 43215-5677
614-228-6525 • Fax 614-228-8776

WASTE KING COMMERCIAL
4240 E La Palma Ave
Anaheim, CA 92807-1816
www.wasteking.com
714-524-7811 • Fax 714-996-0572

WATCO MANUFACTURING
1220 S Powell Rd
Independence, MO 64057-2724
800-821-8576

WATER DOCTER/CVB INC
P.O. Box 3060
Saint Joseph, MO 64503-0060
816-279-0084

WATER LILIES FOOD INC.
136 N 10th Strett
Brooklyn, NY 11211-1103
718-388-6969 • Fax 718-218-6895

WATER TECHNOLOGY
P.O. Box 614
Beaver Dam, WI 53916-0614
info@watertechnologyinc.com
www.watertechnologyinc.com
800-538-8207 • Fax 920-887-8850

WATER WONDERS
3042 Industrial Pkwy
Santa Maria, CA 93455-1808
sales@waterwonders.com
www.waterwonders.com
805-922-3534 • Fax 805-925-3485

**WATERFORD
WEDGWOOD USA** P.O. Box
2298
Asbury Park, NJ 07712-2298
732-938-5800

WATERWISE
2881 W Lake Vista Cir
Fort Lauderdale, FL 33328-1106
garyrosen@earthlink.net
www.thermoplus.com
954-614-7100

WATLOW ELECTRIC
12001 Lackland Rd
Saint Louis, MO 63146-4039
www.watlow.com
314-848-4600 • Fax 314-878-2369

**WATSON FOOD
COMPANY INC**
301 Heffernan Drive
West Ahven, CT 06516-4139
203-932-3000

WATSON SERVICES, INC
75 Pierces Road
Newburgh, NY 12550-3248
845-561-3000

WATSON STEACH & CO
1333 W Pioneer Pkwy, Ste 1
Arlington, TX 76013-6248
800-874-7759

**WAUKESHA COUNTY
TECHNICAL COLLEGE**
800 Main St
Pewaukee, WI 53072-4601
www.waukesha.tec.wi.us
262-691-5254 • Fax 262-691-5155

WAUSAU INSURANCE CO
8905 SW Nimbus Ave
Beaverton, OR 97008-7136
503-626-4100

**WAUSAU INSURANCE
COMPANIES**
P.O. Box 8017
Wausau, WI 54402-8017
ww.wausau.com
888-291-883 • Fax 888-291-9445

WAUSAU TILE, INC
P.O. Box 1520
Wausau, WI 54402-1520
www.wausautile.com
715-359-3121 • Fax 715-355-4627

WAWA INC
260 W Baltimore Pike
Media, PA 19063-5699
610-358-8000 • Fax 610-358-8808

**WAYMAR
INDUSTRIES, INC**
14400 Southcross Dr W
Burnsville, MN 55306-6990
www.waymar.com
800-328-4299 • Fax 800-367-1366

WAYNE FARMS
P.O. Box 2397
Gainesville, GA 30503-2397
800-392-0844 • Fax 770-531-3244

WAYPORT
1609 Shoal Creek Blvd
Austin, TX 78701-1054
877-929-7678

WEATHEREND ESTATE FURNITURE
6 Gordon Dr
Rockland, ME 04841-2137
207-596-6483

WEAVEWOOD INC.
7520 Wayzata Blvd
Minneapolis, MN 55426-1622
612-544-3136 • Fax 612-544-3137

WEBBER COLLEGE
1201 N Scenic Hwy
Babson Park, FL 33827-9751
www.webber.edu
863-638-1431 • Fax 863-638-2823

WEBBER FARMS, INC
P.O. Box 460
Cynthiana, KY 41031-0460
800-467-5154

WEBDONERIGHT, LLC
915 N Cleveland Ave # B
Chicago, IL 60614-5215
www.webdoneright.com
312-335-0384 • Fax 312-335-0736

WEBER MANAGEMENT CONSULTANTS
205 E Main St
Huntington, NY 11743-2923
631-673-4700

WEBLIGHT PRODUCTIONS
125 W Ellsworth Road
Ann Arbor, MI 48108-2206
www.foodhunter.net
734-677-6428 • Fax 734-677-6429

WEBSTER INDUSTRIES
58 Pulaski St
Peabody, MA 01960-1800

WEBSTER UNIVERSITY
7087 Grand National Dr
Orlando, FL 32819-8916
buchankg@webster.edu
www.websterfl.edu
407-345-1139

WEBVERTISING, INC
3100 Richmond Ave
Houston, TX 77098-3000
713-533-9922

WEIN-BAUER, INC
10600 Seymour Ave
Franklin Park, IL 60131-1227
www.weinbauer.com
847-678-0685 • Fax 847-678-0713

WEISS FOODSERVICE VISIONS
300 E 40th Street
New York, NY 10016-2188
212-953-0170 • Fax 917-565-3462

WELBILT CORPORATION
2227 Welbilt Blvd
New Prt Rchy, FL 34655-5130
727-325-8300

WELCHS FOODS
3 Concord Farms Road
Concord, MA 01742-2731
978-371-1000 • Fax 978-371-3737

WELL-PICT BERRIES
P.O. Box 973
Watsonville, CA 95077-0973
805-487-7900

WELLS FARGO BANK
177 Park Ave # 0514-011
San Jose, CA 95113-2224
408-396-7387

WELLS FARGO MERCHANT SERVICES
1200 Montego
Walnut Creek, CA 94598-2876
925-746-4106

WELLS LAMONT
6640 W Touhy Ave
Niles, IL 60714-4587
800-323-2830

WELLS MANUFACTURING
P.O. Box 70
Fond du Lac, WI 54936-0070

WELLS/BLOOMFIELD
P.O. Box 280
Verdi, NV 89439-0280
775-345-0444

WELLSET TABLEWARE MANUFACTURING
201 Water St
Brooklyn, NY 11201-1111
718-624-4490 • Fax 718-596-3959

WENNER BREAD PRODUCTS
44 Rajon Rd
Bayport, NY 11705-1100
631-563-6262

WES DESIGN AND SUPPLY COMPANY
238 Route 109
Farmingdale, NY 11735-1503
wesdesign1@aol.com
www.wesdes.com
631-249-0298 • Fax 631-249-5832

WESLEY BOBER
551 5th Ave Rm 3213
New York, NY 10176-3002
212-986-9521 • Fax 212-986-9545

WESSELS, ARNOLD AND HENDERSON
901 Marquette Avenue, Ste 2700
Minneapolis, MN 55402-3268
612-373-6244

WEST ART LIGHTING
624 Maple St
Conshohocken, PA 19428-1653
610-940-1144 • Fax 610-828-4806

WEST LYNN CREAMERY
626 Lynnway
Lynn, MA 01905-3068
781-599-1300 • Fax 781-599-7810

WEST STAR INDUSTRIES
265 Gandy Dancer Drive
Tracy, CA 95377-9068
www.weststarindustries.com
209-832-2200 • Fax 209-832-2221

WEST WIND TRADERS INC.
48 Bridge Street
Nashua, NH 03060-3564
wstwndtrdr@aol.com
www.westwindtrader.com

WESTCHESTER COMM COLLEGE
75 Grasslands Road
Valhalla, NY 10595-1693
daryl.nosek@sunywcc.edu
www.wcc.co.westchester.ny.us
914-785-6551

WESTERN BAGEL
7814 Sepulveda Blvd
Van Nuys, CA 91405-1062
818-786-5847 • Fax 818-787-3221

WESTERN CULINARY INSTITUTE
1316 SW 13th Avenue
Portland, OR 97201-3355
www.westernculinary.com
503-223-2245 • Fax 503-223-0126

WESTERN EXTERMINATOR
1732 Kaiser Ave
Irvine, CA 92614-5739
www.west-ext.com
949-261-2440 • Fax 949-474-7767

WESTERN FS & HOSPITALITY EXPO
9620 Center Ave

Rancho Cucamonga, CA 91730-5837
800-209-0700

WESTERN PEST SERVICES
225 Broadway Rm 300
New York, NY 10007-3912
www.westernpest.com
212-571-1938 • Fax 212-571-6010

WESTERN PEST SERVICES
400 Fairway Dr Ste 105
Deerfield Beach, FL 33441-1808
954-571-7171 • Fax 954-571-6868

WESTERN RETAIL SERVICES
P.O. Box 1146
Morrison, CO 80465-5146
303-697-5961

WESTERN SPRINGS NATIONAL BANK
4456 Wolf Rd
Western Springs IL 0558-1583
708-246-2200

WESTFORD CHINA CO.
P.O. Box 406
Westford, MA 01886-0406

WESTPOINT STEVENS INC
1221 Avenue Of The Americas
New York, NY 10020-1001
212-382-5000

WESTWEAVE COMMERCIAL
14731 Industry Circle
La Mirada, CA 90638-5818
www.etccarpetmills.com
714-523-2000 • Fax 714-523-5400

WEXLER GROUP
1317 F St NW, Ste 600
Washington, D.C. 20004-1157
202-638-2121

WH SMITH USA TRAVEL RETAIL
3200 Windy Hill Rd SE
Atlanta, GA 30339-5640
derek@bellsouth.net
770-618-4776 • Fax 404-661-9615

WHATABURGER INC
4600 Parkdale Drive
Corpus Christi, TX 78411-2930
361-878-0650

WHEELER RESOURCES
1663 US Highway 8
Saint Croix Falls, WI 54024-7502
715-483-3503

WHEREYAGONNAEAT.COM
P.O. Box 411449
Melbourne, FL 32941-1449
sales@whereyagonnaeat.com
www.whereyagonnaeat.com
321-432-3023 • Fax 407-963-6729

WHIRLEY INDUSTRIES, INC
P.O. Box 988
Warren, PA 16365-0988
www.whirley.com
814-723-7600

WHISKY FEST
3416 Oak Hill Road
Emmaus, PA 18049-4421
610-967-1083

WHITE CASTLE DISTRIBUTING
555 W Goodale St
Columbus, OH 43215-1104
carrollt@whitecastle.com
www.whitecastle.com
614-559-2453 • Fax 614-641-0023

WHITE CLOVER DIARY, INC.
489 Holland Ct
Kaukauna, WI 54130-8953
920-766-5765 • Fax 920-766-0598

WHITE COFFEE CORP.
1835 Steinway Pl
Astoria, NY 11105-1032
www.whitecoffee.com
718-204-7900 • Fax 718-956-8504

WHITE CORP
20 Executive Blvd
Farmingdale, NY 11735-4710
516-293-2211

WHITE DIAMOND SPIRIT
2200 Monumental Ave
Halethorpe, MD 21227-4612
410-242-2000

WHITE HOUSE PROMOTIONS
3805 Jefferson Hwy
New Orleans, LA

WHITE LODGING SERVICES
1000 E 80th Place
Merrillville, IN 46410-5608
219-769-3267

WHITE PLAINES LINEN
4 John Walsh Blvd
Peekskill, NY 10566-5323
wplinen@msn.com
www.whiteplainslinen.com
914-737-2532 • Fax 914-737-2186

WHITE ROCK DISTILLERIES
21 Saratoga St
Lewiston, ME 04240-3527
800-628-5441

WHITE ROCK DISTILLERIES
2181 Lake Marion Dr
Apopka FL 32712-4405
leeatherto@aol.com
407-880-6882

WHITE TOQUE, INC
P.O. Box 5037
Napa, CA 94581-0037
707-252-0921 • Fax 707-252-2347

WHITE WATER CLAMS
P.O. Box 5032
Hialeah. FL 33014-1032
www.whitneyandsonseafoods.com
305-823-2210

WHITE WAVE INC
6123 Arapahoe Rd
Boulder, CO 80303-1401
303-443-3470

WHITEHALL LABS
5 Giralda Farms
Madison, NJ 07940-1021
973-660-5000

WHIZARD PROTECTIVE WEAR
7525 N Oak Park Ave
Niles, IL 60714-3819
www.weuslamont.com
847-647-1231 • Fax 847-647-0755

WI DEPT. OF WORKFORCE DEVELOMENT
201 E Washington Ave Rm P
Madison, WI 53702-0028
www.dwd.state.wi.us
608-264-8166 • Fax 608-267-2392

WI DEPT. OF WORKFORCE DIVISION
P.O. Box 8928
Madison, WI 53708-8928
608-266-3345 • Fax 608-267-4592

WI POTATO GROWERS AUXILIARY
P.O. Box 327
Antigo, WI 54409-0327
715-623-7683 • Fax 715-623-3176

WICK'S PIES, INC.
217 SE Greenville Ave
Winchester, IN 47394-1714
www.wickspies.com
800-642-5880 • Fax 765-584-3700

WIDMER BROTHERS BREWING CO.
929 N Russell St
Portland, OR 97227-1733
obobob@aol.com
800-234-8034 • Fax 503-281-2761

WIKKI STIX COMPANY
432 W Peoria Ave Ste 1188
Phoenix, AZ 85029-4735
wikkistx@uswest.net
www.wikkistix.com
602-870-9937 • Fax 602-870-9877

WILBUR CURTIS CO INC
1781 N Indiana St
Los Angeles, CA 90063-2574
www.wilburcurtis.com
323-269-8121 • Fax 323-269-3288

WILD FRUITZ BEVERAGES & NUTZ
945 E 8th St
Brooklyn, NY 11230-3514
www.wildfruitz.com
718-338-6235 • Fax 718-338-9724

WILDER GROUP
1 Linden Pl Ste 311
Great Neck, NY 11021-2640
516-482-2444

WILDER MANUFACTURING
855 Merrick Avenue
Westbury, NY 11590-6604
www.winholt.com
800-632-7222 • Fax 516-222-0371

WILDER MANUFACTURING
41 Mechanic St
Port Jervis, NY 2771-2829
800-832-1319 • Fax 845-856-1950

WILDLIFE INTERIORS
1090 E Lake Park Drive
Hernando, FL 34442-3148
352-637-9298

WILDMAN & SONS, FREDERICK
307 E 53rd Street
New York, NY 10022-4985
212-355-0700

WILEY PUBLISHING
605 3rd Ave
New York, NY 10158-0180
212-850-6000

WIL-KIL PEST CONTROL
3461 Capitol Dr Ste 3
Sun Prairie, WI 53590-9703
www.wil-kil.com
800-236-8735 • Fax 608-249-2991

WILKINS-ROGERS INC
27 Frederick Rd # 308
Ellicott City, MD 21043-4759
410-465-5800

WILLIAM BLAIR & COMPANY
222 W Adams Street
Chicago, IL 60606-5312
312-364-8825

WILLIAM FISCHER PREMIUM DELI
1860 Mellwood Ave
Louisville, KY 40206-1033
502-896-3248 • Fax 502-896-3316

WILLIAM FOODS INC
13301 W 99th Street
Lenexa, KS 66215-1348
913-888-4343 • Fax 913-888-0727

WILLIAM H LEAHY ASSOCIATES INC
510 Lake Cook Road, Ste 120
Deerfield, IL 60015-4916
847-948-0015 • Fax 847-948-0191

WILLIAMS CHEESE
998 N Huron Road
Linwood, MI 48634-9473
jay@williamscheese.com
989-697-4492 • Fax 989-697-4203

WILLIAMS FOOD MACHINERY
5443 W Crenshaw Street
Tampa, FL 33634-3095
813-884-1968

WILLIAMS SCOTSMAN
P.O. Box 986
Baltimore, MD 21203-0986

WILLIM BOUNDS LTD.
3737 W 240th St
Torrance, CA 90505-6003
310-375-0505

WILLIS CORROON OF NASHVILLE
P.O. Box 305025
Nashville, TN 37230-5025
615-872-3894

WILLOW GROUP
34 Clinton Street
Batavia, NY 14020-2821
585-344-2900 • Fax 585-344-0044

WILLOW SPECIALTIES
68 Nassau Street
Rochester, NY 14605-1982
585-325-6600

WILSHIRE MFG.
645 Myles Standlsh Blvd
Taunton, MA 02780-7331
wilshirelt@aol.com
www.wilshiremfg.com
508-824-1970 • Fax 508-822-7046

WILSONART INTERNATIONAL INC.
1051 Centennial Ave
Piscataway, NJ 08854-4124
732-562-1500 • Fax 732-562-0287

WIMBERLY ALLISON TONG GOO
700 Bishop St
Honolulu, HI 96813-4124
808-521-8888

WINCUP
7980 W Buckeye Rd
Phoenix, AZ 85043-4016
800-292-2877 • Fax 800-628-1070

WINDSOR FROZEN FOODS
5459 Pioneer Blvd
Whittier, CA 90601-2155
562-699-4831 • Fax 562-699-0161

WINDSOR FROZEN FOODS
3355 W Alabama Street, Ste 730
Houston, TX 77098-1797
www.windsorfoods.com
713-960-9637 • Fax 713-960-9709

WINDSOR INDUSTRIES
1351 W Stanford Ave
Englewood, CO 80110-5545
rick.hamilton@windsorind.com
www.windsorind.com
303-762-1800 • Fax 303-762-0817

WINE & DINE ON-LINE
4400 Campus Dr # D
Newport Beach, CA 92660-1813
949-222-0809

WINE ENTHUSIAST COMPANIES
103 Fairview Park Drive
Elmsford, NY 10523-1544
www.wineenthusiast.com
914-789-8022

WINE SHOPPER.COM
665 3rd St
San Francisco, CA 94107-1926

WINE WAREHOUSE
6550 E Washington Blvd
Los Angeles, CA 90040-1800
800-331-2829 • Fax 323-724-4700

WINEKEEPER
625 E Haley Street
Santa Barbara, CA 93103-3168
www.winekeep.com
805-963-3451 • Fax 805-965-5393

WINELIFE INC.
2 Race St
Brookhaven, PA 19015-2414
www.winelife.com
800-220-WINE • Fax 215-929-3032

WINERACKS BY MARCUS
1852 Illinois Street
Costa Mesa, CA 2626-2209
wineracksbymarcus.com
714-546-4922 • Fax 714-549-8238

WINERY ASSOCIATES
1610 Rambling Stone Drive
Richmond, TX 77469-6622
agilberg@wineryassociates.com
281-341-6030 • Fax 281-239-7405

WINERY ASSOCIATES
P.O. Box 910
Healdsburg, CA 95448-0910
707-433-1402

WINES STEINS & COCKTAILS LTD.
700 S 4th St
Youngwood, PA 15697-1171
724-925-7755

WING ENTERPRISES, INC.
P.O. Box 3100
Springville, UT 84663-9001
801-489-3684 • Fax 801-489-3685

WING HING NOODLE CO.
1642 E 23rd Street
Los Angeles, CA 90011-1804
www.winghing.com
323-232-8899 • Fax 323-231-9022

WIN-HOLT
820 Esther Lane
Murfreesboro, TN 37129-5536
615-895-5333 • Fax 615-895-5334

WINKLER USA LP
300 Forge Way
Rockaway, NJ 07866-2032
973-625-4566

WINPAK PORTION PACKAGING, INC.
2558 Pearl Buck Road
Bristol, PA 19007-6809
215-781-8200 • Fax 215-701-0243

WINS PAPER PRODUCTS, INC
P.O. Box 14155
Haltom City, TX 76117-0155
800-733-2420

WINSHAW & ASSOCIATES
17451 SE 192nd Drive
Renton, WA 98058-9617
425-735-3483

WINSTON INDUSTRIES
2345 Carton Drive
Louisville, KY 40299-2513
www.winstonind.com
800-234-5286 • Fax 502-495-5458

WINTER ARCHITECTS, INC.
1024 E 1st St N
Wichita, KS 67214-3903
316-267-7142

WINTER GARDENS QUALITY FOODS
304 Commerce St
New Oxford, PA 17350-1723
800-242-7637 • Fax 717-624-7729

WIREBOUND BOX MFG ASSOCIATION
3263 Sprucewood Lane
Wilmette, II 60091-1110
847-251-5575

WIRELESS EXPRESS USA, INC.
8275 S Eastern Ave
Las Vegas, NV 89123-2591
702-990-8700 • Fax 702-938-1000

WISCO INDUSTRIES, INC
736 Janesville St
Oregon, WI 53575-1607
www.wiscoind.com
608-835-3106 • Fax 608-835-7399

WISCONSIN ALLIED PRODUCTS
4170 N 126th Street
Brookfield, WI 53005-1804
262-781-2038 • Fax 262-781-1448

WISCONSIN BISON PRODUCERS
W2686 Hospital Road
Elkhorn, WI 53121-4461
262-723-6636 • Fax 262-723-6836

WISCONSIN COMMERCIAL DEER & ELK
3591 High Point Road
Spring Green, WI 53588-8935
www.wcdefa.org
888-233-1667 • Fax 888-233-1667

WISCONSIN DEPT. OF AGRICULTURE
P.O. Box 8
Madison, WI 53701-0008
www.datcp.state.wi.us
608-224-5126 • Fax 608-224-5111

WISCONSIN MILK MARKETING BOARD
8418 Excelsior Drive
Madison, WI 53717-1909
608-836-8820 • Fax 608-836-5822

WISCONSIN PORK PRODUCERS
P.O. Box 327
Lancaster, WI 53813-0327
www.wppa.org
608-723-7551 • Fax 608-723-7553

WISCONSIN RED CHERRY GROWERS
P.O. Box 452
Egg Harbor, WI 54209-0452
www.wisconsin-cherries.org
920-839-9414

WISCONSIN RESTAURANT ASSOCIATION
2801 Fish Hatchery Road
Madison, WI 53713-3120
www.wirestaurant.org
800-589-3211 • Fax 608-270-9960

WISCONSIN SPECIALITY CHEESE
P.O. Box 233
Monroe, WI 53566-0233
800-697-8861 • Fax 608-255-4434

WISCONSIN TISSUE
P.O. BOX 489
Menasha, WI 4952-0489
920-725-7030 • Fax 920-727-3743

WISCONSIN GAS
626 E Wisconsin Ave
Milwaukee, WI 53202-4616
www.wisconsingas.com
800-773-6985 • Fax 414-291-6350

WISE FOODS, INC.
6687 Jimmy Carter Blvd
Norcross, GA 30071-1712
678-296-0655 • Fax 770-263-7363

WITT, MARER COMPANY
1 Columbus Center, Ste 1001
Virginia Beach, VA 23462-6764
757-499-2070

WITTCO FOODSERVICE EQUIP.
7737 N 81st St
Milwaukee, WI 53223-3839
414-354-3080 • Fax 414-354-2821

WIU
1 University Cir
Macomb, IL 61455 1390
309-298-1085 • Fax 309-298-2688

WM. BOLTHOUSE FARMS, INC.
7200 E Brundage Lane
Bakersfield, CA 93307-3099
www.bolthouse.com
661-367-7270 • Fax 661-366-2834

WMF HUTSCHENREUTHER
85 Price Pkwy
Farmingdale, NY 11735-1317
516-293-3990 • Fax 516-694-0820

WNA
1135 Samuelson Street
Rowland Heights, CA 91748-1222
626-913-4022 • Fax 626-913-1776

WOLF
P.O. Box 7050
Compton, CA 90224-7050
888-639-9653 • Fax 888-778-1587

WOLF RANGE CO
19600 S Alameda Street
Compton, CA 90221-6291
310-637-3737

WOLFERMAN'S
13400 W 99th St
Lenexa, KS 66215-1365
www.wolfermans.com
913-888-4499 • Fax 913-492-5195

WOLF-GANG & ASSOCIATES
1900 Marconi Ave
Saint Louis, MO 63110-3038
314-771-2231

WOMEN CHEFS/ RESTAURATEURS
304 W Liberty St
Louisville, KY 40202-3012

WOOD COMPANY
6081 Hamilton Blvd
Allentown, PA 18106-9776
800-942-9553

WOOD COMPANY
6081 Hamilton Blvd # O
Allentown, PA 18106-9776
www.woodco.com
610-366-5275 • Fax 610-366-5384

WOOD STONE CORP
530 W Front St
Sumas, WA 98295-9625
800-988-8102

WOOD STONE CORP.
1801 W Bakerview Rd
Bellingham, WA 98226-9105
www.woodstone-corp.com
800-988-8103 • Fax 360-650-1166

WOODARD, INC
P.O. Box 2
Owosso, MI 48867-0002
gvandrie@woodard-furniture.com
www.woodard-furniture.com
989-725-2290 • Fax 989-725-4221

WOODEN VILLAGE
20 S Union Ave
Lansdowne, PA 19050-2239
www.woodenvillage.com
610-394-6727 • Fax 610-394-2399

WOODMAN CO
5224 Snapfinger Woods Drive
Decatur, GA 30035-4023
770-981-5200

WOODSMITHS
2681 NE 4th Ave
Pompano Beach, FL 33064-5405
tables@gate.net
www.woodsmiths.com
954-942-8840

WORCESTER INDUSTRIAL PRODUCTS
7 Brookfield St
Worcester, MA 01605-3901
www.shortening-shuttle.com
508-757-5161 • Fax 508-831-9990

WORKFORCE LOGISTICS
60 Madison Avenue, 7th Floor
New York, NY 10010-1600
www.eroster.com
212- 725-2049 • Fax 212-725-2049

WORLD CAM NETWORK
2432 S Downing St
Denver, CO 80210-5812
800-924-2267

WORLD CINEMA, INC.
9801 Westheimer Road
Houston, TX 77042-3950
800-944-9441

WORLD CLASS BRANDS,LLC
1080 Centre Rd, Ste E
Auburn Hills, MI 48326-2681
248-879-3859 • Fax 248-644-1180

WORLD COMMERCE ONLINE
180 Springwood Trail
Altamonte Spg, FL 32714-3439
877-492-6638

WORLD CRISA CORPORATION
12404 Park Central Dr., Ste 400
Dallas, TX 75251-1800
972-980-1983

WORLD CUISINE
2316 Cotner Ave
Los Angeles, CA 90064-1804
www.world-cuisine.com
310-445-0909 • Fax 310-477-5587

WORLD DIVISION
11929 Denton Dr
Dallas, TX 75234-7235
.worlddivisionusa.com
972-241-2612 • Fax 972-247-8807

WORLD DRYER CORP INC
5700 McDermott Dr.
Berkeley, IL 60163-1196
www.worlddryer.com
708-449-6950 • Fax 708-449-6958

WORLD FINEST CHOCOLATE
4801 S Lawndale Ave
Chicago, IL 60632-3062
773-847-4600 • Fax 773-847-7804

WORLD SIGNATURE
1500 NE 131st St
Miami, FL 33161-4426
800-766-0448

WORLD TABLEWARE INTERNATIONAL
6500 Greenville Ave, Ste 4
Dallas, TX 75206-1014
214-346-1600 • Fax 214-346-1655

WORLD WIDE
2730 W Fullerton Ave
Chicago, IL 60647-3089
wwdistributors.com
773-384-2300 • Fax 773-384-0639

WORLD WIDE FABRIC, INC.
3113 E 26th St
Los Angeles, CA 90023-4206
www.safetynetaccess.com
323-263-1111 • Fax 323-263-1117

WORLDCATCH.COM
1629 Queen Anne Ave N
Seattle, WA 98109-2869
206-284-7400

WORLDCOM
701 Brazos St Ste 600
Austin, TX 78701-2557
sherry.richardson@wcom.com
www.wcom.com
512-495-6775 • Fax 512-495-6798

WORLDS AWAY
397 S Front St
Memphis, TN 38103-4115
www.worlds-away.com
901-529-0844 • Fax 901-527-3406

WORLDWEBEXPO.COM
1905 Aston Ave
Carlsbad, CA 92008-7307
800-646 9790

WORLDWIDE CONCEPTS 2000
561 Jennings Drive
Lake In The Hills, IL 60156-1675
800-259-0040 • Fax 815-356-6682

WORLDWIDE HOTEL SUPPLY CORP
779 Middle Country Rd
Saint James, NY 11780-3221
pineapplegals@aol.com
631-366-2202 • Fax 631-366-2212

WORLDWIDE IMPORTS, INC
6 Ethelbert Pl
Ridgewood, NJ 07450-4229
worldwide@wwiec.com
201-447-3863 • Fax 201-652-6106

WOW PLASTICS, INC
P.O. Box 1726
Richmond, TX 77406-1726
accounting@wowplastics.com
281-238-9977 • Fax 281-232-9299

WTS INTERNATIONAL, INC.
12501 Prosperity Drive
Silver Spring, MD 20904-1689
301-622-7800 • Fax 301-622-3373

WUSTHOF TRIDENT OF AMERICA
525 Executive Blvd
Elmsford, NY 10523-1240
914-347-2185

WWW.BARSUPPLYWARE-HOUSE.COM
9404 North Loop E
Houston, TX 77029-1228
713-673-7676

WYNDHAM HOTELS & RESORTS

2001 Bryan St.
Dallas, TX 75201-3005

WYNDHAM INTERNATIONAL
1950 N Stemmons Fwy, Ste 6001
Dallas, TX 75207-3107
www.wyndham-recruiting.com
214-863-1517 • Fax 214-863-1574

WYNN STARR FLAVOR CO
5 Pearl Ct
Allendale, NJ 07401-1610
201-934-7800

X-PRESS MANUFACTURING
271 FM 306
New Braunfels, TX 8130-2557
www.x-pressmfg.com
830-629-2651 • Fax 830-620-4727

XPRESSO, INC.
5195 Southridge Pkwy
Atlanta, GA 30349-5966
www.jurausa.com
770-996-9992 • Fax 770-996-8352

YAMAHA CORP. OF AMERICA
P.O. Box 470838
Tulsa, OK 74147-0838
918-627-8704 • Fax 918-627-7376

YAMAHA USA GOLF CAR GROUP
1000 Highway 34 E
Newnan, GA 30265-2132
770-254-4000

YAMAN AIR
2034 Cody Lane
Harleysville, PA 19438-3347
610-222-3899

YAMATO CORPORATION
1775 S Murray Blvd
Colorado Springs, CO 80916-4513
www.yamatocorp.com
719-591-1500 • Fax 719-591-1045

YANKEE MARKETERS
5 Birch Rd
Middleton, MA 01949-2261
yankeemktr@erols.com
978-777-9181 • Fax 978-777-5823

YCLIP.COM
8300 N Mo Pac Expy, Ste 100
Austin, TX 78759-8331
www.yclip.com
512-652-1035 • Fax 512-494-1137

YEATTS CONTRACT, INC.
8466 Tyco Rd Ste B
Vienna, VA 22182-2246
703-847-7430 • Fax 703-847-7431

YELLOWPAGES.COM
657 Mission St., Ste 502
San Francisco, CA 94105-4118
www.yellowpages.com
415-344-9694 • Fax 415-371-9332

YO LOGO
249 E 157th St
Gardena, CA 90248-2510
www.yologo.com
310-352-4831 • Fax 310-327-4858

YOHAY
75 Grand Ave
Brooklyn, NY 11205-2592
www.yohay.com
718-857-4514 • Fax 718-230-0759

YORKRAFT INCORPORATED
550 S Pine St
York, PA 17403-2750
www.yorkraft.com
800-872-2044 • 717-845-3666

YOUNG BLOCK ASSOCIATES
514 Main St
Fort Lee, NJ 07024-2543
201-461-3333 • Fax 201-461-3233

YOUNG ELECTRIC SIGN COMPANY
1148 S 300 W
Salt Lake City, UT 84101-3053
dremy@slc.yesco.com
www.yesco.com
800-444-3847 • 801-467-3447

YOUR BEST BAKERY PRODUCTS, LLC
33580 Central Ave
Union City, CA 94587-2097
510-477-9620 • Fax 510-477-9536

YOUR PLACE MENU SYSTEMS
2600 Lockheed Way
Carson City, NV 89706-0717
www.yourplacemenus.com
800-321-8105 • Fax 775-882-5210

YOURSTOREROOM.COM
950 Arthur Ave
Elk Grove Village, IL 60007-5217
847-956-1730 • Fax 847-956-0199

Z SQUARED, INC.
101 Summit St
Oyster Bay, NY 11771-2338
zsquared@optonline.net
516-922-1546 • Fax 516-922-1546

ZACKY KITCHENS
1111 Navy Dr
Stockton, CA 95206-1125
mikekenter@zacky.com
209-948-0129 • Fax 209-948-0109

ZAFARI ART & DECON DESIGN
2606 W Grand Reserve Cir
Clearwater, FL 33759-4900
ghobby@mindspring.com
727-723-1860

ZAFARI ART & DECOR DESIGN
P.O. Box 446
Terra Ceia, FL 34250-0446
ghobby@mindspring.com
941-729-4195 • Fax 941-729-5925

ZAKASPACE
1900 Century Pl NE Ste 108
Atlanta, GA 30345-4302
404-634-7507

ZALDIVA CIGARZ
2805 E Oakland Park Blvd
Fort Lauderdale, FL 33306-1813
954-567-0932

ZARDA BAR-B-Q
214 NW 17th St
Blue Springs, MO 64015-3555
christy@veracpm.net
816-229-3670 • Fax 816-224-3171

ZARTIC
438 Lavender Dr NW
Rome, GA 30165-2200
zartic@zartic.com
www.zartic.com

ZATARAIN'S
82 1st St
Gretna, LA 70053-4745
zatarain.com
504-367-2950 • Fax 504-362-2004

ZAY PRODUCTS, INC.
2174 Meadow Vale Rd.
Longmont, CO 80504-6227
Karend@inteccorp.com
800-666-1611 • Fax 303-833-6650

ZB IND., INC./CONTESSA SHRIMP
P.O. Box 1950
San Pedro, CA 90733-1950
310-832-8000

ZEE MEDICAL
2748 Cavanagh Ct
Hayward, CA 94545-1673
510-783-8250 • Fax 510-783-5517

ZENITH SALES COMPANY 1000
Milwaukee Ave
Glenview, IL 60025-2423
www.zenith.com
847-391-8977 • Fax 847-391-8073

ZENITH SPECIALTY
17625 Railroad St.
Rowland Heights, CA 91748-1195
www.zsb.com
626-912-2481 • Fax 626-810-5136

ZEP
7322 Exchange Dr.
Orlando, FL 32809-6263
www.zepmfg.com
407-851-5610

**ZEP CHEMICAL
MANUFACTURING**
196 Manley St
Brockton, MA 02301-5510
508-583-2440 • Fax 508-559-5028

ZEP MANUFACTURING CO.
3008 Olympic Industrial Dr SE
Smyrna, GA 30080-7325
enrique.francis@zapmfg.com
404-350-3120 • Fax 404-350-0255

ZEPHYR MFG CO
P.O. Box 71
Sedalia, MO 65302-0071

ZERO ZONE
110 N Oakridge Dr
North Prairie, WI 53153-9792
262-392-6400

ZESCO PRODUCTS
640 N Capitol Ave
Indianapolis, IN 46204-1206
317 269 9200

ZIMMERMAN ART GALLERY
225 The Crossroads
Carmel, CA 93923-8649
831-622-9100

ZING ZANG, INC.
50 Milwaukee Ave
Glenview, IL 60025-3710
www.zingzang.com
847-635-8222 • Fax 847-296-6381

ZING ZANG, INC.
P.O. Box 2615
Tupelo, MS 38803-2615
stevem@zingzang.com
662-620-1000 • Fax 662-848-1593

ZINSSER & CO, WM
173 Belmont Dr.
Somerset, NJ 08873-1218
732-469-8100

ZIPSKIN, INC
3108 Baker Rd
Dexter, MI 48130-1119
734-426-5559 • Fax 734-426-0899

ZOHO CORP
1849 Sawtelle Blvd, Ste 543
Los AngelesCA 90025-7011
408-469-4231

**ZOJIRUSHI AMERICA
CORPORATION**
6259 Bandini Blvd
Los Angeles, CA 90040-3113
www.zojirushi.com
323-722-1700 • Fax 323-722-0077

ZONAL RETAIL SYSTEMS
206 W Sybelia Ave

Maitland, FL 32751-4739
407-539-0092

ZOO PIKS/SPIR-IT INC.
3809 Pipestone Road
Dallas, TX 75212-6010
www.spir-it.com
800-321-7667 • Fax 214-634-0242

ZOOM COMMUNICATIONS
1325 Capital Cir Ste C
Lawrenceville, GA 30043-5892
rchandler@brandmakers.com
www.zoomcomm.com
770-277-0414

ZOOMINN.COM
9320 SW Barbur Blvd
Portland, OR 97219-5437
800-634-9248

**ZUCKERMAN FERNANDES
MACDANIELS**
130 Sutter Street, 7th Floor
San Francisco, CA 94104-4024
415-989-0580 • Fax 415-989-0596

ZUMEX OF AMERICA, INC
7382 NW 54th St
Miami, FL 33166-4809
305-887-8332

ZUMOVAL AMERICAS
675 SW 12th Ave, Ste 101
Pompano Beach, FL 33069-4505
pwarren@americasproduce.com

www.pwarrenamericasproduce.com
954-786-0000

ZURICH INSURANCE GROUP
1400 American Ln
Chaumburg, IL 60196-5452
847 605-6000

ZURN INDUSTRIES, INC.
1801 Pittsburgh Ave
Erie, PA 16502-1916
www.zurn.com
814-455-0921 • Fax 814-875-1402

ZYLISS
30161 Avenida De Las Bandera
Margarita, CA 92688-2114
949-858-5005

ZYLISS USA CORP.
19751 Descartes
Foothill Ranch, CA 92610-2620
949-699-1884 • Fax 949-699-1788

Other great books available from Atlantic Publishing:

15 NEW BOOKS AVAILABLE!

This new 15-book series from the editors of the Food Service Professional Magazine are the best and most-comprehensive books for serious food service operators available today. These step-by-step guides on specific management subjects are easy to read, easy to understand and will take the mystery out of the subject. The information is "boiled down" to the essence. They are filled to the brim with up-to-date and pertinent information. These books cover all the bases, providing clear explanations and helpful, specific information. All titles in the series include the phone numbers and Web sites of all companies discussed.

1-800-541-1336 Call toll-free 24 hours a day, 7 days a week. Or fax completed form to: **1-352-622-5836.**
Order Online! Just go to **www.atlantic-pub.com** for fast, easy, secure ordering.

SOFTWARE GUIDE

SAVE 40%
EMPLOYEE HANDBOOK CREATOR GUIDE
Finally, a cost-effective solution for developing your own employee handbook. Simply review the 100-plus policies already written for you and insert your own information when prompted. Complete with table of contents, introduction and a form for each employee to sign. Use with Windows or any word processor.

Item #EHB-CS ~~$99.95~~ **Sale $59.95**

Qty	Order Code	Book Title	Price	Total
	Item # EHB-CS	Employee Handbook Creator Guide	$59.95	
	Item # FS1-01	Restaurant Site Location	$19.95	
	Item # FS2-01	Buying & Selling A Restaurant Business	$19.95	
	Item # FS3-01	Restaurant Marketing & Advertising	$19.95	
	Item # FS4-01	Restaurant Promotion & Publicity	$19.95	
	Item # FS5-01	Controlling Operating Costs	$19.95	
	Item # FS6-01	Controlling Food Costs	$19.95	
	Item # FS7-01	Controlling Labor Costs	$19.95	
	Item # FS8-01	Controlling Liquor Wine & Beverage Costs	$19.95	
	Item # FS9-01	Building Restaurant Profits	$19.95	
	Item # FS10-01	Waiter & Waitress Training	$19.95	
	Item # FS11-01	Bar & Beverage Operation	$19.95	
	Item # FS12-01	Successful Catering	$19.95	
	Item # FS13-01	Food Service Menus	$19.95	
	Item # FS14-01	Restaurant Design	$19.95	
	Item # FS15-01	Increasing Rest. Sales	$19.95	
	Item # FSALL-01	**Entire 15-Book Series**	**$199.95**	
			Subtotal	
			Shipping & Handling	
			Florida 6% Sales Tax	
			TOTAL	

Best Deal! **SAVE 33%**
15 GUIDE TO SERIES books for $199.95

SHIP TO:

Name_____ Phone(____) _____

Company Name _____

Mailing Address _____

City _____ State _____ Zip _____

FAX (____) _____ E-mail _____

❏ My check or money order is enclosed ❏ Please send my order COD ❏ My authorized purchase order is attached

❏ Please charge my: ❏ Mastercard ❏ VISA ❏ American Express ❏ Discover

Card # ☐☐☐☐ – ☐☐☐☐ – ☐☐☐☐ – ☐☐☐☐   Expires ☐☐☐☐

Please make checks payable to: **Atlantic Publishing Company** • 1210 SW 23 Place • Ocala, FL 34474-7014
USPS Shipping/handling: add $5.00 first item, $2.50 each additional or $15.00 for the whole set. Florida residents PLEASE add the appropriate county sales tax.